THE INTERNATIONAL TENNIS FEDERATION

World of Tennis

1991

The year 1990 saw the dawning of a new and exciting event, the *Compaq Grand Slam Cup*. It also marked the first time since 1966 that all eight Grand Slam singles events were won by different players. Ivan Lendl, the Australian Open champion, went on to become the ITF World Champion; Andres Gomez won his first Grand Slam singles title at Roland Garros; Stefan Edberg, the Wimbledon champion, dethroned Lendl from the no. 1 computer ranking closely challenged by Boris Becker; and the youngest US Open champion, 19 year-old Pete Sampras, also went on to become the winner of the inaugural *Grand Slam Cup*. Steffi Graf retained her Australian Open title and her no. 1 ranking; Monica Seles became the youngest French Open champion at 16 and, by winning 9 titles including the Virginia Slims Championships, ended the year as the no. 2 ranked player; Martina Navratilova won her beloved Wimbledon crown for the ninth time, thereby beating Helen Wills-Moody's record of 8 Wimbledon singles titles; and Gabriela Sabatini won her first Grand Slam singles title at the US Open. But it was also an impressive year which saw the rise of many young talented players, especially Jennifer Capriati whose arrival onto the women's circuit has delighted all those who love tennis. These events and more are covered in this twenty-third edition of *World of Tennis*, which provides a comprehensive view of all that is happening in the game. Again published in association with the International Tennis Federation, *World of Tennis* has long been recognised as the sport's foremost reference book. Its pages are packed with photographs, detailed results of all world's major tournaments, including: the four Grand Slams, the *Grand Slam Cup*; the women's International Series; the men's Tour; international team competitions such as the *Davis Cup, Federation Cup* and World Youth Cup, as well as the satellite circuits and junior and veteran tennis. The detailed reference section contains biographies of more than 200 players, with portraits of all the all-time greats, plus the Championship Rolls. And, in a special feature article we look at the Australia and USA Davis Cup Rivalry between 1946 and 1971.

THE INTERNATIONAL TENNIS FEDERATION

World of Tennis

1991

Edited by John Barrett
Compiled by Marijke Volger
Biographies by Christine Forrest

CollinsWillow
An Imprint of HarperCollins*Publishers*

Abbreviations used in this book

ARG	Argentina	**FRA**	France	**NZL**	New Zealand
AUS	Australia	**FRG**	West Germany	**PAK**	Pakistan
AUT	Austria	**GBR**	Great Britain	**PAR**	Paraguay
BAH	Bahamas	**GRE**	Greece	**PER**	Peru
BEL	Belgium	**HAI**	Haiti	**POL**	Poland
BER	Bermuda	**HKG**	Hong Kong	**POR**	Portugal
BOL	Bolivia	**HOL**	Netherlands	**PUR**	Puerto Rico
BRA	Brazil	**HUN**	Hungary	**ROM**	Rumania
BUL	Bulgaria	**INA**	Indonesia	**RSA**	South Africa
CAN	Canada	**IND**	India	**SEN**	Senegal
CHI	Chile	**IRL**	Ireland	**SUI**	Switzerland
CHN	People's Republic	**IRN**	Iran	**SWE**	Sweden
	of China	**ISR**	Israel	**TCH**	Czechoslovakia
COL	Colombia	**ITA**	Italy	**TUR**	Turkey
DEN	Denmark	**JPN**	Japan	**URS**	USSR
ECU	Ecuador	**KOR**	Korea	**URU**	Uruguay
EGY	Arab Republic	**LUX**	Luxembourg	**USA**	United States
	of Egypt	**MEX**	Mexico		of America
ESP	Spain	**NIG**	Nigeria	**YUG**	Yugoslavia
FIN	Finland	**NOR**	Norway	**ZIM**	Zimbabwe

Cover photograph: Stefan Edberg (Professional Sport)

First published in 1991 by
Collins Willow
an imprint of HarperCollins Publishers
London

A CIP catalogue
record for this book
is available from the
British Library

ISBN: 0 00 218403 6

Set in Univers by Phoenix Photosetting, Chatham, Kent
Printed and bound in Great Britain by
Mackays of Chatham PLC, Chatham, Kent

CONTENTS

PREFACE

What a remarkable year it was! After 45 years of confrontation between the super powers, we had a year of change. Yes, 1990 will be remembered as the year when communism in Eastern Europe collapsed under the sheer weight of public opinion. Disenchanted with a system that had been a total failure economically the peoples of the Soviet Union and her satellite neighbours embraced a new form of democracy. In Germany the Berlin Wall came down and the impossible happened – the two Germany's were actually re-united. Even South Africa seemed at last to be prepared to listen to world opinion as Mr. De Klerk announced the end of apartheid.

Meanwhile, the great industrialised nations seemed powerless to halt a slide towards recession and it became a matter of some concern that a failure to deliver the economic goods in Eastern Europe might precipitate a slide back towards totalitarian rule in some of those countries. The year ended with Iraqi forces in control of Kuwait and Sadam Hussein refusing to withdraw, despite the United Nations' threat of invasion from the allied forces led by the United States.

Alongside these momentous international events, the changes that took place in international tennis seem trivial. Indeed they are, and it is necessary to keep a balanced perspective in describing them. To the men players, it was important that the first year of the IBM/ATP Tour should be seen by the outside world as a success. It was encouraging, therefore, to see all the highly ranked men competing strongly through to the end of the season. Later on in these pages the new venture is evaluated and, for the sake of future generations, the full singles results of all the tournaments are printed for the first time, along with the finals of the doubles. Because of the extra space they occupy it has been necessary to dispense with the individual reports of these events. The same approach has been adopted for the new Kraft Geneal Foods womens' tour.

Elsewhere, in this our 23rd edition, it is very much the mixture as before. Or nearly so. As we noted last year, Lance Tingay, the man who since the beginning had contributed some of our key pieces, died just as we were going to press. Accordingly there was insufficient time or space properly to acknowledge the enormous contribution he made to this publication over a span of 22 turbulent years when the game expanded and developed faster than at any time in its history. As the doyen of tennis historians Lance was universally respected and his reports and opinions carried the weight of authority. It is with some trepidation, therefore, that I step into his shoes in providing the reports on Wimbledon, the Players of the Year and the annual Rankings.

I am, as usual, indebted to my colleagues in the press room for some expert contributions on the main Championships and the team events which form the central part of every tennis year. I am equally grateful for another collection of beautiful pictures from those uncomplaining packhorses of our sport, the tennis photographers, who wander the world weighed down by their bulging bags of heavy and expensive equipment. Do you know how you can spot a sports photographer at a distance? One shoulder is always lower than the other! They are a marvellous bunch!

So, too, are the members of the strong team of media executives assembled by the IBM/ATP Tour and the Women's Tennis Association (renamed after four years and two months as the Women's International Tennis Association). On behalf of every member of the working media perhaps I can publicly thank Jay Beck, the Director of Communications for the IBM/ATP Tour and his colleagues for the excellent job they do in keeping us all informed. Richard Evans, Jay's counterpart in Europe, was the ATP Tour's gain and my loss, for he had supplied many of the key stories over the years for these pages. I continue to be impressed by the statistical command of Greg Sharko whose attention to detail and unfailing helpfulness when last minute figures are needed is very much appreciated. In the front line we have been superbly served by Craig Gabriel, George Rubenstein, Caroline Hutton (who has the good sense to escape the treadmill by walking up the aisle – good luck Pidge, and thanks for everything!), Meg Donovan, Lauren Goldberg and Anna Legnani. Thanks to you all.

We are all similarly grateful to Ana Leaird, the WTA's Director of Public Relations and Gene Beckwith, the Director of Management Information Systems, for giving us the support of some truly remarkable people. How Renee Shallouf, Robin Reynolds, Tracey Robinson, Giselle Marrou and Susan Vosburgh maintain their sanity and, more importantly, their charm when dealing with some of the asinine questions that I hear some of my colleagues pose, is beyond me. The hours these ladies keep would drive ordinary mortals to an early grave . . . I am talking strictly about their work!

How lucky we are, also, that the Grand Slam Championships had the good sense to engage Barbara Travers and her omnivorous computer which seems to gobble up every known fact about all the men players . . . well, ALMOST every fact. (We'd rather not know about those, anyway!) Barbara's speed of thought and action have saved many a man hanging on a tight deadline. We love you, Barbara, don't go away!

Love – of tennis, that is – must be responsible for the continuing enthusiasm of Christine Forrest who once again has produced our men's and women's biographies. With two teenage children, it is just as well that her husband Terry is prepared to see her spend the long winter evenings, and even longer weekends, glued to a computer keyboard. At least it gives him time to dismantle his cars in the garage.

The lady who has been cracking the whip over my head this year is the unflappable Judith Newberry. I suspect she did not quite realise what she was taking on but at least she kept smiling to the end. In thanking her, I can only say that I have enjoyed her quiet efficiency – and the occasional company of her baby son Max.

Finally I would like to pay a personal tribute to a departed friend whose obituary appears elsewhere. Ted Tinling, who died last May on the eve of his 80th birthday shortly before Wimbledon, was more than just one of the game's great characters; he was part of the very fabric of tennis. All of us who knew him well will miss him greatly.

JOHN BARRETT
London, March 1991

FOREWORD

It has been another eventful tennis year with continuing growth at all levels, despite signs of a world recession. As I look back upon a lifetime's association with the game, the thing that has continually impressed me is its remarkable resilience. Certainly that has been the case in 1990. The *Davis Cup* by NEC attracted entries from a record number of nations and the *Federation Cup* in Atlanta, also supported by NEC, provided a wonderful showcase for some remarkably talented young women. The fact that the United States claimed both team Championships suggests that this great nation, languishing in the shadows for a few years as the rest of the world overtook them, are back in the sunlight.

The ATP Tour and the Challengers and Satellite event series have provided more opportunities for the men players, while the women's game has expanded under its new sponsor, Kraft General Foods and its associated companies, and the introduction, by the ITF, of a fully intermediate Futures Circuit. With the arrival of the *Compaq Grand Slam Cup*, and the possibility of including the women in future years, we can look forward to a season-ending battle for supremacy worthy of our four great Championships in Australia, France, Britain and the United States. However, almost the most important aspect of this new competition has been the $2 million it has provided for the Grand Slam Development Fund, and will continue to provide each year, for the development of the game in emerging countries.

As I now prepare to hand over the leadership of the International Tennis Federation to others, after 14 years at the helm, I am particularly proud of three things. The first was the inclusion of tennis as a full Olympic sport in 1988. It was the fulfilment of a dream that I had shared with our late General Secretary, David Gray. As we had hoped, this development has provided enormous impetus to the growth of the game, especially in those countries where the funding of all sport is in the hands of the national Olympic Committee. The second was the creation of the Development Department, under the directorship of Doug MacCurdy, to encourage tennis in all our Member Nations. In addition to the Grand Slam Development Fund which provides competitive opportunities around the world, the ITF itself funds the Development Programme which includes educational projects, the distribution of equipment, consultations to National Associations etc. And, thirdly was the decision, also made at the prompting of David Gray in 1981, to adopt *World of Tennis* as the official yearbook of the International Tennis Federation. This latest edition, the 23rd since it started to cover the events of the tennis year with the arrival of open tennis in 1968, is slightly re-arranged to reflect the evolutionary nature of our sport. As usual there is something for everyone – the facts and figures on which the professional commentators rely, the opinions of some of the world's finest tennis writers on the great events of the year, and an abundant variety of pictures from some of the game's most highly skilled photographers which bring everything vividly to life. Enjoy your read!

PHILIPPE CHATRIER
President, International Tennis Federation

Pete Sampras became the youngest-ever winner of the US Open when, aged 19 years 28 days, he beat, in succession, Lendl, McEnroe and Agassi with astonishing maturity at Flushing Meadow. *(R. Adams)*

THE YEAR IN REVIEW

Ronald Atkin

Contrary to what they say in American sport, it *was* over when the fat tenor sang. Or almost over. Placido Domingo's participation in the spectacular opening ceremony of the *Compaq Grand Slam Cup* in Munich's *Olympiahalle* marked the offical start of the final event of 1990 – the richest in the history of tennis and the cause of more bickering and controversy than any other.

There could have been no more soothing end to the season than Domingo's rich rendering of *Be My Love*, a theme which all connected with the *Grand Slam Cup* adhered to throughout a week in which the near-exclusive subject was money. The first prize, as surely they know by now even in the Amazonian rain forest, was $2 million. The winner was Pete Sampras, the 19-year-old Californian who had vaulted into the world's top ten three months previously by becoming the youngest winner of the US Open men's singles.

The dollar-laden success of Sampras was entirely appropriate. For if 1989 had been indisputably the year of the Germans (the supremacy of Boris Becker and Steffi Graf, the demise of the Berlin Wall), 1990 certainly deserved the label 'Year of the Young'. Sampras seized the spotlight from the platoon of other talented American contemporaries, though Andre Agassi continued to present a multi-hued profile, unmissable both for spectators and those anxious to take aim at him.

Despite Sampras, however, it was the women's game which attracted much of the attention in 1990. There was the glorious, high-decibel flowering of Monica Seles and the glittering, much-heralded arrival of Jennifer Capriati, aged 13 on her professional debut in March. Capriati delighted all those who love tennis, with the exception of the fellow-professionals she walloped on her swift climb into the world's elite. Yet the old guard were not eclipsed. The record shows Ivan Lendl, on the brink of his 30th birthday, lifting the Australian Open, Andres Gomez annexing 'Surprise of the Year award' by capturing the French Open at 30 and then Martina Navratilova finally overtaking the long-standing mark of Helen Wills Moody by winning her ninth Wimbledon singles when many thought such a feat beyond a lady of 33 years.

So, on the playing front, 1990 more properly deserves to be entered into the logbook as the opening of a new decade in which the established names fought a stirring rearguard action against the advance of the years and the onrush of eager new talent. There was proof, had it ever been considered proof was needed, that professional tennis has never been stronger: for the first time since 1966 all eight Grand Slam singles titles were won by different players. Lendl, Gomez, Stefan Edberg and Sampras were the male champions; Graf (only one Grand Slam in 1990 after her hat-trick the previous year), Seles, Navratilova and Gabriela Sabatini collected the women's honours. One of the year's sensations was the sight of Sabatini suddenly taking a liking to the volley and winning the US Open in a rousing victory over Graf.

After ninety years the *Davis Cup* continued to exhibit not only excellent health but vigorous growth. The list of nations anxious to tilt for the honours in 1991 soared to a record 88, led by the United States as the proud holders of the *Cup* for the first time since 1982 (this eight-year gap is the longest the Americans have suffered since the thirties). They defeated Australia 3–2 in the final at the superb Florida Suncoast Dome, St. Petersburg, having taken a 3–0 winning lead by the second day. The Americans had been more seriously tested in the semi-finals, where the Austrians laid down a clay court and laid on a hot welcome in a Vienna soccer stadium. Only a typical, gutsy recovery by Michael Chang, battling back from a two-set deficit against Horst Skoff in the deciding rubber, enabled the United States to squeak through.

The triumph in St. Petersburg was only a part of a rousing climax to the year for American tennis. It started with Sampras becoming the first 'home' champion at the US Open since John McEnroe in 1984, continued with Agassi claiming the crown at the ATP Tour Finals in Frankfurt and ended with the modest (but now immensely rich) Sampras as winner of the *Compaq Grand Slam Cup*. No wonder Sampras was able to claim in Munich 'The United States is set to dominate world tennis again.' They had won the *Davis Cup* with the slow court skills of Agassi and Chang – not forgetting the doubles expertise of Rick Leach and Jim Pugh – and still had in reserve such as Sampras, David Wheaton, Jim Courier and Aaron Krickstein, not forgetting a certain J. P. McEnroe jnr. and the astonishing Brad Gilbert, who parlayed his original role as fourth alternate at the *Grand Slam Cup* into a place in the final and a cheque for $1 million.

Sweden, winners or finalists of the *Davis Cup* for the previous seven years, went out in the first round to Italian opposition inspired by playing on home territory. Edberg was injured, Mats Wilander out of form and Kent Carlsson was soon to retire from tennis with chronic knee trouble. It was not the happiest of years for the Swedes until Edberg pulled them round at Wimbledon.

Germany, the holders, could not compensate for Boris Becker's decision to give the *Davis Cup* a miss in 1990. Claiming he was sick of the chauvinism surrounding the team's victory over Sweden in the 1988 and 1989 finals Becker stepped down, ostensibly to pursue his ambition of overtaking the holder of the world No. 1 ranking, Lendl. Instead, it was Edberg who usurped the Czech's reign of 80 consecutive weeks and record overall total of 263 weeks. By year's end Becker, too, had overhauled Lendl but he missed his chance of pipping Edberg when he suffered injury in the Paris Indoor final against the Swede. So Becker, winner of Wimbledon and the US Open in 1989, ended up with a fistful of nothing except money and retreated into morose introspection about the pressures and frustrations of his life.

Steffi Graf's lot was similarly sour. The Golden Grand Slammer of 1988 was first injured, then ill and finally depressed. In the year of her 21st birthday the high-shouldered blonde was suddenly under unexpected assault from girls even younger than herself – and the word was out. Fraulein Forehand (as the US media labelled her) was no longer invincible. Seles proved it, first in Berlin, then in the French final; Zina Garrison proved it at Wimbledon and then Sabatini, unwrapping her volley, proved it once more at Flushing Meadow. The thumb injury she suffered while skiing, the sinus condition which dogged her progress through the French and Wimbledon championships, the continuing distraction of allegations about her father's private life – all combined to drag Graf to the brink of a summit on which she had seemed set to dwell for a long time.

The women's tour flourished under the umbrella of a new overall sponsor, Kraft General Foods, as it embarked on its third decade of professionalism. The Kraft World Tour put up prize money of more than $23 million in 64 tournaments held in a record 21 countries – and promptly benefitted by the level of the young challenge to Graf's supremacy.

On the men's side the ATP Tour suffered a birth pang or two but quickly signed up IBM as a title sponsor, appointed a new executive officer, Mark Miles, in place of Hamilton Jordan, and by the time of its end-of-season Championships in Frankfurt (they replaced the old Masters tournament) the Tour was functioning solidly.

There was the usual sprinkling of innovations. The men staged their first professional event in Moscow. It was called the *Kremlin Cup* and was won, appropriately, by Andrei Cherkasov. The women went to what used to be known as East Germany, playing in Leipzig. Steffi Graf won it then, at her presentation ceremony, broke down and wept at the emotion of it all. The ATP Tour doubles finals were transplanted from the Royal Albert Hall in London to Sanctuary Cove in Australia, where Guy Forget and Jakob Hlasek shaved their heads and swept aside the startled opposition to capture the crown.

The United States, with Jennifer Capriati slotting into the side so smoothly that Chris Evert wasn't even missed, captured the *Federation Cup* in Atlanta, defeating the Soviet Union whose coach, the great Olga Morozova, gave British tennis a shot in the arm by agreeing to tutor its youngsters for the next three years.

The remarkable Czech-born American, Martina Navratilova, created history at Wimbledon when she won a ninth singles title to surpass the record she had shared with the great American champion of the 1930's Helen Wills Moody.   *(Professional Sport)*

The incidence of injuries grew as players of both sexes responded to sponsors' urgings and increased prize money by spending more time on court. It was disturbing to hear bright new talents like Seles and Sampras complaining towards the end of the year that they were exhausted and ailing. Seles, incidentally, had steered clear of the *Federation Cup*, remaining coy when questioned about her intentions of playing either for the country of her birth, Yugoslavia, or her nation of residence, the United States, if and when qualified. Then, quite suddenly, there she was, in Perth, representing Yugoslavia in the *Hopman Cup* – and winning it with Goran Prpic as her partner.

Towards the end of the year the tennis world was alive with rumours that Bjorn Borg was preparing himself for a comeback in 1991. Whether he was, at the age of 34, intending to launch himself and his famous (but outdated) wooden racket back onto the full-time circuit or whether the comeback would be in special events and exhibitions was not clear at the time of writing. But any return would be the biggest media occasion since the Capriati launch. These rumours came to a head during the *Compaq Grand Slam Cup*, fuelled by the comments of Jonas Svensson who had practised with the great man in Milan before travelling on to Munich. They added even more spice to a week never short of a headline – the first round defeats of two Grand Slam champions, Stefan Edberg (Wimbledon) and Andres Gomez (French), the shock exit of Ivan Lendl, the player the other players thought would win, in the quarter-finals and, not least, the confrontation between Lendl's con-queror, David Wheaton, and Brad Gilbert in their semi-final when both were lucky to escape with no more serious a charge than unsportsmanlike conduct and a $5,000 fine.

That unsavoury occasion was obliterated the following day by the calm and sporting fashion in which Sampras accepted his victory and then announced he was donating a quarter of a million dollars of his winnings to research into cerebral palsy. As the new Yugoslav sensation, Goran Ivanisevic, forecast, we shall be seeing much more of him and Sampras in the years ahead.

We shall see no more, alas, of Alice Marble, the 1939 Wimbledon and four-time US champion, who died in December aged 77, or of Ted Tinling, the savant, ace raconteur and skilled couturier of the game who died in a Cambridge hospital just short of his 80th birthday and shortly before the French Open got under way. However, Tinling himself would have insisted that the year belonged to the young ones – to Pete Sampras, to Monica Seles and to Jennifer Capriati.

PLAYERS OF THE YEAR
John Barrett

This has been an historic year. For the first time since 1966 we have eight different singles winners of the four Grand Slam Championships. It would be invidious, therefore to exclude any of our champions from the list of Players of the Year, even though, elsewhere, not all of them maintained a consistently high level of performance.

STEFAN EDBERG

It was a year of mixed fortunes for this quiet and talented Swede who shuns the limelight that inevitably shines on the new world's No. 1 player. In Melbourne at the start of the year, a third Australian title seemed to be within his grasp when he destroyed (there is no other word for it) compatriot Mats Wilander in the semi-finals. But no-one except Stefan and his British coach Tony Pickard knew that in the last game of that match Stefan had torn a stomach muscle. Even when he won the first set of his final against Ivan Lendl few realised why he was not serving at full power. Only when he was broken as he served for the second set and then lost it on a tie-break was it apparent that something was wrong. At 2–5 in the third, Stefan realised it could only do further harm to continue, so he retired.

Perhaps it was as well he did for this 24-year-old super-athlete was about to embark upon his most successful, and yet most erratic, season ever. Wins in Indian Wells and Tokyo were the prelude to a totally inexplicable first round loss in Paris to Sergi Bruguera. Driven hard by Pickard, Stefan bounced back from that disappointment to produce, at Wimbledon, a fabulous display of reflex volleying and controlled service returns that humbled both Lendl and Boris Becker as he claimed his second title there. Further wins in Los Angeles, Cincinnati (where his victory over Chang lifted him past Lendl to the No. 1 world ranking) and Long Island left us all unprepared for another first round loss at Flushing Meadow – where the Russian left-hander Alexander Volkov dismissed him in straight sets. That was hardly the form of a Wimbledon champion. Nevertheless, the best of the 1990 Edberg vintage was very good indeed and there was enough of it to confirm the impression that a new order has arrived in the game, led by this likeable and sensitive Swede.

IVAN LENDL

Always one of the most consistent players of the day, this 30-year-old American-based Czech is finding it increasingly difficult to keep the younger men at bay. It is by no means certain that he would have won a second successive Australian title in 1990 if Stefan Edberg had been fully fit that fateful Sunday afternoon in January. For the Swede had won the first set and had served for the second (which he then lost on a tie-break) before he retired when trailing 2–5 in the third. But win it Ivan did, to bring his tally of Grand Slam crowns to eight.

There was an uneasy transition to a new Japanese-made racket that contributed to Ivan's greatest disappointment last year – namely his failure to win a first Wimbledon title. The preparation had been thorough. He had spent several weeks on grass courts in Australia working with his Australian coach, Tony Roche and chose to miss the French Championships. When, with consummate skill, he beat both McEnroe and Becker to win his second Queen's title in as many years, the prospects for achieving his dream looked good. But, as in 1989, he fell in the semi-finals at Wimbledon, unable to cope with Edberg's

Above (left): *A second Wimbledon title for Edberg and the No. 1 ranking;* (right): *A good start in Australia for Lendl. (M. Cole)* Below (left): *Graf holds on against fierce challenge;* (right): *A fairy-tale finish in Paris for Gomez.* (R. Adams)

greater flexibility on the slicker, lower-bouncing All England Club courts. Despite an unexpected loss to young Pete Sampras in the quarter-finals of the US Open, which prevented him from surpassing the record he shares with Bill Tilden of reaching eight consecutive finals in New York, Ivan Lendl, a proud new father, was most definitely a Player of the Year. It is hard to remember a time when he was not.

ANDRES GOMEZ

A lifetime's dream came true for this amiable giant from Ecuador when, on a hot and humid June afternoon in Paris, with his wife Anna Maria and their young son Juan in the stands, he humbled the 20-year-old American Andre Agassi, the No. 3 seed, to win his first Grand Slam singles crown. In itself this does not seem remarkable for had not the big South American left-hander been recognised as one of the best exponents of the clay court art for more than a decade with 19 tournament titles to his credit? And had he not won the last two of those not one month earlier in Barcelona and Madrid, results that contributed to a number four seeding in Paris? But when you consider that Andres, at 30 years of age, was the second oldest man in the field and that, until this moment, he had never been in a Grand Slam singles final (had never even passed the quarter-finals, in fact) then you begin to understand the enormity of his achievement. On his return home Andres was to experience the most extraordinary week of his life. He was fêted and mobbed wherever he went and the celebrations in Guayaquil lasted a full week. Accordingly, when our hero returned to Europe for Wimbledon he was still floating on cloud nine. The fact that Andres lost in the first round there and at the US Open hardly seemed to matter. Here was a delightful man, as popular with his peers as with the public and nearing the end of his career, basking in his unexpected, but thoroughly deserved, glory. If he never achieves anything else in life, Andres Gomez will always be remembered as one of the finest and most gracious of French Open champions and, without doubt, one of 1990's Players of the Year.

PETE SAMPRAS

For those clever enough to have spotted it there was a clue. When last February the teenage Californian Pete Sampras, then 18, won his first professional title in Philadelphia with wins over Srejber, Agassi, Mayotte, Kratzmann and Gomez, the beaten finalist, Gomez, had said 'Of all the outstanding young Americans in the game today, the best of them is Pete.' That perceptive judgement became an inspired prophecy when young Sampras, just 28 days past his 19th birthday, astonished an admiring audience by beating Agassi again in three devastating sets to become the youngest man ever to win the singles Championship of the United States. En-route to that final Pete had been, if anything, even more impressive in the manner of his dismissal in five sets of eight-times former finalist and three-time winner Lendl, and in three of the four-time champion McEnroe (that last a whirlwind buffeting that had left the older man breathless – and speechless). Has anyone ever served as well as Pete did in those last two matches? McEnroe was aced 17 times and Agassi 13 times. Altogether the Maryland-born teenager delivered 100 aces during his seven winning matches. How refreshing, then, to welcome a new, young champion whose demeanour and bearing are exemplary and one whose coach, Joe Brandi, never has to reprimand or ask for greater effort. How refreshing, too, that Pete is a talented, natural volleyer who hits his groundstrokes in the old fashioned way – early and flat. It is no surprise to discover that Pete's idol when he was growing up was Rod Laver. Let us hope that the next generation of young Americans grow up idolising Pete Sampras. They could not have a better model than our fourth Player of the Year.

STEFFI GRAF

When, last January in Melbourne, Steffi Graf won a third consecutive Australian Open Championship to take her tally of Grand Slam singles titles to nine, it seemed as if the

With a remarkable exhibition of pulverising power from the baseline, the Yugoslav double-hander, Monica Seles, demolished all opposition to win her first Grand Slam title in Paris, at 16 years 9 months, the youngest ever to do so. *(M. Cole)*

20-year-old World Champion was about to embark upon another year of ruthless conquest. But there were three supreme disappointments during the next nine months that turned what might have been another glorious year into (judged by her own high standards), an ordinary one. The first occurred in Paris on the eve of the West German's 21st birthday early in June. It was bad enough to lose in the final for the second year in a row. That her conqueror, the 16-year-old Yugoslav double-hander Monica Seles, was able to out-hit her on a clay court was almost too much to bear because twelve months earlier Steffi had beaten her there in the semi-final, albeit after something of a struggle. Worse was to follow. At Wimbledon Steffi was undoubtedly affected by the scandal surrounding her father's alleged affair with a German model. She lost a tense semi-final to Zina Garrison, who had never beaten her before. She then saw Martina Navratilova claim a ninth singles title, surpassing the total the Czech-born American had shared with Helen Wills Moody.

Despite undergoing a sinus operation to cure a problem that had afflicted Steffi several times before on important occasions, there was no happy ending to the Grand Slam year in New York. There, an inspired Gabriela Sabatini, who had never beaten her in an important final, played attacking tennis of a quality no-one suspected her capable and took away Steffi's title in straight sets. Yet, despite the setbacks, Steffi, with one Grand Slam title, two appearances in the final and one semi-final finish still had a better season than anyone else and can fairly claim to be THE Player of the Year.

MONICA SELES

When, in 1989, Monica Seles, aged 15 and unseeded, pushed the defending champion Steffi Graf to a nine-game final set in a tense semi-final of the French Championships, we all knew that we had witnessed something rather special. Even so, we were not quite ready to believe that a bare 12 months later the precociously gifted Yugoslav would return to Paris and go one better by beating Miss Graf comprehensively in the final. But that is what she did. Furthermore, in the process, Monica, at 16 years 6 months, became the youngest ever winner of this testing Grand Slam Championship, younger by 11 months even than Arantxa Sanchez-Vicario who had been the previous year's winner. Of all previous winners of one of the four Grand Slam Championships only Lottie Dod, who won Wimbledon for the first time in 1887 aged 15 years 10 months, was younger and she competed in a field of only five in the All Comers singles before beating the holder Blanche Bingley in the Challenge Round.

Double-handed on both sides and with early-hit groundstrokes of such aggression that even speedy opponents are often passed at the baseline, Seles has set standards never before seen in women's tennis. A narrow quarter-final loss to Zina Garrison on Wimbledon's fast grass was understandable but the defeat by the lowly ranked Italian Linda Ferrando in the third round at the US Open was more difficult to understand. A change of racket was probably the chief reason. It will be a pity if this most talented of teenagers allows her commercial advisers to blunt the edge of her potential before it has come to full flower.

MARTINA NAVRATILOVA

Just when you thought there was nothing left to say about Martina Navratilova, this remarkable champion, at the age of 33, achieves yet another record! And this one will surely last for a very long time. For, at the 97th Championship meeting that had included women, the 33-year-old Czech-born American scored a ninth Wimbledon singles win, surpassing the record she had shared with the great pre-war champion, Helen Wills Moody of California. Ever since beating Steffi Graf in 1987 for her 8th title, Martina had set her sights on this record. But so dominant had Steffi become in the ensuing years that her dream seemed to be fading. Then the miracle happened. A nervous Graf lost to Zina Garrison in a thrilling semi-final and Martina knew that her hour had come. She had lost only once to Zina in 28 meetings and so was confident from the start. Nor was there ever any doubt about the result. The straight-forward 6–4 6–1 success meant that this amazing left-hander had, for the fourth time, won the world's greatest Championship without dropping a set. She had previously achieved that feat in 1983, 1984 and 1986. Furthermore, this win brought Martina's tally of Grand Slam titles in singles, doubles and mixed to 53 – only nine short of Margaret Court's record. Now that is the sort of challenge that Martina relishes!

GABRIELA SABATINI

It was truly a metamorphosis. Witnessing the transformation of the new US Open champion, Gabriela Sabatini, from moody moonballer into attacking demon, was like watching a colourless chrysalis turning into a beautiful butterfly. Her victim in the New York final, defending champion Steffi Graf who had won 15 of their previous 18 meetings, seemed as surprised as the rest of us. Sabatini, aged 20 and at a stage in her career when we were beginning to wonder if she would ever fulfil the considerable potential she had shown as a French Open semi-finalist at the age of 15, revealed unexpected qualities. The once sullen maiden, trapped in her whirling topspin world on the baseline, had suddenly become a determined aggressor, ruthless in attack and equally confident on volley and passing shot. The lovely face that, so often in the past, used to be contorted with frustration as her looping baseline game was reduced to tatters by the ruthless German machine, was wreathed in smiles. Clearly Gabriela was enjoying herself. At last she was allowing free rein to her all-court talents. The aggressive plan, devised by Gabriela's new coach, the former Brazilian No. 1 Carlos Kirmayr, and bolstered by help from sport's psychologist Jim Loehr, was carried out to perfection. Never did she waver, even as Graf launched one of those fierce counter-attacks in the second set that brought her twice within one point of the set. Although the rest of Gabriela's year was mediocre by comparison, no-one who saw it will ever forget that golden September afternoon at Flushing Meadow. After this performance, there seems no limit to the heights Gabriela might reach.

We saw a new Gabriela Sabatini at the US Open. The 20-year-old Argentine became a hungry killer who devoured the holder, Graf, with ferocious attacking tennis in a fascinating final. (Professional Sport)

THE ITF YEAR

THE ITF YEAR
DAVIS CUP
FEDERATION CUP

In a year clouded by allegations about her father's private life and by physical problems, Steffi Graf nevertheless won a third Australian Open title and reached two other Grand Slam finals. (M. Cole)

The dream came true for Brad Gilbert who only got into the Compaq Grand Slam Cup *when Agassi withdrew and then reached the final to win a cool $1 million.* (T. Hindley)

THE ITF YEAR

John Parsons

Obviously it was the launch of the *Compaq Grand Slam Cup* that attracted the most attention among the activities of the International Tennis Federation during 1990. The fact that the end of year tournament, based on performances achieved solely in Grand Slam tournaments, was to offer record prize money of $6m, inevitably provoked much excitement among some and criticism from others. Some even went so far as to suggest – particularly when it was thought that some of the leading players might boycott the tournament because the Association of Tennis Professionals Tour disapproved of a competition they feared might harm their own Championships in Frankfurt – that the *Grand Slam Cup* may never get off the ground. In fact, despite all the problems, including the fact that not all the 8,000 seats sold for each day were filled, due, perhaps, to the absence on the court – though not within the *Olympiahalle* in Munich – of Germany's favourite tennis son, Boris Becker, the inaugural *Grand Slam Cup* suggested that the event is here to stay.

The concept itself is appealing. After all, Ivan Lendl, who was to finish the year by being named as the ITF's official world champion by the independent selection panel of Fred Perry, Frank Sedgman and Tony Trabert, has often said that it is the Grand Slam tournaments which 'separate the men from the boys'. And it was Lendl's greater consistency in Grand Slam events, in which he won 16 matches in three events, including the Australian Open title, which persuaded the panel to nominate him fractionally ahead of Wimbledon champion, Stefan Edberg, who lost in the first round of the French and US Open tournaments and the *Grand Slam Cup*, to finish with 13 match wins in four Grand Slam tournaments. Curiously enough though, Lendl was about the only critic of the decision taken by the Grand Slam Committee during the Australian Open, to broaden the format of the *Grand Slam Cup* from eight players, starting with two groups of four in a round-robin to a 16 man straight knock-out. This move also helped make it possible to have the best of five sets in both the semi-finals and final, thus bringing it more into line with a normal Grand Slam tournament. However, experience has since demonstrated that the starting time between those matches will have to be reviewed, in order that the winner of the second semi-final might be allowed more recovery time.

The real benefit of the *Grand Slam Cup* is, of course, the $2m dollar windfall it provides for the newly named Grand Slam Development Fund. This began life as the Grand Slam Trust Fund with donations from Wimbledon, the Australian Open, French Open and US Open. And to make sure no time was lost in putting the extra money to good use, extensive consultations were held between Doug MacCurdy, the ITF's Director of Development and development advisers, regional associations and several national assciations. They drew up a blueprint which was then approved by the Committee of Management.

Development of the game, in its various guises, is an integral part of the Federation's remit. Obviously a major part of this work concentrates on providing greater opportunities for youngsters, by introducing them to tennis and then helping them to fulfil their potential, in parts of the world where, without such help, it may never have been possible. The opening of the first ITF Training Centre in the Ivory Coast under the direction of the former Canadian national coach, Josef Brabenec – a project funded jointly by the ITF, Olympic Solidarity and the Grand Slam Development Fund – was one of the highlights of this work in 1990.

Funding from the ITF and the Grand Slam Development Fund has proved to be essential in maintaining a world-wide network of junior teams and circuits. By giving travel grants and special development grants the ITF has helped to increase both the number of youngsters who play tennis around the world and the quality of their performances. Their help ranges from introducing youngsters in remote African villages to tennis, to providing help for regional and international touring teams as well as helping those who still need and deserve assistance to bridge the gap between junior and open tennis in the 19–22 age group. The changing way of life in Eastern Europe has also provided the ITF with the opportunity to play its part in broadening tennis involvment in that part of the world. Romania and Czechoslovakia were two of the first of these countries to receive grants, based along the lines of those that have proved so successful in Asia, Africa and South and Central America.

Naturally it would be marvellous if some of the youngsters who have been directly helped by the ITF Grand Slam Development Fund were to become top ten players or even Grand Slam tournament winners. The success of India's Leander Paes in reaching the final of the junior boys singles at the Australian Open and then winning the junior title at Wimbledon, is the sort of progress that fuels the enthusiasm of those involved in the various development programmes still further.

Development is not confined to helping junior players. Just as essential are the courses funded by the ITF for coaches and tournament officials. The arrival, in the New Year, of Ken Farrar who took charge of the ITF officials' department, led to the launching of the most comprehensive training programme in the game's history. For the first time, plans were made to help make sure that referees, umpires and linesmen all over the world, and at all levels, follow uniform procedures and techniques, thus ensuring a consistent interpretation of the rules and the ITF Code of Conduct. Such an outcome will not only be of value to the referees, umpires and linesmen but also to the players, the public and the image of the game.

Several of the world's leading umpires were offered contracts to help the ITF ensure that the most experienced officials available were present at Grand Slam tournaments, *Davis Cup* and *Federation Cup* matches as well as some satellite circuits in order that they could also pass on their knowledge to others. Umpiring schools were held in Sweden, Paraguay, Venezuela, Nairobi, Poland, London and two in Asia.

Some of the Grand Slam Development Fund resources, generated by the *Grand Slam Cup*, will also be used to support the enormous growth of Veterans tennis. The 1990 ITF World Veterans' Championships in Umag, Yugoslavia, needed 32 courts to complete its many events, while the 14th European Indoor Veterans Championships in Austria, alone, attracted 430 entries.

As far as the public are concerned however, it is what happens in major international tennis that leaves the lasting impression. All the major individual tournaments and events such as the *Davis Cup* and *Federation Cup* lived up to their reputations by providing quality and excitement. Indeed, for the first time in Open tennis history, all four singles titles in the Grand Slam tournaments, for both men and women, were won by diferent players. This helped to make the men's world champions panels' task of nominating the men's world champion very difficult. However, in the women's game, Steffi Graf's pre-eminence, both in terms of titles and matches won, remained strong enough to keep her out in front of the Kraft/General Foods-Virginia Slims points table and she became a worthy women's world champion for a fourth consecutive year.

Once again the unrivalled appeal and credibility of the Grand Slams was demonstrated by the number of entries and record attendances in Australia, France and the United States. However, Wimbledon, which remains one of the 'hottest tickets' among all the world's major sporting occasions, showed a drop of nearly 15% but that was almost entirely due to the stringent crowd safety regulations that have been introduced at all sports stadiums in Britain which sharply reduced the capacity.

In the *Davis Cup* by NEC, there were several major shocks along the way, especially Italy's first round victory over Sweden, finalists for the previous seven years, and Argentina's second round victory over the holders who, without Boris Becker, who were playing as West Germany for the last time.

Several leading players, including Steffi Graf, Martina Navratilova and Monica Seles were disappointingly absent from the *Federation Cup* in Atlanta but one clear message given from both competitions was the re-emergence of the United States as the leading tennis nation. Their *Davis Cup* final triumph over Australia was clearly an emotional moment for team captain, Tom Gorman, who, like Neale Fraser, his opposite number, had thereby experienced the joy of winning the *Davis Cup* both as a player and team captain, guiding others from the side of the court.

In the *Federation Cup*, no-one contributed more to the United States success, with her endeavours both on and off the court, than Jennifer Capriati, aged 14, who, as she continued an altogether remarkable first year on the women's circuit, was unbeaten in her five matches and was also number one cheer leader. As the late Ted Tinling, whose death was one of the saddest events of the tennis year, said after watching Miss Capriati, then still 13, make her senior debut in Boca Raton in March: 'I've just seen a glimpse of tennis in the 1990's . . . and I liked what I saw. Now I shall die happy.'

Miss Capriati has opted out of junior events altogether. Others, such as Magdalena Maleeva, the youngest of the three sisters, combined both but despite winning the junior titles in Australia, Paris and at the US Open, she did not play in the required number of six out of 94 events on the ITF World Junior Circuit to qualify as the world junior champion. Instead the title went to Karina Habsudova.

In the World Youth Cup, Holland, where the number of promising tennis girls aged 16 and under is considerable, scored their first success in their section. In the boys' section, the USSR ended Australia's run of success over the three previous years in an event that is increasingly taking on the guise of being the junior *Davis Cup* and *Federation Cup*.

This review can only scratch the surface of the range of ITF activities. Away from the courts, one of the most important decisions during the year was the introduction of a truly comprehensive and random drug testing programme, adhering to Olympic procedures, which almost certainly helped to encourage both the ATP and WTA to agree upon a much more realistic drug testing policy of their own. It was also agreed that the Wheelchair Tennis Association, which is becoming increasingly active in many parts of the world, should become affiliated to the ITF, and their administrative offices be based with us at Baron's Court, where the necessary work of providing wheelchair ramps, etc has already been carried out. It is just one more happy example of the ITF's determination to offer as many people as possible, whatever their ages, circumstances or abilities, as many opportunities as possible to play tennis to their full potential. In this way at least, tennis, so riddled by political power-play, can also remain a sport.

ITF WORLD CHAMPIONS

The ITF men's World Champion is decided by the men's world champions panel. The ITF Women's World Champion title is awarded to the player who heads the Kraft General Foods points table for the year.

MEN				WOMEN			
1978	Bjorn Borg	1985	Ivan Lendl	1978	Chris Evert	1985	Martina Navratilova
1979	Bjorn Borg	1986	Ivan Lendl	1979	Martina Navratilova	1986	Martina Navratilova
1980	Bjorn Borg	1987	Ivan Lendl	1980	Chris Evert Lloyd	1987	Steffi Graf
1981	John McEnroe	1988	Mats Wilander	1981	Chris Evert Lloyd	1988	Steffi Graf
1982	Jimmy Connors	1989	Boris Becker	1982	Martina Navratilova	1989	Steffi Graf
1983	John McEnroe	1990	Ivan Lendl	1983	Martina Navratilova	1990	Steffi Graf
1984	John McEnroe			1984	Martina Navratilova		

Above: *The victorious American team with the trophy they last held in 1982 (l to r) Andre Agassi, Jim Pugh, Tom Gorman (Capt.), Rick Leach, Michael Chang. (R. Adams)* **Below:** *The vanquished Australians (l to r) Darren Cahill, John Fitzgerald, Neale Fraser (Capt.), Pat Cash, Richard Fromberg.* *(R. Adams)*

THE *DAVIS CUP* by NEC

Andrew Longmore

The story of the USA's victory in the 1990 *Davis Cup* was a mixture of farce, intrigue and fairytale, an episode of *Dallas* written by Hans Christian Anderson. In the end, the American team of Andre Agassi, Michael Chang, Rick Leach and Jim Pugh walked happily off into the Florida sunset clutching the huge trophy which the Americans had waited eight long and painful years to reclaim. But the year had been marked by internal dissent in the team, which reached its height when the ever unpredictable Agassi refused to play in the second round tie against Czechoslovakia and publicly called for the head of Tom Gorman, the mild and gentle team captain. Agassi's suggestion as Gorman's successor was John McEnroe. He was serious too. 'At least he would argue all the linecalls', said Agassi.

The final, in which the USA beat Australia 3–2, was also preceded and, to some extent, soured by dispute. The Australians complained loudly to the International Tennis Federation not just about the United States Tennis Association's decision to play the tie on clay indoors, but about their delay in announcing the surface and the timing of the singles on the first day and the doubles on the second, all of which were designed to give the home team a considerable advantage. Given that, by a stroke of luck, the Australians had played all their matches on grass at home against France, New Zealand and Argentina, there was limited sympathy for much of their criticism, but equally there was no doubt that the USTA gave the spirit of the competition a hefty kick in their desperate attempts to beat their oldest and deadliest rivals.

But first, the happy ending. In front of 50,962 patriotic fans, a record attendance for a *Davis Cup* tie in America, the home team exploited their advantage to the full with Agassi narrowly and Chang easily winning the two singles on the opening day and the doubles pair of Leach and Pugh, who had been a model of solidity all year, applying the finishing touches on the second day. As Leach swept away the winning crosscourt volley to end a courageous fightback by Pat Cash and John Fitzgerald, all the emotions of a torrid year were unleashed. Flags were waved, tears were shed, and another chorus of *God bless America* swelled the futuristic awnings of the Suncoast Dome in St Petersburg. The celebrations were tinged with relief, too, not just at beating an Australian team, which made up for its lack of class by its lust for combat, but at memories of the desperate victory over Austria in the semi-finals.

In the imposing surroundings of the Prater Stadium in Vienna, the Americans had reached the point of no return, with Chang two sets down in the deciding rubber against the ebullient Horst Skoff. Typically, the Asian-American refused to bow to the wishes of 15,000 Viennese and won the third set before bad light and drizzle stopped play for the day. Both players seemed to sense that the momentum of the match had changed and Chang completed his remarkable – and almost inevitable – recovery the following day to win 3–6 6–7 6–4 6–4 6–3. No wonder he led the chorus of sobs when the Cup was won.

While Germany's victory the previous year had been due almost solely to Boris Becker, the USA's victory, their 29th in the *Davis Cup*, was a tribute to strength in depth as well as to the low-key diplomacy of their captain. Gorman used 5 singles players during the year. When Agassi was sulking because he could not take all his entourage with him to Czechoslovakia, Aaron Krickstein came in and calmly won both his singles matches. In the opening round against Mexico, Brad Gilbert and Jay Berger had shouldered the duties.

Australia had been forced to chop and change as well. Their most consistent performer was Wally Masur, who won all six of his singles, three of them – against the Frenchmen Yannick Noah and Henri Leconte in the first round and the Argentine Martin Jaite in the semi-final – in five sets. Neale Fraser was never able to field the same team twice, but, celebrating his fifth decade of *Davis Cup* tennis as player and captain, he has a remarkable ability to make the sum of his teams far greater than its individual parts.

It was true again in the final. Including Chang and Agassi, seven American players were ranked higher than the best Australian, Richard Fromberg, a tall gangling figure from Tasmania, had won two tournaments on clay during an impressive season and was, in Fraser's words, the Australian's 'secret weapon'. With Pat Cash still struggling to find his form after returning from an achilles tendon injury in April and Darren Cahill, who was chosen to play singles, much happier on a faster surface, Fromberg was thrust into the role of No. 1 in his first *Davis Cup* tie. It was a tribute to his confidence and his maturity at the age of 20 that he more than matched Agassi, the world No. 4, for pace and power during three and a half hours of slogging claycourt tennis in the opening singles. Only inexperience when he lost momentum after the ten-minute break and allowed the American just the glimpse of salvation that he needed, and tiredness deprived Fromberg of a remarkable victory and Australia of a precious morale-boosting first point. Until the break, Fromberg had controlled the match, serving solidly, timing his approaches to the net intelligently and surprising Agassi with the power and consistency of his huge forehand. But, to his credit, Agassi, who said he had almost pulled out of the tie with a virus earlier in the week, shook off his lethargy and showed a strength of character his critics – and, for that matter, his recent *Davis Cup* record of played four, lost three – had suggested he did not possess. Crucially, he broke in the first game of the fourth set and as the crowd belatedly found their voices, recovered to win only the second five-set match of his career 4–6 6–2 4–6 6–2 6–4. He had lost four of the previous five and, by his own admission, would have lost that one not long ago, too.

On a surface which reminded him of Roland Garros, Chang was never seriously in danger of defeat by Darren Cahill in the second of the singles on the first day. The Australian did have a point to take the second set, but once that had gone and Chang had taken the tie-break, resistence crumbled. Chang won 6–2 7–6 6–0 in two hours and eleven minutes to leave the Australians in the shadow of a very tall mountain.

Fraser's summary at the end of the first day was accurate enough. 'What's the position? We have to win the doubles to stay in the *Davis Cup*. That's the position'. If John Fitzgerald had found his range on his service returns to convert one of a harvest of break points, if he had held his nerve just long enough to serve out for the fourth set and level the match, they might just have done so, but, in the unheralded Leach, the Australians faced a player who found inspiration at just the right time. The left-hander, who had served the best of the quartet throughout the match, produced an ace and a service winner to take the tie-break 7–2 and the match 6–4 6–2 3–6 7–6. It brought the Americans their first *Davis Cup* since they beat France in Grenoble, also on clay, in 1982, and only two years after they had been relegated from the world group. It also ended the recent domination of the *Davis Cup* by Sweden and West Germany, who had won five of the last six finals but, without Edberg and Becker respectively, failed to go beyond the second round this year.

Sweden were surprisingly and ecstatically defeated by Italy in the first round and had to suffer the indignity of beating Finland to avoid relegation. Germany did rather better. Without Becker, who had decided to take a rest from the pressures of *Davis Cup* after his exertions in 1988 and 1989, an inexperienced German team went into the lion's den against Argentina and very nearly emerged intact. Leading by two rubbers to one, Michael Stich had to be drafted in to play his first 'live' *Davis Cup* singles in place of Jens Wohrmann, who was unwell. Stich made a pretty good fist of it too, stretching Jaite deep into the fifth set before Argentina levelled the tie. Carl-Uwe Steeb, however, could find none of his customary fighting spirit and his straight sets loss to Alberto Mancini ended Germany's run of eight wins, stretching back to early 1987. Like Sweden, France had to win a relegation match, which they did with some ease against Britain. Switzerland and The Netherlands were relegated from the world group and replaced by Belgium and Canada, promoted for the first time.

Other mentions in dispatches should go to Thomas Muster, who won all his six singles matches in taking Austria to the brink of their first final and to a young New Zealander called

Brett Steven, who lost the first two sets 6–0 6–1 to Fitzgerald in the second round and recovered to win the next three.

War and politics permitting, 88 nations will compete in the 1991 *Davis Cup* when, for the first time, singles players will be ranked according to the computer, the No. 1 player meeting the opposition's No. 2 on the opening day and the two No. 1s playing the third singles. The aim of the new ruling is to ensure that more ties go into the third day.

THE *DAVIS CUP* by NEC, 1990

WORLD GROUP

FIRST ROUND – **F.R. Germany d. Netherlands 3–2, Bremen** (C. Steeb d. M. Schapers 6–1 4–6 6–3 6–3; E. Jelen d. T. Nijssen 7–6 7–5 3–6 6–3; Jelen/M. Stich d. Nijssen/Schapers 6–4 6–2 5–7 6–4; Stich lost to Nijssen 6–7 5–7 1–6; Jelen lost to Schapers 4–6 4–6 4–6); **Argentina d. Israel 3–0, Buenos Aires** (A. Mancini d. G. Bloom 6–2 7–6 6–2; M. Jaite d. A. Mansdorf 6–4 6–3 6–2; J. Frana/G. Luza d. Mansdorf/S. Perkiss 6–3 6–0 7–6; Jaite vs Bloom and Mancini vs Mansdorf cancelled dued to rain); **New Zealand d. Yugoslavia 3–2, Christchurch** (K. Evernden d. S. Zivojinovic 6–7 3–6 6–3 6–2 6–4; B. Steven d. G. Prpic 6–4 6–2 6–4; Ivanisevic/S. Zivojinovic d. Evernden/S. Guy 7–5 6–3 6–7 7–5; Evernden d. Prpic 6–0 2–6 6–7 6–3 6–2; Steven lost to Zivojinovic 7–5 7–6 7–5); **Australia d. France 3–2, Perth** (D. Cahill lost to H. Leconte 3–6 5–7 3–6; W. Masur d. Y. Noah 4–6 6–3 4–6 6–3 6–2; P. Cash/J. Fitzgerald d. G. Forget/Noah 7–6 6–4 6–4; Masur d. Leconte 6–4 3–6 6–3 2–6 6–4; Cahill lost to Noah 6–4 4–6); **Czechoslovakia d. Switzerland 5–0, Prague** (M. Srejber d. M. Rosset 6–3 6–2 6–4; M. Mecir d. J. Hlasek 7–6 6–2 6–1; P. Korda/Srejber d. H. Guenthardt/Hlasek 6–4 2–6 7–6 7–6; Mecir d. Rosset 6–7 6–1 6–3; Srejber d. Hlasek 3–6 6–4 7–5); **USA d. Mexico 4–0, Carlsbad** (J. Berger d. J. Lozano 6–7 6–4 6–3 6–3; B. Gilbert d. L. Lavalle 6–3 6–1 7–6; R. Leach/J. Pugh d. Lavalle/Lozano 6–4 6–7 7–5 6–1; Gilbert d. Lozano 4–6 6–2 6–3; Berger vs Lavalle 4–1 2–30/0, rained off); **Austria d. Spain 3–2, Barcelona** (T. Muster d. E. Sanchez 1–6 6–2 4–6 6–3 6–4; H. Skoff d. S. Bruguera 6–4 7–5 6–0; A. Antonitsch/Muster lost to S. Casal/Sanchez 6–1 3–6 6–7 4–6; Muster d. Bruguera 7–5 6–1 7–6; Skoff lost to Sanchez 3–6 3–6); **Italy d. Sweden 3–2, Cagliari** (P. Cane d. J. Svensson 3–6 2–6 6–3 6–3 6–1; O. Camporese lost to M. Wilander 4–6 4–6 7–5 7–6 4–6; D. Nargiso/Cane d. J. Gunnarsson/A. Jarryd 7–5 6–1 7–5; Camporese lost to Svensson 7–6 1–6 3–6 1–6; Cane d. Wilander 6–4 3–6 4–6 7–5 7–5).

QUARTER FINALS – **Argentina d. F.R. Germany 3–2, Buenos Aires** (A. Mancini d. J. Wohrmann 7–5 4–6 7–6 7–6; M. Jaite lost to C. Steeb 3–6 7–6 4–6 3–6; J. Frana/G. Luza lost to M. Stich/E. Jelen 2–6 6–7 2–6; Jaite d. Stich 4–6 6–4 6–1 1–6 6–3; Mancini d. Steeb 7–6 6–3 6–4); **Australia d. New Zealand 3–2, Milton** (J. Fitzgerald lost to B. Steven 6–1 6–0 3–6 4–6 2–6; W. Masur d. K. Evernden 6–3 7–6 6–1; D. Cahill/M. Kratzmann d. Evernden/D. Lewis 5–6 3 7–6; Masur d. Steven 7–5 6–2 6–4; Fitzgerald lost to Evernden 5–7 7–6 1–6); **USA d. Czechoslovakia 4–1, Prague** (A. Krickstein d. M. Srejber 4–6 7–6 7–6 6–2; B. Gilbert lost to P. Korda 2–6 3–6 3–6; R. Leach/J. Pugh d. Srejber/Korda 6–4 6–4; Krickstein d. Korda 6–2 6–3 1–6 6–3; Gilbert d. K. Novacek 6–2 6–1); **Austria d. Italy 5–0, Vienna** (H. Skoff d. D. Nargiso 6–0 6–0 6–2; T. Muster d. P. Cane 7–5 7–5 1–6 4–6 6–3; A. Antonitsch/Muster d. Nargiso/Cane 7–6 1–6 6–2 6–2; Skoff d. C. Pistolesi 6–4 6–1; Muster d. Nargiso 6–3 6–2).

SEMI-FINALS – **Australia d. Argentina 5–0, Sydney** (P. Cash d. A. Mancini 6–1 6–1 6–2; W. Masur d. M. Jaite 3–6 6–7 6–4 6–0 6–2; D. Cahill/M. Kratzmann d. J. Frana/C. Miniussi 3–6 7–6 7–6 4–6 15–13; Cash d. Jaite 7–5 6–2; Masur d. Frana 6–2 6–2); **USA d. Austria 3–2, Vienna** (M. Chang lost to T. Muster 6–4 2–6 2–6 4–6; A. Agassi d. H. Skoff 7–6 6–0 6–1; R. Leach/J. Pugh d. Muster/A. Antonitsch 7–6 3–6 4–0 7–5; Agassi lost to Muster 2–6 6–7; Chang d. Skoff 3–6 6–7 6–4 6–4 6–3).

FINAL – **USA d. Australia 3–2, St. Petersburg** (A. Agassi d. R. Fromberg 4–6 6–2 4–6 6–2 6–4; M. Chang d. D. Cahill 6–2 7–6 6–0; R. Leach/J. Pugh d. P. Cash/J. Fitzgerald 6–4 6–2 3–6 7–6; Agassi lost to Cahill 4–6 6–4 (ret); Chang lost to Fromberg 5–7 6–2 3–6).

QUALIFYING ROUND FOR WORLD GROUP 1991

Spain d. USSR 4–1, Moscow (S. Bruguera d. A. Chesnokov 6–2 6–7 6–2 6–3; E. Sanchez d. A. Cherkasov 6–3 6–7 6–3 6–4; S. Casal/Sanchez d. A. Volkov/V. Gabrichidze 4–6 6–3 6–3 4–6 6–3; Bruguera lost to Cherkasov 4–6 6–7; Sanchez d. Chesnokov 7–6 7–5); **Mexico d. Uruguay 5–0, Mexico City** (L. Lavalle d. D. Perez 6–7 6–2 4–6 6–3 6–2; J. Lozano d. M. Filippini 6–4 6–4 6–2; Lozano/L. Herrera d. Perez/Filippini 6–4 7–6 4–6 7–5; Lozano d. V. Caldarelli 3–6 6–3 6–1; O. Fernandez d. Filippini 7–5 6–3); **Canada d. Netherlands 3–2, Toronto** (C. Pridham lost to M. Koevermans 6–7 4–6 3–6; G. Connell d. P. Haarhuis 7–6 6–4 6–4; Connell/G. Michibata d. Haarhuis/Koevermans 7–6 7–6 6–2; Pridham lost to Haarhuis 6–4 3–6 0–6 5–7; Connell d. Koevermans 7–6 7–6 6–3); **Yugoslavia d. Switzerland 3–2, Split** (G. Ivanisevic d. M. Rosset 6–4 4–6 6–7 6–3 6–2; G. Prpic lost to J. Hlasek 6–3

6–4 6–7 4–6; Ivanisevic/Prpic d. Rosset/Hlasek 3–6 6–3 6–4 6–2; Ivanisevic d. C. Mezzadri 6–1 6–4 6–2; Prpic lost to Rosset 4–6 6–7); *Sweden d. Finland 5–0, Vasteras* (S. Edberg d. A. Rahunen 6–1 6–1 7–6; J. Svensson d. V. Paloheimo 6–1 6–1 6–1; Edberg/P. Lundgren d. Paloheimo/O. Rahnasto 6–2 6–1 6–2; Edberg d. Paloheimo 3–6 6–4 6–0; Svensson d. Rahunen 6–4 6–0); *France d. Great Britain 5–0, London* (H. Leconte d. N. Brown 6–3 7–6 6–2; G. Forget d. J. Bates 2–6 7–6 6–4 6–1; Leconte/Forget d. A. Castle/Bates 6–1 6–4 6–4; Leconte d. Bates 7–6 6–0; Forget d. Brown 6–3 6–2); *Belgium d. Korea 4–1, Brussels* (B. Wuyts d. N. Bae 3–6 3–6 6–0 6–1 6–2; E. Masso d. J. Kim 6–3 6–1 6–3; E. Masso/X. Daufresne lost to Kim/J. Yoo 6–7 6–2 3–6 4–6; Masso d. Bae 6–4 6–1 6–1; Wuyts d. Kim 7–5 6–4); *Israel d. China 5–0, Tel Aviv* (A. Mansdorf d. L. Xiaocheng 6–4 6–2 6–0; G. Bloom d. L. Di 6–1 6–0 6–1; Mansdorf/S. Perkiss d. Xiaocheng/Z. Jiaheng 6–4 6–4 7–5; Bloom d. Xiaocheng 6–3 6–1; Mansdorf d. Di 6–3 6–3).

ZONAL COMPETITION

GROUP 1

EURO/AFRICAN ZONE

FIRST ROUND – Portugal d. Ghana 5–0, Accra (J. Cunhaesilva d. K. Atiso 6–4 6–4 6–0; N. Marques d. F. Ofori 7–6 6–4 6–3; Cunhaesilva/Marques d. Atiso/Ofori 6–3 6–4 6–3; Cunhaesilva d. Ofori 4–6 7–6 15–13; Marques d. Atiso 6–1 7–5); *Romania d. Ireland 3–2, Dublin* (G. Cosac lost to E. Collins 4–6 4–6 6–3 6–3 7–9; A. Marcu lost to P. Wright 4–6 6–2 3–6 6–7; Cosac/F. Segarceanu d. O. Casey/Wright 6–1 7–6 4–6 7–6; Marcu d. Collins 7–6 6–7 6–1 6–4; Cosac d. Wright 3–6 4–6 6–3 6–4 6–3); *Finland d. Nigeria 4–1, Lagos* (V. Paloheimo d. S. Akinloye 6–0 6–3 6–3; A. Rahunen d. O. Odizor 7–6 6–1 6–0; Paloheimo/O. Rahnasto d. Odizor/Y. Suleiman 6–3 2–6 6–7 6–4 6–4; Rahunen d. Akinloye 7–6 6–3; Paloheimo lost to Odizor 6–2 2–6 2–6).

FINAL PLAY-OFFS – USSR d. Portugal 4–1, Kiev (A. Cherkasov lost to N. Marques 7–6 6–2 2–6 3–6 4–6; A. Chesnokov d. J. Cunha E. Silva 6–3 6–2 7–5; Chesnokov/Poliakov d. Cunha E. Silva/Marques 7–6 6–3 7–6; Chesnokov d. Marques 6–4 3–6 6–3 6–4; Cherkasov d. Cunha E Silva 6–2 6–2); *Great Britain d. Romania 3–2, Bucharest* (D. Sapsford d. G. Cosac 4–6 6–1 6–2 6–3; J. Bates lost to F. Segarceanu 5–7 1–6 1–6; Bates/A. Castle d. Cosac/Segarceanu 6–3 6–3 6–2; Bates d. Cosac 3–6 6–1 6–2 6–2; Sapsford lost to Segarceanu 3–6 6–4 3–6); *Belgium d. Hungary 4–1, Brussels* (E. Masso d. S. Noszaly 6–7 6–2 6–4 7–6; B. Wuyts d. A. Lanyi 6–1 6–1 6–2; X. Daufresne/D. Langaskens lost to Lanyi/L. Markovits 4–6 3–6 6–4 6–7; Masso d. Lanyi 6–2 4–6 7–5 6–3; Wuyts d. Noszaly 6–1 6–1); *Finland d. Denmark 3–2, Aarhus* (A. Rahunen d. M. Christensen 7–5 7–6 6–3; V. Paloheimo lost to M. Tauson 1–6 5–7 6–3 6–4 3–6; Paloheimo/O. Rahnasto d. M. Mortensen/Tauson 6–4 6–4 6–4; Paloheimo d. Christensen 1–6 4–6 6–3 7–5 6–4; Rahunen lost to Tauson 3–6 2–6).

PLAY-OFF FOR RELEGATION – Ireland d. Ghana 3–2, Accra (P. Wright d. K. Dowuona 6–4 6–7 6–3 6–1; E. Collins d. F. Ofori 7–6 7–6 3–6 6–3; Collins/Wright d. Dowuona/Ofori 1–6 5–7 6–2 6–2 11–9; Wright lost to Ofori 2–6 3–6; M. Nugent lost to Dowuona 4–6 1–6).

ASIA/OCEANIA ZONE

PRELIMINARY ROUND – China d. Pakistan 5–0, Guangzhou (P. Bing d. H. Ul Haq 6–0 6–2 6–0; Z. Jiuhua d. R. Malik 6–1 6–3 6–0; X. Jiaping/L Shuhua d. Ul Haq/Malik 6–2 6–1 6–2; Jiuhua d. Ul Haq 6–4 6–2; Bing d. Malik 7–5 6–1).

FIRST ROUND – China d. Philippines 5–0, Shanghai (X. Jiaping d. R. So 4–6 5–7 6–4 6–3 6–2; P. Bing d. D. Pila 6–0 6–0 6–0; Bing/L. Shuhua d. So/F. Barrientos 6–4 6–4 2–6 7–6; Bing d. So 6–4 6–3; Jiaping d. Pila 6–2 6–4); *India d. Japan 4–1, Chandigarh* (Z. Ali d. H. Tanizawa 6–4 6–2 6–3; S. Vasudevan d. S. Matsuoka 6–4 6–4 1 7–6; Ali/L. Paes d. S. Matsuoka/S. Ota 4–6 6–3 6–4 4–6 18–16; Vasudevan d. Tanizawa 6–2 6–2; Ali lost to Shuzo 1–6 6–7).

FINAL PLAY-OFFS – China d. Indonesia 4–1, Beijing (X. Jiaping d. D. Heryanto 3–6 6–3 7–5 2–6 6–3; P. Bing d. Suharyadi 3–6 3–6 6–4 6–1 6–3; Bing/L. Shuhua lost to Heryanto/Wiryawan 6–2 4–6 6–7 6–3 4–6; Bing d. Heryanto 6–3 6–1 6–2; Jiaping d. Suharyadi 7–5 6–0); *Korea d. India 5–0, Seoul* (B. Kim d. S. Vasudevan 6–7 3–6 6–4 6–0 7–5; J. Kim d. Z. Ali 6–3 6–2 6–4; J. Yoo/N. Bae d. Ali/L. Paes 2–6 6–0 6–1 3–6 9–7; J. Kim d. R. Rajpal 6–1 6–2; B. Kim d. Paes 7–6 6–0).

AMERICAN ZONE

FIRST ROUND – Canada d. Brazil 4–1, Vancouver (G. Connell d. D. Marcelino 7–5 6–3 6–4; A. Sznajder d. L. Mattar 6–4 3–6 7–6 6–4; Connell/G. Michibata d. Mattar/F. Roese 6–4 7–5 7–5; Connell lost to Mattar 7–6 5–7 6–8; Sznajder d. Marcelino 6–4 6–2); *Uruguary d. Chile 3–2, Montevideo* (D. Perez lost to P. Rebolledo 6–3 4–6 2–6 0–6; M. Filippini d. S. Cortes 7–5 6–1 6–2; V. Caldarelli/Filippini lost to C. Araya/Rebolledo 3–6 4–6 4–6; Perez d. Cortes 6–3 6–2 6–2; Filippini d. Rebolledo 6–1 7–5 6–0).

FINAL PLAY-OFFS – Canada d. Paraguay 5–0, Asuncion (A. Sznajder d. H. Chapacu 6–2 6–4 6–2; M. Wostenholme d. V. Pecci 6–4 6–2 3–6 6–0; G. Connell/G. Michibata d. Pecci/Chapacu 6–1 6–2 6–2;

Wostenholme d. R. Mena 6–1 6–0; Sznajder d. R. Alvarenga 6–4 6–1); **Uruguay d. Peru 4–1, Montevideo** (D. Perez d. J. Yzaga 6–4 6–2 3–6 1–6 9–7; M. Filippini d. A. Aramburu 5–7 6–0 6–1 6–2; N. Zurmendi/D. Montes de Oca lost to Yzaga/C. Di Laura 4–6 2–6 5–7; Filippini d. Yzaga 6–1 6–3 6–4; Perez d. Aramburu 6–1 2–6 6–2).
PLAY-OFF FOR RELEGATION – Brazil d. Chile 4–1, Brasilia (F. Roese d. J. Fernandez 6–1 6–3 6–2; L. Mattar d. G. Vacarezza 7–6 6–3 6–3; M. Menezes/D. Marcelino d. P. Rebolledo/C. Araya 6–7 6–4 7–6 6–4; Roese d. Vacarezza 6–2 6–2; Menezet lost to Fernandez 4–6 4–6).

GROUP II

EUROPEAN ZONE

FIRST ROUND – Bulgaria d. Cyprus 5–0, Nicosia (R. Rainov d. Y. Hadjigeorgiou 6–1 6–2 6–3; I. Keskinov d. A. Papamichael 6–4 7–5 6–1; Keskinov/M. Velev d. Hadjigeorgiou/N. Neocleous 6–1 6–1 6–4; Rainov d. Papamichael 6–3 6–4; Keskinov d. Hadjigeorgiou 6–1 6–1).
QUARTER-FINALS – Bulgaria d. Greece 5–0, Sofia (M. Velv d. G. Kalovelonis 6–3 6–4 6–0; I. Keskinov d. C. Efremoglou 6–3 7–5 6–1; S. Tzvetkov/Velev d. Kalovelonis/T. Rigas 6–7 1–6 6–2 6–1 6–3; Velev d. Efremoglou 6–2 7–5; Keskinov d. Kalovelonis 6–2 6–3); **Turkey d. Malta 3–2, Izmir** (A. Karagoz d. G. Asciak 6–0 6–1 6–4; M. Ertunga lost to C. Gatt 5–7 3–6 0–6; Karagoz/Ertunga lost to Asciak/Gatt 4–6 4–6 7–5 4–6; Karagoz d. Gatt 6–7 7–6 6–3 4–6 8–6; Ertunga d. Asciak 5–7 6–1 1–6 6–3 6–2); **Poland d. Luxembourg 4–1, Luxembourg** (T. Iwanski d. J. Radoux 6–7 6–3 7–6 4–6 6–3; W. Kowalski d. J. Goudenbour 6–3 6–4 6–2; Kowalski/L. Sidor lost to Goudenbour/Radoux 4–6 6–7 1–6; Kowalski d. Radoux 6–1 6–4 6–3; Iwanski d. Goudenbour 7–5 6–4); **Norway d. Monaco 4–1, Monte Carlo** (A. Haaseth d. J. Seguin 6–7 6–3 6–4 3–6 6–2; C. Ruud d. G. Ganancia 5–7 6–3 6–2 6–2; Ruud/A. Rofsen d. C. Boggetti/J. Vincileoni 6–4 6–7 5–7 6–2 6–3; Ruud d. Seguin 6–4 4–6 7–5; Haaseth lost to Ganancia 0–6 5–7).
SEMI-FINALS – Poland d. Bulgaria 4–1, Warsaw (T. Iwanski d. M. Velev 6–3 6–2 6–3; W. Kowalski d. I. Keskinov 6–3 6–4 1–6 7–6; Kowalski/Iwanski d. Velev/Tzvetkov 3–6 6–4 6–1 6–2; Iwanski lost to Keskinov 6–7 2–6; Kowalski d. Velev 7–6 7–5); **Norway d. Turkey 3–2, Izmir** (A. Haaseth lost to A. Karagoz 3–6 6–0 2–6 4–6; B.-O. Pedersen d. M. Ertunga 6–2 6–1 6–1; Pedersen/Rolfsen d. Askara/Karagoz 7–6 7–6 6–1; Haaseth d. Ertunga 6–0 6–1 6–4; Karagoz d. Raabe 6–3 6–4).
FINAL – Poland d. Norway 4–1, Warsaw (W. Kowalski d. B.-O. Pedersen d. 7–6 6–0 6–4 6–4; Iwanski d. C. Ruud 6–2 6–4 6–3; Fibak/Kowalski lost to Pedersen/Rolfsen 3–6 6–3 6–7 6–2 4–6; Kowalski d. Ruud 6–3 6–0 6–0; Iwanski d. B.-O. Pedersen 1–6 7–6 8–6).

AFRICAN ZONE

FIRST ROUND – Togo w/o Libya; Egypt d. Algeria 4–1, Algiers (A. El-Mehelmy lost to R. Galou 6–4 5–7 6–7 6–1 4–6; T. El-Sawy d. M. Zehar 6–3 6–7 7–6 6–1; El Aroussy/K. El-Sawy d. Galou/Zehar 7–6 6–2 7–6; El-Sawy d. Galou 6–1 6–3 6–1; El-Salawy d. A. Hamerlaine 7–5 3–6 6–2 6–4); **Côte d'Ivoire d. Kenya 4–1, Abidjan** (C. N'Goran d. E. Polo 6–4 6–3 6–2; C.-J. Nabi d. K. Bhardwaj 6–3 6–2 6–2; E. N'Goran/N'Goran d. Bhardwaj/N. Oduor 6–1 6–3 6–4; N'Goran d. Bhardwaj 7–5 6–2; Nabi lost to Polo 4–6 5–7).
QUARTER-FINALS – Togo d. Senegal 5–0, Lome (G. Gbedey d. N. Kabaz 6–2 6–2 6–2; M. Segbeaya d. A. Berthe 6–3 6–3 6–2; Gbedey/Segbeaya d. Berthe/F. Berthe 6–3 6–7 5–7 6–4 7–5; Segbeaya d. Kabaz 6–1 6–2; Gbedey d. A. Berthe 6–1 6–2); **Morocco d. Egypt 5–0, Cairo** (O. Khalid d. T. El Sawy 7–5 6–4 6–1; A. Karim d. A. El Mihelmy 6–4 1–6 6–3 6–7 6–3; Khalid/Karim d. El Mihelmy/El Sawy 6–7 7–6 6–3 6–4; R. Mohamed d. K. El Sallawy 6–2 6–1; Karim d. El Sawy 4–6 6–4 7–5); **Côte d'Ivoire d. Cameroon 5–0, Abidjan** (J.-J. Kouassi d. Y. Auzoux 6–2 6–1 6–2; C. N'Goran d. L. Kemajou 6–2 6–0 1–0 (ret.); N'Goran/E. N'Goran d. Auzoux/J. Ekono 6–3 3–4 6–6 3; C. N'Goran d. Auzoux 6–1 6–2; Kouassi d. J. Oyebog 6–2 6–1); **Zimbabwe d. Zambia 4–1, Lusaka** (G. Rodger d. S. Kangwa 6–2 3–6 3–6 6–4 6–2; G. Thomson lost to F. Kangwa 3–6 6–3 4–6 3–6; M. Birch/M. Lock d. F. Kangwa/T. Simunyola 6–2 6–3 7–6; Rodger d. F. Kangwa 7–6 7–6 7–6; Thomson d. S. Kangwa 6–4 6–3).
SEMI-FINALS – Morocco d. Togo 5–0, Casablanca (M. Ridaoui d. G. Gbedey 6–2 6–1 3–6 6–4; K. Outaleb d. M. Segbeaya 7–6 3–6 6–1 6–4; Outaleb/Ridaoui d. Segbeaya/Gbedey 6–1 6–0 1–6 6–0; Ridaoui d. Segbeaya 6–7 6–3 6–2; Outaleb d. Gbedey 6–0 6–1); **Zimbabwe d. Côte d'Ivoire 5–0, Harare** (O. Lourenco d. J.-C. Nabi 6–2 6–2 4–6 2–6 7–5; B. Black d. E. N'Goran 6–0 6–2, 6–1; Black/Rodger d. N'Goran/Ilou 6–3 6–3 6–0; C. Wilson d. N'Goran 6–2 6–3; Black d. L. Ilou 6–1 6–0).
FINAL – Morocco d. Zimbabwe 4–1, Casablanca (K. Alami d. O. Lourenco 2–6 6–1 6–3 7–5; K. Outaleb lost to B. Black 6–2 5–7 2–6 2–6; Alami/Ridaoui d. Black/Lourenco 6–4 6–4 7–6; Y. El Aynaoui d. O. Lourenco 6–1 6–4 7–5; Alami d. Black 7–6 6–3).

AMERICAN ZONE

FIRST ROUND – Haiti d. Trinidad & Tobago 5–0, Port-of-Spain (R. Agenor d. M. Webster 6–1 6–1 6–0; B. Lacombe d. O. Adams 6–1 6–4 6–4; Agenor/B. Lamothe d. Adams/D. Attong 6–1 6–4 7–6;

Agenor d. Adams 6–0 6–3; Lacombe d. Webster 6–1 7–6); *Venezuela d. Jamaica 5–0, Caracas* (C. Claverie d. D. Burke 6–3 6–4 3–6 6–4; M. Ruah d. P Campbell 4–6 6–3 6–0 6–1; A. Mora/Ruah d. Burke/Campbell 6–3 7–6 7–6; Claverie d. Campbell 6–2 6–2; Ruah d. Burke 6–3 6–3); *Colombia d. Guatemala 4–1, Cali* (M. Hadad d. D. Chavez 6–0 6–2 6–3; A. Jordan d. F. Sical 6–4 6–1 7–5; J. Cortes/M. Tobon lost to Chavez/Sical 6–4 1–6 4–6 6–4 4–6; Jordan d. Chavez 7–6 7–5 6–1; Hadad d. Sical 6–1 6–4); *Dominican Republic d. Costa Rica 3–2, Santo Domingo* (G. de Leon lost to K. Thome 6–1 3–6 4–6 1–6; R. Moreno d. R. Brenes 6–1 6–2 6–1; Moreno/M. Olivares lost to K. Thome/F. Thome 2–6 6–4 3–6 4–6; de Leon d. Brenes 6–1 6–2 6–2; Moreno d. K. Thome 3–6 6–4 3–6 6–4 6–1); *Barbados d. Bolivia 3–2, St. Michael* (H. Ashby d. J. Medrano 4–6 7–5 6–1 6–0; A. Clarke lost to O. Blacutt 6–7 3–6 4–6; Ashby/B. Frost d. R. Aguirre/Blacutt 6–2 6–3 6–7 6–4; J. Jacker Jnr lost to Medrano 2–6 7–5 1–6 4–6; Ashby d. Blacutt 6–2 6–4 6–2).

QUARTER-FINALS – Ecuador d. Haiti 3–2, Port-au-Prince (R. Viver d. B. Lacombe 6–4 3–6 6–4 6–3; G. Carneade lost to R. Agenor 2–6 6–4 3–6 6–4 3–6; Agenor/R. Lamothe lost to Carneade/Campana 5–7 6–7 3–6; Viver lost to Agenor 4–6 6–3 5–7 1–6; Carneade d. Lacombe 6–2 6–3 6–3); *Cuba d. Venezuela 4–1, Matanzas* (M. Tabares Perez d. M. Ruah 6–4 6–1 6–2; J. Pino Perez lost to C. Claverie 3–6 3–6 4–7–6 6–3; Tabares Perez/Pino Perez d. Claverie/A. Mora 3–6 6–4 6–4 6–1; Tabares Peres d. Claverie 6–7 6–2 6–3 6–2; Pino Perez d. Ruah 6–1 6–4); *Colombia d. Dominican Republic 4–1, Santo Domingo* (A. Jordan d. G. de Leon 6–2 6–3 6–2; M. Hadad lost to R. Moreno 6–3 3–6 6–2 2–6 2–6; Jordan/Hadad d. Moreno/A. Schad 6–2 6–3 6–4; Hadad d. de Leon 6–2 6–2 6–2; Jordan d. Moreno 6–2 6–3); *Barbados d. Bahamas 4–1, St. Michael* (R. Ashby d. R. Smith 7–6 6–3 6–2; J. Tasker lost to J. Farrington 1–6 2–6 0–6; Ashby/B. Frost d. Smith/Farrington 7–5 4–6 4–6 7–6 6–4; Ashby d. Farrington 6–2 5–7 6–4 6–2; Frost d. S. Cartwright 6–1 6–4).

SEMI-FINALS – Cuba d. Ecuador 4–1, Havana (M. Tabares d. A. Alarcon 6–1 6–0 6–2; J. Pino d. G. Carneade 6–0 6–1 7–5; Tabares/Pino d. Carneade/Linger 6–4 6–7 6–4 2–1 (ret); W. Henry lost to Alarcon 4–6 4–6; Tabares d. P. Campana 6–2 7–6); *Colombia d. Barbados 4–1, St. Peter* (A. Jordan d. R. Ashby 4–6 6–3 7–6 6–3; M. Tobon d. R. Taylor 6–7 6–0 6–3 6–4; Cortes/Jordan d. Ashby/Frost 6–4 6–4 6–4; Jordan d. Taylor 6–3 6–2; Tobon lost to Ashby 6–7 3–6).

FINAL – Cuba d. Colombia 3–2, Havana (M. Tabares d. M. Tobon 7–5 7–5 6–4; J. Pino lost to A. Jordan 2–6 6–3 2–6 4–6; Tabares/Pino d. Jordan/Cortez 6–1 7–5 6–3; Pino d. Tobon 6–4 6–3 3–6 6–1; Tabares lost to Jordan 6–7 6–1 10–12).

ASIA/OCEANIA ZONE

FIRST ROUND – Malaysia d. Jordan 5–0, Amman (A. Malik d. A. Abujaber 6–1 6–0 6–1; V. Selvam d. H. Alali 6–3 7–6 6–2; Malik/Selvam d. Alali/E. Shahadeh 6–2 6–1 6–4; K. Vhei d. F. Hammadi 6–1 6–2 6–1; U. Muralidharan d. Abujaber 6–4 6–1); *Chinese Taipei d. Singapore 5–0, Singapore* (L. Chung-Hsing d. H. Sidek 7–5 7–6 6–2; L. Yu-Hui d. V. Pereira 4–6 6–3 7–5 6–1; H.-J. Hsu/Yu-Hui d. Pereira/Sidek 6–2 6–4 6–4; Chung-Hsing d. Pereira 6–4 6–3; Yu-Hui d. S. Liu 6–1 6–2)); *Bahrain d. Iraq 3–2, Manama* (M. Ahmed Saleh lost to A. Hussain Kadum 2–6 5–7 3–6; E. Jaffar Abdul Aal d. K. Hussain Kadum 6–2 7–6 2–6 6–1; Jaffar Abdul Aal/A. Rashid Shehad d. A. Hussain Kadum/K. Hussain Kadum 6–4 7–6 7–6; M. Ahmed Saleh lost to K. Hussain Kadum 0–6 4–6 2–6; Jaffar Abdul Aal d. A. Hussain Kadum 6–4 6–4 6–1 6–0); *Kuwait d. Syria 4–1, Hawalli* (K. Ashkanani d. S. Mourad 7–5 6–4 2–6 6–2; K. Hassan Rashed d. D. Dawoodian 7–6 7–6 6–2; A. Alashwak/Ashkanani d. Dawoodian/A. Hafez 6–4 6–4 6–1; T. Hadeed lost to Dawoodian 3–6 3–6; Hassan Rashed d. S. Mourad 6–7 6–3 6–3).

QUARTER-FINALS – Hong Kong d. Malaysia 4–1, Kuala Lumpur) (M. Bailey d. V. Selvam 0–6 6–2 6–4 2–6 8–6; C. Grant d. M. Dharan 6–3 6–2 6–2; R. Harrison/P. Lui d. Selvam/K. Ka Vhei 7–6 3–6 6–3 6–0; Grant lost to Selvam 6–7 4–6; Bailey d. Dharan 6–4 6–2); *Chinese Taipei d. Bangladesh 5–0, Dhaka* (L. Yu-Hui d. Hiralal 6–1 6–1 6–4; L. Chung-Hsing d. F. Rahman 6–2 6–3 7–5; H.-J. Hsu/Chung Tse Ming d. F. Rahman/M. Rahman 6–2 6–1 4–6 7–6; Chung-Hsing d. Hiralal 6–1 6–1; Yu-Hui d. F. Rahman 6–1 6–3); *Sri Lanka d. Bahrain 4–1, Colombo* (U. Walloopillai d. E. Jaffar Abdul Aal 6–1 6–2 6–1; A. Fernando d. N. Jafar Ali Abdul A'al 6–0 6–0 6–1; Fernando/R. de Silva d. E. Jaffar Abdul Aal/A. Rashid Shehad 6–2 6–0 6–0; Walloopillai d. N. Jafar Ali Abdul A'al 6–1 6–0; S. Wijemanne lost to E. Jafar Ali Abdul A'al 6–1 6–7 5–7); *Thailand d. Kuwait 5–0, Hawalli* (W. Thongkamchoo d. K. Rashed 6–4 6–1 6–0; T. Srichaphan d. A. Al-Ashwak 7–5 6–4 6–4; N. Srichaphan/V. Sumrey d. K. Ashkanani/Rashed 6–4 6–2 2–6 6–1; T. Srichaphan d. Rashed 6–2 6–2; Thongkamchoo d. Al-Ashwak 6–4 6–0).

SEMI-FINALS – Hong Kong d. Chinese Taipei 4–1, Kowloon (M. Bailey d. L. Chung-Hsing 1–6 6–3 7–6 6–0; C. Grant d. L. Yu-Hui 3–6 7–6 6–2 6–1; Lui/Harrison lost to Chung-Hsing/Huang-Jang 6–4 3–6 6–7 6–3 6–3 6–8; Bailey d. Yu-Hui 3–6 7–6 6–3; Grant d. Chung-Hsing 6–3 6–4); *Thailand d. Sri Lanka 4–1, Colombo* (S. Thanakorn d. U. Walloopillai 6–2 7–5 7–5; T. Woraphol d. A. Fernando 6–7 5–7 6–0 6–3 6–2; Phnomkorn/Vittaya d. Fernando/R. de Silva 7–5 7–6 7–6; Thanakorn lost to de Silva 4–6 6–7 6–3 6–7; Woraphol d. J. Wijeyesekara 6–4 6–4 6–1).

FINAL – Thailand d. Hong Kong 3–2, Bangkok (W. Thongkamchoo lost to C. Grant 1–6 6–3 3–6 3–6; T. Srichapan d. M. Bailey 6–2 6–3 6–2; Pladchurnil/Samrej lost to Bailey/Grant 5–7 3–6 0–6; Thongkamchoo d. Bailey 7–5 3–6 6–3 6–2; Srichapan d. Grant 4–6 7–5 6–3 6–1).

DAVIS CUP **PRIZE MONEY** (provided by NEC)

WORLD GROUP COMPETITION: Champion Nation $316,000. Runner-up $158,000. Semi-finalists $119,000. Quarter-finalists $71,000. First-round winners $26,000. Qualifying-round winners $20,000. Qualifying-round losers $14,000.
ZONAL COMPETITION: Group 1: $4,500 per tie. ***Bonuses:*** Second-round winners $3,000. First-round winners $2,000. Play-off/preliminary round winners $1,000. ***Group II:*** $3,000 per tie. ***Bonuses:*** Winners $3,500. Semi-finalists $2,000. Quarter-finalists $1,000. First round winners $1,000.

Qualifying Round

Zonal Winners and World Group First Round Losers	Promoted to World Group 1991
FRANCE	FRANCE
Great Britain	5–0
Canada	Canada
Netherlands	3–2
SPAIN	SPAIN
USSR	4–1
Uruguay	Mexico
Mexico	5–0
SWEDEN	SWEDEN
Finland	5–0
Israel	Israel
China	5–0
YUGOSLAVIA	YUGOSLAVIA
Switzerland	3–2
Belgium	Belgium
Korea	4–1

DAVIS CUP by NEC 1990
World Group

FIRST ROUND	QUARTER-FINALS	SEMI-FINALS	FINAL	CHAMPION
F.R. GERMANY	F.R. GERMANY			
Netherlands	3–2	ARGENTINA		
ARGENTINA	ARGENTINA	3–2		
Israel	3–0		Australia	
YUGOSLAVIA	New Zealand		5–0	
New Zealand	3–2	Australia		
FRANCE	Australia	3–2		
Australia	3–2			USA
Switzerland	CZECHOSLOVAKIA			3–2
CZECHOSLOVAKIA	5–0	USA		
Mexico	USA	4–1		
USA	4–0		USA	
Spain	AUSTRIA		3–2	
AUSTRIA	3–2	AUSTRIA		
Italy	Italy	5–0		
SWEDEN	3–2			

Capital letters denote seeded nations.

Zonal Competition
Group 1
EURO-AFRICAN ZONE A

FIRST ROUND	FINAL	WINNERS
USSR		
Bye	USSR	USSR
Portugal	Portugal	4–1
Ghana	5–0	
Ireland	Romania	
Romania	3–2	GREAT BRITAIN
Bye		3–2
GREAT BRITAIN	GREAT BRITAIN	

EURO-AFRICAN ZONE B

FIRST ROUND	FINAL	WINNERS
HUNGARY		
Bye	HUNGARY	Belgium
Belgium	Belgium	4–1 .
Bye		
Finland	Finland	
Nigeria	4–1	Finland
Bye		3–2
DENMARK	DENMARK	

AMERICAN ZONE

FIRST ROUND	FINAL	WINNERS
PARAGUAY		
Bye	PARAGUAY	Canada
Canada	Canada	5–0
Brazil	4–1	
Uruguay	Uruguay	
Chile	3–2	Uruguay
Bye		4–1
PERU	PERU	

ASIA/OCEANIA ZONE

PRELIMINARY ROUND	FIRST ROUND	FINAL	WINNERS
	INDONESIA		
	Bye	INDONESIA	
China	China		China
Pakistan	5–0	China	4–1
	Philippines	5–0	
	Japan		
	India	India	
	Bye	4–1	KOREA
	KOREA	KOREA	5–0

Group II

EUROPEAN ZONE

FIRST ROUND	QUARTER-FINALS	SEMI-FINALS	FINAL	WINNERS
GREECE				
Bye	GREECE	Bulgaria		
Bulgaria	Bulgaria	5–0		
Cyprus	5–0		Poland	
LUXEMBOURG			4–1	
Bye	LUXEMBOURG	Poland		Poland
Poland	Poland	4–1		4–1
Bye				(Promoted to
Bye				Euro/African
Malta	Malta			Zone Group I
Bye		TURKEY		1991)
TURKEY	TURKEY	3–2		
Bye			Norway	
Norway	Norway	Norway	3–2	
Bye		4–1		
MONACO	MONACO			

AFRICAN ZONE

FIRST ROUND	QUARTER-FINALS	SEMI-FINALS	FINAL	WINNERS
SENEGAL	SENEGAL			
Bye		Togo		
Togo	Togo W/O	5–0		
Libya			MOROCCO	
MOROCCO	MOROCCO		5–0	
Bye		MOROCCO		MOROCCO
Algeria	Egypt	5–0		4–1
Egypt	4–1			(Promoted to
Kenya	Côte d'Ivoire			Euro/African
Côte d'Ivoire	4–1	Côte d'Ivoire		Zone Group I
Bye		5–0		1991)
CAMEROON	CAMEROON		ZIMBABWE	
Bye			5–0	
Zambia	Zambia	ZIMBABWE		
Bye		4–1		
ZIMBABWE	ZIMBABWE			

AMERICAN ZONE

FIRST ROUND	QUARTER-FINALS	SEMI-FINALS	FINAL	WINNERS
ECUADOR	ECUADOR			
Bye		ECUADOR		
Haiti	Haiti	3–2		
Trinidad & Tob	5–0		CUBA	
CUBA	CUBA		4–1	
Bye		CUBA		CUBA
Jamaica	Venezuela	4–1		3–2
Venezuela	5–0			(Promoted to
Colombia	Colombia			American Zone
Guatemala	4–1	Colombia		Group I, 1991)
Costa Rica	DOMINICAN REP	4–1		
DOMINICAN REP	3–2		Colombia	
Barbados	Barbados		4–1	
Bolivia	3–2	Barbados		
Bye		4–1		
BAHAMAS	BAHAMAS			

ASIA/OCEANIA ZONE

FIRST ROUND	QUARTER-FINALS	SEMI-FINALS	FINAL	WINNERS
HONG KONG	HONG KONG			
Bye		HONG KONG		
Jordan	Malaysia	4–1		
Malaysia	5–0		HONG KONG	
BANGLADESH	BANGLADESH		4–1	
Bye		Chinese Taipei		THAILAND
Singapore	Chinese Taipei	5–0		3–2
Chinese Taipei	5–0			(Promoted to
Iraq	Bahrain			Asia/Oceania
Bahrain	3–2	SRI LANKA		Zone Group I
Bye		4–1		1991)
SRI LANKA	SRI LANKA		THAILAND	
Kuwait	Kuwait		4–1	
Syria	4–1	THAILAND		
Bye		5–0		
THAILAND	THAILAND			

Capital letters denote seeded nations.

Eleven years after his last Davis Cup appearance Rod Laver, the only man to achieve a Grand Slam twice, returned to the Australian team and led them to a 5–0 victory over the ancient foe in the 1973 Challenge Round. (R & A. Photofeatures)

THE GOLDEN YEARS

Alan Trengove

The 1990 Davis Cup final at St Petersburg evoked memories of the greatest and longest rivalry the competition has known: that between Australia and the United States of America. So dramatically has the tennis strength of other nations grown in recent years that it came as a surprise to realise that not since 1973 had Australia and the USA fought out a final.

Going a little further back, to a time when Boris Becker and Stefan Edberg had not even learned how to grip a rattle, some of us can recall the years when it was almost unthinkable that neither America nor Australia would fail to make their annual rendezvous.

Between 1946 and 1971 these two tennis giants met 17 times in the Challenge Round, as the Davis Cup final was then dubbed, with Australia's 9 victories giving them a slight edge. Overall Australia had much the better record, winning the cup 15 times in those 26 years, and losing only 4 times between 1950 and 1968.

Those long-ago years have been called Australia's golden age (in other sports as well as tennis). The world of tennis was much less complex than it is today, and the yearly Davis Cup confrontation between Uncle Sam's boys and the lads from Down Under was one of life's certainties, like death and taxes.

Right through the late 1940s, the 1950s and 1960s up to 1964, cup matches between America and Australia were always played on grass. If the grass got a bit damp, the players put on black shoes bearing spikes, and the court finished up looking like a soccer pitch in winter. There was no sponsorship, no advertising signs and no prize-money. But there was a lot of chivalry. One or two players may have got a little uptight occasionally, but over the years they all became good mates. The host country provided the umpires and referee without question, and any suggestion of a code of conduct would have seemed bizarre.

I watched my first challenge round in 1953 as a cub reporter in Melbourne. It was a good one to start with because it had so much drama. Two 19-year-old rookies, Lew Hoad and Ken Rosewall, turned back the reigning Wimbledon and US title-holders, Vic Seixas and Tony Trabert respectively, in front of 17,500 fans, many of them perched high up in swaying temporary stands.

The nation came to a standstill as Hoad did battle with Trabert in the fourth rubber, trying to keep the contest alive. Television and transistor radios were then unknown in Australia, and most people had to rely on their wireless sets for knowledge of what was happening. Outside the Kooyong stadium in Glenferrie Road a tram conductor clambered on top of his tram so that he could peer over the eastern stand (where there was no temporary seating) and yell out the score to his passengers.

Hoad won in drizzling rain, 7–5 in the fifth, and my notebook was saturated and useless, but I didn't need any notes. The Rosewall-Seixas match was postponed overnight. The next day Ken looked as pale and frail as a consumptive schoolboy but when he won a huge roar went up and hundreds of seat cushions were hurled onto the court.

The era had begun on this same court in 1946 when Jack Kramer and Ted Schroeder had savaged the old guard of John Bromwich and Adrian Quist, who had wrested the cup from America so heroically in Philadelphia on the eve of the Second World War. Kramer's game was an eye-opener to the Australians; so efficient, so relentless, so overpowering. Schroeder was an instinctive hustler too – and what a competitor!

The cup went back to America. It seemed clear that Bromwich and Quist, who had lost their best tennis years to the war, as well as the other leading Australians of the immediate post-war years, were a bit outclassed by the likes of Kramer, Schroeder and, later, Pancho

Gonzales. In the four Challenge Rounds up to 1950, Australia managed to win only two doubles.

Then Harry Hopman regained the captaincy of the Australian team. He first led the team in America in 1938 and 1939, but after the war had concentrated on his work as a sports-writer while seeking and grooming the kind of talent he believed was necessary to build a new and powerful team in his spare time. The conjunction of Hopman and two athletic young players, Frank Sedgman and Ken McGregor, set in train the wonderful Australian tennis dynasty that extended over the next two decades.

Hopman, a former Davis Cup player whose main achievements were in doubles, imposed high standards in fitness, athleticism and self-discipline. He wanted aggressive players who could go five sets without weakening and who would fight to the bitter end. Sedgman was the perfect example. He had impressed Hopman as a boy because he never got tired of chasing the ball, and as he grew up and put in hours of training he became very fast and very adept at volleying. McGregor, a tall, husky fellow, was more interested in Australian Rules football than tennis, but he could unleash a pretty formidable net-rushing game.

Hopman's reputation as an 'old fox' – a term first applied by Trabert in 1953 – began when he chose McGregor instead of Bromwich for the 1950 Challenge Round at Forest Hills. The Americans were completely misled. Bromwich had played in the inter-zone final against Sweden a few weeks before and was the Wimbledon finalist of 1948, whereas McGregor was inexperienced and hardly known. But McGregor whipped Schroeder in straight sets after Sedgman had beaten Tom Brown, and the Australians then combined to win the doubles.

While McGregor was the trump that Hopman held up his sleeve, Sedgman, was the dependable match winner year-in, year-out, and the real trail-blazer of Australian tennis in those years. He was the sheet-anchor when the Australian selectors insisted that Hopman should choose Mervyn Rose instead of McGregor for singles duty in the 1951 Challenge Round at Sydney. Frank filled the same role in Adelaide the following year when McGregor returned. In six Challenge Round singles, he dropped but one set.

Sedgman and McGregor came from working-class backgrounds, as did most of the best Australian players who followed them. They were products of the post-depression 1930s when tennis became a cheap recreation in the suburbs and in the bush. Their American opponents were usually college graduates, more mature and articulate. The Australians were employed by sporting goods companies from the time they left school and were part of a tightly controlled system that became geared to winning the cup year after year and thus filling the coffers of the Lawn Tennis Association of Australia. The money was spent on facilities and team tours.

The Australians loved to beat the Americans, and I am sure the reverse was also true. Nobody enjoyed a tennis clash between the two nations more than Sir Norman Brookes, who was the LTAA's president and who remembered the tennis wars he himself had once waged against America as a player, beginning as far back as 1905. Behind the intensity of American-Australian contests was a deep respect held by each country for the competitive ardour and the sportsmanship of its opponent. Oh yes, there was some needling, some hard words expressed at times. Hopman might try to undermine an American player's confidence by questioning in his newspaper column whether he was a flagrant foot-faulter; and the Americans might poke fun at Harry's 'chain gang' and his system of fines for petty misdemeanours, such as swearing or breaking curfew. But on the court the fight was clean and unsullied by tantrums, and the fans in each country were as fair as you could honestly expect them to be.

When Sedgman and McGregor turned professional after the 1952 challenge round, they set up a pattern. Thereafter, the top Australians (with the notable exception of Neale Fraser) would sooner or later be enticed by promoter Jack Kramer to join his troupe. Yet always, it seemed, there were adequate replacements. Of course, Kramer recruited his countrymen as well for his professional tours, but his greatest reservoir was Australia. In retrospect, one wonders whether players of the calibre of Neale Fraser, Ashley Cooper, Mal Anderson and even Roy Emerson would have ever played in the Davis Cup if, for instance, Sedgman, Hoad and Rosewall had remained available for selection.

In Australia, the Challenge Round was always played at Christmas time, usually starting on Boxing Day. Crowds would turn up at the courts on Christmas Day just to watch the final practice sessions. The peak year was undoubtedly 1954, when Hoad and Rosewall defended the cup at White City in Sydney. Davis Cup fever was at its most virulent. Temporary stands helped to swell the crowd to 25,578, a world record (for a legitimate tennis match) that still stands; and £90,000 had to be returned to disappointed ticket-seekers. From an Australian viewpoint, the occasion developed into something of an anti-climax, because a very determined Seixas and Trabert turned the tables on their young tormenters of a year previously, winning the first three rubbers.

Seixas, who, like Fraser, resisted all professional overtures, was possibly the most popular American Davis Cup stalwart of all-time. He played against Australia in six straight Challenge Rounds. He was (and remains) a very handsome man, with an attractive game built around spin and variety and a deft touch on volleys. One Australian columnist admiringly headed a story, *Good Gracious, Vic Seixas*. His Nemesis in cup play was Rosewall, and if you ask Vic today for his favourite match he will surely nominate that 1954 victory; it was the only time in four Challenge Round matches that he got the better of Ken's line-splitting ground-strokes.

With Hoad and Rosewall approaching their peaks as amateur players, Australia regained the cup in 1955 with a 5–0 victory at Forest Hills. The next two Challenge Rounds – at Adelaide and Melbourne – were also one-sided. Trabert had joined Kramer, and there were no adequate US replacements to back up the ageing Seixas. By 1957 Hoad and Rosewall had also departed, but Cooper and Anderson in the singles, and Cooper and Rose in the doubles, were too strong for the Americans.

Having lost a Challenge Round only once in eight years, a certain complacency descended on Australian tennis. As if pre-ordained, Cooper won the Wimbledon and US crowns in 1958, beating his compatriots in the finals. It was no secret that he and Anderson were going to turn pro at the end of the year, but who cared? Australia had Fraser, Laver, Emerson and others waiting to get their chance.

The events in Brisbane came as a shock. Perry Jones, a roly-poly, short-sighted and elderly man who was then the czar of Californian tennis, came to Australia as the new US team captain and brought with him his protege, the Peruvian Alejandro Olmedo. Alex – or 'The Chief', as Olmedo became known because of his Aztec blood – did to the Aussies what McGregor had done to the Yanks in 1950. His selection was controversial on two counts. He was not a US national; simply an expatriate South American enrolled at an American college, and the more experienced and higher ranked Ham Richardson expected to play the singles along with Barry MacKay.

But Olmedo fully justified his patron's confidence, beating both Anderson and Cooper in singles, and partnering Richardson to victory in a marathon doubles over Anderson and Fraser. The first Challenge Round ever held in the sub-tropical city of Brisbane was an extraordinary affair, with Richardson and his captain not on speaking terms, the 'fox' outsmarted by an old man who, if anything, resembled a rumpled teddy bear, and Olmedo and Jones drowning each other in tears at the end.

As in 1954, America had less than 12 months in which to savour its triumph, for Hopman quickly promoted a few of his apprentices, Fraser, Laver and Emerson, and reclaimed the silverware at Forest Hills in 1959. This was Fraser's finest hour; the Melbourne left-hander, destined to become his country's longest serving team-captain in the 1970s, 1980s and 1990s, beat Olmedo (by now the Wimbledon champion) and, in the decisive fifth rubber, Barry MacKay. In between, he partnered Emerson to a doubles victory.

The 1960s marked the beginning of the end of the Australian-American saga, for other nations were by then producing outstanding players (such as Santana, Pietrangeli and Osuna), and the US could not always reach the Challenge Round. Italy, Mexico, Spain and India won the right to tilt at Australian supremacy, but found the fast, sun-baked grass courts and the rock-hard players Down Under too tough a combination to master. It is fair to say that many Australians regarded a Challenge Round without Americans as the sporting equivalent of a pub with no beer.

Ironically, the only two times the Americans campaigned in Australia in the 1960s they took the Cup home. At Adelaide in 1963, the late Chuck McKinley was the hero, beating rookie John Newcombe in the last match to register a 3–2 victory. Five years later, also at Adelaide, Arthur Ashe and Clark Graebner, with Stan Smith and Bob Lutz in the doubles, got the better of Bill Bowrey, Ray Ruffles and John Alexander. (Adelaide has never been given the right to host the Americans since!)

The only other occasion on which the two countries met in that decade was in 1964 at Cleveland, Ohio, on a clay court put down by a private promoter who had acquired the staging rights from the USLTA. Down 1–2 after the doubles, Australia was saved first by Fred Stolle beating Dennis Ralston in a long five-setter, and then by Emerson defeating McKinley in the clincher.

By the late 1960s, Australia's overwhelming tennis might was broken. The advent of open tennis severely disrupted the Australian tennis machine, and tennis in other countries, stimulated by the new conditions, continued to develop. Another blow to Australia was the end, in 1972, of the Challenge Round format, whereby the defending nation could stand above the fray until there emerged a challenger who had then to attempt to storm the citadel. When Australia held the cup, that meant a long trip Down Under and playing on grass.

Hopman went to live in America, where he coached, among others, youngsters such as John McEnroe and Vitas Gerulaitis, who would confound Australian teams later on. Some of the Aussie greats – Emerson, Laver, Stolle – also settled in America, where the pickings for professionals were richer, while Hoad set up a tennis camp in Spain.

The glorious American-Australian battles of Christmases past are memories now, fond memories of another time, another age. But for participants and spectators alike, the memories are certainly not fading. Indeed, they form an enduring part of the rich tradition of our game.

After five years in winning US teams, the last a magnificent 3–2 success against the Rumanians in Bucharest in 1972, Stan Smith was brought to earth the following year by Laver and Newcombe. *(R & A Photofeatures)*

Above: *The successful American team in Atlanta: (l to r) Capt. Marty Riessen, Patty Fendick, Zina Garrison, Gigi Fernandez, Jennifer Capriati.* *(R. Adams)*

Left: *Natalia Zvereva who led the Soviet team to the final and beat Garrison as the USA won 2–1.* *(M. Cole)*

THE *FEDERATION CUP* by NEC

Henry Wancke

The people of Atlanta were out to make an impression. They were in the throes of bidding for the 1996 Olympics and were determined that the *Federation Cup* by NEC would play a part in showing the world that they could successfully host major international events. That they did, and subsequently they learnt that Atlanta had won the necessary votes at the IOC meeting in Tokyo. Whether the 1990 *Federation Cup* actually helped, will never be known. What can be confirmed is that Southern hospitality is all that is rumoured, and the WCT Peachtree venue did the city proud.

For the 28th *Federation Cup*, 47 nations (a record) competed with the defending champions, the USA, favourites to retain the title on home soil. The team, however, had a very new look about it with Zina Garrison playing in the No. 1 spot and Jennifer Capriati making her debut. Gigi Fernandez and Patty Fendick completed the line up with Marty Riessen carrying the responsibility of team captain. Apart from Garrison and the captain, the team were inexperienced but in the final analyses, it proved their strength as a great team spirit evolved during the course of the week. With a personality like Capriati involved, it was only natural!

Spain, with the services of top tenners Arantxa Sanchez-Vicario and Conchita Martinez, were seeded 2 and many felt they would provide the main threat to the Americans. Austria were the surprise third seeds but with Judith Wiesner and Barbara Paulus impressing on the world circuit, their rise in international terms was well justified. That placed the Soviet Union (Natalia Zvereva and Larisa Savchenko) in fourth spot, France 5, Italy 6, and because they couldn't field their top players, Czechoslovakia 7 and West Germany 8.

The ommision of the German No. 1 Steffi Graf, the Czech leader Helen Sukova plus Monica Seles from the Yugoslav line up and Gabriela Sabatini from Argentina's, proved an early topic of discussion. Their presence would have undoubtedly increased public aware-ness and increased the gate, but it didn't detract from the on court competition as other players grasped the opportunity of representing their countries. In many ways, Capriati's debut helped to fill the void for she became the focal point of attention and the fourteen-year-old thrived on it. She was the American mascot off court and she doubled up as cheerleader when the US team was locked in combat. Here was one player who took her team duties seriously! Not only did she provide the US with a winning performance by always giving them a 1–0 lead everytime she always came back in support of her team mates and ensured the crowd got behind the local representatives. Indeed, Capriati's *Federation Cup* debut was impressive. She won all five singles without dropping a set, though she had a tendency to lose concentration and allow her opponents back into the match. But she always recovered. Her on-court contribution to the team effort was to prove decisive.

The US progressed confidently through the early stages with 3–0 victories over both Poland and Belgium. They met their first real challenge in the quarter-finals when they came up against Czechoslovakia. Capriati gave them the start they expected by beating Regina Rajchrtova but Garrison then faltered. Jana Novotna, playing at No. 1 for the Czechs, outplayed her to record a 6–3 6–3 victory over the Wimbledon finalist and level the tie score. The Czechs then further embarrassed their hosts by grabbing a 5–2 lead in the first set of the deciding doubles but Garrison and Fernandez managed to stem the tide and save the tie by eventually winning through 7–6 (10–8) 6–4 over Novotna and Rajchrtova. With that win the USA set a new milestone in *Federation Cup* play by winning their 100th tie. But it had been close!

A 3–0 American victory over Austria (who had defeated Great Britain in the quarter-finals 2–1) secured their expected place in the final where their opponents were not the expected second seeds, Spain, but the Soviets, captained by the experienced Olga Morozova. The Spaniards who had opened their *Federation Cup* challenge by dropping a rubber to Canada then settled to record 3–0 victories over Israel and France. They were getting into their stride but regretably for them, the resilience of the Soviets in the semi-finals proved too big an obstacle for them to overcome. Martinez opened the Spanish account with a 6–3 7–5 victory over Leila Meskhi but fate was against the Spaniards. Zvereva went on court clearly determined to outlast Arantxa Sanchez-Vicario and to achieve that objective set about keeping the ball deep and in play thus keeping the Spaniard on the move and forcing her to go for outright winners. It seemed to work and she won the first set 6–4. Zvereva continued with these tactics but while retrieving once again, Sanchez-Vicario twisted her ankle badly. An injury time-out was called and after treatment she valiantly attempted to play on but was forced to retire. The doubles favoured the Soviets. The experience of Zvereva and Savchenko was enough to take the USSR into the final as they won the deciding tie 6–2 6–3 over Martinez and Pilar Perez. It was a sad day for Spain, but the team is young and once they have a bit more depth with an experienced doubles pair behind their talented singles players, they should go all the way. But that remains in the future.

The final, whilst unexpected, provided a confrontation worthy of the occasion. Capriati maintained her unbeaten record in front of a full house. She was tested in the first set by Meskhi and had to come back from 2–4 down before claiming the first rubber 7–6 (7–3) 6–3. Zvereva, on behalf of the visitors, then upset Garrison who, having taken the first set, crumbled before the Russian's consistent play. That 4–6 6–3 6–3 Soviet victory should have launched the challengers towards the winners rostrum, for in Zvereva and Savchenko they had a doubles combination equal to, if not better, than Garrison and Fernandez. Perhaps over-confidence was the cause, for in the 100°F heat and high humidity, and having already played a two hour match, Zvereva returned to the fray without any head protection. Garrison, on the other hand, took precautionary measures and played herself back in, allowing Fernandez to take the strain in the initial stages. Zvereva, affected by the sun, could not rally to the cause despite Savchenko's brave attempts to take control. As a match it was a disappointment bearing in mind how much depended on it. With Capriati in full voice leading the partisan crowd, the defending champions romped home 6–4 6–3, settling the tie 2–1 in their favour and ensuring that the *Federation Cup* remained in the USA for the 14th time.

The American victory proved once again what an incredible depth of players the United States can call on. Whilst West Germany is the proud birthplace of Steffi Graf, the World Champion and World No. 1, without her services they couldn't get past the second round, losing 1–2 to the Netherlands. The US may not have the top woman player, but they remain the top team in the world. However in Jennifer Capriati, they may well have a future No. 1. For her, Atlanta 1990 was a personal triumph. The All-American teenager, embarking on her chosen career, had given us a glimpse of future greatness – and the populace just love her!

QUALIFYING ROUND – Malta d. Sri Lanka 3–0 (K. Camilleri d. V. Premaratne 6–3 5–7 6–3; C. Curmi d. L. Weerasuriya 6–1 6–4; Camilleri/Curmi d. Premaratne/S. de Silva 6–1 6–0; **Chinese Taipei d. Bahamas 3–0** (S. Lai d. R. Farrington 6–0 6–1; S. Wang d. K. Griffith 6–2 6–1; Lai/Wang d. Farrington/Griffith 6–2 6–3); **Philippines d. Trinidad & Tobago 2–1** (J. Saret d. M. Ward 6–1 6–1; S. Castillejo lost to B. Corbie 4–6 3–6; D. Castillejo/N. Castillejo d. Corbie/D. Millington 6–1 6–3).
PRELIMINARY ROUND – People's Republic of China d. Mexico 2–1 (L. Fang d. A. Gallardo 6–4 6–1; T. Min lost to A. Gavaldon 1–6 4–6; Fang/Min d. Gavaldon/G. Novelo 6–4 6–4); **Indonesia d. Yugoslavia 2–1** (S. Wibowo lost to G. Matic 4–6 4–6; Y. Basuki d. N. Ercegovic 6–0 6–7 8–6; Wibowo/I. Moerid d. S. Goles/Matic 6–4 6–3); **Finland d. Jamaica 3–0** (P. Thoren d. H. Harris 6–1 6–1; N. Dahlman d. J. Van Rick de Groot 6–1 6–1; Thoren/Dahlman d. Van Rick de Groot/Harris 6–1 6–2); **Denmark d. Norway 2–0** (S. Albinus d. C. Instebo 6–3 6–2; T. Scheuer-Larsen d. A. Jonsson 3–6 6–4 6–3; doubles not played); **Poland d. Uruguay 2–1** (M. Mroz d. C. Brause 6–2 6–1; K. Nowak lost to P.

Miller 6–2 4–6 0–2 (ret); Mroz/R. Skrzypzynska d. Miller/Brause 6–2 6–4); **Republic of Korea d. Luxembourg 2–1** (M. Park d. C. Goy 6–1 6–0; I. Kim lost to K. Kschwendt 2–6 2–6; Kim/J. Myung Lee d. Kschwendt/Goy 7–5 6–7 6–4); **Bulgaria d. Philippines 3–0** (D. Ranguelova d. J. Saret 6–2 6–3; E. Pampoulova d. S. Castillejo 6–2 6–0; Ranguelova/G. Angelova d. D. Castillejo/N. Castillejo 3–6 6–1 7–5); **Dominican Republic d. Thailand 2–0** (J. Schad d. T. Summa 6–1 7–6; M. Sanchez d. O. Thampensri 6–3 6–3; doubles not played); **Hong Kong d. Malaysia 3–0** (E. Lightbody d. L. Sze May 6–0 6–0; P. Moreno d. N. Su Peng 6–2 6–0; Lightbody/P. Sheung d. K. Lin/L. Singarajah 6–1 6–1); **Chinese Taipei d. Venezuela 2–1** (S. Lai lost to E. Leonardi 0–6 1–6; S. Wang d. M. Vento 7–5 6–3; Lai/Wang d. Leonardi/Vento 5–7 6–2 6–4); **Greece d. Malta 3–0** (O. Tsarbopoulou d. K. Camilleri 6–1 6–2; A. Kanellopoulou d. C. Curmi 6–3 6–3; Tsarbopoulou/Kanellopoulou d. Camilleri/Curmi 6–4 6–0); **Israel d. Ireland 2–0** (I. Berger d. J. Thornton 6–2 6–2; Y. Segal d. L. O'Halloran 6–1 6–3; doubles not played).
FIRST ROUND – USA d. Poland 3–0 (J. Capriati d. M. Mroz 6–3 6–1; Z. Garrison d. K. Nowak 6–0 6–1; Garrison/G. Fernandez d. R. Skrzypzynska/Mroz 6–0 6–0); **Belgium d. Sweden 2–1** (S. Wasserman d. M. Strandlund 6–4 6–4; S. Appelmans lost to C. Lindqvist 5–7 5–7; Wasserman/Appelmans d. Strandlund/Lindqvist 6–2 6–2); **Australia d. Indonesia 2–0** (E. Smylie d. S. Wibowo 5–7 6–4 6–0; R. McQuillan d. Y. Basuki 6–3 3–6 6–3; doubles cancelled due to rain); **Czechoslovakia d. Republic of Korea 3–0** (R. Rajchrtova d. M. Park 6–4 6–1; J. Novotna d. S. Im 6–1 6–0; Rajchrtova/E. Svglerova d. I. Kim/J. Myung Lee 6–2 6–3); **Austria d. Bulgaria 3–0** (B. Paulus d. D. Ranguelova 6–2 6–3; J. Wiesner d. E. Pampoulova 6–0 6–0; Paulus/Wiesner d. Ranguelova/G. Angelova 6–0 6–2; **Japan d. People's Republc of China 3–0** (K. Date d. L. Fang 6–3 6–0; N. Sawamatsu d. T. Min 6–2 6–0; M. Kidowaki/N. Miyagi d. Fang/Min 6–1 6–1); **Great Britain d. Dominican Republic 3–0** (M. Javer d. J. Schad 6–2 6–3; S. Loosemore d. M. Sanchez 6–2 6–1; J. Durie/C. Wood d. J. Schad/Sanchez 6–2 6–0); **Italy d. Finland 3–0** (C. Caverzasio d. P. Thoren 6–2 6–3; R. Reggi d. N. Dahlman 6–2 6–2; Reggi/L. Golarsa d. Thoren/A. Aallonen 6–2 6–3); **F.R. Germany d. Argentina 2–1** (A. Huber d. B. Fulco 6–1 6–2; C. Porwik d. F. Labat 6–0 6–3; I. Cueto/W. Probst lost to Fulco/Labat 4–6 2–6); **Netherlands d. Switzerland 2–1** (B. Schultz d. C. Bartos 7–6 6–0; M. Bollegraf lost to E. Zardo 7–6 5–7 2–6; Bollegraf/Schultz d. E. Krapl/C. Cohen 6–0 6–1); **Hong Kong d. Hungary 2–1** (E. Lightbody d. A. Noszaly 7–6 7–5; P. Moreno d. A. Temesvari 6–0 6–1; Lightbody/P. Sheung lost to Noszaly/R. Szikszai 2–6 4–6); **USSR d. Brazil 3–0** (L. Meshki d. A. Vieira 6–7 6–1 6–2; N. Zvereva d. C. Chabalgoity 6–0 6–1; N. Zvereva/L. Savchenko d. Chabalgoity/L. Corsato 6–2 6–1); **France d. Chinese Taipei 3–0** (J. Halard d. S. Lai 6–2 6–1; N. Tauziat d. S. Wang 6–3 6–2; I. Demongeot/M. Pierce d. S. Lai/Y. Lin 6–2 6–2); **New Zealand d. Greece 3–0** (C. Toleafoa d. O. Tsarbopoulou 6–3 7–6; B. Cordwell d. A. Kanellopoulou 7–5 6–3; Cordwell/J. Richardson d. Kanellopoulou/Tsarbopoulou 6–1 6–0); **Israel d. Denmark 2–1** (I. Berger d. S. Albinus 6–3 6–3; Y. Segal lost to T. Scheuer-Larsen 2–6 6–4 5–7; Berger/L. Zaltz d. Albinus/Scheuer-Larsen 6–3 6–2); **Spain d. Canada 2–1** (C. Martinez d. J. Hetherington 6–1 6–4; A. Sanchez-Vicario d. H. Kelesi 6–3 6–2; Martinez/P. Perez lost to R. Simpson/Hetherington 7–5 2–6 2–6).
SECOND ROUND – USA d. Belgium 3–0 (J. Capriati d. S. Wasserman 6–0 7–6; Z. Garrison d. S. Appelmans 6–4 6–1; Garrison/G. Fernandez d. Appelmans/Wasserman 6–1 6–3); **Czechoslovakia d. Australia 2–1** (R. Rajchrtova d. E. Smylie 6–4 6–4; J. Novotna d. R. McQuillan 6–4 6–4; Rajchrtova/E. Svglerova lost to J. Thompson/K. Godridge 2–6 3–6); **Austria d. Japan 2–1** (B. Paulus d. K. Date 6–3 7–6; J. Wiesner d. N. Sawamatsu 6–2 6–2; Paulus/B. Reinstadler lost to N. Miyagi/M. Kidowaki 0–6 0–6); **Great Britain d. Italy 2–1** (M. Javer lost to L. Golarsa 2–6 2–6; S. Loosemore d. R. Reggi 2–6 7–5 7–5; J. Durie/C. Wood d. Reggi/L. Garrone 6–4 6–1); **Netherlands d. F.R. Germany 2–1** (B. Schultz d. A. Huber 6–3 6–2; M. Bollegraf lost to C. Porwick 2–6 4–6; Schultz/Bollegraf d. Porwick/W. Probst 7–6 7–6); **USSR d. Hong Kong 3–0** (L. Savchenko d. E. Lightbody 6–3 6–1; N. Zvereva d. P. Moreno 6–3 7–6; Zvereva/Savchenko d. Moreno/P. Sheung 6–3 6–0); **France d. New Zealand 3–0** (J. Halard d. C. Toleafoa 6–2 7–5; N. Tauziat d. B. Cordwell 6–1 6–2; I. Demongeot/M. Pierce d. Cordwell/J. Richardson 6–3 6–4); **Spain d. Israel 3–0** (C. Martinez d. I. Berger 6–3 6–2; A. Sanchez-Vicario d. Y. Segal 6–0 6–0; Martinez/Sanchez-Vicario d. Berger/L. Zaltz 6–3 6–4).
QUARTER-FINALS – USA d. Czechoslovakia 2–1 (J. Capriati d. R. Rajchrtova 6–2 7–6; Z. Garrison lost to J. Novotna 3–6 3–6; Garrison/G. Fernandez d. Novotna/Rajchrtova 7–6, 6–4); **Austria d. Great Britain 2–1** (B. Paulus d. J. Durie 7–6 5–7 6–4; J. Wiesner d. S. Loosemore 7–6 2–6 8–6; Paulus/B. Reinstadler lost to Durie/C. Wood 2–5 retired); **USSR d. Netherlands 2–1** (L. Meshki lost to B. Schultz 7–6 4–6 3–6; N. Zvereva d. M. Bollegraf 6–1 6–3; Zvereva/L. Savchenko d. Schultz/Bollegraf 7–6 6–3); **Spain d. France 3–0** (C. Martinez d. J. Halard 6–0 6–3; A. Sanchez-Vicario d. N. Tauziat 7–6 6–1; Martinez/Sanchez-Vicario d. I. Demongeot/M. Pierce 6–4 6–4).
SEMI-FINALS – USA d. Austria 3–0 (J. Capriati d. B. Paulus 6–3 6–4; Z. Garrison d. J. Wiesner 6–3 6–4; P. Fendick/G. Fernandez d. Paulus/Wiesner 6–2 6–3); **USSR d. Spain 2–1** (L. Meshki lost to C. Martinez 3–6 5–7; N. Zvereva d. A. Sanchez-Vicario 6–4 2–0 (ret); Zvereva/L. Savchenko d. Martinez/P. Perez 6–2 6–3).
FINAL – USA d. USSR 2–1 (J. Capriati d. L. Meshki 7–6 6–2; Z. Garrison lost to N. Zvereva 6–4 3–6 3–6; Garrison/G. Fernandez d. Zvereva/L. Savchenko 6–4 6–3).

FEDERATION CUP by NEC 1990

PRELIMINARY ROUND	FIRST ROUND	SECOND ROUND	QUARTER-FINALS	SEMI-FINALS	FINAL	
Poland / Uruguay	USA (1)	USA 3–0	USA 3–0	USA 2–1	USA 3–0	USA 2–1
	Poland 2–1					
	Sweden / Belgium / Australia	Belgium 2–1				
Indonesia / Yugoslavia	Indonesia 2–1	Australia 2–0	CZECHOSLOVAKIA 2–1			
Republic of Korea / Luxembourg	Republic of Korea 2–1	CZECHOSLOVAKIA 3–0				
	CZECHOSLOVAKIA (7)					
Philippines / Bulgaria	AUSTRIA (3)	AUSTRIA 3–0	AUSTRIA 2–1	AUSTRIA 2–1		
	Bulgaria 3–0					
Japan / P.R. China	Japan 2–1	Japan 3–0				
P.R. China / Mexico	P.R. China / Dominican Republic / Great Britain	Great Britain 3–0	Great Britain 2–1			
Finland / Jamaica	Finland 3–0	ITALY 3–0				
	ITALY (6)					
	F.R. GERMANY (8)	F.R. GERMANY 2–1	Netherlands 2–1			
	Argentina / Netherlands / Switzerland	Netherlands 2–1		USSR 2–1	USSR 2–1	
Malaysia / Hong Kong	Hong Kong 3–0	Hong Kong 2–1	USSR 3–0			
	Hungary / Brazil / USSR (4)	USSR 3–0				
Venezuela / Chinese Taipei	FRANCE (5)	FRANCE 3–0	FRANCE 3–0	SPAIN 3–0		
	Chinese Taipei 2–1					
Malta / Greece	New Zealand	New Zealand 3–0				
Israel	Greece 3–0					
	Israel 2–0	Israel 2–1	SPAIN 3–0			
Norway / Denmark	Denmark 2–0	SPAIN 2–1				
	Canada / SPAIN (2)					

Capital letters denote seeded countries. Number following countries' names gives seeding order.

NEC WORLD YOUTH CUP

The 6th NEC World Youth Cup Finals held in the Netherlands, in September, proved to be a great success for the host nation both on and off the court. There were 16 boys' and 16 girls' teams that qualified from the five regional qualifying zones held on all continents and in total, 25 nations were represented in these finals held at the Victoria Tennis Club, Rotterdam. But it is the European teams that traditionally achieve good results in the NEC World Youth Cup Finals and indeed, this year: the top two placed nations in the boys' and girls' European qualifying zones were awarded the 1st and 2nd seeded positions in their respective events.

In the boys' event, top seeded USSR were led by Andrei Medvedev, who had helped his team to the runner-up position the previous year. On their way to victory in the European zone, USSR had narrowly beaten both France and Sweden, seeded 2nd and 3rd/4th respectively, in the final. The other 3rd/4th seeded position was awarded to Mexico, winners of the North and Central American zone, albeit only in the deciding doubles against both USA and Canada. Seeded 5–8, and drawn for position, were Argentina, Australia, Italy and USA.

In the girls' event, defending champions, FR Germany, again led by Anke Huber who had swept all before her the previous year, were seeded 1. Their beaten European zone opponents, USSR, headed by Tatiana Ignatieva and Irina Soukhova, a formidable doubles team on the Junior World Ranking Circuit, were seeded 2. The 3rd/4th seeded positions went to USA and Yugoslavia respectively and positions 5–8 to People's Republic of China, Czechoslovakia, Netherlands and Paraguay. China had caused an upset in their qualifying zone by beating the 2nd seeded Australian side in their quarter-final match, and proving that this was no fluke, going on to beat the top seeded side, Japan, in the final. They were an unknown quantity in the NEC World Youth Cup Finals but were to most certainly justify their claim to a seeded position.

All the girls first round matches were played on day one of the competition and there was only one seeded casualty – Paraguay. Fielding the same team that had represented them in the previous final, they were defeated by France which was rather a disappointing result for them. In fact, all three South American teams were forced to fight for consolation places after their initial matches. One half of the boys' first round was also played on the first day with the seeded nations coming through fairly comfortably. Argentina however, gave themselves a scare by losing their opening singles match to the Republic of Korea, but they recovered to win the remaining two matches.

The second day caused a little concern for the organisers since poor weather delayed the start of play. Excellent on-site organisation, however, meant that play was able to commence almost as soon as the weather improved and the day's schedule was completed. Spain made the best use of their time by defeating Mexico and causing the second upset of the boys' first round. The Cote d'Ivoire, in their first appearance in the finals, had a very exciting encounter with the USA. Their opening singles player, Lonfo Ilou pushed his opponent Adam Peterson to the limit before losing out 9–7 in the third set. The second singles also went in favour of the USA, but the Cote d'Ivoire managed a very creditable win in the doubles, displaying the good teamwork that had brought them through their regional qualifying zone.

The Girls' quarter-final matches brought about one or two surprises as well. To the delight of the home spectators, the Netherlands comfortably beat Yugoslavia with both Linda Niemantsverdriet and Petra Kamstra looking ominously powerful in their singles matches. China also continued their unbeaten ways by beating the USA in the deciding doubles. The boys' quarter-finals provided differing fortunes for European teams. Top seeded USSR had a comfortable win over Italy, and Sweden, led by the impressive Thomas Enqvist, managed to overcome Argentina despite dropping the opening set of the crucial doubles match. Once again living up to their title of giant-killers, Spain defeated the USA to earn their semi-final place and were joined there by Australia. Although not highly fancied, Australia, winners from 1985–1987, combined solid singles play with a strong doubles formation and this was sufficient to bring them through against the second seeded French team.

The Semi-finals in both events produced more surpises. Medvedev was unable to capitalise on a strong start to his rubber and lost in three sets to the hard working Alex Corretja, to level the match against Spain at one all. The deciding doubles was an enthralling match for the spectators. USSR gained the initiative by taking the first set on a tie-break, only for the Spanish boys to level by winning the next. However, an early break of serve in the third was enough to give victory to USSR and a place in the final. Sweden, their expected opponents in the final, found the going tough against Australia in the second semi-final. After dropping their first rubber, Enqvist again came to their rescue with an emphatic whitewash of the Australian No. 1, Grant Doyle. Demonstrating his determination and fighting ability however, Doyle then teamed up with Bradley Sceney to defeat Enqvist and Thomas Johansson in the doubles and so claim a place in the final.

The girls' semi-finals, although not as close as the boys', provided the main interest for the crowds. In the first, China's good run was finally ended at the hands of the more experienced team from USSR. It was, however, the second semi-final which saw strong favourites, FR Germany, off to a bad start by losing their opening rubber to the Netherlands when Petra Kamstra defeated the resilient Marketa Kochta that attracted the crowds. The FR Germany would have expected to draw level after the second rubber with Anke Huber playing at No. 1, but nothing Huber could do was able to deter the Dutch No. 1 Niemantsverdriet. To the delight of the large crowds straining for a view on the centre court she gained a straight sets victory, in a high quality match which ensured their appearance in the final.

Before the finals took place, the bronze medal matches were played. With three out of four teams European, the placings came as little surprise. In the boys' event, Sweden defeated Spain, and in the girls' event, FR Germany defeated China. Both the matches were comfortable wins for the victors.

The finals of each event were anything but comfortable wins for the champions, and produced some of the best tennis of the week. In the girls' final there was, understandably, great local support for the home team and Kamstra excited the sell-out crowd of more than 1,000 by beating Soukhova 6–1 7–6 in the opening rubber. Matters were soon levelled, however, when a hard-hitting performance by French Open junior champion, Ignatieva, earned her a 6–0 1–6 6–4 success against local heroine Niemantsverdriet. The final result was decided by the doubles in which Kamstra and Niemantsverdriet battled to a 6–3 4–6 6–1 victory against the more experienced pair, Ignatieva and Soukhova.

The USSR had the second chance of a title in the boys' event and they made a good start when their opening match was won by Dimitri Tomashevitch, a 6–3 6–2 victor over Taso Vasiliadis. Victory looked assured in the second singles match when Medvedev led by a set and 2–0 against Doyle. However, the latter again displayed his resilience, and fought back to take a 2–6 6–4 7–5 victory and so level the score. The deciding doubles was a close match with both Medvedev and Doyle yet to lose a doubles rubber in the competition. Medvedev, partnered by Evgeni Kafelnikov, finally prevailed for a 7–6 6–3 victory to secure the title of champion nation for USSR.

In order to ensure that all the players remembered the Netherlands, not just for the tennis and the good administration of the local organisers, a sightseeing tour of Amsterdam was arranged for the following day. This gave the teams a welcome chance to enjoy the customs and culture of their host nation.

NEC WORLD YOUTH CUP 1990

Boys' and Girls' 16 & Under International Team Championship
52 nations competed, 51 taking part in the boys' event and 44 in the girls' event. Final stages took place in Rotterdam, Netherlands 11–16 September.

FINAL POSITIONS – BOYS: Champion nation – USSR; runners-up – Australia; 3rd – Sweden; 4th – Spain; 5th – Argentina; 6th – Italy; 7th – USA; 8th – France; 9th – Republic of Korea; 10th – Mexico; 11th – Brazil; 12th – Israel; 13th – Chile; 14th – Netherlands; 15th – Japan; 16th – Cote d'Ivoire. **GIRLS:** Champion nation – Netherlands; runners-up – USSR; 3rd – West Germany; 4th – P. R. China; 5th – Czechoslovakia; 6th – USA; 7th – Yugoslavia; 8th – France; 9th – Japan; 10th – Paraguay; 11th – Republic of Korea; 12th – Canada; 13th – Argentina; 14th – Thailand; 15th – Brazil; 16th – Zimbabwe.

BOYS' CHAMPIONSHIP – Semi-finals: USSR d. Spain 2–1 (A. Medvedev lost to A. Corretja 6–2 6–7 3–6; D. Tomashevitch d. J. Velasco 6–4 6–1; E. Kafelnikov/Medvedev d. Corretja/Velasco 7–6 4–6 6–3); **Australia d. Sweden 2–1** (G. Doyle lost to T. Enqvist 0–6 0–6; T. Vasiliadis d. T. Johansson 7–5 3–6 6–2; Doyle/B. Sceney d. Enqvist/Johansson 7–5 3–6 6–2). **3rd place play-off: Sweden d. Spain 3–0** (T. Enqvist d. A. Corretja 3–0 (ret); T. Johansson d. J. Velasco 6–4 6–1; doubles not played). **Final: USSR d. Australia 2–1** (A. Medvedev lost to G. Doyle 6–2 4–6 5–7; D. Tomashevitch d. T. Vasiliadis 6–3 6–2; E. Kafelnikov/Medvedev d. Doyle/B. Sceney 7–6 6–3).

GIRLS' CHAMPIONSHIP – Semi-finals: Netherlands d. West Germany 3–0 (L. Niemantsverdriet d. A. Huber 6–3 6–3; P. Kamstra d. M. Kochta 6–2 3–6 6–3; Kamstra/Niemantsverdriet d. M. Babel/Kochta 6–3 6–1; **USSR d. P. R. China 3–0** (T. Ignatieva d. Q. Huang 6–0 6–1; I. Soukhova d. Y. Cai 6–4 6–4; Ignatieva/Soukhova d. Cai/J-Q. Yi 6–2 7–5). **3rd place play-off: West Germany d. P. R. China 3–0** (A Huber d. J-Q. Yi 6–3 6–3; M. Kochta d. Y. Cai 6–0 6–1; M. Babel/Kochta d. Cai/Yi 7–5 6–3). **Final: Netherlands d. USSR 2–1** (L. Niemantsverdriet lost to T. Ignatieva 0–6 6–1 4–6; P. Kamstra d. I. Soukhova 6–1 7–6; Kamstra/Niemantsverdriet d. Ignatieva/Soukhova 6–3 4–6 6–1).

The following tennis manufacturers
and other groups whose interest
lie in the sport are members of the
ITF FOUNDATION

Any commercial tennis organisation is welcome to
apply for membership – details of the
I.T.F. Foundation and the benefits it brings
to both sport and member can be obtained from:-

The ITF Foundation
International Tennis Federation
Palliser Road
Barons Court
London W14 9EN.

GRAND SLAM CHAMPIONSHIPS

AUSTRALIAN OPEN CHAMPIONSHIPS
FRENCH OPEN CHAMPIONSHIPS
WIMBLEDON CHAMPIONSHIPS
US OPEN CHAMPIONSHIPS

A frustrating year for Germany's Boris Becker who lost his Wimbledon and US titles and narrowly failed to displace Edberg from the No. 1 ranking. *(Professional Sport)*

Suitably attired for an Antipodean summer, Ivan Lendl won the first Grand Slam of the year in Melbourne when Stefan Edberg was forced to retire in the final. (Professional Sport)

AUSTRALIAN OPEN CHAMPIONSHIPS

Alan Trengove

One disappointment followed another at the Australian Open, with the greatest letdown coming at the end when Stefan Edberg was forced to retire from the men's singles final because of a torn stomach muscle. The score in favour of his opponent, Ivan Lendl, was 4–6 7–6 (7–3) 5–2. Thus, for the second successive Sunday, the centre court crowd of 15,000 at Flinders Park, as well as television audiences around the world, were stunned by the blow fate had dealt them. On the previous Sunday, John McEnroe, whose brilliant tennis had aroused everyone's expectations, was disqualified for misbehaviour while playing Mikael Pernfors.

Earlier in the tournament, Gabriela Sabatini, the No. 2 women's seed, sprained an ankle while playing Claudia Porwik and had to default. On the same day, Australia's Mark Woodforde did likewise against David Wheaton on Court 1. Two other players, Veli Paloheimo in the men's singles, and 15-year-old Anke Huber, in the women singles, also went over on their ankles and lost whatever chance they had of beating Mats Wilander and Raffaella Reggi respectively. In addition, the men's semi-finals, which had looked likely to be exciting, were complete fizzers. Edberg gave Wilander the worst thrashing of his career, dropping only four games, and Lendl crushed the revitalised Yannick Noah 6–4 6–1 6–2. In fact, the Open was almost devoid of memorable matches, and, as in 1989, the best match – this time a cliff-hanger in the third round between Wilander and Wally Masur – finished in the small hours of the morning. To make matters worse for Australian fans, not one Aussie won a title, even in the junior doubles.

The tragedy of the men's singles was that Edberg had hit perhaps the best form of his life and was poised to capture his third Australian crown. Despite his injury, he won the first set convincingly and served for the second set at 6–5.

The stylish Swede had dropped only one set on his way to the final – to Wheaton on a very windy day – and seemed destined to make up for his bad luck in Melbourne the previous year when he injured his back while playing Pat Cash in the quarter-finals and had to withdraw. As was the case then, it was Edberg's beautifully synchronised and sinuous service action that probably proved his undoing. His serving imposes an enormous strain on many of his muscles, and he thought he probably hurt himself in the last service game of his match with Wilander. In his first service game of the final, he realised that an abdominal muscle on his left side was stiff, and as the match progressed it got progressively more painful. That he survived as long as he did is testimony to his courage, for Lendl was also in very good form, having lost only one set in his previous matches – to fellow Czech Karel Novacek.

Only twice before has a Grand Slam singles final ended in default. At Wimbledon in 1911, H. Roper Barrett was forced to retire when two-sets-all against Anthony Wilding; and in 1931, also at Wimbledon, Frank Shields gave Sidney Wood a walkover after injuring his knee in the semi-finals.

It was a sad irony that this tournament should prove to be so anti-climactic, since not for many years had it presented such a fascinating array of talent. Besides Lendl, the defending champion, and his leading challengers, Boris Becker and Edberg, players of the calibre of Noah, McEnroe, Wilander, Mecir and Muster were in good enough form to entertain hopes of winning. All grimly departed.

Though Becker has a Melbourne-born coach in Bob Brett, this windswept city is not one of his favourite places. In four previous visits, he had never advanced beyond the quarter-finals, and this time, in a night match, he had to dig deep into his strength, stamina and nervous energy to survive a fourth round against Mecir. The 'Big Cat', with his velvet touch and deceptive changes of pace, led Becker 6–4 7–6 3–1 before the German, in yet another of his narrow escapes, turned the match around to seize the last three sets from his exhausted opponent 6–4 6–1 6–1.

But the effort took its toll. In the next round, Becker was only a shadow of the player who, in 1989, so resolutely won Wimbledon and the US Open and led his country to another *Davis Cup* triumph. A few weeks earlier, in the *Davis Cup* final which was held on an indoor carpet, Becker had allowed Wilander only four games and even though, in the early rounds here, Mats – a three-time Open champion – regained some of his confidence and 'feel' for the game, his cause looked doomed. However, a hot, blustery wind played havoc with Becker's timing, and the long battle with Mecir had depleted his physical and nervous resources. In deference to the sun, he played in a cap that made him look like a train driver, and was soon derailed by Wilander's passing shots, losing 6–4 6–4 6–2.

McEnroe's exit was the most dramatic occurrence in the history of the Open. He had won his first three matches easily, but after a fine start against Pernfors his temper frayed and he became involved in a series of incidents. He received a warning for intimidating a lineswoman. Then, at 2–3, and break-point in the fourth set, he was penalised a point for cracking his racquet by flinging it to the ground. Then, at the end of an argument with umpire Gerry Armstrong, supervisor Ken Farrar and referee Peter Bellenger, McEnroe verbally abused the officials, and Farrar instructed Armstrong to default him. McEnroe said later that he did not realise the tournament was governed by the new three-step disciplinary code – warning, penalty point, default – and that he was expecting, if anything, a game penalty under the old four-step code. He was fined a total of $6,500.

Wilander, unlike McEnroe, is widely admired in Australia, and everybody sympathised with him in his 'free fall' from the No. 1 ranking to beyond the top 10. He and Masur, the No. 1 ranked Australian, had a gripping struggle in which the doughty Swede pitted his once flawless but still formidable groundstrokes against Masur's persistent aggression. It was nip-and-tuck all the way, and in the end one service-break and a net-cord on match point decided it, with Wilander a 6–4 5–7 6–4 1–6 6–3 winner. How shattering then was his defeat two matches later when Edberg, playing, as he himself said, 'near perfect' tennis, blasted him off the court in 82 minutes!

Noah and Muster were the two in-form dark horses. Both had won a lead-up tournament on *Rebound Ace*; Noah in Sydney, Muster in Adelaide. Buoyed up by his new coach, Dennis Ralston, and exhilarated by a new romance, Noah electrified the crowds with his swashbuckling tennis. He almost went out in the first round to Goran Prpic, but then whipped Ronald Agenor, Gilad Bloom, Pete Sampras and Mikael Pernfors to raise the prospect of becoming the first Frenchman since Jean Borotra in 1928 to capture the Australian crown. Alas, poor Yannick! Lendl's heavy artillery blew holes in his net attack after a fairly even first set.

As for Muster, the iron-man from Leibnitz who had made a remarkable recovery from the car accident that left him with a smashed knee, he fell victim to Australia's Simon Youl in the third round. A semi-finalist in 1989, Muster was exhausted by his 1–6 7–5 7–5 2–6 8–6 win over Christo Van Rensburg on a very hot day in the second round. He found Youl's steady ground play and polished net attack too much to counter and went down 3–6 6–4 6–3 6–2. It was typical of a jinxed tournament that Youl, the only Aussie to reach the fourth round, aggravated his chronic back trouble in that match, and was merely cannon fodder for Lendl in the next round. But let's not take anything away from Ivan. As usual, he prepared himself meticulously, arriving in Australia many weeks before the Open started. He acquired new headgear, resembling a foreign legionaire's cap and cape, and wore it for every match, even when the weather wasn't particularly hot, so that he could get used to it. And it turned out, it was not required in the final when the coolness of the day may have contributed to Edberg's disability.

Not all was gloom and despair in the men's events. In the men's doubles, Pat Cash made a cautious return to competition following his achilles tendon rupture and, paired with Edberg, pushed the defending champions, Rick Leach and Jim Pugh, to five sets. The winners were duly toppled by the unseeded Canadians, Grant Connell and Glenn

Michibata, in another five-setter. Meanwhile, South Africans Pieter Aldrich and Danie Visser survived the longest match in the history of the tournament, beating Scott Davis and Robert Van't Hof 6–4 4–6 7–6 4–6 23–21 in 5 hours and 29 minutes. They went on to become the first South African pair to win the title by defeating Connell and Michibata 6–4 4–6 6–1 6–4.

The women had little chance of compensating for the mishaps of the men's singles, as such leading players as Martina Navratilova, Arantxa Sanchez-Vicario and Monica Seles chose not to play. In their absence, and after Sabatini's lamentable injury, Steffi Graf was thought likely to have a cakewalk. She duly won the title comfortably enough for a third consecutive time, beating Mary Joe Fernandez 6–3 6–4 in the final, though her form was not quite as impressive as hitherto, perhaps because of the perceived lack of any real challenge.

Fernandez gave the world champion a good match while lacking the penetration to put her under serious pressure. Two other opponents, Patty Fendick, in the quarter-finals, and Helena Sukova, in the semis, pressed her closer. Down a set, Fendick went for her shots boldly and reached set point at 5–2 in the second set, but then faded. Sukova's aggression also drew dividends. After losing the first set, she won the second set when her forehand actually eclipsed Graf's. An upset seemed distinctly possible when the tall Czech broke the champion's service early in the third set, but Graf immediately broke back. And finally, when serving at 4–5, Sukova made a series of nervous, unforced errors, losing on a double-fault.

Sabatini's exit had left the bottom half of the draw up for grabs, presenting seventh seed Hana Mandlikova, in particular, with a golden opportunity to reach the semi-finals. However, as so often in the past, Mandlikova's flashes of brilliance were not enough to allow her to survive. She paid the price for her erratic play by losing to the 16-year-old qualifier, Angelica Gavaldon, by the bewildering score 6–1 1–6 6–1. Gavaldon, an amateur, got to the quarters before losing to Claudia Porwik.

The key match in the bottom half was that between Fernandez, the sixth seed, and Zina Garrison, the third. Nerves, as much as Mary Joe's steadiness beat Zina; she twice served for the match, and finally lost it 8–6 in the third. Fernandez scored an easy win over Porwik to reach her first Grand Slam final and, at the same time, won many admirers with her Evert-like grace and aplomb. She also finished runner-up in the women's doubles, losing with Fendick in two close sets to Sukova and Jana Novotna.

MEN'S SINGLES

Holder: M. Wilander (SWE)

4-6 7-6 5-2 retd

FIRST ROUND | SECOND ROUND | THIRD ROUND | FOURTH ROUND | QUARTER-FINALS | SEMI-FINALS | FINAL

First Round

1 I. LENDL (TCH) (1)
2 J. Pugh (USA)
3 C. Carbonell (ESP)
4 K. Suk (TCH)
5 K. Novacek (TCH)
6 M. Brown (AUS) (Q)
7 E. Winogradsky (FRA)
8 T. Wilkison (USA)
9 S. Youl (AUS) (WC)
10 M. Laurendeau (CAN)
11 C. Poline (FRA) (Q)
12 B. Drewett (AUS) (WC)
13 C. Van Rensburg (RSA)
14 J. Potier (FRA)
15 J. Vissel (FRG) (Q)
16 T. MUSTER (AUT) (15)
17 A. GOMEZ (ECU) (9)
18 D. Cahill (AUS)
19 T. Witsken (USA)
20 B. Oresar (YUG)
21 M. Stich (FRG)
22 P. Doohan (AUS) (Q)
23 J. Bates (GBR)
24 L. Lavalle (MEX)
25 A. Cherkasov (URS)
26 S. Matsuoka (JAP) (Q)
27 B. Lavendecker (USA)
28 B. Benhabiles (FRA)
29 J. Brown (USA)
30 A. Volkov (URS)
31 J. Fleurian (FRA)
32 J. SANCHEZ (ESP) (7)
33 J. McENROE (USA) (4)
34 T. Tulasne (FRA)
35 A. Mansdorf (ISR)
36 A. Antonisch (AUT)
37 N. Pereira (VEN)
38 G. Pondrahan (CAN) (Q)
39 D. Goldie (USA)
40 D. Patten (AUS) (WC)
41 P. Korda (TCH)
42 J. Hlasek (SUI)
43 H. Leconte (FRA)
44 F. Roig (ESP)
45 M. Pernfors (SWE)
46 S. Zivojinovic (YUG)
47 J. Shiras (USA)
48 S. BRUGUERA (ESP) (13)
49 Y. NOAH (FRA) (12)
50 G. Prpic (YUG)
51 R. Reneberg (USA)
52 R. Agenor (HAI)
53 P. Aldrich (RSA)
54 G. Bergstrom (SWE)
55 G. Bloom (ISR)
56 J. Fitzgerald (AUS)
57 N. Broad (RSA) (Q)
58 C. Pistolesi (ITA)
59 M. Schapers (HOL)
60 T. Woodbridge (AUS)
61 J. Arrese (ESP)
62 N. Brown (GBR) (Q)
63 P. Sampras (USA)
64 T. MAYOTTE (USA) (2)

Second Round

LENDL (1) 6-3 6-2 6-4
Carbonell 6-4 7-5 6-3
Novacek 6-3 6-1 2-6 6-2
Winogradsky 6-2 7-6 6-3
Youl 4-6 7-6 6-2 6-2
Drewett
Van Rensburg 6-7 6-3 5-7 6-3
MUSTER (15) 6-2 5-7 7-5 6-3
GOMEZ (9)
Oresar 6-4 6-1 6-4
Stich 6-3 6-1 6-2
Lavalle 6-7 6-1 6-4 6-2
Cherkasov 6-2 6-4 6-6 0-6 2
Lavendecker 7-6 7-6 6-3
Volkov
Fleurian 6-3 6-3 6-1
McENROE (4) 6-2 6-1 6-1
Antonisch 4-6 6-4 6-4 6-7 6-3
Pereira 7-6 4-6 6-3
Goldie 6-3 6-4 6-4
Korda
Leconte 6-1 6-7 7-5 6-4
Pernfors 6-2 6-1 6-2
BRUGUERA (13) 6-1 6-4 6-3
NOAH (12) 6-4 7-6 2-4 6-1
Agenor 6-2 6-4 3-6 6-1
Bergstrom
Bloom 7-6 7-6 4-6 6-2
Pistolesi 5-7 6-4 6-4 6-1
Woodbridge 4-6 6-0 6-3 6-1
Sampras 7-6 6-7 4-6 7-5 12-10

Third Round

LENDL (1) 6-4 6-2 6-3
Novacek 6-4 6-1 4-6 6-3
Youl 6-4 7-6 6-0
MUSTER (15) 1-6 7-5 2-6 8-6
GOMEZ (9) 6-4 3-6 6-3 6-2
Stich 6-4 6-4 2-0 retd
Cherkasov 6-4 5-7 7-5 6-0
Fleurian 6-4 1-6 7-5 2-6 6-2
McENROE (4) 6-1 6-2 6-1
Goldie 6-3 6-4 6-3
Leconte 6-2 4-6 6-3 7-4
Pernfors 6-4 6-3 1-6 6-4
NOAH (12) 7-6 6-3 6-3
Bloom 2-6 5-7 6-2 6-4 6-2
Woodbridge 6-3 6-2 6-2
Sampras 0-6 6-2 3-6 6-1 6-3

Fourth Round

LENDL (1) 6-4 3-6 6-4 6-1
Youl 3-6 6-4 6-3 6-2
GOMEZ (9) 6-4 6-3 3-6 7-6
Cherkasov 6-4 6-4 7-5
McENROE (4) 6-3 6-2 6-2
Pernfors 6-4 6-1 6-3
NOAH (12) 6-3 6-3 6-3
Sampras 7-5 6-4 6-2

Quarter-Finals

LENDL (1) 6-1 6-3 6-1
Cherkasov 2-6 6-3 7-6 7-6
Pernfors 1-6 6-4 5-7 4-2 def
NOAH (12) 6-3 6-4 3-6 6-2

Semi-Finals

LENDL (1) 6-3 6-2 6-3
NOAH (12) 6-3 7-5 6-2

Final

LENDL (1) 6-4 6-1 6-2

I. LENDL (TCH) (1)

EDBERG (3)
6-1 6-1 6-2

EDBERG (3)
7-5 7-6 3-6 6-2

WILANDER (8)
6-4 6-4 6-2

Wheaton
7-6 6-4 6-3

EDBERG (3)
6-2 6-2 6-4

WILANDER (8)
7-5 6-4 6-0

BECKER (2)
4-6 7-6 4-6 1-6-1

KRICKSTEIN (12)
6-7 6-2 6-3 6-2

Wheaton
6-3 4-5 retd

Svensson
6-4 7-5 3-6 4-6 6-2

EDBERG (3)
6-3 6-4 6-1

WILANDER (8)
6-4 5-7 6-4 1-6 6-3

Paloheimo
7-5 6-4 3-6 6-1

MECIR (16)
2-6 6-1 6-0 6-2

BECKER (2)
4-6 6-7 6-4 6-1 6-1

KRICKSTEIN (5) 6-1 4-6 6-3 6-1	Wahlgren 4-6 7-5 7-5 6-3
Wheaton 6-3 6-2 3-6 6-1	Woodforde 6-3 6-2 7-5
Svensson 2-6 6-2 3-6-2	Jonsson 6-1 6-2 6-2
Chamberlin 6-7 7-5 6-3 6-4	EDBERG (3) 6-2 6-2 6-4
WILANDER (8) 6-3 7-5 6-3	Masur 7-6 6-7 6-3 6-1
Sanchez 6-1 7-6 6-3	Paloheimo 6-4 3-6 6-3 6-3
MECIR (16) 2-6 6-1 6-0 6-2	Riglewski 6-2 6-2 6-2
Delaitre 6-3 4-6 6-3 6-4	BECKER (2) 6-3 7-6 4-6 6-2

KRICKSTEIN (5) 6-4 6-7 6-4 7-5	Wahlgren 4-6 7-5 6-4 5-7 6-1
Wohmann 6-3 6-1 6-3	Wheaton 6-3 2-6 6-3 6-1
Larsson 6-4 6-4 6-1	Woodforde
CHESNOKOV (11) 3-6 6-7 6-6 3-6-2	Courier 6-3 6-1
Svensson 6-2 7-5 7-5	Gustafsson 2-2 retd
Jonsson	Pescosolido 6-3 6-2 7-6
Chamberlin 6-0 6-7 6-3 6-4	Kuhnen 6-3 6-7 2-6 7-6 6-2
EDBERG (3) 7-6 6-3 6-4	WILANDER (8) 7-6 7-5 7-5
Wostenholme 6-3 5-7 7-6 6-1	Odizor
Masur 6-2 6-1 6-2	Sanchez 6-0 6-3 6-1
Annacone 6-3 6-4 6-7 2-6 6-3	Forget 2-6 6-4 6-4 6-2
Paloheimo 5-7 6-3 0-6 6-2 6-2	MECIR (16)
Schapper 7-6 6-3 7-6	Borwick 6-3 6-1
Riglewski 6-2 6-3 2-6 6-2	Delaitre 2-6 6-3 3-6 4-6-3
Jones 6-3 5-7 2-6 6-2 6-3	Davis
BECKER (2) 6-1 6-2 6-1	

65	A. KRICKSTEIN (USA) (5)
66	G. Pozzi (ITA) (Q)
67	R. Krishnan (IND)
68	M. Zoecke (FRG)
69	L. Wahlgren (SWE)
70	H. De La Pena (ARG)
71	A. Vysand (URS)
72	J. Wohmann (FRG)
73	G. Ivanisevic (YUG)
74	D. Wheaton (USA)
75	M. Larsson (SWE) (Q)
76	M. Rosset (SUI)
77	J. Altur (ESP)
78	M. Woodforde (AUS)
79	M. Krazman (AUS)
80	A. CHESNOKOV (URS) (11)
81	J. COURIER (USA) (14)
82	J. Anas (USA)
83	J. Svensson (SWE)
84	T. Hogstedt (SWE)
85	M. Gustafsson (SWE)
86	M. Kulti (SWE)
87	T. Nijssen (HOL)
88	J. Jonsson (SWE)
89	J. Gunnarsson (SWE)
90	S. Pescosolido (ITA) (Q)
91	S. Barr (AUS) (WC)
92	P. Chamberlin (USA)
93	K. Kumen (FRG)
94	K. Kroon (SWE)
95	J. Anderson (AUS)
96	S. EDBERG (SWE) (3)
97	M. WILANDER (SWE) (8)
98	R. Fromberg (AUS)
99	D. Macpherson (AUS) (WC)
100	M. Wostenholme (CAN)
101	N. Odizor (NIG) (Q)
102	I. Peter-Budge (AUS) (WC)
103	W. Masur (AUS)
104	E. Jelen (FRG)
105	A. Rahunen (FIN)
106	J. Sanchez (ESP)
107	P. Annacone (USA)
108	G. Muller (USA)
109	G. Forget (FRA)
110	C. Cornel (CAN)
111	V. Paloheimo (FIN)
112	C. STEEB (FRG) (10)
113	M. MECIR (TCH) (16)
114	M. Koevermans (HOL)
115	L. Nemecek (TCH) (Q)
116	A. Schapper (CAN)
117	N. Borwick (AUS) (WC)
118	K. Evernden (NZL)
119	U. Riglewski (FRG) (Q)
120	P. Cane (ITA)
121	O. Delaitre (FRA)
122	C. Campese (ITA)
123	K. Jones (USA)
124	K. Tauson (DEN)
125	S. Davis (USA)
126	J. Morgan (AUS) (WC)
127	S. Razbun (HOL)
128	B. BECKER (FRG) (2)

Capital letter denotes seeded players. Number following players' name gives seeding order. (Q) – Qualifier, (WC) – Wild Card, (LL) – Lucky Loser

WOMEN'S SINGLES

Holder: S. Graf (FRG)

FIRST ROUND	SECOND ROUND	THIRD ROUND	FOURTH ROUND	QUARTER-FINALS	SEMI-FINALS	FINAL

6-3 3-6 6-4

GRAF (1)
6-3 3-6 6-4

GRAF (1)
6-3 7-5

SUKOVA (4)
6-4 6-3

GRAF (1)
6-2 6-3

Fendick
7-5 6-2

SUKOVA (4)
6-4 6-3

MALEEVA (9)
3-6 6-4 6-1

GRAF (1)
6-4 6-1

REGGI (13)
7-5 4-6 6-4

PAULUS (16)
6-4 6-3

Fendick
1-6 7-6 6-4

SUKOVA (4)
6-3 4-6 6-3

Date
6-4 6-3

MALEEVA (9)
6-0 6-4

McQuillan
6-2 7-6

GRAF (1)
6-1 6-2

Meskhi
2-6 6-1 6-3

Huber
6-2 6-0

REGGI (13)
6-4 6-4

Smylie
6-2 6-4

Fendick
7-5 6-2

NOVOTNA (5)
6-1 6-1

SUKOVA (4)
6-2 6-0

Loosemore
6-3 6-3

Date
7-5 7-6

SHRIVER (11)
1-6 6-2 9-7

MALEEVA (9)
6-3 6-2

Jagerman
6-1 6-2

McQuillan
6-3 6-0

KELESI (8)
6-2 6-4

GRAF (1)
6-2 7-5
De Lone
6-4 7-6-1
Meskhi
6-4 6-4
Dahlman
7-6 6-1
Huber
6-1 6-1
Burgin
2-7 7-6 6-3
Durie
7-5 7-6
REGGI (13)
6-1 6-0
PAULUS (16)
6-3 6-1
Miyagi
7-5 6-4
Smylie
6-3 7-5
Reinstadler
6-1 6-2
Fendick
6-1 6-3
Keller
3-6 7-6 6-4
Temesvari
0-6 6-3 6-2
NOVOTNA (5)
6-7 6-0 6-0
SUKOVA (4)
6-4 6-3
Medvedeva
6-4 7-5
Loosemore
6-3 7-5
Pampoulova
4-6 6-4 6-2
Date
6-3 7-6
Schultz
6-4 6-3
Provis
7-5 7-6
SHRIVER (11)
6-3 6-4
MALEEVA (9)
6-2 6-1
McDonald
6-4 6-4
Jagerman
6-4 2-6 6-1
Jagerman
6-4 7-6
Sharpe
7-5 3-6 6-3
McQuillan
6-1 6-2
Meir
6-4 6-2
KELESI (8)
6-2 6-3

1 S. **GRAF** (FRG) (1)
2 C. Cunningham (USA)
3 L. Stacey (AUS) (WC)
4 E. De Lone (USA) (Q)
5 L. Golarsa (ITA)
6 L. Meskhi (URS)
7 K. Kessaris (USA)
8 C. Dahlman (SWE)
9 A. Huber (FRG)
10 M. Laval (FRA)
11 E. Burgin (USA)
12 S. Stafford (USA)
13 P. Paradis (FRA)
14 J. Durie (GBR)
15 J. Hodder (AUS) (WC)
16 R. **REGGI** (ITA) (13)
17 B. **PAULUS** (AUT) (16)
18 R. Rajchrtova (TCH)
19 R. Zrubakova (TCH)
20 N. Miyagi (JAP)
21 E. Smylie (AUS)
22 J. Hetherington (CAN)
23 B. Reiss (USA)
24 B. Reinstadler (AUT)
25 A. Nishiya (JAP)
26 P. Fendick (USA)
27 A. Keller (USA)
28 S. Meinng (FRG)
29 J. Stubbs (AUS) (WC)
30 A. Temesvari (HUN)
31 S. Martin (USA)
32 J. **NOVOTNA** (TCH) (5)
33 H. **SUKOVA** (TCH) (4)
34 K. McDonald (AUS) (WC)
35 N. Medvedeva (URS)
36 L. Gregory (RSA) (Q)
37 S. Loosemore (GBR) (Q)
38 J. Faull (AUS)
39 E. Pampoulova (BUL)
40 A. Grossman (USA) (WC)
41 P. Etchemendy (FRA)
42 K. Date (JAP)
43 B. Schultz (HOL)
44 N. Pawlik (FRG)
45 N. Provis (AUS)
46 A. Schurhoff (FRG) (Q)
47 E. Sviglerova (TCH)
48 P. **SHRIVER** (USA) (11)
49 K. **MALEEVA** (BUL) (9)
50 L. McNeil (USA)
51 J. Allen (USA)
52 K. McDonald (AUS) (WC)
53 K. Okamoto (JAP)
54 M. Drake (CAN)
55 C. Kohde-Kilsch (FRG)
56 J. Jagerman (AUS)
57 L. Field (AUS)
58 K. Sharpe (AUS)
59 F. Bonsignori (ITA)
60 R. McQuillan (AUS)
61 S. Meir (FRG)
62 J. Smoller (USA) (Q)
63 W. Probst (FRG)
64 H. **KELESI** (CAN) (8)

S. GRAF (FRG) (1)

First round (draw positions 65–128):

65 M. FERNANDEZ (USA) (6)
66 M. Jaggard (AUS)
67 K. Rinaldi (USA)
68 E. White (USA)
69 M. Wedell (USA)
70 A. Henricksson (USA)
71 A. Devries (BEL)
72 J. Halard (FRA)
73 D. Faber (USA)
74 E. Pfaff (FRG)
75 D. Balestrat (AUS)
76 A. Leand (USA)
77 C. Bakkum (HOL)
78 K. Radford (AUS)
79 R. FAIRBANK NIDEFFER (USA) (14)
80 L. SAVCHENKO (URS) (12)
81 B. Benjamin (USA)
82 C. Tanvier (FRA)
83 B. Bowes (USA)
84 E. Inoue (JAP)
85 H. Ludloff (USA)
86 N. Pratt (AUS) (WC)
87 S. Gomer (GBR)
88 S. Appelmans (BEL)
89 K. Adams (USA)
90 I. Demongeot (FRA)
91 K. Kidowaki (JAP)
92 F. Kapl (SUI)
93 P. Thoren (FIN)
94 T. Scheuer-Larsen (DEN)
95 A. Kimura (JAP)
96 Z. GARRISON (USA) (3)
97 H. MANDLIKOVA (AUS) (7)
98 A. Minter (AUS)
99 C. MacGregor (USA)
100 C. Wood (GBR) (Q)
101 L. Ponin (USA)
102 A. Gavaldon (USA) (Q)
103 A. Dechaume (FRA) (LL)
104 K. Kschwendt (LUX)
105 C. Suire (FRA)
106 T. Whitlinger (USA)
107 J. Thompson (AUS)
108 T. Phelps (USA)
109 J. Pospisilova (TCH)
110 E. Zardo (SUI)
111 K. Quentrec (FRA)
112 G. FERNANDEZ (USA) (15)
113 N. ZVEREVA (URS) (10)
114 N. Herreman (FRA)
115 S. Wasserman (BEL)
116 P. Langrova (TCH)
117 P. Ritter (AUT)
118 D. Van Rensburg (RSA)
119 C. Cioffi (USA)
120 G. Bartos (SUI)
121 S. Goles (YUG)
122 J. Wiesner (AUT)
123 C. Cohen (SUI)
124 C. Porwick (FRG)
125 A. Grossman (USA)
126 M. Bollegraf (HOL)
127 A. Frazier (USA)
128 G. SABATINI (ARG) (2)

Second round:
FERNANDEZ (6) 6-1 6-3
Rinaldi 6-4 3-6 6-4
Henricksson 4-6 6-4 6-4
Halard 7-5 6-2
Faber 6-3 6-0
Leand 6-2 4-6 6-4
Bakkum 6-3 6-2
FAIRBANK NIDEFFER (14) 6-3 6-3
Tanvier 4-6 6-1 12-10
Inoue 6-3 7-6
Pratt 6-1 6-7 10-8
Appelmans 6-1 6-0
Demongeot 4-6 6-2 6-2
Kidowaki 6-2 6-2
Thoren 3-6 6-3 6-1
GARRISON (3) 6-2 6-0
MANDLIKOVA (7) 6-1 6-2
MacGregor 6-4 6-2
Gavaldon 6-3 6-3
Dechaume 6-4 7-5
Whitlinger 6-1 6-2
Phelps 6-4 6-3
Pospisilova 6-4 6-1
FERNANDEZ (15) 6-3 6-4
ZVEREVA (10) 6-7 7-5 7-5
Wasserman 7-6 0-6 6-3
Van Rensburg 6-0 6-0
Cioffi 7-5 6-4
Wiesner 7-5 6-2
Porwick 6-4 6-1
Bollegraf 6-2 6-3
SABATINI (2) 7-5 6-1

Third round:
FERNANDEZ (6) 6-4 6-4
Halard 7-6 6-2
Faber 6-1 6-3
FAIRBANK NIDEFFER (14) 7-6 6-4
Tanvier 6-3 7-6
Appelmans 6-2 6-3
Demongeot 6-4 6-1
GARRISON (3) 5-7 6-3 6-4
MANDLIKOVA (7) 7-6 6-3
Gavaldon 6-4 4-6 7-5
Whitlinger 7-5 6-3
FERNANDEZ (15) 6-4 7-6
Wasserman 7-5 6-1
Van Rensburg 6-0 6-4
Porwick 6-3 7-6
SABATINI (2) 6-1 6-1

Fourth round:
FERNANDEZ (6) 6-4 6-0
Faber 6-3 6-4
Tanvier 7-6 6-0
GARRISON (3) 6-2 6-0
Gavaldon 6-1 1-6 6-1
FERNANDEZ (15) 7-6 6-3
Van Rensburg 6-4 6-2
Porwick 2-6 0-1 retd

Round of 16:
FERNANDEZ (6) 6-4 6-2
GARRISON (3) 6-2 2-0 retd
Gavaldon 6-3 1-6 6-2
Porwick 7-6 3-6 6-4

Quarter-finals:
FERNANDEZ (6) 1-6 6-2 8-6
Porwick 6-4 6-3

Semi-final:
FERNANDEZ (6) 6-2 6-1

MEN'S DOUBLES

Holders: R. Leach (USA)/J. Pugh (USA)

Winner: ALDRICH (RSA)/VISSER (RSA) (2) 6–4 4–6 6–1 6–4

FIRST ROUND	SECOND ROUND	THIRD ROUND	QUARTER-FINALS	SEMI-FINALS	FINAL
1 LEACH/PUGH (1)	LEACH/PUGH (1)	LEACH/PUGH (1)	LEACH/PUGH (1)	LEACH/PUGH (1)	
2 Page/Schmidt	6–4 6–2	6–4 6–2	6–4 6–4	3–6 7–5 7–6 2 6 6–4	
3 Dyke/Warner	Brown/Gunthardt				
4 N. Brown/Gunthardt	6–4 2–6 6–4				
5 Nelson/R. Smith	Jones/Rive				
6 Jones/Rive	6–2 6–2	LAYENDECKER/RENEBERG (16)			
7 Mansdorf/Pimc	LAYENDECKER/RENEBERG (16)	5–7 6–4 10–8			
8 LAYENDECKER/RENEBERG (16)	6–7 6–2 6–2				
9 EVERNDEN/J. SANCHEZ (9)	EVERNDEN/SANCHEZ (9)		Cash/Edberg	CONNELL/MICHIBATA (13)	
10 Bates/Nyssen	7–6 4–6 6–4	Woodbridge/Youl	w/o	3–6 6–3 6–1 2 6 6–4	
11 Woodbridge/Youl	Woodbridge/Youl	6–4 6–4			
12 Derlin/Guy	6–4 6–3				
13 Jarrison/Kinnear	Korda/Suk				
14 Korda/Suk	6–2 6–2	Cash/Edberg			
15 Cash/Edberg (W)	Cash/Edberg	7–6 3–7 6–4			
16 PAWSAT/WARDER (7)	7–6 6–2				
17 ANNACONE/FITZGERALD (3)	ANNACONE/FITZGERALD (3)	ANNACONE/FITZGERALD (3)	CONNELL/MICHIBATA (13)		
18 Mota/Petten (WC)	6–3 6–3	6–3 7–6	6–4 4–6 6–4		
19 Kuhnen/Lavalle	Kuhnen/Lavalle				
20 Macpherson/Shiras	6–3 7–8–6				
21 Novacek/Osterthun	Novacek/Osterthun				
22 Custer/Tyson	6–3 3–7	CONNELL/MICHIBATA (13)			
23 Beckman/Cannon	CONNELL/MICHIBATA (13)	6–2 6–1			
24 CONNELL/MICHIBATA (13)	6–4 6–4				
25 CASALE/SANCHEZ (11)	CASAL/SANCHEZ (11)			CONNELL/MICHIBATA	
26 Mora/Schor	6–1 6–2	Fleurian/Leconte	Fleurian/Leconte	4–6 7–5 7–5 6–2	
27 Fleurian/Leconte (WC)	Fleurian/Leconte	6–3 4–6 7–5	6–2 7–6		
28 Baur/Saceanu	2–6 6–2 7–5				
29 Forget/Noah	Forget/Noah				
30 Broom/Goldie	6–3 6–4	HLASEK/WINOGRADSKY (5)			
31 Benhabiles/Poline	HLASEK/WINOGRADSKY (5)	w/o			
32 HLASEK/WINOGRADSKY (5)	6–2 4–6 19–17				
33 CAHILL/KRATZMANN (6)	CAHILL/KRATZMANN (6)	CAHILL/KRATZMANN (6)	CAHILL/KRATZMANN (6)		
34 Ballauf/Wahlgren	4–6 7–5 10–8	6–3 6–3	6–3 6–4		
35 Jensen/Wheaton	Jensen/Wheaton				
36 Ridgewood/Stoll	6–3 7–5				
37 Drewett/Masur	Drewett/Masur				
38 Mronz/Schapers	6–3 6–4	Drewett/Masur			
39 Galbraith/Van Emburgh	Drewett/Masur	6–3 6–3			
40 LOZANO/WITSKEN (12)	6–4 4–6 14–12			Broad/Muller	
41 DOHMAN/AROCZY (14)	LOZANO/WITSKEN (12)		Broad/Muller	6–4 3–6 3–7–6	
42 Haarhuis/Koevermans	3–6 6–1 7–5	Henricksson/Utgren	6–4 4–6 6–3		
43 Henricksson/Utgren	Haarhuis/Koevermans	7–6 7–6			
44 Castle/Odzor	6–2 7–5				
45 Broad/Muller	Henricksson/Utgren				
46 Bathman/Svensson	Broad/Muller	Broad/Muller			
47 Arnaud/Mutel	6–3 6–4	6–4 7–6			
48 VAN RENSBURG/WOODFORDE (4)	VAN RENSBURG/WOODFORDE (4)				
49 COURIER/SAMPRAS (8)	6–4 6 7 9–7				
50 Cassidy/Pozzi	Cassidy/Pozzi	Cassidy/Pozzi	Davis/Van 't Hof		
51 Artese/Clavet	6–4 6–4	6–2 6–4	7–5 3–6 6–2		
52 Adams/Altur	Adams/Altur				
53 Gomez/Pereira	6–4 5–7 6–4				
54 Barr/Borwick (WC)	Barr/Borwick				
55 CARBONELL/NARGISO (10)	6–4 6–2	Davis/Van 't Hof			
56 Davis/Van 't Hof	Davis/Van 't Hof	6–1 6–4			ALDRICH/VISSER (2)
57 IVANISEVIC/ZIVOJINOVIC (15)	6–3 5–4				7–6 7–6 2–6 6–4
58 Engel/Gustafsson	IVANISEVIC/ZIVOJINOVIC (15)		Chamberin/Wilkison		
59 Chamberin/Wilkison	4–6 6–4 6–3	Chamberin/Wilkison	6–3 6–4		
60 Kroon/Larsson	Chamberin/Wilkison	7–6 3–6 6–4			
61 Delaitre/Laurendeau	Delaitre/Laurendeau				
62 Anderson/Fromberg	4–6 6–4			ALDRICH/VISSER (2)	
63 Pagg/Scherman	ALDRICH/VISSER (2)	ALDRICH/VISSER (2)	ALDRICH/VISSER (2)	6–4 4–6 7–6 4–6 23–21	
64 ALDRICH/VISSER (2)	6–3 6–4	7–5 6–3	6–3 6–4		

Capital letters denote seeded pairings. Number following players' names give seeding order. (Q) – Qualifier, (WC) – Wild Card, (LL) – Lucky Loser

WOMEN'S DOUBLES

Holders: M. Navratilova (USA)/P. H. Shriver (USA)

J. NOVOTNA (TCH)/H. SUKOVA (TCH) (1) 7–6 7–6

FIRST ROUND	SECOND ROUND	THIRD ROUND	QUARTER-FINALS	SEMI-FINALS	FINAL
1 NOVOTNA/SUKOVA (1)	NOVOTNA/SUKOVA (1) 6-2 6-3	NOVOTNA/SUKOVA (1) 6-4 6-1	NOVOTNA/SUKOVA (1) 6-3 6-4	NOVOTNA/SUKOVA (1) 7-5 6-2	NOVOTNA/SUKOVA (1) 6-1 4-6 8-6
2 Bakkum/Van Rensburg					
3 Godridge/Sharpe (WC)	Skalstad/Benjamin 6-4 6-2				
4 Skalstad/Benjamin					
5 Ito/Mizokuchi	Scott/Walsh	Minter/Richardson 3-6 7-6 6-2			
6 Scott/Walsh					
7 Minter/Richardson	Minter/Richardson 6-2 6-2				
8 PORWICK/REGGI (16)					
9 BOLLEGRAF/DURIE (11)	Macgregor/Macgregor 6-4 3-6 6-3	Macgregor/Macgregor 6-4 6-4	Macgregor/Macgregor 0-6 6-4 6-3		
10 Macgregor/Macgregor					
11 Vanborg/Wood	Dechaume/Krapl 6-3 7-6				
12 Dechaume/Krapl					
13 Henricksson/Scheuer-Larsen	Field/Gregory	ADAMS/McNEIL (6) 6-4 6-3			
14 Fendick/Gregory					
15 Fewless/Grossman	ADAMS/McNEIL (6) 6-3 6-2				
16 ADAMS/McNEIL (6)					
17 G. FERNANDEZ/WHITE (4)	FERNANDEZ/WHITE (4) 6-2 7-6	FERNANDEZ/WHITE (4) 6-0 6-2	FERNANDEZ/WHITE (4) 6-2 6-2	FERNANDEZ/WHITE (4) 6-3 6-1	
18 Exstrand/Simpkin					
19 Ida/Schuerhoff	Croft/Frazier 6-3 6-4				
20 Croft/Frazier					
21 Faber/Werdel	Lindstrom/Ludloff 6-4	Lindstrom/Ludloff			
22 Lindstrom/Ludloff					
23 McDonald/Radford	McDonald/Radford 7-6 6-1				
24 HETHERINGTON/PROVIS (9)					
25 MEDVEDEVA/MESKHI (14)	MEDVEDEVA/MESKHI (14) 6-3 2-6 6-4	MEDVEDEVA/MESKHI (14) 6-1 6-3	MEDVEDEVA/MESKHI (14) 4-6 6-3 7-5		
26 Demess/Wasserman					
27 Herreman/Sure	Halard/Leand 6-2 6-3				
28 Halard/Leand					
29 Keller/Zambrzycki	Grousbeck/Miyagi 6-3 6-2	THOMPSON/TURNBULL (8) 6-2 6-3			
30 Grousbeck/Miyagi					
31 Cohen/O'Neill	THOMPSON/TURNBULL (8) 6-0 6-2				
32 THOMPSON/TURNBULL (8)					
33 GRAF/SABATINI (7)	GRAF/SABATINI (7) 6-2 6-4	Goles Maleeva w/o	SCHULTZ/TEMESVARI (13) 7-5 6-3	SCHULTZ/TEMESVARI (13) 6-4 6-2	FENDICK/FERNANDEZ (5) 6-3 6-3
34 Golarsa/Wiesner					
35 Garrison/Rinaldi	Goles/Maleeva 6-2 6-4				
36 Goles/Maleeva					
37 Okorawa/Sato	Paulus/Zrubakova 6-2 6-3	SCHULTZ/TEMESVARI (13) 7-6 6-4			
38 Paulus/Zrubakova					
39 Pratt/Woolcock (WC)	SCHULTZ/TEMESVARI (13) 6-3 6-1				
40 SCHULTZ/TEMESVARI (13)					
41 JORDAN/SMYLIE (12)	JORDAN/SMYLIE (12) 6-3 6-1	JORDAN/SMYLIE (12) 6-1 6-0	Faull/McQuillan 5-7 6-4 6-4		
42 Date/Kendrowski					
43 Meier/Pampoulova	Kschwendt/Toleafoa 7-6 7-6				
44 Kschwendt/Toleafoa					
45 Rees/Stafford	Bowrey/Hodder	Faull/McQuillan 5-7 7-5 6-2			
46 Bowrey/Hodder					
47 Faull/McQuillan	Faull/McQuillan 7-5				
48 MANDLIKOVA/SHRIVER (3)					
49 FENDICK/M-J. FERNANDEZ (5)	FENDICK/FERNANDEZ (5) 6-2 6-4	FENDICK/FERNANDEZ (5) 6-3 6-3	FENDICK/FERNANDEZ (5) 2-6 7-5 6-3	FENDICK/FERNANDEZ (5) 5-7 7-6 6-2	
50 Jagerman/Vis					
51 Pfaff/Stubbs	Pfaff/Stubbs 6-2 6-4				
52 Pospisilova/Rajchtova					
53 Dahlman/Probst	Allen/Jappard 6-1 6-3	DEMONGEOT/TANVIER (15) 6-4 6-3			
54 Aller/Jappard					
55 Frankl/Seeman	DEMONGEOT/TANVIER (15) 6-0 6-2				
56 DEMONGEOT/TANVIER (15)					
57 BURGIN/FAIRBANK NIDEFFER (10)	BURGIN/FAIRBANK NIDEFFER (10) 6-0 6-2	BURGIN/FAIRBANK NIDEFFER (10) 6-2 6-3	SAVCHENKO/ZVEREVA (2) 6-2 7-6		
58 Stacey/Taylor					
59 Pawlik/Sprung	Pawlik/Sprung 6-2 6-1				
60 Takagi/Thoren					
61 Jones/McNamara	Collins/Smoller 7-5 7-6	SAVCHENKO/ZVEREVA (2) 6-1 6-3			
62 Collins/Smoller					
63 Langtova/Svglerova	SAVCHENKO/ZVEREVA (2) 6-2 6-3				
64 SAVCHENKO/ZVEREVA (2)					

Capital letters denote seeded pairings. Number following players' names give seeding order. (Q) – Qualifier. (WC) – Wild Card. (LL) – Lucky Loser

MIXED DOUBLES

Holders: J. Pugh (USA)/J. Novotna (TCH)

Winner: J. PUGH (USA)/N. ZVEREVA (URS) (1) 4–6 6–2 6–3

FIRST ROUND	SECOND ROUND	QUARTER-FINALS	SEMI-FINALS	FINAL
1 PUGH/ZVEREVA (1)	PUGH/ZVEREVA (1) 6–2 6–2	PUGH/ZVEREVA (1) 6–2 6–2	PUGH/ZVEREVA (1) 7–5 4–6 6–2	PUGH/ZVEREVA (1) 3–6 6–2 6–3
2 Borwick/McDonald (WC)				
3 N. Brown/D. Van Rensburg	Smith/Adams 6–3 3–6 6–1			
4 R. Smith/K. Adams				
5 Cannon/R. White	Cannon/White 6–4 2–6 6–4	Cannon/White 6–1 7–6		
6 Van Emburgh/Smoller				
7 Broad/Fairbank Nideffer	KRATZMANN/THOMPSON (7) 1–6 6–4 6–3			
8 KRATZMANN/THOMPSON (7)				
9 CAHILL/TURNBULL (4)	Wheaton/Fernandez 6–1 6–4	Warder/Durie 6–3 7–6	Warder/Durie 6–4 6–2	
10 Wheaton/M. J. Fernandez				
11 Suk/Rajchrtova	Warder/Durie 6–3 6–2			
12 Warder/Durie				
13 Odizor/Lindstrom	Woodbridge/Faull 6–4 6–2	Lozano/Fernandez 7–6 6–3		
14 Woodbridge/Faull (WC)				
15 Lozano/G. Fernandez	Lozano/Fernandez 7–6 6–4			
16 DAVIS/FENDICK (6)				
17 DOOHAN/HETHERINGTON (8)	DOOHAN/HETHERINGTON (8) 6–3 6–7 6–4	Bates/Provis 6–4 7–6	FITZGERALD/SMYLIE (3) 6–2 6–2	LEACH/GARRISON (2) 6–1 6–3
18 C. Van Rensburg/Stafford				
19 Nelson/Allen	Bates/Provis 6–3 6–7 6–2			
20 Bates/Provis				
21 Witsken/Benjamin	Witsken/Benjamin 6–2 7–6	FITZGERALD/SMYLIE (3) w-o		
22 Warner/Reis				
23 Zivojinovic/Temesvari	FITZGERALD/SMYLIE (3) 7–6 7–6			
24 FITZGERALD/SMYLIE (3)				
25 PAWSAT/McNEIL (5)	Stich/Porwick 6–1 6–2	Castle/Reggi w-o	LEACH/GARRISON (2) 6–4 6–4	
26 Stich/Porwick				
27 Castle/Reggi	Castle/Reggi 6–2 6–4			
28 Jensen/Phelps				
29 Lavendecker/Burgin	Antonisch/Paulus 6–3 6–4	LEACH/GARRISON (2) 6–7 6–1 6–2		
30 Antonisch/Paulus				
31 Beckman/Ludloff	LEACH/GARRISON (2) 6–7 6–1 6–2			
32 LEACH/GARRISON (2)				

Capital letters denote seeded pairings. Number following players' names gives seeding order. (Q) – Qualifier. (WC) – Wild Card. (LL) – Lucky Loser.

JUNIOR EVENTS

BOYS' SINGLES – Final: Dirk Dier (FRG) (2) d. Leander Paes (IND) 6–4 7–6.
GIRLS' SINGLES – Final: Magdelena Maleeva (BUL)(3) d. Louise Stacey (AUS)(9) 7–5 6–7 6–1.
BOYS' DOUBLES – Final: Roger Pettersson (SWE)/Marten Renstroem (SWE) d. Robert Janecek (CAN)/Ernesto Munoz de Cote (MEX) 4–6 7–6 6–1.
GIRLS' DOUBLES – Final: Limor Zaltz (ISR)/Rona Mayer (ISR)(8) d. Justine Hodder (AUS)/Nicole Pratt (AUS)(2) 6–4 6–4.

AUSTRALIAN OPEN CHAMPIONSHIPS PRIZE MONEY – AUS$

MEN'S SINGLES – Winner $320,000. Runner-up $160,000. Semi-finalists $80,000. Quarter-finalists $40,000. Fourth-round losers $21,000. Third-round losers $12,000. Second-round losers $7,500. First-round losers $4,600.
Total: $1,694,400.
WOMEN'S SINGLES – Winner $320,000. Runner-up $160,000. Semi-finalists $80,000. Quarter-finalists $40,000. Fourth-round losers $21,000. Third-round losers $12,000. Second-round losers $7,500. First-round losers $4,600.
Total: $1,694,400.
MEN'S DOUBLES (per team) – Winners $125,000. Runners-up $62,500. Semi-finalists $32,000. Quarter-finalists $16,000. Third-round losers $9,000. Second-round losers $4,800. First-round losers $2,900.
Total: $557,100.
WOMEN'S DOUBLES (per team) – Winners $125,000. Runners-up $62,500. Semi-finalists $32,000. Quarter-finalists $16,000. Third-round losers $9,000. Second-round losers $4,800. First-round losers $2,900.
Total: $557,100.
MIXED DOUBLES (per team) – Winners $40,000. Runners-up $20,000. Semi-finalists $10,000. Quarter-finalists $5,200. Second-round losers $2,600. First-round losers $1,400.
Total: $144,000.

At the age of 30, Andres Gomez achieved a lifetime's ambition when he became the first player from Ecuador to win the French Open. He was also the oldest winner since another Andres – Gimeno of Spain – had won in 1972, aged 34. *(R. Adams)*

FRENCH OPEN CHAMPIONSHIPS

David Irvine

'Too late. Too soon'. Had anyone seriously suggested Andres Gomez and Monica Seles as a win-double before the 1990 French Open began, that is the likely response that would have been elicited from most observers. So much for informed opinion. As the song reminds us *it's never too late and it's never too soon*. Never.

Paris, which in recent years has become probably the most predictable among the four Grand Slams, may have opened with the odds on those with a proven track record but it could hardly have closed in less likely circumstances, with a 30-year-old journeyman from Ecuador being hailed as the oldest men's champion for 18 years and a mere 16-year-old from Yugoslavia emerging in a fit of giggles as the youngest women's title-winner ever.

'I suppose it's the sort of ending you dream about but never really expect to see'. That's how one veteran of Roland Garros summed it up. And it certainly offered a timely reminder that the star system is not infallible.

For the left-hander Gomez, whose dream had taken 11 long and arduous years to become reality, the sheer unexpectedness of it all – winning, that is, at an age when most players have given up on the serious pursuit of the game's highest honours – was what invested his triumph with added lustre. A year earlier, he revealed, he had gone back to his home in Guayaquil after his second-round loss and, though declining an offer to comment on the final for television, decided it was the sort of role for which he would perhaps be more suited in 1990. Then he heard that his *bête noir*, Ivan Lendl, had decided not to enter. 'And he was the only one that really bothered me. I thought maybe I had a chance. So instead of doing TV, I came to play.' Came, saw – and conquered. And in the final, moreover, he conquered the American Andre Agassi, an opponent 10 years his junior, by 6–3 2–6 6–4 6–4.

Seles repeated her Berlin triumph of a mere three weeks earlier (there she had ended Steffi Graf's 66-match winning streak) by beating the favourite, again in straight sets, by 7–6 6–4. Many had expected Graf to have learned enough in Berlin to devise a match-winning strategy; instead it was as if she seemed to have difficulty concentrating.

For Agassi, who had taken an outrageous gamble in limiting his preparation to just two matches (one of which he lost to Sweden's Magnus Gustafsson) at the German Open, it was a bitter blow. On his way to the final he had grown steadily into the favourite's role as one by one his rivals departed – Stefan Edberg and Boris Becker at the very first hurdle; the defending champion, Michael Chang, at Agassi's hand in the quarters; and Austria's Thomas Muster, arguably the best of the clay-courters, in the semis.

'Andres is going to have to work for this one' he had predicted before the final. 'I'm ready physically. That's the big difference in my game now'. He was convinced his time had come. But in the end fitness, on which Agassi continued to set such store even at the post-mortem, had little bearing on the outcome. It was on a cerebral level that the issue was resolved. And in that area Gomez was out on his own. Gomez had the variety to force Agassi to play on his terms. As a result the young American's limitations (but tactical, not physical) were exposed. Agassi wanted pace to feed off. Gomez declined to give it to him. Long rallies would have suited the American too. But the wily Gomez kept the exchanges brief and varied. Chip, slice, loop, whack. That was how Gomez played it. 'Whenever I had the chance to go in I took it. That put pressure on him'.

Even when down, Gomez kept his head. His failure in the past, he suggested, had been due to not playing the important points confidently. 'And I guess that's what big tennis is all about. Today was different. Even when I was down 0–30 in the final game I was able to come up with big serves'. A break in the eighth game was enough to give Gomez the first set and, though Agassi levelled in the second, it was less in the American's favour than the score suggested. In the third and fourth sets Gomez was supreme – and no-one enjoyed it more than Ecuador's ambassador, whose uninhibited support in the presidential box was a source of much amusement to a packed and delighted crowd.

As Gomez received the crowd's acclaim a near-to-tears Agassi, clad in his pink 'hot lava' outfit, stood on the court looking for all the world like a street urchin who had just had his packet of sweets confiscated. Team Agassi, all six in dark glasses, looked on gloomily, with coach Nick Bolletieri (foiled again on the brink) probably remembering the Rome final back in 1984 when another of his proteges, Aaron Krickstein, had also lost to Gomez. Even Seles' victory seemed to rub salt in the Florida coach's wounds. It was on account of Bollettieri favouring Agassi instead of her, she said, that the young Yugoslav had broken with him. Yet there could be no doubt his influence was a significant contributory factor.

It was entirely in keeping with events as they had unfolded throughout the two weeks of competition that neither final should end in the way the seedings had predicted – though in the men's event, as it happened, they were never much of a guide after day two.

Lendl's decision to by-pass Paris and, instead, devote lengthy preparation to his grass-court game, had opened up the draw intriguingly but the unprecedented exit of the top seeds Edberg and Becker brought total confusion.

As the beaten finalist in 1989 and the official favourite, Edberg's humiliation at the hands of the 19-year-old Spaniard, Sergi Bruguera, was perhaps the more complete (after leading 4–2 in the first set he won only three more games) yet Becker was a set up before some awesomely powerful serving from Yugoslavia's Goran Ivanisevic brought him down. 'I really didn't think he could keep it up' admitted Becker 'but he kept on serving and hitting. In the fourth set no-one in the world could have stopped him'. In all Ivanisevic, who the previous week had led Yugoslavia to ATP's World Team Cup in Dusseldorf, fired in 18 aces – one for each year of his life.

Emilio Sanchez (seeded 6) and Jay Berger (seeded 9) were other notable first round failures – going out to Nicklas Kulti and Alberto Mancini respectively – and by the time the quarter-finalists emerged, the cast included a qualifier and a wild card (the French pair Thierry Champion and Henri Leconte), two outsiders but only four seeds – Agassi, Chang, Gomez and Muster.

Local hopes were dashed when Leconte was unable to sustain a good start and lost in four sets to Jonas Svensson and Champion, handicapped by injury, had no chance against a fresh and eager Gomez, who had had a walkover in the previous round, and he was beaten in three sets.

Agassi's march to the final was never in doubt once he removed the defending champion Chang, for Svensson's semi-final challenge was much too erratic to worry him, but few expected Muster to fall so easily to Gomez.

Then again it was not a tournament for making assumptions as Graf's supporters learned in a fascinating women's final. Like a true champion she battled from 1–4 to 6–6 in the first set, dominated the tie-break by taking the first five points, had four set points and still lost it.

Seles's response to the crisis (though watching her there was little evidence that she saw it was such) was an object lesson in maturity. She denied Graf her first set point with a fierce backhand service return, the second on a service winner, and the third with a negotiated smash. And it was Graf's nerve that went. On set point number four she double faulted to bring the score to 6–6. Seles was in such a daze she forgot to change ends. 'But I knew I had her' she said. And she did. Graf had a last chance to take it to a third set when she forced two break points at 4–4. Again, however Seles was equal to the challenge. Graf suggested later that had she won the first set, the title would have been hers. But there was little evidence to support her assertion. Seles was always one jump ahead of her. She was as quick around the court and even more deadly than the German on her ground game. It was a chilling statement of intent for the future.

Of the two Graf, who was hampered by a respiratory problem, had had the easier run to the final, losing only 22 games in six matches, whereas Seles had become battle-hardened by having to fight her way through tough tests against Helen Kelesi in round two, Leila Meskhi in round three and Manuela Maleeva Fragnière in the quarter-finals.

Interest inevitably built and focussed on what everyone had been waiting for – a semi-final between Seles and the new American sensation, 14-year-old Jennifer Capriati but, though the Centre Court was treated to an explosive display of power-hitting, Seles always carried the greater fire-power and won 6–2 6–2.

From the start Seles knew she must not let Capriati take the initiative, as the youngster had done in all her previous matches, and concentrated on pinning her to the baseline. 'She's got the game to win' Seles acknowledged. 'She hits the ball really hard. I can tell you at 14 I'd never have made the semi-finals'.

Capriati, though disappointed, was quite realistic. A more memorable Grand Slam debut would be hard to imagine – after all there had never been a younger semi-finalist. 'I think it's been great' she said. It had taken the second seed and eventual champion to stop her and she had beaten a number of experienced campaigners such as Judith Wiesner and Mary-Joe Fernandez.

Nevertheless there was one cautionary note that would not have been lost on either the Seles or Capriati camps. Just 12 months after becoming the youngest Parisian winner Arantxa Sanchez-Vicario became the first defending champion to lose in the second round. Success, then, can be fleeting and must always be worked for. Ironically it was Sanchez-Vicario's doubles partner, a new slimline Mercedes Paz, who did the dirty deed, the Argentine winning 7–5 3–6 6–1, but later they reached the quarter-finals of the doubles together. It was the top-seeded Czech pairing of Helena Sukova and Jana Novotna, however, who subsequently added the French to their Australian title while the men's crown went to the experienced Spaniards Sergio Casal and Emilio Sanchez over newcomers Goran Ivanisevic and Petr Korda.

MEN'S SINGLES

Holder: M. Chang (USA)

FIRST ROUND · SECOND ROUND · THIRD ROUND · FOURTH ROUND · QUARTER-FINALS · SEMI-FINALS · FINAL

FIRST ROUND

1. S. **EDBERG** (SWE) (1)
2. J. Bruguera (ESP)
3. T. Svensson (SWE)
4. J. Potier (FRA)
5. R. Azar (ARG) (Q)
6. L. Duncan (USA)
7. M. Strelba (TCH)
8. K. Jones (USA)
9. C. Pioline (FRA) (WC)
10. A. Schnaider (CAN)
11. Y. Noah (FRA)
12. F. Clavet (ESP) (Q)
13. F. Vitoux (FRA) (Q)
14. O. Cherkasov (URS)
15. G. Soules (FRA) (WC)
16. G. **PEREZ-ROLDAN** (ARG) (15)
17. J. **BERGER** (USA) (9)
18. A. Mancini (ARG)
19. F. Maciel (MEX) (Q)
20. E. Jelen (FRG)
21. D. Davin (ARG)
22. B. Oresar (YUG)
23. H. Leconte (FRA) (WC)
24. R. Agenor (HAI)
25. J. Arrese (ESP)
26. M. Zoecke (FRG) (LL)
27. F. Santoro (FRA) (WC)
28. E. Raoux (FRA) (WC)
29. J. Fleurian (FRA)
30. M. Vajda (TCH)
31. J. Riglewski (FRG)
32. A. **CHESNOKOV** (URS) (8)
33. A. **AGASSI** (USA) (3)
34. M. Wostenholme (CAN)
35. M. Bahrami (IRN) (WC)
36. T. Woodbridge (AUS) (Q)
37. G. Bloom (ISR)
38. R. Fromberg (AUS)
39. M. Kratzmann (AUS)
40. A. Boetsch (FRA) (Q)
41. N. Marques (POR)
42. O. Mniussi (ARG)
43. O. Delaitre (FRA)
44. J. Anderson (AUS)
45. M. Srejber (TCH)
46. D. Wheaton (USA)
47. J. Altur (ESP)
48. J. **COURIER** (USA) (13)
49. M. **CHANG** (USA) (11)
50. C. Motta (BRA)
51. M. Rosset (SUI)
52. F. Roig (ESP)
53. C. Bergstrom (SWE) (Q)
54. T. Witsken (USA)
55. T. Wilkison (USA)
56. M. Mercir (TCH)
57. M. Ingaramo (ARG) (Q)
58. J. Sanchez (ESP)
59. S. Youl (AUS)
60. P. Rebolledo (CHI) (Q)
61. P. Lundgren (SWE)
62. J. Hlasek (SUI)
63. M. Kuhl (SWE) (Q)
64. E. **SANCHEZ** (ESP) (6)

SECOND ROUND

- Bruguera 6-4 6-2 6-1
- Svensson 6-4 3-6 6-1 6-2
- Azar 6-3 6-1 6-1
- Strelba 6-1 6-3 4-6 6-3
- Schnaider 7-6 6-3 6-1
- Noah 6-4 4-6 6-4 1-6 7-5
- Cherkasov 3-6 6-4 6-4
- PEREZ-ROLDAN (15) 6-7 6-1 6-3 6-2
- Mancini 6-4 6-2 6-2
- Davin 6-2 6-1 6-2
- Oresar 7-6 4-6 2-6 6-1 6-4
- Leconte 6-4 6-2 6-4
- Arrese 6-4 3-6 6-3 6-1
- Santoro 6-1 6-4 6-4
- Fleurian 6-2 4-6-1
- CHESNOKOV (8) 6-1 6-1 6-3
- AGASSI (3)
- Woodbridge
- Bloom 2-6 6-1 4-6 3-8-6
- Boetsch 5-7 7-5 1-6 6-3 6-2
- Boetsch 6-4 6-0 6-3
- Marques 6-1 7-6 6-2
- Anderson 6-4 7-5 6-1
- Srejber 3-6 7-6 3-7 6-6-3
- COURIER (13) 6-1 4-6 6-3 6-4
- CHANG (11) 6-2 7-6 6-1
- Rosset 3-6 3-6 4-6-4
- Bergstrom 6-1 6-2 6-0
- Wilkison 6-4 1-4 6-4
- Sanchez 6-4 6-2 7-6
- Rebolledo 6-1 3-6 6-2 7-6
- Hlasek 7-5 6-3 6-1
- Kuhl 3-6 7-6 2-6 7-5 6-2
- SANCHEZ (6) 4-6 6-4 6-7 6-2 6-1

THIRD ROUND

- Svensson 2-6 2-6 6-4 6-4 6-0
- Azar 3-6 6-4 4-6 6-3 6-4
- Noah 6-4 5-7 6-4 6-4
- PEREZ-ROLDAN (15) 7-5 6-4 6-3
- Davin 6-3 5-7 7-5 6-1
- Leconte 6-4 6-2 6-1
- Arrese 4-6 6-3 6-2 6-2
- CHESNOKOV (8) 7-6 6-2 6-0
- AGASSI (3) 7-5 6-1 6-3
- Boetsch 6-2 6-1 6-0
- Anderson 7-5 6-3 6-1
- COURIER (13) 7-6 1-2-6 6-2
- CHANG (11) 7-5 4-6 6-4 6-3
- Bergstrom 6-4 6-2 6-1
- Sanchez 6-4 7-6 6-2
- Kuhl 6-2 6-4 6-4

FOURTH ROUND

- Svensson 5-7 6-4 6-1 7-6
- PEREZ-ROLDAN (15) 7-6 6-4 4-6 6-3
- Leconte 6-3 7-6 6-4
- CHESNOKOV (8) 7-5 6-4 6-2
- AGASSI (3) 6-3 6-2 6-0
- COURIER (13) 6-0 6-2 6-1
- CHANG (11) 2-6 5-7 6-0 6-2 6-4
- Sanchez 6-4 6-4 6-3

QUARTER-FINALS

- Svensson 2-5 6-4 6-2 6-2
- Leconte 6-4 6-3 4-6 2-6 6-6-3
- AGASSI (3) 6-7 6-1 6-4 6-0
- CHANG (11) 6-4 6-4 6-2

SEMI-FINALS

- Svensson 3-6 7-5 6-3 6-4
- AGASSI (3) 6-2 6-1 4-6 6-2

FINAL

- AGASSI (3) 6-1 6-4 3-6 6-3

6-3 2-6 6-4 6-4

A. GOMEZ (ECU) (4)

Entrants (lower half)

65	A. KRICKSTEIN (USA) (5)
66	J. Yzaga (PER)
67	S. Grenier (FRA) (Q)
68	J. Bates (GBR)
69	R. Matuszewski (USA)
70	L. Mattar (BRA)
71	S. Davis (USA)
72	K. Novacek (TCH)
73	D. Rostagno (USA)
74	A. Antonitsch (AUT)
75	R. Reneberg (USA)
76	G. Forget (FRA)
77	T. Champion (FRA) (Q)
78	G. Prpic (YUG)
79	M. Washington (USA)
80	J. AGUILERA (ESP) (12)
81	M. GUSTAFSSON (SWE) (14)
82	T. Carbonell (ESP)
83	P. Korda (TCH)
84	Y. Benhabiles (FRA) (WC)
85	O. Camporese (ITA)
86	T. Hogstedt (SWE)
87	D. Perez (URU)
88	N. Pereira (VEN)
89	A. Volkov (URS)
90	J. Arias (USA)
91	N. Filippini (URU)
92	D. Riki (TCH) (Q)
93	M. Filippini (URU)
94	L. Wahlgren (SWE)
95	E. Lundt (ESP)
96	A. GOMEZ (ECU) (4)
97	T. MUSTER (AUT) (7)
98	L. Jonsson (SWE)
99	E. Winogradsky (FRA) (WC)
100	R. Schwaier (FRG) (Q)
101	S. Haarhuis (HOL)
102	J. Grabb (USA)
103	J. Pugh (USA)
104	T. Tulasne (FRA)
105	G. Connell (CAN)
106	A. Rahunen (FIN)
107	S. Shiras (USA)
108	S. Zivojinovic (YUG)
109	J. Rive (USA)
110	M. Stich (FRG)
111	C. Pistolesi (ITA)
112	M. JAITE (ARG) (10)
113	M. Tabares (CUB) (LL)
114	A. Mansdorf (ISR)
115	F. Cancellotti (ITA)
116	R. Krishnan (IND)
117	N. Kroon (SWE)
118	K. Goble (USA)
119	M. Schapers (HOL)
120	J. Stoltenberg (AUS)
121	M. Koevermans (HOL)
122	J. Gunnarsson (SWE)
123	C. Engel (SWE) (Q)
124	P. Kuhnen (FRG)
125	D. Cahill (AUS)
126	A. Jarryd (SWE)
127	G. Ivanisevic (YUG)
128	B. BECKER (FRG) (2)

First round

- KRICKSTEIN (5) 6-0 2-6 6-3 6-3
- Grenier 6-2 6-4 6-2
- Mattar 6-4 6-1 6-4
- Novacek 6-3 6-2 6-2
- Antonitsch 6-7 7-6 6-3
- Forget 3-6 6-4 6-4 6-4
- Champion 3-6 6-4 6-4 6-4
- AGUILERA (12) 7-5 4-6 1-6 6-2
- GUSTAFSSON (14) 3-6 7-6 1-6 6-1 9-7
- Korda 6-2 6-3 4-6 6-2
- Camporese 6-2 6-3 6-4
- Perez 6-1 6-4 1-0 retd
- Volkov 6-2 0-4 6-4 6-1
- Arias 6-2 6-1 3-6 6-2
- Filippini 4-6 0-6 6-1 6-0 6-1
- GOMEZ (4) 6-3 6-7 6-3 4-6 6-2
- MUSTER (7) 7-5 6-3 6-2
- Winogradsky 6-4 6-1 6-3
- Haarhuis 6-4 6-3
- Pugh 6-4 6-3 1-0 retd
- Rahunen 1-6 6-1 6-4 6-0
- Shiras 6-4 3-6 3-6 6-4
- Stich 6-4 6-1 6-1
- JAITE (10) 6-7 6-4 6-7 6-4 6-3
- Mansdorf 6-3 4-6 6-4 6-4
- Cancellotti 6-4 6-4 3-6 7-6
- Kroon 6-0 6-3 6-1
- Stoltenberg 6-4 6-3 6-1
- Koevermans 6-3 2-6 7-6 3-6 7-5
- Kuhnen 6-3 6-1 6-2
- Jarryd 6-2 4-6 6-1 6-7 6-3
- Ivanisevic 5-7 6-4 7-5 6-2

Second round

- KRICKSTEIN (5) 6-3 6-4 7-5
- Novacek 5-7 6-3 6-2 6-1
- Forget 6-1 6-1 6-1
- Champion 3-6 6-3 6-2
- GUSTAFSSON (14) 6-1 4-6 6-1 6-3
- Perez 6-2 7-5 4-6 6-3
- Volkov 1-6 3-6 3-4 retd
- GOMEZ (4) 6-2 6-1 6-0
- MUSTER (7) 7-6 3-6 6-2 7-6
- Haarhuis 6-4 7-6 6-7 7-5
- Rahunen 1-6 6-1 6-4 6-0
- JAITE (10) 6-4 6-1 6-1
- Mansdorf 6-3 4-6 6-4 6-4
- Kroon 6-0 6-3 6-1
- Kuhnen 6-3 2-6 6-4 6-2
- Ivanisevic 6-3 6-0 6-2

Third round

- Novacek 6-2 6-3 3-6 7-6
- Champion 6-4 6-7 6-4 5-7 6-3
- GUSTAFSSON (14) 6-1 4-6 1-6 6-3
- GOMEZ (4) 6-2 7-5 4-6 6-3
- MUSTER (7) 3-6 7-5 6-2 7-6
- JAITE (10) 7-6 6-2 6-1
- Kroon 6-4 7-6 6-1
- Ivanisevic 7-6 6-1 7-5

Fourth round

- Champion 6-3 4-6 3-6 7-6 6-3
- GOMEZ (4) w/o
- MUSTER (7) 7-6 3-6 6-2
- Ivanisevic 6-2 6-4 7-5

Quarter-finals

- GOMEZ (4) 6-3 6-3 6-4
- MUSTER (7) 6-2 4-6 6-4 6-3

Semi-final

- GOMEZ (4) 7-5 6-1 7-5

Capital letter denote seeded players. Number following players' name gives seeding order. (Q) – Qualifier. (WC) – Wild Card. (LL) – Lucky Loser

WOMEN'S SINGLES

Holder: A. Sanchez (ESP)

FIRST ROUND · SECOND ROUND · THIRD ROUND · FOURTH ROUND · QUARTER-FINALS · SEMI-FINALS · FINAL

#	First round	Second round	Third round	Fourth round	Quarter-finals	Semi-finals	Final
1	S. GRAF (FRG) (1)	GRAF (1) 6-0 6-2	GRAF (1) 6-1 6-2	GRAF (1) 6-2 6-3	GRAF (1) 6-1 6-4	GRAF (1) 6-1 6-3	GRAF (1) 6-1 6-2
2	P Parada (FRA)						
3	J Santrock (USA) (LL)	Santrock 6-2 6-4					
4	J Loosemore (GBR)						
5	S Amiach (FRA)	Amiach 7-5 6-7 6-2	Cecchini 6-2 6-1				
6	F Haumuller (ARG)						
7	N Guerree (FRA) (WC)	Cecchini 7-5 6-0					
8	S Cecchini (ITA)						
9	B Reinstadler (AUT)	Lapi	Lapi 6-1 6-1	TAUZIAT (15) 6-1 2-6 6-1			
10	Lapi (ITA)						
11	M Javer (GBR)	Javer 4-6 6-4 7-5					
12	A Kanellopoulou (GRE)						
13	E Krapl (SUI)	Hack 6-2 6-1	TAUZIAT (15) 6-2 3-6 6-3				
14	S Hack (FRG)						
15	K Godridge (AUS)	TAUZIAT (15) 6-3 7-5					
16	N TAUZIAT (FRA) (15)						
17	C. MARTINEZ (ESP) (9)	MARTINEZ (9) 7-5 6-1	MARTINEZ (9) 7-6 6-3	MARTINEZ (9) 6-1 6-3	MARTINEZ (9) 3-6 6-3		
18	J Thompson (AUS)						
19	P Etchemendy (FRA) (WC)	Etchemendy					
20	P Fendick (USA)						
21	A Strandlund (SWE)	Strandlund 6-3 3-6 6-0	Zubakova 6-1 7-6				
22	S Wasserman (BEL)						
23	R Zubakova (TCH)	Zubakova 6-1 6-2					
24	S Meier (FRG)						
25	C Benjamin (USA)	Benjamin 6-2 6-1	Benjamin 7-6 6-3	Probst 6-2 6-2			
26	S Rihter (AUT) (Q)						
27	H Na (USA)	Na 0-6 7-6 6-2					
28	K Nowak (POL) (Q)						
29	J Pospisilova (TCH)	Romano 6-3 6-1	Probst 6-2 4-6 7-5				
30	B Romano (ITA)						
31	Probst (FRG)	Probst 6-1 1-6 7-5					
32	Z. GARRISON (USA) (5)						
33	G. SABATINI (ARG) (4)	SABATINI (4) 6-0 7-6	SABATINI (4) 6-0 5-7 6-1	SABATINI (4) 6-0 6-1	NOVOTNA (11) 6-4 7-5	NOVOTNA (11) 4-6 6-2 6-4	
34	A Vieira (BRA)						
35	S Sloane (USA)	Sloane 6-4 6-3					
36	A Coetzer (RSA)						
37	N Sawamatsu (JPN)	Sawamatsu 6-1 4-6 6-2	Herreman 6-1 6-3				
38	L Harvey-Wild (USA)						
39	M Laval (FRA) (WC)	Herreman 6-3 6-3					
40	N Herreman (FRA)						
41	D Van Rensburg (RSA)	Van Rensburg 6-4 6-2	Svigierova 6-3 7-5	NOVOTNA (11) 7-5 6-2			
42	S La Fratta (ITA)						
43	S Rinaldi (USA)	Svigierova 6-2 5-5 retd					
44	E Svigierova (TCH)						
45	R Garrone (ITA)	Schultz	NOVOTNA (11) 6-3 6-1				
46	B Schultz (HOL)						
47	P Demongeot (FRA)	NOVOTNA (11) 6-4 7-6					
48	J. NOVOTNA (TCH) (11)						
49	R. FAIRBANK-NIDEFFER (USA) (13)	Simpson 6-0 6-7 10-8	Temesvari 7-6 6-2	Provis 2-6 6-3 6-3	K. MALEEVA (8) 3-6 6-3 6-3		
50	R Simpson (CAN)						
51	C Dahlman (SWE)	Temesvari 6-1 6-2					
52	A Temesvari (HUN)						
53	S Sabas (FRA) (WC)	Pampoulova 6-2 6-1	Provis 6-4 6-2				
54	E Pampoulova (BUL)						
55	E Smylie (AUS)	Provis 6-3 6-3					
56	N Provis (AUS)						
57	B Bowes (USA)	Medvedeva 6-1 6-3	Halard 6-2 4-6 6-4	K. MALEEVA (8) 6-2 6-1			
58	N Medvedeva (URS)						
59	N Nagelsen (USA)	Halard 6-2 4-6 6-4					
60	J Halard (FRA)						
61	D Faber (USA)	Faber 6-1 6-4	K. MALEEVA (8) 7-5 6-1				
62	P Langrova (TCH)						
63	S Appelmans (BEL)	K. MALEEVA (8) 6-3 6-3					
64	K. MALEEVA (BUL) (8)						

7-6 6-4

M. SELES (YUG) (2)

First round

#	Player	Result
65	M. FERNANDEZ (USA) (7)	FERNANDEZ (7) 6-4 6-2
66	K. McDonald (AUS) (Q)	
67	M. Pierce (FRA) (WC)	Pierce 6-0 6-1
68	B. Fulco (ARG)	
69	S. Hanika (FRG)	Hanika 6-3 6-2
70	M. Kidowaki (JPN)	
71	I. Cueto (FRG)	Cueto 7-6 6-0
72	E. Zardo (SUI)	
73	S. Goles (YUG)	Grossman 6-0 6-2
74	A. Grossman (USA)	
75	N. Miyagi (JPN)	Miyagi 6-3
76	M. Pawlik (FRG)	
77	K. Sharpe (AUS) (Q)	Sharpe 6-3
78	T. Phelps (USA)	
79	A. Gavaldon (USA)	REGGI (14) 1-6 7-6 6-2
80	R. REGGI (ITA) (14)	
81	J. WIESNER (AUT) (12)	WIESNER (12) 4-6 6-0
82	L. Meyers (USA)	
83	M. Bollegraf (HOL)	Jaggard 7-6 3-2 retd
84	M. Jaggard (AUS)	
85	S. Testud (FRA) (WC)	Capriati 6-1 6-1
86	J. Capriati (USA)	
87	C. Suire (FRA) (WC)	Macgregor 6-7 7-6 6-3
88	C. Macgregor (USA)	
89	A. Dechaume (FRA)	Cohen 6-4 7-6
90	C. Cohen (SUI) (Q)	
91	K. Keller (USA)	Ferrando 3-6 6-0 6-4
92	L. Ferrando (ITA)	
93	L. Quentrec (FRA)	Paz 6-4 2-6 6-3
94	M. Paz (ARG)	
95	N. Van Lottum (FRA) (WC)	SANCHEZ VICARIO (3) 6-1 6-3
96	A. SANCHEZ VICARIO (ESP) (3)	
97	M. MALEEVA FRAGNIÈRE (SUI) (6)	MALEEVA FRAGNIÈRE (6) 6-1 6-0
98	J. Stafford (USA)	
99	A. Minter (AUS)	Minter 7-5 6-3
100	F. Romano (ITA)	
101	P. Tarabini (ARG)	Tarabini 6-0 6-4
102	J. Faull (AUS)	
103	C. Kohde-Kilsch (FRG)	Kohde-Kilsch 6-1 6-1
104	K. Okamoto (JPN)	
105	N. Jagerman (HOL)	Caverzasio 6-4 6-2
106	C. Caverzasio (ITA)	
107	S. Martin (USA)	Martin 6-2 6-2
108	L. Field (AUS)	
109	I. Budarova (TCH)	Budarova 6-2 7-6
110	J. Hy (CAN)	
111	C. TANVIER (FRA)	ZVEREVA (10) 6-4 7-6
112	N. ZVEREVA (URS) (10)	
113	L. GILDEMEISTER (PER) (16)	GILDEMEISTER (16) 6-3 6-4
114	K. McNeil (USA)	
115	E. Burgin (USA)	Burgin 6-3 3-6 6-4
116	M. Werdel (USA)	
117	T. Whitlinger (USA)	Rajchtrova 6-2 6-0
118	R. Rajchtrova (TCH)	
119	F. Labat (ARG)	Maleeva 6-7 6-4 6-3
120	M. Maleeva (BUL)	
121	L. Meskhi (URS)	Meskhi
122	R. McQuillan (AUS)	
123	L. Savchenko (URS)	Savchenko 6-7 4-6 6-4
124	L. Corsato (BRA) (Q)	
125	C. Lindqvist (SWE)	Kelesi 6-3 6-0
126	H. Kelesi (CAN)	
127	K. Rinaldi (ITA)	SELES (2) 6-0 6-0
128	M. SELES (YUG) (2)	

Second round

- FERNANDEZ (7) 6-4 6-4
- Cueto 6-3 4-6 6-0
- Grossman 6-2 6-3
- Sharpe 6-4 6-2
- WIESNER (12) 6-3 6-1
- Capriati 6-1 6-0
- Cohen 6-1 6-0
- Paz 7-5 3-6 6-4
- MALEEVA FRAGNIÈRE (6) 6-1 6-0
- Tarabini 3-6 6-1 6-4
- Martin 6-3 7-5
- ZVEREVA (10) 6-1 6-3
- GILDEMEISTER (16) 6-3 6-4
- M. Maleeva 6-2 6-3
- Meskhi 3-0 retd
- SELES (2) 7-6 7-6

Third round

- FERNANDEZ (7) 7-6 6-2
- Grossman 6-2 4-6 6-1
- Capriati 6-1 6-0
- Paz 6-1 7-5
- MALEEVA FRAGNIÈRE (6) 2-6 7-5 6-0
- ZVEREVA (10) 6-4 6-1
- GILDEMEISTER (16) 6-1 6-3
- SELES (2) 6-4 6-0

Fourth round

- FERNANDEZ (7) 6-3 6-2
- Capriati 6-0 6-3
- MALEEVA FRAGNIÈRE (6) 6-4 6-2
- SELES (2) 6-4 6-0

Quarter-final

- Capriati 6-2 6-4
- SELES (2) 6-2 6-2

Semi-final

- SELES (2) 6-2 6-2

Capital letters denote seeded players. Number following player's name gives seeding order. (Q) – Qualifier, (WC) – Wild Card, (LL) – Lucky Loser.

MEN'S DOUBLES

Holders: J. Grabb (USA)/J. P. McEnroe (USA)

Winner: S. CASAL (ESP)/E. SANCHEZ (ESP) (7) 7–5 6–3

FIRST ROUND

1. LEACH/PUGH (1)
2. Masso/Vajda
3. Engel/Nydahl
4. Cannon/Jones
5. Rive/Shiras
6. Derlin/Fulwood
7. Henricsson/Utgren
8. IVANISEVIC/KORDA (16)
9. FORGET/HLASEK (9)
10. Delaitre/Raoux (WC)
11. Bruguera/Pereira
12. Aerts/Roese
13. Bathman/Bergh
14. Beckman/Jensen
15. Stoltenberg/Woodbridge
16. CAHILL/KRATZMANN (8)
17. GRABB/McENROE (4)
18. Depalmer/Talbot
19. Frana/Minussi
20. Di Laura/Filippini
21. Albano/De La Pena
22. Shelton/Youl
23. Tarczy/Wilkison
24. RIGLEWSKI/STICH (14)
25. BAHRAMI/WINOGRADSKY (11)
26. Brown/Schapers
27. Rikl/Zdrazila
28. Odizor/Vekesa
29. Clavet/Nido
30. Boetsch/Champion (WC)
31. Baguena/Roig
32. LOZANO/WITSKEN (6)
33. DAVIS/PATE (5)
34. Mortensen/Nijssen
35. Haarhuis/Koevermans
36. Fleurian/Rostagno
37. Mattar/Perez
38. Bates/Castle
39. Carbonell/Costa
40. FLACH/SEGUSO (12)
41. PAWSAT/SMID (13)
42. De Palmer/Nargiso
43. Jansson/Warner
44. Benhabiles/Grenier (WC)
45. Foster/Tulasne (WC)
46. Kuhnen/Van Emburgh
47. Novacek/Sreiber
48. FITZGERALD/JARRYD (3)
49. CASAL/SANCHEZ (7)
50. Menezes/Pimek
51. Chaksuk
52. Pawson/Reneberg
53. Mancini/Rosset
54. Dyke/Warder
55. Galbraith/Macpherson
56. CONNELL/MICHIBATA (10)
57. LUZA/MOTTA (15)
58. Pioline/Santoro (WC)
59. Mora/Page
60. Devries/Kinnear
61. Nelson/Smith
62. Dosvis/Kruger
63. Sanchez/Wheaton
64. ALDRICH/VISSER (2)

SECOND ROUND

- LEACH/PUGH (1) 4–6 6–0 7–5
- Cannon/Jones
- Rive/Shiras 6–4 6–4
- IVANISEVIC/KORDA (16) 6–3 3–6 6–3
- Delaitre/Raoux 6–3 6–3
- Bruguera/Pereira 6–3 6–4
- Beckman/Jensen 6–4 4–6 7–5
- Stoltenberg/Woodbridge 5–7 7–5 6–4
- GRABB/McENROE (4) 6–2 6–4
- Frana/Minussi
- Shelton/Youl 5–7 6–0 7–5
- RIGLEWSKI/STICH (14) 6–3 6–4
- Brown/Schapers 6–7 7–6 6–4
- Rikl/Zdrazila 6–3 7–6
- Clavet/Nido
- LOZANO/WITSKEN (6) 6–3 6–2
- Mortensen/Nijssen 3–6 6–1 6–4
- Haarhuis/Koevermans 6–4 6–0
- Mattar/Perez 2–6 6–2 6–1
- FLACH/SEGUSO (12)
- PAWSAT/SMID (13) 2–6 7–6 6–1
- Benhabiles/Grenier 6–4 6–4
- Novacek/Sreiber 7–6 7–6
- CASAL/SANCHEZ (7) 6–2 6–4
- Dyke/Warder 3–6 6–0 8–6
- CONNELL/MICHIBATA (10) 6–3 6–3
- LUZA/MOTTA (15) 6–1 4–6 6–1
- Mora/Page 7–5 7–6
- Davis/Kruger
- ALDRICH/VISSER (2) 7–6 6–3

THIRD ROUND

- LEACH/PUGH (1) 6–4 6–2
- IVANISEVIC/KORDA (16) 6–4 6–4
- Bruguera/Pereira 4–6 6–4 7–5
- Stoltenberg/Woodbridge 6–4 6–7 6–4
- GRABB/McENROE (4) 6–4 6–4
- Shelton/Youl 6–4 4–6 7–5
- Rikl/Zdrazila 6–1 6–1
- LOZANO/WITSKEN (6) 6–4 6–1
- Haarhuis/Koevermans 2–6 6–3 10–8
- Mattar/Perez 6–3 6–2
- PAWSAT/SMID (13) 6–1 7–6
- Novacek/Sreiber 7–5 6–4
- CASAL/SANCHEZ (7) 4–6 6–3 6–2
- CONNELL/MICHIBATA (10) 6–3 6–3
- LUZA/MOTTA (15) 6–2 6–2
- ALDRICH/VISSER (2) 7–6 7–6

QUARTER-FINALS

- IVANISEVIC/KORDA (16) 6–4 6–4
- Stoltenberg/Woodbridge 6–4 6–2
- GRABB/McENROE (4) 7–5 6–4
- LOZANO/WITSKEN (6) 2–6 6–0 6–4
- Haarhuis/Koevermans 3–6 6–3 6–4
- Novacek/Sreiber 6–4 6–1
- CASAL/SANCHEZ (7) 6–4 5–7 6–2
- ALDRICH/VISSER (2) 4–6 6–3 6–2

SEMI-FINALS

- IVANISEVIC/KORDA (16) 7–6 7–6
- GRABB/McENROE (4) 6–1 6–3
- Haarhuis/Koevermans 6–2 6–3 15–13
- CASAL/SANCHEZ (7) 4–6 6–4 6–3

FINAL

- IVANISEVIC/KORDA (16) 6–2 6–3
- CASAL/SANCHEZ (7) 7–6 6–4

Capital letters denote seeded pairings. Numbers following players' names gives seeding order. (Q) – Qualifier, (WC) – Wild Card, (LL) – Lucky Loser

WOMEN'S DOUBLES

Holders: L. Savchenko (URS)/N. Zvereva (URS)

Winner: J. NOVOTNA (TCH)/H. SUKOVA (TCH) (1) 6–4 7–5

FIRST ROUND	SECOND ROUND	THIRD ROUND	QUARTER-FINALS	SEMI-FINALS	FINAL

FIRST ROUND

1 NOVOTNA/SUKOVA (1)
2 Demongeot/Tanvier
3 Gildemeister/Scheuer-Larsen
4 Bakkum/Schimper
5 Kapfer/Sager-Herr
6 Phelps/Stafford
7 McDonald/Morton
8 GREGORY/MAGERS (11)
9 BOLLEGRAF/REGGI (13)
10 Faber/Minter
11 Dechaume/Derly (WC)
12 Etcheverry/Guerre (WC)
13 Meier/Pospisilova
14 Bowes/Werdel
15 Rajchrtova/Temesvari
16 Vasquez/Villanueva
17 PAZ/SANCHEZ VICARIO (4)
18 Romano Svigler
19 Jaggard Na
20 Field/Thomas
21 Anadari/Inteman
22 Lindqvist/Lindstrom
23 Budarova/Wasserman
24 MEDVEDEVA/MESKHI (10)
25 FAULL/McQUILLAN (15)
26 Caverzasio Garrone
27 Maleeva Maleeva
28 Halard/Quentrec (WC)
29 Sabas/Testud (WC)
30 Jagerman/Van Rensburg
31 Capriati/Garrison
32 PROVIS/REINACH (6)
33 ADAMS/McNEIL (5)
34 Cosato/Sprung
35 Byrne/Thompson
36 Ferrando/Goles
37 Paradis/Suire
38 Fernandez/Villagran-Reami
39 Langrova/Zubakova
40 TAUZIAT/WIESNER (14)
41 KOHDE KILSCH/SCHULTZ (16)
42 Collins/Smoller
43 Kidowaki/Scott
44 Kelesi/Fendick
45 Radford/Spadea
46 Castro/Martinez
47 Foltz/Mvagi
48 JORDAN/SMYLIE (3)
49 BURGIN/FAIRBANK-NIDEFFER (8)
50 Allen/Benjamin
51 Pampoulova/Probst
52 Aallonen/Schilder
53 Strandlund/Stubbs
54 Bassett-Seguso/Grossman
55 Brioukhovets/Laxova
56 CECCHINI/TARABINI (9)
57 NAGELSEN/SELES (12)
58 Macgregor/Macgregor
59 Szkszay/Vis
60 Groubeck/Simpson
61 Barnard/Field
62 Albinus/Van Lottum
63 Fulco/Labat
64 SAVCHENKO/ZVEREVA (2)

SECOND ROUND

- NOVOTNA/SUKOVA (1) 6-4 6-1
- Gildemeister/Scheuer-Larsen 6-0 6-1
- Phelps/Stafford 6-1 4-6 6-3
- GREGORY/MAGERS (11) 6-0 6-4
- BOLLEGRAF/REGGI (13) 6-4 6-1
- Dechaume/Derly 5-3 6-3
- Bowes/Werdel 6-2 6-4
- Rajchrtova/Temesvari 6-1 7-6
- PAZ/SANCHEZ VICARIO (4) 6-2 6-4
- Jaggard Na 6-7 6-3 6-2
- Lundqvist/Lindstrom 3-6 6-3 6-2
- MEDVEDEVA/MESKHI (10) 6-0 6-3
- FAULL/McQUILLAN (15) 7-5 7-5
- Maleeva Maleeva 6-3 6-3
- Sabas/Testud 6-7 6-0 6-1
- PROVIS/REINACH (6) 6-4 6-3
- ADAMS/McNEIL (5) 6-4 6-3
- Byrne/Thompson 3-6 6-2 6-3
- Paradis/Suire 6-4 6-3
- TAUZIAT/WIESNER (14) 7-5 6-3
- KOHDE KILSCH/SCHULTZ (16) 6-1 6-2
- Kidowaki/Scott 6-2 6-1
- Castro/Martinez 6-3 3-6 6-1
- JORDAN/SMYLIE (3) 6-4 6-2
- BURGIN/FAIRBANK-NIDEFFER (8) 6-4 6-2
- Pampoulova/Probst
- Bassett-Seguso/Grossman 6-4 6-2
- CECCHINI/TARABINI (9) 7-6 6-3
- NAGELSEN/SELES (12) 6-3 6-1
- Szkszay/Vis 5-1 6-2
- Albinus/Van Lottum 6-3 4-6 6-2
- SAVCHENKO/ZVEREVA (2) 6-0 6-3

THIRD ROUND

- NOVOTNA/SUKOVA (1) 6-1 7-6
- GREGORY/MAGERS 6-1 6-7 6-2
- BOLLEGRAF/REGGI (13) 6-3 7-6
- Rajchrtova/Temesvari 6-0 7-6
- PAZ/SANCHEZ VICARIO (4) 6-1 6-2
- MEDVEDEVA/MESKHI (10) 6-1 6-3
- FAULL/McQUILLAN (15) 4-6 7-5 6-6
- PROVIS/REINACH (6) 6-0 6-1
- Adams/McNeil 1-6 6-4 8-6
- TAUZIAT/WIESNER (14) 6-4 6-4
- KOHDE KILSCH/SCHULTZ (16) 3-7 7-6 6-1
- Castro-Martinez 7-5 1-6 6-1
- Pampoulova Probst 6-2 6-3
- CECCHINI/TARABINI (9) 0-6 6-2 6-3
- NAGELSEN/SELES (12) 6-2 6-3
- SAVCHENKO/ZVEREVA (2) 6-3 6-7 6-3

QUARTER-FINALS

- NOVOTNA/SUKOVA (1) 7-6 3-6 6-2
- PAZ/SANCHEZ VICARIO (4) 6-4 6-3
- PROVIS/REINACH (6) 6-3 6-4
- TAUZIAT/WIESNER (14) 3-6 6-2 6-1
- KOHDE/KILSCH-SCHULTZ (16) 7-5 6-3
- CECCHINI/TARABINI (9) 6-2 6-1
- SAVCHENKO/ZVEREVA (2) 6-3 1-6 6-1

SEMI-FINALS

- NOVOTNA/SUKOVA (1) 4-6 7-6 6-4
- PROVIS/REINACH (6) 6-4 6-4
- TAUZIAT/WIESNER (14) 6-2 5-7 6-3
- SAVCHENKO/ZVEREVA (2) 6-4 6-3

FINAL

- NOVOTNA/SUKOVA (1) 6-4 6-0
- SAVCHENKO/ZVEREVA (2) 6-2 6-2

Capital letters denote seeded pairings. Number following players' names gives seeding order. (Q) – Qualifier, (WC) – Wild Card, (LL) – Lucky Loser

MIXED DOUBLES

Holders: J. Lozano (MEX)/L. McNeil (USA)

Winner: J. LOZANO (MEX)/A. SANCHEZ-VICARIO (ESP) (4) 7-6 7-6

FIRST ROUND	SECOND ROUND	THIRD ROUND	QUARTER-FINALS	SEMI-FINALS	FINAL

FIRST ROUND

1 ALDRICH/REINACH (1)
2 Galbraith/Smoller
3 Jansson/Lindstrom
4 Mattar/Vieira (WC)
5 Potier/Etchemendy (WC)
6 Filabert/Deri
7 Pimek/Krajl
8 SCHAPERS/SCHULTZ (16)
9 JONES/MEDVEDEVA (10)
10 Deppe/Van Rensburg
11 Masso/Fulco
12 Clavet/Scott
13 Perez/Paz
14 Beckman/Stubbs
15 De La Pena Temesvari
16 CASAL/NAGELSEN (7)
17 LOZANO/SANCHEZ-VICARIO (4)
18 Koemans/Ter Riet
19 Cherkasov/Savchenko
20 Stoltenberg/Faull
21 Mora/MacGregor
22 Benhabiles/Herreman
23 Woodbridge/McQuillan
24 WARDER/BARG MAGER (13)
25 NIJSSEN/BOLLEGRAF (11)
26 Nelson/Magers
27 Campbell/Pierce
28 Bale/Fairbank-Nideffer
29 Haarhuis/Bakkum
30 Albano/Labat
31 Dzelde/Mesthki
32 SMID/SMYLIE (6)
33 WITSKEN/BURGIN (5)
34 Youl/Field
35 Sobell/Gregory
36 Stewart/Garrison (WC)
37 Winogradsky/Testud (WC)
38 Van Emburgh/MacGregor
39 Fennau/Field
40 FRANA/GILDEMEISTER (12)
41 BAHRAMI/TANVIER (14)
42 MacPherson/Byrne
43 Delaitre/Sure
44 Shelton/Benjamin
45 Aerts/Fernandez
46 Perlin/Thompson
47 Dyke/Jaggard
48 McENROE/JORDAN (3)
49 SEGUSO/McNEIL (8)
50 Mortensen/Scheue-Larsen
51 Kruger/Bonves
52 Smith/Adams
53 Pawsat/Herr
54 Roese/Corsato
55 Jensen/Phelps
56 MUZA/TARABINI (9)
57 PUGH/ACOLLINS (15)
58 Flach/Bassett-Seguso
59 Zdrazilia/Langrova
60 Wilkson/Stafford
61 Raoux/Quemtrec (WC)
62 Nargiso/Grousbeck
63 Boetsch/Van Lottum (WC)
64 VISSER/PROVIS (2)

SECOND ROUND

ALDRICH/REINACH (1) 6-4 6-4
Mattar/Vieira 6-3 6-3
Potier/Etchemendy 6-7 6-3 6-1
SCHAPERS/SCHULTZ (16) 6-0 7-5
JONES/MEDVEDEVA (10) 1-6 6-3 9-7
Masso/Fulco 7-5 5-6
Perez/Paz 6-2 7-6
De La Pena Temesvari 6-2 7-6
LOZANO/SANCHEZ-VICARIO (4) 6-3 6-1
Stoltenberg/Faull 0-6 6-3 6-1
Benhabiles/Herreman 2-6 6-3 13-11
Woodbridge/McQuillan 6-3 6-2
NIJSSEN/BOLLEGRAF (11) 7-6 4-6 6-1
Campbell/Pierce 6-2 6-1
Haarhuis/Bakkum 5-7 6-3 6-2
SMID/SMYLIE (6) 6-1 6-4
Youl/Field 6-1 7-6
Stewart/Garrison 6-3 7-5
Winogradsky/Testud 6-3 7-5
FRANA/GILDEMEISTER (12) 6-1 6-3
BAHRAMI/TANVIER (14) 6-4 7-6
Delaitre/Sure 6-2 6-2
No match played
Dyke/Jaggard 4-6 6-4 7-5
Mortensen/Scheue-Larsen 6-2 6-3
Smith/Adams 6-3 6-4
Pawsat/Herr 6-4 6-7 6-3
LUZA/TARABINI (9) 6-2 7-5
Flach/Bassett-Seguso 6-4 6-4
Wilkson/Stafford 6-4 1-6 6-1
Nargiso/Grousbeck 6-1 7-5
VISSER/PROVIS (2) 6-2 6-3

THIRD ROUND

ALDRICH/REINACH (1) 7-6 7-5
SCHAPERS/SCHULTZ (16) w/o
JONES/MEDVEDEVA (10) 6-4 6-4
Perez/Paz 2-6 7-5 6-3
LOZANO/SANCHEZ-VICARIO (4) 6-1 1-6 6-1
Woodbridge/McQuillan 6-7 6-4 7-5
Campbell/Pierce 7-6 6-4
SMID/SMYLIE (6) 6-1 6-4
Youl/Field 3-6 6-3 6-2
FRANA/GILDEMEISTER (12) 6-1 6-3
Delaitre/Sure 6-3 6-4
Dyke/Jaggard w/o
Mortensen/Scheue-Larsen 7-6 6-4
Flach/Bassett-Seguso 6-4 6-2
VISSER/PROVIS (2) 6-1 6-4

QUARTER-FINALS

SCHAPERS/SCHULTZ (16) 7-5 3-6 7-5
JONES/MEDVEDEVA (10) 4-6 6-2 6-2
LOZANO/SANCHEZ VICARIO (4) 6-1 1-6 6-1
Campbell/Pierce 6-2 6-2
Youl/Field 6-3 6-2
Delaitre/Sure 6-3 6-2
Mortensen/Scheue-Larsen 6-3 6-3
VISSER/PROVIS (2) 4-6 7-5 6-3

SEMI-FINALS

JONES/MEDVEDEVA (10) 6-2 6-3
LOZANO/SANCHEZ VICARIO (4) 6-1 6-1
Youl/Field 6-3 6-2
VISSER/PROVIS (2) 7-5 6-4

FINAL

LOZANO/SANCHEZ VICARIO (4) 6-2 6-4
VISSER/PROVIS (2) 7-5 6-4

Capital letters denote seeded pairings. Number following players' names gives seeding order. (Q) – Qualifier, (WC) – Wild Card. (LL) – Lucky Loser

JUNIOR EVENTS

BOYS' SINGLES – Final: Andrea Gaudenzil (ITA) d. Thomas Enqvist (SWE) 2–6 7–6 6–4.
GIRLS' SINGLES – Final: Magdalena Maleeva (BUL) d. Tatiana Ignatieva (URS) 6–2 6–3.
BOYS' DOUBLES – Final: Sebastien Lareau (CAN)/Sebastian Leblanc (CAN) d. Clinton Marsh (RSA)/Marcos Andruska (RSA) 7–6 6–7 9–7.
GIRLS' DOUBLES – Final: Ruxandra Dragomir (ROM)/Irina Spirlea (ROM) d. Tatiana Ignatieva (URS)/Irina Soukhova (URS) 6–3 6–1.

FRENCH OPEN CHAMPIONSHIPS PRIZE MONEY – US$5,350,000

MEN'S SINGLES – Winner $370,000. Runner-up $185,000. Semi-finalists $95,500. Quarter-finalists $48,000. Fourth-round losers $26,000. Third-round losers $15,000. Second-round losers $9,250. First-round losers $5,500.
Total: $2,026,400.
WOMEN'S SINGLES – Winner $293,000. Runner-up $146,500. Semi-finalists $73,500. Quarter-finalists $36,800. Fourth-round losers $19,300. Third-round losers $10,700. Second-round losers $6,300. First-round losers $4,000.
Total: $1,747,580.
MEN'S DOUBLES (per team) – Winners $151,000. Runners-up $75,500. Semi-finalists $37,750. Quarter-finalists $19,300. Third-round losers $11,000. Second-round losers $5,500. First-round losers $3,700.
Total: $673,600.
WOMEN'S DOUBLES (per team) – Winners $103,080. Runners-up $51,540. Semi-finalists $25,760. Quarter-finalists $13,090. Third-round losers $6,736. Second-round losers $3,584. First-round losers $2,074.
Total: $502,420.
MIXED DOUBLES (per team) – Winners $30,000. Runners-up $18,000. Semi-finalists $10,800. Quarter-finalists $6,600. Second-round losers $3,600. First-round losers $1,575.
Total: $150,000.
QUALIFYING EVENTS
Men's total (128 draw) $1,333,440. Women's total (64 draw) $66,720.

A second Wimbledon title in three years for Stefan Edberg, the quiet achiever from Sweden, who was to end the year as the top ranked player in the world.

(Professional Sport)

WIMBLEDON CHAMPIONSHIPS
John Barrett

The 1990 Championship meeting, the 104th for men and the 97th for women, became an historic one when Martina Navratilova, playing at Wimbledon for the 18th time since she first appeared in 1973, achieved a ninth singles success. This one-sided 6–4 6–1 win over Zina Garrison gave the 33-year-old Czech-born American sole possession of the record that, since her eighth win in 1987, she had shared jointly with the great American champion of the 1930's, Helen Wills Moody.

It was unfortunate, therefore, that this historic moment was celebrated in a rather subdued atmosphere – the result of replacing the free-standing areas on each side of the Centre Court with seats. Even the frequent appearances of a pair of pied wagtails, who seemed to be nesting just below the Royal Box, could not make up for 2,000 absent young fans.

The Fire Safety and *Safety at Places of Sport Act* enforced following the Hillsborough disaster had made this regrettable action necessary even though there had never been any threat to public safety in Wimbledon's proud history. The argument that tennis crowds, spending 5–6 hours at Wimbledon, behaved rather differently from football crowds attending a match for 1½ hours, was not heeded by the officials at Merton Council. Without the alterations they would not have issued a safety certificate, and without that there would have been no tournament. The alterations provided 608 new seats to bring the Centre Court total to 13,110. Without the standing fans there were, therefore, approximately 1,392 fewer spectators each day. In the past this group of enthusiasts had always been most demonstrative. They were missed.

Several other changes were imposed. The standing area for 1,000 on Court No. 1 became an all-ticket enclosure but there were no alterations to the 6,508 seats. However, the total number of individuals in the ground at any time was limited to 28,000. People leaving the ground were encouraged to leave their tickets in special boxes for re-sale to the late afternoon fans. It was eerie to be able to move between the courts in comparative comfort but sad to note that, without the customary crush, there was a noticeable reduction of atmosphere. Inevitably there was also a reduction in the total attendance, down from 403,706 in 1989 to 347,979, the lowest since 1979's 343,091 and 1981's 358,250.

The decision to make the spectator accommodation around courts 2, 3, 13 and 14 reserved-ticket stands backfired. People would sit through a match and then wander off for tea or to watch matches on other courts. Accordingly the stands were half empty for much of the day, thus defeating the object of the exercise – namely to keep the footpaths as clear as possible. Also the players seemed to be affected by this flat atmosphere and produced some colourless matches on these courts.

There was no lack of colour or excitement in the men's singles final. After a fluctuating battle of majestic serve-and-volley tennis, Stefan Edberg, seeded three, beat the No. 2 seed Boris Becker 6–2 6–2 3–6 3–6 6–4 to regain the title he had first won in 1988 by beating the West German in four sets. Thus, after 2 hours and 28 minutes of athletic endeavour, the 24-year-old Swede was avenged for the straight sets loss he had suffered at Becker's hands in the previous year's final.

This was the first time since the abolition of the Challenge Round in 1922 that the same two men had faced each other in three successive title rounds. In the early days of The Championships, William Renshaw had beaten Herbert Lawford in the Challenge Round three years in a row (1884, '85, '86) before Lawford had at last won the title in 1887 when, with Renshaw unfit to defend, he had beaten William's brother, Ernest, in the final of the All-Comers tournament. Four years later, in 1891, Wilfred Baddeley and Joshua Pym had played the first of the four consecutive Challenge Rounds they would dispute. When Baddeley won the first of these at the age of 19 years, 5 months and 21 days he became Wimbledon's youngest men's champion, a distinction he retained until Becker won in 1985 at the age of 17 years, 7 months.

Although the decision of the committee to give the world No. 1 Ivan Lendl the top seeding position ahead of Becker and Edberg was questioned by some, their placing of three-times former champion John McEnroe at No. 4 instead of the No. 7 position his ATP ranking would have earned him, was generally applauded. Unfortunately the 31-year-old American could not live up to their expectations and was bundled out of the tournament in the first round by the free-wheeling Californian Derrick Rostagno who won 7–5 6–4 6–4 on a still green and soft Centre Court. In 37 Grand Slam appearances this was only the fourth time McEnroe had lost in the first round. The last time that had happened at Wimbledon was 1978 when Erik Van Dillen had surprised him. For Rostagno it was some consolation for failing on two match points against Becker at the 1989 US Open. The American sustained his challenge as far as the third round when the tall young Yugoslav, Goran Ivanisevic beat him en route to the semi-finals.

There were five other first round casualties among the men's seeds – Andres Gomez (5), Tim Mayotte (6), Pete Sampras (12), Petr Korda (14), and Yannick Noah (16). In addition Aaron Krickstein (8) withdrew through injury before a ball had been struck. Not since full seeding was introduced in 1927 had so many of the fancied runners fallen at the first hurdle.

Gomez, the 30-year-old Ecuadorian, had still not recovered from the celebrations in Guayaquil that had followed his dramatic French Open victory over Andre Agassi. He lost predictably in straight sets to the powerful American Jim Grabb. Mayotte, the 1982 semi-finalist and four times a quarter-finalist, had been seeded at No. 6, ahead of fellow Americans Brad Gilbert (7) and Aaron Krickstein (8) who were ranked higher. But Mayotte could not harness his serve-and-volley game and was beaten in his opening match by the left-handed South African Gary Muller. Gilbert was to justify his ranking. In a torrid fourth round battle on Court No. 1 against the tall, 21-year-old American David Wheaton, the Californian saved two match points before clinching the final set 13–11. Nor was Gilbert disgraced in losing his quarter-final against Becker in straight sets. He was simply out-played. Sampras, the winner in Manchester the previous week, fell unexpectedly 7–5 7–6 7–6 to the wily South African Christo Van Rensburg and the left-handed Korda went down in four sets against Gilad Bloom of Israel who had been the beaten finalist in Manchester. Noah was completely outplayed by the highly promising South African Wayne Ferreira, an 18-year-old from Johannesburg who had been the world's No. 1 junior in doubles in 1989. He was too swift and sure for a strangely lethargic Frenchman whose record at Wimbledon is miserable. In his four appearances in the past 11 years, Noah has reached the third round once and the second round once. This was his second first round defeat. It is all such a bewildering waste of talent.

The best of the four unseeded quarter-finalists was Ivanisevic. Before beating Rostagno he had been hard pressed by the versatile Frenchman Olivier Delaitre and afterwards by the Dutchman Mark Koevermans. These tough tests had hardened him for his quarter-final against the 32-year-old finalist of 1985, Kevin Curren, also unseeded, who saved a match point in a close fourth set tie-break of 18 points before being ousted 4–6 6–4 6–4 6–7 6–3. Curren served 15 aces, the Yugoslav 26, to bring his tally for the tournament to 79, more than the other three survivors Becker, Lendl and Edberg.

Brad Pearce, 24, a gritty American who had lost his opening match in 1986 and had failed in the qualifying tournament for three years in a row, detained Lendl for four sets on a slippery Centre Court. Lendl's appeal to referee Alan Mills that it was unfit to continue was refused. Had Pearce converted his 4–1 lead in the second set the match might have been closer still. The other unseeded survivor, Christian Bergstrom, broke the serve of fellow Swede Edberg three times in the third set, a commendable effort. Unfortunately he could hold his own only once and went down quickly on Court 14 were the match had been transferred on account of programme congestion because of rain the previous day.

Lendl was playing in the semi-finals for the seventh time in eight years but despite his greater experience he could not repeat the win he had scored over Edberg at the same stage in 1987. The Swede returned so well that Lendl's serve was always under threat and his own relentless attacking game brought him many easy service games. With Lendl holding only one break point in the entire match, Edberg swept through impressively to his third successive appearance in the final. It was all very disappointing for Lendl who had prepared so professionally. He had spent three April weeks on grass in Australia with his coach Tony Roche and had missed the European clay court season to concentrate on his build-up in England. Beating both McEnroe and Becker to retain his Queen's Club title had seemed to make all that effort worthwhile but the lower, faster bounce of the ball at Wimbledon, plus the natural fast-court skills of Edberg, had finally defeated him.

Becker had no easy ride against Ivanisevic who had put him out of the French Open in the first round with some spectacular serving. The stringy 18-year-old Yugoslav, looking even taller than his official height of 6'4" continued to blast down his thunderbolts. He served 14 aces altogether to bring his total for six matches to a record 94, only six fewer than Sampras would serve in seven matches two months later to win the US Open. When Ivanisevic won the first set 6–4 and broke to lead 6–5 in the second, a major upset seemed likely. But youthful impetuosity cost him his serve and in the tie-break Becker remained rock-like. It was effectively the end. Watched by an enthusiastic Duchess of York, Becker swept through the third set without loss in 17 minutes (the fastest set of the Championships) and clinched the tie-break of the fourth without ever being seriously threatened. The players both deserved their standing ovation.

A momentous year for the Czechs, Helena Sukova and Jana Novotna, whose bid for a doubles Grand Slam was thwarted only at the last hurdle in the US Open final.

(R. Adams)

Becker was playing Edberg for the 24th time since their first professional meeting in 1984. Edberg had won that one but, since then, Becker had built a lead of 15 to 8. This was their fifth meeting on grass and again Becker was ahead 3–1, the last occasion being in the Queen's Club semi-final three weeks earlier.

For two sets Edberg was almost faultless. He broke Becker four times, twice in each set, and in 56 minutes he led 6–2 6–2. A first loss of serve by Edberg in the second game of the third set was all the encouragement Becker needed. Although he was slipping and sometimes falling, the German could now see a way back. He took the third set 6–3 and the fourth by the same score with two breaks of a now rather tentative Swedish serve. When, in the gusty wind, Edberg served his 6th and 7th double faults, the last on game point, to concede his serve and give Becker a 3–1 lead in the fifth, it seemed the German would, after all, retain his title. But, unusually, Becker froze on a high forehand volley when break point down in the next game. He pushed it wide of the sideline and grimaced with pain. With a new spring in his step Edberg surged back into top gear. At 4–4 he had Becker at 15–40 with two glorious backhand returns and a volley that Becker was forced to volley into the net. On game point he hit a killing lob that Becker could only watch as it spun over his head just out of reach. It was the end. Two backhand volleys and two winning serves brought Edberg a second title and a prize of £230,000. More than that, it brought Stefan and his British coach Tony Pickard the satisfaction of a fourth Grand Slam title after the disappointment of having had to retire to Lendl in the final of the Australian Open when most observers felt he would have won.

As usual the women seeds were more reliable than their male counterparts and allowed no interlopers to reach the quarter-finals. There were, however, three who lost in the first round, the most notable being Arantxa Sanchez-Vicario (6) who was beaten 1–6 7–6 9–7 by the 33-year-old American Betsy Nagelsen, the wife of sports entrepreneur Mark McCormack. The other two seeds were both victims of British players, itself a notable fact. Sara Gomer, a wild card entry, did well to overpower Manuela Maleeva Fragnière (8) 6–2 6–3 and Sara Loosemore was equally impressive in dismissing the Austrian Barbara Paulus (16) 6–2 3–6 6–4. Predictably both English girls lost their next matches – Gomer to the young American Angelica Gavaldon, Loosemore to Elna Reinach of South Africa.

Apart from Miss Navratilova's ultimate triumph, the most impressive performance came from her victim in the final, Zina Garrison. The 26-year-old Houston resident, playing in her eighth Wimbledon, beat in succession Helena Sukova (10), Monica Seles (3) the new French Champion, and Steffi Graf (1), the holder of the title since 1988 and the overwhelming favourite to record her 10th Grand Slam success. The most exciting of these was unquestionably the 3–6 6–3 9–7 victory in the quarter-finals against Seles who had won her last 6 tournaments in 36 consecutive winning matches. Court No. 1, so often the scene of drama, was the stage for this stunning upset which was voted the best match of the Championships. The battle fluctuated wildly and was in doubt until the last shot. Garrison began by rushing forward, trying to impose her considerable volleying skills against the double-fisted baseliner. Seles thrived on the pace and fired her passing shots unerringly past the American to claim the first set. Sensibly Garrison changed her tactics. In order to deny Seles the pace on which she thrives, moonballs and floaters were interspersed with some fierce drives to the lines. Errors started to creep in as the 16-year-old Yugoslav lost her rhythm and the second set was lost. The momentum carried Garrison to 4–1 in the decider. The two service breaks were quickly recovered and Seles went ahead 5–4 with one of those familiar surges that usually blasts the opposition from the court. There were thoughts of all those close matches that Garrison has lost over the years because she had never really believed in herself. But this was a new Garrison. Her coach of five months, Sherwood Stewart, had helped her to believe. He was there with Zina's husband Willard Jackson to see her fight on magnificently. Serving at 6–7 Garrison faced a match point but saved it with a fearless drive to the sideline. It was the signal for a burst of confident driving and volleying that won the American twelve of the next thirteen points. It had been a splendid victory against the odds.

The odds against Garrison in the semi-final were even longer. Although Graf had been deeply disturbed by the scandal surrounding her father's alleged affair with a German model, the champion had sailed through five matches for the loss of a mere 23 games. The last of those, a 6–2 6–4 victory over the American prodigy Jennifer Capriati had ended the speculation that this phenomenal 14-year-old from Florida was ready to become the youngest Wimbledon winner of all time. The one-sided match was a non-event. Though not disgraced, Jennifer was nervous and was simply outplayed.

Against Garrison it was Graf who looked nervous. The famous forehad was misfiring and accordingly her confidence was dented (especially when she lost her serve in the third game despite delivering three aces). Some of Garrison's driving was glorious in its uninhibited accuracy and she was serving well too. Garrison's 4/1 lead became 6/3 – a pattern that was repeated in the second set, but in reverse. A single break in the third game of the final set was enough to give Garrison the best victory of her life. It was a bitter disappointment for Graf who had failed to reach a Grand Slam final for the first time since the French Open of 1987, her first major success. Furthermore, after losses in her two previous tournaments in Berlin and Paris, Steffi was losing her third tournament in a row, something that had not happened since 1986. It also marked only her third loss before the finals since she became the World No. 1 on 17th August 1987. The other losses, both at the semi-final stage in 1988, had occurred at Amelia Island (to Sabatini) and at the Virginia Slims Championships (to Shriver).

From the moment Garrison lost her serve in the third game, the final became a procession. Understandably, in her first Grand Slam final Garrison was nervous and failed to produce her best tennis. Navratilova started well and got better. She also stayed cool, safe in the knowledge that she had achieved 27 previous wins against Garrison, who had beaten her only once – in a superb roller coaster quarter-final at the US Open in 1988. Martina never put a foot wrong as she pounded down her swinging left-handed serve and darted across the net to cut off the passes. With impressively athletic professionalism she swept imperiously to victory, winning seven of the last eight games of a one-sided match that lasted only 76 minutes. As the games mounted the smile got broader and the gestures to Billie Jean King, who had prepared her mentally, coach Craig Kardon and long-time friend Judy Nelson, were more frequent. Martina knew that she was about to break a record that had stood for 51 years. She was also creating a new one that will probably last for ever. The winner's cheque for £207,000 was almost irrelevant to someone whose career prize money now totalled more than $16 million.

In a service-dominated men's doubles final, remarkable for the fact that there were no breaks of serve, the finalists of 1989 and No. 1 seeds this time, Rick Leach and Jim Pugh of the United States, beat the reigning Australian Open champions, Peter Aldrich and Danie Visser (2) of South Africa, 7–6 7–6 7–6. Over the entire 140-odd minutes there were only seven break points in three separate games – three against Leach in the 10th game of the first set, two against Visser, in the 8th game of the second and two against Pugh in the 12th game of the third. It was all hugely efficient but a trifle tedious.

The women's doubles fell to the all-conquering Czechs, Jana Novotna and Helena Sukova (1), the holders of the Australian and French titles. They won 6–3 6–4 against the American-Australian pair, Kathy Jordan and Elizabeth Smylie (6), who had won in 1985 to end Navratilova and Shriver's winning streak of 109 matches.

Leach became the only double winner for 1990 when he won his first mixed doubles title with Zina Garrison, the champion in 1988 with her present coach Sherwood Stewart. The 7–5 6–2 win by the No. 3 seeds over the Australians John Fitzgerald and Smylie (4) was thus some consolation for Garrison who completed her finest Wimbledon on a high note.

MEN'S SINGLES

Holder: B. Becker (FRG)

6-2 6-2 3-6 6-3 6-4

FIRST ROUND	SECOND ROUND	THIRD ROUND	FOURTH ROUND	QUARTER-FINALS	SEMI-FINALS	FINAL

FIRST ROUND

1 I. LENDL (TCH) (1)
2 C. Miniussi (ARG)
3 C. Costa (ESP) (LL)
4 J. Hlasek (SUI)
5 B. Shelton (USA)
6 H. Hogstedt (SWE)
7 S. Bruguera (ESP)
8 A. N. Castle (GBR) (WC)
9 C. Pistoles (ITA)
10 D. Pate (USA)
11 G. Raoux (FRA) (Q)
12 J. M. Turner (GBR) (WC)
13 A. Antonitsch (AUT)
14 M. Roberston (RSA) (Q)
15 S. Youl (AUS)
16 H. LECONTE (FRA) (15)
17 J. COURIER (USA) (9)
18 M. Kaplan (RSA)
19 J. Woodbridge (AUS) (LL)
20 J. Stoltenberg (AUS)
21 U. Riglewski (FRG)
22 V. Paloheimo (FIN)
23 J. B. Fitzgerald (AUS)
24 C. Woodforde (AUS) (WC)
25 B. Garrow (USA)
26 J. Wohrmann (FRG)
27 M. Srejber (TCH)
28 R. A. Reneberg (USA)
29 B. Pearce (USA)
30 R. Bathman (SWE) (Q)
31 L. Mattar (BRA)
32 S. Matsuoka (JPN) (Q)
33 S. EDBERG (SWE) (3)
34 B. Dyke (AUS) (LL)
35 J. Meori (TCH)
36 T. Carboneli (ESP)
37 J. Fleunan (FRA)
38 R. Fromberg (AUS)
39 A. Mandorf (ISR)
40 H. Holm (SWE)
41 M. Kratzmann (AUS)
42 C. Motta (BRA)
43 R. Leach (USA) (Q)
44 A. Jarryd (SWE)
45 J. Gunnarsson (SWE)
46 J. Pugh (USA)
47 J. Altur (ESP)
48 M. CHANG (USA) (13)
49 G. FORGET (FRA) (11)
50 L. A. Wahlgren (SWE)
51 P. Kuhnen (FRG)
52 R. Jelen (FRG)
53 A. Rahunen (FIN)
54 K. Evernden (NZL)
55 M. Stich (FRG)
56 D. Dier (FRG) (Q)
57 N. Broad (GBR) (Q)
58 C. Duncan (USA)
59 U. Bergstrom (SWE)
60 T. Wilkison (USA)
61 M. R. J. Petchev (GBR) (WC)
62 P. Chamberlin (USA)
63 J. Grabb (USA)
64 A. GOMEZ (ECU) (5)

SECOND ROUND

LENDL (1) 3-6 6-4 6-3 6-4
Hlasek 6-3 6-4 6-1
Shelton 7-6 5-7 7-6 6-4
Bruguera 6-7 6-4 6-3 6-1
Pate 6-3 6-4 6-4
Raoux 6-3 6-4 7-5
Antonitsch 7-6 6-3 3-6 4-6 6-4
LECONTE (15)
COURIER (9) 6-4 6-3
Stoltenberg 6-3 6-4
Riglewski 6-4 7-5
Woodforde 6-4 6-4
Srejber 6-7 3-6 7-6 6-3 6-2
Pearce 7-6 6-3
Matsuoka 7-6 6-3 6-1
EDBERG (3) 4-6 6-1 6-3 6-1
Meori 6-4 6-1
Fromberg 7-6 5-7 4-6 6-1 6-4
Mandorf 6-1 1-6 5-7 6-3 6-2
Kratzmann 6-1 6-3 6-1
Jarryd 6-2 6-1 6-3
Pugh 6-3 1-6 5-7 6-3 6-4
CHANG (13) 6-2 6-2
FORGET (11) 5-7 6-4 6-3 7-5
Jelen 6-3 6-1
Rahunen
Stich 5-3
Bergstrom 6-2 6-2
Broad 6-2 7-6 8-6
Chamberlin 3-6 6-0 7-6 6-3
Grabb 6-4 6-2 6-2

THIRD ROUND

LENDL (1) 6-1 6-3 6-0
Shelton 5-7 2-6 6-4 6-4 6-3
Pate 3-6 6-2 6-4 6-3
Antonitsch 2-6 4-7-6 2-6 6-3
COURIER (9) 6-2 7-6 6-4
Woodforde 6-7 6-4 6-4 7-5
Srejber 6-2 6-7 6-3 6-2
Pearce 7-6 7-5 6-3
EDBERG (3) 6-2 6-3 6-2
Mansdorf 6-4 7-6 6-1
Kratzmann w/o
CHANG (13) 6-3 6-2
FORGET (11) 7-6 6-7 6-1 6-2
Stich 6-2 7-5 6-3
Bergstrom 4-6 7-6 6-2 6-2
Grabb 6-2 6-7 7-6 3-6 6-3

FOURTH ROUND

LENDL (1) 7-6 6-7 6-4 6-4
Antonitsch 6-4 6-4 7-6
Woodforde 7-5 5-7 7-5 6-4
Pearce 6-3 6-3 6-1
EDBERG (3) 6-4 5-7 3-6 6-2 9-7
CHANG (13) 3-6 4-6 6-4 6-2 6-2
FORGET (11) 3-6 7-5 6-2 4-6 6-3
Bergstrom 7-6 6-4 6-2

QUARTER-FINALS

LENDL (1) 3-6 6-4 6-3 6-4
Pearce 6-4 6-4 6-4
EDBERG (3) 6-3 6-2 6-1
Bergstrom 6-4 3-6 6-3 7-5

SEMI-FINALS

LENDL (1) 6-4 6-4 5-7 6-4
EDBERG (3) 6-3 6-2 6-4

FINAL

EDBERG (3) 6-1 7-6 6-3

S. EDBERG (SWE) (3)

First round (players 65–128)

No.	Player	Round 1 winner & score
65	T. S. MAYOTTE (USA) (6)	Muller 4-6 7-6 7-5 6-3
66	G. Muller (RSA)	
67	K. Curren (USA)	Curren 6-1 6-4 6-1
68	J. Tarango (USA)	
69	K. Novacek (TCH)	Novacek 6-4 6-7 0-6 6-4 6-0
70	G. Lavendecker (USA)	
71	J. Rive (USA)	Rive 5-7 6-4 6-4 5-7 6-4
72	V. Amritraj (IND) (Q)	
73	K. Jones (USA)	Jones 6-3 3-6 6-4 6-4
74	D. E. Sapsford (GBR) (WC)	
75	S. E. Davis (USA)	Rosset 7-6 7-5 6-3
76	M. Rosset (SUI)	
77	S. Zivojinovic (YUG)	Volkov 6-7 7-6 7-6 6-1
78	A. Volkov (URS)	
79	C. J. Van Rensburg (RSA)	Van Rensburg 7-6 7-5 7-6
80	P. SAMRAS (USA) (12)	
81	P. KORDA (TCH) (14)	Bloom 6-0 6-4 4-6 6-2
82	G. Bloom (ISR)	
83	R. Krishnan (IND)	Koevermans 7-5 4-6 6-2
84	M. Koevermans (HOL)	
85	T. Benhabiles (FRA)	Kroon 6-3 6-2 5-7 3-6 6-3
86	N. Kroon (SWE)	
87	D. Perez (URU)	Krishnan 6-4 6-2 6-4
88	R. Krishnan (IND)	
89	O. Delaitre (FRA)	Delaitre 7-5 6-4 3-6 6-2
90	M. Zoecke (FRG)	
91	A. Lesch (FRG) (Q)	Ivanisevic 6-4 6-0 6-4
92	G. Ivanisevic (YUG)	
93	J. Lundgren (SWE)	Bates 6-7 6-4 6-4 6-0
94	M. Bates (GBR)	
95	D. Rostagno (USA)	Rostagno 7-5 6-4 6-4
96	J. P. McENROE (USA) (4)	
97	B. GILBERT (USA) (7)	GILBERT (7)
98	B. Oresar (YUG)	
99	G. Connell (CAN)	Visser 6-4 6-4 6-4
100	D. Visser (RSA) (Q)	
101	D. Cahill (AUS)	Cahill 6-2 6-2 6-0
102	M. Wostenholme (CAN)	
103	T. Nijssen (HOL)	Haarhus 7-6 6-3 6-3
104	P. Haarhus (HOL)	
105	M. Larsson (SWE)	Wheaton 7-6 6-2
106	D. Wheaton (USA)	
107	P. Annacone (USA)	Annacone 2-6 3-6 6-3 6-3 8-6
108	L. Shiras (USA)	
109	L. Jonsson (SWE)	Washington 6-2 6-3 6-1
110	M. Washington (USA)	
111	M. Santoro (FRA)	SVENSSON (10) 6-2 6-3 6-1
112	J. B. SVENSSON (SWE) (10)	
113	Y. NOAH (FRA) (16)	Ferreira 6-4 6-3 6-2
114	W. Ferreira (RSA) (Q)	
115	W. Strelba (TCH)	Aguilera 6-3 7-5 6-3
116	J. Aguilera (ESP)	
117	P. Cash (AUS) (WC)	Cash 4-6 7-5 7-6 4-6 6-1
118	D. Poliakov (URS) (Q)	
119	N. Brown (GBR) (WC)	Anderson 6-4 6-2 7-6
120	J. Anderson (AUS)	
121	D. Goldie (USA)	Goldie 7-5 6-1 7-5
122	B. Kok (HOL) (Q)	
123	K. Flach (USA) (Q)	Flach 6-4 7-6 6-3
124	M. Schapers (HOL)	
125	W. Masur (AUS)	Masur 6-3 6-4 6-2
126	A. Cherkasov (URS)	
127	L. E. Herrera (MEX) (Q)	BECKER (2) 7-6 7-6 7-5
128	B. BECKER (FRG) (2)	

Second round
- Curren 6-7 6-4 7-6 6-3
- Novacek 5-7 6-4 6-4 7-6
- Rosset 3-6 6-7 6-3 7-5 6-3
- Volkov 6-3 6-4 7-5
- Koevermans 7-5 6-4 6-3
- Kroon 6-3 2-6 6-3 6-3
- Ivanisevic 6-2 6-2 6-4
- Rostagno 6-1 3-6 6-4 6-1
- GILBERT (7) 5-7 6-3 6-2 6-2
- Haarhus 7-5 5-7 7-6 4-6 6-3
- Wheaton 6-4 1-6 6-4 6-7 6-4
- SVENSSON (10) 6-3 6-4
- Aguilera 6-3 7-6 7-5
- Cash 6-2 6-3 7-6
- Goldie 6-3 6-4 6-4
- BECKER (2) 6-7 6-2 (6-3) 6-2

Third round
- Curren 6-2 4-6 1-6 7-5 6-3
- Volkov 6-3 6-4 7-5
- Koevermans 6-7 6-4 6-7 6-4 6-3
- Ivanisevic 6-2 6-2 6-4
- GILBERT (7) 6-1 3-6 6-1 6-2
- Wheaton 2-6 6-7 6-1 6-0 6-4
- Cash 6-1 6-1 6-4
- BECKER (2) 6-3 6-4 4-6 7-5

Fourth round
- Curren 6-4 7-6 7-6
- Ivanisevic 4-6 6-3 6-4 7-6
- GILBERT (7) 6-7 3-6 6-1 6-4 13-11
- BECKER (2) 7-6 6-1 6-4

Quarter-finals
- Ivanisevic 4-6 6-4 6-7 6-3
- BECKER (2) 6-4 6-4 6-1

Semi-final
- BECKER (2) 4-6 7-6 6-0 7-6

Capital letters denote seeded players. Number following player's name gives seeding order. (Q) – Qualifier. (WC) – Wild Card. (LL) – Lucky Loser.

WOMEN'S SINGLES

Holder: S. Graf (FRG)

FIRST ROUND	SECOND ROUND	THIRD ROUND	FOURTH ROUND	QUARTER-FINALS	SEMI-FINALS	FINAL
1 S. GRAF (FRG) (1)	GRAF (1) 6–1 6–2	GRAF (1) 6–3 6–0	GRAF (1) 6–0 6–4	GRAF (1) 6–2 6–4	GRAF (1) 7–5 6–2	
2 C. Porwik (FRG)						
3 E. Brioukhovets (URS) (Q)	McGrath 6–1 6–2					
4 M. McGrath (USA)						
5 C. Kohde-Kilsch (FRG)	Kohde-Kilsch 4–6 6–1 6–1	Kohde-Kilsch 6–2 6–0				
6 M. Paz (ARG)						
7 R. Stubbs (AUS) (Q)	Faber 5–7 7–5 8–6					
8 D. L. Faber (USA)						
9 N. Miyagi (JPN)	White 6–2 6–1	White 4–6 7–5 6–4	CAPRIATI (12) 7–5 6–7 6–3			
10 R. M. White (USA)						
11 M. Maleeva (BUL)	Maleeva 6–4 4–6 6–2					
12 C. Lindqvist (SWE)						
13 J. Halard (FRA)	Halard 7–5 6–2	CAPRIATI (12) 6–2 7–6				
14 K. Jordan (USA) (WC)						
15 H. Kelesi (CAN)	CAPRIATI (12) 6–3 6–1					
16 J. CAPRIATI (USA) (12)						
17 H. NOVOTNA (TCH) (13)	NOVOTNA (13) 6–3 6–1	NOVOTNA (13) 6–2 6–1	NOVOTNA (13) 6–2 6–1	NOVOTNA (13) 6–2 6–4		
18 L. Golarsa (ITA)						
19 B. A. Bonneo (GBR) (WC)	Cunningham 3–6 7–6 6–2					
20 C. E. Cunningham (USA)						
21 J. A. Faull (AUS)	Faull 4–6 6–2 11–9	Faull 6–2 6–3				
22 R. Langrova (TCH)						
23 R. Fairbank (RSA) (Q)	Whitlinger 6–2 6–1					
24 T. S. Whitlinger (USA)						
25 S. P. Sloane (USA)	Sloane 6–3 6–2	Fendick 6–2 6–4	Fendick 6–1 6–1			
26 L. Ferrando (ITA)						
27 Hu Na (USA)	Fendick 1–6 7–6 6–3					
28 A. Fendick (USA)						
29 J. Pospisilova (TCH)	Gavaldon 7–5 7–5	Gavaldon 7–5 0–6 7–5				
30 A. Gavaldon (USA)						
31 S. L. Gomer (GBR) (WC)	Gomer 6–2 6–3					
32 **M. MALEEVA FRAGNIÈRE** (SUI) (8)						
33 M. SELES (YUG) (3)	SELES (3) 6–2 6–3	SELES (3) 6–3 7–5	SELES (3) 6–3 6–3	SELES (3) 6–1 6–0		GARRISON (5) 6–3 6–6 6–4
34 M. Strandlund (SWE)						
35 C. Benjamin (USA)	Benjamin 6–3 6–1					
36 A. M. Cecchini (ITA)						
37 T. Phelps (USA)	Phelps 6–2 2–6 6–2	Minter 6–0 6–1				
38 B. J. Cordwell (NZL)						
39 A. L. Minter (AUS)	Minter 6–2 6–2					
40 J. A. Salmon (GBR) (WC)						
41 H. Mandlikova (AUS)	Mandlikova 6–3 3–6 11–9	Henricksson 6–3 6–3	Henricksson 3–6 6–3 6–3			
42 L. Lapi (ITA)						
43 M. Werdel (USA)	Henricksson 7–5 6–2					
44 A. B. Henricksson (USA)						
45 K. Inoue (JPN)	Reinach 6–0 6–4	Reinach 6–3 7–5				
46 E. Reinach (RSA)						
47 S. J. Loosemore (GBR)	Loosemore 6–2 3–6 6–4					
48 **B. PAULUS** (AUT) (16)						
49 H. SUKOVA (TCH) (10)	SUKOVA (10) 7–5 6–2	SUKOVA (10) 6–4 4–6 7–5	SUKOVA (10) 6–4 6–3	GARRISON (5) 6–3 6–3	GARRISON (5) 3–6 6–3 9–7	
50 M. M. Bollegraf (HOL)						
51 N. A. M. Jagerman (HOL)	Jagerman 6–4 6–1					
52 R. Zrubakova (TCH)						
53 V. Martinek (FRG)	Provis 6–1 6–0	Dechaume 3–6 6–3 6–2				
54 N. Provis (AUS)						
55 N. Sawamatsu (JPN)	Dechaume 7–5 2–6 6–3					
56 A. Dechaume (FRA)						
57 L. Garrone (ITA)	Garrone 6–2 6–4	Leand 5–7 6–4 7–5				
58 S. La Fratta (ITA)						
59 A. Vieira (BRA)	Leand 6–3 7–5					
60 A. L. Leand (USA) (LL)						
61 J. J. Santrock (USA) (LL)	Dahlman 6–4 6–1	GARRISON (5) 6–2 6–1	GARRISON (5) 6–0 6–3			
62 C. Dahlman (SWE)						
63 S. L. Smith (GBR) (WC)	GARRISON (5) 6–2 6–1					
64 Z. L. GARRISON (USA) (5)						

FINAL: 6–4 6–1

M. NAVRATILOVA (USA) (2)

Draw (lower half)

65	A. SANCHEZ VICARIO (ESP) (6)
66	B. Nagelsen (USA)
67	D. S. Van Rensburg (RSA)
68	W. E. Prausa (USA)
69	A. Temesvari (HUN)
70	B. Schultz (HOL)
71	R. Reggi (ITA)
72	R. McQuillan (AUS)
73	S. W. Magers (USA)
74	P. D. Smylie (AUS)
75	K. M. Adams (USA)
76	L. Savchenko (URS)
77	G. Fernandez (USA)
78	F. Labat (ARG)
79	T. A. Harper (USA)
80	R. D. FAIRBANK NIDEFFER (USA) (15)
81	N. ZVEREVA (URS) (11)
82	R. Baranski (POL) (LL)
83	A. Frazier (USA)
84	I. Demongeot (FRA)
85	N. Tauziat (FRA)
86	N. Field (AUS)
87	M. Javer (GBR)
88	E. S. Pfaff (FRG) (Q)
89	C. Tanvier (FRA)
90	E. Svigilerova (TCH)
91	C. Probst (FRG)
92	H. A. Ludloff (USA) (Q)
93	A. Huber (FRG)
94	J. M. Durie (GBR) (WC)
95	E. M. Burgin (USA)
96	G. SABATINI (ARG) (4)
97	M. MALEEVA (BUL) (7)
98	B. Romano (ITA)
99	K. Date (JPN)
100	S. C. Stafford (USA)
101	S. Meier (FRG)
102	L. M. Harvey-Wild (USA)
103	A. Simpkin (GBR) (WC)
104	A. Devries (BEL) (Q)
105	L. M. McNeil (USA)
106	K. Piccolini (ITA)
107	N. Medvedeva (URS)
108	A. J. Coetzer (RSA)
109	A. Grossman (USA)
110	P. F. Daniels (USA)
111	H. Herreman (FRA)
112	A. Ivan (USA) (LL)
113	K. W. WIESNER (AUT) (14)
114	K. Wasserman (BEL)
115	K. Quentrec (FRA)
116	L. Meskhi (URS)
117	L. Gildemeister (PER)
118	M. Kidowaki (JPN)
119	R. Rajchrtova (TCH)
120	A. A. Keller (USA)
121	C. MacGregor (USA)
122	P. Etchemendy (FRA) (LL)
123	K. S. Rinaldi (USA)
124	K. Kschwendt (LUX) (Q)
125	E. Smith (USA)
126	C. J. Wood (GBR) (WC)
127	S. Amiach (FRA)
128	M. NAVRATILOVA (USA) (2)

Round 1

- Nagelsen 1-6 7-6 9-7
- Van Rensburg 6-2 7-6
- Schultz 6-2 6-0
- McQuillan 7-6 7-6
- Magers 6-1 7-6
- Savchenko 5-7 6-4 6-3
- Fernandez 6-2 6-2
- FAIRBANK NIDEFFER (15) 6-2 3-6 6-2
- ZVEREVA (11) 6-3 6-3
- Frazier 6-1 6-4
- Tauziat 6-2 6-1
- Pfaff 7-5 6-1
- Tanvier 6-2 6-4
- Ludloff 2-6 6-4 7-5
- Huber 7-5 4-6 6-2
- SABATINI (4) 6-2 7-6
- MALEEVA (7) 6-2 6-4
- Date 7-6 6-3
- Harvey-Wild 6-2 6-1
- Devries 7-5 6-2
- McNeil 6-1 3-6 6-1
- Coetzer 4-6 6-2 6-1
- Grossman 6-2 6-1
- Herreman 6-0 6-2
- WIESNER (14) 6-3 6-0
- Quentrec 3-6 6-3 6-2
- Gildemeister 6-3 6-3
- Rajchrtova 7-5 6-7 6-4
- Etchemendy 6-3 3-6 6-2
- Kschwendt 6-3 3-6 6-3
- Smith 6-3 4-6 6-2
- NAVRATILOVA (2) 6-1 6-1

Round 2

- Nagelsen 2-6 6-4 6-2
- Schultz 6-4 3-6 7-5
- Magers 6-3 6-4
- ZVEREVA (11) 7-6 6-4
- Frazier 6-4 6-3
- Tauziat 6-2 6-1
- Tanvier 6-3 6-4
- SABATINI (4) 6-2 7-6
- MALEEVA (7) 6-1 6-4
- Devries 7-5 6-2
- McNeil 6-3 6-2
- Herreman 6-0 6-2
- WIESNER (14) 6-3 6-3
- Gildemeister 6-2 6-2
- Kschwendt 7-6 1-6 6-0
- NAVRATILOVA (2) 6-2 6-3

Round 3

- Schultz 6-1 6-4
- ZVEREVA (11) 2-6 6-2 6-4
- Tauziat 3-6 6-2 7-5
- SABATINI (4) 6-4 6-2
- MALEEVA (7) 6-2 6-0
- Herreman 6-4 6-3
- WIESNER (14) 6-2 7-6
- NAVRATILOVA (2) 6-3 6-3

Round 4

- ZVEREVA (11) 6-2 6-2
- SABATINI (4) 6-2 7-6
- MALEEVA (7) 6-3 6-0
- NAVRATILOVA (2) 6-3 6-3

Quarter-finals

- SABATINI (4) 6-2 6-8 8-6
- NAVRATILOVA (2) 6-1 6-1

Semi-final

- NAVRATILOVA (2) 6-3 6-4

Capital letters denote seeded players. Number following player's name gives seeding order. (Q) – Qualifier. (WC) – Wild Card. (LL) – Lucky Loser.

MEN'S DOUBLES

Holders: J. B. Fitzgerald (AUS)/A. Jarryd (SWE)

Winner: R. LEACH (USA)/J. PUGH (USA) (1) 7-6 7-6 7-6

FIRST ROUND	SECOND ROUND	THIRD ROUND	QUARTER-FINALS	SEMI-FINALS	FINAL
1 R. LEACH/J. PUGH (1)	LEACH/PUGH (1) 6-4 6-4 7-6	LEACH/PUGH (1) 6-4 3-6 7-5 7-6	LEACH/PUGH (1) 3-6 6-1 6-4 7-5	LEACH/PUGH (1) 7-6 7-6 7-6	LEACH/PUGH (1) 4-6 6-4 7-6 6-3
2 T. Nelson/R. Smith					
3 R. Bergh/H. Holm (LL)	Fleurian/Nargiso 6-1 7-6 6-3				
4 J. Fleurian/D. Nargiso					
5 M. Mortensen/P. Nyborg	Mortensen/Nyborg 7-5 6-7 3-6 7-6 6-4	Ferreira/Norval 6-4 6-7 6-7 6-9 7			
6 M. Abahano/T. Papel					
7 W. Ferreira/P. Norval (Q)	Ferreira/Norval 6-4 6-3 6-4				
8 G. LAYENDECKER/R. A. RENEBERG (15)					
9 D. CAHILL/M. KRATZMANN (9)	Stoltenberg/Woodbridge 6-4 6-4 6-4	Stoltenberg/Woodbridge 6-4 6-1 7-6	Stoltenberg/Woodbridge 6-4 6-3 7-6		
10 J. Pawsat/R. Wheaton					
11 J. Pawsat/R. Wheaton	Pawsat/Wheaton 6-2 6-2 6-4				
12 C. B. Bailey/D. P. son (WC)					
13 M. Bahrami/E. Winogradsky	Petchey/Sapsford 3-6 7-5 6-2 6-4	FORGET/HLASEK (7) 6-3 6-4 6-4			
14 M. R. J. Petchey/D. E. Sapsford (WC)					
15 J. Novacek/E. Pimek	FORGET/HLASEK (7) 6-7 5-6 7-6 6-0				
16 G. FORGET/J. HLASEK (7)					
17 S. E. DAVIS/D. PATE (4)	DAVIS/PATE (4) 7-6 6-4 6-4	Kruger/Van Emburgh 7-6 6-3 6-4	Kruger/Van Emburgh 6-4 6-3 6-2	Kruger/Van Emburgh 7-6 6-7 6-2 4-6 6-4	
18 P. Annacone/C. J. Van Rensburg					
19 T. Hand/C. Wilkinson (Q)	Kruger/Van Emburgh 7-6 6-4 6-4				
20 S. Kruger/G. Van Emburgh					
21 M. Bahrami/M. Turner (WC)	Botfield/Turner 7-6 6-4 6-4	Botfield/Turner 6-2 6-2 5-7 7-6			
22 P. Chamberlin/T. Wilkinson					
23 G. Ivanisevic/B. Taroczy	LUZA/MOTTA (13) 7-5 7-5 1-0 retd	Drewett/Masur 6-2 6-2 6-7 7-6			
24 G. LUZA/C. MOTTA (13)					
25 U. RIGLEWSKI/M. STICH (12)	RIGLEWSKI/STICH (12) 6-2 7-5 6-2				
26 B. Dyke/B. Talbot (LL)					
27 D. Drewett/W. Masur	Drewett/Masur 7-6 7-5 6-2	CONNELL/MICHIBATA (6) 7-6 7-5 6-7 4-6 10-8	CONNELL/MICHIBATA (6) 3-6 6-3 7-6 7-6		
28 A. Antonitsch/A. N. Castle					
29 J. M. Goodall/U. Nganga (WC)	Evernden/Pereira 6-4 1-6 6-3				
30 K. Evernden/N. Pereira					
31 P. Haarhuis/M. Koevermans	CONNELL/MICHIBATA (6) 6-3 5-7 6-4 7-6				
32 G. CONNELL/G. MICHIBATA (6)					
33 P. KORDA/T. SMID (5)	KORDA/SMID (5) 7-6 6-4 6-2	Cannon/Garrett 3-6 7-6 7-6 4-6 15-13	Frana/Lavalle 6-3 6-3 6-3	Frana/Lavalle 6-3 2-6 7-5 6-1	
34 N. Aerts/F. Roese					
35 B. Garrow/S. Salumaa	Cannon/Garrett 6-4 5-7 7-5 6-4				
36 S. Cannon/B. Garrett					
37 J. Frana/L. Lavalle	Frana/Lavalle 6-4 4-7 2-6 6-1	Frana/Lavalle 6-4 5-7 6-2 3-6 8-6			
38 C. Mezzadri/C. Minussi					
39 A. Mora/B. Page	BROAD/MULLER (11) 7-6 7-6 5-7 4-6 9-7				
40 N. BROAD/G. MULLER (11)					
41 M. J. BATES/K. CURREN (14)	BATES/CURREN (14) 6-4 6-2 6-2	BATES/CURREN (14) 7-6 6-3 5-6 6-7 6-4	BATES/CURREN (14) 6-2 6-1 6-4		
42 D. Rikl/T. Zdrazila					
43 J. Donohoe/J. Vardel	Donohoe/Vardel 6-3 3-6 6-7 6-4				
44 S. Colombo/G. Pozzi					
45 C. Beckman/L. B. Jensen	Devries/Rive 3-6 6-3 7-6 6-3	Canter/Derlin 7-6 3-6 6-3 6-4			
46 S. Devries/J. Rive					
47 J. Canter/B. Derlin	Canter/Derlin 3-6 3-6 6-4 1-0 retd				
48 J. B. FITZGERALD/A. JARRYD (3)					
49 K. FLACH/R. SEGUSO (8)	FLACH/SEGUSO (8) 6-4 6-1 6-3	FLACH/SEGUSO (8) 6-2 7-6 6-3	FLACH/SEGUSO (8) 1-6 6-4 7-5 7-6	ALDRICH/VISSER (2) 6-4 6-3 6-2	
50 R. Bathman/J. Gunnarsson					
51 K. Kinnear/B. Pearce	Kinnear/Pearce 7-6 6-3 6-7 6-3				
52 N. Odizor/P. Wekesa					
53 Baur/C. Saceanu (Q)	Fulwood/Lundgren 7-6 6-3 6-7 6-3 8-6	GRABB/McENROE (10) 6-1 6-7 6-3 6-3			
54 A. Fulwood/P. Lundgren (WC)					
55 A. Boetsch/G. Raoux (Q)	GRABB/McENROE (10) 5-7 7-6 7-6 6-4				
56 J. GRABB/P. McENROE (10)					
57 R. GALBRAITH/D. MacPHERSON (16)	GALBRAITH/MacPHERSON (16) 6-0 6-4 7-5	Brown/Schapers 4-6 7-5 6-2 6-3	ALDRICH/VISSER (2) 7-6 6-3 7-6		
58 B. Dyke/S. Youl					
59 M. Brown/M. Schapers	Brown/Schapers 3-4 6-4 6-7 7-5				
60 G. Pritzner/T. Thane (Q)					
61 J. Courier/M. Davis	Courier/Davis 4-6 6-7 7-6 6-3 6-3	ALDRICH/VISSER (2) 7-6 6-4 7-5			
62 J. Chlak/C. Suk					
63 K. Jones/R. W. Van 't Hof	ALDRICH/VISSER (2) 7-6 6-3 6-4				
64 P. ALDRICH/D. T. VISSER (2)					

Capital letters denote seeded pairings. Number following players' names give seeding order. (Q) – Qualifier. (WC) – Wild Card. (LL) – Lucky Loser.

WOMEN'S DOUBLES

Holders: J. Novotna (TCH)/H. Sukova (TCH)

Winner: J. NOVOTNA (TCH)/H. SUKOVA (TCH) (1) 6–3 6–4

Columns: FIRST ROUND · SECOND ROUND · THIRD ROUND · QUARTER-FINALS · SEMI-FINALS · FINAL

First Round

1. J. NOVOTNA/H. SUKOVA (1)
2. C. Bakkum/K. Radford
3. J. M. Durie/J. A. Richardson
4. C. Lindqvist/T. Scheuer-Larsen
5. S. L. Gomer/J. A. Salmon (WC)
6. N. Pratt/K. Sharp (Q)
7. K. L. McDonald/T. J. Morton (Q)
8. A. E. SMITH/W. M. TURNBULL (13)
9. P. F. DANIELS/W. E. PRAUSA (15)
10. S. L. Collins/J. B. Smoller
11. S. J. Loosemore/A. Simpkin (WC)
12. C. Porwick/W. Probst
13. M. Lindstrom/H. A. Ludloff
14. A. A. Fairbank/R. D. McQuillan
15. J. Durie/N. C. M. Vis (Q)
16. M. PAZ/A. SANCHEZ-VICARIO (7)
17. A. Devries/K. Godridge (LL)
18. H. Kelesi/M. Seles
19. E. Krapl/M. Werdel
20. H. Brandt/J. Field
21. M. Javer/A. H. White (WC)
22. S. L. Smith/H. Tier Riet
23. E. S. Pfaff/R. P. Stubbs
24. P. A. FENDICK/Z. L. GARRISON (10)
25. J. M. HETHERINGTON/R. M. WHITE (12)
26. A. Hu...
27. P. Langrova/J. Pospisilova
28. L. K. Allen/S. Amiach
29. J. M. Byrne/J. G. Thompson
30. C. Kohde-Kilsch/B. Schultz
31. B. Bowes/E. Manokova
32. N. PROVIS/E. REINACH (5)
33. S. GRAF/G. SABATINI (8)
34. I. Demongeot/C. Tanvier
35. C. MacGregor/C. B. MacGregor
36. A. Dechaume/N. Herreman
37. M. Kotkowska/A. Scott
38. E. A. Herr/T. Phelps
39. S. Albinus/N. Van Lottum
40. E. M. BURGIN/R. D. FAIRBANK NIDEFFER (11)
41. K. M. ADAMS/L. M. McNEIL (9)
42. R. Baranski/R. Zrubakova
43. B. Capriati/M. McGrath
44. C. K. Bassett-Seguso/A. Grossman
45. A. M. Cecchini/L. Gildemeister
46. A. B. Henricksson/D. S. Van Rensburg
47. B. Romano/R. Svobbnova
48. L. SAVCHENKO/N. M. ZVEREVA (3)
49. K. JORDAN/P. D. SMYLIE (6)
50. B. A. Borneo/C. J. Wood (WC)
51. A. H. Grousbeck/N. Miyagi
52. L. Garrone/L. Golarsa
53. L. Tauziat/H. W. Wiesner
54. N. J. Gustafsson/I. Hodder (Q)
55. L. Antonoplis/M. Standiund (LL)
56. L. J. MEDVEDEVA/N. MESKHI (14)
57. L. J. GREGORY/S. W. MAGERS (16)
58. K. Maleeva/M. Maleeva
59. M. M. Bollegraf/B. J. Cordwell
60. T. A. Harper/H. L. Mager
61. P. Paradis/C. Suire
62. L. Ferrando/S. Goles
63. C. Benjamin/A. L. Minter
64. G. FERNANDEZ/M. NAVRATILOVA (2)

Second Round

- NOVOTNA/SUKOVA (1) 6–1 6–2
- Durie/Richardson 7–6 6–4
- Pratt/Sharpe 6–0 3–6 6–2
- SMITH/TURNBULL (13) 6–4 3–6 6–2
- DANIELS/PRAUSA (15) 7–6 6–3
- Porwick/Probst 6–2 6–1
- Lindstrom/Ludloff 6–1 6–3
- PAZ/SANCHEZ-VICARIO (7) 6–1 6–3
- Devries/Godridge 6–2 6–3
- Barnard/Field 7–6 6–2
- Javer/White 6–2 6–3
- FENDICK/GARRISON (10) 6–1 6–3
- HETHERINGTON/WHITE (12) 6–1 6–2
- Langrova/Pospisilova 7–5 6–4
- Kohde-Kilsch/Schultz 3–6 6–2
- PROVIS/REINACH (5) 7–6 6–1
- GRAF/SABATINI (8) 2–6 6–3 7–5
- Dechaume/Herreman 6–3 6–3
- Herr/Phelps 6–3 6–3
- BURGIN/FAIRBANK NIDEFFER (11) 6–3 6–4
- ADAMS/McNEIL (9) 3–6 6–0 11–9
- Capriati/McGrath 6–1 6–4
- SAVCHENKO/ZVEREVA (3) 6–3 4–6 6–2
- JORDAN/SMYLIE (6) 6–2 6–2
- Garrone/Golarsa 6–0 6–4
- Tauziat/Wiesner 6–3 6–3
- MEDVEDEVA/MESKH (14) 6–3 6–4
- GREGORY/MAGERS (16) 6–2 3–6 9–7
- Harper/Mager 6–3 6–4
- Paradis/Suire 7–5 7–5
- FERNANDEZ/NAVRATILOVA (2) 6–0 6–1

Third Round

- NOVOTNA/SUKOVA (1) 2–6 6–3 6–0
- SMITH/TURNBULL (13) 6–3 6–2
- DANIELS/PRAUSA (15) 7–5 7–5
- PAZ/SANCHEZ-VICARIO (7) 6–4 6–1
- FENDICK/GARRISON (10) 6–3 5–7 6–1
- HETHERINGTON/WHITE (12) 6–1 6–2
- PROVIS/REINACH (5) 7–6 6–3
- GRAF/SABATINI (8) 6–0 6–3
- BURGIN/FAIRBANK NIDEFFER (11) 6–3 6–4
- ADAMS/McNEIL (9) 3–6 6–0 11–9
- SAVCHENKO/ZVEREVA (3) 6–1 7–5
- JORDAN/SMYLIE (6) 6–2 6–0
- GREGORY/MAGERS (16) 6–4 6–1
- FERNANDEZ/NAVRATILOVA (2) 6–3 6–3

Quarter-Finals

- NOVOTNA/SUKOVA (1) 7–5 7–6
- PAZ/SANCHEZ-VICARIO (7) 6–4 6–3
- FENDICK/GARRISON (10) 6–4 6–0
- HETHERINGTON/WHITE (12) 6–4 6–1
- GRAF/SABATINI (8) 7–6 6–4
- SAVCHENKO/ZVEREVA (3) 6–3 6–3
- JORDAN/SMYLIE (6) 4–6 6–3 6–1
- FERNANDEZ/NAVRATILOVA (2) 3–6 6–2 6–1

Semi-Finals

- NOVOTNA/SUKOVA (1) 6–4 6–1
- FENDICK/GARRISON (10) 6–1 6–7 6–1
- SAVCHENKO/ZVEREVA (3) 6–4 1–6 7–5
- JORDAN/SMYLIE (6) 6–3 2–6 6–4

Final

- NOVOTNA/SUKOVA (1) 7–6 6–4
- JORDAN/SMYLIE (6) 6–2 7–6

Capital letters denote seeded pairings. Number following players' names give seeding order. (Q) – Qualifier, (WC) – Wild Card, (LL) – Lucky Loser.

MIXED DOUBLES

Holders: J. Pugh (USA)/J. Novotna (TCH)

R. LEACH (USA)/Z. L. GARRISON (USA) (3) 7–5 6–2

FIRST ROUND | SECOND ROUND | THIRD ROUND | QUARTER-FINALS | SEMI-FINALS | FINAL

Winner: LEACH/GARRISON (3) 7–6 7–6

FITZGERALD/SMYLIE (4) 7–6 7–5

SEMI-FINALS:
- PUGH/NOVOTNA (1) 6–1 6–3
- LEACH/GARRISON (3) 2–6 6–4 7–5
- FITZGERALD/SMYLIE (4) 7–5 6 7–6 4
- Nelson/Magers 6–2 7–6

QUARTER-FINALS:
- PUGH/NOVOTNA (1) 7–6 6–4
- Cannon/White 7–5 7–6
- LEACH/GARRISON (3) 7–5 6–7 6–4
- VISSER/FAIRBANK NIDEFFER (6) 6–4 7–6
- Bates/Durie 6–2 6–3
- FITZGERALD/SMYLIE (4) 6–2 6–1
- Nelson/Magers 2–6 6–3 9–7
- ALDRICH/REINACH (2) 3–6 6–4 6–0

THIRD ROUND:
- PUGH/NOVOTNA (1) 7–5 7–5
- SEGUSO/McNEIL (10) 6–3 6–7 6–3
- Norval/De Swardt 6–2 6–4
- Cannon/White 5–2 retd
- LEACH/GARRISON (3) 3–6 6–3 9–7
- NIJSSEN/BOLLEGRAF (16) 6–3 6–2
- Michibata/Huber 6–7 7–6 6–1
- VISSER/FAIRBANK NIDEFFER (6) 6–2 7–6
- Galbraith/Mvagi 6–4 6–4
- BATES/DURIE 6–2 6–3
- CAHILL/FERNANDEZ (9) 6–7 6–4 6–4
- FITZGERALD/SMYLIE (4) 6–4 6–1
- Nelson/Magers 7–6 6–4
- ANNACONE/SANCHEZ-VICARIO (13) 6–2 7–5
- WOODBRIDGE/PROVIS (14) 7–6 6–4
- ALDRICH/REINACH (2) 6–3 6–3

SECOND ROUND:
- PUGH/NOVOTNA (1) 7–6 6–0
- Warder/Thompson 7–5 6–2
- SEGUSO/McNEIL (10) 6–7 6–3 6–4
- JONES/BURGIN (12) 2–6 6–4 6–2
- Norval/De Swardt 6–3 6–2
- Cannon/White 6–6 6–4
- MOTTA/JORDAN (7) 6–6 6–4
- LEACH/GARRISON (3) 6–3 6–4
- Dyke/Jaggard 5–7 6–2 6–2
- NIJSSEN/BOLLEGRAF (16) 7–5 6–2
- WOODFORDE/MANDLIKOVA (15) 6–1 6–3
- Michibata/Huber 6–3 6–7 6–3
- Page/Smoller 6–4 5–7 6–4
- VISSER/FAIRBANK NIDEFFER (6) 6–2 7–6
- Galbraith/Mvagi 2–6 6–3 6–3
- Bates/Durie 7–5 6–2
- McENROE/McGRATH (11) 6–3 7–5
- CAHILL/FERNANDEZ (9) 7–6 6–2
- Delin/Richardson 7–5 6–7 6–3
- Petchey/Loosemore 7–6 7–6
- FITZGERALD/SMYLIE (4) 6–3 7–5
- Nelson/Magers 6–3 7–5
- Wilkison/Stafford 7–6 6–4
- Koevermans/Ter Riet 6–2 6–2
- ANNACONE/SANCHEZ-VICARIO (13) 7–6 6–2
- WOODBRIDGE/PROVIS (14) 7–5 4–6 6–3
- Van Rensburg/Savchenko 6–3 6–2
- Kruger/Field 7–5 5–7 11–9
- ALDRICH/REINACH (2) 6–3 6–2

FIRST ROUND:
1. J. PUGH/J. NOVOTNA (1)
2. J. Stottenberg/R. McQuillan
3. M. Bahrami/T. Tanvier
4. W. Van Emburgh/S. L. Col ns
5. C. Suk/R. Raichrtova
6. L. Warder/J. G. Thompson
7. N. Odizor/E. S. Pfaff
8. B. SEGUSO/L. M. McNEIL (10)
9. K. JONES/K. M. BURGIN (12)
10. A. Morai/L. Gildemeister
11. P. Norval/M. De Swardt (LL)
12. M. Mortensen/T. Scheuer-Larsen
13. N. Brown/H. A. Ludloff
14. S. Cannon/R. M. White
15. A. Antonitsch/A. M. Cecchini
16. C. MOTTA/K. JORDAN (7)
17. R. LEACH/Z. L. GARRISON (3)
18. D. MacPherson/J. M. Byrne
19. C. Beckman/L. J. Gregory
20. N. Dyke/M. Jaggard
21. N. Brode/L. Phebs
22. S. Devries/H. L. Maper
23. S. E. Stewart/S. L. Smith (WC)
24. T. NIJSSEN/M. M. BOLLEGRAF (16)
25. M. WOODFORDE/H. MANDLIKOVA (15)
26. K. Jensen/M. Werdel
27. K. Kinnear/T. Fendick (LL)
28. G. Michibata/A. Hubel (LL)
29. B. Page/J. B. Smoller
30. R. Smith/K. M. Adams
31. A. Reneberg/C. J. Harper
32. T. VISSER/R. D. FAIRBANK NIDEFFER (6)
33. T. SMID/H. SUKOVA (5)
34. P. Galbraith/N. Mvagi
35. D. Nargiso/A. H. Grossbeck
36. S. You/A. L. Minter
37. J. Bates/J. M. Durie
38. T. Pawsat/E. A. Herr
39. J. Bale/J. Thomas (LL)
40. P. McENROE/M. McGRATH (11) (Q)
41. D. CAHILL/J. FERNANDEZ (9)
42. J. Chaku/J. Pospisilova
43. P. Derlin/J. A. Richardson (Q)
44. B. P. Derlin/J. A. Richardson (Q)
45. R. P. J. Petchey/S. J. Loosemore (WC)
46. D. P. Ison/A. Simpen (WC)
47. J. Rive/C. Benjamin
48. B. FITZGERALD/P. D. SMYLIE (4)
49. M. KRATZMANN/D. SCHULTZ (8)
50. T. Nelson/S. W. Magers
51. T. Wilkison/S. C. Safford
52. R. Deppe/D. S. Van Rensburg
53. M. Koevermans/H. Ter Riet
54. A. Fukuwoka/J. E. Salmon
55. H. Leconte/B. Nagelsen
56. P. ANNACONE/A. SANCHEZ-VICARIO (13)
57. T. WOODBRIDGE/N. PROVIS (14)
58. B. Talbot/L. Barned
59. C. J. Van Rensburg/L. Savchenko
60. G. Donnan/J. M. Hetherington
61. N. Pereira/N. Zvereva
62. S. Kruger/K. Field
63. B. Garnett/K. Radford (Q)
64. P. ALDRICH/E. REINACH (2)

Capital letters denotes seeded pairings. Number following players' names gives seeding order (Q) – Qualifier, (WC) – Wild Card, (LL) – Lucky Loser.

JUNIOR EVENTS

BOYS' SINGLES – Final: Leander Paes (IND) d. Marcos Ondruska (RSA) 7–5 2–6 6–4.
GIRLS' SINGLES – Final: Andrea Strnadova (TCH) d. Kirrily Sharpe (AUS) 6–2 6–4.
BOYS' DOUBLES – Final: Sebastien Lareau (CAN)/Sebastian Leblanc (CAN) d. Clinton Marsh (RSA)/Marcos Andruska (RSA) 7–6 4–6 6–3.
GIRLS' DOUBLES – Final: K. Habsudova (TCH)/A. Strnadova (TCH) d. N. Pratt (AUS)/K. Sharpe (AUS) 6–3 6–2.

OVER 35 INVITATION EVENTS

MEN'S SINGLES – Final: T. R. Gullikson (USA) d. T. E. Gullikson (USA) 4–6 6–2 7–6.
MEN'S DOUBLES – Final: P. McNamara (AUS)/P. McNamee (AUS) d. T. E. Gullikson (USA)/T. R. Gullikson (USA) 6–7 7–6 13–11.
WOMEN'S DOUBLES – Final: W. M. Turnbull (AUS)/S. V. Wade (GBR) d. R. Casals (USA)/Mrs M. H. Pete (USA) 6–2 6–4.

WIMBLEDON CHAMPIONSHIPS PRIZE MONEY – £3,874,450

MEN'S SINGLES – Winner £230,000. Runner-up £115,000. Semi-finalists £57,550. Quarter-finalists £29,990. Fourth-round losers £16,100. Third-round losers £9,310. Second-round losers £5,635. First-round losers £3,450.
Total: £1,258,480.
WOMEN'S SINGLES – Winner £207,000. Runner-up £103,500. Semi-finalists £50,315. Quarter-finalists £25,415. Fourth-round losers £12,880. Third-round losers £7,215. Second-round losers £4,370. First-round losers £2,675.
Total: £1,042,310.
MEN'S DOUBLES (per team) – Winners £94,230. Runners-up £47,110. Semi-finalists £24,180. Quarter-finalists £12,560. Third-round losers £6,680. Second-round losers £3,630. First-round losers £2,130.
Total: £419,620.
WOMEN'S DOUBLES (per team) – Winners £81,510. Runners-up £40,750. Semi-finalists £19,350. Quarter-finalists £10,050. Third-round losers £5,010. Second-round losers £2,780. First-round losers £1,540.
Total: £334,040.
MIXED DOUBLES (per team) – Winners £40,000. Runners-up £20,000. Semi-finalists £10,000. Quarter-finalists £4,600. Third-round losers £2,300. Second-round losers £1,150. First-round losers £520.
Total: £151,840.
OVER 35 MEN'S INVITATION SINGLES – Winner £15,000. Runner-up £12,000. Semi-finalists £7,500. Quarter-finalists £4,500. First-round losers £3,000.
Total: £84,000.
OVER 35 MEN'S INVITATION DOUBLES (per team) – Winners £12,000. Runners-up £9,000. Semi-finalists £6,000. First-round losers £3,000.
Total: £45,000.
OVER 35 WOMEN'S INVITATION DOUBLES (per team) – Winners £9,000. Runners-up £7,200. Semi-finalists £4,800. First-round losers £2,400.
Total: £36,000.
QUALIFYING – MEN – Round of 32 £2,300, round of 64 £1,150, First-round losers £575.
Total: £110,400.
QUALIFYING – WOMEN – Round of 16 £1,785, round of 32 £890, First-round losers £445.
Total: £42,760.

Per Diem Allowance (estimate) £350,000

With an astonishing display of consistent attacking tennis the Argentine beauty, Gabriela Sabatini, won her first Grand Slam singles title by destroying the holder, Steffi Graf, in the final. *(R. Adams)*

US OPEN CHAMPIONSHIPS

Bud Collins

A proverb from Russia: 'If you fear the wolf, don't go into the forest.'

Could unwary Stefan Edberg have imagined that a left-pawed Volkov (meaning wolf in Russian) would transform Flushing Meadow into an unsurvivable forest for him? That opened a path through the wilderness for a kid who cudgeled every dangerous creature in his way – Pete Sampras, a most unexpected champion of a US Open that Edberg was seeded to win. And could the champ of the previous two years, Steffi Graf, have suspected that her pet lamb of most finals – Gabriela Sabatini – would suddenly turn wolfish attacker to seize her title?

Sabatini and Sampras as champions crowned the most startling US Open of the 22-year-old Open era. As far as young championship pairs go – he 19, she 20 – they were second only to the Tracy Austin (16) – John McEnroe (20) double of 1979. Moreover they were the lowest seeds to triumph in many years, he 12th, she 5th. And did anyone expect that four-time monarch McEnroe, first round flop at Wimbledon and unimpressive all summer, would make an unseeded resurgence in his hometown? John's semi-final finish was his best since he last won in 1984.

As surprising to some was Boris Becker's inability to retain the title. He seemed ready to take the throne again, especially after winning the most gripping set of the fortnight, a 12–10 semi-final tie-breaker over Andre Agassi. However, Boris receded sharply to lose in four, strangely failing to press his advantage. The German was no match for 'Kid Glitter' from the baseline.

There was much talk of 1966 after Sampras flattened Agassi, 6–4 6–3 6–2, and Sabatini, with a last gasp match-point-forehand that pinked a sideline, lunged past Graf, 6–2 7–6 (7–4). Twenty-four years had passed since the major titles had been split four ways among both women and men. That year Roy Emerson and Margaret Smith won their native Australian; Briton Ann Haydon-Jones and Aussie Tony Roche, the French; American Billie Jean King and Spaniard Manolo Santana, Wimbledon and Brazilian Maria Bueno and Aussie Fred Stolle won the US. This time the winners at the first three were Graf and Ivan Lendl, Monica Seles and Andres Gomez, Martina Navratilova and Edberg. Bueno had been the last Latin female to win the US Open, and Sampras was the most remotely placed since the unseeded Stolle. Actually Pete was the longest shot in the 33 years since the startling success of unseeded Aussie Mal Anderson. The failure to seed Stolle, one of the world leaders and fresh from winning the German title, had been clearly an instance of committee negligence.

For a century 19-year-old college boy Oliver Cambell had stood as the greenest of US champs. Sampras undercut Campbell's record by five months with probably the most astounding of all runs to the American title – through two ex-champs and three high seeds. In 1957 Anderson had plucked seeds 2, 3 and 1 (American Dick Savitt, Swede Sven Davidson and countryman Ashley Cooper), none of them champs, in his victorious rush. Sampras, behind the humming serve that accounted for 102 tournament aces, took out seeds 6 and 3, Thomas Muster and Lendl, a four-time champ, the resuscitated McEnroe, and No. 4 seed Agassi.

Sampras was a point from trailing the puissant lefty, Muster, by two sets and was given up on by most after squandering a two-set lead over Lendl. How could a kid stop the fifth set charge of a champion trained for such ordeals? But Sampras asserted right there that it was to be his tournament. A driving 6–2 fifth over Lendl launched him into overdrive, and neither McEnroe nor Agassi could cope with his firepower and balance.

By then Edberg, he of the curious record in majors (two finals, two first round fades), was long gone. Though mercurial Alexander Volkov held together for three strong sets, it was 20-year-old Andrei Cherkasov who registered the best Open by a Soviet, a quarter-final finish to Agassi. Included was a third round overpowering of the No. 11 seed Chang.

Mistreating a Wimbledon champ and No. 1 seed in the opening round, 52nd ranked Volkov had pulled possibly the most astounding upset in tourney annals. Aussie John Newcombe, with similar credentials fell at the outset in 1971, but that was to Czechoslovak Jan Kodes, hardly an outsider. French champion, Kodes had been another example of lame seeding at Forest Hills.

The first round contained more grief for Sweden. The deflated Mats Wilander, champion only 24 months before (and beaten by Sampras a year ago), toppled in four sets to No. 8 seed Brad Gilbert. Never recovering from the joys of winning the French, No. 5 seed Gomez also disappeared fast, to Luis Mattar. And Volkov's moment was brief, his flame immediately snuffed by Todd Witsken, while Gilbert was spiked in the third round by Amos Mansdorf.

Immediate area beneficiary of Edberg's misfortune was gangling 21-year-old David Wheaton, who became one of five Americans in the quarter-finals. Once there, Wheaton, who as a boy had marvelled at McEnroe via TV, learned first-hand about his 31-year-old foe's revival.

Sampras's quarter-final win over Lendl left Ivan in a tie with Big Bill Tilden (1920–26) for the most consecutive US final-round appearances (eight). But the greatest roars were provoked by McEnroe's victory that boosted him to the quarters: winning a five set beauty over No. 7 seed Emilio Sanchez.

Becker appeared to get the hard work he needed by battling in five sets to beat Darren Cahill in the fourth round, and four sets to nail the No. 9 seed Aaron Krickstein. Dispelling five Agassi set points, three of them in the tingling breaker, Boris looked to be in control after 71 minutes. But Agassi refused to wilt as he had in the 1988–89 semis against Lendl. Andre's heavy artillery from the backcourt tamed the customarily assault-minded Becker, 6–7 (10–12) 6–3 6–2 6–3. That deed arranged the first all-American final since McEnroe beat Vitas Gerulaitis in 1979, and the tourney's youngest ever, Agassi the elder at 20.

Once into his second major final, Agassi seemed as paralysed by Sampras's clout as he had been by Gomez's in Paris.

By the time Steffi Graf got off the floor and cleared her head from Gabriela Sabatini's rousing and relentless first set offensive, it was too late. Perhaps only one shot too late, but that was enough.

Sabatini, seeded No. 6 and the least regarded victor since No. 8 seed Virgina Wade came through in 1968, had been fortunate to get past Mary-Joe Fernandez in a demanding 2-hour 43-minute semi, 7–5 5–7 6–3. But the divine Argentine, despite a 4–1 deficit in the first, stuck to her new chip-and-charge philosophy. Fernandez had two points for 5–1 on serve, and was two points from set at 6–5, 30–15, but Gaby wouldn't budge. An unflinching, and eventually rewarding, reliance on volleying, under newly hired coach Carlos Kirmayr, was an abrupt reversal of Gaby's familiar waves of topspinning groundies, so laborious and ennervating.

Graf, appearing much sharper than at Wimbledon, lost her edge momentarily in a 6–4 3–6 6–1, third rounder with Elna Reinach, but whizzed through the next three impediments: youngest seed ever No. 13 Jennifer Capriati, 6–1 6–2; No. 12 seed Jana Novotna 6–3 6–1 and No. 6 seed Arantza Sanchez-Vicario 6–1 6–2.

Yet 16 minutes into the final Steffi was behind 0–4 before she could adjust to the reconstituted Sabatini. That set was gone in 32 minutes. Gaby would need 67 minutes more to close because Steffi fought back stubbornly, and seemingly dammed the Sabatini tide with a service break in match game to 5–5. The flaxen-haired German held to 6–5. Though Sabatini, the first Argentine woman to win a major, warded off two set points in the next game, Graff appeared about to force a third set by taking a 3–1 tie-breaker lead.

There seemed little doubt that Steffi's fitness and resolve would carry a third set – but it never arrived. Visibly weary, Sabatini sensed it was now-or-never – 'I needed to win in two sets' – and she competed better than ever before against Graf, snatching six of the remaining seven points, four of them winners. A stupendous twirling backhand drop volley made it 6–4, and Gaby closed on the desperately mashed forehand down the line.

Although 16-year-old French champ Monica Seles pulled herself together in the third set to serve for the match at 5–4, and, two games later, squelched three match points, an unswerving Italian attacker, Linda Ferrando, wouldn't let up. Ferrando, ranked 82nd and a first round loser in the Italian Open which Seles won, took their third rounder, 1–6 6–1 7–6 (7–3). 'I got scared,' Seles admitted.

Gracing her 18th Open, 33-year-old Navratilova, had reason to believe she could win a fifth time. However, she couldn't keep 9th seeded Manuela Maleeva Fragnière down forever. Jittery and wild in the crunches, Martina, who had been 9–0 against the 23-year-old Bulgarian, was beaten, 7–5 3–6 6–3, in the fourth round. Same place, same opponent, one year earlier, Martina had rolled a double-bagel over the elder of the Sofia Sisters, 6–0 6–0, and even led 4–1 on two breaks this time.

With 15-year-old Magdalena Maleeva making her Open debut (unluckily drawn against her 21-year-old sister Katerina in the opening round), the three set a tourney record for sisters. However, they couldn't improve on the family record for singles set in 1987 by the two male Sanchez's (Emilio and Javier) plus their sister, Arantxa.

Taking care of countrywoman, 14th seed Natalia Zvereva in the second round, and later Ferrando, Soviet Leila Meskhi was the lone unseeded quarter-finalist. No. 4 seed Zina Garrison got that far too, but there hopes of duplicating her Wimbledon-finalist glory gave way quickly to a gimpy ankle and Sanchez-Vicario, 6–2 6–2.

The singles setback didn't prevent Navratilova from solidifying her second place position among the all-time champions. Martina's ninth US doubles victory, this time alongside Gigi Fernandez, raised her aggregate to 54 major titles in singles, doubles and mixed (only eight behind Margaret Court) and gave her fans hope that if she hangs around long enough the record will be hers. She and Fernandez, seeded No. 2, were spoilers, wrecking the Grand Slam revery of Jana Novotna and Helena Sukova, 6–2 6–4. The Czechoslovaks, victors at Melbourne, Paris and Wimbledon, had won all their 44 matches and eight tournaments of 1990 before colliding with Martina and Gigi.

Favourites Rick Leach and Jim Pugh fainted away amazingly in the first round of the men's doubles to Brazilians Nelson Aerts and Danilo Marcelino, 7–6 (7–5) 7–6 (7–5), easing the way for the first male triumph by a South African pair. Second seeded Pieter Aldrich and lefty Danie Visser stopped unseeded Paul Annacone and David Wheaton and took the crown, 6–2 7–6 (7–3) 6–2.

Nineteen-year-old Todd Woodbridge became the youngest ladies man to master the mixed, coalescing with fellow Aussie Liz Smylie for a 6–4 6–2, triumph over top seeds Natalia Zvereva and Jim Pugh.

Sabatini, Sampras, Aldrich, Visser and Woodbridge were all fresh faces in the winners circle, but maybe the hero of Flushing Meadow was an enthusiastic hacker named Dinkins. New York Mayor David Dinkins, he of the suspect backhand and popcorn ball serve, nevertheless tamed the most oppressive element of Flushing Meadow – high-decible air traffic noise. At his behest, traffic patterns were altered for the fortnight, and the Meadow's 13th Open was its most pleasant.

MEN'S SINGLES

Holder: B. Becker (FRG)

6-4 6-3 6-2

FIRST ROUND	SECOND ROUND	THIRD ROUND	FOURTH ROUND	QUARTER-FINALS	SEMI-FINALS	FINAL
1 S. EDBERG (SWE) (1)	Volkov 6-3 7-6 6-2	Witsken 6-2 6-3	Curren 6-4 6-3 6-3	Wheaton 7-5 7-6 4-6 6-4	J McEnroe 6-1 6-4 6-4	SAMPRAS (12) 6-2 6-4 3-6 6-3
2 A. Volkov (URS)						
3 D. Nargiso (ITA) (LL)	Witsken 6-3 6-7 7-6 6-4					
4 T. Witsken (USA)						
5 A. Mancini (ARG)	Washington 6-2 6-4 6-3	Curren 7-6 7-6 6-4				
6 M. Washington (USA)						
7 K. Curren (USA)	Curren 6-4 6-1					
8 S. Perkiss (ISR) (Q)						
9 T. Woodbridge (AUS) (Q)	Svensson 7-6 6-2 3-6 6-2	Wheaton 6-4 7-5	Wheaton 6-2 7-6 6-3			
10 J. Svensson (SWE)						
11 D. Wheaton (USA)	Wheaton 6-3 6-1 6-0					
12 J. Arrese (ESP)						
13 P. Annacone (USA)	JAITE (16) 6-3 6-4 6-3	Annacone 7-6 6-2 6-2				
14 R. Ahonen (FRG)						
15 M. Blackman (USA) (Q)						
16 M. JAITE (ARG) (16)						
17 A. CHESNOKOV (URS) (10)	CHESNOKOV (10) 6-4 5-6 6-3	CHESNOKOV (10) 6-7 6-3 6-1 6-3	J McEnroe 6-3 7-5 6-4	J McEnroe 7-6 3-6 4-6 6-4 6-3		
18 C. Delaitre (FRA)						
19 S. Matsuoka (JAP) (Q)	Matsuoka 7-5 6-4 6-2					
20 D. Witt (USA) (Q)						
21 D. Engel (SWE)	Engel 6-4 6-2 6-2	J McEnroe 7-6 5-6 6-4				
22 M. Rincon (COL) (LC)						
23 J. McEnroe (USA)	J. McEnroe 7-6 7-6 6-4					
24 J. Sanchez (ESP)						
25 J. Grabb (USA)	Grabb 6-4 6-2 6-4	Santoro 7-6 6-4 7-6	E. SANCHEZ (7) 6-3 6-4 5-7 3-6 7-5			
26 L. Duncan (USA)						
27 L. Baron (USA) (WC)	Santoro 6-2 6-4 6-4					
28 F. Santoro (FRA)						
29 J. Pugh (USA)	Pugh 2-6 6-4 7-5 7-6	E. SANCHEZ (7) 6-1 6-2 6-2				
30 R. Fromberg (AUS)						
31 B. Garrow (USA) (WC)	E. SANCHEZ (7) 7-6 6-4 6-4					
32 E. SANCHEZ (ESP) (7)						
33 I. LENDL (TCH) (3)	LENDL (3) 7-5 6-2 6-2	LENDL (3) 6-4 5-6 6-3 6-3	LENDL (3) 7-6 6-1 6-2	LENDL (3) 6-0 6-3 6-4	SAMPRAS (12) 6-4 7-6 3-6 4-6 6-2	
34 M. Laurendeau (CAN) (Q)						
35 L. Jonsson (SWE)	Srich 6-4 6-2 7-5					
36 M. Srich (FRG)						
37 M. Filippini (URU)	Limberger 6-3 7-5 6-4	Antonitsch 6-1 5-7 6-4 6-3				
38 C. Limberger (AUS) (Q)						
39 A. Antonitsch (AUT)	Antonitsch 3-6 6-2 6-1 6-0					
40 M. Kaplan (USA) (Q)						
41 J-F. Altur (ESP)	Anderson 7-5 6-0 7-5	Bloom 6-3 6-3 4-6 1-6 7-6	Bloom 6-2 6-3 6-4			
42 J. Anderson (AUS)						
43 B. Pearce (USA)	Bloom 7-5 6-7 7-5 6-0					
44 B. Bloom (ISR)						
45 R. Azar (ARG)	Muller 7-5 3-6 6-1 6-2	Muller 4-6 6-4 7-6 7-6				
46 G. Muller (RSA)						
47 W. Masur (AUS)	COURIER (14) 6-4 6-0 5-7 6-1					
48 J. COURIER (USA) (14)						
49 P. SAMPRAS (USA) (12)	SAMPRAS (12) 6-1 7-5 6-1	SAMPRAS (12) 6-4 6-3	SAMPRAS (12) 6-3 6-4 6-1	SAMPRAS (12) 6-7 7-6 4-6 6-3		
50 D. Goldie (USA)						
51 P. Garner (USA)	Lundgren 6-7 6-2					
52 P. Lundgren (SWE) (Q)						
53 N. Odizor (NIG) (LL)	Ho 6-2 4-6 6-2 3-6 7-5	Hlasek 6-3 6-2 7-6				
54 T. Ho (USA) (WC)						
55 R. Reneberg (USA)	Hlasek 3-6 7-6 6-4 6-0					
56 K. Hlasek (SUI)						
57 T. Champion (FRA)	Champion 7-5 3-6 6-3 7-5	Yzaga 6-1 3-6 6-3 6-2	MUSTER (6) 6-2 6-2 4-6 5-7 7-6			
58 T. Mayotte (USA)						
59 J. Yzaga (PER)	Yzaga 7-5 7-6 6-3					
60 K. Novacek (TCH)						
61 A. Jarryd (SWE)	Jarryd 2-6 7-5 retd	MUSTER (6) 6-4 6-3 4-6 6-1				
62 A. Youl (AUS) (LL)						
63 A. Rahunen (FIN)	MUSTER (6) 5-7 6-4 6-3 0-3 retd					
64 T. MUSTER (AUT) (6)						

P. SAMPRAS (USA) (12)

Draw (players 65–128)

Entrants / First round

#	Player	First-round result
65	A. GOMEZ (ECU) (5)	Mattar 6-3 6-3 6-3
66	L. Mattar (BRA)	
67	J. Bates (GBR)	Palomino 6-3 7-5 6-4
68	P. Palomino (FIN)	
69	P. McEnroe (USA) (WC)	P. McEnroe 6-3 6-4 1-6 2-6 7-5
70	J. Tarango (USA)	
71	M. Strelba (TCH)	Van Rensburg 7-6 7-6 6-2
72	C. Van Rensburg (RSA)	
73	R. Krishnan (IND)	Leconte 6-4 6-1 6-1
74	H. Leconte (FRA)	
75	A. Cherkasov (URS)	Cherkasov 6-0 6-7 6-2 6-3
76	R. Seguso (USA) (WC)	
77	G. Forget (FRA)	Anas 7-6 6-4 3-6 6-4
78	J. Anas (USA)	
79	M. Pernfors (SWE)	CHANG (11) 6-0 6-2 6-3
80	M. CHANG (USA) (11)	
81	J. BERGER (USA) (13)	BERGER (13) 6-4 6-1 3-6 6-4
82	R. Agenor (HAI)	
83	J. Carlsson (SWE) (Q)	Carlsson 3-6 6-2 6-1 6-2
84	R. Matuszewski (USA) (Q)	
85	S. Bryan (USA) (WC)	Caratti 6-2 7-5 2-6 6-2
86	C. Caratti (ITA) (Q)	
87	D. Rostagno (USA)	Rostagno 6-4 6-2 6-2
88	T. Benhabiles (FRA)	
89	G. Layendecker (USA)	Layendecker 6-4 6-2 6-2
90	G. Bosse (RSA) (Q)	
91	F. Davin (ARG)	Davin 6-4 6-4 7-6
92	F. Rive (USA)	
93	E. Jelen (FRG)	Korda 2-6 6-3 6-0 6-3
94	J. Korda (TCH)	
95	G. Connell (CAN)	AGASSI (4) 6-2 6-2
96	A. AGASSI (USA) (4)	
97	B. GILBERT (USA) (8)	GILBERT (8) 6-4 3-6 6-3 7-5
98	M. Wilander (SWE)	
99	R. Leach (USA) (WC)	Leach 6-4 7-6 6-1
100	T. Chamberlin (USA)	
101	J. Bruguera (ESP)	Bruguera 6-3 6-2
102	T. Hogstedt (SWE)	
103	A. Mansdorf (ISR)	Mansdorf 3-6 3-6 6-3 6-3 6-0
104	B. Dyke (AUS) (Q)	
105	M. Rosset (SUI)	Cash 2-6 2-6 6-3 6-3 6-3
106	P. Cash (AUS)	
107	M. Kratzmann (AUS)	Kratzmann 6-7 6-3 6-3 6-4
108	P. Shelton (USA)	
109	U. Riglewski (FRG)	Stoltenberg 4-6 1-6 6-0 2-1 retd
110	J. Stoltenberg (AUS)	
111	A. Snajder (TCH)	KRICKSTEIN (9) 6-1 4-6 7-6 1-6 6-1
112	A. KRICKSTEIN (USA) (9)	
113	G. IVANISEVIC (YUG) (15)	IVANISEVIC (15) 1-6 6-4 6-1 7-6
114	O. Camporese (ITA)	
115	T. Martin (USA) (Q)	Fleurian 7-6 6-3 7-6
116	J-P. Fleurian (FRA)	
117	K. Jones (USA)	Cahill 6-3 3-6 6-2 6-0
118	D. Cahill (AUS)	
119	C-U. Steeb (FRG)	Sreiber 7-5 7-6 6-3
120	M. Sreiber (TCH)	
121	P. Carbonell (ESP)	Carbonell 6-7 7-6 4-6 6-0
122	P. Haarhuis (HOL)	
123	S. Davis (USA)	S. Davis 5-5 1-6 3
124	K. Evernden (NZL)	
125	Y. Noah (FRA)	Noah 7-6 6-4 6-7 4-6 6-2
126	D. Pate (USA)	
127	J. Aguilera (ESP)	BECKER (2) 7-5 6-3 6-2
128	B. BECKER (FRG) (2)	

Second round

Mattar 6-4 6-0 3-6 2-6 6-3
Van Rensburg 6-1 6-4 7-5
Cherkasov 1-6 6-1 6-4 6-3
CHANG (11) 7-6 3-6 2
BERGER (13) 3-6 6-1 6-4 6-2
Caratti 3-6 7-6 6-4 1-6 7-6
Davin 6-7 6-3 6-2 6-4
AGASSI (4) 7-5 6-0 6-4
GILBERT (8) 7-6 6-4 6-2
Mansdorf 5-7 5-7 6-3 7-5 6-1
Cash 6-4 2-6 2-6 6-1 6-4
KRICKSTEIN (9) 6-4 6-2 6-4
IVANISEVIC (15) 6-4 6-2 3-6 6-1
Cahill 6-3 2-0 retd
Carbonell 6-4 6-2
BECKER (2) 6-4 6-2 7-6

Third round

Van Rensburg 6-4 3-6 2-6 6-3
Cherkasov 6-4 6-3
BERGER (13) 4-6 2-6 6-4 6-3 6-4
AGASSI (4) 7-5 6-0 6-2
Mansdorf 7-6 6-3 7-5 6-1
KRICKSTEIN (9) 6-4 6-2
Cahill 4-6 4-6 6-2 7-6 6-0
BECKER (2) 6-4 6-2

Fourth round

Cherkasov 6-4 6-4 7-5
AGASSI (4) 7-5 6-0 6-2
KRICKSTEIN (9) 6-3 6-4 6-4
BECKER (2) 2-6 6-2 6-3 3-6 6-4

Quarter-finals

AGASSI (4) 6-2 6-2 6-3
BECKER (2) 3-6 6-3 6-2 6-3

Semi-final

AGASSI (4) 6-7 6-3 6-2 6-3

Capital letters denote seeded players. Number following player's name gives seeding order. (Q) – Qualifier. (WC) – Wild Card. (LL) – Lucky Loser.

WOMEN'S SINGLES

Holder: S. Graf (FRG)

FIRST ROUND	SECOND ROUND	THIRD ROUND	FOURTH ROUND	QUARTER-FINALS	SEMI-FINALS	FINAL
1 S. GRAF (FRG) (1)	GRAF (1) 6-1 6-1	GRAF (1) 6-1 6-3	GRAF (1) 6-4 3-6 6-1	GRAF (1) 6-1 6-2	GRAF (1) 6-3 6-1	GRAF (1) 6-1 6-2
2 M. Drake (CAN) (Q)						
3 L. Harvey-Wild (USA)	McQuillan 7-6 7-5					
4 R. McQuillan (AUS)						
5 F. Dechaume (FRA)	Dechaume 6-2 6-1	Reinach 6-3 6-0				
6 F. Bonsignori (ITA)						
7 S. Hack (FRG)	Reinach 6-1 6-2					
8 E. Reinach (RSA)						
9 G. Magers (USA)	Bollegraf 6-2 6-1	Strandlund 4-6 1-7-5				
10 M. Bollegraf (BEL)						
11 M. Strandlund (SWE)	Strandlund 6-4 1-6 6-2					
12 B. Bowers (USA)						
13 P. Hy (CAN)	Hy 6-3 6-3	CAPRIATI (13) 6-3 6-1	CAPRIATI (13) 6-1 6-4			
14 L. Golarsa (ITA)						
15 A. Huber (FRG)	CAPRIATI (13) 7-5 7-5					
16 J. CAPRIATI (USA) (13)						
17 H. NOVOTNA (TCH) (12)	NOVOTNA (12) 6-3 6-1	NOVOTNA (12) 6-4 6-3	NOVOTNA (12) 6-3 6-1	NOVOTNA (12) 6-4 6-2		
18 Lapi (ITA)						
19 F. Labat (ARG)	Rinaldi 6-4 4-6 6-3					
20 K. Rinaldi (USA)						
21 L. Gildemeister (PER)	Gildemeister 7-5 6-3	Gildemeister 7-5 6-3				
22 M. McGrath (USA)						
23 N. Sawamatsu (JAP)	Sawamatsu 6-1 6-3					
24 P. Tarabini (ARG)						
25 N. Herreman (FRA)	Reggi 6-1 4-6 7-6	Reggi 6-2 6-2	K. MALEEVA (7) 6-4 6-0			
26 R. Reggi (ITA)						
27 S. Wasserman (BEL)	Wasserman 1-6 6-3 6-3					
28 L. Farley (USA) (Q)						
29 L. Raymond (USA) (W...)	Kschwendt 6-2 6-3	K. MALEEVA (7) 7-5 6-1				
30 K. Kschwendt (LUX)						
31 M. Maleeva (BUL)	K. MALEEVA (7) 6-3 6-1					
32 K. MALEEVA (BUL) (7)						
33 Z. GARRISON (USA) (4)	GARRISON (4) 6-1 6-3	GARRISON (4) 6-4 6-0	GARRISON (4) 6-4 6-3	GARRISON (4) 6-1 7-5	SANCHEZ-VICARIO (6) 6-2 6-2	
34 B. Reinstadler (AUT)						
35 D. Faber (USA)	Gavaldon 6-3 6-2					
36 A. Gavaldon (USA)						
37 J. Santrock (USA) (W...)	Javer 6-1 6-1	Meier 7-5 7-5				
38 M. Javer (GBR)						
39 M. Meir (FRG)	Meir 6-2 6-5 5-2 retd					
40 C. Porwick (FRG)						
41 C. Dahlman (SWE)	Tauziat 7-5 6-2	Tauziat 6-4 4-6 6-2	Tauziat 6-2 6-1			
42 N. Tauziat (FRA)						
43 E. Zardo (SUI)	Zardo 6-1 4-6 6-1					
44 C. Caverzasio (ITA)						
45 C. Burgin (USA)	Burgin 6-4 4-6 6-4	MARTINEZ (10) 6-0 6-4				
46 S. Bartos (SUI)						
47 M. Wendel (USA)	MARTINEZ (10) 2-6 7-5 6-2					
48 C. MARTINEZ (ESP) (10)						
49 B. PAULUS (AUT) (16)	PAULUS (16) 7-5 6-1	PAULUS (16) 6-2 4-6 6-4	PAULUS (16) 6-4 6-3	SANCHEZ-VICARIO (6) 6-4 6-3		
50 E. Smylie (AUS)						
51 K. McNeil (USA)	McNeil 6-4 6-3					
52 E. Keller (USA)						
53 P. Louie Harper (USA)	Grossman 2-6 6-4 6-4	Grossman 6-2 6-3				
54 A. Grossman (USA)						
55 B. Cordwell (NZL)	Cordwell 6-3 7-6					
56 C. Adams (USA) (W...)						
57 R. Zrubakova (TCH)	Zrubakova 7-5 6-2	Fendick 6-2 6-3	SANCHEZ-VICARIO (6) 6-2 6-1			
58 T. Whitlinger (USA)						
59 P. Fendick (USA)	Fendick 6-7 6-4 7-5					
60 M. Kidowaki (JAP)						
61 C. Kuhlman (USA) (W C)	Kuhlman 6-2 6-4	SANCHEZ-VICARIO (6) 6-1 6-2				
62 C. Rubin (USA) (WC)						
63 N. Provis (AUS)	SANCHEZ-VICARIO (16) 6-0 6-3					
64 A. SANCHEZ-VICARIO (ESP) (6)						

6-2 7-6

G. SABATINI (ARG) (5)

Seed	Player	R1	R2	R3	R4	R5	Final
65	G. SABATINI (ARG) (5)	SABATINI (5) 6-1 6-1	SABATINI (5) 6-1 6-1	SABATINI (5) 6-2 6-4	SABATINI (5) 6-2 6-1	SABATINI (5) 7-6 6-4	SABATINI (5) 7-6 6-4
66	K. Jordan (USA) (WC)	Demongeot					
67	I. Demongeot (FRA)		Appelmans 6-4 6-4				
68	S. Collins (USA) (Q)	Appelmans 6-4 7-6 4					
69	C. Lindqvist (SWE)	Probst 6-0 6-2					
70	S. Appelmans (BEL)		Stafford 4-6 6-3 7-5				
71	A. Leand (USA)	Kelesi 7-5 4-6 6-3					
72	W. Probst (FRG)						
73	A. Coetzer (RSA)	Stafford 6-1 6-3					
74	H. Kelesi (CAN)		SUKOVA (11) 6-1 6-3	SUKOVA (11) 7-5 6-1			
75	S. Stafford (USA) (WC)	Garrone 6-4 7-6					
76	A. Minter (AUS)						
77	G. Fernandez (USA)	SUKOVA (11) 6-1 retd					
78	L. Garrone (ITA)		Meskhi 6-4 6-0				
79	J. Dune (GBR)	Meskhi 6-4 6-2					
80	H. SUKOVA (TCH) (11)						
81	N. ZVEREVA (URS) (14)	ZVEREVA (14) 1-6 7-6 7-6			Meskhi 6-2 4-6 7-6	Meskhi 7-6 6-1	
82	K. Quentrec (FRA)	Cecchini 6-3 6-1	Piccolini 4-6 7-5 6-4				
83	L. Meskhi (URS)						
84	A. Kijimuta (TCH) (LL)	Piccolini 7-6 6-3					
85	J. Pospisilova (TCH)						
86	C. Cecchini (ITA)	Benjamin 6-7 6-3 6-2	Piccolini 4-6 7-5 6-4	Piccolini 1-6 6-1 7-6			
87	A. Kanellopoulo (GRE)						
88	K. Piccolini (ITA)	Ferrando 6-4 2-6 7-6					
89	C. Benjamin (USA)		Ferrando 7-6 6-2	Ferrando 1-6 6-1 7-6			
90	N. Miyagi (JAP)						
91	L. Ferrando (ITA)	Fairbank-Nideffer 3-6 6-1 6-2					
92	M. Paz (ARG)						
93	P. Langrova (TCH)	SELES (3) 6-0 6-0	SELES (3) 6-0 6-0				
94	R. Fairbank-Nideffer (USA)						
95	E. Pampoulova (TCH)						
96	M. SELES (YUG) (3)	M-J. FERNANDEZ (8) 7-6 6-1	M-J. FERNANDEZ (8) 6-4 6-1	M-J. FERNANDEZ (8) 6-1 6-2	M-J. FERNANDEZ (8) 6-3 6-2	M-J. FERNANDEZ (8) 6-2 2-6 6-1	
97	M-J. FERNANDEZ (USA) (8)	Oremans 6-3 6-2					
98	A. Henricksson (HOL) (Q)						
99	M. Oremans (HOL) (Q)	Halard 6-2 6-4	R. White 6-4 6-3				
100	S. Martin (USA)						
101	B. Schultz (HOL)	R. White 4-6 6-2					
102	J. Halard (FRA)						
103	R. White (USA)	Savchenko 6-3 1-6 6-3	Savchenko 6-4 6-4				
104	A. Temesvari (HUN)						
105	R. Rajchtrova (TCH)	Cunningham 6-1 1-6 6-2					
106	L. Savchenko (URS)						
107	W. White-Prausa (USA)	Date 6-0 6-3	WIESNER (15) 6-1 6-3	WIESNER (15) 6-1 6-3			
108	C. Cunningham (USA)						
109	C. MacGregor (USA)	WIESNER (15) 6-3 6-1					
110	K. Date (JAP)						
111	M-L. Daniels (USA)	MALEEVA-FRAGNIÈRE (9) 6-1 6-3	MALEEVA-FRAGNIÈRE (9) 6-0 6-2	MALEEVA-FRAGNIÈRE (9) 6-1 6-0	MALEEVA-FRAGNIÈRE (9) 7-5 3-6 6-3		
112	J. WIESNER (AUT) (15)	Graham 6-4 6-0					
113	M. MALEEVA-FRAGNIÈRE (SUI) (9)						
114	E. Frazier (USA)	Hanika 6-3 1-6 6-4	van Rensburg 6-3 6-3				
115	D. Graham (USA) (WC)						
116	E. Rossides (USA)	van Rensburg 6-3 6-3					
117	S. Hanika (FRG)						
118	B. Fulco (ARG)	Cioffi 7-6 6-2	Cioffi 7-5 6-2	NAVRATILOVA (2) 6-2 6-2			
119	D. van Rensburg (RSA)						
120	D. Spirlea (ITA)	Medvedeva 6-4 6-2					
121	S. Sloane (USA)						
122	H. Cioffi (USA)	Wood 6-0 6-0	NAVRATILOVA (2) 6-0 6-4				
123	T. Phelps (USA)						
124	N. Medvedeva (URS)	NAVRATILOVA (2) 6-4 6-0					
125	M. Bananski (USA) (Q)						
126	C. Wood (GBR) (Q)						
127	F. Haumuller (ARG)						
128	M. NAVRATILOVA (USA) (2)						

Capital letters denote seeded players. Number following player's name gives seeding order. (Q) – Qualifier. (WC) – Wild Card. (LL) – Lucky Loser.

MEN'S DOUBLES

Holders: J. P. McEnroe (USA)/M. Woodforde (AUS)

P. ALDRICH (RSA)/D. VISSER (RSA) 6–2 7–6 6–2

FIRST ROUND	SECOND ROUND	THIRD ROUND	QUARTER-FINALS	SEMI-FINALS	FINAL

1 LEACH/PUGH (1)
2 Aerts/Marcelino
3 Eisenmann/Lucena
4 Delaitre/Rosset
5 Pozzi/Tarozzy
6 Bruguera/Carbonell
7 Evernden/Pereira
8 STOLTENBERG/WOODBRIDGE (16)
9 RIGLEWSKI/STICH (10)
10 Annacone/Wheaton
11 Pearce/Kinnear
12 Nelson/Shelton
13 Courier/Sampras
14 J. Brown/Melville
15 Beckman/Jensen
16 LOZANO/WITSKEN (8)
17 CONNELL/MICHIBATA (4)
18 Hombrecher/Washington
19 Cannon/Canter
20 Mattar/Roese
21 Galbraith/K. Jones
22 Mortensen/Novacek
23 Talbot/Youl
24 BATES/CURREN (13)
25 BROAD/MULLER (11)
26 Doohan/Warder
27 Davids/Haarhuis
28 Frana/Minussi
29 DeVries/MacPherson
30 Rive/Van 't Hof
31 Jarryd/Van Rensburg
32 S. DAVIS/PATE (5)
33 CAHILL/KRATZMANN (6)
34 Cash/Masur
35 Castle/R. Smith
36 Kruger/M. Davis
37 Deppe/Garnett
38 Nilsson/Svantesson
39 Smid/Suk
40 CAMPORESE/J. SANCHEZ (12)
41 P. McENROE/RENEBERG (14)
42 Lavalle/Yzaga
43 Chamberlain/Wilkison
44 Odizor/Wekesa
45 Berger/D. Flach
46 Garrow/Salumaa
47 Mora/Page
48 CASAL/E. SANCHEZ (3)
49 FORGET/HLASEK (7)
50 J. McEnroe/Woodforde
51 Bryan/Martin
52 N. Brown/Pimek
53 Ferreira/Norval
54 Arend/Bramand
55 Carati/Nargiso
56 IVANISEVIC/KORDA (9)
57 FLACH/SEGUSO (15)
58 Albano/Jaite
59 Bergh/Henriksson
60 Jarsson/Sobel
61 Bahrami/Fleurian
62 Baron/Flanagan
63 Dyke/Lundgren
64 ALDRICH/VISSER (2)

SECOND ROUND

Aerts/Marcelino
7–6 7–6
Delaitre/Rosset
6–4 6–4
Bruguera/Carbonell
2–6 6–0 6–4
STOLTENBERG/WOODBRIDGE (16)
7–6 6–7 6–1
Annacone/Wheaton
6–1 6–2
Pearce/Kinnear
6–3 6–4
J. Brown/Melville
3–6 7–6 6–4
Beckman/Jensen
6–1 6–4
CONNELL/MICHIBATA (4)
7–6 4–6 6–4
Mattar/Roese
4–6 6–2
Galbraith/K. Jones
6–3 5–7 6–3
BATES/CURREN (13)
6–4 6–3
Doohan/Warder
7–5
Frana/Minussi
6–3 6–2
DeVries/MacPherson
4–6 6–3 7–5
Jarryd/Van Rensburg
6–4 3–6 6–3
Cash/Masur
6–4 6–2
Castle/R. Smith
6–3 5–7 6–2
CAMPORESE/J. SANCHEZ (12)
6–4 6–4
P. McENROE/RENEBERG (14)
6–3 7–6
Garrow/Salumaa
7–5 6–4
CASAL/E. SANCHEZ (3)
6–4 4–6 6–4
FORGET/HLASEK (7)
7–5 7–6
Ferreira/Norval
6–3 7–5
IVANISEVIC/KORDA (9)
6–3 6–3
K. FLACH/SEGUSO (15)
7–6 3–6 6–3
Bergh/Henriksson
3–6 6–3 7–6
ALDRICH/VISSER (2)
5–7 6–2 6–0

THIRD ROUND

Aerts/Marcelino
6–2 6–3
Bruguera/Carbonell
1–6 7–6 6–4
Annacone/Wheaton
4–6 6–2 7–6
J. Brown/Melville
6–2 6–7 6–3
CONNELL/MICHIBATA (4)
6–4 6–4
Galbraith/K. Jones
6–4 6–7 7–6
Doohan/Warder
7–5 5–7 7–5
Jarryd/Van Rensburg
4–6 6–2
Castle/R. Smith
2–6 6–3 6–4
Deppe/Garnett
7–6 4
P. McENROE/RENEBERG (14)
7–5 5–2
Garrow/Salumaa
6–3 6–2
FORGET/HLASEK (7)
6–3 6–3
Ferreira/Norval
0–6 7–5 6–4
K. FLACH/SEGUSO (15)
6–4 7–5
ALDRICH/VISSER (2)
7–6 6–4

QUARTER-FINALS

Bruguera/Carbonell
7–6 6–4
Annacone/Wheaton
6–1 6–4
Galbraith/K. Jones
4–6 7–6 6–4
Jarryd/Van Rensburg
6–4 3–6 6–2
Castle/Smith
6–4 6–4
Garrow/Salumaa
6–3 7–6
FORGET/HLASEK (7)
6–3 6–2
ALDRICH/VISSER (2)
w/o

SEMI-FINALS

Annacone/Wheaton
7–5 6–7 4–6 6–3
Galbraith/K. Jones
7–6 6–3 4–6 6–1
Garrow/Salumaa
6–3 7–5 5–7 3–6 6–3
ALDRICH/VISSER (2)
7–6 2–6 3–6 7–6 6–2

FINAL

Annacone/Wheaton
7–6 7–6 6–7 7–6
ALDRICH/VISSER (2)
4–6 7–6 3–6 7–6 6–2

Capital letters denote seeded pairings. Numbers following players' names gives seeding order. (Q) – Qualifier. (WC) – Wild Card. (LL) – Lucky Loser

WOMEN'S DOUBLES

Holders: H. Mandlikova (AUS)/M. Navratilova (USA)

Winner: G. FERNANDEZ (USA)/M. NAVRATILOVA (USA) (2) 6–2 6–4

FIRST ROUND

1 NOVOTNA/SUKOVA (1)
2 Amabh/Hy
3 Delone/Raymond
4 Phelps/Stafford
5 Budarova/Laskova
6 Ferrando/Fulco
7 Albinus/Van Lottum
8 BOLLEGRAF/SCHULTZ (15)
9 GREGORY/MAGERS (11)
10 Fuchs/Strandlund
11 Lindstrom/Ludloff
12 Romano/Svigierova
13 McClellan/Thompson
14 Kelesi/Seles
15 Dure/Richardson
16 SANCHEZ-VICARIO/R. WHITE (5)
17 SAVCHENKO/ZVEREVA (3)
18 Meier/Pampoulova
19 Ghabaipur/Corsato
20 Hetherington/Rinaldi
21 Pierce/Spadea
22 MacGregor/Hu Na
23 Brioukhovets/Manokova
24 PAZ/SABATINI (9)
25 MEDVEDEVA/MESKHI (14)
26 Langrova/Pospisilova
27 Cordwell/Henricksson
28 Collins/Smoller
29 Birch/Graham
30 Porwick/Probst
31 MacGregor/Werdel
32 FENDICK/GARRISON (7)
33 Foxworth/Whittington
34 Byrne/A. White
35 Graf/McNeil
36 S. Smith/Ter Riet
37 Garrone/Golarsa
38 Faull/Turnbull
39 Paulus/Zrubakova
40 CECCHINI/TARABINI (13)
41 BURGIN/FAIRBANK-NIDEFFER (12)
42 Barg Mager/Louie Harper
43 Benjamin/Minter
44 Teri Whitlinger/Tami Whitlinger
45 Kschwendt/Morton
46 Tauziat/Wiesner
47 Parad/Suire
48 JORDAN/SMYLIE (4)
49 PROVIS/REINACH (8)
50 Field/Toleafoa
51 Barnard/Van Rensburg
52 Rajchrtova/Temesvari
53 Cioworzasol/Labat
54 Grossman/Stubbs
55 Kidowaki/Miyagi
56 DANIELS/WHITE-PRAUSA (10)
57 ADAMS/GILDEMEISTER (16)
58 Endross/Scott
59 Demongeot/Pfaff
60 M. Maleeva/Maleeva-Fragniere
61 Dechaume/Herreman
62 Cioffi/Frazier
63 Capriati/McGrath
64 G. FERNANDEZ/NAVRATILOVA (2)

SECOND ROUND

NOVOTNA/SUKOVA (1) 6-4 6-2
delone/Raymond 3-6 6-3 6-3
Ferrando/Fulco
BOLLEGRAF/SCHULTZ (15) 6-1 6-2
GREGORY/MAGERS (11) 6-3 6-4
Lindstrom/Ludloff 7-5 6-2
Kelesi/Seles 7-6 6-1
SANCHEZ-VICARIO/R. WHITE (5)
SAVCHENKO/ZVEREVA (3) 6-0 6-4
Hetherington/Rinaldi 6-3 6-1
Pierce/Spadea
PAZ/SABATINI (9) 2-6 7-5 6-0
MEDVEDEVA/MESKHI (14) 6-3 6-1
Cordwell/Henricksson
Porwick/Probst 6-2 6-2
FENDICK/GARRISON (7) 6-7 6-3 6-1
Byrne/A. White 6-4 6-1
Graf/McNeil
Faull/Turnbull 6-2 6-4
CECCHINI/TARABINI (13)
BURGIN/FAIRBANK-NIDEFFER (12) 6-2 6-3
Whitlinger/Whitlinger 1-6 6-3 6-1
Tauziat/Wiesner 6-1 6-0
JORDAN/SMYLIE (4) 6-4 5-7 6-3
PROVIS/REINACH (8) 6-1 6-0
Barnard/Van Rensburg 6-3 6-1
Grossman/Stubbs 6-4 6-7 6-3
DANIELS/WHITE-PRAUSA (10) 7-5 6-4
ADAMS/GILDEMEISTER (16) 6-2 6-4
Demongeot/Pfaff 7-6 6-3
Cioffi/Frazier 6-1 6-0
FERNANDEZ/NAVRATILOVA (2) 7-5 6-4

THIRD ROUND

NOVOTNA/SUKOVA (1) 6-0 6-0
BOLLEGRAF/SCHULTZ (15) 6-4 6-3
GREGORY/MAGERS (11) 1-7 7-6 7-5
SANCHEZ-VICARIO/R. WHITE (5) 6-1 6-3
SAVCHENKO/ZVEREVA (3) 6-1 5-7 6-3
PAZ/SABATINI (9) 4-6 6-4 7-5
MEDVEDEVA/MESKHI (14) 6-4 6-2
FENDICK/GARRISON (7) 7-5 7-5
Graf/McNeil 4-6 7-5 7-6
CECCHINI/TARABINI (13) 6-2 6-4
BURGIN/FAIRBANK-NIDEFFER (12) 6-4 6-1
JORDAN/SMYLIE (4) 6-2 6-3
PROVIS/REINACH (8) 6-7 6-1 6-2
DANIELS/WHITE-PRAUSA (10) 2-6 6-4 6-4
ADAMS/GILDEMEISTER (16) 6-4 6-3
FERNANDEZ/NAVRATILOVA (2) 6-2 6-1

QUARTER-FINALS

NOVOTNA/SUKOVA (1) 6-1 6-7 6-4
SANCHEZ-VICARIO/R. WHITE (5) 6-3 6-1
SAVCHENKO/ZVEREVA (3) 6-7 6-4 6-4
MEDVEDEVA/MESKHI (14) w/o
Graf/McNeil 6-3 2-6 6-0
JORDAN/SMYLIE (4) 6-1 7-6
PROVIS/REINACH (8) 6-4 6-3
FERNANDEZ/NAVRATILOVA (2) 0-6 6-2 6-2

SEMI-FINALS

NOVOTNA/SUKOVA (1) 7-6 6-3
SAVCHENKO/ZVEREVA (3) 6-3 6-7 6-3
JORDAN/SMYLIE (4) 6-2 5-7 6-1
FERNANDEZ/NAVRATILOVA (2) 7-6 4-6 6-0

FINAL

NOVOTNA/SUKOVA (1) 6-2 6-3
FERNANDEZ/NAVRATILOVA (2) 6-4 7-5

Capital letters denote seeded pairings. Number following players' names gives seeding order. (Q) – Qualifier, (WC) – Wild Card, (LL) – Lucky Loser

MIXED DOUBLES

Holders: S. Cannon (USA)/R. White (USA)

Winner: T. WOODBRIDGE (AUS)/E. SMYLIE (AUS) (8) 6–4 6–2

FIRST ROUND

1 PUGH/ZVEREVA (1)
2 M. Davis/Frazier
3 Van't Hof/Daniels
4 Jones/Medvedeva
5 Mortensen/Bollegraf
6 Kinnear/W. White
7 Warder/Burgin
8 K. FLACH/FENDICK (7)
9 VISSER/PROVIS (4)
10 Woodforde/McGrath
11 Nelson/Magers
12 Kruger/Gregory
13 Odizor/Pfaff
14 Smid/Schultz
15 Connell/Hetherington
16 LOZANO/SANCHEZ-VICARIO (5)
17 Evernden/McQuillan
18 DeVries/Kuhlman
19 MacPherson/Richardson
20 Jensen/Tarabini
21 Beckman/Louie Harper
22 Seguso/McNeil
23 Witsken/Collins
24 ALDRICH/REINACH (3)
25 WOODBRIDGE/SMYLIE (8)
26 Baron/Raymond
27 Smith/Adams
28 Washington/McCarthy
29 Cannon/R. White
30 Van Rensburg/Jordan
31 Aerts/Van Lottum
32 LEACH/GARRISON (2)

SECOND ROUND

PUGH/ZVEREVA (1) 6–1 7–6
Jones/Medvedeva 7–5 4–6 6–4
Mortensen/Bollegraf 7–5 6–2
Woodforde/McGrath 6–7 7–6 4–2 retd
Nelson/Magers 6–4 7–6
Smid/Schultz 6–3 7–6
LOZANO/SANCHEZ-VICARIO (5) 2–6 7–6 6–2
Evernden/McQuillan 6–0 6–1
MacPherson/Richardson 7–5 6–3
Beckman/Louie Harper 6–4 6–3
ALDRICH/REINACH (3) 6–3 6–3
WOODBRIDGE/SMYLIE (8) 6–4 6–2
Washington/McCarthy 6–4 3–6 6–1
Cannon/R. White 6–7 6–4 7–5
LEACH/GARRISON (2) 6–4 6–2

QUARTER-FINALS

PUGH/ZVEREVA (1) 6–1 7–5
Mortensen/Bollegraf 6–3 6–3
Woodforde/McGrath 6–2 7–5
LOZANO/SANCHEZ-VICARIO (5) 7–6 7–6
Evernden/McQuillan 4–6 6–2 6–3
ALDRICH/REINACH (3) 6–1 1–6 6–4
WOODBRDIGE/SMYLIE (8) 7–5 7–6
LEACH/GARRISON (2) 3–6 6–1 6–3

SEMI-FINALS

PUGH/ZVEREVA (1) 6–0 6–4
Woodforde/McGrath 5–7 6–2 6–4
Evernden/McQuillan 7–6 3–6 6–3
WOODBRIDGE/SMYLIE (8) 7–6 6–4

FINAL

PUGH/ZVEREVA (1) 2–6 6–2 6–3
WOODBRIDGE/SMYLIE (8) 7–5 6–4

Capital letters denote seeded pairings. Number following players' names gives seeding order. (Q) – Qualifier; (WC) – Wild Card; (LL) – Lucky Loser.

JUNIOR EVENTS

BOYS' SINGLES – *Final:* Mikael Tillstroem (SWE) d. Andrea Gaudenzi (ITA) 2–6 6–4 7–6.
GIRLS' SINGLES – *Final:* Magdalena Maleeva (BUL) d. Noelle Van Lottum (FRA) 7–5 6–2.
BOYS' DOUBLES – *Final:* Marten Renstroem (SWE)/Mikael Tillstroem (SWE) d. Sebastian Leblanc (CAN)/Greg Rusedski (CAN) 6–7 6–3 6–4.
GIRLS' DOUBLES – *FINAL:* Kristin Godridge (AUS)/Kirrily Sharpe (AUS) d. Erika deLone (USA)/Lisa Raymond (USA) 4–6 7–5 6–2.

SENIOR EVENTS

MEN'S INVITATIONAL SINGLES – *FINAL:* A. Mayer (USA) d. Tom Gullikson (USA) 6–4 6–4.
MEN'S INVITATIONAL DOUBLES – *FINAL:* Tom Gullikson (USA)/R. Stockton (USA) d. M. Edmondson (AUS)/S. Stewart (USA) 6–7 7–6 6–4.
WOMEN'S INVITATIONAL DOUBLES – *FINAL:* R. Casals (USA)/B. J. King (USA) d. W. Turnbull (AUS)/V. Wade (GBR) 2–6 6–4 6–3.

US OPEN CHAMPIONSHIPS PRIZE MONEY – US$6,349,250

MEN'S AND WOMEN'S SINGLES – Winners $350,000. Runners-up $175,000. Semi-finalists $87,000. Quarter-finalists $45,378. Fourth-round losers $24,590. Third-round losers $14,166. Second-round losers $8,697. First-round losers $5,195.
Total for each event: $1,915, 672.
MEN'S AND WOMEN'S DOUBLES (per team) – Winners $142,861. Runners-up $71,431. Semi-finalists $35,715. Quarter-finalists $18,258. Third-round losers $10,414. Second-round losers $5,224. First-round losers $3,529.
Total for each event: $638,578.
MIXED DOUBLES (per team) – Winners $42,500. Runners-up $20,000. Semi-finalists $10,000. Quarter-finalists $5,625. Second-round losers $3,125. First-round losers $1,250.
Total: $150,000.
QUALIFYING COMPETITIONS
Men's total (128 draw) $156,000. Women's total (64 draw) $78,000.

Total for senior events $275,000.
Player per diem and other $581,750.

A compassionate Pete Sampras donated $250,000 of his record $2 million winner's prize at the Compaq Grand Slam Cup *to research into cerebral palsy, a disease that had claimed two of his aunts.* (Professional Sport)

COMPAQ GRAND SLAM CUP

John Barrett

It was entirely appropriate that the first *Compaq Grand Slam Cup*, plus the first prize of $2 million from the record purse of $6 million, should have been won by Pete Sampras. The 19-year-old Californian had undoubtedly been the most impressive of the season's four Grand Slam Champions when, three months earlier, he had become the youngest-ever winner of the US Open.

The devastating manner of Sampras's 6–3 6–4 6–2 victory over fellow American Brad Gilbert in a final that lasted a bare 103 minutes was uncannily like his equally brief dismissal of Andre Agassi in the Flushing Meadow final. In both cases, the star of the show reduced a helpless opponent to a walk-on part by dictating the outcome of most of the rallies.

With the Slazenger Wimbledon ball on a pacey Supreme Court carpet in Munich's cavernous *Olympiahalle*, the stinging Sampras serve, so innocently fast, so difficult to read, was the foundation of his success. In four rounds it produced a total of 51 aces and 75 other service winners. The confidence engendered by such superiority gave Sampras the freedom to unleash the full power of his groundstrokes – not recklessly – but with increasing awareness of when to take calculated risks. Some of the winning forehands and backhands he had produced in the middle of a routine rally, taken on the rise and timed with such natural precision that they literally passed his opponents at the baseline, made you gasp with surprise. Their sheer audacity left you wide-eyed with disbelief. One could understand just how humiliated his vanquished foes must have felt. Yet, at the start of the week, there had been little to suggest that Pete would produce such devastating form. Inactive after some disappointing performances in the ATP Tour finals in Frankfurt four weeks earlier where he suffered from sore shins, Sampras had arrived in Munich via two exhibition matches in Europe where he had filled in for the injured Andre Agassi. In retrospect that was probably the best thing that could have happened to him. The enforced rest had left him eager and the exhibitions had given him a taste of match play.

Another who had Agassi to thank was Gilbert whose original role in Munich was as one of the two alternates, the other being Thierry Champion of France. Agassi's injury had occurred when playing Darren Cahill in the first 'dead' rubber of America's 3–2 triumph over Australia in the final of the *Davis Cup*. It had been diagnosed later as a torn rib cartilage and had caused Agassi to withdraw from the *Grand Slam Cup* for the second time.

The biggest surprise of the week occurred on the opening night when the 18-year-old Chinese-American, Michael Chang, upset the new world No. 1 Stefan Edberg 6–4 4–6 7–5. Edberg had been the firm favourite to win this end-of-year spectacular. The 24-year-old Swede could and should have won. He had beaten Chang three times in 1990 and had suffered the second of his two losses in seven meetings against the diminutive Californian in that memorable French Open final in 1989. After three successive breaks of serve at the start of the final set Edberg held for 3–1 and then served for the match at 5–4. A fourth double-fault put him break point down and another of those early returns from Chang, which he seems able to find when it most matters, gave him the break back. From that moment Edberg looked a tired and beaten man, one for whom the end of the year could not come soon enough. It arrived two games later. Another double fault contributed to his demise as Chang ran off 10 of the last 12 points for a surprising victory after 2 hrs 17 minutes, his first win indoors against the Swede who was philosophical about his loss. 'It has been a long year and I was probably not as motivated as I should have been – but it is hard to push yourself. . . . I made a lot of mistakes. I think this event has the potential to become one of the greatest. . . . I mean where else in the world does a player have his own changing room?'

There were three other excellent first round matches. In the first Sampras beat the Soviet No. 2 Andrei Cherkasov 5–7 6–2 7–5 thanks to delivering 39 service winners and scoring with 64% of his approaches to the net. In the second, Goran Ivanisevic, the tall left-hander from Yugoslavia, repeated his Wimbledon win over Kevin Curren in two tie-break sets. A code violation seemed to have a salutary effect on Ivanisevic who was always the more dangerous of the two heavy servers. Curren had led 3–1 in the second set but found Ivanisevic's early double-handed backhand almost as difficult to read as his lethal forehand and lost his serve in the 8th game after saving five break points. The second tie-break, won by the Yugoslav 9–7 after being denied on two match points, was a thrilling affair, full of powerful shots hit without compromise.

The third battle resulted in a spirited 7–6 6–7 6–3 victory for David Wheaton over the acrobatic Frenchman Yannick Noah. It was a thoroughly entertaining match thanks to the cheerful way Noah accepted the greater power and consistency of his younger opponent. One break of serve in the final set, at 4–3 to Wheaton, was all that separated them.

There had been straightforward wins for the second Frenchman Henri Leconte over Thomas Muster of Austria 6–3 6–4 and, eventually, for Gilbert over Sweden's Jonas Svensson who faded after taking the opening set and went down 2–6 6–3 6–4. The two-handed American Aaron Krickstein easily dismissed Ecuador's French Open champion Andres Gomez whose season seemed to have ended on 3rd June – and who could blame him – whilst Ivan Lendl, the No. 2 seed and many people's choice as the likely winner, sent home Christian Bergstrom for the loss of four games, all of them in the first set. It was a total suprise, then, when Wheaton completely outplayed Lendl to win their quarter-final 6–2 7–6 in less than an hour and a half. The tall American was charging towards the net at every opportunity and preventing his opponent from getting into a rhythm. He was successful with 57% of his approaches to the net in the first set and 61% in the second. This pressure induced 13 forced errors from the usually imperturbable Lendl who, towards the closing stages was looking tense and tight. Perhaps the thought of all that loot was too much for him or perhaps the great man is beginning to experience what every champion must face, the infinitesimal slowing of his reaction time and speed of court coverage. It begins to show first against the big hitters like Wheaton. However, after saving two break points at 4–4 in the second set one felt that Lendl's greater experience of these tight situations would save him. Furthermore, he had beaten Wheaton comfortably in their only previous meeting at Washington. But that had been back in 1987 when Wheaton had been a green 18-year-old, a talented but fragile US Junior champion. Now, supported by his two brothers John and Mark, he believed in himself and to his credit he did not panic when Lendl charged back from 0–3 to 3–4 in the tie-break. Forcing errors from the now desperate Lendl, Wheaton stole both Lendl's service points to lead 6–3 and clinched the match on his second match point.

With Lendl out of the way the fates seemed to be smiling once again on Gilbert, as they had done in 1989 when he had suddenly been summoned to Dallas for the WCT finals and had beaten Edberg and Pernfors before losing narrowly to McEnroe in the final by 6–3 3–6 7–6. Although Krickstein held a 4–3 career advantage against him, Gilbert had won their only previous meeting on carpet. He repeated that success with a 6–7 6–4 6–3 win that brought him to a semi-final against Wheaton in the lower-half.

In the two quarter-finals in the top-half, Chang got the better of Leconte 7–6 6–3 by allowing the Frenchman to hit himself to destruction and Sampras survived magnificently against Ivanisevic 7–6 6–7 8–6. This was a match to savour, a match between the two best servers in the men's game that gave us a glimpse of the future. Until the 11th game of the second set there was no break of serve. In fact so sound and well disguised were the two serves, so effective and skilful the first volleys, that neither man had faced a break point. When Sampras at last found a way past the Yugoslav's racket to break for 6–5 in the second set the match seemed to be over. But Ivanisevic, remembering the advice of his Hungarian coach Balazs Taroczy, went for his shots in the crisis and contrived his first break of the match with some glorious returns. The second tie-break was always his. A lead of 3–1 became 5–2 and then, as a Sampras charge was repulsed, 7–5.

The first break points in the final set were against Sampras. At 15–40 in the 9th game he was as solid as a rock. He saved two more break points that would have allowed Ivanisevic to serve for the match and looked totally in command of himself. Five games later, by contrast, Ivanisevic became edgy as he served at 6–7 and at 15–40 it was hardly a surprise to see the Yugoslav deliver a double-fault to concede the match. Once again the slight question mark about his temperament had been raised. But he remained confident about his future. 'I playcd really well . . . Sampras served very well at important points . . . in a few years time we will be the two best players in the world. This week was very good for me, too, (to the tune of $300,000!) now I'll practise harder because I want to play even better next year', he said.

The two semi-finals, played over the best-of-five sets distance, were both excellent contests between four Americans who had proved to be the most competitive of the 16 original starters. Sampras was always a little too powerful for Chang and beat him in straight sets 6–3 6–4 6–4. For all that, it was a close match with a high level of skill from both men and it was surprising to discover that in five previous meetings as seniors, Sampras had never beaten Chang. It seemed that, as at Flushing Meadow, Sampras was gaining confidence with every round. The two blistering forehands he delivered to secure the only break of serve in the fifth game of the second set were awesome in their power and control. His serve always posed problems – even for a man who excels on early-hit returns. In the first set Sampras conceded only 8 points on his delivery, in the second just 6. Even though he did at last concede his serve in the 8th game of the third set he immediately broke Chang again and served out the match after one deuce. The only problem for Sampras was a blood blister that had developed on the ball of his left foot. Twice he removed his shoe and sock, but because there was no bleeding, he could not receive treatment from the trainer. When he finished the match limping there were doubts about his ability to play a five-set final on the morrow.

The other match was much more competitive, in fact over competitive. With the first two sets evenly divided, the third was boiling up to a fitting climax in an excellent tie-break when at, 6 points all, the British umpire Stephen Winyard over-ruled Gilbert's shot to the far sideline that had been called out. Wheaton, for whom this was a set point at 6–5 saw the chance of scoring a first ever-win against Gilbert disappearing and was incensed. Later he said 'There's no way that the umpire could have sworn on the bible that the ball was good'. Gilbert, not hearing the over-rule and furious with himself for missing a playable shot, thrashed the top of the net with his racket and was lucky not to be penalised for racket abuse. Meanwhile, in the hubbub that ensued, Wheaton's brother John raced from one side of the court to the other to protest to the umpire and referee Ken Farrar. Eventually calm was restored and Wheaton, facing now a set point, hit a service winner for 7–7. Perhaps because of all the confusion Wheaton immediately delivered a double fault to give Gilbert a second set point. Gilbert duly put in a deep first serve and saw the return land in the net. Then, as the players changed ends a nasty incident occurred. Wheaton, resentful for what Gilbert had said about his brother's involvement made a remark as Gilbert passed his chair. There was an immediate response from Gilbert and the two men confronted each other menacingly. 'I would not have been disappointed if he had thrown the first blow', said Wheaton later. Certainly if Farrar and umpire Bruno Rebeuh had not sprung forward to part them there may have been physical violence and it was right that the two men were later fined. Whether the $5,000 apiece it cost them was enough when the loser would take home $450,000 and the winner would earn either $1 million or $2 million is another matter.

Just as suddenly it was all over and calm was restored. Icy calm now, Wheaton stormed through the fourth set 6–2 but crucially lost his opening delivery in the fifth to go 0–1 down. Gilbert, experienced match-player that he is, never allowed him to escape. The only chance the younger man had came in the 6th game but a safe, deep serve at 30–40 and another at advantage out, saved the day. When Gilbert served an ace to hold for 4–2 you knew it was as good as over. Four games later it was and here was Gilbert, all smiles now, at the age of 29, unexpectedly in another final and about to win the biggest cheque of his career. He made light of the controversy. 'We are out there for 3hrs and 53 minutes and we have a flare up that lasts a few seconds. No it shouldn't have happened, it was't good for the sport but we're both competitive guys, neither of us likes to lose. But don't make too much of it. There was nothing said before the incident and nothing afterwards.'

It was unlucky for Gilbert that he had played second and had had such a long match. Certainly during the next day's final he looked mentally tired, and also a little jaded physically. A tournament of this stature should provide a day's rest between matches which should all be played over the best of five sets. If the women were included, or perhaps a world junior championship, then this could be achieved.

The final itself is barely worth reporting in detail simply because it was so one-sided. You could hardly believe that Gilbert had twice beaten Sampras in 1990 – by 6–0 6–3 on a hard court in Toronto and by 6–7 6–2 6–3 indoors on carpet in Stockholm. For the record Sampras lost only 22 points on serve – 10 in the first set, 5 in the second and 7 in the third. He hit a total of 57 winners to Gilbert's 35, 28 of those on serve, 14 from the forehand wing and only 8 on the volley. Such was his dominance from the back of the court that Sampras only came to the net to finish a rally.

Perhaps the most surprising thing was the way Sampras moved. There was no sign of discomfort from the blistered foot. 'I put new-skin on it and had it taped', he said. 'Once you are into the match you just don't think about it . . . not when there's a million dollars at stake', he added with a smile. It was the nearest he got to a show of emotion. There was an air of quiet authority in all that Sampras did which suggests that here is a potential world champion. On this form only Edberg, Becker and occasionally Lendl could expect to live with him.

So ended the first *Compaq Grand Slam Cup* which had opened in fine theatrical style with a memorable performance from Placido Domingo, supported by the Norwegian pop group a-ha. The decision to sell only series tickets for every day was a mistake and accounted for the poor attendance figures – considerably less than the 50,000 or so tickets that were supposed to have been sold. In an arena that seats 11,000, a crowd of 6,000 looks rather meagre. The ITF were understandably delighted that the Grand Slam Development Fund will benefit by $2 million to improve programmes of training and competition in third world countries. They were also gratified by the fact, thanks to the sales expertise of Dr. Axel Meyer-Woelden, the man whose company, ISPR GmbH, had promoted the tournament, some 70 television networks around the world were taking the pictures supplied by the host broadcaster Sat 1.

It was felt from the attitude of the players that everyone who qualifies for inclusion next year will play. If that happens, the German public will surely be encouraged to attend in large numbers and so provide the atmosphere that such an ambitious tournament deserves.

MUNICH, 11–16 DECEMBER
1st round: M. Chang (USA) d. S. Edberg (SWE) (1) 6–4 4–6 7–5; H. Leconte (FRA) d. T. Muster (AUT) (7) 6–3 6–4; P. Sampras (USA) (4) d. A. Cherkasov (URS) 5–7 6–2 7–5; G. Ivanisevic (YUG) (5) d. K. Curren (USA) 7–6 7–6; B. Gilbert (USA) d. J. Svensson (SWE) (6) 2–6 6–3 6–4; A. Krickstein (USA) d. A. Gomez (ECU) (3) 6–3 6–4; D. Wheaton (USA) (8) d. Y. Noah (FRA) 7–6 6–7 6–3; I. Lendl (TCH) (2) d. C. Bergstrom (SWE) 6–4 6–0.
Quarter-finals: Chang d. Leconte 7–6 6–3; Sampras (4) d. Ivanisevic (5) 7–6 6–7 8–6; Gilbert d. Krickstein 6–7 6–4 6–3; Wheaton (8) d. Lendl (2) 6–2 7–6.
Semi-finals: Sampras (4) d. Chang 7–6 6–7 8–6; Gilbert d. Wheaton 6–3 3–6 7–6 2–6 6–4.
Final: Sampras (4) d. Gilbert 6–3 3–6 7–6 2–6 6–4.
Prize Money: Winner $2m; Finalist $1m; Semi-finalists $400,000; Quarter-finalists $300,000; First round $100,000; Alternates $50,000.

THE GRAND SLAM DEVELOPMENT FUND

The Grand Slam Development Fund, formerly the Grand Slam Trust fund began in 1985 when the Championships at Wimbledon made a contribution of £100,000 to assist with the development of competitive tennis in areas of the world where opportunity was lacking. The French and the US Open Championships followed suit in 1986 and now the *Compaq Grand Slam Cup* will make an annual contribution of $2 million. This will transform the ITF's ability to foster the growth of the game in Third World Countries. To date the Grand Slam Development Fund has helped launch the entry level of professional tournaments for men and women in dozens of countries. Through travel grants, the Fund had given countless juniors the opportunity to test their skills internationally. While ITF junior teams compete at the highest levels of the junior game, regional circuits have been established to provide competition closer to home in various regions of the world. Special grants to develop facilities have also been awarded and the $2,000,000 per year income from the *Compaq Grand Slam Cup* will have an immediate and significant impact on both the quantity and quality of international play.

After extensive consultation with the Development Advisors, Regional Associations and numerous National Association Officials, a blueprint was approved by the ITF Committee of Management which maps out plans for the use of the new Grand Slam Development Fund in 1991. As a result, the *Compaq Grand Slam Cup* will bring together the best male players in the world. It is appropriate that many hundreds of aspiring young male players will benefit from the $395,000 to be allocated to Men's Satellite Circuits. Our aim is to ensure that opportunity exists for young players worldwide to express their talent.

Women's tennis will also benefit enormously from the *Grand Slam Cup*. Whereas a Satellite or Development Circuit consists of four tournaments, the ITF Futures' Rules allow for one-off tournaments offering $10,000 in prize money. This gives numerous smaller tennis countries the opportunity to conduct a professional tournament without having the expense and difficulty of organising four events. $330,000 will be spent on the expansion of Women's Competition.

Junior teams from Africa, Asia, the South Pacific, South America, Central America and the Caribbean will play in ITF Junior World Ranking tournaments around the globe. Junior circuits involving players from over 100 countries will be played. Travel grants will be issued to National Asscocations for the competitive development of their most promising players.

To date we have been very effective in helping to develop junior players but have been very limited in our ability to assist good players in the 19–22 age group that bridges the gap between junior and open tennis. We hope to establish young professional or world class development teams to assist in those areas where National Associations are unable to provide the guidance and/or programme to help their players reach their full potential.

The first ITF Training Centre has just opened in Abidjan, Ivory Coast under the direction of the former national coach of Canada, Josef Brabenec. This project will be jointly funded by the ITF, Olympic Solidarity and the Grand Slam Development Fund. For the first time National Associations in Africa will have a top notch training facility to which they can send their best players at a moderate cost. Players will stay at the centre for visits ranging from two weeks to nine months. But perhaps the fastest growing area of competitive tennis lies not with the young lions but the old foxes . . . the veterans. With hundreds of players entering ITF events and many nations wishing to initiate international events, $50,000 will be earmarked to help ensure that this growth area continues to develop in a professional fashion.

In light of the number of new events coming onto the international calendar, there is a definite need for more qualified officials. In order to ensure that international standards are maintained, a portion of the Development Fund will be allocated to producing on-court officials. Furthermore, special grants to assist with the development of facilities will be made – a small injection of funds from the ITF frequently serves as a catalyst for further fund raising! These grants are particularly effective in developing nations. A reserve of $222,500 or 11% of the budget will also be maintained at this time, with a possible view to assisting with the World Youth Cup in 1991.

The International Tennis Federation is pleased that these new funds will aid in its firm commitment to the worldwide development of tennis.

Wimbledon finalist Zina Garrison came from John Wilkerson's public parks programme in Houston, just the sort of scheme that the Grand Slam Trust fund will now be supporting in less privileged lands. *(Professional Sport)*

IBM/ATP TOUR

TOUR REVIEW
POINTS EXPLANATION
IBM/ATP TOUR TOURNAMENTS
ATP TOUR WORLD CHAMPIONSHIP

For the tall young Yugoslav left-hander, Goran Ivanisevic, 1990 was a year of significant progress when he reached the Wimbledon semi-final, helped his country to win the World Team Cup and ended the year ranked No. 9.   *(M. Cole)*

Love him or hate him, you could certainly never ignore Andre Agassi in 1990 as he swept through the year dressed in various highly coloured outfits whose exotic details were slavishly copied by the young everywhere. *(R. Adams)*

IBM/ATP TOUR REVIEW

John Parsons

In an increasingly exciting race which, as they say, went right down to the wire, Stefan Edberg proved to be the most consistently successful competitor on the inaugural IBM/ATP Tour. After displacing Ivan Lendl from the No. 1 spot on August 13th the 24-year-old Swede held on gamely to finish 1990 on top of the men's world rankings.

Entering the final event, the ATP Tour Championships, which, for the first time – and controversially – offered ranking points whereas its predecessor, The Masters, had not, Edberg knew that mathematically, at least, Boris Becker, who had made a strong autumnal challenge, was breathing down his neck. Indeed, in the end, Becker went ahead of Edberg in Frankfurt but despite that, the vast majority agreed that the Swede, who had ended Lendl's 80 weeks reign as world number one, deserved to retain the new status he was clearly enjoying.

Edberg's year had begun with despair at the Australian Open. After injuring a stomach muscle in the final game of his winning semi-final against Mats Wilander, he became the first player to withdraw from a Grand Slam tournament final since Frank Shields at Wimbledon in 1931. Edberg then went on to claim six Tour events – at Indian Wells, the Japan Open, Los Angeles, Cincinnati, Long Island and the Paris Indoor, in addition, of course, to the greatest of all his 1990 triumphs, his second win at Wimbledon. His nearest rival was Becker, appropriately enough, with five titles and then Lendl with four to add to his Australian Open crown which, like the other Grand Slam tournaments, is completely independent of the players' own tour. And, if further justification was needed of Edberg's claim to be number one, his overall match record for the year, 70–14 (83.33%) was superior to that of all his rivals. Becker's win-loss record, for instance, was 71–15 (82.56%) which was not quite so impressive, while Lendl finished with 53–11 (82.81%) and Andre Agassi with 45–10 (81.82%).

One of the many claims made by The Association of Tennis Professionals when they began planning their breakaway from the now defunct Grand Prix, which had been jointly administered by players, tournament directors and the ITF, was that they would create an atmosphere and structure within their circuit which would not only prove more rewarding for sponsors, players and the public but would also encourage the top players to enter more tournaments. Indeed, in some ways ATP officials could claim to have been successful. In others the progress they claim was, in effect, merely maintaining a momentum which had been equally evident under the old regime.

The ATP Tour, in their first end of year review, reported that 'From almost every perspective, tournament fields in 1990 have been considerably stronger than ever before. Championship Series cutoffs have improved 35% . . . top ten players played 25% more in 1990 . . . and that 120 players, compared with only 70 this time last year (the final number was 85), earned £100,000 or more in prize money.' They produced a broad range of statistics to support their claims but, as is so often the case with statistics, they are open to wildly different interpretations. After all, the phrase 'top ten players', on which much of the ATP analysis is based, does not literally mean players ranked within the top ten. That phrase actually refers to the ten players chosen by a ballot among tournament directors as being the ones they regard the most marketable, plus others not included, who were in the top ten at that time or when the mid-year review took place. In other words 'top ten' meant never less than 14 players and often more. If, for instance, you made a strict mathematical comparison of the records of the top eight players in the world going into the ATP Championships in 1990 with those of the top eight going into the Grand Prix Masters in

1989, you would find that on average, they actually played more under the old system than the new. They also played more matches against each other, as a top eight elite, than in 1990. In 1989 the top eight collectively played 532 matches. In 1990 the total was 524. The total number of matches which top eight players took part in against other top eight players was 44 in 1989 compared with 36 in 1990.

It was most significant that no less than half the eight-man field in Frankfurt had not played the required minimum of major events on the tour, as they had signed so to do. These men either had to pay fines or agree to increase their commitment for 1991. As politicians have long since discovered, the value of statistics lies not in the figures themselves but how they are presented.

However, the IBM/ATP tour was outstandingly succcessful in providing tournaments with considerably stronger fields in the weeks immediately after the US Open. In the past this has tended to be something of a barren period when it was always dangerous to draw too many conclusions from unexpected results. In fact, Sydney and Tokyo both had semi-finals featuring the top three players in the world. In Stockholm, where ATP officials took a strong and persuasive stand against threats to prevent players who had competed in South Africa in the previous 15 months from taking part, the entry included 13 of the top 15. At the indoor event in Paris the field was even stronger, boasting 27 of the top 30. There was also the triumphant launching of the first tour event in Moscow, The Kremlin Cup, won, appropriately enough, in front of a capacity 15,000 crowd, by Andrei Cherkasov.

Cherkasov was one of 15 players who won tour titles for the first time during the year. The first was Pete Sampras in February at Philadelphia. By also winning at Manchester on grass and at the US Open on hard courts, Sampras shared with Edberg and Lendl the distinction of being the only players during the year to win tournaments on three different surfaces. Apart from Sampras, the only other newcomers who collected their first titles in a Championship Series event, were Derrick Rostagno in New Haven and Goran Ivanisevic, in Stuttgart. Ivanisevic, still a teenager, was another who also demonstrated his versatility and ability on a variety of surfaces, finishing the year with a 23–6 match record on clay, which was equalled only by Andres Gomez, the French Open champion and by the leading Russian, Andrei Chesnokov.

Other first time tour winners were Michael Stich (Memphis), Alex Antonitsch (Seoul), David Wheaton (Kiawah Island), Goran Prpic (Umag), Richard Fromberg (Bologna), Magnus Larsson (Florence), Pieter Aldrich (Newport), Francisco Clavet (Hilversum), Jordi Arrese (San Remo), Mark Koevermans (Athens) and Robbie Weiss (Sao Paulo). Of the 74 tournaments on the ATP Tour, most of which had been carried over from the Grand Prix fixture list, all but four produced a different champion. The only repeat winners were Gomez in Barcelona, Edberg at the Japan Open, where he is virtually a national hero, Kelly Jones in Singapore and Lendl at Queen's Club.

One of the most controversial innovations on the tour during 1990, was the introduction of the 'Best 14' rule, whereby a player's ranking was assessed solely on his best 14 tournament performances thus enabling him to discard results from his worst weeks. This change was made with the best of intentions and it certainly helped to persuade some players to enter more tournaments than perhaps would otherwise have been the case. On the other hand, when set in conjunction with the legalising of appearance money which occured for the first time in all tour events bar the Championship Series, it did lead to considerable scepticism in the early part of the year when early round losses for top ten players in lower-graded tournaments seemed disappointingly numerous.

Several leading players, including Edberg and Lendl have strongly questioned the ethicacy of the Best 14 rule. The ATP Tour, again with figures based on that misleading 'top ten', insist that the new system is working. They claim that the 'top ten' players lost 8% fewer early round matches than in 1989. What is inescapable is that only 18 of the 74 tournaments were won by top seeds and that the top eight at the end of the year had collectively won 27 tour titles, compared with 26 by the top eight a year earlier. The ranking of winners stretched all the way down from one, of course, to the 243rd place which Pat Cash held when he won Hong Kong as part of his steady comeback from injury during the year. There were also 47 different winners of titles, three more than in 1989, which was not only a record but must be a healthy sign. On the other hand the number of countries they represented went down by two from 21 to 19.

In 1989, Czechoslovakia, thanks principally to Lendl, claimed the most individual titles other than the United States, with 12. In 1990, behind the United States whose ten different players collected 16 titles between them, came Sweden, with five players, (principally Edberg with seven successes) earning them eleven titles. Spain overtook both Czechoslovakia and Germany with seven titles divided between four players one of whom, Juan Aguilera, had triumphed at both Nice and Hamburg in a year when he had lifted his ranking back into the top 20 from the 166 it had been two years earlier. His awesome, as well as clinical 6–1 6–0 7–6 defeat of Becker in the Hamburg final in May was second only to the success of Andres Gomez at the French Open as one of the finest clay court performances of the year.

The breadth of international involvement and progress in tennis was again impressively illustrated by the representation of 25 different countries – three more than last year but by no means a record – among the list of the top 100 rankings. Perhaps even more encouraging was that eight countries ended the year with a player among the top ten. These were Sweden, Germany, Czechoslovakia, the United States, Ecuador, Austria, Spain and Yugoslavia.

American representation among the top 100, which ten years ago amounted to 41, including six in the top ten, has slipped again from 27 in 1989 to 24 now, followed by Sweden with 11, Australia, France and Spain with seven each, Germany with six and Czechoslovakia with five. Once again the European influence was impressive, accounting for just over 50%.

The average prize money earned by the top 200 players, according to ATP, showed an increase of 46% over the previous year and Agassi's success in Frankfurt enabled him to join Edberg, with $1,995,901 and Lendl with $1,537,000, on the seven figure mark. Agassi, who had collected the relatively modest $478,901 in 1989 more than doubled what he had won in the rest of 1990 when he was handed a cheque for $950,000 as the winner of the ATP World Championships.

Strangely enough, while so many players saw their incomes soar, not only because of increased prize money on the Tour but also because it had risen in the four Grand Slam Championships too, the abolition of the bonus pool meant that two of the top three in the rankings, Becker and Lendl, saw their prize money earnings reduced. In 1989, Lendl and Becker both surpased John McEnroe's single year record set in 1984, with figures of $2,344,367 and $1,216,823 respectively. Not that they finished 1990 looking for financial sympathy!

Of those who entered 1990 ranked among the world's top ten, only five were still there at the end of the year. Lendl and Edberg changed places so far as first and third in the rankings were concerned, leaving an often perplexed Becker in second position. Agassi climbed from seventh to fourth, while Brad Gilbert dropped from six to ten. The most spectacular rise at this highest level came from Sampras. He improved his ranking by 76 places from 81st to fifth, a record. Meanwhile the Argentine, Alberto Mancini, failed to sustain the exciting progress he had made in 1989 and slid from ninth to 127.

Others among the most impressive ranking improvements were Richard Fromberg, 20, the Australian who crowned a fine year by being given his *Davis Cup* debut in the final against the United States – up from 126 to 32 – and two Frenchmen, Thierry Champion, who rose from 404 to 59 and teenager, Fabrice Santoro, who climbed from 235 to 62. And although they were beaten in the ATP Doubles Championships in Sanctuary Cove, where Guy Forget and Jakob Hlasek took the title, after both had shaved their heads immediately before the event, as a joke, there was no doubt that the South Africans, Danie Visser and Aldrich were the most consistently successful doubles team of the year. Indeed, having won the Australian and US Open titles and then finished as runners-up at Wimbledon to Rick Leach and Jim Pugh on three tie-break sets, they not only finished as the No. 1 team but were also joint No. 1 individually – the first time this has happened at the top of the doubles ranking list. Forget and Hlasek finished second on the team list, followed by Scott Davis and David Pate, Grant Connell and Glenn Michibata and Leach and Pugh.

IBM/ATP TOUR 1990

DATE	VENUE	SINGLES FINAL	DOUBLES WINNERS
1–7 Jan	Wellington	E. Sanchez d. R. Reneberg 6–7 6–4 6–0	K. Evernden/N. Pereira
1–7 Jan	Adelaide	T. Muster d. J. Arias 3–6 6–2 7–5	A. Castle/N. Odizor
8–14 Jan	Sydney	Y. Noah d. C. Steeb 5–7 6–3 6–4	P. Cash/M. Kratzmann
8–14 Jan	Auckland	S. Davis d. A. Chesnokov 4–6 6–3 6–3	K. Jones/R. Van't Hof
15–28 Jan	Melbourne (Australian Open)	I. Lendl d. S. Edberg 4–6 7–6 5–2 retd	P. Aldrich/D. Visser
5–11 Feb	Milan	I. Lendl d. T. Mayotte 6–3 6–2	O. Camporese/D. Nargiso
5–11 Feb	San Francisco	A. Agassi d. T. Witsken 6–1 6–3	K. Jones/R. Van't Hof
5–11 Feb	Brazil	M. Jaite d. L. Mattar 3–6 6–4 6–3	J. Frana/G. Luza
12–18 Feb	Toronto	I. Lendl d. T. Mayotte 6–3 6–0	P. Galbraith/D. MacPherson
12–18 Feb	Brussels	B. Becker d. C. Steeb 7–5 6–2 6–2	E. Sanchez/S. Zivojinovic
19–25 Feb	Philadelphia	P. Sampras d. A. Gomez 7–6 7–5 6–2	R. Leach/J. Pugh
19–25 Feb	Stuttgart	B. Becker d. I. Lendl 6–2 6–2	J. Hlasek/G. Forget
26 Feb–4 March	Memphis	M. Stich d. W. Masur 6–7 6–4 7–6	D. Cahill/M. Kratzmann
26 Feb–4 March	Indian Wells	B. Gilbert d. J. Svensson 6–1 6–3	J. Lozano/L. Lavalle
5–11 March		S. Edberg d. A. Agassi 6–4 5–7 7–6 7–6	B. Becker/G. Forget
5–11 March	Casablanca	T. Muster d. G. Perez-Roldan 6–1 6–7 6–2	T. Woodbridge/S. Youl
16–25 March	Key Biscayne	A. Agassi d. S. Edberg 6–1 6–4 0–6 6–2	R. Leach/J. Pugh
2–8 April	Orlando	B. Gilbert d. C. Van Rensburg 6–2 6–1	S. Davis/D. Pate
2–8 April	Rio de Janeiro	L. Mattar d. A. Sznajder 6–4 6–4	B. Garrow/S. Salumaa
2–8 April	Lisbon	E. Sanchez d. F. Davin 6–3 6–1	S. Casal/E. Sanchez
9–15 April	Tokyo	S. Edberg d. A. Krickstein 6–4 7–5	M. Kratzmann/W. Masur
9–15 April	Barcelona	A. Gomez d. G. Perez-Roldan 6–0 7–6 3–6 0–6 6–2	A. Gomez/J. Sanchez
16–22 April	Nice	J. Aguilera d. G. Forget 2–6 6–3 6–2	A. Mancini/Y. Noah
16–22 April	Seoul	A. Antontsch d. P. Cash 7–6 6–3	G. Connell/G. Michibata
23–29 April	Monte-Carlo	A. Chesnokov d. T. Muster 7–5 6–3 6–3	P. Korda/T. Smid
23–29 April	Hong Kong	P. Cash d. A. Antontsch 6–3 6–4	P. Cash/W. Masur
30 April–6 May	Munich	K. Novacek d. T. Muster 6–4 6–2	U. Riglewski/M. Stich
30 April–6 May	Madrid	A. Gomez d. M. Rosset 6–3 7–6	J. Baguena/O. Camporese
30 April–6 May	Singapore	K. Jones d. R. Fromberg 6–4 2–6 7–6	M. Kratzmann/J. Stoltenberg
7–13 May	Hamburg	J. Aguilera d. B. Becker 6–1 6–0 7–6	S. Bruguera/J. Courier
7–13 May	Kiawah Island	D. Wheaton d. M. Kaplan 6–4 6–4	S. Davis/D. Pate
14–20 May	Rome	T. Muster d. A. Chesnokov 6–1 6–3 6–1	S. Casal/E. Sanchez
14–20 May	Umag	G. Prpic d. G. Ivanisevic 6–4 4–6 6–4	V. Flegl/D. Vacek
21–27 May	Bologna	R. Fromberg d. M. Rosset 4–6 6–4 7–6	G. Luza/U. Riglewski
28 May–10 June	Paris (French Open)	A. Gomez d. A. Agassi 6–3 2–6 6–4 6–4	S. Casal/E. Sanchez
11–17 June	Queen's Club	I. Lendl d. B. Becker 6–3 6–2	J. Bates/K. Curren
11–17 June	Rosmalen	A. Mansdorf d. A. Volkov 6–3 7–6	J. Hlasek/M. Stich
11–17 June	Florence	M. Larsson d. L. Duncan 6–7 5–6 0	S. Bruguera/H. De La Pena
18–24 June	Genova	R. Agenor d. T. Benhabiles 3–6 6–4 6–3	T. Carbonell/U. Riglewski
18–24 June	Manchester	P. Sampras d. G. Bloom 7–6 7–6	M. Kratzmann/J. Stoltenberg
25 June–8 July	London (Wimbledon)	S. Edberg d. B. Becker 6–2 6–2 3–6 3–6 6–4	R. Leach/J. Pugh
9–15 July	Newport	P. Aldrich d. D. Cahill 7–6 1–6 6–1	D. Cahill/M. Kratzmann

DATE	VENUE	SINGLES FINAL	DOUBLES WINNERS
9-15 July	Gstaad	M. Jaite d. S. Bruguera 6-3 6-7 6-2 6-2	S. Casal/E. Sanchez
9-15 July	Bastad	R. Fromberg d. M. Larsson 6-2 7-6	R. Bergh/R. Bathman
16-22 July	Stuttgart	G. Ivanisevic d. G. Perez-Roldan 6-7 6-1 6-4 7-6	P. Aldrich/D. Visser
16-22 July	Washington	A. Agassi d. J. Grabb 6-1 6-4	G. Connell/G. Michibata
23-29 July	Toronto	M. Chang d. J. Berger 4-6 6-3 7-6	P. Annacone/D. Wheaton
23-29 July	Hilversum	F. Clavet d. E. Masso 3-6 6-4 6-2 6-0	S. Casal/E. Sanchez
30 July-5 Aug	Kitzbuhel	H. De La Pena d. K. Novacek 6-4 7-6 2-6 6-2	E. Sanchez/E. Winogradsky
30 July-5 Aug	San Remo	J. Arrese d. J. Aguilera 6-2 6-2	I. Nastase/G. Prpic
30 July-5 Aug	Los Angeles	S. Edberg d. M. Chang 7-6 2-6 7-6	S. Davis/D. Pate
6-12 Aug	Cincinnati	S. Edberg d. B. Gilbert 6-1 6-1	D. Cahill/M. Kratzmann
6-12 Aug	Prague	J. Arrese d. N. Kulti 7-6 7-6	V. Flegl/D. Vacek
13-19 Aug	Indianapolis	B. Becker d. P. Lundgren 6-3 6-4	S. Davis/D. Pate
13-19 Aug	New Haven	D. Rostagno d. T. Woodbridge 6-3 6-3	S. Brown/S. Melville
20-26 Aug	Schenectady	R. Krishnan d. K. Evernden 6-1 6-1	R. Fromberg/B. Pearce
20-26 Aug	San Marino	G. Perez-Roldan d. O. Camporese 6-3 6-3	V. Flegl/D. Vacek
20-26 Aug	Long Island	S. Edberg d. G. Ivanisevic 7-6 6-3	P. Aldrich/D. Visser
27 Aug-9 Sept	New York (US Open)	P. Sampras d. A. Agassi 6-4 6-3 6-2	T. Carbonell/L. Pimek
10-16 Sept	Bordeaux	G. Forget d. G. Ivanisevic 6-4 6-3	C. Van Rensburg/S. Kruger
10-16 Sept	Geneva	H. Skoff d. S. Bruguera 7-6 7-6	J. Stoltenberg/T. Woodbridge
24-30 Sept	Basle	J. McEnroe d. G. Ivanisevic 6-7 4-6 7-6 6-3 6-4	S. Casal/E. Sanchez
24-30 Sept	Brisbane	B. Gilbert d. A. Krickstein 6-3 6-1	B. Dyke/P. Lundgren
24-30 Sept	Palermo	F. Davin d. J. Aguilera 6-1 6-1	N. Broad/G. Muller
1-7 Oct	Sydney	B. Becker d. S. Edberg 7-6 4-6 6-4	S. Casal/E. Sanchez
1-7 Oct	Toulouse	J. Svensson d. F. Santoro 7-6 6-2	G. Forget/J. Hlasek
1-7 Oct	Athens	M. Koevermans d. F. Davin 5-7 6-4 6-4	P. Aldrich/D. Visser
8-14 Oct	Tokyo	I. Lendl d. B. Becker 4-6 6-3 7-6	N. Odizor/C. Van Rensburg
8-14 Oct	Berlin	R. Agenor d. A. Volkov 4-6 6-4 7-6	P. Galbraith/K. Jones
8-13 Oct	Tel Aviv	A. Chesnokov d. A. Mansdorf 6-4 6-3	U. Riglewski/M. Stich
15-21 Oct	Lyon	M. Rosset d. M. Wilander 6-3 6-2	G. Forget/J. Hlasek
15-21 Oct	Vienna	J. Jarryd d. H. Skoff 6-3 6-3 6-1	G. Forget/J. Hlasek
22-28 Oct	Stockholm	B. Becker d. S. Edberg 6-4 6-0 6-3	S. Cannon/A. Mora
22-28 Oct	Sao Paulo	R. Weiss d. J. Yzaga 6-3 6-7 8-6	S. Davis/D. Pate
29 Oct-4 Nov	Paris	S. Edberg d. B. Becker 3-3 retd	H.-J. Davids/P. Haarhuis
5-11 Nov	Berlin	A. Cherkasov d. T. Mayotte 6-2 6-1	M. Menezes/F. Roese
5-11 Nov	Itaparica	M. Wilander d. M. Filippini 6-1 6-2	J. Grabb/P. McEnroe
5-11 Nov	Wembley	J. Hlasek d. M. Chang 7-6 6-3	
12-18 Nov	Frankfurt (ATP Finals)	A. Agassi d. S. Edberg 5-7 7-6 7-5 6-2	G. Forget/J. Hlasek
21-25 Nov	Sanctuary Cove (ATP Doubles Finals)		
11-16 Dec	Munich (Grand Slam Cup)	P. Sampras d. B. Gilbert 6-3 6-4 6-2	

IBM/ATP TOUR 1990 – POINTS EXPLANATION

The ATP TOUR came into existence in September 1988 when the Association of Tennis Professionals (ATP) announced that their three representatives on the Men's Tennis Council would no longer attend meetings of that body. Until that time the MTC, with three representatives each from the players, the International Tennis Federation and International Tournament Directors, had been responsible for the management of all professional tennis for men.

The ATP TOUR, a new alliance between players and tournament directors, is an independent Corporation with a Board of Directors and a Player's Council. It replaced the ATP which ceased to exist as a player's association. Before the end of 1988, the ATP TOUR announced a 1990 circuit of 76 tournaments in 28 countries on six continents. There were to be two categories – Championship Series and World Series – and 12 levels of prize money. As the following tables show, points are awarded according to the round reached in these events, as well as at the four Grand Slam Championships, to determine an order of ranking, which is used as the basis of entry for all tournaments.

Below the main Championship Series and World Series events are the Challenger tournaments, administered by the ATP TOUR and having minimum prize money of $25,000. These tournaments also carry ranking points, as do the Masters events of the many Satellite circuits (3 tournaments plus a Masters) which are administered by the National Tennis Associations or Federations in most tennis playing countries of the world.

IBM/ATP TOUR POINTS TABLES Identical ranking points are awarded for singles and doubles. No points are awarded until a player has completed a match. Anyone who reaches the second round via a bye and then loses is considered to have lost in the first round and receives one point, but he does receive second round prize money. There are also additional 'Bonus Points' awarded for beating players ranked between 1 and 200 in singles, or a team ranked between 2 and 400 in doubles. In addition to the points won in any tournament, a player or doubles team winning a place in the main draw via a qualifying event also receives half the points awarded to the second round singles loser in that tournament. Lucky Losers receive no qualifying points.

Category	Total Prize Money	Computer Points							
		W	F	S	Q	16	32	64	128
Grand Slams	$2 million	400	300	200	100	50	25	13	1
	$1 million	360	270	180	90	45	23	12	1
Championship	$2 million	300	225	150	75	38	19	10	1
Series	$1,750,000	285	214	143	72	36	18	9	1
	$1,500,000	265	199	133	67	34	17	9	1
	$1,250,000	250	188	125	63	32	16	1	–
	$1,000,000	230	173	115	58	29	15	1	–
	$750,000	205	164	103	52	26	13	1	–
	$500,000	180	135	90	45	23	12	1	–
World Series	$625,000	150	113	75	38	19	10	1	
	$500,000	133	100	67	34	17	9	1	
	$375,000	115	87	58	29	15	8	1	
	$250,000	103	78	52	26	13	7	1	
	$150,000	90	68	45	28	12	1	–	
Challenger	$100,000+H	70	53	35	18	9	1		
Series	$100,000	60	45	30	15	8	1		
	$75,000	50	38	25	13	7	1		
	$50,000	40	30	20	10	5	1		
	$25,000	30	23	15	8	4	1		

Note: Any Challenger providing hospitality will receive the points of the next highest prize money level (see the example above for 100,000+H).

BONUS POINTS

Singles		*Doubles* Team	
Ranking	Bonus Points	Ranking	Bonus Points
2–3	50	2–3	50
4–10	45	4–10	45
11–20	36	11–20	36
21–30	18	21–40	24
31–50	12	41–60	18
51–75	6	61–100	12
76–100	3	101–150	6
101–150	2	151–200	3
151–200	1	201–300	2
		300–400	1

David Wheaton of the United States won his first career title at the US Clay Courts in Kiawah Island and was a quarter-finalist in Australia and at the US Open where he reached the doubles final. *(R. Adams)*

CHAMPIONSHIP SERIES

SKYDOME TORONTO INDOOR ($1,005,000)

TORONTO, 12–18 FEBRUARY

MEN'S SINGLES – 1st round: I. Lendl (TCH) (1) – bye; J. Brown (USA) d. M. Washington (USA) 6–4 6–7 6–4; P. Haarhuis (HOL) d. P. McEnroe (USA) 6–3 4–1 ret.; K. Evernden (NZL) d. P. Sampras (USA) (15) 7–6 ret.; J. Courier (USA) (9) d. D. Cahill (AUS) 6–0 6–3; G. Connell d. D. Goldie (USA) 6–4 2–6 6–3; A. Sznajder d. O. Jonsson (SWE) 6–0 6–4; K. Curren (USA) (8) – bye; J. McEnroe (USA) (3) – bye; P. Chamberlin (USA) d. D. Rostagno (USA) 6–4 7–5; R. Matuszewski (USA) d. C. Pridham 6–1 6–2; L. Shiras (USA) d. S. Davis (USA) (14) 6–3 7–5; P. Lundgren (SWE) d. D. Wheaton (USA) (11) 6–3 6–7 6–2; R. Reneberg (USA) d. T. Wilkison (USA) 6–2 6–3; R. Krishnan (IND) d. G. Layendecker (USA) 6–1 7–5; J. Berger (USA) (5) – bye; T. Mayotte (USA) (6) – bye; J. Pugh (USA) d. J. Bates (GBR) 6–2 2–0 ret.; J. Lozano (MEX) d. R. Seguso (USA) 7–6 1–0 ret.; M. Vajda (TCH) d. J. Grabb (USA) (12) 1–6 7–6 6–3; J. Fitzgerald (AUS) d. W. Masur (AUS) (13) 4–6 7–6 6–3; M. Wostenholme d. T. Witsken (USA) 6–7 6–4 7–5; T. Nijssen (HOL) d. L. Duncan (USA) 6–3 6–3; A. Krickstein (USA) (4) – bye; A. Gomez (ECU) (7) – bye; P. Korda (TCH) d. M. Laurendeau 6–2 6–2; S. Devries (USA) d. J. Potier (FRA) 7–6 7–6; J. Yzaga (PER) (10) d. N. Kroon (SWE) 6–4 6–1; M. Srejber (TCH) d. J. Fleurian (FRA) (16) 3–6 7–6 7–5; B. Oresar (YUG) d. G. Van Emburgh (USA) 6–4 6–7 6–2; A. Antonitsch (AUT) d. J. Arias (USA) 6–4 7–6; B. Gilbert (USA) (2) – bye.

2nd round: Lendl d. Brown 7–5 6–1; Haarhuis d. Evernden 6–4 6–7 6–1; Connell d. Courier (9) 6–3 7–5; Curren (8) d. Sznajder 6–0 7–5; McEnroe (3) d. Chamberlin 6–3 6–3; Shiras d. Matuszewski 7–6 4–2 ret.; Reneberg d. Lundgren 7–5 6–1; Berger (5) d. Krishnan 7–6 6–3; Mayotte (6) d. Pugh 7–5 5–7 6–3; Lozano d. Vajda 7–5 4–6 7–5; Fitzgerald d. Wostenholme 6–1 6–1; Krickstein (4) d. Nijssen 6–2 6–2; Korda d. Gomez (7) 6–3 6–4; Yzaga (10) d. Devries 6–4 6–2; Srejber d. Oresar 4–6 6–4 6–2; Gilbert (2) d. Antonitsch 6–3 6–3.

3rd round: Lendl (1) d. Haarhuis 7–5 6–2; Curren (8) d. Connell 7–6 2–6 6–1; McEnroe (3) d. Shiras 6–4 6–3; Berger (5) d. Reneberg 6–4 7–6; Mayotte (6) d. Lozano 6–2 4–6 6–2; Krickstein (4) d. Fitzgerald 6–2 6–2; Korda d. Yzaga 6–4 6–4; Gilbert (2) d. Srejber 6–2 6–2.

Quarter-finals: Lendl (1) d. Curren (8) 6–7 7–6 6–3; McEnroe (3) d. Berger (5) 6–4 6–0; Mayotte (6) d. Krickstein (4) 4–6 6–4 7–6; Gilbert (2) d. Korda 3–6 7–6 6–2.

Semi-finals: Lendl (1) d. McEnroe (3) 6–3 6–2; Mayotte (6) d. Gilbert (2) 6–3 7–6.

Final: Lendl (1) d. Mayotte (6) 6–3 6–0.

MEN'S DOUBLES – Final: P. Galbraith (USA)/D. MacPherson (AUS) d. N. Broad (RSA)/Curren (6) 2–6 6–4 6–3.

BELGIAN INDOOR CHAMPIONSHIPS ($465,000)

BRUSSELS, 12–18 FEBRUARY

MEN'S SINGLES – 1st round: B. Becker (FRG) (1) d. K. Novacek (TCH) 7–6 6–2; G. Forget (FRA) d. A. Boetsch (FRA) 6–3 6–4; J. Aguilera (ESP) d. M. Strelba (TCH) 6–2 6–7 6–3; P. Cane (ITA) (7) d. O. Camporese (ITA) 6–3 6–3; J. Hlasek (SUI) (4) d. M. Koevermans (HOL) 6–4 6–1; J. Svensson (SWE) d. A. Volkov (URS) 6–4 7–6; A. Mansdorf (ISR) d. T. Nelson (USA) 6–3 3–6 6–4; M. Gustafsson (SWE) (6) d. J. Gunnarsson (SWE) 6–2 6–2; R. Agenor (HAI) (5) d. M. Schapers (HOL) 6–4 6–4; B. Wuyts d. X. Daufresne 4–6 6–2 6–1; A. Rahunen (FIN) d. A. Cherkasov (URS) 4–6 7–6 6–2; M. Mecir (TCH) d. E. Sanchez (ESP) (3) 6–4 3–6 6–4; G. Ivanisevic (YUG) (8) d. J. Wohrmann (FRG) 6–4 2–6 6–3; G. Prpic (YUG) d. H. Leconte (FRA) 6–3 5–7 6–1; T. Hogstedt (SWE) d. M. Rosset (SUI) 6–4 6–2; C. Steeb (FRG) (2) d. E. Jelen (FRG) 6–3 7–6.

2nd round: Becker (1) d. Forget 3–6 6–3 7–6; Cane (7) d. Aguilera 6–3 6–7 6–4; Svensson d. Hlasek (4) 5–7 6–2 7–6; Gustafsson (6) d. Mansdorf 6–4 6–4; Agenor (5) d. Wuyts 6–4 6–4; Mecir d. Rahunen 7–6 6–4; Ivanisevic (8) d. Prpic 6–3 6–7 6–2; Steeb (2) d. Hogstedt 6–4 6–6 6–2.

Quarter-finals: Becker (1) d. Cane (7) 6–4 3–2 ret.; Gustafsson (6) d. Svensson 6–7 7–6 6–3; Mecir d. Agenor (5) 6–3 6–2; Steeb (2) d. Ivanisevic (8) 6–3 3–6 6–4.

Semi-finals: Becker (1) d. Gustafsson (6) 6–4 7–6; Steeb (2) d. Mecir 6–2 6–3.

Final: Becker (1) d. Steeb (2) 7–5 6–2 6–2.
MEN'S DOUBLES – *Final:* E. Sanchez/S. Zivojinovic (YUG) (4) d. Ivanisevic/B. Taroczy (3) 7–5 6–3.

EBEL US PRO INDOOR CHAMPIONSHIPS ($825,000)

PHILADELPHIA, PA, 19–25 FEBRUARY
MEN'S SINGLES – *1st round:* J. McEnroe (1) – bye; R. Reneberg d. J. Pugh 6–3 3–6 6–3; M. Kratzmann (AUS) d. B. Pearce 7–5 6–4; S. Davis (15) – bye; C. Van Rensburg (RSA) (10) – bye; P. Annacone d. N. Kroon (SWE) 6–7 6–2 6–4; K. Evernden (NZL) d. J. Brown 6–3 7–5; J. Courier (8) – bye; A. Agassi (3) – bye; J. Fleurian (FRA) d. K. Flach 7–6 4–6 6–4; M. Srejber (TCH) d. J. Wohrmann (FRG) 3–6 7–6 6–2; P. Sampras (13) – bye; D. Wheaton (12) – bye; G. Layendecker d. P. Lundgren (SWE) 6–3 6–2; D. Rostagno d. M. Washington 7–6 5–6 7–6; T. Mayotte (5) – bye; A. Chesnokov (URS) (6) – bye; P. Korda (TCH) d. L. Duncan 6–3 6–1; C. Garner d. D. Cassidy 7–5 2–6 7–5; J. Yzaga (PER) (11) – bye; W. Masur (AUS) (14) – bye; D. Goldie d. P. Chamberlin 2–6 6–4 6–4; M. Schapers (HOL) d. D. Cahill (AUS) 6–7 6–3 7–6; J. Berger (4) – bye; A. Gomez (ECU) (7) – bye; A. Sznajder (CAN) d. J. Fitzgerald (AUS) 6–2 4–6 7–6; R. Krishnan (IND) d. T. Witsken 6–2 6–2; K. Curren (9) – bye; M. Pernfors (SWE) (16) – bye; P. Haarhuis (HOL) d. J. Potier (FRA) 6–3 6–4; T. Wilkison d. R. Leach 6–4 7–6; B. Gilbert (2) – bye.
2nd round: Reneberg d. McEnroe (1) 6–7 6–3 6–3; Kratzmann d. Davis (15) 7–5 4–6 6–1; Van Rensburg (10) d. Annacone 0–6 7–6 6–4; Courier (8) d. Evernden 7–6 6–4; Agassi (3) d. Fleurian 2–6 6–0 6–1; Sampras (13) d. Srejber 6–3 6–7 6–3; Layendecker d. Wheaton (12) 6–3 4–6 6–4; Mayotte (5) d. Rostagno 6–2 3–6 7–6; Korda d. Chesnokov (6) 6–2 6–4; Yzaga (11) d. Garner 6–0 6–4; Masur (14) d. Goldie 2–6 7–6 6–2; Berger (4) d. Schapers 7–6 6–7 6–4; Gomez (7) d. Sznajder 7–5 6–2; Curren (9) d. Krishnan 6–2 4–6 6–3; Haarhuis d. Pernfors 4–6 7–6 7–5; Gilbert (2) d. Wilkison 6–2 7–5.
3rd round: Kratzmann d. Reneberg 6–4 6–4; Courier (8) d. Van Rensburg (10) 6–3 5–7 6–4; Sampras (13) d. Agassi (3) 5–7 7–5 ret.; Mayotte (5) d. Layendecker 4–6 6–3 7–6; Korda d. Yzaga (11) 2–6 6–3 7–5; Berger (4) d. Masur (14) 6–2 6–4; Gomez (7) d. Curren (9) 6–7 6–3 6–4; Haarhuis d. Gilbert (2) 7–5 6–7 6–4.
Quarter-finals: Kratzmann d. Courier (8) 4–6 6–3 7–6; Sampras (13) d. Mayotte (5) 6–4 4–6 6–3; Korda d. Berger (4) 7–6 6–1; Gomez (7) d. Haarhuis 7–6 7–6 4.
Semi-finals: Sampras (13) d. Kratzmann 4–6 7–6 1 6–4; Gomez (7) d. Korda 6–2 6–0.
Final: Sampras (13) d. Gomez (7) 7–6 7–5 6–2.
MEN'S DOUBLES – *Final:* Leach/Pugh (2) d. G. Connell (CAN)/G. Michibata (CAN) (8) 3–6 6–4 6–2.

EUROCARD STUTTGART INDOOR ($825,000)

STUTTGART, 19–25 FEBRUARY
MEN'S SINGLES – *1st round:* I. Lendl (TCH) (1) d. O. Camporese (ITA) 6–4 6–2; G. Prpic (YUG) d. K. Novacek (TCH) 6–3 4–6 6–4; M. Strelba (TCH) d. J. Arrese (ESP) 7–5 6–3; P. Kuhnen d. T. Muster (AUT) (7) 4–6 7–6 6–1; A. Mansdorf (ISR) d. C. Steeb (4) 6–2 6–1; A. Rahunen (FIN) d. J. Sanchez (ESP) 7–6 6–3; M. Gustafsson (SWE) d. G. Ivanisevic (YUG) 4–6 7–6 6–4; E. Sanchez (ESP) (5) d. J. Gunnarsson (SWE) 6–4 6–1; H. Skoff (AUT) (6) d. M. Zoecke 6–4 3–6 6–3; T. Hogstedt (SWE) d. E. Jelen 6–4 2–6 6–2; J. Svensson (SWE) d. M. Stich 7–6 7–5; Y. Noah (FRA) (3) d. G. Forget (FRA) 4–7 6–4 7–6; M. Mecir (TCH) d. R. Agenor (HAI) (8) 7–5 6–4; P. Cane (ITA) d. J. Hlasek (SUI) 6–4 7–5; A. Volkov (URS) d. S. Zivojinovic (YUG) 6–3 7–5; B. Becker (2) d. B. Dyke (AUS) 7–6 6–4.
2nd round: Lendl (1) d. Prpic 7–6 6–2; Kuhnen d. Strelba 6–1 6–2; Rahunen d. Mansdorf 6–2 6–4; Gustafsson d. E. Sanchez (5) 6–3 6–0; Skoff (6) d. Hogstedt 6–2 1–6 6–3; Svensson d. Noah (3) 6–2 6–4; Mecir d. Cane 6–0 6–4; Becker (2) d. Volkov 6–4 3–6 6–3.
Quarter-finals: Lendl (1) d. Kuhnen 6–3 6–3; Gustafsson d. Rahunen 6–7 6–1 6–2; Svensson d. Skoff (6) 6–4 6–2; Becker (2) d. Mecir 6–4 6–2.
Semi-finals: Lendl (1) d. Gustafsson 6–4 6–7 6–3; Becker (2) d. Svensson 7–5 6–2.
Final: Becker (2) d. Lendl (1) 6–2 6–2.
MEN'S DOUBLES – *Final:* Forget/J. Hlasek (SUI) d. M. Mortensen (DEN)/T. Nijssen (HOL) 6–3 6–2.

NEWSWEEK'S CUP ($750,000)

INDIAN WELLS, CA, 5–11 MARCH
MEN'S SINGLES – *1st round:* B. Becker (FRG) (1) – bye; J. Sanchez (ESP) d. J. Grabb 6–1 6–2; J. Fleurian (FRA) d. W. Masur (AUS) 6–2 6–3; H. Skoff (AUT) (16) d. R. Bergh (SWE) 4–6 6–3 7–5; G. Ivanisevic (YUG) d. M. Jaite (ARG) (10) 6–1 6–4; F. Clavet (ESP) d. K. Novacek (TCH) 7–5 6–2; G. Forget (FRA) d. D. Pate 6–2 7–6; J. Berger (8) – bye; B. Gilbert (3) – bye; N. Kroon (SWE) d. P. Chamberlin 7–5 6–2; S. Matsuoka (JPN) d. M. Filippini (URU) 1–6 6–4 7–5; E. Sanchez (ESP) (14) d. P. Annacone 6–3 3–6 6–2; M. Schapers (HOL) d. A. Mancini (ARG) (11) 6–4 6–1; K. Curren d. R. Agenor (HAI) 6–3 6–4; J. Arias d. D. Visser (RSA) 0–6 7–6 6–4; A. Agassi (6) – bye; K. Jones – bye; J. Courier d. S. Bryan 7–5 6–1; C. Van Rensburg (RSA) d. J. Arrese (ESP) 6–1 6–3; D. Cahill (AUS) d. A. Gomez (ECU) (12) 7–5 6–4; P. Sampras (13) d. R. Krishnan (IND) 6–3 6–2; R. Reneberg d. M. Mecir (TCH) 5–7 6–3 6–3; B. Dyke (AUS)

d. L. Duncan 4–6 6–1 6–2; A. Krickstein (4) – bye; T. Mayotte (7) – bye; J. Pugh d. A. Volkov (URS) 4–6 6–2 7–6; K. Flach d. T. Witsken 6–2 6–3; J. Gunnarsson (SWE) d. M. Wilander (SWE) (19) 7–6 6–4; B. Pearce d. A. Chesnokov (URS) (15) 6–4 3–6 6–4; S. Bruguera (ESP) d. J. Yzaga (PER) 7–6 6–2; S. Davis d. J. Aguilera (ESP) 6–2 6–4; S. Edberg (SWE) (2) – bye.
2nd round: Becker (1) d. J. Sanchez 7–6 6–3; Skoff (16) d. Fleurian 6–3 6–3; Ivanisevic d. Clavet 6–2 6–4; Berger (8) d. Forget 6–2 7–5; Gilbert (3) d. Kroon 6–4 6–2; E. Sanchez (14) d. Matsuoka 6–0 6–3; Schapers d. Curren 7–6 6–4; Agassi (6) d. Arias 6–1 7–6; Courier d. Jones 6–2 6–3; Cahill d. Van Rensburg 6–1 6–3; Reneberg d. Sampras 4–6 6–4 6–2; Krickstein (4) d. Dyke 4–6 6–3 6–2; Pugh d. Mayotte (7) 6–2 4–6 6–4; Gunnarsson d. Flach 4–6 6–3 6–2; Bruguera d. Pearce 7–6 7–5; Edberg (2) d. Davis 6–3 6–2.
3rd round: Becker (1) d. Skoff (16) 6–4 1–6 7–6; Berger (8) d. Ivanisevic 6–4 7–6; E. Sanchez (14) d. Gilbert (3) 6–3 6–3; Agassi (6) d. Schapers 6–4 7–5; Courier d. Cahill 6–4 6–2; Krickstein (4) d. Reneberg 6–2 6–4; Gunnarsson d. Pugh 6–3 4–6 6–0; Edberg (2) d. Bruguera 6–0 6–3.
Quarter-finals: Becker (1) d. Berger 6–1 6–2; Agassi (6) d. E. Sanchez (14) 6–1 7–6; Courier d. Krickstein (4) 6–2 7–6; Edberg (2) d. Gunnarsson 6–2 6–2.
Semi-finals: Agassi (6) d. Becker (1) 6–4 6–1; Edberg (2) d. Courier 6–4 6–1.
Final: Edberg (2) d. Agassi (6) 6–4 5–7 7–6 7–6.
MEN'S DOUBLES – Final: Becker/Forget d. J. Grabb/P. McEnroe (3) 4–6 6–4 6–3.

LIPTON INTERNATIONAL PLAYER'S CHAMPIONSHIPS ($1,200,000)

KEY BISCAYNE, FL, 16–25 MARCH
MEN'S SINGLES – 1st round: I. Lendl (TCH) (1) – bye; J. Wohrmann (FRG) d. R. Matuszewski 4–6 7–6 6–4; N. Kroon (SWE) d. L. Shiras 6–2 7–6; M. Filippini (URU) (31)– bye; H. Skoff (AUT) (18) – bye; S. Zivojinovic (YUG) d. T. Carbonell (ESP) 6–3 6–4; L. Duncan d. F. Cancellotti (ITA) 6–1 7–6; E. Sanchez (ESP) (15) – bye; M. Jaite (ARG) (10) – bye; K. Novacek (TCH) d. J. Kriek 4–6 6–0 6–4; M. Stich (FRG) d. L. Wahlgren (SWE) 6–4 6–2; C. Van Rensburg (RSA) (23) – bye; R. Reneberg (25) – bye; R. Krishnan (IND) d. J. Aguilera (ESP) 6–7 6–2 6–2; A. Volkov (URS) d. J. Brown 4–6 7–6 6–1; T. Mayotte (8) – bye; S. Edberg (SWE) (3) – bye; R. Smith (BAH) d. K. Evernden (NZL) 7–5 7–5; A. Mansdorf (ISR) d. D. Rostagno 7–6 6–1; S. Davis (29) – bye; K. Curren (19) – bye; P. Lundgren (SWE) d. J. Bates (GBR) 7–6 6–2; G. Raoux (FRA) d. U. Riglewski (FRG) 6–1 6–0; C. Steeb (FRG) (13) – bye; A. Mancini (ARG) (11) – bye; B. Shelton d. D. Goldie 6–3 7–5; J. Tarango d. H. Leconte (FRA) 7–5 4–6 6–3; S. Bruguera (ESP) (22) – bye; J. Arrese (ESP) (27) – bye; A. Jarryd (SWE) d. P. Aldrich (RSA) 6–2 6–4; J. Hlasek (SUI) d. M. Schapers (HOL) 6–4 6–7 6–4; A. Krickstein (6)– bye; A. Agassi (5) – bye; K. Jones d. A. Sznajder (CAN) 6–3 6–1; M. Srejber (TCH) d. T. Nijssen (HOL) 6–1 5–7 7–6; J. Gunnarsson (SWE) (28) – bye; J. Yzaga (PER) (21) – bye; G. Connell (CAN) d. J. Fitzgerald (AUS) 6–4 6–4; B. Oresar (YUG) d. P. Cash (AUS) 6–2 6–2; A. Gomez (ECU) (12) – bye; J. Courier (14) – bye; K. Thorne d. G. Layendecker 7–5 7–6; T. Witsken d. T. Wilkison 7–5 6–4; P. Korda (TCH) (20) – bye; J. Sanchez (ESP) (30) – bye; C. Motta (BRA) d. A. Cherkasov (URS) 6–4 6–3; G. Bloom (ISR) d. N. Pereira (VEN) 2–6 6–4 6–2; B. Gilbert (4) – bye; J. Berger (7) – bye; D. Engel (SWE) d. D. Perez (URU) 2–6 7–6 6–2; M. Zoecke (FRG) d. J. Arias 6–4 6–4; G. Ivanisevic (YUG) (26) – bye; R. Agenor (HAI) (24) – bye; E. Jelen (FRG) d. J. Lozano (MEX) 6–4 6–3; M. Kratzmann (AUS) d. D. Cahill (AUS) 6–3 4–6 6–2; Y. Noah (FRA) (9) – bye; P. Sampras (16) – bye; P. Chamberlin d. F. Roese (BRA) 6–4 6–4; G. Forget (FRA) d. P. Annacone 6–3 7–5; A. Chesnokov (URS) (17) – bye; J. Fleurian (FRA) (32) – bye; J. Pugh d. M. Pernfors (SWE) 6–7 6–3 6–4; F. Santoro (FRA) d. M. Rosset (SUI) 6–4 6–1; B. Becker (FRG) (2) – bye.
2nd round: Lendl (1) d. Wohrmann 6–7 6–2 6–1; Filippini (31) d. Kroon 2–6 6–4 7–6; Skoff (18) d. Zivojinovic 6–2 6–2; E. Sanchez (15) d. Duncan 6–4 6–1; Jaite (10) d. Novacek 6–4 6–4; Van Rensburg (23) d. Stich 6–3 6–4; Reneberg (25) d. Krishnan 6–3 7–5; Volkov d. Mayotte (8) 6–1 6–4; Edberg (3) d. Smith 6–2 2–6 6–4; Mansdorf d. Davis (29) 6–2 6–2; Curren (19) d. Lundgren 6–0 7–6; Steeb (13) d. Raoux 2–6 4–6 6–3; Shelton d. Mancini (11) 2–6 6–4 6–3; Tarango d. Bruguera (22) 6–3 6–4; Arrese (27) d. Jarryd 7–6 6–2; Hlasek d. Krickstein (6) 1–6 7–6 6–3; Agassi (5) d. Jones 6–1 6–2; Gunnarsson (28) d. Srejber 6–2 7–6; Yzaga (21) d. Connell 7–6 4–6 7–6; Gomez (12) d. Oresar 2–6 6–2 6–3; Courier (14) d. Thorne 6–3 6–3; Witsken d. Korda (20) 6–2 2–6 6–4; J. Sanchez (30) d. Motta 5–7 7–6 6–4; Gilbert (4) d. Bloom 6–3 6–3; Berger (7) d. Engel 7–6 6–4; Ivanisevic (26) d. Zoecke 4–6 5–1 ret.; Agenor (24) d. Jelen 7–6 6–1; Kratzmann d. Noah (9) 6–4 2–6 7–6; Sampras (16) d. Chamberlin 2–6 7–6 6–1; Forget d. Chesnokov 6–7 6–3 6–3; Fleurian (32) d. Pugh 6–2 7–5; Becker (2) d. Santoro 6–3 5–7 6–2.
3rd round: Lendl (1) d. Filippini (31) 6–0 6–2; E. Sanchez (15) d. Skoff 3–6 6–3 6–3; Jaite (10) d. Van Rensburg (23) 4–6 6–4 6–4; Volkov d. Reneberg (25) 6–3 3–6 6–2; Edberg (3) d. Mansdorf 6–2 6–1; Steeb (13) d. Curren (19) 3–6 6–3 6–2; Shelton d. Tarango 3–6 6–3 6–3; Hlasek d. Arrese (27) 7–6 6–2; Agassi (5) d. Gunnarsson (28) 6–1 6–3; Gomez (12) d. Yzaga (21) 7–6 3–6 7–6; Courier (14) d. Witsken 6–0 6–1; J. Sanchez (30) d. Gilbert (4) 6–3 6–7 7–6; Berger (7) d. Ivanisevic (26) 4–6 6–3 6–4; Kratzmann d. Agenor (24) 7–6 7–5; Sampras (16) d. Forget 6–1 6–3; Fleurian (32) d. Becker (2) 7–6 6–1.
4th round: E. Sanchez (15) d. Lendl (1) 6–3 6–7 6–4; Jaite (10) d. Volkov 6–1 6–1; Edberg (3) d. Steeb

(13) 6–2 4–6 6–3; Hlasek d. Shelton 6–3 6–4; Agassi (5) d. Gomez (12) 6–7 6–2 6–3; Courier (14) d. J. Sanchez (30) 7–6 6–3; Berger (7) d. Kratzmann 6–0 6–1; Sampras (16) d. Fleurian (32) 5–7 6–4 6–1.
Quarter-finals: E. Sanchez (15) d. Jaite (10) 6–3 6–3; Edberg (3) d. Hlasek 6–7 7–6 7–6; Agassi (5) d. Courier (14) 4–6 6–3 6–1; Berger (7) d. Sampras (16) W/O.
Semi-finals: Edberg (3) d. E. Sanchez (15) 6–1 7–5; Agassi (5) d. Berger (7) 5–7 6–1 6–1.
Final: Agassi (5) d. Edberg (3) 6–1 6–4 0–6 6–2.
MEN'S DOUBLES – Final: R. Leach/Pugh (2) d. Becker/Motta (13) 6–4 3–6 6–3.

SUNTORY TOKYO OUTDOOR ($825,000)

TOKYO, 9–15 APRIL
MEN'S SINGLES – 1st round: I. Lendl (TCH) (1) – bye; S. Matsuoka d. A. Castle (GBR) 6–2 6–3; J. Russell (USA) d. T. Nijssen (HOL) 7–5 ret.; D. Goldie (USA) (16) d. B. Derlin (NZL) 6–4 6–1; A. Mansdorf (ISR) (10) d. C. Garner (USA) 6–2 6–2; D. Lewis (NZL) d. S. Youl (AUS) 6–3 6–4; S. Zivojinovic (YUG) d. B. Drewett (AUS) 6–1 6–1; S. Davis (USA) (8) – bye; A. Krickstein (USA) (4) – bye; D. Pate (USA) d. T. Tsuchihashi 6–2 6–3; G. Connell (CAN) d. H. Tanizawa 6–3 6–2; T. Hogstedt (SWE) (14) d. P. Vojtisek (FRG) 7–5 6–3; P. Kuhnen (FRG) d. K. Evernden (NZL) (11) 7–6 6–3; T. Woodbridge (AUS) d. R. Matuszewski (USA) 6–4 4–6 7–5; K. Jones (USA) d. C. Saceanu (FRG) 6–2 7–6; M. Chang (USA) (5) – bye; W. Masur (AUS) (6) – bye; J. Carlsson (SWE) d. J. Tarango (USA) 6–2 6–3; P. McEnroe (USA) d. N. Pereira (VEN) 6–2 7–6; P. Chamberlin (USA) (12) d. G. Bloom (ISR) 7–6 7–5; M. Srejber (TCH) (13) d. K. Masuda 6–2 6–4; A. Mronz (FRG) d. M. Laurendeau (CAN) 6–3 7–5; B. Pearce (USA) d. L. Wahlgren (SWE) 6–1 6–0; B. Gilbert (USA) (3) – bye; J. Grabb (USA) (7) – bye; J. Rive (USA) d. M. Nido (USA) 1–6 6–3 6–4; J. Canter (USA) d. D. Sapsford (GBR) 6–4 7–6; M. Kratzmann (AUS) (9) d. P. Cash (AUS) 6–4 6–7 6–4; A. Antonitsch (AUT) (15) d. J. Stoltenberg (AUS) 7–6 5–7 6–2; A. Jarryd (SWE) d. D. Cassidy (USA) 6–0 6–3; L. Shiras (USA) d. B. Garnett (USA) 6–7 7–6 6–4 6–1; S. Edberg (SWE) (2) – bye.
2nd round: Lendl (1) d. Matsuoka 6–4 6–2; Russell d. Goldie (16) 6–4 6–3; Mansdorf (10) d. Lewis 6–3 7–5; Davis (8) d. Zivojinovic 6–3 7–6; Krickstein (4) d. Pate 6–4; Connell d. Hogstedt (14) 6–4 7–6; Kuhnen d. Woodbridge 3–6 6–2 6–2; Chang (5) d. Jones 1–6 6–0 6–1; Masur (6) d. Carlsson 6–1 6–0; McEnroe d. Chamberlin (12) 3–6 6–3 7–5; Mronz d. Srejber (13) 4–6 6–3 6–3; Gilbert (3) d. Pearce 1–6 6–1 6–0; Grabb (7) d. Rive 6–1 6–4; Kratzmann (9) d. Canter 1–6 6–2 6–4; Antonitsch (15) d. Jarryd 6–2 7–6; Edberg (2) d. Shiras 6–0 6–2.
3rd round: Lendl (1) d. Russell 7–6 6–2; Mansdorf (10) d. Davis (8) 7–6 6–7 6–2; Krickstein (4) d. Connell 6–3 6–2; Chang (5) d. Kuhnen 7–5 6–2; Masur (6) d. McEnroe 6–2 7–6; Gilbert (3) d. Mronz 7–6 6–1; Grabb (7) d. Kratzmann (9) 6–4 6–2; Edberg (2) d. Antonitsch (15) 6–2 6–7 6–1.
Quarter-finals: Lendl (1) d. Mansdorf (10) 6–4 6–2; Krickstein (4) d. Chang (5) 7–6 6–1; Gilbert (3) d. Masur (6) 6–1 7–6; Edberg (2) d. Grabb (7) 6–3 6–3.
Semi-finals: Krickstein d. Lendl (1) 6–3 5–7 6–4; Edberg (2) d. Gilbert (3) 6–1 7–6.
Final: Edberg (2) d. Krickstein (4) 6–4 7–5.
MEN'S DOUBLES – Final: Kratzmann/Masur (5) d. K. Kinnear (USA)/Pearce 3–6 6–3 6–4.

INTERNATIONAL CHAMPIONSHIPS OF SPAIN ($375,000)

BARCELONA, 9–15 APRIL
MEN'S SINGLES – 1st round: J. Berger (USA) (1) – bye; O. Camporese (ITA) d. U. Riglewski (FRG) 6–2 6–3; M. Stich (FRG) d. R. Fromberg (AUS) 4–6 7–6 7–6; J. Arrese (15) d. S. Casal 6–4 7–6; C. Costa d. P. Korda (9) (TCH) 6–3 2–6 6–2; A. Cherkasov (URS) d. F. Roig 6–3 6–3; R. Azar (ARG) d. L. Duncan (USA) 6–2 6–4; A. Chesnokov (URS) (7) – bye; A. Gomez (ECU) (4) – bye; M. Schapers (HOL) d. B. Oresar (YUG) 6–4 6–7 4–5; M. Vajda (TCH) d. J. Wohrmann (FRG) 6–1 6–2; G. Lopez d. R. Agenor (HAI) (13) 6–2 3–6 7–5; P. Cane (ITA) (12) d. C. Pistolesi (ITA) 6–2 6–7 6–3; D. Perez (URU) d. D. Leppen (FRG) 6–4 6–4; A. Rahunen (FIN) d. D. De Miguel (ESP) 7–5 7–6; A. Mancini (ARG) (5) – bye; H. Skoff (AUT) (6) – bye; M. Strelba (TCH) d. H. Leconte (FRA) 6–7 6–4 6–4; M. Filippini (URU) d. J. Avendano (ESP) 5–7 6–3 6–4; S. Bruguera (11) d. T. Carbonell 7–5 6–4; J. Fleurian (FRA) (14) d. P. Haarhuis (HOL) 3–1 ret.; V. Paloheimo (FIN) d. J. Aguilera 7–6 4–6 6–3; F. Davin (ARG) d. E. Bengoechea (ARG) 6–1 6–2; E. Sanchez (3) – bye; T. Muster (AUT) (8) – bye; G. Prpic (YUG) d. V. Solves (ESP) 6–4 6–4; M. Koevermans (HOL) d. J. Anderson (AUS) 6–3 6–3; G. Perez-Roldan (ARG) (10) d. A. Volkov (URS) 6–4 6–2; J. Sanchez (16) d. J. Potier (FRA) 6–4 6–2; K. Novacek (TCH) d. M. Rosset (SUI) 6–3 6–2; M. Zoecke (FRG) d. J. Clavet 7–6 6–4; M. Jaite (ARG) (2) – bye.
2nd round: Berger (1) d. Camporese 5–7 6–3 7–6; Arrese (15) d. Stich 6–3 3–6 7–5; Costa d. Cherkasov 6–3 6–2; Chesnokov (7) d. Azar 6–4 1–6 6–3; Gomez (4) d. Schapers 6–4 7–6; Lopez d. Vajda 6–4 7–6; Perez d. Cane (12) 6–2 2–0 ret.; Mancini (5) d. Rahunen 7–6 0–6 6–4; Skoff (6) d. Strelba 6–3 4–6 6–1; Bruguera (11) d. Filippini 7–5 6–3; Paloheimo d. Fleurian (14) 6–2 6–2; E. Sanchez (3) d. Davin 6–3 6–1; Prpic d. Muster (8) 3–6 6–1 6–2; Perez-Roldan (10) d. Koevermans 6–3 6–4; J. Sanchez (16) d. Novacek 7–6 6–2; Jaite (2) d. Zoecke 6–2 7–6.
3rd round: Berger (1) d. Arrese (15) 3–6 6–3 6–3; Chesnkov (7) d. Costa 6–4 6–0; Gomez (4) d. Lopez

6–1 6–4; Perez d. Mancini (5) 6–4 6–1; Bruguera (11) d. Skoff (6) 6–2 6–3; E. Sanchez (3) d. Paloheimo W/O; Perez-Roldan (10) d. Prpic 6–2 7–5; Jaite (2) d. J. Sanchez (16) 6–3 3–6 6–3.
Quarter-finals: Chesnokov (7) d. Berger (1) 6–2 6–4; Gomez (4) d. Perez 3–6 6–3 7–6; E. Sanchez (3) d. Bruguera (11) 5–7 6–4 6–4; Perez-Rolden (10) d. Jaite (2) 6–4 6–4.
Semi-finals: Gomez (4) d. Chesnokov (7) 6–3 7–5; Perez-Roldan (10) d. E. Sanchez (3) 7–5 7–6.
Final: Gomez (4) d. Perez-Roldan (10) 6–0 7–6 3–6 0–6 6–2.
MEN'S DOUBLES – Final: Gomez/J. Sanchez (2) d. S. Casal (ESP)/E. Sanchez (1) 7–6 7–5.

VOLVO MONTE CARLO OPEN ($750,000)

MONTE CARLO, 23–29 APRIL
MEN'S SINGLES – 1st round: S. Edberg (SWE) (1) – bye; J. Arias (USA) d. G. Muller (RSA) 6–1 6–3; J. Aguilera (ESP) d. D. Nargiso (ITA) 6–1 6–3; S. Bruguera (ESP) (16) d. J. Fleurian (FRA) 6–4 6–4; J. Courier (USA) (9) d. M. Stich (FRG) 6–3 4–6 6–4; G. Ivanisevic (YUG) d. C. Bergstrom (SWE) 4–6 6–2 6–4; T. Muster (AUT) d. M. Filippini (URU) 6–2 6–2; M. Jaite (ARG) (8) – bye; A. Krickstein (USA) (4) – bye; J. Arrese (ESP) d. P. Cane (ITA) 7–6 7–5; K. Novacek (TCH) d. L. Mattar (BRA) 6–4 6–1; H. Skoff (AUT) (14) d. N. Kroon (SWE) 6–0 6–4; A. Mancini (ARG) (11) d. C. Van Rensburg (RSA) 6–2 6–4; H. Leconte (FRA) d. T. Witsken (USA) 6–1 6–4; J. Sanchez (ESP) d. F. Santoro (FRA) 6–2 6–4; A. Gomez (ECU) (6) – bye; J. Berger (USA) (5) – bye; J. Yzaga (PER) d. L. Jonsson (SWE) 6–3 6–1; T. Carbonell (ESP) d. J. Hlasek (SUI) 6–3 6–1; A. Chesnokov (URS) (12) d. G. Prpic (YUG) 7–5 6–3; G. Perez-Roldan (ARG) (13) d. D. Perez (URU) 6–2 6–3; M. Rosset (SUI) d. S. Cortes (CHI) 6–4 6–4; D. Engel (SWE) d. J. Gunnarsson (SWE) 6–0 3–0 ret.; G. Markus (ARG) – bye; E. Sanchez (ESP) (7) – bye; M. Vajda (TCH) d. M. Strelba (TCH) 6–4 6–2; G. Forget (FRA) d. P. Haarhuis (HOL) 6–3 7–5; J. Svensson (SWE) d. C. Steeb (10) (FRG) 7–6 6–3; R. Agenor (HAI) d. M. Gustafsson (SWE) (15) 6–2 6–2; P. Korda (TCH) d. Y. Noah (FRA) 6–1 3–6 6–2; C. Pioline (FRA) d. M. Srejber (TCH) 6–1 6–1; B. Becker (FRG) (2) – bye.
2nd round: Edberg (1) d. Arias 7–6 6–3; Aguilera d. Bruguera (16) 6–7 6–4 ret.; Courier (9) d. Ivanisevic 6–3 6–1; Muster d. Jaite (8) 6–3 6–2; Arrese d. Krickstein (4) 7–5 6–2; Skoff (14) d. Novacek 6–3 6–7 6–4; Leconte d. Mancini (11) 6–4 6–4; Gomez (6) d. J. Sanchez 7–6 6–4; Yzaga d. Berger (5) 1–6 6–4 6–1; Chesnokov (12) d. Carbonell 4–1 ret.; Rosset d. Perez-Roldan 6–1 7–6; Engel d. Markus 7–5 6–4; E. Sanchez (7) d. Vajda 6–1 6–1; Forget d. Svensson 6–4 5–7 6–1; Agenor d. Korda 6–3 6–2; Becker (2) d. Pioline 7–5 6–4.
3rd round: Aguilera d. Edberg (1) 7–6 7–6; Muster d. Courier (9) 6–4 6–4; Skoff (14) d. Arrese 6–7 6–4 7–5; Leconte d. Gomez (6) 6–3 6–4; Chesnokov (12) d. Yzaga 6–2 6–1; Rosset d. Engel 6–0 6–4; E. Sanchez (7) d. Forget 6–2 6–2; Becker (2) d. Agenor 6–2 4–6 6–4.
Quarter-finals: Muster d. Aguilera 6–3 6–4; Leconte d. Skoff (14) 6–2 6–7 6–4; Chesnokov (12) d. Rosset 6–3 6–2; E. Sanchez (7) d. Becker (2) 4–6 7–5 7–6.
Semi-finals: Muster d. Leconte 6–2 6–3; Chesnokov (12) d. E. Sanchez (7) 4–6 6–1 7–6.
Final: Chesnokov (12) d. Muster 7–5 6–3 6–3.
MEN'S DOUBLES – Final: P. Korda (TCH)/T. Smid (TCH) (8) d. Gomez/J. Sanchez (4) 6–4 7–6.

BMW GERMAN OPEN ($750,000)

HAMBURG, 7–13 MAY
MEN'S SINGLES – 1st round: B. Becker (1) – bye; P. Cane (ITA) d. K. Curren (USA) 7–6 6–4; A. Cherkasov (URS) d. M. Zoecke 6–2 6–2; J. Wohrmann d. A. Mancini (ARG) (16) 6–0 6–2; J. Arias (USA) d. M. Jaite (ARG) (9) 3–6 7–5 6–3; J. Hlasek (SUI) d. M. Stich 7–6 6–4; U. Riglewski d. J. Apell (SWE) 6–1 6–2; L. Jonsson (SWE) – bye; A. Krickstein (USA) (3) – bye; J. Yzaga (PER) d. M. Srejber (TCH) 6–2 6–3; H. Leconte (FRA) d. T. Witsken (USA) 7–6 2–6 6–2; J. Arrese (ESP) d. H. Skoff (AUT) (13) 3–1 ret.; F. Davin (ARG) d. C. Bergstrom (SWE) 7–5 6–2; R. Agenor (HAI) d. E. Jelen (FRG) 7–5 6–4; L. Mattar (BRA) d. C. Pistolesi (ITA) 6–4 7–5; A. Gomez (ECU) (6) – bye; J. Berger (USA) (5) – bye; P. Kuhnen d. T. Champion (FRA) 6–7 6–2 6–4; R. Azar (ARG) d. J. Fleurian (FRA) 7–6 1–6 6–4; C. Steeb (11) d. J. Sanchez (ESP) 6–4 2–6 6–4; G. Prpic (YUG) d. G. Perez-Roldan (ARG) (14) 6–0 6–3; G. Forget (FRA) d. K. Novacek (TCH) 6–4 7–5; F. Santoro (FRA) d. P. Korda (TCH) 6–2 3–6 7–6; E. Sanchez (ESP) (4) – bye; M. Chang (USA) (7) – bye; J. Aguilera (ESP) d. G. Ivanisevic (YUG) 6–4 6–1; P. Haarhuis (HOL) d. A. Mansdorf (ISR) 6–0 6–3; J. Courier (USA) (10) d. J. Gunnarsson (SWE) 6–7 6–4 6–2; M. Gustafsson (SWE) (15) d. S. Bruguera (ESP) 6–2 6–4; M. Filippini (URU) d. A. Volkov (URS) 6–2 7–5; D. Perez (URU) d. J. Svensson (SWE) 6–3 3 6 7–6; A. Agassi (USA) (2) – bye.
2nd round: Becker (1) d. Cane 7–5 6–1; Cherkasov d. Wohrmann 6–4 6–1; Arias d. Hlasek 6–4 2–6 6–2; Jonsson d. Riglewski 6–0 6–4; Krickstein (3) d. Yzaga 7–6 6–2; Leconte d. Arrese 6–4 1–6 6–2; Davin d. Agenor 6–3 2–6 6–2; Mattar d. Gomez (6) 6–7 7–6 6–3; Berger (5) d. Kuhnen 6–2 6–2; Azar d. Steeb (11) 6–2 6–7 6–4; Forget d. Prpic 7–6 3–6 6–4; E. Sanchez (4) d. Santoro 4–6 6–1 6–1; Aguilera d. Chang (7) 6–2 6–2; Courier (10) d. Haarhuis 6–1 6–1; Gustafsson (15) d. Filippini 6–3 5–7 6–3; Agassi (2) d. Perez 6–1 1–0 ret.
3rd round: Becker (1) d. Cherkasov 6–2 6–3; Arias d. Jonsson 6–1 6–2; Leconte d. Krickstein (3) 6–4

6–4; Davin d. Mattar 6–0 6–2; Berger (5) d. Azar 3–6 6–2 6–3; Forget d. E. Sanchez (4) 7–6 6–4; Aguilera d. Courier (10) 1–6 6–4 6–4; Gustafsson (15) d. Agassi (2) 7–6 7–6.
Quarter-finals: Becker (1) d. Arias 6–3 6–1; Leconte d. Davin 6–3 6–3; Forget d. Berger (5) 6–3 3–6 6–4; Aguilera d. Gustafsson (15) 6–1 6–4.
Semi-finals: Becker (1) d. Leconte 6–3 3–6 6–3; Aguilera d. Forget 7–5 7–6.
Final: Aguilera d. Becker (1) 6–1 6–0 7–6.
MEN'S DOUBLES – Final: Bruguera/Courier d. Riglewski/Stich 7–6 6–2.

INTERNATIONAL CHAMPIONSHIPS OF ITALY ($1,002,000)

ROME, 14–20 MAY
MEN'S SINGLES – 1st round: B. Gilbert (USA) (1) d. J. Pugh (USA) 1–6 6–4 6–4; L. Mattar (BRA) d. D. Wheaton (USA) 6–2 6–3; H. Leconte (FRA) d. T. Champion (FRA) 6–2 6–4; A. Mancini (ARG) (16) d. C. Miniussi (ARG) 4–6 7–6 6–4; J. Courier (USA) (9) d. F. Davin (ARG) 6–1 1–6 6–4; J. Yzaga (PER) d. J. Sanchez (ESP) 6–4 4–6 6–4; P. Cane d. F. Mordegan 4–6 7–5 6–2; A. Chesnokov (URS) (8) d. J. Arias (USA) 7–6 6–3; E. Sanchez (ESP) (4) d. A. Sznajder (CAN) 6–2 6–1; M. Filippini (URU) d. T. Witsken (USA) 6–4 3–6 6–4; T. Carbonell (ESP) d. G. Pozzi 6–1 6–3; J. Svensson (SWE) (13) d. L. Jensen (USA) 6–2 3–6 6–2; G. Perez-Roldan (ARG) (12) d. R. Agenor (HAI) 6–7 6–2 6–4; J. Fleurian (FRA) d. R. Reneberg (USA) 4–6 6–3 7–5; R. Furlan d. M. Strelba (TCH) 6–3 6–3; M. Jaite (ARG) (6) d. D. Leppen (FRG) 6–3 6–1; J. Berger (USA) (5) d. A. Mansdorf (ISR) 3–6 6–1 6–0; O. Camporese d. A. Boetsch (FRA) 6–4 6–4; M. Cierro d. C. Pistolesi 6–3 7–6; P. Haarhuis (HOL) d. S. Casal (ESP) 6–1 6–4; M. Gustafsson (SWE) (14) d. J. Arrese (ESP) 3–6 6–4 6–3; S. Pescosolido d. L. Duncan (USA) 6–2 6–3; D. Nargiso d. C. Motta (BRA) 6–3 6–2; A. Gomez (ECU) (3) d. Y. Noah (FRA) 6–1 6–7 6–3; J. Gunnarsson (SWE) d. M. Chang (USA) (7) 6–3 6–3; S. Bruguera (ESP) d. M. Srejber (TCH) 7–6 6–7 6–3; A. Jarryd (SWE) d. N. Kroon (SWE) 6–3 6–3; T. Muster (AUT) (10) d. J. Hlasek (SUI) 6–3 6–4; G. Forget (FRA) d. P. Korda (TCH) (15) 6–3 6–2; A. Volkov (URS) d. J. Aguilera (ESP) 6–3 1–6 6–4; K. Novacek (TCH) d. T. Theine (FRG) 6–4 1–6 6–4; A. Krickstein (USA) (2) d. J. Grabb (USA) 6–1 6–3.
2nd round: Gilbert (1) d. Mattar 7–6 6–4; Mancini (16) d. Leconte 6–4 6–4; Courier (9) d. Yzaga 6–3 6–4; Chesnokov (8) d. Cane 4–6 6–3 6–3; E. Sanchez (4) d. Filippini 4–6 6–1 6–2; Svensson (13) d. Carbonell 6–3 6–1; Perez-Roldan (12) d. Fleurian 6–3 6–4; Jaite (6) d. Furlan 6–4 6–4; Camporese d. Berger (5) 6–4 6–4; Haarhuis d. Cierro 6–4 6–4; Gustafsson (14) d. Pescosolido 6–4 6–7 6–2; Gomez (3) d. Nargiso 7–6 6–4; Gunnarsson d. Bruguera 6–4 6–2; Muster (10) d. Jarryd 5–1 ret.; Forget d. Volkov 6–1 3–6 6–2; Krickstein (2) d. Novacek 6–2 6–2.
3rd round: Mancini (16) d. Gilbert (1) 6–2 6–1; Chesnokov (8) d. Courier (9) 4–6 7–6 6–3; E. Sanchez (4) d. Svensson (13) 6–3 6–2; Perez-Roldan (12) d. Jaite (6) 6–4 6–3; Camporese d. Haarhuis 6–4 6–1; Gomez (3) d. Gustafsson (14) 6–4 7–5; Muster (10) d. Gunnarsson 6–3 6–2; Forget d. Krickstein (2) 6–4 7–6.
Quarter-finals: Chesnokov (8) d. Mancini (16) 7–6 6–0; E. Sanchez (4) d. Perez-Roldan (12) 7–6 6–2; Gomez (3) d. Camporese 6–1 6–2; Muster (10) d. Forget 6–2 3–6 6–3.
Semi-finals: Chesnokov (8) d. E. Sanchez (4) 6–7 6–4 7–6; Muster (10) d. Gomez (3) 5–7 6–4 7–6.
Final: Muster (10) d. Chesnokov (8) 6–1 6–3 6–1.
MEN'S DOUBLES – Final: Casal/E. Sanchez (5) d. Courier/Davis 7–6 7–5.

MERCEDES STUTTGART OUTDOOR ($825,000)

STUTTGART, 16–22 JULY
MEN'S SINGLES – 1st round: A. Gomez (ECU) (1) – bye; L. Mattar (BRA) d. M. Sinner 6–3 6–7 7–5; J. Arias (USA) d. A. Mancini (ARG) 6–4 6–3; H. Skoff (AUT) (16) – bye; G. Perez-Roldan (ARG) (9) – bye; S. Bruguera (ESP) d. U. Riglewski 7–5 6–4; G. Prpic (YUG) d. F. Clavet (ESP) 7–6 7–5; G. Forget (FRA) (8) – bye; M. Jaite (ARG) (4) – bye; K. Novacek (TCH) d. J. Bates (GBR) 6–1 6–2; A. Cherkasov (URS) d. J. Gunnarsson (SWE) 6–2 5–7 6–4; P. Korda (TCH) – bye; H. Leconte (FRA) (12) – bye; J. Windahl (SWE) d. A. Antonitsch (AUT) 4–0 ret.; J. Yzaga (PER) d. J. Fleurian (FRA) 5–7 6–4 7–6; A. Chesnokov (URS) (5) – bye; J. Courier (USA) (6) – bye; M. Filippini (URU) d. R. Agenor (HAI) 6–4 7–6; T. Carbonell (ESP) d. H. Schwaier 2–6 7–6 6–3; C. Steeb (11) – bye; M. Rosset (SUI) (14) – bye; R. Fromberg (AUS) d. T. Tulasne (FRA) 4–6 6–2 7–5; J. Wohrmann d. P. Haarhuis (HOL) 6–4 6–4; E. Sanchez (ESP) (3) – bye; J. Aguilera (ESP) (7) – bye; W. Masur (AUS) d. J. Arrese (ESP) 6–7 4–6 6–3; J. Sanchez (ESP) d. R. Vogel (TCH) 7–6 6–2; G. Ivanisevic (YUG) (10) – bye; M. Wilander (SWE) (15) – bye; F. Davin (ARG) d. C. Bergstrom (SWE) 5–7 6–2 6–4; E. Jelen d. O. Delaitre (FRA) 6–7 6–1 7–5; T. Muster (AUT) (2) – bye.
2nd round: Gomez (1) d. Mattar 7–5 6–4; Skoff (16) d. Arias 6–2 6–4; Perez-Roldan (9) d. Bruguera 6–2 6–4; Prpic d. Forget (8) 6–2 7–6; Novacek d. Jaite (4) 7–6 5–7 6–1; Cherkasov d. Korda (13) 7–6 6–1; Leconte (12) d. Windahl 6–4 6–2; Chesnokov (5) d. Yzaga 6–3 6–3; Filippini d. Courier (6) 6–3 6–2; Carbonell d. Steeb 6–3 7–5; Fromberg d. Rosset (14) 6–1 6–3; E. Sanchez (3) d. Wohrmann 4–6 6–3 6–3; Masur d. Aguilera (7) 7–6 7–5; Ivanisevic (10) d. J. Sanchez 6–2 6–3; Davin d. Wilander (15) 6–1 4–6 6–2; Jelen d. Muster (2) 4–6 6–2 2–0 ret.

3rd round: Skoff (16) d. Gomez (1) 7–5 0–6 6–4; Perez-Roldan (9) d. Prpic 6–4 6–3; Cherkasov d. Novacek 7–5 3–6 6–4; Leconte (12) d. Chesnokov (5) 7–5 6–3; Filippini d. Carbonell 6–2 6–4; E. Sanchez (3) d. Fromberg 6–3 2–6 6–2; Ivanisevic (10) d. Masur 6–2 6–7 6–4; Jelen d. Davin 4–6 7–6 6–3.
Quarter-finals: Perez-Roldan (9) d. Skoff (16) 2–6 6–3 7–6; Leconte (12) d. Cherkasov 4–6 6–4 6–4; E. Sanchez (3) d. Filippini 7–6 6–2; Ivanisevic (10) d. Jelen 6–2 6–3.
Semi-finals: Perez-Roldan (9) d. Leconte (12) 6–7 6–3 7–6; Ivanisevic (10) d. E. Sanchez (3) 6–4 6–4.
Final: Ivanisevic (10) d. Perez-Roldan (9) 6–7 6–1 6–4 7–6.
MEN'S DOUBLES – Final: P. Aldrich (RSA)/D. Visser (RSA) (1) d. P. Henricsson (SWE)/N. Utgren (SWE) 6–3 6–4.

SOVRAN NATIONAL BANK CLASSIC ($420,000)

WASHINGTON, DC, 16–22 JULY
MEN'S SINGLES – 1st round: A. Agassi (1) – bye; B. Pearce d. B. Shelton 6–4 3–6 6–2; J. Palmer d. T. Hogstedt (SWE) 6–7 6–4 6–4; G. Bloom (ISR) (15) d. L. Herrera (MEX) 6–4 6–3; D. Cahill (AUS) d. C. Van Rensburg (RSA) (7) 6–4 6–0; M. Nido d. M. Laurendeau (CAN) 6–4 6–3; J. Stoltenberg (AUS) d. M. Kaplan (RSA) 5–7 6–3 6–0; R. Reneberg (7) – bye; T. Mayotte (4) – bye; R. Krishnan (IND) d. K. Evernden (NZL) 6–3 6–1; D. Goldie d. P. Kuhnen (FRG) 6–2 6–2; T. Witsken (14) d. M. Washington 7–5 6–2; S. Youl (AUS) d. M. Kratzmann (AUS) (11) 6–3 6–4; R. Weiss d. P. Lundgren (SWE) 6–0 6–2; S. Bryan d. K. Jones 6–3 6–3; M. Chang (5) – bye; J. Grabb (6) – bye; M. Woodforde (AUS) d. P. Annacone 6–7 6–3 6–1; J. Brown d. J. Rive 7–6 6–4; G. Connell (CAN) d. M. Srejber (TCH) (12) 6–3 7–6; G. Muller (RSA) d. S. Stolle 6–3 6–3; D. Rostagno d. M. Wostenholme (CAN) 6–3 6–7 6–1; P. Chamberlin d. D. Pate 6–4 6–4; J. McEnroe (3) – bye; A. Volkov (URS) (8) – bye; M. Stich (FRG) d. G. Stafford (RSA) 7–6 6–0; N. Pereira (VEN) d. J. Ross 7–6 6–2; J. Hlasek (SUI) (10) d. A. Mronz (FRG) 6–4 7–5; A. Sznajder (CAN) (16) d. K. Flach 6–4 5–7 6–4; M. Ondruska (RSA) d. P. Baur (FRG) 4–6 6–1 6–0; E. Teltscher d. J. Tarango 6–4 4–6 6–3; B. Gilbert (2) – bye.
2nd round: Agassi (1) d. Pearce 7–6 6–3; Bloom (15) d. Palmer 6–2 6–4; Cahill d. Nido 4–6 6–0 6–2; Reneberg (7) d. Stoltenberg 3–6 6–2 6–3; Mayotte (4) d. Krishnan 6–2 6–1; Witsken (14) d. Goldie 6–3 6–4; Youl d. Weiss 6–3 3–6 7–6; Chang (5) d. Bryan 6–2 7–6; Grabb (6) d. Woodforde 6–2 6–2; Connell d. Brown 6–3 7–6; Rostagno d. Muller (13) 4–6 6–3 6–2; McEnroe (3) d. Chamberlin 6–2 6–3; Stich (FRG) d. Volkov (8) 6–4 7–5; Hlasek (10) d. Pereira 7–6 6–3; Sznajder (16) d. Ondruska 6–3 6–0; Gilbert (2) d. Teltscher 6–1 7–5.
3rd round: Agassi (1) d. Bloom (15) 6–1 7–5; Reneberg (7) d. Cahill 6–4 2–6 7–5; Witsken (14) d. Mayotte (4) 2–6 6–4 7–5; Chang (5) d. Youl 6–1 6–1; Grabb (6) d. Connell 6–4 6–4; Rostagno d. McEnroe (3) 6–3 1–6 6–1; Stich d. Hlasek (10) 7–6 7–6; Gilbert (2) d. Sznajder (16) 6–2 6–3.
Quarter-finals: Agassi (1) d. Reneberg (7) 7–6 6–0; Chang (5) d. Witsken (14) 6–3 6–4; Grabb (6) d. Rostagno 6–4 6–3; Gilbert (2) d. Stich 6–3 6–4.
Semi-finals: Agassi (1) d. Chang (5) 6–3 6–1; Grabb (6) d. Gilbert (2) 7–5 0–6 6–4.
Final: Agassi (1) d. Grabb (6) 6–1 6–4.
MEN'S DOUBLES – Final: Connell/G. Michibata (CAN) (2) d. J. Lozano (MEX)/Witsken (1) 6–3 6–7 6–2.

PLAYERS LTD INTERNATIONAL CANADIAN OPEN TENNIS CHAMPIONSHIPS ($930,000)

TORONTO, 23–29 JULY
MEN'S SINGLES – 1st round: A. Agassi (USA) (1) – bye; M. Stich (FRG) d. T. Hogstedt (SWE) 6–4 6–2; B. Pearce (USA) d. P. Lundgren (SWE) 7–6 6–2; D. Cahill (AUS) d. A. Volkov (URS) (15) 5–7 7–5 6–3; D. Wheaton (USA) (9) d. M. Washington (USA) 6–4 6–4; E. Velez (MEX) d. D. Goldie (USA) 6–4 6–4; B. Dyke (AUS) d. J. Tarango (USA) 6–2 6–2; M. Chang (USA) (7) – bye; J. McEnroe (USA) (3) – bye; G. Connell d. K. Evernden (NZL) 6–1 4–6 7–6; J. Stoltenberg (AUS) d. M. Woodforde (AUS) 4–6 6–3 6–0; A. Mansdorf (ISR) (13) d. B. Shelton (USA) 7–6 4–6 6–1; A. Sznajder d. K. Curren (12) (USA) 7–5 6–7 6–4; P. Wekesa (KEN) d. G. Pozzi (ITA) 6–2 6–7 6–2; M. Wostenholme d. K. Jones (USA) 4–6 6–2 6–4; P. Sampras (USA) (5) – bye; T. Mayotte (USA) (6) – bye; C. Garner (USA) d. B. Gyetko 6–4 6–4; P. Chamberlin (USA) d. J. Rive (USA) 6–3 7–6; R. Reneberg (USA) (11) d. G. Bloom (ISR) 2–6 6–2 6–1; J. Fleurian (FRA) (14) d. G. Michibata 7–6 6–2; D. Rostagno (USA) d. B. Derlin (NZL) 2–6 6–0 6–1; L. Shiras (USA) d. P. Annacone (USA) 6–1 6–4; J. Berger (USA) (4) – bye; P. Korda (TCH) (8) – bye; J. Hlasek (SUI) d. S. Davis (USA) 6–3 6–2; J. Arias (USA) d. L. Nemecek (TCH) 6–1 7–5; J. Grabb (USA) (10) d. U. Riglewski (FRG) 6–4 7–6; M. Kratzmann (AUS) (16) d. S. Youl (AUS) 3–6 6–4 6–3; R. Krishnan (IND) d. C. Pridham 7–6 6–4; T. Witsken (USA) d. M. Srejber (TCH) 3–6 7–6 6–4; B. Gilbert (USA) (2) – bye;
2nd round: Agassi (1) d. Stich 6–3 6–7 6–3; Cahill d. Pearce 6–4 6–4; Wheaton (9) d. Velez 6–2 6–4; Chang (7) d. Dyke 6–2 6–3; McEnroe (3) d. Connell 7–6 6–1; Mansdorf (13) d. Stoltenberg 6–2 6–2; Sznajder d. Wekesa 7–6 6–3; Sampras (5) d. Wostenholme 6–3 6–2; Mayotte (6) d. Garner 6–3 6–2; Reneberg (11) d. Chamberlin 6–3 2–6 6–2; Rostagno d. Fleurian (14) 6–2 6–2; Berger (4) d. Shiras 6–2

6–4; Hlasek d. Korda (8) 5–7 6–4 6–4; Arias d. Grabb (10) 4–1 ret.; Krishnan d. Kratzmann (16) 2–6 7–5 6–2; Witsken d. Gilbert (2) 7–5 4–6 6–2.
3rd round: Agassi (1) d. Cahill 6–2 6–4; Chang (7) d. Wheaton (9) 6–0 6–3; McEnroe (3) d. Mansdorf (13) 6–2 6–4; Sampras (5) d. Sznajder 4–6 6–3 6–2; Mayotte (6) d. Reneberg (11) 6–3 4–6 6–3; Berger (4) d. Rostagno 4–6 6–4 6–1; Hlasek d. Arias 7–5 6–1; Witsken d. Krishnan 6–4 6–4.
Quarter-finals: Chang (7) d. Agassi (1) 4–6 7–5 7–5; Sampras (5) d. McEnroe (3) 7–6 4–6 6–3; Berger (4) d. Mayotte (6) 7–6 6–4; Hlasek d. Witsken 6–4 6–2.
Semi-finals: Chang (7) d. Sampras (5) 3–6 7–6 7–5; Berger (4) d. Hlasek 3–6 6–2 6–2.
Final: Chang (7) d. Berger (4) 4–6 6–3 7–6.
MEN'S DOUBLES – Final: Annacone/Wheaton d. Dyke/Lundgren 6–1 7–6.

THRIFTWAY ATP CHAMPIONSHIPS ($1,020,000)

CINCINNATI, OH, 6–12 AUGUST
MEN'S SINGLES – 1st round: S. Edberg (SWE) (1) – bye; M. Srejber (TCH) d. J. Ross 6–4 7–6; A. Sznajder (CAN) d. R. Seguso 4–6 6–4 6–4; M. Ondruska (RSA) d. P. Korda (TCH) (16) 6–3 4–6 7–5; P. Sampras (10) d. D. Pate 7–6 6–4; J. Pugh d. M. Kratzmann (AUS) 3–6 7–5 6–0; A. Mansdorf (ISR) d. A. Antonitsch (AUT) 6–4 6–1; M. Chang (7) – bye; A. Gomez (ECU) (3) – bye; D. Goldie d. P. Chamberlin 6–4 6–4; M. Wilander (SWE) d. G. Connell (CAN) 6–4 3–6 6–3; D. Cahill (AUS) d. T. Mayotte (14) 1–6 6–4 7–5; J. Courier (11) d. K. Jones 6–3 6–7 6–3; J. Stoltenberg (AUS) d. T. Hogstedt (SWE) 6–2 3–6 6–4; N. Pereira (VEN) d. G. Pozzi (ITA) 6–1 6–3; J. Berger (6) – bye; A. Krickstein (5) – bye; J. Carlsson (SWE) d. T. Champion (FRA) 7–6 7–5; J. Arias d. A. Rahunen (FIN) 7–6 6–7 6–1; J. Hlasek (SUI) d. J. Svensson (SWE) (12) 6–4 4–6 7–5; G. Forget (FRA) (13) d. K. Curren 6–3 6–4; T. Witsken d. T. Woodbridge (AUS) 6–2 6–4; D. Wheaton d. L. Shiras 6–4 7–6; B. Gilbert (4) – bye; J. McEnroe (8) – bye; J. Fleurian (FRA) d. C. Van Rensburg (RSA) 6–3 3–6 6–3; S. Davis d. G. Muller (RSA) 2–6 6–1 6–1; A. Chesnokov (URS) (9) d. R. Krishnan (IND) 6–4 6–7 6–2; R. Fromberg (AUS) (15) d. K. Novacek (TCH) 3–6 6–4 6–4; J. Rive d. J. Bates (GBR) 7–5 3–6 6–4; R. Reneberg d. G. Layendecker 6–3 6–2; A. Agassi (2) – bye.
2nd round: Edberg (1) d. Srejber 6–4 6–7 6–4; Sznajder d. Ondruska 6–3 4–6 6–4; Sampras (10) d. Pugh 6–1 1–6 7–6; Chang (7) d. Mansdorf 6–0 6–4; Gomez (3) d. Goldie 6–3 7–6; Cahill d. Wilander 6–3 6–2; Courier (11) d. Stoltenberg 6–2 2–6 7–6; Berger (6) d. Pereira 6–2 6–7 6–4; Krickstein (5) d. Carlsson 6–2 7–6; Hlasek d. Arias 3–6 6–2 6–3; Forget (13) d. Witsken 4–6 6–3 6–3; Gilbert (4) d. Wheaton 6–3 6–2; McEnroe (8) d. Fleurian 7–6 6–2; Davis d. Chesnokov (9) 6–3 6–2; Fromberg (15) d. Rive 6–3 6–2; Agassi (2) d. Reneberg 6–4 6–3.
3rd round: Edberg (1) d. Sznajder 6–1 6–0; Chang (7) d. Sampras (10) 7–5 6–4; Gomez (3) d. Cahill 7–6 6–3; Courier (11) d. Berger (6) 6–2 6–2; Hlasek d. Krickstein (5) 6–4 6–2; Gilbert (4) d. Forget (13) 6–2 6–1; Davis d. McEnroe (8) 6–3 5–7 6–4; Fromberg (15) d. Agassi (2) 6–4 3–6 6–3.
Quarter-finals: Edberg (1) d. Chang (7) 3–6 6–3 6–4; Gomez (3) d. Courier (11) 6–1 6–4; Gilbert (4) d. Hlasek 2–6 6–1 7–5; Davis d. Fromberg (15) 4–6 6–4 7–6.
Semi-finals: Edberg (1) d. Gomez (3) 7–5 6–3; Gilbert (4) d. Davis 6–3 6–4.
Final: Edberg (1) d. Gilbert (4) 6–1 6–1.
MEN'S DOUBLES – Final: Cahill/Kratzmann (7) d. N. Broad (RSA)/Muller 7–6 6–2.

GTE US HARD COURT CHAMPIONSHIPS ($825,000)

INDIANAPOLIS, IN, 13–19 AUGUST
MEN'S SINGLES – 1st round: B. Becker (FRG) (1) – bye; B. Garrow d. D. Pate 5–7 6–2 6–3; K. Kinnear d. A. Antonitsch (AUT) 6–0 7–5; K. Curren (15) d. J. Tarango 4–6 6–4 7–6; J. Stoltenberg (AUS) d. G. Forget (FRA) (9) 4–6 6–3 6–2; K. Jones d. A. Rahunen (FIN) 7–5 6–7 7–5; R. Krishnan (IND) d. W. Ferreira (RSA) 7–6 6–7 6–4; J. Courier (8) – bye; J. Berger (4) – bye; D. Cahill (AUS) d. S. Davis 3–6 6–4 6–2; P. Wekesa (KEN) d. S. Zivojinovic (YUG) 6–4 6–4; J. Hlasek (SUI) (13) d. J. Rive 6–3 6–4; K. Evernden (NZL) d. Y. Noah (FRA) (12) 7–5 6–2; M. Laurendeau (CAN) d. M. Kaplan (RSA) 6–4 7–6; G. Connell (CAN) d. K. Flach 7–5 1–6 6–1; J. McEnroe (6) – bye; P. Sampras (6) – bye; A. Volkov (URS) d. O. Delaitre (FRA) 4–6 6–4 6–0; T. Witsken d. P. Kuhnen (FRG) 6–4 6–1; B. Dyke (AUS) d. C. Steeb (FRG) (11) 6–7 6–4 6–0; R. Reneberg (14) d. M. Kratzmann (AUS) 6–0 6–3; L. Shiras d. R. Weiss 6–2 6–4; M. Ondruska (RSA) d. S. Youl (AUS) 7–6 6–3; A. Krickstein (3) – bye; M. Jaite (ARG) (7) – bye; P. Lundgren (SWE) d. G. Failla 6–3 6–1; S. Matsuoka (JPN) d. J. Fleurian (FRA) 2–6 6–2 6–4; T. Champion (FRA) d. K. Novacek (TCH) (10) 6–2 3–1 ret.; L. Lavalle (MEX) d. G. Muller (RSA) (16) 6–4 6–4; T. Martin d. S. Bryan 4–6 6–4 7–5; R. Seguso d. J. Bates (GBR) 6–4 7–6; A. Agassi (2) – bye.
2nd round: Becker (1) d. Garrow 6–2 6–4; Curren (15) d. Kinnear 6–4 2–6 7–5; Stoltenberg d. Jones 7–5 7–5; Courier (8) d. Krishnan 6–3 6–3; Berger (4) d. Cahill 1 0–6 7–5; Hlasek (13) d. Wekesa 6–4 6–2; Evernden d. Laurendeau 4–6 6–1 7–5; McEnroe d. Connell 6–4 6–4; Sampras (6) d. Volkov 6–2 7–6; Witsken d. Dyke 7–5 6–3; Reneberg (14) d. Shiras 6–0 6–1; Krickstein (3) d. Ondruska 6–1 6–1; Lundgren d. Jaite (7) 4–6 6–3 6–3; Matsuoka d. Champion 2–6 6–2 6–1; Martin d. Lavalle 6–1 6–4; Agassi (2) d. Seguso 6–2 6–3.

3rd round: Becker (1) d. Curren (15) 7–6 6–4; Courier (8) d. Stoltenberg 4–6 6–3 6–2; Berger (4) d. Hlasek (13) 6–4 6–2; Evernden d. McEnroe (5) 6–2 6–4; Sampras (6) d. Witsken 6–7 6–3 6–4; Reneberg (14) d. Krickstein (3) 6–4 6–2; Lundgren d. Matsuoka 6–4 1–6 7–5; Agassi (2) d. Martin 7–6 6–4.
Quarter-finals: Becker (1) d. Courier (8) 4–6 7–5 3–1 ret.; Berger (4) d. Evernden 5–7 6–1 6–3; Reneberg (14) d. Sampras (6) 3–6 6–1 7–6; Lundgren d. Agassi (2) 6–4 6–0.
Semi-finals: Becker (1) d. Berger (4) 6–4 6–3; Lundgren d. Reneberg (14) 6–4 6–4.
Final: Becker (1) d. Lundgren 6–3 6–4.
MEN'S DOUBLES – Final: Davis/Pate d. Connell/G. Michibata (CAN) 7–6 7–6.

VOLVO NEW HAVEN ($825,000)

NEW HAVEN, CT, 13–19 AUGUST
MEN'S SINGLES – 1st round: I. Lendl (TCH) (1) – bye; M. Washington d. D. Marcelino (BRA) 6–3 7–5; B. Shelton d. C. Pistolesi (ITA) 6–3 7–6; D. Wheaton (15) d. M. Srejber (TCH) 6–1 6–2; R. Fromberg (AUS) (9) d. N. Borwick (AUS) 6–3 6–0; M. Woodforde (AUS) d. J. Fitzgerald (AUS) 6–4 6–2; T. Ho d. E. Teltscher 6–4 4–6 7–6; J. Svensson (SWE) (7) – bye; M. Chang (4) – bye; T. Woodbridge (AUS) d. T. Hogstedt (SWE) 6–1 6–0; B. Pearce d. P. Johnson 7–5 6–0; P. Cash (AUS) d. M. Wilander (SWE) (14) 1–6 7–5 6–3; W. Masur (AUS) (11) d. M. Schapers (HOL) 1–6 6–3 6–4; D. Goldie d. G. Layendecker 7–6 6–4 6–3; P. Chamberlin d. T. Benhabiles (FRA) 6–3 3–6 6–2; G. Ivanisevic (YUG) (6) – bye; A. Chesnokov (URS) (5) – bye; J. Anderson (AUS) d. S. Barr (AUS) 7–6 6–3; A. Jarryd (SWE) d. D. Cassidy 7–6 5–7 6–1; J. Grabb (12) d. G. Bloom (ISR) 6–3 7–5; A. Mansdorf (ISR) (13) d. M. Nido 6–1 6–1; C. Claverie (VEN) d. C. Adams 6–3 7–6; C. Caratti (ITA) d. T. Wilkison 6–4 6–2; B. Gilbert (3) – bye; T. Mayotte (8) – bye; D. Rostagno d. P. Annacone 4–6 7–6 6–2; J. Arias d. J. Yzaga (PER) 6–1 6–3; J. Pugh d. P. Korda (10) (TCH) 3–6 6–4 6–1; C. Van Rensburg (RSA) (16) d. M. Zeile (SWE) 6–4 6–1; M. Wostenholme (CAN) d. C. Pridham (CAN) 6–2 3–6 6–1; L. Herrera (MEX) d. M. Strelba (TCH) 6–3 6–3; A. Gomez (ECU) (2) – bye.
2nd round: Washington d. Lendl (1) 6–2 6–3; Shelton d. Wheaton (15) 6–2 6–4; Woodforde d. Fromberg (9) 6–1 2–6 6–4; Svensson (7) d. Ho 4–6 6–4 7–6; Woodbridge d. Chang (4) 6–3 1–6 6–3; Pearce d. Cash 3–6 7–6 6–3; Masur (11) d. Goldie 4–6 7–6 7–5; Chamberlin d. Ivanisevic (6) 6–1 7–6; Chesnokov (5) d. Anderson 6–2 6–2; Grabb (12) d. Jarryd 6–3 6–2; Mansdorf (13) d. Claverie 6–3 6–2; Caratti d. Gilbert (3) 6–4 6–4; Rostagno d. Mayotte (8) 4–6 6–4 6–3; Pugh d. Arias 6–4 6–2; Van Rensburg (16) d. Wostenholme 6–1 6–4; Gomez (2) d. Herrera 7–5 5–7 6–1.
3rd round: Shelton d. Washington 6–4 3–6 7–6; Woodforde d. Svensson (7) 6–3 3–6 6–4; Woodbridge d. Pearce 6–4 6–4;. Masur (11) d. Chamberlin 6–7 6–3 6–3; Chesnokov (5) d. Grabb (12) 7–6 6–3; Caratti d. Mansdorf (13) 5–7 7–6 6–3; Rostagno d. Pugh 6–2 6–2; Van Rensburg (16) d. Gomez (2) 7–5 6–7 7–6.
Quarter-finals: Woodforde d. Shelton 7–5 6–2; Woodbridge d. Masur (11) 7–6 3–6 7–5; Chesnokov (5) d. Caratti 6–2 6–1; Rostagno d. Van Rensburg (16) 7–5 6–0.
Semi-finals: Woodbridge d. Woodforde 1–6 6–4 6–3; Rostagno d. Chesnokov (5) 7–6 6–3.
Final: Rostagno d. Woodbridge 6–3 6–3.
MEN'S DOUBLES – Final: N. Brown (GBR)/S. Melville (USA) d. Korda/Ivanisevic 2–6 7–5 6–0.

AUSTRALIAN INDOOR CHAMPIONSHIPS ($750,000)

SYDNEY, 1–7 OCTOBER
MEN'S SINGLES – 1st round: S. Edberg (SWE) (1) – bye; N. Kroon (SWE) d. L. Wahlgren (SWE) 6–4 6–3; S. Youl d. T. Hogstedt (SWE) 6–1 6–4; M. Kratzmann (15) – bye; D. Wheaton (USA) (9) – bye; S. Stolle (USA) d. P. Chamberlin (USA) 6–3 6–3; P. Kuhnen (FRG) d. E. Jelen (FRG) 6–3 6–0; R. Fromberg (7) – bye; I. Lendl (TCH) (3) – bye; A. Rahunen (FIN) d. J. Stoltenberg 6–4 6–4; S. Davis (USA) d. S. Matsuoka (JPN) 6–7 6–3 6–4; J. Grabb (USA) (14) – bye; C. Steeb (FRG) (11) – bye; P. Lundgren (SWE) d. D. Goldie (USA) 6–2 6–4; T. Witsken (USA) d. T. Nelson (USA) 6–3 2–6 6–4; M. Chang (USA) (6) – bye; A. Krickstein (USA) (5) – bye; G. Connell (CAN) d. C. Eagle (RSA) 7–6 6–4; P. Haarhuis (HOL) d. A. Jarryd (SWE) 6–7 6–2; D. Rostagno (USA) (12) – bye; D. Cahill (13) – bye; B. Pearce (USA) d. D. Engel (SWE) 2–6 6–1 7 5; T. Woodbridge d. K. Jones (USA) 6–4 6–0; B. Gilbert (USA) (4) – bye; R. Reneberg (USA) (8) – bye; D. Pate (USA) d. B. Shelton (USA) 6–2 6–3; P. Cash d. J. Fitzgerald 6–7 7–6 6–2; W. Masur (10) – bye; K. Evernden (NZL) (16) – bye; J. Rive (USA) d. J. Anderson 7–6 6–3; M. Wilander (SWE) d. M. Woodforde 6–3 6–4; B. Becker (FRG) (2) – bye.
2nd round: Edberg (1) d. Kroon 6–3 6–2; Kratzmann (15) d. Youl 6–2 3–6 6–3; Wheaton (9) d. Stolle 4–6 6–0 6–2; Kuhnen d. Fromberg (7) 7–6 6–2; Lendl (3) d. Rahunen 6–0 3–6 6–3; Davis d. Grabb 3–6 6–3 6–3; Lundgren d. Steeb 7–5 6–3; Chang (6) d. Witsken 4–6 6–1 6–4; Connell d. Krickstein (5) 7–6 6–0; Haarhuis d. Rostagno (12) 7–6 6–4; Pearce d. Cahill (13) 6–4 6–1; Woodbridge d. Gilbert (4) 7–6 6–3;

Reneberg (8) d. Pate 6–2 6–3; Masur (10) d. Cash 4–6 6–4 6–3; Evernden (16) d. Rive 6–3 2–6 7–6; Becker (2) d. Wilander 6–2 7–5.
3rd round: Edberg (1) d. Kratzmann (15) 6–2 7–6; Wheaton (9) d. Kuhnen 7–5 3–6 6–3; Lendl (3) d. Davis 7–6 4–6 6–2; Lundgren d. Chang (6) 6–2 6–4; Connell d. Haarhuis 5–7 7–5 6–4; Woodbridge d. Pearce 6–3 4–6 6–3; Reneberg (8) d. Masur (10) 7–5 6–3; Becker (2) d. Evernden (16) 6–4 6–3.
Quarter-finals: Edberg (1) d. Wheaton (9) 6–2 7–6; Lendl (3) d. Lundgren 6–2 7–6; Woodbridge d. Connell 7–6 2–6 6–1; Becker (2) d. Reneberg (8) 6–4 6–4.
Semi-finals: Edberg (1) d. Lendl (3) 3–6 7–6 6–3; Becker (2) d. Woodbridge 7–5 6–4.
Final: Becker (2) d. Edberg (1) 7–6 6–4 6–4.
MEN'S DOUBLES – Final: B. Dyke/Lundgren d. Edberg/Lendl 6–2 6–4.

SEIKO TOKYO INDOOR ($750,000)

TOKYO, 8–14 OCTOBER
MEN'S SINGLES – 1st round: S. Edberg (SWE) (1) – bye; T. Woodbridge (AUS) d. E. Furusho 6–3 7–6; P. Kuhnen (FRG) d. S. Youl (AUS) 6–3 7–6; D. Cahill (AUS) (16) – bye; J. Hlasek (SUI) (9) – bye; P. Haarhuis (HOL) d. J. Grabb (USA) 6–3 6–4; B. Garrow (USA) d. K. Evernden (NZL) 6–3 6–4; R. Fromberg (AUS) (8) – bye; I. Lendl (TCH) (3) – bye; M. Woodforde (AUS) d. S. Matsuoka 6–7 7–6 ret.; D. Rostagno (USA) d. G. Connell (CAN) 7–6 6–4; W. Masur (AUS) (12) – bye; D. Wheaton (USA) (12) – bye; A. Rahunen (FIN) d. P. Chamberlin (USA) 7–5 6–2; S. Davis (USA) d. M. Kratzmann (AUS) 7–5 7–6; A. Krickstein (USA) (5) – bye; G. Forget (FRA) (6) – bye; B. Pearce (USA) d. D. Goldie (USA) 6–7 6–4 6–3; J. Stoltenberg (AUS) d. P. Lundgren (SWE) 4–2 ret.; R. Reneberg (USA) (11) – bye; C. Steeb (FRG) (14) – bye; E. Jelen (FRG) d. K. Jones (USA) 6–4 6–4; T. Hogstedt (SWE) d. B. Shelton (USA) 7–6 7–6; A. Gomez (ECU) (4) – bye; M. Chang (USA) (7) – bye; P. Cash (AUS) d. N. Kroon (SWE) 6–2 7–6; R. Leach (USA) d. D. Pate (USA) 7–6 7–6; A. Cherkasov (URS) (10) – bye; T. Mayotte (USA) (15) – bye; T. Witsken (USA) d. K. Masuda 6–2 6–3; R. Tsujino d. J. Rive (USA) 2–6 7–6 6–4; B. Becker (FRG) (2) – bye.
2nd round: Edberg (1) d. Woodbridge 6–3 6–1; Cahill (16) d. Kuhnen 6–4 6–3; Hlasek (9) d. Haarhuis 4–6 6–0 6–3; Garrow d. Fromberg (8) 3–6 6–3 7–6; Lendl (3) d. Woodforde 6–2 7–6; Masur (13) d. Rostagno 6–4 6–4; Wheaton (12) d. Rahunen 7–5 6–4; Davis d. Krickstein (5) 6–3 6–1; Forget (6) d. Pearce 6–7 6–3 6–3; Reneberg (11) d. Stoltenberg 6–1 6–4; Jelen d. Steeb)14) 6–3 3–6 7–5; Hogstedt d. Gomez (4) 6–4 6–4; Cash d. Chang (7) 3–6 7–6 6–4; Cherkasov (10) d. Leach 6–1 6–4; Witsken d. Mayotte (15) 2–6 7–6 6–4; Becker (2) d. Tsujino 6–4 7–6.
3rd round: Edberg (1) d. Cahill (16) 6–4 6–2; Hlasek (9) d. Garrow 6–4 6–4; Lendl (3) d. Masur (13) 6–4 3–6 6–3; Davis d. Wheaton (12) 6–4 7–6; Reneberg (11) d. Forget (6) 7–6 7–6; Hogstedt d. Jelen 4–6 6–4 6–2; Cherkasov (10) d. Cash 7–6 6–3; Becker (2) d. Witsken 6–2 6–3.
Quarter-finals: Edberg (1) d. Hlasek (9) 6–4 3–6 7–6; Lendl (3) d. Davis 7–6 6–2; Reneberg (11) d. Hogstedt 6–3 6–2; Becker (2) d. Cherkasov (10) 7–6 6–2.
Semi-finals: Lendl (3) d. Edberg (1) 7–5 6–3; Becker (2) d. Reneburg (11) 7–6 6–2.
Final: Lendl (3) d. Becker (2) 4–6 6–3 7–6.
MEN'S DOUBLES – Final: Forget/Hlasek d. Davis/Pate 7–6 7–5.

STOCKHOLM INDOOR ($840,000)

STOCKHOLM, 22–28 OCTOBER
MEN'S SINGLES – 1st round: S. Edberg (1) – bye; M. Wilander d. T. Woodbridge (AUS) 7–5 6–7 6–0; M. Rosset (SUI) d. D. Rostagno (USA) 2–6 6–2 6–2; J. Svensson (15) – bye; A. Chesnokov (URS) (10) – bye; J. Courier (USA) d. B. Dyke (AUS) 6–1 6–3; J. Hlasek (SUI) d. A. Cherkasov (URS) 6–3 6–4; B. Gilbert (USA) (7) – bye; A. Agassi (USA) (3) – bye; N. Kulti d. T. Mayotte (USA) 6–4 7–6; M. Larsson d. D. Engel 6–3 6–4; G. Forget (FRA) (13) – bye; A. Krickstein (USA) (11) – bye; M. Gustafsson d. R. Fromberg (AUS) 7–6 6–1; A. Volkov (URS) d. C. Steeb (FRG) 4–6 6–4 6–3; E. Sanchez (ESP) (6) – bye; A. Gomez (ECU) (5) – bye; D. Wheaton (USA) d. C. Wedenby 7–6 6–3; M. Jaite (ARG) d. M. Filippini (URU) 6–4 6–3; M. Chang (USA) (12) – bye; G. Perez-Roldan (ARG) (14) – bye; P. Korda (TCH) d. J. Gunnarsson 4–6 6–4 7–5; R. Bergh d. P. Lundgren 6–4 7–6; P. Sampras (USA) (4) – bye; J. McEnroe (USA) (8) – bye; K. Novacek (TCH) d. W. Masur (AUS) 7–6 3–6 6–3; L. Lavalle (MEX) d. H. Holm 6–2 3–6 6–3; G. Ivanisevic (YUG) (9) – bye; J. Berger (USA) (16) – bye; R. Reneberg (USA) d. S. Bruguera (ESP) 6–1 6–4; D. Cahill (AUS) d. K. Curren (USA) 6–3 6–3; B. Becker (FRG) (2) – bye.
2nd round: Edberg (1) d. Wilander 6–4 6–3; Rosset d. Svensson (15) 6–7 7–6 7–6; Chesnokov (10) d. Courier 3–6 6–3 7–5; Gilbert (7) d. Hlasek 6–3 7–6; Kulti d. Agassi (3) 6–3 7–5; Forget (13) d. Larsson 6–3 3–6 6–3; Gustafsson d. Krickstein (11) 6–2 6–3; Volkov d. E. Sanchez (6) 7–6 7–6; Wheaton d. Gomez 6–7 6–3 6–1; Chang (12) d. Jaite 6–4 6–3; Korda d. Perez-Roldan (14) 6–3 6–4; Sampras (4) d. Bergh 7–6 6–7 6–3; McEnroe (8) d. Novacek 6–2 6–7 7–5; Ivanisevic (9) d. Lavalle 7–6 6–3; Reneberg d. Berger (16) 6–3 6–3; Becker (2) d. Cahill 6–2 6–0.

3rd round: Ebderg (1) d. Rosset 6–4 6–4; Gilbert (7) d. Chesnokov (10) 6–3 6–4; Kulti d. Forget (13) 6–4 6–2; Volkov d. Gustafsson 6–3 7–6; Wheaton d. Chang (12) 6–7 6–2 6–3; Sampras (4) d. Korda 6–3 3–6 7–6; Ivanisevic (9) d. McEnroe (8) 6–4 6–4; Becker (2) d. Reneberg 6–4 6–3.
Quarter-finals: Edberg (1) d. Gilbert (7) 6–4 3–6 6–1; Volkov d. Kulti 6–2 6–1; Sampras (4) d. Wheaton 7–6 5–7 6–4; Becker (2) d. Ivanisevic (9) 6–4 6–2.
Semi-finals: Edberg (1) d. Volkov 7–6 6–2; Becker (2) d. Sampras (4) 6–4 6–4.
Final: Becker (2) d. Edberg (1) 6–4 6–0 6–3.
MEN'S DOUBLES – Final: Forget/Hlasek d. J. Fitzgerald (AUS)/A. Jarryd 6–4 6–2.

PARIS INDOOR ($1,650,000)

PARIS, 29 OCTOBER–4 NOVEMBER
MEN'S SINGLES – 1st round: S. Edberg (SWE) (1) – bye; A. Cherkasov (URS) d. F. Santoro 3–6 6–3 6–2; Y. Noah d. K. Novacek (TCH) 6–3 3–6 7–6; A. Krickstein (USA) (15) – bye; G. Ivanisevic (YUG) (9) – bye; M. Gustafsson (SWE) d. D. Wheaton (USA) 7–6 7–6; J. Hlasek (SUI) d. M. Wilander (SWE) 6–3 6–2; J. McEnroe (USA) (7) – bye; P. Sampras (USA) (4) – bye; C. Steeb (FRG) d. W. Masur (AUS) 6–2 7–6; G. Raoux d. M. Filippini (URU) 2–6 6–4 6–3; G. Perez-Roldan (ARG) (13) – bye; M. Chang (USA) (11) – bye; M. Rosset (SUI) d. J. Arrese (ESP) 6–3 6–1; S. Bruguera (ESP) d. H. Leconte 1–6 6–2 5–2 ret.; A. Gomez (ECU) (5) – bye; E. Sanchez (ESP) (6) – bye; P. McEnroe (USA) d. R. Fromberg (AUS) 7–6 6–7 7–5; R. Agenor (HAI) d. A. Volkov (URS) 2–6 7–5 7–5; G. Forget (12) – bye; J. Svensson (SWE) (14) – bye; T. Champion d. T. Mayotte (USA) 4–6 6–3 6–3; K. Curren (USA) d. P. Korda (TCH) 6–2 6–2; I. Lendl (TCH) (3) – bye; B. Gilbert (USA) (8) – bye; A. Mansdorf (ISR) d. M. Jaite (ARG) 6–7 6–3 6–0; M. Stich (FRG) d. H. Skoff (AUT) 6–1 1–0 ret.; A. Chesnokov (URS) (10) – bye; J. Aguilera (ESP) (16) – bye; J. Courier (USA) d. J. Grabb (USA) 7–5 6–7 6–3; R. Reneberg (USA) d. E. Winogradsky 7–6 6–3; B. Becker (FRG) (2) – bye.
2nd round: Edberg (1) d. Cherkasov 6–2 6–3; Krickstein (15) d. Noah 6–3 6–2; Ivanisevic (9) d. Gustafsson 6–2 6–4; Hlasaek d. J. McEnroe (7) 3–6 6–3 7–6; Sampras (4) d. Steeb 7–6 3–6 7–6; Raoux d. Perez-Roldan (13) 7–5 6–4; Rosset d. Chang (11) 7–6 6–4; Bruguera d. Gomez (5) 7–6 4–6 6–1; E. Sanchez (6) d. P. McEnroe 6–4 7–6; Forget (12) d. Agenor 7–6 6–2; Svensson (14) d. Champion 6–2 6–2; Lendl (3) d. Curren 6–3 6–4; Gilbert (8) d. Mansdorf 6–3 7–6; Stich d. Chesnokov (10) 7–6 6–4; Courier d. Aguilera 6–1 6–2; Becker (2) d. Reneberg 4–6 6–3 6–2.
3rd round: Edberg (1) d. Krickstein (15) 6–3 6–2; Hlasek d. Ivanisevic (9) 6–3 6–4; Raoux d. Sampras (4) 3–6 6–3 6–3; Bruguera d. Rosset 4–6 6–1 6–3; E. Sanchez (6) d. Forget (12) 7–5 6–3; Svensson (14) d. Lendl (3) 3–6 6–4 6–2; Stich d. Gilbert (8) 6–4 6–4; Becker (2) d. Courier 6–1 7–5.
Quarter-finals: Edberg (1) d. Hlasek 6–3 6–4; Bruguera d. Raoux 4–6 6–1 6–3; Svensson (14) d. E. Sanchez (6) 7–5 6–4; Becker (2) d. Stich 6–1 6–2.
Semi-finals: Edberg (1) d. Bruguera 6–3 6–3; Becker (2) d. Svensson (14) 4–6 7–6 6–1.
Final: Edberg (1) d. Becker (2) 3–3 ret.
MEN'S DOUBLES – Final: S. Davis (USA)/D. Pate (USA) d. D. Cahill (AUS)/M. Kratzmann (AUS) 5–7 6–3 6–4.

WORLD SERIES

BP NATIONAL CHAMPIONSHIPS ($125,000)

WELLINGTON, 1–7 JANUARY
MEN'S SINGLES – Quarter-finals: E. Sanchez (ESP) (1) d. R. Fromberg (AUS) 6–4 6–3; P. Cane (ITA) (5) d. G. Bloom (ISR) 7–6 2–6 6–3; K. Novacek (TCH) d. L. Wahlgren (SWE) 6–3 6–1; R. Reneberg (USA) (8) d. A. Chesnokov (URS) (2) 2–6 6–0 6–0.
Semi-finals: Sanchez (1) d. Cane (5) 7–5 6–2; Reneberg (8) d. Novacek 6–7 6–4 6–0.
Final: Sanchez (1) d. Reneberg (8) 6–7 6–4 4–6 6–4 6–1.
MEN'S DOUBLES – Final: K. Evernden/N. Pereira (VEN) d. S. Casal (ESP)/Sanchez (2) 6–4 7–6.

AUSTRALIAN HARD COURT CHAMPIONSHIPS ($125,000)

ADELAIDE, 1–7 JANUARY
MEN'S SINGLES – Quarter-finals: S. Bruguera (ESP) (1) d. M. Stich (FRG) 6–7 6–0 6–4; T. Muster (AUT) (3) d. M. Kratzmann 7–5 6–4; J. Arias (USA) d. M. Koevermans (HOL) (6) 6–3 6–4; J. Fleurian (FRA) d. J. Potier (FRA) 6–3 3–6 6–1.
Semi-finals: Muster (3) d. Bruguera (1) 2–6 6–2 7–6; Arias d. Fleurian 6–2 6–3.
Final: Muster (3) d. Arias 3–6 6–2 7–5.
MEN'S DOUBLES – Final: A. Castle (GBR)/N. Odizor (NGR) d. A. Mronz (FRG)/M. Schapers (HOL) 7–6 6–2.

NEW SOUTH WALES OPEN CHAMPIONSHIPS ($150,000)

SYDNEY, 8–14 JANUARY
MEN'S SINGLES – Quarter-finals: Y. Noah (FRA) (8) d. I. Lendl (TCH) (1) 6–1 6–4; A. Krickstein (USA) (3) d. D. Wheaton (USA) 6–1 7–6; M. Wilander (SWE) (5) d. P. Sampras (USA) 6–7 7–5 6–0; C. Steeb (FRG) (7) d. B. Becker (FRG) (2) 7–6 6–3.
Semi-finals: Noah (8) d. Krickstein (3) 6–4 7–5; Steeb (7) d. Wilander (5) 6–3 6–2.
Final: Noah (8) d. Steeb (7) 5–7 6–3 6–4.
MEN'S DOUBLES – Final: P. Cash/M. Kratzmann d. P. Aldrich (RSA)/D. Visser (RSA) (1) 6–4 7–5.

BENSON & HEDGES NEW ZEALAND OPEN ($125,000)

AUCKLAND, 8–14 JANUARY
MEN'S SINGLES – Quarter-finals: A. Chesnokov (URS) (1) d. G. Connell (CAN) 2–6 6–4 6–3; A. Mansdorf (ISR) (5) d. J. Arias (USA) 6–3 7–6; R. Krishnan (IND) d. M. Gustafsson (SWE) (3) 7–6 6–2; S. Davis (USA) (8) d. S. Guy 6–2 7–6.
Semi-finals: Chesnokov (1) d. Mansdorf (5) 7–6 6–2; Davis (8) d. Krishnan 5–7 6–3 6–4.
Final: Davis (8) d. Chesnokov (1) 4–6 6–3 6–3.
MEN'S DOUBLES – Final: K. Jones (USA)/R. Van't Hof (USA) d. G. Bloom (ISR)/P. Haarhuis (HOL) 7–6 6–0.

STELLA ARTOIS INDOOR CHAMPIONSHIPS ($540,000)

MILAN, 5–11 FEBRUARY
MEN'S SINGLES – Quarter-finals: I. Lendl (TCH) (1) d. J. Courier (USA) (8) 6–2 6–4; P. Sampras (USA) d. M. Srejber (TCH) 6–7 6–4 6–4; T. Mayotte (USA) (5) d. J. Hlasek (SUI) 7–5 6–7 7–5; J. McEnroe (USA) (2) d. E. Jelen (FRG) 6–3 6–3.
Semi-finals: Lendl (1) d. Sampras 3–6 6–0 6–3; Mayotte (5) d. McEnroe (2) 6–4 6–4.
Final: Lendl (1) d. Mayotte (5) 6–3 6–2.
MEN'S DOUBLES – Final: O. Camporese (ITA)/D. Nargiso (ITA) d. T. Nijssen (HOL)/U. Riglewski (FRG) 6–4 6–4.

VOLVO SAN FRANCISCO INDOOR ($225,000)

SAN FRANCISCO, CA, 5–11 FEBRUARY
MEN'S SINGLES – Quarter-finals: T. Witsken d. R. Reneberg (7) 7–6 6–4; J. Rive d. J. Arias 2–6 6–4 6–2; J. Grabb (5) d. C. Van Rensburg (RSA) (4) 4–6 6–2 7–6; A. Agassi (2) d. P. Annacone (8) 6–4 6–2.
Semi-finals: Witsken d. Rive 6–4 7–6; Agassi (2) d. Grabb (5) 6–2 6–2.
Final: Agassi (2) d. Witsken 6–1 6–3.
MEN'S DOUBLES – Final: K. Jones/R. Van't Hof d. G. Layendecker/R. Reneberg 2–6 7–6 6–3.

CHEVROLET CLASSIC ($125,000)

GUARUJA, 5–11 FEBRUARY
MEN'S SINGLES – Quarter-finals: E. Bengoechea (ARG) (7) d. J. Berger (USA) (1) 7–5 6–0; L. Mattar (4) d. I. Kley 6–3 6–2; A. Hocevar d. C. Motta (6) 6–4 6–1; M. Jaite (ARG) (2) d. P. Vojtisek (FRG) 7–5 6–2.
Semi-finals: Mattar (4) d. Bengoechea (7) 6–4 6–2; Jaite (2) d. Hocevar 6–2 3–6 6–3.
Final: Jaite (2) d. Mattar (4) 3–6 6–4 6–3.
MEN'S DOUBLES – Final: J. Frana (ARG)/G. Luza (ARG) (1) d. Mattar/Motta (2) 7–6 7–6.

ABN WORLD INDOOR TOURNAMENT ($450,000)

ROTTERDAM, 26 FEBRUARY–4 MARCH
MEN'S SINGLES – Quarter-finals: B. Gilbert (USA) (1) d. A. Mansdorf (ISR) (8) 6–1 7–6; M. Tauson (DEN) d. M. Gustafsson (SWE) (5) 6–3 1–6 7–6; J. Hlasek (SUI) (6) d. A. Antonitsch (AUT) 7–5 6–1; J. Svensson (SWE) (7) d. T. Hogstedt (SWE) 6–3 6–7 7–5.
Semi-finals: Gilbert (1) d. Tauson 6–3 6–3; Svensson (7) d. Hlasek (6) 6–4 7–5.
Final: Gilbert (1) d. Svensson (7) 6–1 6–3.
MEN'S DOUBLES – Final: L. Lavalle (MEX)/J. Lozano (MEX) d. D. Nargiso (ITA)/N. Pereira (VEN) 6–3 7–6.

VOLVO MEMPHIS INDOOR ($225,000)

MEMPHIS, TN, 26 FEBRUARY–4 MARCH
MEN'S SINGLES – Quarter-finals: G. Muller (RSA) d. D. Visser (RSA) 7–5 7–5; M. Stich (FRG) d. M. Washington 6–4 7–6; W. Masur (AUS) (6) d. P. Korda (TCH) (13) 6–4 7–5; G. Layendecker d. V. Paloheimo (FIN) 5–7 7–6 6–4.
Semi-finals: Stich d. Muller 7–5 7–6; Masur (6) d. Layendecker 6–3 6–2.
Final: Stich d. Masur (6) 6–7 6–4 7–6.
MEN'S DOUBLES – Final: D. Cahill (AUS)/M. Kratzmann (AUS) (3) d. U. Riglewski (FRG)/Stich (8) 7–5 6–2.

HASSAN II TROPHY ($125,000)

CASABLANCA, 5–11 MARCH
MEN'S SINGLES – Quarter-finals: G. Perez-Roldan (ARG) (1) d. T. Tulasne (FRA) 6–2 7–5; T. Carbonell (6) d. R. Azar (ARG) 7–5 2–6 6–3; G. Prpic (YUG) (3) d. J. Anderson (SWE) 6–3 6–1; T. Muster (AUT) (2) d. M. Koevermans (HOL) (7) 6–4 7–6.
Semi-finals: Perez-Roldan (1) d. Carbonell (6) 6–1 6–1; Muster (2) d. Prpic (3) 6–1 6–3.
Final: Muster (2) d. Perez-Roldan (1) 6–1 6–7 6–2.
MEN'S DOUBLES – Final: T. Woodbridge (AUS)/S. Youl (AUS) d. P. Haarhuis (HOL)/Koevermans (3) 6–3 6–1.

ESTORIL OPEN ($225,000)

LISBON, 2–8 APRIL
MEN'S SINGLES – Quarter-finals: J. Arrese (ESP) d. J. Berger (USA) (1) 4–6 6–3 7–5; E. Sanchez (ESP) (3) d. O. Camporese (ITA) 6–3 6–3; J. Aguilera (ESP) d. T. Muster (AUT) (5) 6–3 6–0; F. Davin (ARG) d. P. Haarhuis (HOL) 6–4 7–5.
Semi-finals: Sanchez (3) d. Arrese 6–2 6–1; Davin d. Aguilera 6–4 6–3.
Final: Sanchez (3) d. Davin 6–3 6–1.
MEN'S DOUBLES – Final: S. Casal (ESP)/Sanchez d. Camporese/P. Cane (ITA) 7–5 4–6 7–5.

PRUDENTIAL-BACHE CLASSIC ($225,000)

ORLANDO, FL, 2–8 APRIL
MEN'S SINGLES – Quarter-finals: B. Gilbert (1) d. J. Rive 6–3 6–3; M. Washington d. S. Davis (4) 6–3 7–5; C. Van Rensburg (RSA) (3) d. J. Stoltenberg (AUS) 6–4 4–6 6–1; D. Pate d. A. Hombrecher 6–4 7–6.

Semi-finals: Gilbert (1) d. Washington 6–2 7–5; Van Rensburg (3) d. Pate 6–7 6–3 7–5.
Final: Gilbert (1) d. Van Rensburg (3) 6–2 6–1.
MEN'S DOUBLES – Final: Davis/Pate (1) d. A. Mora/B. Page 6–3 7–6.

BANESPA RIO DE JANEIRO OPEN ($225,000)

RIO DE JANEIRO, 2–8 APRIL
MEN'S SINGLES – Quarter-finals: L. Mattar (1) d. P. Vojtisek (FRG) 4–6 6–1 6–3; M. Wostenholme (CAN) (6) d. S. Colombo (ITA) 6–2 6–2; B. Garrow (USA) d. M. Laurendeau (CAN) (5) 6–3 6–3; A. Sznajder (CAN) (2) d. P. Baur (FRG) 7–5 6–1.
Semi-finals: Mattar (1) d. Wostenholme (6) 6–3 6–1; Sznajder (2) d. Garrow 6–4 1–6 6–4.
Final: Mattar (1) d. Sznajder (2) 6–4 6–4.
MEN'S DOUBLES – Final: Garrow/S. Salumaa (USA) d. N. Aerts/F. Roese 7–5 6–3.

PHILIPS NICE OPEN ($225,000)

NICE, 16–22 APRIL
MEN'S SINGLES – Quarter-finals: A. Cherkasov (URS) d. J. Berger (USA) (1) 2–6 6–2 6–3; G. Forget d. G. Prpic (YUG) 7–6 6–2; M. Rosset (SUI) d. F. Santoro 6–0 5–7 6–2; J. Aguilera (ESP) d. J. Hlasek (SUI) 6–4 6–4.
Semi-finals: Forget d. Cherkasov 4–6 7–6 6–4; Aguilera d. Rosset 6–3 6–0.
Final: Aguilera d. Forget 2–6 6–3 6–4.
MEN'S DOUBLES – Final: A. Mancini (ARG)/Y. Noah d. M. Filippini (URU)/H. Skoff (AUT) 6–4 7–6.

KAL CUP ($140,000)

SEOUL, 16–22 APRIL
MEN'S SINGLES – Quarter-finals: G. Bloom (ISR) (8) d. R. Matuszewski (USA) 6–2 6–2; P. Cash (AUS) d. M. Srejber (TCH) (5) 6–2 6–3; D. Goldie (USA) (6) d. S. Matsuoka (JPN) 7–5 6–2; A. Antonitsch (AUT) d. P. Kuhnen (FRG) 6–4 6–4.
Semi-finals: Cash d. Bloom (8) 6–3 6–3; Antonitsch d. Goldie (6) 4–6 6–3 7–6.
Final: Antonitsch d. Cash 7–6 6–3.
MEN'S DOUBLES – Final: G. Connell (CAN)/G. Michibata (CAN) (1) d. J. Stoltenberg (AUS)/T. Woodbridge (AUS) 7–6 6–4.

SALEM HONG KONG OPEN ($185,000)

HONG KONG, 23–29 APRIL
MEN'S SINGLES – Quarter-finals: J. Canter (USA) d. T. Nijssen (HOL) 6–1 6–4; A. Antonitsch (AUT) d. P. McEnroe (USA) 6–7 6–1 7–6; P. Kuhnen (FRG) d. B. Pearce (USA) 6–2 6–2; P. Cash (AUS) d. G. Connell (CAN) 6–2 7–6.
Semi-finals: Antonitsch d. Canter 3–6 6–3 6–4; Cash d. Kuhnen 6–7 7–5 6–1.
Final: Cash d. Antonitsch 6–3 6–4.
MEN'S DOUBLES – Final: Cash/W. Masur (AUS) d. K. Curren (USA)/J. Rive (PUR) 6–3 6–3.

MADRID GRAND PRIX ($279,000)

MADRID, 30 APRIL–6 MAY
MEN'S SINGLES – Quarter-finals: J. Sanchez d. J. Baguena 6–3 6–1; M. Rosset (SUI) d. M. Gorriz 6–2 2–6 7–5; M. Jaite (ARG) (4) d. A. Mancini (ARG) (5) 6–3 3–6 6–2; A. Gomez (ECU) (2) d. M. Koevermans (HOL) 7–5 3–6 6–3.
Semi-finals: Rosset d. Sanchez 7–5 2–6 6–2; Gomez (2) d. Jaite (4) 6–3 6–4.
Final: Gomez (2) d. Rosset 6–3 7–6.
MEN'S DOUBLES – Final: Baguena/O. Camporese (ITA) d. Gomez/Sanchez (2) 6–4 3–6 6–3.

BMW MUNICH OPEN ($225,000)

MUNICH, 30 APRIL–6 MAY
MEN'S SINGLES – Quarter-finals: T. Muster (AUT) d. M. Strelba (TCH) 4–3 ret.; P. Korda (TCH) d. J. Wohrmann 6–3 7–5; J. Svensson (SWE) d. J. Courier (USA) (4) 3–6 6–3 6–4; K. Novacek (TCH) d. C. Bergstrom (SWE) 6–1 6–1.
Semi-finals: Muster d. Korda 6–3 6–1; Novacek d. Svensson 6–1 2–6 6–1.
Final: Novacek d. Muster 6–4 6–2.
MEN'S DOUBLES – Final: U. Riglewski/M. Stich d. Korda/T. Smid (TCH) (4) 6–1 6–4.

EPSON SINGAPORE ($225,000)

SINGAPORE, 30 APRIL–6 MAY
***MEN'S SINGLES** – Quarter-finals:* R. Fromberg (AUS) (7) d. W. Masur (AUS) (1) 6–4 6–4; D. Goldie (USA) (5) d. J. McEnroe (USA) 3–6 6–1 7–6; J. Siemerink (HOL) d. K. Evernden (NZL) (6) 6–2 6–1; K. Jones (USA) d. T. Hogstedt (SWE) 7–6 2–6 6–2.
Semi-finals: Fromberg (7) d. Goldie (5) 6–4 7–6; Jones d. Siemerink 6–1 6–4.
Final: Jones d. Fromberg (7) 6–4 2–6 7–6.
***MEN'S DOUBLES** – Final:* M. Kratzmann (AUS)/J. Stoltenberg (AUS) (3) d. B. Drewett (AUS)/T. Woodbridge (AUS) 6–1 6–0.

US CLAY COURT CHAMPIONSHIPS ($197,000)

KIAWAH ISLAND, SC, 7–13 MAY
***MEN'S SINGLES** – Quarter-finals:* A. Mronz (FRG) d. D. Rostagno (7) 6–3 6–2; D. Wheaton (3) d. T. Tarango 6–2 6–7 7–6; M. Kaplan (RSA) d. T. Wilkison 6–4 6–2; M. Washington (8) d. M. Wostenholme (FRG) 6–4 4–6 6–3.
Semi-finals: Wheaton (3) d. Mronz 2–6 7–5 6–2; Kaplan d. Washington (8) 6–2 6–3.
Final: Wheaton (3) d. Kaplan 6–4 6–4.
***MEN'S DOUBLES** – Final:* S. Davis/D. Pate (1) d. J. Grabb/L. Lavalle (MEX) (2) 6–2 6–3.

INTERNATIONAL CHAMPIONSHIPS OF YUGOSLAVIA ($147,500)

UMAG, 14–20 MAY
***MEN'S SINGLES** – Quarter-finals:* G. Prpic (1) d. R. Azar (ARG) 6–4 6–4; H. De La Pena (ARG) d. A. Rahunen (FIN) (6) 5–7 7–6 6–1; A. Cherkasov (URS) (5) d. E. Jelen (FRG) 6–2 6–0; G. Ivanisevic (2) d. T. Benhabiles (FRA) 6–4 7–6.
Semi-finals: Prpic (1) d. De La Pena 7–6 7–6; Ivanisevic (2) d. Cherkasov (5) 6–3 5–7 6–4.
Final: Prpic (1) d. Ivanisevic (2) 6–3 4–6 6–4.
***MEN'S DOUBLES** – Final:* V. Flegl (TCH)/D. Vacek (TCH) d. Cherkasov/A. Olhovskiy (URS) 6–4 6–4.

BOLOGNA SAVINGS BANK TROPHY ($225,000)

BOLOGNA, 21–27 MAY
***MEN'S SINGLES** – Quarter-finals:* R. Fromberg (AUS) d. G. Perez-Roldan (ARG) (1) 6–0 1–6 6–4; J. Potier (FRA) d. T. Tulasne (FRA) 7–5 1–0 ret.; F. Davin (ARG) (4) d. T. Witsken (USA) 6–4 6–0; M. Rosset (SUI) (2) d. L. Duncan (USA) 6–2 6–3.
Semi-finals: Fromberg d. Potier 7–6 6–3; Rosset (2) d. Davin (4) 6–2 6–4.
Final: Fromberg d. Rosset (2) 4–6 6–4 7–6.
***MEN'S DOUBLES** – Final:* G. Luza (ARG)/U. Riglewski (FRG) (4) d. Potier/J. Pugh (USA) 7–6 4–6 6–1.

STELLA ARTOIS GRASS COURT CHAMPIONSHIPS ($450,000)

QUEEN'S, LONDON, 11–17 JUNE
***MEN'S SINGLES** – Quarter-finals:* I. Lendl (TCH) (1) d. D. Pate (USA) 6–2 6–4; J. McEnroe (USA) (4) d. R. Fromberg (USA) (12) 6–7 6–3 7–5; B. Becker (FRG) (3) d. D. Wheaton (USA) (11) 6–3 6–3; S. Edberg (SWE) (2) d. C. Van Rensburg (RSA) (9) 7–5 6–3.
Semi-finals: Lendl (1) d. McEnroe (4) 6–2 6–4; Becker (3) d. Edberg (2) 6–4 6–4.
Final: Lendl (1) d. Becker (3) 6–3 6–2.
***MEN'S DOUBLES** – Final:* J. Bates (GBR)/K. Curren (USA) d. H. Leconte (FRA)/Lendl 6–2 7–6.

FLORENCE INTERNATIONAL TOURNAMENT ($225,000)

FLORENCE, 11–17 JUNE
***MEN'S SINGLES** – Quarter-finals:* M. Larsson (SWE) d. G. Perez-Roldan (ARG) (1) 7–5 6–4; A. Rahunen (FIN) d. J. Sanchez (ESP) (5) 6–4 4–6 7–5; L. Duncan (USA) d. T. Carbonell (ESP) 7–5 6–3; O. Camporese d. F. Luna (ESP) 6–1 7–6.
Semi-finals: Larsson d. Rahunen 6–4 6–4; Duncan d. Camporese 6–2 6–3.
Final: Larsson d. Duncan 6–7 7–5 6–0.
***MEN'S DOUBLES** – Final:* S. Bruguera (ESP)/H. De La Pena (ARG) d. L. Mattar (BRA)/D. Perez (URU) 3–6 6–3 6–4.

CONTINENTAL GRASS COURT CHAMPIONSHIPS ($225,000)

ROSMALEN, 11–17 JUNE
MEN'S SINGLES – Quarter-finals: I. Mansdorf (ISR) d. H. Holm (SWE) 6–3 6–4; R. Reneberg (USA) (5) d. D. Engel (SWE) 7–6 6–4; A. Volkov (URS) d. G. Layendecker (USA) 6–3 6–4; P. McEnroe (USA) d. R. Weiss (USA) 6–3 6- 4.
Semi-finals: Mansdorf d. Reneberg (5) 6–4 6–4; Volkov d. McEnroe 6–3 4–6 6–3.
Final: Mansdorf d. Volkov 6–3 7–6.
MEN'S DOUBLES – Final: J. Hlasek (SUI)/M. Stich (FRG) (2) d. J. Grabb (USA)/McEnroe 7–6 6–3.

INTERNATIONAL CHAMPIONSHIPS OF PUGLIA ($225,000)

GENOA, 18–24 JUNE
MEN'S SINGLES – Quarter-finals: C. Pioline (FRA) d. U. Riglewski (FRG) 6–1 6–7 6–3; T. Benhabiles (FRA) d. M. Koevermans (HOL) 6–3 6–3; O. Camporese d. L. Mattar (BRA) (5) 6–1 6–1; R. Agenor (HAI) (8) d. H. Skoff (AUT) (2) 3–6 6–1 6–0.
Semi-finals: Benhabiles d. Pioline 6–4 6–4; Agenor (8) d. Camporese 4–6 6–3 6–3.
Final: Agenor (8) d. Benhabiles 3–6 6–4 6–3.
MEN'S DOUBLES – Final: T. Carbonell/Riglewski (1) d. C. Carratti/F. Mordegan 7–6 7–6.

DIRECT LINE MANCHESTER OPEN ($225,000)

MANCHESTER, 18–24 JUNE
MEN'S SINGLES – Quarter-finals: G. Bloom (ISR) d. K. Jones (USA) 3–6 7–5 6–1; N. Brown d. M. Kratzmann (AUS) 6–1 6–3; E. Jelen (FRG) d. C. Van Rensburg (RSA) (5) 6–2 6–4; P. Sampras (USA) (2) d. K. Evernden (NZL) 6–3 7–6.
Semi-finals: Bloom d. Brown 6–4 7–6; Sampras (2) d. Jelen 6–7 6–4 6–4.
Final: Sampras (2) d. Bloom 7–6 7–6.
MEN'S DOUBLES – Final: Kratzmann/J. Stoltenberg (AUS) (2) d. Brown/Jones 6–3 2–6 6–4.

RADO SWISS OPEN ($275,000)

GSTAAD, 9–15 JULY
MEN'S SINGLES – Quarter-finals: R. Agenor (HAI) d. C. Steeb (FRG) (7) 3–6 6–2 6–2; M. Jaite (ARG) (3) d. J. Courier (USA) (5) 3–6 7–6 6–4; S. Bruguera (ESP) d. A. Chesnokov (URS) (4) 6–2 6–3; M. Rosset (8) d. E. Sanchez (ESP) (2) 6–4 3–6 6–3.
Semi-finals: Jaite (3) d. Agenor 7–5 6–1; Bruguera d. Rosset (8) 6–3 7–5.
Final: Jaite (3) d. Bruguera 6–3 6–7 6–2 6–2.
MEN'S DOUBLES – Final: S. Casal (ESP)/Sanchez (1) d. O. Camporese (ITA)/J. Sanchez (ESP) (2) 6–3 3–6 7–5.

SWEDISH OPEN ($225,000)

BASTAD, 9–15 JULY
MEN'S SINGLES – Quarter-finals: L. Jonsson d. V. Paloheimo (FIN) 6–1 6–2; R. Fromberg (AUS) (4) d. D. Perez (URU) 7–5 6–3; M. Larsson d. G. Prpic (YUG) (3) 6–3 4–6 6–3; M. Filippini (URU) d. A. Rahunen (FIN) (8) 6–1 6–3.
Semi-finals: Fromberg (4) d. Jonsson 6–4 6–2; Larsson d. Filippini 6–4 6–1.
Final: Fromberg (4) d. Larsson 6–2 7–6.
MEN'S DOUBLES – Final: R. Bergh/R. Bathman d. J. Gunnarsson/U. Riglewski (FRG) (1) 6–1 6–4.

VOLVO HALL OF FAME CHAMPIONSHIPS ($150,000)

NEWPORT, RI, 9–15 JULY
MEN'S SINGLES – Quarter-finals: P. Aldrich (RSA) d. R. Weiss 6–4 6–1; G. Muller (RSA) (4) d. J. Pugh (5) 6–3 6–7 6–3; D. Cahill (AUS) (6) d. M. Kratzmann (AUS) (3) 6–2 6–4; E. Jelen (FRG) (7) d. P. Lundgren (SWE) 6–2 6–2.
Semi-finals: Aldrich d. Muller (4) 6–4 7–6; Cahill (6) d. Jelen (7) 7–6 6–3.
Final: Aldrich d. Cahill (6) 7–6 1–6 6–1.
MEN'S DOUBLES – Final: Cahill/Kratzmann (3) d. T. Nelson/B. Shelton 7–6 6–2.

INTERNATIONAL CHAMPIONSHIPS OF NETHERLANDS ($215,000)

HILVERSUM, 23–29 JULY
MEN'S SINGLES – Quarter-finals: E. Sanchez (ESP) (1) d. O. Delaitre (FRA) 6–2 7–6; E. Masso (BEL)

d. S. Bruguera (ESP) 4–6 7–5 6–0; O. Camporese (ITA) d. R. Agenor (HAI) 7–5 7.–6; F. Clavet (ESP) d. M. Jaite (ARG) (2) 5–7 6–1 6–2.
Semi-finals: Masso d. Sanchez (1) 6–4 7.–5; Clavet d. Camporese 4–6 7–6 7–6.
Final: Clavet d. Masso 3–6 6–4 6–2 6–0.
MEN'S DOUBLES – Final: S. Casal (ESP)/Sanchez (1) d. P. Haarhuis (HOL)/M. Koevermans (HOL) (4) 7–5 7–5.

PHILIPS' AUSTRIAN OPEN ($337,000)

KITZBUHEL, 30 JULY–5 AUGUST
MEN'S SINGLES – Quarter-finals: K. Novacek (TCH) (7) d. B. Becker (FRG) (1) 6–3 6–3; H. Skoff (6) d. T. Muster (4) 6–4 6–2; E. Sanchez (ESP) (3) d. A. Cherkasov (URS) (11) 6–1 6–4; H. De La Pena (ARG) d. S. Bruguera (ESP) (8) 6–4 6–1.
Semi-finals: Novacek (7) d. Skoff (6) 6–4 4–6 6–4; De La Pena d. Sanchez (3) 7–5 7–6.
Final: De La Pena d. Novacek (7) 6–4 7–6 2–6 6–2.
MEN'S DOUBLES – Final: Sanchez/E. Winogradsky (FRA) (2) d. F. Clavet (ESP)/Skoff 7–6 6–2.

VOLVO LOS ANGELES ($225,000)

LOS ANGELES, CA, 30 JULY–5 AUGUST
MEN'S SINGLES – Quarter-finals: S. Edberg (SWE) (1) d. J. Tarango 6–4 6–4; P. Sampras (3) d. J. Stoltenberg (AUS) 6–3 6–4; M. Chang (4) d. D. Goldie 6–1 7–5; G. Muller (RSA) (7) d. B. Garrow 6–3 6–4.
Semi-finals: Edberg (1) d. Sampras (3) 6–2 6–7 6–1; Chang (4) d. Muller (7) 7–6 6–2.
Final: Edberg (1) d. Chang (4) 7–6 2–6 7–6.
MEN'S DOUBLES – Final: S. Davis/D. Pate (3) d. P. Lundgren (SWE)/P. Wekesa (KEN) 3–6 6–1 6–3.

SAN REMO TOURNAMENT ($225,000)

SAN REMO, 30 JULY–5 AUGUST
MEN'S SINGLES – Quarter-finals: J. Arrese (ESP) (7) d. G. Perez-Roldan (ARG) (1) 6–4 6–2; M. Filippini (URU) (4) d. R. Furlan 6–1 6–3; R. Azar (ARG) d. C. Mezzadri (SUI) 7–6 7–6; J. Aguilera (ESP) (2) d. O. Camporese (8) 6–3 6–2.
Semi-finals: Arrese (7) d. Filippini (4) 6–2 6–3; Aguilera (2) d. Azar 7–6 6–2.
Final: Arrese (7) d. Aguilera (2) 6–2 6–2.
MEN'S DOUBLES – Final: I. Nastase/G. Prpic (YUG) d. L. Jonsson (SWE)/Nilsson (SWE) (4) 3–6 7–5 6–3.

CEDOK CZECHOSLOVAKIAN CHAMPIONSHIPS ($148,400)

PRAGUE, 6–12 AUGUST
MEN'S SINGLES – Quarter-finals: H. De La Pena (ARG) d. T. Benhabiles (FRA) 6–2 7–6; N. Kulti (SWE) d. F. Davin (ARG) (5) 6–3 1–6 6–2; G. Prpic (YUG) (6) d. H. Skoff (AUT) (3) 2–6 6–3 7–6; J. Arrese (ESP) (8) d. C. Saceanu (FRG) W/O.
Semi-finals: Kulti d. De La Pena 6–3 1–0 ret.; Arrese (8) d. Prpic (6) 7–5 6–4.
Final: Arrese (8) d. Kulti 7–6 7–6.
MEN'S DOUBLES – Final: V. Flegl/D. Vacek d. G. Cosac/Segarceanu 5–7 6–4 6–3.

NORSTAR BANK CHALLENGE CUP ($225,000)

LONG ISLAND, NY, 20–26 AUGUST
MEN'S SINGLES – Quarter-finals: S. Edberg (SWE) (1) d. Svenson (SWE) (7) 6–4 6–2; J. McEnroe (6) d. B. Gilbert (3) 6–3 6–2; G. Ivanisevic (YUG) (5) d. P. Sampras (4) 7–6 6–3; G. Forget (FRA) (8) d. A. Gomez (ECU) (2) 6–7 6–0 7–5.
Semi-finals: Edberg (1) d. McEnroe (6) 6–1 6–4; Ivanisevic (5) d. Forget (8) 6–2 1–6 6–3.
Final: Edberg (1) d. Ivanisevic (5) 7–6 6–3.
MEN'S DOUBLES – Final: Forget/J. Hlasek (SUI) d. U. Riglewski (FRG)/M. Stich (FRG) 6–4 2–6 7–6.

OTB INTERNATIONAL ($125,000)

SCHENECTADY, NY, 20–26 AUGUST
MEN'S SINGLES – Quarter-finals: M. Jaite (ARG) (1) d. A. Olhovskiy (URS) 4–6 7–5 6–4; R. Krishnan (IND) d. C. Adams 6–3 6–1 6–4; B. Pearce d. S. Guy (NZL) 7–5 7–6; K. Evernden (NZL) (7) d. A. Mansdorf (ISR) (2) 7–5 7–6.
Semi-finals: Krishnan d. Jaite (1) 1–6 6–3 7–5; Evernden (7) d. Pearce 6–2 3–6 6–4.
Final: Krishnan d. Evernden 6–1 6–1.
MEN'S DOUBLES – Final: R. Fromberg (AUS)/Pearce d. B. Garrow/S. Salumaa 6–2 3–6 7–6.

INTERNATIONAL CHAMPIONSHIPS OF SAN MARINO ($125,000)

SAN MARINO, 20–26 AUGUST
MEN'S SINGLES – Quarter-finals: G. Perez-Roldan (ARG) (1) d. R. Furlan (ITA) 6–2 6–3; M. Filippini (URU) (3) d. P. Arraya (PER) 6–3 6–2; O. Camporese (ITA) (6) d. F. Davin (ARG) 6–2 0–6 6–3; N. Kulti (SWE) d. P. Vojtisek (FRG) 6–4 6–2.
Semi-finals: Perez-Roldan (1) d. Filippini (3) 1–6 6–2 6–4; Camporese (6) d. Kulti 6–3 1–6 6–3.
Final: Perez-Roldan (1) d. Camporese (6) 6–3 6–3.
MEN'S DOUBLES – Final: V. Flegl (TCH)/D. Vacek (TCH) d. Burillo (ESP)/M.-A. Gorriz (ESP) 6–1 4–6 7–6.

PASSING SHOT GRAND PRIX ($270,000)

BORDEAUX, 10–16 SEPTEMBER
MEN'S SINGLES – Quarter-finals: R. Agenor (HAI) (8) d. T. Nydahl (SWE) 6–0 6–1; G. Forget (4) d. L. Duncan (USA) 6–1 6–7 6–0; G. Perez-Roldan (ARG) (3) d. T. Champion 4–6 6–2 6–1; G. Ivanisevic (YUG) (2) d. F. Santoro 6–2 6–3.
Semi-finals: Forget (4) d. Agenor (8) 6–3 6–4; Ivanisevic (2) d. Perez-Roldan (3) 6–4 6–4.
Final: Forget (4) d. Ivanisevic (2) 6–4 6–3.
MEN'S DOUBLES – Final: T. Carbonell (ESP)/L. Pimek (BEL) d. M. Bahrami/Y. Noah 6–3 6–7 6–2.

BARCLAY GENEVA OPEN ($225,000)

GENEVA, 10–16 SEPTEMBER
MEN'S SINGLES – Quarter-finals: M. Tauson (DEN) d. H. Leconte (FRA) (1) 6–4 6–3; S. Bruguera (ESP) (6) d. H. De La Pena (ARG) 6–0 6–2; M. Rosset (4) d. O. Camporese (ITA) (5) 7–6 7–6; H. Skoff (AUT) (2) d. R. Furlan (ITA) 7–6 7–6.
Semi-finals: Bruguera (6) d. Tauson 6–1 6–2; Skoff (2) d. Rosset (4) 4–6 6–3 6–2.
Final: Skoff (2) d. Bruguera (6) 7–6 7–6.
MEN'S DOUBLES – Final: P. Albano (ARG)/D. Engel (SWE) d D. Lewis (NZL)/N. Borwick (AUS) 6–3 7–6.

SWISS INDOOR CHAMPIONSHIPS ($450,000)

BASLE, 24–30 SEPTEMBER
MEN'S SINGLES – Quarter-finals: S. Melville (USA) d. Y. Noah (FRA) 7–6 6–7 6–4; J. McEnroe (USA) (3) d. A. Cherkasov (URS) 6–3 7–5; V. Paloheimo (FIN) d. M. Gustafsson (SWE) (6) 7–6 6–4; G. Ivanisevic (YUG) (2) d. M. Stich (FRG) 7–6 7–6.
Semi-finals: McEnroe (3) d. Melville 6–2 2–6 6–3; Ivanisevic (2) d. Paloheimo 6–2 6–4.
Final: McEnroe (3) d. Ivanisevic (2) 6–7 4–6 7–6 6–3 6–4.
MEN'S DOUBLES – Final: C. Van Rensburg (RSA)/S. Kruger (RSA) d. G. Muller (RSA)/N. Broad (RSA) (3) 4–6 7–6 6–3.

INTERNATIONAL CHAMPIONSHIPS OF SICILY ($270,000)

PALERMO, 24–30 SEPTEMBER
MEN'S SINGLES – Quarter-finals: F. Davin (ARG) (7) d. M. Strelba (TCH) 6–2 6–4; T. Champion (FRA) d. H. De La Pena (ARG) 6–7 6–1 6–3; J. Aguilera (ESP) (3) d. C. Pistolesi 6–4 6–4; G. Perez-Roldan (ARG) (2) d. M. Vajda (TCH) 6–4 7–6.
Semi-finals: Davin (7) d. Champion 6–1 4–6 7–5; Aguilera (3) d. Perez-Roldan (2) 6–2 6–3.
Final: Davin (7) d. Aguilera (3) 6–1 6–1.
MEN'S DOUBLES – Final: S. Casal (ESP)/E. Sanchez (ESP) d. De La Pena/C. Costa (ESP) 6–3 6–4.

QUEENSLAND INDOOR ($225,000)

BRISBANE, 24–30 SEPTEMBER
MEN'S SINGLES – Quarter-finals: B. Gilbert (USA) (1) d. C. Limberger 6–2 6–4; C. Steeb (FRG) (4) d. N. Kroon (SWE) 7–5 7–5; J. Fitzgerald d. R. Weiss (USA) 2–6 6–3 6–4; A. Krickstein (USA) (2) d. E. Jelen (FRG) (8) 6–2 6–1.
Semi-finals: Gilbert (1) d. Steeb (4) 5–7 6–3 6–4; Krickstein (2) d. Fitzgerald 6–2 6–0.
Final: Gilbert (1) d. Krickstein (2) 6–3 6–1.
MEN'S DOUBLES – Final: J. Stoltenberg/T. Woodbridge d. M. Woodforde/B. Garrow (USA) 2–6 6–4 6–4.

TOULOUSE INDOOR ($260,000)

TOULOUSE, 1–7 OCTOBER
MEN'S SINGLES – Quarter-finals: F. Santoro d. C. Bergstrom (SWE) 7–5 6–4; R. Agenor (HAI) (6) d. A. Volkov (URS) 6–4 6–4; J. Svensson (SWE) d. M. Larsson (SWE) 6–4 6–7 6–3; A. Mansdorf (ISR) (8) d. Y. Noah 6–4 6–4.
Semi-finals: Santoro d. Agenor (6) 7–6 6–3; Svensson (4) d. Mansdorf (8) 6–7 6–4 6–3.
Final: Svensson (4) d. Santoro 7–6 6–2.
MEN'S DOUBLES – Final: N. Broad (RSA)/G. Muller (RSA) d. M. Mortensen (DEN)/M. Schapers (HOL) 7–6 6–4.

ATHENS GRAND PRIX ($125,000)

ATHENS, 1–7 OCTOBER
MEN'S SINGLES – Quarter-finals: M. Vajda (TCH) d. T. Carbonell (ESP) 6–3 6–3; F. Davin (ARG) (5) d. G. Perez-Roldan (ARG) (2) 6–2 6–1; J. Arrese (ESP) (4) d. J. Sanchez (ESP) (6) 6–2 6–3; M. Koevermans (HOL) (7) d. F. Roig (ESP) 3–6 6–1 6–2.
Semi-finals: Davin (5) d. Vajda 7–6 2–6 6–3; Koevermans (7) d. Arrese (4) 6–2 7–6.
Final: Koevermans (7) d. Davin (5) 5–7 6–4 6–4.
MEN'S DOUBLES – Final: S. Casal (ESP)/E. Sanchez (ESP) d. T. Kempers (HOL)/Krajicek (HOL) 6–4 6–3.

EUROPEAN INDOOR ($260,000)

BERLIN, 8–14 OCTOBER
MEN'S SINGLES – Quarter-finals: M. Sinner d. M. Srejber (TCH) 6–4 5–7 6–2; R. Agenor (HAI) (6) d. K. Curren (USA) 7–6 6–4; L. Mattar (BRA) d. J. Fleurian (FRA) 7–6 6–4; A. Volkov (URS) (8) d. J. Svensson (SWE) (2) 6–3 6–0.
Semi-finals: Agenor (6) d. Sinner 6–1 7–6; Volkov (8) d. Mattar 6–3 6–2.
Final: Agenor (6) d. Volkov (8) 4–6 6–4 7–6.
MEN'S DOUBLES – Final: P. Aldrich (RSA)/D. Visser (RSA) d. K. Curren (USA)/P. Galbraith (USA) 7–6 7–6.

RIKLIS ISRAEL CENTRE CLASSIC ($125,000)

TEL AVIV, 8–13 OCTOBER
MEN'S SINGLES – Quarter-finals: A. Chesnokov (URS) (1) d. L. Jonsson (SWE) 6–3 6–1; G. Bloom (5) d. C. Van Rensburg (RSA) (3) 2–6 7–6 7–5; J. Tarango (USA) d. M. Koevermans (HOL) (4) 7–6 6–1; A. Mansdorf (2) d. N. Odizor (NGR) 7–5 6–1.
Semi-finals: Chesnokov (1) d. Bloom (5) 6–3 6–3; Mansdorf (2) d. Tarango 6–1 6–2.
Final: Chesnokov (1) d. Mansdorf (2) 6–4 6–3.
MEN'S DOUBLES – Final: Odizor/Van Rensburg d. R. Bathman (SWE)/R. Bergh (SWE) 6–3 6–4.

LYON INDOOR ($450,000)

LYON, 15–21 OCTOBER
MEN'S SINGLES – Quarter-finals: A. Mronz (FRG) d. A. Krickstein (USA) (1) 6–4 2–6 6–4; M. Wilander (SWE) d. J. Svensson (SWE) (3) 4–6 6–4 6–3; M. Rosset (SUI) (6) d. R. Agenor (HAI) (4) 7–6 7–5; D. Pate (USA) d. G. Muller (RSA) 7–6 4–6 6–3.
Semi-finals: Wilander d. Mronz 6–2 7–6; Rosset (6) d. Pate 6–4 1–6 6–4.
Final: Rosset (6) d. Wilander 6–3 6–2.
MEN'S DOUBLES – Final: P. Galbraith (USA)/K. Jones (USA) d. J. Grabb (USA)/Pate 7–6 6–4.

VIENNA INDOOR ($225,000)

VIENNA, 15–21 OCTOBER
MEN'S SINGLES – Quarter-finals: T. Muster (1) d. A. Olhovskiy (URS) 0–6 6–4 7–6; H. Skoff (4) d. L. Jonsson (SWE) 6–3 6–4; A. Volkov (URS) (6) d. M. Jaite (ARG) (3) 6–2 6–1; A. Jarryd (SWE) d. J. McEnroe (USA) (2) 7–6 6–2.
Semi-finals: Skoff (4) d. Muster (1) 6–3 7–6; Jarryd d. Volkov (6) 6–2 7–5.
Final: Jarryd d. Skoff (4) 6–3 6–3 6–1.
MEN'S DOUBLES – Final: U. Riglewski (FRG)/M. Stich (FRG) d. J. Lozano (MEX)/T. Witsken (USA) 6–4 6–4.

PHILIPS SAO PAULO OPEN ($125,000)

SAO PAULO, 22–28 OCTOBER
MEN'S SINGLES – Quarter-finals: R. Weiss (USA) (7) d. M. Nido (USA) 6–4 6–3; J. Eltingh (HOL) d. J. Cunha-Silva (POR) 7–5 7–6; J. Yzaga (PER) (4) d. C. Garner (USA) 7–5 7–5; D. Marcelino d. L. Mattar (2) 6–7 6–2 7–6.
Semi-finals: Weiss (7) d. Eltingh 7–6 4–6 7–6; Yzaga (4) d. Marcelino 6–4 3–6 7–6.
Final: Weiss (7) d. Yzaga (4) 6–3 6–7 8–6.
MEN'S DOUBLES – Final: S. Cannon (USA)/A. Mora (USA) d. Mattar/M. Koevermans (HOL) 6–7 6–3 7–6.

DIET PEPSI INDOOR CHAMPIONSHIPS ($297,000)

WEMBLEY, LONDON, 5–11 NOVEMBER
MEN'S SINGLES – Quarter-finals: C. Bergstrom (SWE) d. P. McEnroe (USA) 6–2 6–4; M. Chang (USA) (3) d. P. Lundgren (SWE) 3–6 6–3 6–4; D. Nargiso (ITA) d. M. Larsson (SWE) 6–3 3–6 6–3; J. Hlasek (SUI) (7) d. G. Ivanisevic (YUG) (2) 4–1 ret.
Semi-finals: Chang (3) d. Bergstrom 6–3 3–6 7–6; Hlasek (7) d. Nargiso 7–6 6–2.
Final: Hlasek (7) d. Chang (3) 7–6 6–3.
MEN'S DOUBLES – Final: J. Grabb (USA)/P. McEnroe (USA) d. R. Leach (USA)/J. Pugh (USA) 7–6 6–3.

BAYER KREMLIN INDOOR CUP ($297,000)

MOSCOW, 5–11 NOVEMBER
MEN'S SINGLES – Quarter-finals: P. Korda (TCH) d. A. Jarryd (SWE) 7–5 7–6; T. Mayotte (USA) d. A. Volkov (5) 6–3 6–2; U. Riglewski (FRG) d. S. Casal (ESP) 4–6 7–6 6–3; A. Cherkasov (8) d. E. Sanchez (ESP) (2) 6–3 6–3.
Semi-finals: Mayotte d. Korda 7–6 3–6 6–3; Cherkasov (8) d. Riglewski 6–1 7–6.
Final: Cherkasov (8) d. Mayotte 6–2 6–1.
MEN'S DOUBLES – Final: H.-J. Davids (HOL)/P. Haarhuis (HOL) d. J. Fitzgerald (AUS)/A. Jarryd (SWE) 6–4 7–6.

CITIBANK ITAPARICA OPEN ($225,000)

ITAPARICA, 5–11 NOVEMBER
MEN'S SINGLES – Quarter-finals: M. Filippini (URU) (7) d. N. Marques (POR) 6–3 3–6 2–6; T. Carbonell (ESP) d. C. Motta 6–3 7–5; M. Wilander (SWE) (5) d. A. Sznajder (CAN) 6–1 6–0; M. Koevermans (HOL) d. M. Ruah (VEN) 7–6 6–3.
Semi-finals: Filippini (7) d. Carbonell 7–6 6–4; Wilander (5) d. Koevermans 6–4 6–3.
Final: Wilander (5) d. Filippini (7) 6–1 6–2.
MEN'S DOUBLES – Final: M. Menezes/F. Roese d. Carbonell/M.-A. Gorriz (ESP) 7–6 7–5.

Guillermo Perez-Roldan of Argentina won his sixth career title last year in San Marino to finish the year ranked No. 14, his best ever. (Professional Sport)

The colourful American, Andre Agassi, who had competed sparingly in 1990 and had lost in two Grand Slam finals, ended the year spectacularly by beating Becker and Edberg to claim the first ATP Tour Championship. *(R. Adams)*

ATP TOUR WORLD CHAMPIONSHIP
John Barrett

At the end of a season that had brought him major disappointments in the finals of the French and US Opens, Andre Agassi at last enjoyed his hour of glory. To the delight of the 8,500 fans packed into Frankfurt's *Festhalle*, the colourful, 20-year-old American became the first ATP Tour World Champion as he outhit the world's No. 1, Stefan Edberg of Sweden, to win their hard-fought final in 3¼ hours, 5–7 7–6 7–5 6–2.

This reversed their round-robin result of four days earlier and revealed once more the anomalies that can occur in a group system. Ironically, the previous year in New York it was Edberg who had won the last Nabisco Masters by beating Boris Becker in the final after losing to him in round-robin play. It is also interesting to recall that Agassi, playing then for the second time in the Masters and facing derision for his psychedelic pink bicycling shorts and a long pink fingernail, had lost easily to Edberg and Becker and had won only one set (against Brad Gilbert) in finishing fourth in his group.

The Las Vegas showman had come a long way in twelve months. Without a false fingernail but dressed now in bright lime-green and black, Agassi was as colourful as ever. But he was also a much better player. This, he said, was mainly due to his greatly improved physique. 'Gil Reyes has helped me to put on 20 pounds since last December. I've worked a lot with weights to help my strength and quickness. A year ago I would not have been able to lift 135 pounds from the bench 1 or 2 times. Before coming here I lifted 245 pounds 3 times.' The result was there for all to see. Not only was he quicker than ever and hitting his groundstrokes with as much pace as before, but he was now serving with astonishing power for a man of 5'10". He was also lasting better and at the end of the final it was Edberg who was tiring, not Agassi.

The presence of Becker among the exclusive eight who gathered in Frankfurt for the season-ending showdown – the first time since Stockholm in 1975 that it had been held in Europe – was in doubt until the last moment. A leg injury that had forced the German No. 1 to retire during the first set of his final against Edberg in Paris eight days earlier was requiring intensive physiotherapy treatment from the national football trainer Hans Montag in Munich.

Becker, whose late season bid to oust Edberg from the No. 1 ranking spot had brought him to a magnificent peak in Stockholm the week before Paris, had requested a Wednesday start so that he could have a late fitness test on the Tuesday. Accordingly he was absent when the other seven men, plus the alternate, Goran Ivanisevic of Yugoslavia, gathered on the Monday at the *Festhalle* to meet the media.

The two groups, named after the first two ATP Presidents, contained the top eight men on the IBM/ATP Tour ranking list at the end of a gruelling 11-month season that had included 74 tournaments plus the World Team Cup in 26 countries on 6 continents. In the Arthur Ashe group, along with Edberg (1) and Agassi (4), were the Californian Pete Sampras (5), who two months earlier had beaten Agassi to become the youngest ever US Open champion, and the lone Spaniard, Emilio Sanchez (8). In the Cliff Drysdale group with Becker (2) were Ivan Lendl (3) the Greenwich-based Czech, Andres Gomez (6), the left-hander from Ecuador who at 30 years, 8 months and 14 days was 7 days Lendl's senior and the oldest of the competitors, plus the Austrian left-hander, Thomas Muster (7). In practice Lendl had looked sharp and fast, his confidence truly restored after beating Edberg and Becker back-to-back to win the Seiko title in Tokyo a month earlier. Gomez, the reigning French champion, had become the uncrowned king of Ecuador as a result of that remarkable win over Agassi, but had done nothing of note since. The gritty

Muster was the subject of everyone's admiration. Here he was, miraculously back in the top ten only 20 months after having the ligaments in his left knee severed by a hit-and-run drunk driver in Miami. He is a living example of what courage and determination can achieve.

Besides the prize money of $2,020,000, there were also ranking points at stake for the first time at a season ending play-off. The fairness of this innovation is questionable. It merely makes the positions of the leading players more secure and further increases suspicions among the rank and file membership that their interests are being ignored.

The first day of round-robin play on the Tuesday produced a surprisingly hard 6–7 6–3 6–1 victory for Edberg over Sanchez, and two one-sided wins. Agassi simply outhit Sampras, who was suffering from shin splints, to win 4–2 4–2 and Lendl overpowered Muster 6–3 6–3. On the Wednesday a much improved Sampras served too well for Sanchez and beat him 6–2 6–4 thus keeping his hopes alive. Becker, competing for the first time after his break, started slowly against Gomez but came back strongly to win 4–6 6–3 6–3. Then Edberg, moving like a lithe panther, produced his finest tennis of the year to thwart an inspired Agassi 7–6 4–6 7–6. This was the match of the tournament, played at a blinding pace by two men who were determined to end their year on a high note. They had met twice in 1990. Edberg had won the Indian Wells final in four sets and 10 days later the American had gained his revenge in the title round at Key Biscayne.

Agassi's serve was a revelation, transformed from the rather ordinary delivery we had seen at Flushing Meadow. He served countless unreturnable first serves in the early part of the match and 5 aces altogether. Thus he was able to take advantage of the fast Supreme Court carpet and the fast *Dunlop* balls to show us just how well he can volley. The American was also timing his returns so well and taking them so early, that Edberg, normally the finest first volleyer in the business, was increasingly forced to stay back on his second deliveries. Nevertheless, when the issue became critical in the final set the athletic Swede was masterly in his ability to hit his winners on the full run. A 2–0 lead to Agassi became 3–1, then 3–2 as Edberg held to 30. Agassi's wild backhand return when ahead 15–30 on Edberg's serve and another unforced error signalled a tightening of his arm. It was no surprise when, in the next game two flailing forehands and another reckless backhand cost him his serve. Edberg gave a little skip of determination as he headed towards the chair, knowing he had his man. It still took a determined effort in the tie-break finally to quell him. Agassi actually led 4 points to 2 but Edberg stormed back. He delivered his third ace and forced three errors from Agassi's now desperate racket. Leading 6–4, Edberg shook his head as yet another blazing return shot past him. After 2 hours and 34 sweating minutes the dripping Edberg threw in one last heavy serve – and it was over. The two players thoroughly deserved their standing ovation.

The Thursday matches were quite straightforward. Lendl dismissed Gomez 6–4 6–1 and Becker seemed to be finding his touch as he inflicted a 7–5 6–4 defeat on the plucky Muster. Agassi reacted well from his defeat the previous day and thrashed a now resigned Sanchez 6–0 6–3.

There were two key encounters on the Friday, as well as Muster's battle with Gomez to decide who would receive the wooden spoon in the Drysdale group. The first, between Becker and Lendl who were both undefeated, would decide the leadership of that group. The second, between Edberg and Sampras, would settle the outcome of the Ashe group. If Edberg won then he and Agassi would go through to the semi-finals; furthermore, the Swede's position as the No. 1 ranked player for 1990 would be unassailable, regardless of what Becker did. If Edberg lost it would be Agassi and Sampras who would proceed.

Again Becker started slowly against Lendl. After losing the opening set 1–6 the German began to hit his serve better and lost only 7 points on it in the next six service games. In the tie-break he was rock-solid and won it 7–2. The final set produced some great tennis from both men who were now serving with impressive authority. Suddenly, at 4–4, Becker struck. As Lendl served at 15–0 Becker smote a fierce crosscourt backhand return. '15-all', called umpire Gerry Armstrong. Another fierce return forced Lendl's backhand volley into the net. '15–30'. Running now to his forehand, Becker smote a full-blooded forehand which clipped the top of the net and flew past Lendl for a winner. '15–40', called

Armstrong. Another winning forehand return completed the job. Once again Becker had found the winning formula at just the right moment. It was, perhaps, unlucky for Lendl that in the next game Becker, serving at 40–15, should deliver his 13th ace. Thus Becker won his group and waited to see who he would play in the semi-finals. And Edberg made no mistake against a much improved Sampras. Serving near his best, the Swede inflicted a 7–5 6–4 defeat on the young Californian whom he had beaten in July in the semi-finals at Los Angeles, their only previous meeting. So it was that Edberg confirmed his status as the world's No. 1, a position he had first achieved on 13th August.

The last of the round-robin matches, in which Muster defeated Gomez 7–5 5–7 6–4, was a difficult one for both men to play. They were both striving to avoid a whitewash and the tennis was scrappy. Financially, though, there was a lot at stake – $50,000 to be precise, the sum awarded for each round robin win. The alternate, Ivanisevic, received $20,000 for the inconvenience of standing by while the eight main contenders were guaranteed a sum of $50,000 as a starting fee. The two semi-final winners would each receive a further $200,000 and the winner of the final would earn another $600,000. Thus, an undefeated winner would take home a prize of $1 million.

The favourite to do that was Edberg. Like Lendl and Becker, he was playing in the semi-finals of the season-ending play-off for the fourth time in five years. As the Nabisco Champion there was an extra incentive and the manner of his win against Agassi, who was in the last four for the first time, had suggested he would dismiss the challenge of Lendl relatively easily. So it proved. The Swede's powerful game flowed with easy confidence to deny Lendl the time he needs to make his shots. From his opening service game, which was lost to 30, the former world champion was made to look ponderous as he went down 6–4 6–2 in 76 brief minutes. In the first four games of the second set, during which golden spell Edberg won 16 of the first 18 points, the tall Swede seemed to have supernatural powers of anticipation. He was everywhere, hitting winning passes on the run, volleying to sharp angles or returning the Lendl serves brutally early. It was the masterly performance of a man relishing his secure position atop the world rankings. Thus Edberg went ahead 5–4 in his 1990 encounters against Lendl and reduced to 9–11 his career deficit against his old rival.

Earlier in the day Becker had faced Agassi in the first semi-final. During 1990 the German had won 25 of the 27 matches he had played on an indoor carpet and many thought he would add to that tally. After his humiliating defeat at the American's hands in the semi-final of the US Open when, as holder, he had attempted, without success, to play Agassi from the back of the court, everyone expected to see Becker launch an all-out net attack. For a while he attempted to do just that. But so fierce and so early were the Agassi returns, so accurate his early-ball counter-hitting passes – single-handed on the forehand, double-handed on the backhand – that the German was simply forced to stay back. Losing two of his first three service games, Becker looked shell-shocked. When Agassi wrapped up the set 6–2 in 33 minutes the American had lost only 3 points in his four service games – and one of those had been a double-fault!

Agassi's serve continued to embarrass Becker in the second set. Breaking for 2–1 the American held to love, served two consecutive aces in the 6th game as another love game took him to 4–2 and then held service twice more to complete his 6–2 6–4 win in 78 minutes. Altogether Agassi had served eight aces in 9 service games which had cost him a miserly eight points, three of which had been lost in the last game of the match. It had been an awesome display by a man who was coming to a peak at exactly the right moment, as his long-time coach Nick Bollettieri had forecast and as his brother Philip, sitting alongside Bollettieri and Gil Reyes in the courtside box, had hoped he would.

After such a thrashing it was not altogether surprising that Becker refused to attend the obligatory post match press conference. He preferred to pay the fine of $1,000 to the humiliation of exposing his bruised ego to public analysis.

The final between Edberg and Agassi, though not quite as good technically as their round-robin match had been, was a triumph for the American. His lightning fast thrust that took him to 4–1 in the first set had been parried by Edberg who broke twice to lead 5–4. All sorts of doubts about Agassi's belief were resurrected. If Edberg had closed out the set there and then, he might have won. As it was he lost his serve and only clinched the set two games later. Again, if the 1989 Master had converted one of the three points he held to break Agassi in the opening game of the second set, he might have kept the momentum going. But the little American was bouncing back from each threat with great spirit. He survived another break point in the 11th game and then won the tie-break 7 points to 5 with a glorious crosscourt forehand volley.

There were two early breaks in the third set, one each way, and then Agassi again held off two break points in the 8th game. When, three games later, Edberg was trapped by a perfect lob to go 0–30 down he looked anxious. The two consecutive double faults he delivered to lose his serve and go 5–6 down, were just the encouragement Agassi needed. Two aces by the American launched his successful bid for the third set and from that moment a tiring Edberg looked a beaten man. From 1–2 in the fourth set Agassi reeled off four games in a row to claim the most important title of his young life. He had beaten the Nos. 1 and 2 players in the world on a fast surface that should have suited them, and he did it by outpacing them!

It was a pity, then, that this controversial figure should have listened to bad advice and used the platform of the ATP Tour Championships to announce his withdrawal from the *Compaq Grand Slam Cup.*

Agassi said he was aware that by breaking a signed contract he would face a possible fine of $25,000, plus debarment from one or more of the four Grand Slam Championships in 1991 as well as from next Year's *Grand Slam Cup.* 'I hope you don't think I'm that stupid!', he had said. However, many people were not sure about that. If Agassi was not aware that a signed contract should be honoured, how else should he be viewed?

There were three other announcements during the week that promised a stronger and healthier world circuit in 1991 and beyond. After meetings with the Women's Tennis Association, Mark Miles, the Chief Executive Officer of the ATP Tour, explained that the two bodies had formed a joint scheduling committee that would prevent a clash between the two season-ending Championships, as had occurred in 1990. Furthermore there would be a unified approach to the rules and to testing for drugs, the latter in collaboration with the International Tennis Federation. In 1991 the 25 second rule between points, the 90 second rule at change-overs and the three-step rule towards disqualification for on-court code violations (not including time violations) would apply to both tours.

The second announcement concerned an initiative to raise millions of dollars for selected charities. Edberg was nominated by his peers to serve as the International Chairman of an IBM/ATP Tour Charity Programme that would guarantee a minimum of $250,000 in direct contributions, thanks to generous support from IBM. In addition individual players would be encouraged to create their own fund-raising activities, as Edberg himself had done with the North Shore hospital on Long Island and Yannick Noah had done with his *Enfants de la Terre* organisation in France.

Finally there was news about an IBM initiative that would revolutionize the statistical coverage of the men's Tour. From January 1st 1991 the IBM *MatchFacts* system would go into effect at every one of the 3,000 or so matches that would be played in the 75 tournaments of the 1991 IBM/ATP Tour. By having the umpire fill in a newly designed scoresheet, which would then be scanned by computer, it would be possible to analyze the performance of every player in 10 main categories. These would all be matters of fact, like the number of aces and double faults served, the percentage of points won against an opponent's first serve, the number of break points converted, and so on. By eliminating personal judgements the data collected will be as accurate as the efficiency of the umpire when he makes his entries. In time there would be a database of information that would enable us to compare the great players of every era – a fascinating prospect and a technical triumph. All in all, the first year of the ATP Tour had been a qualified success.

ATP TOUR WORLD CHAMPIONSHIP ($2,020,000)

FRANKFURT, 12–18 NOVEMBER
ROUND ROBIN SECTION – *Arthur Ashe Group:* **1st:** S. Edberg (SWE) d. E. Sanchez 6–7 6 .3 6–1, d. Agassi 7–6 4–6 7–6, d. Sampras 7–5 6–4; **2nd:** A. Agassi (USA) d. Sampras 6–4 6–2, d. E. Sanchez 6–0 6–3; **3rd:** P. Sampras (USA) d. E. Sanchez 6–2 6–4; **4th:** E. Sanchez (ESP). *Cliff Drysdale Group:* **1st:** B. Becker (FRG) d. Gomez 4–6 6–3 6–3, d. Muster 7–5 6–4, d. Lendl 1–6 7–6 6–4; **2nd:** I. Lendl (TCH) d. Muster 6–3 6–3, d. Gomez 6–4 6–1; **3rd:** T. Muster (AUT) d. Gomez 7–5 5–7 6–4; **4th:** A. Gomez (ECU).
PLAY-OFFS – *Semi-finals:* Edberg d. Lendl 6–4 6–2; Agassi d. Becker 6–2 6–4. *Final:* Agassi d. Edberg 5–7 7–6 7–5 6–2.

ATP TOUR WORLD DOUBLES FINAL ($1,000,000)

SANCTUARY COVE, 19–25 NOVEMBER
ROUND ROBIN SECTION – *Newcombe/Roche Group:* **1st:** G. Forget (FRA)/J. Hlasek (SUI) d. Connell/Michibata 6–3 7–6, d. Aldrich/Visser 6–3 7–5, d. Cahill/Kratzmann 6–2 7–6; **2nd:** G. Connell (CAN)/G. Michibata (CAN) d. Cahill/Kratzmann 6–4 5–7 6–4, d. Aldrich/Visser 6–2 7–6; **3rd:** P. Aldrich (RSA)/D. Visser (RSA) d. Cahill/Kratzmann 6–4 6–2; **4th:** D. Cahill (AUS)/M. Kratzmann (AUS). *Hoad/Rosewall Group:* **1st=:** S. Davis (USA)/D. Pate (USA) d. Broad/Muller 6–2 6–2, d. Leach/Pugh 7–6 3–6 6–4; **1st=;** S. Casal (ESP)/E. Sanchez (ESP) d. Broad/Muller 6–7 6–3 7–6, d. Davis/Pate 6–3 7–6; **3rd=:** R. Leach (USA)/J. Pugh (USA) d. Casal/E. Sanchez 6–4 6–2; **3rd=:** N. Broad (RSA)/G. Muller (RSA) d. Leach/Pugh 6–7 6–4 7–6.
PLAY-OFFS – *Semi-finals:* Casal/E. Sanchez d. Connell/Michibata 6–4 6–7 6–4 6–7 6–3; Forget/Hlasek d. Davis/Pate 3–6 4–6 6–4 7–6 6–4. *Final:* Forget/Hlasek d. Casal/E. Sanchez 6–4 7–6 5–7 6–4.

Jakob Hlasek (left) of Switzerland teamed with Frenchman Guy Forget to win the inaugural ATP Tour Doubles Championship at Sanctuary Cove, Australia, for which event they shaved their heads. (M. Cole)

By special dispensation, Jennifer Capriati competed on the women's tour shortly before her 14th birthday and proceeded to terrorize her seniors as she shot to No. 8 in the world rankings by the year's end. *(Professional Sport)*

KRAFT GENERAL FOODS WORLD TOUR

TOUR REVIEW
POINTS EXPLANATION
KRAFT GENERAL FOODS SERIES TOURNAMENTS
VIRGINIA SLIMS CHAMPIONSHIPS

The 19-year-old American Mary Joe Fernandez had victories in Tokyo and Filderstadt in 1990 as she lifted her ranking to a career high of No. 4 by the year's end.   *(R. Adams)*

After the excitement of 1989 when she had won the French Open, Arantxa Sanchez-Vicario of Spain had a year of consolidation in 1990 when she reached seven finals and won two of them – in Barcelona and Newport. (M. Cole)

THE KRAFT GENERAL FOODS WORLD TOUR
Barry Wood

The first year in which overall sponsorship of the women's circuit came under the umbrella of Kraft General Foods was arguably the most exciting in the game's history. For the first time since 1981 four different players claimed the Grand Slams titles, and the challenge from the younger generation reached new heights with the emergence of 14-year-old Jennifer Capriati as a player of world class.

Monica Seles confirmed herself as a major force despite a disasterous start to the year in which she won only two matches in her first three tournaments. At least part of the reason for her run of defeats was that she had grown much taller in a short space of time, and was unfamiliar with the new court dimensions the extra inches presented to her. Once she had become reorientated she was almost invincible. Titles at the Lipton International, the US Hardcourts, the Eckerd Open, the Italian Open and the German Open all followed, all without the loss of a set. Then came the French Championships and she took that title too, the youngest player ever to do so. The European events were especially interesting, for Seles brushed aside Martina Navratilova in the Italian final (admittedly on the American's least favourite surface), before going on to defeat Steffi Graf in both Berlin and Paris. The first of those wins ended Graf's bid to overtake Navratilova's winning streak of 74 matches, set in 1984. Instead, Graf had to be satisfied with a run of 66 matches, stretching from the 1989 French Open final which she had lost to Arantxa Sanchez-Vicario.

Seles slipped up only briefly during her remaining tournaments, but two of those defeats came in Grand Slams. She was beaten by Zina Garrison in the quarter-finals at Wimbledon and by Linda Ferrando in the 3rd round of the US Open, and she fell to Amy Frazier in Tokyo in September. But she also defeated Navratilova for the Los Angeles title, and beat her again in Oakland in the Virginia Slims of California final. Monica rounded off 1990 by defeating Gabriela Sabatini in five sets at the Virginia Slims Championships and by reaching the semi-finals of that event she replaced Navratilova as the world's number 2.

Navratilova was missing from New York that week. Calcium deposits on both knees had almost forced her to miss the Oakland final, and for the first time in her career she had to succumb to surgery. It marked a disappointing end to a wonderful year in which she had become the first player ever to win nine Wimbledon titles. She also won a further five singles titles and five double titles, including the US Open with Gigi Fernandez. That particular result, over Jana Novotna and Helena Sukova, ended the Grand Slam hopes of the Czech pair, who until that point had remained undefeated in 1990. Their aura of invincibility was gone after that, and the year ended on a sour note as they suffered early losses in their remaining three tournaments. The partnership split, with Novotna ironically linking up with her conqueror at Flushing Meadow, Gigi Fernandez.

While Seles was on the acendency, Graf was struggling and she greeted the end of the year with relief. Victory at the Australian Open and then the Pan Pacific event in Tokyo had suggested she would continue to dominate the game in her usual manner, but she suffered her first setback shortly afterwards, breaking her right thumb in a skiing accident. Upon her return, she won in Amelia Island and Hamburg, but a storm was gathering over her father's private life which was to cloud the remainder of her summer. Distracted by the publicity, Graf struggled to give her entire attention to tennis and was beaten in Berlin, Paris, and then in the Wimbledon semi-finals by Garrison. A serious sinus condition had also dogged Graf, and required not only a desperate return to Germany for treatment during the middle weekend of Wimbledon, but surgery afterwards.

Announcing herself fully fit, Graf came back to win the Canadian Open and San Diego, and looked magnificent at the US Open until perhaps her most surprising defeat of the year, to Sabatini in an intriguing final. That setback affected her very badly. Then came Leipzig, the first – and with unification coming a few days later – the only tournament to be held in East Germany. Although the crowds were disappointing, the event could still be considered a success. Graf won, and in an emotional presentation ceremony broke down in tears as she donated her prize money to assist the development of tennis in East Germany. Wins in Zurich, Brighton, and New England took her into the Virginia Slims Championships, where again disaster struck. She was suffering from a virus, and one suspects that had Navratilova not already done so then Graf would have withdrawn. Instead, she just survived against Capriati, retired to her sick bed, and was eventually beaten, again by Sabatini, in the semi-finals. However, there was one record Graf could be proud of in a comparatively disappointing year. On 3 September she acheived the longest consecutive period as the number 1 ranked player in either men's or women's tennis, surpassing Jimmy Connors' record of 159 weeks and Navratilova's record of 156.

It was an interesting year for supporters of Sabatini who saw here restructure her game under the guidance of Carlos Kirmayr. He replaced Angel Gimenez as her coach just before Wimbledon. Kirmayr made Sabatini rely less on her heavy topspin and encouraged her to become more aggressive. Indeed, as the year progressed, the Argentine developed a far more rounded game. Having thought, at the beginning of 1990, that she had peaked and was increasingly a spent force, one was eventually left with the feeling that Sabatini's best was still to come. We saw a glimpse of this with her victory at the US Open; the first by a woman from Argentina and her first title since March, when she had turned aside the precocious challenge of Capriati at the Virginia Slims of Florida. That tournament marked Capriati's professional debut, a few days short of her 14th birthday.

With many of the world's top tennis media in attendance, creating an atmosphere which Capriati so perceptively described as 'slightly out of control', she defeated Mary Lou Daniels, Claudia Porwik, Nathalie Tauziat, Sukova and Laura Gildemeister, before Sabatini stopped her run with a 6–4 7–5 victory in the final. The following week at the Lipton International she defeated Sukova again, but fell to qualifier Nathalie Herreman in the 4th round. In her third tournament, at Hilton Head, she reached the final again, losing only two games to Sanchez-Vicario, a set to Helen Kelesi, and four games to Natalia Zvereva. In the final she was beaten 6–2 6–4 by an opponent she nicknamed 'The Lege' (legend). It was an accolade that made Navratilova smile.

With three tournaments played, Capriati was given a world ranking and debuted at 25. She went on to reach the quarter-finals at the Italian Open, losing again to Sabatini, and then to become the youngest ever Grand Slam semi-finalist in Paris, conceeding to eventual champion Seles 6–2 6–2. At Wimbledon, where she reached the 4th round, losing in her first encounter with Graf, she became the youngest player ever to be seeded (at number 12), and the youngest player to win a match there.

Shortly after that Jennifer, still giggling infectiously at all the wonderful things that were happening to her, played a major role in helping the United States to their 14th Federation Cup win. She won all her matches. Grand Slam history repeated itself at the US Open when she lost to Graf in the 4th round, but the following month she claimed her first career title by defeating Garrison in the final of the Puerto Rican Open.

Capriati finished the year at number 8, and with wins over five top 10 players could be more than satisfied with her first year as a professional. Although losing to Graf again, at the Virginia Slims Championships, she confirmed that she has the game to challenge the best, and no one would argue with Graf's prediction that she would reach the top 5 in 1991.

Sanchez-Vicario, considered one of the main challengers to Graf, slipped back in 1990, ending the year at number 7. Poor performances in the Grand Slams were to blame. She didn't play the Australian, lost in the 2nd round of the French (where she was the title holder) to doubles partner Mercedes Paz, and the 1st round of Wimbledon to Betsy Nagelsen. A semi-final finish at the US Open was the only bright spot. Although she reached seven other finals, her only titles came at Barcelona out of a modest field, and at Newport, Rhode Island, where she rallied in typical fashion from 2–5 in the final set to defeat a re-juvenated Jo Durie. That win was significant, however, for it occured on grass, a surface which the Spaniard once treated with caution. It also helped to explain her modest year, for she was attempting to change her game from that of a baseliner into more of an all-court player. By the end of the year she was looking much more impressive, and her match against Seles at the Virginia Slims Championships was one of the best of 1990.

It was an interesting year for the Maleeva sisters. Magdalena who turned 15 on 1st April joined the senior tour, while at the same time winning the Australian, French and US Open junior titles. One of her most significant victories occured at Wimbledon where, playing her first ever match on grass, she overcame 1989 semi-finalist Catarina Lindqvist. She also faced both her sisters, a situation that none of them liked. Manuela, playing in the same tournament as Maggie for the first time, met her at the Canadian Open and was leading 4–1 when Maggie was forced to retire with a pulled muscle. The following month, Maggie played Katerina at the US Open, losing that encounter 6–3 6–1.

Katerina, 21, in fact had a better year than her 23-year-old sister, overtaking her on the rankings for the first time when Manuela, having won the title the previous year, failed to advance beyond the 2nd round of the European Open. But Katerina's best week came in Houston, where she defeated both Navratilova and Sanchez-Vicario on her way to the title, and she consolidated her position by beating the Spaniard again at the Eckerd Open. She also enjoyed wins over Sabatini, Capriati and Sukova. Manuela also produced two wins over Navratilova towards the end of the year, including the 4th round of the US Open.

Conchita Martinez, as the year before, chose her tournaments carefully and won in Scottsdale and Indianapolis, and at the Clarins Open in Paris. Although she now had seven titles to her credit, none of them had come in major events, but her consistency nevertheless earned her a year-end ranking of 11, down 4 from 1989.

The Soviets were highly successful. Zvereva won her first ever titles at Brisbane and Sydney, Leila Meskhi claimed Auckland and Moscow, and Natalia Medvedeva, Nashville.

As well as Zvereva and Medvedeva (and Capriati), several other players won titles for the first time. Federica Haumuller was the first ever winner on the Kraft General Foods world tour at the Rainha Cup in Brazil, and Dinky Van Rensburg won in Wichita. Wiltrud Probst claimed Wellington, while Federica Bonsignori won the Estoril Open in Portugal. Nathalie Tauziat improved throughout the year, and won her first tournament in Bayonne, and Mary Joe Fernandez was successful in both the Tokyo Indoors and Filderstadt. Indeed, one was left to wonder what Fernandez might have achieved had she been fully fit, for she finished 1990 ranked number 4, a rise of 8 places. She was a finalist at the Australian Open, and a semi-finalist at six other events. But she missed two major tournaments (the Lipton International and Wimbledon) through injury. In all, Fernandez was injured at the Pan Pacific (shoulder), Boca Raton and Lipton (pulled hamstring), Barcelona and Berlin (back) and Eastbourne (knee), as well as at an exhibition event in Essen, but she assured us she was trying to strengthen her body with the help of Tim Gullikson who was now coaching her.

Another to make a breakthrough was Anke Huber, considered by many to be potentially in the same class as Graf. Indeed, she benefits from coaching by Boris Breskvar, who had guided Graf and Boris Becker in their early days. As a qualifier, she won Schenectady after upsetting top seed Gildemeister, and then produced a win over Garrison on the way to the final in Bayonne (losing to Tauziat).

Naoko Sawamatsu excelled by reaching the semi-finals of the Japan Open, and then the following week won in Singapore. Solid performances at the Canadian Open, where she defeated Barbara Paulus and pushed Katerina Maleeva to three sets, made her a candidate for the WTA's Most Impressive Newcomer award, improving her ranking from 256 to 31.

Although she failed to win a title, Sabine Appelmans also caught the eye, rising from 149 to 22. She was a finalist at Auckland, a semi-finalist the following week in Wellington, and then in Singapore. In October, she defeated Judith Wiesner in Filderstadt, and then took eventual champion Mary Joe Fernandez to the brink of defeat. The product of a special tennis academy in Belgium, she plays left-handed but does everything else with her right!

Two players who have known better times proved they are still a force to be reckoned with. Claudia Kohde-Kilsch defeated Australian Rachel McQuillan to win the Austrian Open in Kitzbuhel, her first title in more than two years, while Catarina Lindqvist won her first tournament since 1986 when she overcame Elizabeth Smylie at the Japan Open.

KRAFT GENERAL FOODS WORLD TOUR 1990

DATE	VENUE	SINGLES FINAL	DOUBLES WINNERS
1–7 Jan	Brisbane	N. Zvereva d. R. McQuillan 6–4 6–0	J. Novotna/H. Sukova
8–14 Jan	Sydney	N. Zvereva d. B. Paulus 4–6 6–1 6–3	J. Novotna/H. Sukova
15–28 Jan	Melbourne (Australian Open)	S. Graf d. M.-J. Fernandez 6–3 6–4	J. Novotna/H. Sukova
29 Jan–4 Feb	Tokyo	S. Graf d. A. Sanchez-Vicario 6–1 6–2	G. Fernandez/E. Smylie
29 Jan–4 Feb	Auckland	L. Meskhi d. S. Appelmans 6–1 6–0	N. Medvedeva/L. Meskhi
5–11 Feb	Kansas	D. Van Rensburg d. N. Tauziat 2–6 7–5 6–2	M. Bollegraf/M. McGrath
5–11 Feb	Wellington	W. Probst d. L. Meskhi 1–6 6–4 6–0	N. Medvedeva/L. Meskhi
12–18 Feb	Chicago	M. Navratilova d. M. Maleeva-Fragnière 6–3 6–2	M. Navratilova/A. Smith
19–25 Feb	Washington	M. Navratilova d. Z. Garrison 6–1 6–0	Z. Garrison/M. Navratilova
19–25 Feb	Oklahoma City	A. Frazier d. M. Bollegraf 6–4 6–2	M.-L. Daniels/R. White
26 Feb–4 March	Indian Wells	M. Navratilova d. H. Sukova 6–2 5–7 6–1	J. Novotna/H. Sukova
5–11 March	Boca Raton	G. Sabatini d. J. Capriati 6–4 7–5	J. Novotna/H. Sukova
16–25 March	Key Biscayne	M. Seles d. J. Wiesner 6–1 6–2	J. Novotna/H. Sukova
28 March–1 April	San Antonio	M. Seles d. M. Maleeva-Fragnière 6–4 6–3	K. Jordan/E. Smylie
27 March–1 April	Houston	K. Maleeva d. A. Sanchez-Vicario 6–1 1–6 6–4	
2–8 April	Hilton Head	M. Navratilova d. J. Capriati 6–2 6–4	M. Navratilova/A. Sanchez-Vicario
9–15 April	Amelia Island	S. Graf d. A. Sanchez-Vicario 6–1 6–0	M. Paz/A. Sanchez-Vicario
9–15 April	Tokyo	C. Lindqvist d. E. Smylie 6–3 6–2	K. Jordan/E. Smylie
16–22 April	Tampa	M. Seles d. K. Maleeva 6–1 6–0	M. Paz/A. Sanchez-Vicario
16–22 April	Singapore	N. Sawamatsu d. S. Loosemore 7–6 3–6 6–4	J. Durie/J. Hetherington
23–29 April	Barcelona	A. Sanchez-Vicario d. I. Cueto 6–4 6–2	M. Paz/A. Sanchez-Vicario
30 Apr–6 May	Hamburg	S. Graf d. A. Sanchez-Vicario 5–7 6–0 6–1	G. Fernandez/M. Navratilova
1–6 May	Taranto	R. Reggi d. A. Dechaume 3–6 6–0 6–2	E. Brioukhovets/E. Maniokova
7–13 May	Rome	M. Seles d. M. Navratilova 6–1 6–1	H. Kelesi/M. Seles
14–20 May	Berlin	M. Seles d. S. Graf 6–4 6–3	N. Provis/E. Reinach
21–27 May	Geneva	B. Paulus d. H. Kelesi 2–6 7–5 7–6	L. Field/D. Van Rensburg
21–27 May	Strasbourg	M. Paz d. A. Grossman 6–2 6–3	N. Provis/E. Reinach
28 May–10 June	Paris (French Open)	M. Seles d. S. Graf 7–6 6–4	J. Novotna/H. Sukova
11–17 June	Birmingham	Z. Garrison d. H. Sukova 6–4 6–1	L. Savchenko/N. Zvereva
18–23 June	Eastbourne	M. Navratilova d. G. Magers 6–0 6–2	L. Savchenko/N. Zvereva
24 June–8 July	London (Wimbledon)	M. Navratilova d. Z. Garrison 6–4 6–1	J. Novotna/H. Sukova

DATE	VENUE	SINGLES FINAL	DOUBLES WINNERS
9–13 July	Palermo	I. Cueto d. B. Paulus 6–2 6–2	L. Garrone/K. Kschwendt
9–15 July	Bastad	S. Cecchini d. C. Bartos 6–1 6–2	M. Paz/T. Scheuer-Larsen
16–22 July	Newport	A. Sanchez-Vicario d. J. Durie 7–6 4–6 7–5	L. Gregory/G. Magers
16–22 July	Estoril	F. Bonsignori d. L. Garrone 2–6 6–3 6–3	S. Cecchini/P. Tarabini
30 Jul–5 August	Montreal	S. Graf d. M. Maleeva-Fragnière 6–1 6–7 6–3	B. Nagelsen/G. Sabatini
6–12 August	San Diego	S. Graf d. M. Maleeva-Fragnière 6–3 6–2	P. Fendick/Z. Garrison
6–12 August	Albuquerque	J. Novotna d. L. Gildemeister 6–4 6–4	M. McGrath/A. Smith
13–19 August	M'hattan Beach	M. Seles d. M. Navratilova 6–4 3–6 7–6	G. Fernandez/J. Novotna
20–25 August	Schenectady	A. Huber d. M. Werdel 6–1 5–7 6–4	A. May/N. Miyagi
26 August–9 Sept	New York (US Open)	G. Sabatini d. S. Graf 6–2 7–6	G. Fernandez/M. Navratilova
10–16 Sept	Kitzbuhel	C. Kohde-Kilsch d. R. McQuillan 7–6 6–4	P. Langrova/R. Zrubakova
10–16 Sept	Athens	C. Dahlman d. K. Piccolini 7–5 7–5	L. Garrone/K. Kschwendt
17–23 Sept	Paris	C. Martinez d. P. Tarabini 7–5 6–3	K. Godridge/K. Sharpe
24–30 Sept	Bayonne	N. Tauziat d. A. Huber 6–3 7–6	L. Field/C. Tanvier
24–30 Sept	Tokyo	M.J Fernandez d. A. Frazier 3–6 6–2 6–3	M.-J. Fernandez/R. White
24–30 Sept	Leipzig	S. Graf d. A. Sanchez-Vicario 6–1 6–1	L. Gregory/G. Magers
1–7 Oct	Moscow	L. Meskhi d. E. Brioukhovets 6–4 6–4	G. Magers/R. White
8–14 Oct	Zurich	S. Graf d. G. Sabatini 6–3 6–2	M. Bollegraf/E. Pfaff
15–21 Oct	Filderstadt	M.J Fernandez d. B. Paulus 6–1 6–3	M.-J. Fernandez/Z. Garrison
15–21 Oct	Phoenix	C. Martinez d. M. Werdel 7–5 6–1	E. Burgin/H. Kelesi
22–28 Oct	San Juan	J. Capriati d. Z. Garrison 5–7 6–4 6–2	E. Brioukhovets/N. Medvedeva
22–28 Oct	Brighton	S. Graf d. H. Sukova 7–5 6–3	H. Sukova/N. Tauziat
29 Oct–4 Nov	Oakland	M. Seles d. M. Navratilova 6–3 7–6	M. McGrath/A. Smith
29 Oct–4 Nov	Nashville	N. Medvedeva d. S. Sloane 6–3 7–6	K. Jordan/L. Savchenko
5–11 Nov	Worcester	S. Graf d. G. Sabatini 7–6 6–3	G. Fernandez/H. Sukova
5–11 Nov	Indianapolis	C. Martinez d. L. Meskhi 6–4 6–2	P. Fendick/M.McGrath
12–18 Nov	New York (Virginia Slims Championships)	M. Seles d. G. Sabatini 6–4 5–7 3–6 6–4 6–2	K. Jordan/E. Smylie

KRAFT GENERAL FOODS WORLD TOUR 1990 – POINTS EXPLANATION

The Kraft General Foods World Tour is the equivalent of the men's ATP TOUR. The 1990 women's Tour began in December 1989 with the tournament in Guaruja, Brazil and ended with the $1 million Virginia Slims Championships at Madison Square Garden, New York in November 1990. Altogether 59 tournaments (including the four Grand Slams) were staged in 19 countries, plus the season-ending Championships for the top 16 singles players and the top eight doubles pairs on the Kraft General Foods points table.

Events carrying points on the 1990 Kraft General Foods World Tour included:

Grand Slam Championships: The Championships of Australia, France, Great Britain and the United States of America.

Virginia Slims Championships: With $1 million in prize money and $2 million in the Virginia Slims Bonus Pool.

Lipton International Players Championships: A ten-day event with minimum prize money for women of $750,000 and a main singles draw of 96.

Tier I: Five tournaments approved by the Women's International Professional Tennis Council (WIPTC) and having prize money of $500,000.

Tier II: Fourteen tournaments approved by the WIPTC and having prize money of $350,000.

Tier III: Seven tournaments approved by the WIPTC and having prize money of $225,000.

Tier IV: Thirteen designated tournaments approved by the WIPTC and having prize money of $150,000 and receiving guaranteed WTA player commitment, plus three non-designated tournaments approved by the WIPTC but receiving no WTA player commitment.

Tier V: Twelve tournaments having prize money of $75,000 and approved by the WIPTC.

POINTS TABLE (Equal points are awarded for singles and doubles)

Category	Winner	Finalist	Semi-finalist	Quarter-finalist	9–16	17–32	33–64	Round of 128
Grand Slams	820	575	370	190	100	50	25	13
VS Champs(s)	820	575	370	190	100	—	—	—
Lipton Int.	470	330	210	110	55	25	13	6
Tier I	375	265	170	85	45	23	11	—
Tier II	300	210	135	70	35	18	9	—
Tier III	240	170	110	55	30	14	7	—
Tier IV	190	135	85	45	20	10	5	—
Tier V	110	75	50	25	10	6	3	—

Note: In both singles and doubles, no points are awarded to a player until she has completed a match.

1990 BONUS POOLS ($US) TOTAL $2 million)

Singles ($1,510,000) **1** 500,000; **2** 350,000; **3** 200,000; **4** 100,000; **5** 50,000; **6** 40,000; **7** 35,000; **8** 30,000; **9** 25,000; **10** 20,000; **11** 17,500; **12** 15,000; **13** 12,000; **14** 10,000; **15** 7,500; **16** 6,000; **17** 5,500; **18** 5,000; **19** 4,500; **20** 4,000.
Players 21–30: $3,500 each
Players 31–40: $2,500 each
Players 41–50: $1,300 each

Doubles ($115,000) **1** 50,000; **2** 25,000; **3** and **4** 10,000; **5** to **8** 5,000 each.

Special Incentive Fund ($375,000)
This fund is designed to encourage Top 20 players to play tournaments above their minimum commitment when a tournament does not have a player commitment. Payments are made as follows: Players listed 1 and 2 – $75,000; Players listed 3 and 4 – $50,000; Players listed 5 to 8 – up to $25,000; Players listed 9 to 12 – up to $10,000; Players listed 13 to 20 – up to $5,000.

FINAL 1990 BONUS POOL PAYOUTS

Steffi Graf finished first in the 1990 $2 Million Virginia Slims Bonus Pool Earnings with $614,783 following the conclusion of the Virginia Slims Championships at Madison Square Garden.

A total of $1,965,044 was paid of a possible $2 million to the top eligible players on the year-long Kraft General Foods World Tour, a total of 60 events. The Bonus Pool is broken down into three categories: Singles, Doubles and Special Incentive Fund.

Of players who accumulated the most Kraft General Foods World Tour points in 1990 and met Bonus Pool eligibility requirements, Graf finished first, Seles was second ($430,348) and Navratilova was third ($250,914).

	Player	Singles	Doubles	Special Incentive Fund	Total
1.	Graf, Steffi	$512,139	–	$102,644	$614,783
2.	Seles, Monica	358,497	–	71,851	430,348
3.	Navratilova, Martina	204,856	$ 5,000	41,058	250,914
4.	Sabatini, Gabriela	102,428	–	20,529	122,957
5.	Sanchez-Vicario, Arantxa	30,728	–	57,185	87,913
6.	Novotna, Jana	20,486	50,000	5,132	75,618
7.	Sukova, Helena	17,925	25,000	29,106	72,031
8.	Garrison, Zina	40,971	–	10,264	51,235
9.	Maleeva, Katerina	35,850	–	8,212	44,062
10.	Maleeva-Fragnière, Manuela	25,607	–	6,159	31,766
11.	Zvereva, Natalia	15,364	10,000	3,593	28,957
12.	Tauziat, Nathalie	10,243	–	3,079	13,322
13.	Savchenko, Larisa	–	10,000	–	10,000
14.	Lindqvist, Catarina	2,561	–	6,129	8,690
15.	Wiesner, Judith	6,146	–	2,463	8,609
16.	Paz, Mercedes	3,585	5,000	–	8,585
17.	Capriati, Jennifer	7,682	–	–	7,682
18.	Frazier, Amy	5,121	–	2,053	7,174
19.	Fernandez, Gigi	1,280	5,000	–	6,280
20.	Kelesi, Helen	3,585	–	1,540	5,125
21.	Smylie, Liz	–	5,000	–	5,000
22.	Sloane, Susan	3,585	–	1,232	4,817
23.	Meshki, Leila	4,609	–	–	4,609
24.	Fairbank-Nideffer, Rosalyn	4,097	–	–	4,097
25.	McNeil, Lori	2,561	–	1,026	3,587
T26.	Gildemeister, Laura	3,585	–	–	3,585
	Porwik, Claudia	3,585	–	–	3,585
	Magers, Gretchen	3,585	–	–	3,585
	Cecchini, Sandra	3,585	–	–	3,585
	McQuillan, Rachel	3,585	–	–	3,585
	Van Rensburg, Dinky	3,585	–	–	3,585
27.	Fendick, Patty	2,561	–	924	3,485
28.	Paulus, Barbara	2,817 (50%)	–	–	2,817
T29.	Grossman, Ann	2,561	–	–	2,561
	Cueto, Isabel	2,561	–	–	2,561
	Bollegraf, Manon	2,561	–	–	2,561
	Herreman, Nathalie	2,561	–	–	2,561
	Schultz, Brenda	2,561	–	–	2,561
	Provis, Nicole	2,561	–	–	2,561
30.	Kohde-Kilsch, Claudia	1,332	–	821	2,153
T31.	Gavaldon, Angelica	1,332	–	–	1,332
	Werdel, Marianne	1,332	–	–	1,332
	Smith, Anne	1,332	–	–	1,332
	Probst, Wiltrud	1,332	–	–	1,332
	Halard, Julie	1,332	–	–	1,332
	Minter, Anne	1,332	–	–	1,332
	Tarabini, Patricia	1,332	–	–	1,332
	Medvedeva, Natalia	1,332	–	–	1,332
32.	Reggi, Raffaella	896 (25%)	–	–	896
	TOTAL				$1,965,044

NOTE: Mary Joe Fernandez and Conchita Martinez were ineligible for Bonus Pool distribution because they did not meet eligibility requirements pertaining to minimum number of primary tournaments played. Barbara Paulus and Raffaella Reggi were eligible but only received a certain percentage of their bonus pool distribution due to the fact that Paulus was one tournament short and Reggi two tournaments short of the minimum requirement.

* Numbers above are rounded off to the nearest dollar.

KRAFT GENERAL FOODS WORLD TOUR

Tournaments with prize money of $225,000 and above

HOLDEN NSW OPEN ($225,000)

SYDNEY, 8–14 JANUARY

WOMEN'S SINGLES – 1st round: H. Sukova (TCH) (1) – bye; A. Grossman (USA) d. M. Jaggard 6–0 6–4; A. Henricksson (USA) d. A. Nishiya (JPN) 3–6 7–5 6–2; R. Zrubakova (TCH) (13) d. D. Van Rensburg (RSA) 6–1 6–0; B. Paulus (AUT) (10) d. C. Cunningham (USA) 5–7 6–1 6–4; B. Schultz (HOL) d. J-A. Faull 6–3 6–2; N. Provis d. C. Tanvier (FRA) 6–0 6–3; R. Fairbank Nideffer (USA) (8) – bye; H. Mandlikova (4) – bye; E. Smylie d. L. Field 7–5 6–7 6–4; M. Bollegraf (HOL) d. A. Temesvari (HUN) 6–3 6–2; J. Wiesner (AUT) (16) d. K. Quentrec (FRA) 7–5 6–4; C. Porwik (FRG) d. P. Fendick (USA) (12) 5–7 7–5 6–2; E. Burgin (USA) d. C. Kohde-Kilsch (FRG) 6–2 7–5; J. Pospisilova (TCH) d. R. Rajchrtova (TCH) 7–6 6–1; P. Shriver (USA) (5) – bye; L. Savchenko (URS) (6) – bye; J. Halard (FRA) d. L. McNeil (USA) 6–2 1–6 7–5; T. Phelps (USA) d. S. Martin (USA) 6–2 0–6 7–5; P. Langrova (TCH) d. A. Minter (15) 6–4 6–4; N. Zvereva (URS) (11) d. A. Kijimuta (JPN) 6–3 6–1; L. Golarsa (ITA) d. K. Radford 6–3 6–2; I. Demongeot (FRA) d. K. Adams (USA) 6–2 6–2; H. Kelesi (CAN) (3) – bye; R. Reggi (ITA) (7) – bye; S. Stafford (USA) d. E. Inoue (JPN) 6–4 4–6 7–5; Cam. MacGregor (USA) d. N. Miyagi (JPN) 6–4 6–3; G. Fernandez (USA) (9) d. H. Cioffi (USA) 6–3 6–1; A. Frazier (USA) (14) d. N. Jagerman (HOL) 3–6 6–4 6–3; N. Herreman (FRA) d. T. Whitlinger (USA) 1–6 6–3 6–1; R. McQuillan d. R. White (USA) 4–6 6–2 6–4; J. Novotna (TCH) (2) – bye.
2nd round: Sukova (1) d. Grossman 6–2 6–4; Zrubakova (13) d. Henricksson 6–1 1–6 6–3; Paulus (10) d. Schultz 7–6 6–7 6–1; Provis d. Fairbank Nideffer (8) 6–2 7–6; Mandlikova (4) d. Smylie 6–2 6–2; Wiesner (16) d. Bollegraf 6–3 6–2; Porwik d. Burgin 6–3 6–3; Pospisilova d. Shriver (5) 6–4 6–7 7–5; Halard d. Savchenko (6) 6–4 7–5; Langrova d. Phelps 7–5 6–3; Zvereva (11) d. Golarsa 6–4 6–3; Demongeot d. Kelesi (3) 6–2 4–6 7–6; Reggi (7) d. Stafford 6–4 5–7 6–1; Fernandez (9) d. MacGregor 6–0 4–6 6–3; Frazier (14) d. Herreman 6–4 6–0; Novotna (2) d. MacQuillan 6–1 6–4.
3rd round: Zrubakova (13) d. Sukova (1) 6–1 1–6 6–3; Paulus (10) d. Provis 7–6 6–2; Wiesner (16) d. Mandlikova (4) 7–6 6–3; Porwik d. Pospisilova 6–1 6–0; Halard d. Langrova 6–2 0–6 6–4; Zvereva (11) d. Demongeot 6–1 6–1; Reggi (7) d. Fernandez (9) 6–1 7–5; Frazier (14) d. Novotna (2) 6–3 6–4.
Quarter-finals: Paulus (10) d. Zrubakova (13) 6–2 6–1; Wiesner (16) d. Porwik 6–3 4–6 6–3; Zvereva (11) d. Halard 4–6 6–2 6–4; Frazier (14) d. Reggi (7) 6–3 7–5.
Semi-finals: Paulus (10) d. Wiesner (16) 6–4 3–6 6–1; Zvereva (11) d. Frazier (14) 6–3 2–6 6–2.
Final: Zvereva (11) d. Paulus (10) 4–6 6–1 6–3.
WOMEN'S DOUBLES – Final: Novotna/Sukova (1) d. Savchenko/Zvereva (2) 6–3 7–5.

TORAY PAN PACIFIC OPEN ($350,000)

TOKYO, 29 JANUARY–4 FEBRUARY

WOMEN'S SINGLES – 1st round: S. Graf (FRG) (1) – bye; N. Jagerman (HOL) d. C. Benjamin (USA) 6–3 6–3; P. Louie-Harper (USA) d. S. Collins (USA) 2–6 6–4 6–2; L. Savchenko (URS) (5) d. C. Porwik (FRG) 6–4 6–4; M. Maleeva Fragnière (SUI) (3) – bye; T. Phelps (USA) d. A. Nishiya 7–5 6–1; B. Schultz (HOL) d. R. McQuillan (AUS) 6–3 7–5; E. Inoue d. A. Minter (AUS) (8) 6–2 7–6; A. Kijimuta d. L. McNeil (USA) (7) 6–3 3–6 6–3; Cam. MacGregor (USA) d. H. Ludloff (USA) 6–4 6–2; N. Miyagi d. K. Adams (USA) 6–2 3–6 6–3; R. Hiraki – bye; G. Fernandez (USA) d. K. Date 6–1 6–4; M. Kidowaki d. K. Okamoto 6–3 6–3; J-A. Faull (AUS) d. E. Smylie (AUS) 1–6 6–2 ret.; A. Sanchez-Vicario (ESP) (2) – bye.
2nd round: Graf (1) d. Jagerman 6–0 6–1; Savchenko (5) d. Louie-Harper 4–6 7–6 7–6; Maleeva Fragnière (3) d. Phelps 6–2 6–1; Schultz d. Inoue 6–1 6–2; Kijimuta d. MacGregor 6–1 3–6 6–1; Miyagi d. Hiraki 7–6 6–2; Fernandez (6) d. Kidowaki 6–3 6–2; Sanchez-Vicario (2) d. Faull 6–1 6–0.
Quarter-finals: Graf (1) d. Savchenko (5) 6–0 6–3; Maleeva Fragnière (3) d. Schultz 6–2 6–0; Kijimuta d. Miyagi 7–6 2–6 6–2; Sanchez-Vicario (2) d. Fernandez (6) 1–6 6–1 6–2.
Semi-finals: Graf (1) d. Maleeva Fragnière (3) 6–4 6–4; Sanchez-Vicario (2) d. Kijimuta 6–4 6–2.
Final: Graf (1) d. Sanchez-Vicario (2) 6–1 6–2.
WOMEN'S DOUBLES – Final: Fernandez/Smylie (2) d. Faull/McQuillan 6–2 6–2.

VIRGINIA SLIMS OF CHICAGO ($500,000)

CHICAGO, IL, 12–18 FEBRUARY

WOMEN'S SINGLES – 1st round: M. Navratilova (1) d. A. Temesvari (HUN) 6–1 6–3; A. White d. A. Keller 7–6 7–6; T. Whitlinger d. Hu Na 3–6 6–3 6–1; K. Rinaldi d. N. Zvereva (URS) (6) 7–5 3–6 6–1; L. Harvey-Wild d. A. Sanchez-Vicario (ESP) (3) 6–3 7–6; N. Provis (AUS) d. A. Grossman 1–6 6–1 7–6; S. Sloane d. L. Ferrando (ITA) 7–5 7–6; P. Shriver (8) d. A. Henricksson 6–2 6–2; M. Maleeva Fragnière (SUI) (5) d. Lou. Allen 6–3 6–3; P. Fendick d. A. Smith 6–3 1–6 6–4; C. Kohde-Kilsch (FRG) d. A. Minter (AUS) 3–6 6–3 6–1; R. Fairbank Nideffer d. M. Seles (YUG) (4) 6–3 6–4; L. Gildemeister (PER) (7) d. G. Magers 6–1 6–7 6–4; N. Tauziat (FRA) d. I. Cueto (FRG) 6–4 6–1; L. McNeil d. T. Phelps 7–5 7–6; Z. Garrison (2) d. M. Pierce (FRA) 6–4 6–4.

2nd round: Navratilova (1) d. White 6–0 6–0; Whitlinger d. Rinaldi 0–6 6–4 6–3; Harvey-Wild d. Provis 6–4 6–4; Shriver (8) d. Sloane 6–3 6–4; Maleeva Fragnière (5) d. Fendick 6–4 7–5; Fairbank Nideffer d. Kohde-Kilsch 6–3 3–6 6–3; Tauziat d. Gildemeister (7) 6–1 6–7 7–5; Garrison (2) d. McNeil 6–3 6–2.

Quarter-finals: Navratilova (1) d. Whitlinger 6–0 6–1; Shriver (8) d. Harvey-Wild 6–1 6–2; Maleeva Fragnière (5) d. Fairbank Nideffer 6–1 6–0; Garrison (2) d. Tauziat 6–3 7–5.

Semi-finals: Navratilova (1) d. Shriver (8) 6–4 6–3; Maleeva Fragnière (5) d. Garrison (2) 6–2 6–0.

Final: Navratilova (1) d. Maleeva Fragnière (5) 6–3 6–2.

WOMEN'S DOUBLES – Final: Navratilova/Smith d. Sanchez-Vicario/Tauziat 6–7 6–4 6–3.

VIRGINIA SLIMS OF WASHINGTON ($350,000)

WASHINGTON, 19–25 FEBRUARY

WOMEN'S SINGLES – 1st round: M. Navratilova (1) – bye; A. Grossman d. R. Fairbank Nideffer 3–6 6–2 7–6; C. Kohde-Kilsch (FRG) d. D. Van Rensburg (RSA) 6–1 4–6 6–3; A. Smith d. H. Kelesi (CAN) (5) 6–1 6–2; M. Seles (YUG) (3) – bye; S. Martin d. K. Adams 7–6 4–6 7–5; P. Fendick d. A. Henricksson 6–2 6–1; P. Shriver (7) d. E. Burgin 6–0 6–2; L. Gildemeister (PER) (6) d. S. Hanika (FRG) 4–6 6–4 6–2; N. Provis (AUS) d. A. Temesvari (HUN) 6–3 7–6; H. Cioffi d. J. Ingram 6–3 6–3; N. Zvereva (URS) (4) – bye; N. Tauziat (FRA) (8) d. K. Rinaldi 7–5 6–3; L. Ferrando (ITA) d. E. Rossides 6–0 6–3; E. Smylie (AUS) d. L. McNeil 6–2 4–6 7–6; Z. Garrison (2) – bye.

2nd round: Navratilova (1) d. Grossman 6–0 6–0; Smith d. Khode-Kilsch 6–3 6–3; Seles (3) d. Martin default; Shriver (7) d. Fendick 6–3 3–6 6–4; Provis d. Gildemeister (6) 6–3 6–3; Zvereva (4) d. Cioffi 4–6 6–2 6–3; Tauziat (8) d. Ferrando 6–2 6–4; Garrison (2) d. Smylie 6–0 6–1.

Quarter-finals: Navratilova (1) d. Smith 6–4 6–2; Seles (3) d. Shriver (7) 6–2 7–6; Zvereva (4) d. Provis 5–7 6–3 6–4; Garrison (2) d. Tauziat 3–6 7–6.

Semi-finals: Navratilova (1) d. Seles (3) 6–3 6–0; Garrison (2) d. Zvereva (4) 6–2 3–6 6–3.

Final: Navratilova (1) d. Garrison (2) 6–1 6–0.

WOMEN'S DOUBLES – Final: Garrison/Navratilova (1) d. Henricksson/Van Rensburg 6–0 6–3.

VIRGINIA SLIMS OF INDIAN WELLS ($350,000)

INDIAN WELLS, CA, 26 FEBRUARY–4 MARCH

WOMEN'S SINGLES – 1st round: M. Navratilova (1) – bye; N. Provis (AUS) d. E. Pfaff (FRG) 1–6 6–3 6–3; T. Phelps d. A. Minter (AUS) 6–4 7–6; J. Wiesner (AUT) (12) d. L. Bonder-Kreiss 7–6 6–0; C. Lindqvist (SWE) (13) d. C. Benjamin 7–5 6–3; N. Herreman (FRA) d. L. Poruri 6–4 6–0; E. Inoue (JPN) d. N. Iaccarino (ITA) 5–7 6–4, 6–1; L. Savchenko (URS) (7) – bye; J. Novotna (TCH) (4) – bye; Y. Koizumi (JPN) d. Hu Na 6–4 4–6 6–2; M. McGrath d. B. Cordwell (NZL) 6–3 6–3; A. Coetzer (RSA) d. P. Fendick (16) 6–3 6–3; G. Fernandez (9) d. J. Pospisilova (TCH) 6–1 6–3; E. Rossides d. P. Louie Harper 1–6 7–5 6–1; K. Rinaldi d. S. Collins 6–3 6–0; K. Maleeva (BUL) (5) – bye; H. Mandlikova (AUS) (6) – bye; K. Gompert d. K. Schimper (RSA) 6–2 6–3; A. Keller d. L. Golarsa (ITA) 7–6 6–4; I. Demongeot (FRA) d. K. Jordan 6–3 2–6 6–0; G. Magers (10) d. P. Vasquez (PER) 6–3 7–6; A. Gavaldon (MEX) d. S. Stafford 6–0 6–3; M. Javer (GBR) d. A. Leand 6–2 6–4; H. Sukova (TCH) (3) – bye; R. Fairbank Nideffer (8) – bye; N. Miyagi (JPN) d. L. Tanner 7–6 6–1; R. White d. A. Kijimuta (JPN) 6–2 6–1; C. Porwik (FRG) (14) d. K. Shin 6–1 3–6 7–6; A. Frazier (11) d. E. Reinach (RSA) 7–6 6–3; K. Quentrec (FRA) d. A. Henricksson 3–6 7–5 7–6; Cam. MacGregor d. R. Reis 7–5 6–2; C. Martinez (ESP) (2) – bye.

2nd round: Navratilova (1) d. Provis 6–2 6–0; Wiesner (12) d. Phelps 6–0 6–0; Herreman d. Lindqvist (13) 6–2 6–1; Inoue d. Savchenko (7) 6–4 6–1; Novotna (4) d. Koizumi 6–0 6–0; McGrath d. Coetzer 6–2 7–6; Fernandez (9) d. Rossides 4–6 6–3 6–2; Maleeva (5) d. Rinaldi 6–1 6–3; Mandlikova (6) d. Gompert 6–4 6–2; Demongeot d. Keller 6–3 6–2; Magers (10) d. Gavaldon 6–2 6–4; Sukova (3) d. Javer 4–6 7–6 6–0; Fairbank Nideffer (8) d. Miyagi 6–4 6–1; Porwik (14) d. R. White 5–7 7–5 7–6; Frazier (11) d. Quentrec 3–6 6–1 6–4; Martinez (2) d. MacGregor 6–1 6–2.

3rd round: Navratilova (1) d. Wiesner (12) 6–3 6–2; Herreman d. Inoue 4–6 6–4 6–3; McGrath d. Novotna (4) 3–6 7–5 6–3; Maleeva (5) d. Fernandez (9) 6–3 6–2; Demongeot d. Mandlikova (6) 7–5 0–6 6–3; Sukova (3) d. Magers (10) 6–4 5–7 7–6; Fairbank Nideffer (8) d. Porwik (14) 5–7 6–2 6–3; Frazier (11) d. Martinez (2) 1–6 6–4 6–2.
Quarter-finals: Navratilova (1) d. Herreman 6–2 6–1; Maleeva (5) d. McGrath 6–1 6–2; Sukova (3) d. Demongeot 6–4 6–3; Frazier (11) d. Fairbank (8) 6–2 6–3.
Semi-finals: Navratilova (1) d. Maleeva (5) 7–6 6–1; Sukova (3) d. Frazier (11) 7–5 6–4.
Final: Navratilova (1) d. Sukova (3) 6–2 5–7 6–1.
WOMEN'S DOUBLES – Final: Novotna/Sukova (1) d. Fernandez/Navratilova (2) 6–2 7–6.

VIRGINIA SLIMS OF FLORIDA ($350,000)

BOCA RATON, FL, 5–11 MARCH

WOMEN'S SINGLES – 1st round: G. Sabatini (ARG) (1) – bye; E. Inoue (JPN) d. J. Pospisilova (TCH) 6–2 6–0; J. Halard (FRA) d. M. Strandlund (SWE) 6–2 6–0; R. Reggi (ITA) (9) d. S. Wasserman (BEL) 7–6 6–4; N. Guerree (FRA) d. R. Zrubakova (TCH) (13) 4–6 6–4 6–4; D. Van Rensburg (RSA) d. W. Probst (FRG) 6–1 6–3; S. Loosemore (GBR) d. E. Reinach (RSA) 6–3 6–1; P. Shriver (7) – bye; M-J. Fernandez (3) – bye; N. Provis (AUS) d. I. Demongeot (FRA) 6–4 6–3; B. Fulco (ARG) d. K. Quentrec (FRA) 7–5 6–3; J. Wiesner (AUT) (12) d. T. Phelps 6–1 6–4; S. Hanika (FRG) (16) d. E. De Lone 6–4 6–1; A. Coetzer (RSA) d. Lou. Allen 7–5 6–3; N. Herreman (FRA) d. E. Pfaff (FRG) 6–2 6–4; H. Mandlikova (AUS) (6) – bye; N. Tauziat (FRA) (8) – bye; S. Martin d. F. Labat (ARG) 6–1 6–4; J. Capriati d. M-L. Daniels 7–6 6–1; C. Porwik (FRG) (15) d. E. Burgin 6–1 4–6 6–2; A. Smith d. L. Golarsa (ITA) 4–6 6–3 7–6; H. Cioffi d. N. Miyagi (JPN) 6–3 6–3; R. Simpson (CAN) d. P. Vasquez (PER) 6–1 6–4; H. Sukova (TCH) (4) – bye; J. Novotna (TCH) (5) – bye; T. Whitlinger d. S. Hack (FRG) 6–1 5–7 6–2; A. Gavaldon (MEX) d. A. Huber (FRG) 6–4 6–0; P. Louie Harper d. S. Sloane (14) 2–6 6–2 6–0; L. Gildemeister (PER) d. A. Kijimuta (JPN) 6–1 7–6; A. Grossman d. B. Cordwell (NZL) 6–3 6–3; N. Jagerman (HOL) d. S. Stafford 6–4 6–3; M. Seles (YUG) (2) – bye.
2nd round: Sabatini (1) d. Inoue 6–2 7–5; Reggi (9) d. Halard 6–2 5–7 6–2; Van Rensburg d. Guerree 7–5 7–6; Shriver (7) d. Loosemore 6–3 6–0; Fernandez (3) d. Provis 6–2 4–6 7–6; Wiesner (12) d. Fulco 7–5 6–2; Coetzer d. Hanika (16) 6–1 2–6 6–2; Mandlikova (6) d. Herreman 6–3 6–0; Tauziat (8) d. Martin 6–2 6–1; Capriati d. Porwik (15) 7–5 0–6 6–2; Cioffi d. Smith 2–6 6–3 7–6; Sukova (4) d. Simpson 6–1 6–3; Novotna (5) d. Whitlinger 6–0 6–3; Gavaldon d. Louie Harper 7–6 4–6 6–2; Gildemeister (10) d. Grossman 6–2 3–6 6–2; Seles (2) d. Jagerman 6–2 6–0.
3rd round: Sabatini (1) d. Reggi (9) 6–2 6–1; Van Rensburg d. Shriver (7) 7–5 6–1; Fernandez (3) d. Wiesner (12) 6–4 6–1; Coetzer d. Mandlikova (6) 2–6 6–2 6–3; Capriati d. Tauziat (8) 6–4 6–2; Sukova (4) d. Cioffi 6–4 4–6 6–1; Novotna (5) d. Gavaldon 6–1 6–0; Gildemeister (10) d. Seles (2) 6–1 7–6.
Quarter-finals: Sabatini (1) d. Van Rensburg 6–2 7–6; Fernandez (3) d. Coetzer 6–0 6–1; Capriati d. Sukova (4) 6–1 6–4; Gildemeister (10) d. Novotna (5) 3–6 6–3 6–3.
Semi-finals: Sabatini (1) d. Fernandez (3) 4–4 ret.; Capriati d. Gildemeister (10) 7–6 7–6.
Final: Sabatini (1) d. Capriati 6–4 7–5.
WOMEN'S DOUBLES – Final: Novotna/Sukova (1) d. E. Burgin/W. Turnbull (4) 6–4 6–2.

LIPTON INTERNATIONAL PLAYERS CHAMPIONSHIPS ($750,000)

KEY BISCAYNE, FL, 16–25 MARCH

WOMEN'S SINGLES – 1st round: G. Sabatini (ARG) (1) – bye; S. Wasserman (BEL) d. C. Bassett-Seguso (CAN) 6–0 6–2; M. Kidowaki (JPN) d. E. Reinach (RSA) 6–1 6–3; B. Cordwell (NZL) (25) – bye; S. Sloane (20) – bye; A. Grossman d. B. Schultz (HOL) 6–4 6–1; R. White d. M. Paz (ARG) 6–4 2–6 6–1; A. Frazier (11) – bye; G. Magers (14) – bye; W. Probst (FRG) d. E. Burgin 6–2 6–1; E. Smylie (AUS) d. B. Baranski (POL) 6–4 4–6 6–2; B. Nagelsen (29) – bye; S. Hanika (FRG) (23) – bye; K. Quentrec (FRA) d. B. Bowes 6–3 6–3; D. Van Rensburg (RSA) d. S. Collins 6–4 6–1; C. Martinez (ESP) (5) – bye; M. Maleeva Fragnière (SUI) (4) – bye; D. Faber d. S. Stafford 6–2 6–1; C. Benjamin d. H. Cioffi 7–5 6–4; C. Lindqvist (SWE) (17) – bye; M. Bollegraf (HOL) (28) – bye; S. Hack (FRG) d. T. Zambrzycki (BRA) 6–2 7–5; A. Coetzer (RSA) d. M. Javer (GBR) 6–1 6–3; R. Reggi (ITA) (10) – bye; J. Wiesner (AUT) (15) – bye; M. Werdel d. A. Kijimuta (JPN) 7–6 7–6; T. Phelps d. A. Henricksson 4–6 6–3 7–6; I. Demongeot (FRA) (22) – bye; K. Rinaldi (32) – bye; E. Inoue (JPN) d. S. Martin 7–6 0 6–3; L. Bonder-Kreiss d. H. Ter Riet (HOL) 6–2 6–2; J. Novotna (TCH) (7) – bye; H. Sukova (TCH) (6) – bye; J. Capriati d. L. Spadea 7–5 6–3; A. Vieira (BRA) d. C. Tanvier (FRA) 6–3 6–4; P. Fendick (31) – bye; A. Minter (AUS) (26) – bye; C. Caverzasio (ITA) d. N. Medvedeva (URS) 7–6 2–0 ret.; N. Herreman (FRA) d. P. Vasquez (PER) 6–0 6–0; L. Gildemeister (PER) (12) – bye; R. Fairbank Nideffer (13) – bye; C. Cunningham d. K. Adams 7–5 6–3; L. McNeil d. M. Strandlund (SWE) 6–3 7–5; A. Temesvari (HUN) (27) – bye; R. Rajchrtova (TCH) (30) – bye; L. Lapi (ITA) d. J. Pospisilova (TCH) 6–2 6–3; L. Harvey-Wild d. L. Gavaldon (MEX) 7–5 6–4; M.

Seles (YUG) (3) – bye; H. Kelesi (CAN) (8) – bye; F. Labat (ARG) d. M. McGrath 2–6 7–6 6–3; S. Loosemore (GBR) d. K. Gompert 3–4 ret.; C. Porwik (FRG) (21) – bye; B. Fulco (ARG) (24) – bye; J. Santrock d. L. Garrone (ITA) 6–0 6–7 6–1; T. Whitlinger d. N. Guerree (FRA) 6–3 6–2; A. Smith (16) – bye; N. Tauziat (FRA) (9) – bye; Cam. MacGregor d. B. Romano (ITA) 6–1 6–2; N. Miyagi (JPN) d. P. Tarabini (ARG) 6–0 6–2; R. Zrubakova (TCH) (18) – bye; L. Savchenko (URS) (19) – bye; A. Keller d. A. Reis 7–5 6–2; J. Halard (FRA) d. P. Louie Harper 6–1 6–4; Z. Garrison (2) – bye.

2nd round: Sabatini (1) d. Wasserman 6–3 6–4; Kidowaki d. Cordwell (25) 7–5 4–6 6–2; Sloane (20) d. Grossman 6–1 6–3; White d. Frazier (11) 7–6 7–6; Magers (14) d. Probst 6–2 6–3; Smylie d. Nagelsen (29) 6–2 6–4; Quentrec d. Hanika (23) 5–7 6–3 6–4; Martinez (5) d. Van Rensburg 3–6 7–6 7–6; Maleeva Fragnière (4) d. Faber 6–0 6–2; Benjamin d. Lindqvist (17) 2–6 6–4 7–5; Bollegraf (28) d. Hack 6–0 6–1; Reggi (10) d. Coetzer 6–2 3–6 7–6; Wiesner (15) d. Werdel 7–6 0–6 6–3; Phelps d. Demongeot (22) 7–6 6–1; Rinaldi (32) d. Inoue 7–6 6–1; Novotna (7) d. Bonder-Kreiss 6–0 1–6 6–1; Capriati d. Sukova (6) 6–3 6–2; Fendick (31) d. Vieira 6–3 6–4; Caverzasio d. A. Minter (26) 7–5 2–6 6–0; Herreman d. Gildemeister (17) 6–1 6–1; Fairbank Nideffer (13) d. Cunningham 6–2 6–4; McNeil d. Temesvari (27) 4–6 6–4 7–5; Lapi d. Rajchrtova (30) 6–1 7–6; Seles (3) d. Harvey-Wild 6–1 6–4; Kelesi (8) d. Labat 6–4 6–2; Porwik (21) d. Loosemore 6–2 6–3; Fulco (24) d. Garrone 6–4 4–6 6–1; Whitlinger d. Smith (16) 6–1 6–4; Tauziat (9) d. Cam. MacGregor 6–2 4–6 6–3; Miyagi d. Zrubakova (18) 6–1 6–2; Keller d. Savchenko (19) 6–3 7–5; Halard d. Garrison (2) 2–6 6–3 6–4.

3rd round: Sabatini (1) d. Kidowaki 6–2 6–3; Sloane (20) d. White 6–3 6–3; Magers (14) d. Smylie 6–2 6–4; Martinez (5) d. Quentrec 6–3 6–4; Maleeva Fragnière (4) d. Benjamin 6–1 6–2; Reggi (10) d. Bollegraf (28) 6–7 6–3 6–1; Wiesner (15) d. Phelps 6–1 5–7 6–2; Novotna (7) d. Rinaldi (32) 6–0 1–6 6–1; Capriati d. Fendick (31) 2–4 ret.; Herreman d. Caverzasio 6–3 6–4; Fairbank Nideffer (13) d. McNeil 6–2 2–6 6–3; Seles (3) d. Lapi 6–1 6–1; Porwik (21) d. Kelesi 6–4 6–1; Fulco (24) d. Whitlinger 7–6 3–6 7–6; Tauziat (9) d. Miyagi 6–1 6–4; Halard d. Keller 6–3 4–6 6–0.

4th round: Sabatini (1) d. Sloane (20) 6–2 6–2; Martinez (5) d. Magers (14) 4–6 7–5 6–4; Maleeva Fragnière (4) d. Reggi (10) 6–1 3–6 6–2; Wiesner (15) d. Novotna (7) 7–5 5–7 6–3; Herreman d. Capriati 6–2 6–4; Seles (3) d. Fairbank Nideffer (13) 6–3 6–4; Porwik d. Fulco (24) 6–2 6–3; Tauziat (9) d. Halard 6–4 6–3.

Quarter-finals: Martinez (5) d. Sabatini (1) 7–6 6–2; Wiesner (15) d. Maleeva Fragnière (4) 2–6 6–1 6–2; Seles (3) d. Herreman 6–3 6–1; Tauziat (9) d. Porwik (21) 6–3 4–6 6–3.

Semi-finals: Wiesner (15) d. Martinez (5) 6–2 6–1; Seles (3) d. Tauziat (9) 6–3 6–1.

Final: Seles (3) d. Wiesner (15) 6–1 6–2.

WOMEN'S DOUBLES – Final: Novotna/Sukova (1) d. Nagelsen/White (5) 6–4 6–3.

VIRGINIA SLIMS OF HOUSTON ($225,000)

HOUSTON, TX, 27 MARCH–1 APRIL

WOMEN'S SINGLES – 1st round: M. Navratilova (1) d. B. Fulco (ARG) 6–0 6–1; A. Temesvari (HUN) d. N. Iaccarino (ITA) 6–2 6–1; K. Maleeva (BUL) (4) d. L. Meskhi (URS) 7–6 6–1; L. Gildemeister (PER) d. I. Cueto (FRG) 6–2 7–5; M-L. Daniels d. S. Hanika (FRG) 6–4 6–4; A. Sanchez-Vicario (ESP) (3) d. G. Magers 6–3 6–3; S. Cecchini (ITA) d. S. Sloane 3–6 6–2 6–3; Z. Garrison (2) d. N. Zvereva (URS) 4–6 6–3 6–3.

Quarter-finals: Navratilova (1) d. Temesvari 7–5 6–2; Maleeva (4) d. Gildemeister 6–2 7–6; Sanchez-Vicario (3) d. Daniels 7–5 6–2; Garrison (2) d. Cecchini 6–1 6–3.

Semi-finals: Maleeva (4) d. Navratilova (1) 6–4 2–6 6–1; Sanchez-Vicario (3) d. Garrison (2) 6–7 6–3 7–6.

Final: Maleeva (4) d. Sanchez-Vicario (3) 6–1 1–6 6–4.

WOMEN'S DOUBLES – Cancelled.

POST CEREALS US HARDCOURT ($225,000)

SAN ANTONIO, TX, 28 MARCH–1 APRIL

WOMEN'S SINGLES – 1st round: L. McNeil d. G. Sabatini (ARG) (1) 6–3 6–4; G. Fernandez d. C. Lindqvist (SWE) 6–1 6–0; M. Maleeva Fragnière (SUI) (3) d. E. Reinach (RSA) 6–2 6–0; C. Cunningham d. K. Rinaldi 4–6 6–1 6–4; R. Fairbank Nideffer d. R. White 6–1 6–2; J. Novotna (TCH) (4) d. A. Minter (AUS) 6–4 6–1; H. Mandlikova (AUS) d. L. Savchenko (URS) 6–4 7–5; M. Seles (YUG) (2) d. A. Smith 6–3 7–5.

Quarter-finals: McNeil d. Fernandez 6–2 6–0; Maleeva Fragnière (3) d. Cunningham 6–1 6–1; Fairbank Nideffer d. Novotna (4) 6–1 2–6 7–5; Seles (2) d. Mandlikova 6–4 6–4.

Semi-finals: Maleeva (3) d. McNeil 6–0 6–4; Seles (2) d. Fairbank Nideffer 6–3 6–0.

Final: Seles (2) d. Maleeva Fragnière (3) 6–4 6–3.

WOMEN'S DOUBLES – Final: K. Jordan/E. Smylie d. Fernandez/White 7–5 7–5.

FAMILY CIRCLE MAGAZINE CUP ($500,000)

HILTON HEAD ISLAND, SC, 2–8 APRIL

WOMEN'S SINGLES – 1st round: M. Navratilova (1) – bye; H. Cioffi d. R. Casals 6–3 6–4; L. Garrone (ITA) d. B. Romano (ITA) 7–5 4–6 6–2; I. Cueto (FRG) (12) d. T. Phelps 6–2 6–3; C. Kohde-Kilsch (FRG) d. S. Cecchini (ITA) (9) 6–3 6–1; L. Lapi (ITA) d. W. White 6–1 6–4; L. Harvey-Wild d. H. Ter Riet (HOL) 6–0 6–1; K. Maleeva (BUL) (5) – bye; Z. Garrison (3) – bye; B. Bowes d. K. Shin 4–6 6–2 6–2; T. Whitlinger d. S. Collins 3–6 6–1 6–2; L. Ferrando (!TA) (15) d. K. Schimper (RSA) 6–4 6–1; A. Keller d. B. Fulco (ARG) (14) 6–1 4–0 ret.; R. Rajchrtova (TCH) d. H. Brioukhovets (URS) 2–6 6–4 6 3; A. Gooden d. P. Vasquez (PER) 6–4 6–3; L. Gildemeister (PER) (7) – bye; N. Zvereva (URS) (6) – bye; P. Tarabini (ARG) d. E. Rossides 6–1 7–6; P. Langrova (TCH) d. D. Faber 2–6 6–4 6–1; L. Meshki (URS) (11) d. B. Baranski (POL) 3–6 6–2 6–0; C. Caverzasio (ITA) (16) d. I. Budarova (TCH) 6–2 6–3; S. Martin d. J. Santrock 6–4 6–3; C. Benjamin d. A. Vieira (BRA) 6–4 6–2; C. Martinez (ESP) (4) – bye; H. Kelesi (CAN) (8) – bye; S. Goles (YUG) d. A. Temesvari (HUN) 6–2 2–6 7–5; M. Paz (ARG) d. V. Martinek (FRG) 6–4 3–6 7–5; G. Magers (10) d. E. Pampoulova (BUL) 6–3 6–3; J. Capriati d. S. Sloane (13) 6–4 6–1; A. Kanellopoulou (GRE) d. L. Corsato (BRA) 6–2 6–4; M-L. Daniels d. C. MacGregor 6–3 6–4; A. Sanchez-Vicario (ESP) (2) – bye.

2nd round: Navratilova (1) d. Cioffi 6–2 6–1; Cueto (12) d. Garrone 6–1 6–3; Lapi d. Kohde-Kilsch 6–3 7–6; Maleeva (5) d. Harvey-Wild 6–1 6–2; Garrison (3) d. Bowes 6–2 6–2; Ferrando (15) d. Whitlinger 6–2 6–1; Rajchrtova d. Keller 4–6 6–2 6–1; Gildemeister (7) d. Gooden 6–1 6–4; Zvereva (6) d. Tarabini 6–4 6–2; Meskhi (11) d. Langrova 4–6 6–2 7–6; Caverzasio (16) d. Martin 6–1 6–2; Martinez (4) d. Benjamin 7–6 6–0; Kelesi (8) d. Goles 6–2 6–2; Magers (10) d. Paz 6–4 4–6 6–3; Capriati d. Kanellopoulou 6–1 6–3; Sanchez-Vicario (2) d. Daniels 6–2 6–2.

3rd round: Navratilova (1) d. Cueto (12) 6–3 6–2; Maleeva (5) d. Lapi 7–5 6–3; Garrison (3) d. Ferrando (15) 6–1 4–6 7–5; Rajchrtova d. Gildemeister (7) 6–4 6–2; Zvereva (6) d. Meskhi (11) 6–2 6–1; Martinez (4) d. Caverzasio (16) 6–3 7–5; Kelesi (8) d. Magers (10) 6–1 7–6; Capriati d. Sanchez-Vicario (2) 6–1 6–1.

Quarter-finals: Navratilova (1) d. Maleeva (5) 6–0 6–1; Rajchrtova d. Garrison (3) 4–6 6–3 6–1; Zvereva (6) d. Martinez (4) 7–6 6–0; Capriati d. Kelesi (8) 6–2 4–6 6–1.

Semi-finals: Navratilova (1) d. Rajchrtova 6–4 6–3; Capriati d. Zvereva (6) 6–0 6–4.

Final: Navratilova (1) d. Capriati 6–2 6–4.

WOMEN'S DOUBLES – Final: Navratilova/Sanchez-Vicario (1) d. Paz/Zvereva (2) 6–2 6–1.

BAUSCH & LOMB CHAMPIONSHIPS ($350,000)

AMELIA ISLAND, FL, 9–15 APRIL

WOMEN'S SINGLES – 1st round: S. Graf (FRG) (1) – bye; P. Langrova (TCH) d. P. Barg-Mager 6–0 6–0; A. Keller d. S. Meier (FRG) 7–6 6–4; A. Temesvari (HUN) (13) d. E. Pampoulova (BUL) 7–5 7–5; L. Ferrando (ITA) (12) d. C. Dahlman (SWE) 6–3 6–3; A. Gooden d. H. Ter Riet (HOL) 6–2 7–6; C. Basset-Seguso (CAN) d. A. Schwartz 6–2 6–1; S. Cecchini (ITA) (7) – bye; Z. Garrison (3) – bye; B. Romano (ITA) d. S. Stafford 6–1 2–6 6–4; S. Collins d. S. Goles (YUG) 4–6 4 2–6 7–5; V. Martinek (FRG) d. R. Rajchrtova (TCH) 6–1 6–3; L. Meshki (URS) (9) d. N. Sodupe 6–2 6–2; A. Kanellopoulou (GRE) d. C. MacGregor 6–3 6–7 6–4; A. Grossman d. L. Garrone (ITA) 6–3 6–3; N. Zvereva (URS) (5) – bye; H. Kelesi (CAN) (6) – bye; M. Paz (ARG) d. A. Vieira (BRA) 1–6 6–3 6–1; L. Harvey-Wild d. T. Whittington 3–6 6–1 6–2; B. Fulco (ARG) (11) d. I. Budarova (TCH) 4–6 6–1 6–0; K. Rinaldi d. R. Simpson (CAN) 5–7 6–2 6–1; D. Faber d. S. La Fratta (ITA) 6–2 6–1; L. Lapi (ITA) d. B. Herr 7–6 6–2; A. Sanchez-Vicario (ESP) (3) – bye; G. Magers (8) – bye; C. Benjamin d. T. Whitlinger 3–6 7–6 6–4; A. Farley d. B. Baranski (POL) 6–2 6–0; I. Cueto (FRG) (10) d. P. Tarabini (ARG) 6–4 6–2; C. Caverzasio (ITA) (14) d. B. Bowes 2–6 6–1 7–6; L. Spadea d. A. Leand 6–4 6–4; C. Kohde-Kilsch (FRG) d. J. Santrock 6–3 4–6 6–3; G. Sabatini (ARG) (2) – bye.

2nd round: Graf (1) d. Langrova 6–1 6–0; Temesvari (13) d. Keller 6–4 6–2; Ferrando (12) d. Gooden 3–6 6–4 6–2; Basset-Seguso d. Cecchini (7) 6–4 3–6 6–4; Garrison (4) d. Romano 6–3 6–7 6–0; Martinek d. Collins 6–0 7–5; Kanellopoulou d. Meskhi (9) 0–6 7–6 6–4; Zvereva (5) d. Grossman 6–3 6–2; Kelesi (6) d. Paz 6–3 6–4; Fulco (11) d. Harvey-Wild default; Rinaldi d. Faber 6–4 6–2; Sanchez-Vicario (3) d. Lapi 6–3 7–5; Magers (8) d. Benjamin 6–1 6–4; Cueto (10) d. Farley 6–3 6–1; Caverzasio (14) d. Spadea 6–4 6–2; Sabatini (2) d. Kohde-Kilsch 6–2 6–4.

3rd round: Graf (1) d. Temesvari (13) 6–0 6–1; Basset-Seguso d. Ferrando (12) 6–4 6–2; Garrison (4) d. Martinek 6–4 6–4; Zvereva (5) d. Kanellopoulou 6–1 6–3; Kelesi (6) d. Fulco (11) 6–2 7–6; Sanchez-Vicario (3) d. Rinaldi 6–0 6–1; Cueto (10) d. Magers (8) 6–1 6–4; Sabatini (2) d. Caverzasio (14) 6–4 6–0.

Quarter-finals: Graf (1) d. Bassett-Seguso 6–4 6–4; Zvereva (5) d. Garrison (4) 6–1 2–6 7–6; Sanchez-Vicario (3) d. Kelesi (6) 7–5 6–4; Sabatini (2) d. Cueto (10) 6–3 6–3.

Semi-finals: Graf (1) d. Zvereva (5) 7–6 6–7 6–1; Sanchez-Vicario (3) d. Sabatini (2) 6–4 6–0.

Final: Graf (1) d. Sanchez-Vicario (3) 6–1 6–0.

WOMEN'S DOUBLES – Final: Paz/Sanchez-Vicario (3) d. Rajchrtova/Temesvari (7) 7–6 6–4.

ECKERD TENNIS OPEN ($225,000)

TAMPA, FL, 16–22 APRIL

WOMEN'S SINGLES – 1st round: M. Seles (YUG) (1) d. S. Collins 6–1 6–1; D. Faber d. J. Byrne (AUS) 6–3 6–2; M-L. Daniels d. A. Vieira (BRA) 6–4 6–2; S. Sloane (8) d. S. Stafford 6–4 2–6 7–5; C. Martinez (ESP) (3) d. B. Fulco (ARG) 6–1 7–6; A. Gavaldon (MEX) d. A. Kanellopoulou (GRE) 6–1 6–4; Cam. MacGregor d. B. Bowes 6–4 6–4; S. Meier (FRG) d. L. Gildemeister (PER) (5) 6–1 6–4; S. Cecchini (ITA) (7) d. A. Grossman 7–5 6–2; H. Ter Riet (HOL) d. P. Casale 6–2 6–0; L. Ferrando (ITA) d. L. Corsato (BRA) 6–2 3–6 6–1; K. Maleeva (BUL) (4) d. S. La Fratta (ITA) 6–1 6–0; H. Kelesi (CAN) (6) d. M. Paz (ARG) 7 –6 5–7 7–6; S. Smith (GBR) d. P. Langrova (TCH) 4–6 6–4 6–1; C. Dahlman (SWE) d. S. Foltz 6–2 6–0; A. Sanchez-Vicario (ESP) (2) d. T. Whitlinger 6–4 6–2.
2nd round: Seles (1) d. Faber 6–0 6–1; Sloane (8) d. Daniels 6–2 6–4; Martinez (3) d. Gavaldon 6–3 6–1; MacGregor d. Meier 2–6 6–2 7–6; Cecchini (7) d. Ter Riet 6–4 6–2; Maleeva (4) d. Ferrando 6–2 6–1; Kelesi (6) d. Smith 6–2 6–4; Sanchez-Vicario (2) d. Dahlman 3–6 6–3 6–0.
Quarter-finals: Seles (1) d. Sloane (8) 6–2 6–0; Martinez (3) d. MacGregor 6–2 6–3; Maleeva (4) d. Cecchini (7) 6–4 6–2; Sanchez-Vicario (2) d. Kelesi (6) 6–3 6–2.
Semi-finals: Seles (1) d. Martinez (3) 6–4 6–0; Maleeva (4) d. Sanchez-Vicario (2) 6–4 6–2.
Final: Seles (1) d. Maleeva (4) 6–1 6–0.
WOMEN'S DOUBLES – Final: Paz/Sanchez-Vicario (1) d. Cecchini/Gildemeister (4) 6–2 6–0.

CITIZEN CUP ($350,000)

HAMBURG, 30 APRIL–6 MAY

WOMEN'S SINGLES – 1st round: S. Graf (1) – bye; L. Lapi (ITA) d. L. Field (AUS) 4–6 6–3 6–1; J. Halard (FRA) d. B. Schultz (HOL) 5–7 6–0 6–1; N. Provis (AUS) d. R. Zrubakova (TCH) (14) 6–4 1–6 6–1; R. Rajchrtova (TCH) d. S. Cecchini (ITA) (10) 6–0 2–6 6–4; A. Coetzer (RSA) d. C. Dahlman (SWE) 0–6 6–1 6–3; S. Meier d. A. Huber 0–6 6–2 6–3; H. Sukova (TCH) (5) – bye; K. Maleeva (BUL) (4) – bye; I. Demongeot (FRA) d. M. Kochta 6–3 7–5; P. Langrova (TCH) d. A. Vieira (BRA) 6–4 6–4; C. Caverzasio (ITA) (15) d. S. Goles (YUG) 7–5 6–1; C. Tanvier (FRA) d. L. Savchenko (URS) (12) 6–0 2–6 6–4; W. Probst d. M. Strandlund (SWE) 6–1 6–2; S. Frankl d. N. Herreman (FRA) 6–1 6–1; J. Wiesner (AUT) (8) – bye; N. Tauziat (FRA) (6) – bye; S. Martin (USA) d. S. Hack 3–6 6–4 6–1; N. Jagerman (HOL) d. E. Reinach (RSA) 6–4 6–4; T. Morton (AUS) d. K. Duell 6–4 6–1; S. Hanika (16) d. F. Labat (ARG) 6–4 6–4; E. Pampoulova (BUL) d. M. Pawlik 4–6 7–6 6–2; B. Rittner d. E. Krapl (SUI) 6–0 6–1; A. Sanchez-Vicario (ESP) (3) – bye; L. Gildemeister (PER) (7) – bye; A. Kanellopoulou (GRE) d. J-A. Faull (AUS) 6–1 6–1; R. Baranski (POL) d. N. Medvedeva (URS) 7–6 6–1; L. Meskhi (URS) (11) d. B. Fulco (ARG) 6–2 2–0 ret.; I. Cueto (9) d. M. Jaggard (AUS) 6–0 6–2; M. Paz (ARG) d. A. Temesvari (HUN) 6–2 6–2; R. McQuillan (AUS) d. P. Tarabini (ARG) 6–7 6–0 7–6; M. Navratilova (USA) (2) – bye.
2nd round: Graf (1) d. Lapi 6–1 6–2; Provis d. Halard 6–4 7–6; Rajchrtova d. Coetzer 6–4 3–6 6–1; Sukova (5) d. Meier 6–1 4–6 7–5; Demongeot d. Maleeva (4) default; Langrova d. Caverzasio (15) 6–3 6–4; Probst d. Tanvier 3–6 6–2; Wiesner (8) d. Frankl 6–1 6–0; Tauziat (6) d. Martin 4–6 6–3 6–3; Jagerman d. Morton 6–3 7–5; Hanika (16) d. Pampoulova 6–4 6–0; Sanchez-Vicario (3) d. Rittner 6–4 6–1; Gildemeister (7) d. Kanellopoulou 7–5 6–4; Meskhi (11) d. Baranski 5–7 6–1 6–2; Cueto (9) d. Paz 3–6 6–4 6–4; Navratilova (2) d. McQuillan 3–6 6–1 6–1.
3rd round: Graf (1) d. Provis 6–0 6–2; Sukova (5) d. Rajchrtova 7–6 6–2; Langrova d. Demongeot 6–4 6–4; Wiesner (8) d. Probst 6–3 6–2; Jagerman d. Tauziat (6) 6–4 2–6 6–3; Sanchez-Vicario (3) d. Hanika (16) 6–1 6–1; Meskhi (11) d. Gildemeister (7) 1–6 6–3 6–1; Navratilova (2) d. Cueto (9) 6–2 6–2.
Quarter-finals: Graf (1) d. Sukova (5) 6–1 6–2; Wiesner (8) d. Langrova 6–3 6–1; Sanchez-Vicario (3) d. Jagerman 6–3 6–0; Navratilova (2) d. Meskhi (11) 6–3 6–4.
Semi-finals: Graf (1) d. Wiesner (8) 6–4 6–2; Sanchez-Vicario (3) d. Navratilova (2) 6–1 6–7 6–2.
Final: Graf (1) d. Sanchez-Vicario (3) 5–7 6–0 6–1.
WOMEN'S DOUBLES – Final: G. Fernandez/Navratilova (2) d. Savchenko/Sukova (1) 6–2 6–3.

XLVII CAMPIONATI INTERNAZIONALI D'ITALIA PEUGEOT OPEN CUP ($500,000)

ROME, 7–13 MAY

WOMEN'S SINGLES – 1st round: M. Navratilova (USA) (1) – bye; R. McQuillan (AUS) d. C. Kohde-Kilsch (FRG) 6–2 7–6; K. Kschwendt (LUX) d. S. Wasserman (BEL) 6–3 6–2; S. Cecchini (14) d. B. Fulco (ARG) 6–7 6–0 6–2; C. Caverzasio (16) d. M. Jaggard (AUS) 6–3 6–1; J. Halard (FRA) d. K. Piccolini 6–2 6–2; D. Faber (USA) d. L. Garrone 6–4 6–4; C. Martinez (ESP) (6) – bye; G. Sabatini (ARG) (4) – bye; A. Grossman (USA) d. H. Ter Riet (HOL) 6–4 6–2; R. Rajchrtova (TCH) d. A. Kanellopoulou (GRE) 5–7 6–4 6–4; L. Gildemeister (PER) (9) d. N. Provis (AUS) 6–2 7–5; J. Capriati (USA) (12) d. L. Laskova (TCH) 6–0

6–3; S. Sloane (USA) d. J. Byrne (AUS) 6–3 6–0; L. Golarsa d. L. Ferrando 3–6 7–5 4–1 ret.; N. Tauziat (FRA) (7) – bye; J. Wiesner (AUT) (8) – bye; A. Vieira (BRA) d. B. Romano 6–3 6–4; P. Tarabini (ARG) d. I. Demongeot (FRA) 6–1 6–4; C. Lindqvist (SWE) (13) d. N. Jagerman (HOL) 7–5 6–7 6–2; H. Kelesi (CAN) (11) d. J-A. Faull (AUS) 6–4 6–1; L. Lapi d. A. Temesvari (HUN) 6–2 2–1 ret.; K. Godridge (AUS) d. S. Smith (GBR) 3–6 6–1 6–4; A. Sanchez-Vicario (ESP) (3) – bye; M. Maleeva Fragnière (SUI) (5) – bye; S. La Fratta d. S. Martin (USA) 2–6 6–2 6–2; A. Coetzer (RSA) d. F. Romano 7–5 1–6 7–5; R. Reggi (10) d. N. Medvedeva (URS) 6–0 6–3; L. Meskhi (URS) (15) d. E. Reinach (RSA) 6–2 6–2; M. Paz (ARG) d. P. Langrova (TCH) 6–1 7–6; R. Zrubakova (TCH) d. L. McNeill (USA) 7–6 6–2; M. Seles (YUG) (2) – bye.

2nd round: Navratilova (1) d. McQuillan 6–2 3–6 6–2; Cecchini (14) d. Kschwendt 6–1 1–6 6–3; Caverzasio (16) d. Halard 7–5 6–2; Martinez (6) d. Faber 6–0 6–2; Sabatini (4) d. Grossman 7–6 6–0; Rajchrtova d. Gildemeister (9) 6–4 7–6; Capriati (12) d. Sloane 6–4 7–6; Golarsa d. Tauziat (7) 6–3 7–6; Vieira d. Wiesner (8) 5–7 7–5 6–2; Lindqvist (13) d. Tarabini 4–6 6–3 6–1; Kelesi (11) d. Lapi 6–2 6–0; Sanchez-Vicario (3) d. Godridge 6–1 6–1; Maleeva Fragnière (5) d. La Fratta 6–2 6–2; Reggi (10) d. Coetzer 6–4 6–1; Paz d. Meskhi (15) 6–4 7–5; Seles (2) d. Zrubakova 6–4 6–1.

3rd round: Navratilova (1) d. Cecchini (14) 6–4 3–6 6–3; Martinez (6) d. Caverzasio (16) 6–2 6–2; Sabatini (4) d. Rajchrtova 6–0 6–1; Capriati (12) d. Golarsa 6–3 6–7 6–2; Lindqvist (13) d. Vieira 6–4 6–2; Kelesi (11) d. Sanchez-Vicario (3) 6–4 7–5; Maleeva Fragnière (5) d. Reggi (10) 6–3 6–3; Seles (2) d. Paz 6–1 6–1.

Quarter-finals: Navratilova (1) d. Martinez (6) 6–2 6–0; Sabatini (4) d. Capriati (12) 6–2 7–5; Kelesi (11) d. Lindqvist (13) 6–4 6–3; Seles (2) d. Maleeva Fragnière (5) 6–0 6–2.

Semi-finals: Navratilova (1) d. Sabatini (4) 7–6 7–5; Seles (2) d. Kelesi (1) 6–1 6–2.

Final: Seles (2) d. Navratilova (1) 6–1 6–1.

WOMEN'S DOUBLES – Final: Kelesi/Seles d. Garrone/Golarsa 6–3 6–4.

LUFTHANSA CUP GERMAN OPEN ($500,000)

BERLIN, 14–20 MAY

WOMEN'S SINGLES – 1st round: S. Graf (1) – bye; M. Paz (ARG) d. S. Loosemore (GBR) 6–4 3–6 7–5; K. Piccolini (ITA) d. S. Smith (GBR) 6–3 6–1; F. Labat (ARG) d. I. Cueto (12) 4–6 7–6 6–1; L. Meskhi (URS) (14) d. A. Coetzer (RSA) 6–0 6–0; R. Rajchrtova (TCH) d. S. Martin (USA) 6–4 7–5; W. Probst d. B. Fulco (ARG) 6–3 4–6 6–2; K. Maleeva (BUL) (5) – bye; M-J. Fernandez (USA) (4) – bye; S. Hack d. S. Hanika 6–2 6–4; A. Huber d. T. Whitlinger (USA) 6–4 6–2; J. Wiesner (AUT) (9) d. V. Martinek 6–2 6–4; C. Lindqvist (SWE) (15) d. S. Meier 7–6 6–0; R. Zrubakova (TCH) d. J. Byrne (AUS) 6–2 6–3; A. Grossman (USA) d. I. Demongeot (FRA) 6–4 6–3; N. Zvereva (URS) (8) – bye; J. Novotna (TCH) (7) – bye; C. Dahlman (SWE) d. J-A. Faull (AUS) 6–4 6–1; N. Provis (AUS) d. R. McQuillan (AUS) 6–0 6–1; N. Tauziat (FRA) (10) d. M. Kochta 7–6 6–4; S. Cecchini (ITA) (11) d. R. Simpson (CAN) 6–4 7–6; J. Thompson (AUS) d. L. McNeill (USA) 7–6 1–6 6–3; E. Burgin (USA) d. E. Reinach (RSA) 1–6 6–3 6–1; G. Sabatini (ARG) (3) – bye; C. Martinez (ESP) (6) – bye; N. Medvedeva (URS) d. K. Rinaldi (USA) 7–5 7–6; L. Savchenko (URS) d. C. Kohde-Kilsch 6–1 6–7 6–1; H. Mandlikova (AUS) (16) d. S. Stafford (USA) 6–4 6–3; H. Kelesi (CAN) (13) d. K. Duell 6–1 6–4; M. Maleeva (BUL) d. A. Temesvari (HUN) 6–2 6–1; N. Jagerman (HOL) d. P. Tarabini (ARG) 0–0 ret.; M. Seles (YUG) (2) – bye.

2nd round: Graf (1) d. Paz 6–1 6–2; Piccolini d. Labat 3–6 6–4 6–3; Meskhi (14) d. Rajchrtova 6–1 6–1; Maleeva (5) d. Probst 6–1 6–0; Fernandez (4) d. Hack 6–3 6–3; Wiesner (9) d. Huber 6–4 6–7 6–4; Zrubakova d. Lindqvist (15) 6–0 6–3; Zvereva (8) d. Grossman 4–6 6–3 6–2; Novotna (7) d. Dahlman 7–5 6–4; Tauziat (10) d. Provis 6–4 6–7 6–4; Cecchini (11) d. Thompson 3–6 6–3 7–5; Sabatini (3) d. Burgin 6–2 6–1; Martinez (6) d. Medvedeva 6–4 6–3; Savchenko d. Mandlikova (16) 6–3 6–0; Maleeva d. Kelesi (13) 6–0 ret.; Seles (2) d. Jagerman 6–1 6–0.

3rd round: Graf (1) d. Piccolini 6–0 6–1; Meskhi (14) d. Maleeva (5) 4–6 6–2 6–0; Wiesner (9) d. Fernandez (4) 0–1 ret.; Zvereva (8) d. Zrubakova 7–5 6–1; Tauziat (10) d. Novotna (7) 2–6 7–5 7–5; Cecchini (11) d. Sabatini (3) 6–4 3–6 6–4; Martinez (6) d. Savchenko 6–3 6–1; Seles (2) d. Maleeva 6–2 6–3.

Quarter-finals: Graf (1) d. Meskhi (14) 6–4 6–1; Zvereva (8) d. Wiesner (9) 6–7 6–0 6–4; Cecchini (11) d. Tauziat (10) 7–6 6–3; Seles (2) d. Martinez (6) 6–0 6–3.

Semi-finals: Graf (1) d. Zvereva (8) 6–4 6–2; Seles (2) d. Cecchini (11) 6–1 6–3.

Final: Seles (2) d. Graf (1) 6–4 6–3.

WOMEN'S DOUBLES – Final: Provis/Reinach (6) d. Mandlikova/Novotna (2) 6–2.

PILKINGTON GLASS LADIES CHAMPIONSHIPS ($350,000)

EASTBOURNE, 18–23 JUNE

WOMEN'S SINGLES – 1st round: M. Navratilova (USA) (1) d. C. Benjamin (USA) 6–2 6–1; A. Minter (AUS) d. J-A. Faull (AUS) 6–4 6–4; S. Smith d. A. Gavaldon (MEX) 6–4 6–1; R. Reggi (ITA) (12) d. H. Mandlikova (AUS) 7–5 6–2; N. Tauziat (FRA) (9) d. S. Loosemore 6–1 7–5; N. Provis (AUS) d.

C. Kohde-Kilsch (FRG) 6–1 6–1; B. Nagelsen (USA) d. L. Ferrando (ITA) 2–6 6–3 6–2; N. Zvereva (URS) (5) d. N. Sawamatsu (JPN) 6–4 6–1; H. Sukova (TCH) (4) d. D. Van Rensburg (RSA) 6–4 6–2; E. Reinach (RSA) d. P. Harper (USA) 7–5 4–6 6–0; R. White (USA) d. B. Schultz (HOL) 7–5 6–2; C. Lindqvist (SWE) (15) d. M. Kidowaki (JPN) 6–3 6–2; L. Meskhi (URS) (14) d. D. Faber (USA) 6–2 6–2; K. Quentrec (FRA) d. N. Herreman (FRA) 6–3 6–1; M. Javer d. J. Salmon 6–2 5–7 6–2; J. Novotna (TCH) (7) d. L. Field (AUS) 6–4 6–2; J. Capriati (USA) (6) d. A. Smith (USA) 6–3 7–5; G. Magers (USA) d. E. Smylie (AUS) 6–1 7–6; J. Durie d. C. Wood 6–3 6–4; S. Gomer d. G. Fernandez (USA) (13) 2–6 7–6 9–7; A. Frazier (USA) (10) d. J. Halard (FRA) 2–6 6–2 6–4; N. Medvedeva (URS) d. N. Miyagi (JPN) 6–2 6–3; P. Fendick (USA) d. I. Demongeot (FRA) 7–5 6–3; M-J. Fernandez (USA) (3) d. C. Tanvier (FRA) 6–4 6–1; M. Bollegraf (HOL) d. B. Paulus (AUT) (8) 7–5 3–6 6–3; R. McQuillan (AUS) d. S. Amaich (FRA) 6–4 6–3; L. Savchenko (URS) d. A. Henricksson (USA) 6–2 6–3; R. Fairbank Nideffer (USA) (11) d. E. Inoue (JPN) 6–1 6–1; L. McNeil (USA) d. C. Porwik (FRG) (16) 4–6 6–2 7–6; C. Dahlman (SWE) d. T. Phelps (USA) 7–6 7–6; L. Golarsa (ITA) d. S. Stafford (USA) 6–4 5–7 6–0; Z. Garrison (USA) (2) d. E. Burgin (USA) 6–1 4–0 ret.

2nd round: Navratilova (1) d. Minter 6–2 6–3; Smith d. Reggi (12) 2–6 7–6 6–4; Tauziat (9) d. Provis 4–6 6–3 6–0; Zvereva (5) d. Nagelsen 7–5 7–6; Sukova (4) d. Reinach 6–4 6–3; White d. Lindqvist)15) 6–2 7–5; Meskhi (14) d. Quentrec 6–2 2–6 7–5; Novotna (7) d. Javer 6–2 6–2; Magers d. Capriati (6) 2–6 6–4 6–2; Durie d. Gomer 7–5 6–0; Medvedeva d. Frazier (10) 7–5 7–6; Fernandez (3) d. Fendick 6–7 7–6 3–0 ret.; Bollegraf d. McQuillan 6–3 6–0; Fairbank Nideffer (11) d. Savchenko 6–2 6–2; McNeil d. Dahlman 6–1 6–2; Golarsa d. Garrison (2) 6–2 7–5.

3rd round: Navratilova (1) d. Smith 6–3 6–2; Zvereva (5) d. Tauziat (9) 6–2 6–0; Sukova (4) d. White 6–3 6–3; Novotna (7) d. Meskhi (14) 6–4 6–1; Magers d. Durie 6–4 3–6 6–3; Fernandez (3) d. Medvedeva 6–1 6–3; Bollegraf d. Fairbank Nideffer 7–5 6–4; McNeil d. Golarsa 6–3 6–3.

Quarter-finals: Navratilova (1) d. Zvereva (5) 7–6 6–1; Novotna (7) d. Sukova (4) 7–5 6–4; Magers d. Fernandez 6–2 2–2 ret.; McNeil d. Bollegraf 6–3 1–1 ret.

Semi-finals: Navratilova (1) d. Novotna (7) 7–6 3–6 6–3; Magers d. McNeil 7–6 6–2.

Final: Navratilova (1) d. Magers 6–0 6–2.

WOMEN'S DOUBLES – Final: Savchenko/Zvereva (3) d. Fendick/Garrison (8) 6–4 6–3.

VIRGINIA SLIMS OF NEWPORT ($225,000)

RHODE ISLAND, 16–22 JULY

WOMEN'S SINGLES – 1st round: A. Sanchez-Vicario (ESP) (1) d. G. Helgeson 6–3 6–3; B. Schultz (HOL) d. E. Burgin 6–7 7–6 7–5; W. White d. A. Henricksson 4–6 6–4 7–5; M. McGrath d. D. Van Rensburg (RSA) (8) 6–4 6–4; G. Magers (5) d. L. Golarsa (ITA) 6–4 7–6; J. Richardson (NZL) d. A. Farley 6–3 1–6 6–4; E. De Lone d. B. Cordwell (NZL) 6–3 6–2; L. Field (AUS) d. P. Fendick 6–4 6–4; A. Leand d. M. Bollegraf (HOL) (6) 6–3 6–2; J. Durie (GBR) d. R. Baranski (POL) 6–0 6–1; A. Keller d. J. Salmon (GBR) 6–4 6–4; R. Fairbank Nideffer (4) d. J. Smoller 6–1 6–2; A. Smith (7) d. T. Phelps 6–2 6–3; Hu Na d. C. Toleafoa (NZL) 6–2 6–1; R. Field (RSA) d. K. Gompert 6–4 6–1; E. Smylie (AUS) d. L. Gildemeister (PER) (2) 2–6 7–6 6–3.

2nd round: Sanchez-Vicario (1) d. Schultz 4–6 6–2 6–2; McGrath d. White 6–3 6–2; Magers (5) d. Richardson 6–1 6–1; Field d. De Lone 6–3 6–2; Durie d. Leand 7–6 6–0; Fairbank Nideffer (4) d. Keller 6–2 2–6 6–3; Smith (7) d. Hu Na 6–0 6–3; Smylie d. Field 7–5 6–3.

Quarter-finals: Sanchez-Vicario (1) d. McGrath 6–4 7–5; Magers (5) d. Field 6–0 7–6; Durie d. Fairbank Nideffer (4) 7–5 6–0; Smith (7) d. Smylie 6–1 7–6.

Semi-finals: Sanchez-Vicario (1) d. Magers (5) 6–3 6–2; Durie d. Smith (7) 6–4 6–1.

Final: Sanchez-Vicario (1) d. Durie 7–6 4–6 7–5.

WOMEN'S DOUBLES – Final: L. Gregory/Magers (4) d. Fendick/Smith (3) 7–6 6–1.

PLAYER'S CANADIAN OPEN ($500,000)

MONTREAL, 30 JULY–5 AUGUST

WOMEN'S SINGLES – 1st round: S. Graf (FRG) (1) – bye; M. Javer (GBR) d. L. Spadea (USA) 6–1 6–1; R. Baranski (POL) d. B. Fulco (ARG) 6–4 6–2; L. McNeil (USA) (15) d. R. Simpson 6–1 6–1; L. Savchenko (URS) (13) d. H. Cioffi (USA) 0–6 6–1 6–0; J. Durie (GBR) d. S. Martin (USA) 7–6 6–3; S. Loosemore (GBR) d. N. Miyagi (JPN) 6–4 6–7 6–2; N. Zvereva (URS) (5) – bye; M. Maleeva Fragnière (SUI) (4) – bye; M. Maleeva (BUL) d. K. Jordan (USA) 6–4 6–3; A. Minter (AUS) d. Y. Segal (ISR) 6–3 6–0; H. Kelesi (9) d. C. Cunningham (USA) 7–6 6–3; C. Porwik (FRG) (11) d. E. Burgin (USA) 6–2 7–6; P. Hy d. C. Chabalgoity (BRA) 6–0 5–7 6–0; B. Bowes (USA) d. E. Smylie (AUS) 6–1 2–6 7–6; N. Tauziat (FRA) (7) – bye; B. Paulus (AUT) (8) – bye; T. Phelps (USA) d. M. Strandlund (SWE) 6–3 6–1; L. Field (AUS) d. A. Leand (USA) 6–3 7–5; N. Sawamatsu (JPN) d. J. Halard (FRA) (14) 6–3 6–3; S. Gomer (GBR) d. R. Rajchrtova (TCH) (16) 6–7 6–4 7–5; J. Richardson (NZL) d. L. Allen (USA) 6–0 6–4; B. Cordwell (NZL) d. J. Hetherington 6–2 3–6 6–4; K. Maleeva (BUL) (3) – bye; J. Capriati (USA) (6) – bye; L. Green (USA) d.

M. Mraz 6–4 6–0; C. Benjamin (USA) d. B. Nagelsen (USA) 2–6 6–3 7–6; M. Bollegraf (HOL) (12) d. A. Grossman (USA) 5–7 6–4 7–6; R. Reggi (ITA) (10) d. I. Demongeot (FRA) 6–4 6–3; M. Werdel (USA) d. S. Italiano 7–5 6–2; K. Rinaldi (USA) d. C. Toleafoa (NZL) 6–4 6–1; G. Sabatini (ARG) (2) – bye.
2nd round: Graf (1) d. Javer 6–1 6–2; McNeil (15) d. Baranski 6–4 6–0; Durie d. Savchenko (13) 6–2 4–2 ret.; Zvereva (5) d. Loosemore def.; Maleeva Fragnière (4) d. M. Maleeva 4–1 ret.; Kelesi (9) d. Minter 6–4 6–4; Hy d. Porwik (11) 6–1 6–1; Tauziat (7) d. Bowes 6–4 4–6 7–6; Paulus (8) d. Phelps 6–7 6–4 6–4; Sawamatsu d. Field 6–1 6–3; Richardson d. Gomer 7–5 6–2; K. Maleeva (3) d. Cordwell 6–0 6–2; Capriati (6) d. Green 6–4 6–0; Benjamin d. Bollegraf (12) 4–2 ret.; Reggi d. Werdel 6–1 6–0; Sabatini (2) d. Rinaldi 6–0 6–3.
3rd round: Graf (1) d. McNeil (15) 7–5 6–3; Zvereva (5) d. Durie 6–4 6–2; Maleeva Fragnière (4) d. Kelesi (9) 6–3 2–6 6–2; Tauziat (7) d. Hy 6–1 6–0; Sawamatsu d. Paulus (8) 6–2 1–6 6–3; Maleeva (3) d. Richardson 6–0 6–0; Capriati (6) d. Benjamin 6–3 6–2; Sabatini (2) d. Reggi 6–1 6–0.
Quarter-finals: Graf (1) d. Zvereva (5) 6–0 6–4; Tauziat (7) d. Maleeva Fragnière (4) 6–3 6–2; Maleeva (3) d. Sawamatsu 6–7 6–2 6–4; Sabatini (2) d. Capriati (6) 3–6 6–1 6–4.
Semi-finals: Graf (1) d. Tauziat (7) 6–2 6–2; Maleeva (3) d. Sabatini (2) 6–3 6–4.
Final: Graf (1) d. Maleeva (3) 6–1 6–7 6–3.
WOMEN'S DOUBLES – Final: Nagelsen/Sabatini (4) d. Kelesi/Reggi (7) 3–6 6–2.

GREAT AMERICAN BANK TENNIS CLASSIC ($225,000)

SAN DIEGO, CA, 6–12 AUGUST

WOMEN'S SINGLES – 1st round: S. Graf (FRG) (1) d. S. Rehe 6–0 6–3; K. Rinaldi d. L. Allen 6–3 6–2; S. Martin d. H. Ludloff 6–4 6–3; N. Tauziat (FRA) (5) d. A. Schwartz 6–1 6–2; Z. Garrison (3) d. G. Fernandez 6–2 6–2; N. Herreman (FRA) d. I. Demongeot (FRA) 4–6 6–2 6–2; R. Baranski (POL) d. C. Lindqvist (SWE) 0–6 6–4 6–1; T. Phelps d. G. Magers (7) 3–6 6–3 6–2; R. Reggi (ITA) (8) d. L. Gregory (RSA) 6–2 6–2; A. Grossman d. L. McNeil 6–1 6–4; P. Fendick d. E. Burgin 7–6 6–3; M. Maleeva Fragnière (SUI) (4) d. A. May 6–4 7–6; B. Paulus (AUT) (6) d. M. Javer (GBR) 6–3 6–1; E. Pfaff (FRG) d. A. Temesvari (HUN) 6–2 6–2; A. Gavaldon (MEX) d. C. Porwik (FRG) 7–5 6–4; R. Fairbank Nideffer d. L. Spadea 7–5 6–1.
2nd round: Graf (1) d. Rinaldi 6–3 6–4; Tauziat (5) d. Martin 6–4 6–2; Garrison (3) d. Herreman 6–2 6–1; Phelps d. Baranski 6–2 6–1; Grossman d. Reggi (8) 6–2 2–6 6–1; Maleeva Fragnière (4) d. Fendick 6–1 6–2; Paulus (6) d. Pfaff 5–7 6–2 6–2; Fairbank Nideffer d. Gavaldon 4–6 7–5 6–0.
Quarter-finals: Graf (1) d. Tauziat (5) 6–3 6–2; Garrison (3) d. Phelps 6–0 6–3; Maleeva Fragnière (4) d. Grossman 7–5 6–1; Paulus (6) d. Fairbank Nideffer 7–5 6–3.
Semi-finals: Graf (1) d. Garrison (3) 6–4 7–5; Maleeva Fragnière (4) d. Paulus (6) 6–0 4–6 6–1.
Final: Graf (1) d. Maleeva Fragnière (4) 6–3 6–2.
WOMEN'S DOUBLES – Final: Fendick/Garrison (2) d. Burgin/Fairbank Nideffer (4) 6–4 7–6.

VIRGINIA SLIMS OF LOS ANGELES ($350,000)

MANHATTAN BEACH, CA, 13–19 AUGUST

WOMEN'S SINGLES – 1st round: M. Navratilova (1) – bye; D. Graham d. R. White 7–5 7–5; B. Cordwell (NZL) d. S. Sloane 7–6 3–6 6–2; C. Lindqvist (SWE) d. L. McNeil 6–1 6–2; F. Labat (ARG) d. C. Porwik (FRG) (16) 2–6 6–2 7–5; K. Rinaldi d. N. Miyagi (JPN) 6–3 7–6; M. Pierce (FRA) d. A. Temesvari (HUN) 6–0 6–2; J. Novotna (TCH) (7) – bye; Z. Garrison (4) – bye; B. Fulco (ARG) d. K. Quentrec (FRA) 6–2 5–7 6–1; I. Demongeot (FRA) d. T. Takagi (JPN) 6–4 6–3; R. Fairbank Nideffer (13) d. M. Javer (GBR) 7–6 3–6 7–6; P. Louie Harper d. G. Magers (12) 6–4 6–1; A. Coetzer (RSA) d. C. Dahlman (SWE) 6–3 6–2; D. Van Rensburg (RSA) d. A. Grossman 6–1 6–3; K. Maleeva (BUL) (5) – bye; M-J. Fernandez (6) – bye; C. Toleafoa (NZL) d. A. Gavaldon (MEX) 6–3 6–4; P. Tarabini (ARG) d. S. Gomer (GBR) 6–2 6–4; L. Gildemeister (PER) (11) d. A. May 6–0 6–1; G. Fernandez (15) d. N. Herreman (FRA) 7–5 6–1; S. Rehe d. B. Nagelsen 6–4 6–3; H. Cioffi d. S. Hanika (FRG) 4–6 6–3 6–0; G. Sabatini (ARG) (3) – bye; N. Tauziat (FRA) (8) – bye; R. Baranski (POL) d. E. Burgin 6–3 3–6 6–2; T. Whitlinger d. E. Reinach (RSA) 6–0 6–4; A. Frazier (9) d. M. Paz (ARG) 6–2 3–6 6–1; A. Smith (14) d. D. Faber 6–2 6–2; N. Provis (AUS) d. A. Minter (AUS) 6–2 3–6 7–5; A. Keller d. P. Fendick 6–3 1–1 ret.; M. Seles (YUG) (2) – bye.
2nd round: Navratilova (1) d. Graham 6–1 6–2; Lindqvist d. Cordwell 6–4 5–7 6–3; Rinaldi d. Labat 6–0 6–7 6–2; Novotna (7) d. Pierce 6–4 7–5; Garrison (4) d. Fulco 6–0 6–4; Fairbank Nideffer (13) d. Demongeot 6–3 6–4; Coetzer d. Louie Harper 6–1 1–6 7–5; Maleeva (5) d. Van Rensburg 6–1 6–1; Fernandez (6) d. Toleafoa 6–2 6–2; Gildemeister (11) d. Tarabini 4–6 6–3 6–2; Rehe d. Fernandez (15) 6–3 6–3; Sabatini (3) d. Cioffi 6–2 6–0; Tauziat (8) d. Baranski 6–2 6–1; Frazier (9) d. Whitlinger 7–5 6–3; Smith (14) d. Provis 6–2 2–6 6–4; Seles (2) d. Keller 6–2 6–2.
3rd round: Navratilova (1) d. Lindqvist 6–1 6–1; Rinaldi d. Novotna (7) 3–6 6–3 6–4; Garrison (4) d. Fairbank Nideffer (13) 6–2 6–0; Maleeva (5) d. Coetzer 6–2 6–0; Fernandez (6) d. Gildemeister (11) 6–3

6–2; Rehe d. Sabatini (3) 5–7 6–4 6–4; Frazier (9) d. Tauziat (8) 3–6 6–1 6–1; Seles (2) d. Smith (14) 6–3 6–3.
Quarter-finals: Navratilova (1) d. Rinaldi 6–0 6–1; Garrison (4) d. Maleeva (5) 6–1 6–1; Fernandez (6) d. Rehe 7–5 6–2; Seles (2) d. Frazier (9) 2–6 6–2 7–5.
Semi-finals: Navratilova (1) d. Garrison (4) 6–0 6–7 6–4; Seles (2) d. Fernandez (6) 6–1 6–0.
Final: Seles (2) d. Navratilova (1) 6–4 3–6 7–6.
WOMEN'S DOUBLES – Final: Fernandez/Novotna (1) d. Paz/Sabatini 6–3 4–6 6–4.

NICHIREI INTERNATIONAL LADIES TENNIS CHAMPIONSHIPS ($350,000)

TOKYO, 25–30 SEPTEMBER

WOMEN'S SINGLES – 1st round: M. Navratilova (USA) (1) – bye; S. Rehe (USA) d. R. White (USA) 4–6 6–0 6–1; P. Louie-Harper (USA) d. C. MacGregor (USA) 6–3 6–2; M. Maleeva Fragnière (SUI) (5) d. T. Takagi 6–0 6–2; M-J. Fernandez (USA) (4) – bye; C. Tessi (ARG) d. M. Javer (GBR) 6–3 6–2; M. Werdel (USA) d. P. Vasquez (PER) 6–4 6–2; H. Sukova (TCH) (7) d. A. Leand (USA) 6–2 6–2; J. Capriati (USA) (6) d. M. Miyauchi 6–4 7–6; M. Maleeva (BUL) d. K. Okamoto 6–3 6–4; G. Fernandez (USA) d. M. Kidowaki 6–0 6–2; K. Maleeva (BUL) (3) – bye; A. Frazier (USA) (8) d. B. Schultz (HOL) 7–6 6–1; E. Sviglerova (TCH) d. J. Richardson (NZL) 7–5 6–3; E. Pfaff (FRG) d. M. Jaggard (AUS) 6–3 6–4; M. Seles (YUG) (2) – bye.
2nd round: Navratilova (1) d. Rehe 6–1 6–3; Maleeva Fragnière (5) d. Louie-Harper 6–2 6–2; Fernandez (4) d. Tessi 6–3 6–1; Sukova (7) d. Werdel 6–7 6–3 6–2; Capriati (6) d. Maleeva 6–2 6–4; Maleeva (3) d. Fernandez 6–7 6–2 6–2; Frazier (8) d. Sviglerova 6–2 7–5; Seles (2) d. Pfaff 6–1 6–0.
Quarter-finals: Maleeva Fragnière (5) d. Navratilova (1) 7–5 4–6 6–3; Fernandez (4) d. Sukova (7) 6–3 6–4; Maleeva (3) d. Capriati (6) 7–6 3–6 7–6; Frazier (8) d. Seles (2) 5–7 7–5 6–2.
Semi-finals: Fernandez (4) d. Maleeva Fragnière 4–6 7–5 6–4; Frazier (8) d. Maleeva (3) 7–5 6–4.
Final: Fernandez (4) d. Frazier (8) 3–6 6–2 6–3.
WOMEN'S DOUBLES – Final: M-J. Fernandez/White (2) d. G. Fernandez/Navratilova (1) 4–6 6–3 7–6.

VOLKSWAGEN DAMEN GRAND PRIX ($225,000)

LEIPZIG, 24–30 SEPTEMBER

WOMEN'S SINGLES – 1st round: S. Graf (1) – bye; L. Golarsa (ITA) d. L. Gregory (RSA) 6–4, 6–4; K. Rinaldi (USA) d. M. Kochta 1–6 7–5 6–0; M. Bollegraf (HOL) (7) d. A. Devries (BEL) 5–7 6–3 6–2; C. Martinez (ESP) (3) – bye; C. Lindqvist (SWE) d. S. Menning 6–4 6–0; C. Kohde-Kilsch d. K. Quentrec (FRA) 6–2 6–2; B. Rittner d. G. Magers (USA) (6) 3–6 7–6 7–5; B. Paulus (AUT) (5) d. J. Salmon (GBR) 6–4 6–4; A. Minter (AUS) d. N. Herreman (FRA) 6–2 7–5; D. Krajcovicova (TCH) d. W. Probst 4–6 6–4 7–6; J. Wiesner (AUT) (4) – bye; A. Strnadova (TCH) d. J. Halard (8) (FRA) 6–1 7–6; R. Zrubakova (TCH) d. R. Rajchrtova (TCH) 4–6 6–4 6–4; M. Paz (ARG) d. J. Durie (GBR) 4–6 7–6 6–3; A. Sanchez-Vicario (ESP) (2) – bye.
2nd round: Graf (1) d. Golarsa 6–3 6–2; Bollegraf (7) d. Rinaldi 6–4 6–0; Martinez (3) d. Lindqvist 6–3 6–3; Kohde-Kilsch d. Rittner 6–1 6–0; Paulus (5) d. Minter 6–1 6–0; Wiesner (4) d. Krajcovicova 6–1 6–1; Strnadova d. Zrubakova 6–2 6–4; Sanchez-Vicario d. Paz 7–6 6–3.
Quarter-finals: Graf (1) d. Bollegraf (7) 6–1 6–2; Martinez (3) d. Kohde-Kilsch 6–3 2–6 6–1; Paulus (5) d. Wiesner (4) 6–3 5–7 6–4; Sanchez-Vicario (2) d. Strnadova 6–7 6–2 6–1.
Semi-finals: Graf (1) d. Martinez (3) 7–6 7–6; Sanchez-Vicario (2) d. Strnadova 6–7 6–2 6–1.
Final: Graf (1) d. Sanchez-Vicario 6–1 6–1.
WOMEN'S DOUBLES – Final: Gregory/Magers (2) d. Bollegraf/Durie (3) 6–2 4–6 6–3.

BMW EUROPEAN OPEN ($350,000)

ZURICH, 8–14 OCTOBER

WOMEN'S SINGLES – 1st round: S. Graf (FRG) (1) d. A. Leand (USA) 6–1 6–4; D. Van Rensburg (RSA) d. N. Herreman (FRA) 7–6 5–7 6–4; N. Guerree (FRA) d. C. Suire (FRA) 6–1 3–6 7–6; N. Tauziat (FRA) (7) d. R. McQuillan (AUS) 6–7 6–2 6–1; M. Maleeva Fragnière (3) d. M. Bollegraf (HOL) 6–1 3–6 6–2; C. Porwik (FRG) d. J. Salnikova (URS) 6–2 6–2; B. Schultz (HOL) d. P. Tarabini (ARG) 6–4 6–4; J. Wiesner (AUT) (6) d. C. Caverzasio (ITA) 2–6 6–2 6–0; W. Probst (FRG) d. R Fairbank Nideffer (8) 6–2 6–3; L. Golarsa (ITA) d. S. Appelmans (BEL) 6–4 7–5; M. Paz (ARG) d. J. Halard (FRA) 6–4 4–6 7–6; J. Novotna (TCH) (4) d. J. Durie (GBR) 6–4 6–0; H. Sukova (TCH) (3) d. L. Ferrando (ITA) 6–2 6–2; E. Zardo (FRG) d. A. Mueller (FRG) 6–1 6–2; C. Kohde-Kilsch d. E. Pfaff (FRG) 7–5 6–2; G. Sabatini (ARG) (2) d. S. Menning (FRG) 6–2 6–1.

2nd round: Graf (1) d. Van Rensburg 6–1 6–4; Tauziat (7) d. Guerree 6–4 6–2; Maleeva Fragnière (3) d. Porwik 6–1 3–6 6–2; Schultz d. Wiesner (6) 6–7 6–4 7–6; Probst d. Golarsa 7–5 7–6; Novotna (4) d. Paz 6–2 6–2; Sukova (3) d. Zardo 6–4 7–5; Sabatini (2) d. Kohde-Kilsch 6–4 7–5.
Quarter-finals: Graf (1) d. Tauziat (7) 6–4 6–1; Maleeva Fragnière (3) d. Schultz 6–3 6–2; Novotna (4) d. Probst 6–0 6–1; Sabatini (2) d. Sukova (3) 6–4 7–5.
Semi-finals: Graf (1) d. Maleeva Fragnière (3) 6–7 6–2 6–3; Sabatini (2) d. Novotna (4) 6–7 7–5 7–6.
Final: Graf (1) d. Sabatini (2) 6–3 6–2.
WOMEN'S DOUBLES – Final: Bollegraf/Pffaf d. Suire/Van Rensburg 7–5 6–4.

PORSCHE TENNIS GRAND PRIX ($350,000)

FILDERSTADT, 15–21 OCTOBER

WOMEN'S SINGLES – 1st round: G. Sabatini (ARG) (1) d. J. Halard (FRA) 6–4 6–3; M. Paz (ARG) d. H. Thoms 7–6 6–1; B. Rittner d. M. Bollegraf (HOL) 6–2 4–6 3–0 ret.; H. Sukova (TCH) (6) d. N. Tauziat (FRA) 6–4 6–4; Z. Garrison (USA) (4) d. R. Zrubakova (TCH) 7–5 6–2; N. Guerre (FRA) d. W. Probst 6–3 1–6 6–2; R. Fairbank Nideffer (USA) d. K. Oeljeklaus 1–6 6–4 6–4; B. Paulus (AUT) (8) d. P. Paradis (FRA) 2–6 7–5 6–4; J. Novotna (TCH) (5) d. P. Etchemendy (FRA) 6–4 6–0; D. Van Rensburg (RSA) d. C. Kohde-Kilsch 1–6 6–4 6–2; C. Porwik d. C. Lindqvist (SWE) 3–6 6–2 6–0; K. Maleeva (BUL) (3) d. I. Cueto 6–0 6–1; J. Wiesner (AUT) (7) d. L. Golarsa (ITA) 6–2 6–4; S. Appelmans (BEL) d. E. Pfaff 2–6 6–4 6–4; R. McQuillan (AUS) d. A. Huber 2–6 6–3 6–4; M. Fernandez (USA) (2) d. P. Tarabini (ARG) 6–1 6–1.
2nd round: Sabatini (1) d. Paz 7–6 6–1; Sukova (6) d. Rittner 6–2 6–4; Garrison (4) d. Guerree 7–5 6–3; Paulus (8) d. Fairbank Nideffer 6–4 6–3; Novotna (5) d. Van Rensburg 6–2 7–5; Maleeva (3) d. Porwik 6–3 6–1; Appelmans d. Wiesner (7) 6–4 6–4; Fernandez (2) d. McQuillan 6–3 6–3.
Quarter-finals: Sabatini (1) d. Sukova (6) 6–2 6–7 6–2; Maleeva (3) d. Novotna (5) 7–6 6–3; Paulus (8) d. Garrison (4) 2–6 7–5 6–4; Fernandez (2) d. Appelmans 2–6 7–6 6–1.
Semi-finals: Paulus (8) d. Sabatini (1) 6–3 6–4; Fernandez (2) d. Maleeva (3) 7–5 6–0.
Final: Fernandez (2) d. Paulus (8) 6–1 6–3.
WOMEN'S DOUBLES – Final: Fernandez/Garrison (3) d. Paz/A. Sanchez-Vicario (ESP) (2) 7–5 6–3.

VIRGINIA SLIMS OF CALIFORNIA ($350,000)

OAKLAND, CA, 29 OCTOBER–4 NOVEMBER

WOMEN'S SINGLES – 1st round: M. Navratilova (1) – bye; R. White d. P. Tarabini (ARG) 6–3 6–4; R. Zrubakova (TCH) d. D. Faber 6–1 6–1; J. Wiesner (AUT) (6) d. A. Henricksson (USA) 7–6 6–4; B. Paulus (AUT) (4) – bye; M. McGrath d. S. Martin 6–1 7–5; R. Fairbank Nideffer d. A. May 7–6 7–5; A. Smith (8) d. P. Louie-Harper 6–3 6–2; A. Frazier (5) d. A. Leand 6–0 4–6 6–2; M. Werdel d. M. Paz (ARG) 4–6 6–3 6–3; M-L. Daniels d. M. Javer (GBR) 3–6 6–2 6–4; Z. Garrison (3) – bye; L. Gildemeister (PER) (7) d. P. Fendick 7–5 6–0; S. Rehe d. M. Pierce (FRA) 6–7 6–1 6–2; A. Temesvari (HUN) d. F. Labat (ARG) 6–2 6–0; M. Seles (YUG) (2) – bye.
2nd round: Navratilova (1) d. White 6–2 6–3; Zrubakova d. Wiesner (6) 6–2 6–1; McGrath d. Paulus (4) 6–7 6–1 6–0; Fairbank Nideffer d. Smith (8) 7–6 6–1; Werdel d. Frazier (5) 7–6 6–7 6–4; Garrison (3) d. Daniels 6–2 7–5; Rehe d. Gildemeister (7) 7–5 6–0; Seles (2) d. Temesvari 6–1 6–2.
Quarter-finals: Navratilova (1) d. Zrubakova 6–2 6–0; McGrath d. Fairbank Nideffer 6–3 4–6 6–3; Garrison (3) d. Werdel 6–7 6–1 6–2; Seles (2) d. Rehe 6–1 6–2.
Semi-finals: Navratilova (1) d. McGrath 6–4 6–3; Seles (2) d. Garrison (3) 6–1 3–6 6–2.
Final: Seles (2) d. Navratilova (1) 6–3 7–6.
WOMEN'S DOUBLES – Final: McGrath/Smith (1) d. Fairbank Nideffer/White (2) 2–6 6–0 6–4.

MIDLAND BANK CHAMPIONSHIP ($350,000)

BRIGHTON, 22–28 OCTOBER

WOMEN'S SINGLES – 1st round: S. Graf (FRG) (1) d. C. Dahlman (SWE) 6–2 6–2; N. Herreman (FRA) d. C. Kohde-Kilsch (FRG) 7–6 7–5; C. Suire (FRA) d. A. Devries (BEL) 6–4 7–5; N. Tauziat (FRA) (5) d. S. Loosemore 6–1 6–2; C. Wood d. N. Zvereva (URS) (4) 6–3 6–3; C. Lindqvist (SWE) d. J. Durie 3–6 6–4 6–2; C. Caverzasio (ITA) d. C. Tanvier (FRA) 6–2 7–5; S. Appelmans (BEL) (7) d. L. Garrone (ITA) 2–6 6–4 6–2; S. Gomer d. R. McQuillan (AUS) (8) 6–1 6–1; P. Vasquez (PER) d. J. Salmon 4–6 7–6 6–3; M. Maleeva (BUL) d. D. Faber (USA) 6–4 6–2; H. Sukova (TCH) (3) d. V. Milvidskaia (URS) 6–4 7–6; S.

Cecchini (ITA) (6) d. B. Borneo 6–3 6–4; S. Dopfer (AUT) d. D. Krajcovicova (TCH) 7–5 6–3; K. Hand d. B. Schultz (HOL) 7–6 7–6; K. Maleeva (BUL) (2) d. P. Thoren (FIN) 6–3 5–7 6–3.
2nd round: Graf (1) d. Herreman 6–4 6–2; Tauziat (5) d. Suire 7–6 6–4; Lindqvist d. Wood 6–2 6–0; Caverzasio d. Appelmans (7) 6–2 7–5; Gomer d. Vasquez 6–7 6–4 6–4; Sukova (3) d. Maleeva 6–4 6–1; Cecchini (6) d. Dopfer 7–6 6–3; Maleeva (2) d. Hand 6–2 6–2.
Quarter-finals: Graf (1) d. Tauziat (5) 6–2 6–4; Lindqvist d. Caverzasio 6–2 6–3; Sukova (3) d. Gomer 6–1 6–1; Maleeva (2) d. Cecchini (6) 7–5 6–0.
Semi-finals: Graf (1) d. Lindqvist 6–2 7–5; Sukova (3) d. Maleeva (2) 6–4 6–7 6–3.
Final: Graf (1) d. Sukova (3) 7–5 6–3.
WOMEN'S DOUBLES – Final: Sukova/Tauziat (1) d. Durie/Zvereva (2) 6–1 6–4.

VIRGINIA SLIMS OF NEW ENGLAND ($350,000)

WORCESTER, NE, 5–11 NOVEMBER

WOMEN'S SINGLES – 1st round: S. Graf (FRG) (1) – bye; A. Smith d. M-L. Daniels 7–6 6–2; R. Baranski d. K. Greenman 6–2 6–4; N. Zvereva (URS) (7) d. M. Werdel 6–4 6–3; A. Sanchez-Vicario (ESP) (4) – bye; M. Paz (ARG) d. A. Henricksson 6–3 7–6; E. Smylie (AUS) d. A. Leand 6–0 6–1; Maleeva Fragnière (SUI) (5) d. R. Zrubakova (TCH) 6–2 6–0; H. Sukova (TCH) (6) d. R. Fairbank Nideffer 6–3 6–3; S. Rehe d. G. Magers 6–7 6–4 6–3; L. Gildemeister (PER) d. A. Coetzer (RSA) 6–1 7–6; G. Sabatini (ARG) (3) – bye; A. Frazier (8) d. L. Savchenko (URS) 6–3 5–7 6–4; A. Temesvari (HUN) d. G. Fernandez 2–6 7–6 6–4; F. Labat (ARG) d. E. Pfaff (FRG) 6–1 2–6 7–6; M-J. Fernandez (2) – bye.
2nd round: Graf (1) d. Smith 6–0 6–4; Zvereva (7) d. Baranski 6–2 6–3; Paz d. Sanchez-Vicario (4) 4–6 7–5 6–4; Maleeva Fragnière (5) d. Smylie 6–1 6–1; Sukova (6) d. Rehe 4–6 6–2 6–2; Sabatini (3) d. Gildemeister 6–0 6–3; Frazier (8) d. Temesvari 6–3 7–5; Ferandez (2) d. Labat 6–1 6–3.
Quarter-finals: Graf (1) d. Zvereva (7) 6–0 6–1; Maleeva Fragnière (5) d. Paz 6–1 6–3; Sabatini (3) d. Sukova (6) 6–3 6–2; Fernandez (2) d. Frazier (8) 6–3 6–4.
Semi-finals: Graf (1) d. Maleeva Fragnière (5) 7–6 6–7 6–3; Sabatini (3) d. Fernandez (2) 6–2 6–4.
Final: Graf (1) d. Sabatini (3) 7–6 6–3.
WOMEN'S DOUBLES – Final: G. Fernandez/Sukova (1) d. M-J. Fernandez/J. Novotna (TCH) (2) 3–6 6–3 6–3.

KRAFT GENERAL FOODS WORLD TOUR

Tournaments with prize money below $225,000

DANONE WOMEN'S OPEN ($150,000)

BRISBANE, 1–7 JANUARY

WOMEN'S SINGLES – Quarter-finals: N. Zvereva (URS) (6) d. H. Sukova (TCH) (1) 6–3 6–4; B. Schultz (HOL) d. K. Godridge 7–5 6–3; R. McQuillan d. K. Date (JPN) 6–0 6–4; J. Wiesner (AUT) (10) d. J. Novotna (TCH) (2) 7–6 6–3.
Semi-finals: Zvereva (6) d. Schultz 6–4 6–1; McQuillan d. Wiesner (10) 6–3 7–6.
Final: Zvereva (6) d. McQuillan 6–4 6–0.
WOMEN'S DOUBLES – Final: Novotna/Sukova (1) d. H. Mandlikova/P. Shriver (USA) (2) 6–3 6–1.

NUTRI-METICS INTERNATIONAL ($75,000)

AUCKLAND, 29 JANUARY– 4 FEBRUARY

WOMEN'S SINGLES – Quarter-finals: B. Cordwell (1) d. B. Bowes (USA) 1–6 7–6 7–5; S. Appelmans (BEL) d. A. Leand (USA) 6–3 6–3; R. White (USA) (8) d. J. Durie (GBR) 6–2 6–4; L. Meskhi (URS) (2) d. S. Wasserman (BEL) (6) 6–0 6–2.
Semi-finals; Appelmans d. Cordwell (1) 6–1 6–2; Meskhi (2) d. White (8) 6–4 6–2.
Final: Meskhi (2) d. Appelmans 6–1 6–0.
WOMEN'S DOUBLES – Final: N. Medvedeva (URS)/Meskhi (2) d. J. Hetherington/White (CAN) (1) 3–6 6–3 7–6.

BREYERS TENNIS CLASSIC ($150,000)

WICHITA, KA, 5–11 FEBRUARY

WOMEN'S SINGLES – Quarter-finals: N. Tauziat (FRA) (1) d. M. Bollegraf (HOL) (7) 6–1 6–2; P. Louie Harper d. A. Minter (AUS) (5) 6–3 6–3; D. Van Rensburg (RSA) d. M-L. Daniels 6–1 4–6 6–2; S. Sloane (6) d. A. Frazier (2) 7–5 3–6 6–3.
Semi-finals: Tauziat (1) d. Louie Harper 6–3 6–2; Van Rensburg d. Sloane 6–2 7–6.
Final: Van Rensburg d. Tauziat (1) 2–6 7–5 6–2.
WOMEN'S DOUBLES – Final: Bollegraf/M. McGrath (1) d. Daniels/R. White (3) 6–0 6–2.

FERNLEAF INTERNATIONAL CLASSIC ($75,000)

WELLINGTON, 5–11 FEBRUARY

WOMEN'S SINGLES – Quarter-finals: W. Probst (FRG) (6) d. E. Zardo (SUI) 7–5 6–3; S. Appelmans (BEL) d. M. Maleeva (BUL) 6–1 7–5; C. Toleafoa d. S. Wasserman (BEL) (5) 6–7 6–2 6–1; L. Meskhi (URS) (2) d. B. Reinstadler (AUT) 6–4 6–0.
Semi-finals: Probst (6) d. Appelmans 6–4 6–2; Meskhi (2) d. Toleafoa 6–4 6–4.
Final: Probst (6) d. Meskhi (2) 1–6 6–4 6–0.
WOMEN'S DOUBLES – Final: N. Medvedeva (URS)/Meskhi (1) d. M. Jaggard (AUS)/J. Richardson (4) 6–3 2–6 6–4.

VIRGINIA SLIMS OF OKLAHOMA ($150,000)

OKLAHOMA CITY, OK, 19–25 FEBRUARY

WOMEN'S SINGLES – Quarter-finals: M. Maleeva Fragnière (SUI) (1) d. E. Inoue (JPN) (8) 6–2 6–0; A. Frazier (3) d. A. Minter (AUS) (6) 6–2 7–6; M. Bollegraf (HOL) (5) d. J. Santrock 6–4 6–2; A. Gavaldon (MEX) d. B. Schultz (HOL) 3- 6 6–4 7–5.
Semi-finals: Frazier (3) d. Maleeva Fragnière (1) 1–6 6–3 6–3; Bollegraf (5) d. Gavaldon 6–4 7–5.
Final: Frazier (3) d. Bollegraf (5) 6–4 6–2.
WOMEN'S DOUBLES – Final: M. Daniels/R. White (2) d. M. Bollegraf (HOL)/L. Gregory (RSA) (1) 7–5 6–2.

SUNTORY JAPAN OPEN ($150,000)

TOKYO, 9–15 APRIL

WOMEN'S SINGLES** – **Quarter-finals: C. Lindqvist (SWE) (1) d. B. Cordwell (NZL) (5) 6–2 6–2; E. Sviglerova (TCH) d. M. Javer (GBR) 6–1 6–4; E. Smylie (AUS) (6) d. K. Okamoto 6–3 6–2; N. Sawamatsu d. K. Date 6–4 7–6.
Semi-finals: Lindqvist (1) d. Sviglerova 6–1 6–2; Smylie (6) d. Sawamatsu 6–1 6–2.
Final: Lindqvist (1) d. Smylie (6) 6–3 6–2.
WOMEN'S DOUBLES** – **Final: K. Jordan (USA)/Smylie (2) d. Hu Na (USA)/M. Jaggard (USA) 6–0 3–6 6–1.

INTERNATIONAL CHAMPIONSHIPS OF SPAIN ($150,000)

BARCELONA, 23–29 APRIL

WOMEN'S SINGLES** – **Quarter-finals: A. Sanchez-Vicario (1) d. I. Demongeot (FRA) (8) 6–1 6–2; J. Wiesner (AUT) (3) d. R. McQuillan (AUS) (6) 6–0 6–2; I. Cueto (FRG) (4) d. J. Halard (FRA) (7) 6–2 6–4; M-J. Fernandez (USA) (2) d. L. Golarsa (ITA) 6–1 6–1.
Semi-finals: Sanchez-Vicario (1) d. Wiesner (3) 6–2 6–1; Cueto (4) d. Fernandez (2) 7–5 4–6 6–4.
Final: Sanchez-Vicario (1) d. Cueto (4) 6–4 6–2.
WOMEN'S DOUBLES** – **Final: M. Paz (ARG)/Sanchez-Vicario (1) d. S. Goles (YUG)/P. Tarabini (ARG) (4) 6–7 6–2 6–1.

DHL SINGAPORE OPEN ($75,000)

SINGAPORE, 16–22 APRIL

WOMEN'S SINGLES** – **Quarter-finals: M. Kidowaki (JPN) (12) d. P. Vasquez (PER) 6–2 6–3; N. Sawamatsu (JPN) d. T. Takagi (JPN) 6–1 6–3; S. Loosemore (GBR) d. P. Hy (CAN) 6–3 6–4; S. Applemans (BEL) (8) d. M. Werdel (USA) (9) 7–5 3–6 6–3.
Semi-finals: Sawamatsu d. Kidowaki (12) 4–6 7–6 6–3; Loosemore d. Applemans (8) 5–7 6–2 6–3.
Final: Sawamatsu d. Loosemore 7–6 3–6 6–4.
WOMEN'S DOUBLES** – **Final: J. Durie (GBR)/J. Hetherington (CAN) (3) d. P. Paradis (FRA)/C. Suire (FRA) 6–4 6–1.

TROFEO ILVA–COPPA MANTEGAZZA ($75,000)

TARANTO, 1–6 MAY

WOMEN'S SINGLES** – **Quarter-finals: R. Reggi (1) d. T. Scheuer-Larsen (DEN) 5–7 6–2 6–3; P. Etchemendy (FRA) d. A. Grossman (USA) (4) 3–6 6–0 6–2; P. Ritter (AUT) d. K. Piccolini 5–7 6–4 6–3; A. Dechaume (FRA) d. L. Golarsa (2) 7–6 6–2.
Semi-finals: Reggi (1) d. Etchemendy 6–3 2–6 6–4; Dechaume d. Ritter 6–2 6–3.
Final: Reggi (1) d. Dechaume 3–6 6–0 6–2.
WOMEN'S DOUBLES** – **Final: E. Brioukhovets (URS)/E. Maniokova (URS) d. S. Farina/R. Grande 7–6 6–1.

GENEVA EUROPEAN OPEN ($150,000)

GENEVA, 21–27 MAY

WOMEN'S SINGLES** – **Quarter-finals: S. Hack (FRG) d. S. Stafford (USA) 6–1 6–0; H. Kelesi (CAN) (3) d. C. Caverzasio (ITA) (8) 3–6 6–1 6–1; E. Zardo d. L. Garrone (ITA) 4–6 6–4 6–2; B. Paulus (AUT) (2) d. A. Coetzer (RSA) 6–2 6–2.
Semi-finals: Kelesi (3) d. Hack 6–2 6–1; Paulus (2) d. Zardo 7–5 6–3.
Final: Paulus (2) d. Kelesi (3) 2–6 7–5 7–6.
WOMEN'S DOUBLES** – **Final: L. Field (AUS)/D. Van Rensburg (RSA) (3) d. E. Burgin (USA)/B. Nagelsen (USA) (1) 5–7 7–6 7–5.

INTERNATIONAUX DE STRASBOURG ($150,000)

STRASBOURG, 21–27 MAY

WOMEN'S SINGLES** – **Quarter-finals: M. Paz (ARG) d. I. Cueto (FRG) (1) 6–1 6–0; K. Quentrec d. V. Martinek (FRG) 6–7 7–6 6–2; M. Bollegraf (HOL) (3) d. F. Labat (ARG) 6–1 7–6; A. Grossman (USA) d. E. Pampoulova (BUL) 6–1 6–3.
Semi-finals: Paz d. Quentrec 6–1 6–1; Grossman d. Bollegraf (3) 2–6 6–0 6–2.
Final: Paz d. Grossman 6–2 6–3.
WOMEN'S DOUBLES** – **Final: N. Provis (AUS)/E. Reinach (RSA) (3) d. K. Jordan (USA)/E. Smylie (AUS) (1) 6–1 6–4.

THE DOW CLASSIC ($150,000)

BIRMINGHAM, 11–17 JUNE

WOMEN'S SINGLES – Quarter-finals: Z. Garrison (USA) (1) d. B. Cordwell (NZL) 6–1 6–2; N. Tauziat (FRA) (4) d. A. Smith (USA) (7) 6–1 6–2; R. Fairbank Nideffer (USA) (3) d. G. Fernandez (USA) (5) 4–6 6–2 7–5; H. Sukova (TCH) (2) d. L. Savchenko (URS) (8) 3–6 6–3 6–2.
Semi-finals: Garrison (1) d. Tauziat (4) 6–1 3–6 6–0; Sukova (2) d. Fairbank Nideffer (3) 2–6 6–4 7–5.
Final: Garrison (1) d. Sukova (2) 6–4 6–1.
WOMEN'S DOUBLES – Final: Savchenko/N. Zvereva (URS) (1) d. L. Gregory (RSA)/G. Magers (USA) (8) 3–6 6–3 6–3.

TORNEO INTERNAZIONALE ($75,000)

PALERMO, 9–13 JULY

WOMEN'S SINGLES – Quarter-finals: B. Paulus (AUT) (1) d. E. Zardo (SUI) 6–3 6–4; F. Romano d. K. Piccolini 0–6 6–4 6–4; B. Reinstadler (AUT) d. C. Caverzasio (LUX) (3) 6–3 4–6 7–6; I. Cueto (FRG) (2) d. M. Laval (FRA) 6–4 6–1.
Semi-finals: Paulus (1) d. Romano 6–2 2–6 6–1; Cueto (2) d. Reinstadler 6–1 6–1.
Final: Cueto (2) d. Paulus (1) 6–2 6–2.
WOMEN'S DOUBLES – Final: L. Garrone/K. Kschwendt (SUI) (4) d. F. Labat (ARG)/B. Romano 6–2 6–4.

SWEDISH OPEN ($75,000)

BASTAD, 9–15 JULY

WOMEN'S SINGLES – Quarter-finals: S. Cecchini (ITA) (1) d. S. Appelmans (BEL) (5) 6–3 3–6 7–5; E. Pampoulova (BUL) d. M. Paz (ARG) (3) 7–5 6–4; R. Zrubakova (TCH) (4) d. S. Dopfer (AUT) 6–2 6–4; C. Bartos (SUI) d. S. Hack (FRG) (6) 6–0 6–7 6–2.
Semi-finals: Cecchini (1) d. Pampoulova 6–4 6–3; Bartos d. Zrubakova (4) 6–2 6–4.
Final: Cecchini (1) d. Bartos 6–1 6–2.
WOMEN'S DOUBLES – Final: Paz/T. Scheuer-Larsen (DEN) (1) d. C. Bakkum (HOL)/N. Jagerman (HOL) 6–3 6–7 6–2.

ESTORIL LADIES OPEN ($100,000)

ESTORIL, 16–22 JULY

WOMEN'S SINGLES – Quarter-finals: F. Bonsignori (ITA) d. I. Cueto (FRG) (1) 6–2 4–6 6–4; S. Hack (FRG) (3) d. C. Mothes (FRA) 6–3 6–3; L. Garrone (ITA) d. E. Zardo (SUI) 3–6 6–2 6–1; P. Tarabini (ARG) (6) d. K. Piccolini (ITA) 6–2 4–6 6–2.
Semi-Finals: Bonsignori d. Hack 2–6 7–6 6–4; Garrone d. Tarabini (6) 6–2 6–2.
Final: Bonsignori d. Garrone 2–6 6–3 6–3.
WOMEN'S DOUBLES – Final: S. Cecchini (ITA)/Tarabini (1) d. C. Bakkum (HOL)/N. Jagerman (HOL) 1–6 6–2 6–3.

VIRGINIA SLIMS OF ALBUQUERQUE ($150,000)

ALBUQUERQUE, NM, 6–12 AUGUST

WOMEN'S SINGLES – Quarter-finals: J. Novotna (TCH) (1) d. K. Quentrec (FRA) 6–7 6–2 6–1; A. Smith (3) d. A. Coetzer (RSA) (7) 6–2 6–1; S. Sloane (6) d. D. Van Rensburg (RSA) (4) 7–6 6–2; L. Gildemeister (PER) (2) d. A. Minter (AUS) (8) 0–6 6–3 6–2.
Semi-finals: Novotna (1) d. Smith (3) 6–4 6–7 7–5; Gildemeister (2) d. Sloane (6) 6–2 6–2.
Final: Novotna (1) d. Gildemeister (2) 6–4 6–4.
WOMEN'S DOUBLES – Final: M. McGrath (USA)/A. Smith (USA) (3) d. P. Louie Harper (USA)/R. White (USA) (4) 7–6 6–4.

OTB INTERNATIONAL OPEN ($75,000)

SCHENECTADY, NY, 20–25 AUGUST

WOMEN'S SINGLES – Quarter-finals: A. Huber (FRG) d. S. Hanika 4–6 7 6 2–2 ret.; W. Probst (FRG) (7) d. A. Dechaume (FRG) 6–3 5–7 6–1; M. Werdel d. E. Reinach (RSA) 5–7 6–4 6–4; M. Paz (ARG) (6) d. R. Reggi (ITA) (2) 6–1 4–0 ret.
Semi-finals: Huber d. Probst (7) 6–2 6–0; Werdel d. Paz (6) 4–6 7–5 6–3.
Final: Huber d. Werdel 6–1 5–7 6–4.
WOMEN'S DOUBLES – Final: A. May (USA)/N. Miyagi (JPN) d. L. Ferrando (ITA)/Probst (3) 6–4 5–7 6–3.

ATHENS WOMEN'S OPEN ($75,000)

ATHENS, 10–16 SEPTEMBER

WOMEN'S SINGLES – Quarter-finals: F. Bonsignori (ITA) (6) d. S. Hack (FRG) (1) 6–3 3–6 7–6; K. Piccolini (ITA) (7) d. E. Zardo (SUI) (3) 6–7 7–6 6–0; C. Dahlman (SWE) (4) d. S. Smith (GBR) 6–1 6–4; M. Pierce (FRA) d. P. Thoren (FIN) 6–1 6–1.
Semi-finals: Piccolini (7) d. Bonsignori (6) 6–2 6–3; Dahlman (4) d. Pierce 6–4 3–6 6–4.
Final: Dahlman (4) d. Piccolini (7) 7–5 7–5.
WOMEN'S DOUBLES – Final: L. Garrone (ITA)/K. Kschwendt (SUI) (1) d. L. Laskova (TCH)/J. Pospisilova (TCH) (3) 6–0 1–6 7–6.

AUSTRIAN LADIES OPEN ($100,000)

KITZBUHEL, 10–16 SEPTEMBER

WOMEN'S SINGLES – Quarter-finals: J. Wiesner (1) d. P. Langrova (TCH) (7) 6–2 3–6 6–2; R. McQuillan (AUS) (5) d. V. Martinek (FRG) 6–2 7–5; C. Kohde-Kilsch (FRG) (8) d. C. Caverzasio (ITA) (4) 6–1 6–4; S. Cecchini (ITA) (2) d. I. Budarova (TCH) 6–3 6–1.
Semi-finals: McQuillan (5) d. Wiesner (1) 7–6 6–3; Kohde-Kilsch (8) d. Cecchini (2) 6–4 5–7 7–5.
Final: Kohde-Kilsch (8) d. McQuillan (5) 7–6 6–4.
WOMEN'S DOUBLES – Final: P. Langrova (TCH)/R. Zrubakova (TCH) d. Cecchini/P. Tarabini (ARG) 6–0 6–4.

LIGHT AND LIVELY DOUBLES ($175,000)

ORLANDO, FL, 12–16 SEPTEMBER

WOMEN'S DOUBLES – Final: L. Savchenko (URS)/N. Zvereva (URS) (1) d. M. Bollegraf (HOL)/M. McGrath 6–4 6–1.

OPEN CLARINS ($150,000)

PARIS, 17–23 SEPTEMBER

WOMEN'S SINGLES – Quarter-finals: C. Martinez (ESP) (1) d. R. McQuillan (AUS) (5) 6–4 6–3; J. Halard (4) d. D. Graham (USA) 6–7 6–2 6–3; P. Tarabini (ARG) d. P. Langrova (TCH) 6–4 6–3; S. Cecchini (ITA) (2) d. R. Rajchrtova (TCH) (7) 3–6 6–1 6–4.
Semi-finals: Martinez (1) d. Halard (4) 6–1 6–2; Tarabini d. Cecchini (2) 6–4 7–5.
Final: Martinez (1) d. Tarabini 7–5 6–3.
WOMEN'S DOUBLES – Final: K. Godridge (AUS)/K. Sharpe (AUS) (2) d. A. Dechaume/N. Herreman 4–6 6–3 6–1.

TOURNOI DE BAYONNE ($100,000)

BAYONNE, 24–30 SEPTEMBER

WOMEN'S SINGLES – Quarter-finals: A. Huber (FRG) (8) d. Z. Garrison (USA) (1) 7–5 6–3; C. Tanvier d. P. Paradis 7–5 6–4; N. Van Lottum (HOL) d. M. Laval 6–1 7–5; N. Tauziat (2) d. C. Dahlman (SWE) 6–4 6–2.
Semi-finals: Huber (8) d. Tanvier 6–0 6–4; Tauziat (2) d. Van Lottum 6–2 6–1.
Final: Tauziat (2) d. Huber (8) 6–3 7–6.
WOMEN'S DOUBLES – Final: L. Field (AUS)/Tanvier d. J-A. Faull (AUS)/R. McQuillan (AUS) 7–6 6–7 7–6.

MOSCOW OPEN ($100,000)

MOSCOW, 1–7 OCTOBER

WOMEN'S SINGLES – Quarter-finals: L. Meskhi (1) d. K. Habsudova 4–6 6–3 6–1; A. Minter (AUS) d. K. Godridge (AUS) 6–4 6–0; E. Brioukhovets (URS) d. R. McQuillan (AUS) (4) 6–3 6–0; G. Magers (2) d. B. Reinstadler (AUT) 7–5 2–6 6–4.
Semi-finals: Meskhi (1) d. Minter 6–2 6–4; Brioukhovets d. Magers (2) 6–4 6–3.
Final: Meskhi (1) d. Brioukhovets 6–4 6–4.
WOMEN'S DOUBLES – Final: G. Magers/R. White (USA) (2) d. E. Brioukhovets/E. Maniokova (URS) 6–2 6–4.

The American doubles specialist Gigi Fernandez won four Kraft Tour titles in 1990, all with different partners but she teamed with Martina Navratilova for her best win – a second US Open crown which ended the Grand Slam hopes of Novotna and Sukova.

(Professional Sport)

THE ARIZONA CLASSIC ($150,000)

PHOENIX, AZ, 15–21 OCTOBER

WOMEN'S SINGLES – Quarter-finals: C. Martinez (ESP) (1) d. A. Coetzer (RSA) (7) 6–3 6–2; M. Javer (GBR) d. E. Delone 6–1 6–2; M. Werdel d. S. Sloane (4) 6–1 7–5; A. Frazier (2) d. S. Rottier (HOL) 6–3 6–2.
Semi-finals: Martinez (1) d. Javer 6–1 6–1; Werdel d. Frazier (2) 6–4 6–1.
Final: Martinez (1) d. Werdel 7–5 6–1.
WOMEN'S DOUBLES – Final: E. Burgin/H. Kelesi (CAN) (4) d. S. Collins/R. Reis 6–4 6–2.

PUERTO RICO OPEN ($150,000)

SAN JUAN, 22–28 OCTOBER

WOMEN'S SINGLES – Quarter-finals: Z. Garrison (USA) (1) d. A. Grossman (USA) (8) 7–6 3–6 6–1; A. Cunningham (USA) d. F. Labat (ARG) 6–2 6–3; G. Fernandez (USA) (6) d. A. Keller (USA) 6–1 4–6 6–4; J. Capriati (USA) (2) d. A. Strandlund (SWE) 6–1 6–4.
Semi-finals: Garrison (1) d. Cunningham 6–4 6–4; Capriati (2) d. Fernandez (2) d. Fernandez (6) 6–2 6–1.
Final: Capriati (2) d. Garrison (1) 5–7 6–4 6–2.
WOMEN'S DOUBLES – Final: E. Brioukhovets (URS)/N. Medvedeva (URS) d. A. Frazier (USA)/J. Richardson (NZL) 6–4 6–2.

VIRGINIA SLIMS OF NASHVILLE ($150,000)

NASHVILLE, TE, 29 OCTOBER–4 NOVEMBER

WOMEN'S SINGLES – Quarter-finals: N. Medvedeva (URS) d. C. Dahlman (SWE) 6–3 6–4; E. Brioukhovets (URS) d. T. Whitlinger 6–3 5–7 6–1; S. Sloane (5) d. R. Reggi (ITA) (3) 6–3 6–3; E. Reinach (RSA) d. L. Harvey-Wild 6–3 6–3.
Semi-finals: Sloane (5) d. Reinach 6–3 4–6 6–0; Medvedeva d. Brioukhovets 6–3 6–4.
Final: Medvedeva d. Sloane (5) 6–3 7–6.
WOMEN'S DOUBLES – Final: K. Jordan /L. Savchenko (URS) (1) d. L. Schultz (URS)/C. Vis (HOL) 6–1 6–2.

JELLO TENNIS CLASSIC ($150,000)

INDIANAPOLIS, 5–11 NOVEMBER

WOMEN'S SINGLES – Quarter-finals: K. Maleeva (BUL) (1) d. S. Sloane (7) 6–3 7–5; L. Meskhi (URS) (4) d. R. Reggi (ITA) (5) 3–6 7–5 6–3; N. Medvedeva (URS) d. M. McGrath 7–6 6–4; C. Martinez (ESP) (2) d. N. Provis (AUS) (6) 6–2 6–2.
Semi-final: Meskhi (4) d. Maleeva (1) 6–2 6–4; Martinez (2) d. Medvedeva 7–5 6–0.
Final: Martinez (2) d. Meskhi (4) 6–4 6–2.
WOMEN'S DOUBLES – Final: P. Fendick /M. McGrath (1) d. K. Adams /J. Hetherington (CAN) (4) 6–1 6–1.

Any doubts about the skill and versatility of Monica Seles were dispelled in the Virginia Slims Championships in New York when the Yugoslav 16-year-old won the title and overtook Navratilova to become the No. 2 player in the world. *(Professional Sport)*

VIRGINIA SLIMS CHAMPIONSHIPS
Peter Blackman

Monica Seles, the bubbling 16-year-old schoolgirl from Novi Sad, Yugoslavia, enjoyed the greatest week of her meteoric tennis career when she captured the 1990 Virginia Slims singles championship at Madison Square Garden which had over-flowed with tension and drama for seven unforgettable days.

A few days before the curtain rose on the $3,000,000 tournament, the legendary Martina Navratilova pulled out in order to have an operation on both knees. The 7-times former champion's late withdrawal meant that the draw had to be re-done. 'Because of the knee trouble I am only half the player I should be,' she said from her bedside at a Denver, Colorado, hospital. But when the Slims started no one could possibly have predicted a scenario that had the world No. 1 Steffi Graf, becoming seriously ill on court, Seles becoming the youngest champion after getting lost in a New York department store, and the final going the full distance over five punishing sets.

The backcloth to Seles' 6–4 5–7 3–6 6–4 6–2 success over the Argentine Gabriela Sabatini was bizarre as the temperatures in the city soared to 72°F on the Tuesday and then dropped to 38°F on Thursday night. The temperature inside The Garden, though, stayed mainly red hot as the girls gave everything in front of record crowds. In the end Seles was the toast of New York. The French Open champion took a $250,000 winner's cheque back to her Sarasota, Florida, home after dancing the night away with her friends at a noisy end of tournament party off Fifth Avenue. 'It is let my hair down time,' she said. 'I have had a terrific week with everything I wanted actually coming true.' Not only did she win the coveted Slims title but, by beating Mary-Joe Fernandez in the semi-finals, Seles moved to No. 2 in the world after starting the year at No. 6. It was Seles' highest placing and it also marked the first time since 1981 that Navratilova has been out of the top two in the world.

The Final was significant on two counts: it was the first five set ordeal since the US National championships in Philadelphia in 1901 when Elizabeth Moore defeated Myrtle McAteer 6–4 3–6 7–5 2–6 6–2; and it went ahead without Graf, the defending champion. The re-drawn contest had thrown the athletic German against the 14-year-old Florida schoolgirl Jennifer Capriati who was originally scheduled to meet Sabatini, the US Open champion. Graf won 6–3 5–7 6–3 but that scoreline hides a dramatic near-withdrawal by the German who was overcome by gastric-flu and later confined to her bed for 24 hours. With her coach Pavel Slozil and her father, Peter, watching her at courtside, Graf's face went from sweaty red to chalk-white as she sat on her courtside chair hugging her stomach. She drank pints of water and felt sick. But she played on, showing great courage. 'I have never felt so bad on a tennis court,' she said. 'I just wanted to run off to the locker room.' Capriati also was a revelation and in defeat she said: 'I have always wanted to play her in a major tournament like this. I may have lost, but I know that I played well and that I made her fight hard for her victory. My time will come . . .'

Graf advanced towards her second showdown in nine weeks against Sabatini. The Argentine beauty had beaten Graf to land the US Open crown and with Graf still feeling below par the super-confident Sabatini ran out an easy 6–4 6–4 winner. Easy? In the previous round Sabatini had been continually under pressure before beating Conchita Martinez in three tough sets. But Sabatini, the third seed, knew she was playing well after a marathon first round match against Jana Novotna. In many ways this confrontation ranked for quality just below the final with Sabatini coasting one minute and then scrambling for survival the next before winning 6–1 5–7 7–6 (7–3). It was a very close shave.

So, in the top half Sabatini went through in some style. The bottom half of the draw was an electric playground. Seles easily disposed of Barbara Paulus, then ran into major problems against Arantxa Sanchez-Vicario who had earlier eliminated the tired Soviet Natalia Zvereva. Seles beat the Spanish girl 5–7 7–6 (8–6) 6–4 and afterwards Sanchez-Vicario said: 'I should have won. We exchanged some unbelievable shots. I had to be aggressive against her because, if you let her, she tries to hit winners every single time. This time I had the match in my hands and I let it go.' Fernandez, meanwhile, was quietly beating Nathalie Tauziat and Manuela Maleeva-Fragnière. A classic was predicted for her semi-final against Seles. It was a flop. Seles blasted a 6 3 6–4 win and for the first time during the week Fernandez looked worn out.

The Seles-Sabatini showdown had dawned after an exhilarating tournament. Graf versus Capriati had fuelled expectations which had been heightened by an absorbing first round battle in which Zina Garrison, the beaten Wimbledon finalist, had fallen to Martinez in straight sets. That had been a slaughter with the seventh seed winning only three games.

Seles swept into the final after she went missing for 90 minutes at *Bloomingdale's*. She had gone there with her parents looking for Christmas presents. They had split up and when the time came for them to meet again at a pre-arranged meeting point Seles could not find it. 'I went up and down the stairs, in and out of the exits, but I could not find them' she said. 'In the end we were brought together again by the pager service.' Seles didn't lose her way in the Final though. The pair had met once previously with Sabatini winning in 1989 at the Lipton Players championships. This time the stakes were higher and Seles went into the showdown with her confidence sky high after moving to No. 2 in the world.

It was a stupendous final which lasted a punishing three hours 47 minutes with both players proving their fitness, their courage and their blossoming talent. When Seles hit the backhand that won her the title she yelped, clenched her right fist and cried out: 'Oh yeah.'

'When I lost the second set I could have been discouraged,' said Seles. 'But I have learned how to fight back, forget the setbacks.' Sabatini was far from disappointed. 'I have played some of my best tennis and that is what I shall remember as I get ready for next year's matches.' Both Seles and Sabatini crashed with style through the five set barrier. They both agreed: 'We are not physically tired, just a little weary mentally.' The crowd which was close to 20,000 gave them a standing ovation.

Graf, meanwhile, remained a few days longer in New York in order to collect her $500,000 from the Slims Bonus Pool. For her the season had been different: a year in which she had seen the pack below her draw closer to her throne. For Seles and Sabatini it had been a crackerjack year.

Kathy Jordan and Liz Smylie won the doubles and a $90,000 cheque with a 7–6 (7–4) 6–4 win over Mercedes Paz and Sanchez-Vicario. The third seeds were excellent viewing value after battling through a high-class field.

The big first round shock was the exit of the top seeds Jana Novotna and Helena Sukova, the holders of the Australian, French and Wimbledon titles. They were beaten 6–4 1–6 6–3 by Natalia Medvedeva and Leila Meskhi. Slightly less shattering was the defeat of the second favourites Larisa Savchenko and Zvereva by Katrina Adams and Lori McNeil.

MADISON SQUARE GARDEN, NY, 12–18 NOVEMBER ($3,000,000)
1st round: S. Graf (FRG) (1) d. J. Capriati (USA) 6–3 5–7 6–3; K. Maleeva (BUL) (6) d. H. Sukova (TCH) 6–3 6–3; G. Sabatini (ARG) (3) d. J. Novotna (TCH) 6–1 5–7 7–6; Z. Garrison (USA) (7) d. C. Martinez (ESP) 6–3 6–0; M. Maleeva Fragnière (SUI) (8) d. J. Wiesner (AUT) 2–6 6–1 6–0; M-J. Fernandez (USA) (4) d. N. Tauziat (FRA) 6–1 7–6; A. Sanchez-Vicario (ESP) (5) d. N. Zvereva (URS) 6–2 7–5; M. Seles (YUG) (2) d. B. Paulus (AUT) 6–2 6–2.
Quarter-finals: Graf (1) d. Maleeva (6) 6–3 6–0; Sabatini (3) d. Martinez 6–3 6–0; Fernandez (4) d. Maleeva Fragnière (8) 6–1 7–6; Seles (2) d. Sanchez-Vicario (5) 5–7 7–6 6–4.
Semi-finals: Sabatini (3) d. Graf (1) 6–4 6–4; Seles (2) d. Fernandez (4) 6–3 6–4.
Final: Seles (2) d. Sabatini (3) 6–4 5–7 3–6 6–4 6–2.
DOUBLES – Final: K. Jordan/Smylie d. Paz/Sanchez-Vicario 7–6 6–4.

OTHER OFFICIAL PRO TOURNAMENTS

MEN'S CHALLENGER SERIES
MEN'S SATELLITE CIRCUITS
ITF WOMEN'S FUTURES CIRCUIT

The courage and relentless determination of Austria's Thomas Muster as he fought his way back into the top ten following a serious motor accident in March 1989, were universally admired. *(Professional Sport)*

MEN'S CHALLENGER SERIES 1990

Tournaments with minimum prize money of $25,000 that are immediately below the ATP Tour and carry ATP ranking points.

FINALS

JAKARTA 15–21 JANUARY
Singles: H. Skoff d. C. Garner 7–6 4–6 6–1. *Doubles:* E. Amend/T. Mercer d. A. Malik/J. Russell 6–4 6–7 6–3

HEILBRONN 22–28 JANUARY
Singles: M. Srejber d. A. Mronz 7–6 4–6 7–6. *Doubles:* D. Rikl/T. Zdrazila d. B. Talbot/J. Windhal 6–4 6–4

TELFORD 5–11 FEBRUARY
Singles: F. Santoro d. P. Nyborg 6–3 5–7 6–4. *Doubles:* N. Brown/N. Fulwood d. R. Barlow/M. Sinner 6–4 7–5

CROYDON 12–18 FEBRUARY
Singles: C. Saceanu d. U. Riglewski 6–3 6–0. *Doubles:* A. Castle/O. Delaitre d. N. Brown/N. Fulwood 7–6 6–3

SAO PAULO 12–18 FEBRUARY
Singles: M. Nido d. C. Motta 6–3 6–4. *Doubles:* J. Frana/G. Luza d. R. Camargo/I. Kley 6–3 7–6

NAIROBI 12–18 FEBRUARY
Singles: C. Miniussi d. P. Arraya 2–6 6–3 6–4. *Doubles:* E. Masso/Miniussi d. J. Cunha-Silva/M. Oosting 3–6 7–5 7–6

NAIROBI 19–25 FEBRUARY
Singles: C. Miniussi d. M. Oosting 6–2 7–6. *Doubles:* J. Cunha-Silva/E. Masso d. Z. Ali/L. Pimek 6–4 7–5

CAIRO 26 FEBRUARY–4 MARCH
Singles: T. Muster d. J. Altur 6–0 6–4. *Doubles:* D. Rikl/t. Zdrazila d. E. Masso/C. Miniussi 6–3 6–7 7–5

MARTINIQUE 5–11 MARCH
Singles: G. Raoux d. R. Weiss 3–6 6–3 6–3. *Doubles:* O. Delaitre/Raoux d. T. Nelson/R. Smith 6–3 7–5

AGADIR 12–19 MARCH
Singles: T. Muster d. G. Perez-Roldan 6–2 7–5. *Doubles:* J. Cihak/C. Suk d. O. Camporese/D. Nargiso w.o.

JERUSALEM 26 MARCH–1 APRIL
Singles: R. Weidenfeld d. S. Perkiss 5–7 6–4 7–6. *Doubles:* H. Holm/P. Nyborg d. C. Brandi/C. Caratti 6–1 2–6 6–3

ESTORIL 26 MARCH–1 APRIL
Singles: T. Tulasne d. C. Miniussi 6–2 2–3 ret'd. *Doubles:* K. Braasch/H. Davids d. T. Carbonell/U. Riglewski 5–7 7–5 6–2

ZARAGOZA 2–8 APRIL
Singles: C. Costa d. F. Cancellotti 6–3 6–4. *Doubles:* D. Rikl/T. Zdrazila d. Costa/F. Roig 6–3 7–6

PARIOLI 9–15 APRIL
Singles: F. Luna d. M. Larsson 6–3 4–6 6–4. *Doubles:* B. Stankovic/R. Vogel d. N. Bruno/S. Pescosolido 7–5 6–3

BRASILIA 9–15 APRIL
Singles: O. Delaitre d. B. Garrow 7–6 6–1. *Doubles:* N. Aerts/F. Roese d. S. Colombo/C. Kist 6–3 7–5

CAPETOWN 9–15 APRIL
Singles: G. Muller d. J. Bates 5–7 6–2 6–3. *Doubles:* M. Barnard/Bates d. W. Ferreira/P. Norval 6–3 6–1

SAN LUIS POTOSI 9–15 APRIL
Singles: R. Osterthun d. M. Washington 6–4 6–4. *Doubles:* L. Lavelle/J. Lozano d. L. Herrera/F. Perez-Roldan 5–7 6–3 6–2

MEXICO CITY 16–22 APRIL
Singles: F. Maciel d. L. Herrera 2–6 7–6 6–3. *Doubles:* P. Albano/V. Jansson d. N. Odizor/B. Shelton 6–3 6–4

DURBAN 16–22 APRIL
Singles: J. Bates d. G. Stafford 6–4 6–1. *Doubles:* W. Ferreira/P. Norval d. S. Kruger/G. Van Emburgh 6–0 2–6 6–3

OPORTO 16–22 APRIL
Singles: M. Koevermans d. F. Davin 6–3 6–3. *Doubles:* E. Bengoechea/C. Miniussi d. J. Clavet/F. Roig 6–0 6–3

NAGOYA 23–29 APRIL
Singles: R. Krishnan d. B. Garrow 6–2 6–4. *Doubles:* J. Carlsson/D. Lewis d. S. Matsuoka/S. Ota 7–5 6–2

PRETORIA 23–29 APRIL
Singles: M. Sinner d. W. Ferreira 6–4 6–4. *Doubles:* M. Keil/S. Patridge d. S. Kruger/G. Van Emburgh 6–7 6–4 6–4

TAMPA 23–29 APRIL
Singles: B. Shelton d. B. Dyke 6–7 6–2 6–1. *Doubles:* K. Flach/D. Flach d. Dyke/T. Svantesson 3–6 7–6 6–4

LJUBLJANA 7–13 MAY
Singles: M. Larsson d. D. Nargiso 7–5 6–7 7–6. *Doubles:* C. Costa/F. Roig d. O. Camporese/M. Koevermans 6–7 6–4 6–4

KUALA LUMPUR 7–13 MAY
Singles: N. Odizor d. C. Dosedel 6–3 3–6 6–3. *Doubles:* Odizor/P. Wekesa d. J. Canter/B. Derlin 6–3 6–4

BANGKOK 14–20 MAY
Singles: C. Dosedel d. P. Baur 6–3 6–4. *Doubles:* J. Canter/B. Derlin d. N. Borwick/D. Lewis 6–4 6–4

FURTH 28 MAY–3 JUNE
Singles: J. Tarango d. F. Rivera 6–0 6–0. *Doubles:* P. Ballauff/R. Osterthun d. M. Gorriz/A. Olkhovsky 7–6 4–6 6–3

TURIN 25 JUNE–1 JULY
Singles: J. Cunha-Silva d. J. Brown 7–6 6–7 6–4. *Doubles:* N. Borwick/D. Lewis d. C. Allgardh/M. Sinner 6–2 3–6 6–2

SALOU 2–8 JULY
Singles: M. Filippini d. J. Arias 6–3 6–1. *Doubles:* N. Borwick/D. Lewis d. Arias/S. Devries 6–3 5–7 6–3

NEU-ULM 9–15 JULY
Singles: D. Poliakov d. B. Wuyts 3–6 7–5 6–3. *Doubles:* M. Cierro/S. Colombo d. G. Cosac/I. Flegl 0–6 6–2 6–1

BRISTOL 9–15 JULY
Singles: C. Saceanu d. A. Boetsch 6–3 6–7 6–3. *Doubles:* A. Olhovsky/O. Rahnasto d. A. Boetsch/P. Nyborg 7–5 6–4

GRAMADO 16–22 JULY
Singles: P. Rebolledo d. C. Wies 6–2 6–3. *Doubles:* I. Kley/V. Solves d. P. Albano/E. Bengoechea 6–3 7–5

TAMPERE 16–22 JULY
Singles: R. Furlan d. F. Luna 6–3 6–3. *Doubles:* M. Koevermans/J. Siemerink d. M. Cierro/T. Svantesson 6–1 6–2

APTOS 23–29 JULY
Singles: H. Holm d. B. Garrow 1–6 6–3 7–6. *Doubles:* J. Brown/S. Melville d. M. Anger/M. Barnard 6–7 6–4 6–4

HANKO 23–29 JULY
Singles: M. Sinner d. A. Olhovsky 6–3 6–3. *Doubles:* J. Anderson/L. Wahlgren d. T. Nydahl/P. Svensson 6–3 7–6

CAMPOS 23–29 JULY
Singles: J. Oncins d. J. Daher 6–2 6–2. *Doubles:* Daher/Oncins d. N. Aerts/F. Roese 7–6 6–4

WINNETKA 30 JULY–5 AUGUST
Singles: C. Caratti d. C. Garner 7–6 6–1. *Doubles:* Z. Ali/M. Oosting d. D. Flach/L. Herrera 4–6 6–3 6–2

LINS 30 JULY–5 AUGUST
Singles: P. Rebolledo d. J. Zwetsch 7–6 4–6 6–1. *Doubles:* J.-L. Aparisi/J. Clavet d. J. Frana/A. Moreno 7–6 6–3

KNOKKE 6–12 AUGUST
Singles: M.-A. Gorriz d. J. Cihak 7–5 2–6 6–1. *Doubles:* A. Olhovsky/D. Poliakov d. X. Daufresne/D. Langaskens 6–4 4–6 6–3

SAO PAULO 6–12 AUGUST
Singles: J. Cunha-Silva d. C. Motta 6–1 6–2. *Doubles:* J. Frana/Motta d. G. Markus/J. Zwetsch 6–3 3–6 6–1

JAKARTA 6–12 AUGUST
Singles: M. Keil d. S. Patridge 6–4 6–2. *Doubles:* M. Briggs/D. Harkness d. Suharyadi/B. Wijaya 6–2 7–6

BRASILIA 13–19 AUGUST
Singles: C. Motta d. J. Oncins 7–6 6–4. *Doubles:* N. Aerts/F. Roese d. S. Colombo/C. Kist 6–3 7–5

SALZBURG 13–19 AUGUST
Singles: H. Skoff d. J.-F. Altur 6–2 6–2. *Doubles:* H. De la Pena/Skoff d. J. Donar/O. Jonsson 7–5 6–4

PESCARA 13–19 AUGUST
Singles: C. Allgardh d. G. Lopez 4–6 6–3 6–4. *Doubles:* B. Stankovic/R. Vogel d. M. Cierro/A. De Minicis 6–3 6–1

GENEVA 20–26 AUGUST
Singles: R. Arguello d. D. Orsanic 6–3 6–0. *Doubles:* H. Holm/N. Holm d. B. Stankovic/R. Vogel 3–6 7–5 7–6

VERONA 27 AUGUST–2 SEPTEMBER
Singles: R. Krajicek d. J. Eltingh 4–6 6–1 6–4. *Doubles:* C. Dosedel/D. Poliakov d. Eltingh/M. Oosting 6–0 6–7 6–4

HOSSEGOR 3–9 SEPTEMBER
Singles: R. Gilbert d. R. Agenor 6–4 6–4. *Doubles:* M. Gorriz/M. Ingaramo d. E. Bengoechea/E. Masso 7–5 6–2

VENICE 3–9 SEPTEMBER
Singles: B. Oresar d. A. Olhovsky 6–3 6–3. *Doubles:* C. Brandi/P. Mordegan d. H. Holm/N. Holm 6–1 6–4

CANBERRA 10–16 SEPTEMBER
Singles: B. Steven d. A. Kratzmann 6–3 6–4. *Doubles:* P. Doohan/B. Custer d. D. Adams/J. Morgan 6–3 6–4

AZORES 10–16 SEPTEMBER
Singles: F. Roig d. C. Pridham 6–3 2–6 6–4. *Doubles:* B. Haygarth/S. Patridge d. A. Castle/N. Odizor 6–7 7–6 6–3

MESSINA 17–23 SEPTEMBER
Singles: G. Perez-Roldan d. S. Pescosolido 6–1 6–3. *Doubles:* G. Lopez/F. Roig d. P. Arraya/C. Costa 6–3 6–2

GEVREY CHAMBERTIN 17–23 SEPTEMBER
Singles: G. Raoux d. H. Holm 2–6 6–4 6–4. *Doubles:* M. Bahrami/R. Gilbert d. J. Apell/P. Nyborg 7–5 6–2

WHISTLER 17–23 SEPTEMBER
Singles: S. DeVries d. C. Adams 3–6 7–5 7–5. *Doubles:* DeVries/P. Galbraith d. O. Smith/R. Smith 7–5 7–5

BOGOTA 17–23 SEPTEMBER
Singles: A. Jordan d. L. Nemecek 6–3 6–3. *Doubles:* M. Hadad/M. Rincon d. C. Claverie/G. Failla 7–6 7–6

THESSALONIKI 24–30 SEPTEMBER
Singles: C. Geyer d. H. Holm 7–6 6–3. *Doubles:* G. Bloom/A. Hombrecher d. N. Brown/J. Carlsson 6–1 7–6

SINGAPORE 1–7 OCTOBER
Singles: B. Laustroer d. S. Groen 7–6 6–4. *Doubles:* S. Guy/J. Letts d. M. Keil/K. Kinnear 6–1 7–5

MANAUS 1–7 OCTOBER
Singles: L. Herrera d. J. Oncins 6–2 7–5. *Doubles:* S. Cannon/A. Mora d. R. Acioly/M. Menezes 7–6 6–4

CURITIBA 8–14 OCTOBER
Singles: P. Rebolledo d. J. Frana 6–1 7–5. *Doubles:* H. Davids/J. Eltingh d. C. Kist/D. Marcelino 6–4 3–6 6–3

CASABLANCA 8–14 OCTOBER
Singles: R. Krajicek d. C. Dosedel 7–6 6–3. *Doubles:* J. Baguena/F. Roig d. Dosedel/Krajicek 6–4 5–7 7–5

PONTE VEDRA 15–21 OCTOBER
Singles: T. Ho d. C. Pridham 7–6 6–4. *Doubles:* D. Flach/K. Flach d. R. Deppe/B. Garnett 6–3 2–6 6–4

ILHEUS 15–21 OCTOBER
Singles: L. Herrera d. P. Baur 6–2 6–2. *Doubles:* H.-J. Davids/J. Eltingh d. R. Smith/T. Svantesson 4–6 6–3 6–4

BREST 22–28 OCTOBER
Singles: D. Pioline d. R. Krajicek 6–3 6–4. *Doubles:* M. Damm/G. Dzelde d. W. Ferreira/P. Norval 6–4 6–4

BERGEN 29 OCTOBER–4 NOVEMBER
Singles: A. Mronz d. J. Gunnarsson 6–4 6–4. *Doubles:* J. Brown/A. Jarryd d. C. Beckman/L. Jensen 6–3 7–6

RIO DE JANEIRO 29 OCTOBER–4 NOVEMBER
Singles: L. Mattar d. L. Herrera 6–3 3–6 6–3. *Doubles:* R. Smith/T. Svantesson d. S. Cannon/A. Mora 7–5 6–4

THE HAGUE 12–18 NOVEMBER
Singles: A. Jarryd d. M. Vajda 6–1 6–2. *Doubles:* M. Schapers/J. Siemerink d. A. Mronz/A. Olhovsky 6–3 7–5

SAO PAULO 12–18 NOVEMBER
Singles: J. Oncins d. J. Cunha-Silva 6–3 6–3. *Doubles:* R. Lubner/F. Montana d. N. Aerts/D. Marcelino 6–4 7–6

TASMANIA 12–18 NOVEMBER
Singles: S. Youl d. J. Anderson 7–6 7–6. *Doubles:* B. Custer/D. MacPherson d. B. Steven/S. Stolle 6–2 6–7 6–4

BOSSONENS 26 NOVEMBER–2 DECEMBER
Singles: C. Caratti d. M. Schapers 6–4 3–6 7–6. *Doubles:* Schapers/R. Smith d. H. Holm/N. Holm 6–2 7–6

MUNICH 26 NOVEMBER–2 DECEMBER
Singles: A. Jarryd d. R. Krajicek 6–2 6–4. *Doubles:* J. Wohrmann/M. Zoecke d. D. Poliakov/S. Vojinovic 6–4 6–3

GUAM 3–9 DECEMBER
Singles: J. Morgan d. C. Adams 6–2 7–6. *Doubles:* S. DeVries/T. Scherman d. M. Anger/A. Castle 6–1 3–6 7–6

HONG KONG 17–23 DECEMBER
Singles: C. Saceanu d. F. Barrientos 6–4 6–1. *Doubles:* N. Borwick/P. Wekesa d. C. Geyer/Saceanu 6–2 6–2

MEN'S SATELLITE CIRCUITS 1990

CIRCUIT	SINGLES WINNER	DOUBLES WINNERS
Australian	J. Frawley	P. Doohan/R. Rasheed
	J. Stimpson	B. Custer/J. Morgan
	J. Frawley	D. Adams/P. Tramacchi
Austrian	T. Buchmayer	A. Marcu/C. Wedenby
Brazilian	J. Oncins	J. Daher/J. Oncins
	M. Rincon	I. Cappelloni/E. Rossetti
	M. Stringari	J. Pino/M. Tabares
British	C. Caratti	B. Garrow/S. Salumaa
	O. Fuchs	
Canadian	M. Ruah	S. Morse/S. Patridge
Caribbean	L. Herrera	C. Claverie/M. Ruah
Central African	B. Black	B. Black/D. Izaak
Chilean	G.-L. Lobo	G.-L. Lobo/C. Gomez-Diaz
Czechoslovakian	T. Zdrazila	M. Damm/C. Suk
Dutch	J.-A. Fernandez	
Finnish	T. Nydahl	J. Donar/J. Jonsson
French	C. Pioline	T. Kempers/J. Siemerink
	A. Boetsch	A. Boetsch/R. Gilbert
	L. Barthez	B. Devening/J. Sullivan
German	M. Kupferschmid	V. Jansson/K. Thorne
	C. Weis	G. Dzelde/V. Gabrichidze
	F. Fontang	B. Karbacher/W. Kowalski
Hungarian	S. Noszaly	M. Trneny/R. Vasek
Indian	V. Gabrichidze	V. Gabrichidze/D. Poliakov
Indonesian	D. Heryanto	D. Heryanto/B. Wiryawan
Israeli	S. Perkiss	F. Loddenkemper/D. Poliakov
	S. Perkiss	A. Naor/R. Weidenfeld
Italian	F. Santoro	
	P. Pambianco	M. Ardinghi/M. Boscatto
	V. Roubicek	
Japanese	B.-S. Kim	
Korean	N.-J. Bae	Suharyadi/H. Nakano
Malaysian	B. Pan	A. Castle/J. Turner
Mexican	P. Crow	
Moroccan	M. Nastase	A. Beust/P. Gauthier
North African	F. Michelotti	J. Van Duyn/M. Hintermeier
Paraguay/Argentina	G. Schaller/L. Lobo	
Peruvian	D. Varela	I. Cappelloni/D. Varela
Portuguese	S. Patridge	S. Morse/S. Patridge
	V. Gabrichidze	M. Blackman/S. Enrochs
Romanian	A. Pavel	F. Segarceanu/G. Cosac
South East Asian	J.-S. Kim	
Spanish	J. Apell	J. Eltingh/J.-W. Lodder
	G. Lopez	C. Allgardh/J.-W. Lodder
	D. De Miguel	D. De Miguel/J. Burillo
	A. Garizzio	
	D. Prinosil	J. Ireland/A. Sproule
	A. Gutierrez	
Swedish	F. Fetterlein	
Swiss	K. Braasch	
USTA	J. Apell	S. Melville/J. Van Duyn
	G. Lopez	W. Ferreira/P. Norval
	T. Ho	J. Brown/S. Melville
	M. Wolf	K. Thorne/D. Harkness
	M. Robertson	C. Ferreira/D. Randall
West African	C. N'Goran	A. Fernandez-Fermosell/C. N'Goran
Yugoslavian	M. Fiorini	G. Cosac/F. Segarceanu

Austria's Judith Wiesner delighted husband Heinz by reaching the final of the Lipton tournament and ending the year ranked No. 17, her highest ever placing.

(Professional Sport)

ITF WOMEN'S FUTURES CIRCUIT

The Kraft General Foods World Tour was the showcase of the women's professional game in 1990 and consisted of over 60 tournaments offering prize money of $50,000 or more, totalling some $14 million, as authorised by the Women's International Professional Tennis Council (WIPTC). Players must have attained a Virginia Slims ranking of about 300 or higher in order to be able to compete on this circuit. With over 850 players now ranked, it is essential for women to be able to attain an initial ranking and rise up this list, which is computed regularly by the Women's Tennis Association (WTA).

A series of low prize money tournaments worldwide exists as an apprenticeship circuit to the Kraft General Foods World Tour. This level has been in existence for over a decade, funded and co-ordinated by regional and national associations responsible for the development of the grass-roots game in their respective countries. From 1990 this worldwide initiative was renamed as the ITF Women's Futures Circuit, which is run under regulations promulgated by the International Tennis Federation, the governing body of national associations. In 1990 this circuit offered over $2 million in prize money through 150 events worldwide. Eligible for WTA computer credit, ITF Futures events fall into the following categories.

$20,000 Development Circuits:
A circuit of three tournaments, each offering $5,000 in prize money, plus a Masters tournament offering $5,000 in prize money for the most successful players. Total prize money available is $20,000 over four weeks. Players receive computer points for the Masters event only and therefore these circuits, which are suitable for national unranked players, provide essential match-play experience for players under professional conditions to enable them to begin to earn an initial ranking.

$10,000 Satellite Tournaments:
Individual tournaments of $10,000 in prize money. Players receive computer points for the main draw only and these events therefore help them achieve their minimum three tournaments required to appear on the ranking list, and improve the position of players ranked below 150 on the computer.

Satellite Circuits:
A circuit of three tournaments, each of $10,000 in prize money, plus a Masters tournament of $10,000 for the most successful players, offering a total of $40,000 in prize money. Players receive computer credit for each tournament played if they reach the main draw, and these circuits provide essential match-play experience under more international conditions.

$25,000/$50,000 Challenger Tournaments:
Individual tournaments of $25,000 or $50,000 in prize money. Players receive computer points for both qualifying and main draw and these events help those ranked higher than 150 on the computer to improve their ranking towards qualification into Series events of $50,000 or more in prize money.

Further information on ITF Women's Futures events eligible for computer credit is available from the Director of Women's Tennis at the ITF London office, upon request.

DEVELOPMENT CIRCUITS – MASTERS

LEON, 26 FEBRUARY–4 MARCH
SINGLES: I. Concepcion (CUB) d. B. Rodriguez (CUB) 5–7 6–3 6–0.
DOUBLES: R. Pichardo (CUB)/Y. Montesmos (CUB) d. M. Hernandez/A. Meraz 6–0 6–4.

SEOUL, 12–16 JUNE
SINGLES: M-S. Park d. J-S. Choi 6–2 6–0.
DOUBLES: Park/M.-A. Sohn d. E-J. Han/Choi 6–1 6–2.

SATELLITE CIRCUITS

BEDFORD PARK, AUSTRALIA (EVENT I) 14–18 FEBRUARY
SINGLES: K. Sharpe d. N. Pratt 2–6 6–4 6–1.
DOUBLES: C. Barclay/K.-A. Guse d. M. Avotins/J. Limmer 6–0 6–0.

EAST BRIGHTON, AUSTRALIA (EVENT II) 19–25 FEBRUARY
SINGLES: N. Ercegovic (YUG) d. N. Pratt 6–1 7–5.
DOUBLES: H. Hirose (JPN)/Y. Hosoki (JPN) d. D. Jones/S. McNamara 6–3 6–2.

LYNEHAM, AUSTRALIA (EVENT III) 26 FEBRUARY–4 MARCH
SINGLES: J. Thompson d. D. Jones 6–3 6–0.
DOUBLES: D. Deskovic (YUG)/M. Jausovec (YUG) d. V. Elter (FRG)/T. Cerne (YUG) 6–2 6–3.

NEWCASTLE, AUSTRALIA (MASTERS) 7–11 MARCH
SINGLES: K. Sharpe d. J. Taylor 6–0 7–6.
DOUBLES: Sharpe/A. Woolcock d. A. Hirose (JPN)/Y. Hosoki (JPN) 3–6 7–5 6–4.

ASHKELON, ISRAEL (EVENT I) 26 FEBRURAY–3 MARCH
SINGLES: N. Rooimans (HOL) d. M. Oremans (HOL) 6–3 4–6 7–6.
DOUBLES: M. Anderson (RSA)/R. Field (RSA) d. I. Jankovska (TCH)/E. Melicharova (TCH) 6–3 6–4.

HAIFA, ISRAEL (EVENT II) 3–10 MARCH
SINGLES: Y. Segal d. R. Field (RSA) 6–1 6–1.
DOUBLES: M. Anderson (RSA)/Field (RSA) d. I. Jankovska (TCH)/E. Melicharova (TCH) 6–2 6–2.

JAFFA, ISRAEL (EVENT III) 11–17 MARCH
SINGLES: L. Zaltz d. M. Oremans (HOL) 7–6 3–6 6–2.
DOUBLES: M. Anderson (RSA)/R. Field (RSA) d. Oremans/N. Rooimans (HOL) 7–5 6–4.

RAMAT HASHRON, ISRAEL (MASTERS) 18–22 MARCH
SINGLES: R. Field (RSA) d. I. Berger 6–3 3–6 7–5.
DOUBLES: M. Anderson (RSA)/Field (RSA) d. P. Holubova (TCH)/S. Podlahova (TCH) 6–3 6–0.

CHIANG MAI, THAILAND (EVENT I) 20–26 AUGUST
SINGLES: A. Grunfeld (GBR) d. J.-S. Choi (KOR) 7–5 6–4.
DOUBLES: E. Hoogendoorn (HOL)/C. Wegink (HOL) d. P. Moreno (HGK)/O. Thempensri.

KHORAT, THAILAND (EVENT II) 28 AUGUST–2 SEPTEMBER
SINGLES: E. Markestein (HOL) d. S. Lohmann (FRG) 6–4 6–3.
DOUBLES: C. Wegink (HOL)/E. Hoogendoorn (HOL) d. J. Choi/J.-S. Choi (KOR) 7–6 6–2.

HAT YAI, THAILAND (EVENT III) 3–9 SEPTEMBER
SINGLES: J. Choi (KOR) d. E. Markestein (HOL) 6–3 6–4.
DOUBLES: J. Choi/J.-S. Choi (KOR) d. S. Lohmann (FRG)/U. Przysucha (FRG) 6–3 6–4.

BANGKOK, THAILAND (MASTERS) 11–16 SEPTEMBER
SINGLES: J.-S. Choi (KOR) d. J. Choi (KOR) 6–4 6–2.
DOUBLES: E. Hoogendoorn (HOL)/C. Wegink (HOL) d. U. Przysucha (FRG)/S. Lohmann (FRG) 6–0 6–1.

IBARAKI, JAPAN (EVENT I) 24–30 SEPTEMBER
SINGLES: M. Endo d. Y. Kamio 6–2 6–1.
DOUBLES: E. Takahashi/N. Kinoshita d. C. Barclay (AUS)/A. Woolcock (AUS) 6–4 4–6 6–2.

FUSO, JAPAN (EVENT II) 3–7 OCTOBER
SINGLES: J. Emmons (USA) d. A. Kochoff (USA) 6–1 6–1.
DOUBLES: K. Radford (AUS)/K.-A. Guse (AUS) d. R. Hiraki/Y. Kalita 4–6 6–1 7–5.

MATSUYAMA, JAPAN (EVENT III) 10–14 OCTOBER
SINGLES: R. Hiraki d. C. Barclay (AUS) 6–4 6–2.
DOUBLES: K. Radford (AUS)/K.-A. Guse (AUS) d. Barclay/A. Woolcock (AUS) 6–7 6–3 6–4.

KYOTO, JAPAN (MASTERS) 18–21 OCTOBER
SINGLES: K. Radford (AUS) d. R. Hiraki 6–7 6–2 6–3.
DOUBLES: Radford/K.-A. Guse (AUS) d. Y. Kajita/Hiraki 6–3 6–4.

SATELLITE TOURNAMENTS

BAMBERG, 1–7 JANUARY
SINGLES: H. Thoms d. K. Delzeklaus 7–5 6–3.
DOUBLES: Thoms/S. Suer d. A. Seifarth/C. Hofmann 6–4 6–2.

MIDLAND, TX, 9–14 JANUARY
SINGLES: H. Van Den Berg (HOL) d. E. Rossides 7–6 6–3.
DOUBLES: P. Jeffries/L. Tanner d. A. Cooper/E. Rossides 6–3 6–0.

JAKARTA, 15–21 JANUARY
SINGLES: Y. Basuki d. J. Warringa (HOL) 6–2 6–4.
DOUBLES: Basuki/S. Wibowo d. A. Neipel (GBR)/C. Billingham (GBR) W.O.

WACO, TX, 16–21 JANUARY
SINGLES: R. Simpson (CAN) d. J. Ingram 6–7 6–4 6–4.
DOUBLES: L. Bartlett/S. Bartlett d. T. Plunkett/Simpson 6–4 6–3.

HELSINKI, 23–27 JANUARY
SINGLES: A. Jonsson (NOR) d. S. Sabas (FRA) 4–6 6–4 6–3.
DOUBLES: E. Brioukhovets (URS)/E. Maniokova (URS) d. E.-L. Olson (SWE)/N. Eriksson (SWE) 6–1 6–4.

NEW BRAUNFELS, TX, 23–28 JANUARY
SINGLES: M. Pierce d. P. Jefferies 7–5 7–6.
DOUBLES: Pierce/J. Santrock d. S. Lohmann (FRG)/S. Rehmke (FRG) 6–4 6–4.

DANDERYD, 30 JANUARY–3 FEBRUARY
SINGLES: N. Dahlman (FIN) d. M. Strandlund 6–3 6–3.
DOUBLES: E. Briouokhovets (URS)/E. Maniokova (URS) d. C. Schneider (FRG)/C. Franzke (FRG) 6–2 6–0.

STAVANGER, 6–10 FEBRUARY
SINGLES: B. Rittner (FRG) d. A. Jonsson 3–6 7–6 6–4.
DOUBLES: N. Eriksson (SWE)/E. Brioukhovets (URS) d. H. Thoms (FRG)/B. Rittner (FRG) 6–2 6–2.

HORSHOLM, 11–17 FEBRUARY
SINGLES: P. Holubova (TCH) d. B. Rittner (FRG) 6–4 6–2.
DOUBLES: P. Sorensen/M.-B. Stockman d. A. Van Burren (HOL)/G. Coorengel (HOL) 6–4 4–6 7–5.

MANCHESTER, 19–23 FEBRUARY
SINGLES: E. Callens (BEL) d. S. Beglin (HOL) 6–1 6–0.
DOUBLES: M. Anderson (RSA)/V. Humphries-Davies (GBR) d. G. Coorengel (HOL)/A. Van Burren (HOL) 6–2 6–2.

WIGAN, 26 FEBRUARY–3 MARCH
SINGLES: A. Zugasti (FRA) d. T. Hauschildt (FRG) 1–6 6–3 6–3.
DOUBLES: E. Callens (BEL)/C. Wuillot (BEL) d. J. Tielman (SWE)/C. Wegink (HOL) 7–5 6–0.

VALENCIA, 6–11 MARCH
SINGLES: T. Min (CHN) d. F. Perfetti (ITA) 6–2 0–6 6–4.
DOUBLES: S. Gradoen (HOL)/J. Van Wijk (HOL) d. C. Cavina (ITA)/C. Vitali (ITA) 6–4 6–0.

REIMS, 12–18 MARCH
SINGLES: J. Salinkova (URS) d. M.-P. Villani 7–5 4–6 6–0.
DOUBLES: L. Laskova (TCH)/M. Petrova (TCH) d. K. Hand (GBR)/J. Salinkova (TCH) 6–2 3–6 6–3.

MURCIA, 13–18 MARCH
SINGLES: F. Li (CHN) d. S. Lucchi (ITA) 6–2 7–5.
DOUBLES: A. Segura/A. Quintana d. J. Souto/R. Bielsa 7–5 7–5.

GRANADA, 20–25 MARCH
SINGLES: B. Arming (AUT) d. A Fusat (FRA) 6–1 7–6.
DOUBLES: N. Souto/E. Ordinga d. I. Cannadell/B. Navarro 7–5 4–6 6–2.

MADRID, 26 MARCH–1 APRIL
SINGLES: N. Souto d. E. Bes 6–3 6–0.
DOUBLES: K. Kschwendt (LUX)/P. Miller (URU) d. N.Billesikaia (URS)/S. Komleva (URS) 4–6 7–5 6–3.

BARI, 10–15 APRIL
SINGLES: L. Golarsa d. V. Milvidskaia (URS) 6–3 6–4.
DOUBLES: A. Blumberga (URS)/B. Rittner (FRG) d. S. Wibowo (INA)/Y. Basuki (INA) 6–4 4–6 6–2.

MARSA, 16–22 APRIL
SINGLES: N. Ergegovic (YUG) d. J. Salinkova (URS) 6–3 6–2.
DOUBLES: V. Milvidskaya/A. Mirza (URS) d. E. Bes (ESP)/S. Ramon (ESP) 6–2 7–6.

SUTTON, 24–28 APRIL
SINGLES: R. Bobkova (TCH) d. K. Habsudova (TCH) 3–6 7–5 7–6.
DOUBLES: Bobkova/H. Vildova (TCH) d. L. Keller (AUS)/R. Mawdsley (AUS) 7–6 6–3.

LEE-ON-SOLENT, 1–5 MAY
SINGLES: S. Jaquet (SUI) d. D. Herman (USA) 4–6 6–4 6–1.
DOUBLES: C. Bernstein (SWE)/A. Narbe (SWE) d. N. Biletskaya (URS)/S. Komleve (URS) 6–4 6–4.

MANILA, 9–13 MAY
SINGLES: M. Tang (CHN) d. L. Chen (CHN) 7–6 6–0.
DOUBLES: Chen/L. Fang (CHN) d. Tang/N. Lin (CHN) 6–3 6–0.

SWANSEA, 8–12 MAY
SINGLES: R. Bobkova (TCH) d. K. Habsudova (TCH) 7–5 7–5.
DOUBLES: N. Pratt (AUS)/K. Sharpe (AUS) d. C. Barclay/L. Stacey (AUS) 6–1 6–2.

BOURNEMOUTH, 15–19 MAY
SINGLES: J. Kruger (RSA) d. A. Benzon (ITA) 7–6 6–1.
DOUBLES: N. Pratt (AUS)/K. Sharpe (AUS) d. C. Barclay (AUS)/L. Stacey (AUS) 6–1 6–2.

GUADALAJARA, 14–20 MAY
SINGLES: S. Italiano (CAN) d. M.-A. Vento (VEN) 6 -7 6–4 6–3.
DOUBLES: Vento/R. Winebarger (USA) d. B. Rodriguez (CUB)/B. Borbbulla 0–6 7–5 6–4.

AGUASCALIENTES, 21–27 MAY
SINGLES: M.-A. Vento (VEN) d. J.-M. Lozano (USA) 6–3 6–3.
DOUBLES: G. Novelo/Lozano (USA) d. S. Italiano (CAN)/B. Rodriguez (CUB) 6–1 6–1.

LISBON, 28 MAY–3 JUNE
SINGLES: A. Segura (ESP) d. E. Bes (ESP) 6–4 6–0.
DOUBLES: A. Quintana (ESP)/Segura d. I. Dreihuis (HOL)/J. Hodder (AUS) 6–0 6–2.

SAN LUIS POTOSI, 28 MAY–3 JUNE
SINGLES: S. Italiano (CAN) d. J.-M. Lozano (USA) 6–7 6–0 6–2.
DOUBLES: G. Novelo/Lozano d. T. Sambrzycki (BRA)/L. Becerra 6–3 4–6 6–1.

FRANCAVILLA, 28 MAY–3 JUNE
SINGLES: M. De Swardt (RSA) d. S. Witzowa (TCH) 6–7 7–6 6–2.
DOUBLES: J. Trayond (INA)/I. Moerid (INA) d. L. Jachia /Witzowa (TH) 6–7 6–2 6–3.

KEY BISCAYNE, FL, 5–11 JUNE
SINGLES: T. Whittington d. S. McCarthy 3–6 6–3 7–6.
DOUBLES: L. Raymond/R. Reis d. K. Foxworth/V. Procacci 6–4 7–5.

LISBON, 5–10 JUNE
SINGLES: K. Oeljeklaus (FRG) d. D. Leupold (AUT) 0–6 6–2 6–1.
DOUBLES: I. Driehuis (HOL)/J. Hodder (AUS) d. A. Segura (ESP)/A. Quintana (ESP) 6–3 6–3.

LADY LAKE, FL, 12–17 JUNE
SINGLES: N. Ardent d. K. Barry 6–2 6–1.
DOUBLES: Ardent/K. Louthian d. M. Mizokuchi (JPN)/S. Okada (JPN) 6–2 6–4.

CASCAIS, 12–17 JUNE
SINGLES: E. Callens (BEL) d. C. Wegink (HOL) 6–1 6–1.
DOUBLES: Callens/C. Wuillot (BEL) d. L. Pleming (AUS)/I. Driehuis (HOL) 2–6 6–4 7–6.

ST. SIMONS ISLAND, GA, 19–24 JUNE
SINGLES: D. Graham d. K. Il-Soon (KOR) 7–6 6–1.
DOUBLES: Il-Soon/L. Jeong-Myung (KOR) d. S. McCarthy/S. Schefflin 6–2 2–6 6–4.

MADEIRA, 19–24 JUNE
SINGLES: S. Gerke (BEL) d. P. Kamstra (HOL) 6–1 6–1.
DOUBLES: C. Linemann (FRG)/S. Mayorkes (BRA) d. P. Kamstra (HOL)/M. Mraz (CAN) 6–4 7–5.

MOBILE, AL, 3–8 JULY
SINGLES: I.-S. Kim (KOR) d. P. Collantes (ESP) 6–4 6–4.
DOUBLES: Kim/J.-M. Lee (KOR) d. J. Lozano/G. Novelo 6–1 6–0.

CHERBOURG, 2–8 JULY
SINGLES: A. Fusai d. M.-J. Llorca (ESP) 6–3 2–6 6–3.
DOUBLES: L. Pleming (AUS)/C. Linneman (FRG) d. A. Fusai/O. Graveraux 6–4 6–3.

SUBIACO, 10–15 JULY
SINGLES: B. Mulej (YUG) d. I. Watanabe (USA) 6–3 6–1.
DOUBLES: Mulej/K. Johnson (USA) d. V. Csurgo (HUN)/N. Koves (HUN) 7–6 6–0.

FAYETTEVILLE, NC, 10–15 JULY
SINGLES: L. Fang (CHN) d. S.-J. Im (KOR) 6–1 1–6 6–3.
DOUBLES: I.-S. Kim (KOR)/J.-M. Lee (KOR) d. J. Lozano/G. Novelo 4–6 7–6 6–3.

SCHWARZACH, 16–21 JULY
SINGLES: B. Mulej (YUG) d. B. Arming 7–5 6–3.
DOUBLES: I. Driehuis (HOL)/L. Pleming (AUS) d. C. Linemann (FRG)/R. Seeman (NZL) 6–2 6–0.

SEZZE, 17–21 JULY
SINGLES: A. Fusai (FRA) d. S. Woorons (FRA) 6–4 6–3.
DOUBLES: C. Piccini/A. Canapi d. T. Cerne (YUG)/G. Carotenuto 6–2 6–3.

GREENSBORO, NC, 17–22 JULY
SINGLES: C. Kuhlam d. K. Barry 6–4 6–1.
DOUBLES: J. Emmons/M. Geiger d. J. Kaczmarek/V. Sureephong 6–2 6–1.

LA CORUNA, 21–28 JULY
SINGLES: S. Ramon d. S. Rottier (HOL) 7–5 6–3.
DOUBLES: M. Llorca/A. Quintata d. N. Rodriguez (CHI)/V. Vernet (FRA) 3–6 6–3 7–5.

SEMARANG, 30 JULY–5 AUGUST
SINGLES: J. Sutedja d. I. Moerid 6–4 4–6 6–1.
DOUBLES: C. Sely (HOL)/L. Tedjamukti d. Moerid/T. Trayano.

ROANOKE, VA, 31 JULY–5 AUGUST
SINGLES: J. Shiflet d. L. Albano 6–1 6–2.
DOUBLES: M. Dadosh (ISR)/D. Coriat (ISR) d. I. Berger (ISR)/L. Zaltz (ISR) 2–6 6–4 6–4.

CATANIA, 30 JULY–5 AUGUST
SINGLES: J. Watanabe (USA) d. C. Salvi 6–1 6–3.
DOUBLES: C. Piccini/A. Canapi d. Salvi/E. Savoldi 6–3 6–3.

PADERBORN, 6–12 AUGUST
SINGLES: J. Salinkova (URS) d. H. Thoms 6–1 6–0.
DOUBLES: T. Hauschlidt/Thoms d. A. Mirza/J. Salinkova (URS) 6–3 6–1.

JAKARTA, 6–12 AUGUST
SINGLES: Y. Basuki d. S. Wibowo 5–7 6–4 6–3.
DOUBLES: Basuki/Wibowo d. J. Kuswara/M. Irawati 7–5 6–3.

NICOLOSI, 8–11 AUGUST
SINGLES: C. Salvi d. C. Schneider (FRG) 6–7 6–2 6–4.
DOUBLES: J. Hodder (AUS)/S. Lohrmann (FRG) d. Salvi/Schneider 3–6 6–3 6–3.

LEBANON, NJ, 7–12 AUGUST
SINGLES: K. Barry d. S. Okada (JPN) 6–0 6–3.
DOUBLES: K. Foxworth/V. Procacci d. I. Berger (ISR)/L. Zaltz (ISR) 6–4 4–1 ret.

PISTICCI, 15–20 AUGUST
SINGLES: J. Watanabe (USA) d. C. Summers (RSA) 6–3 3–6 7–6.
DOUBLES: I. Concepcion (CUB)/R. Pichardo (CUB) d. Watanabe/D. Chavez (USA) 7–6 6–2.

REBECO, 11–19 AUGUST
SINGLES: R. Dragomir (ROM) d. S. Begijn (HOL) 6–3 7–5.
DOUBLES: E. Callens/C. Wulliot d. Dragomir/I. Spirlea (ROM) 6–4 6–2.

CHATHAM, NJ, 14–19 AUGUST
SINGLES: I. Berger (ISR) d. S. McCarthy 6–2 7–6.
DOUBLES: K. Foxworth/McCarthy d. K. Dreyer/S. Nicholson (IRE) 6–2 7–6.

SPOLETO, 21–26 AUGUST
SINGLES: G. Matic (YUG) d. V. Csurgo (HUN) 3–6 7–6 6–4.
DOUBLES: A. Canapi/C. Piccini d. J. Hodder (AUS)/C. Salvi 6–3 4–6 6–4.

KOKSIDJE, 20–26 AUGUST
SINGLES: D. Monami d. M. Mroz (POL) 6–2 6–1.
DOUBLES: R. Dragomir (ROM)/I. Spirlea (ROM) d. E. Crous (RSA)/L. Ludvigova (TCH) 6–1 2–6 6–3.

PALERMO, 28 AUGUST–2 SEPTEMBER
SINGLES: G. Angelova (BUL) d. C. Vitali 6–4 6–3.
DOUBLES: L. Pleming (AUS)/I. Driehuis (HOL) d. S. Reichels (FRG)/E. Derly (FRA) 6–1 6–1.

AGLIANA, 10–16 SEPTEMBER
SINGLES: T. Stromberg (SWE) d. K. Blahova (TCH) 6–3 6–1.
DOUBLES: G. Carotenuto/C. Salvi d. A. Marbe/C. Bernstein (SWE) 7–5 3–6 7–6.

RABAC, 17–23 SEPTEMBER
SINGLES: R. Dragomir (ROM) d. G. Matic 6–3 6–1.
DOUBLES: Dragomir/I. Spirlea (ROM) d. K. Studenickova (TCH)/G. Vesela (TCH) 1–6 6–3 6–4.

NAPOLI, 18–23 SEPTEMBER
SINGLES: D. Monami (BEL) d. K. Blahova (TCH) 6–3 6–2.
DOUBLES: H. Vildova (TCH)/L. Ludvigova (TCH) d. P. Miller (URU)/M. Alastrue (ESP) 3–6 6–1 6–0.

MALI LOSINJ, 24–30 SEPTEMBER
SINGLES: R. Dragomir (ROM) d. I. Spirlea (ROM) 6–3 6–1.
DOUBLES: Z. Malkova (TCH)/E. Martincova (TCH) d. A. Mirza (URS)/Spirlea 6–1 6–1.

S. MARIA (NAPOLI), 24–30 SEPTEMBER
SINGLES: D. Monami (BEL) d. C. Bernstein (SWE) 4–6 6–4 6–2.
DOUBLES: H. Vildova (TCH)/L. Ludvigova (TCH) d. K. Blahova (TCH)/N. Tschan (SUI) 6–3 6–2.

SIBENIK, 1–7 OCTOBER
SINGLES: B. Mulej d. R. Dragomir (ROM) 7–6 6–4.
DOUBLES: C. Czopek (POL)/K. Teodorowitcz (POL) d. E. Martincova (TCH)/Z. Malkova (TCH) 6–7 7–6 7–6.

BOGOTA, 1–7 OCTOBER
SINGLES: M. Gaidano (ARG) d. J. Watanabe (USA) 0–6 7–5 6–2.
DOUBLES: R. Burzagli (BRA)/E. Neito (VEN) d. Watanabe/D. Chaves (USA) 7–5 6–4.

BOL NA BRACU, 8–14 OCTOBER
SINGLES: B. Mulej d. A. Vanc (ROM) 6–4 6–0.
DOUBLES: I. Spirlea (ROM)/M. Mroz (POL) d. Z. Malkova (TCH)/E. Martincova (TCH) 4–6 6–3 6–1.

LIMA, 8–14 OCTOBER
SINGLES: I. Gorrochategui (ARG) d. M. Miranda (CHI) 6–4 6–3.
DOUBLES: K. Strohmeier/L. Gildemeister d. I. Concepcion (CUB)/R. Pichardo (CUB) 6–4 7–6.

SUPETAR, 15–22 OCTOBER
SINGLES: I. Horvat d. O. Lugina (URS) 6–1 7–5.
DOUBLES: Horvat/E. Martincova (TCH) d. T. Ignatieva (URS)/I. Soukhova (URS) 6–3 6–3.

BURGDORF, 15–22 OCTOBER
SINGLES: D. Monami (BEL) d. S. Lohmann (FRG) 5–7 6–2 6–4.
*DOUBLES:*Lohmann/C. Wegink (HOL) d. M. Strebel/N. Tschann 4–6 6–2 6–4.

LA PAZ, 15–21 OCTOBER
SINGLES: I. Gorrochategui (ARG) d. J. Watanabe (USA) 6–2 3–6 6–1.
DOUBLES: P. Cabezas (CHI)/S. Ugarriza (PAR) d. Gorrochategui/P. Boccia (ARG) 6–2 4–6 6–3.

NEUMUNSTER, 24–28 OCTOBER
SINGLES: C. Singer d. A. Muller 6–4 6–3.
DOUBLES: Singer/A. Marchl d. A. Carlsson (SWE)/M. Linusson (SWE) 6–2 7–5.

LYSS, 23–28 OCTOBER
SINGLES: D. Monami (BEL) d. K. Meichelboeck (FRG) 6–2 6–2.
DOUBLES: C. Wegink (HOL)/S. Lohmann (FRG) d. I. Berger (ISR)/R. Mayer (ISR) 6–1 7–5.

SANTIAGO, 22–28 OCTOBER
SINGLES: I. Gorrochategui (ARG) d. M. Miranda 6–2 6–2.
DOUBLES: Gorrochategui/P. Miller (URU) d. S. Ugarriza (PAR)/ P. Cabezas 3–6 6–1 7–6.

WELS, 31 OCTOBER–4 NOVEMBER
SINGLES: M. Kratochvilova (TCH) d. K. Bueche 7–5 6–3.
DOUBLES: R. Chladkova (TCH)/Kratochvilova d. B. Arming/D. Bauer 6–4 6–4.

PUTIGNANO, 30 OCTOBER–3 NOVEMBER
SINGLES: N. Baudone d. S. Farina 6–2 6–1.
DOUBLES: Baudone/Farina d. D. Deskovic (YUG)/K. Lusnic (YUG) 6–1 6–1.

MEKNES, 30 OCTOBER–4 NOVEMBER
SINGLES: O. Gravereaux (FRA) d. B. Collet (FRA) 6–1 6–2.
DOUBLES: S. Nicholson (IRE)/G. Niland (IRE) d. B. Collet (FRA)/J. Foillard (FRA) 7–5 6–3.

BUENOS AIRES, 30 OCTOBER–4 NOVEMBER
SINGLES: I. Gorrochategui d. G. Mosca 3–6 6–2 6–4.
DOUBLES: Gorrochategui/Mosca d. Val. Falter/Van. Falter 6–2 6–0.

ASUNCION, 4–11 NOVEMBER
SINGLES: J. Watanabe (USA) d. P. Miller (URU) 6–2 6–1.
*DOUBLES:*Watanabe/V. Valdovinos d. M.-J. Gaidano (ARG)/Miller 3–6 6–4 7–6.

HAIFA, 3–10 NOVEMBER
SINGLES: I. Berger d. T. Obziler 6–1 6–3.
DOUBLES: Berger/L. Zalta d. D. Blanke/Y. Shavit 6–2 6–1.

FES, 5–10 NOVEMBER
SINGLES: O. Graveraux (FRA) d. E. Hoogendoorn (HOL) 1–6 6–3 11–9.
DOUBLES: E. Haslinghuis (HOL)/B. Eysvogel (HOL) d. J. Strnadova (TCH)/N. Strnadova (TCH) 6–0 2–6 6–1.

LERIDA, 6–11 NOVEMBER
SINGLES: S. Ramon d. P. Perez 6–3 6–4.
DOUBLES: V. Ruano/E. Bes d. A. Larrakoetxea/Ramon 6–2 1–6 7–5.

ASHKELON, 12–17 NOVEMBER
SINGLES: I. Berger d. D.Coriat 7–5 6–1.
DOUBLES: Berger/L. Zalta d. Coriat/M. Dadoch 4–6 6–1 6–1.

PORTO ALEGRE, 12–18 NOVEMBER
SINGLES: J. Moreno (ARG) d. J. Watanabe (USA) 7–5 6–3.
DOUBLES: C. Chabalgoity/L. Tella d. A. Grousbeck (USA)/L. Weerasuriya (SRI) 6–1 6–1.

ALGIERS, 19–25 NOVEMBER
SINGLES: J. Foillard (FRA) d. E. Haslinghuis (HOL) 7–6 6–5.
DOUBLES: Haslinghuis/B. Eysvogel (HOL) d. Y. Klompenhower (HOL)/H. Leeuwen (HOL) 6–2 7–6.

FLORIANOPOLIS, 19–25 NOVEMBER
SINGLES: A. Viera d. D. Leupold (AUT) 6–4 6–4.
DOUBLES: C. Chabalgoity/C. Rozwadowski d. A. Kaul/T. Buss 6–0 6–1.

LJUSDAL, 26 NOVEMBER–2 DECEMBER
SINGLES: M. Vallin d. C. Linnerman (FRG) 7–6 6–2.
DOUBLES: K. Freyer (FRG)/S. Remke (FRG) d. E.-L. Olsson /Linnerman (FRG) 6–1 7–5.

ERD, 26 NOVEMBER–2 DECEMBER
SINGLES: H. Vildova (TCH) d. K. Blahova (TCH) 6–2 6–3.
DOUBLES: M. Mroz (POL)/K. Teodorowicz (POL) d. L Ludvigova (TCH)/Vildova 5–7 6–4 6–2.

BACHDJARAH, 26 NOVEMBER–2 DECEMBER
SINGLES: E. Haslinghuis (HOL) d. G. Niland (IRE) 6–0 7–6.
DOUBLES: Haslinghuis/B. Eysvogel (HOL) d. Y. Klompenhower (HOL)/H. Leeuwen (HOL) 6–2 1–6 7–5.

BELO HORIZONTE, 3–9 DECEMBER
SINGLES: L. Weerasuriya (SRI) d. S. Okada (JPN) 4–6 6–1 7–5.
DOUBLES: L. Glitz (USA)/S. Kelbert d. S. Reichel (AUT)/Okada 4–6 7–5 6–1.

$25,000 – CHALLENGER TOURNAMENTS

MIDLAND, MI, 30 JANUARY–4 FEBRUARY
SINGLES: L. Ferrando (ITA) d. M. Pierce 6–4 6–1.
DOUBLES: L. Finnerman/L. Seeman d. A. Grossman/M. Pierce 3–6 6–3 6–1.

WELS, 28 FEBRUARY–4 MARCH
SINGLES: M. Maruska (AUT) d. K. Kschwendt (LUX) 3–6 6–1 6–4.
DOUBLES: A. Dechaume/P. Paradis (FRA) d. H. Fukarkova (TCH)/D. Krajcovicova (TCH) 6–3 6–2.

KEY BISCAYNE, FL, 26 FEBRUARY–3 MARCH
SINGLES: L. Spadea d. P. Hy (CAN) 6–1 4–6 6–4.
DOUBLES: J. Fuchs/M. Strandlund (SWE) d. R. Baranski (POL)/L. Barnard (RSA) 6–4 6–4.

MOULINS, 19–25 MARCH
SINGLES: N. Sawamatsu (JPN) d. C. Chabalgoity (BRA) 6–3 6–1.
DOUBLES: M. Maleeva (BUL)/A. Strnadova (TCH) d. P. Paradis/V. Vernet 3–6 6–1 6–1.

LIMOGES, 26 MARCH–1 APRIL
SINGLES: P. Paradis d. K. Habsudova (TCH) 6–4 6–4.
DOUBLES: A. Devries (BEL)/I. Kuczynska (POL) d. C. Tanvier/S. Testud 6–3 3–6 6–4.

TORINO, 2–8 APRIL
SINGLES: S. Dopfer (AUT) d. C. Chabalgoity (BRA) 6–2 ret.
DOUBLES: S. Wibowo (INA)/E. Iida (JPN) d. A. Noszaly (HUN)/F. Bonsignori 7–5 3–6 6–4.

NAPOLI, 15–22 APRIL
SINGLES: K. Piccolini (ITA) d. M. Kochta (FRG) 6–2 6–4.
DOUBLES: Melicharova (TCH)/I. Jankovska (TCH) d. R. Szikszay (HUN)/M. Frimmelova (TCH) 6–3 6–4.

CASERTA, 25–29 APRIL
SINGLES: K. Nowak (POL) d. E. Brioukhovets (URS) 1–6 6–2 6–3.
DOUBLES: Brioukhovets/E. Maniochova (URS) d. R. Skiksay (HUN)/M. Frimmelova (TCH) 4–6 6–3 6–1.

BANGKOK, 30 APRIL–6 MAY
SINGLES: J. Richardson (NZL) d. T. Takagi (JPN) 4–6 6–3 6–2.
DOUBLES: Richardson/J. Thomas (USA) d. I-S. Kim (KOR)/J-M. Lee (KOR) 6–4 6–4.

RAMAT HASHARON, 14–20 MAY
SINGLES: M. De Swardt (RSA) d. P. Thoren (FIN) 6–1 6–4.
DOUBLES: M. Anderson (RSA)/R. Field (RSA) d. K.A. Guse (AUS)/J. Salmon (GBR) 6–3 6–2.

LISBON, 15–20 MAY
SINGLES: C. Mothes (FRA) d. C. Chabalgoity (BRA) 6–3 6–2.
DOUBLES: E. Bes (ESP)/V. Ruano (ESP) d. C. Vis (HOL)/S. Schilder (HOL) 3–6 6–2 6–1.

KATOWICE, 23–27 MAY
SINGLES: K. Habsudova (TCH) d. A.-M. Foeldenyi (HUN) 6–3 6–2.
DOUBLES: A. Van Burren (HOL)/G. Cooengel (HOL) d. K. Balnova (TCH)/J. Dubcova (TCH) 7–5 3–6 6–3.

MANTOVA, 5–10 JUNE
SINGLES: M. De Swardt (RSA) d. F. Bonsignori 6–3 6–7 6–3.
DOUBLES: I. Jankovska (TCH)/E. Melicharova (TCH) d. Y. Basuki (INA)/S. Wibowo (INA) 6–3 7–5.

MODENA, 12–17 JUNE
SINGLES: E. Zardo (SUI) d. K. Piccolini 6–1 4–6 7–5.
DOUBLES: S. Farina/S. Isidori d. M. Oremans (HOL)/H. Van Den Berg (HOL) 6–2 6–3.

ALBANY, GA, 26 JUNE–1 JULY
SINGLES: S. Schefflin d. D. Graham 6–1 6–1.
DOUBLES: K. Foxworth/T. Whittington d. S. McCarthy/S. Schefflin (USA) 6–2 2–6 6–4.

CALTAGIRONE, 26 JUNE–1 JULY
SINGLES: S. Testud (FRA) d. L. Jachia 7–6 7–5.
DOUBLES: J. Fuchs (USA)/E. Iida (JPN) d. C. Nozzoli/S. Isadori 6–1 6–1.

VAIHINGEN, 2–8 JULY
SINGLES: E. Pampoulova (BUL) d. D. Krajcovicova (TCH) 6–3 6–3.
DOUBLES: K.-A. Guse (AUS)/D. Jones (AUS) d. I. Jankovska (TCH)/E. Melicharova (TCH) 6–4 6–7 6–3.

BRINDISI 2–8 JULY
SINGLES: C. Bartos (SUI) d. M. Pierce (FRA) 2–6 6–2 6–2.
DOUBLES: Pierce/S. Testud (FRA) d. S. Shilder (HOL)/J. Fuchs (USA) 6–1 1–6 6–0.

ERLANGEN, 9–15 JULY
SINGLES: A. Popp d. A. Blumberga (URS) 7–6 3–6 7–6.
DOUBLES: E. Pfaff/R. Szikzay (TCH) d. E. Maniokova (URS)/Blumberga 6–3 6–1.

DARMSTADT, 18–22 JULY
SINGLES: C. Tessi (ARG) d. V. Milvidskaya (URS) 6–1 7–6.
DOUBLES: E. Maniokova (URS)/A. Blumberger (URS) d. S. Schilder (HOL)/A. Tiezzi (ARG) 6–4 6–4.

EVANSVILLE, IN, 23–29 JULY
SINGLES: H. Cioffi d. M. Drake (CAN) 6–3 6–4.
DOUBLES: L. Antonoplis/R. Field (RSA) d. D. Graham/J. Lorenzo 3–6 6–2 6–3.

MILAN, 22–29 JULY
SINGLES: F. Romano d. S. Noix Chateau (FRA) 6–4 6–4.
DOUBLES: S. Farina/S. Isidori d. N. Ballet/A. Romand (FRA) 2–6 6–1 6–3.

VIGO, 31 JULY–5 AUGUST
SINGLES: C. Mothes (FRA) d. M.-J. Llorca 4–6 6–1 6–1.
DOUBLES: Llorca/A. Segura d. E. Bes/V. Ruano 6–3 6–4.

RHEDA, 30 JULY–5 AUGUST
SINGLES: A. Blumberger (URS) d. K. Oeljeklaus 3–6 6–4 6–4.
DOUBLES: P. Holubova (TCH)/S. Podlohova (TCH) d. A. Blumberga (URS)/V. Milvidskaja (URS) 6–4 6–4.

BUDAPEST, 6–11 AUGUST
SINGLES: A. Foldenyi d. S. Frankl (FRG) 6–2 4–6 6–4.
DOUBLES: S. Sabas (FRA)/S. Testud (FRA) d. D. Krajcovicova (TCH)/A. Nohacova (TCH) 6–3 6–4.

BRASILIA, 11–19 AUGUST
SINGLES: G. Miro d. S. Guisto 6–1 6–0.
DOUBLES: S. Albinus (DEN)/S. Smith (GBR) d. L. Tella/A. Viera 7–6 4–6 6–3.

KARLOV VARY, 14–19 AUGUST
SINGLES: A. Strnadova d. K. Habsudova 6–3 6–4.
DOUBLES: P. Holubova/S. Podlahova d. K. Kroupovav/M. Stuskova 4–6 6–4 7–6.

ARZACHENA, 3–9 SEPTEMBER
SINGLES: L. Golarsa d. S. Gerke (FRG) 7–6 7–6.
DOUBLES: B. Borneo (GBR)/J. Salmon (GBR) d. L. Pleming (AUS)/E. Derly (FRA) 6–1 4–6 6–3.

CHICAGO, IL, 24–30 SEPTEMBER
SINGLES: L. Allen d. S. Rottier (HOL) 6–4 6–1.
DOUBLES: K. Adams/L. Nabors d. M.-L. Daniels/J. Hetherington (CAN) 6–4 6–4.

YORK, PA, 1–7 OCTOBER
SINGLES: M. Ekstrand (SWE) d. S. Scheflin 6–2 6–1.
DOUBLES: L. Allen/S. Amiach (FRA) d. C. Vis (HOL)/S. Schilder (HOL) 7–6 6–4.

SALISBURY, MD, 8–14 OCTOBER
SINGLES: E. Hakami d. M. Kochta (FRG) 4–6 7–6 6–3.
DOUBLES: J. Hetherington (CAN)/P. Mager d. D. Herman/L. Raymond 6–3 6–1.

NAGASAKI, 24–28 OCTOBER
SINGLES: M. Endo d. Y. Kamio 0–6 6–3 6–2.
DOUBLES: Y. Basuki (INA)/S. Wibowo (INA) d. K.-A. Guse (AUS)/K. Radford (AUS) 6–2 7–6.

SAGA, 29 OCTOBER–4 NOVEMBER
SINGLES: K. Radford (AUS) d. Y. Segal (ISR) 6–3 7–5.
DOUBLES: Y. Basuki (INA)/S. Wibowo (INA) d. K.-A. Guse (AUS)/Radford 6–3 6–2.

EASTBOURNE, 5–9 NOVEMBER
SINGLES:S. Testud (FRA) d. K. Nowak (POL) 2–6 6–3 6–4.
DOUBLES: M. Lindstrom (SWE)/H. Ludloff (USA) d. E. Callens (BEL)/T. Hauschildt (FRG) 7–6 6–1.

MT GAMBIER, 7–11 NOVEMBER
SINGLES: M. Jaggard d. T. Morton 7–6 6–3.
DOUBLES: J.-A. Faull/N. Van Lottum d. K. Guse/J. Hodder 7–5 6–4.

SWINDON, 12–16 NOVEMBER
SINGLES: S. Testud (FRA) d. D. Monami (BEL) 6–4 6–4.
DOUBLES: M. Lindstrom (SWE)/H. Lindstrom (USA) d. A. Aallonen (FIN)/E. Maniokova (URS) 4–6 6–4 7–6.

NURIOOTPA, 14–18 NOVEMBER
SINGLES: S. Wibowo (INA) d. M. Jaggard (AUS) 6–4 6–2.
DOUBLES: Wibowo/Y. Basuki (INA) d. L. Pleming (AUS)/I. Driehuis (HOL) 7–6 7–5.

PERTH, 21–25 NOVEMBER
SINGLES: R. Stubbs d. K. Godridge 6–1 6–1.
DOUBLES: J.-A. Faull/Stubbs d. Godridge/K. Sharpe 6–2 6–4.

OKADA, 26 NOVEMBER–1 DECEMBER
SINGLES: P. Kamstra (HOL) d. S. Bentley (GBR) 6–0 6–4.
DOUBLES: H. Van Den Berg/Y. Grubben (HOL) d. S. Lohrman (FRG)/M. Strebel (SUI) 6–2 7–5.

LE HAVRE, 1–9 DECEMBER
SINGLES: N. Housset d. N. Herreman 4–6 7–6 7–6.
DOUBLES: A. Zugasti/J. Halard d. G. Coorengel (HOL)/A. Van Burren (HOL) 6–3 6–0.

$50,000 – CHALLENGER EVENTS

CHIBA, 19–23 SEPTEMBER
SINGLES: M. Werdell (USA) d. T. Takagi 6–4 4–6 6–2.
DOUBLES: M. Jaggard (AUS)/Werdell d. J. Richardson (NZL)/E. Pfaff (FRG) 6–4 5–7 7–6.

Above: *The successful Yugoslav's who won the World Team Cup for the first time (l to r) Goran Prpic, Goran Ivanisevic and Slobodan Zivojinovic (Capt.).*   *(R. Adams)*

Left: *Jim Courier, a member of the US team that reached the final.*   *(R. Adams)*

INTERNATIONAL TEAM COMPETITIONS

EUROPEAN CUPS
WORLD TEAM CUP
MAUREEN CONNOLLY BRINKER TROPHY

Michael Stich had a great year personally with a first tour win in Memphis and also helped Germany to win the European Cup. *(Professional Sport)*

OTHER INTERNATIONAL TEAM EVENTS

John Parsons and Henry Wancke

EUROPEAN CUP – MEN

The European Cup, rather like the Wightman Cup, though for different reasons, has become something of an anachronism in modern tennis and sadly, this year, despite an exciting final in which Germany beat Russia 2–1, there seemed to be evidence of the event's decline.

When the King's Cup, as the competition is still fondly remembered in many quarters, was launched in 1936, it was a natural extension of men's international tennis. However, this was in the times when there was no prize money and boat and rail offered the most convenient form of European travel. This year, with no sponsorship, particularly after several years in which the players had at least had the opportunity to earn more than simply the match fee and expenses (provided by national associations) there also seemed to be a lack of motivation is some quarters. The European Tennis Association, which has worked hard to make the European Cup an event of real substance, now has to decide whether to continue on an increasingly difficult commercial, but probably impractical, road or accept that it should become a training ground where team captains can assess the prospects of future *Davis Cup* players amidst the pressures of playing for their country.

That was precisely how Nikki Pilic, the West German captain approached the 1990 Group 1 event in Metz, France – and he was well rewarded. 'I clearly told my players that I would be looking closely at their performances here before deciding who would get the singles place alongside Boris Becker in our *Davis Cup* team' he said. He reminded them that with Carl-Uwe Steeb injured and Eric Jelen and Patrick Kuhnen in decline, there was a great *Davis Cup* opportunity ahead of them. The German squad consisted of Udo Riglewski, Michael Stich, Jens Wohrmann and Markus Zoecke. They all played their part in their 3–0 victory over Switzerland and 2–1 defeat of Britain in the group matches but it was Riglewski and Stich, particularly the latter, who earnt the Germans success in the final.

The Russians, who in their group matches had beaten France and Czechoslovakia 2–1, started well in the final against Germany. Dimitri Poliakov recovered from the loss of the first set to beat Riglewski 5–7 6–3 6–2 but Stich then made sure that everything would depend on the doubles with a splendidly determined 6–3 7–6 defeat of Andrei Cherkasov, who was ranked 22 in the world at the time. And, after only a short break, Stich was back on court, still clearly elated by his success in the singles, to partner Riglewski to a 6–3 7–6 defeat of Vladimir Gabrichide and Andrei Olhovskiy.

Britain, who had beaten Switzerland 3–0 in their opening match, finished in third place for the second successive year by beating France 2–1 in a play-off. Having used Jeremy Bates and Nick Brown, his two *Davis Cup* singles men, in the first two matches, team captain, Warren Jacques opted for the two other members of his squad, who had ostensibly been taken along as practice partners and in order that they might benefit from such an atmosphere. Although Paul Hand, 25, who had provided a belated reminder of his abilities at the national championships, went down 6–4 6–1 to Cedric Pioline, Chris Wilkinson, ranked 361 in the world, produced one of the best displays of his career to upset Tarik Benhabiles, ranked 106, in 43 minutes. Together, the British pair then swept past Pioline and Benhabiles to win the doubles 6–2 6–4. – J.P.

Division 1
METZ, 5–7 DECEMBER
Group 1: Great Britain d. Switzerland 3–0 (N. Brown d. S. Mezzadri 6–2 7–5; J. Bates d. C. Mezzadri

6–2 6–2; Bates/Brown d. T. Grin/C. Mezzadri 6–3 6–0); *Germany d. Switzerland 3–0* (U. Riglewski d. Grin 6–4 6–4; M. Stich d. C. Mezzadri 7–6 6–1; J. Wohrmann/M. Zoecke d. C. Mezzadri/R. Stadler 6–7 6–3 6–2); *Germany d. Great Britain 2–1* (Riglewski d. Brown 6–0 6–2; Stich d. Bates 6–0 7–5; Wohrmann/Zoecke lost to Bates/Brown 4–6 4–6).
GROUP 2: USSR d. Czechoslovakia 2–1. (A. Olkhovskiy d. T. Zdrazila 1–6 6–2 6–2; A. Cherkasov d. C. Dosedel 7–6 6–3; V. Gabrichidze/D. Poliakov lost to D. Rikl/Zdrazila 4–6 4–6); *France d. Czechoslovakia 2–1* (C. Pioline d. Rikl 6–3 6–2; G. Raoux lost to Dosedel 6–7 6–2 4–6; Pioline/Raoux d. Rikl/Zdrazila 6–4 6–3); *USSR d. France 3–0* (Poliakov d. Pioline 6–3 7–6; Cherkasov d. Raoux 7–5 6–4; Gabrichidze/Olkhovskiy d. Benhabiles/Raoux 3–6 6–3 6–3).
FINAL: Germany d. USSR 2–1 (Riglewski lost to Poliakov 7–5 3–6 2–6); Stich d. Cherkasov 6–3 7–6; Stich/Riglewski d. Olkhovskiy/Gabrichidze 6–3 7–6).
RELEGATION PLAY-OFF: Czechoslovakia d. Switzerland 2–1 (Zdrazila lost to Grin 3–6 7–6 1–6; Dosedel d. C. Mezzadri 6–1 6–1; Dosedel/Rikl d. Grin/Stadler 4–6 6–1 6–2).

EUROPEAN CUP – WOMEN

The sixth Women's European Cup, proved to be a matter of repeat performances. For the third consecutive year the top division of Europe's flagship event for national women's teams, returned to Nantes. And for the second consecutive year, the finalists were the same, as was the ultimate result. However, it was surprising that both teams reached the championship stage as neither had started as favourites.

That honour fell to Italy who topped the 'Order of Merit', fielding Sandra Cecchini at 20 in the world rankings, Katia Piccolini (47), Laura Golarsa (61) and Linda Ferrando (67). Sweden were second with Catarina Lindqvist (36) backed up by Cecilia Dahlman (80), Maria Strandlund (129) and Maria Lindstrom (336). Belgium, promoted from the second division, followed with Sabine Appelmans (23) and Sandra Wasserman (100) providing their main challenge whilst the defending champions, the Soviet Union, were rated fourth with Natalia Medvedeva (56) and Elena Brioukhovets (76). The host nation, France, was fifth with Julie Halard (41) their leading player and Great Britain sixth had Jo Durie playing in the No. 1 spot with a world ranking of 64 and Monique Javer (101).

With the six nations split into two groups, all played twice to decide which would emerge from each section to contest the final. Great Britain got off to a flying start in their match against Belgium when Javer defeated Wasserman in straight sets. Durie, however, could not close the tie out going down 4–6 4–6 to Appelmans but when she combined with Clare Wood for the deciding doubles, Durie pulled the tie round for Britain to win 2–1. They beat Appelmans and Ann Devries, 6–7 (5–7) 6–1 6–3. The opening match in the other group saw the Soviet Union claim a 2–1 victory over France. Medvedeva came from one set down to claim the tie in the second singles after Brioukhovets had comprehensively disposed of Karine Quentrec in the first.

The second day was to prove crucial in deciding the finalists as the two top rated nations entered the competition against the previous day's winners. First on court were the Soviet Union who overcame Sweden 3–0. Lindqvist put up stern resistance against Medvedeva to try and bring Sweden back into the tie but with her game off form, she eventually capitulated 7–6 0–6, 2–6. Britain, against the odds, also won through 3–0 in their match against Italy. Javer battled long and hard for nearly 2½ hours to set her country on the way with a 6–4 6–7 (1–7) 7–6 (7–2) victory against Ferrando. Then Durie, as she had done last year, defeated Cecchini to secure a winning 2–0 lead. Her 6–3 7–6 (8–6) victory was impressive in that she allowed a 5–3 lead to erode in the second set, and in the tie-break came back from 1–5 down for her straight sets victory. In the doubles, Sara Gomer teamed successfully with Wood to make a clean sweep of it.

With a repeat of the 1989 final now set, the third day saw the losing teams meet to decide which of them would remain in Division 1 without playing the relegation match. France and Belgium both emerged with satisfying 3–0 victories over Sweden and Italy respectively. Ironically this forced the two top rated teams into the embarrassing situation of meeting to decide which would be relegated. The tie began well for Italy when Ferrando beat Dahlman 6–4 6–3. With pride very much at stake, Lindqvist saved the Swedes from the ignomy of being whitewashed by beating Cecchini 2–6 7–5 6–4 to level matters. But then, Lindqvist and Lindstrom could only salvage one game in each set against Ferrando and Golarsa in the deciding doubles, played on the practice court, so that the final could begin on the centre court as scheduled on the fourth day.

Great Britain had high hopes of reversing the previous year's result which they lost 1–2 against the Soviets. The deciding doubles had proved the crucial rubber. The Soviet Union, without Zvereva and Savchenko (their team of '89), seemed weaker but that did not prove to be the case. Brioukhovets found in Javer, a stern opponent for the first set, but having tested her, the Soviet girl applied her speed and solid ground strokes to good effect and won through 7–5 6–3. Durie, attacking in her familiar style, could not find any real weaknesses in Medvedeva and with her serve in ineffective form, went down 3–6, 3–6 to lose the rubber which would have given the British doubles pair a chance of once again trying for overall victory. With the Championship safely regained, the Russians really went through the motions of playing the dead rubber, and once they had lost the first set by 8 points to 6 in the tie-break, they retired with Brioukhovets claiming a strain. The Soviet team were delighted to have retained the title without including their top players in the '90 line-up.

For 1991, Sweden will be replaced by the Netherlands who were relegated last year but who triumphed in the second division when they beat Denmark 2–0 in the final played in Goirle, Holland. Austria lost to Czechoslovakia 1–2 and drop down a division to Division 3 swapping places with Poland who were 2–1 victors over Spain in the final of the bottom division which was played in Sopot, Poland. – H.W.

Division 1
NANTES, 29 NOVEMBER–2 DECEMBER
GROUP 1: Great Britain d. Belgium 2–1 (M. Javer d. S. Wasserman 7–5 7–6; J. Durie lost to S. Appelmans 4–6 4–6; Durie/C. Wood d. Appelmans/A. Devries 6–7 6–1 6–3); **Great Britain d. Italy 3–0** (Javer d. L. Ferrando 6–4 6–7 7–6; Durie d. S. Cecchini 6–3 7–6; S. Gomer/Wood d. L. Golarsa/K. Piccolini 6–1 6–3); **Belgium d. Italy 3–0** (Wasserman d. Piccolini 6–2 6–7 6–1; Appelmans d. Cecchini 6–2 6–1; Appelmans/Wasserman d. Ferrando/Piccolini 6–3 6–2).
GROUP 2: USSR d. France 2–1 (E. Brioukhovets d. K. Quentrec 6–3 6–2; N. Medvedeva d. J. Halard 4–6 6–1 6–2; E. Makarova/Medvedeva lost to P. Paradis/C. Suire 4–6 2–6); **USSR d. Sweden 3–0** (Brioukhovets d. C. Dahlman 6–4 6–3; Medvedeva d. C. Lindqvist 6–7 6–0 6–2; Medvedeva/Brioukhovets d. M. Lindstrom/M. Strandlund 6–2 4–6 6–1); **France d. Sweden 3–0** (Paradis d. Dahlman 6–4 6–3; Halard d. Lindqvist 7–5 7–6; Lindstrom/Strandlund d. Paradis/Suire 5–2 ret.).
FINAL: USSR d. Great Britain 2–1 (Brioukhovets d. Javer 7–5 6–3; Medvedeva d. Durie 6–3 6–3; Brioukhovets/Medvedeva lost to Durie/Wood 6–7, ret.).
RELEGATION PLAY-OFF: Italy d. Sweden 2–1 (Ferrando d. Dahlman 6–4 6–3; Cecchini lost to Lindqvist 6–2 5–7 4–6; Ferrando/Golarsa d. Lindqvist/Lindstrom 6–1 6–1).
Sweden relegated. Netherlands promoted from Division 2.

PEUGEOT WORLD TEAM CUP

This year, Horst Klosterkemper, the assiduous but always understanding director of the Peugeot World Team Cup, was reminded the hard way of both the benefits and problems to be faced when staging an event the week immediately before a Grand Slam tournament. The benefits are that it is not normally difficult to attract a sprinkling of the top box-office names who are happy to have a little more match practice on the same surface that they will be staking their reputations the following week. However, these same players often seem unable, or unwilling, to mask the fact that they are mainly concerned with honing their game for the French Open, sometimes to an extent that their attitude borders on contempt.

What must have galled Klosterkemper even more than the early departure for home by Thomas Muster, citing an arm injury, and the disappointing performances by both Stefan Edberg and Boris Becker (who was twice subject to derisive whistling from the normally admiring crowd in Dusseldorf's *Rochusclub*) was what he called 'unprofessional remarks.' Klosterkemper fully accepts that no player can be at the peak of his or her form every time they step on court and that his event is inevitably part of the build-up for Roland Garros but he was left shaking his head despairingly after hearing Muster, for instance, say that losing did not really matter because it was 'only an exhibition.' As a result, Klosterkemper collated a whole series of newspaper cuttings reporting various player comments, which underlined the basis of his concern, and discussed the problem with Mark Miles, the new executive director of ATP. He hoped that they could persuade the players to take a more professional approach to their role in public relations on such issues.

Whatever doubts there may have been about the degree of commitment demonstrated by some players (despite the fact that this is one of ATP's own events and that there is a waiting list for people to buy tickets) there was no mistaking the desire and dedication of the Yugoslav players, especially in the final when they won both the singles matches in a 2–1 victory over the United States. Goran Prpic provided the bedrock for their success. In the Group victory over Sweden, he beat Edberg 6–1 6–3 and then partnered Goran Ivanisevic, who had been outhit by Magnus Gustafsson in his singles game, to victory in the doubles.

In the final, Prpic beat a determined but seldom confident Brad Gilbert 6–4 6–4. For all his eagerness to learn clay court strategy, Gilbert all too often underlined the fact that he had not played on European clay until the age of 20, by which time his basic tennis ways were set. 'I just wish I could have helped our team a little bit more' he was honest enough to admit. At that stage however, the Americans were still confident of success. They were sure that Jim Courier would repeat his easy win over Ivanisevic in Monte Carlo and then Robert Seguso, who had damaged his arm in practice before the first match of the week, would return with Ken Flach in the doubles for, what they assumed would be, the decisive rubber. Courier actually led 6–3 4–2 but Ivanisevic, inspired by sound tactical advice from team coach, Slobodan Zivojinovic, suddenly lifted his game, to produce some wonderfully inventive and aggressive tennis to take a brilliant 3–6 7–5 6–1 victory.

Apart from their 2–1 victory over Sweden, Yugoslavia had also beaten Argentina 2–1 and Austria 3–0 whilst the United States had reached the final with 2–1 victories over Spain, West Germany and Russia. Yugoslavia were not only worthy winners but, as the capacity crowds made clear, popular winners too. After all they at least had shown, from the first match to the last, that they really cared and that was fully appreciated. – J.P.

DUSSELDORF, 21–27 MAY
ROUND ROBIN BLUE GROUP: Sweden d. Austria 3–0 (J. Svensson d. A. Antonitsch 6–4 6–3; S. Edberg d. T. Muster 6–2 6–4; Edberg/M. Gustafsson d. T. Buchmayer/O. Fuchs 6–4 6–1); ***Yugoslavia d. Argentina 2–1*** (G. Ivanisevic d. A. Mancini 6–4 6–0; G. Prpic d. M. Jaite 7–6 4–6 7–6; Ivanisevic/S. Zivojinovic lost to J. Frana/C. Miniussi 3–6 ret.); ***Argentina d. Sweden 3–0*** (Jaite d. Edberg 3–6 6–2 6–4; Mancini d. Svensson 6–4 6–2; Frana/Miniussi d. Edberg/Gustafsson 6–3 7–6); ***Yugoslavia d. Austria 3–0*** (Ivanisevic d. Fuchs 6–4 6–2; Prpic d. Antonitsch 6–1 6–1; Prpic/Zivojinovic d. Buchmayer/Fuchs 7–6 6–3); ***Yugoslavia d. Sweden 2–1*** (Ivanisevic lost to Gustafsson 4–6 2–6; Prpic d. Edberg 6–1 6–4; Ivanisevic/Prpic d. Edberg/Gustafsson 6–4 6–2); ***Argentina d. Austria 2–1*** (Mancini d. Buchmayer 6–2 6–4; Jaite lost to Antonitsch 4–6 6–7; Frana/Miniussi d. Antonitsch/Buchmayer 6–3 6–3).
1st: Yugoslavia 3 wins. ***2nd:*** Argentina 2 wins. ***3rd:*** Sweden 1 win. ***4th:*** Austria no wins.
ROUND ROBIN RED GROUP: USA d. Spain 2–1 (B. Gilbert lost to J. Arrese 5–7 5–7; J. Courier d. S. Bruguera 7–5 6–1; Courier/K. Flach d. Bruguera/T. Carbonell 7–5 6–1); ***West Germany d. USSR 3–0*** (C-U. Steeb d. A. Volkov 7–5 7–5; B. Becker d. A. Cherkasov 6–4 6–3; E. Jelen/M. Stich d. Cherkasov/V. Gabrichidze 6–4 6–7 6–2); ***USA d. West Germany 2–1*** (Gilbert lost to Becker 1–6 1–6; Courier d. Steeb 6–3 1–6 6–3; Courier/Flach d. Becker/Jelen 6–2 6–2); ***Spain d. USSR 2–1*** (Bruguera d. Volkov 7–5 6–3; J. Arrese d. Cherkasov 6–2 4–6 7–6; Bruguera/Carbonell lost to A. Olhovskiy/Volkov 3–6 6–1 6–7); ***USA d. USSR 2–1*** (Courier d. Volkov 6–4 6–2; Gilbert d. Cherkasov 6–2 6–3; Courier/Flach lost to Babrichidze/Olhovskiy 3–6 6–1 6–7); ***Spain d. West Germany 2–1*** (Burguera d. Steeb 2–6 6–4 6–3; Arrese d. Becker 6–2 6–1; Bruguera/Carbonell lost to Jelen/Stich 3–6 2–6).
1st: USA 3 wins. ***2nd:*** Spain 2 wins. ***3rd:*** West Germany 1 win. ***4th:*** USSR no wins.
FINAL: Yugoslavia d. USA 2–1 (Prpic d. Gilbert 6–4 6–4; Ivanisevic d. Courier 3–6 7–5 6–1; Prpic/Zivojinovic lost to Flach/Seguso 5–7 6–7).

MAUREEN CONNOLLY BRINKER TROPHY

Women's under 21 team competiton between USA and Great Britain
LAKEWAY, TEXAS, 5–7 OCTOBER
USA d. Great Britain 9–2 (S. McCarthy d. S. Bentley 6–4 6–2; C. Cossa lost to V. Humphreys-Davis 3–6 6–7; A. Keller d. A. Simpkin 1–6 6–3 6–1; J. Santrock/Cossa d. Bentley/R. Viollet 6–0 6–4; K. Phebus d. Viollet 6–2 6–3; Santrock lost to S. Smith 2–6 6–2 5–7; Cossa d. Bentley 7–6 6–4; McCarthy d. Humphreys-Davies 6–3 6–2; Santrock d. Simpkin 6–1 6–0; Keller d. Smith 6–2 6–3; Keller/Phebus d. Simpkin/Smith 6–3 6–0).

Today's competitors in the Maureen Connolly Brinker competition all hope that one day they might emulate the great champion whose distinguished career the event commemorates. *(R & A Photofeatures)*

RANKINGS

WORLD RANKINGS
ATP RANKINGS AND PRIZE MONEY
VIRGINIA SLIMS RANKINGS AND PRIZE MONEY

Starting the year as the No. 1 player, Ivan Lendl was overtaken by both Edberg and Becker as he concentrated unavailingly on winning a first Wimbledon title. He was nevertheless selected by the ITF's panel as the official World Champion. *(R. Adams)*

WORLD RANKINGS
John Barrett

1990 WORLD RANKINGS (last year's position in brackets)

MEN	WOMEN
1 Stefan Edberg (SWE) (3)	1 Steffi Graf (FRG) (1)
2 Ivan Lendl (TCH) (2)	2 Monica Seles (YUG) (5)
3 Andre Agassi (USA) (10)	3 Gabriela Sabatini (ARG) (4)
4 Pete Sampras (USA) (–)	4 Martina Navratilova (USA) (2)
5 Boris Becker (FRG) (1)	5 Mary Joe Fernandez (USA) (–)
6 Andres Gomez (ECU) (–)	6 Katerina Maleeva (BUL) (–)
7 Thomas Muster (AUT) (–)	7 Zina Garrison (USA) (7)
8 Goran Ivanisevic (YUG) (–)	8 Arantxa Sanchez-Vicario (ESP) (8)
9 Emilio Sanchez (ESP) (–)	9 Manuela Maleeva Fragnière (BUL) (9)
10 John McEnroe (USA) (4)	10 Jennifer Capriati (USA) (–)

In keeping with a tradition begun with our first publication in 1969 when the late Lance Tingay allowed us to include in these pages the annual ranking list he supplied to the Daily Telegraph, I offer here my own list for 1990 and for previous years which have also appeared in the Financial Times and Tennis Magazine in America.

There is no doubt in my mind that Stefan Edberg and Steffi Graf should head this year's lists although the race was a close one in both categories. As the ATP Tour computer this year rates players only on the evidence of their best 14 results it is more than ever pertinent that there should be an independent assessment of their relative form.

With 7 tournament wins, a second Wimbledon title and an appearance in the final in Melbourne, Edberg has a better record than either Ivan Lendl (one Grand Slam crown in Australia) or Andre Agassi (two Grand Slam finals in Paris and New York plus the ATP Tour title). Sampras, who made himself the youngest-ever US Open winner and was also successful in taking the inaugural *Compaq Grand Slam Cup* was only marginally less consistent than these three and goes in at No. 4.

Becker, last year's No. 1 had a sad and disappointing season in which he could claim no major title and saw his bid to overtake Edberg at the top of the ATP rankings founder because of injury on the last lap. Below them there was a real dog fight with Gomez enjoying his first Grand Slam success in Paris (he did little else of note), Muster showing remarkable resilience now that he has recovered from his awful motoring accident and young Goran Ivanisevic showing great potential. The last two places go to Emilio Sanchez who was most consistent on clay and John McEnroe who enjoyed something of a revival with a semi-final appearance at the US Open.

Graf had started the year in routine fashion with a third win in Australia and looked set to enjoy another season of dominance. Sadly she fell from her normally high standard and did not win another major title all year – although she hardly ever lost elsewhere.

Monica Seles was another who had a good start to the year with seven early titles, including a win over Graf in Berlin to end the German's 66 match-winning streak. Seles also enjoyed a first Grand Slam success in Paris where she beat Graf again. The double-handed Yugoslav also had a spectacular end to the year with a first win in five sets at the Virginia Slims Championships. Gabriela Sabatini was her victim in that final and at last the Argentine beauty overtakes Martina Navratilova for third position by virtue of the other great win she had last year – in the final of the US Open where she produced some wonderfully aggressive tennis to beat Graf. However, for Navratilova nothing will compare with her record 9th Wimbledon win and she will redouble her efforts in 1991 to prevent any of the other youngsters from overtaking her.

Mary Joe Fernandez comes into the list for the first time after an excellent season which saw her reach the final in Australia, the semi-finals in New York and the quarter-finals in Paris. She also won two tour titles. Another newcomer is Katerina Maleeva, the middle of the three Bulgarian sisters, and for the first time she overtakes her older sister Manuela. The 1989 French champion Arantxa Sanchez-Vicario keeps her place at No. 8, as does Manuela Maleeva Fragnière at No. 9 but in tenth place is the remarkable 14-year-old Jennifer Capriati of whom, I fancy, we shall be hearing much more in the years to come.

JOHN BARRETT'S WORLD RANKINGS 1973–1990

MEN

1973		1974		1975		1976	
1	Smith	1	Nastase	1	Connors	1	Ashe
2	Nastase	2	Newcombe	2	Rosewall	2	Orantes
3	Rosewall	=3	Kodes	3	Newcombe	3	Borg
4	Laver	=3	Smith	4	Borg	4	Connors
5	Newcombe	5	Connors	5	Smith	5	Nastase
6	Ashe	6	Okker	6	Vilas	6	Vilas
7	Orantes	7	Rosewall	7	Nastase	7	Ramirez
8	Okker	8	Ashe	8	Orantes	8	Laver
9	Drysdale	9	Laver	9	Ashe	9	Tanner
10	Riessen	10	Orantes	=10	Tanner	10	Roche
				=10	Kodes		

1977		1978		1979		1980	
1	Connors	1	Borg	1	Connors	1	Borg
2	Borg	2	Vilas	2	Borg	2	McEnroe
3	Nastase	3	Connors	3	Gerulaitis	3	Connors
4	Vilas	4	Gottfried	4	McEnroe	4	Gerulaitis
5	Panatta	5	Stockton	5	Ramirez	5	Tanner
6	Dibbs	6	Gerulaitis	6	Dibbs	6	Vilas
7	Ramirez	7	Orantes	7	Gottfried	7	DuPre
8	Solomon	8	Dent	8	Barazzutti	8	Dibbs
9	Tanner	9	Ramirez	9	Vilas	9	Pecci
10	Orantes	10	Nastase	10	Solomon	10	Solomon

1981		1982		1983		1984	
1	Borg	1	McEnroe	1	Connors	1	McEnroe
2	McEnroe	2	Borg	2	Lendl	2	Connors
3	Connors	3	Connors	3	McEnroe	3	Wilander
4	Lendl	4	Lendl	4	Vilas	4	Lendl
5	Mayer G.	5	Clerc	5	Wilander	5	Noah
6	Vilas	6	Mayer G.	6	Gerulaitis	=6	Arias
7	Solomon	7	Vilas	7	Mayer G.	=6	Higueras
8	Gerulaitis	8	Gerulaitis	8	Noah	8	Solomon
9	Gottfried	9	Pecci	9	Clerc	9	Clerc
10	Clerc	10	Tanner	10	Higueras	10	Teltscher

1985		1986		1987		1988	
1	McEnroe	1	Lendl	1	Lendl	1	Lendl
2	Lendl	2	Wilander	2	Becker	2	Edberg
3	Connors	3	Edberg	3	Edberg	3	Wilander
4	Wilander	4	Becker	4	Leconte	4	Cash
5	Gomez	5	McEnroe	5	Nystrom	5	Mecir
6	Cash	6	Connors	6	Mecir	6	Connors
7	Sundstrom	7	Jarryd	7	Wilander	7	Becker
8	Jarryd	8	Leconte	8	Noah	8	Noah
9	Nystrom	9	Nystrom	9	McEnroe	9	Mayotte
10	Arias	=10	Gunthardt	10	Gomez	10	Gomez
		=10	Noah				

WOMEN

1989
1. Wilander
2. Edberg
3. Lendl
4. Becker
5. Agassi
6. Mayotte
7. Mecir
8. Carlsson K.
9. Cash
=10. Leconte
=10. Svensson

1973
1. King
2. Court
3. Evert
4. Goolagong
5. Gunter
6. Melville
7. Casals
8. Wade
9. Durr
10. Stove

1974
1. Court
2. Evert
=3. Goolagong
=3. King
5. Melville
6. Masthoff
7. Casals
8. Wade
9. Morozova
10. Gunter

1975
1. Evert
2. King
3. Goolagong
4. Morozova
5. Wade
6. Melville
7. Navratilova
8. Heldman
9. Masthoff
10. Casals

1976
1. Evert
2. King
3. Goolagong
4. Navratilova
5. Wade
6. Court
7. Morozova
8. Melville Reid
9. Stove
10. Sawamatsu

1977
1. Evert
2. Goolagong
3. Wade
4. Barker
5. Casals
6. Navratilova
7. Jausovec
8. Durr
9. Fromholtz
10. Tomanova

1978
1. Evert Lloyd
2. Wade
3. King
4. Stove
5. Navratilova
6. Barker
7. Turnbull
8. Casals
9. Jausovec
10. Melville Reid

1979
1. Evert Lloyd
2. Navratilova
3. Goolagong
4. Wade
5. Turnbull
6. Ruzici
7. King
=8. Austin
=8. Shriver
10. Jausovec

1980
1. Navratilova
2. Austin
3. Evert Lloyd
4. Goolagong
5. King
6. Fromholtz
7. Wade
8. Turnbull
9. Melville Reid
10. Ruzici

1981
1. Evert Lloyd
2. Austin
3. Navratilova
4. Goolagong
5. Mandlikova
6. Jaeger
7. Turnbull
8. Ruzici
9. Fromholtz
10. Shriver

1982
=1. Evert Lloyd
=1. Austin
3. Mandlikova
4. Navratilova
5. Jaeger
6. Turnbull
7. Shriver
8. Ruzici
9. Hanika
10. Jausovec

1983
1. Navratilova
2. Evert Lloyd
3. Jaeger
4. Mandlikova
5. Austin
6. Ruzici
7. Bunge
8. Shriver
9. Potter
=10. Garrison
=10. Turnbull

1984
1. Navratilova
2. Evert Lloyd
3. Jaeger
4. Durie
5. Shriver
6. Mandlikova
7. Turnbull
8. Hanika
9. Temesvari
10. Potter

1985
1. Navratilova
2. Evert Lloyd
3. Mandlikova
4. Shriver
5. Bassett
6. Maleeva M.
7. Garrison
8. Jordan K.
9. Turnbull
10. Kohde-Kilsch

1986
1. Navratilova
2. Evert Lloyd
3. Mandlikova
4. Garrison
5. Kohde-Kilsch
6. Sukova
7. Shriver
8. Graf
9. Maleeva M.
=10. Rinaldi
=10. Sabatini

1987
1. Navratilova
2. Evert
3. Graf
4. Sukova
5. Mandlikova
6. Sabatini
7. Shriver
8. Garrison
9. Maleeva M.
10. Rinaldi

1988
1. Graf
2. Navratilova
3. Evert
4. Mandlikova
5. Sabatini
6. Shriver
7. Sukova
8. Kohde-Kilsch
9. Maleeva M.
10. McNeil

1989
1. Graf
2. Sabatini
3. Navratilova
4. Evert
5. Shriver
6. Sukova
7. Zvereva
8. Garrison
9. Maleeva M.
10. Kohde-Kilsch

IBM/ATP TOUR RANKINGS AND PRIZE MONEY 1990

The following tables show the year-end rankings for 1990 of the top 200 in singles, the top 100 in doubles and the top 200 men on the prize-money list.

The basis for ranking the men in 1990 was different from the one in use up to the end of 1989. Since the start of the ATP rankings in 1973 each player's total points won at recognized events with prize money of $25,000 or above were divided by the number of tournaments he had played over a moving 12 month period to produce an average. The minimum divisor was 12, even if he had played fewer tournaments than that. Certain refinements were added in an attempt to encourage players to compete in the lower prize money tournaments but they were not altogether successful. A new ranking list was produced each week to be used as the basis for acceptance in all official tournaments.

Starting in 1990, the Tour was reconstructed with two main categories of tournament – Championship Series and World Series – and below them Challenger Series tournaments and Satellite circuits (organised by the National Associations of the countries in which they were held). All were eligible to count towards a player's ranking which was now based on his best 14 results over a moving 12 month period. The object of this change, as before, was to encourage players to enter lower prize-money tournaments, but this time without their ranking being threatened, as it had been previously. Furthermore it now became 'legal' to offer appearance money at tournaments in the World Series group. The tournament directors of these events liked the change because they could now sign up one or two 'star' players in advance to satisfy sponsors, obtain television coverage and encourage ticket sales. This was all part of the Tour's attempt to market the game more professionally. The International Management Group was engaged to carry out this function.

(Standings supplied by IBM/ATP Tour)

SINGLES

1	Stefan Edberg (SWE)	19	3889	24	Alexander Volkov (URS)	26	929
2	Boris Becker (FRG)	19	3528	25	Jim Courier (USA)	21	923
3	Ivan Lendl (TCH)	15	2581	26	Horst Skoff (AUT)	25	899
4	Andre Agassi (USA)	13	2398	27	David Wheaton (USA)	20	893
5	Pete Sampras (USA)	21	1888	28	Sergi Bruguera (ESP)	24	886
6	Andres Gomez (ECU)	26	1680	29	Ronald Agenor (HAI)	29	864
7	Thomas Muster (AUT)	20	1654	30	Henri Leconte (FRA)	16	860
8	Emilio Sanchez (ESP)	23	1564	31	Magnus Gustafsson (SWE)	17	810
9	Goran Ivanisevic (YUG)	22	1514	32	Richard Fromberg (AUS)	26	809
10	Brad Gilbert (USA)	21	1451	33	Amos Mansdorf (ISR)	24	800
11	Jonas Svensson (SWE)	19	1365	34	Karel Novacek (TCH)	31	792
12	Andrei Chesnokov (URS)	22	1361	35	Franco Davin (ARG)	25	774
13	John McEnroe (USA)	16	1210	36	Martin Jaite (ARG)	21	747
14	Guillermo Perez-Roldan (ARG)	23	1190	37	Tim Mayotte (USA)	19	737
15	Michael Chang (USA)	19	1119	38	Petr Korda (TCH)	26	706
16	Guy Forget (FRA)	24	1101	39	Jordi Arrese (ESP)	27	691
17	Jakob Hlasek (SUI)	23	1089	40	Yannick Noah (FRA)	21	676
18	Jay Berger (USA)	18	1066	41	Mats Wilander (SWE)	14	669
19	Juan Aguilera (ESP)	21	1042	42	Michael Stich (FRG)	24	652
20	Aaron Krickstein (USA)	25	1025	43	Luiz Mattar (BRA)	22	645
21	Andrei Cherkasov (URS)	26	1003	44	Scott Davis (USA)	23	638
22	Marc Rosset (SUI)	26	977	45	Omar Camporese (ITA)	24	613
23	Richey Reneberg (USA)	25	967	46	Carl-Uwe Steeb (FRG)	21	611

		T'MENTS	POINTS			T'MENTS	POINTS
47	Derrick Rostagno (USA)	19	604	105	Cassio Motta (BRA)	27	331
48	Mark Koevermans (HOL)	27	601	106	Roberto Azar (ARG)	25	328
49	Marcelo Filippini (URU)	24	597	107	Tarik Benhabiles (FRA)	29	324
50	Todd Woodbridge (AUS)	20	569	108	Jason Stoltenberg (AUS)	20	315
51	Nicklas Kulti (SWE)	18	563	109	Paolo Cane (ITA)	17	313
52	Gary Muller (RSA)	22	557	110	Fernando Luna (ESP)	24	310
53	Wally Masur (AUS)	21	555	111	Martin Sinner (FRG)	20	309
54	Paul Haarhuis (HOL)	28	554	112	Jose Francisco Altur (ESP)	26	309
55	Goran Prpic (YUG)	22	553	113	Jaime Oncins (BRA)	18	302
56	Magnus Larsson (SWE)	17	551	114	Claudio Pistolesi (ITA)	30	301
57	Darren Cahill (AUS)	20	541	115	Joao Cunha-Silva (POR)	24	299
58	Todd Witsken (USA)	19	535	116	Miloslav Mecir (TCH)	8	297
59	Thierry Champion (FRA)	23	534	117	David Engel (SWE)	19	294
60	Jimmy Arias, (USA)	28	529	118	Cedric Pioline (FRA)	18	293
61	Christo Van Rensburg (RSA)	21	527	119	Niclas Kroon (SWE)	19	293
62	Fabrice Santoro (FRA)	23	526	120	Patrick McEnroe (USA)	12	289
63	Horacio De La Pena (ARG)	19	518	121	Jim Pugh (USA)	15	285
64	Alex Antonitsch (AUT)	22	516	122	Francisco Roig (ESP)	20	284
65	Peter Lundgren (SWE)	18	510	123	Bryan Shelton (USA)	24	282
66	Gilad Bloom (ISR)	26	508	124	Pedro Rebolledo (ARG)	15	280
67	Jean-Philippe Fleurian (FRA)	30	506	125	Eduardo Masso (ARG)	13	278
68	Eric Jelen (FRG)	23	502	126	Jeremy Bates (GBR)	25	275
69	Veli Paloheimo (FIN)	23	502	127	Alberto Mancini (ARG)	18	274
70	Javier Sanchez (ESP)	24	499	128	Jacco Eltingh (HOL)	19	274
71	Kevin Curren (USA)	18	491	129	Richard Krajicek (HOL)	7	270
72	Jim Grabb (USA)	19	490	130	Martin Strelba (TCH)	29	270
73	Anders Jarryd (SWE)	17	486	131	Jeff Tarango (USA)	23	269
74	Aki Rahunen (FIN)	30	480	132	Diego Perez (URU)	19	263
75	Mark Kratzmann (AUS)	23	479	133	Kelly Jones (USA)	23	262
76	Tomas Carbonell (ESP)	25	474	134	Glenn Layendecker (USA)	14	260
77	Renzo Furlan (ITA)	21	459	135	Jan Siemerink (HOL)	14	258
78	Brad Pearce (USA)	20	453	136	Patrick Baur (FRG)	16	257
79	Ramesh Krishnan (IND)	25	450	137	Henrik Holm (SWE)	17	257
80	Christian Bergstrom (SWE)	20	440	138	Joey Rive (USA)	22	255
81	Pat Cash (AUS)	12	432	139	Michael Tauson (DEN)	18	253
82	Patrik Kuhnen (FRG)	26	430	140	Jens Wohrmann (FRG)	24	251
83	Marian Vajda (TCH)	23	428	141	Stefano Pescosolido (ITA)	25	248
84	Guillaume Raoux (FRA)	18	427	142	Chris Garner (USA)	21	247
85	Milan Srejber (TCH)	28	425	143	Lawson Duncan (USA)	21	246
86	Alexander Mronz (FRG)	23	424	144	Shuzo Matsuoka (JPN)	13	244
87	Jaime Yzaga (PER)	21	406	145	Bart Wuyts (BEL)	20	241
88	Udo Riglewski (FRG)	29	394	146	Ctislav Dosedel (TCH)	14	239
89	Robbie Weiss (USA)	19	393	147	Diego Nargiso (ITA)	17	232
90	Francisco Clavet (ESP)	25	391	148	Andrei Olhovskiy (URS)	11	231
91	Thomas Hogstedt (SWE)	32	387	149	Paul Chamberlin (USA)	23	230
92	Grant Connell (CAN)	21	376	150	Danilo Marcelino (BRA)	18	226
93	Malivai Washington (USA)	20	371	151	Carlos Costa (ESP)	16	224
94	David Pate (USA)	16	364	152	Olivier Delaitre (FRA)	23	223
95	Brian Garrow (USA)	22	364	153	Christian Saceanu (FRG)	18	218
96	Dan Goldie (USA)	26	356	154	Simon Youl (AUS)	21	217
97	Kelly Evernden (NZL)	23	348	155	Chris Pridham (CAN)	15	215
98	Cristiano Caratti (ITA)	13	345	156	Martin Wostenholme (CAN)	25	215
99	Jan Gunnarsson (SWE)	24	342	157	Pablo Arraya (PER)	18	214
100	Lars Jonsson (SWE)	26	342	158	Thierry Tulasne (FRA)	20	214
101	Mark Woodforde (AUS)	13	341	159	Bruno Oresar (YUG)	21	211
102	Nuno Marques (POR)	26	340	160	Rodolphe Gilbert (FRA)	8	203
103	Luis Herrera (MEX)	12	335	161	Jimmy Brown (USA)	20	198
104	Andrew Sznajder (CAN)	23	333	162	Marco Aurelio Gorriz (ESP)	20	196

		T'MENTS	POINTS			T'MENTS	POINTS
163	Christian Miniussi (ARG)	17	195	182	Tommy Ho (USA)	11	154
164	Johan Carlsson (SWE)	14	188	183	Leonardo Lavalle (MEX)	11	154
165	Paul Annacone (USA)	18	187	184	Javier Frana (ARG)	13	154
166	German Lopez (ESP)	11	186	185	Gianluca Pozzi (ITA)	19	152
167	Markus Zoecke (FRG)	17	183	186	Nduka Odizor (NIG)	13	150
168	Christian Geyer (FRG)	20	183	187	Jerome Potier (FRA)	16	149
169	Michiel Schapers (HOL)	15	182	188	John Fitzgerald (AUS)	14	148
170	Daniel Orsanic (ARG)	16	177	189	Neil Borwick (AUS)	19	148
171	Broderick Dyke (AUS)	14	174	190	Scott Melville (USA)	7	145
172	Dimitri Poliakov (URS)	15	168	191	Jonathan Canter (USA)	12	145
173	Wayne Ferreira (RSA)	12	165	192	Pieter Aldrich (RSA)	6	142
174	Johan Anderson (AUS)	23	165	193	Chuck Adams (USA)	9	142
175	Mikael Pernfors (SWE)	6	162	194	Tom Nijssen (HOL)	19	142
176	Arnaud Boetsch (FRA)	10	162	195	Jose Daher (BRA)	14	141
177	Miguel Nido (PUR)	17	162	196	Paolo Pambianco (ITA)	10	139
178	Eduardo Bengoechea (ARG)	15	161	197	Danie Visser (RSA)	6	138
179	Jamie Morgan (AUS)	10	157	198	Paul Vojtischek (FRG)	23	137
180	Mark Kaplan (RSA)	20	156	199	Branislav Stankovic (TCH)	9	134
181	Leif Shiras (USA)	21	156	200	Jan Apell (SWE)	10	133

It was a great year for the No. 1 Spaniard Emilio Sanchez who won two singles and six doubles titles (with Casal) to end the year as a member of the exclusive 'top ten' club in both singles (No. 8) and doubles (No. 9).   *(R. Adams)*

DOUBLES

		T'MENTS	POINTS			T'MENTS	POINTS
1T	Pieter Aldrich (RSA)	18	2192	51	Tomas Carbonell (ESP)	22	829
1T	Danie Visser (RSA)	18	2192	52	Anders Jarryd (SWE)	14	827
3	Jim Pugh (USA)	20	2134	53	Tom Nijssen (HOL)	26	810
4	Guy Forget (FRA)	21	2112	54	Kelly Evernden (NZL)	22	797
5	Rick Leach (USA)	19	2069	55	Gustavo Luza (ARG)	20	790
6	David Pate (USA)	24	2053	56	Andres Gomez (ECU)	15	787
7	Mark Kratzmann (AUS)	25	2031	57	Richey Reneberg (USA)	23	781
8	Scott Davis (USA)	24	2013	58	Scott Melville (USA)	15	772
9	Emilio Sanchez (ESP)	22	1936	59	Sergi Bruguera (ESP)	13	758
10T	Grant Connell (CAN)	25	1925	60	Robert Van't Hof (USA)	21	755
10T	Glenn Michibata (CAN)	25	1925	61	Christo Van Rensburg (RSA)	21	749
12	Jakob Hlasek (SUI)	23	1910	62	Mansour Bahrami (IRN)	28	748
13	Sergio Casal (ESP)	21	1825	63	Jeff Brown (USA)	13	737
14	Neil Broad (RSA)	27	1692	64	Luke Jensen (USA)	34	725
15	Petr Korda (TCH)	26	1505	65	Andrew Castle (GBR)	21	721
16	Gary Muller (RSA)	27	1498	66	Charles Beckman (USA)	32	719
17	Jorge Lozano (MEX)	25	1496	67	Kent Kinnear (USA)	24	709
18	Darren Cahill (AUS)	19	1467	68	Nduka Odizor (NIG)	24	707
19	Udo Riglewski (FRG)	37	1400	69	Luiz Mattar (BRA)	23	701
20	Patrick Galbraith (USA)	28	1382	70	Brian Garrow (USA)	22	699
21	Todd Witsken (USA)	23	1380	71	Steve Devries (USA)	31	698
22	Kelly Jones (USA)	24	1373	72	Nicklas Utgren (SWE)	17	690
23	Patrick McEnroe (USA)	20	1246	73	Javier Frana (ARG)	15	688
24	Jim Grabb (USA)	16	1235	74	Brad Pearce (USA)	20	686
25	Todd Woodbridge (AUS)	21	1219	75	Cyril Suk (TCH)	33	684
26	Kevin Curren (USA)	16	1172	76	Ken Flach (USA)	16	664
27	Michael Stich (FRG)	23	1166	77	Horacio De La Pena (ARG)	22	654
28	Boris Becker (FRG)	11	1136	78	Roger Smith (BAH)	25	639
29	Paul Annacone (USA)	18	1121	79	Leonardo Lavalle (MEX)	18	632
30	Javier Sanchez (ESP)	24	1115	80	Michael Mortensen (DEN)	20	628
31	Goran Ivanisevic (YUG)	22	1113	81	Francisco Roig (ESP)	22	616
32	Broderick Dyke (AUS)	29	1106	82	Karel Novacek (TCH)	27	615
33	Jason Stoltenberg (AUS)	18	1074	83	Laurie Warder (AUS)	26	599
34	Paul Haarhuis (HOL)	27	1059	84	Bryan Shelton (USA)	22	596
35	Tomas Smid (TCH)	26	1021	85	Fernando Roese (BRA)	21	595
36	Peter Lundgren (SWE)	15	998	86	Eric Jelen (FRG)	13	592
37	David MacPherson (AUS)	33	968	87	Wayne Ferreira (RSA)	14	589
38	Cassio Motta (BRA)	21	965	88	Diego Nargiso (ITA)	22	583
39	Wally Masur (AUS)	19	964	89	Piet Norval (RSA)	13	579
40	Jim Courier (USA)	17	937	90	Nelson Aerts (BRA)	20	577
41	Omar Camporese (ITA)	18	932	91	Per Henricsson (SWE)	15	567
42	John Fitzgerald (AUS)	17	903	92	Todd Nelson (USA)	26	553
43	Michiel Schapers (HOL)	22	903	93	Glenn Layendecker (USA)	13	551
44	Mark Koevermans (HOL)	24	865	94	Nick Brown (GBR)	20	550
45	Nicolas Pereira (VEN)	28	862	95	Robert Seguso (USA)	11	546
46	David Wheaton (USA)	12	853	96	Josef Cihak (TCH)	20	544
47	Jeremy Bates (GBR)	18	845	97	Marco Aurelio Gorriz (ESP)	24	540
48	Sven Salumaa (USA)	25	838	98	Shelby Cannon (USA)	29	538
49	Eric Winogradsky (FRA)	23	837	99	Bruce Derlin (NZL)	24	523
50	Stefan Kruger (RSA)	25	837	100	Pat Cash (AUS)	11	521

PRIZE MONEY

In 1990 Stefan Edberg fell just $4,099 short of earning $2 million in prize money on the IBM/ATP Tour alone, a plateau two men had reached in 1989 (Ivan Lendl and Boris Becker). There were four men who exceeded the one million dollar mark – Edberg, Andre Agassi, Becker and Lendl – one more than in 1989.

When the $6 million offered at the inaugural *Compaq Grand Slam Cup* is included, the picture looks like this:

Two above $2 million – Sampras ($2,900,057) and Edberg ($2,095,901)

Five others above $1 million – Agassi ($1,741,382), Becker ($1,587,482), Brad Gilbert ($1,555,733), Ivan Lendl ($1,445,742) and Goran Ivanisevic ($1,020,945).

Even without the earnings from the *Compaq Grand Slam Cup* (which are shown in full as an appendix to the list below) there were 28 men who earned more than $300,000, four more than in the previous record year, 1988. A further 38 won between $200,000 and $300,000, 19 more than in 1989.

In all 132 men carried their earnings above the $100,000 mark, an indication of the growing rewards available in the game as more tournaments join the Tour and the levels of prize money rise.

Note: The prize money figures include earnings from tournaments, circuit bonuses and play-offs, plus team events where entry is based purely on merit. They do not include earnings from *Davis Cup* ties, invitation tournaments, exhibitions or special events, nor do they include income from commercial contracts or endorsements.

The following tables show the top 200 men on the IBM/ATP Tour and the final earnings of the 16 men and two alternates who were involved in the *Compaq Grand Slam Cup*.

		PRIZE MONEY			PRIZE MONEY
1	Stefan Edberg (SWE)	$1,995,901	35	Karel Novacek (TCH)	282,730
2	Andre Agassi (USA)	1,741,382	36	Rick Leach (USA)	282,355
3	Boris Becker (FRG)	1,587,482	37	Marc Rosset (SUI)	282,048
4	Ivan Lendl (TCH)	1,145,742	38	Sergio Casal (ESP)	281,481
5	Pete Sampras (USA)	900,057	39	Michael Stich (FRG)	280,823
6	Andres Gomez (ECU)	872,613	40	Martin Jaite (ARG)	271,498
7	Emilio Sanchez (ESP)	734,286	41	Tim Mayotte (USA)	263,156
8	Goran Ivanisevic (YUG)	720,945	42	Gary Muller (RSA)	261,675
9	Jakob Hlasek (SUI)	661,671	43	Alexander Volkov (URS)	259,417
10	Guy Forget (FRA)	638,358	44	Kevin Curren (USA)	257,542
11	Thomas Muster (AUT)	605,267	45	Derrick Rostagno (USA)	257,285
12	Brad Gilbert (USA)	555,733	46	Goran Prpic (YUG)	251,018
13	Jonas Svensson (SWE)	441,745	47	Todd Witsken (USA)	250,624
14	Jim Courier (USA)	437,390	48	Todd Woodbridge (AUS)	248,992
15	Andrei Chesnokov (URS)	423,863	49	Horst Skoff (AUT)	247,239
16	Scott Davis (USA)	422,390	50	Amos Mansdorf (ISR)	246,286
17	Michael Chang (USA)	416,072	51	Ronald Agenor (HAI)	243,950
18	John McEnroe (USA)	372,505	52	Wally Masur (AUS)	243,266
19	Aaron Krickstein (USA)	350,183	53	Peter Lundgren (SWE)	241,333
20	Jay Berger (USA)	349,354	54	Paul Haarhuis (HOL)	238,564
21	Mark Kratzmann (AUS)	346,366	55	Jim Grabb (USA)	237,612
22	Jim Pugh (USA)	342,672	56	Henri Leconte (FRA)	235,590
23	David Pate (USA)	342,637	57	Richard Fromberg (AUS)	228,987
24	Sergi Bruguera (ESP)	342,423	58	Javier Sanchez (ESP)	226,368
25	David Wheaton (USA)	341,240	59	Magnus Gustafsson (SWE)	224,554
26	Pieter Aldrich (RSA)	331,652	60	Yannick Noah (FRA)	222,732
27	Petr Korda (TCH)	331,404	61	Udo Riglewski (FRG)	218,928
28	Danie Visser (RSA)	322,665	62	Jordi Arrese (ESP)	218,212
29	Guillermo Perez-Roldan (ARG)	317,538	63	Omar Camporese (ITA)	214,402
30	Juan Aguilera (ESP)	311,806	64	Kelly Jones (USA)	211.782
31	Grant Connell (CAN)	307,589	65	Christo Van Rensburg (RSA)	210,540
32	Richey Reneberg (USA)	307,336	66	Alex Antonitsch (AUT)	208,090
33	Darren Cahill (AUS)	292,899	67	Eric Jelen (FRG)	206,631
34	Andrei Cherkasov (URS)	292,171	68	Glenn Michibata (CAN)	203,541

69	Mark Koevermans (HOL)	202,883	132	Paolo Cane (ITA)	100,765
70	Luiz Mattar (BRA)	200,016	133	Marian Vajda (TCH)	99,972
71	Franco Davin (ARG)	197,673	134	David Engel (SWE)	97,369
72	Tomas Carbonell (ESP)	195,984	135	Robert Seguso (USA)	96,989
73	Milan Srejber (TCH)	191,197	136	Leonardo Lavalle (MEX)	96,528
74	Slobodan Zivojinovic (YUG)	189,671	137	Jose Francisco Altur (ESP)	95,453
75	Mats Wilander (SWE)	187,435	138	Eric Winogradsky (FRA)	95,323
76	Anders Jarryd (SWE)	184,518	139	Leif Shiras (USA)	94,623
77	Carl-Uwe Steeb (GER)	184,050	140	Olivier Delaitre (FRA)	94,308
78	Jean-Philippe Fleurian (FRA)	180,718	141	Lars Jonsson (SWE)	93,936
79	Brad Pearce (USA)	179,189	142	Javier Frana (ARG)	92,029
80	Neil Broad (RSA)	169,453	143	Roberto Azar (ARG)	88,299
81	Paul Annacone (USA)	169,290	144	Tomas Smid (TCH)	87,495
82	Marcelo Filippini (URU)	168,729	145	Lawson Duncan (USA)	86,886
83	Jason Stoltenberg (AUS)	166,467	146	Jeff Tarango (USA)	85,191
84	Patrick McEnroe (USA)	160,605	147	Renzo Furlan (ITA)	84,581
85	Jimmy Arias (USA)	156,709	148	Francisco Roig (ESP)	84,543
86	Kelly Evernden (NZL)	155,598	149	Martin Wostenholme (CAN)	82,598
87	Broderick Dyke (AUS)	153,872	150	Miloslav Mecir (TCH)	82,293
88	Patrik Kuhnen (FRG)	153,039	151	Tim Wilkison (USA)	81,012
89	Horacio de la Pena (ARG)	149,936	152	Luke Jensen (USA)	81,008
90	Aki Rahunen (FIN)	148,738	153	Claudio Pistolesi (ITA)	79,737
91	Gilad Bloom (ISR)	148,399	154	Johan Anderson (AUS)	79,662
92	Cassio Motta (BRA)	148,027	155	Mansour Bahrami (IRN)	79,065
93	Jorge Lozano (MEX)	147,993	156	Jens Wohrmann (FRG)	76,712
94	Jeremy Bates (GBR)	147,543	157	Cedric Pioline (FRA)	76,243
95	Thierry Champion (FRA)	145,007	158	Nduka Odizor (NIG)	75,144
96	Christian Bergstrom (SWE)	144,238	159	Bruno Oresar (YUG)	73,330
97	Jan Gunnarsson (SWE)	143,256	160	Cristiano Caratti (ITA)	72,671
98	Alberto Mancini (ARG)	140,732	161	Marco Aurelio Gorriz (ESP)	71,808
99	Bryan Shelton (USA)	138,952	162	Carlos Costa (ESP)	71,550
100	Pat Cash, (AUS)	137,916	163	Scott Melville (USA)	70,814
101	Dan Goldie (USA)	136,848	164	Stefano Pescosolido (ITA)	70,215
102	Thomas Hogstedt (SWE)	131,666	165	Thierry Tulasne (FRA)	69,769
103	Jaime Yzaga (PER)	131,300	166	Christian Miniussi (ARG)	69,623
104	Ramesh Krishnan (IND)	128,898	167	Nuno Marques (POR)	69,114
105	Fabrice Santoro (FRA)	127,027	168	Cyril Suk (TCH)	69,041
106	Mark Woodforde (AUS)	125,842	169	Fernando Luna (ESP)	67,137
107	Paul Chamberlin (USA)	124,604	170	Markus Zoecke (FRG)	67,116
108	Brian Garrow ( )	123,511	171	Jerome Potier (FRA)	67,024
109	Joey Rive (USA)	121,679	172	Shuzo Matsuoka (JPN)	66,605
110	Magnus Larsson (SWE)	120,972	173	Robbie Weiss (USA)	66,559
111	Patrick Galbraith (USA)	120,347	174	Lars Wahlgren (SWE)	65,987
112	Andrew Sznajder (CAN)	120,150	175	Steve Devries (USA)	65,173
113	Veli Paloheimo (FIN)	119,973	176	Stefan Kruger (RSA)	64,772
114	John Fitzgerald (AUS)	117,274	177	Charles Beckman (USA)	63,252
115	Francisco Clavet (ESP)	117,005	178	Christian Saceanu (FRG)	61,089
116	Ken Flach (USA)	116,019	179	Martin Sinner (FRG)	60,958
117	Niclas Kroon (SWE)	116,009	180	Nick Brown (GBR)	60,382
118	Diego Nargiso (ITA)	113,060	181	Eduardo Masso (ARG)	58,708
119	Nicolas Pereira (VEN)	112,900	182	Michael Tauson (DEN)	58,285
120	Tom Nijssen (HOL)	112,225	183	Joao Cunha-Silva (POR)	57,776
121	Simon Youl (AUS)	111,012	184	Andrew Castle (GBR)	57,362
122	Tarik Benhabiles (FRA)	110,648	185	Jonathan Canter (USA)	57,002
123	Alexander Mronz (FRG)	108,942	186	Gianluca Pozzi (ITA)	56,188
124	Guillaume Raoux (FRA)	108,245	187	Henrik Holm (SWE)	55,267
125	Michiel Schapers (HOL)	107,957	188	Nicklas Utgren (SWE)	55,257
126	Martin Strelba (TCH)	107,223	189	Michael Mortensen (DEN)	54,832
127	Diego Perez (URU)	106,965	190	Chris Garner (USA)	54,608
128	Nicklas Kulti (SWE)	106,809	191	Laurie Warder (AUS)	54,372
129	David Macpherson (AUS)	106,062	192	Danilo Marcelino (BRA)	53,900
130	Malivai Washington (USA)	105,611	193	Jimmy Brown (USA)	53,865
131	Glenn Layendecker (USA)	103,771	194	Fernando Roese (BRA)	53,657

195	Kent Kinnear (USA)	52,911	198	Martin Laurendeau (CAN)	51,465
196	Simone Colombo (ITA)	52,548	199	Sven Salumaa (USA)	51,363
197	Mark Kaplan (RSA)	52,345	200	Gustavo Luza (ARG)	51,253

COMBINED EARNINGS

The combined earnings of the 16 men who contested the inaugural *Compaq Grand Slam Cup*, plus the two alternates, were:

		IBM/ATP TOUR	*COMPAQ GRAND SLAM CUP*	TOTAL
1	Pete Sampras (USA)	$ 900,057	$2,000,000	$2,900,057
2	Stefan Edberg (SWE)	1,995,901	100,000	2,095,901
3	Brad Gilbert (USA)	555,733	1,000,000	1,555,733
4	Ivan Lendl (TCH)	1,145,742	300,000	1,445,742
5	Goran Ivanisevic (YUG)	720,945	300,000	1,020,945
6	Andres Gomez (ECU)	872,613	100,000	972,613
7	Michael Chang (USA)	416,072	450,000	866,072
8	David Wheaton (USA)	341,240	450,000	791,240
9	Thomas Muster (AUT)	605,267	100,000	705,267
10	Aaron Krickstein (USA)	350,183	300,000	650,183
11	Jonas Svensson (SWE)	441,745	100,000	541,745
12	Henri Leconte (FRA)	235,590	300,000	535,590
13	Andrei Cherkasov (URS)	292,171	100,000	392,171
14	Kevin Curren (USA)	257,542	100,000	357,542
15	Karel Novacek (TCH)	282,730	50,000	332,730
16	Yannick Noah (FRA)	222,732	100,000	322,732
17	Christian Bergstrom (SWE)	144,238	100,000	244,238
18	Thierry Champion (FRA)	145,007	50,000	195,007

Players who, by December 31st 1990, had won more than $1 million in prize money

1	Ivan Lendl	$16,772,078	29	Peter Fleming	1,986,529
2	John McEnroe	11,265,336	30	Jose-Luis Clerc	1,984,461
3	Stefan Edberg	8,633,696	31	Guy Forget	1,917,312
4	Boris Becker	8,160,207	32	John Fitzgerald	1,845,891
5	Jimmy Connors	8,107,685	33	Aaron Krickstein	1,815,383
6	Mats Wilander	7,310,656	34	Harold Solomon	1,799,230
7	Guillermo Vilas	4,897,967	35	Stan Smith	1,774,811
8	Andres Gomez	3,958,682	36	Roscoe Tanner	1,696,108
9	Tomas Smid	3,665,330	37	Eliot Teltscher	1,653,997
10	Bjorn Borg	3,607,206	38	Sherwood Stewart	1,602,562
11	Andre Agassi	3,342,838	39	Ken Rosewall	1,600,300
12	Anders Jarryd	3,233,489	40	Arthur Ashe	1,584,909
13	Yannick Noah	3,228,947	41	Robert Seguso	1,579,382
14	Brad Gilbert	3,217,946	42	Jimmy Arias	1,570,625
15	Brian Gottfried	2,782,514	43	Martin Jaite	1,568,336
16	Vitas Gerulaitis	2,778,748	44	Rod Laver	1,564,213
17	Wojtek Fibak	2,724,948	45	Heinz Gunthardt	1,550,007
18	Miloslav Mecir	2,632,538	46	Pat Cash	1,534,968
19	Kevin Curren	2,593,669	47	Scott Davis	1,447,597
20	Emilio Sanchez	2,575,082	48	Mark Edmondson	1,450,890
21	Tim Mayotte	2,564,901	49	Paul Annacone	1,440,612
22	Johan Kriek	2,331,367	50	Balazs Taroczy	1,437,443
23	Jakob Hlasek	2,319,320	51	Bill Scanlon	1,427,007
24	Raul Ramirez	2,213,581	52	Brian Teacher	1,426,244
25	Henri Leconte	2,203,821	53	Jose Higueras	1,406,355
26	Ilie Nastase	2,076,761	54	Manuel Orantes	1,398,303
27	Joakim Nystrom	2,074,947	55	Jim Pugh	1,384,705
28	Eddie Dibbs	2,016,426	56	Gene Mayer	1,381,562

57	David Pate	1,358,678	72	Andrei Chesnokov	*1,157,163
58	Jonas Svensson	*1,333,933	73	Guillermo Perez-Roldan	*1,155,435
59	Vijay Amritraj	1,385,833	74	Ramesh Krishnan	1,139,370
60	Ken Flach	1,304,625	75	Wally Masur	*1,135,527
61	Thomas Muster	*1,304,201	76	Tim Gullikson	1,120,570
62	Michael Chang	*1,297,486	77	Pete Sampras	*1,103,725
63	Slobodan Zivojinovic	1,285,690	78	Steve Denton	1,082,214
64	Tim Wilkison	1,281,578	79	Rick Leach	*1,067,175
65	Sergio Casal	*1,271,335	80	Dick Stockton	1,063,385
66	Tom Okker	1,257,200	81	John Newcombe	1,062,408
67	Christo van Rensburg	1,237,419	82	Alexander Mayer	1,057,783
68	Paul McNamee	1,238,825	83	Peter NcNamara	1,046,145
69	Amos Mansdorf	*1,216,279	84	Thierry Tulasne	*1,038,817
70	John Alexander	1,214,079	85	Jan Gunnarsson	*1,035,971
71	Robert Lutz	1,165,276	86	Darren Cahill	*1,034,329

These players passed the $1 million mark during 1990.

ATP TOUR BOARD OF DIRECTORS

Tournament Representatives:
Franco Bartoni (Europe)
Graham Lovett (International Group)
Charlie Pasarell (North America)

Player Representatives:
Vijay Amritraj
Steven Meister
Larry Scott

ATP TOUR COUNCIL

President:
Vijay Amritraj
Vice-President:
Larry Scott
Members:
Andrew Castle
Brad Gilbert
Cassio Motta
Emilio Sanchez
Fred Stolle
Bryon Talbot
Robert Van't Hof
Todd Witsken

Address:
ATP Tour
Four Sawgrass Village,
Suite 240
Ponte Vedra Beach,
FL 32082
Tel: 904 285 8000
Fax: 904 285 5966

VIRGINIA SLIMS RANKINGS AND PRIZE MONEY 1990

RANKINGS

The following tables show the season-ending rankings in singles and doubles. The rankings, updated each week, are based on points won at official events on the Kraft General Foods World Tour.

SINGLES

		T'MENTS	AVGE POINTS			T'MENTS	AVGE POINTS
1	Steffi Graf (FRG)	15	278.10	42	Patty Fendick (USA)	15	24.20
2	Monica Seles (YUG)	15	203.75	43	Brenda Schultz (HOL)	17	23.56
3	Martina Navratilova (USA)	13	199.42	44	Cathy Caverzasio (ITA)	14	23.25
4	Mary Joe Fernandez (USA)	12	147.03	45	Sabine Hack (FRG)	13	22.46
5	Gabriela Sabatini (ARG)	16	137.02	46	Claudia Kohde-Kilsch (FRG)	17	22.35
6	Katerina Maleeva (BUL)	16	115.84	47	Katia Picolini (ITA)	13	22.10
7	Arantxa Sanchez-Vicario (ESP)	16	112.60	48	Marianne Werdel (USA)	21	22.07
8	Jennifer Capriati (USA)	12	103.41	49	Nicole Provis (AUS)	19	21.97
9	Manuela Maleeva Fragnière	16	103.15	50	Ann Grossman (USA)	22	21.23
10	Zina Garrison (USA)	19	100.52	51	Angelica Gavaldon (MEX)	17	21.21
11	Conchita Martinez (ESP)	13	98.56	52	Lori McNeil (USA)	20	21.17
12	Natalia Zvereva (URS)	17	77.50	53	Elizabeth Smylie (AUS)	16	20.16
13	Jana Novotna (TCH)	17	77.26	54	Regina Rajchrotova (TCH)	16	19.25
14	Helena Sukova (TCH)	17	77.14	55	Patricia Tarabini (ARG)	17	19.23
15	Barbara Paulus (AUT)	15	69.93	56	Natalia Medvedeva (URS)	18	19.14
16	Amy Frazier (USA)	15	64.07	57	Radka Zrubakova (TCH)	18	19.00
17	Judith Wiesner (AUT)	19	62.78	58	Stephanie Rehe (USA)	6	18.83
18	Nathalie Tauziat (FRA)	21	60.35	59	Robin White (USA)	15	18.78
19	Leila Meskhi (URS)	16	53.75	60	Mary Lou Daniels (USA)	12	18.66
20	Sandra Cecchini (ITA)	15	41.80	61	Laura Golarsa (ITA)	17	18.65
21	Laura Gildemeister (PER)	19	35.34	62	Nathalie Herreman (FRA)	21	18.54
22	Sabine Applemans (BEL)	12	35.04	63	Emanuela Zardo (SUI)	13	18.10
23	Raffaella Reggi (ITA)	17	34.71	64	Jo Durie (GBR)	17	17.84
24	Ros. Fairbank-Nideffer (USA)	20	33.92	65	Laura Garrone (ITA)	15	17.80
25	Helen Kelesi (CAN)	17	33.62	66	Pam Shriver (USA)	5	17.79
26	Isabel Cueto (FRG)	15	33.60	67	Linda Ferrando (ITA)	17	17.38
27	Susan Sloane (USA)	16	31.81	68	Nicole Jagerman (HOL)	13	17.35
28	Meredith McGrath (USA)	13	30.38	69	Kathy Rinaldi (USA)	18	16.58
29	Claudia Porwik (FRG)	17	29.26	70	Carrie Cunningham (USA)	13	16.42
30	Dinky Van Rensburg (RSA)	17	29.04	71	Etsuko Inoue (JPN)	13	16.42
31	Naoko Sawamatsu (JPN)	11	28.79	72	Magdalena Maleeva (BUL)	14	16.13
32	Manon Bollegraf (HOL)	16	28.72	73	Elena Brioukhovets (URS)	14	16.06
33	Anne Smith (USA)	14	28.71	74	Peanut Louie-Harper (USA)	15	15.75
34	Anke Huber (FRG)	12	28.61	75	Amanda Coetzer (RSA)	19	15.53
35	Gretchen Magers (USA)	19	28.60	76	Federica Bonsignori (ITA)	18	15.42
36	Gigi Fernadez (USA)	14	28.53	77	Isabelle Demongeot (FRA)	17	15.18
37	Mercedes Paz (ARG)	23	27.52	78	Kimiko Date (JPN)	7	14.67
38	Catarina Lindqvist (SWE)	17	26.65	79	Petra Langrova (TCH)	15	14.47
39	Rachel McQuillan (AUS)	21	26.17	80	Cecilia Dahlman (SWE)	21	14.40
40	Wiltrud Probst (FRG)	16	25.28	81	Tami Whitlinger (USA)	16	14.26
41	Julie Halard (FRA)	16	24.41	82	Sarah Loosemore (GBR)	17	14.20

		T'MENTS	AVGE POINTS			T'MENTS	AVGE POINTS
83	Linda Harvey-Wild (USA)	16	13.81	142	Andrea Leand (USA)	15	7.47
84	Alexia Dechaume (FRA)	18	13.74	143	Claudia Chabalgoity (BRA)	13	7.45
85	Anne Minter (AUS)	22	13.73	144	Andrea Strnadova (TCH)	18	7.40
86	Elna Reinach (RSA)	18	13.58	145	Petra Ritter (AUT)	9	7.34
87	Larisa Savchenko (URS)	18	13.56	146	Michelle Jaggard (AUS)	16	7.33
88	Sara Gomer (GBR)	11	13.53	147	D Krajcovicova-Szabova (TCH)	13	7.29
89	Maya Kidowaki (JPN)	13	13.50	148	Clare Wood (GBR)	17	7.18
90	Csilla Bartos (SUI)	13	13.33	149	Beverly Bowes (USA)	13	6.92
91	Belinda Cordwell (NZL)	14	13.18	150	Elise Burgin (USA)	19	6.79
92	Betsy Nagelsen (USA)	12	12.92	151	Shaun Stafford (USA)	19	6.63
93	Terry Phelps (USA)	17	12.76	152	Pilar Vasquez (PER)	18	6.61
94	Audra Keller (USA)	20	12.76	153	Eva Pfaff (FRG)	14	6.31
95	Eva Sviglerova (TCH)	15	12.74	154	Jennifer Santrock (USA)	12	6.30
96	Catherine Tanvier (FRA)	13	12.72	155	Wendy White-Prausa (USA)	10	6.29
97	Beate Reinstadler (AUT)	12	12.33	156	Stephanie Rottier (HOL)	9	6.10
98	Elena Pampoulova (BUL)	16	12.23	157	Carling Bassett-Seguso (CAN)	5	6.05
99	Catherine Mothes (FRA)	11	12.19	158	Mariaan De Swardt (RSA)	11	5.96
100	Sandra Wasserman (BEL)	17	11.65	159	Barbara Romano (ITA)	13	5.85
101	Monique Javer (GBR)	18	11.63	160	Silke Frankl (FRG)	12	5.80
102	Laura Lapi (ITA)	13	11.61	161	Andrea Vieira (BRA)	18	5.73
103	Patricia Hy (CAN)	11	11.57	162	Pascale Etchemendy (FRA)	18	5.62
104	Karine Quentrec (FRA)	17	11.53	163	Kumiko Okamoto (JPN)	10	5.58
105	Stacey Martin (USA)	18	11.50	164	Kirrily Sharpe (AUS)	16	5.49
106	Mary Pierce (FRA)	12	11.42	165	Luciana Corsato (BRA)	19	5.47
107	Barbara Rittner (FRG)	12	11.39	166	Hellas Ter Riet (HOL)	20	5.47
108	Halle Cioffi (USA)	14	11.32	167	Jana Pospisilova (TCH)	14	5.43
109	Francesca Romano (ITA)	10	11.12	168	Celine Cohen (SUI)	12	5.39
110	Nana Miyagi (JPN)	16	11.07	169	Pascale Paradis (FRA)	17	5.39
111	Veronika Martinek (FRG)	12	10.94	170	Petra Thoren (FIN)	17	5.36
112	Ann Henricksson (USA)	19	10.79	171	Kataryna Nowak (POL)	15	5.11
113	Akiko Kijimuta (JPN)	11	10.75	172	Marketa Kochta (FRG)	10	5.01
114	Donna Faber (USA)	17	10.59	173	Nanne Dahlman (FIN)	11	4.94
115	Karin Kschwendt (LUX)	12	10.39	174	Jo-Anne Faull (AUS)	19	4.83
116	Renata Baranski (USA)	19	10.10	175	Agnese Blumberga (URS)	13	4.77
117	Andrea Temesvari (HUN)	19	10.10	176	Anna-Maria Foeldenyi (HUN)	12	4.77
118	Florencia Labat (ARG)	19	10.00	177	Anouschka Popp (FRG)	12	4.76
119	Angeliki Kanellopoulou (GRE)	12	9.96	178	Viktoria Milvidskaia (URS)	12	4.76
120	Cammy Macgregor (USA)	16	9.87	179	Marion Maruska (AUT)	9	4.69
121	Debbie Graham (USA)	7	9.79	180	Rene Simpson-Alter (CAN)	10	4.65
122	Karina Habsudova (TCH)	9	9.46	181	Yukie Koizumi (JPN)	10	4.58
123	Sylvia Hanika (FRG)	10	9.12	182	Tine Scheuer-Larsen (DEN)	11	4.54
124	Claudine Toleafoa (NZL)	20	8.96	183	Maria Ekstrand (SWE)	20	4.51
125	Louise Field (AUS)	18	8.93	184	Iva Budarova (TCH)	13	4.37
126	Cristina Tessi (ARG)	12	8.85	185	Sandrine Testud (FRA)	18	4.36
127	Bettina Fulco (ARG)	21	8.70	186	Catherine Suire (FRA)	17	4.29
128	Hu Na (USA)	13	8.67	187	Maureen Drake (CAN)	16	4.27
129	Kristin Godridge (AUS)	20	8.64	188	Sabrina Giusto (BRA)	16	4.26
130	Maria Strandlund (SWE)	16	8.44	189	Louise Allen (USA)	19	4.23
131	Samantha Smith (GBR)	20	8.43	190	Luanne Spadea (USA)	20	4.13
132	Federica Haumuller (ARG)	14	8.40	191	Miriam Oremans (HOL)	13	4.12
133	Sandra Dopfer (AUT)	15	8.37	192	Silvia Farina (ITA)	12	4.09
134	Silke Meier (FRG)	15	8.32	193	Kate McDonald (AUS)	12	4.08
135	Nathalie Guerree (FRA)	13	8.32	194	Julie Salmon (GBR)	12	4.06
136	Tamaka Takagi (JPN)	11	8.32	195	Silvia La Fratta (ITA)	11	4.03
137	Camille Benjamin (USA)	21	7.99	196	Akemi Nishiya (JPN)	12	3.90
138	Noelle Van Lottum (FRA)	18	7.77	197	Mana Endo (JPN)	9	3.89
139	Julie Richardson (NZL)	16	7.77	198	Andrea Tiezzi (ARG)	13	3.81
140	Erika De Lone (USA)	14	7.76	199	Katja Oeljeklaus (FRG)	10	3.81
141	Maider Laval (FRA)	11	7.56	200	Eva Krapl (SUI)	14	3.76

		T'MENTS	AVGE POINTS			T'MENTS	AVGE POINTS
201	Robyn Field (RSA)	18	3.68	226	Rika Hiraki (JPN)	12	2.94
202	Akiko Gooden (USA)	12	3.64	227	Sabrina Lucchi (ITA)	13	2.93
203	Ann Devries (BEL)	15	3.63	228	Il-Soon Kim (KOR)	9	2.91
204	Sabrina Goles (YUG)	12	3.62	229	Sandrine Jaquet (SUI)	12	2.91
205	Kathy Jordan (USA)	10	3.57	230	Sybille Niox-Chateau (FRA)	13	2.88
206	Leona Laskova (TCH)	11	3.57	231	Lorenza Jachia (ITA)	15	2.77
207	Julija Salnikova (URS)	14	3.52	232	Rennae Stubbs (AUS)	20	2.75
208	Andrea Farley (USA)	6	3.51	233	Luciana Tella (BRA)	14	2.73
209	Caroline Vis (HOL)	17	3.50	234	Inmaculada Varas (ESP)	10	2.72
210	Heather Ludloff (USA)	16	3.49	235	Amy Schwartz (USA)	15	2.66
211	Sandy Collins (USA)	16	3.42	236	Ilana Berger (ISR)	12	2.56
212	Stacey Schefflin (USA)	16	3.41	237	Kaye Hand (GBR)	19	2.55
213	Janine Thompson (AUS)	13	3.41	238	Shannan McCarthy (USA)	9	2.55
214	Carin Bakkum (HOL)	11	3.37	239	Elly Hakami (USA)	3	2.53
215	Tracey Morton (AUS)	17	3.35	240	Heidi Sprung (AUT)	26	2.53
216	Maya Palaversic (YUG)	14	3.27	241	Helen Van Den Berg (HOL)	14	2.50
217	Sabine Gerke (FRG)	10	3.26	242	Ginger Helgeson (USA)	7	2.48
218	Nicole Pratt (AUS)	19	3.17	243	Jill Hetherington (CAN)	16	2.48
219	Gisele Miro (BRA)	8	3.17	244	Katharina Duell (FRG)	14	2.47
220	Jane Taylor (AUS)	13	3.11	245	Andrea Mueller (FRG)	9	2.44
221	Natalia Baudone (ITA)	9	3.09	246	Belinda Borneo (GBR)	15	2.44
222	Eleni Rossides (USA)	18	3.07	247	Jolene Watanabe (USA)	13	2.43
223	Sophie Amiach (FRA)	16	3.02	248	Ana Segura (ESP)	13	2.40
224	Ulrike Priller (AUT)	12	3.01	249	Yael Segal (ISR)	16	2.39
225	Martina Pawlik (FRG)	6	2.98	250	Sofie Albinus (DEN)	21	2.39

DOUBLES

		T'MENTS	AVGE POINTS			T'MENTS	AVGE POINTS
1	Helena Sukova (TCH)	16	413.69	26	Nicole Provis (AUS)	24	113.35
2	Jana Novotna (TCH)	17	387.31	27	Elise Burgin (USA)	19	112.07
3	Gigi Fernandez (USA)	13	335.68	28	Mary Lou Daniels (USA)	13	106.81
4	Martina Navratilova (USA)	12	309.41	29	Gabriela Sabatini (ARG)	6	104.60
5	Natalia Zvereva (URS)	17	243.76	30	Helen Kelesi (CAN)	15	102.73
6	Mary Joe Fernandez (USA)	10	237.40	31	Leila Meskhi (URS)	18	101.00
7	Larisa Savchenko (URS)	19	231.90	32	Katerina Maleeva (BUL)	10	92.80
8	Arantxa Sanchez-Vicario (ESP)	15	222.83	33	Sandra Cecchini (ITA)	14	90.43
9	Kathy Jordan (USA)	17	219.19	34	Brenda Schultz (HOL)	19	87.53
10	Elizabeth Smylie (AUS)	19	218.02	35	Ros. Fairbank-Nideffer (USA)	21	87.41
11	Patty Fendick (USA)	15	199.35	36	Nathalie Tauziat (FRA)	20	83.40
12	Robin White (USA)	14	194.94	37	Dinky Van Rensburg (RSA)	17	79.41
13	Zina Garrison (USA)	13	178.74	38	Eva Pfaff (FRG)	17	78.71
14	Mercedes Paz (ARG)	23	166.31	39	Jo Durie (GBR)	17	78.35
15	Betsy Nagelsen (USA)	10	164.05	40	Monica Seles (YUG)	11	76.55
16	Meredith McGrath (USA)	13	161.35	41	Andrea Temesvari (HUN)	20	75.72
17	Anne Smith (USA)	15	148.39	42	Patricia Tarabini (ARG)	18	75.44
18	Gretchen Magers (USA)	20	134.95	43	Jill Hetherington (CAN)	17	75.24
19	Elna Reinach (RSA)	19	128.56	44	Wendy Turnbull (AUS)	10	74.20
20	Lise Gregory (RSA)	23	125.91	45	Jo-Anne Faull (AUS)	18	73.22
21	Katrina Adams (USA)	20	123.63	46	Hana Mandlikova (AUS)	6	71.80
22	Lori McNeil (USA)	20	122.39	47	Elena Brioukhovets (URS)	12	69.50
23	Wendy White-Prausa (USA)	15	116.88	48	Louise Field (AUS)	18	69.11
24	Manon Bollegraf (HOL)	19	114.67	49	Julie Richardson (NZL)	20	68.64
25	Natalia Medvedeva (URS)	19	113.74	50	Catherine Tanvier (FRA)	14	67.36

PRIZE MONEY

The following table shows the prize money (including bonuses) won at all recognized tournaments which adopt the WTA guidelines and where direct entry is based solely on merit. Standings supplied by VIRGINIA SLIMSTAT SYSTEM.

		PRIZE MONEY			PRIZE MONEY
1	Steffi Graf (FRG)	$1,921,853	51	Elise Burgin (USA)	92,441
2	Monica Seles (YUG)	1,637,222	52	Wiltrud Prost (FRG)	91,076
3	Martina Navratilova (USA)	1,330,794	53	Susan Sloane (USA)	88,349
4	Gabriela Sabatini (ARG)	975,490	54	Linda Ferrando (ITA)	88,049
5	Jana Novotna (TCH)	645,500	55	Jo Durie (GBR)	87,984
6	Zina Garrison (USA)	602,203	56	Patricia Tarabini (ARG)	87,768
7	Helena Sukova (TCH)	562,715	57	Regina Rajchrtova (TCH)	86,140
8	Mary Joe Fernandez (USA)	518,366	58	Radka Zrubakova (TCH)	85,265
9	Arantxa Sanchez-Vicario (ESP)	517,662	59	Anne Minter (AUS)	84,303
10	Natalia Zvereva (URS)	462,770	60	Kathy Rinaldi (USA)	82,349
11	Katerina Maleeva (BUL)	418,475	61	Ann Henricksson (USA)	78,974
12	Manuela Maleeva-Fragnière (SUI)	360,215	62	Isabel Cueto (FRG)	77,161
13	Nathalie Tauziat (FRA)	300,103	63	Julie Halard (FRA)	76,865
14	Jennifer Capriati (USA)	283,597	64	Lise Gregory (RSA)	76,376
15	Elizabeth Smylie (AUS)	258,904	65	Angelica Gavaldon (USA)	76,236
16	Judith Wiesner (AUT)	251,446	66	Mary Lou Daniels (USA)	74,377
17	Conchita Martinez (ESP)	248,184	67	Isabelle Demongeot (FRA)	73,155
18	Gigi Fernandez (USA)	231,500	68	Laura Garrone (ITA)	71,591
19	Mercedes Paz (ARG)	220,513	69	Naoko Sawamatsu (JAP)	69,710
20	Larisa Savchenko (URS)	217,984	70	Betsy Nagelsen (USA)	69,144
21	Leila Meskhi (URS)	210,438	71	Laura Golarsa (ITA)	69,036
22	Barbara Paulus (AUT)	184,164	72	Cammy MacGregor (USA)	68,007
23	Gretchen Magers (USA)	175,652	73	Camille Benjamin (USA)	67,377
24	Nicole Provis (AUS)	165,022	74	Peanut Louie-Harper (USA)	67,230
25	Rosalyn Fairbank-Nideffer (USA)	163,582	75	Terry Phelps (USA)	65,820
26	Lori McNeil (USA)	162,939	76	Jo-Anne Faull (AUS)	65,067
27	Patty Fendick (USA)	160,713	77	Eva Pfaff (FRG)	64,308
28	Amy Frazier (USA)	160,620	78	Sabine Appelmans (BEL)	63,696
29	Kathy Jordan (USA)	155,932	79	Cecilia Dahlman (SWE)	63,159
30	Laura Gildemeister (PER)	151,619	80	Cathy Caverzasio (USA)	62,198
31	Helen Kelesi (CAN)	144,847	81	Catherine Tanvier (FRA)	62,129
32	Robin White (USA)	135,910	82	Wendy White-Prausa (USA)	60,477
33	Natalia Medvedeva (URS)	135,497	83	Tami Whitlinger (USA)	60,379
34	Elna Reinach (RSA)	135,171	84	Alexia Dechaume (FRA)	59,872
35	Manon Bollegraf (HOL)	134,012	85	Louise Field (AUS)	58,950
36	Dinky Van Rensburg (RSA)	131,803	86	Nana Miyagi (JAP)	58,349
37	Sandra Cecchini (ITA)	131,699	87	Shaun Stafford (USA)	57,971
38	Brenda Schultz (HOL)	126,330	88	Donna Faber (USA)	57,886
39	Rachel McQuillan (AUS)	124,758	89	Bettina Fulco (ARG)	57,495
40	Claudia Porwik (FRG)	118,934	90	Monique Javer (GBR)	57,010
41	Ann Grossman (USA)	115,923	91	Magdalena Maleeva (BUL)	56,907
42	Raffaella Reggi (ITA)	113,404	92	Petra Langrova (TCH)	56,901
43	Anne Smith (USA)	113,042	93	Amanda Coetzer (RSA)	55,895
44	Meredith McGrath (USA)	110,124	94	Florencia Labat (ARG)	55,855
45	Catarina Lindqvist (SWE)	109,994	95	Maria Strandlund (SWE)	55,085
46	Nathalie Herreman (FRA)	107,460	96	Anke Huber (FRG)	53,412
47	Andrea Temesvari (HUN)	102,632	97	Maya Kidowaki (JAP)	53,186
48	Katrina Adams (USA)	99,775	98	Halle Cioffi (USA)	51,720
49	Claudia Kohde-Kilsch (FRG)	96,677	99	Audra Keller (USA)	51,235
50	Marianne Werdel (USA)	95,322	100	Pam Shriver (USA)	50,976

Players who have won more than $1 million in prize money

1	Martina Navratilova	$16,674,607	17	Evonne Goolagong	1,399,431
2	Chris Evert	8,896,195	18	Lori McNeil	1,392,083
3	Steffi Graf	7,173,198	19	Andrea Jaeger	1,379,066
4	Pam Shriver	4,323,497	20	Barbara Potter	1,376,580
5	Gabriela Sabatini	3,656,136	21	Rosie Casals	1,363,455
6	Helena Sukova	3,473,097	22	Jana Novotna	1,350,104
7	Hana Mandlikova	3,340,959	23	Sylvia Hanika	1,296,560
8	Zina Garrison	2,783,770	24	Arantxa Sanchez-Vicario	1,260,417
9	Wendy Turnbull	2,769,024	25	Rosalyn Fairbank-Nideffer	1,230,295
10	Claudia Kohde-Kilsch	2,034,541	26	Virginia Ruzici	1,183,728
11	Manuela Maleeva-Fragnière	1,966,679	27	Natalia Zvereva	1,148,133
12	Billie Jean King	1,966,487	28	Bettina Bunge	1,126,424
13	Tracy Austin	1,925,415	29	Katerina Maleeva	1,087,419
14	Monica Seles	1,891,283	30	Elizabeth Smylie	1,080,589
15	Virginia Wade	1,542,278	31	Anne Smith	1,071,022
16	Kathy Jordan	1,539,395	32	Betty Stove	1,047,356

WTA ANNUAL AWARDS 1990

PLAYER OF THE YEAR	Steffi Graf
DOUBLES TEAM OF THE YEAR	Jana Novotna/Helena Sukova
MOST IMPROVED PLAYER	Monica Seles
MOST IMPRESSIVE NEWCOMER	Jennifer Capriati
COMEBACK PLAYER OF THE YEAR	Elizabeth Smylie
MEDIA PERSON OF THE YEAR	John Parsons
KAREN KRANTZCKE SPORTSMANSHIP	Mercedes Paz
PLAYER SERVICE	Wendy Turnbull
DAVID GRAY SPECIAL SERVICE	Marvin Koslow

WTA BOARD OF DIRECTORS (Voted in 26th August 1990)

PRESIDENT	Chris Evert	**ADDRESS**	
VICE-PRESIDENT	Pam Shriver	133 First Street N.E.	
SECRETARY	Wendy Turnbull	St. Petersburg, FL	
TREASURER	Elise Burgin	33701, U.S.A.	
Members	Manon Bolegraf	Tel: 813–895 5000	
	Zina Garrison	Fax: 813–894 1982	
	Kathy Jordan	Telex: 441761	
	Martina Navratilova		
	Candy Reynolds		
	Elizabeth Smylie		
	Catherine Suire		
	Natalia Zvereva		
	Marvin Koslow		
	Loretta McCarthy		
	Gerard Smith		

WTA EXECUTIVE STAFF:

EXECUTIVE DIRECTOR AND C.E.O.	Gerard Smith
DIRECTOR OF INTERNATIONAL OPERATIONS	Peachy Kellmeyer
CHIEF FINANCIAL OFFICER	Gregory A. Pangburn
DIRECTOR OF PUBLIC RELATIONS	Ana Leaird
DIRECTOR OF MANAGEMENT INFORMATION SYSTEMS	Gene Beckwith
DIRECTOR OF EUROPEAN OPERATIONS	Georgina Clark

WOMEN'S INTERNATIONAL PROFESSIONAL TENNIS COUNCIL

ADDRESS: 100 Park Avenue, Second Floor, New York, N.Y., 10017 USA.
Tel: 212–878 2250; FAX: 212–599 5190

MANAGING DIRECTOR:	Jane Brown (Appointed August 1989)
ITF REPRESENTATIVES:	Robert A. Cookson Heinz Grimm Brian Tobin Debbie Jevans
PLAYER REPRESENTATIVES:	Peachy Kellmeyer Candy Reynolds Gerard Smith Wendy Turnbull
TOURNAMENT REPRESENTATIVES:	William Goldstein (United States) Jack Jones (United States) George Hendon (Europe) Geoffrey Pollard (Rest of the World)
KRAFT GENERAL FOODS REPRESENTATIVES:	Tom Keim, Edy McGoldrick
VIRGINIA SLIMS REPRESENTATIVES:	Ina Broeman, Leo McCullagh

Key Biscayne, Florida, site of the Lipton Players International, a tournament created by former US No. 1 Butch Buccholz in a co-operative venture with the two players' Associations. A new Stadium, already approved, will make this one of the finest tennis centres in the world. *(T. Hindley)*

REFERENCE SECTION

BIOGRAPHIES
ALL-TIME GREATS
CHAMPIONSHIP ROLLS

A tournament finalist in her first tournament when still aged 13, the American prodigy, Jennifer Capriati, enjoyed unprecedented attention in her first year as a professional winning her first title in Puerto Rico and ending the year ranked No. 8 in the world.

(M. Cole)

Recovering from a stress fracture of the hip sustained the previous December, Michael Chang took time to settle in 1990 and had only one tournament win (in Toronto) as his ranking slipped from No. 5 to No. 15. *(M. Cole)*

BIOGRAPHIES

Christine Forrest

Abbreviations used in this section:

f	final	D Cup	Davis Cup
sf	semi-final	Fed Cup	Federation Cup
qf	quarter-final	W Cup	Wightman Cup
r/u	runner-up	FC Cup	Family Circle Cup
def	defaulted	GS Cup	Grand Slam Cup
ret'd	retired	Champ	Championship/Champion
fs	final set	Int	International
rr	round-robin	Inv	Invitation
b-p	break-point	Jun	Junior
s-p	set-point	Nat	National
m-p	match-point	Pro	Professional
t-b	tie-break	Tourn	Tournament
1 r	first round	CS	Colgate Series
2 s	second set	TS	Toyota Series
RH	right-handed	HC	Hard Court
LH	left-handed	VS	Virginia Slims
2HB	2-handed backhand	KGF	Kraft General Foods
2HF	2-handed forehand	WCT	World Championship Tennis
US CC	US Clay Court	WTT	World Team Tennis
	Championships	GP	Grand Prix
LIPC	Lipton International		
	Players Championships		

Men and women who appear in the top 100 on the ATP and WTA computer rankings are included below, as well as leading doubles players, a few prominent players who compete less than usual nowadays, plus some newcomers. We gratefully acknowledge the assistance of the ATP Tour, Virginia Slims and WTA in supplying additional biographical information.

The final ranking for each year is shown in brackets following the date.

1990 doubles ranking is shown in brackets after 1990 ranking where applicable.

Note: 1990 rankings for women are season-end rankings, and those for men are year-end rankings.

ANDRE AGASSI (USA)
Born Las Vegas, 29 April 1970, and lives there; RH; 2HB; 5ft 11in; 155lb; final 1990 ATP ranking 4; 1990 prize money $1,741,382; career prize money $3,342,838
Suffered from Osgood Schlatter's disease, which causes a bone in the knee to grow improperly. Coached from age 13 by Nick Bollettieri and from 1989 by Pat Etchenbery for movement; trained by Gil Reyes in 1990. **1984:** Ranked 4 in US Boys' 14s and won Nat 14s. **1985:** (618) Receiving expert council from brother-in-law Pancho Gonzales, he tested the waters of men's circuit. **1986:** (91) Downed Mayotte and S. Davis on way to qf Stratton Mountain. **1987:** (25) Reached first GP f at Seoul, won his 1st GP title at Itaparica at end of season and d. Jarryd *en route* to sf Basel. **1988:** (3) Began the year by winning 2nd consecutive tourn at Memphis, adding US CC, Tourn of Champs, Stuttgart, Stratton Mountain and Livingston during the year. After reaching 1st GS sf in Paris, he took a month's rest, missing Wimbledon. Made D Cup début and qualified for Masters, but was

restricted by a hand injury. *1989:* (7) Could not maintain the high standards of 1988, having to wait until Orlando in Oct. for his 1st title for 14 months. R/u Italian Open; reached 2nd GS sf at US Open and appeared in 4 other sf to qualify for Masters, but won no match there. *1990:* His year finished on a high note when he beat world No. 1, Edberg, to win ATP Tour World Champ in Nov. Reached 1st GP f at French Open, where he shocked traditionalists with his lurid outfits, which included luminous cycling shorts under black denim shorts. Did not play Wimbledon or Australian Open, but was also r/u at US Open, where he was fined $3,000 for his conduct in 3r match v Korda. In autumn was fined 20% of total earnings on ATP tour (excluding GS) for falling 2 tourns short of his commitment to the tour. Won San Francisco, LIPC, Washington; r/u Indian Wells; and played in US D Cup team that d. Australia 3–2 in f but withdrew with pulled stomach muscle in 4th rubber v Cahill, after d. Fromberg in 5s in 1st. Withdrew from GS Cup after submitting an entry and was fined $25,000. *1990 HIGHLIGHTS – SINGLES: r/u French Open* seed 3 (d. Wostenholme 4–6 7–6 6–0 6–1, Woodbridge 7–5 6–1 6–3, Boetsch 6–3 6–2 6–0, Courier [seed 13] 6–7 6–1 6–4 6–0, Chang [seed 11] 6–1 6–2 4–6 6–2, Svensson 6–1 6–4 3–6 6–3, lost Gomez [seed 4] 6–3 2–6 6–4 6–4), *r/u US Open* seed 4 (d. Connell 6–4 6–2 6–2, Korda 7–5 5–7 6–0 6–4, Davin 7–5 6–4 6–0, Berger [seed 13] 7–5 6–0 6–2, Cherkasov 6–2 6–2 6–3, Becker [seed 2] 6–7 6–3 6–2 6–3, lost Sampras [seed 12] 6–4 6–3 6–2); *won* San Francisco (d. Krishnan 6–2 6–7 6–0, Goldie 2–6 6–0 6–1, Annacone 6–4 6–2, Grabb 6–2 6–2, Witsken 6–1 6–3), *won* LIPC (d. Jones 6–1 6–2, Gunnarsson 6–1 6–3, Gomez 6–7 6–2 6–3, Courier 4–6 6–3 6–1, Berger 5–7 6–1 6–1, Edberg 6–1 6–4 0–6 6–2), *won* Washington (d. Pearce 7–6 6–3, Bloom 6–1 7–5, Reneberg 7–6 6–0, Chang 6–3 6–1, Grabb 6–1 6–4), *won* ATP World Champ (d. Sampras, E. Sanchez, lost Edberg in rr; d. Becker 6–2 6–4 in sf, d. Edberg 5–7 7–6 7–5 6–2 in f); *r/u* Indian Wells (d. Arias 6–1 7–6, Schapers 6–4 7–5, E. Sanchez 6–1 7–6, Becker 6–4 6–1, lost Edberg 6–4 5–7 7–6 7–6). *CAREER HIGHLIGHTS – SINGLES: French Open – r/u 1990, sf 1988* (d. Perez Roldan 6–2 6–2 6–4, lost Wilander 4–6 6–2 7–5 5–7 6–0); *US Open – r/u 1990, sf 1988* (d. Chang 7–5 6–3 6–2, Connors 6–2 7–6 6–1, lost Lendl 4–6 6–2 6–3), *sf 1989* (d. Weiss, Broad, Johnson 6–1 7–5 6–2, Grabb 6–1 7–5 6–3, Connors 6–1 4–6 0–6 6–3 6–4, lost Lendl 7–6 6–1 3–6 6–1). *LIPC – won 1990*.

RONALD AGENOR (Haiti)
Born Rabat, Morocco, 13 November 1964; lives Bordeaux, France and Monte Carlo; RH; 5ft 11in; 163lb; final 1990 ATP ranking 29; 1990 prize money $243,950.
Lived some time in Zaire. Works with Patrice Hagelauer. *1985:* (50) With a stream of steady results including six qf showings on GP tour, he moved up 366 places on ATP computer. *1986:* (74) Performing solidly on clay again, he beat Pate, Arias, Tulasne and Jaite among others and reached sf Bordeaux. *1987:* (44) Took Lendl to 4s French Open before reaching his 1st GP f at Gstaad and being r/u again in Bordeaux and Basel. *1988:* (28) Last 16 French Open (d. Gomez) and US Open; r/u Bordeaux (d. Noah), sf Italian Open (d. Wilander). *1989:* (37) Won his 1st GP title at Athens, upset Agassi at Tokyo Seiko and was a surprise quarter-finalist at French Open. *1990:* Won Genova and at Berlin took his 1st title on a surface other than clay; sf Gstaad (upset Gomez), Bordeaux and Toulouse. *1990 HIGHLIGHTS – SINGLES: Australian Open* 2r (d. Reneberg 6–2 6–4 3–6 6–1, lost Noah [seed 12] 7–6 6–3 6–3), *French Open* 1r (lost Leconte 6–4 6–2 6–4), *US Open* 1r (lost Berger [seed 13] 6–4 6–4 3–6 6–4); *won* Genova (d. Motta 5–7 7–5 6–4, Altur 7–5 6–3, Skoff 3–6 6–1 6–0, Camporese 4–6 6–3 6–3, Benhabiles 3–6 6–4 6–3), *won* Berlin (d. Champion 6–1 6–2, Wohrmann 6–2 6–3, Curren 7–6 6–4, Sinner 6–1 7–6, Volkov 4–6 6–4 7–6); *sf* Gstaad (d. Wostenholme 6–4 6–7 6–3, Gomez 1–6 7–5 6–3, Steeb 3–6 6–2 6–2, lost Jaite 7–5 6–1), *sf* Bordeaux (d. Boetsch 6–4 7–5, Benhabiles 4–6 6–3 6–2, Nydahl 6–0 6–1, lost Forget 6–3 6–4, *sf* Toulouse (d. Connors 6–4 6–4, Raoux 3–6 6–3 6–2, Volkov 6–4 6–4, lost Santoro 7–6 6–3). *CAREER HIGHLIGHTS – SINGLES: French Open – qf 1989* unseeded (d. Limberger, Mayotte 3–6 7–5 5–7 7–5 6–2, Pistolesi 1–6 6–1 6–4 6–3, Bruguera 2–6 6–3 6–1 6–2, lost Chang 6–4 2–6 6–3 6–3).

JUAN AGUILERA (Spain)
Born Barcelona, 22 March 1962 and lives there; RH; 6ft; 150lb; final 1990 ATP ranking 19; 1990 prize money $311,806
Coached by Joel Figueras and Alberto Tous. Plays guitar and drums in a rock band, Palo. Wife Paula. *1982:* (277). *1983:* (64) R/u Bordeaux. *1984:* (19) Won Hamburg and Aix-en-Provence. *1985:* (79) Sf Geneva. *1986:* (255). *1987:* (141) Sf Buenos Aires. *1988:* (166) Sf

Buenos Aires again. *1989:* (64) Broke left clavicle bone at qf Athens in April, returning in June to win Bari for his 1st title in 5 years and was r/u St Vincent. Upset Mancini 1r Itaparica. *1990:* Two titles and some big upsets during the year took him into the top 20. Won Nice and Hamburg (d. Chang and Becker); r/u San Remo and Palermo; sf Estoril (d. Gomez and Muster), and upset Edberg *en route* to qf Monte Carlo. *1990 HIGHLIGHTS – SINGLES: French Open* 2r, seed 12 (d. Washington 7–5 4–6 6–1 6–2, lost Champion 3–6 6–3 6–3 6–2), *Wimbledon* 3r (d. Strelba 6–3 7–5 6–3, Ferreira 6–3 7–6 7–5, lost Cash 6–1 6–1 6–4), *US Open* 1r (lost Becker [seed 2] 7–5 6–3 6–2); *won* Nice (d. J. Sanchez 6–4 2–6 6–1, Rahunen 6–2 2–6 6–4, Hlasek 6–4 6–4, Rosset 6–3 6–0, Forget 4–6 7–6 6–4), *won* Hamburg (d. J. Sanchez 6–4 6–1, Chang 6–3 6–2, Courier 1–6 6–4 6–4, Gustafsson 6–1 6–4, Forget 7–5 7–6, Becker 6–3 3–6 6–3); *r/u* San Remo (d. Nastase 6–0 6–3, Yunis 3–6 6–4 6–0, Camporese 6–3 6–2, lost Arrese 6–2 6–2), *r/u* Palermo (d. Pescosolido 6–3 4–6 3–1 ret'd, J. Sanchez 7–6 6–4, Pistolesi 6–4 6–4, Perez Roldan 6–2 6–3, lost Davin 6–1 6–1); *sf* Estoril (d. Gomez 4–6 7–6 6–1, Cane 6–2 6–7 6–4, Muster 6–3 6–0, lost Davin 6–4 6–3).

PIETER ALDRICH (South Africa)
Born Johannesburg, 7 September 1965; lives Vereeniging and Palm Desert, Cal.; RH; 5ft 11in; 165lb; final 1990 ATP ranking 192 singles, 1 doubles; 1990 prize money $331,652
1986: (275). *1987:* (134) Won East London and Cape Town on Challenger circuit. *1988:* (68) Sf Newport and Johannesburg, and in doubles won 2 titles with Visser, qualifying for Masters. *1989:* (125) In doubles with Visser reached 6 f, winning 3 and qualifying for Masters again, where they lost sf to Grabb and P. McEnroe. *1990:* With Visser won 1st GS title at Australian Open, following with US Open and r/u Wimbledon plus 2 other doubles titles to qualify for IBM/ATP World Doubles. In singles won his 1st tour title in his 1st singles f at Newport. *1990 HIGHLIGHTS – SINGLES: Australian Open* 1r (lost Bergstrom 6–2 6–4 6–2); *won* Newport (d. Shiras 6–3 6–4, Rive 2–6 6–1 6–4, Weiss 6–4 6–1, Muller 6–4 7–6, Cahill 7–6 1–6 6–1). *1990 HIGHLIGHTS – DOUBLES:* (with Visser) *won Australian Open* (d. Connell/Michibata 6–4 4–6 6–1 6–4), *r/u Wimbledon* (lost R. Leach/Pugh 7–6 7–6 7–6), *won US Open* (d. Annacone/Wheaton 6–2 7–6 6–2); *won* Stuttgart (d. Henricsson/Utgren 6–3 6–4), *won* Berlin (d. Curren/Galbraith 7–6 7–6); *r/u* Sydney (lost Cash/Kratzmann 6–4 7–5). *CAREER HIGHLIGHTS – DOUBLES:* (with Visser) *Australian Open – won 1990; US Open – won 1990; Wimbledon – r/u 1990.*

PAUL ANNACONE (USA)
Born Southampton, NY, 20 March 1963; lives East Hampton, NY; RH; 6ft 1in; 175lb; final 1990 ATP ranking 165 singles, 29 doubles; 1990 prize money $162,290; career prize money $1,441,327.
Wife Tracy, son Nicholas (born 2 June 1987). Coached by Carlos Borja and Nick Bollettieri, advised by sports psychologist Noel Blundell. *1982:* (389) All-American at Univ. of Tennessee (and again in 1983). *1984:* (94) Surprisingly lost qf NCAA Champ but as qualifer reached qf first Wimbledon. *1985:* (13) Surged into top 20 with sizzling autumn including two GP victories in LA and Brisbane, and won Australian Open doubles with Van Rensburg. Married Tracy Kohr Nov. *1986:* (43) Joined American D Cup squad and contributed to only victory in 3–1 sf lost to Australia, taking doubles in 5s with Flach over Cash/McNamee. Upset McEnroe 1r US Open. *1987:* (32) Last 16 Australian Open; qf Philadelphia and Forest Hills. *1988:* (38) Upset Svensson *en route* to last 16 Wimbledon and r/u Stratton Mountain. *1989:* (65) Having won only 1 singles match all year, he reached sf Queen's, where he d. Wilander and took Lendl to 3s, then in autumn won Vienna for his 1st title for 4 years. In doubles with Van Rensburg won Memphis and US Pro Indoor, qualifying for Masters. *1990:* In singles upset Jaite at US Open and reached qf San Francisco. In doubles with Wheaton was r/u US Open and won Canadian Open. *1990 HIGHLIGHTS – SINGLES: Australian Open* 2r (d. Muller 6–3 6–4 6–7 2–6 6–3, lost J. Sanchez 6–1 7–6 6–3), *Wimbledon* 2r (d. Shiras 7–6 6–4 6–3), *US Open* 3r (d. Kuhnen 7–6 7–5 6–4, Jaite [seed 16] 7–6 6–2 6–2, lost Wheaton 6–2 7–6 6–3). *1990 HIGHLIGHTS – DOUBLES:* (with Wheaton) *r/u US Open* (lost Aldrich/Visser 6–2 7–6 6–2); *won* Canadian Open (d. Dyke/Lundgren 6–1 7–6). *CAREER HIGHLIGHTS – DOUBLES:* (with Van Rensburg unless stated) *Australian Open – won 1985* (d. Edmondson/Warwick 3–6 7–6 6–4 6–4); *LIPC – won 1985* (d. Stewart/Warwick 7–5 7–5 6–4), *won 1987* (d. Flach/Seguso 6–2 6–4 6–4); [Wheaton] *US Open – r/u 1990.*

ALEX ANTONITSCH (Austria)
Born Villach, 6 February 1966, and lives there; RH; 6ft 2in; 188lb; final 1990 ATP ranking 64; 1990 prize money $208,090
Coached by Stan Franker. Left-handed for everything except tennis, in which he switched to the right hand after breaking his left arm playing ice-hockey. *1982:* Nat Jun Champ. *1986;* (217) Qf St Vincent. *1987:* (115) Sf Livingston and Young Masters. *1988:* Won Graz Challenger but failed to reach any qf on GP circuit. *1989:* (83) Qf Stuttgart. *1990:* Beat Cash to win Seoul, then lost f Hong Kong to the same player the following week. Upset Leconte *en route* to last 16 Wimbledon, unseeded. *1990 HIGHLIGHTS – SINGLES: Australian Open* 2r (d. Mansdorf 4–6 6–4 6–4 6–7 6–3, lost J. McEnroe [seed 4] 6–1 6–2 6–1), *French Open* 2r (d. Reneberg 6–3 7–6 6–3, lost Forget 6–1 6–1 6–1), *Wimbledon* last 16, unseeded (d. Robertson 7–6 6–4 3–6 4–6 6–4, Leconte [seed 15] 2–6 6–4 7–6 2–6 6–3, Pate 6–4 6–4 7–6, lost Lendl [seed 1] 3–6 6–4 6–3 6–4), *US Open* 3r (d. Kaplan 3–6 6–2 6–1 6–0, Limberger 6–1 5–7 6–4 6–3, lost Lendl [seed 3] 7–6 6–1 6–2); *won* Seoul (d. Jones 6–4 6–4, Shiras 6–1 6–0, Kuhnen 6–4 6–4, Van Rensburg 4–6 6–3 7–6, Cash 6–3 6–3); *r/u* Hong Kong (d. Matuszewski 6–2 6–4, Stoltenburg 7–6 6–1, P. McEnroe 6–7 6–1 7–6, Canter 3–6 6–3 6–4, lost Cash 6–3 6–4).

SABINE APPELMANS (Belgium)
Born Aalst, 22 April 1972; lives Erembonegen; LH; 2HB; 5ft 5in; 120lb; 1990 WTA ranking 22; 1990 prize money $63,696.
1987: (283). *1988:* (215) Enjoyed some success on the European satellite circuits and upset Burgin 1r French Open. *1989:* (149) Reached her 1st primary circuit qf at Taipei. *1990:* R/u Auckland (d. Cordwell) and reached sf Wellington and Singapore, breaking into top 100 and finishing the year in the top 25. *1990 HIGHLIGHTS – SINGLES: Australian Open* 3r (d. Gomer 6–1 6–0, Pratt 6–2 6–3, lost Tanvier 7–6 6–0), *French Open* 1r (lost K. Maleeva [seed 8] 6–3 6–3), *US Open* 3r (d. Lindqvist 6–4 6–4, Probst 6–4 6–4, lost Sabatini [seed 5] 6–2 6–4); *r/u* Auckland (d. Probst 4–6 6–4 6–2, Toleafoa 6–3 3–6 6–2, Leand 6–3 6–3, Cordwell 6–1 6–2, lost Meskhi 6–1 6–0); *sf* Wellington (d. Bakkum 6–2 6–0), Medvedeva 6–0 6–0; M. Maleeva 6–1 7–5, lost Probst 6–4 6–2), *sf* Singapore (d. Jones 6–4 6–1, Javer 6–3 3–6 7–5, Werdel 7–5 3–6 6–3, lost Loosemore 5–7 6–2 6–3).

JIMMY ARIAS (USA)
Born Buffalo, NY, 16 August 1964, and lives there; RH; 5ft 9in; 145lb; final 1990 ATP ranking 60; 1990 prize money $156,709; career prize money $1,571,340.
Married 16 Dec. 1989 (wife Gina). Does not employ a coach, preferring to work alone. *1981:* (81) Under guidance of Nick Bollettieri, climbed into top 100, beat Teltscher on USTA Penn circuit and won French Open mixed doubles with A. Jaeger. *1982:* (20) Beaten in 1r of 6 of first 8 tournaments, he then made tremendous surge to reach f Washington and US CC and won his first GP event (Japan Asian Open) in autumn. *1983:* (6) Won 4 tournaments, including Italian Open and US CC; sf US Open. *1984:* (14) Reached qf French Open and 6 sf. *1985:* (21) Had disappointing results until end of year when he reached sf Canadian Open, f Japan Open and sf South African Open. *1986:* (48) Helped US past Ecuador in D Cup. *1987:* (34) After D Cup loss in Paraguay he consulted sports psychologist Jim Loehe, who helped him to improve his attitude, enjoy his tennis more and reach f Monte Carlo. Yet, still lacking motivation, he took 3 months off from Aug. *1988:* (106) Still only a shadow of his former self, he lost 1r 5 consecutive tourns before reaching f US CC. *1989:* (92) Qf Memphis. *1990:* R/u Adelaide; qf Auckland, San Francisco and Hamburg. *1990 HIGHLIGHTS – SINGLES: Australian Open* 1r (lost Courier [seed 14] 6–3 6–3 6–1), *French Open* 2r (d. Rikl 6–2 6–1 3–6 6–2, lost Volkov 1–6 6–3 6–3 4–6 6–1), *US Open* 2r (d. Forget 7–6 6–4 3–6 6–4, lost Chang [seed 11] 7–6 6–3 6–2); *r/u* Adelaide (d. Woodforde 7–6 6–3, Volkov 6–4 7–6, Koevermans 6–3 6–4, Fleurian 6–2 6–3, lost Muster 3–6 6–2 7–5). *CAREER HIGHLIGHTS – MIXED DOUBLES:* (with A. Jaeger) *French Open – won 1981* (d. Gonzalez/Teeguarden 4–6 6–3 11–9, McNair/Stove [seed 2] 7–6 6–4).

JORDI ARRESE (Spain)
Born Barcelona 29 August 1964, and lives there; RH; 5ft 9in; 165lb; final 1990 ATP ranking 39; 1990 prize money $218,212.
Coached by Roberto Vizcairio. *1986:* (97) With a sf showing in his first tournament of the season at Nice, he set the tone for a successful year. *1987:* (128) Qf Palermo. *1988:* (33)

Won 2 Challenger titles before reaching 1st SS sf at Hamburg and qf Kitzbuhel. *1989:* (44) Reached 1st GP f at Madrid despite being restricted by a back injury during the last 3 matches, for which he wore a neck brace. Upset Krickstein *en route* to sf Italian Open. *1990:* Won San Remo in Aug., following with Prague the next week; sf Estoril and Athens. *1990 HIGHLIGHTS – SINGLES: Australian Open* 2r (d. Brown 4–6 6–4 6–1 6–3, lost Sampras 0–6 6–2 3–6 6–1 6–3), *French Open* 3r (d. Zoecke 6–4 3–6 6–3 6–1, Santoro 4–6 6–3 6–2 6–2, lost Chesnokov [seed 8] 7–5 6–4 6–2), *US Open* 1r (lost Wheaton 6–3 6–1 6–0); *won* San Remo (d. Pioline 6–4 6–2, Pescosolido 5–7 6–2 6–2, Perez Roldan 6–4 6–2, Filippini 6–2 6–3, Aguilera 6–2 6–3), *won* Prague (d. Dosedel 6–4 6–4, J. Kodes Jnr 2–6 6–0 6–2, Saceanu w.o., Prpic 7–5 6–4, Kulti 7–6 7–6); *sf* Estoril (d. Clavet 6–1 6–3, Cherkasov 6–2 6–2, Berger 4–6 6–3 7–5, lost E. Sanchez 6–2 6–1), *sf* Athens (d. Lopez 6–2 6–1, Brown 6–3 7–6, J. Sanchez 6–2 6–3, lost Koevermans 6–2 7–6).

CSILLA BARTOS (Switzerland)
Born Cairo, Egypt, 29 March 1966; lives Zurich, Switzerland; RH; 2HB; 5ft 11in; 147lb; final 1990 WTA ranking 90; 1990 prize money $26,710.
1981: Played Fed Cup for Hungary. *1983:* (197) Played Fed Cup again and for next 3 years. *1984:* (167) Won 2 titles on the satellite circuits. *1985:* (150) Married Danny Cserepy, a Swiss national. *1986:* (109) Won Queen's on British satellite circuit and reached f Perugia on primary circuit. *1987:* (152) Achieved her highest career ranking of 76 in July, but then underwent two knee operations, which kept her out for a year. *1988:* (417). *1989:* (194). *1990:* Upset Lindqvist at Bastad as she swept to her 1st f for 4 years, finishing the year back in the top 100. *1990 HIGHLIGHTS – SINGLES: Australian Open* 1r (lost Cioffi 7–5 6–4), *US Open* 2r (d. Burgin 6–4 4–6 6–4, lost Martinez 6–0 6–4); *r/u* Bastad (d. Martinek 6–1 6–2, Lindqvist 3–6 6–2 6–4, Hack 6–0 6–7 6–2, Zrubakova 6–2 6–4, lost Cecchini 6–1 6–2).

JEREMY BATES (Great Britain)
Born Solihull, 19 June 1962; lives London; RH; 5ft 11in; 160lb; final 1990 ATP ranking 126; 1990 Prize money $147,543.
Coached by Warren Jacques. *1982:* (329) Joined British D Cup squad. *1983:* (256). *1984:* (185). *1985:* (99) Sf Tel Aviv, qf Bristol. *1986:* (187) Qf Bristol. *1987:* (89) Sf Hong Kong and won Wimbledon mixed doubles with Durie. *1988:* (152) Qf Guaruja, Lyon and Rye Brook; r/u Australian Open doubles with Lundgren. *1989:* (96) Reached sf Johannesburg and qf Nancy; upset Gilbert at Tel Aviv. *1990:* Won Durban Challenger and in doubles won Queen's with Curren. *1990 HIGHLIGHTS – SINGLES: Australian Open* 1r (lost Lavalle 6–7 6–1 6–4 6–2), *French Open* 1r (lost Grenier 6–2 6–4 6–2), *Wimbledon* 2r (d. Lungren 6–7 6–7 6–4 6–4 6–0 lost Rostagno 6–1 3–6 6–4 6–1), *US Open* 1r (lost Paloheimo 6–3 7–5 6–4); *won* Durban Challenger (d. Stafford 6–4 6–1). *1990 HIGHLIGHTS – DOUBLES:* [Curren] *won* Queen's (d. Leconte/Lendl 6–2 7–6). *CAREER HIGHLIGHTS – DOUBLES:* (with Lundgren) *Australian Open – r/u 1988* (lost R. Leach/Pugh 6–3 6–2 6–3). *MIXED DOUBLES:* (with Durie) *Wimbledon – won 1987* (d. Cahill/Provis 7–6 6–3).

BORIS BECKER (Germany)
Born Leimen, 22 November 1967; lives there and Monte Carlo; RH; 6ft 3in; 187lb; final 1990 ATP ranking 2 singles, 28 doubles; 1990 prize money $1,587,482; career prize money $8,160,187.
Coached by Bob Brett. *1982:* Won first of three consecutive German Nat Jun Champs. *1983:* (564) R/u Orange Bowl 16s. *1984:* (65) R/u US Open Jun and qf Australian Open in first big men's showing. *1985:* (6) Won Queen's Club, Wimbledon, at 17 yrs 7 mths becoming youngest men's titlist, the first German, and the first unseeded player to capture the world's most prestigious event. Won Cincinnati and closed year with D Cup wins over Edberg and Wilander in f as Germany lost 3–2 to Sweden. Won inaugural Young Masters and was voted ATP Most Improved Player. *1986:* (2) Won tournaments in Chicago, Toronto, Sydney, Tokyo and Paris Indoor, but most notably won Wimbledon again in even more convincing fashion, dismissing Lendl in f without loss of a set and still younger than any other champ. Closed year with streak of 3 straight tournaments and 21 matches in a row before losing Masters f to Lendl. Won Young Masters in Jan. and Dec. *1987:* (5) Split with coach Gunther Bosch Jan; trained by Frank Dick. At end of year Bob Brett became coach. Missed LIPC suffering from a form of typhus which seemed to weaken him and

restrict his performance for several weeks, and he was further restricted by tendonitis of left knee for last 5 months of year. Won only 3 titles all year and going for his third consecutive Wimbledon singles title, fell 2r to Doohan. After US Open took time off in Germany with his family, returning refreshed in Oct. and qualified for Masters where he extended Lendl to 3s, but lost his Young Masters title. *1988:* (4) He was again plagued by injury problems, withdrawing from Toronto and the Olympics and playing Masters only 10 days after his foot had been removed from plaster following injury in Stockholm sf. He still won Indian Wells, WCT Finals, Queen's, Indianapolis, Tokyo Seiko and Stockholm and finished the year by taking his 1st Masters title in a thrilling f v Lendl, as well as leading West Germany to victory over Sweden in D Cup f in Gothenburg. At Wimbledon he was r/u to Edberg and reached last 16 in French Open. *1989:* (2) The high spot of his year was a convincing third title at Wimbledon where he beat Lendl in a stirring sf and Edberg in f, followed by his first triumph at US Open, where he d. Lendl in f, and r/u spot at Masters to Edberg. He won in Milan and on clay reached the f in Monte Carlo and sf in French Open. He also won 3 other titles and led FRG to victory in World Team Cup, and in D Cup where he won 2 singles and doubles (with Jelen) as Germany d. Sweden 3–2 in Stuttgart. Voted ATP Player of the Year. *1990:* R/u Wimbledon to Edberg, sf US Open, qf Australian Open, but his 1r loss to Ivanisevic at French Open was his 1st at that stage in GS. Strongly challenged Edberg for the No. 1 spot at end of year, especially after a stunning performance at Stockholm where he d. the Swede in f, a result that took his indoor match record since 1988 to 77–5. However, in f Paris Open he had to withdraw v the same player with a pulled left thigh, which was still undergoing treatment when he began play on 2nd day of ATP World Champ, where he fell to Agassi in sf. Won Brussels, Stuttgart, Indianapolis, Sydney Indoor and Stockholm, reaching 4 more f. *1990 HIGHLIGHTS – SINGLES: Australian Open* qf, seed 2 (d. Haarhuis 6–1 6–2 6–1, S. Davis 6–3 7–6 4–6 6–2, Delaitre 6–3 6–1 6–4, Mecir [seed 16] 4–6 6–7 6–4 6–1 6–1, lost Wilander [seed 8] 6–4 6–4 6–2), *French Open* 1r, seed 2 (lost Ivanisevic 5–7 6–4 7–5 6–2), *r/u Wimbledon* seed 3 (d. Herrera 7–6 7–6 7–5, Masur 6–7 6–2 6–3 6–2, Goldie 6–3 6–4 4–6 7–5, Cash 7–6 6–1 6–4, Gilbert [seed 7] 6–4 6–4 6–1, Ivanisevic 4–6 7–6 6–0 7–6, lost Edberg 6–2 6–2 3–6 3–6 6–4), *US Open* sf, seed 2 (d. Aguilera 7–5 6–3 6–2, Noah 6–4 6–2 7–6, Carbonell 6–4 6–2 6–2, Cahill 2–6 6–2 6–3 3–6 6–4, Krickstein [seed 9] 3–6 6–3 6–3 6–3, lost Agassi [seed 4] 6–7 6–3 6–2 6–3); *won* Brussels (d. Novacek 7–6 6–2, Forget 3–6 6–3 7–6, Cane 6–4 3–2 ret'd, Gustafsson 6–4 7–6, Steeb 7–5 6–2 6–2), *won* Stuttgart (d. Dyke 7–6 6–4, Volkov 6–4 3–6 6–3, Mecir 6–4 6–2, Svensson 7–5 6–2, Lendl 6–2 6–2), *won* Indianapolis (d. Garrow 6–2 6–4, Curren 7–6 6–4, Courier 4–6 7–5 3–1 ret'd, Berger 6–4 6–3, Lundgren 6–3 6–3), *won* Sydney Indoor (d. Wilander 6–2 7–5, Evernden 6–4 6–3, Reneberg 6–4 6–4, Woodbridge 7–5 6–4, Edberg 7–6 6–4 6–4), *won* Stockholm (d. Cahill 6–2 6–0, Reneberg 6–4 6–3, Ivanisevic 6–4 6–2, Sampras 6–4 6–4, Edberg 6–4 6–0 6–3); *r/u* Hamburg (d. Cane 7–5 6–1, Cherkasov 6–2 6–3, Arias 6–3 6–1, Leconte 6–3 3–6 6–3, lost Aguilera 6–1 6–0 7–6), *r/u* Queen's (d. Chamberlin 6–4 6–4, Antonitsch 3–6 6–1 9–7, Wheaton 6–3 6–3, Edberg 6–4 6–4, lost Lendl 6–3 6–2), *r/u* Tokyo Seiko (d. Tsujino 6–4 7–6, Witsken 6–2 6–3, Cherkasov 6–4 6–4, Reneberg 7–6 6–2, lost Lendl 4–6 6–3 7–6), *r/u* Paris Open (d. Reneberg 4–6 6–3 6–2, Courier 6–1 7–5, Stich 6–1 6–2, Svensson 4–6 7–6 6–1, lost Edberg 3–3 ret'd); *sf* Indian Wells (d. J. Sanchez 7–6 6–3, Skoff 6–4 1–6 7–6, Berger 6–1 6–2, lost Agassi 6–4 6–1), *sf* ATP World Champ (d. Gomez, Muster, Lendl in rr, lost Agassi 6–2 6–4 in sf). *1990 HIGHLIGHTS – DOUBLES:* [Forget] *won* Indian Wells (d. Grabb/P. McEnroe 4–6 6–4 6–3); [Motta] *r/u* LIPC (lost R. Leach/Pugh 6–4 3–6 6–3). *CAREER HIGHLIGHTS – SINGLES: Wimbledon – won 1985* unseeded (d. Nystrom 3–6 7–6 6–1 4–6 9–7, Mayotte 6–3 4–6 6–7 7–6 6–2, Leconte 7–6 3–6 6–3 6–4, Jarryd 2–6 7–6 6–3 6–3, Curren 6–3 6–7 7–6 6–4), *won 1986* (d. Bengoechea, Tom Gullikson, McNamee, Pernfors 6–3 7–6 6–2, Mecir 6–4 6–2 7–6, Leconte 6–2 6–4 6–7 6–3, Lendl 6–4 6–3 7–5), *won 1989* (d. Shelton 6–1 6–4 7–6, Matuszewski 6–3 7–5 6–4, Gunnarsson 7–5 7–6 6–3, Krickstein 6–4 6–4 7–5, Chamberlin 6–1 6–2 6–0, Lendl 7–6 6–7 2–6 6–4 6–3, Edberg 6–0 7–6 6–4), *r/u 1988* (d. Annacone, Cash 6–4 6–3 6–4, Lendl 6–4 6–3 6–7 6–4, lost Edberg 4–6 7–6 6–4 6–2), *r/u 1990; US Open – won 1989* (d. Pate 6–1 6–3 6–1, Rostagno 1–6 6–7 6–3 7–6 6–3, Mecir 6–4 3–6 6–4 6–3, Pernfors 5–7 6–3 6–2 6–1, Noah 6–3 6–3 6–2, Krickstein 6–4 6–3 6–4, Lendl 7–6 1–6 6–3 7–6), *sf 1986* (d. Michibata, Motta, Casal, Donnelly 6–4 6–3 6–7 6–4, Srejber 6–3 6–2 6–1, lost Mecir 4–6 6–3 6–4 3–6 6–3), *sf 1990; Nabisco Masters – won 1988* (d. Wilander, Leconte, lost Edberg in rr. d. Hlasek 7–6 7–6, Lendl 5–7 7–6 3–6 6–2

7–6), *r/u 1985* (lost Lendl 6–2 7–6 6–1), *r/u 1986* (d. Nystrom, Leconte, Wilander 6–3 fs, Edberg 6–4 6–4, lost Lendl 6–4 6–4 6–4), *r/u 1989* (d. Gilbert, Agassi, Edberg in rr, J. McEnroe 6–4 6–4, lost Edberg 2–6 7–6 6–3 6–1); *French Open – sf 1987* (d. Connors 6–3 6–3 7–5, lost Wilander 6–4 6–1 6–2), *sf 1989* (d. Pugh, Winogradsky, Bates, Perez Roldan 3–6 6–4 6–2 4–6 7–5, Berger 6–3 6–4 6–1, lost Edberg 6–3 6–4 5–7 3–6 6–2), *qf 1986* (d. Potier, Oresar, Teltscher, E. Sanchez 6–0 4–6 4–6 6–4 6–2, lost Pernfors 2–6 6–4 6–2 6–0).

JAY BERGER (USA)
Born Fort Dix, NJ, 26 November 1966; lives Weston, Fla.; 5ft 11in; 165lb; RH; final 1990 ATP ranking 18; 1990 prize money $349,354.
Coached by Brian Gottfried. Fiancée Nadia Stastny. *1984:* R/u Orange Bowl 18s. *1985:* (249) Won US Boys' 18, US Boys' 18 CC, Florida State Open and Florida State Jun titles as well as reaching last 16 US Open all before his jun year at Clemson, where he was an All-American. *1986:* (82) Made the most of his 8 tournament appearances, winning Buenos Aires at end of year. *1987:* (47) Qf LIPC (d. Gomez), r/u Buenos Aires where he retired v Perez Roldan with ankle injury, sf Sao Paulo. *1988:* (34) Won Sao Paulo in singles and doubles, upset Wilander *en route* to sf Orlando and reached 4 other qf. *1989:* (10) Won US CC, r/u Indianapolis and Itaparica. Reached qf French Open and US Open and scored some big upsets during the year, removing Connors at French Open, Becker *en route* to sf Indian Wells, Wilander to reach qf Italian Open, and Edberg at Indianapolis. Took a 3-month break from Nov. *1990:* R/u Canadian Open; sf LIPC and Indianapolis. *1990 HIGHLIGHTS – SINGLES: French Open* 1r, seed 9 (lost Mancini 6–4 6–2 6–2), *US Open* last 16, seed 13 (d. Agenor 3–6 6–2 3–6 6–4, J. Carlsson 3–6 6–1 6–4 6–2, Caratti 4–6 2–6 6–4 6–3 6–4, lost Agassi [seed 4] 7–5 6–0 6–2); *r/u* Canadian Open (d. Shiras 6–2 6–4, Rostagno 4–6 6–4 6–1, Mayotte 7–6 6–4, Hlasek 3–6 6–2 6–2, lost Chang 4–6 6–3 7–6); *sf* LIPC (d. Engel 7–6 6–4, Ivanisevic 4–6 6–3 6–4, Kratzmann 6–0 6–1, Sampras w.o., lost Agassi 5–7 6–1 6–1), *sf* Indianopolios (d. Cahill 6–1 0–6 7–5, Hlasek 6–4 6–2, Evernden 5–7 6–1 6–3, lost Becker 6–4 6–3).

CHRISTIAN BERGSTROM (Sweden)
Born Gothenburg, 19 July 1967; lives there and Monte Carlo; RH; 5ft 11in; 147lb; final 1990 ATP ranking 80; 1990 prize money $244,238.
Coached by Tim Klein. *1984:* (606) Nat Jun Champ. *1985:* (410) European Jun Champ and No. 2 in ITF Jun rankings. *1986:* (120) Won Tampere Challenger. *1987:* (69) Qf Nancy; won Porto Challenger. *1988:* (71) Working with sports psychologist Lars Ryberg, he reached 1st GP sf at Bastad and upset Leconte *en route* to same stage at Toulouse. *1989:* (106) Qf Milan, Bastad and Toulouse. *1990:* A qualifier at the French Open, he was 2 sets up v Chang before losing 3r; at Wimbledon he upset Forget *en route* to qf, unseeded, and in sf Wembley was 4–0 up fs v Chang but lost 7–2 on t-b. Played GS Cup, lost 1r Lendl (2) 6–4 6–0. *1990 HIGHLIGHTS – SINGLES: Australian Open* 2r (d. Aldrich 6–2 6–4 6–2, lost Bloom 2–6 5–7 6–2 6–4 6–2), *French Open* 3r (d. Witsken 6–1 6–2 6–0, Wilkison 6–4 6–2 6–1, lost Chang [seed 11] 2–6 5–7 6–0 6–2 6–4), *Wimbledon* qf, unseeded (d. Wilkison 6–4 6–3 6–4, Broad 4–6 7–6 6–2 6–2, Grabb 7–6 6–4 6–2, Forget [seed 11] 6–4 3–6 6–3 7–5, lost Edberg [seed 3] 6–3 6–2 6–4); *sf* Wembley (d. Masso 6–4 6–4, Sampras w.o., P. McEnroe 6–2 6–4, lost Chang 6–3 3–6 7–6). *CAREER HIGHLIGHTS – SINGLES: Wimbledon – qf 1990.*

GILAD BLOOM (Israel)
Born Tel Aviv, 1 March 1967; lives Ramat Hasharon; LH; 5ft 8in; 150lb; final 1990 ATP ranking 66; 1990 prize money $148,399.
Coached by Shlomo Zoreff. *1984:* (385). *1985:* (452) Nat Jun Champ for 2nd year. *1986:* (152). *1987:* (139) Won Estoril Challenger. *1988:* (210) Won Jerusalem Challenger and upset Jaite at Tourn of Champs. *1989:* (105) Won 2 Challenger titles, then in autumn reached f Tel Aviv, where he took Connors to 3s. *1990:* R/u Manchester; sf Seoul and Tel Aviv; appeared unexpectedly in last 16 US Open. *1990 HIGHLIGHTS – SINGLES: Australian Open* 3r (d. Fitzgerald 7–6 7–6 3–6 6–2, Bergstrom 2–6 5–7 6–2 6–4 6–2, lost Noah [seed 12] 6–3 6–3 6–3), *French Open* 2r (d. Fromberg 5–7 7–5 1–6 6–3 6–2, lost Boetsch 6–2 6–1 6–0), *Wimbledon* 2r (d. Korda 6–0 6–4 4–6 6–2, lost Koevermans 7–5 6–4 6–3), *US Open* last 16, unseeded (d. Pearce 7–5 6–7 7–5 6–0, Anderson 6–3 6–3 4–6 1–6 7–6, Muller 6–2 6–3 6–4, lost Lendl [seed 3] 6–0 6–3 6–4); *r/u* Manchester (d. Pugh 6–4 4–6

7–6, Rahunen 6–2 7–5, Jones 3–6 7–5 6–1, N. Brown 6–4 7–6, lost Sampras 7–6 7–6); *sf* Seoul (d. Youl 6–3 6–1, Nido 6–4 6–3, Matuszewski 6–2 6–2, lost Cash 6–3 6–3), *sf* Tel Aviv (d. Pozzi 6–2 6–1, Norval 6–1 6–4, Van Rensburg 2–6 7–6 7–5, lost Chesnokov 6–3 6–3). *1990 HIGHLIGHTS – DOUBLES:* (with Haarhuis) *r/u* Auckland (lost Jones/Van't Hof 7–6 6–0).

MANON BOLLEGRAF (Netherlands)
Born Den Bosch, 10 April 1964; lives Ermelo; RH; 2HB; 5ft 8in; 140lb; final 1990 WTA ranking 32 singles, 24 doubles; 1990 prize money $134,012.
Coached by Anke Dijkstra. *1986:* (148) Qf Singapore. *1987:* (120) Qf Little Rock. *1988:* (117) Qf Brisbane. *1989:* (38) In singles won 1st primary circuit title at Oklahoma, reached sf Brussels and Nashville and upset McNeil 2r French Open. In doubles won 4 women's titles plus French Open mixed with Nijssen. *1990:* In singles r/u VS Oklahoma and reached sf Strasbourg. Appeared in 5 doubles f with various partners, winning Wichita with McGrath and Zurich with Pfaff. *1990 HIGHLIGHTS – SINGLES: Australian Open* 1r (lost Daniels 6–7 6–3 6–4), *French Open* 1r (lost Jaggard 7–6 3–2 ret'd), *Wimbledon* 1r (lost Sukova [seed 10] 7–5 6–2), *US Open* 2r (d. Magers 6–2 6–1, lost Strandlund 4–6 6–1 7–5); *r/u* VS Oklahoma (d. Coetzer 6–1 6–3, Cunningham 6–4 6–2, Santrock 6–4 6–2, Gavaldon 6–4 7–5, lost Frazier 6–4 6–2); *sf* Strasbourg (d. Herreman 6–4 2–6 6–4, Dechaume 6–2 6–3, Labat 6–1 7–6, lost Grossman 2–6 6–0 6–2). *1990 HIGHLIGHTS – DOUBLES:* (with McGrath unless stated) *won* Wichita (d. Daniels/W. White 6–0 6–2), [Pfaff] *won* Zurich (d. Suire/Van Rensburg 7–5 6–4); [Gregory] *r/u* VS Oklahoma (lost Daniels/W. White 7–5 6–2), *r/u* Orlando (lost Savchenko/Zvereva 6–4 6–1), [Durie] *r/u* Leipzig (lost Gregory/ Magers 6–4 4–6 6–3).

FEDERICA BONSIGNORI (Italy)
Born Rome, 20 November 1967 and lives there; RH; 2HB; 5ft 4in; 117lb; final 1990 WTA ranking 76; 1990 prize money $41,307.
Coached by Martin Simek. *1984:* (145). *1985:* (188) Sf Bastad. *1986:* (123) Qf Athens. *1987:* (88) Reached sf Paris Open and upset M. Maleeva *en route* to qf Belgian Open. *1988:* (99) Upset McNeil 1r LIPC. *1989:* (141) Upset Cueto at Athens. *1990:* Won her first primary circuit title at Estoril, reached sf Athens and returned to the top 100 in July. *1990 HIGHLIGHTS – SINGLES: Australian Open* 1r (lost McQuillan 6–1 6–2), *US Open* 1r (lost Dechaume 6–2 6–1); *won* Estoril (d. Ruano 6–2 6–7 6–0, Kanellopoulou 6–3 6–1, Cueto 6–2 4–6 6–4, Hack 2–6 7–6 6–4, Garrone 2–6 6–3 6–3); *sf* Athens (d. Godridge 6–0 6–7 6–0, B. Romano 7–6 6–4, Hack 6–3 3–6 7–6, lost Piccolini 6–2 6–3).

ELENA BRIOUKHOVETS (USSR)
Born Odessa, 8 June 1971 and lives there; RH; 5ft 4in; 132lb; final 1990 WTA ranking 73; 1990 prize money $49,369.
1990: Upset Magers to reach her 1st tour f at Moscow, taking her place in the top 100 in Oct. and won 2 doubles titles. *1990 HIGHLIGHTS – SINGLES: Wimbledon* 1r (lost McGrath 6–1 6–2); *r/u* Moscow (d. Biletskaia 6–3 6–0, Kschwendt 7–6 6–4, McQuillan 6–3 6–0, Magers 6–4 6–3, lost Meskhi 6–4 6–4); *sf* VS Nashville (d. Reinstadler 7–5 7–5, Vis 3–6 6–2 6–2, Whitlinger 6–3 5–7 6–1, lost Medvedeva 6–3 6–4). *1990 HIGHLIGHTS – DOUBLES:* (with Maniokova unless stated) *won* Taranto (d. Farina/Grande 7–6 6–1), [Medvedeva] *won* Puerto Rico (d. Frazier/Richardson 6–4 6–2); *r/u* Moscow (lost Magers/ R. White 6–2 6–4).

NEIL BROAD (South Africa)
Born Cape Town, 20 November 1966, and lives there; RH; 6ft 3in; 185lb; final 1990 ATP ranking 366 singles; 14 doubles; 1990 prize money $189,453.
With a British father and grandparents, he holds a British passport and has applied for British nationality. Has not played D Cup for S Africa and played at Wimbledon 1990 under British nationality. A former All-American at Texas Christian Univ. *1986:* (668). *1987:* (348). *1988:* (131) Won 2 Challenger titles and reached qf Johannesburg. *1989:* (176) In doubles won Adelaide with Kruger and Washington with Muller. *1990:* In doubles won Toulouse and reached 3 other f to qualify for IBM/ATP World Doubles with Muller. *1990 HIGHLIGHTS – SINGLES: Australian Open* 1r (lost Pistolesi 5–7 6–4 6–4 6–1), *Wimbledon* 2r (d. Duncan 6–4 6–2 7–6, lost Bergstrom 4–6 7–6 6–2 6–2). *1990 HIGHLIGHTS – DOUBLES:* (with Muller unless stated) *won* Toulouse (d. Mortensen/Schapers 7–6 6–4);

[Curren] *r/u* Toronto (lost Galbraith/MacPherson 2–6 6–4 6–3), *r/u* Cincinnati (lost Cahill/ Kratzman 7–6 6–2), *r/u* Basel (lost Kruger/Van Rensburg 4–6 7–6 6–3).

SERGI BRUGUERA (Spain)
Born Barcelona, 16 January 1971 and lives there; RH; 6ft 1in; 160lb; final 1990 ATP ranking 28; 1990 prize money $342,423.
Coached by his father, Luis. **1987:** (333) Won Nat Jun Champ. **1989:** (26) Upset Gomez and Connors *en route* to 1st GP sf at Italian Open, following with his 2nd and 3rd at Gstaad and Stuttgart, as well as reaching last 16 French Open. Voted ATP Newcomer of the Year. **1990:** Recorded some big upsets during the year. Removed top seed Edberg in ss 1r French Open; r/u Gstaad (d. Chesnokov) and Geneva; sf Adelaide (took Muster to 3s and Paris Open (d. Gomez). Won 2 doubles titles. *1990 HIGHLIGHTS – SINGLES:* **Australian Open** 2r, seed 13 (d. Shiras 6–1 6–4 6–3, lost Pernfors 6–4 6–3 1–6 6–4), **French Open** 2r (d. Edberg [seed 1] 6–4 6–2 6–1, lost Svensson 2–6 2–6 6–4 6–4 6–0), **Wimbledon** 2r (d. Castle 6–7 6–4 6–3 6–1, lost Shelton 5–7 2–6 6–4 6–4 6–4), **US Open** 2r (d. Hogstedt 6–3 6–2 6–2, lost Mansdorf 7–6 6–2 2–6 6–3); *r/u* Gstaad (d. Mancini 6–3 6–4, Aguilera 6–3 6–4, Chesnokov 6–2 6–3, Rosset 6–3 7–5, lost Jaite 6–3 6–7 6–2 6–2), *r/u* Geneva (d. Azar 6–1 6–3, Gunnarsson 7–5 6–2, de la Pena 6–0 6–2, Tauson 6–1 6–2, lost Skoff 7–6 7–6); *sf* Adelaide (d. Hericsson 7–6 6–2, Dyke 6–7 6–2 6–3, Stich 6–7 6–0 6–4, lost Muster 2–6 6–2 7–6), *sf* Paris Open (d. Leconte 1–6 6–2 5–2 ret'd, Gomez 7–6 4–6 6–1, Rosset 4–6 6–1 6–3, Raoux 4–6 6–1 6–3, lost Edberg 6–3 6–3). *1990 HIGHLIGHTS – DOUBLES:* [Courier] **won** Hamburg 7–6 6–2), [de la Pena] **won** Florence (d. Mattar/Perez 3–6 6–3 6–4).

ELISE BURGIN (USA)
Born Baltimore, Md, 5 March 1962 and lives there; LH; 2HB; 5ft 5in; 120lb; final 1990 WTA ranking 150 singles, 26 (25) doubles; 1990 prize money $92,441.
Coached by Lenny Scheuermann. **1980:** Always among the top American jun in her age group, she capped a successful jun career by beating Horvath *en route* to f US Open jun. **1981:** (85) Moved into world top 100. **1982:** (48) Reached qf Wimbledon doubles with Stanford Univ. friend, Moulton, and beat Bunge on way to last 16 of US Open singles. **1983:** (42) Sf Canadian Open with upset of K. Jordan. **1984:** (51) Returned to circuit after 6 months out with back injury; graduated from Stanford and won NCAA doubles. **1985:** (27) Had best year in singles, including r/u showings at VS Houston and Indianapolis. Played Fed Cup. **1986:** (43) Won Wild Dunes in singles, made debut as US W Cup captain and proved to be a born leader as the Americans routed British 7–0 at Albert Hall. Sf Wimbledon and US Open doubles with Fairbank. **1987:** (65) Best singles showing was qf Strasbourg, but reached 5 f in doubles, winning 2. Suffered a knee injury at end of year. **1988:** Out of action March to May following surgery on left knee. Sf Arizona was best showing. **1989:** (62) At Phoenix played 1st singles f since Charleston 1986 and reached 6 doubles f, winning San Diego. **1990:** Reached 3 doubles f with different partners. *1990 HIGHLIGHTS – SINGLES:* **Australian Open** 2r (d. Stafford 2–6 7–6 6–3, lost Huber 6–2 6–0), **French Open** 2r (d. Werdel 6–3 3–6 6–4, lost Gildemeister 6–3 6–4), **Wimbledon** 1r (lost Sabatini [seed 4] 6–3 6–3), **US Open** 1r (lost Bartos 6–4 4–6 6–4). *1990 HIGHLIGHTS – DOUBLES:* [Turnbull] *r/u* VS Florida (lost Novotna/Sukova 6–4 6–2), [Nagelsen] *r/u* Geneva (lost Field/Van Rensburg 5–7 7–6 7–5), [Fairbank Nideffer] *r/u* San Diego (lost Fendick/Garrison 6–4 7–6). *CAREER HIGHLIGHTS – DOUBLES:* (with Fairbank Nideffer) **Wimbledon – sf 1986** (lost Navratilova/Shriver [seed 1] 6–4 6–3).

DARREN CAHILL (Australia)
Born Adelaide, 2 October 1965 and lives there; RH; 6ft 1in; 154lb; final 1990 ATP ranking 57 singles, 18 doubles; 1990 prize money $292,899.
1985: (132). **1986:** (132) Formed an effective doubles partnership with Kratzmann, reaching f Queens. **1987:** (82) Sf Kitzbuhel and Hong Kong. Broke into top 100 in Aug. and underwent a knee operation at end of year. **1988:** (20) Upset Krickstein and Becker to reach sf US Open; won 1st GP title at Gstaad and reached sf Stratton Mountain and Queen's (d. Cash and Curren back-to-back). Won 4 doubles titles with 3 different partners. **1989:** (53) Sf Rotterdam and Tokyo Seiko; upset Hlasek 1r Australian Open and took J. McEnroe to 8–6 5s at the same stage at Wimbledon. In doubles was r/u Australian Open with Kratzmann and won 3 titles, qualifying for Masters, where they lost sf to Jarryd and Fitzgerald. **1990:** R/u Newport then, unseeded, he upset Ivanisevic to reach last 16 US

Open, where he extended Becker to 5s. In doubles with Kratzmann won 3 titles and qualified for IBM/ATP World Doubles. Member of Aust. D Cup team beaten 3–2 by USA in f. In final Chang beat him in ss. *1990 HIGHLIGHTS – SINGLES: Australian Open* 1r (lost Gomez [seed 9] 4–6 6–3 1–6 6–2 6–3), *French Open* 1r (lost Jarryd 6–3 6–1 6–2), *Wimbledon* 2r (d. Wostenholme 6–2 6–2 6–0), *US Open* last 16, unseeded (d. Jones 6–3 3–6 6–2 6–0, Srejber 6–3 2–0 ret'd, Ivanisevic [seed 15] 4–6 4–6 6–2 7–6 6–0, lost Becker [seed 2] 2–6 6–2 6–3 3–6 6–4); *r/u* Newport (d. Dyke 6–3 6 3, Martin w.o., Kratzmann 6–2 6–4, Jelen 7–6 6–3, lost Aldrich 7–6 1–6 6–1). *1990 HIGHLIGHTS – DOUBLES:* (with Kratzmann) *won* Memphis (d. Riglewski/Stich 7–5 6–2), *won* Newport (d. Nelson/Shelton 7–6 6–4), *won* Cincinnati (d. Broad/Muller 7–6 6–2); *r/u* Paris Open (lost S. Davis/Pate 5–7 6–3 6–4). *CAREER HIGHLIGHTS – SINGLES: US Open – sf 1988* (d. Becker 6–3 6–3 6–2, Krickstein 6–2 5–7 7–6 5–7 6–3, lost Wilander 6–4 6–4 6–2). *CAREER HIGHLIGHTS – DOUBLES:* (with Kratzmann) *Australian Open – r/u 1989* (lost R. Leach/Pugh 6–4 6–4 6–4).

OMAR CAMPORESE (Italy)
Born Bologna, 8 May 1968 and lives there; RH; 6ft 2in; 172lb; final 1990 ATP ranking 45; 1990 prize money $214,402.
1986: (766) Won Italian Jun and r/u European Jun Champs. *1987:* (283) R/u Mediterranean Games. *1988:* (216) Qf Bologna and won Vienna Challenger. *1989:* (49) Won Vienna Challenger again and upset Mecir *en route* to qf Italian Open. *1990:* Reached 1st tour f at San Marino; sf Florence, Genova and Hilversum and upset Berger *en route* to qf Italian Open. In doubles with various partners reached 4 f, winning Milan and Madrid. *1990 HIGHLIGHTS – SINGLES: Australian Open* 1r (lost Delaitre 2–6 6–3 3–6 6–4 6–3), *French Open* 2r (d. Benhabiles 6–2 6–3 6–4, lost Perez 3–6 7–6 6–3 4–6 6–2), *US Open* 1r (lost Ivanisevic [seed 15] 1–6 6–4 6–1 7–6); *r/u* San Marino (d. Bruno 6–3 7–5, Pioline 6–4 3–6 6–3, Davin 6–2 0–6 6–3, Kulti 6–3 1–6 6–3, lost Perez Roldan 6–3 6–3); *sf* Florence (d. Skoff 6–2 6–0, de la Pena 6–3 6–4, Luna 6–1 7–6, lost Duncan 6–2 6–3), *sf* Genova (d. Perez 6–2 1–6 6–2, Furlan 6–1 6–1, Mattar 6–1 6–1, lost Agenor 4–6 6–3 6–3), *sf* Hilversum (d. Santoro 6–3 7–5, Filippini 6–7 6–1 7–6, Agenor 7–5 7–6, lost Clavet 4–6 7–6 7–6). *1990 HIGHLIGHTS – DOUBLES:* [Nargiso] *won* Milan (d. Nijssen/Riglewski 6–4 6–4), [Baguena] *won* Madrid (d. Gomez/J. Sanchez 6–4 3–6 6–3); [Cane] *r/u* Estoril (lost Casal/E. Sanchez 7–5 4–6 7–5), [J. Sanchez] *r/u* Gstaad (lost Casal/E. Sanchez 6–3 3–6 7–5).

PAOLO CANE (Italy)
Born Bologna, 9 April 1965 and lives there; RH; 5ft 11in; 150lb; final 1990 ATP ranking 109; 1990 prize money $100,765.
Coached by Fabio Avogadri. *1983:* (353) R/u Italian Nat Champs. *1984:* (552) Won bronze medal at Olympics in LA. *1985:* (197) Played nine tourns in singles, but performed better in doubles, earning a ranking of 44. *1986:* (44) Burst out of the pack on GP tour, winning Bordeaux, reaching f Bologna, and beating Nystrom to reach qf Bastad. Played D Cup. *1987:* (51) Sf Bologna and St Vincent. Began 1 year's military service in June, but was granted special leave to play Wimbledon, where he extended Lendl to 5s, and US Open. *1988:* (81) Upset E. Sanchez *en route* to qf Olympics and Edberg to appear at same stage Stockholm. Won 2 Challenger tourns and reached sf Bastad. *1989:* (33) Won Bastad, r/u Palermo and sf Hilversum. *1990:* Won all 3 of his matches as Italy upset Sweden in D Cup. Reached sf Wellington and qf Brussels. *1990 HIGHLIGHTS – SINGLES: Australian Open* 1r (lost Riglewski 6–2 6–3 2–6 6–2); *sf* Wellington (d. Krishnan 6–4 5–7 6–3, Derlin 7–6 6–4, Bloom 7–6 2–6 6–3, lost E. Sanchez 7–5 6–2). *1990 HIGHLIGHTS – DOUBLES:* [Camporese] *r/u* Estoril (lost Casal/E. Sanchez 7–5 4–6 7–5).

JENNIFER CAPRIATI (USA)
Born New York, 28 March 1976; lives Saddlebrook, Fla.; RH; 2HB; 5ft 7in; 135lb; 1990 WTA ranking 8; 1990 prize money $283,597.
Coached by her father, Stefano; formerly coached by Jimmy Evert. *1988:* Won Nat 18s. *1989:* Won French Open Jun (lost no set and d. Sviglerova 6–4 6–0 in f), US Open Jun (d. McQuillan 6–2 6–3), plus Wimbledon and US Open Jun doubles with McGrath as well as US 18s HC and CC. At 13 yrs 6 mths was youngest to play W Cup, making a sparkling début with a 6–0 6–0 drubbing of Wood, but was still too young to compete on the pro tour until

March 1990. **1990:** At age 13 she became the first female to reach f of her first pro tourn at VS Florida, Boca Raton. She upset Sukova there and at LIPC, where she reached last 16, stunned Sanchez-Vicario and Zvereva *en route* to 2nd tour f at FC Cup, and in Oct. beat Garrison at Puerto Rico to win her 1st tour title. Reached sf in 1st GS tourn at French Open, becoming youngest (at 14 yrs 66 days) to reach that stage; youngest seed at Wimbledon, where she reached last 16; youngest to win singles match at US Open where she reached same stage; and youngest to qualify for VS Champs, where she lost 1r to Graf. She was a member of the winning US Fed Cup team and won WTA Most Impressive Newcomer award. **1990 HIGHLIGHTS – SINGLES: French Open** sf, unseeded (d. Testud 6–1 6–1, Cammy MacGregor 6–1 6–0, Wiesner 6–4 6–4, Paz 6–0 6–3, M-J. Fernandez 6–2 6–4, lost Seles 6–2 6–2), **Wimbledon** last 16, seed 12 (d. Kelesi 6–3 6–1, Halard 6–2 7–6, R. White 7–5 6–7 6–3, lost Graf [seed 1] 6–2 6–4), **US Open** last 16, seed 13 (d. A. Huber 7–5 7–5, Hy 6–3 6–1, Strandlund 6–1 6–4, lost Graf [seed 1] 6–1 6–2); **won** Puerto Rico (d. Strnadova 6–0 7–6, McGrath 6–3 6–2, Strandlund 6–1 6–4, G. Fernandez 6–2 6–1, Garrison 5–7 6–4 6–2); **r/u** VS Florida (d. Daniels 7–6 6–1, Porwik 7–5 0–6 6–2, Tauziat 6–4 6–2, Sukova 6–1 6–4, Gildemeister 7–6 7–6, lost Sabatini 6–4 7–5), **r/u** FC Cup (d. Sloane 6–4 6–1, Kanellopoulou 6–1 6–3, Sanchez 6–1 6–1, Kelesi 6–2 4–6 6–1, Zvereva 7–6 6–0, lost Navratilova 6–2 6–4). **CAREER HIGHLIGHTS – SINGLES: French Open – sf 1990.**

TOMAS CARBONELL (Spain)
Born Barcelona, 23 August 1968; lives Cabrera de Mar; RH; 5ft 10in; 163lb; final 1990 ATP ranking 76; 1990 prize money $195,984.
Coached by Pato (Bill) Alvarez. **1985:** Nat Jun champ. **1986:** No. 1 in ITF Jun Doubles World Rankings. Won US Open Jun (with J. Sanchez), Wimbledon Jun (with Korda) and r/u French Open Jun (with J. Sanchez). **1987:** (242) Qf Barcelona and won Buenos Aires doubles with Casal. **1988:** Qf Bologna and Athens. **1989:** (77) Reached 1st GP sf at Hilversum, following with St Vincent, and won 2 doubles titles. **1990:** Reached sf Casablanca and Itaparica and won 2 doubles titles again. **1990 HIGHLIGHTS – SINGLES: Australian Open** 2r (d. Suk 6–4 7–5 6–3, lost Lendl [seed 1] 6–4 6–2 6–3), **French Open** 1r (lost Gustafsson [seed 14] 6–4 5–7 4–6 6–4 6–2), **Wimbledon** 1r (lost Mecir 6–4 6–4 6–1), **US Open** 3r (d. Haarhuis 6–7 7–6 6–4 6–0, S. Davis 6–4 6–4 6–2, lost Becker [seed 2] 6–4 6–2 6–2); **sf** Casablanca (d. Roig 6–4 6–2, Wostenholme 6–1 6–4, Azar 7–5 2–6 6–3, lost Perez Roldan 6–1 6–1), **sf** Itaparica (d. Davin 7–6 6–0, Altur 4–6 6–1 6–2, Motta 6–3 7–5, lost Filippini 7–6 6–4). **1990 HIGHLIGHTS – DOUBLES:** [Riglewski] **won** Genova (d. Caratti/Mordegan 7–6 7–6), [Pimek] **won** Bordeaux (d. Bahrami/Noah 6–3 6–7 6–2]; [Gorriz] **r/u** Itaparica (lost Menezes/Roese 7–6 7–5).

SERGIO CASAL (Spain)
Born Barcelona, 8 September 1962, and lives there; RH; 6ft 2in; 155lb; final 1990 ATP ranking 263 singles; 13 doubles; 1990 prize money $281,481.
Coached by Pato (Bill) Alvarez. **1980:** Stopped S. Giammalva and Wilander to reach qf Orange Bowl. **1982:** (159) Joined Spanish D Cup squad. **1985:** (38) Won first GP at Florence and reached sf Kitzbuhel. Started successful partnership with E. Sanchez, winning Kitzbuhel, Geneva and Barcelona and reaching 4 other f. **1986:** (62) Had great run to final of new Paris tourn, won 5 doubles titles with E. Sanchez, and won US Open mixed doubles with Reggi. **1987:** (92) Qf Munich and Itaparica; with E. Sanchez won 6 doubles titles, r/u Wimbledon and sf Masters. **1988:** (77) Underwent wrist surgery after French Open, returning in July. Sf Gstaad and qf Madrid in singles. In doubles with E. Sanchez won US Open and r/u Masters, winning 7 other titles plus Olympic silver medal. **1989:** (184) In singles reached sf Madrid, upsetting E. Sanchez. In doubles, injuries to his regular partner E. Sanchez prevented the success of previous years, but he teamed with J. Sanchez to win Bologna. **1990:** In action again with E. Sanchez, won French Open and 5 other titles, plus a 7th with J. Sanchez. R/u IBM/ATP World Doubles with E. Sanchez. **1990 HIGHLIGHTS – DOUBLES:** (with E. Sanchez unless stated) **won French Open** (d. Ivanisevic/Korda 7–5 6–3); **won** Estoril (d. Camporese/Cane 7–5 4–6 7–5), **won** Italian Open (d. Courier/M. Davis 7–6 7–6), **won** Gstaad (d. Camporese/J. Sanchez 6–3 3–6 7–5), **won** Hilversum (d. Haarhuis/Koevermans 7–5 7–5), **won** Palermo (d. Costa/de la Pena 6–3 6–4). [J. Sanchez] **won** Athens (d. Kempers/Krajicek 4–6 7–6 6–3); **r/u** Wellington (lost Evernden/Pereira 6–4 7–6), **r/u** Barcelona (lost Gomez/J. Sanchez 7–6 7–5), **r/u** IBM/ATP World Doubles (d. Connell/Michibata 6–4 6–7 6–4 6–7 6–3, lost Forget/Hlasek 6–4 7–6 5–7 6–4). **CAREER**

HIGHLIGHTS – DOUBLES: (with E. Sanchez) *French Open – won 1990; US Open – won 1988* (d. R. Leach/Pugh w.o.); *Wimbledon – r/u 1987* (lost Flach/Seguso 7–6 6–1 6–4); *Masters – r/u 1988* (lost R. Leach/Pugh 6–4 6–3 2–6 6–0); *IBM/ATP World Doubles r/u 1990; Olympics – silver medal 1988* (lost Flach/Seguso 6–3 6–4 6–7 6–7 9–7). *MIXED DOUBLES:* (with Reggi) *US Open – won 1986* (d. Navratilova/Fleming 6–4 6–4).

PAT CASH (Australia)
Born Melbourne, 27 May 1965; lives there and London; RH; 5ft 11in; 170lb; final 1990 ATP ranking 81; 1990 prize money $137,916; career prize money $1,534,968.
Coached by Ian Barclay, trainer Anne Quinn. Separated from former girlfriend Anne-Britt Kristiansen May 1989; son Daniel born May 1986, daughter Mia born April 1988. Married Emily Bendit in Jamaica, 22 July 1990. *1982:* (44) In Melbourne he became the youngest to win a GP title (Krickstein broke the record the following year); earlier in year he won Wimbledon and US Open Jun. *1983:* (38) Won Brisbane and led Australia to victory in D Cup. *1984:* (8) Sf Wimbledon and US Open, where he had m-p in sf with Lendl, upset Connors in dead rubber D Cup match and reached f Melbourne. *1985:* (67) Sidetracked by back injuries, he achieved his best effort to reach sf Brussels. R/u Wimbledon doubles 2nd straight year. *1986:* (24) Only 3 weeks after having emergency appendectomy he reached qf Wimbledon with win over Wilander and later in year he led Australia to victory over Sweden in D Cup f. *1987:* (7) After reaching f Australian Open (d. Lendl sf), where he took Edberg to 5s, won Nancy for 1st title since 1983. He followed in tremendous style by winning 1st GS title at Wimbledon (d. Lendl in ss in f), becoming 1st Australian to win the singles there since Newcombe in 1971 and the only player to d. Lendl twice in 1987. Won Johannesburg and qualified for Masters 1st time. *1988:* (20) Began the year in style as r/u Australian Open, losing 8–6 5s to Wilander, but after arthroscopic surgery on right knee in Feb., fell in last 16 French Open, qf Wimbledon and missed US Open with Achilles tendon injury. In other tourns reached sf Indian Wells and qf Toronto. *1989:* (368) Feb. injury to right elbow kept him off court until Suntory Tokyo in April where, v Scanlon in 2r and leading 4–2 1st set, he ruptured Achilles' tendon and was sidelined for 7 months. *1990:* Returned to action in Jan. playing doubles only at Sydney and winning the title with Kratzmann. In his 4th tourn he was r/u Seoul and the following week won both singles and doubles (with Masur) at Hong Kong. It was his 1st singles title since Johannesburg in Nov. 1987 and, at 243, he became the lowest-ranked player to win a tour title. At Wimbledon, still not ranked high enough to be seeded, he reached qf. *1990 HIGHLIGHTS – SINGLES: Wimbledon* qf, unseeded (d. Azar 4–6 7–6 5–7 6–4 6–1, Anderson 6–2 6–3 7–6, Aguilera 6–1 6–1 6–4, lost Becker [seed 2] 7–6 6–1 6–4), *US Open* 3r (d. Rosset 2–6 2–6 6–3 6–3 6–3, Kratzmann 6–4 2–6 2–6 6–1 6–4, lost Krickstein [seed 9] 6–4 7–6 7–6), *won* Hong Kong (d. Curren 6–1 6–4, Jelen 6–2 7–6, Connell 6–2 7–6, Kuhnen 6–7 7–5 6–1, Antonitsch 6–3 6–4); *r/u* Seoul (d. Laurendeau 6–4 6–3, Connell 6–7 7–5 6–2, Srejber 6–2 6–3, Bloom 6–3 6–3, lost Antonitsch 7–6 6–3). *1990 HIGHLIGHTS – DOUBLES:* [Kratzmann] *won* Sydney (d. Aldrich/Visser 6–4 7–5). [Masur] *won* Hong Kong (d. Curren/Rive 6–3 6–3). *CAREER HIGHLIGHTS – SINGLES: Wimbledon – won 1987* (d. Freeman, McNamee, Schapers, Forget 6–2 6–3 6–4, Wilander 6–3 7–5 6–4, Connors 6–4 6–4 6–1, Lendl 7–6 6–2 7–5), *sf 1984* unseeded (d. Wilander, Motta, Curren, Gomez, lost McEnroe 6–3 7–6 6–4), *qf 1986* unseeded (d. Vilas, Simpson, Lapidus, Wilander 4–6 6–4 7–5 6–3, lost Leconte 4–6 7–6 7–6 6–3), *qf 1988* (d. Fitzgerald, Olhovsky, lost Becker 6–4 6–3 6–4), *qf 1990; Australian Open – r/u 1987* (d. Pistolesi, Testerman, Annacone, Noah 6–4 6–2 2–6 6–0, Lendl 7–6 5–7 7–6 6–4, lost Edberg 6–3 6–4 3–6 5–7 6–3), *r/u 1988* (d. Muster, Svensson 6–1 6–4 6–1, Schapers 6–1 6–4 6–2, Lendl 6–4 2–6 6–2 4–6 6–2, lost Wilander 6–3 6–7 2–6 6–1 8–6), *qf 1984* (lost Kriek 7–5 6–1 7–6); *US Open – sf 1984* (d. Wilander, lost Lendl [seed 2] 3–6 6–3 6–4 6–7 7–6 after having 1 m-p). *CAREER HIGHLIGHTS – DOUBLES:* (with Fitzgerald unless stated) [McNamee] *Wimbledon – r/u 1984* (lost McEnroe/Fleming 6–2 5–7 6–2 3–6 6–3), *r/u 1985* (d. McEnroe/Fleming, lost Gunthardt/Taroczy 6–4 6–3 4–6 6–3); *Australian Open – sf 1984* (lost Nystrom/Wilander 6–4 6–4 2–6 6–3).

CATHY CAVERZASIO (Italy)
Born Geneva, Switzerland, 28 September 1972 and lives there; RH; 2HB; 5ft 4½in; 124lb; final 1990 WTA ranking 44; 1990 prize money $62,198.
Coached by Massino Di Domenico; trains in Italy. *1987:* (284). *1988:* (108) R/u US Open Jun doubles with Lapi. *1989:* (58) R/u Taranto and sf Paris Open. *1990:* Qf Geneva,

Birmingham, Palermo and Brighton. ***1990 HIGHLIGHTS – SINGLES: French Open*** 2r (d. Jagerman 6–4 6–2, lost Martin 6–3 7–5), US Open 1r (lost Zardo 6–1 4–6 6–1).

ANNA MARIA (SANDRA) CECCHINI (Italy)
Born Bologna, 27 February 1965; lives Ceriva; RH; 5ft 6½in; 130lb; final 1990 WTA ranking 20; 1990 Prize money $131,699.
Prefers to be known by her nickname Sandra. ***1983:*** R/u to Spence at Orange Bowl 18s, ranked second among world juniors and third among Italy's women. ***1984:*** (49) Won Rio de Janeiro. ***1985:*** (49) Reached qf French Open and won Barcelona, restoring herself after 8 consecutive 1r losses early in year. ***1986:*** (76) Produced the upset of the year when she stunned Evert Lloyd in Fed Cup, the first time the American had lost in the international team competition. ***1987:*** (18) Extended Graf to 3s sf Berlin, won VS Arkansas and reached f Strasbourg. ***1988:*** (21) Won Strasbourg and Nice and reached f Bastad. ***1989:*** (26) Won Paris Open in singles and doubles; r/u Estoril, sf Tampa and Bastad in singles and won 2 other doubles titles with Tarabini. ***1990:*** Won Bastad; sf Berlin (upset Sabatini), Kitzbuhel and Clarins. ***1990 HIGHLIGHTS – SINGLES: French Open*** 3r (d. Guerree 7–5 6–0, Amiach 6–2 6–1, lost Graf [seed 1] 6–2 6–3), ***Wimbledon*** 1r (lost Benjamin 6–3 6–1), ***US Open*** 2r (d. Pospisilova 6–3 6–1, lost Piccolini 4–6 7–5 6–4); ***won*** Bastad (d. Thoren 6–0 6–4, Vieira 3–6 6–1 6–1, Appelmans 6–3 3–6 7–5, Pampoulova 6–4 6–3, Bartos 6–1 6–2); ***sf*** Berlin (d. Simpson 6–4 7–6, J. Thompson 3–6 6–3 7–5, Sabatini 6–4 3–6 6–4, Tauziat 7–6 6–3, lost Seles 6–1 6–3), ***sf*** Kitzbuhel (d. Nohakova 6–0 6–7 6–0, Heelgeson 6–2 6–0, Budarova 6–3 6–1, lost Kohde-Kilsch 6–4 5–7 7–5), ***sf*** Clarins (d. Wasserman 5–7 6–4 7–5, Dechaume 6–4 7–5, Rajchrtova 3–6 6–1 6–4, lost Tarabini 6–4 7–5). ***1990 HIGHLIGHTS – DOUBLES:*** (with Tarabini unless stated) ***won*** Estoril (d. Bakkum/Jagerman 1–6 6–2 6–3); [Gildemeister] ***r/u*** Tampa (lost Paz/Sanchez-Vicario 6–2 6–0), ***r/u*** Kitzbuhel (lost Langrova/Zrubakova 6–0 6–4). ***CAREER HIGHLIGHTS – SINGLES: French Open – qf 1985*** (lost Navratilova 6–2 6–2).

THIERRY CHAMPION (France)
Born Bagnol sur Seine, 31 August 1966; lives Paris; RH; 5ft 11½in; 155lb; final 1990 ATP ranking 59; 1990 prize money $195,007.
Coached by Bernard Pestre. Won Nat 16s and 18s. ***1985:*** (190). ***1986:*** (128) Qf Bordeaux. ***1987:*** (105) Qf Bordeaux again. ***1988:*** (125) Appeared in 1st GP singles f at St Vincent (d. Jaite) and sf Bari. Broke into top 100 briefly in late summer. ***1989:*** (404) Reached qf Athens but then was sidelined for months with a broken wrist and was close to retiring. ***1990:*** Became the first qualifier to reach qf French Open in the open era, despite being hampered by right hip injury. Reached sf Palermo and finished the year at his highest-ever ranking. ***1990 HIGHLIGHTS – SINGLES: French Open*** qf, unseeded (d. Prpic 6–4 3–6 6–3 6–3, Aguilera 3–6 6–3 6–3 6–2, Forget 6–4 6–7 6–4 5–7 6–3, Novacek 6–4 4–6 3–6 7–6 6–3, lost Gomez [seed 4] 6–3 6–3 6–4), ***US Open*** 2r (d. Mayotte 7–5 3–6 6–3 7–5, lost Yzaga 6–1 3–6 6–3 6–2); ***sf*** Palermo (d. Azar 6–3 6–3, Clavet 6–4 6–2, de la Pena 6–7 6–1 6–3, lost Davin 6–1 4–6 7–5). ***CAREER HIGHLIGHTS – SINGLES: French Open – qf 1990.***

MICHAEL CHANG (USA)
Born Hoboken, NJ, 22 February 1972; lives Placentia, Cal.; RH; 5ft 8in; 135lb; final 1990 ATP ranking 15; 1990 prize money $866,072.
Parents from Taipei. Coached by his father, Joe, and José Higueras and at end of 1990 by Phil Dent. ***1987:*** (163) At 15 yrs 6 mths was youngest player to compete in men's singles at US Open since 1918, and was the youngest ever to win a match in GS tourn, having been granted a wild card after winning US 18s at Kalamazoo. At 15 yrs 7 mths was youngest to win a pro tourn at Las Vegas Challenger and was youngest-ever GP semi-finalist at Scottsdale. ***1988:*** (30) At 16 yrs 4 mths he was the youngest for 60 years to win a match in Wimbledon main draw, and when he won his 1st title at San Francisco at 16 yrs 7 mths, he was youngest to win a SS event and second-youngest after Krickstein to win a GP title. Upset Svensson *en route* to last 16 US Open and reached qf Washington and Cincinnati. ***1989:*** (5) The highlight of his career to date came at the French Open where, at 17 yrs 3 mths, he became the youngest known male winner of a GS tourn and the 1st American since Trabert in 1955 to win that title. In 5s of his 4r match v Lendl, he was so badly affected with cramp that he had to serve underarm. Won Wembley and r/u Los Angeles, last 16 Wimbledon and US Open to qualify for 1st Masters, where he failed to win a match. Was

the youngest to play D Cup for USA, making his début v Paraguay, and the youngest to break into top 5. *1990:* Out until March with stress fracture of cup of left hip suffered Dec. 1989. He did not reach the heights of the previous year, but won 1st HC title at Canadian Open, was r/u Los Angeles and Wembley and reached sf Washington. His best showing in GS was qf French Open. In winning US D Cup team, in sf coming back from 2 sets to 1 down v Skoff to take US into f where he d. Cahill in 2nd rubber in 3–2 win v Australia. Reached sf GS Cup. *1990 HIGHLIGHTS – SINGLES: French Open* qf, seed 11 (d. Motta 6–2 7–6 6–1, Rosset 7–5 4–6 6–4 6–3, Bergstrom 2–6 5–7 6–0 6–2 6–4, E. Sanchez [seed 6] 6–4 6–4 6–2, lost Agassi [seed 3] 6–1 6–2 4–6 6–2), *Wimbledon* last 16, seed 13 (d. Altur 5–7 6–4 6–3 7–5, Pugh 6–3 6–2 6–2, Kratzmann 3–6 4–6 6–4 6–2 6–2, lost Edberg [seed 3] 6–3 6–2 6–1), *US Open* 3r, seed 11 (d. Pernfors 6–0 6–2 6–3, Arias 7–6 6–3 6–2, lost Cherkasov 6–4 6–4 6–3); *won* Canadian Open (d. Dyke 6–2 6–3, Wheaton 6–0 6–3, Agassi 4–6 7–5 7–5, Sampras 3–6 7–6 7–5, Berger 4–6 6–3 7–6); *r/u* Los Angeles (d. S. Davis 7–5 4–6 6–4, Sznajder 6–2 6–3, Goldie 6–1 7–5, Muller 7–6 6–2, lost Edberg 7–6 2–6 7–6), *r/u* Wembley (d. Kratzmann 6–0 6–0, Bates 6–3 6–3, Lundgren 3–6 6–3 6–4, Bergstrom 6–3 3–6 7–6, lost Hlasek 7–6 6–3); *sf* Washington (d. Bryan 6–2 7–6, Youl 6–1 6–1, Witsken 6–3 6–4, lost Agassi 6–3 6–1); *sf* GS Cup (d. Edberg (1) 6–4 4–6 7–5, Leconte 7–6 6–3; lost Sampras (4) 6–3 6–4 6–4. *CAREER HIGHLIGHTS – SINGLES: French Open – won 1989* (d. Masso 6–7 6–3 6–0 6–3, Sampras 6–1 6–1 6–1, Roig 6–0 7–5 6–3, Lendl 4–6 4–6 6–3 6–3 6–3, Agenor 6–4 2–6 6–4 7–6, Chesnokov 6–1 5–7 7–6 7–5, Edberg 6–1 2–6 4–6 6–4 6–2), *qf 1990.*

ANDREI CHERKASOV (USSR)

Born Ufa, 4 July 1970; lives Moscow; RH; 5ft 11in; 160lb; final 1990 ATP ranking 21; 1990 prize money $392,171.
1986: (870) Coached by Natalia Rogova. R/u to Courier at Orange Bowl. *1987:* (409) No. 3 in ITF Jun rankings; r/u to Wheaton at US Open Jun and to Courier at Orange Bowl again. *1988:* (236). *1989:* (82) Broke into top 100 after qf showing at Milan and top 50 after winning 2 Challenger titles. At Sydney reached f, having never before reached GP qf. *1990:* Upset Gomez *en route* to his 1st GS qf at Australian Open, and Chang *en route* to same stage at US Open, unseeded both times. Won his 1st tour title at Moscow in Oct.; sf Nice (d. Berger) and Umag. Played GS Cup, lost 1r Sampras (4) 5–7 6–2 7–5. *1990 HIGHLIGHTS – SINGLES: Australian Open* qf, unseeded (d. Matsuoka 6–2 4–6 4–6 6–0 6–2, Layendecker 6–4 5–7 7–5 6–0, Fleurian 6–4 6–4 7–5, Gomez [seed 9] 2–6 6–3 7–6 7–6, lost Lendl [seed 1] 6–3 6–2 6–3), *French Open* 2r (d. Vitoux 6–0 6–4 6–4, lost Perez Roldan [seed 15] 7–5 6–4 6–3), *Wimbledon* 1r (lost Masur 6–3 6–4 6–2), *US Open* qf, unseeded (d. Seguso 6–0 6–7 6–2 6–3, Leconte 1–6 6–1 6–4 6–3, Chang [seed 11] 6–4 6–4 6–3, Van Rensburg 6–4 6–4 7–5, lost Agassi [seed 4] 6–2 6–2 6–3); *won* Moscow (d. Mansdorf 6–2 6–0, Bloom 6–3 6–3, E. Sanchez 6–3 6–3, Riglewski 6–1 7–6, Mayotte 6–2 6–1); *sf* Nice (d. Korda 0–6 7–5 7–5, Stich 6–4 6–4, Berger 2–6 6–2 6–3, lost Forget 4–6 7–6 6–4), *sf* Umag (d. Clavet 6–2 6–4, Roig 6–3 6–4, Jelen 6–2 6–0, lost Ivanisevic 6–3 5–7 6–4). *1990 HIGHLIGHTS – DOUBLES:* [Olkhovskiy] *r/u* Umag (lost Flegl/Vacek 6–4 6–4). *CAREER HIGHLIGHTS – SINGLES: Australian Open – qf 1990; US Open – qf 1990.*

ANDREI CHESNOKOV (USSR)

Born Moscow, 2 February 1966 and lives there; RH; 2HB; 6ft 2in; 167lb; final 1990 ATP ranking 12; 1990 prize money $423,863.
Coached by Tatiana Naoumko. *1980:* Won Russian Nat Jun Champ. *1982:* Won Russian Nat Jun Champ again. *1984:* Beat Glickstein and Perkis in D Cup. *1985:* (136) Upset Teltscher at French Open. *1986:* (36) Reached qf French Open, upsetting No. 2 seed Wilander in 3r, and last 16 US Open. *1987:* (52) Reached last 16 US Open and won his 1st GP title in his 1st f at Florence, becoming 1st from his country to win a title since Metreveli won S Orange in 1974. *1988:* (14) Won Orlando, r/u Wellington, Sydney and Toulouse. In GS reached qf both Australian Open and French Open (d. Cash). *1989:* (22) Upset Wilander *en route* to sf French Open after winning Nice and Munich back-to-back in spring. *1990:* Won Monte Carlo (d. E. Sanchez and Muster) and Tel Aviv; r/u Auckland and Italian Open (d. E. Sanchez again); sf Barcelona and New Haven. *1990 HIGHLIGHTS – SINGLES: Australian Open* 2r, seed 11 (d. Kratzmann 3–6 6–7 7–6 6–3 6–2, lost Woodforde 6–3 6–2 7–5), *French Open* last 16, seed 8 (d. Riglewski 6–1 6–1 6–3, Fleurian 7–6 6–2 6–0, Arrese 7–5 6–4 6–2, lost Leconte 6–4 6–3 4–6 2–6 6–3), *US Open* 3r, seed 10 (d. Delaitre 6–4 7–5

6–3, Matsuoka 6–7 6–3 6–1 6–3, lost J. McEnroe 6–3 7–5 6–4); **won** Monte Carlo (d. Prpic 7–5 6–3, Carbonell 4–1 ret'd, Rosset 6–3 6–2, E. Sanchez 4–6 6–1 7–6, Muster 6–2 6–3), **won** Tel Aviv (d. Perreira 6–3 6–2, Robertson 7–5 6–4, Jonsson 6–3 6–1, Bloom 6–3 6–3, Mansdorf 6–4 6–3); **r/u** Auckland (d. Zoecke 7–6 6–7 7–5, Reneberg 6–4 6–4, Connell 2–6 6–4 6–3, Mansdorf 7–6 6–2, lost S. Davis 4–6 6–3 6–3), **r/u** Italian Open (d. Arias 7–6 6–3, Cane 4–6 6–3 6–3, Courier 4–6 7–6 6–3, Mancini 7–6 6–0, E. Sanchez 6–7 6–4 7–6, lost Muster 6–1 6–3 6–1); **sf** Barcelona (d. Azar 6–4 1–6 6–3, Costa 6–4 6–0, Berger 6–2 6–4, lost Gomez 6–3 7–5), **sf** New Haven (d. Anderson 6–2 6–2, Grabb 7–6 6–3, Caratti 6–2 6–1, lost Rostagno 7–6 6–3). **CAREER HIGHLIGHTS – SINGLES: French Open – sf 1989** unseeded (d. Arraya, Steeb 3–6 6–1 7–5 6–3, Courier 2–6 3–6 7–6 6–2 7–5, Wilander 6–4 6–0 7–5, lost Chang 6–1 5–7 7–6 7–5), **qf 1986** unseeded (d. Svensson 6–3 2–6 6–4 6–2, Osterthun, Wilander 6–2 6–3 6–2, Maciel, lost Leconte 6–3 6–4 6–3), **qf 1988** (d. Cash, lost Leconte 6–2 6–3 7–6); **Australian Open – qf 1988** (d. Mansdorf 6–3 4–6 7–5 6–2, Benhabiles, Kratzmann, Steeb, lost Edberg 4–6 7–6 6–4 6–4).

FRANCISCO CLAVET (Spain)
Born Aranjuez, 24 October 1968; lives Madrid; LH; 6ft; 156lb; final 1990 ATP ranking 90; 1990 prize money $117,005.
Elder brother of José. **1987:** (638). **1988:** (290). **1989:** (188) Qf Kitzbuhel. **1990:** Won his 1st tour title at Hilversum as a lucky loser, upsetting Jaite on the way. **1990 HIGHLIGHTS – SINGLES: French Open** 1r (lost Noah 6–4 4–6 6–4 1–6 7–5); **won** Hilversum (d. Novacek 7–6 7–6, Haarhuis 7–5 6–2, Jaite 5–7 6–1 6–2, Camporese 4–6 7–6 7–6, Masso 3–6 6–4 6–2 6–0). **1990 HIGHLIGHTS – DOUBLES:** [Skoff] **r/u** Kitzbuhel (lost J. Sanchez/Winogradsky 7–6 6–2).

AMANDA COETZER (South Africa)
Born Hoopstad, 22 October 1971 and lives there; RH; 2HB; 5ft 2in; 115lb; final 1990 WTA ranking 75; 1990 prize money $55,895.
1987: (442). **1988:** (153) Won 4 titles on the satellite circuits. **1989:** (63) Made an unexpected appearance in last 16 French Open and reached sf VS Arizona. **1990:** Qf VS Florida, Geneva and VS Albuquerque. **1990 HIGHLIGHTS – SINGLES: French Open** 1r (lost Sloane 6–4 6–3), **Wimbledon** 2r (d. Medvedeva 4–6 6–2 6–1, lost McNeil 6–3 6–2), **US Open** 1r (lost Kelesi 7–5 4–6 6–3).

GRANT CONNELL (Canada)
Born Regina, Saskatchewan, 17 November 1965; lives Toronto; LH; 6ft 1in; 175lb; final 1990 ATP ranking 92 singles; 10T doubles; 1990 prize money $307,589.
1983: Nat Jun Singles Champ. **1985:** (570) All American at Texas A & M. **1986:** (191) Won 1st of 3 straight Nat doubles titles. **1987:** (123) Won Vancouver Challenger and r/u Nancy doubles with Scott. **1988:** (134) Qf Sydney and Tokyo Seiko; won Livingston in doubles with his D Cup partner, Michibata. **1989:** (94) Reached qf Montreal and broke into top 100 Aug. **1990:** In singles reached f Auckland, Hong Kong and Sydney Indoor. In doubles with Michibata r/u Australian Open, won 2 titles and reached 2 other f to qualify for IBM/ATP World Doubles. **1990 HIGHLIGHTS – SINGLES: Australian Open** 1r (lost Forget 2–6 6–4 6–4 6–2), **French Open** 1r (lost Rahunen 1–6 6–1 6–4 6–0), **Wimbledon** 1r (lost Visser 6–4 6–4 6–4), **US Open** 1r (lost Agassi [seed 4] 6–4 6–2 6–2). **1990 HIGHLIGHTS – DOUBLES:** (with Michibata) **r/u Australian Open** (lost Aldrich/Visser 6–4 4–6 6–1 6–4); **won** Seoul (d. Stoltenburg/Woodbridge 7–6 6–4), **won** Washington (d. Lozano/Witsken 6–3 6–7 6–2); **r/u** Philadelphia (lost R. Leach/Pugh 3–6 6–4 6–2), **r/u** Indianapolis (lost S. Davis/Pate 7–6 7–6). **CAREER HIGHLIGHTS – DOUBLES:** (with Michibata) **Australian Open – r/u 1990.**

JIM COURIER (USA)
Born Sanford, Fla., 17 August 1970; lives Dade City, Fla.; RH; 6ft 1in; 173lb; final 1990 ATP ranking 25; 1990 prize money $437,390.
Started at Nick Bollettieri Tennis Academy. Coach now Sergio Cruz. **1986:** Played on US Jun World Cup team r/u to AUS. **1987:** Won French Open Jun doubles with Stark and was ranked 4 in Jun singles, winning Orange Bowl. **1988:** (43) Sf US CC and Stockholm (d. Jarryd and Pernfors back-to-back); qf Stratton Mountain and Detroit. R/u US Nat 18s to Chang. **1989:** (24) Upset Agassi *en route* to last 16 French Open and beat Edberg to win his 1st GP title at Basle in autumn. In doubles won Italian Open and qualified for Masters with

Sampras. *1990:* Sf Indian Wells; qf Milan, Philadelphia, LIPC, Munich, Gstaad and Cincinnati. *1990 HIGHLIGHTS – SINGLES: Australian Open* 2r, seed 14 (d. Arias 6–3 6–3 6–1, lost Svensson 2–6 6–2 6–3 6–2), *French Open* last 16, seed 13 (d. Altur 6–1 4–6 6–3 6–4, Srejber 7–6 6–1 2–6 6–2, Anderson 6–0 6–2 6–1, lost Agassi [seed 3] 6–7 6–1 6–4 6–0), *Wimbledon* 3r, seed 9 (d. Kaplan 6–1 6–4 6–4, Stoltenberg 6–2 7–6 6–4, lost Woodforde 7–5 5–7 7–5 6–4), *US Open* 2r, seed 14 (d. Masur 6–4 6–0 5–7 6–1, lost Muller 4–6 6–4 7–6 7–6); *sf* Indian Wells (d. Bryan 7–5 6–1, Jones 6–2 6–3, Cahill 6–4 6–2, Krickstein 6–2 7–6, lost Edberg 6–4 6–1). *1990 HIGHLIGHTS – DOUBLES:* [Bruguera] *won* Hamburg (d. Riglewski/Stich 7–6 6–2); [M. Davis] *r/u* Italian Open (lost Casal/E. Sanchez 7–6 7–5).

BELINDA CORDWELL (New Zealand)
Born Wellington, 21 September 1965 and lives there; LH; 5ft 9in; 147lb; final 1990 WTA ranking 91; 1990 prize money $47,549.
Coached by Mark Cox. *1982:* Won Nat HC and Indoor 18s. *1984:* (211) Won 4 USTA doubles titles with Richardson. *1985:* (70) Qf Newport. *1986:* (216). *1987:* (124) Won Canberra and Brisbane on Australian satellite circuit. *1988:* (62) Last 16 Australian Open, unseeded, and reached qf Wellington, Taipei and Birmingham. *1989:* (18) Upset Potter and Lindqvist *en route* to sf Australian Open, unseeded, where she took Sukova to 3s. Won Singapore in singles and doubles, r/u Auckland and sf Tokyo. *1990:* Reached sf Auckland plus qf Tokyo Suntory and Birmingham. *1990 HIGHLIGHTS – SINGLES: Wimbledon* 1r (lost Phelps 6–2 2–6 6–2), *US Open* 2r (d. Adams 6–3 7–6, lost Grossman 6–2 6–3); *sf* Auckland (d. J. Thompson 6–3 6–0, O'Neil 1–6 6–1 6–1, Bowes 1–6 7–6 7–5, lost Appelmans 6–1 6–2). *CAREER HIGHLIGHTS – SINGLES: Australian Open – sf 1989* unseeded (d. Potter, Bowes 3–6 6–3 12–10, Temesvari 1–6 7–6 6–1, Schultz 6–3 6–1, Lindqvist 6–2 2–6 6–1, lost Sukova 7–6 4–6 6–2).

ISABEL CUETO (Germany)
Born Kehl, Rhein, 3 December 1968; lives Aspach; LH; 2HB; 5ft 7in; 124lb; final 1990 WTA ranking 29; prize money $77,181.
1984: Won Valencia. *1985:* Won Nat 18s for 2nd time; qf Taranto and Bregenz. *1986:* (96) Qf Athens, Bregenz and Perugia. *1987:* (32) At Hamburg reached first f since 1984. *1988:* (30) Won her 1st primary circuit title at Bastad, following with her 2nd 3 weeks later at Athens Open. *1989:* (28) Won Estoril and Sofia and upset K. Maleeva *en route* to sf Berlin. *1990:* Upset Tarabini and Magers at Amelia Island, surprised M-J. Fernandez *en route* to f Barcelona 2 weeks later, and won Palermo in July. *1990 HIGHLIGHTS – SINGLES: French Open* 3r (d. Zardo 7–6 6–0, Hanika 6–3 4–6 6–0, lost M-J. Fernandez [seed 7] 7–6 6–2); *won* Palermo (d. Ritter 6–1 7–6, Laskova 6–4 6–7 6–1, Laval 6–4 6–1, Reinstadler 6–1 6–1, Paulus 6–2 6–2); *r/u* Barcelona (d. Herreman 6–3 6–0, Halard 6–2 6–4, M-J. Fernandez 7–5 4–6 6–4, lost Sanchez-Vicario 6–4 6–2).

CARRIE CUNNINGHAM (USA)
Born Southfield, Mich., 28 April 1972; lives Livonia, Mich.; LH; 5ft 5in; 112lb; final 1990 WTA ranking 70; 1990 prize money $44,622.
Coached by Joe Fodell. *1986:* Won Nat 14s. *1987:* Won Nat 16s. *1988:* (138) Won US Open Jun over McQuillan. Qf Schenectady. *1988:* (88) Upset K. Maleeva *en route* to sf VS Houston. *1990:* Reached sf Puerto Rico and qf San Antonio. *1990 HIGHLIGHTS – SINGLES: Australian Open* 1r (lost Graf [seed 1] 6–2 7–5), *Wimbledon* 2r (d. Borneo 4–6 6–2 11–9, lost Novotna 6–2 6–1), *US Open* 2r (d. White Prausa 6–1 1–6 6–3, lost Savchenko 6–4 6–4); *sf* Puerto Rico (d. Hy 5–1 ret'd, Reinach 2–6 7–5 6–1, Labat 6–2 6–3, lost Garrison 6–4 6–4).

KEVIN CURREN (USA)
Born Durban, South Africa, 2 March 1958; lives Austin, Tex.; RH: 2HB; 6ft 1in; 170lb; final 1990 ATP ranking 71 singles, 26 doubles; 1990 prize money $357,542; career prize money $2,693,669.
Coached by Robert Trogolo. Became US citizen in 1985. *1979:* (195) A huge server with a two-handed forehand (a shot he since has abandoned), he won NCAA champs while attending University of Texas. *1980:* (47) Last 16 Wimbledon. *1981:* (57) Won Johannesburg in spring; last 16 US Open. *1982:* (17) Won Cologne singles, US Open doubles with Steve Denton and 2nd straight US Open mixed and Wimbledon mixed with A. Smith. *1983:* (9) R/u Milan and reached sf Wimbledon, upsetting Connors in last 16. *1984:* (15) R/u

to Wilander at Australian Open (d. Lendl). *1985:* (10) R/u to Becker at Wimbledon (d. McEnroe and Connors) and won Toronto Indoor. *1986:* (18) Won his 1st SS title in Atlanta and was one of only four players to beat Lendl, upsetting world No. 1 at Canadian Open. *1987:* (37) Reached qf only 3 times in singles but won 3 doubles titles. *1988:* (23) At Toronto reached 1st GP f since Scottsdale 1986, and appeared in sf Mephis, LA, Scottsdale and Vienna. Out with torn calf muscle from March to June, and then again with twisted ankle from Wimbledon to end Aug. *1989:* (20) Won his 1st title for 3 years at Frankfurt, despite being restricted all autumn by knee problems, and reached sf Memphis, LIPC, Singapore and San Francisco. In doubles with various partners reached 5 f, winning Tokyo Seiko. *1990:* Reached qf Wimbledon and last 16 US Open, both unseeded. In doubles with various partners reached 4 f, winning Queen's with Bates. Played GS Cup, lost 1r Ivanisevic (5) 7–6 7–6. *1990 HIGHLIGHTS – SINGLES: Wimbledon* qf, unseeded (d. Tarango 6–1 6–4 6–1, Muller 6–7 6–4 7–6 6–7 6–4, Novacek 6–2 4–6 1–6 7–5 6–3, Volkov 6–4 7–6 7–6, lost Ivanisevic 4–6 6–4 6–4 6–7 6–3), *US Open* last 16, unseeded (d. Perkiss 6–4 6–4 6–1, Washington 7–5 7–6 6–4, Witsken 6–4 6–3 6–3, lost Wheaton 7–5 7–6 4–6 6–4). *1990 HIGHLIGHTS – DOUBLES:* [Bates] *won* Queen's (d. Leconte/Lendl 6–2 7–6); [Broad] *r/u* Toronto World Tennis (lost Galbraith/MacPherson 2–6 6–4 6–3), [Rive] *r/u* Hong Kong (d. Cash/Masur 6–3 6–3), [Galbraith] *r/u* Berlin (lost Aldrich/Visser 7–6 7–6). *CAREER HIGHLIGHTS – SINGLES: Wimbledon – r/u 1985* (d. Edberg 7–6 6–3 7–6, McEnroe 6–2 6–2 6–4, Connors 6–2 6–2 6–1, lost Becker 6–3 6–7 7–6 6–4), *sf 1983* (d. Connors 6–3 6–7 6–3 7–6, Mayotte, lost C. Lewis 6–7 6–4 7–6 6–7 8–6); *Australian Open – r/u 1984* (d. Lendl, S. Davis, Testerman, lost Wilander 6–7 6–4 7–6 6–2). *CAREER HIGHLIGHTS – DOUBLES:* (with Denton) *US Open – won 1982* (d. Amaya/Pfister 6–2 6–7 5–7 6–2 6–4); *US CC – won 1980* (d. Fibak/Lendl 3–6 7–6 6–4), *won1981* (d. Ramirez/Winitsky 7–5 fs); *US Pro Indoor – won 1983* (d. McEnroe/Fleming 6–4 7–6); *Wimbledon – sf 1982* (lost McEnroe/Fleming 6–2 6–4 2–6 6–3), *sf 1983* (lost Tim/Tom Guillikson 7–6 6–7 7–6 6–3); *Australian Open – sf 1981* (lost Edmondson/Warwick). *MIXED DOUBLES:* (with A. Smith) *Wimbledon – won 1982* (d. Lloyd/Turnbull 2–6 6–3 7–5); *US Open – won 1981* (d. Denton/Russell 6–4 7–6), *won 1982* (d. Taygan/Potter 6–3 7–6).

CECILIA DAHLMAN (Sweden)
Born Lund, 24 July 1968; lives Svalov; RH; 2HB; 5ft 10in; 138lb; final 1990 WTA ranking 80; 1900 prize money $63,159.
Coached by Ralf Henriksson and Michael Brobeck. *1986:* (211). *1987:* (377). *1988:* (163) Qf Bastad. *1989:* (98) Qf Bastad and Sofia, then in autumn won her 1st primary circuit title in Athens. *1990:* Won Athens again and reached qf Bayonne and Nashville. *1990 HIGHLIGHTS – SINGLES: Australian Open* 2r (d. Kessaris 7–5 6–1, lost Meskhi 2–6 6–1 6–3), *French Open* 1r (lost Temesvari 6–2 6–1), *Wimbledon* 2r (d. Santrock 6–4 6–1, lost Garrison [seed 5] 6–2 6–1), *US Open* 1r (lost Tauziat 7–5 6–2); *won* Athens (d. Hofmann 6–1 6–0, F. Romano 6–3 3–6 6–3, S. Smith 6–1 6–4, Pierce 6–4 3–6 6–4, Piccolini 7–5 7–5).

MARY LOU PIATEK DANIELS (USA)
Born Whiting, Ind., 6 August 1961; lives Chicago, Ill.; RH; 2HB; 5ft 6in; 125lb; final 1990 WTA ranking 60; 1990 prize money $74,377.
Husband Paul Daniels (married 19 Oct. 1987). Coached by her father, Joseph. *1979:* Ranked 1 in US 18s, she won Wimbledon and Italian Jun titles and was r/u at US and French Open Jun. *1980:* (23) Turned pro after an impressive season for Trinity Univ in Texas. R/u Richmond. *1981:* (17) Won Richmond. *1982:* (37) Sf French Open doubles with Walsh. *1983:* (64) Sf Washington. *1984:* (60). *1985:* (61) Qf VS Denver. *1986:* (98). *1987:* (90). *1988:* (83) Qf VS Dallas. *1989:* (116). *1990:* In singles reached qf Wichita and VS Houston; in doubles won VS Oklahoma with W. White. *1990 HIGHLIGHTS – SINGLES: Wimbledon* 1r (lost Grossman 6–2 6–1), *US Open* 1r (lost Wiesner [seed 15] 6–3 6–1). *1990 HIGHLIGHTS – DOUBLES:* (with W. White) *won* VS Oklahoma (d. Bollegraf/Gregory 7–5 6–2); *r/u* Wichita (lost Bollegraf/McGrath 6–0 6–2).

KIMIKO DATE (Japan)
Born Kyoto, 28 September 1970; lives Amagasaki City; RH; 5ft 4in; 113lb; final 1990 WTA ranking 78; 1990 prize money $40,388.
Coached by Takeshi Koura. Although she plays right-handed, she writes and eats left-

handed. *1988:* (321) Won 2 titles on Japanese satellite circuit. *1989:* (120) Qf Tokyo Suntory and Birmingham; won 3 titles on British satellite circuit in May, and played Fed Cup. *1990:* Upset Fairbank Nideffer at Brisbane and then surprised Shriver at Australian Open to become the 1st Japanese woman since 1973 to reach last 16 there, a performance which took her into the top 100. Appeared in qf Tokyo Suntory again. *1990 HIGHLIGHTS – SINGLES: Australian Open* last 16, unseeded (d. Etchemendy 6–3 7–6, Schultz 7–5 7–6, Shriver [seed 11] 6–3 6–4, lost Sukova [seed 4] 6–4 6–3), *Wimbledon* 2r (d. Stafford 7–6 6–3, lost K. Maleeva [seed 7] 6–1 6–4, *US Open* 2r (d. Cammy MacGregor 6–0 6–3, lost Wiesner [seed 15] 7–6 6–1).

FRANCO DAVIN (Argentina)
Born Buenos Aires, 11 January 1970 and lives there; LH; 5ft 8in; 140lb; final 1990 ATP ranking 35; 1990 prize money $197,673.
Coached by Raul Perez Roldan. *1985:* (508). *1986:* (111) R/u Buenos Aires. *1987:* (166) Qf Bari and Bologna. *1988:* (94) Qf St Vincent and won Marrakech Challenger. *1989:* (73) Won St Vincent, r/u Bologna, sf Athens and Prague. *1990:* Won Palermo (d. Aguilera), r/u Estoril (d. Aguilera again) and Athens; sf Bologna. *1990 HIGHLIGHTS – SINGLES: French Open* 3r (d. Maciel 6–2 6–1 6–2, Mancini 6–3 5–7 7–5 6–1, lost Leconte 6–3 7–6 6–4), *US Open* 3r (d. Rive 6–4 6–4 7–6, Layendecker 6–7 6–3 6–2 6–4, lost Agassi [seed 4] 7–5 6–4 6–0); *won* Palermo (d. de Minicis 6–4 6–1, Cane 6–3 6–4, Strelba 6–2 6–4, Champion 6–1 4–6 7–5, Aguilera 6–1 6–1); *r/u* Estoril (d. Ozer 6–1 6–4, Bruguera 7–5 6–4, Haarhuis 6–4 7–5, Aguilera 6–4 6–3, lost E. Sanchez 6–3 6–1), *r/u* Athens (d. Furlan 6–3 6–1, Luna 7–5 6–3, Perez Roldan 6–2 6–1, Vajda 7–6 2–6 6–3, lost Koevermans 5–7 6–4 6–4)); *sf* Bologna (d. Nargiso 6–4 6–4, Camporese 1–6 7–6 7–6, Witsken 6–4 6–0, lost Rosset 6–2 6–4).

SCOTT DAVIS (USA)
Born Santa Monica, Cal., 27 August 1962; lives Largo, Fla.; RH; 6ft 2in; 170lb; final 1990 ATP ranking 44 singles, 8 doubles; 1990 prize money $422,390.
1977–80: No. 1 US Jun in his age group. *1980:* (457) Broke Dick Stockton's previous record of 20 US Nat Jun titles, concluding jun career with 24. *1983:* (24) Graduated from Stanford, turned pro, won Maui (first GP title), r/u Seiko Tokyo (d. Leconte, Gomez, Connors, lost Lendl 6–4 fs), Newport and Taipei. Won Columbus doubles with Teacher. *1984:* (48) Married Suzy Jaeger (sister of Andrea). Reached last 16 Wimbledon, extending Lendl to 7–5 in 5s, and qf Australian Open. *1985:* (17) Finalist LIPC and sf at US Pro Indoor and Chicago; won Japan Open and qualified for Masters first time. Won doubles at Stratton Mountain, Japan Open (with Pate) and LA (with Van't Hof). *1986:* (39) An off year in which injuries and bad draws contributed to his woes. Began working with Australian Bob Brett in autumn in effort to build up stamina and confidence and finished on a high note as r/u WCT Houston. *1987:* (59) Beat Mecir and Connors to reach sf Tokyo. Continued to work with Bob Brett until end of year. *1988:* (111) Qf Tel Aviv and won Cherbourg Challenger. *1989:* (70) R/u Schenectady and sf Los Angeles. In doubles won 3 titles with different partners. *1990:* Started the year by winning Auckland for his 1st singles title since 1985, then upset Chesnokov for a 2nd time and J. McEnroe *en route* to sf Cincinnati. In doubles with Pate won 5 titles to qualify for IBM/ATP World Doubles. *1990 HIGHLIGHTS – SINGLES: Australian Open* 2r (d. Morgan 6–2 6–2 6–2, lost Becker [seed 2] 6–3 7–6 4–6 6–2), *French Open* 1r (lost Novacek 6–3 6–2 6–2), *Wimbledon* 1r (lost Rosset 7–6 7–5 6–3), *US Open* 2r (d. Evernden 7–5 6–1 6–3, lost Carbonell 6–4 6–4 6–2); *won* Auckland (d. Bergstrom 1–6 6–4 6–2, Goldie 6–1 6–7 6–2, Guy 6–2 7–6, Krishnan 5–7 6–3 6–4, Chesnokov 4–6 6–3 6–3); *sf* Cincinnati (d. Muller 2–6 6–1 6–1, Chesnokov 6–3 6–2, J. McEnroe 6–3 7–6, Fromberg 4–6 6–4 7–6, lost Gilbert 6–3 6–4). *1990 HIGHLIGHTS – DOUBLES:* (with Pate) *won* Orlando (d. Mora/Page 6–3 7–6), *won* US CC (d. Grabb/Lavalle 6–2 6–3), *won* Los Angeles (d. Lundgren/Wekesa 3–6 6–1 6–3), *won* Indianapolis (d. Connell/Michibata 7–6 7–6), *won* Paris Open (d. Cahill/Kratzmann 5–7 6–3 6–4); *r/u* Tokyo Seiko (lost Forget/Hlasek 7–6 7–5)

HORACIO de la PENA (Argentina)
Born Buenos Aires, 1 August 1966, and lives there; LH; 5ft 11in; 138lb; final 1990 ATP ranking 63; 1990 prize money $149,936.
Has twin sister, Nuria. Coached by Roy Emerson whose daughter Heidi, he married 8 March 1990. *1984;* (90) Won two satellite events, beginning to fulfil promise he had

exhibited in sweeping Nat 12, 14, 16 and 18 jun crowns. *1985:* (70) Joined Argentine D Cup team. Won GP Marbella and reached sf Buenos Aires. *1986:* (38) Producing superior CC results, he reached last 16 at French Open, was r/u at Bari, and reached sf Boston (d. Tulasne). *1987:* (88) Sf Bari, qf Buenos Aires and stunned McEnroe 1r French Open. *1988:* (52) R/u Sao Paulo, sf Rye Brook, Geneva and Boston, where he upset Wilander in ss. *1989:* As a qualifier he won Florence for his 1st title since 1985 but thereafter suffered bouts of patellar tendonitis and bursitis. *1990:* Returning from injury, he was obliged to play qualifying in the early tourns. Won Kitzbuhel in Aug, upsetting Gilbert and E. Sanchez, and reached sf Umag and Prague. *1990 HIGHLIGHTS – SINGLES: Australian Open* 1r (lost Wahlgen 6–3 6–1 6–3); *won* Kitzbuhel (d. Maciel 6–2 2–6 6–1, Gilbert 6–2 6–4, Strelba 6–2 6–1, Bruguera 6–4 6–1, E. Sanchez 7–5 7–6, Novacek 6–4 7–6 2–6 6–2); *sf* Umag)d. Bengoechea 5–7 6–2 6–0, Koevermans 7–6 6–3, Rahunen 5–7 7–6 6–1, lost Prpic 7–6 7–6), *sf* Prague (d. Larsson 6–0 6–2; Pescosolido 6–3 6–1, Benhabiles 6–2 7–6, lost Kulti 6–3 1–0 ret'd). *1990 HIGHLIGHTS – DOUBLES:* [Bruguera] *won* Florence (d. Mattar/ Perez 3–6 6–3 6–4); [Costa] *r/u* Palermo (lost Casal/E. Sanchez 6–3 6–4).

ALEXIA DECHAUME (France)
Born La Rochelle, 3 May 1970; lives Bologne; 5ft 4½in; 124lb; RH; 2HB; final 1990 WTA ranking 84; 1990 prize money $59,872.
Coached by Patrick Favière. *1986:* (225). *1987:* (127) Qf Athens. *1988:* (127) Qf Taranto and won Bayonne on French satellite circuit, breaking into top 100 in June. In doubles with Derly won Paris Open, French Open Jun and r/u Wimbledon Jun. *1989:* (173). *1990:* Reached her first primary circuit f at Taranto and broke into the top 100 in Sept. *1990 HIGHLIGHTS – SINGLES: Australian Open* 2r (d. Kschwendt 6–4 7–5, lost Gavaldon 6–4 4–6 7–5), *French Open* 1r (lost Cohen 6–4 7–6), *Wimbledon* 3r (d. Sawamatsu 7–5 2–6 6–3, Provis 3–6 6–3 6–2, lost Sukova [seed 10] 6–4 6–3), *US Open* 2r (d. Bonsignori 6–2 6–1, lost Reinach 6–3 6–0); *r/u* Taranto (d. Thoren 6–4 6–2, La Fratta 4–6 7–6 6–4, Golarsa 7–6 6–2, Ritter 6–2 6–3, lost Reggi 3–6 6–0 6–2). *1990 HIGHLIGHTS – DOUBLES:* (with Herreman) *r/u* Clarins (lost Godridge/Sharpe 4–6 6–3 6–1).

ISABELLE DEMONGEOT (France)
Born Gassin, 18 September 1966; lives St Tropez; RH; 5ft 7in; 134lb; final 1990 WTA ranking 77; 1990 prize money $73,155.
Coached by Regis DeCamaret. *1983:* (245) No. 1 player on Israeli satellite circuit. *1984:* (165) No. 15 in ITF World Jun rankings. R/u French Nat. *1985:* (135) Won Chicago on USTA satellite circuit and reached sf Hilversum. *1986:* (64) Reached last 16 Wimbledon and qf Mahwah. *1987:* (54) Played Fed Cup; qf San Francisco and San Diego. *1988:* (44) Sf Geneva (d. M. Maleeva) and Nice. In doubles with Tauziat won Berlin and Zurich and qualified for VS Champs. *1989:* (46) Upset Manuela Maleeva Fragnière to reach qf LIPC and in doubles with Tauziat won Hamburg. *1990:* Qf Indian Wells and Barcelona. *1990 HIGHLIGHTS – SINGLES: Australian Open* 3r (d. Adams 4–6 6–2 6–3, Kidowaki 6–4 6–1, lost Garrison [seed 3] 5–7 6–3 6–4), *French Open* 1r (lost Novotna [seed 11] 6–0 6–7 10–8), *Wimbledon* 1r (lost Frazier 6–1 6–4), *US Open* 2r (d. Collins 6–3 6–3, lost Sabatini [seed 5] 6–1 6–1).

RUXANDRA DRAGOMIR (Rumania)
Born 24 October 1972.
1990: Won French Open Jun doubles with Spirlea.

JO DURIE (Great Britain)
Born Bristol, 27 July 1960; lives London; RH; 6ft; 150lb; final 1990 WTA ranking 64; 1990 prize money $87,984.
Coached by Alan Jones. *1978:* Top-ranked British jun. *1979:* (73) Sf Wimbledon Plate. *1980:* (53) Out of action 8 months following back surgery. Sf German Indoor Open. *1981:* (31) Last 16 US Open; won British HC. *1982:* (28) No. 1 in Great Britain, taking over from Wade. *1983:* (6) Best year of career when she reached sf US and French Opens, qf Australian Open, and won Sydney and Mahwah. *1984:* (24). *1985:* (26) Sf Brighton (d. Graf). *1986:* (23) Played 17 tournaments and W and Fed Cups, winning 24 of 44 matches, beating McNeil, Lindqvist and K. Jordan, but best showing was sf Mahwah in summer. *1987:* (73) In W Cup ended 23-match winning streak by US when she d. Garrison, and won Wimbledon mixed doubles with Bates, but otherwise suffered a poor year. *1988:* (61) Qf

San Diego and California Open. Missed Fed Cup with shoulder injury. *1989:* Sf Auckland. A back injury forced her to withdraw from Wimbledon. *1990:* An appearance in f VS Newport was her best showing since Brighton 1983. *1990 HIGHLIGHTS – SINGLES: Australian Open* 2r (d. Paradis 6–3 7–6, lost Reggi [seed 13] 6–4 6–4), *Wimbledon* 1r (lost A. Huber 7–5 4–6 6–2), *US Open* 1r (lost Sukova [seed 11] 1–6 7–6 7–6); *r/u* Newport (d. Baranski 6–0 6–1, Leand 7–6 6–0, Fairbank Nideffer 7–5 6–0, A. Smith 6–4 6–1, lost Sanchez-Vicario 7–6 4–6 7–5). *1990 HIGHLIGHTS – DOUBLES:* [Hetherington] *won* Singapore (d. Paradis/Suire 6–4 6–1); [Bollegraf] *r/u* Leipzig (lost Gregory/Magers 6–2 4–6 6–3), [Zvereva] *r/u* Brighton (lost Sukova/Tauziat 6–1 6–4). *CAREER HIGHLIGHTS – SINGLES: US Open – sf 1983* (d. Madruga Osses 6–2 6–2, lost Evert Lloyd 6–4 6–4); *French Open – sf 1983* (d. Moulton, Shriver, Rinaldi, Austin 6–0 fs, lost Jausovec 6–2 fs); *Australian Open – qf 1983* (lost Navratilova 4–6 6–3 6–4). *CAREER HIGHLIGHTS – DOUBLES:* (with Hobbs unless stated) *Wimbledon – sf 1983* (lost Navratilova/Shriver 6–3 7–5), [Evert Lloyd] *qf 1985* (d. Bunge/Pfaff, lost Navratilova/Shriver [seed 1] 6–4 6–2); *French Open – sf 1983* (lost Fairbank/Reynolds 6–3 6–2); *Australian Open – sf 1985* (lost Navratilova/Shriver 7–6 6–2). *MIXED DOUBLES:* (with Bates) *Wimbledon – won 1987* (d. Cahill/Provis 7–6 6–3).

STEFAN EDBERG (Sweden)
Born Vastervik, 19 January 1966; lives there, London and Mougins, France; RH; 6ft 2in; 170lb; final 1990 ATP ranking 1; 1990 prize money $2,095,901; career prize money $8,733,696.
Coached by Tony Pickard. Girlfriend Annette Olssen. *1983:* (53) Won jun Grand Slam, proving prowess on 3 different surfaces, and played 11 events on men's tour. *1984:* (20) Won Milan and contributed crucial triumph in D Cup f as Sweden d. USA with doubles win alongside Jarryd over McEnroe/Fleming, repeating their success over that duo at US Open, where they were r/u. *1985:* (5) Reached top 5 with first GS men's success, upending Lendl and Wilander for Australian Open title. Also won San Francisco, Basle and Memphis. *1986:* (5) Won Gstaad, Basle and Stockholm, lost four other finals (two to Becker, one to McEnroe, one to Gilbert) and reached sf US Open. In doubles with Jarryd won Masters and r/u French Open. *1987:* (2) Won 2nd Australian singles title, sf Wimbledon and US Open, won titles in Memphis, Rotterdam, Tokyo (2), Cincinnati and Stockholm, reached 4 more f and achieved win-loss singles record of 70–11 going into Masters, where he reached sf. In doubles with Jarryd won Australian and US Opens, and reached sf Masters. *1988:* (5) Won Wimbledon over Becker, sf Australian Open and last 16 French and US Opens. Won Rotterdam and Basel, reached 4 other f and took Olympic bronze medal. Played virtually no doubles and was restricted at Masters by tendonitis in left knee, falling to Lendl in sf. *1989:* (3) Finished the year in triumph with his 1st Masters title, beating Lendl in sf and Becker in f. R/u French Open and Wimbledon, but fell last 16 US Open to Connors and withdrew qf Australian Open with back injury which kept him out for 5 weeks. His only other title came at Tokyo Suntory, but he reached f Scottsdale, Cincinnati, Basle and Paris Open. *1990:* Won a 2nd Wimbledon title and on 13 Aug took over No. 1 ranking for 1st time from Lendl, holding off a strong late challenge from Becker to finish the year in that position. He was forced to retire during f Australian Open with stomach muscle injury, suffered during sf match, which kept him out for 4 weeks. He was without his coach, Pickard, who was recovering from a hip operation, from end Australian Open to beginning French, where, as top seed, he lost 1r to Bruguera, suffering similarly at the hands of Volkov at the same stage US Open. Altogether in 1990 won 7 titles and reached 5 other finals including ATP World Champ, where he lost to Agassi, having beaten him in rr. Fined 15% of total earnings on ATP tour (excluding GS) for falling 2 tourns short of commitment to the tour. Seeded No. 1 GS Cup but lost 1r Chang 6–4 4–6 7–5. *1990 HIGHLIGHTS – SINGLES: r/u Australian Open*, seed 3 (d. Anderson 7–6 6–3 6–4, Kuhnen 6–2 6–2 6–4, Chamberlin 6–3 6–4 6–1, Svensson 6–2 6–2 6–4, Wheaton 7–5 7–6 3–6 6–2, Wilander 6–1 6–1 6 2, lost Lendl [seed 1] 4–6 7–6 5–2 ret'd), *French Open* 1r, seed 1 (lost Brugera 6–4 6–2 6–1), *won Wimbledon* seed 3 (d. Dyke 4–6 6–1 6–3 6–1, Mecir 6–2 6–3 6–2, Mansdorf 6–4 5–7 3–6 6–2 9–7, Chang [seed 13] 6–3 6–2 6–1, Bergstrom 6–3 6–2 6–4, Lendl [seed 1] 6–1 7–6 6–3, Becker [seed 2] 6–2 6–2 3–6 3–6 6–4), *US Open* 1r, seed 1 (lost Volkov 6–3 7–6 6–2); *won* Indian Wells (d. S. Davis 6–3 6–2, Bruguera 6–0 6–3, Gunnarsson 6–2 6–2, Courier 6–4 6–1, Agassi 6–4 5–7 7–6 7–6), *won* Tokyo Suntory (d. Shiras 6–0 6–2, Antonitsch 6–2 6–7 6–1, Grabb 6–3 6–3, Gilbert 6–1 7–6,

Krickstein 6–4 7–5), **won** Los Angeles (d. Washington 6–2 6–4, Matsuoka 7–5 6–4, Tarango 6–4 6–4, Sampras 6–2 6–7 6–1, Chang 7–6 2–6 7–6), **won** Cincinnati (d. Srejber 6–4 6–7 6–4, Sznajder 6–1 6–0, Chang 3–6 6–3 6–4, Gomez 7–5 6–3, Gilbert 6–1 6–1), **won** Long Island (d. Wheaton 3–6 6–1 6–2, Svensson 6–4 6–2, J. McEnroe 6–1 6–4, Ivanisevic 7–6 6–3), **won** Paris Open (d. Cherkasov 6–2 6–3, Krickstein 6–3 6–2, Hlasek 6–3 6–4, Bruguera 6–3 6–3, Becker 3–3 ret'd); **r/u** LIPC (d. Smith 6–2 2–6 6–4, Mansdorf 6–2 6–1, Steeb 6–2 4–6 6–3, Hlasek 6–7 7–6 7–6, E. Sanchez 6–1 7–5, lost Agassi 6–1 6–4 0–6 6–2), **r/u** Sydney Indoor (d. Kroon 6–3 6–2, Kratzmann 6–2 7–6, Wheaton 6–2 7–6, Lendl 6–2 7–6, lost Becker 7–6 6–4 6–4), **r/u** Stockholm (d. Wilander 6–4 6–3, Rosset 6–4 6–4, Gilbert 6–4 3–6 6–1, Volkov 7–6 6–2, lost Becker 6–4 6–0 6–3), **r/u** ATP World Champ (d. E. Sanchez, Agassi, Sampras in rr, Lendl 6–4 6–2 in sf, lost Agassi 5–7 7–6 7–5 6–2 in f); **sf** Queen's (d. Zoecke 6–0 6–3, Kroon 6–3 6–0, Van Rensburg 7–5 6–3, lost Becker 6–4 6–4), **sf** Tokyo Seiko (d. Woodbridge 6–3 6–1, Cahill 6–4 6–2, Hlasek 6–4 3–6 7–6, lost Lendl 7–5 6–3). **1990 HIGHLIGHTS – DOUBLES:** [Lendl] **r/u** Sydney Indoor (lost Dyke/Lundgren 6–2 6–4). **CAREER HIGHLIGHTS – SINGLES: Australian Open – won 1985** (d. Masur 6–7 2–6 7–6 6–4 6–2 [saving 2 mps], Schapers, Lendl 6–7 7–5 6–1 4–6 9–7, Wilander 6–4 6–3 6–3), **won 1987** (d. Mecir 6–1 6–4 6–4, Masur 6–2 6–4 7–6, Cash 6–3 6–4 3–6 5–7 6–3), **r/u 1990, sf 1988** (d. Chesnokov 4–6 7–6 6–4 6–4, lost Wilander 6–0 6–7 6–3 3–6 6–1); **Wimbledon – won 1988** (d. Forget, Reneberg, K. Flach, Youl 6–2 6–4 6–4, Kuhnen 6–3 4–6 6–1 7–6, Mecir 4–6 2–6 6–4 6–3 6–4, Becker 4–6 7–6 6–4 6–2), **won 1990, r/u 1989** (d. Pridham, Woodbridge 6–4 6–4 1–6 7–6, S. Davis 6–3 6–4 4–6 6–2, Mansdorf 6–4 6–3 6–2, Mayotte 7–6 7–6 6–3, J. McEnroe 7–5 7–6 7–6, lost Becker 6–0 7–6 6–4). **sf 1987** (lost Lendl 3–6 6–4 7–6 6–4); **Masters – won 1989** (d. Agassi, Gilbert, Becker in rr, Lendl 7–6 7–5, Becker 4–6 7–6 6–3 6–1); **ATP World Champ – r/u 1990; French Open – r/u 1989** (d. Vajda, Pereira, Arias 6–4 6–4 6–4, Ivanisevic 7–5 6–3 6–3, Mancini 6–1 6–3 7–6, Becker 6–3 6–4 5–7 3–6 6–2, lost Chang 6–1 3–6 4–6 6–4 6–2); **US Open – sf 1986** (d. Curren, Krishnan, Goldie, Wilkison 6–3 6–3 6–3, lost Lendl 7–6 6–2 6–3), **sf 1987** (lost Wilander 6–4 3–6 6–3 6–4); **LIPC – r/u 1990; Olympics – bronze medal 1988** (d. Skoff, Moreno, Hlasek 6–2 6–4 7–6, Cane 6–1 7–5 6–4, lost Mecir 3–6 6–0 1–6 6–4 6–2). **CAREER HIGHLIGHTS – DOUBLES:** (with Jarryd) **US Open – won 1987** (d. Flach/Seguso 7–6 6–2 4–6 5–7 7–6), **r/u 1984** (d. McEnroe/Fleming 3–6 7–6 5–7 7–6, lost Fitzgerald/Smid 7–6 6–3 6–3); **Australian Open – won 1987** (d. Doohan/Warder 6–4 6–4 7–6); **Masters – won 1985** (d. Wilander/Nystrom 4–6 6–2 6–3), **won 1986** (d. Forget/Noah 6–3 7–6 6–3); **French Open – r/u 1986** (lost Fitzgerald/Smid 6–3 4–6 6–3 6–7 14–12).

TOMAS ENQVIST (Sweden)
Born 13 March, 1974.
1990: R/u French Open Jun (lost Gaudenzi 2–6 7–6 6–4).

KELLY EVERNDEN (New Zealand)
Born Gisborne, 21 September 1961; lives Naples, Fla.; RH; 5ft 9in; 155lb; final 1990 ATP ranking 97; 1990 prize money $155,598.
Coached by Jeff Simpson. Has only a left lung following a serious motor accident when he was 16. While at Univ. of Arkansas where he was All American (1984), started rock and roll band 'Out of Bounds' at Fayetteville, Ark. Turned pro 1985. **1983:** (527). **1984:** (255). **1985:** (86) R/u Brisbane and Sydney. Joined New Zealand D Cup squad. **1986:** (289). **1987:** (36) Began the year well by reaching qf Australian Open, unseeded; won his 1st GP title at Bristol following with Brisbane singles and doubles in Oct. **1988:** (119) Sf Wellington and Detroit in singles and qualified for Masters doubles with Kriek. **1989:** (38) Won Wellington r/u Vienna, sf Seoul and San Francisco (d. Chang). Underwent eye surgery in summer. **1990:** R/u Schenectady; qf Singapore, Manchester and Indianapolis. **1990 HIGHLIGHTS – SINGLES: Australian Open** 1r (lost Borwick 6–3 6–1 6–1), **Wimbledon** 1r (lost Rahunen 3–6 4–6 6–1 7–6 6–3), **US Open** 1r (lost S. Davis 7–5 6–1 6–3); **r/u** Schenectady (d. Goldberg 6–4 4–6 6–2, Bates 5–7 7–6 7–6, Mansdorf 7–5 7–6, Pearce 6–2 3–6 6–4, lost Krishnan 6–1 6–1). **1990 HIGHLIGHTS – DOUBLES:** (with Pereira) **won** Wellington (d. Casal/E. Sanchez 6–4 7–6).

ROSALYN FAIRBANK NIDEFFER (USA)
Born Durban, South Africa, 2 November 1960; lives San Diego, Cal.; RH; 5ft 8in; 140lb; final 1990 WTA ranking 24; 1990 prize money $163,582; career prize money $1,230,295.

Married her coach, sports psychologist Rod Nideffer, 6 May 1989 and became a US citizen. *1978:* Seemingly shy and somewhat portly, she displayed extraordinary court sense and a fine flat forehand in her drive to f Orange Bowl, losing to A. Jaeger. *1979:* Established herself firmly on women's tour, winning 22 of 23 matches on Australian satellite tour and reaching f NSW Open. *1980:* (33) Won Wimbledon Plate. *1981:* (43) Won French Open doubles with Hartford. *1982:* (17) Won Indianapolis, sf Detroit and Fort Myers. *1983:* (26) Won Richmond. *1984:* (32) Sf VS LA. *1985:* (38) Beat Rehe in San Diego. *1986:* (30) Sf Canadian Open (d. Sabatini) and Brighton, r/u French Open mixed doubles with Edmondson, and sf Wimbledon and US Open doubles with Burgin. *1987:* (37) Reached last 16 Wimbledon, extending Evert to 7–5 fs. *1988:* (37) Reached qf Wimbledon, upsetting McNeil and Zvereva and extending Navratilova to 7–5 3s; sf San Diego and Newport. *1989:* (22) Unseeded, she reached qf Wimbledon again (upset Sabatini and M-J. Fernandez) and last 16 US Open. Sf Eastbourne and Newport in singles and in doubles reached 6 f, winning San Diego. *1990:* Surprised Novotna *en route* to sf San Antonio and G. Fernandez in reaching the same stage at Birmingham. *1990 HIGHLIGHTS – SINGLES: Australian Open* 3r, seed 14 (d. Benjamin 6–3 6–3, Bakkum 7–6 6–4, lost Faber 6–3 6–4), *French Open* 1r (lost Simpson 6–1 6–2), *Wimbledon* 2r, seed 15 (d. Baranski 6–2 3–6 6–2, lost Frazier 6–4 6–3), *US Open* 2r (d. Langrova 3–6 6–1 6–2, lost Seles [seed 3] 6–2 6–2; *sf* San Antonio (d. R. White 6–1 6–2, Novotna 6–1 2–6 7–5, lost Seles 6–4 6–3), *sf* Birmingham (d. Salmon 6–1 6–3, Nagelsen 6–3 6–3, G. Fernandez 4–6 6–2 7–5, lost Sukova 2–6 6–4 7–5). *1990 HIGHLIGHTS – DOUBLES:* [Burgin] *r/u* San Diego (lost Fendick/Garrison 6–4 7–6), [R. White] *r/u* VS California (lost McGrath/A. Smith 2–6 6–0 6–4). *CAREER HIGHLIGHTS – DOUBLES:* (with Harford unless stated) *French Open – won 1981* (d. K. Jordan/A. Smith, Reynolds/P. Smith 6–1 6–3), [Reynolds] *won 1983* (d. Durie/Hobbs, K. Jordan/A. Smith 5–7 7–5 6–2); *US Open –* [Reynolds] *r/u 1983* (d. Burgin/Russell 7–5 fs, King/Walsh 7–5 fs, lost Navratilova/Shriver 6–7 6–1 6–3). *MIXED DOUBLES:* (with Edmondson) *French Open – r/u 1986* (lost Flach/K. Jordan 3–6 7–6 6–3).

PATTY FENDICK (USA)
Born Sacramento, Cal., 31 March 1965, and lives there; RH: 5ft 5in; 117lb; final 1990 WTA ranking 42 singles, 11 (15) doubles; 1990 prize money $160,713.
Scar tissue in her eye from an old injury expands and restricts her vision in brightness, obliging her to wear a baseball cap to play tennis. *1983:* Won Wimbledon Jun doubles with Hy, and Orange Bowl 18s singles and doubles. *1984:* Member US Jun Fed Cup team. All-American for Stanford, playing No. 1 on that team. *1985:* (83). *1986:* (94) Sf Wimbledon doubles with Hetherington and won NCAA singles. *1987:* (78) NCAA Champ for second time. While out of action at end of year with intestinal flu, she worked on the mental aspect of her game with John Whittlinger. *1988:* (22) Won her 1st pro title in Auckland, following with Japan Open, and reached sf on 5 other occasions. Last 16 US Open singles, and r/u in doubles with Hetherington, with whom she won 5 of 6 titles during the year and qualified for VS Champs. *1989:* (31) Out 3 months March–June with shoulder injury, returning to reach last 16 Wimbledon. Won Auckland in both singles and doubles with Hetherington, with whom she was r/u Australian Open and won VS California. *1990:* In singles she upset Novotna and Paulus to reach qf Australian Open and, again unseeded, appeared in last 16 Wimbledon. In doubles was r/u Australian Open with M-J. Fernandez, but was less fortunate at US Open, where both her women's and mixed partners withdrew. With various partners she reached 4 other doubles f, winning 2. Played in winning US Fed Cup team. *1990 HIGHLIGHTS – SINGLES: Australian Open* qf, unseeded (d. Nishiya 6–1 6–3, Keller 7–5 6–2, Novotna [seed 5] 1–6 7–6 6–4, Paulus [seed 16] 7–5 6–2, lost Graf [seed 1] 6–3 7–5), *Wimbledon* last 16, unseeded (d. Hu Na 7–5 7–5, Sloane 6–2 6–4, Gavaldon 6–1 6–1, lost Novotna 6–2 6–4), *US Open* 3r (d. Kidowaki 6–7 6–4 7–5, Zrubakova 6–2 6–3, lost Sanchez-Vicario [seed 6] 6–2 6–1. *1990 HIGHLIGHTS – DOUBLES:* (with Garrison unless stated) [M-J. Fernandez] *r/u Australian Open* (lost Novotna/Sukova 7–6 7–6); *won* San Diego (d. Burgin/Fairbank Nideffer 6–4 7–6); *r/u* Eastbourne (lost Savchenko/Zvereva 6–4 6–3), [A. Smith] *r/u* VS Newport (lost Gregory/Magers 7–6 6–1), [McGrath] *won* Indianapolis (d. Adams/Hetherington 6–1 6–1). *CAREER HIGHLIGHTS DOUBLES:* (with Hetherington unless stated) *Australian Open – r/u 1989* (lost Navratilova/Shriver 3–6 6–3 6–2), [M-J. Fernandez] *r/u 1990*; *US Open – r/u 1988* (lost G. Fernandez/R. White 6–4 6–1).

GIGI FERNANDEZ (USA)

Born Puerto Rico, 22 February 1964; lives Miami, Fla and Aspen, Col.; 5ft 7in; 145lb; final 1990 WTA ranking 36 singles, 3(7) doubles; 1990 prize money $231,500.
Coached by Julie Anthony. **1983:** (84) Narrowly beaten 7–6 fs by Herr in f AIAW. **1984:** (27) Buoyed by praise she received from Navratilova after coming within two points of upsetting Shriver at Wimbledon, she reached f Newport as 'Lucky Loser' and pushed Navratilova to 2s tb. **1985:** (64) Won LIPC doubles with Navratilova. **1986:** (62) Qualified with R. White for VS Champ doubles in Nov. **1987:** (39) Reached last 16 Wimbledon unseeded, qf VS Florida and San Diego and won 3 doubles titles with McNeil. **1988:** (52) In doubles won US Open and Japan Open with R. White, reaching 7 other f with various partners and qualifying for VS Champs. **1989:** (23) R/u Puerto Rico, sf Eastbourne and Newport in singles; in doubles with various partners reached 8 f, winning 4. **1990:** In singles appeared in last 16 US Open plus sf Puerto Rico and qf Tokyo, San Antonio and Birmingham. In doubles won US Open with Navratilova and with various partners took 4 other titles, reaching 3 more f. Played in winning US Fed Cup team. **1990 HIGHLIGHTS – SINGLES: Australian Open** last 16, seed 15 (d. Quentrec 6–3 6–4, Pospisilova 6–4 7–6, Whitlinger 7–6 6–3, lost Gavaldon 6–3 1–6 6–2), Wimbledon 2r (d. Labat 6–2 6–2, lost Zvereva [seed 11] 7–6 6–4), **US Open** 1r (lost Garrone 6–4 7–6); **sf** Puerto Rico (d. Bowes 7–6 6–3, Provis 6–4 7–6, Keller 6–1 4–6 6–4, lost Capriati 6–2 6–1). **1990 HIGHLIGHTS – DOUBLES:** (with Navratilova unless stated) **won US Open** (d. Novotna/Sukova 6–2 6–4); [Smylie] **won** Tokyo Toray (d. Faul/McQuillan 6–2 6–2), **won** Hamburg (d. Savchenko/Sukova 6–2 6–3), [Novotna] **won** VS Los Angeles (d. Kelesi/Reggi 6–3 4–6 6–4). [Sukova] **won** VS New England (d. M-J. Fernandez/Novotna 6–4 7–6); **r/u** Indian Wells (lost Novotna/Sukova 6–2 7–6), [R. White] **r/u** San Antonio (lost K. Jordan/Smylie 7–5 7–5), **r/u** Tokyo Nicherei (lost M-J. Fernandez/R. White 4–6 6–3 7–6). **CAREER HIGHLIGHTS – DOUBLES: US Open** – [R. White] **won 1988** (d. Fendick/Hetherington 6–4 6–1), [M. Navratilova] **won 1990**.

MARY-JOE FERNANDEZ (USA)

Born Dominican Republic, 19 August 1971; lives Miami, Fla.; RH; 2HB; 5ft 10in; 130lb; final 1990 WTA ranking 4 singles, 6(8) doubles; 1990 prize money $518,366.
Original coach Fred Stolle. Now advised by Tim Gullikson who is paid by USTA. **1982:** Won Orange Bowl 12s, beating Sabatini in f. **1983:** Won Orange Bowl 14s, beating Sabatini in sf. **1984:** Won Orange Bowl 16s, US Nat 16, US 16 CC and was ranked 1 in US 16s. **1985:** (99) Won Orange Bowl 18s, ranked second behind Rehe in US 18s. **1986:** (27) Demonstrating her uncanny court sense, her excellent anticipation, her extraordinary determination and formidable flat forehand and two-handed backhand, she stopped 4th-seeded Kohde-Kilsch to reach qf French Open; had other good CC wins over Rehe and Sabatini during year. **1987:** (20) Reached last 16 Wimbledon, qf Geneva and Filderstadt. **1988:** (15) Last 16 Wimbledon and upset Sabatini *en route* to sf both LIPC and Eastbourne. **1989:** (12) Upset Sabatini *en route* to sf French Open; r/u Filderstadt and sf Pan Pacific Open. In doubles r/u US Open with Shriver, and with various partners reached 4 other f, winning VS Dallas. Qualified for VS Champs for 1st time but lost 1r to Navratilova. **1990:** Her year began on a high note at Australian Open, where she was r/u to Graf in singles and r/u with Fendick in doubles. She continued to do well in GS, reaching qf French Open and sf US Open, having missed Wimbledon. In Sept, won her 1st career title at Tokyo Nicherei, following with Filderstadt in Oct. In other tourns she reached sf VS Florida, Barcelona, VS Los Angeles, VS New England and VS Champs to finish the year in the top 5, ahead of Sabatini. **1990 HIGHLIGHTS – SINGLES: r/u Australian Open** seed 6 (d. Jaggard 6–1 6–3, Rinaldi 6–4 6–4, Halard 6–0 3–6 6–3, Faber 6–4 6–2, Garrison [seed 3] 1–6 6–2 8–6, Porwik 6–2 6–1, lost Graf 6–3 6–4), **French Open** qf, seed 7 (d. McDonald 6–4 6–2, Pierce 6–4 6–4, Cueto 7–6 6–2, Grossman 6–3 6–2, lost Capriati 6–2 6–4), **US Open** sf, seed 8 (d. Henricksson 6–1 6–1, Oremans 6–4 6–1, R. White 6–1 6–2, Wiesner [seed 15] 6–3 6–2, Maleeva Fragnière [seed 9] 7–5 3–6 6–3, lost Sabatini [seed 5] 7–5 5–7 6–3); **won** Tokyo Nicherei (d. Tessi 6–3 6–1, Sukova 6–3 6–4, Maleeva Fragnière 4–6 7–5 6–4, Frazier 3–6 6–2 6–3), **won** Filderstadt (d. Tarabini 6–1 6–1, McQuillan 6–3 6–3, Appelmans 2–6 7–6 6–1, K. Maleeva 7–5 6–0, Paulus 6–3 6–4); **sf** VS Florida (d. Provis 6–2 4–6 7–6, Wiesner 6–4 6–1, Coetzer 6–0 6–1, lost Sabatini 4–4 ret'd), **sf** Barcelona (d. Varas 6–1 6–2, Golarsa 6–1 6–1, lost Cueto 7–5 4–6 6–4), **sf** VS Los Angeles (d. Toleafoa 6–2 6–2, Gildemeister 6–3 6–2, Rehe 7–5 6–2, lost Seles 6–1 6–0), **sf** VS New England (d. Labat 6–1 6–3, Frazier 6–3 6–4,

lost Sabatini 6–2 6–4), **sf** VS Champs (d. Tauziat 6–1 7–6, Maleeva Fragnière 6–2 6–4, lost Seles 6–3 6–4). **1990 HIGHLIGHTS – DOUBLES:** [Fendick] **r/u Australian Open** (lost Novotna/Sukova 7–6 7–6); [R. White] **won** Tokyo Nicherei (d. G. Fernandez/Navratilova 4–6 6–3 7–6), [Garrison] **won** Filderstadt (d. Paz/Sanchez-Vicario 7–5 6–3); [Novotna] **r/u** VS New England (lost G. Fernandez/Sukova 3–6 6–3 6–3). **CAREER HIGHLIGHTS – SINGLES: Australian Open – r/u 1990; French Open – sf 1989** (d. Herreman, Farley, Dias, Sabatini 6–4 6–4, Kelesi 6–2 7–5, lost Sanchez-Vicario [seed 7] 6–2 6–2), **qf 1986** (d. Temesvari, Hobbs, Kohde-Kilsch 7–6 7–5, lost Sukova 6 2 6–4), **qf 1990; US Open – sf 1990; VS Champs – sf 1990. CAREER HIGHLIGHTS – DOUBLES: Australian Open –** [Fendick] **r/u 1990;** [Shriver] **US Open – r/u 1989** (lost Mandlikova/Navratilova 5–7 6–4 6–4).

LINDA FERRANDO (Italy)
Born Genova, 12 January 1966, and lives there; RH; 5ft 7in; 127lb; final 1990 WTA ranking 67, 1990 prize money $88,049.
Coached by Maurizio Bonaiti. **1984:** (294). **1985:** (217) Qf Bastad. **1986:** (253). **1987:** (154). **1988:** (67) Sf Taranto. **1989:** (44) Sf Mahwah; qf Tampa and US HC, where she upset Zvereva. **1990:** Having never before passed 2s in GS, she upset Seles at US Open and advanced to last 16, unseeded. **1990 HIGHLIGHTS – SINGLES: French Open** 2r (d. Keller 3–6 6–0 6–4, lost Cohen 2–6 7–5 6–4), **Wimbledon** 1r (lost Sloane 1–6 7–6 6–3), **US Open** last 16, unseeded (d. Paz 6–4 2–6 7–6, Benjamin 7–6 6–2, Seles [seed 3] 1–6 6–1 7–6, lost Meskhi 7–6 6–1). **1990 HIGHLIGHTS – DOUBLES:** [Probst] **r/u** Schenectady (lost May/Miyagi 6–4 5–7 6–3).

MARCELO FILIPPINI (Uruguay)
Born Montevideo, 4 August 1967, and lives there; RH; 5ft 10in; 145lb; final 1990 ATP ranking 49; 1990 prize money $168,729.
1986: (415). **1987:** (118) Won Sao Paulo Challenger and reached qf there on GP circuit. **1988:** (53) Won 1st GP singles title at Bastad in July – the 1st time he had passed qf in a GP tourn – r/u Bari, sf St Vincent and Barcelona. **1989:** (43) Won Prague and reached 5 more qf, finishing the year with an upset of Hlasek at Itaparica. **1990:** R/u Itaparica; sf Bastad (upset Wilander) San Remo and San Marino. **1990 HIGHLIGHTS – SINGLES: French Open** 2r (d. Wahlgren 4–6 6–0 6–1 6–0, lost Gomez [seed 4] 7–6 6–2 6–1), **US Open** 1r (lost Limberger 6–3 7–5 6–4); **won** Salou Challenger (d. Arias 6–3 6–1); **r/u** Itaparica (d. Zdrazila 6–2 6–3, Yzaga 6–2 6–2, Marques 6–3 3–6 7–6, Carbonell 7–6 6–4, lost Wilander 6–1 6–2); **sf** Bastad (d. Orsear 6–3 6–2, Wilander 6–2 3–6 7–6, Rahunen 6–1 6–3, lost Larsson 6–4 6–1), **sf** San Remo (d. Champion 6–2 2–6 7–6, Benhabiles 2–6 6–4 7–5, Furlan 6–1 6–3, lost Arrese 6–2 6–3), **sf** San Marino (d. Cunha-Silva 6–7 6–3 6–0, Altur 6–2 7–5, Arraya 6–3 6–2, lost Perez Roldan 1–6 6–2 6–4). **1990 HIGHLIGHTS – DOUBLES:** (with Skoff) **r/u** Nice (lost Mancini/Noah 6–4 7–6).

JOHN FITZGERALD (Australia)
Born Cummins, 28 December 1960; lives Newport Beach, Cal.; RH; 6ft 1in; 170lb; final 1990 ATP ranking 188 singles, 42 doubles; 1990 prize money $117,274; career prize money $1,846,271.
Wife Jenny, daughters Elizabeth Jean (born July 1988) and Bridget (born Aug. 1990). **1979:** (301). **1980:** (136) Won $25,000 tourn in Tokyo. **1981:** (60) Last 16 Wimbledon and won Kitzbuhel over Vilas. **1982:** (78) Won Australian Open doubles with Alexander, and in singles won Hawaii and r/u Sydney. **1983:** (35) Last 16 Australian Open, where he won mixed doubles with Sayers, and won Newport and Stowe. Member of winning Australian D Cup team. **1984:** (29) Won Sydney NSW and r/u Melbourne; sf Australian Open doubles with Cash. **1985:** (91) In doubles won Auckland with C. Lewis, Las Vegas and Sydney Indoor with Jarryd, also reaching f Wimbledon (d. McEnroe/Fleming) and Queens Club, both with Cash. **1986:** (102) Won French Open doubles with Smid. In victorious Australian D Cup squad, winning doubles in f over Edberg/Jarryd with Cash. Married Jenny Harper 18 Nov. **1987:** (73) Underwent shoulder surgery in Feb. Reached 1st f in 3 years at Hong Kong and d. Connors 2r Tokyo Seiko. **1988:** (25) Finally free from his nagging shoulder injury, he enjoyed his best season, winning Sydney. *En route* to f Philadelphia, he upset Lendl, being the 1st player outside the top 50 to do so since F. Gonzalez in Aug. 1984. Beat Gomez and Edberg back-to-back to reach f Tokyo Seiko and appeared in sf Adelaide,

Wembley and Brussels. In doubles r/u French Open and Wimbledon with Jarryd, won 4 titles with different partners and qualified for Masters doubles with Jarryd, losing sf to Casal/E. Sanchez. Missed US Open with calf injury. *1989:* (117) Took a 2-month break mid Feb. to April, returning to reach sf Seoul. The high spot of his year came at Wimbledon, where he upset Gilbert to reach last 16 singles and won the doubles with Jarryd, with whom he was also r/u Masters. *1990:* Out 4 weeks April-May with torn calf muscle. In singles reached sf Brisbane; in doubles reached 2 f with Jarryd and was r/u Wimbledon mixed with Smylie. Won doubles (with Cash) in Aust. D Cup wins over France, New Zealand and Argentina but lost vital 3rd rubber in f during 2/3 loss to USA. *1990 HIGHLIGHTS – SINGLES: Australia Open* 1r (lost Bloom 7–6 7–6 3–6 6–2), *Wimbledon* 1r (lost Woodforde 7–5 6–2 6–4); *sf* Brisbane (d. Anderson 6–4 4–6 7–5, Woodbridge 6–4 2–6 6–4, Weiss 2–6 6–3 6–4, lost Krickstein 6–2 6–0). *1990 HIGHLIGHTS – DOUBLES:* (with Jarryd) *r/u* Stockholm (lost Forget/Hlasek 6–4 6–2), *r/u* Moscow (lost Davids/Haarhuis 6–4 7–6). *1990 HIGHLIGHTS – MIXED DOUBLES:* (with Smylie) *r/u Wimbledon* (lost R. Leach/Garrison 7–5 6–2). *CAREER HIGHLIGHTS – DOUBLES:* (with Jarryd unless stated) *French Open* – [Smid] *won 1986* (d. Edberg/Jarryd 6–3 4–6 6–3 6–7 14–12), *r/u 1988* (lost Gomez/E. Sanchez 6–3 6–7 6–4 6–3); *Wimbledon – won 1989* (d. R. Leach/Pugh 3–6 7–6 6–4 7–6), [Cash] *r/u 1985* (d. McEnroe/Fleming, lost Gunthardt/Taroczy), *r/u 1988* (lost Flach/Seguso 6–4 2–6 6–4 7–6); *Australian Open* – [Alexander] *won 1982* (d. Taygan/Rennert, Andrews/Sadri 6–4 7–6), [Cash] *sf 1984* (lost Nystrom/Wilander 6–4 6–4 2–6 6–3); *Masters – r/u 1989* (lost Grabb/P. McEnroe 7–5 7–6 5–7 6–3); *LIPC – won 1988* (d. Flach/Seguso 7–6 6–1 7–5).

JEAN-PHILIPPE FLEURIAN (France)
Born Paris, 11 September 1965, and lives there; RH; 6ft 1in; 170lb; final 1990 ATP ranking 67; 1990 prize money $180,718.
1985: (151). *1986:* (78) R/u Itaparica in 1st GP f. *1987:* (129) Sf Seoul. *1988:* (108) Gained his best results on the Challenger circuit. *1989:* (78) Sf Bordeaux and Sao Paulo. *1990:* Reached sf Adelaide and scored 2 big upsets, removing E. Sanchez 1r Australian Open and Becker 3r LIPC. *1990 HIGHLIGHTS – SINGLES: Australian Open* 3r (d. E. Sanchez [seed 7] 6–2 6–4 6–4, Volkov 6–4 1–6 7–5 2–6 6–2, lost Cherkasov 6–4 6–4 7–5), *French Open* 2r (d. Vajda 6–2 6–4 6–1, lost Chesnokov 7–6 6–2 6–0), *Wimbledon* 1r (lost Fromberg 7–6 5–7 4–6 6–1 6–4), *US Open* 2r (d. Martin 7–6 6–3 7–6, lost Ivanisevic 6–4 6–2 3–6 6–1); *sf* Adelaide (d. Nijssen 6–3 6–0, Riglewski 6–3 6–4, Potier 6–3 3–6 6–1, lost Arias 6–2 6–3).

GUY FORGET (France)
Born Casablanca, Morocco, 4 January 1965; lives Marseilles and London; LH; 6ft 1in; 160lb; final 1990 ATP ranking 16 singles, 4 doubles; 1990 prize money $638,358; career prize money $1,917,312.
Wife Isabelle (married May 1989); son Mathieu (born 30 Oct. 1989). *1982:* (70) Was world's second best jun, winning Orange Bowl in Dec. and making presence felt on GP tour. *1983:* (188) String of 1r losses as he joined men's tour. *1984:* (36) Confidence restored by reaching 3r Wimbledon and last 16 Australian Open where he beat V. Amritraj (seed 15). Qf Queens, Bordeaux, Stockholm and Wembley where he beat Jarryd and Becker. *1985:* (61) Despite sf appearance in Gstaad and Toulouse, he suffered a hard year. *1986:* (25) Reached last 16 French Open where he held m-p before bowing to Vilas. Won Toulouse, as his grandfather (1946) and father (1966) had done, and lifted his ranking again. R/u Masters doubles with Noah. *1987:* (54) Last 16 Wimbledon, d. his doubles partner Noah, with whom he was r/u French Open and won 5 titles. *1988:* (48) Sf Nice and Queen's and upset Zivojinovic at Olympics. In doubles won 3 titles with different partners. *1989:* (36) Won Nancy for 1st title since Toulouse 1986. Underwent surgery on his left knee in April, returning to action at Geneva in Sept. and upset J. McEnroe *en route* to f Wembley in Nov. *1990:* Broke into top 20 in his most successful year to date in which he reached qf Wimbledon and won Bordeaux, overcoming the trauma of the death of his father before qf and funeral before sf playing on at the insistence of his mother. Also reached f Nice and sf Hamburg and Long Island. In Feb. formed a successful doubles duo with Hlasek, with whom he won IBM/ATP World Doubles (for which both shaved their heads) and 4 other titles (plus a 6th with Becker). *1990 HIGHLIGHTS – SINGLES: Australian Open* 2r (d. Connell 2–6 6–4 6–4 6–2, lost Paloheimo 6–4 3- 6 6–3 6–3), *French Open* 3r (d. Reneberg 3–6 6–4 6–4 6–4, Antonitsch 6–1 6–1 6–1, lost Champion 6–4 6–7 6–4 5–7 6–3),

Wimbledon qf, seed 11 (d. Wahlgren 6–2 6–1 6–4, Jelen 7–6 6–7 6–1 6–2, Stich 3–6 7–5 6–2 4–6 6–3, lost Bergstrom 6–4 3–6 6–3 7–5), *US Open* 1r (lost Arias 7–6 6–4 3–6 6–4); *won* Bordeaux (d. Fleurian 7–5 3–6 6–2, Costa 6–4 3–6 6–4, Duncan 6–1 6–7 6–0, Agenor 6–3 6–4, Ivanisevic 6–4 6–3); *r/u* Nice (d. Paloheimo 6–2 7–5, Kroon 7–6 6–1, Prpic 7–6 6–2, Cherkasov 4–6 7–6 6–4, Aguilera 2–6 6–3 6–4); *sf* Hamburg (d. Novacek 6–4 7–5, Prpic 7–6 3–6 6–4, E. Sanchez 7–6 6–4, Berger 6–3 3–6 6–4, lost Aguilera 7–5 7–6), *sf* Long Island (d. Muller 7–6 7–6, Haarhuis 6–3 6–3, Gomez 6–7 6–0 7–5, lost Ivanisevic 6–2 1–6 6–3). *1990 HIGHLIGHTS – DOUBLES:* (with Hlasek unless stated) *won* Stuttgart (d. Mortensen/Nijssen 6–3 6–2), [Becker] *won* Indian Wells (d. Grabb/P. McEnroe 4–6 6–4 6–3), *won* Long Island (d. Riglewski/Stich 2–6 6–3 6–4), *won* Tokyo Seiko (d. S. Davis/Pate 7–6 7–5), *won* Stockholm (d. Fitzgerald/Jarryd 6–4 6–2), *won* IBM/ATP World Doubles (d. S. Davis/Pate 3–6 4–6 6–4 7–6 6–4, Casal/E. Sanchez 6–4 7–6 5–7 6–4). *CAREER HIGHLIGHTS – DOUBLES:* (with Noah) *French Open – r/u 1987* (lost Jarryd/Seguso 6–7 6–7 6–3 6–4 6–2).

AMY FRAZIER (USA)
Born St Louis, Mo., 19 September 1972; lives Rochester Hills, Mich.; RH; 2HB; 5ft 8in; 130lb; final 1990 WTA ranking 16; 1990) prize money $160,620.
Won 7 Nat Jun titles. *1986:* (331). *1987:* (202) Won Kona on USTA circuit. *1988:* (55) Sf Guaruja; qf LA (d. Shriver and Magers), Kansas and Indianapolis (d. Kelesi). *1989:* (33) Won 1st primary circuit singles title at VS Kansas; sf Albuquerque (d. Maleeva Fragnière) and VS Indianapolis. *1990:* Won VS Oklahoma and was r/u Tokyo Nicherei, where she beat Seles and K. Maleeva back-to-back and extended M-J. Fernandez to 3s. In other tourns reached sf Indian Wells and Sydney, where she upset Novotna and took Zvereva to 3s, and upset Fairbank Nideffer at Wimbledon. *1990 HIGHLIGHTS – SINGLES: Australian Open* 1r (lost Sabatini [seed 2] 6–4 7–6), *Wimbledon* 3r (d. Demongeot 6–1 6–4, Fairbank Nideffer [seed 15] 6–4 6–3, lost Tauziat 3–6 6–2 7–5), *US Open* 1r (lost Maleeva Fragnière 6–1 6–3); *won* VS Oklahoma (d. Hy 6–3 1–6 7–6, Miyagi 6–2 6–0. A. Minter 6–2 7–6, Maleeva Fragnière 1–6 6–3 6–3, Bollegraf 6–4 6–2); *r/u* Tokyo Nicherei (d. Schultz 7–6 6–1, Sviglerova 6–2 7–5, Seles 5–7 7–5 6–2, K. Maleeva 7–5 6–4, lost M-J. Fernandez 3–6 6–2 6–3); *sf* Sydney (d. Jagerman 3–6 6–4 6–3, Herreman 6–4 6–0, Novotna 6–3 6–4, Reggi 6–3 7–5, lost Zvereva 4–6 6–2 6–2), *sf* Indian Wells (d. E. Reinach 7–6 6–3, Quentrec 3–6 6–1 6–4, Martinez 1–6 6–4 6–2, Fairbank Nideffer 6–2 6–3, lost Sukova 7–5 6–4). *1990 HIGHLIGHTS – DOUBLES:* (with Richardson) *r/u* Puerto Rico (lost Brioukhovets/ Medvedeva 6–4 6–2).

RICHARD FROMBERG (Australia)
Born Ulvestone, Tas., 28 April 1970; lives Newtown, Tas.; RH; 6ft 3in; 168lb; final 1990 ATP ranking 32; 1990 prize money $228,987.
Played in winning World Youth Cup team in 1985 and 1986. Member BP Achiever Squad. Coach Ray Ruffels. *1988:* (103) Qf Brisbane and r/u Australian Open Jun doubles with J. Anderson. *1989:* (126) Won Bahia Challenger. *1990:* Reached f Singapore then won 1st tour title at Bologna, following with Bastad. Joined Australian D Cup squad for f v USA, where he took Agassi to 5s in 1st rubber and beat Chang in dead 5th rubber. *1990 HIGHLIGHTS – SINGLES: Australian Open* 1r (lost Wilander [seed 8] 7–6 7–5 7–5), *French Open* 1r (lost Bloom 5–7 7–5 1–6 6–3 6–2), *Wimbledon* 2r (d. Fleurian 7–5 5–7 4–6 6–1 6–4, lost Mansdorf 6–4 7–6 6–1), *US Open* 1r (lost Pugh 2–6 6–4 7–5 7–6); *won* Bologna (d. Mattar 6–1 6–3, Pistolesi 3–6 6–0 6–3, Perez Roldan 6–0 1–6 6–4, Potier 7–6 6–3, Rosset 4–6 6–4 7–6), *won* Bastad (d. Vajda 7–6 7–5, Utgren 6–7 6–3 7–6, Perez 7–5 6–3, Jonsson 6–4 6–2, Larsson 6–2 2–7 6); *r/u* Singapore (d. Saceanu 6–3 7–6, Pridham 6–7 7–6 7–5, Masur 6–4 6–4, Goldie 6–4 7–6, lost Jones 6–4 2–6 7–6). *1990 HIGHLIGHTS – DOUBLES:* [Pearce] *won* Schenectady (d. Strelba/Triguiero 6–2 3–6 7–6).

RENZO FURLAN (Italy)
Born Conegliano, 17 May 1970; lives Codogne; RH; 5ft 8in; 150lb; final 1990 ATP ranking 77; 1990 prize money $84,581.
1988: (374). *1989:* (222) Qf San Marino. *1990:* Won Tampere Challenger; qf San Remo (d. Agenor 1r, San Marino and Geneva). *1990 HIGHLIGHTS – SINGLES: won* Tampere Challenger (d. Luna 6–3 6–3).

PATRICK GALBRAITH (USA)
Born Tacoma, Wash., 16 April 1967, and lives there; RH; 6ft; 160lb; final 1990 ATP ranking 581 singles, 20 doubles; 1990 prize money $120,347.
A 3-time All-American at UCLA in doubles with Garrow, with whom he won NCAA doubles in 1988. *1989:* (438) Won Newport doubles with Garrow. *1990:* Playing with various partners, he reached 3 doubles f, winning 2. *1990 HIGHLIGHTS – DOUBLES:* [MacPherson] *won* Toronto World Tennis (d. Broad/Curren 2–6 6–4 6–3), [Jones] *won* Lyon (d. Grabb/Pate 7–6 6–4); [Curren] *r/u* Berlin (lost Adlrich/Visser 7–6 7–6).

ZINA GARRISON (USA)
Born Houston, 16 November 1963 and lives there; RH; 5ft 4½in; 128lb; final 1990 WTA ranking 10 singles, 13(9) doubles; 1990 prize money $802,203; career prize money $2,783,770.
Married Willard Jackson Jr 23 Sept. 1989. Coached by Willis Thomas until Aug. that year when Angel Lopez took over. During 1990 Sherwood Stewart took on that role. Discovered by John Wilkerson in public parks programme in Houston. *1981:* Won Wimbledon and US Open Jun. *1982:* (16) Qf French Open and last 16 Wimbledon. *1983:* (10) Sf Australian Open, Eastbourne and Detroit. *1984:* (9) Won Zurich; r/u VS Washington and New Orleans. *1985:* (8) Won WTA Champs (d. Mandlikova and Evert Lloyd), sf Wimbledon and r/u US CC. *1986:* (11) Won 48 of 69 matches as she won VS Indianapolis, reached f Tampa and sf Canadian Open. *1987:* (9) Suffering stress fracture to foot, was obliged to pull out of French Open and missed Wimbledon. Won NSW Open and VS California, reached f Canadian Open, 5 sf, and qf Australian Open. In doubles was r/u Australian Open with McNeil and won Australian Open mixed with Stewart. Qualified for VS Champs in singles and doubles. *1988:* (9) Qf Wimbledon, where she won mixed doubles with Stewart, and sf US Open, where she d. Navratilova for 1st time in 22 meetings. At Olympics won bronze medal in singles and gold in doubles with Shriver. Qualified for VS Champs singles, but lost 1r to Sukova. *1989:* (4) Won first singles title for 2 years at VS Cal, following with Newport and Chicago as well as reaching 4 more f. At US Open ended Evert's GS career *en route* to sf, reached qf Australian Open and at VS Champs fell qf to Sabatini. In doubles won 4 titles with K. Adams and in mixed was r/u Australian Open with Stewart. *1990:* The high point of her career came at Wimbledon, where she beat Seles and Graf back-to-back before losing f to Navratilova, becoming the 1st black woman to reach f there since Althea Gibson in 1950. Reached qf Australian Open and US Open; won Birmingham; r/u VS Washington and Puerto Rico; sf VS Chicago, Houston, San Diego, Los Angeles and VS California. In doubles won Washington with Navratilova, San Diego with Fendick and Filderstadt with M-J. Fernandez; in mixed with Leach won Wimbledon and r/u Australian Open. Played in winning US Fed Cup team and qualified for VS Champs, where she lost 1r to Martinez. *1990 HIGHLIGHTS – SINGLES: Australian Open* qf, seed 3 (d. Kijimuta 6–1 6–2, Thoren 6–2 6–0, Demongeot 5–7 6–3 6–4, Tanvier 6–2 2–0 ret'd, lost M-J. Fernandez 1–6 6–2 8–6), **French Open** 1r, seed 5 (lost Probst 6–1 1–6 7–5), *r/u Wimbledon* seed 5 (d. S. Smith 6–2 6–1, Dahlman 6–2 6–1, Lendl 6–0 6–3, Sukova [seed 10] 6–3 6–3, Seles [seed 3], Graf [seed 1] 6–3 3–6 6–4, lost Navratilova [seed 2] 6–4 6–1, *US Open* qf, seed 4 (d. Reinstadler 6–1 6–3, Gavaldon 6–4 6–0, Meier 6–4 6–3, Tauziat 6–1 7–5, lost Sanchez-Vicario [seed 6] 6–2 6–2; *won* Birmingham (d. Suire 7–5 6–2, Kidowaki 6–7 6–2 6–1, Cordwell 6–1 6–2, Tauziat 6–1 3–6 6–0, Sukova 6–4 6–1); *r/u* VS Washington (d. Smylie 6–0 6–1, Tauziat 6–0 7–6, Zvereva 6–2 3–6 6–3, lost Navratilova 6–1 6–0), *r/u* Puerto Rico (d. Pampoulova 6–3 7–5, S. Smith 7–5 6–1, Grossman 7–6 3–6 6–1, Cunningham 6–4 6–4, lost Capriati 5–7 6–4 6–2); *sf* VS Chicago (d. Pierce 6–4 6–4, McNeil 6–3 6–2, Tauziat 6–3 7–5, lost Maleeva Fragnière 6–2 6–0), *sf* Houston (d. Zvereva 4–6 6–3 6–3, Cecchini 6–1 6–3, lost Sanchez-Vicario 6–7 6–3 7–6), *sf* San Diego (d. G. Fernandez 6–2 6–2, Herreman 6–2 6–1, Phelps 6–3 6–3, lost Graf 6–4 7–5), *sf* VS Los Angeles (d. Fulco 6–0 6–4, Fairbank Nideffer 6–2 6–0, K. Maleeva 6–1 6–1, lost Navratilova 6–0 6–7 6–4), sf VS California (d. Daniels 6–2 7–5, Werdel 6–7 6–1 6–2, lost Seles 6–1 3–6 6–2). *1990 HIGHLIGHTS – DOUBLES:* (with Fendick unless stated) [Navratilova] *won* VS Washington (d. Henricksson/Van Rensburg 6–0 6–3), *won* San Diego (d. Burgin/Fairbank Nideffer 6–4 7–6), [M-J. Fernandez] *won* Filderstadt (d. Paz/Sanchez-Vicario 7–5 6–3); *r/u* Eastbourne (lost Savchenko/Zvereva 6–4 6–3). *1990 HIGHLIGHTS – MIXED DOUBLES:* (with R. Leach) *r/u Australian Open* (lost Pugh/Zvereva 4–6 6–2 6–3), *won Wimbledon* (d.

Smylie/Fitzgerald 7–6 6–2). *CAREER HIGHLIGHTS – SINGLES: Wimbledon – r/u 1990*, *sf 1985* (d. Tanvier, Van Nostrand, lost Navratilova [seed 1] 6–4 7–6), *qf 1988* (d. Sabatini 6–1 3–6 6–2, lost Shriver 6–4 6–4); *USCC – r/u 1983* (lost Temesvari 6–2 6–2), *r/u 1985* (lost Temesvari 7–6 6–3); *Olympics – bronze medal 1988* (lost Graf 6–2 6–0); *Australian Open – sf 1983* (d. Pfaff, Turnbull 6–2 7–6, lost K. Jordan), *qf 1985* (d. Henricksson, lost Mandlikova [seed 3] 2–6 6–3 6–3), *qf 1989* (lost Sabatini 6–4 2–6 6–4), *qf 1990; US Open – sf 1988* (d. Sanchez 4–6 7–5 6–2, Navratilova 6–4 6–7 7–5, lost Sabatini 6–4 7–5), *sf 1989* (d. G. Fernandez, Fendick 6–3 7–5, Faber, Evert 7–6 6–2, lost Navratilova 7–6 6–2), *qf 1985* (d. Gompert, lost Navratilova [seed 1] 6–2 6–3), *qf 1990; French Open – qf 1982* unseeded (d. Bunge, Herr, Jausovec 7–5 6–1, lost Navratilova 6–3 6–2). *CAREER HIGHLIGHTS – DOUBLES: Olympics –* [Shriver] *gold medal 1988* (d. Novotna/Suire 4–6 6–2 10–8); *Australian Open –* [McNeil] *r/u 1987* (lost Navratilova/Shriver 6–1 6–0); *US Open –* [Rinaldi] *qf 1985* unseeded (d. Bassett/Evert Lloyd, lost Kohde-Kilsch/Sukova 5–7 6–4 6–3). *MIXED DOUBLES:* (with Stewart unless stated) *Australian Open – won 1987* (d. Castle/Hobbs 3–6 7–6 6–3), [R. Leach] *r/u 1990; Wimbledon – won 1988* (d. Magers/Jones 6–1 7–6), [R. Leach] *won 1990.*

LAURA GARRONE (Italy)
Born Milan, 15 November 1967, and lives there; RH; 5ft 5in; 125lb; final 1990 WTA ranking 65; 1990 prize money $71,591.
1985: (108) Won French Open Jun and US Open Jun, was ranked 1 in ITF Jun World Rankings, and 3 in her country behind Reggi and Cecchini. *1986:* (38) Reached last 16 French Open, unseeded, and f Barcelona. *1987:* (87) Sf Belgian Open. *1988:* (60) R/u Taranto. *1989:* (92) Sf Geneva and Athens. *1990:* Still looking for a 1st primary circuit singles title, she reached 3rd f of career at Estoril in July. In doubles with Kschwendt won Palermo and Athens. *1990 HIGHLIGHTS – SINGLES: French Open* 1r (lost Schultz 6–4 7–6), *Wimbledon* 2r (d. La Fratta 6–2 6–4, lost Leand 5–7 6–4 7–5), *US Open* 2r (d. G. Fernandez 6–4 7–6, lost Sukova [seed 11] 6–3 6–0); *r/u* Estoril (d. Cueto 6–2 6–3, Guerree 6–3 6–4, Zardo 3–6 6–2 6–1, Tarabini 6–2 6–2, lost Bonsignori 2–6 6–3 6–3). *1990 HIGHLIGHTS – DOUBLES:* (with Kschwendt unless stated) *won* Palermo (d. Labat/B. Romano 6–2 6–4), *won* Athens (d. Laskova/Pospisilova 6–0 1–6 7–6); [Golarsa] *r/u* Italian Open (lost Kelesi/Seles 6–3 6–4).

BRIAN GARROW (USA)
Born Santa Clara, Cal., 8 April 1968; lives Los Altos Hills, Cal.; RH; 5ft 8in; 160lb; final 1990 ATP ranking 95 singles, 70 doubles; 1990 prize money $123,511.
A 3-times singles and doubles (with Galbraith) All-American at UCLA. *1988:* (533) Won NCAA doubles with Galbraith and was r/u in singles to Weiss. *1989:* (290) Won Winnetka Challenger singles and Newport doubles with Galbraith. *1990:* Reached 1st tour sf at Rio de Janeiro, where he won the doubles with Alumaa. *1990 HIGHLIGHTS – SINGLES: Wimbledon* 1r (lost Wohrmann 6–4 6–4 6–4), *US Open* 1r (lost E. Sanchez [seed 7] 7–6 6–4 6–4); *sf* Rio de Janeiro (d. Bengoechea 6–0 4–6 6–3, Pridham 2–6 7–5 6–1, Laurendeau 6–3 6–3, lost Sznajder 6–4 1–6 6–4). *1990 HIGHLIGHTS – DOUBLES:* [Alumaa] *won* Rio de Janeiro (d. Aerts/Roese 7–5 6–3); [Woodforde] *r/u* Brisbane (lost Stoltenberg/Woodbridge 2–6 6–4 6–4).

ANDREA GAUDENZI (Italy)
Born 30 July 1973.
1990: Ranked No. 1 in ITF Jun singles Rankings. Won French Open Jun (d. Enqvist 2–6 7–6 6–4) and r/u US Open Jun (lost Tillstroem 2–6 6–4 7–6).

ANGELICA GAVALDON (USA)
Born El Centro, Cal., 3 October 1973; lives Coronado, Cal.; RH; 5ft 2½in; 115lb; final 1990 WTA ranking 51; 1990 prize money $76,236.
Coached by Lee Merry. *1988:* (265). *1989:* (182) Upset Fairbank Nideffer at San Diego. Ranked 3 in Nat 16s. *1990:* Played through the qualifying to reach qf Australian Open, upsetting Mandlikova and G. Fernandez on the way. This took her into the top 100 and was followed by sf showing at Oklahoma the next month. *1990 HIGHLIGHTS – SINGLES: Australian Open* qf, unseeded (d. Poruri 6–3 6–3, Dechaume 6–4 4–6 7–5, Mandlikova [seed 7] 6–1 1–6 6–1, G. Fernandez [seed 6] 6–3 1–6 6–2, lost Porwik 6–4 6–3), *French Open* 1r (lost Reggi [seed 14] 1–6 7–6 6–2), *Wimbledon* 3r (d. Pospisilova 6–3 7–5, Gomer

7–5 0–6 7–5, lost Fendick 6–1 6–1), **US Open** 2r (d. Faber 6–3 6–2, lost Garrison [seed 4] 6–4 6–0); **sf** Oklahoma (d. Nagelsen 6–3 7–6, Louie Harper 6–1 6–4, Schultz 3–6 6–4 7–5, lost Bollegraf 6–4 7–5).

BRAD GILBERT (USA)

Born Oakland, Cal., 9 August 1961, and lives there; RH; 6ft 1in; 175lb; final 1990 ATP ranking 10; 1990 prize money $1,555,733; career prize money $4,217,946.

Coached by Tom Shivington; trained by Mark Grabow. Wife Kim, son Zachary (born 1988). **1982:** (54) The brother of 1978 US CC titlist Dana Gilbert he played for Allan Fox's Pepperdine team in California and reached f NCAA, losing to M. Leach. Won Taipei. **1983:** (62). **1984:** (23) Won Columbus and Taipei and reached last 16 Australian Open. **1985:** (18) Moved into top 20 winning Livingston, Cleveland and Tel Aviv and capping best year with 1r victory over McEnroe at Masters. **1986:** (11) Made further strides, downing Connors and Edberg for US Indoor crown, adding GP titles in Livingston, Israel and Vienna, reaching last 16 Wimbledon and US Open, and playing D Cup. **1987:** (13) Qf US Open, won Scottsdale and reached 4 more f to qualify for Masters, where he d. Connors and Becker. **1988:** (21) Out of action Jan–March with ankle injury and again, missing Wimbledon, after X-rays revealed a massive build-up of scar tissue on the tendon of left ankle as well as ligament damage from a sprain suffered in 1982, Won his 1st tourn of year at Tel Aviv, was Olympic bronze medallist, and reached f Paris Open plus 3 sf. **1989:** (6) Won Memphis, then in late summer captured Stratton Mountain, Livingston and Cincinnati back-to-back, becoming the first player to win 3 titles in consecutive weeks since Becker in 1986. Reached qf or better in 17 of 20 tourns – exceptions being 1r losses at Wimbledon, US Open and Tel Aviv – and qualified for Masters, where he won only one match. **1990:** Won Rotterdam, Orlando and Brisbane; r/u Cincinnati; sf Toronto World Tennis, Tokyo Suntory and Washington; and reached 2nd GS qf at Wimbledon. Finalist at GS Cup where he competed as alternate when Agassi withdrew and won $1m. **1990 HIGHLIGHTS – SINGLES: Wimbledon** qf, seed 7 (d. Oresar 6–1 3–6 4–6 6–1 6–2, Visser 5–7 6–3 6–2 6–2, Haarhuis 6–1 3–6 6–1 6–2, Wheaton 6–7 3–6 6–1 6–4 13–11, lost Becker [seed 2] 6–4 6–4 6–1), **US Open** 3r, seed 8 (d. Wilander 6–4 3–6 6–3 7–5, R. Leach 7–6 6–4 6–2, lost Mansdorf 5–7 5–7 6–3 7–5 6–1); **won** Rotterdam (d. Cherkasov 7–5 4–6 6–4, Camporese 6–3 6–3, Mansdorf 6–1 7–6, Tauson 6–3 6–3, Svensson, 6–1 6–3), **won** Orlando (d. Saceanu 6–4 6–4, J. Brown 6–2 6–1, Rive 6–3 6–3, Washington 6–2 7–5, Van Rensburg 6–2 6–1), **won** Brisbane (d. Doohan 6–0 6–1, Kuhnen 6–3 6–2, Limberger 6–2 6–4, Steeb 5–7 6–3 6–4, Krickstein 6–2 6–0); **r/u** Cincinnati (d. Wheaton 6–3 6–2, Forget 6–2 6–1, Hlasek 2–6 6–1 7–5, S. Davis 6–3 6–4, lost Edberg 6–1 6–1); **r/u** GS Cup (d. Svensson (6) 2–6 6–3 6–4, Krickstein 6–7 6–4 6–3, Wheaton (8) 6–3 3–6 7–6 2–6 6–4, lost Sampras (4) 6–3 6–4 6–2); **sf** Toronto World Tennis (d. Antonitsch 6–3 6–3, Srejber 6–2 6–2, Korda 3–6 7–6 6–2, lost Mayotte 6–3 7–6), **sf** Tokyo Suntory (d. Pearce 1–6 6–1 6–0, Mronz 4–6 7–5 6–1, Masur 6–1 7–6, lost Edberg 6–1 7–6), **sf** Washington (d. Teltscher 6–1 7–5, Sznajder 6–2 6–3, Stich 6–3 6–4, lost Grabb 7–5 0–6 6–4). **CAREER HIGHLIGHTS – SINGLES: US Indoor – won 1986** (d. Connors 6–4 fs, Jarryd 6–3 6–0, Edberg 7–5 7–6); **Olympics – bronze medal 1988** (d. Jaite, lost Mayotte 6–4 6–4 6–3); **Wimbledon – qf 1990; US Open – qf 1988** (d. Doohan, Berger 4–6 6–2 6–4 6–3, Forget 6–4 6–7 7–5 6–4, Becker 2–6 6–7 7–6 7–5 6–1, lost Connors 4–6 6–3 6–4 6–0); **Masters – qf 1985** (d. McEnroe 5–7 6–4 6–1, lost Jarryd 6–1 6–2).

LAURA ARRAYA GILDEMEISTER (Peru)

Born Cordoba, Argentina, 12 January 1964; lives Lima, Peru and Miami, Fla.; RH; 2HB; 5ft 8in; 125lb; final 1990 WTA ranking 21; 1990 prize money $151,619.

Coached by her husband, Heinz Gildemeister (married 1984); son Heinz Andre born June 1988. Having lived in Argentina until age 7, she moved with her family to Peru and became a citizen of that country. **1982:** (69) Burst into her own, beating Bonder, Nagelsen, Temesvari and Horvath. **1983:** (86) R/u Freiburg, qf Hilton Head. **1984:** (34) R/u Tourn of Champs. **1985:** (63) Sf VS Utah and Japan Open; played Fed Cup. **1986:** (31) Upset Lindqvist, M. Maleeva and Kohde-Kilsch during year. **1987:** (46). **1988:** (—) Did not play all year, taking a 9-month break after the birth of her son in June. **1989:** (19) Returned to action at LIPC in March and at Schenectady won 1st primary circuit title for 7 years, following with Puerto Rico (d. Zvereva and G. Fernandez) in Oct. **1990:** R/u Albuquerque and upset Seles in ss *en route* to sf VS Florida. **1990 HIGHLIGHTS – SINGLES: French Open** last 16, seed

16 (d. McNeil 7–6 6–3, Burgin 6–3 6–4, M. Maleeva 6–1 6–3, lost Seles 6–4 6–0), **Wimbledon** 3r (d. Kidowaki 6–3 6–3, Rajchrtova 6–2 6–2, lost Wiesner [seed 14] 6–2 7–6), **US Open** 3r (d. McGrath 7–5 6–3, Sawamatsu 7–5 6–3, lost Novotna [seed 12] 6–3 6–1); **r/u** VS Albuquerque (d. Gomer 6–4 7–6, Fulco 6–7 6–2 6–2, Minter 0–6 6–3 6–2, Sloane 6–2 6–2, lost Novotna 6–4 6–4); **sf** VS Florida (d. Kijimuta 6–1 7–6, Grossman 6–2 3–6 6–2, Seles 6–1 7–5, Novotna 3–6 6–3 6–3, lost Capriati 7–6 7–6). **1990 HIGHLIGHTS – DOUBLES:** [Cecchini] **r/u** Tampa (lost Paz/Sanchez-Vicario 6–2 6–0).

KRISTIN GODRIDGE (Australia)
Born Taralgon, 7 February 1973 and lives there; RH; 2HB; 5ft 4in; 120lb; final 1990 WTA ranking 129; 1990 prize money $35,746.
1990: Qf Brisbane. In doubles with Sharpe won US Open Jun and Clarins. **1990 HIGHLIGHTS – SINGLES: Australian Open** 1r (lost Pampoulova 4–6 6–4 6–2), **French Open** 1r (lost Tauziat 6–3 7–5). **1990 HIGHLIGHTS – DOUBLES:** (with Sharpe) **won** Clarins (d. Dechaume/Herreman 4–6 6–3 6–1).

LAURA GOLARSA (Italy)
Born Milan, 27 November 1967 and lives there; RH; 2HB; 5ft 5in; 125lb; final 1990 WTA ranking 61; 1990 prize money $69,036.
Coached by Aldo Mei. **1985:** (162). **1986:** (208). **1987:** (106) Qf Taipei and Argentine Open. **1988:** (79) R/u Athens Open. **1989:** (59) Unseeded, she reached qf Wimbledon, where she took Evert to 7–5 fs; qf Moscow. **1990:** Qf Barcelona and Taranto. **1990 HIGHLIGHTS – SINGLES: Australian Open** 1r (lost Meskhi 6–4 6–4), **Wimbledon** 1r (lost Novotna [seed 13] 3–6 7–6 6–2), **US Open** 1r (lost Hy 6–3 6–3). **1990 HIGHLIGHTS – DOUBLES:** [Garrone] **r/u** Italian Open (lost Kelesi/Seles 6–3 6–4). **CAREER HIGHLIGHTS – SINGLES: Wimbledon – qf 1989** unseeded (d. Paz, Strandlund, L. Field, Novotna 7–6 2–6 6–4, lost Evert 6–3 2–6 7–5).

DAN GOLDIE (USA)
Born Sioux City, Iowa, 3 October 1963; lives Redwood City, Cal.; RH; 6ft 2in; 175lb; final 1990 ATP ranking 96; 1990 prize money $136,848.
Wife Christine Marie Matthews; married Nov. 1988. Coached by Jack Shore and Dick Gould. **1983:** (794). **1984:** (102) Broke into top 100 during year. **1985:** (265). **1986:** (113) Last 16 US Open and won NCAA singles playing for Stanford. **1987:** (50) Last 16 Australian Open, won 1st pro title in singles and doubles at Newport and broke into top 50. **1988:** (29) Won Seoul, sf Stratton Mountain and Stockholm, where he d. Wilander in ss 3r. **1989:** (67) Upset Connors 2r Wimbledon en route to qf, unseeded, and reached sf Schenectady. **1990:** Reached sf Seoul and Singapore. **1990 HIGHLIGHTS – SINGLES: Australian Open** 3r (d. Patten 6–3 6–4 6–4, Pereira 6–2 6–4 6–3, lost J. McEnroe [seed 4] 6–3 6–2 6–2), **French Open** 1r (lost Kroon 7–6 6–3 6–1), **Wimbledon** 3r (d. Kok 7–5 6–1 7–5, Flach 6–3 6–4 6–4, lost Becker [seed 2] 6–3 6–4 4–6 7–5), US Open 1r (lost Sampras [seed 12] 6–1 7–5 6–1); **sf** Seoul (d. Woodbridge 6–4 2–6 6–4, Rive 7–5 6–2, Matsuoka 6–4 4–6 6–1, lost Antonitsch 4–6 6–3 7–6), **sf** Singapore (d. Garrow 6–2 6–4, Woodbridge 6–4 5–7 6–0, P. McEnroe 3–6 6–1 7–6, lost Fromberg 6–4 7–6). **CAREER HIGHLIGHTS – SINGLES: Wimbledon – qf 1989** unseeded (d. Evernden, Connors 7–6 5–7 6–4 6–2, Masur 7–6 7–6 3–6 7–6, Zivojinovic 6–4 6–4 7–6, lost Lendl 7–6 7–6 6–0).

SARA GOMER (Great Britain)
Born Torquay, 13 May 1964 and lives there; LH; 6ft 2in; 165lb; final 1990 WTA ranking 88; 1990 prize money $30,081.
1985: (77) One of the tallest players on the tour, this former member of the British Annie Soisbault and Maureen Connolly Brinker Cup teams won USTA San Antonio and was named first time to W Cup squad. **1986;** (56) With a record of 15 wins, 15 losses for the year, she demonstrated her prowess and improvement with wins over Reggi, R. White and Burgin. **1987:** (71). **1988:** (50) Won her 1st tour title at N California Open and r/u Auckland. **1989:** (124) Was ranked No. 1 in Great Britain for first time. At Wimbledon she took Shriver to 8–6 3s. **1990:** A mystery virus at the beginning of the year threatened to keep her out for 2 years, but at Wimbledon she had recovered sufficiently to upset Maleeva Fragnière 1r and in Oct. she reached qf Brighton. **1990 HIGHLIGHTS – SINGLES: Australian Open** 1r (lost Appelmans 6–1 6–0), **Wimbledon** 2r (d. Maleeva Fragnière [seed 8] 6–2 6–3, lost Gavaldon 7–5 0–6 7–5).

ANDRES GOMEZ (Ecuador)
Born Guayaquil, 27 February 1960 and lives there; LH; 6ft 4in; 185lb; final 1990 ATP ranking 6 singles, 56 doubles; 1990 prize money $972,613; career prize money $4,058,685.
Coached by Patricio Rodriguez. Wifc Ana Maria Estrada (married June 1986); son, Juan Andres, born Dec. 1987. *1980:* (43). *1981:* (37) Won first GP title in Bordeaux. *1982:* (15) Won Italian Open and Quito, showing the talent that had been blossoming under the guidance of Harry Hopman. *1983:* (14) Won Dallas GP event. *1984:* (5) Qf French and US Opens and Wimbledon. Won second Italian, US CC, Washington, Nice and Hong Kong. *1985:* (15) Won Hong Kong again and r/u US CC. *1986:* (10) Won US CC, Florence, US Pro and Itaparica in singles and US Open doubles with Zivojinovic *1987:* (11) Qf French Open, won Tourn of Champs, r/u Frankfurt and reached sf on 5 other occasions, but failed to qualify for Masters. *1988:* (24) Having reached 6 qf, was r/u Stuttgart and Washington back-to-back in July. Won French Open doubles with E. Sanchez. *1989:* (17) Upset Lendl on his way to the title in Barcelona and Wilander to take US Pro; sf Florence and Basle. *1990:* His best tennis came at the beginning of the year, reaching a climax at French Open when, aged 30, he became the 1st Ecuadorian to win a GS title, reaching an all-time high at No. 4 on the computer. Also won Barcelona and Madrid, r/u Philadelphia and sf Italian Open and Cincinnati. Qualified for ATP World Champ at end of year, but failed to reach sf. In doubles with J. Sanchez reached 3 f, winning Barcelona. Seeded 3 GS Cup, lost 1r Krickstein 6–3 6–4. *1990 HIGHLIGHTS – SINGLES: Australian Open* last 16, seed 9 (d. Cahill 4–6 6–3 1–6 6–2 6–3, Oresar 6–4 3–6 6–3 6–2, Stich 6–4 6–3 3–6 7–6, lost Cherkasov 2–6 6–3 7–6 7–6), *won French Open* seed 4 (d. Luna 7–6 6–1 7–6, Filippini 7–6 6–2 6–1, Volkov 6–2 7–5 4–6 6–3, Gustafsson [seed 14] w.o., Champion 6–3 6–3 6–4, Muster [seed 7] 7–5 6–1 7–5, Agassi [seed 3] 6–1 6–4 3–6 6–3), *Wimbledon* 1r, seed 5 (lost Grabb 6–4 6–2 6–2), *US Open* 1r, seed 5 (lost Mattar 6–3 3–6 6–3 6–3); *won* Barcelona (d. Schapers 6–4 7–6 7–6, Lopez 6–1 6–4, Perez 3–6 6–3 7–6, Chesnokov 6–3 7–5, Perez Roldan 6–0 7–6 3–6 0–6 6–2), *won* Madrid (d. Sznajder 6–1 6–3, Perez 3–6 7–6 6–0, Koevermans 7–5 3–6 6–3, Jaite 6–3 6–4, Rosset 6–3 7–6); *r/u* Philadelphia (d. Sznajder 7–5 6–2, Curren 6–7 6–3 6–4, Haarhuis 7–6 6–7 6–4, Korda 6–2 6–2, lost Sampras 7–6 7–5 6–2); *sf* Italian Open (d. Noah 6–1 6–7 6–3, Nargiso 7–6 6–4, Gustafsson 6–4 7–5, Camporese 6–1 6–2, lost Muster 5–7 6–4 7–6), *sf* Cincinnati (d. Goldie 6–3 7–6, Cahill 7–6 6–3, Courier 6–1 6–4, lost Edberg 7–6 6–3). *1990 HIGHLIGHTS – DOUBLES:* (with J. Sanchez) *won* Barcelona (d. Casal/E. Sanchez 7–6 7–5); *r/u* Monte Carlo (lost Korda/Smid 6–4 7–6), r/u Madrid (lost Baguera/Camporese 6–4 3–6 6–3). *CAREER HIGHLIGHTS – SINGLES: French Open – won 1990; qf 1984* (lost Lendl [seed 2] 6–3 6–7 6–4 6–3), *qf 1986* (lost Lendl [seed 1] 6–7 7–0 6–0 6–0), *qf 1987* (lost Lendl 5–7 6–4 6–1 6–1); *Italian Open – won 1982* (d. Noah 6–0 fs, Higueras 6–3 fs. Wilander 5–7 6–4 6–3, Teltscher 6–2 6–3 6–2), *won 1984* (d. Krickstein 2–6 6–1 6–2 6–2); *Wimbledon – qf 1984* (lost Cash 6–4 6–4 6–7 7–6); *US Open – qf 1984* (lost Lendl [seed 2] 6–4 6–4 6–1). *CAREER HIGHLIGHTS – DOUBLES: French Open* – [E. Sanchez] *won 1988* (d. Fitzgerald/Jarryd 6–3 6–7 6–4 6–3); *US Open* – [Zivojinovic] *won 1986* (d. Nystrom/Wilander 4–6 6–3 6–3 4–6 6–3); *Italian Open* – [Gildemeister] *won 1981* (d. Manson/Smid 7–5 6–2).

JIM GRABB (USA)
Born Tucson, Arizona, 14 April 1964, and lives there; RH; 6ft 4in; 180lb; final 1990 ATP ranking 72 singles, 24 doubles; 1990 prize money $237,612.
1984: (313) Sf NCAA Champs. *1985:* (250) Senior year at Stanford; reached sf Livingston. *1986:* (94) Qf San Francisco and Scottsdale. *1987:* (66) Won 1st GP title at Seoul. *1988:* (91) Qf Memphis (d. Edberg) and Philadelphia. In doubles, with 6 different partners, won Stockholm and reached 5 f. *1989:* (35) Sf Stratton Mountain then upset E. Sanchez to make an unexpected appearance in last 16 US Open. In doubles with P. McEnroe won French Open and Masters, r/u LIPC and Washington. *1990:* In singles was r/u Washington (d. Gilbert) and reached sf San Francisco. In doubles with 3 different partners appeared in 5 f, winning Wembley. *1990 HIGHLIGHTS – SINGLES: French Open* 1r (lost Haarhuis 6–3 6–3 6–2), *Wimbledon* 3r (d. Gomez [seed 5] 6–4 6–2 6–2, Chamberlin 6–2 6–7 7–6 3–6 6–3, lost Bergstrom 7–6 6–4 6–2), *US Open* 2r (d. Duncan 6–4 6–2 6–4, lost Santoro 7–6 6–4 7–6); *r/u* Washington (d. Woodforde 6–2 6–2, Connell 6–4 6–4, Rostagno 6–4 6–3, Gilbert 7–5 0–6 6–4, lost Agassi 6–1 6–4); *sf* San Francisco (d. J. Brown 6–3 7–6, Rostagno

6–2 6–7 6–4, Van Rensburg 4–6 6–2 7–6, lost Agassi 6–2 6–2). *1990 HIGHLIGHTS –
DOUBLES:* (with P. McEnroe unless stated) *won* Wembley (d. R. Leach/Pugh 7–6 4–6
6–3); *r/u* Indian Wells (lost Becker/Forget 4–6 6–4 6–3), [Lavalle] *r/u* US CC (lost S.
Davis/Pate 6 2 6–3), *r/u* Rosmalen (lost Hlasek/Stich 7–6 6–3), [Pate] *r/u* Lyon (lost
Galbraith/Jones 7–6 6–4). *CAREER HIGHLIGHTS – DOUBLES:* (with P. McEnroe) *French
Open – won 1989* (d. Bahrami/Winogradsky 6–4 2–6 6–4 7–6); *Masters – won 1989* (d.
Jarryd/Fitzgerald 7–5 7–6 5–7 6–3); *LIPC – r/u 1989* (lost Hlasek/Jarryd 6–3 ret'd).

STEFFI GRAF (Germany) **Official World Champion**
Born Bruehl, 14 June 1969; lives there and Delray Beach, Fla.; RH; 5ft 9in; 132lb; final
1989 WTA ranking 1; 1990 prize money $1,921,853; career prize money $7,173,198.
Coached by her father, Peter. Trained by Pavel Slozil. *1981:* Won Orange Bowl 12s. *1982:*
(214) At the time the youngest to receive a WTA ranking at 13 years, 4 months; won
European 14-and-under and European circuit Masters. *1983:* (98) Sf Freiburg. *1984:* (22)
Won Olympic Demonstration event in LA and reached last 16 Wimbledon. *1985:* (6) Sf US
Open and LIPC; last 16 French Open and Wimbledon. *1986:* (3) Won 8 of her last 11 tourns
and 52 of her last 55 matches. Won her first pro tourn by beating Evert Lloyd in Hilton Head
f, then beat Navratilova in German Open f and had 3 mps in memorable US Open sf loss to
Navratilova. Won 4 straight tourns and 23 consecutive matches in the spring. A virus
infection affected her performance in Paris and kept her out of Wimbledon, and a freak
accident in Prague (a heavy umbrella stand blew over and broke a toe) prevented her from
playing in Fed Cup. *1987:* (1) After a 2-month break Dec Jan, missing Australian Open, she
took over No. 2 ranking from Evert Lloyd end Feb, and No. 1 from Navratilova 16 Aug. Won
her first GS title at French Open, becoming, at 17 years 11 months and 23 days, the
youngest-ever winner of the women's singles there. Unbeaten from 23 Nov 1986 (VS
Champs) until Wimbledon f, where she fell to Navratilova, losing to her again in f US Open
when suffering from flu. She won 75 of 77 matches to take 11 titles, confirming her No. 1
ranking by taking the VS Champs and being named Official World Champion by virtue of
her position at head of VS points table. She became only the 2nd player after Navratilova to
earn more than 1m in prize money in a year. *1988:* (1) At the age of 19 she achieved a
unique 'Golden Slam', becoming only the 3rd woman, after Connolly and Court, to achieve
the traditional Grand Slam, and topping her exceptional year with a gold medal at the
Olympics in Seoul. She won 6 other titles, and 71 of 74 matches, losing only to Sabatini – at
VS Florida (following a 6-week break) and at Amelia Island – and to Shriver (when suffering
from flu) at VS Champs, ending run of 46 winning results. Became the 2nd German woman
to win Wimbledon after Cilly Aussem in 1931. In doubles won Wimbledon and LIPC with
Sabatini, but was forced to default qf VS Champs. *1989:* (1) A second consecutive GS
slipped from her grasp when, feeling unwell after suffering from food poisoning, she lost f
French Open to Sanchez–Vicario. However, she retained her titles at Australian Open,
Wimbledon and US Open, won VS Champs and took 10 other singles titles. With a record
of 82 wins and 2 defeats, losing just 12 sets all year, she was beaten only by Sanchez-
Vicario at French Open and Sabatini at Amelia Island in spring. In doubles was r/u French
Open with Sabatini. *1990:* Began the year in her usual style by winning Australian Open
and recorded a 66–match winning streak (the 2nd-highest in women's tennis), which was
broken when she lost to Seles in f Berlin. She lost f French Open (her 13th consecutive GS
final) to the same player, Garrison upset her in sf Wimbledon and Sabatini beat her in f US
Open and sf VS Champs. These were the only players to beat her in a year in which she
won 9 titles. She was out of action from Feb to April after breaking her thumb ski-ing, and
was hampered through the year by allegations concerning her father and by sinus problems, which caused her to withdraw from the Fed Cup team and required an operation
after Wimbledon. On 13 Aug went into her 157th consecutive week at No. 1, (starting 17
Aug, 1987, overtaking Navratilova's women's record of 156 (14 June 1982 – 9 June 1985);
3 weeks later she passed Jimmy Connor's all-time record of 159 weeks. *1990
HIGHLIGHTS – SINGLES: won Australian Open* seed 1 (d. Cunningham 6–2 7–5, de
Lone 6–1 6–2, Meskhi 6–4 6–1, Reggi [seed 13] 6–2 6–3, Fendick 6–3 7–5, Sukova [seed 4]
6–3 3–6 6–4, M-J. Fernandez 6–3 6–4), *r/u French Open* seed 1 (d. Paradis 6–0 6–2,
Santrock 6–1 6–2, Cecchini 6–2 6–3, Tauziat 6–1 6–4, Martinez [seed 9] 6–1 6–3, Novotna
[seed 11] 6–1 6–2, lost Seles 7–6 6–4, *Wimbledon* sf, seed 1 (d. Porwik 6–1 6–2, McGrath
6–3 6–0, Kohde-Kilsch 6–0 6–4, Capriati [seed 12] 6–2 6–4, , Novotna [seed 13] 7–5 6–2,

lost Garrison [seed 5] 6–3 3–6 6–4, *r/u US Open* seed 1 (d. Drake 6–1 6–1, McQuillan 6–1 6–3, Reinach 6–4 3–6 6–1, Capriati [seed 13] 6–1 6–2, Novotna [seed 12] 6–3 6–1, Sanchez-Vicario [seed 6] 6–1 6–2, lost Sabatini 6–2 7–6); *won* Tokyo Toray (d. Jagerman 6–0 6–1, Savchenko 6–0 6–3; Maleeva Fragnière 6–4 6–4, Sanchez-Vicario 6–1 6–2), *won* Amelia Island (d. Langrova 6–1 6–0, Temesvari 6–0 6–1, Bassett Seguso 6–4 6–4, Zvereva 7–6 6–7 6–1, Sanchez-Vicario 6–1 6–0), *won* Hamburg (d. Lapi 6–1 6–2, Provis 6–0 6–2, Sukova 6–1 6–2, Wiesner 6–4 6–2, Sanchez-Vicario 5–7 6–0 6–1), *won* Canadian Open (d. Javer 6–1 6–2, McNeil 7–5 6–3, Zvereva 6–0 6–4, Tauziat 6–2 6–2, K. Maleeva 6–1 6–7 6–3), *won* San Diego (d. Rehe 6–0 6–3, Rinaldi 6–3 6–4, Tauziat 6–3 6–2, Garrison 6–4 7–5, Maleeva Fragnière 6–3 6–2), *won* Leipzig (d. Golarsa 6–3 6–2, Bollegraf 6–1 6–2, Martinez 7–6 7–6, Sanchez-Vicario 6–1 6–1), *won* Brighton (d. Dahlman 6–2 6–2, Herreman 6–4 6–2, Tauziat 6–2 6–4, Lindqvist 6–2 7–5, Sukova 7–5 6–3), *won* VS New England (d. A. Smith 6–0 6–4, Zvereva 6–0 6–1, Maleeva Fragnière 7–6 6–7 6–3, Sabatini 7–6 6–3), *won* Zurich (d. Leand 6–1 6–4, Van Rensburg 6–1 6–4, Tauziat 6–4 6–1, Maleeva Fragnière 6–7 6–2 6–3, Sabatini 6–3 6–2); *r/u* Berlin (d. Paz 6–1 6–2, Piccolini 6–0 6–1, Meskhi 6–4 6–1, Zvereva 6–4 6–2, lost Seles 6–4 6–3); *sf* VS Champs (d. Capriati 6–3 5–7 6–3, K. Maleeva 6–3 6–0, lost Sabatini 6–4 6–4). *CAREER HIGHLIGHTS – SINGLES: Olympics – gold medal 1988* (d. Garrison 6–2 6–0, Sabatini 6–3 6–3); *Australian Open – won 1988* (d. Lindqvist 6–0 7–5, Mandlikova 6–2 6–2, Kohde-Kilsch 6–2 6–3, Evert 6–1 7–6), *won 1989* (d. Guse, Simpson, Werdel, Provis 6–4 6–0, Kohde-Kilsch 6–2 6–3, Sabatini 6–3 6–0, Sukova [seed 5] 6–4 6–4), *won 1990; French Open – won 1987* (d. Novotna, Kelesi, M. Maleeva 6–4 6–1, Sabatini 6–4 4–6 7–5, Navratilova 6–4 4–6 8–6) *won 1988* (d. Tauziat, Fulco, Sabatini 6–3 7–6, Zvereva 6–0 6–0), *r/u 1989* (d. Benjamin, Fulco, Jagerman, La Fratta, Martinez 6–0 6–4, Seles 6–3 3–6 6–3, lost Sanchez-Vicario 7–6 3–6 7–5), *r/u 1990; Wimbledon – won 1988* (d. M-J. Fernandez 6–2 6–2, Paradis 6–3 6–1, Shriver 6–1 6–2, Navratilova 5–7 6–2 6–1), *won 1989* (d. Salmon, Kessaris, A. Minter, Seles 6–4 6–3, Sanchez-Vicario 7–5 6–1, Evert 6–2 6–1, Navratilova 6–2 6–7 6–1), *r/u 1987* (d. Gildemeister, Novotna, Sabatini 4–6 6–1 6–1, Shriver 6–0 6–2, lost Navratilova 7–5 6–3), *sf 1990; US Open – won 1988* (d. Fendick 6–4 6–2, K. Maleeva 6–3 6–0, Evert w.o., Sabatini 6–3 3–6 6–1), *won 1989* (d. Inoue, Herreman, Phelps, Fairbank Nideffer 6–4 6–0, Sukova 6–1 6–1, Sabatini 3–6 6–4 6–2, Navratilova 3–6 7–5 6–1), *r/u 1987* (d. Tarabini, Hanika 7–5 6–2, Shriver 6–4 6–3, McNeil 4–6 6–2 6–4, lost Navratilova 7–6 6–1), *r/u 1990, sf 1985* (d. M. Maleeva 6–4 6–2, Shriver 7–6 6–7 7–6, lost Navratilova [seed 2] 6–2 6–3), *sf 1986* (d. Mascarin, Temesvari, Bowes, Reggi 6–1 3–6 6–0, Gadusek 6–3 6–1, lost Navratilova [seed 1] 6–1 6–7 7–6); *VS Champs – won 1987* (d. Garrison 6–0 6–3, Sukova 6–2 6–0, Hanika 6–1 6–4, Sabatini 4–6 6–4 6–0 6–4), *won 1989* (d. Novotna 6–3 6–4, Sukova 6–2 6–1, Sabatini 6–3 5–7 6–1, Navratilova 6–4 7–5 2–6 6–2), *r/u Nov. 1986* (d. McNeil 6–3 fs, M. Maleeva 7–5 fs, Sukova 6–1 fs, lost Navratilova 7–6 6–3 6–2), *sf March 1986* (lost Navratilova 6–3 6–2), *sf 1988* (lost Shriver 6–3 7–6), *sf 1990; LIPC – won 1988* (d. Kohde-Kilsch 6–3 6–0, Rehe 6–3 6–1, Evert 6–4 6–4). *CAREER HIGHLIGHTS – DOUBLES:* (with Sabatini) *Wimbledon – won 1988* (d. Savchenko/Zvereva 6–3 1–6 12–10); *LIPC – won 1988* (d. G. Fernandez/Garrison 7–6 6–3); *French Open – r/u 1986* (lost Navratilova/Temesvari 6–1 6–2), *r/u 1987* (lost Navratilova/Shriver 6–2 6–1), *r/u 1989* (lost Savchenko/Zvereva 6–4 6–4).

LISE GREGORY (South Africa)
Born Durban, 29 August 1963; lives there and Miami, Fla.; LH; 5ft 10in; 140lb; final 1990 WTA ranking 275 singles, 20 doubles; 1990 prize money $76,376.
1986: (322) Won NCAA doubles with Reis, playing for Univ. of Miami. *1987:* (168) Won Puerto Rico doubles with Reis. *1988:* (216) Again with Reis won North California Open doubles. *1989:* (251) Won Wichita doubles with Bollegraf. *1990:* In doubles reached 4 f, winning Newport and Leipzig with Magers, with whom she qualified for VS Champs. *1990 HIGHLIGHTS – SINGLES: Australian Open* 1r (lost Medvedeva 6–4 7–5). *1990 HIGHLIGHTS DOUBLES:* (with Magers unless stated) *won* VS Newport (d. Fendkick/A. Smith 7–6 6–1), *won* Leipzig (d. Bollegraf/Durie 6–2 4–6 6–3); [Bollegraf] *r/u* VS Oklahoma (lost Daniels/W. White 7–5 6–2), *r/u* Birmingham (lost Savchenko/Zvereva 3–6 6–3 6–3).

ANN GROSSMAN (USA)
Born Grove City, Ohio, 13 October 1970 and lives there; RH; 2HB; 5ft 3in; 110lb; final 1990 WTA ranking 50; 1989 prize money $115,923.

1986: Won US Int GC 16s. *1987:* (378) Won Nat 18s. *1988:* (48) Upset Fairbank *en route* to f San Diego. *1989:* (55) Reached qf San Diego and last 16 LIPC and French Open. *1990:* Reached last 16 French Open, unseeded, and upset Magers *en route* to f Strasbourg. *1990 HIGHLIGHTS – SINGLES: Australian Open* 1r (lost Daniels 6–7 6–3 6–4), *French Open* last 16, unseeded (d. Goles 6–0 6–2; Myagi 6–2 6–3, Sharpe 6–2 4–6 6–1, lost M-J. Fernandez 6–3 6–2), *Wimbledon* 2r (d. Daniels 6–2 6–1, lost Herreman 6–0 6–2), *US Open* 3r (d. Louie Harper 2–6 6–4 6–4, Cordwell 6–2 6–3, lost Paulus 6–4 6–3); *r/u* Strasbourg (d. Strandlund 0–6 6–2 6–0, Magers 6–3 6–4, Pampoulova 6–1 6–3, Bollegraf 2–6 6–0 6–2, lost Paz 6–2 6–3).

JAN GUNNARSSON (Sweden)
Born Olofstroem, 30 May 1962; lives Monte Carlo; RH; 6ft 1in; 176lb; final 1990 ATP ranking 99; 1990 prize money $?143,256.
Girlfriend Catharin; daughter Anna; twins Elin and Johan born Sept. 1989. *1979:* (392) R/u US Open Jun. *1980:* (247) Sf Pepsi GS Jun; finished 3rd Swedish satellite circuit. *1983:* (100) Qf Bastad and Barcelona. R/u doubles Nancy with Jarryd and Rome with Leach-.*1984:* (47) Won Vienna ($25,000), r/u Metz, qf 4 tourns and last 16 French Open. Won doubles at Nice, Bastad, Toulouse with Mortensen. *1985:* (25) Won Vienna and sf LIPC. *1986:* (57) Sf Gstaad and Vienna, last 16 Boca West. *1987:* (39) R/u Stuttgart and d. Wilander, E. Sanchez and Gilbert during the year. *1988:* (84). *1989:* (29) Upset Leconte and Svensson to reach sf Australian Open, unseeded; sf Gstaad. *1990:* His best showing was qf Indian Wells, where he upset Wilander 1r. *1990 HIGHLIGHTS – SINGLES: Australian Open* 1r (lost Pescosolido 6–2 6–7 6–0 6–2), *French Open* 1r (lost Koevermans 6–3 2–6 6–7 6–3 7–5), *Wimbledon* 1r (lost Pugh 6–3 1–6 5–7 6–3 6–4). *1990 HIGHLIGHTS – DOUBLES:* (with Riglewski) *r/u* Bastad (lost Bergh/Bathman 6–1 6–4). *CAREER HIGHLIGHTS – SINGLES: Australian Open – sf 1989,* unseeded (d. Leconte [seed 6] 6–4 6–3 6–2, Saceanu 6–1 6–2 6–7 4–6 6–1, Keretic 6–3 6–4 3–6 6–3, Schapers 7–6 6–1 6–2, Svensson 6–0 6–3 4–6 6–4, lost Mecir 7–5 6–2 6–2).

MAGNUS GUSTAFSSON (Sweden)
Born Lund, 3 January 1967; lives Lindome; RH; 6ft 1in; 172lb; final 1990 ATP ranking 31; 1990 prize money $224,554.
Coached by Tim Klein. *1986:* (273) Nat 18 Champ. *1987:* (53) Reached 1st GP sf at Stockholm, won Tampere Challenger and broke into top 50. *1988:* (51) Upset Mayotte to reach last 16 French Open; sf Hilversum and Barcelona (d. Jaite and Leconte). *1989:* (34) Reached last 16 Australian Open; played 1st GP f at Gstaad, then in autumn upset Wilander and Agassi *en route* to 1st SS f at Stockholm. *1990:* Took a break in March, suffering from shin splints. Reached sf Brussels, Stuttgart (d. E. Sanchez and took Lendl to 3s) and upset Agassi at Hamburg. Reached last 16 French Open, but was forced to default to Gomez owing to a knee injury. *1990 HIGHLIGHTS – SINGLES: Australian Open* 2r (d. Kulti 2–2 ret'd, lost Jonsson 6–1 6–2 6–2), *French Open* last 16, seed 14 (d. Carbonell 6–4 5–7 4–6 6–4 6–2, Korda 3–6 7–6 1–6 6–1 9–7, Perez 6–1 4–6 6–1 6–3, lost Gomez [seed 4] w.o.); *sf* Brussels (d. Gunnarsson 6–2 6–2, Mansdorf 6–4 6–4, Svensson 6–7 7–6 6–3, lost Becker 6–4 7–6), *sf* Stuttgart)d. Ivanisevic 4–6 7–6 6–4, E. Sanchez 6–3 6–0, Rahunen 7–6 6–1 6–2, lost Lendl 6–4 6–7 6–3).

PAUL HAARHUIS (Netherlands)
Born Eindhoven, 19 February 1966, and lives there; RH; 6ft 2in; 177lb; final 1990 ATP ranking 54; 1990 prize money $238,564.
Coached by Henk van Hulst. *1987:* (397) Finished 2nd on Dutch Satellite Circuit. *1988:* (462). *1989:* (57) After winning Lagos Challenger qualified for French Open, where he upset Zivojinovic 1r, and again as a qualifier upset J. McEnroe at US Open, going on to last 16. Qf Hilversum (d. K. Carlsson) and Itaparica. *1990:* Qf Philadelphia (d. Gilbert and took Gomez to 3s) and Estoril. Reached 4 f in doubles with various partners, winning Moscow. *1990 HIGHLIGHTS – SINGLES: Australian Open* 1r (lost Becker [seed 2] 6–1 6–2 6–1), *French Open* 3r (d. Grabb 6–3 6–3 6–2, Pugh 6–4 7–6 6–7 6–7 7–5, lost Muster [seed 7] 3–6 7–5 6–2 7–6), *Wimbledon* 3r (d. Nijssen 7–6 6–3 6–3, Cahill 7–5 5–7 7–6 4–6 6–3, lost Gilbert [seed 7] 6–1 3–6 6–1 6–2), *US Open* 1r (lost Carbonell 6–7 7–6 6–4 6–0). *1990 HIGHLIGHTS – DOUBLES:* (with Koevermans unless stated) [Davids] *won* Moscow (d. Fitzgerald/Jarryd 6–4 7–6); [Bloom] *r/u* Auckland (lost Jones/Van't Hof 7–6 6–0, *r/u*

Casablanca (lost Woodbridge/Youl 6–3 6–1), *r/u* Hilversum (lost Casal/E. Sanchez 7–5 7–5).

KARINA HABSUDOVA (Czechoslovakia)
Born Bojnice, 2 August 1973 and lives Bratislava; RH; 2HB; 5ft 7in; 132lb; final 1990 WTA ranking 122; 1990 prize money $14,591
1990: Ranked No. 1 in ITF Jun singles and doubles Rankings. Won Wimbledon Jun with Strnadova.

SABINE HACK (Germany)
Born Ulm, 7 December 1969; lives Ravemburg; RH; 5ft 7in; 130lb; final 1990 WTA ranking 45; 1990 prize money $39,283.
1985: (187) Enjoyed some success on the satellite circuits. *1986:* (263). *1987:* (234).*1988:* (141) Qf Athens and Paris Open. *1989:* (73) Reached 1st tour f at Bastad and broke into top 100. *1990:* Upset Maleeva Fragnière *en route* to sf Geneva and reached same stage Estoril. *1990 HIGHLIGHTS – SINGLES: French Open* 2r (d. Krapl 6–0 6–1, lost Tauziat 6–2 3–6 6–3), *US Open* 1r (lost Reinach 6–1 6–2); *sf* Geneva (d. Field 6–3 6–3, Maleeva Fragnière 6–2 6–1, Stafford 6–1 6–0, lost Kelesi 6–2 6–1); *sf* Estoril (d. Martinek 6–2 6–1, Ritter 6–2 6–2, Mothes 6–3 6–3, lost Bonsignori 2–6 7–6 6–4).

JULIE HALARD (France)
Born Versailles, 10 September 1970; lives La Baule; RH; 2HB; 5ft 7in; 110lb; final 1990 WTA ranking 41; 1990 prize money $76,865
1986: Won French Open Jun. *1987:* (62) Turned pro June. R/u Wimbledon Jun to Zvereva and reached f Athens. *1988:* (75) Won French Open Jun over Farley. *1989:* (119) Upset Shriver *en route* to qf Moscow. *1990:* Sf Clarins, qf Sydney and Barcelona, and upset Garrison *en route* to last 16 LIPC. *1990 HIGHLIGHTS – SINGLES: Australian Open* 3r (d. Devries 7–5 6–2, Henricksson 7–6 6–2, lost M-J. Fernandez [seed 6] 6–0 3–6 6–3), *French Open* 3r (d. Nagelsen 6–1 6–4, Medvedeva 6–2 4–6 6–4, lost K. Maleeva 6–2 6–1), *Wimbledon* 2r (d. K. Jordan 7–5 6–2, lost Capriati [seed 12] 6–2 7–6), *US Open* 2r (d. Schultz 6–2 6–4, lost R. White 6–4 6–3); *sf* Clarins (d. Lapi 6–4 6–2, Kanellopoulou 4–6 6–3 6–3, Graham 6–7 6–2 6–3, lost Martinez 6–1 6–2).

MAREEN 'PEANUT' LOUIE HARPER (USA)
Born San Francisco, 15 August 1960 and lives there; RH; 2HB; 5ft 5in; 120lb; final 1990 WTA ranking 74; 1990 prize money $67,230.
1977: One of five children including Marcie Louie (ranked 5 in US in 1975), she was r/u Wimbledon Jun. *1978:* (36) Won San Carlos. *1979:* (80). *1980:* (35) Won Columbus. *1981:* (32) Qf Chicago, Boston. *1982:* (90). *1983:* (52) Qf Hershey. *1984:* (53) Won Durban. *1985:* (22) Her best year, in which she reached sf Fort Lauderdale, sf VS Florida and won VS Denver (d. Sabatini and Garrison). *1986:* (65) Married Tim Harper 31 May. Overcame four consecutive 1r losses at start of season to beat Kelesi and Spence. *1987:* (97). *1988:* (56) Qf VS Kansas and Pan Pacific Open. *1989:* (115) In doubles won VS Arizona with Barg, and in singles upset Kohde-Kilsch 1r US HC. *1990:* Returned to top 100 with sf showing at Wichita. *1990 HIGHLIGHTS – SINGLES: Wimbledon* 1r (lost Zvereva [seed 11] 6–3 6–3), *US Open* 1r (lost Grossman 2–6 6–4 6–4); *sf* Wichita (d. Cioffi 6–1 6–3, Cueto 6–4 7–6, A. Minter 6–3 6–3, lost Tauziat 6–3 6–2). *1990 HIGHLIGHTS – DOUBLES:* [White Prausa] *r/u* VS Albuquerque (lost McGrath/A. Smith 7–6 6–4).

LINDA HARVEY-WILD (USA)
Born Arlington Heights, Ill., 11 February 1971; lives Hawthorn Woods, Ill.; RH; 5ft 7in; 135lb; final 1990 WTA ranking 83; 1990 prize money $46,068
Coached by her stepfather, Steve Wild. At Univ. of S. Cal. *1987:* (338). *1988:* (428). *1989:* (153) Won 2 consec. USTA circuit events. *1990:* Qf VS Chicago (upsetting Sanchez-Vicario) and VS Nashville (d. Provis); broke into top 100 in Aug. *1990 HIGHLIGHTS – SINGLES: French Open* 1r (lost Sawamatsu 6–1 4–6 6–2), *Wimbledon* 2r (d. Meier 6–2 6–1, lost DeVries 7–5 6–2), *US Open* 1r (lost McQuillan 7–6 7–5).

NATHALIE HERREMAN (France)
Born St Adresse, 28 March 1966; lives Paris; LH; 5ft 4in; 132lb; final 1990 WTA ranking 62; 1990 prize money $107,460.
Coached by Patrick Faviere. *1983:* Won French Nat Champs and reached sf Wimbledon

Jun singles and doubles and qf Tokyo. *1985:* (126) Qf Hewlett-Packard Trophy. *1986:* (42) Won first title at Perugia and surprised Rinaldi 1r Wimbledon. Wore a cast to correct wrist injury for 2 months at end of year. *1987:* (85) Stunned Mandlikova in ss at French Open, reached sf Belgian Open and qf San Diego. Ranked No. 1 in her country. *1988:* (95) R/u Moulins on French Satellite circuit. *1989:* (133) Reached 2 doubles f with Suire. *1990:* Became 1st qualifier to reach qf LIPC, having appeared at same stage at Indian Wells, and then reached last 16 Wimbledon, unseeded. *1990 HIGHLIGHTS – SINGLES: Australian Open* 1r (lost Zvereva [seed 10] 6–7 7–5 7–5), **French Open** 3r (d. Laval 6–3 6–3, Sawamatsu 6–1 6–3, lost Sabatini [seed 4] 6–0 6–1), **Wimbledon** last 16, unseeded (d. Ivan 7–5 6–3, Grossman 6–0 6–2, McNeil 6–4 6–3, lost K. Maleeva [seed 7] 6–3 6–0), *US Open* 1r (lost Reggi 6–1 4–6 7–6). *1990 HIGHLIGHTS – DOUBLES:* (with Dechaume) *r/u* Clarins (lost Godridge/Sharpe 4–6 6–3 6–1).

JAKOB HLASEK (Switzerland)
Born Prague, Czechoslovakia, 12 November 1964; lives Zurich; 6ft 2in; 165lb; final 1990 ATP ranking 17 singles, 12 doubles; 1990 prize money $661,671; career prize money $2,319,320.
Ex-coach Georges Deniau. Family moved to Zurich in 1968. Speaks 6 languages. *1984:* (88) Joined both Olympic and D Cup squads for Switzerland and played prolific schedule including 22 tournaments. *1985:* (33) R/u Rotterdam, sf Milan, Hong Kong and qf 4 times. Won Toulouse doubles with Acuna. *1986:* (32) Played consistent tennis all season, reaching f Hilversum and 8 qf. *1987:* (23) Reached last 16 Wimbledon with 2nd win over Nystrom, sf Toulouse and Wembley (d. Mecir). *1988:* (8) Out of action 3½ months after breaking right wrist and 3 ribs in car accident Jan., when he fell asleep at the wheel. Enjoyed a spectacular 2nd half of year, reaching last 16 US Open, f Gstaad and Basel (d. Connors), before taking 1st GP title at Wembley and following with Johannesburg and r/u finish at Brussels to qualify for 1st Masters, where he reached sf. *1989:* (30) Won Rotterdam and r/u Lyon in singles; in doubles won Milan, Indian Wells, LIPC and Wembley with various partners. Out of action with wrist injury July–Oct. *1990:* In singles won Wembley (d. Chang) and reached sf Rotterdam and Canadian Open. Formed a successful doubles duo with Forget in Feb.; together they won 5 titles, including IBM/ATP World Doubles for which both shaved their heads and he took another with Stich. *1990 HIGHLIGHTS – SINGLES: Australian Open* 1r (lost Korda 7–6 6–0 6–3), **French Open** 2r (d. Lundgren 3–6 7–6 2–6 7–5 6–2, lost Kulti 6–2 6–4 6–4), **Wimbledon** 2r (d. Costa 6–3 6–4 6–1, lost Lendl [seed 1] 6–1 6–3 6–0), *US Open* 3r (d. Reneberg 3–6 7–6 6–4 6–0, Ho 6–3 6–2 7–6, lost Sampras [seed 12] 6–3 6–4 6–1); *won* Wembley (d. Woodbridge 6–1 6–7 6–3, Muller 7–5 7–5, Ivanisevic 4–1 ret'd, Nargiso 7–6 6–2, Chang 7–6 6–3); *sf* Rotterdam (d. Jelen 7–6 7–6, Pereira 6–2 6–3, Antonitsch 7–5 6–1, lost Svensson 6–4 7–5), *sf* Canadian Open (d. Nemecek 6–3 6–2, Korda 5–7 6–4 6–4, Arias 7–5 6–1, Witsken 6–4 6–2, lost Berger 3–6 6–2 6–2). *1990 HIGHLIGHTS – DOUBLES:* (with Forget unless stated) *won* Stuttgart (d. Mortensen/Nijssen 6–3 6–2). [Stich] *won* Rosmalen (d. Grabb/P. McEnroe 7–6 6–3), *won* Long Island (d. Riglewski/Stich 2–6 6–3 6–4), *won* Tokyo Seiko (d. S. Davis/Pate 7–6 7–5), *won* Stockholm (d. Fitzgerald/Jarryd 6–4 6–2), *won* IBM/ATP World Doubles (d. S. Davis/Pate 3–6 4–6 6–4 7–6 6–4, Casal/E. Sanchez 6–4 7–6 5–7 6–4). *CAREER HIGHLIGHTS – DOUBLES:* [Jarryd] *LIPC – won 1989* (d. Grabb/P. McEnroe 6–3 ret'd); [Forget] *IBM/ATP World Doubles – won 1990.*

TOMMY HO (USA)
Born Winter Haven, Fla., 17 June 1973, and lives there; RH; 5ft 11in; 158lb; final 1990 ATP ranking 182; 1990 prize money $30,391
1988: (625) Became youngest to win a pro tourn when he took Rye Brook at age 15 yrs 2 mths. Won USTA Nat Champs. *1989:* (641). *1990:* won Ponte Vedra Challenger. *1990 HIGHLIGHTS – SINGLES: US Open* 2r (d. Odizor 6–2 4–6 6–2 3–6 7–5, lost Hlasek 6–3 6–2 7–6); *won* Ponte Vedra Challenger (d. Pridham 7–6 6–4).

TOMAS HOGSTEDT (Sweden)
Born Mariestad, 21 September 1963; lives Stockholm; RH; 6ft 3in; 170lb; final 1990 ATP ranking 91; 1990 prize money $131,666
1980: (549). *1981:* (240) Won US Open Jun over Schwaier. *1982:* (88) Upset Wilander at Cincinnati, Edberg at Stockholm and Gomez *en route* to sf Basle, reaching same stage at

Bastad. *1983:* (62) Won Ferrara. *1984:* (85) Won Italian Indoor and reached qf Milan. *1985:* (210) Sf Brussels (d. Teltscher) and qf San Francisco. *1986:* (124). *1987:* (179) Sf Schenectady. *1988:* (159) Out of action for the early months, recovering from pneumonia. Reached sf Schenectady again. *1989:* (133) Qf Rio de Janeiro and Sydney Indoor; upset Hlasek 1r Wimbledon. *1990:* Reached qf Rotterdam, Singapore and Tokyo Seiko. *1990 HIGHLIGHTS – SINGLES: Australian Open* 1r (lost Svensson 6–2 7–5 7–5), *French Open* 1r (lost Perez 6–1 6–4 1–0 ret'd), *Wimbledon* 1r (lost Shelton 7–6 5–7 7–6 6–4), *US Open* 1r (lost Bruguera 6–3 6–2 6–2).

ANKE HUBER (Germany)
Born Bruchsal, 4 December 1974 and lives Karlsdorf; RH; 2HB; 5ft 8in; 120lb; final 1990 WTA ranking 34; 1990 prize money $53,412
Coached by Boris Breskvar, who coached both Becker and Graf in the early stages of their development. *1990:* Coming from nowhere, she showed great fighting spirit in extending Sabatini to 2s tb in their 2r encounter at Wimbledon. At end Aug. won her 1st tour title at Schenectady after qualifying and followed with r/u Bayonne, upsetting Garrison and breaking into top 100, then shooting up to top 50 by Oct. *1990 HIGHLIGHTS – SINGLES: Australian Open* 3r (d. Laval 6–1 6–1, Burgin 6–2 6–0, lost Reggi [seed 13] 7–5 4–6 6–4), *Wimbledon* 2r (d. Durie 7–5 4–6 6–2, lost Sabatini [seed 4] 6–2 7–6, *US OPEN* 1r (lost Capriati [seed 13] 7–5 7–5); *won* VS Schenectady (d. Quentrec 2–6 7–6 6–0, Gildemeister 6–3 6–1, Hanika 4–6 7–6 2–2 ret'd, Probst 6–2 6–0, Werdel 6–1 5–7 6–4; *r/u* Bayonne (d. Guerre 6–2 6–3, Field 6–4 6–3, Garrison 7–5 6–3, Tanvier 6–0 6–4, lost Tauziat 6–3 7–6).

TATIANA IGNATIEVA (USSR)
Born 11 June 1974; final 1990 WTA ranking 576.
1990: R/u French Open Jun (lost M. Maleeva 6–2 6–3).

ETSUKO INOUE (Japan)
Born Tokyo, 18 October 1964 and lives there; RH; 5ft 4in; 114lb; final 1990 WTA ranking 70; 1990 prize money $34,211.
Coached by Jun Kuki. *1983:* (81) Ranked first in Japan and won Japan/Asian Open. *1984:* (68) Won Borden Classic in Tokyo over Herr. *1985:* (98) Had wins over Mesker, Schropp and Scheuer-Larsen. *1986:* (81) Played exceptional grass-court tennis to reach qf Birmingham and Eastbourne, producing wins over Durie, Pfaff, Gildemeister and Nagelsen. *1987:* (29) Sf Japan/Asian Open, Singapore and Edgbaston. *1988:* (51) Qf Sydney, US HC and Pan Pacific Open. *1989:* (68) Sf Oklahoma; qf Japan Open and Eastbourne (d. Garrison). *1990:* Reached qf VS Oklahoma. *1990 HIGHLIGHTS – SINGLES: Australian Open* 2r (d. Bowes 6–3 7–6, lost Tanvier 6–4 6–4), *Wimbledon* 1r (lost E. Reinach 6–0 6–4).

GORAN IVANISEVIC (Yugoslavia)
Born Split, 13 September 1971, and lives there; LH; 6ft 4in; 161lb; final 1990 ATP ranking 9; 1990 prize money $1,020,945.
Coached originally by Ladislav Kacek and Nikki Pilic and from Sept 1989 by Balazs Taroczy. They parted company end 1990. *1987:* (954) Won US Open Jun doubles with Nargiso. *1988:* (371) Joined Yugoslav D Cup squad. R/u French Open Jun doubles with Coratti and was ranked No. 3 in ITF Jun singles rankings. *1989:* (40) Qf Australian Open after qualifying and last 16 French Open, unseeded. Upset Leconte *en route* to 1st GP sf at Nice, following with 2nd at Palermo and f Florence. *1990:* Helped his country to win World Team Cup in May, then upset Becker 1r French Open *en route* to qf, following with sf appearance at Wimbledon, both unseeded. Won his 1st career title at Stuttgart; r/u Umag, Long Island, Bordeaux and Basel and broke into the top 10. R/u French Open doubles with Korda. Reached 2r GS Cup as No. 5 seed, d. Curren 7–6 7–6, lost Sampras 7–6 6–7 8–6. *1990 HIGHLIGHTS – SINGLES: Australian Open* 1r (lost Wheaton 7–5 7–5 6–0), *French Open* qf, unseeded (d. Becker [seed 2] 5–7 6–4 7–5 6–2, Jarryd 6–3 6–0 6–2, Kuhnen 7–6 6–1 7–5, Kroon 6–2 6–4 7–5, lost Muster [seed 7] 6–2 4–6 6–4 6–3), *Wimbledon* sf, unseeded (d. Leach 6–4 6–0 6–4, Delaitre 6–2 6–0 4–6 6–7 6–3, Rostagno 6–2 6–2 6–4, Koevermans 4–6 6–3 6–4 7–6, Curren 4–6 6–4 6–4 6–7 6–3, lost Becker [seed 3] 4–6 7–6 6–0 7–6), *US Open* 3r, seed 15 (d. Camporese 1–6 6–4 6–1 7–6, Fleurian 6–4 6–2 3–6 6–1, lost Cahill 4–6 4–6 6–2 7–6 6–0); *won* Stuttgart (d. J. Sanchez 6–2 6–3, Masur 6–2 6–7 6–4, Jelen 6–2 6–3; E. Sanchez 6–4 6–4, Perez Roldan 6–7 6–1 6–4 7–6); *r/u* Umag (d.

Pereira 6–1 6–4, Luna 6–2 6–3, Benhabiles 6–4 7–6, Cherkasov 6–3 5–7 6–4, lost Prpic 6–3 4–6 6–4), *r/u* Long Island (d. Pozzi 6–3 6–1, Ferreira 6–2 2–6 6–3, Sampras 7–6 6–3, Forget 6–2 1–6 6–3, lost Edberg 7–6 6–3), *r/u* Bordeaux (d. Aparisi 6–7 6–1 6–3, Luna 3–6 7–6 6–0, Santoro 6–2 6–3, Perez Roldan 6–4 6–4, lost Forget 6–4 6–3), *r/u* Basel (d. Volkov 7–6 6–1, Korda 6–1 6–2, Stich 7–6 7–6, Paloheimo 6–2 6–4, lost J. McEnroe 6–7 4–6 7–6 6–3 6–4). *1990 HIGHLIGHTS – DOUBLES:* [Korda] *r/u* French Open (lost Casal/E. Sanchez 7–5 6–3); [Taroczy] *r/u* Brussels (lost E. Sanchez/Zivojinovic 7–5 6–3), [Korda] *r/u* New Haven (lost J. Brown/Melville 2–6 7–5 6–0). *CAREER HIGHLIGHTS – SINGLES: Wimbledon – sf 1990; Australian Open – qf 1989* unseeded (d. Larsson, Fitzgerald 6–3 4–6 6–3 6–4, Nijssen 6–4 6–4 6–0, Lavelle 3–6 3–6 6–3 6–4 6–1, lost Mecir 7–5 6–0 6–3); *French Open – qf 1990. CAREER HIGHLIGHTS – DOUBLES:* (with Korda) *French Open – r/u 1990.*

NICOLE JAGERMAN (Netherlands)
Born Amstelveen, 23 July 1967, and lives there; RH; 5ft 10in; 148lb; final 1990 WTA ranking 68; 1990 prize money $47,875.
Coached by Frits Don. *1985:* (259). *1986:* (134) Qf Brazilian Open, Argentine Open (d. Garrison in ss) and Hilversum. *1987:* (146) Joined Fed Cup team. *1988:* (72) Last 16 French Open. *1989:* (83) Sf Archachon and Brussels. *1990:* In singles reached qf Hamburg and in doubles 2 f with Bakkum. *1990 HIGHLIGHTS – SINGLES: Australian Open* 3r (d. Kohde-Kilsch 6–4 7–6, Okamoto 6–1 6–2, lost K. Maleeva [seed 9] 6–0 6–4), *French Open* 1r (lost Caverzasio 6–4 6–2), *Wimbledon* 2r (d. Zrubakova 6–4 6–1, lost Sukova [seed 10] 6–4 4–6 7–5. *1990 HIGHLIGHTS – DOUBLES:* (with Bakkum) *r/u* Bastad (lost Paz/Scheuer-Larsen 6–3 6–7 6–2), *r/u* Estoril (lost Cecchini/Tarabini 1–6 6–2 6–3).

MARTIN JAITE (Argentina)
Born Buenos Aires, 9 October 1964 and lives there; RH; 5ft 11in; 155lb; final 1990 ATP ranking 36; 1990 prize money $271,498.
Coached by Daniel Garcia. Lived in Spain 1976–83. *1984:* (54) Burst into top 100 with upset of Gerulaitis at French Open and qf appearances at US CC and Barcelona. *1985:* (20) Won his first tournament of year in Buenos Aires, r/u Boston and Washington, and reached qf French Open over Mecir and Gunthardt. *1986:* (17) Won Bologna and Stuttgart, r/u Boston, sf Forest Hills (d. Becker) and US CC and last 16 French Open. Married Beatrice Kleinman 1 Nov. *1987:* (14) Last 16 French Open, r/u Italian Open (d. Nystrom), won Barcelona (d. Wilander) and Palermo back-to-back in autumn. Underwent ankle surgery at end of year. *1988:* (54) R/u Monte Carlo, sf Bologna and Itaparica. *1989:* (11) Won Stuttgart, Madrid, Sao Paulo and Itaparica; r/u Rio de Janeiro and Kitzbuhel. *1990:* Won Guaruja and Gstaad; sf Madrid and Schenectady; reached last 16 French Open and broke into top 10 in July. *1990 HIGHLIGHTS – SINGLES: French Open* last 16, seed 10 (d. Pistolesi 6–2 7–6 6–2, Stich 6–7 6–4 6–7 6–4 6–3, Rahunen 7–6 6–2 6–1, lost Muster [seed 7] 7–6 6–3 6–2), *US Open* 2r, seed 16 (d. Blackman 7–6 7–5 6–4, lost Annacone 7–6 6–2 6–2); *won* Guaruja (d. Frana 7–6 6–3, Sobel 6–1 6–2, Vojtesek 7–5 6–2, Hocevar 6–2 3–6 6–3, Mattar 3–6 6–4 6–3), *won* Gstaad (d. Zoecke 7–5 6–4, Motta 7–6 6–1, Courier 3–6 7–6 6–4, Agenor 7–5 6–1, Bruguera 6–3 6–7 6–2 6–2); *sf* Madrid (d. Haarhuis 5–7 6–0 6–3, Davin 6–3 7–6, Mancini 6–3 3–6 6–2, lost Gomez 6–3 6–4), *sf* Schenectady (d. Santoro 7–5 7–5, Olkhovskiy 4–6 7–5 6–4, lost Krishnan 1–6 6–3 7–5). *CAREER HIGHLIGHTS – SINGLES: French Open – qf 1985* (d. Mecir 2–6 7–6 6–3 6–4, Gunthardt 6–1 6–2 6–3, lost Lendl 6–4 6–2 6–4).

ANDERS JARRYD (Sweden)
Born Lidkoping, 13 July 1961 and lives there, London and Bastad; RH; 2HB; 5ft 11in; 155lb; final 1990 ATP ranking 73 singles, 52 doubles; 1990 prize money $184,518; career prize money $3,234,189.
Girlfriend Lotta Sundgren; son Niklas born Feb. 1988. *1981:* (100). *1982:* (60) Playing second singles in D Cup v US, he stunned Gottfried in straight sets. Won Linz and Ancona. *1983:* (19) Won French Open doubles with H. Simonsson, d. McEnroe in sf Canadian Open, losing f to Lendl, and was r/u Bastad. *1984:* (6) Won 2 GP tourns, including Australian Indoor at Sydney where he d. Lendl in f and was r/u US Open doubles with Edberg. Played on winning Swedish D Cup team, contributing decisive win in doubles with Edberg over McEnroe/Fleming. *1985:* (8) Sf Wimbledon, won Brussels over Wilander; r/u

Toronto, Milan and Stockholm and won Masters doubles with Edberg. *1986:* (19) Won WCT Finals win Dallas over Wilander and Becker, and r/u French Open doubles, but slowed down after knee surgery, returning to win Masters doubles with Edberg again in Dec. *1987:* (15) In singles reached qf Australian Open and Wimbledon, r/u Wembley; in doubles won Australian and US Opens with Edberg and French Open with Seguso and sf Masters with Edberg. *1988:* (32) Underwent knee surgery early in year. Qf Australian Open; sf Cincinnati and Frankfurt. In doubles with Fitzgerald r/u French Open and Wimbledon, won LIPC and qualified for Masters, losing sf to Casal/E. Sanchez. *1989:* (31) In singles reached f Rotterdam and San Francisco. In doubles won Wimbledon and r/u Masters with Fitzgerald, taking 3 other titles with various partners. *1990:* Restricted for much of the year by a shoulder injury and persistent cough. However, he upset J. McEnroe and Skoff to win Vienna for his 1st title for 4½ years and won The Hague Challenger. *1990 HIGHLIGHTS – SINGLES: French Open* 2r (d. Cahill 6–2 4–6 6–1 6–7 6–3, lost Ivanisevic 6–3 6–0 6–2), *Wimbledon* 2r (d. R. Leach 6–3 3–6 7–5 7–5, lost Kratzmann w.o.), *US Open* 2r (d. Youl 2–6 7–5 ret'd lost Muster [seed 6] 6–4 6–3 4–6 6–1); *won* Vienna (d. Stich 7–5 6–2, Kuhnen 6–3 6–4, J. McEnroe 7–6 6–2, Volkov 6–2 7–5, Skoff 6–3 6–3 6–1), *won* The Hague Challenger (d. Vajda 6–1 6–2). *1990 HIGHLIGHTS – DOUBLES:* (with Fitzgerald) *r/u* Stockholm (lost Forget/Hlasek 6–4 6–2), *r/u* Moscow (lost Davids/Haarhuis 6–4 7–6). *CAREER HIGHLIGHTS – SINGLES: Wimbledon – sf 1985* (d. Visser, Gunthardt 6–4 6–3 6–2, lost Becker 2–6 7–6 6–3 6–3). *CAREER HIGHLIGHTS – DOUBLES:* (with Edberg unless stated) *Australian Open – won 1987* (d. Doohan/Warder 6–4 6–4 7–6); *French Open* – [H. Simonsson] *won 1983*, seed 8 (d. Edmondson/Stewart 7–6 6–4 6–2), [Seguso] *won 1987* (d. Forget/Noah 6–7 6–7 6–3 6–4 6–2), *r/u 1986* (lost Fitzgerald/Smid 6–3 4–6 6–3 6–7 14–12), [Fitzgerald] *r/u 1988* (lost Gomez/E. Sanchez 6–3 6–7 6–4 6–3), *sf 1985* (d. Annacone/Van Rensburg, lost Glickstein/H. Simonsson 6–3 6–4 6–1); *Wimbledon* – [Fitzgerald] *won 1989* (d. R. Leach/Pugh 3–6 7–6 6–4 7–6), [Fitzgerald] *r/u 1988* (lost Flach/Seguso 6–4 2–6 6–4 7–6); *US Open – won 1987* (d. Flach/Seguso 7–6 6–2 4–6 5–7 7–6), *r/u 1984* (d. McEnroe/Fleming 3–6 7–6 7–5 7–6, lost Fitzgerald/Smid 7–6 6–3 6–3); *Masters – won 1985* (d. Nystrom/Wilander 4–6 6–2 6–3), *won 1986* (d. Forget/Noah 6–3 7–6 6–3), [Fitzgerald] *r/u 1989* (lost Grabb/P. McEnroe 7–5 7–6 5–7 6–3); *LIPC* – [Fitzgerald] *won 1988* (d. Flach/Seguso 7–6 6–1 7–5), [Hlasek] *won 1989* (d. Grabb/P. McEnroe 6–3 ret'd).

ERIC JELEN (Germany)
Born Trier, 11 March 1965, and lives there; RH; 5ft 11in; 170lb; final 1990 ATP ranking 68; 1990 prize money $206,631.
Coached by Wolfgang Popp. *1981:* Won Nat 16s. *1985:* (192) Qf Tel Aviv. *1986:* (31) Ousted 1985 r/u Curren 1r Wimbledon *en route* to last 16, sf Rotterdam, and had wins during year over Wilander, Zivojinovic and Krishnan. *1987:* (40) Underwent surgery in Jan. to relieve severe sinus condition. R/u Brisbane in 1st GP f. *1988:* (76) Sf Lorraine, qf Queen's, Bristol and Brussels. Finished the year in triumph, when he joined with Becker to beat Edberg and Jarryd in D Cup to give FRG a decisive 3–0 lead over SWE in Gothenburg. *1989:* (47) Won Bristol; sf Milan. *1990:* Sf Manchester and Newport; qf Milan, Umag and Stuttgart. *1990 HIGHLIGHTS – SINGLES: Australian Open* 1r (lost Masur 6–2 6–1 6–2), *French Open* 1r (lost Oresar 7–6 4–6 2–6 6–1 6–4), *Wimbledon* 2r (d. Kuhnen 6–3 6–3 6–1, lost Forget [seed 11] 7–6 6–7 1–6 2), *US Open* 1r (lost Korda 2–6 6–3 6–0 6–3); *sf* Manchester (d. Paloheimo 1–6 6–2 6–3, Muller 7–6 7–6, Van Rensburg 6–2 6–4, lost Sampras 6–7 6–4 6–4), *sf* Newport (d. Kaplan 6–1 6–3, R. Leach 6–0 6–2, Lundgren 6–2 6–2, lost Cahill 7–6 6–3).

KELLY JONES (USA)
Born Fort Gordon, Ga., 31 March 1964; lives San Diego, Cal.; RH; 6ft 1in; 165lb; final 1990 ATP ranking 133 singles, 22 doubles; 1990 prize money $211,782.
Brother of former touring pro Kim Jones Shaefer. *1983:* (409) All-American at Pepperdine for 1st of 4 years. *1984:* (741) Won NCAA doubles with Jerome Jones. *1985:* (489) Won NCAA doubles again with DiLaura. *1986:* (168). *1987:* (156) Sf Lyon in singles and won Auckland doubles with Pearce. *1988:* (366) Won Newport doubles with Lundgren. *1989:* (110) Working with Nick Bollettieri and Jim Loehr at the beginning of the year, he won his 1st career GP title at Singapore after qualifying. *1990:* Won Singapore again and reached qf

Manchester in singles; in doubles took Auckland and San Francisco with Van't Hof and Lyon with Galbraith. *1990 HIGHLIGHTS – SINGLES: Australian Open* 2r (d. Tauson 6–3 5–7 2–6 6–2 6–3, lost Delaitre 6–3 4–6 6–3 6–4), *French Open* 1r (lost Strelba 6–3 6–1 6–1), *Wimbledon* 2r (d. Sapsford 6–3 3–6 6–4 6–4, lost Rosset 3–6 6–7 6–3 7–5 6–3), *US Open* 1r (lost Cahill 6–3 3–6 6–2 6–0); *won* Singapore (d. Zoecke 6–4 6–2, Kratzmann 7–6 6–1, Hogstedt 7–6 2–6 6–2, Siemerink 6–1 6–4, Fromberg 6–4 2–6 7–6). *1990 HIGHLIGHTS – DOUBLES:* (with Van't Hof unless stated) *won* Auckland (d. Bloom/Haarhuis 7–6 6–0), *won* San Francisco (d. Layendecker/Reneberg 2–6 7–6 6–3), [Galbraith] *won* Lyon (d. Grabb/Pate 7–6 6–4).

LARS JONSSON (Sweden)
Born Goteborg, 27 June 1970; lives Onsala; RH; 6ft 1½in; 148lb; final 1990 ATP ranking 100; 1990 prize money $93,936.
Coached by Tim Klein. *1984:* Nat Jun champ. *1987:* (897). *1988:* (452). *1989:* Qf Geneva; won Dublin and Tampere Challengers. *1990:* Upset Perez Roldan *en route* to 1st tour sf at Bastad. *1990 HIGHLIGHTS – SINGLES: Australian Open* 3r (d. Nijssen 6–3 6–2 7–6, Gustafsson 6–1 6–2 6–2, lost Svensson 6–4 7–5 3–6 4–6 6–2), *French Open* 1r (lost Muster [seed 7] 7–5 6–3 6–2), *Wimbledon* 1r (lost Washington 6–2 6–3 6–1), *US Open* 1r (lost Stich 6–4 6–2 7–5); *sf* Bastad (d. Kroon 7–5 3–6 6–3, Perez Roldan 6–4 5–7 6–3, Paloheimo 6–1 6–2, lost Fromberg 6–4 6–2). *1990 HIGHLIGHTS – DOUBLES:* (with Nilsson) *r/u* San Remo (lost Nastase/Prpic 3–6 7–5 6–3).

KATHY JORDAN (USA)
Born Bryn Mawr, Pa., 3 December 1959; lives King of Prussia, Pa.; RH; 5ft 8in; 130lb; final 1990 WTA ranking 205 singles, 9 doubles; 1990 prize money $155,932; career prize money $1,539,395.
1977: R/u US Nat 18 Champs. *1979:* (11) Won AIAW Champs while at Stanford and came within 2 points of beating eventual champ Tracy Austin in last 16 US Open. *1980:* (13) Won Wimbledon and French Open doubles with A. Smith. *1981:* (15) Won US and Australian doubles with A. Smith. *1982:* (21) Won Boston indoors over Turnbull. *1983:* (14) Reached qf Wimbledon, upsetting Evert Lloyd in 3r to hand her fellow-American her first pre-semi final defeat in 35 GS events. R/u Australian Open to Navratilova. *1984:* (10) Ranked 5 for 9 months in her finest year, reaching sf Wimbledon with upset of Shriver and f Eastbourne with win over Evert Lloyd. *1985:* (19) Won Wimbledon doubles again with Smylie, ending the 109-match winning streak of Navratilova/Shriver in memorable 3s f. *1986:* (15) Had first career win in 13 meetings with Navratilova in sf VS Oakland and won French Open and Wimbledon mixed doubles with Flach. *1987:* (36) Out of action for first half of year with a string of injuries, returning to form in autumn to be r/u US Open doubles with Smylie and d. Garrison to reach sf Brighton. *1988:* (—) Underwent knee surgery in July and was out of action for the next 12 months. *1989:* (—) Returned to action at San Diego, playing doubles only and wearing a knee brace; played her first singles match at Albuquerque, where she lost 1r to Reggi. *1990:* Again concentrating mainly on doubles, was r/u Wimbledon and won VS Champs plus 2 other titles with Smylie, taking a 4th with Savchenko. *1990 HIGHLIGHTS – SINGLES: Wimbledon* 1r (lost Halard 7–5 6–2), *US Open* 1r (lost Sabatini [seed 5] 6–1 6–1). *1990 HIGHLIGHTS – DOUBLES:* (with Smylie unless stated) *r/u Wimbledon* (lost Novotna/Sukova 6–3 6–4); *won* San Antonio (d. G. Fernandez/R. White 7–5 7–5), *won* Tokyo Suntory (d. Hu Na/Jaggard 6–0 3–6 6–1), [Savchenko] *won* VS Nashville (d. Schultz/Vis 6–1 6–2), *won* VS Champs (d. Paz/Sanchez-Vicario 7–6 6–4); *r/u* Strasbourg (lost Provis/E. Reinach 6–1 6–4). *CAREER HIGHLIGHTS – SINGLES: Wimbledon – qf 1983* (d. Evert Lloyd 6–1 7–6, lost King), *sf 1984* (d. Shriver 2–6 6–3 6–4, lost Navratilova 6–3 6–4). *CAREER HIGHLIGHTS – DOUBLES:* (with A. Smith unless stated) *French Open – won 1980* (d. Madruga/Villagran 6–1 6–0); *Wimbledon – won 1980* (d. Casals/Turnbull 3–6 7–6 6–1), [Smylie] *won 1985* (d. Kohde-Kilsch/Sukova, Navratilova/Shriver 5–7 6–3 6–4), *r/u 1981* (d. Fairbank/Harford, lost Navratilova/Shriver 6–3 7–6), *r/u 1982* (lost Navratilova/Shriver 6–4 6–1), *r/u 1984* (d. Potter/Walsh, lost Navratilova/Shriver 6–3 6–1), [Smylie] *r/u 1990*, [Jausovec] *qf 1983* (lost Navratilova/Shriver 3–6 6–3 6–3); *US Open – won 1981* (d. Casals/Turnbull 6–3 6–3), [Smylie] *r/u 1987* (lost Navratilova/Shriver 5–7 6–4 6–2), [Jausovec] *sf 1983* (lost Navratilova/Shriver 6–3 6–2); *Australian Open – won 1981* (d. Navratilova/Shriver 6–2 7–5); *VS Champs –* [Smylie] *won 1990. CAREER HIGHLIGHTS – MIXED DOUBLES:* (with Flach] *French Open – won 1986* (d.

Edmondson/Fairbank 4–6 7–5 6–3); ***Wimbledon – won 1986*** (d. Navratilova/Gunthardt 6–3 7–6).

HELEN KELESI (Canada)
Born Victoria, 15 November 1969; lives Toronto; RH; 2HB; 5ft 5in; 130lb; final 1990 WTA ranking 25; 1990 prize money $144,847.
Coached by her father, Milan. **1985:** (48) The daughter of Czech parents who left that country for Canada a year before her birth, this feisty, gritty backcourt player made her mark on the tour, reaching f VS Central NY. **1986:** (40) Won her first pro event – Japan Open – and d. Mandlikova VS New England. **1987:** (33) Upset Kohde-Kilsch at Amelia Island and Lindqvist at French Open, where she held sp against Graf last 16. Reached qf Canadian Open, played Fed Cup and took over No. 1 ranking in Canada from Bassett Seguso. **1988:** (19) Extended Sabatini to 3s qf French Open and f Italian Open. Upset M. Maleeva twice; won Taranto, r/u Cincinnati and qualified for VS Champs 1st time. **1989:** (13) Qf French Open, r/u Barcelona and VS Nashville, sf Berlin and San Juan to qualify for VS Champs. **1990:** In singles was r/u Geneva and upset Sanchez-Vicario *en route* to sf Italian Open, where she won the doubles with Seles, reaching 2 other f with Reggi. **1990 HIGHLIGHTS – SINGLES: Australian Open** 3r, seed 8 (d. Probst 6–2 6–3, Meier 6–2 6–4, lost McQuillan 6–2 7–6), **French Open** 2r (d. Lindqvist 6–3 6–0, lost Seles 4–6 6–4 6–4), **Wimbledon** 1r (lost Capriati [seed 12] 6–3 6–1), **US Open** 2r (d. Coetzer 7–5 4–6 6–3, lost Stafford 4–6 6–3 7–5); **r/u** Geneva (d. C. Cohen 6–3 5–7 6–4, Harvey-Wild 6–1 6–4, Caverzasio 3–6 6–1 6–1, Hack 6–2 6–1, lost Paulus 2–6 7–5 7–6); **sf** Italian Open (d. Faull 6–4 6–1, Lapi 6–2 6–0, Sanchez-Vicario 6–4 7–5, Lindqvist 6–4 6–3, lost Seles 6–1 6–2). **1990 HIGHLIGHTS – DOUBLES:** (with Reggi unless stated) [Seles] **won** Italian Open (d. Garrone/Golarsa 6–3 6–4); **r/u** Canadian Open (lost Hagelsen/Sabatini 3–6 6–2 6–2), **r/u** VS Los Angeles (lost G. Fernandez/Novotna 6–3 4–6 6–4). **CAREER HIGHLIGHTS – SINGLES: French Open – qf 1988** (d. Manuela Maleeva 6–4 6–2, Jagerman, lost Sabatini 4–6 6–1 6–3), **qf 1989** (d. Zrubakova, Temesvari, Magers 6–4 2–6 6–3, Grossman 6–1 6–2, lost M-J. Fernandez 6–2 7–5).

AUDRA KELLER (USA)
Born Macon, Ga., 17 November 1971; lives Memphis Tenn.; RH; 2HB; 5ft 8in; 132lb; final 1990 WTA ranking 94; 1990 prize money $51,235.
Coached by Phil Chamberlain. **1989:** (154) Enjoyed some success in doubles on the USTA circuit. **1990:** A qf appearance at Puerto Rico, upsetting Kelesi, took her into the top 100 in autumn. **1990 HIGHLIGHTS – SINGLES: Australian Open** 2r (d. Menning 3–6 7–6 6–4, lost Fendick 6–5 6–2), **French Open** 1r (lost Ferrando 3–6 6–0 6–4), **Wimbledon** 1r (lost Rajchrtova 7–5 6–7 6–4), US Open 1r (lost McNeil 6–4 6–3).

MAYA KIDOWAKI (Japan)
Born Kyoto, 17 May 1969, and lives there; RH; 5ft 6in; 125lb; final 1990 WTA ranking 89; 1990 prize money $53,186.
1985: (263). **1986:** (304). **1987:** (219). **1988:** (243) Won 3 titles back-to-back on Japanese satellite circuit. **1989:** (136) Won singles and doubles titles again on the Japanese satellite circuit. **1990:** Made her mark on the primary circuit and broke into the top 100 in April after reaching sf Singapore, where she took Sawamatsu to 3s. **1990 HIGHLIGHTS – SINGLES: Australian Open** 2r (d. Krapl 7–5 6–2, lost Demongeot 6–4 6–1), **Wimbledon** 1r (lost Gildemeister 6–3 6–3), **US Open** 1r (lost Fendick 6–7 6–4 7–5); **sf** Singapore (d. Suire 6–4 7–5, Kiozumi 6–2 6–2, Jaggard 6–3 6–2, Vasquez 6–2 6–1, lost Sawamatsu 4–6 7–6 6–3).

MARK KOEVERMANS (Netherlands)
Born Rotterdam, 3 February 1968 and lives there; RH; 6ft 1in; 175lb; final 1990 ATP ranking 48; 1990 prize money $202,883.
1987: (524). **1988:** (139) Won Salou Challenger and joined the Dutch D Cup squad. **1989:** (63) Broke into top 100 March after being r/u Casablanca and Agadir Challengers. Reached 1st GP sf at Sao Paulo and upset K. Carlsson 1r Italian Open, where he reached qf despite playing with a broken toe suffered two weeks earlier. **1990:** Having appeared in qf Adelaide, Casablanca, Madrid and Genova and won Porto Challenger, he took his 1st tour title at Athens and reached sf Sao Paulo. In GS he reached last 16 Wimbledon, unseeded. **1990 HIGHLIGHTS – SINGLES: Australian Open** 1r (lost Mecir [seed 16] 6–2 6–4 7–6),

French Open 2r (d. Gunnarsson 6–3 2–6 6–7 6–3 7–5, lost Kuhnen 6–3 2–6 6–4 6–2), **Wimbledon** last 16, unseeded (d. Bailey 6–4 6–4 6–2, Bloom 7–5 6–4 6–3, Kroon 6–7 6–4 6–7 6–4 6–3, lost Ivanisevic 4–6 6–3 6–4 7–6); **won** Athens (d. Cunha Silva 6–4 6–2, Bavelas 6–3 4–6 6–2, Roig 3–6 6–1 6–2, Arrese 6–2 7–6, Davin 7–6 2–6 6–3), **won** Porto Challenger (d. Davin 6–3 6–3); **sf** Sao Paulo (d. Jaite 6–3 6–7 6–2, Wuyts 3–6 6–3 7–5, Ruah 7–6 6–3, lost Wilander 6–4 6–3). **1990 HIGHLIGHTS – DOUBLES:** (with Haarhuis unless stated) **r/u** Casablanca (lost Woodbridge/Youl 6–3 6–1), **r/u** Hilversum (lost Casal/ E. Sanchez 7–5 7–5), [Mattar] **r/u** Sao Paulo (lost Cannon/Mora 6–7 6–3 7–6).

CLAUDIA KOHDE-KILSCH (Germany)
Born Saarbrucken, 11 December 1963; lives there and Monte Carlo; RH; 6ft 0½in; 150lb; final 1990 WTA ranking 46; 1990 prize money $96,677; career prize money $2,034,541. Coached by Bob Rheinberger. **1979:** Ranked in top 10 jun, she won German Int Jun event. **1980:** (78). **1981:** (20) Upset Navratilova 1r VS Oakland and won Swiss Open. **1982:** (19) Won Avon Futures Champs, reached sf Mahwah and r/u Australian Open doubles. **1983:** (24) Adopted by her step-father, Jurgen Kilsch, and added his name to hers. **1984:** (8) Won German Open and r/u Australian and French Open doubles. **1985:** (5) Reached sf French and Australian Opens; upset Navratilova in qf on way to f Canadian Open, won US Open doubles, and r/u French Open and Australian Open doubles with Sukova. **1986:** (7) R/u WTA Champs. **1987:** (10) Sf Australian Open, qf Wimbledon and French and US Opens; won Wimbledon doubles with Sukova and qualified for VS Champs in singles and doubles. **1988:** (12) Sf Australian Open, won Birmingham and reached 5 other sf, qualifying for VS Champs in both singles and doubles again. R/u French Open doubles with Sukova and reached 6 other f with various partners. Underwent knee operation in June, missing Wimbledon. **1989:** (36) Still plagued by injuries, she was inconsistent but reached qf Australian Open and sf Birmingham. **1990:** Still struggling to regain her form, she won Kitzbuhel for her 1st title since 1988. **1990 HIGHLIGHTS – SINGLES: Australian Open** 1r (lost Jagerman 6–4 7–6), **French Open** 2r (d. Okamoto 6–1 6–1,lost Tarabini 3–6 6–1 6–4), **Wimbledon** 3r (d. Paz 4–6 6–1 6–1, Faber 6–2 6–0, lost Graf [seed 1] 6–0 6–4); **won** Kitzbuhel (d. Dopler 6–1 6–3, Vasquez 4–6 6–4 7–6, Caverzasio 6–1 6–4, Cecchini 6–4 5–7 7–5, McQuillan 7–6 6–4). **CAREER HIGHLIGHTS – SINGLES: French Open – sf 1985** (d. Mandlikova [seed 3] 6–4 6–4, lost Navratilova [seed 1] 6–4 6–4); **Australian Open – sf 1985** (lost Evert Lloyd [seed 1] 6–1 7–6), **sf 1987** (d.Hanika, Smylie 7–6 4–6 6–2, lost Mandlikova 6–1 0–6 6–3), **sf 1988** (d. Zrubakova 3–6 6–0 6–3, A. Minter 6–2 6–4, lost Graf 6–2 6–3); **US Open sf 1985** (lost Evert Lloyd [seed 1] 6–3 6–3). **CAREER HIGHLIGHTS – DOUBLES:** (with Sukova unless stated) **Wimbledon – won 1987** (d. Nagelsen/Smylie 6–4 6–7 6–4), [Bunge] **sf 1982** (d. Barker/Kiyomura 6–3 3–6 6–4, Piatek/W. White, Blackwood/ Leo, lost Navratilova/Shriver 6–3 6–4), **sf 1985** (lost Jordan/Smylie 5–7 6–1 6–4); **US Open – won 1985** (d. Navratilova/Shriver 6–7 6–2 6–3), [Bunge] **sf 1982** (d. K. Jordan/A. Smith 6–3 fs, lost Casals/Turnbull 6–4 6–1); **French Open –** [Mandlikova] **r/u 1984** (lost Navratilova/Shriver 5–7 6–3 6–2), **r/u 1985** (lost Navratilova/Shriver 4–6 6–2 6–2), **r/u 1988; Australian Open –** [Pfaff] **r/u 1982** (d. Casals/Turnbull 6–3 5–7 6–2, Potter/Walsh 7–6 fs, lost Navratilova/Shriver 6–4 6–2), **r/u 1984** (lost Navratilova/Shriver 6–3 6–4), **r/u – 1985** (lost Navratilova/Shriver 6–3 6–4); **VS Champs – r/u 1984–85** (lost Navratilova/ Shriver 6–7 6–4 7–6), **r/u 1985–86** (lost Mandlikova/Turnbull 6–4 6–7 6–3), **r/u Nov. 1986** (lost Navratilova/Shriver 7–6 6–3), **r/u 1987** (lost Navratilova/Shriver 6–1 6–1).

PETR KORDA (Czechoslovakia)
Born Prague, 23 January 1968, and lives there; LH; 6ft 3in; 145lb; final 1990 ATP ranking 38 singles, 15 doubles; 1990 prize money $331,404.
1986: (511) Won Wimbledon Jun doubles with Carbonell. **1987:** (87) Won Budapest Challenger; qf Prague (d. Srejber). **1988:** (188) Broke into top 100 in May and upset E. Sanchez in his 1st tourn on grass at Wimbledon. In doubles won Gstaad and Prague. Out of action with shoulder and ankle injuries following a car accident. **1989:** (59) Reached his 1st GP f at Frankfurt in autumn after sf showing at Vienna. In doubles won Stuttgart and reached 3 other f. **1990:** Reached f Philadelphia, Munich (d. Chang) and Moscow, and upset Gomez at Toronto World Tennis. In doubles r/u French Open with Ivanisevic and reached 3 more f, winning Monte Carlo with Smid. **1990 HIGHLIGHTS – SINGLES: Australian Open** 2r (d. Hlasek 7–6 6–0 6–3, lost Leconte 6–2 4–6 6–3 6–4), **French Open** 2r (d. Paloheimo 6–4 6–1 2–6 6–3, lost Gustafsson [seed 14] 3–6 7–6 1–6 6–1 9–7),

Wimbledon 1r, seed 14 (lost Bloom 6–0 6–4 4–6 6–2), US Open 2r (d. Jelen 2–6 6–3 6–0 6–3); *sf* Philadelphia (d. Duncan 6–3 6–1, Chesnokov 6–2 6–4, Yzaga 2–6 6–3 7–5, Berger 7–6 6–1, lost Gomez 6–2 6–2), *sf* Munich (d. Chang 6–7 7–5 7–6, Curren 7–5 6–1, Wohrmann 6–3 7–5, lost Muster 6–3 6–1), *sf* Moscow (d. Masur 7–5 6–4, Gunnarsson 6–1 6–7 6–2, Jarryd 7–6 7–6, lost Mayotte 7–6 3–6 6–3). *1990 HIGHLIGHTS – DOUBLES:* (with Ivanisevic unless stated) *r/u French Open* (lost Casal/E. Sanchez 7–5 6–3); [Smid] *won* Monte Carlo (d. Gomez/J. Sanchez 6–4 7–6); [Smid] *r/u* Munich (lost Riglewski/Stich 6–1 6–4), *r/u* New Haven (lost J. Brown/Melville 2–6 7–5 6–0). *CAREER HIGHLIGHTS – DOUBLES:* (with Ivanisevic) *French Open – r/u 1990.*

MARK KRATZMANN (Australia)

Born Murgon, 17 May 1966, and lives there; LH; 5ft 8in; 145lb; final 1990 ATP ranking 75 singles, 7 doubles; 1990 prize money $346,366.
Developed as member of BP Achievers Squad under Bob Carmichael. *1982:* (616). *1983:* (340) Ranked No. 1 in ITF Jun Doubles Rankings after winning French Open, Wimbledon and US Open. *1984:* (245) Won US Open Jun and r/u French Open Jun to take No. 1 singles position in ITF Jun Rankings. *1985:* (209). *1986:* (142) Broke into top 100 1st time in Aug. *1987:* (182) Played his best tennis at beginning of year when he reached last 16 Australian Open and qf Sydney. *1988:* (150) Took 4 months out in autumn to allow torn tendons in shoulder to heal. Won Sydney and Adelaide doubles with Cahill. *1989:* (122) Qf Adelaide was his best showing in singles, but in doubles won 3 titles and was r/u Australian Open with Cahill, with whom he qualified for Masters, where they lost sf to Jarryd and Fitzgerald. *1990:* Reached 1st tour singles sf at Philadelphia. In doubles with various partners reached 8 f, winning 7, and qualified for IBM/ATP World Doubles with Cahill. *1990 HIGHLIGHTS – SINGLES: Australian Open* 1r (lost Chesnokov [seed 11] 3–6 6–7 7–6 6–3 6–2), *French Open* 1r (lost Boetsch 6–4 6–0 6–3), *Wimbledon* 3r (d. Motta 6–2 6–1 6–3, Jarryd w.o., lost Chang 3–6 4–6 6–4 6–2 6–2), *US Open* 2r (d. Shelton 6–7 6–3 6–3 6–4, lost Cash 6–4 2–6 2–6 6–1 6–4); *sf* Philadelphia (d. Pearce 7–5 6–4, S. Davis 7–5 4–6 6–1, Reneberg 6–4 6–4, Courier 4–6 6–3 7–6, lost Sampras 4–6 6–1 6–4). *1990 HIGHLIGHTS – DOUBLES:* (with Cahill unless stated) [Cash] *won* Sydney (d. Aldrich/Visser 6–4 7–5), *won* Memphis (d. Riglewski/Stich 7–5 6–2), [Masur] *won* Tokyo Suntory (d. Pearce/Kinnear 3–6 6–3 6–4), [Stoltenberg] *won* Singapore (d. Drewett/Woodbridge 6–1 6–0), [Stoltenberg] *won* Manchester (d. N. Brown/Jones 5–7 7–6 6–4), *won* Newport (d. Nelson/Shelton 7–6 6–2), *won* Cincinnati (d. Broad/Muller 7–6 6–2); *r/u* Paris Open (lost S. Davis/Pate 5–7 6–3 6–4). *CAREER HIGHLIGHTS – DOUBLES:* (with Cahill) *Australian Open – r/u 1989* (lost R. Leach/Pugh 6–4 6–4 6–4).

AARON KRICKSTEIN (USA)

Born Ann Arbor, Mich., 2 August 1967; lives Grosse Pointe, Mich.; RH; 2HB; 5ft 10in; 150lb; final 1990 ATP ranking 20; 1990 prize money $650,183.
Attended Nick Bollettieri Tennis Academy. Coached by Tim Gullikson from 1989. *1982:* Won US Nat 16 at Kalamazoo. *1983:* (94) Won Nat 18 at Kalamazoo and turned pro in autumn, after arriving in last 16 at US Open where he upended Edberg and Gerulaitis in 5s before Noah stopped him. He won his first pro event in Tel Aviv to become youngest ever to capture GP tournament at 16 years, 2 months, 13 days. *1984:* (12) Won US Pro and two other GP titles and reached f Italian Open, including Wilander among his major victims. *1985:* (30) Despite r/u showing in Hong Kong and last 16 French Open, he did not live up to promise of previous two years. *1986:* (26) Made history at US Open with two straight triumphs from two-sets-to-love down against Novacek and Annacone, and added a straight-sets dismissal of Purcell to reach last 16. R/u Tel Aviv and contributed to US D Cup win over Ecuador with win over Viver. *1987:* (61) Reached qf 3 times, but progressed no further. Stress fracture of left tibia kept him out Aug–Sept, and before he could return to action, a rib injury sustained in a motor accident sidelined him until Feb. 1988. *1988:* (15) Qf US Open, upsetting Gomez and Edberg back-to-back, r/u Tel Aviv and Detroit and reached 3 other sf. *1989:* (8) Regained his old form, returning to top 10 in Oct. after sf appearance at US Open. At Sydney in Jan. he won his 1st title since Geneva in Sept. 1984. At Los Angeles in Sept. took his 1st SS title since US Pro in July 1984 and followed with Tokyo Seiko in Oct. (d. Edberg). Qualified for Masters. *1990: En route* to f Tokyo Suntory had back-to-back wins v Chang and Lendl (for the 1st time), despite nursing a hamstring injury that forced him to withdraw from Orlando. Also appeared in f Brisbane and sf Sydney, and in GS reached qf

US Open. Reached 2r GS Cup, d. Gomez (3) 6–3 6–4, lost Gilbert 6–7 6–4 6–3. *1990 HIGHLIGHTS – SINGLES: Australian Open* last 16, seed 5 (d. Pozzi 6–4 6–7 6–4 7–5, Krishnan 6–1 4–6 6–3 6–1, Wahlgren 6–7 6–2 6–3 6–2, lost Wheaton 7–6 6–4 6–3), *French Open* 3r, seed 5 (d. Yzaga 6–0 2–6 6–3 6–3, Grenier 6–3 6–4 7–5, lost Novacek 6–2 6–3 3–6 7–6), *US Open* qf, seed 9 (d. Sznajder 6–1 4–6 6–7 6–1 6–1, Stoltenberg 6–4 6–2 6–4, Cash 6–4 7–6 7–6, Mansdorf 6–3 6–4 6–4, lost Becker [seed 2] 3–6 6–3 6–3 6–3); *r/u* Tokyo Suntory (d. Pate 6–4 7–6, Connell 6–3 6–2, Chang 7–6 6–1, Lendl 6–3 5–7 6–4, lost Edberg 6–4 7–5), *r/u* Brisbane (d. Jarryd 2–1 ret'd, Goldie 6–2 6–3, Jelen 6–2 6–1, Fitzgerald 6–2 6–0, lost Gilbert 6–3 6–1); *sf* Sydney (d. Gunnarsson 7–6 6–2, Annacone 6–3 7–6, Wheaton 6–1 7–6, lost Noah 6–4 7–5). *CAREER HIGHLIGHTS – SINGLES: US Open – sf 1989* (d. Matuszewski, Masur 2–6 6–4 7–6 6–3, Volkov 3–6 3–6 6–4 6–2 6–3, Haarhuis 6–2 6–4 7–5, Berger 3–6 6–4 6–2 1–0 ret'd, lost Becker 6–4 6–3 6–4), *qf 1990.*

RAMESH KRISHNAN (India)
Born Madras, 5 June 1961; lives there; RH; 5ft 7in; 160lb; final 1990 ATP ranking 79; 1990 prize money $128,898; career prize money $1,139,370.
Wife Priya, daughter Gayatri (born 29 July 1989). *1979:* (179) Became top jun in world, sweeping French and Wimbledon Jun. *1981:* (66) Had long slump brought about by playing with injuries but rebounded to win Manila and reach qf US Open, taking 1s from eventual champion McEnroe. *1982:* (100) Won Stuttgart. *1983:* (84). *1984:* (24) Upset Wilander to reach sf Seiko Tokyo and won Metz. *1985:* (40) Got married a few weeks before Wimbledon. R/u Cologne. *1986:* (35) Reached qf Wimbledon, and won Tokyo and Hong Kong. *1987:* (58) Reached qf US Open, sf Nancy and Rye Brook and helped India to f D Cup for 1st time since 1966, when his father played. Troubled by recurring knee injury. *1988:* (40) Won Wellington and r/u Auckland, Bristol and Rye Brook. *1989:* (72) Won Auckland and upset Wilander 2r Australian Open. *1990:* Reached sf Auckland, then upset Jaite on his way to the title at Schenectady, and won Nagoya Challenger. *1990 HIGHLIGHTS – SINGLES: Australian Open* 2r (d. Zoecke 4–6 7–5 6–4 5–7 6–1, lost Krickstein 6–1 4–6 6–3 6–1), *French Open* 1r (lost Cancellotti 6–4 6–4 3–6 7–6), *Wimbledon* 2r (d. Perez 6–4 6–2 6–4, lost Kroon 6–3 2–6 6–3 6–3), *US Open* 1r (lost Leconte 6–4 6–1 6–1); *won* Schenectady (d. Kodes 6–0 6–4, Srejber 6–3 4–6 6–4, Adams 6–3 6–1, Jaite 1–6 6–3 7–5, Evernden 6–1 6–1), *won* Nagoya Challenger (d. Garrow 6–2 6–4); *sf* Auckland (d. Cane 6–1 6–1, Derlin 7–6 7–5, Gustafsson 7–6 6–2, lost S. Davis 5–7 6–3 6–4). *CAREER HIGHLIGHTS – SINGLES: Wimbledon – qf 1986*, unseeded (d. Maciel, Bauer, Nystrom [seed 6] 6–7 6–2 7–6 6–4, Jelen, lost Zivojinovic 6–2 7–6 4–6 6–3); *US Open – qf 1981* (d. S. Smith 6–4 6–3 6–3, M. Davis 6–2 7–5 6–7 6–4, G. Mayer [seed 7] 4–6 1–6 7–6 7–5 ret'd, lost McEnroe [seed 1] 6–7 7–6 6–4 6–2), *qf 1987* (d. Annacone, Nystrom 6–4 7–5 6–2, Kriek 6–3 6–4 6–3, Chesnokov 6–4 6–1 6–2, lost Edberg 6–2 6–2 6–2).

PATRICK KUHNEN (Germany)
Born Puttlingen, 11 February 1966, and lives there; RH; 6ft 2in; 170lb; final 1990 ATP ranking 82; 1990 prize money $153,039.
1987: (83) Qf Indianapolis and won Bergen on satellite circuit. *1988:* (61) Sprung one of the surprises of the year at Wimbledon, where he upset Connors to reach qf. Sf Brussels and qf Frankfurt. *1989:* (69) R/u Adelaide. *1990:* Sf Hong Kong, qf Stuttgart and Seoul. *1990 HIGHLIGHTS – SINGLES: Australian Open* 2r (d. Kroon 6–3 6–7 2–6 7–6 6–2, lost Edberg [seed 3] 6–2 6–2 6–4), *French Open* 3r (d. Engel 6–3 6–1 6–2, Koevermans 6–3 2–6 6–4 6–2, lost Ivanisevic 7–6 6–1 7–5), *Wimbledon* 1r (lost Jelen 6–3 6–3 6–1), *US Open* 1r (lost Annacone 7–6 7–5 6–4); *sf* Hong Kong (d. Rive 6–1 6–4, Fromberg 7–5 7–5, Pearce 6–2 6–2, lost Cash 6–7 7–5 6–1).

NICKLAS KULTI (Sweden)
Born Stockholm, 22 April 1971 and lives there; RH; 6ft 3in; 172lb; final 1990 ATP ranking 57; 1990 prize money $106,809.
Coached by Martin Bohm. Won 11 nat junior titles. *1988:* (176) R/u US Open Jun to Pereira. *1989:* (118) In Jun tennis won Australian Open and Wimbledon, r/u US Open to Stark and finished the year ranked No. 1 in ITF Jun Rankings. On the senior tour reached sf Bastad. *1990:* Reached 1st tour f at Prague and sf San Marino. *1990 HIGHLIGHTS – SINGLES: Australian Open* 1r (lost Gustafsson 2–2 ret'd), *French Open* 1r (lost E. Sanchez [seed 6] 4–6 6–4 6–7 6–1 6–2); *r/u* Prague (d. Mronz 6–3 6–2, Filippini 6–1 6–3, Davin 6–3 1–6 6–2,

de la Pena 6–3 1–0 ret'd, lost Arrese 7–6 7–6); *sf* San Marino (d. Pescosolido 5–2 ret'd, Skoff 6–7 7–6 6–2, Vojtisek 6–4 6–2, lost Camporese 6–3 6–1 6–3).

PETRA LANGROVA (Czechoslovakia)

Born Prostejov, 27 June 1970 and lives there; RH; 2HB; 5ft 8in; 143lb; final 1990 WTA ranking 79; 1990 prize money $56,901.
Coached by Radim Paveler. *1987:* (412). *1988:* (106) Won satellite events in Bournemouth and Oporto and took 1st title on main tour at Paris Open in Sept. Won European Champs doubles. *1989:* (78) Sf Paris Open and qf Tampa (d. Zvereva). *1990:* Reached qf Hamburg, Clarins and Kitzbuhel, where she won the doubles with Zrubakova. *1990 HIGHLIGHTS – SINGLES: Australian Open* 1r (lost Wasserman 7–6 7–5), *French Open* 1r (lost Faber 7–5 7–5), *Wimbledon* 1r (lost Faull 6–2 6–1), *US Open* 1r (lost Fairbank Nideffer 3–6 6–1 6–2). *1990 HIGHLIGHTS – DOUBLES:* (with Zrubakova) *won* Kitzbuhel (d. Cecchini/ Tarabini 6–0 6–4).

SEBASTIAN LaREAU (Canada)

Born 27 April 1973.
1990: Won Wimbledon Jun doubles with LeBlanc.

MAGNUS LARSSON (Sweden)

Born Olofstrom, 25 March 1970; lives Vaxjo; RH; 6ft 3in; 172lb; final 1990 ATP ranking 56; 1990 prize money $120,972.
Coached by Martin Bohm. *1986:* Won European Jun doubles with Kulti. *1988:* (381) R/u French Open Jun to Pereira. *1989:* (145) Won Genova Challenger. *1990:* Won Florence after qualifying, r/u Bastad and won Ljubliana Challenger. *1990 HIGHLIGHTS – SINGLES: Australian Open* 2r (d. Rosset 6–4 6–1 6–1, lost Wheaton 6–3 6–2 3–6 6–1), *Wimbledon* 1r (lost Wheaton 7–6 6–4 6–2). *1990:* won Florence (d. Mattar 6–3 6–2, Koevermans 3–6 6–3 7–6, Perez Roldan 7–5 6–4, Rahunen 6–4 6–4, Duncan 6–7 7–5 6–0), *won* Ljubliana Challenger (d. Nargiso 7–5 6–7 7–6); *r/u* Bastad (d. Santoro 6–3 6–1, J. Carlsson 6–4 6–4, Prpic 6–3 4–6 6–3, Filippini 6–4 6–1, lost Fromberg 6–2 7–6).

RICK LEACH (USA)

Born Arcadia, Cal., 28 December 1964; lives Laguna Beach, Cal.; LH; 6ft 2in; 165lb; final 1990 ATP ranking 279 singles, 5 doubles; 1990 prize money $282,355.
1986: (201) Coached by father, Dick, at USC, when he was All American; won NCAA doubles with Pawsat and 3 singles titles on USTA circuit. *1987:* (148) Won NCAA doubles again (with Melville) and won 2 GP doubles titles. *1988:* (258) In doubles with Pugh won Australian Open and Masters doubles on 1st appearance there but, suffering from flu and food poisoning, was forced to default US Open doubles f. Won 6 other titles (1 with Goldie). *1989:* (195) In doubles with Pugh won Australian Open, r/u Wimbledon and took 4 other titles to qualify for Masters, where they surprisingly took only 6th place. *1990:* In doubles with Pugh won a 1st Wimbledon title, plus LIPC and Philadelphia, to qualify for IBM/ATP World Doubles Final, where they failed to reach sf. In mixed doubles with Garrison won Wimbledon and r/u US Open. Played dbls (with Pugh) in winning US D Cup team. *1990 HIGHLIGHTS – SINGLES: Wimbledon* 1r (lost Jarryd 6–3 3–6 7–5 7–5), *US Open* 2r (d. Chamberlin 6–4 7–6 6–1, lost Gilbert [seed 8] 7–6 6–4 6–2). *1990 HIGHLIGHTS – DOUBLES:* (with Pugh) *won* Wimbledon (d. Aldrich/Visser 7–6 7–6 7–6); *won* Philadelphia (d. Connell/Michibata 3–6 6–4 6–2), *won* LIPC (d. Becker/Motta 6–4 3–6 6–3); *r/u* Wembley (lost Grabb/P. McEnroe 7–6 4–6 6–3). *1990 HIGHLIGHTS – MIXED DOUBLES:* (with Garrison) *r/u Australian Open* (lost Pugh/Zvereva 4–6 6–2 6–3), *won* Wimbledon (d. Smylie/Fitzgerald 7–5 6–2). *CAREER HIGHLIGHTS – DOUBLES:* (with Pugh) *Australian Open – won 1988* (d. Bates/Lundgren 6–3 6–2 6–3), *won 1989* (d. Cahill/Kratzmann 6–4 6–4 6–4); *Wimbledon – won 1990; r/u 1989* (lost Fitzgerald/Jarryd 3–6 7–6 6–4 7–6); *Masters – won 1988* (d. Casal/E. Sanchez 6–4 6–3 2–6 6–0); *US Open – r/u 1988* (lost Casal/E. Sanchez def.). *MIXED DOUBLES:* (with Garrison) *Wimbledon – won 1990.*

SEBASTIAN LeBLANC (Canada)

Born 27 December, 1973.
1990: Won Wimbledon Jun doubles with LaReau.

HENRI LECONTE (France)
Born Lilliers, 4 July 1963; lives Geneva, Switzerland; LH; 6ft 1in; 175lb; final 1990 ATP ranking 30; 1990 prize money $535,590; career prize money $2,503,821.
Coached by Patrice Hagelauer. Separated from wife Brigitte 1989; son Maxim born 6 March 1986. **1982:** (28) Won Stockholm Open over Wilander and played No. 2 singles on D Cup team behind Noah as France lost to US in f. Beat Borg in 2r Monte Carlo as the Swede attempted a come-back. **1983:** (30) Beat Lendl twice (on clay at WCT Forest Hills and indoors at Sydney) and was r/u at Kitzbuhel and Sydney. **1984:** (27) Won Stuttgart (d. Borg in 2r), r/u to Connors at Memphis and won French Open doubles with Noah. **1985:** (16) Won Nice and Sydney NSW as well as reaching qf French Open and Wimbledon and last 16 US Open. R/u US Open doubles with Noah. **1986:** (6) Won Geneva and Hamburg, qualified for Masters first time, reached sf French Open and Wimbledon and qf US Open, finally arriving as expected in world's top 10. **1987:** (21) Underwent laser surgey Feb. to repair herniated disc, and was not fully fit until Wimbledon, where he reached qf again and followed with last 16 US Open. But then he was sidelined again in Oct. suffering from an illness similar to mononucleosis, returning to reach 1st sf of year at Paris Open. **1988** (9) At Nice won 1st GP title title since 1986 and finished the year by taking Brussels to qualify for Masters, where he retired v Becker in 1r with injured ankle. Delighted and disappointed the Paris crowds as he swept to f French Open, where he lost to Wilander; reached last 16 Wimbledon and was r/u Hamburg. **1989:** (115) Out of action from May, when he underwent back surgery again to repair disc hernia, returning in Sept. to reach qf Barcelona, Bordeaux and Tokyo Seiko. **1990:** A wild-card entry at French Open, he upset Chesnokov *en route* to qf. Reached sf Monte Carlo (d. Gomez), Stuttgart (d. Chesnokov again) and Hamburg, where he extended Becker to 3s. Reached 2r GS Cup, d. Muster (7) 6–3 6–4, lost Chang 7–6 6–3. **1990 HIGHLIGHTS – SINGLES: Australian Open** 3r (d. Roig 6–1 4–6 7–5 6–4, Korda 6–2 4–6 6–3 6–4, lost Pernfors 6–4 6–1 6–3), **French Open** qf, unseeded (d. Agenor 6–4 6–2 6–4, Oresar 6–4 6–2 6–1, Davin 6–3 7–6 6–4, Chesnokov [seed 8] 6–4 6–3 4–6 2–6 6–3, lost Svensson 3–6 7–5 6–3 6–4), **Wimbledon** 2r, seed 15 (d. Youl 6–4 6–3 6–3, lost Antonitsch 2–6 6–4 7–6 2–6 6–3), **US Open** 2r (d. Krishnan 6–4 6–1 6–1, lost Cherkasov 1–6 6–1 6–4 6–3); **sf** Monte Carlo (d. Witsken 6–1 6–4, Mancini 6–4 6–4, Gomez 6–3 6–4, Skoff 6–2 6–7 6–4, lost Muster 6–2 6–3), **sf** Hamburg (d. Witsken 7–6 2–6 6–2, Arrese 6–4 1–6 6–2, Krickstein 6–4 6–4, Davin 6–3 6–3, lost Becker 6–3 3–6 6–3), **sf** Stuttgart (d. Windahl 6–4 6–2, Chesnokov 7–5 6–3, Cherkasov 4–6 6–4 6–4, lost Perez Roldan 6–7 6–3 7–6). **1990 HIGHLIGHTS – DOUBLES:** [Lendl] **r/u** Queens's (lost Bates/ Curren 6–2 7–6). **CAREER HIGHLIGHTS – SINGLES: French Open – r/u 1988** (d. de la Pena 6–4 7–5 6–1, Becker 6–7 6–3 6–1 5–7 6–4, Chesnokov 6–3 6–2 7–6, Svensson 7–6 6–2 6–1, lost Wilander 7–5 6–2 6–1), **sf 1986** (d. Chesnokov 6–3 6–4 6–3, lost Pernfors 2–6 7–5 7–6 6–3), **qf 1985** (d. Gomez, Noah 6–3 6–4 6–7 4–6 6–1, lost Wilander 6–4 7–6 6–7 7–5), **qf 1990; Wimbledon – sf 1986** (d. Fitzgerald, Cash 4–6 7–6 7–6 6–3, lost Becker 6–2 6–4 6–7 6–3), **qf 1985** (d. Lendl 3–6 6–4 6–3 6–1, lost Becker 7–6 3–6 6–3 6–4), **qf 1987** (d. Gomez, lost Lendl 7–6 6–3 7–6); **US Open – qf 1986** (d. Krickstein 6–3 7–5 6–4, lost Lendl 7–6 6–1 1–6 6–1). **CAREER HIGHLIGHTS – DOUBLES:** (with Noah) **French Open – won 1984** (d. Slozil/Smid 6–4 2–6 3–6 6–3 6–2). **US Open – r/u 1985** (lost Flach/Seguso 7–6 6–7 7–6 6–0).

IVAN LENDL (Czechoslovakia) **Official World Champion**
Born Ostrava, 7 March 1960; lives Greenwich, Conn.; RH; 6ft 2in; 175lb; final 1990 ATP ranking 3; 1990 prize money $1,445,742; career prize money $17,072,078.
Coached by Tony Roche. Hitting partner Chris Lewis from Jan 1991. Wife Samantha Frankl (married 16 Sept. 1989); daughter, Marike Lee, born 4 May 1990. **1977:** (Won Orange Bowl 18. **1978:** (74) Won Wimbledon, French, Italian Jun and became first ITF world jun champ. **1979:** (20) R/u Brussels. **1980:** (6) Won Houston, Toronto, Barcelona, Basel, Tokyo, Hong Kong, Taipei, beating world No. 1 Borg in Toronto and Basel. **1981:** (2) Won Stuttgart, Las Vegas, Montreal, Madrid, Barcelona, Basel, Vienna, Cologne, Buenos Aires, Masters, closing season with seven straight tourn wins and 35 straight matches, a streak which ended at 44 in Feb. 1982. **1982:** (3) Won 15 of 23 tourns and 106 of 115 matches, taking Frankfurt, Washington, North Conway, Cincinnati, WCT Delray Beach, WCT Genoa, WCT Munich, Strasbourg, Houston, Dallas, Forest Hills, LA, Naples, Hartford, Masters and r/u US Open. **1983:** (2) Won Detroit, Milan, Houston, Hilton Head, Montreal, San Francisco,

Tokyo, r/u US Open and Australian Open. *1984:* (3) Won French Open for first GS success in 5 finals, coming from two-sets-to-love down to oust McEnroe in f. Won Wembley and Luxembourg and reached sf Wimbledon and f US Open. *1985:* (1) Won 84 of 91 matches (31 consecutively from US Open to sf Australian Open) and 11 of 18 tournaments, capturing first US Open in fourth straight f and third Masters to cement his status as No. 1 in the world. *1986:* (1) Won 74 of 80 matches and 9 of 15 tournaments to take second consecutive US Open, second French Open, second consecutive Nabisco Masters and fourth in all, being beaten by only Becker, Noah, Edberg and Curren all year. *1987:* (1) Underwent arthroscopic knee surgery March, returning to win Hamburg in May. Still vulnerable on grass, he fell in sf Australian Open and 2nd consecutive Wimbledon f, both to Cash. However, he won 3rd French Open, 3rd US Open crown, a record 5th Masters, 5 other titles and finished the year undisputed No. 1 for 3rd consecutive year. *1988:* (2) In an injury-plagued year, a fractured bone in his right foot kept him out for 6 weeks in spring, and he underwent arthoscopic surgery on his right shoulder after US Open, returning for Masters, where he lost thrilling f to Becker. Won no GS, losing sf Australian Open to Cash, qf French Open to Svensson, sf Wimbledon to Becker and f US Open to Wilander. Lost to Fitzgerald in Philadelphia – the 1st time he had been beaten by a player outside the top 50 since losing to F. Gonzalez Aug. 1984 – and then to R. Smith at Stratton Mountain in July – the 1st time he'd lost to a player ranked as low as 150 since losing 1r Wimbledon to Fancutt in 1981. After US Open he lost the No. 1 ranking to Wilander, having held that position continuously for 156 weeks, just 3 weeks short of Connors's record of 159 weeks. However, he won Monte Carlo, Italian Open and Toronto during the year. *1989:* (1) Regained the No. 1 ranking after winning his 1st Australian Open. At Queen's won his 1st GP title on grass but failed again to win Wimbledon, lost 5s sf to Becker, and was r/u to the same player at US Open. Won a total of 10 titles and in autumn he achieved the highest No. 1 average ever in the history of the ATP computer rankings (208.5385). Was the 1st to qualify for Masters, but failed for 1st time in 10 appearances to reach f, falling in sf to an inspired Edberg. *1990:* Won Australian Open but missed French Open (1st GS he'd missed since Australian Open 1982) to prepare for Wimbledon. He looked to be on course to achieve his greatest ambition of winning there when he beat Becker for 1st time on grass to win Queen's, but at Wimbledon he never looked secure and fell to Edberg in sf. On 13 Aug. lost No. 1 ranking to Edberg, having held that position for 80 weeks since 30 Jan. 1989, and on 20 Aug. slipped to No. 3 behind Becker for 1st time since 1 April 1985. At US Open, seeded 3 for 1st time since 1983, he fell to Sampras in qf. Won a total of 5 titles, reached 1 other f and 3 sf, including ATP World Champ, where he lost to Becker in rr and Edberg in sf. Fined 15% of total earnings on ATP tour (excluding GS) for falling 2 tourns short of commitment to ATP. Reached 2r GS Cup as No. 2 seed, d. Bergstrom 6–4 6–0, lost Wheaton (8) 6–2 7–6. *1990 HIGHLIGHTS – SINGLES: won Australian Open* seed 1 (d. Pugh 6–3 6–2 6–4, Carbonell 6–4 6–2 6–3, Novacek 6–4 3–6 6–4 6–1, Youl 6–1 6–3 6–1, Cherkasov 6–3 6–2 6–3, Noah [seed 12] 6–4 6–1 6–2, Edberg [seed 3] 4–6 7–6 5–2 ret'd). *Wimbledon* sf, seed 1 (d. Miniussi 3–6 6–4 6–3 6–4, Hlasek 6–1 6–3 6–0, Shelton 7–6 6–7 6–4 6–4, Antonitsch 3–6 6–4 6–3 6–4, Pearce 6–4 6–4 5–7 6–4, lost Edberg [seed 3] 6–1 7–6 6–3), *US Open* qf, seed 3 (d. Laurendeau 7–5 6–2 6–2, Stich 6–4 5–7 6–4 6–3, Antonitsch 7–6 6–1 6–2, Bloom 6–0 6–3 6–4, lost Sampras 6–4 7–6 3–6 4–6 6–2); *won* Milan (d. Nargiso 6–3 6–3, Volkov 6–2 2–6 6–1, Courier 6–2 6–4, Sampras 3–6 6–0 6–3, Mayotte 6–3 6–2), *won* Toronto World Tennis (d. J. Brown 7–6 6–1, Haarhuis 7–5 6–2, Curren 6–7 7–6 6–3, J. McEnroe 6–3 6–2, Mayotte 6–3 6–0), *won* Queen's (d. Youl 6–4 6–2, S. Davis 6–4 6–2, Pate 6–2 6–4, J. McEnroe 6–2 6–4, Becker 6–3 6–2), *won* Tokyo Seiko (d. Woodforde 6–2 7–6, Masur 6–4 3–6 6–3, S. Davis 7–6 6–2, Edberg 7–5 6–3, Becker 4–6 6–3 7–6); *r/u* Stuttgart (d. Camporese 6–4 6–2, Prpic 7–5 6–4, Kuhnen 6–3 6–3, Gustafsson 6–4 6–7 6–3, lost Becker 6–2 6–2); *sf* Tokyo Suntory (d. Matsuoka 6–4 6–2, Russell 7–6 6–2, Mansdorf 6–4 6–2, lost Krickstein 6–3 5–7 6–4), *sf* Sydney Indoor (d. Rahunen 6–0 3–6 6–3, S. Davis 7–6 4–6 6–2, Lundgren 6–2 7–6, lost Edberg 3–6 7–6 6–3), *sf* ATP World Champ (d. Muster 6–3 6–3, Gomez 6–4 6–1, lost Becker 1–6 7–6 6–4 in rr, lost Edberg 6–4 6–2 in sf). *1990 HIGHLIGHTS – DOUBLES:* [Leconte] *r/u* Queen's (lost Bates/Curren 6–2 7–6), [Edberg] *r/u* Sydney Indoor (lost Dyke/Lundgren 6–2 6–4). *CAREER HIGHLIGHTS – SINGLES: Australian Open – won 1989* (d. Mronz, Steeb, Kulti, Mansdorf 7–6 6–4 6–2, J. McEnroe 7–6 6–2 7–6, Muster 6–2 6–4 5–7 7–5, Mecir 6–2 6–2 6–2), *won 1990, r/u 1983* (d. Mayotte 6–1 7–6 6–3, lost Wilander 6–1 6–4 6–4), *sf 1985* (lost Edberg 6–7 7–5 6–1 4–6 9–7), **sf 1987** (d. Jarryd 7–6 6–1 6–3, lost Cash 7–6 5–7 7–6 6–4), **sf 1988** (d. Woodforde, Masur 7–5 6–4 6–4, Witsken 6–2 6–1 7–6, lost Cash 6–4 2–6 6–2 4–6 6–2); **French Open – won 1984** (d. Wilander, J. McEnroe 3–6 2–6 6–4 7–5 7–5), **won 1986** (d. Westphal, Hlasek, Miniussi, Keretic, Gomez 6–7 7–6 6–0 6–0, Kriek 6–2 6–1 6–0, Pernfors 6–3 6–2 6–4), **won 1987** (d. Agenor, Canter, Tulasne, Nystrom 2–6 6–1 5–7 6–0 6–2, Gomez 5–7 6–4 6–1 6–1, Mecir 6–3 6–3 7–6), **r/u 1981** (d. McNamee 6–2 4–6 7–6 7–6, J. McEnroe 6–4 6–4 7–5, Clerc 3–6 6–4 4–6 7–6 6–2, lost Borg 6–1 4–6 6–2 3–6 6–1), **r/u 1985** (lost Wilander 3–6 6–4 6–2 6–2), **qf 1988** (lost Svensson 7–6 7–5 6–2); **US Open – won 1985** (d. Noah, Connors 6–2 6–3 7–5, J. McEnroe [seed 1] 7–6 6–3 6–4), **won 1986** (d. Svensson, Gilbert, Leconte, Edberg 7–6 6–2 6–3, Mecir 6–4 6–2 6–0), **won 1987** (d. Moir, Fleurian, Pugh, Jarryd 6–2 7–6 6–4, J. McEnroe 6–4 7–6 6–3, Connors 6–4 6–2 6–2), **r/u 1982** (d. J. McEnroe 6–4 6–4 7–6, lost Connors 6–3 6–2 0–6 6–4), **r/u 1983** (d. Wilander, Arias 6–2 7–6 6–1, lost Connors 6–3 6–7 7–5 6–0), **r/u 1984** (d. Cash 3–6 6–3 6–4 6–7 7–6 [saving 1 mp], lost J. McEnroe 6–3 6–4 6–4), **r/u 1988** (d. Hlasek, Rostagno, Agassi 4–6 6–2 6–3 6–4, lost Wilander 6–4 4–6 6–3 5–7 6–4), **r/u 1989** (d. Perez, Fitzgerald, Courier, Chesnokov 6–3 4–6 1–6 6–4 6–3, Mayotte 6–4 6–0 6–1, Agassi 7–6 6–1 3–6 6–1, lost Becker 7–6 1–6 6–3 7–6), **qf 1990; Masters – won 1981** (d. Gerulaitis, Vilas in rr, J. McEnroe 6–4 6–2, Gerulaitis 6–7 2–6 7–6 6–2 6–4), **won 1982** (d. Noah 6–4 7–5, Connors 6–3 6–1, J. McEnroe 6–4 6–4 6–2), **won 1985** (d. Becker 6–2 7–6 6–3), **won 1986** (d. Gomez, Edberg, Noah 6–4 6–4, Wilander 6–4 6–2, Becker 6–4 6–4 6–4), **won 1987** (d. Gilbert 6–2 6–4, Wilander 6–2 6–2 6–3), **r/u 1980** (d. Mayer 6–3 6–4, lost Borg 6–4 6–2 6–2), **r/u 1983** (d. Connors 6–3 6–4, lost J. McEnroe 6–3 6–4 6–4), **r/u 1984** (d. Connors, lost J. McEnroe 7–5 6–0 6–4), **r/u 1988** (d. Edberg 6–3 7–6, lost Becker 5–7 7–6 3–6 6–2 7–6), **sf 1989** (d. Chang, Krickstein, J. McEnroe in rr, lost Edberg 7–6 7–5), **Wimbledon – r/u 1986** (d. Lavelle, Freeman, Mansdorf, Anger, Mayotte 6–4 4–6 6–4 3–6 9–7, Zivojinovic 6–2 6–7 6–3 6–7 6–4, lost Becker 6–4 6–3 7–5), **r/u 1987** (d.Saceanu, Cane, Reneberg, Kreik, Leconte 7–6 6–3 7–6, Edberg 3–6 6–4 7–6 6–4, lost Cash 7–6 6–2 7–5), **sf 1983** (d. Tanner, lost J. McEnroe 7–6 6–4 6–4), **sf 1984** (lost Connors 6–7 6–3 7–5 6–1), **sf 1988** (d. Woodforde 7–5 6–7 6–7 7–5 10–8, Mayotte 7–6 7–6 6–3, lost Becker 6–4 6–3 6–7 6–4), **sf 1989** (d. Pereira 7–6 4–6 6–3 6–7 6–1, Bathman 6–7 6–3 6–2 6–2, Carbonell 7–6 6–3 6–1, Lundgren 1–6 7–6 6–2 6–4, Goldie 7–6 7–6 6–0, lost Becker 7–5 6–7 2–6 6–4 6–3), **sf 1990; D Cup – 1980 winning team** TCH.

CATARINA LINDQVIST (Sweden)
Born Kristinehamn, 13 June 1963; lives Holviksnas and London; RH; 5ft 5in; 125lb; final 1990 WTA ranking 38; 1990 prize money $109,994.
Husband Bill Ryan of IMG (married 16 July 1988). **1983:** (114). **1984:** (18) Won Hershey and Filderstadt and reached sf Canadian Open. **1985:** (13) Won Ginny Champs, and using superior topspin groundstrokes off both sides she upset Shriver at Australian Open, to reach qf, and Mandlikova at Key Biscayne. **1986:** (16) R/u to Graf at Brighton, had 4mps v Navratilova qf Filderstadt, reached first Wimbledon qf and won Bastad. **1987:** (16) Sf Australian Open, last 16 Wimbledon and US Open, r/u Bastad and qualified for VS Champs. **1988:** (42) Last 16 Australian Open; sf Oklahoma and Taipei, and upset Shriver and Manuela Maleeva during the year. **1989:** (16) Upset Shriver *en route* to qf Australian Open, and at Wimbledon upset Zvereva and Sukova *en route* to sf, becoming the first Swedish woman to reach that stage. At Sydney reached 1st f since Bastad 1987 and qualified for VS Champs, but fell 1r to Sanchez-Vicario. **1990:** At Tokyo Suntory she won her 1st primary circuit title since 1984, also reaching sf Brighton and qf Italian Open. **1990 HIGHLIGHTS – SINGLES: French Open** 1r (lost Kelesi 6–3 6–0), **Wimbledon** 1r (lost M. Maleeva 6–7 6–4 6–2), **US Open** 1r (lost Appelmans 6–4 6–7 6–4); **won** Tokyo Suntory (d. Durie 6–4 6–4, Appelmans 7–5 6–2, Cordwell 6–2 6–2, Sviglerova 6–1 6–2, Smylie 6–3 6–2); **sf** Brighton (d. Durie 3–6 6–4 6–2, Wood 6–2 6–0, Caverzasio 6–2 6–3, lost Graf 6–2 7–5). **CAREER HIGHLIGHTS – SINGLES: Australian Open – sf 1987** (d. Manuela Maleeva 6–3 6–3, Shriver 6–3 6–1, lost Navratilova 6–3 6–2), **qf 1985** (d. Shriver, lost Kohde-Kilsch [seed 5] 6–4 6–0), **qf 1989** (d. Shriver 1–6 6–3 6–4, Wiesner 7–5 6–2, lost Cordwell 6–2 2–6 6–1); **Wimbledon – sf 1989** (d. Cammy MacGregor, Demongeot, Zvereva 7–6 4–6 6–4, Sukova 6–4 7–6, Fairbank Nideffer 7–5 7–5, lost Navratilova 7–6 6–2), **qf 1986** (d. Rush, Kelesi, E. Minter, Balestrat 6–2 7–5, lost Sabatini 6–2 6–3).

SARAH LOOSEMORE (Great Britain)
Born Cardiff, 15 June 1971, and lives there; RH; 5ft 9in; 140lb; final 1990 WTA ranking 82; 1990 prize money $50,153.
Coached by Simon Jones and Ken Fletcher. **1987:** (367) R/u Telford on the British satellite circuit. Played Jun Wightman Cup. **1988:** (159). **1989:** (298) Out most of year owing to injuries and A levels. **1990:** Broke into the top 100 after reaching her lst tour f at Singapore in April; upset Paulus 1r Wimbledon and played Fed Cup. Taking the year to decide whether to continue playing the circuit or to take up her place at Oxford Univ. in 1991. **1990 HIGHLIGHTS – SINGLES: Australian Open** 3r (d. Faull 6–3 7–5, Pampoulova 6–3 6–3, lost Sukova [seed 4] 6–3 4–6 6–3), **French Open** 1r (lost Santrock 6–2 6–4), **Wimbledon** 2r (d. Paulus [seed 16] 6–2 3–6 6–4, lost E. Reinach 6–3 7–5); **r/u** Singapore (d. Strnadova 6–3 6–4, Pawlik 6–0 6–1, Toleafoa 5–7 6–4 6–2, Hy 6–3 6–4 Appelmans 5–7 6–2 6–3, lost Sawamatsu 7–6 3–6 6–4).

JORGE LOZANO (Mexico)
Born San Luis Potosi, 17 May 1963; lives Guadalajara; RH; 5ft 11in; 159lb; final 1990 ATP ranking 248 singles, 17 doubles; 1990 prize money $147,993.
1980: Nat Jun champ. **1981:** Played D Cup. **1985:** (493) 3rd year as All-American at Univ. of Southern Cal. **1986:** (391). **1987:** (107) Won Lagos Challenger as lucky loser. **1988:** (62) Reached his 1st GP sf at Philadelphia and appeared unexpectedly in last 16 US Open. In doubles won 3 titles and reached 5 more f with Witsken to qualify for Masters, where they lost sf to R. Leach and Pugh. Won French Open mixed doubles with McNeil. **1989:** (350) In singles won San Luis Challenger. In doubles with Witsken won 2 titles and qualified for Masters, where they took 5th place. **1990:** In doubles won Rotterdam with Lavalle, reached 2 more f with Witsken and took a second French Open mixed title, with Sanchez-Vicario. **1990 HIGHLIGHTS – DOUBLES:** (with Witsken unless stated) [Lavalle] **won** Rotterdam (d. Nargiso/Pereira 6–3 7–6); **r/u** Washington (lost Connell/Michibata 6–3 6–7 6–2), **r/u** Vienna (lost Riglewski/Stich 6–4 6–4). **1990 HIGHLIGHTS – MIXED DOUBLES:** (with Sanchez-Vicario) **won French Open** (d. Provis/Visser 7–6 7–6). **CAREER HIGHLIGHTS – MIXED DOUBLES: French Open** – [McNeil] **won 1988** (d. Schultz/Schapers 7–5 6–2), [Sanchez-Vicario] **won 1990.**

PETER LUNDGREN (Sweden)
Born Sundsvall, 29 January 1965; lives there and Monte Carlo; RH; 6ft 1in; 167lb; final 1990 ATP ranking 65; 1990 prize money $241,333.
Coached by Per Hjertqvist. **1985:** (27) The most improved player among the Swedes, he won first GP title in Cologne. **1986:** (98) Won only 7 matches in first 13 tournaments, with best showing sf Los Angeles, and dropped in the rankings. **1987:** (26) After a poor start in which he failed to pass 2r in all tournaments until end July, he had his best season yet, upsetting Wilander 2r Cincinnati, winning Rye Brook to break into top 50, stunning Cash 3r Canadian Open and 1r US Open and beating Lendl *en route* to 1st SS title in San Francisco. **1988:** (66) Having reached qf only at Adelaide and Newport, he upset Mecir at Stockholm and swept to f, where he lost to Becker. R/u Australian Open doubles with Bates. **1989:** (71) R/u Newport and upset Pernfors *en route* to last 16 Wimbledon. **1990:** Upset Jaite and Agassi *en route* to f Indianapolis. Reached 3 doubles f, winning Sydney Indoor with Dyke. **1990 HIGHLIGHTS – SINGLES: French Open** 1r (lost Hlasek 3–6 7–6 2–6 7–5 6–2), **Wimbledon** 1r (lost Bates 6–7 6–7 6–4 6–4 6–0), **US Open** 2r (d. Garner 6–1 6–2 6–2, lost Sampras [seed 12] 6–4 6–3 6–3); **r/u** Indianapolis (d. Failla 6–3 6–1, Jaite 3–6 6–3 6–3, Matsuoka 6–4 1–6 7–5, Agassi 6–4 6–0, Reneberg 6–4 6–4, lost Becker 6–3 6–4). **1990 HIGHLIGHTS – DOUBLES:** (with Dyke unless stated) **won** Sydney Indoor (d. Edberg/Lendl 6–2 6–4); **r/u** Canadian Open (lost Annacone/Wheaton 6–1 7–6), [Wekesa] **r/u** Los Angeles (lost S. Davis/Pate 3–6 6–1 6–3). **CAREER HIGHLIGHTS – DOUBLES:** (with Bates) **Australian Open – r/u 1988** (lost R. Leach/Pugh 6–3 6–2 6–3).

JOHN McENROE (USA)
Born Wiesbaden, West Germany, 16 February 1959; lives New York and Malibu, Cal.; LH; 5ft 11in; 165lb; final 1990 ATP ranking 13; 1990 prize money $372,505; career prize money $11,265,336.
Wife Tatum O'Neal (married Aug. 1986); sons Kevin (born May 1986) and Sean Timothy (born Sept. 1987). As youth, coached at Pt. Washington Tennis Academy by Harry

Hopman. Later by Tony Palafox. *1976:* (264) R/u to Larry Gottfried at US Nat 18 Champs and won Orange Bowl 18s. *1977:* (21) Stunned tennis world by reaching sf Wimbledon as qualifier and taking set off Connors. *1978:* (4) Turned pro in June after winning NCAA title as Stanford freshman. Won Hartford, San Francisco, Stockholm and Wembley in autumn, led US D Cup triumph, and closed year by saving 2 mps to beat Ashe in Masters f. *1979:* (3) Won US Open, WCT Finals, New Orleans, Milan, San José, Queens Club, South Orange, San Francisco, Stockholm and Wembley and again led US D Cup triumph. *1980:* (2) Lost epic Wimbledon f to Borg after saving 7 mps in 4s, finally falling 8–6 5s. Won second straight US Open with 5s triumph over Borg as well as Richmond, Memphis, Milan, Queens Club, Brisbane, Sydney, Wembley and WCT Montreal. *1981:* (1) Became first male player since Connors in 1974 to win Wimbledon and US Open in same year, stopping Borg in both f to replace the Swede as the No. 1 player in the world. Led US to D Cup victory. *1982:* (1) Lost to Connors in 5s Wimbledon f, coming within three points of victory at 4–3 in 4s tb. After losing to Lendl in sf US Open and f Masters, he was regarded by many experts as No. 3 behind Connors and Lendl. Led US to D Cup victory for 4th time in 5 years and won US Pro Indoor, San Francisco, Sydney, Tokyo and Wembley. *1983:* (1) Won his second Wimbledon and Masters titles, beating Lendl in sf former and f latter. Also won US Pro Indoor, WCT Dallas, Forest Hills, Sydney and Wembley to become undisputed No. 1. *1984:* (1) Won 13 of 15 tournaments and 79 of 82 matches, losing only to Lendl in f French Open, V. Amritraj at Cincinnati and Sundstrom in D Cup f. For the second time he won Wimbledon and US Open, producing glorious form to rout Connors in Wimbledon f and dismissing Lendl with relative ease 6–3 6–4 6–1 in US Open f. Only his loss to Lendl from 2 sets to 0 ahead in f French Open spoiled a nearly perfect year. *1985:* (2) Won Philadelphia, Houston, Chicago, Milan, Atlanta, Stratton, Montreal and Stockholm, but was soundly beaten by Curren in qf Wimbledon and Lendl in f US Open. When he lost to Gilbert in 1r Masters, he elected to take a 6-month sabbatical from the game. *1986:* (14) Returning to competition in Stratton Mountain in July, he lost to Becker in sf after holding 4 mps, then lost to Seguso in 3r Canadian Open and suffered his first 1r defeat at US Open to Annacone. He rebounded with three straight tourn wins (LA, San Francisco and Scottsdale), but was beaten thereafter by Casal in qf of Paris Indoor and Cash in 1r Wembley. *1987:* (10) In f World Team Cup v Mecir he walked off the court following two disputed umpiring decisions, later claiming that a back injury had prompted his withdrawal, and avoided threatened suspension when MIPTC accepted that he was indeed injured. However, following US Open, when he accumulated fines exceeding $7,500 for the second time in the year, he was suspended for 2 months from 28 Sept. Continuing to be plagued by injuries, and missing Wimbledon with a leg injury, he began working with physical trainers Dae-Shik Seo and Chuck Debus. Reached f 5 times but won no title. *1988:* (11) Won Tokyo for his 71st title and his 1st since Oct. 1986, following with Detroit, and was r/u Indianapolis. Formed a successful partnership with Woodforde in autumn. Coached by Peter Fleming until end of year. *1989:* (4) Playing with renewed confidence he won WCT Finals for record fifth time (d. Lendl for 1st time in 4 years), Lyon and Indianapolis. Missed French Open with back trouble and prepared enthusiastically for Wimbledon, where he reached sf, but fell 2r US Open to qualifier Haarhuis. However, he won the doubles title there with Woodforde. Played Masters for 1st time since losing to Gilbert 1r in 1985, and reached sf (lost Becker). *1990:* At Australian Open became the 1st player since Willy Alvarez at French Open in 1963 to be disqualified from a GS tourn, following a third code of conduct warning for verbal abuse in 4r match v Pernfors. He was fined $6,000 for extreme verbal abuse, although he claimed that he believed GS events were still run on the basis of four warnings. Out nearly 4 months to June with a shoulder injury and lacking motivation, and fell 1r Wimbledon to Rostagno. His ranking dropped to 21 until, unseeded for the 1st time in 12 years, he reached sf US Open. Returned to top 10 for a while, having also won Basel, to become only the 2nd player after Sherwood Stewart to win titles in 3 decades. Sf Milan, Toronto World Tennis, Queen's and Long Island, Reunited during the year with his former coach, Tony Palafox. *1990 HIGHLIGHTS – SINGLES: Australian Open* last 16, seed 4 (d. Tulasne 6–2 6–1 6–1, Antonitsch 6–1 6–2 6–1, Goldie 6–3 6–2 6–2, lost Pernfors 1–6 6–4 5–7 4–2 def.), *Wimbledon* 1r, seed 4 (lost Rostagno 7–5 6–4 6–4), *US Open* sf, unseeded (d. J. Sanchez 7–6 7–6 6–4, Engel 6–2 6–3 7–5, Chesnokov [seed 10] 6–3 7–5 6–4, E. Sanchez 7–6 3–6 4–6 6–4 6–3, Wheaton 6–1 6–4 6–4, lost Sampras 6–2 6–4 3–6 6–3); *won* Basel (d. Srejber 6–4 6–3, Kulti 6–1 6–2, Cherkasov 6–3

7–5, Melville 6–2 2–6 6–3, Ivanisevic 6–7 4–6 7–6 6–3 6–4); *sf* Milan (d. Cherkasov 6–1 4–6 6–4, Cane 6–4 6–1, Jelen 6–3 6–3, lost Mayotte 6–4 6–4), *sf* Toronto World Tennis (d. Chamberlin 6–3 6–3, Shiras 6–4 6–3, Berger 6–4 6–0, lost Lendl 6–3 6–2), *sf* Queen's (d. Krishnan 4–6 6–4 6–2, Paloheimo 6–0 6–7 7–5, Fromberg 6–7 6–3 7–5, lost Lendl 6–2 6–4), *sf* Long Island (d. Borwick 6–4 6–1, Stich 6–3 7–5, Gilbert 6–3 6–2, lost Edberg 6–1 6–4). *CAREER HIGHLIGHTS – SINGLES: Wimbledon – won 1981*, seed 2 (d. Ramirez, Smith, Kriek, Frawley 7–6 6–4 7–5, Borg 4–6 7–6 7–6 6–4), *won 1983* (d. Lendl 7–6 6–4 6–4, C. Lewis 6–2 6–2 6–2), *won 1984* (d. Connors 6–1 6–1 6–2), *r/u 1980*, seed 2 (d. Connors 6–3 3–6 6–3 6–4, lost Borg 1–6 7–5 6–3 6–7 8–6), *r/u 1982* (lost Connors 3–6 6–3 6–7 7–6 6–4), *sf 1977*, unseeded after qualifying (lost Connors 6–3 3–6 6–3 4–6 6–4), *sf 1989* (d. Cahill 4–6 4–6 6–2 6–3 8–6, Reneberg 6–3 3–6 6–3 7–5, Pugh 6–3 6–4 6–2, Fitzgerland 6–3 0–6 6–4 6–4, Wilander 7–6 3–6 6–3 6–4, lost Edberg 7–5 7–6 7–6); *US Open – won 1979* (d. Connors 6–3 6–3 7–5, Gerulaitis 7–5 6–4 6–3), *won 1980*, seed 2 (d. Lendl 4–6 6–3 6–2 7–5, Connors 6–4 5–7 0–6 6–3 7–6, Borg 7–6 6–1 6–7 5–7 6–4), *won 1981* (d. Gerulaitis 5–7 6–3 6–2 4–6 6–3, Borg 4–6 6–2 6–4 6–3), *won 1984* (d. Connors 6–4 4–6 7–5 4–6 6–3, Lendl 6–3 6–4 6–4), *r/u 1985* (d. Wilander 3–6 6–4 4–6 6–3 6–3, lost Lendl 7–6 6–3 6–4), *sf 1982* (lost Lendl 6–4 6–4 7–6), *sf 1990; WCT Finals – won 1979* (d. Connors 6–1 6–4 6–4, Borg 7–5 4–6 6–2 7–6), *won 1981* (d. Kriek 6–1 6–2 6–4), *won 1983* (d. Lendl 6–2 4–6 6–7 7–6), *won 1984* (d. Connors 6–1 6–2 6–3), *won 1989* (d. Lendl 6–7 7–6 6–2 7–6, Gilbert 3 6–3 7–6); *Masters – won 1979* (d. Ashe 6–7 6–3 7–5), *won 1983* (d. Wilander 6–2 7–5, Lendl 6–3 6–4 6–4), *won 1984* (d. Wilander 6–1 6–1, Lendl 7–5 6–0 6–4), *r/u 1982* (d. Vilas, lost Lendl 6–4 6–4 6–2), *sf 1981* (lost Lendl 6–4 6–2), *sf 1989* (d. Krickstein, Chang, lost Lendl in rr, lost Becker 6–4 6–4); *French Open – r/u 1984* (lost Lendl 3–6 2–6 6–4 7–5 7–5); *sf 1985* (lost Wilander 6–1 7–5 7–5). *CAREER HIGHLIGHTS – DOUBLES:* (with Fleming) *Wimbledon – won 1979* (d. Gottfried/Ramirez 6–2 4s), *won 1981* (d. Smith/Lutz 6–4 6–4 6–4), *won 1983* (d. Tim/Tom Gullikson 6–4 6–3 6–4), *won 1984* (d. Cash/McNamee 6–2 5–7 6–2 3–6 6–3), *r/u 1978* (lost Hewitt/McMillan 6–1 6–4 6–2), *r/u 1982* (lost McNamara/McNamee 6–3 6–1), *sf 1980* (lost McNamara/McNamee 6–3 6–3 6–3), *sf 1985* (lost Cash/Fitzgerald 7–6 2–6 6–1 6–4), *US Open – won 1979* (d. Smith/Lutz), *won 1981* (d. Newcombe/Stolle 6–2 6–2 6–7 5–7 7–6, McNamara/Gunthardt def.), *won 1983* (d. Buehning/Winitsky 6–3 6–4 6–2), [Woodforde] *won 1989* (d. Flach/Seguso 6–4 4–6 6–3 6–3); *Masters – won 1978* (d. Lutz/Smith 6–4 6–2 6–4), *won 1979* (d. Fibak/Okker 6–4 6–2 6–4), *won 1980* (d. McNamara/McNamee 6–4 6–4), *won 1981* (d. Curren/Denton 6–3 6–3), *won 1982* (d. Stewart/Taygan 7–5 6–3), *won 1983* (d. Slozil/Smid 6–2 6–2), *won 1984* (d. Edmondson/Stewart 6–3 6–1).

PATRICK McENROE (USA)

Born Manhasset, NY, 7 July 1966; lives Oyster Bay, NY; RH; 2HB; 6ft; 160lb; final 1990 ATP ranking 120 singles, 23 doubles; 1990 prize money $160,605.
Brother of John. **1983:** R/u US Nat 18s. **1984:** Won Nat GC 18s. **1987:** (452) Won San Francisco doubles with Grabb. **1988:** (494) Graduated from Stanford and in winning NCAA team. 3 times All-American in singles (1986–8). R/u US Open mixed doubles with Smylie. **1989:** (356) Won French Open and Masters doubles with Grabb. Elected ATP Tour Council. **1990:** In singles reached qf Hong Kong and Singapore before appearing in his 1st tour sf at Rosmalen. In doubles with Grabb won Wembley and reached 2 more f. *1990 HIGHLIGHTS – SINGLES: US Open* 2r (d. Tarango 6–3 6–4 1–6 2–6 7–5, lost Van Rensburg 6–4 6–4 7–5); *sf* Rosmalen (d. Kempers 6–0 6–3, Siemerink 6–2 6–3, Weiss 6–3 6–4, lost Volkov 6–3 4–6 6–3). *1990 HIGHLIGHTS – DOUBLES:* (with Grabb) *won* Wembley (d. R. Leach/Pugh 7–6 4–6 6–3); *r/u* Indian Wells (lost Becker/Forget 4–6 6–4 6–3), *r/u* Rosmalen (lost Hlasek/Stich 7–6 6–3). *CAREER HIGHLIGHTS – DOUBLES:* (with Grabb) *French Open – won 1989* (d. Bahrami/Winogradsky 6–4 2–6 6–4 7–6); *Masters – won 1989* (d. Jarryd/Fitzgerald 7–5 7–6 5–7 6–3); *LIPC – r/u 1989* (lost Hlasek/Jarryd 6–3 ret'd).

MEREDITH McGRATH (USA)

Born Midland, Mich., 28 April 1971 and lives there; RH; 2HB; 5ft 7in; 130lb; final 1990 WTA ranking 28 singles, 16 doubles; 1990 prize money $110,124.
Coached by Glenn William. **1987:** Won US Open Jun doubles with Po. **1988:** Won US Jun doubles with Po again and was No. 3 in ITF Jun Doubles Rankings. **1989:** (94) Upset Reggi *en route* to sf VS Kansas. R/u Wimbledon Jun to Strnadova and won Jun doubles at

Wimbledon and US Open with Capriati. *1990:* In singles reached sf VS California plus qf VS Indian Wells and Newport; in doubles won 4 titles with 3 different partners. *1990 HIGHLIGHTS – SINGLES: Wimbledon* 2r (d. Brioukhovets 6–1 6–2, lost Graf [seed 1] 6–3 6–0), *US Open* 1r (lost Gildemeister 7–5 6–3); *sf* VS California (d. S. Martin 6–1 7–5, Paulus 6–7 6–1 6–0, Fairbank Nideffer 6–3 4–6 6–3, lost Navratilova 6–4 6–3). *1990 HIGHLIGHTS – DOUBLES:* (with Bollegraf unless stated) *won* Wichita (d. Daniels/W. White 6–0 6–2). [A. Smith] *won* VS Albuquerque (d. Louie Harper/White Prausa 7–6 6–4), [A. Smith] *won* VS California (d. Fairbank Nideffer/R. White 2–6 6–0 6–4), [Fendick] *won* Indianapolis (d. Adams/Hetherington 6–1 6–1); *r/u* Orlando (lost Savchenko/Zvereva 6–4 6–1).

LORI McNEIL (USA)
Born San Diego, Cal., 18 December 1963; lives Houston, Texas; 5ft 7in; 135lb; RH; final 1990 WTA ranking 52 singles, 22 (16) doubles; 1990 prize money $162,939; career prize money $1,392,083.
Coached by Willis Thomas. *1983:* Member US Jun Fed Cup team, ranked 8 US Intercollegiate list and 4 on USTA satellite circuit. *1984:* (97) Reached last 16 US Open and led Mandlikova by a set and 4–2 before losing. *1985:* (93). *1986:* (14) Burst out of the pack and established herself as one of top 15 players in world. Won Tampa – over Garrison in first VS Series final between two black women – and VS Tulsa back-to-back in Sept. Ably coached by John Wilkerson, who was also Garrison's instructor, she reached qf Wimbledon unseeded and qualified first time for VS Champs in Nov., clearly the most improved fast-court player in the world. *1987:* (11) Qf Australian Open and sf US Open, where she spoiled Evert's record of winning at least one GS event each year by beating her in qf. Won no singles title but reached f Oklahoma, New Orleans and New Jersey. In doubles r/u Australian Open with Garrison, won 6 titles and r/u 7 more with 5 different partners. Qualified for VS Champs in singles and doubles. *1988:* (13) Won Oklahoma and Newport in singles, took 5 doubles titles with different partners, and won French Open mixed with Lozano. Qualified for VS Champs in both singles and doubles. *1989:* (37) Upset Evert *en route* to f Pan Pacific Open in Tokyo, where she took Navratilova to 3s tb, then won her first singles title for 13 months at Albuquerque. In doubles with various partners she reached 8 f, winning 5. *1990:* Upset Sabatini and G. Fernandez *en route* to sf San Antonio and reached the same stage at Eastbourne. Qualified for VS Champs doubles with K. Adams, upsetting Savchenko/Zvereva to reach sf. *1990 HIGHLIGHTS – SINGLES: Australian Open* 1r (lost K. Maleeva [seed 9] 6–2 6–2), *French Open* 1r (lost Gildemeister 7–6 6–3), *Wimbledon* 3r (d. Piccolini 6–1 3–6 6–1, Coetzer 6–3 6–2, lost Herreman 6–4 6–3), *US Open* 2r (d. Keller 6–4 6–3, lost Paulus [seed 16] 6–2 4–6 6–4); *sf* San Antonio (d. Sabatini 6–3 6–4, G. Fernandez 6–2 6–0, lost Maleeva Fragnière 6–0 6–4), *sf* Eastbourne (d. Porwik 4–6 6–2 7–6, Dahlman 6–1 6–2, Golarsa 6–3 6–3, Bollegraf 6–3 1–1 ret'd, lost Magers 7–6 6–2). *CAREER HIGHLIGHTS – SINGLES: US Open – sf 1987* (d. Provis, Garrison 7–6 3–6 7–5, Evert 3–6 6–2 6–4, lost Graf 4–6 6–2 6–4); *Wimbledon – qf 1986,* unseeded (d. Bryant, Mesker, Burgin 6–3 6–2, Nagelsen 7–5 6–1, lost Mandlikova [seed 3] 6–7 6–0 6–2); *Australian Open – qf 1987* (lost Mandlikova 6–0 6–0). *CAREER HIGHLIGHTS – DOUBLES:* (with Garrison) *Australian Open – r/u 1987* (lost Navratilova/Shriver 6–1 6–0). *MIXED DOUBLES:* (with Lozano) *French Open – won 1988* (d. Schultz/Schapers 7–5 6–2).

RACHEL McQUILLAN (Australia)
Born Waratah, NSW, 2 December 1971; lives Newcastle, NSW; RH; 2HB; 5ft 7in; 132lb; final 1990 WTA ranking 39; 1990 prize money $124,758.
Coached by Ken Richardson and Terry Rocavert. *1987:* (448) In winning World Youth Cup team. *1988:* (202) Won Australian Open and Wimbledon Jun doubles with Faull; r/u US Open Jun to Cunningham. Ranked No. 2 in ITF Jun doubles and No. 5 in singles. *1989:* (79) Qf Adelaide and Hamburg, then upset Cecchini *en route* to f Athens. R/u US Open Jun to Capriati. *1990:* Upset Wiesner twice to make surprise appearances in f Brisbane and Kitzbuhel. In GS overturned Kelesi *en route* to last 16 Australian Open, unseeded, and in doubles reached 2 f with Faull. *1990 HIGHLIGHTS – SINGLES: Australian Open* last 16, unseeded (d. Bonsignori 6–1 6–2, Sharpe 6–3 6–0, Kelesi [seed 8] 6–2 6–4, lost K. Maleeva [seed 9] 3–6 6–4 6–1), *French Open* 1r (lost Meskhi 6–4 6–1), *Wimbledon* 2r (d. Reggi 7–6 7–6, lost Schultz 6–4 3–6 7–5), *US Open* 2r (d. Harvey-Wild 7–6 7–5, lost Graf [seed 1] 6–1 6–3); *r/u* Brisbane (d. Temesvari 6–1 6–1, Smylie 6–1 3–6 6–1, Martin 6–1 6–4, Date 6–0

6–4, Wiesner 6–3 7–6, lost Zvereva 6–4 6–0), *r/u* Kitzbuhel (d. Krajcovicova 2–6 7–5 6–2, Giusto 6–2 6–1, Martinek 6–2 7–5, Wiesner 7–6 6–3, lost Kohde-Kilsch 7–6 6–4). *1990 HIGHLIGHTS – DOUBLES:* (with Faull) *r/u* Tokyo Toray (lost G. Fernandez/Smylie 6–2 6–2), *r/u* Bayonne (lost Field/Tanvier 7–6 6–7 7–6).

GRETCHEN RUSH MAGERS (USA)
Born Pittsburgh, Pa, 7 February 1964; lives San Diego, Cal.; RH; 5ft 7in; 135lb; final 1990 WTA ranking 35 singles, 18 doubles; 1990 prize money $175,652.
1981: Won US CC 18s. *1982:* Qf US Open (d. Jausovec and Turnbull). Top of ITF Jun World Rankings, r/u US Open Jun, won Italian Open Jun and US 18 GC and played Jun W Cup. *1983:* (55) Qf French Open. At Trinity, won NCAA doubles with Louise Allen. Won 3 doubles titles on US circuit and played Jun Fed Cup. *1984:* (81) All-American for 2nd year and played W Cup. *1985:* (176) R/u NCAA Champs singles and doubles with Sassano. *1986:* (74) Married Stephen Magers Dec. *1987:* (53) Won Auckland. *1988:* (40) Won Schenectady and reached 6 other qf. Upset Lindqvist at Bastad. *1989:* (29) At Wimbledon upset Shriver (12–10 fs) *en route* to qf, unseeded. Won Moscow, reached sf Schenectady and qualified for VS Champs, where she fell 1r to Sabatini. Received Karen Krantzcke Sportsmanship award. *1990:* In singles upset Capriati *en route* to f Eastbourne and reached sf VS Newport and Moscow. Won 3 doubles titles and qualified for VS Champs with Gregory. *1990 HIGHLIGHTS – SINGLES: French Open* 1r (lost Wiesner 6–4 6–0), *Wimbledon* 3r (d. Smylie 6–1 7–6, Savchenko 6–3 6–4, lost Zvereva [seed 11] 2–6 6–2 6–4), *US Open* 1r (lost Bollegraf 6–2 6–1); *r/u* Eastbourne (d. Smylie 6–1 7–6, Capriati 2–6 6–4 6–2, Durie 6–4 3–6 6–3, M-J. Fernandez 6–2 2–2 ret'd, McNeil 7–6 6–2, lost Navratilova 6–0 6–2); *sf* VS Newport (d. Golarsa 6–4 7–6, Richardson 6–1 6–1, Field 6–0 7–6, lost Sanchez-Vicario 6–3 6–2), *sf* Moscow (d. Wasserman 6–3 4–6 6–2, Loosemore 6–3 6–3, Reinstadler 7–5 2–6 6–4, lost Brioukhovets 6–4 6–3). *1990 HIGHLIGHTS – DOUBLES:* (with Gregory unless stated) *won* VS Newport (d. Fendick/A. Smith 7–6 6–1), *won* Leipzig (d. Bollegraf/Durie 6–2 4–6 6–3), [R. White] *won* Moscow (d. Brioukhovets/Maniokova 6–2 6–4); *r/u* Birmingham (lost Savchenko/Zvereva 3–6 6–3 6–3). *CAREER HIGHLIGHTS – SINGLES: French Open – qf 1983* (d. Manuela Maleeva, Madruga Osses, lost Jaeger 6–2 6–2); *Wimbledon – qf 1989* (d. Bollegraf, Lake, Shriver 2–6 6–2 12–10, Faull 6–7 6–1 6–0, lost Navratilova 6–1 6–2); *US Open – qf 1982* (d. Jausovec 7–5 2–6 6–4, Mundel, Turnbull 6–3 4–6 6–2, lost Jaeger 3–6 6–1 6–0).

KATERINA MALEEVA (Bulgaria)
Born Sofia, 7 May 1969 and lives there; RH; 2HB; 5ft 6in; 122lb; final 1990 WTA ranking 6; 1990 prize money $418,475.
Coached by her mother, 9 times Bulgarian champion Yulia Berberian. Sister of Manuela and Magdalena. *1984:* (93) Won US Open Jun and was r/u to Sabatini at both Orange Bowl and French Open Jun while making her mark in women's play as well. *1985:* (28) Won Seabrook Island and Hilversum and stopped some of the big names in the sport like Shriver, Sukova and Garrison. *1986:* (28) Did not pass qf in 20 tournaments but won 26 of 47 matches. Played Fed Cup again with sister and mother. *1987:* (13) Beat Sukova 3r Mahwah, won Japan/Asian Open for first title since 1985, following with Athens and qualifying for VS Champs 1st time. *1988:* (11) Upset Sukova to reach f US HC and again *en route* to qf Hamburg. After reaching f Hamburg, won 1st primary circuit title at Indianapolis, beating Garrison in f. Qualified for VS Champs again. *1989:* (15) Won Bastad, Bayonne and VS Indianapolis; r/u Sofia. *1990:* Won VS Houston (d. Navratilova and Sanchez-Vicario back-to-back), r/u Tampa (d. Sanchez-Vicario) and Canadian Open (d. Sabatini and took Graf to 3s), and appeared in 5 more sf. In GS reached qf Australian Open, French Open and Wimbledon. Broke into the top 10, overtaking her elder sister in the rankings in June, and qualified for VS Champs, where she lost qf to Graf. *1990 HIGHLIGHTS – SINGLES: Australian Open* qf, seed 9 (d. McNeil 6–2 6–2, McDonald 6–3 6–2, Jagerman 6–0 6–4, McQuillan 3–6 6–4 6–1, lost Sukova [seed 4] 6–4 6–3), *French Open* qf, seed 8 (d. Appelmans 6–3 6–3, Faber 7–5 6–1, Halard 6–2 6–1, Provis 3–6 6–3 6–3, lost Novotna [seed 11] 4–6 6–2 6–4), *Wimbledon* qf, seed 7 (d. B. Romano 6–2 6–4, Date 6–1 6–4, DeVries 6–2 6–0, Herreman 6–3 6–0, lost Navratilova [seed 2] 6–1 6–1), *US Open* last 16, seed 7 (d. M. Maleeva 6–3 6–1, Kschwendt 7–5 6–1, Reggi 6–4 6–0, lost Novotna [seed 12] 6–4 6–2); *won* VS Houston (d. Meskhi 7–6 6–1, Gildemeister 6–2 7–6, Navratilova 6–4 2–6 6–1, Sanchez-Vicario 6–1 1–6 6–4); *r/u* Tampa (d. La Fratta 6–1 6–0, Ferrando 6–2

6–1, Cecchini 6–4 6–2, Sanchez-Vicario 6–4 6–2, lost Seles 6–1 6–0), **r/u** Canadian Open (d. Cordwell 6–0 6–2, Richardson 6–0 6–0, Sawamatsu 6–7 6–2 6–4, Sabatini 6–3 6–4, lost Graf 6–1 6–7 6–3); **sf** VS Indian Wells (d. Rinaldi 6–1 6–3, G. Fernandez 6–3 6–2, McGrath 6–1 6–2, lost Navratilova 7–6 6–1), **sf** Tokyo Nicherei (d. G. Fernandez 6–7 6–2 6–2, Capriati 7–6 3–6 7–6, lost Frazier 7–5 6–4), **sf** Filderstadt (d. Cueto 6–0 6–1, Porwik 6–3 6–1, Novotna 7–6 6–3, lost M-J. Fernandez 7–5 6–0), **sf** Brighton (d. Thoren 6–3 5–7 6–3, Hand 6–2 6–2, Cecchini 7–5 6–0, lost Sukova 6–4 6–7 6–3), **sf** Indianapolis (d. Wasserman 6–2 6–1, Pampoulova 6–1 6–2, Sloane 6–3 7–5, lost Meskhi 6–2 6–4). **CAREER HIGHLIGHTS – SINGLES: Australian Open – qf 1990; French Open – qf 1990; Wimbledon – qf 1990; US Open – qf 1988** (d. Sukova 6–1 6–3, lost Graf 6–3 6–0).

MAGDALENA MALEEVA (Bulgaria)
Born Sofia, 1 April 1975, and lives there; RH; 2HB; 5ft 6in; 109lb; final 1990 WTA ranking 72; 1990 prize money $56,907.
Coached by Jan Kurtz and her mother, Yulia Berberian. Sister of Manuela and Katerina. **1988:** Won Orange Bowl 12s. **1989:** (211) R/u Bari on Italian satellite circuit in first pro tourn. **1990:** In Jun singles won Australian Open (d. Stacey 7–5 6–7 6–1), French Open (d. Ignatieva 6–2 6–3) and US Open (d. Van Lottum 7–5 6–2). On the senior tour reached qf Wellington and after upsetting Lindqvist at Wimbledon she moved into the top 100. **1990 HIGHLIGHTS – SINGLES: French Open** 3r (d. Labat 6–7 6–4 6–3, Rajchrtova 6–2 6–3, lost Gildemeister 6–1 6–3), **Wimbledon** 2r (d. Lindqvist 6–7 6–4 6–2, lost R. White 4–6 7–5 6–4), **US Open** 1r (lost K. Maleeva 6–3 6–1).

MANUELA MALEEVA FRAGNIÈRE (Switzerland)
Born Sofia, Bulgaria, 14 February 1967; lives Bourg-Dessous; RH; 2HB; 5ft 8in; 127lb; final 1990 WTA ranking 9; 1990 prize money $360,215; career prize money $1,966,679.
Coached by her husband, Swiss coach François Fragnière (married Dec. 1987). Daughter of Yulia Berberian, 9 times Bulgarian women's champion; sister of Katerina and Magdalena. Played for Switzerland Jan. 1990. **1981:** Won Orange Bowl 14s. **1982:** (60) This stylish groundstroker made inroads in women's events but concluded jun career on sad note when her mother ordered her off the court as she trailed Bassett 3–6 3–4 in Orange Bowl f at Miami Beach. **1983:** (31) Upsets of Mandlikova and Bunge signalled her swift advance. **1984:** (6) In her most productive season, she won 5 tourns, including Italian Open, on the last day of which she completed qf win over Ruzici and then dismissed Bassett and Evert Lloyd. Voted Most Impressive Newcomer. **1985:** (7) Won Tokyo Pacific to close year with her only singles title. **1986:** (8) Reached qf or better in 11 of 22 tournaments entered, including US Open qf, and joined sister Katerina and mother Yulia to represent Bulgaria in Fed Cup at Prague. **1987:** (8) Upset Evert FC Cup and at Wild Dunes won 1st tourn since 1985, qualifying for VS Champs, where she reached sf. **1988:** (6) Won Kansas and Arizona, qf US Open and VS Champs and won Olympic bronze medal. **1989:** (9) Won Indian Wells and Geneva; sf VS Dallas, Brighton and VS Chicago. At VS Champs lost qf to Sanchez-Vicario. In GS reached qf French Open and US Open. **1990:** Reached qf French Open, where she took Seles to 3s and same stage US Open, upsetting Navratilova on the way. R/u VS Chicago, San Antonio and San Diego and appeared in 5 more sf. Qualified for VS Champs, where she fell in qf to M-J. Fernandez. **1990 HIGHLIGHTS – SINGLES: French Open** qf, seed 6 (d. Stafford 6–2 6–3, A. Minter 6–1 6–0, Tarabini 2–6 7–5 6–0, Zvereva [seed 10] 6–4 6–2, lost Seles 3–6 6–1 7–5), **Wimbledon** 1r, seed 8 (lost Gomer 6–2 6–3), **US Open** qf, seed 9 (d. Frazier 6–1 6–3, Graham 6–4 6–0, Van Rensburg 6–1 6–0, Navratilova 7–5 3–6 6–3 [seed 2], lost M-J. Fernandez [seed 8] 6–2 2–6 6–1); **r/u** VS Chicago (d. Louise Allen 6–3 6–3, Fendick 6–4 7–5, Fairbank Nideffer 6–1 6–0, Garrison 6–2 6–0, lost Navratilova 6–3 6–2), **r/u** San Antonio (d. Reinach 6–2 6–0, Cunningham 6–1 6–1, McNeil 6–0 6–4, lost Seles 6–4 6–3), **r/u** San Diego (d. May 6–4 7–6, Fendick 6–1 6–2, Grossman 7–5 6–1, Paulus 6–0 4–6 6–1, lost Graf 6–3 6–2); **sf** Tokyo (d. Phelps 6–2 6–1, Schultz 6–2 6–0, lost Graf 6–4 6–4), **sf** VS Oklahoma (d. S. Smith 6–2 6–1, K. Jordan 6–1 6–2, Inoue 6–2 6–0, lost Frazier 1–6 6–3 6–3), **sf** Tokyo Nicherei (d. Takagi 6–0 6–2, Louie Harper 6–2 6–2, Navratilova 7–5 4–6 6–3, lost M-J. Fernandez 4–6 7–5 6–4), **sf** Zurich (d. Bollegraf 6–1 3–6 6–2, Porwik 6–1 3–6 6–2, Schultz 6–3 6–2, lost Graf 6–7 6–2 6–3), **sf** VS New England (d. Zrubakova 6–2 6–0, Smylie 6–1 6–1, Paz 6–1 6–3, lost Graf 7–6 6–7 6–3). **CAREER HIGHLIGHTS – SINGLES: Olympics – bronze medal 1988** (d. Reggi 6–3 6–4, lost Sabatini 6–1 6–1); **VS Champs – sf 1987** (lost Sabatini 6–3 4–6 6–3); **French Open –**

qf 1985 (lost Sabatini 6–3 3–6 6–1), *qf 1989* (d. Smylie, Wasserman, Savchenko 6–1 6–2, J. Thompson 7–6 6–2, lost Seles 6–3 7–5; *Wimbledon – qf 1984* (lost Navratilova [seed 1] 6–3 6–2); *US Open – qf 1986* (d. Kohde-Kilsch 6–2 2–6 7–6, lost Evert Lloyd [seed 2] 6–2 6–2), *qf 1988* (d. Potter 6–3 6–2, lost Evert 3–6 6–4 6–2), *qf 1989* (d. Werdel, Cueto, Tauziat, Zvereva 6–2 6–0, lost Navratilova 6–0 6–0); *Australian Open – qf 1985* (lost Evert Lloyd 6–3 6–3).

HANA MANDLIKOVA (Australia)
Born Prague, Czechoslovakia, 19 February 1962; lives there and Sanctuary Cove; RH; 5ft 8in; 132lb; final 1990 WTA ranking 31 singles, 46 doubles; 1990 prize money $49,773; career prize money $3,340,959.
Coached by Mike Estep. Became a naturalised Australian 1 Jan. 1988. *1977:* Won Orange Bowl 16s in Miami Beach, already flashing brilliant range of strokes at age 15. *1978:* (45) R/u to Austin at Wimbledon Jun, she was ITF World Jun Champ with countryman Lendl. *1979:* (17) Won 5 tourns. *1980:* (5) Won 6 of 24 tourns including Australian Open, Mahwah, Atlanta and Stockholm and was r/u US Open. *1981:* (4) Won French Open (d. Evert Lloyd in sf), and was r/u at Wimbledon but won only 3 of 18 tourns. *1982:* (7) Played only 13 tourns and won none, although r/u Italian Open. *1983:* (12) Reached f only twice in 15 events. *1984:* (3) Won 5 of 16 events. *1985:* (3) Won third GS title with back-to-back triumphs over Evert Lloyd and Navratilova at US Open, the first player since Tracy Austin at TS Champs 1981 to beat both in same tourn. Since Austin won 1981 US Open, Navratilova or Evert Lloyd had won the intervening 15 GS titles. Won 3 of 18 tourns and 59 of 73 matches, defeating Evert Lloyd and Navratilova twice each. *1986:* (4) Won no tournament in 15 appearances but was r/u Wimbledon to Navratilova, reached sf French Open and was r/u at VS Champs March. Married Sydney restaurant owner Jan Sedlak during Fed Cup in Prague in July. *1987:* (5) Won Australian Open for 1st title since 1985, but missed Wimbledon owing to foot injury and retired 1r VS Champs with pulled hamstring. *1988:* (29) Won no title, her best showings being qf Australian Open and sf Washington, and finished the year outside the top 20 for the 1st time since 1978. Took a break at end of year in an attempt to regain fitness and enthusiasm, both of which had been adrift since Aug. Divorced. *1989:* (14) Restricted again by a variety of injuries and her old lack of consistency, she reached sf Sydney, US HC and Indian Wells but played no singles f and at VS Champs fell 1r to Maleeva Fragnière. In doubles with Navratilova won US Open. *1990:* Having failed in her aim to return to the top 5, she retired from singles after Wimbledon, playing only doubles, and by end of year had announced her retirement from doubles, too. *1990 HIGHLIGHTS – SINGLES: Australian Open* 3r [seed 7] (d. Minter 4–6 6–2 6–3, Cammy MacGregor 7–6 6–3, lost Gavaldon 6–1 1–6 6–1), *Wimbledon* 2r (d. Lapi 6–3 3–6 11–9, lost Henricksson 6–3 6–3). *1990 HIGHLIGHTS – DOUBLES:* [Shriver] *r/u* Brisbane (lost Novotna/Sukova 6–3 6–1), [Novotna] *r/u* Berlin (lost Provis/E. Reinach 6–2 6–1). *CAREER HIGHLIGHTS – SINGLES: French Open – won 1981* (d. Romanov, Casals, Vasquez, Rinaldi, Evert Lloyd [seed 1], Hanika 6–2 6–4), *sf 1980* seed 7 (d. Redondo, Fairbank, Delhees, Madruga, lost Evert Lloyd [seed 1] 6–7 6–2 6–2), *sf 1982* (d. Austin 7–6 6–7 6–2, lost Navratilova 6–0 6–2), *sf 1984* (lost Navratilova 3–6 6–2 6–2), *sf 1986* (d. Goles, Paquet, Marsikova 6–1 6–2, Gildemeister 6–1 6–3, Graf [seed 3] 2–6 7–6 6–1, lost Evert Lloyd 6–1 6–1); *US Open – won 1985* (d. Evert Lloyd 4–6 6–2 6–3, Navratilova 7–6 1–6 7–6), *r/u 1980* seed 9 (d. Collins, Guissani, P. Smith, Navratilova [seed 2] 7–6 6–4, Hallquist, Jaeger [seed 8] 6–1 3–6 7–6, lost Evert Lloyd 5–7 6–1 6–1), *r/u 1982* (d. Austin 4–6 6–4 6–4, Shriver 6–4 2–6 6–2, lost Evert Lloyd 6–3 6–1), *qf 1981* seed 5 (lost Evert Lloyd 6–1 6–3), *qf 1983* (lost Evert Lloyd 6–4 6–3), *qf 1984* (lost Bassett 6–4 6–3); *Australian Open – won 1980*, seed 3 (d. Little, Hallquist, Ruzici [seed 6] 6–1 3–6 6–4, Jausovec 6–4 6–1, Turnbull [seed 4] 6–0 7–5), *won 1987* (d. Bassett, McNeil 6–0 6–0, Kohde-Kilsch 6–1 0–6 6–3, Navratilova 7–5 7–6), *qf 1981* (d. Sukova 6–4 7–6, lost Evert Lloyd 6–4 7–6), *qf 1988* (d. Tanvier 6–4 6–3, McNeil 6–2 6–4, lost Graf 6–2 6–2); *Wimbledon – r/u 1981* seed 2 (d. Turnbull, Navratilova, lost Evert Lloyd [seed 1] 6–2 6–2), *r/u 1986* (d. Tacon, Tanvier, Budarova, Bassett 6–4 [7–6, McNeil 6–7 6–0 6–2, Evert Lloyd [seed 2] 7–6 7–5, lost Navratilova [seed 1] 7–6 6–3), *sf 1984* (lost Evert Lloyd 6–1 6–2); *VS Champs – r/u 1985–86* (d. Evert Lloyd 6–3 7–5, lost Navratilova 6–2 6–0 3–6 6–1). *CAREER HIGHLIGHTS – DOUBLES:* (with Turnbull unless stated) *US Open –* [Navratilova] *won 1989* (d. M-J. Fernandez/Shriver 5–7 6–4 6–4), *r/u 1986* (lost Navratilova/Shriver 6–4 3–6 6–3), *sf 1985* (lost Navratilova/Shriver 6–3 6–4); *VS*

Champs – won 1985–86 (d. Kohde-Kilsch/Sukova 6–4 6–7 6–3); **French Open –** [Kohde-Kilsch] **r/u 1984** (lost Navratilova/Shriver 5–7 6–3 6–2); **Wimbledon – r/u 1986** (lost Navratilova/Shriver 6–1 6–3), **sf 1985** (lost Navratilova/Shriver 6–4 6–2).

AMOS MANSDORF (Israel)
Born Tel Aviv, 20 October 1965, and lives there; RH; 5ft 9in; 158lb; final 1990 ATP ranking 33; 1990 prize money $246,286.
Coached by Peter Fishbach. **1984:** (268) Joined Israeli Olympic team; qf US Open Jun.**1985:** (84) R/u Tel Aviv. **1986:** (37) Won first GP title in Johannesburg. **1987:** (27) Beat Mecir and Novacek as he led his country to major upset of TCH in D Cup, d. Connors and Gilbert to win Tel Aviv, and appeared in top 20 in Nov. **1988:** (26) Won Auckland and Paris Open, sf Tel Aviv; upset Becker at Orlando and took Lendl to 5s 1r US Open. **1989:** (39) R/u Auckland and Singapore; last 16 Australian Open and Wimbledon. **1990:** Won his 1st title on grass at Rosmalen, r/u Tel Aviv, sf Auckland and Toulouse. Upset Gilbert *en route* to last 16 US Open, and in 3r Wimbledon took eventual champion Edberg to 9–7 5s. **1990 HIGHLIGHTS – SINGLES: Australian Open** 1r (lost Antonitsch 4–6 6–4 6–4 6–7 6–3), **French Open** 3r (d. Tabares 6–3 4–6 6–4 6–4, Cancellotti 6–2 2–6 6–1 7–5, lost Kroon 6–4 7–6 6–1), **Wimbledon** 3r (d. Holm 6–1 1–6 5–7 6–3 6–2, Fromberg 6–4 7–6 6–1, lost Edberg [seed 3] 6–4 5–7 3–6 6–2 9–7), **US Open** last 16, unseeded (d. Dyke 3–6 3–6 6–3 6–3 6–0, Bruguera 7–6 6–2 2–6 6–3, Gilbert [seed 8] 5–7 5–7 6–3 7–5 6–1, lost Krickstein [seed 9] 6–3 6–4 6–4); **won** Rosmalen (d. Evernden 6–4 6–3, Goldie 7–6 1–6 7–6, Holm 6–3 6–4, Reneberg 6–4 6–4, Volkov 6–3 7–6); **r/u** Tel Aviv (d. Weidenfeld 6–3 6–1, Perkis 7–6 6–4, Odizor 7–5 6–1, Tarango 6–1 6–2, lost Chesnokov 6–4 6–3); **sf** Auckland (d. Novacek 6–4 6–1, Delaitre 6–2 7–5, Arias 6–3 7–6, lost Chesnokov 7–6 6–2), **sf** Toulouse (d. Kulti 6–0 6–3, Arias 6–2 6–0, Noah 6–4 6–4, lost Svensson 3–6 7–6 4 6–3).

CONCHITA MARTINEZ (Spain)
Born Monzon, 16 April 1972; lives Barcelona and Lueggern, Switzerland; RH; 5ft 7in; 132lb; final 1990 WTA ranking 11; 1990 prize money $248,184.
Coached by Eric van Harpen in Switzerland. **1988:** (40) Upset McNeil *en route* to last 16 French Open after qualifying and won 1st pro title in both singles and doubles (with Paulus) at Sofia. Won Nat Champs over Sanchez and played Fed Cup. **1989:** (7) Won her 2nd tour singles title at Wellington, following with Tampa (d. Sabatini) and VS Arizona; r/u Geneva and Bayonne; qf French Open and qualified for 1st VS Champs. Voted WTA Most Impressive Newcomer. **1990:** Won Clarins and Indianapolis; sf LIPC (d. Sabatini), Tampa and Leipzig; qf French Open again. **1990 HIGHLIGHTS – SINGLES: French Open** qf, seed 9 (d. Thompson 7–5 6–1, Etchemendy 7–6 6–3, Zrubkova 6–1 6–3, Probst 6–3 6–3, lost Graf [seed 1] 6–1 6–3), **US Open** 3r, seed 10 (d. Werdel 2–6 7–5 6–2, Bartos 6–4 4–6 6–4, lost Tauziat 6–2 6–1); **won** Clarins (d. Quentrec 6–1 6–3, Herreman 6–1 6–3, McQuillan 6–4 6–3, Halard 6–1 6–2, Tarabini 7–5 6–3), **won** Indianapolis (d. Fulco 6–1 6–2, Reinach 6–1 5–7 6–2, Provis 6–2 6–2, Medvedeva 7–5 6–0, Meskhi 6–2 6–4); **sf** LIPC (d. Van Rensburg 3–6 7–6 7–6, Quentrec 6–3 6–4, Magers 4–6 7–5 6–4, Sabatini 7–6 6–2, lost Wiesner 6–2 6–1), **sf** Tampa (d. Fulco 6–1 7–6, Gavaldon 6–3 6–1, Cammy MacGregor 6–2 6–3, lost Seles 6–4 6–0), **sf** Leipzig (d. Lindqvist 6–3 6–3, Khode-Kilsch 6–3 2–6 6–1, lost Graf 7–6 7–6). **CAREER HIGHLIGHTS – SINGLES: French Open – qf 1989** (d. Herr, Pospisilova, Amiach 6–3 6–3, K. Maleeva 6–0 6–1, lost Graf 6–0 6–4), **qf 1990**.

WALLY MASUR (Australia)
Born Southampton, England, 13 May 1963; lives Sydney; RH; 5ft 11in; 175lb; final 1990 ATP ranking 53; 1990 prize money $243,266.
Wife Sue Steel (married 17 Dec. 1989). **1981:** (287) Won Australian Open Jun. **1982:** (125). **1983:** (66) Qf Australian Open and won Hong Kong. **1984:** (106) R/u Taipei. **1985:**(101) R/u Auckland. **1986:** (87) Sf Livingston and Auckland. **1987:** (35) In Adelaide won first tourn since 1983, then upset Becker *en route* to sf Australian Open. **1988:** (46) Won Newport, r/u Adelaide and reached last 16 Australian Open and Wimbledon (d. McEnroe 2r). **1989:** (42) Sf Singapore, Brisbane and Wembley. **1990:** In singles was r/u Memphis; in doubles won Tokyo Suntory with Kratzmann and Hong Kong with Cash, won singles during Aust D Cup. Wins over France, N. Zealand and Argentina but dropped from team that lost 2–3 in f to USA. **1990 HIGHLIGHTS – SINGLES: Australian Open** 3r (d. Jelen 6–2 6–1 6–2, Odizor 7–6 6–7 6–3 6–1, lost Wilander [seed 8] 6–4 5–7 6–4 1–6 6–3), **Wimbledon** 2r (d.

Cherkasov 6–3 6–4 6–2, lost Becker [seed 2] 6–7 6–2 6–3 6–2). *US Open* 1r (lost Courier [seed 14] 6–4 6–0 5–7 6–1); *r/u* Memphis (d. Perez 6–2 6–3, Fleurian 6–7 6–1 7–6 Korda 6–4 7–5, Layendecker 6–3 6–2, lost Stich 6–7 6–4 7–6). *1990 HIGHLIGHTS – DOUBLES:* [Kratzmann] *won* Tokyo Suntory (d. Pearce/Kinnear 3–6 6–3 6–4), [Cash] *won* Hong Kong (d. Curren/Rive 6–3 6–3). *CAREER HIGHLIGHTS – SINGLES: Australian Open – sf 1987* (d. Becker 4–6 7–6 6–4 6–7 6–2, Evernden, lost Edberg 6–2 6–4 7–6), *qf 1983* (d. Flach, Jarryd 6–3 6–3 4–6 6–1, lost J. McEnroe 6–2 6–1 6–2).

LUIZ MATTAR (Brazil)
Born Sao Paulo, 18 August 1963, and lives there; RH; 6ft; 167lb; final 1990 ATP ranking 43; 1990 prize money $200,016.
Married Ornella Sennati 18 April 1990. Coach Paolo Cleto. Nickname 'Nico'. 5 years at Mackenzie Univ. studying engineering. *1985:* (230). *1986:* (95) Qf Madrid. Played D Cup. *1987:* (38) Won Guaruja, r/u Sao Paulo and Itaparica. *1988:* (44) Won Guaruja again plus 2 Challenger titles; sf Tourn of Champs and Kitzbuhel. Took a few months off at end of year to rest his injured back and to train. *1989:* (62) Returned in Feb. and won Guaruja for 3rd straight year before taking his 4th career title (all won in Brazil) at Rio de Janeiro. Upset Noah 1r French Open. *1990:* Won both Challenger and main tour titles at Rio de Janeiro; r/u Guaruja, sf Berlin, upset Gomez 1r US Open, and reached 3 doubles f with different partners. *1990 HIGHLIGHTS – SINGLES: French Open* 2r (d. Matuszewski 6–4 6–1 6–4, lost Novacek 5–7 6–3 6–2 6–1), *Wimbledon* 1r (lost Matsuoka 7–6 6–3 6–4), *US Open* 3r (d. Gomez [seed 5] 6–3 3–6 6–3 6–3, Paloheimo 6–4 6–0 3–6 2–6 6–3, lost Van Rensburg 6–1 6–4 5–7 6–4); *won* Rio de Janeiro (d. Oncins 1–6 7–5 6–1, Arguello 6–3 6–3, Vojtisek 4–6 6–1 6–3, Wostenholme 6–3 6–1, Sznajder 6–4 6–4), *won* Rio de Janeiro Challenger (d. Herrera 6–3 3–6 6–3); *r/u* Guaruja (d. Roese 7–5 6–3, Rittersbacher 4–6 7–6 6–4, Kley 6–3 6–2, Bengoechea 6–4 6–2, lost Jaite 3–6 6–4 6–3); *sf* Berlin (d. Kodes Jun. 6–3 6–1, Skoff 6–1 4–6 6–3, Fleurian 7–6 6–4, lost Volkov 6–3 6–2). *1990 HIGHLIGHTS – DOUBLES:* [Motta] *r/u* Guaruja (lost Frana/Luza 7–6 7–6), [Perez] *r/u* Florence (lost Bruguera/de la Pena 3–6 6–3 6–4), [Koevermans] *r/u* Sao Paulo (lost Cannon/Mora 6–7 6–3 7–6).

RONA MAYER (Israel)
Born 11 July 1973.
1990: Won Australian Open Jun doubles with Zaltz.

TIM MAYOTTE (USA)
Born Springfield, Mass., 3 August 1960; lives Bradenton, Fla.; RH; 6ft 3in; 185lb; final 1990 ATP ranking 37; 1990 prize money $263,156; career prize money $2,564,901.
Coached first by Bill Drake then Jeff Arons. Starting working with B-J. King 1991. *1978:* Top-ranked player in US Boys' 18. *1981:* (30) Won NCAA Champs while playing for Stanford, reached qf Wimbledon and Australian Open and f Maui to be named ATP Newcomer of the Year. *1982:* (29) Reached sf Wimbledon, f WCT Strasbourg and Bristol. *1983* (16) Qf Wimbledon, sf Australian Open. *1984:* (44) R/u Newport. *1985:* (12) Won inaugural LIPC Champs and r/u to Lendl at WCT Dallas. *1986:* (15) Won Queens Club (d. Becker, Edberg, Connors), qf Wimbledon, r/u US Pro Indoor and D Cup début for US, winning crucial 5s match over Lavalle to lead US into sf v Australia. *1987:* (9) Took a 2-month break at beginning of year to concentrate on improving his backcourt game, returning to win US Pro Indoor, Chicago, Toulouse, Paris Open and Frankfurt. *1988:* (10) Qf Wimbledon, Olympic silver medal and won Philadelphia, Schenectady, Brisbane and Frankfurt to qualify for Masters. *1989:* (13) Reached only 2 f, winning Washington and being r/u to Becker at US Pro. *1990:* Having parted from his former coach, Bill Drake, and working with Jeff Arons from April, he began to change his game, working on his serve and groundstrokes. R/u Milan, Toronto World Tennis and Moscow, but suffered a poor year in GS, losing 1r French Open, Wimbledon and US Open to finish with his lowest ranking for 6 years. *1990 HIGHLIGHTS – SINGLES: Australian Open* 1r, seed 6 (lost Sampras 7–6 6–7 4–6 7–5 12–10), *Wimbledon* 1r, seed 6 (lost Muller 4–6 7–6 7–5 6–3), *US Open* 1r (lost Champion 7–5 3–6 6–3 7–5); *r/u* Milan (d. Strelba 6–1 6–1, Champion 6–2 6–1, Hlasek 7–5 6–7 7–5, J. McEnroe 6–4 6–4, lost Lendl 6–3 6–2), *r/u* Toronto World Tennis (d. Pugh 7–5 5–7 6–3, Lozano 6–2 4–6 6–2, Krickstein 4–6 6–4 7–6, Gilbert 6–3 7–6, lost Lendl 6–3 6–0), *r/u* Moscow (d. Gustafsson 4–6 7–6 7–5, Kuhnen 6–3 7–6, Volkov 6–3 6–2, Korda 7–6 3–6 6–3, lost Cherkasov 6–2 6–1). *CAREER HIGHLIGHTS – SINGLES: LIPC – won*

1985 (d. Becker 6–2 6–3, S. Davis 4–6 4–6 6–3 6–2 6–4); *Olympics – silver medal 1988* (d. Mansdorf, Steeb, Gilbert 6–4 6–4 6–3, lost Mecir 3–6 6–2 6–4 6–2); *Wimbledon – sf 1982* (d. Mayer 3–6 6–7 6–4 6–2 6–4, Mottram 6–2 7–5 6–3, Teacher 6–7 7–6 7–5 3–6 6–1, lost McEnroe [seed 1] 6–1 6–3 6–2), *qf 1981* (d. Mitton, Fancutt, Sadri, A. Mayer 6–3 6–4 7–6, lost Frawley 4–6 7–6 6–3 6–3), *qf 1983* (d. Dickson, Teacher, McCurdy, lost Curren 4–6 7–6 6–2 7–6), *qf 1986* (d. Canter, Smid, Edwards, lost Lendl [seed 1] 6–4 4–6 6–4 3–6 9–7), *qf 1988* (d. Nystrom 6–4 4–6 6–2 6–4, Leconte 6–4 7–6 4–6 6–2, lost Lendl 7–6 7–6 6–3); *Australian Open – sf 1983* (d. Nystrom, Teltscher, lost Lendl 6–1 7–6 6–3), *qf 1981* (d. Van't Hof, DuPre, lost Kriek 7–6 6–3 7–5).

MILOSLAV MECIR (Czechoslovakia)
Born Bojnice, 19 May 1964; lives Prague; RH; 2HB; 6ft 3in; 180lb; 1990 ATP ranking 116; 1990 prize money $82,293; career prize money $2,632,538.
Wife Petra (married Aug. 1987); son Miloslav born 20 Jan. 1988. *1982:* (215). *1983:* (101) Immensely talented, deceptive with his lethal forehand down the line and sharp two-handed backhand crosscourt, he won Czech Closed Champs and r/u Adelaide. *1984:* (60) R/u Palermo and Cologne. *1985:* (9) Won Rotterdam and Hamburg, r/u to McEnroe at US Pro Indoor following win over Connors and r/u Italian Open (d. Wilander, lost Noah). *1986:* (9) Played his best tennis in the two biggest tournaments, upsetting Edberg at Wimbledon *en route* to qf and downing Wilander, Nystrom and Becker to reach US Open f. Won Kitzbuhel over Gomez. Missed Masters owing to knee injury. *1987:* (6) Was the first since McEnroe in 1984 to win GP titles on all four surfaces – Auckland and LIPC on HC, Sydney on GC, WCT Finals on carpet, Stuttgart and Hilversum on CC – and was one of the few players to beat Lendl all year. Sf French Open, qf Australian and US Opens, won LIPC mixed doubles with Novotna, and qualified for Masters in singles and doubles, winning doubles with Smid. *1988:* (13) Suffered a slipped disc in April, missing French Open, and wore a corset at Wimbledon, where he reached sf, losing in 5s to Edberg. Saved his best performance for Olympics in Seoul, where he won a gold medal. R/u Rotterdam and Orlando. *1989:* (18) R/u Australian Open and won Indian Wells, but withdrew 2r LIPC with a back injury which prevented him playing D Cup v FRG and restricted him at French Open, where he fell 1r to Tulasne. *1990:* Still restricted by injuries, he suffered a poor year in which sf Brussels was his best showing. Underwent back surgery after Wimbledon and has not competed since. *1990 HIGHLIGHTS – SINGLES: Australian Open* last 16, seed 16 (d. Koevermans 6–2 6–4 7–6, Sznajder 2–6 6–1 6–0 6–2, Riglewski 6–4 6–2 6–0, lost Becker [seed 2] 4–6 6–7 6–4 6–1 6–1), *French Open* 1r (lost Wilkison 6–4 6–1 4–6 6–4), *Wimbledon* 2r (d. Carbonell 6–4 6–4 6–1, lost Edberg 6–2 6–3 6–2); *sf* Brussels (d. E. Sanchez 6–4 3–6 6–4, Rahunen 7–4 6–4, Agenor 6–3 6–2, lost Steeb 6–2 6–3). *CAREER HIGHLIGHTS – SINGLES: Olympics – gold medal 1988* (d. Forget, Schapers 3–6 7–6 6–2 6–4, Edberg 3–6 6–0 1–6 6–4 6–2, Mayotte 3–6 6–2 6–4 6–2); *Australian Open – r/u 1989* (d. Champion, Kratzmann, Stoltenberg, Van Rensburg 6–4 6–1 6–0, Ivanisevic 7–5 6–0 6–3, Gunnarsson 7–5 6–2 6–2, lost Lendl 6–2 6–2 6–2); *US Open – r/u 1986* (d. Tim Gullikson, Forget, Edwards, Wilander 6–7 6–3 6–3 6–4, Nystrom 6–4 6–2 3–6 6–2, Becker [seed 3] 4–6 6–3 6–4 3–6 6–3, lost Lendl 6–4 6–2 6–0), *qf 1987* (lost Wilander 6–3 6–7 6–4 7–6); *French Open – sf 1987* (d. Novacek, lost Lendl 6–3 6–3 7–6); *Wimbledon – sf 1988* (d. Moreno, Volkov, Acuna, Masur 4–6 6–2 6–4 6–2, Wilander 6–3 6–1 6–3, lost Edberg 4–6 2–6 6–4 6–3 6–4), *qf 1986*, unseeded (d. Edberg 6–4 6–4 6–4, Gilbert [seed 12] 3–6 7–6 6–1 6–2, lost Becker 6–4 6–2 7–6. *CAREER HIGHLIGHTS – DOUBLES:* (with Smid) *Masters – won 1987* (d. Flach/Seguso 6–4 7–5 6–7 6–3). *MIXED DOUBLES:* (with Novotna) *LIPC – won 1987* (d. Van Rensburg/M. Reinach).

NATALIA MEDVEDEVA (USSR)
Born Kiev, 15 November 1971 and lives there; RH; 2HB; 5ft 8in; 142lb; final 1990 WTA ranking 56; 1990 prize money $135,497.
Known as Natasha in USSR. *1987:* (196) ITF Jun Champ in doubles; won French Open and Wimbledon Jun doubles with Zvereva. In autumn won 3 consec. titles on LTA British circuit. *1988:* (305). *1989:* (66) Sf Moscow and extended Sanchez-Vicario to 3s at French Open. *1990:* In singles won her 1st tour title at VS Nashville in Oct. and followed the next week with sf showing at Indianapolis. In doubles won Auckland and Wellington at the beginning of the year with Meskhi, with whom she upset Novotna/Sukova at VS Champs, and also took Puerto Rico with Brioukhovets in Oct. *1990 HIGHLIGHTS – SINGLES:*

Australian Open 2r (d. Gregory 6–4 7–5, lost Sukova [seed 4] 6–2 6–0), ***French Open*** 2r (d. Bowes 6–3 3–6 6–2, lost Halard 6–2 4–6 6–4), ***Wimbledon*** 1r (lost Coetzer 4–6 6–2 6–1), ***US Open*** 2r (d. Phelps 6–4 6–2, lost Cioffi 7–5 6–2); ***won*** VS Nashville (d. De Lone 7–6 6–2, Ferrando 6–7 6–2 6–3, Dahlman 6–3 6–4, Brioukhovets 6–3 6–4, Sloane 6–3 7–6); ***sf*** Indianapolis (d. S. Martin 6–1 1–6 6–4, Fendick 6–3 6–3, McGrath 7–6 6–4, lost Martinez 7–5 6–0). ***1990 HIGHLIGHTS – DOUBLES:*** (with Meskhi unless stated) ***won*** Auckland (d. Hetherington/R. White 3–6 6–3 7–6), ***won*** Wellington (d. Jaggard/Richardson 6–3 2–6 6–4), ***won*** Puerto Rico (d. Frazier/Richardson 6–4 6–2).

LEILA MESKHI (USSR)
Born Tbilisi, 5 January 1968 and lives there; RH; 2HB; 5ft 4½in; 120lb; final 1990 WTA ranking 19; 1990 prize money $210,438.
Coached by Kakulia and Olga Morozova. Husband Pavil Nadibaidze (married 1989). ***1986:*** (241) No. 1 in ITF Jun doubles world rankings. In singles r/u Wimbledon Jun; in doubles won French Open Jun (with Zvereva), r/u Wimbledon (with Zvereva) and US Open Jun (with Brioukhovets). ***1987:*** (44) Reached 1st sf at VS Indianapolis, qf Athens and Chicago, and upset Bunge 2r Hamburg. ***1988:*** (46) R/u Singapore, sf Japan Open and Nashville (d. Potter), and stunned Shriver 2r US Open. ***1989:*** (30) Won VS Nashville (d. K. Maleeva and Kelesi); r/u VS Oklahoma. Joined her country's Fed Cup team. ***1990:*** In singles she won Auckland and Moscow, was r/u Wellington and Indianapolis (upset K. Maleeva) and, after surprising Zvereva *en route* to qf US Open, she broke into the top 20. In doubles with Medvedeva won 2 titles and upset Novotna/Sukova at VS Champs. ***1990 HIGHLIGHTS – SINGLES: Australian Open*** 3r (d. Golarsa 6–4 6–4, Dahlman 2–6 6–1 6–3, lost Graf 6–4 6–1), ***French Open*** 3r (d. McQuillan 6–4 6–1, Savchenko 3–0 ret'd, lost Seles 7–6 7–6). ***Wimbledon*** 1r (lost Quentrec 3–6 6–3 6–2), ***US Open*** qf (d. Kijimuta 6–4 6–2, Zvereva [seed 14] 6–4 6–0, Piccolini 6–2 4–6 7–6, Ferrando 7–6 6–1, lost Sabatini [seed 5] 7–6 6–4); ***won*** Auckland (d. Bonsignori 6–1 6–2, Richardson 6–2 6–1, Wasserman 6–0 6–2, R. White 6–4 6–2, Appelmans 6–1 6–0), ***won*** Moscow (d. Krajcovicova 6–3 6–0, M. Maleeva 6–2 6–1, Habsudova 4–6 6–3 6–1, Minter 6–2 6–4, Brioukhovets 6–4 6–4); ***r/u*** Wellington (d. Segal 6–0 6–2, Huber 7–5 6–2, Reinstadler 6–4 6–0, Toleafoa 6–4 6–4, lost Probst 1–6 6–4 6–0) ***r/u*** Indianapolis (d. Reinbold 6–1 6–2, Stafford 6–2 6–1, Reggi 3–6 7–5 6–3, K. Maleeva 6–2 6–3, lost Martinez 6–4 6–2). ***1990 HIGHLIGHTS – DOUBLES:*** (with Medvedeva) ***won*** Auckland (d. Hetherington/R. White 3–6 6–3 7–6), ***won*** Wellington (d. Jaggard/Richardson 6–3 2–6 6–4). ***CAREER HIGHLIGHTS – SINGLES: US Open – qf 1990.***

GLENN MICHIBATA (Canada)
Born Toronto, 13 June 1962; lives Islington, Ontario; RH; 5ft 9in; 152lb; final 1990 ATP ranking 481 singles, 10T doubles; 1990 prize money $203,541.
Wife Angie. Nat champ in 14s, 16s, 18s and 21s. ***1982:*** (172) Qf Japan Open. ***1983:*** (79) Nat Jun champ for 3rd year. Qf Tokyo Seiko, Maui and Taipei. ***1984:*** (163). ***1985:*** (76). ***1986:*** (206) Broke into top 50 in April. ***1987:*** (178) Qf Adelaide. ***1988:*** (102) Won Livingston doubles with Connell. ***1989:*** (152) Sf Wellington and Schenectady. ***1990:*** In doubles with Connell r/u Australian Open, won Seoul and Washington and reached 2 more f, qualifying for IBM/ATP World Doubles Final. ***1990 HIGHLIGHTS – DOUBLES:*** (with Connell) ***r/u Australian Open*** (lost Aldrich/Visser 6–4 4–6 6–1 6–4); ***won*** Seoul (d. Stoltenberg/Woodbridge 7–6 6–4), ***won*** Washington (d. Lozano/Witsken 6–3 6–7 6–2); ***r/u*** Philadelphia (lost R. Leach/Pugh 3–6 6–4 6–2), ***r/u*** Indianapolis (lost S. Davis/Pate 7–6 7–6). ***CAREER HIGHLIGHTS – DOUBLES:*** (with Connell] ***US Open – r/u 1990.***

ANNE MINTER (Australia)
Born Ballarat, 4 March 1963; lives Melbourne and Deerfield Beach, Fla.; RH; 5ft 5in; 120lb; final 1990 WTA ranking 85; 1990 prize money $84,303.
Married her coach Graeme Harris, 27 Nov. 1988. Sister of Elizabeth. Plays flute to state orchestra standard. ***1980:*** Won Australian Open Jun and was ranked 5 on ITF world Jun list. ***1981:*** Australian Jun champ. ***1982:*** (77) Won Goldair on Australian satellite circuit. ***1983:*** (95). ***1984:*** (43) Sf Salt Lake City and Newport in singles, qf Australian Open doubles with her sister. Joined Fed Cup team. ***1985:*** (72) Qf Marco Island. ***1986:*** (82) Won 20 of 40 matches, upsetting Lindqvist 1r VS LA. ***1987:*** (38) Won her first major title at Taipei, following with Singapore a week later and d. Sukova 2r Canadian Open. ***1988:*** (26) Upset

Shriver to reach qf Australian Open and Mandlikova to reach last 16 Wimbledon; won Puerto Rico, sf Wellington. **1989:** (34) Won Taipei, sf Tokyo and Toronto (upset Evert). **1990:** Sf Moscow; qf Wichita, VS Oklahoma and Albuquerque. **1990 HIGHLIGHTS – SINGLES: Australian Open** 1r (lost Mandlikova [seed 7] 4–6 6–2 6–3), **French Open** 2r (d. Romano 7–5 6–3, lost Maleeva Fragnière 6–1 6–0), **Wimbledon** 3r (d. Salmon 6–2 6–2, Phelps 6–0 6–1, lost Seles [seed 3] 6–3 6–3), **US Open** 1r (lost Stafford 6–1 6–3); **sf** Moscow (d. Sharpe 6–0 7–5, Golarsa 7–5 6–3, Godridge 6–4 6–0, lost Meskhi 6–2 6–4). **CAREER HIGHLIGHTS – SINGLES: Australian Open – qf 1988** (d. Shriver 6–2 6–4, lost Kohde-Kilsch 6–2 6–4).

CATHERINE MOTHES (France)
Born Begles, 7 June 1970, and lives there; RH; 2HB; 5ft 5in; 109lb; final 1990 WTA ranking 99; 1990 prize money $17,630.
1987: (302) Reached f Bayonne on French satellite circuit. **1988:** (299) Reached 2 f on Spanish satellite circuit. **1989:** (148) Won Vigo on Spanish satellite circuit. **1990:** Emerged from satellite circuits to appear in qf Estoril on main tour and broke into the top 100 in autumn.

ALEXANDER MRONZ (Germany)
Born Cologne, 7 April 1965, and lives there; RH; 6ft 2in; 175lb; final 1990 ATP ranking 86; 1990 prize money $108,942.
Coached by Tilo Busch. **1986:** (481) Nat doubles champ. **1987:** (190). **1988:** (278) Qf Tel Aviv and in doubles won Schenectady with Van Emburgh. **1989:** (148) Underwent knee surgery in Feb, returning Sept. **1990:** Reached 1st career sf at US CC, and upset Krickstein *en route* to same stage Lyon. Won Bergen Challenger. **1990 HIGHLIGHTS – SINGLES: won** Bergen Challenger (d. Gunnarsson 6–4 6–4); **sf** US CC (d. Van't Hof 6–3 6–3, Reneberg 6–4 6–2, Rostagno 6–3 6–2, lost Wheaton 2–6 7–5 6–2), **sf** Lyon (d. Fleurian 3–6 6–3 6–0, Winogradsky 6–7 6–4 6–4, Krickstein 6–4 2–6 6–4, lost Wilander 6–2 7–6). **1990 HIGHLIGHTS – DOUBLES:** [Schapers] **r/u** Adelaide (lost Castle/Odizor 7–6 6–2).

GARY MULLER (South Africa)
Born Durban, 24 December 1964; lives Johannesburg and Los Angeles, Cal.; LH; 6ft 2in; 180lb; final 1990 ATP ranking 52 singles, 16 doubles; 1990 prize money $261,675.
Coached by José Higueras. **1985:** (186). **1986:** (236) Qf Basle, sf US Open doubles with Nelson. **1987:** (68) Qf Indianapolis (d. Gomez) Schenectady and Johannesburg. **1988:** (133) Upset Cash 2r Cincinnati and reached qf Johannesburg. **1989:** (90) Qf Queen's and Johannesburg. Out of action for 6 weeks after pulling hamstring at Cincinnati. **1990:** Sf Memphis (upset Edberg), Newport and Los Angeles; upset Mayotte 1r Wimbledon and Courier 2r US Open. In doubles with Broad reached 3 f, winning Toulouse and qualifying for IBM/ATP World Doubles Final. **1990 HIGHLIGHTS – SINGLES: Australian Open** 1r (lost Annacone 6–3 6–4 6–7 2–6 6–3), **Wimbledon** 2r (d. Mayotte [seed 6] 4–6 7–6 7–5 6–3, lost Curren 6–4 7–6 6–7 6–6), **US Open** 3r (d. Azar 6–3 3–6 6–1 6–1, Courier [seed 14] 4–6 6–4 7–6 7–6, lost Bloom 6–2 6–3 6–4); **won** Cape Town Challenger (d. Bates 5–7 6–2 6–3); **sf** Memphis (d. Aldrich 7–6 6–3, Edberg 6–1 7–5, Arias 4–6 7–5 6–3, Visser 7–5 7–5, lost Stich 7–5 7–6), **sf** Newport (d. J. Brown 6–3 3–6 7–6, Baur 6–3 6–3, Pugh 6–3 6–7 6–3, lost Aldrich 6–4 7–6), **sf** Los Angeles (d. Adams 6–4 3–6 6–3, Rive 2–6 6–3 6–1, Garrow 6–3 6–4, lost Chang 7–6 6–2). **1990 HIGHLIGHTS – DOUBLES:** (with Broad) **won** Toulouse (d. Mortensen/Schapers 7–6 6–4); **r/u** Cincinnati (lost Cahill/Kratzmann 7–6 6–2), **r/u** Basel (lost Kruger/Van Rensburg 4–6 7–6 6–3).

THOMAS MUSTER (Austria)
Born Leibnitz, 2 October 1967; lives there and Monte Carlo; LH; 5ft 11in; 165lb; final 1990 ATP ranking 7; 1990 prize money $705,267.
Coached by Ronald Leitgeb until end 1990 when he became business manager only. **1985:** (98) Won Banana Bowl, r/u French Open Jun and Rolex. Became a member of Austrian D Cup squad and finished 6 on Austrian satellite circuit. **1986:** (47) Won first GP title in Hilversum. **1987:** (56) Sf Vienna (d. E. Sanchez) and won Young Masters. **1988:** (16) Upset Jaite 1r Italian Open and then in the space of 5 weeks won Boston (playing in his 1st GP f), Bordeaux and Prague, following with Bari later in year. **1989:** (21) Reached 1st GS sf at Australian Open. On 1 April, 2 hours after beating Noah to reach f LIPC, which took him into top 10 for 1st time, he was knocked down by a drunken driver in Miami and suffered 2 torn

ligaments and torn cartilage in his left knee, requiring reconstructive surgery. In plaster 1½ months and was expected to be out of action for about 10 months, but in May he was already practising in a specially designed wheelchair. In Sept., after only 4 months' rehabilitation, he played doubles at Geneva then reached qf Barcelona in singles, following with sf Vienna. *1990:* At Adelaide in Jan. won 1st tour title since injury 10 months earlier, following with Casablanca in March, Italian Open in May and reaching sf French Open to regain his place in the top 10. R/u Monte Carlo and Munich, sf Vienna and qualified for ATP World Champ but failed to reach sf. Still in pain and advised by doctors to concentrate on CC tourns in 1990. Suspended 5 weeks from 22 Oct. and fined $15,000 (reduced on appeal from a ten-week suspension from US Open plus $25,000 fine) by ATP for 'violation of best efforts' and 'unsportsmanlike conduct' – after accepting guarantee to play at Prague he pulled out after just 1 game, having previously expressed his intention to do so. Competed GS Cup as No. 7 seed, lost 1r Leconte 6–3 6–4. *1990 HIGHLIGHTS – SINGLES: Australian Open* 3r, seed 15 (d. Vojtisek 6–3 6–2 6–4, Van Rensburg 1–6 7–5 7–5 2–6 8–6, lost Youl 3–6 6–4 6–3 6–2), *French Open* sf, seed 7 (d. Jonsson 7–5 6–3 6–2, Winogradsky 6–2 6–3 6–1, Haarhuis 3–6 7–5 6–2 7–6, Jaite [seed 10] 7–6 6–3 6–2, Ivanisevic 6–2 4–6 6–4 6–3, lost Gomez [seed 4] 7–6 6–1 7–5), *US Open* last 16, seed 6 (d. Rahunen 5–7 6–4 6–0 3–0 ret'd, Jarryd 6–4 6–3 4–6 6–1, Yzaga 6–2 6–2 4–6 5–7 7–6, lost Sampras [seed 12] 6–7 7–6 6–4 6–3); *won* Adelaide (d. Pistolesi 6–4 4–6 6–3, Fitzgerald 6–2 7–6, Kratzmann 7–5 6–4, Bruguera 2–6 6–2 7–6, Arias 3–6 6–2 7–5), *won* Casablanca (d. Vysand 6–2 7–5, Benhabiles 4–6 6–1 6–2, Koevermans 6–4 7–6, Prpic 6–1 6–3, Perez Roldan 6–1 6–7 6–2), *won* Italian Open (d. Hlasek 6–3 6–4, Jarryd 5–1 ret'd, Gunnarsson 6–3 6–2, Forget 6–2 3–6 6–3, Gomez 5–7 6–4 7–6, Chesnokov 6–1 6–3 6–1), *won* Agadir Challenger (d. Perez Roldan 6–2 7–5); *r/u* Monte Carlo (d. Filippini 6–2 6–2, Jaite 6–3 6–2, Courier 6–4 6–4, Aguilera 6–3 6–4, Leconte 6–2 6–3, lost Chesnokov 7–5 6–3 6–3), *r/u* Munich (d. Perez Roldan 6–4 6–4, Gustafsson 7–5 6–2, Strelba 4–3 ret'd, Korda 6–3 6–1, lost Novacek 6–4 6–2); *sf* Vienna (d. Strelba 7–6 6–4, Annacone 3–6 7–6 7–6, Olkhovskiy 0–6 6–4 7–6, lost Skoff 6–2 7–6). *CAREER HIGHLIGHTS – SINGLES: LIPC – r/u 1989* (d. Odizor, Michibata 7–5 7–6 6–2, Sznajder 6–1 3–6 6–3 7–6, Bengoechea 6–1 6–1, Grabb 7–5 7–6 1–6 6–0, Noah 5–7 3–6 6–3 6–3 6–2, lost Lendl def.); *Australian Open – sf 1989* (d. Rive, Wekesa, Visser 6–3 3–6 6–3 11–9, Gustafsson 6–3 6–2 7–5, Edberg w.o., lost Lendl 6–2 6–4 5–7 7–5); *French Open – sf 1990.*

BETSY NAGELSEN (USA)

Born St Petersburg, Fla., 23 October 1956; lives Maui, Hawaii; RH; 5ft 9in; 135lb; final 1990 WTA ranking 92 singles, 15 (23) doubles; 1990 prize money $69,144.
Husband Mark McCormack of IMG (married 1 March 1986). *1974:* At 17, she stunned Morozova and Wade to reach f Newport, displaying superior serve-and-volley skills and delighting the galleries. *1975:* (51) Beset by back injuries which plagued her for several years. *1977:* (30) Won first Avon Futures Champ. *1978:* (87) R/u Australian Open. *1981:* (23) Won Surbiton, d. Navratilova in sf. *1982:* (54) Achieved highest career ranking of 17 in March. *1984:* (77) Reached sf US Open doubles with A. White. *1985:* (45) Reached sf French Open doubles with A. White. *1986:* (47) Married Mark McCormack in March. R/u VS Kansas and last 16 Wimbledon (d. Shriver for first time in 1r). *1987:* (61) Sf Brisbane and Japan/Asian Open in singles; r/u Wimbledon doubles with Smylie and r/u US Open mixed with Annacone. *1988:* (107) Qf Taipei in singles, and in doubles won Brisbane, Brighton and Chicago to qualify for VS Champs. *1989:* (45) Returning after knee surgery, she upset McNeil at Oklahoma, Sanchez-Vicario *en route* to sf Albuquerque and reached qf Eastbourne and Birmingham, as well as winning 3 doubles titles. *1990:* Upset Sanchez-Vicario 1r Wimbledon. In doubles won Canadian Open with Sabatini; r/u LIPC with R. White and Geneva with Burgin. *1990 HIGHLIGHTS – SINGLES: French Open* 1r (lost Halard 6–1 6–4), *Wimbledon* 3r (d. Sanchez-Vicario [seed 6] 1–6 7–6 9–7, Van Rensburg 2–6 6–4 6–2, lost Schultz 6–1 6–4). *1990 HIGHLIGHTS – DOUBLES:* [Sabatini] *won* Canadian Open (d. Kelesi/Reggi 3–6 6–2 6–2); [R. White] *r/u* LIPC (lost Novotna/Sukova 6–4 6–3), [Burgin] *r/u* Geneva (lost Field/Van Rensburg 5–7 7–6 7–5). *CAREER HIGHLIGHTS – SINGLES: Australian Open – r/u 1978* (d. Tomanova 6–4 6–4, Matison 7–5 6–4, lost C. O'Neill 6–3 7–6). *CAREER HIGHLIGHTS – DOUBLES: Australian Open* – [Tomanova] *won 1978* (d. Sato/Whytcross 7–5 6–2), [Reid] *r/u 1977* [Jan.] (lost Fromholtz/H. Cawley 5–7 6–1 7–5); *Wimbledon* [Smylie] *r/u 1987* (lost Kohde-Kilsch/Sukova 7–5 7–5); *Italian Open* – [Mihai]

r/u 1978 (lost Jausovec/Ruzici 6–2 2–6 7–5); *French Open* [Navratilova] *sf 1981* (d. Evert Lloyd/Ruzici [seed 6], lost Reynolds/P.Smith [seed 2] 6–4 7–5), [A. White] *sf 1985* (lost Navratilova/Shriver 6–3 6–4); *US Open* [Shriver] *sf 1978* (d. Stove/Evert [seed 3] 6–3 6–2, lost Reid/Turnbull [seed 2] 6–4 1–6 7–5), [A. White] *sf 1984* (d. Evert Lloyd/King 7–6 4–6 6–3, lost Navratilova/Shriver 6–4 7–5).

MARTINA NAVRATILOVA (USA)
Born Prague, 18 October 1956; lives Fort Worth, Texas and Aspen, Colo.; LH; 5ft 8in; 145lb; final 1990 WTA ranking 3 singles, 4 (1) doubles; 1990 prize money $1,330,794; career prize money $16,674,607.
Coached by Craig Kardon and B-J. King (1990). *1973:* Displaying enormous promise, she reached qf French Open and extended Goolagong to 7–6 6–4 in memorable match after eliminating 1968 champion Nancy Richey. *1974:* Won first major tournament in Orlando and was r/u to Evert at Italian Open. *1975:* (3) Led Czechoslovakia to Fed Cup title (d. Goolagong in f), and was r/u to Evert at VS Champs, French and Italian Opens, reaching f in 13 of 25 tourns. The day after losing to Evert in US Open sf Forest Hills she announced her defection from Czechoslovakia. *1976:* (4) Reached first sf at Wimbledon and won first doubles there with Evert, but made tearful exit from US Open after losing 1r. *1977:* (3) Won 6 tourns and reached f of 5 other events in 20 appearances. *1978:* (1) Ranked 1 on computer in close race with Evert, whom she beat to win first Wimbledon singles title. Won 80 of 89 matches and 11 of 20 tourns, including 37-match winning streak as she won 7 straight VS tourns in winter. *1979:* (1) Defended Wimbledon title safely and won 11 of 23 tourns, reaching f of 19 events and closing year with resounding victory over Austin at TS Champs. *1980:* (3) Won 11 of 24 tourns but no majors. *1981:* (3) Linking with Renee Richards at US Open, she received sound technical and tactical advice, leading to sf win there over Evert Lloyd, another f Australian Open, and sucess in 8 of 19 tourns. Became US citizen 21 July. *1982:* (1) Won 15 of 18 tourns 90 of 93 matches, including 41 straight from March until September, with third Wimbledon singles and first French Open. *1983:* (1) Won 16 of 17 tourns, including first US Open and fourth Wimbledon, and 86 of 87 matches, closing season with streak of 50 straight match victories, her only defeat being by Kathleen Horvath in last 16 of French Open. Her .988 winning percentage set an 'Open Tennis' record for men and women. *1984:* (1) Won 78 of 80 matches, 13 of 15 tourns, and set modern pro record of 74 straight matches won, beginning immediately after her 54-match streak was broken at start of season by Mandlikova at VS Oakland. Won bonus of $1m from ITF for achieving a modern GS, culminating with French Open where she played possibly the best match of her career to beat Evert Lloyd in f. She extended her GS streak to six with her fifth Wimbledon and second US Open victories, but her bid for traditional GS, as well as her 74-match winning streak, were stopped by Sukova in sf Australian Open. *1985:* (1) Won her 6th Wimbledon and 3rd Australian titles, 84 of 89 matches and 12 of 17 tourns. Was challenged for No. 1 ranking by Evert Lloyd, who took over top spot for virtually half the year, but Martina clinched No. 1 with 3s triumph over Chris in Australian f. *1986:* (1) Won 14 of 17 tourns and 89 of 92 matches, including 5th straight Wimbledon (the first since Lenglen 1919–23 to achieve that feat) and her 3rd US Open. Won two VS Champs and closed season with streak of 53 straight matches. Won 1,000th match in Filderstadt. *1987:* (2) Coached by Randy Crawford Jan. to March, Virginia Wade Jan. to May and by Renee Richards to end of year. Losing Australian Open f to Mandlikova, French Open f to Graf, who also beat her in sf LIPC, she won no singles tournament from Nov. 1986 until triumphing over Graf at Wimbledon. This was her longest spell without a win since mid 1970s and cost her the No. 1 computer ranking which she had held continuously since July 1985. However, she won her 1st triple crown at US Open, her 2 GS singles titles confirming her as No. 1 in some eyes until she fell to Sabatini in qf VS Champs. In doubles, won 3rd GS with Shriver in Paris and their 6th VS Champs together. *1988:* (2) Coached by Tim Gullikson, with Craig Kardon taking over for 1989. For the first time in 8 years she won no GS title, falling in sf Australian Open to Evert, last 16 French Open to Zvereva, f Wimbledon to Graf and qf US Open to Garrison. Nor did she find consolation at VS Champs, where she fell in qf to Sukova. In doubles won Australian, French Open and VS Champs with Shriver, but failed in both women's and mixed at Wimbledon, leaving there empty handed for the first time since 1981. However, she won 9 singles titles and her 1,100th career victory at Amelia Island, remaining firmly in the No. 2 position. *1989:* (2) Again won

no GS singles title, falling qf Australian Open to Sukova, missing French Open to prepare for Wimbledon, where she was r/u to Graf, and losing f US Open also to Graf, despite having been ahead 6–3 4–2. However, she won 8 singles titles, was r/u VS Champs to Graf and lost to no one else from April. Took 7 doubles titles, including Australian Open and VS Champs with Shriver and US Open with Mandlikova after ending her partnership with Shriver in July. Called on Bille Jean King mid-season to help her overcome a crisis of confidence and to 'get the fun back' into her game. *1990:* Acheived her primary aim of winning a 9th Wimbledon – without dropping a set – to pass Helen Wills Moody's record, and setting a new record of 99 singles victories there, passing Chris Evert's 97. In her only other GS tourn, at US Open, found motivation hard to maintain and lost in last 16 to Maleeva Fragnière, who beat her again in qf Tokyo Nicherei. Won her 150th title at FC Cup in April, also taking VS Chicago, Washington, Indian Wells and Eastbourne; r/u Italian Open, Los Angeles and VS California, losing each time to Seles, while Sanchez-Vicario beat her in sf Hamburg and K. Maleeva at same stage Houston. She was overtaken in the rankings by Seles and finished the year ranked 3 for the first time since 1981. In doubles she won US Open with G. Fernandez and took four other titles with various partners. *1990 HIGHLIGHTS – SINGLES: won Wimbledon* seed 2 (d. Amiach 6–1 6–1, A. Smith 6–2 6–3, Kschwendt 6–1 6–1, Wiesner [seed 14] 6–3 6–3, K. Maleeva [seed 7] 6–1 6–1, Sabatini [seed 4] 6–3 6–4, Garrison [seed 5] 6–4 6–1), *US Open* qf, seed 2 (d. Haumuller 6–4 6–0, Wood 6–0 6–4, Cioffi 6–2 6–2, lost Maleeva Fragnière [seed 9] 7–5 3–6 6–3); *won* VS Chicago (d. Temesvari 6–1 6–3, A. White 6–0 6–0, Whitlinger 6–0 6–1, Shriver 6–4 6–3, Maleeva Fragnière 6–3 6–2), *won* VS Washington (d. Grossman 6–0 6–0, A. Smith 6–4 6–2, Seles 6–3 6–0, Garrison 6–1 6–0), *won* Indian Wells (d. Provis 6–2 6–0, Wiesner 6–3 6–2, Herreman 6–2 6–1, K. Maleeva 7–6 6–1, Sukova 6–2 5–7 6–1), *won* FC Cup (d. Cioffi 6–2 6–1, Cueto 6–3 6–2, K. Maleeva 6–0 6–1, Rajchrtova 6–4 6–3, Capriati 6–0 6–4), *won* Eastbourne (d. Benjamin 6–2 6–1, A. Minter 6–2 6–3, S. Smith 6–3 6–2, Zvereva 7–6 6–1, Novotna 7–6 3–6 6–3), Magers 7–6 6–2); *r/u* Italian Open (d. McQuillan 6–2 3–6 6–2, Cecchini 6–4 3–6 6–3, Martinez 6–2 6–0, Sabatini 6–2 7–5, lost Seles 6–1 6–1), *r/u* VS Los Angeles (d. Graham 6–1 6–2, Lindqvist 6–1 6–1, Rinaldi 6–0 6–1, Garrison 6–0 6–7 6–4, lost Seles 6–4 3–6 7–6), *r/u* VS California (d. R. White 6–2 6–3, Zrubakova 6–2 6–0, McGrath 6–4 6–3, lost Seles 6–3 7–6); *sf* VS Houston (d. Fulco 6–0 6–1, Temesvari 7–5 6–2, lost K. Maleeva 6–4 2–6 6–1), *sf* Hamburg (d. McQuillan 3–6 6–1 6–1, Cueto 6–2 6–2, Meskhi 6–3 6–4, lost Sanchez-Vicario 6–1 6–7 6–2). *1990 HIGHLIGHTS – DOUBLES:* (with G. Fernandez unless stated) *won US Open* (d. Novotna/Sukova 6–2 6–4); [A. Smith] *won* VS Chicago (d. Sanchez-Vicario/Tauziat 6–4 7–6). [Garrison] *won* VS Washington (d. Henricksson/Van Rensburg 6–0 6–3), [Sanchez-Vicario] *won* FC Cup (d. Paz/Zvereva 6–2 6–1), *won* Hamburg (d. Savchenko/Sukova 6–2 6–3); *r/u* VS Indian Wells (lost Novotna/Sukova 6–2 7–6), *r/u* Tokyo Nicherei (lost M-J. Fernandez/R. White 4–6 6–3 7–6). *CAREER HIGHLIGHTS – SINGLES: Australian Open – won 1981* seed 3 (d. Tobin, K. Jordan, Goolagong Cawley, Shriver, Evert Lloyd [seed 1] 6–7 6–4 7–5), *won 1983* (d. Durie 4–6 6–3 6–4, Shriver 6–4 6–3, K.Jordan 6–2 7–6), *won 1985* (d. Mandlikova 6–7 6–1 6–4, Evert Lloyd 6–2 4–6 6–2), *r/u 1982* (d. Shriver 6–3 6–4, lost Evert Lloyd 6–3 2–6 6–3), *r/u 1987* (d. Garrison 6–0 6–3, Lindqvist 6–3 6–2, lost Mandlikova 7–5 7–6); *French Open – won 1982* (d. Mandlikova 6–6 2, Jaeger 7–6 6–1), *won 1983* (d. Mandlikova 3–6 6–2 6–2, Evert Lloyd 6–3 6–1), *r/u 1975* (lost Evert 2–6 6–2 6–0), *r/u 1985* (lost Evert Lloyd 6–3 6–7 7–5), *r/u 1986* (d. Cecchini, Savchenko, Porwik, Garrone 6–1 6–2, Rinaldi 7–5 6–4, Sukova 4–6 7–6 6–2, lost Evert Lloyd 2–6 6–3 6–3), *r/u 1987* (d. Huber, Hanika, Kohde-Kilsch 6–1 6–2, Evert 6–2 6–2, lost Graf 6–4 4–6 8–6); *Wimbledon – won 1978* (d. Goolagong Cawley 2–6 6–4 6–4, Evert 2–6 6–4 7–5), *won 1979* (d. Austin 7–5 6–1, Evert Lloyd 6–4 6–4), *won 1982* (d. Russell 6–3 6–4, Bunge 6–2 6–2, Evert Lloyd 6–1 3–6 6–2), *won 1983* (d. Vermaak 6–1 6–1, Jaeger 6–0 6–3), *won 1984* (d. Evert Lloyd 7–6 6–2), *won 1985* (d. Garrison 6–4 7–6, Evert Lloyd 4–6 6–3 6–2), *won 1986* (d. Dingwall, Forman, Kinney, Demongeot 6–3 6–3, Bunge 6–1 6–3, Sabatini 6–2 6–2, Mandlikova 7–6 6–3), *won 1987* (d. G. Fernandez 6–3 6–1, Balestrat, Evert 6–2 5–7 6–4, Graf 7–5 6–3), *won 1990, r/u 1988* (d. Savchenko 6–4 6–2, Fairbank 4–6 6–4 7–5, Evert 6–1 4–6 7–5, lost Graf 5–7 6–2 6–1), *r/u 1989* (d. Hetherington, Radford 3–6 6–3 6–3, Provis, Mandlikova 6–3 6–2, Magers 6–1 6–2, Lindqvist 7–6 6–2, lost Graf 6–2 6–7 6–1); *US Open – won 1983* (d. Hanika 6–0 6–3, Shriver 6–2 6–1, Evert Lloyd 6–1 6–3), *won 1984* (d. Evert Lloyd 4–6 6–4 6–4), *won 1986* (d. Holikova, Nagelsen, Horvath, Sabatini 6–4 6–2, Shriver 6–2 6–4, Graf 6–1 6–7 7–6,

Sukova 6–3 6–2), **won 1987** (d. Lindqvist 6–0 6–4, Sabatini 7–5 6–3, Sukova 6–2 6–2, Graf 7–6 6–1), **r/u 1981** (d. K. Jordan, A. Smith, Evert Lloyd [seed 1], lost Austin [seed 3] 1–6 7–6 7–6), **r/u 1985** (d. Garrison, Graf, lost Mandlikova 7–6 1–6 7–6), **r/u 1989** (d. Iida, Halard 6–1 6–0, Goles 6–4 6–0, Rajchrtova 6–2 6–0, M. Maleeva 6–0 6–0, Garrison 7–6 6–2, lost Graf 3–6 7–5 6–1). **VS Champs – won 1978** (d. Goolagong Cawley 7–6 6–4), **won 1984** (d. Evert Lloyd 6–3 7–5 6–1), **won 1985** (d. Mandlikova, Sukova 6–3 7–5 6–4), **won 1985–86** (d. Mandlikova 6–2 6–0 3–6 6–1), **won 1986** (d. Shriver 6–2 4–6 6–4, Graf 7–6 6–3 6–2), **r/u 1975** (lost Evert Lloyd 6–4 6–2), **r/u 1989** (d. M-J. Fernandez 6–2 6–3, Seles 6–3 5–7 7–5, Sanchez-Vicario 6–2 6–2, lost Graf 6–4 7–5 2–6 6–2); **Avon Champs – won 1979** (d. Austin 6–3 3–6 6–2), **won 1981** (d. Jaeger 6–3 7–6), **r/u 1982** (lost Hanika 1–6 6–3 6–4); **TS Final – won 1982** (d. Evert Lloyd 4–6 6–1 6–2), **r/u 1981** (lost Austin 2–6 6–4 6–2); **Italian Open – r/u 1974** (lost Evert 6–3 6–3), **r/u 1975** (lost Evert 6–1 6–0); **CS Finals – r/u 1978** (lost Evert 6–3 6–3). **CAREER HIGHLIGHTS – DOUBLES:** (with Shriver unless stated) **Australian Open** [Nagelsen] **won 1980** (d. Kiyomura/Reynolds), **won 1982** (d. Kohde/Pfaff 6–4 6–2), **won 1983** (d. Hobbs/Turnbull 6–4 6–7 6–2), **won 1984** (d. Kohde-Kilsch/Sukova 6–3 6–4), **won 1987** (d. Garrison/McNeil 6–1 6–0), **won 1988** (d. Evert/Turnbull 6–0 7–5), **won 1989** (d. Fendick/Hetherington 3–6 6–3 6–2), [Tomanova] **r/u 1974, r/u 1981** (lost K. Jordan/A. Smith 6–2 7–5); **French Open –** [Evert] **won 1975** (d. Anthony/Morozova, [A. Smith] **won 1982** (d. Casals/Turnbull 6–3 6–4), **won 1984** (d.Kohde-Kilsch/Mandlikova 5–7 6–3 6–2), **won 1985** (d. Kohde-Kilsch/Sukova 4–6 6–2 6–2), [Temesvari] **won 1986** (d. Graf/Sabatini 6–1 6–2), **won 1987** (d. Graf/Sabatini 6–2 6–1), **won 1988** (d. Kohde-Kilsch/Sukova 6–2 7–5); **Wimbledon –** [Evert] **won 1976** (d.King/Stove 6–1 3–6 7–5), [King] **won 1979** (d. Stove/Turnbull 5–7 6–3 6–2), **won 1981** (d. K. Jordan/A. Smith 6–3 7–6), **won 1982** (d. K. Jordan/A. Smith 6–4 6–1), **won 1983** (d. Casals/Turnbull 6–2 6–2), **won 1984** (d. K. Jordan/A. Smith 6–3 6–4), **won 1986** (d. Mandlikova/Turnbull 6–1 6–3), **r/u 1985** (lost K. Jordan/Smylie 5–7 6–3 6–4); **US Open –** [Stove] **won 1977** (d. Richards/Stuart), [King] **won 1978** (d. Stove/Turnbull 7–6 6–4), [King] **won 1980** (d. Shriver/Stove 7–6 7–5), **won 1983** (d. Reynolds/Fairbank 6–7 6–1 6–3), **won 1984** (d. Turnbull/Hobbs 6–2 6–4), **won 1986** (d. Mandlikova/Turnbull 6–4 3–6 6–3), **won 1987** (d. K. Jordan/Smylie 5–7 6–4 6–2), [Mandlikova] **won 1989** (d. M-J. Fernandez/Shriver 5–7 6–4 6–4), [G. Fernandez] **won 1990**, [King] **r/u 1979** (lost Stove/Turnbull), **r/u 1985** (lost Kohde-Kilsch/Sukova 6–7 6–2 6–3); **Italian Open –** [Evert] **won 1975** (d. Barker/Coles), [Tomanova] **r/u 1973** (lost Wade/Morozova 7–5 fs); **CS Finals –** [King] **won 1978** (d. Reid/Turnbull), [King] **won 1979** (d. Casals/Evert Lloyd); **TS Champs – won 1981** (d. Casals/Turnbull 6–3 6–4), **won 1982** (d. Reynolds/P. Smith); **VS Champs – won 1984** (d. Durie/Kiyomura 6–3 6–1), **won 1985–86** (d. Kohde-Kilsch/Sukova 6–7 6–4 7–6), **won 1986** (d. Kohde-Kilsch/Sukova 7–6 6–3), **won 1987** (d. Kohde-Kilsch/Sukova 6–1 6–1), **won 1988** (d. Savchenko/Zvereva 6–3 6–4), **won 1989** (d. Savchenko/Zvereva 6–3 6–2), **US Indoor –** [King] **won 1979** (d. Stove/Turnbull), **won 1984** (d. Durie/Kiyomura Hayashi 6–4 6–3); **Avon Champs – won 1980** (d. Casals/Turnbull 6–3 fs), [King] **won 1981** (d. Potter/Walsh 6–0 7–6), **won 1982** (d. K. Jordan/A. Smith). **MIXED DOUBLES:** (with J. Sanchez) **US Open – won 1987** (d. Nagelsen/Annacone 6–4 6–7 7–6).

YANNICK NOAH (France)

Born Sedan, 18 May 1960; lives Paris and Montreux, Switzerland; RH; 6ft 4in; 187lb; final 1990 ATP ranking 40; 1990 prize money $322,732; career prize money $3,328,950.
Son Joakim Simon (born Dec. 1984), daughter Yelenah Tara (born April 1986). Coached by Patrice Hagelauer until US Open 1989 when Dennis Ralston replaced him and parted from Ralston after US Open 1990. **1977:** Won French Open Jun and r/u to Lendl Orange Bowl 18s. **1978:** (49) R/u Nice, won Manila and Calcutta. **1979:** (25) Won Nancy, Madrid and Bordeaux. **1980:** (23) R/u to Vilas Italian Open. **1981:** (12) Won Nice and Richmond WCT, r/u Gstaad, qf French Open. **1982:** (9) Won Palm Springs (d. Lendl to end 44-match winning streak), South Orange, Basle, Toulouse, r/u Nice, qf French Open and led France into D Cup f with crucial win over Lendl. **1983:** (5) Became first from his country to win French Open since Marcel Bernard in 1946. Also won Madrid and Hamburg, was r/u Lisbon and reached qf US Open. **1984:** (10) R/u La Quinta to Connors. **1985:** (7) Won Italian Open, Washington, Toulouse and was r/u Memphis and Basle. **1986:** (4) Played 15 tourns, winning WCT Forest Hills and Wembley, was r/u to Nystrom at La Quinta and Monte Carlo and was one of only four players to beat Lendl (at WCT Forest Hills). **1987:** (8) Won Lyon but lost 1r Italian Open

to K. Carlsson, fell 2r Wimbledon to his doubles partner, Forget, and further discouraged by 1r loss to Bates at Bordeaux, he pulled out of French D Cup tie v Sweden, talking of retiring from competitive tennis. However, he returned refreshed ten weeks later to win Basel, but a torn stomach muscle in the autumn sidelined him for rest of year. Qf Australian and French Opens and r/u French Open doubles with Forget. *1988:* (12) Tendonitis in both knees prevented him from playing at Wimbledon, restricted him through the summer and forced him to retire v Stoltenberg 2r US Open. Last 16 Australian Open and sf LIPC, Lyon, WCT Finals, Monte Carlo and Bordeaux. *1989:* (16) Once again tendonitis in both knees restricted his schedule until spring, when he consulted a witch doctor on a visit to his native Cameroons; thereafter he had no further problems with his knees. In French Open lost 1r (to Mattar) for 1st time since 1977 but at US Open reached qf, unseeded. Sf Rotterdam and LIPC. *1990:* At Sydney upset Lendl *en route* to 1st title for 2 years, following with sf showing at Australian Open, but went into French Open on a run of 6 1r losses and did nothing else of note. Competed GS Cup, lost 1r Wheaton (8) 7–6 6–7 6–3. *1990 HIGHLIGHTS – SINGLES: Australian Open* sf, seed 12 (d. Prpic 4–6 7–6 6–2 4–6 7–5, Agenor 7–6 6–3 6–3, Bloom 6–3 6–3 6–3, Sampras 6–3 6–4 3–6 6–2, Pernfors 6–3 7–5 6–2, lost Lendl 6–4 6–1 6–2), *French Open* 3r (d. Clavet 6–4 4–6 6–4 1–6 7–5, Sznajder 6–4 5–7 6–4 6–4, lost Perez Roldan [seed 15] 7–6 6–4 4–6 6–3), *Wimbledon* 1r, seed 16 (lost Ferreira 6–4 6–3 6–2), *US Open* 2r (d. Pate 7–6 6–4 5–7 6–4 6–2, lost Becker [seed 2] 6–4 6–2 7–6); *won* Sydney (d. Agenor 6–4 6–3, Cherkasov 6–1 6–4, Lendl 6–1 6–4, Krickstein 6–4 7–5, Steeb 5–7 6–3 6–4). *1990 HIGHLIGHTS – DOUBLES:* [Mancini] *won* Nice (d. Filippini/Skoff 6–4 7–6); [Bahrami] *r/u* Bordeaux (lost Carbonell/Pimek 6–3 6–7 6–2). *CAREER HIGHLIGHTS – SINGLES: Australian Open –* sf *1990, qf 1987* (lost Cash 6–4 6–2 2–6 6–0). *French Open – won 1983* (d. Jarryd 6–1 6–0 6–2, Pecci, DuPre, Alexander, Lendl 7–6 6–2 5–7 6–0, Roger-Vasselin, Wilander 6–2 7–5 7–6), *qf 1981* seed 11 (d. Vilas [seed 6], lost Pecci 3–6 6–4 6–4 6–4), *qf 1982* (d. Fibak 4–6 6–7 6–4 6–4 6–3, lost Vilas 7–6 6–3 6–4), *qf 1984* (lost Wilander 7–6 3–6 2–6 6–3 6–3), *qf 1987* (lost Wilander 6–4 6–3 6–2); *Italian Open – won 1985* (d. Becker, Mecir 6–3 3–6 6–2 7–6), *r/u 1980* (d. Dibbs, Barazzutti, Smid 6–1 6–1, lost Vilas 6–0 6–4 6–4); *US Pro Indoor – sf 1981* (d. Gerulaitis 6–3 fs, lost Fibak 6–2 4s); *US Open – qf 1983* (lost Arias 7–5 fs), *f 1985* (lost Lendl 6–2 6–2 6–4), *qf 1989. CAREER HIGHLIGHTS – DOUBLES:* (with Leconte unless stated) *French Open – won 1984* (d. Slozil/Smid 6–4 2–6 3–6 6–3 6–2), [Forget] *r/u 1987* (lost Jarryd/Seguso 6–7 6–7 6–3 6–4 6–2); *US Open – r/u 1985* (lost Flach/Seguso 7–6 6–7 7–6 6–0); *Nabisco Masters –* [Forget] *r/u 1986* (lost Edberg/Jarryd 6–3 7–6 6–3).

KAREL NOVACEK (Czechoslovakia)
Born Prostejov, 30 March 1965; lives Prevov; RH; 6ft 3in; 180lb; final 1990 ATP ranking 34; 1990 prize money $332,730.
Won Nat 12s, 14s, 18s. *1984:* Joined Olympic team. *1985:* (158) Sf Madrid. *1986:* (33) R/u Vienna and captured his first GP title in Washington. Czech Nat champ. *1987:* (76) Reached qf French Open unseeded (d. Jaite); r/u Palermo. *1988:* (127) Qf Nice, Athens and Bastad. *1989:* (74) After splitting with former coach Petr Hutka, he won his 2nd GP title at Hilversum (d. E. Sanchez). *1990:* Scored some major upsets during the year, beating Krickstein and Muster to win Munich, upsetting Krickstein again to reach last 16 French Open and removing Antonitsch, Becker and Skoff back-to-back to reach f Kitzbuhel, as well as appearing in sf Wellington. *1990 HIGHLIGHTS – SINGLES: Australian Open* 3r (d. M. Brown 6–3 6–1 2–6 6–2, Winogradsky 6–4 6–1 4–6 6–3, lost Lendl [seed 1] 6–4 3–6 6–4 6–1), *French Open* last 16, unseeded (d. S. Davis 6–3 6–2 6–2, Mattar 5–7 6–3 6–2 6–1, Krickstein [seed 5] 6–2 6–3 3–6 7–6, lost Champion 6–4 4–6 3–6 7–6 6–3), *Wimbledon* 3r (d. Layendecker 6–4 6–7 0–6 6–4 6–0, Rive 6–1 6–4 7–6, lost Curren 6–2 4–6 1–6 7–5 6–3), *US Open* 1r (lost Yzaga 7–5 7–6 6–3); *won* Munich (d. Schwaier 6–3 6–4, Krickstein 6–2 7–6, Bergstrom 6–1 6–1, Svensson 6–1 2–6 6–1, Muster 6–4 6–2); *r/u* Kitzbuhel (d. Cierro 6–4 6–4, Antonitsch 6–3 6–7 6–4, Becker 6–3 6–3, Skoff 6–4 4–6 6–4, lost de la Pena 6–4 7–6 2–6 6–2); *sf* Wellington (d. Clavet 6–2 6–3, Anderson 6–3 4–6 6–3, Wahlgren 6–3 6–1, lost Reneberg 6–7 6–4 6–0).

JANA NOVOTNA (Czechoslovakia)
Born Brno, 2 October 1968, and lives there; RH; 5ft 8½in; 145lb; final 1990 WTA ranking 13 singles, 2 (5) doubles; 1990 prize money $645,500.
Coached by Mike Estep until after 1990 Wimbledon when Hana Mandlikova took over.

1986: (182) Won US Open Jun doubles with Zrubakova. *1987:* (49) Reached last 16 Wimbledon and US Open, qf VS Kansas. In doubles formed a formidable partnership with Suire, qualifying for VS Champs and taking a set off Navratilova/Shriver. *1988:* (45) Reached her 1st VS final at Brisbane and upset Sabatini 1r Filderstadt. In doubles won Olympic silver medal with Sukova and took 5 titles with 3 different partners. In mixed doubles with Pugh won Australian and US Open. *1989:* (11) In singles won Adelaide, Eastbourne, Strasbourg, r/u Hamburg and Zurich and reached 4 more sf as well as qf French Open to qualify for VS Champs in both singles (lost Graf 1r) and doubles for 1st time. In doubles won 6 women's titles, including Wimbledon and LIPC with Sukova, plus Australian Open and Wimbledon mixed with Pugh. *1990:* She continued her successful doubles partnership with Sukova, with whom she won 8 of her 9 titles across the year. The duo were unbeaten until US Open, but, having won Australian Open, French Open and Wimbledon, failed in their bid for a GS when they lost f US Open to Navratilova/G. Fernandez. They were also disappointed at VS Champs, where they fell 1r to Medvedeva/Meskhi. In singles she upset Sabatini and K. Maleeva *en route* to her 1st GS sf at French Open and followed with qf Wimbledon and US Open. Won VS Albuquerque and extended Navratilova to 3s *en route* to sf Eastbourne, Qualified to VS Champs in both singles and doubles, losing 1r singles to Sabatini. *1990 HIGHLIGHTS – SINGLES: Australian Open* 3r, seed 5 (d. Martin 6–7 6–0 6–0, Temesvari 6–1 6–1, lost Fendick 1–6 7–6 6–4), *French Open* sf, seed 11 (d. Demongeot 6–0 6–7 10–8, Schultz 6–3 6–1, Sviglerova 7–5 6–2, Sabatini [seed 4] 6–4 7–5, K. Maleeva [seed 8] 4–6 6–2 6–4, lost Graf 6–1 6–2), *Wimbledon* qf, seed 13 (d. Golarsa 3–6 7–6 6–2, Cunningham 6–2 6–1, Faull 6–2 6–1, Fendick 6–2 6–4, lost Graf [seed 1] 7–5 6–2), *US Open* qf, seed 12 (d. Lapi 6–3 6–1, Rinaldi 6–4 6–3, Gildemeister 6–3 6–1, K. Maleeva [seed 7] 6–4 6–2, lost Graff 6–3 6–1); *won* VS Albuquerque (d. Cunningham 6–0 6–1, Toleafoa 6–2 6–3, Quentrec 6–7 6–2 6–1, A. Smith 6–4 6–7 7–5, Gildemeister 6–4 6–4); *sf* Eastbourne (d. Field 6–4 6–2, Javer 6–2 6–2, Meskhi 6–4 6–1, Sukova 7–5 6–4, lost Navratilova 7–6 3–6 6–3), *sf* Zurich (d. Durie 6–4 6–0, Paz 6–2 6–2, Probst 6–0 6–1, lost Sabatini 6–7 7–5 7–6). *1990 HIGHLIGHTS – DOUBLES:* (with Sukova unless stated) *won Australian Open* (d. Fendick/M-J. Fernandez 7–6 7–6), *won French Open* (d. Savchenko/Zvereva 6–4 7–5), *won Wimbledon* (d. K. Jordan/Smylie 6–3 6–4), *r/u* US Open (lost G. Fernandez/Navratilova 6–2 6–4); *won* Brisbane (d. Mandlikova/Shriver 6–3 6–1), *won Sydney* (d. Savchenko/Zvereva 6–3 7–5), *won* VS Indian Wells (d. G. Fernandez/Navratilova 6–2 7–6), *won* VS Florida (d. Burgin/Turnbull 6–4 6–2), *won* LIPC (d. Nagelsen/R. White 6–4 6–3), [G. Fernandez] *won* VS Los Angeles (d. Kelesi/Reggi 6–3 4–6 6–4); [Mandlikova] *r/u* Berlin (lost Provis/Reinach 6–2 6–1), [M-J. Fernandez] *r/u* VS New England (lost G. Fernandez/Sukova 3–6 6–3 6–3). *CAREER HIGHLIGHTS – SINGLES: French Open – sf 1990, qf 1989* (d. Halard, Porwik 6–3 7–5, Simpson 6–1 6–0, Hanika 6–1 6–4, lost Sanchez-Vicario 6–2 6–2); *Wimbledon – qf 1990; US Open – qf 1990. CAREER HIGHLIGHTS – DOUBLES:* (with Sukova) *Australian Open – won 1990; French Open – won 1990; Wimbledon – won 1989* (d. Savchenko/Zvereva 6–1 6–2), *won 1990; LIPC – won 1989* (d. G. Fernandez/McNeil 7–6 6–4), *won 1990; US Open – r/u 1990; Olympics – silver medal 1988* (lost Shriver/Garrison 4–6 6–2 10–8). *MIXED DOUBLES:* (with Pugh) *Australian Open – won 1988* (d. Navratilova/Gullikson 5–7 6–2 6–4), *won 1989* (d. Stewart/Garrison 6–3 6–4); *Wimbledon – won 1989* (d. Kratzmann/Byrne 6–4 5–7 6–4); *US Open – won 1988* (d. Smylie/P. McEnroe 7–5 6–3).

MARCOS ONDRUSKA (South Africa)
Born Blomfontein, 18 December, 1972; lives Pretoria; RH; 5ft 10in; 150lb; final 1990 ATP ranking 256; 1990 prize money $16,805.
1989: Won Durban Challenger. *1990:* Reached 2r Washington (d. Baur, lost Sznajder); 2r Cincinatti (d. Korda, lost Sznajder); 2r Indianapolis (d. Youl, lost Krickstein). R/u Wimbledon Jun (lost Paes 7–5 2–6 6–4).

LEANDER PAES (India)
Born 16 June 1973.
1990: Won Wimbledon Jun (d. Ondruska 7–5 2–6 6–4).

VELI PALOHEIMO (Finland)
Born Tampere, 13 December 1967, and lives there; RH; 6ft; 168lb; final 1990 ATP ranking 69; 1990 prize money $119,973.
Coached by Jari Hedman. Has won 4 Nat singles titles. *1986:* (418) Joined Finnish D Cup

squad. *1987:* (515). *1988:* (117) Won Helsinki Challenger. *1989:* (109) Sf Adelaide and won 2 Challenger titles. *1990:* Sf Basel, qf Memphis and Bastad. Upset Steeb 1r *en route* to last 16 Australian Open, unseeded, becoming the first Finn to appear at that stage of any GS tourn. *1990 HIGHLIGHTS – SINGLES: Australian Open* last 16, unseeded (d. Steeb [seed 10] 5–7 6–3 0–6 6–2 6 2, Forget 6–4 3–6 6–3 6–3, J. Sanchez 7–5 6–4 3–6 6–1, lost Wilander [seed 8] 7–5 6–4 6–0), *French Open* 1r (lost Korda 6–4 6–1 2–6 6–3), *Wimbledon* 1r (lost Riglewski 6–4 7–5 7–5), *US Open* 2r (d. Bates 6–3 7–5 6–4); *sf* Basel (d. Filippini 6–2 5–7 6–3, Chesnokov 2–6 6–2 7–5, Gustafsson 7–6 6–4, lost Ivanisevic 6–2 6–4).

ELENA PAMPOULOVA (Bulgaria)
Born Sofia, 17 May 1972 and lives there; RH; 2HB; 5ft 5½in; 111lb; final 1990 WTA ranking 98; 1990 prize money $48,880.
Coached by her parents, Emil and Lubka. Father and uncle played D Cup and mother played Fed Cup. *1988:* Played Fed Cup. *1989:* (122) Qf Paris Open and won 3 titles on satellite circuits. *1990:* Reached sf Bastad and qf Strasbourg, upsetting Tarabini 1r. *1990 HIGHLIGHTS – SINGLES: Australian Open* 2r (d. Godridge 4–6 6–4 6–2, lost Loosemore 6–3 6–3), *French Open* 2r (d. Sabas 6–3 6–3, lost Provis 6–4 6–2), *US Open* 1r (lost Seles [seed 3] 6–0 6–0); *sf* Bastad (d. Mothes 6–3 6–2, Jagerman 6–1 6–2, Paz 7–5 6–4, lost Cecchini 6–4 6–3).

DAVID PATE (USA)
Born Los Angeles, 16 April 1962; lives Las Vegas; RH; 6ft; 170lb; final 1990 ATP ranking 94 singles, 6 doubles; 1990 prize money $342,637.
Coached, as a young man, by Pancho Gonzales. Wife Debra. *1981:* (662) A two-time All-American at Texas Christian University, he won NCAA doubles title with Richter. *1983:* (103). *1984:* (31) Won first GP event – Japan Open in Tokyo. *1985:* (26) R/u La Quinta to Stefanki and sf Newport and Wembley where he d. Edberg and Nystrom. *1986:* (30) Sf Atlanta and Scottsdale and 7 qfs. *1987:* (18) Had his biggest wins of the year at Tokyo, where he beat Lendl on his way to f, and at LA where he beat Edberg *en route* to his first title since Tokyo 1984. *1988:* (47) Upset Connors *en route* to sf Orlando; qf Memphis and Tokyo. *1989:* (157) Reached 4 doubles f winning 2. *1990:* Sf Orlando and Lyon in singles. In doubles reached 7 f, winning 5 titles with S. Davis, with whom he qualified for IBM/ATP World Doubles Final. *1990 HIGHLIGHTS – SINGLES: Wimbledon* 3r (d. Pistolesi 6–3 6–4 6–4, Raoux 3–6 6–2 6–4 6–3, lost Antonitsch 6–4 6–4 7–6), *US Open* 1r (lost Noah 7–6 6–4 6–7 4–6 6–2); *sf* Orlando (d. Mronz 6–4 6–4, Krishnan 6–2 3–6 6–3, Hombrecher 6–4 7–6, lost Van Rensburg 6–7 6–3 7–5), *sf* Lyon (d. Forget 7–6 4–6 7–6, Champion 6–3 3–6 6–3, Muller 7–6 4–6 6–3, lost Rosset 6–4 1–6 6–4). *1990 HIGHLIGHTS – DOUBLES:* (with S. Davis unless stated) *won* Orlando (d. Mora/Page 6–3 7–6), *won* US CC (d. Grabb/Lavalle 6–2 6–3), *won* Los Angeles (d. Lundgren/Wekesa 3–6 6–1 6–3), *won* Indianapolis (d. Connell/Michibata 7–6 7–6) *won* Paris Open (d. Cahill/Kratzmann 5–7 6–3 6–4); *r/u* Tokyo-Seiko (lost Forget/Hlasek 7–6 7–5), [Grabb] *r/u* Lyon (lost Galbraith/Jones 7–6 6–4).

BARBARA PAULUS (Austria)
Born Vienna, 1 September 1970; lives Hinterbruehl; RH; 5ft 9½in; 134lb; final 1990 WTA ranking 15; 1990 prize money $184,164.
Coached by Peter Eipeldauer. *1982:* Won Nat 12s 2nd time. *1985:* Won Nat 18s. *1986:* (187) Won Nat Indoor and Outdoor; qf Bregenz and played Fed Cup. *1987:* (96). *1988:* (25) Won her 1st primary circuit title at Geneva over McNeil, r/u Sofia and upset Kohde-Kilsch 1r Filderstadt. *1989:* (24) R/u Arcachon, sf Geneva (d. Evert) and surprised Novotna *en route* to last 16 US Open. *1990:* Won Geneva; r/u Sydney, Palermo and Filderstadt (d. Garrison and Sabatini); sf San Diego and Leipzig and reached last 16 Australian Open. *1990 HIGHLIGHTS – SINGLES: Australian Open* last 16, seed 16 (d. Rajchrtova 6–3 6–1, Miyagi 7–6 4–6 6–0, Smylie 6–4 6–3, lost Fendick 7–5 6–2), *Wimbledon* 1r, seed 16 (lost Loosemore 6–2 3–6 6–4), *US Open* last 16, seed 16 (d. Smylie 7–5 6–1, McNeil 6–2 4–6 6–4, Grossman 6–4 6–3, lost Sanchez-Vicario [seed 6] 6–4 6–3); *won* Geneva (d. Castro 6–3 6–1, Werdel 6–2 6–3, Coetzer 6–2 6–2, Zardo 7–5 6–3, Kelesi 2–6 7–5 7–6); *r/u* Sydney (d. Cunningham 5–7 6–1 6–4, Schultz 7–6 6–7 6–1, Provis 7–6 6–2, Zrubakova 6–2 6–1, Wiesner 6–4 3–6 6–1, lost Zvereva 4–6 6–1 6–3), *r/u* Palermo (d. Pierce 6–1 6–3, Farina 3–6 6–4 6–2, Zardo 6–3 6–4, F. Romano 6–2 2–6 6–1, lost Cueto 6–2 6–2), *r/u*

Born in Vienna, Barbara Paulus waltzed through to four finals in 1990, winning one, and went to the fourth round of the US Open to lift her year-end ranking to No. 15, a personal best. *(Professional Sport)*

Filderstadt (d. Paradis 2–6 7–5 6–4, Fairbank Nideffer 6–4 6–3, Garrison 2–6 7–5 6–4, Sabatini 6–3 6–4, lost M-J. Fernandez 6–1 6–3); *sf* San Diego (d. Javer 6–3 6–1, Pfaff 5–7 6–2 6–2, Fairbank Nideffer 7–5 6–3, lost Maleeva Fragnière 6–0 4–6 6–1), *sf* Leipzig (d. Salmon 6–4 6–4, Minter 6–1 6–0, Wiesner 6–3 5–7 6–4, lost Sanchez-Vicario 6–0 7–5).

MERCEDES PAZ (Argentina)
Born Tucuman, 27 June 1966, and lives there; RH; 5ft 10in; 164lb; final 1990 WTA ranking 37 singles, 14 doubles; 1990 prize money $220,513.
Coached by Patricio Apey. *1984:* Won Rolex Jun Port Washington and US Open Jun doubles and Orange Bowl 18 doubles with Sabatini. *1985:* (115) Won Sao Paulo and was ranked 2 in Argentina. *1986:* (59) Last 16 French Open, r/u Singapore, sf USCC. *1987:* (91) Qf Belgian Open. *1988:* (43) Won Guaruja at end of year, r/u Puerto Rico and reached 5 other qf. *1989:* (87) R/u Brussels and sf Arcachon in singles; won 4 doubles titles with different partners. Won WTA Player Service award. *1990:* Following a new fitness regime from early in year, she won Strasbourg and then upset Sanchez-Vicario *en route* to last 16 French Open, unseeded. In doubles won 5 titles with 3 different partners and was r/u VS Champs with Sanchez-Vicario. Won Karen Krantzcke Sportsmanship award. *1990 HIGHLIGHTS – SINGLES: French Open* last 16, unseeded (d. Quentrec 6–4 2–6 6–3, Sanchez-Vicario [seed 3] 7–5 3–6 6–1, Cohen 6–1 7–5, lost Capriati 6–0 6–3), *Wimbledon* 1r (lost Kohde-Kilsch 4–6 6–1 6–1), *US Open* 1r (lost Ferrando 6–4 2–6 7–6); *won* Strasbourg (d. Provis 7–5 7–6, Fulco 6–1 6–4, Cueto 6–1 6–0, Quentrec 6–1 6–1, Grossman 6–2 6–3); *sf* Schenectady (d. Date 6–1 7–5, Kijimuta 6–1 6–4, Reggi 6–1 4–0 ret'd, lost Werdel 4–6 7–5 6–3). *1990 HIGHLIGHTS – DOUBLES:* (with Sanchez-Vicario unless stated) [Tarabini] *won* Guaruja (d. Chabalgoity/Corsato 6–2 6–2), *won* Amelia Island (d. Rajchrotova/Temesvari 7–6 6–4), *won* Tampa (d. Cecchini/Gildemeister 6–2 6–0), *won* Barcelona (d. Goles/Tarabini 6–7 6–2 6–1), [Scheuer-Larsen] *won* Bastad (d. Bakkum/ Jagerman 6–3 6–7 6–2); [Zvereva] *r/u* FC Cup (lost Navratilova/Sanchez-Vicario 6–2 6–1), *r/u* Filderstadt (lost M-J. Fernandez/Garrison 7–5 6–3), *r/u* VS Champs (lost K. Jordan/ Smylie 7–6 6–4). *CAREER HIGHLIGHTS – DOUBLES:* (with Sanchez-Vicario) *VS Champs – r/u 1990.*

BRAD PEARCE (USA)
Born Provo, Utah, 21 March 1966, and lives there; RH; 5ft 9in; 155lb; final 1990 ATP ranking 78; 1990 prize money $179,189.
Wife Cindi; daughter Jordan (born 12 Dec. 1988). *1985:* (287) Member of US Jun D Cup team, and was All-American in singles and doubles for UCLA for 1st of 2 years. *1986:* (92) Reached sf NCAA Champs and won 2 Challenger titles. *1987:* (288) Won Auckland doubles with Jones. *1988:* (302). *1989:* (161). *1990:* Qf Hong Kong. His best performance came at Wimbledon when, ranked 120, he reached qf. Reached sf Schenectady and qf Hong Kong. *1990 HIGHLIGHTS – SINGLES: Wimbledon* qf, unseeded (d. Bathman 6–3 3–6 6–2 6–3, Matsuoka 7–6 7–5 6–3, Srejber 6–3 6–3 6–1, Woodforde 6–4 6–4 6–4, lost Lendl [seed 1] 6–4 6–4 5–7 6–4), *US Open* 1r (lost Bloom 7–5 6–7 7–5 6–0); sf Schenectady (d. Hogstedt 6–2 7–5, Yzaga 6–3 6–3, Guy 7–5 7–6, lost Evernden 6–3–3 6–4). *1990 HIGHLIGHTS – DOUBLES:* [Fromberg] *won* Schenectady (d. Strelba/Triguiero 6–4 6–3); [Kinnear] *r/u* Tokyo Suntory (lost Kratzmann/Masur 3–6 6–3 6–4).

GUILLERMO PEREZ-ROLDAN (Argentina)
Born Tandil, Buenos Aires, 20 October 1969 and lives there; RH; 5ft 9in; 170lb; final 1990 ATP ranking 14; 1990 prize money $317,538.
Coached by his father, Raul. Won Nat. and S American 14s, 16s, 18s. Brother of Mariana. *1985:* (485). *1986:* (109) Sf St Vincent and Buenos Aires and won French Open Jun singles and doubles. *1987:* (19) When he won Munich aged 17 years, 6 months, 10 days he became the second-youngest at the time (after Krickstein) to win a GP title, following with Athens 7 weeks later and Buenos Aires in Nov to take him into top 20. Won French Open Jun singles again over Stoltenberg. *1988:* (18) Confirmed his CC ability by winning Munich again, taking Lendl to 5s f Italian Open, upsetting Edberg *en route* to qf French Open and also reaching f Hilversum, Prague and Buenos Aires. *1989:* (32) Won Palermo in autumn, r/u Geneva and sf Bologna. *1990:* Won San Marino; r/u Casablanca, Barcelona and Stuttgart; sf Bordeaux and Palermo and reached last 16 French Open. *1990 HIGHLIGHTS – SINGLES: French Open* last 16, seed 15 (d. Soules 6–7 6–1 6–3 6–2, Cherkasov 7–5 6–4

6–3, Noah 7–6 6–4 4–6 6–3, lost Svensson 2–6 6–4 6–2 6–2); **won** San Marino (d. Cierro 4–6 6–3 6–4, Pambianco 7–6 6–1, Furlan 6–2 6–3, Filippini 1–6 6–2 6–4, Camporese 6–3 6–3), **won** Messina Challenger (d. Pescosolido 6–1 6–3); **r/u** Casablanca (d. Woodbridge 7–6 6–1, Fromberg 3–6 6–3 6–3, Tulasne 6–2 7–5, Carbonell 6–1 6–1, lost Muster 6–1 6–7 6–2), **r/u** Barcelona (d. Volkov 6–4 6–2, Koevermans 6–3 6–4, Prpic 6–2 7–5, Jaite 6–4 6–4, E. Sanchez 7–5 7–6, lost Gomez 6–0 7–6 3–6 0–6 6–2), **r/u** Stuttgart (d. Bruguera 6–2 6–4, Prpic 6–4 6–3, Skoff 2–6 6–3 7–6, Leconte 6–7 6–3 7–6, lost Ivanisevic 6–7 6–1 6–4 7–6); **sf** Bordeaux (d. Bahrami 7–6 6–2, Carbonell 4–6 6–4 6–2, Champion 4–6 6–2 6–1, lost Ivanisevic 6–4 6–4), **sf** Palermo (d. Tarango 6–1 6–2, Carbonell 7–6 6–4, Vajda 6–4 7–6, lost Aguilera 6–2 6–3).

TERRY PHELPS (USA)
Born Larchmont, NY, 18 December 1966 and lives there; RH; 2HB; 5ft 10in; 135lb; final 1990 WTA ranking 93; 1990 prize money $65,820.
Coached by Art Byron. **1982:** (107) Ranked 4 in US 16s. **1983:** (54) Won US 16 Nat; ranked 4 in 18s; turned pro. **1984:** (26) Played 27 tournaments and reached sf Filderstadt. **1985:** (29) Reached qf French Open, beat Rehe and Potter at US Open and took a set off Navratilova in Fort Lauderdale. **1986:** (22) Qualified for VS Champ in both March and Nov., demonstrating her consistency and high standards. **1987:** (48) R/u Auckland and qf San Diego. **1988:** (49) R/u Schenectady and reached last 16 US Open. **1989:** (48) Upset Shriver at Sydney to reach sf, where she extended Lindqvist to 3s tb. **1990:** Upset Magers *en route* to qf San Diego. **1990 HIGHLIGHTS – SINGLES: Australian Open** 2r (d. Thompson 6–4 6–3, lost Whitlinger 7–5 6–3), **French Open** 1r (lost Sharpe 6–3 6–3), **Wimbledon** 2r (d. Cordwell 6–2 2–6 6–2, lost A. Minter 6–0 6–1), **US Open** 1r (lost Medvedeva 6–4 6–2).

KATIA PICCOLINI (Italy)
Born L'Aquile, 15 January 1973, and lives there; RH; 5ft 11in; 107lb; final 1990 WTA ranking 47; 1990 prize money $49,970.
1988: (300) On Italian satellite circuit reached 3 consec. f, winning Subiaco. **1989:** (171) Sf Estoril. **1990:** Qf Taranto, Palermo and Estoril (upset Cecchini), then in Sept. reached her first tour f at Athens. Broke into top 100 in June and top 50 in Sept. **1990 HIGHLIGHTS – SINGLES: French Open** 1r (lost Seles [seed 2] 6–0 6–0), **Wimbledon** 1r (lost McNeil 6–1 3–6 6–1), **US Open** 3r (d. Kanellopoulou 7–6 6–3, Cecchini 4–6 7–5 6–4, lost Meskhi 6–2 4–6 7–6); **r/u** Athens (d. Dahlman 6–0 7–6, Pospisilova 6–4 6–4, Zardo 6–7 7–6 6–0, Bonsignori 6–2 6–3, lost Dahlman 7–5 7–5).

CLAUDIO PISTOLESI (Italy)
Born Rome, 25 August 1967 and lives there; RH; 5ft 11½in; 167lb; final 1990 ATP ranking 114; 1990 prize money $79,737.
1985: (211) ITF Jun Champ and won Orange Bowl 18s. **1986:** (179). **1987:** (97) Won 1st GP title at Bari (d. Krickstein). **1988:** (112) Upset Krickstein and Wilander *en route* to qf Monte Carlo after qualifying. **1989:** (95) Sf St Vincent, won Salerno Challenger and upset K. Carlsson *en route* to qf Nice. **1990:** Qf Palermo was his best showing. **1990 HIGHLIGHTS – SINGLES: Australian Open** 2r (d. Broad 5–7 6–4 6–4 6–1, lost Woodbridge 6–3 6–2 6–2), **French Open** 1r (lost Jaite 6–2 7–6 6–2), **Wimbledon** 1r (lost Pate 6–3 6–4 6–4).

CLAUDIA PORWIK (Germany)
Born Coburg, 14 November 1968; lives Furth; RH; 5ft 10in; 138lb; final 1990 WTA ranking 29; 1990 prize money $118,934.
Works with Nic Marschand. **1985:** (244) Won Mexico. **1986:** (95) Won 20 of 28 matches. Underwent operation to remove cysts from right wrist end of year. **1987:** (103) Reached first f at Taipei. **1988:** (68) Beat Potter to make an unscheduled appearance in qf Australian Open. **1989:** (74) Qf Oklahoma and Bayonne. **1990:** Taking advantage of an injury to Sabatini, who had to retire when a set up in their 3r match, she reached her 1st GS sf at Australian Open, unseeded, Qf LIPC and Sydney. **1990 HIGHLIGHTS – SINGLES: Australian Open** sf, unseeded (d. Cohen 6–4 6–1, Wiesner 6–3 7–6, Sabatini 2–6 0–1 ret'd, Van Rensburg 7–6 3–6 6–4, Gavaldon 6–4 6–3, lost M-J. Fernandez [seed 6] 6–2 6–1), **Wimbledon** 1r (lost Graf [seed 1] 6–1 6–2). **US Open** 1r (lost Meier 6–4 2–6 5–2 ret'd). **CAREER HIGHLIGHTS – SINGLES: Australian Open – sf 1990, qf 1988** (d. Potter 7–6 7–5, lost Evert 6–3 6–1).

WILTRUD PROBST (Germany)
Born Nuremburg, 29 May 1969; lives Neunkirchen; RH; 5ft 6in; 129lb; final 1990 WTA ranking 40; 1990 prize money $91,076.
1987: (98) Qf Wild Dunes and Hamburg. ***1988:*** (80) Qf Tampa. ***1989:*** (91) Reached sf Strasbourg and upset Magers at Auckland. ***1990:*** Won 1st career singles title at Wellington, reached sf Schenectady and upset Garrison *en route* to last 16 French Open, unseeded. ***1990 HIGHLIGHTS – SINGLES: Australian Open*** 1r (lost Kelesi [seed 8] 6–2 6–3), ***French Open*** last 16, unseeded (d. Garrison 6–1 1–6 7–5, B. Romano 6–2 4–6 7–5, Benjamin 6–2 6–2, lost Martinez 6–3 6–3), ***Wimbledon*** 1r (lost Ludloff 2–6 6–4 7–5), ***US Open*** 2r (d. Leand 6–0 6–2, lost Appelmans 6–4 6–4); ***won*** Wellington (d. Bartos 6–0 6–4, Strnadova 5–7 6–1 6–0, Zardo 7–5 6–3, Appelmans 6–4 6–2, Meskhi 1–6 6–4 6–0); ***sf*** Schenectady (d. Coetzer 7–6 6–1, Fulco 6–4 7–5, Dechaume 6–3 5–7 6–1, lost A. Huber 6–2 6–0). ***1990 HIGHLIGHTS – DOUBLES:*** (with Ferrando) ***r/u*** Schenectady (lost May/Miyagi 6–4 5–7 6–3).

NICOLE PROVIS (Australia)
Born Melbourne, 22 September 1969; lives Sandringham, Vic.; RH; 5ft 9in; 141lb; final 1990 WTA ranking 49; 1990 prize money $165,022.
Coached by Ken Richardson. ***1986:*** (105) R/u French Open Jun. ***1987:*** (77) R/u Australian Open Jun to Jaggard; won doubles with Devries. On senior tour qf Auckland and r/u Wimbledon mixed doubles with Cahill. ***1988:*** (33) Reached sf Strasbourg and qf North California and Berlin, but the high spot of her year came at the French Open, where, unseeded, she upset Kohde-Kilsch, Hanika and Sanchez, before taking Zvereva to 7–5 3s in sf. ***1989:*** (61) Reached last 16 Australian Open and sf VS Arizona. ***1990;*** Reached last 16 French Open, unseeded, and qf VS Washington and Indianapolis. In doubles won Berlin and Strasbourg with Reinach, with whom she qualified for VS Champs, and was r/u French Open mixed with Visser. ***1990 HIGHLIGHTS – SINGLES: Australian Open*** 2r (d. Schuerhoff 7–5 7–6, lost Shriver [seed 11] 1–6 6–2 9–7), ***French Open*** last 16, unseeded (d. Smylie 6–1 6–3, Pampoulova 6–4 6–2, Temesvari 7–6 6–2, lost K. Maleeva [seed 8] 3–6 6–3 6–3), ***Wimbledon*** 2r (d. Martinek 6–1 6–0, lost Dechaume 3–6 6–3 6–2), ***US Open*** 1r (lost Sanchez-Vicario [seed 6] 6–0 6–3). ***1990 HIGHLIGHTS – DOUBLES:*** (with E. Reinach) ***won*** Berlin (d. Mandlikova/Novotna 6–2 6–1), ***won*** Strasbourg (d. K. Jordan/Smylie 6–1 6–4). ***1990 HIGHLIGHTS – MIXED DOUBLES:*** (with Visser) ***r/u French Open*** (lost Sanchez-Vicario/Lozano 7–6 7–6). ***CAREER HIGHLIGHTS – SINGLES: French Open – sf 1988*** (d. Kohde-Kilsch 1–6 6–4 7–5, Hanika 7–6 7–6, Sanchez 7–5 3–6 6–4, lost Zvereva 6–3 6–7 7–5).

GORAN PRPIC (Yugoslavia)
Born Zagreb, 4 May 1964, and lives there; RH; 5ft 11in; 165lb; final 1990 ATP ranking 55; 1990 prize money $251,018.
Wife Andrea, one son. ***1980:*** Nat Jun champ. ***1982:*** Won Rolex Jun. ***1985:*** (139) Qf Bologna (d. Vilas), Bastad (d. Svensson) and Palermo. Upset Noah and Leconte in D Cup. ***1986:*** (870) Severe leg injury suffered at LIPC sidelined him for nearly 2 years. ***1988:*** (226) Returned to play D Cup. ***1989:*** (28) Broke into top 100 in April after success on the Challenger circuit, upset Mecir *en route* to 1st GP f at Stuttgart and reached sf Kitzbuhel. Voted ATP Comeback Player of the Year. ***1990:*** Played a major part in Yugoslavia winning first World Team Cup with a 4–0 singles record. Won 1st career title at Umag (d. Ivanisevic) and reached sf Casablanca and Prague. ***1990 HIGHLIGHTS – SINGLES: Australian Open*** 1r (lost Noah [seed 12] 4–6 7–6 6–2 4–6 7–5), ***French Open*** 1r (lost Champion 6–4 3–6 6–3 6–3); ***won*** Umag (d. Masso 6–7 6–4 6–0, Perez 6–2 6–0, Azar 6–4 6–4, de la Pena 7–6 7–6, Ivanisevic 6–3 4–6 6–4); ***sf*** Casablanca (d. El Aynaoui 6–2 7–6, Champion 7–5 7–6, Anderson 6–3 6–1, lost Muster 6–1 6–3); ***sf*** Prague (d. Vojtisek 4–6 6–3 6–1, Paloheimo 7–5 6–0, Skoff 2–6 6–3 7–6, lost Arrese 7–5 6–4). ***1990 HIGHLIGHTS – DOUBLES:*** [Nastase] ***won*** San Remo (d. Jonsson/Nilsson 3–6 7–5 6–3).

JIM PUGH (USA)
Born Burbank, Cal., 5 February 1964; lives Rancho Palos Verdes, Cal.; RH; 2HF and 2HB; 6ft 4in; 180lb; final 1990 ATP ranking 121 singles, 3 doubles; 1990 prize money $342,672; career prize money $1,385,070.
1982: Suffered severe shoulder injury, amazingly cured by taking thyroid tablets. ***1983:*** All-

American at UCLA. *1985:* (344). *1986:* (99) Won Istanbul Challenger. *1987:* (45) Stunned Cash 1r French Open and reached first GP f at Schenectady, following with San Francisco (d. Mayotte). *1988:* (63) Sf Auckland, Scottsdale and Frankfurt in singles. Was a major force in doubles with R. Leach, winning Australian Open and Masters, and being forced to default US Open f to Casal/E. Sanchez because of Leach's illness. Took 5 other titles, and in mixed doubles with Novotna won Australian and US Opens. *1989:* (60) Won his 1st GP singles title at Newport and reached f Stratton Mountain. He continued his success in doubles with R. Leach, winning Australian Open, r/u Wimbledon and taking 4 other titles to qualify for Masters, where they surprisingly took only 6th place. In mixed doubles with Novotna won Australian Open and Wimbledon. *1990:* In singles reached qf Newport and upset Mayotte at LIPC. In doubles with R. Leach won 1st Wimbledon title, plus LIPC and Philadelphia to qualify for IBM/ATP World Doubles Final. In mixed doubles with Zvereva won Australian Open and r/u US Open. Was a member of the victorious US D Cup team winning dbls with Leach. *1990 HIGHLIGHTS – SINGLES: Australian Open* 1r (lost Lendl [seed 1] 6–3 6–2 6–4), *French Open* 2r (d. Tulasne 6–4 6–3 1–0 ret'd, lost Haarhuis 4–6 6–7 7–6 7–6 5–7), *Wimbledon* 2r (d. Gunnarsson 6–3 1–6 5–7 6–3 6–4, lost Chang [seed 13] 6–3 6–2 6–2), *US Open* 2r (d. Fromberg 2–6 6–4 7–5 7–6, lost E. Sanchez [seed 7] 6–1 6–2 6–2). *1990 HIGHLIGHTS – DOUBLES:* (with R. Leach unless stated) *won Wimbledon* (d. Aldrich/Visser 7–6 7–6 7–6); *won* Philadelphia (d. Connell/Michibata 3–6 6–4 6–2), *won* LIPC (d. Becker/Motta 6–4 3–6 6–3); [Potier] *r/u* Bologna (lost Luza/Riglewski 7–6 4–6 6–1), *r/u* Wembley (lost Grabb/P. McEnroe 7–6 4–6 6–3). *1990 HIGHLIGHTS – MIXED DOUBLES:* (with Zvereva) *won Australian Open* (d. R. Leach/Garrison 4–6 6–2 6–3), *r/u US Open* (lost Smylie/Woodbridge 6–4 6–2). *CAREER HIGHLIGHTS – DOUBLES:* (with R. Leach) *Australian Open – won 1988* (d. Bates/Lundgren 6–3 6–2 6–3), *won 1989* (d. Cahill/Kratzmann 6–4 6–4 6–4); *Wimbledon – won 1990, r/u 1989* (lost Fitzgerald/Jarryd 3–6 7–6 6–4 7–6); *Masters – won 1988* (d. Casal/E. Sanchez 6–4 6–3 2–6 6–0); *LIPC – won 1990; US Open – r/u 1988* (lost Casal/Sanchez def.). *MIXED DOUBLES:* (with Novotna unless stated) *Australian Open – won 1988* (d. Navratilova/Gullikson 5–7 6–2 6–4), *won 1989* (d. Stewart/Garrison 6–3 6–4), [Zvereva] *won 1990; Wimbledon – won 1989* (d. Kratzmann/Byrne 6–4 5–7 6–4); *US Open – won 1988* (d. Smylie/P. McEnroe 7–5 6–3), [Zvereva] *r/u 1990.*

AKI RAHUNEN (Finland)
Born Helsinki, 24 December 1971; lives Espoo; RH; 5ft 9in; 132lb; final 1990 ATP ranking 74; 1990 prize money $148,738.
1988: (634) Joined Finnish D Cup squad. *1989:* (138) Won Hanko Challenger. *1990:* Broke into top 100 in Feb. after reaching 1st tour qf at Stuttgart as a qualifier, upsetting Mansdorf *en route.* Followed with sf showing at Florence and qf Umag and Bastad. *1990 HIGHLIGHTS – SINGLES: Australian Open* 1r (lost J. Sanchez 6–0 6–3 6–1), *French Open* 3r (d. Connell 1–6 6–1 6–4 6–0, Shiras 6–0 6–1 6–1, lost Jaite 7–6 6–2 6–1), *Wimbledon* 2r (d. Evernden 3–6 4–6 6–1 7–6 6–3, lost Stich 6–2 7–5 6–3), *US Open* 1r (lost Muster [seed 6] 5–7 6–4 6–0 3–0 ret'd); *sf* Florence (d. Motta 6–4 7–5, Mancini 2–6 6–2 6–3, J. Sanchez 6–4 4–6 7–5, lost Larsson 6–4 6–4).

REGINA RAJCHRTOVA (Czechoslovakia)
Born Havlickuv Brod, 5 February 1968; lives Prague; RH; 6ft; 148lb; final 1990 WTA ranking 54; 1990 prize money $86,140.
Coached by Zdenek Zofka and Jan Soukup. *1985:* (282). *1986:* (226). *1987:* (89) Reached 4 f on satellite circuits, winning Mald. *1988:* (217). *1989:* (40) Reached her 1st tour f at Paris Open and made an unexpected appearance in last 16 US Open. *1990:* Upset Gildemeister and Garrison to reach sf FC Cup. *1990 HIGHLIGHTS – SINGLES: Australian Open* 1r (lost Paulus [seed 16] 6–3 6–1), *French Open* 2r (d. Whitlinger 6–2 6–0, lost M. Maleeva 6–2 6–3), *Wimbledon* 2r (d. Keller 7–5 6–7 6–4, lost Gildemeister 6–2 6–2), *US Open* 1r (lost Savchenko 6–3 1–6 6–3); *sf* FC Cup (d. Brioukhouvets 2–6 6–4 6–3, Keller 4–6 6–2 6–1, Gildemeister 6–4 6–2, Garrison 4–6 6–3 6–1, lost Navratilova 6–4 6–3). *1990 HIGHLIGHTS – DOUBLES:* (with Temesvari) *r/u* Amelia Island (lost Paz/Sanchez-Vicario 7–6 6–4).

GUILLAME RAOUX (France)
Born Bagnol-sur-Cèze, 14 February 1970; lives Paris; RH; 5ft 11in; 165lb; final 1990 ATP ranking 84; 1990 prize money $108,245.

1987: (938). *1988:* (448) R/u Wimbledon Jun to Pereira and was ranked 3 on ITF Jun list. Won Nat 18s. *1989:* (220) Won Guadeloupe Challenger. *1990:* Upset Sampras at Paris Open and won Martinque and Gevrey-Chambertin Challengers. *1990 HIGHLIGHTS – SINGLES: French Open* 1r (lost Santoro 6–1 6–4 6–4), Wimbledon 2r (d. Turner 6–3 6–4 7–5, lost Pate 3–6 6–2 6–4 6–3); *won* Martinique Challenger (d. Weiss 3–6 6–3 6–3), *won* Gevrey-Chambertin Challenger (d. Holm 2–6 6–4 6–4).

RAFFAELLA REGGI (Italy)
Born Faenza, 27 November 1965; lives Monte Carlo; RH; 2HB; 5ft 7in; 127lb; final 1990 WTA ranking 23; 1990 prize money $113,404.
Coached by Ferruccio Bonetti; fitness coach Daniele Gatti. *1981:* One of the most spirited performers in the sport, an unwavering competitor, she won Orange Bowl 16s and was ranked No. 1 in Italian 16s. *1982:* (127) Moved up to No. 3 among Italian women and joined Fed Cup team. *1983:* (48) No. 1 in Italy. *1984:* (62) Sf Swiss Open and qf for Italian Open and Lugano with victories over Bunge and M. Maleeva, reached last 16 Wimbledon and US Open both unseeded, and won US Open mixed doubles with Casal. Qualified for VS Champ Nov. *1987:* (17) Beat Sukova *en route* to qf French Open, reached last 16 Wimbledon and won VS San Diego. Qualified for VS Champs again. *1988:* (23) f At Olympics upset Kohde-Kilsch and Evert to reach qf; r/u Brussels, sf Oklahoma and Filderstadt. *1989:* (21) In GS reached last 16 Australian Open, upset 1988 finalist Zvereva at French Open and held 2 mps v Sanchez at Wimbledon. R/u Eastbourne and VS Indianapolis, sf Oklahoma and Bayonne to qualify for VS Champs (lost Sukova 1r), and in doubles reached 3 f. *1990:* Won Taranto and reached last 16 Australian Open. *1990 HIGHLIGHTS – SINGLES: Australian Open* last 16, seed 13 (d. Hodder 6–1 6–0, Durie 6–4 6–4, Huber 7–5 4–6 6–4, lost Graf 6–2 6–3), *French Open* 2r, seed 14 (d. Gavaldon 1–6 7–6 6–2, lost Sharpe 6–4 6–2), *Wimbledon* 1r (lost McQuillan 7–6 7–6), *US Open* (d. Herreman 1–6 6–3 6–3, Wasserman 6–2 6–2, lost K. Maleeva [seed 7] 6–4 6–0); *won* Taranto (d. Devries 6–1 4–6 6–2, Chabalgoity 6–3 6–0, Scheuer-Larsen 5–7 6–2 6–3, Etchemendy 6–3 2–6 6–4, Dechaume 3–6 6–0 6–2). *1990 HIGHLIGHTS – DOUBLES:* (with Kelesi) *r/u* Canadian Open (lost Nagelsen/Sabatini 3–6 6–2 6–2), *r/u* VS Los Angeles (lost G. Fernandez/ Novotna 6–3 4–6 6–4). *CAREER HIGHLIGHTS – SINGLES: French Open – qf 1987* (lost Evert 6–2 6–2). *MIXED DOUBLES:* (with Casal) *US Open – won 1986* (d. Navratilova/ Fleming 6–4 6–4).

STEPHANIE REHE (USA)
Born Fontana, Cal., 5 November 1969; lives Oceanside, Cal.; RH; 2HB; 5ft 11in; 140lb; final 1990 WTA ranking 58; 1990 prize money $30,663.
Coached by Olaf Merkel. *1981:* Won US Nat 12 singles. *1982:* Youngest to compete in VS tourn at 13 years 1 month. Won US Nat 14 indoor singles and Orange Bowl 14s. *1983:* At 13 years 2 months, youngest to receive computer ranking. Won US Nat 14 and Nat 16 Clay. *1984:* Won 18 Clay and 18 Nat Indoor. *1985:* (18) Won Nat 18, VS Utah and Tampa, and climbed into top 20 with wins over Sabatini and Bassett. *1986:* (17) Consolidated position in game, doing better early in season. *1987:* (28) Won Puerto Rico and reached last 16 French Open. Out of action 6 weeks in late summer with pulled stomach muscle. *1988:* (14) Won Taipei and San Diego, r/u Japan Open and reached 5 other sf. Upset Kohde-Kilsch to reach last US Open and Shriver at Chicago. Qualified for VS Champs but withdrew with an ankle injury. *1989:* (–) Did not play at all owing to back injury for which she underwent back surgery in late summer. *1990:* Returned in Aug. after an absence of 18 months to upset Sabatini in reaching qf VS Los Angeles and Gildemeister *en route* to the same stage at VS California.

ELNA REINACH (South Africa)
Born Pretoria, 2 December 1968 and lives there; RH; 5ft 11½in; 145lb; final 1990 WTA ranking 86 singles, 19 (20) doubles; 1990 prize money $135,171.
Coached by her mother, Elna. Sister of Monica. *1984:* R/u Wimbledon Jun, won South African Int jun event and South African satellite circuit Masters. *1985:* Won Wimbledon Plate and 2 tourns on satellite circuits. *1986:* (55) Upset Rinaldi at Mahwah. *1987:* (93). *1988:* (28) Qf Birmingham, Oklahoma, Filderstadt and LIPC, where she upset Garrison, and reached last 16 US Open with upset of M-J. Fernandez. *1989:* (57) Sf Birmingham and reached 3 doubles f, winning Albuquerque. Ranked No. 1 in her country for 3rd straight

year. *1990:* In singles reached sf VS Nashville and qf Schenectady; in doubles with Provis won Berlin and Strasbourg, qualifying for VS Champs. *1990 HIGHLIGHTS – SINGLES: French Open* 1r (lost Etchemendy 7–5 6–1), *Wimbledon* 3r (d. Inoue 6–0 6–4, Loosemore 6–3 7–5, lost Henricksson 3–6 6–3 6–3), *US Open* 3r (d. Hack 6–1 6–2, Dechaume 6–3 6–0, lost Graf [seed 1] 6–4 3–6 6–1); *sf* VS Nashville (d. Grossman 6–1 6–3, Schultz 4–6 6–1 6–4, Harvey-Wild 6–3 6–3, lost Sloane 6–3 4–6 6–0). *1990 HIGHLIGHTS – DOUBLES:* (with Provis) *won* Berlin (d. Mandlikova/Novotna 6–2 6–1), *won* Strasbourg (d. K. Jordan/Smylie 6–1 6–4).

BEATE REINSTADLER (Germany)
Born Stuttgart, 20 May 1967; lives Thaur, Aut; RH; 2HB; 5ft 6in; 125lb; Final 1990 WTA ranking 54; 1990 prize money $25,761.
1990: Reached sf Palermo and qf Wellington, breaking into the top 100 in July. *1990 HIGHLIGHTS – SINGLES: Australian Open* 2r (d. Reis 6–1 6–2, lost Smylie 6–2 6–4), *French Open* 1r (lost Lapi 6–4 6–2), *US Open* 1r (lost Garrison [seed 4] 6–1 6–3); *sf* Palermo (d. Kschwendt 3–6 6–4 7–6, Bonsignori 6–1 2–6 6–3, Caverzasio 6–3 4–6 7–6, lost Cueto 6–1 6–1).

RICHEY RENEBERG (USA)
Born Phoenix, Ariz., 5 October 1965; lives Laporte, Texas; RH; 5ft 11in; 170lb; final 1990 ATP ranking 23; 1990 prize money $307,336.
1985: (794) All American at Southern Methodist Univ. for 1st of 3 straight years. *1986:* (337) R/u NCAA singles to Goldie. *1987:* (79) Qf Indianapolis and was voted ATP Newcomer of the Year. *1988:* (103) Qf US CC and Vienna. *1989:* (80) Reached 1st GP sf at Auckland and upset Noah *en route* to the same stage at Washington. *1990:* Shot up the rankings into the top 25 with r/u showing at Wellington (d. Chesnokov), plus sf Rosmalen, Indianapolis (d. Sampras) and Tokyo Seiko, and an upset of J. McEnroe at Philadelphia. *1990 HIGHLIGHTS – SINGLES: Australian Open* 1r (lost Agenor 6–2 6–4 3–6 6–1), *French Open* 1r (lost Forget 3–6 6–4 6–4 6–4), *Wimbledon* 1r (lost Srejber 6–7 3–6 7–6 6–3 6–2), *US Open* 1r (lost Hlasek 3–6 7–6 6–4 6–0); *r/u* Wellington (d. Casal 6–4 4–6 7–5, Bergstrom 6–4 6–3, Chesnokov 2–6 6–0 6–0, Novacek 6–7 7–4 6–0, lost E. Sanchez 6–7 6–4 4–6 6–4); *sf* Rosmalen (d. Woodforde 6–2 6–4, Stich 5–7 6–3 6–3, Engel 7–6 6–4, lost Mansdorf 6–4 6–4), *sf* Indianapolis (d. Kratzmann 6–0 6–3, Shiras 6–0 6–1, Krickstein 6–4 6–2, Sampras 3–6 6–1 7–6, lost Lundgren 6–4 6–4), *sf* Tokyo Seiko (d. Stoltenberg 6–1 6–4, Forget 7–6 7–6, Hogstedt 6–3 6–2, lost Becker 7–6 6–2). *1990 HIGHLIGHTS – DOUBLES:* [Layendecker] *r/u* San Francisco (lost Jones/Van't Hof 2–6 7–6 6–3).

MARTEN RENSTROEM (Sweden)
Born 3 February 1962.
1990: Ranked No. 1 in ITF Jun doubles Rankings. Won US Open Jun doubles with Tillstroem.

UDO RIGLEWSKI (Germany)
Born Lauffen, 28 July 1966; lives Gemmingen; RH; 6ft 1in; 177lb; final 1990 ATP ranking 88 singles, 19 doubles; 1990 prize money $218,928.
Married Sabine Koanig 8 April 1989. *1987:* (338) In doubles with Popp won Florence and 3 Challenger titles. *1988:* (93) Qf Bastad and upset Chesnokov 1r Wimbledon. *1989:* (142) Qf Rotterdam and Gstaad in singles and won 3 doubles titles with different partners. *1990:* In singles reached sf Moscow and qf Genova. In doubles with various partners reached 9 f, winning 4. *1990 HIGHLIGHTS – SINGLES: Australian Open* 3r (d. Cane 6–2 6–3 2–6 6–2, Borwick 6–2 6–4 6–2, lost Mecir [seed 16] 6–4 6–2 6–0), *French Open* 1r (lost Chesnokov [seed 8] 6–1 6–1 6–3), *Wimbledon* 2r (d. Paloheimo 6–4 7–5 7–5, lost Woodforde 6–7 6–4 6–4 7–5), *US Open* 1r (lost Stoltenberg 4–6 6–1 6–0 2–1 ret'd); *sf* Moscow (d. Shelton 7–6 6–7 6–2, Reneberg 1–6 6–3 6–2, Casal 4–6 7–6 6–3, lost Cherkasov 6–1 7–6). *1990 HIGHLIGHTS – DOUBLES:* (with Stich unless stated) *won* Munich (d. Korda/Smid 6–1 6–4), [Luza] *won* Bologna (d. Potier/Pugh 7–6 4–6 6–1), [Carbonell] *won* Genova (d. Caratti/Mordecan 7–6 7–6), *won* Vienna (d. Lozano/Witsken 6–4 6–4); [Nijssen] *r/u* Milan (lost Camporese/Nargiso 6–4 6–4), *r/u* Memphis (lost Cahill/Kratzmann 7–5 6–2), *r/u* Hamburg (lost Bruguera/Courier 7–6 6–2), [Gunnarsson] *r/u* Bastad (lost Bergh/Bathman 6–1 6–4), *r/u* Long Island (lost Forget/Hlasek 2–6 6–3 6–4).

KATHY RINALDI (USA)
*Born Stuart, Fla, 24 March 1967; lives Amelia Island, Fla; RH; 2HB; 5ft 6in; 121lb; final
1990 WTA ranking 69; 1990 prize money $82,349.*
Coached by Andy Brandi. **1979:** Quietly precocious, she became first to win a US Girls' 12
GS, winning Indoor, HC, CC and Nat Champ. **1980:** Won Nat Girls' 14 CC and was ranked
3rd in division. **1981:** (33) Youngest to reach qf French Open and youngest to win a match
at Wimbledon (14 years and 3 months). Turned pro in July. Voted WTA Most Impressive
Newcomer. **1982:** (12) R/u German Open and San Diego. **1983:** (16) Sf US CC and WTA
Champs, last 16 Wimbledon and French Open, and played W Cup. **1984:** (23) Sf Fort
Lauderdale. **1985:** (11) Sf Wimbledon, won Mahwah over Graf and had wins over Sukova,
Kohde-Kilsch and Mandlikova. **1986:** (9) Had a strong start with qf French Open, overcame
mid-season injuries and returned to win VS Arkansas at end of year. **1987:** (26) Qf
Washington. Suffered a fractured thumb at French Open, which kept her out of action for
11 months. **1988:** (88) Returned at Amelia Island, playing only doubles and losing 1r. **1989:**
(52) Reached sf Bayonne and was voted WTA Comeback Player of Year. **1990:** Suffered a
poor year in which she reached no qf. **1990 HIGHLIGHTS – SINGLES: Australian Open**
2r (d. R. White 6–4 3–6 6–4, lost M-J. Fernandez 6–4 6–4), **French Open** 1r (lost Sviglerova
6–2 5–5 ret'd), **Wimbledon** 1r (lost Kschwendt 7–6 1–6 6–0), **US Open** 2r (d. Labat 6–4
4–6 6–3, lost Novotna [seed 12] 6–4 6–3) **CAREER HIGHLIGHTS – DOUBLES:** (with
Garrison) **US Open – sf 1985** (lost Kohde-Kilsch/Sukova 6–3 fs).

JOEY RIVE (USA)
*Born Santurce, Puerto Rico, 8 July 1963; lives West Palm Beach, Fla.; LH; 6ft 1in; 180lb;
final 1990 ATP ranking 138; 1990 prize money $121,679.*
Coached by Craig Wittus. **1985:** (497). **1986:** (363). **1987:** (102) Qf Newport and Stratton
Mountain (d. Mayotte). **1988:** (80) Reached his 1st GP sf at Sydney; qf Adelaide and Seoul.
1989: (149) Plagued by injuries, he slipped from the top 100, but salvaged his year with sf
appearance at Johannesburg. **1990:** Reached sf San Francisco and qf Orlando. **1990
HIGHLIGHTS – SINGLES: French Open** 1r (lost Stich 6–4 6–1 6–1), **Wimbledon** 2r (d.
Amritraj 5–7 6–4 6–4 5–7 6–4, lost Novacek 6–1 6–4 7–6), **US Open** 1r (lost Davin 6–4 6–4
7–6); **sf** San Francisco (d. Curren 6–2 7–5, Duncan 4–6 6–3 6–3, Arias 2–6 6–4 6–2, lost
Witsken 6–4 7–6). **1990 HIGHLIGHTS – DOUBLES:** [Curren] **r/u** Hong Kong (lost Cash/
Masur 6–3 6–3).

MARC ROSSET (Swizerland)
*Born Geneva, 7 November 1970, and lives there; RH; 6ft 5in; 184lb; final 1990 ATP ranking
22; 1990 prize money $282,048.*
Coached by Stephane Oberer. **1988:** Won Orange Bowl and was No. 4 on ITF Jun
Rankings. **1989:** (45) On Challenger circuit reached qf or better in 10 tourns, winning 2.
Broke into top 100 after winning Geneva in Sept. **1990:** Broke into the top 25 in autumn,
following some big upsets during the year. Won his 1st tour title at Lyon (d. Wilander); r/u
Madrid (d. E. Sanchez) and Bologna; sf Nice (d. Noah), Gstaad (d. E. Sanchez) and Geneva.
1990 HIGHLIGHTS – SINGLES: Australian Open 1r (lost Larsson 6–4 6–1 6–1), **French
Open** 2r (d. Roig 3–6 6–3 6–4 6–4, lost Chang [seed 11] 7–5 4–6 6–4 6–3), **Wimbledon** 3r
(d. S. Davis 7–6 7–5 6–3, Jones 3–6 6–7 6–3 7–5 6–3, lost Volkov 6–3 6–4 7–5), **US Open**
1r (lost Cash 2–6 2–6 6–3 6–3 6–3); **won** Lyon (d. Srejber 7–6 6–7 7–6, Jelen 6–1 3–6 6–3,
Agenor 7–6 7–5, Pate 6–4 1–6 6–4, Wilander 6–3 6–2); **r/u** Madrid (d. Camporese 4–6 7–6
6–3, E. Sanchez 4–6 6–4 6–4, Gorriz 6–2 2–6 7–5, J. Sanchez 7–5 2–6 6–2, lost Gomez 6–3
7–6), **r/u** Bologna (d. Bloom 6–2 3–6 6–1, de la Pena 7–6 3–6 6–4, Duncan 6–2 6–3, Davin
6–2 6–4, lost Fromberg 4–6 6–4 7–6); **sf** Nice (d. Noah 5–7 6–3 6–3, Carbonell 7–6 4–6
6–4, Santoro 6–0 5–7 6–2, lost Aguilera 6–3 6–0), **sf** Gstaad (d. Novacek 7–6 5–7 6–2,
Masur 6–4 5–7 7–6, E. Sanchez 6–4 3–6 6–3, lost Bruguera 6–3 7–5), **sf** Geneva (d. Albano
6–4 6–2, Mronz 6–4 6–2, Camporese 7–6 7–6, lost Skoff 4–6 6–3 6–2).

DERRICK ROSTAGNO (USA)
*Born Los Angeles, 25 October 1965; lives Pacific Palisades, Cal. and St Augustine, Fla.;
RH; 6ft 1in; 165lb; final 1990 ATP ranking 47; 1990 prize money $257,285.*
1983: Won New Zealand Masters satellite circuit. **1984:** Played in Olympic demonstration
event in Los Angeles. **1985:** (427). **1986:** (70) Sf Houston, qf LA. **1987:** (60) Reached last
16 Australian Open, sf Auckland and Frankfurt, with wins across the year over Gilbert,

Becker and Gomez. *1988:* (36) Upset Mayotte *en route* to an unexpected appearance in qf US Open, took Connors to 7–5 fs Wimbledon and reached sf Bristol and Washington. *1989:* (89) Sf Queen's. *1990:* Upset Mayotte and Chesnokov *en route* to his 1st tour title at New Haven and removed J. McEnroe 1r Wimbledon. *1990 HIGHLIGHTS – SINGLES: French Open* 1r (lost Antonitsch 6–3 7–6 6–3), *Wimbledon* 3r (d. J. McEnroe 7–5 6–4 6–4, Bates 6–1 3–6 6–4 6–1, lost Ivanisevic 6–2 6–2 6–4), *US Open* 2r (d. Benhabiles 6–4 6–2 6–2, lost Caratti 3–6 7–6 6–4 1–6 7–6); *won* New Haven (d. Annacone 4–6 7–6 6–2, Mayotte 4–6 6–4 6–3, Pugh 6–2 6–2, Van Rensburg 7–5 6–0, Chesnokov 7–6 6–3, Woodbridge 7–6 6–3).

GABRIELA SABATINI (Argentina)
Born Buenos Aires, 16 May 1970; lives there and Key Biscayne, Fla.; 5ft 8in; 130lb; final 1990 WTA ranking 5; 1990 prize money $975,490; career prize money $3,656,136.
Coached by Angel Gimenez for 5 years until, in June 1990 she turned to the Brazilian, Carlos Kirmayr who restored her joy in the game. Trained by Omar Carminatti. *1984:* (74) Top of ITF Jun rankings, she won French and Italian Jun and Orange Bowl 18s, where she conceded only 9 games in 6 matches. Meanwhile she tested the waters in women's tennis and reached 3r US CC and US Open, where she was youngest to win a match. *1985:* (12) Youngest sf at French Open, won Japan Open and was r/u to Evert Lloyd at Hilton Head, following big wins over Garrison, Shriver and M. Maleeva. *1986:* (10) Youngest sf Wimbledon and qf or better in 12 of 21 tournaments. Established a successful doubles partnership with Graf, r/u French Open. *1987:* (6) With a win-loss record of 56–16, she was one of the few players to trouble Graf during the year, frequently taking her to 3s but never beating her. Sf French Open, r/u Italian Open and won her first major titles at Tokyo and Brighton in autumn. R/u VS Champs where she d. Navratilova in ss and took Graf to 4s. R/u French Open doubles with Graf. *1988:* (4) Won VS Champs over Shriver, Argentine Open, Italian Open, Montreal and VS Florida, where she beat Evert and achieved a first-ever win over Graf, ending the No. 1's 30-match winning streak. She upset her again at Amelia Island, and was the only player to inflict 2 defeats on the World Champion during the year. Reached sf French Open and last 16 Wimbledon, then at US Open became 1st Argentine to reach GS f where she took Graf to 3s, following with Olympic silver medal. In doubles with Graf won Wimbledon and LIPC, but they were forced to default sf VS Champs owing to Graf's illness. *1989:* (3) Did not progress beyond sf in any GS, reaching that stage in Australian Open and US Open but falling to M-J. Fernandez in last 16 French Open and to Fairbank 2r Wimbledon. However, she won US doubles with Graf. In singles won LIPC, Italian Open, Amelia Island (d. Navratilova and Graf) and Filderstadt, reaching 3 other f and sf VS Champs. Was 1 of only 2 players to beat Graf during the year. *1990:* Following her loss to Novotna in last 16 French Open, she sacked her coach, Angel Gimenez, and working with new coach Carlos Kirmayr and sports psychologist Jim Lohr, she developed a serve and volley game with which she beat Graf at US Open to win a 1st GS title in her 8th f. Earlier had snapped a tendon in her ankle 3r Australian Open, which kept her out until March, when she returned to win VS Florida at Boca Raton, following with sf Wimbledon, r/u VS New England and Zurich, plus 4 more sf showings. At VS Champs she beat Graf again in sf, but lost f in 5s to Seles. *1990 HIGHLIGHTS – SINGLES: Australian Open* 3r, seed 2 (d. Frazier 6–4 7–6, Daniels 7–5 6–1, lost Porwik 2–6 0–1 ret'd), *French Open* last 16, seed 4 (d. Vieira 6–0 7–6, Sloane 6–0 5–7 6–1, Herreman 6–0 6–1, lost Novotna [seed 11] 6–4 7–5), *Wimbledon* sf, seed 4 (d. Burgin 6–3 6–3, A. Huber 6–2 7–6, Tanvier 6–4 6–2, Tauziat 6–2 7–6, Zvereva [seed 11] 6–2 2–6 8–6, lost Navratilova 6–3 6–4), *won US Open* seed 5 (d. Jordan 6–1 6–1, Demongeot 6–1 6–1, Appelmans 6–2 6–4, Sukova [seed 11] 6–2 6–1, Meskhi 7–6 6–4, M-J. Fernandez [seed 8] 7–5 5–7 6–3, Graf [seed 1] 6–2 7–6); *won* VS Florida (d. Inoue 6–2 7–5, Reggi 6–2 6–1, Van Rensburg 6–2 7–6, M-J. Fernandez 4–4 ret'd, Capriati 6–4 7–5); *r/u* Zurich (d. Menning 6–2 6–1, Khode-Kilsch 6–4 7–5, Sukova 6–4 7–5, Novotna 6–7 7–5 7–6, lost Graf 6–3 6–2), *r/u* VS New England (d. Gildemeister 6–0 6–3, Sukova 6–3 6–2, M-J. Fernandez 6–2 6–4, lost Graf 7–6 6–3), *r/u* VS Champs (d. Novotna 6–1 5–7 7–6, Martinez 6–4 1–6 6–1, Graf 6–4 6–4, lost Seles 6–4 5–7 4–6 6–4 6–2); *sf* Amelia Island (d. Kohde-Kilsch 6–2 6–1, Caverzasio 6–4 6–0, Cueto 6–3 6–3, lost Sanchez-Vicario 6–4 6–0), *sf* Italian Open (d. Grossman 7–6 6–0, Rajchrtova 6–0 6–1, Capriati 6–2 7–5, lost Navratilova 7–6 7–5), *sf* Canadian Open (d. Rinaldi 6–0 6–3, Reggi 6–1 6–0, Capriati 3–6 6–1 6–4, lost K. Maleeva 6–3 6–4), *sf* Filderstadt (d. Halard 6–4

6–3, Paz 6–2 6–2, Sukova 6–2 6–7 6–2, lost Paulus 6–3 6–4). *1990 HIGHLIGHTS –* *DOUBLES:* [Nagelsen] *won* Canadian Open (d. Kelesi/Reggi 3–6 6–2 6–2). *CAREER HIGHLIGHTS – SINGLES: US Open – won 1990, r/u 1988* (d. Rehe, Savchenko 4–6 6–4 6–1, Garrison 6–4 7–5, lost Graf 6–3 3–6 6–1), *sf 1989* (d. Porwik, Caverzasio, Meskhi 6–2 6–0, Martinez 6–1 6–1, Sanchez-Vicario 3–6 6–4 6–1, lost Graf 3–6 6–4 6–2); *VS Champs – won 1988* (d. K. Maleeva, Zvereva 6–1 6–1, Sukova 6–4 6–2, Shriver 7–5 6–2 6–2), *r/u 1987* (d. Bunge, Navratilova 6–4 7–5, lost Graf 7–5 4–6 6–0), *r/u 1990, sf 1989* (d. Magers 6–4 6–1, Garrison 6–3 5–7 6–3, lost Graf 6–3 5–7 6–1); *Olympics – silver medal 1988* (d. Zvereva, Manuela Maleeva 6–1 6–1, lost Graf 6–3 6–3); *Australian Open – sf 1989* (d. Dahlman, Martinez 3–6 6–1 6–2, Benjamin 6–0 6–0, Reggi 6–0 4–6 6–1, Garrison 6–4 2–6 6–4, lost Graf 6–3 6–0); *French Open – sf 1985* (d. Manuela Maleeva 6–1 fs, lost Evert Lloyd 6–4 6–1), *sf 1987* (d. Schimper, Sanchez, lost Graf 6–4 4–6 7–5), *sf 1988* (d. Kelesi 4–6 6–1 6–3, lost Graf 6–3 7–6); *Wimbledon – sf 1986* (d. Jolissaint, Suire, Gerken, Reggi 6–4 1–6 6–3, Lindqvist 6–2 6–3, lost Navratilova [seed 1] 6–2 6–2), *sf 1990. CAREER HIGHLIGHTS – DOUBLES:* (with Graf) *Wimbledon – won 1988* (d. Savchenko/Zvereva 6–3 1–6 12–10); *LIPC – won 1988* (d. G. Fernandez/Garrison 7–6 6–3); *French Open – r/u 1986* (lost Navratilova/Temesvari 6–1 6–2), *r/u 1987* (lost Navratilova/Shriver 6–2 6–1), *r/u 1989* (lost Savchenko/Zvereva 6–4 6–4).

PETE SAMPRAS (USA)
Born Potomac, Md, 12 August 1971; lives Rancho Palos Verdes, Cal.; RH; 6ft; 160lb; final 1990 ATP ranking 5; 1990 prize money $2,900,057.
Mother Georgia, father Sam, son of Greek immigrants. Brother Gus sometimes trains with him. In 1985 changed from 2HB to 1HB on the advice of his then coach, Dr Pete Fischer, with whom he split in 1989. Robt. Lansdof had coached him on forehand, Larry Easley on volleying and Del Little for footwork. Went to Bollettieri Academy and worked with Joe Brandi but parted in Dec. 1990 and started working with Pat Etchenbury for strength at Bolliettieri Academy. Reunited with Brandi Jan. 1991. *1988:* (97) Sf Schenectady and upset Mayotte *en route* to qf Detroit. *1989:* (81) Reached qf Adelaide and upset Wilander *en route* to last 16 US Open. In doubles with Courier won Italian Open, and took 7th place at Masters. *1990:* Upset Mayotte in 70-game struggle 1r Australian Open *en route* to last 16, unseeded, and in Feb. won his 1st tour title at Philadelphia, which took him into top 20. He followed with Manchester, but the crescendo of his year came in Sept. when he won his 1st GS title at US Open and moved into the top 10. At 19 years 28 days he was the youngest champion there (the previous youngest was Oliver Campbell, who won in 1890 aged 19 years 6 months). Also reached sf Milan, Canadian Open, Los Angeles and Stockholm, but withdrew from Paris Open suffering from shin splints, which had been troubling him since US Open. He was able to play ATP World Champ, but did not progress beyond rr. Won inaugural GS Cup and first prize $2m. *1990 HIGHLIGHTS – SINGLES: Australian Open* last 16, unseeded (d. Mayotte [seed 6] 7–6 6–7 4–6 7–5 12–10, Arrese 0–6 6–2 3–6 6–1 6–3, Woodbridge 7–5 6–4 6–2, lost Noah [seed 12] 6–3 6–4 3–6 6–2), *Wimbledon* 1r (lost Van Rensburg 7–6 7–5 7–6), *won US Open* seed 12 (d. Goldie 6–1 7–5 6–1, Lundgren 6–4 6–3 6–3, Hlasek 6–3 6–4 6–1, Muster [seed 6] 6–7 7–6 6–4 6–3, Lendl [seed 3] 6–4 7–6 3–6 4–6 6–2, J. McEnroe 6–2 6–4 3–6 6–3, Agassi 6–4 6–3 6–2); *won* Philadelphia (d. Srejber 6–3 6–7 6–3, Agassi 5–7 7–5 ret'd, Mayotte 6–4 4–6 6–3, Kratzmann 4–6 6–1 6–4, Gomez 7–6 7–5 6–2), *won* Manchester (d. Volkov 4–6 7–6 7–6, Rive 4–6 6–3 6–2, Evernden 6–3 7–6, Jelen 6–7 6–4, Bloom 7–6 7–6), *won* GS Cup seed 4 (d. Cherkasov 5–7 6–2 7–5, Ivanisevic 7–6 6–7 8–5, Chang 6–3 6–4 6–4, Gilbert 6–3 6–4 6–2), *sf* Milan (d. Jarryd 6–1 6–3, Zoecke 6–1 7–6, Srejber 6–7 6–4 6–4, lost Lendl 3–6 6–0 6–3), *sf* Canadian Open (d. Wostenholme 6–3 6–2, Sznajder 4–6 6–3 6–2, J. McEnroe 7–6 4–6 6–3, lost Chang 3–6 7–6 7–5), *sf* Los Angeles (d. R. Leach 7–5 6–3, Pearce 6–2 2–6 6–4, Stoltenberg 6–3 6–4, lost Edberg 6–2 6–7 6–1), *sf* Stockholm (d. Bergh 7–6 6–7 6–3, Korda 6–3 3–6 7–6, Wheaton 7–6 7–5 6–4, lost Becker 6–4 6–4). *CAREER HIGHLIGHTS – SINGLES: US Open – won 1990.*

ARANTXA SANCHEZ-VICARIO (Spain)
Born Barcelona, 18 December 1971, lives Andorra; RH; 2HB; 5ft 6½in; 110lb; final 1990 WTA ranking 7 singles, 8 doubles; 1990 prize money $517,662.
Sister of Emilio and Javier. Coached by Mike Estep to end 1990, then by Eduardo Osta. Travels with her mother, Marisa, whose family name, Vicario, she added to her own after

1989 French Open. *1986:* (124) Emerging from satellite circuit, she reached sf Spanish Open and played Fed Cup. *1987:* (47) Qf French Open in first GS appearance. *1988:* (18) Upset Evert (suffering from a foot injury) at French Open *en route* to qf again and reached last 16 US Open. Won her 1st pro singles title at Brussels and was r/u Tampa. *1989:* (5) At 17 yrs 6 mths became the youngest woman and the first Spaniard to win French Open women's title. Qf Wimbledon and US Open, won Barcelona and was r/u Italian Open and Canadian Open, qualifying for 1st VS Champs, where she reached sf. Voted WTA Most Improved Player for 2nd year running. *1990:* In some disappointing performances she fell to Harvey-Wild 1r VS Chicago, to Paz 2r French Open and to Nagelsen 1r Wimbledon. Her 1st singles title came at Barcelona in April, followed by VS Newport; r/u Tokyo Toray, VS Houston, Amelia Island, Leipzig and Hamburg, where she d. Navratilova and took Graf to 3s. She lost 1r VS Champs to K. Maleeva and in GS her best showing was sf US Open, but she won French Open mixed doubles with Lozano. In women's doubles won 1 title with Navratilova and 3 with Paz, with whom she was r/u VS Champs. *1990 HIGHLIGHTS – SINGLES: French Open* 2r, seed 3 (d. Van Lottum 6–1 6–3, lost Paz 7–5 3–6 6–1), *Wimbledon* 1r, seed 6 (lost Nagelsen 1–6 7–6 9–7), *US Open* sf, seed 6 (d. Provis 6–0 6–3, Kuhlman 6–1 6–2, Fendick 6–2 6–1, Paulus [seed 16] 6–4 6–3, Garrison [seed 4] 6–2 6–2, lost Graf [seed 1] 6–1 6–2); *won* Barcelona (d. Hack 6–2 6–4, Demongeot 6–1 6–2, Wiesner 6–2 6–1, Cueto 6–4 6–2), *won* VS Newport (d. Helgeson 6–3 6–3, Schultz 4–6 6–2 6–2, McGrath 6–4 7–5, Magers 6–3 6–2, Durie 7–6 4–6 7–5); *r/u* Tokyo Toray (d. Faull 6–1 6–0, G. Fernandez 1–6 6–1 6–2, Kijimuta 6–4 6–2, lost Graf 6–1 6–2), *r/u* VS Houston (d. Magers 6–3 6–3, Daniels 7–5 6–2, Garrison 6–7 6–3 7–6, lost K. Maleeva 6–1 1–6 6–4), *r/u* Amelia Island (d. Lapi 6–3 7–5, Rinaldi 6–0 6–1, Kelesi 7–5 6–4, Sabatini 6–4 6–0, lost Graf 6–0 6–1), *r/u* Hamburg (d. Rittner 6–4 6–1, Hanika 6–1 6–1, Jagerman 6–3 6–0, Navratilova 6–1 6–7 6–2, lost Graf 5–7 6–0 6–1); *r/u* Leipzig (d. Paz 7–6 6–3, Strnadova 6–7 6–2 6–1, Paulus 6–0 7–5, lost Graf 6–1 6–1); *sf* Tampa (d. Whitlinger 6–4 6–2, Dahlman 3–6 6–3 6–0, Kelesi 6–3 6–2, lost K. Maleeva 6–4 6–2). *1990 HIGHLIGHTS – DOUBLES:* (with Paz unless stated) [Navratilova] *won* FC Cup (d. Paz/Zvereva 6–2 6–1), *won* Amelia Island (d. Rajchrtova/Temesvari 7–6 6–4), *won* Tampa (d. Cecchini/Gildemeister 6–2 6–0), *won* Barcelona (d. Goles/Tarabini 6–7 6–2 6–1); [Tauziat] *r/u* VS Chicago (lost Navratilova/A. Smith 6–7 6–4 6–3), *r/u* Filderstadt (lost M-J. Fernandez/Garrison 7–5 6–3), *r/u* VS Champs (lost K. Jordan/Smylie 7–6 6–4). *1990 HIGHLIGHTS – MIXED DOUBLES:* (with Lozano) *won French Open* (d. Provis/Visser 7–6 7–6). *CAREER HIGHLIGHTS – SINGLES: French Open – won 1989*, (d. Rajchrtova, Demongeot, Medvedeva 6–0 3–6 6–2, Coetzer 6–3 6–2, Novotna 6–2 6–2, M-J. Fernandez 6–2 6–2, Graf 7–6 3–6 7–5), *qf 1987* (lost Sabatini 6–4 6–0), *qf 1988* (d. Evert 6–1 7–6, Tanvier 6–2 6–0, lost Provis 7–5 3–6 6–4); *Wimbledon – qf 1989* (d. Pospisilova, Halard, Reggi 4–6 6–3 7–5, McNeil 6–3 2–6 6–1, lost Graf 7–5 6–1); *US Open – sf 1990, qf 1989* (d. Faull, Cammy MacGregor, Wasserman 6–1 2–6 6–4, Paulus 6–2 6–2, lost Sabatini 3–6 6–4 6–1). *CAREER HIGHLIGHTS – DOUBLES:* (with Paz) *VS Champs – r/u 1990. CAREER HIGHLIGHTS – MIXED DOUBLES:* (with Lozano) *French Open – won 1990.*

EMILIO SANCHEZ (Spain)

Born Madrid, 29 May 1965; lives Barcelona; RH; 5ft 11in; 155lb; final 1990 ATP ranking 8 singles, 9 doubles; 1990 prize money $734,286; career prize money $2,575,077.

Coached by Pato (Bill) Alvarez. Brother of Javier and Arantxa. *1983:* (208) R/u Orange Bowl and won Spanish Champs. *1984:* (112) Last 16 French Open. *1985:* (64) Upset Nystrom and Jarryd and reached 7 f doubles with Casal, winning 3 titles. *1986:* (16) Emerged as the most improved slow-court player, winning Nice, Munich and Bastad, r/u Italian Open reaching 5 sfs and twice stopping Wilander and also claiming Becker and Edberg as his victims. *1987:* (17) In singles won Gstaad, Bordeaux, Kitzbuhel, Madrid and reached last 16 French Open and Wimbledon. In doubles with Casal r/u Wimbledon, won 6 titles and qualified for Masters, reaching sf. In mixed doubles won French Open with Shriver and US Open with Navratilova. *1988:* (17) In doubles won French Open with Gomez and Bologna with his brother Javier, while regular partner Casal was undergoing wrist surgery. With Casal won US Open and 7 other titles, plus Olympic silver medal and r/u Masters to R. Leach and Pugh. In singles won Hilversum, reached 3 more f, upset Noah *en route* to qf French Open and d. Mecir to reach same stage at US Open. *1989:* (19) Missed French Open with knee injury which kept him out for 2 months. Won Kitzbuhel in singles and doubles and was r/u Hilversum and Bordeaux. *1990:* In singles won Wellington and Estoril; sf LIPC (d. Lendl), Barcelona, Monte Carlo (d. Becker), Italian Open, Stuttgart, Hilversum and Kitzbuhel. Qualified for ATP World Champ, but won no match there. In doubles reached 9 f, winning 5 with Casal, including French Open, and 1 with Zivojinovic. Qualified with Casal for IBM/ATP World Doubles Final, where they were r/u to Forget/Hlasek. *1990 HIGHLIGHTS – SINGLES: Australian Open* 1r, seed 7 (lost Fleurian 6–2 6–4 6–4), *French Open* 1r, seed 6 (lost Kulti 4–6 6–4 6–7 6–2 6–1), *US Open* last 16, seed 7 (d. Garrow 7–6 6–4 6–4, Pugh 6–1 6–2 6–2, Santoro 6–3 6–4 5–7 3–6 7–5, lost J. McEnroe 7–6 3–6 4–6 6–4 6–3); *won* Wellington (d. Guy 4–6 6–1 6–4, Jonsson 4–6 6–3 7–5, Fromberg 6–4 6–3, Cane 7–5 6–2, Reneberg 6–7 6–4 4–6 6–4 6–1), *won* Estoril (d. Fromberg 6–4 7–5, Carbonell 6–4 6–3, Camporese 6–3 6–3, Arrese 6–2 6–1, Davin 6–4 6–3); *sf* LIPC (d. Duncan 6–4 6–1, Skoff 3–6 6–3 6–3, Lendl 6–3 6–7 6–4, Jaite 6–3 6–3, lost Edberg 6–1 7–5), *sf* Barcelona (d. Davin 6–3 6–1, Paloheimo ret'd, Bruguera 5–7 6–4 6–4, lost Perez Roldan 7–5 7–6), *sf* Monte Carlo (d. Vajda 6–1 6–1, Forget 6–3 6–2, Becker 4–6 7–5 7–6, lost Chesnokov 4–6 6–1 7–6), *sf* Italian Open (d. Sznajder 6–2 6–1, Filippini 4–6 6–1 6–2, Svensson 6–3 6–2, Perez Roldan 7–6 6–2, lost Chesnokov 6–7 6–4 7–6), *sf* Stuttgart (d. Wohrmann 4–6 6–3 6–3, Fromberg 6–3 2–6 6–2, Filippini 7–6 6–2, lost Ivanisevic 6–4 6–4), *sf* Hilversum (d. Nijssen 6–3 5–7 6–4, Masur 4–6 7–6 6–4, Delaitre 6–2 7–6, lost Masso 6–4 7–5), *sf* Kitzbuhel (d. Roig 6–2 0–6 7–5, Riglewski 6–3 7–6, Cherkasov 6–1 6–4, lost de la Pena 7–5 7–6). *1990 HIGHLIGHTS – DOUBLES:* (with Casal unless stated) *won* French Open (d. Ivanisevic/Kulti 7–5 6–3); [Zivojinovic] *won* Brussels (d. Ivanisevic/Taroczy 7–5 6–3), *won* Estoril (d. Camporese/Cane 7–5 4–6 7–5), *won* Italian Open (d. Courier/M. Davis 7–6 7–5), *won* Gstaad (d. Camporese/J. Sanchez 6–3 3–6 7–5), *won* Hilversum (d. Haarhuis/Koevermans 7–5 7–5), *won* Palermo (d. Costa/de la Pena 6–3 6–4); *r/u* Wellington (lost Evernden/Pereira 6–4 7–6), *r/u* Barcelona (lost Gomez/J. Sanchez 7–6 7–5), *r/u* IBM/ATP World Doubles Final (d. Connell/Michibata 6–4 6–7 6–4 6–7 6–3, lost Forget/Hlasek 6–4 7–6 5–7 6–4). *CAREER HIGHLIGHTS – DOUBLES:* (with Casal unless stated) *French Open* – [Gomez] *won 1988* (d. Fitzgerald/Jarryd 6–3 6–7 6–4 6–3), *won 1990*; *US Open – won 1988* (d. R. Leach/Pugh w.o.); *Wimbledon – r/u 1987* (lost Flach/Seguso 3–6 6–7 7–6 6–1 6–4); *Olympics – silver medal 1988* (lost Flach/Seguso 6–3 6–4 6–7 6–7 9–7); *Masters – r/u 1988* (lost R. Leach/Pugh 6–4 6–3 2–6 6–0). *IBM/ATP World Doubles Final – r/u 1990. MIXED DOUBLES: French Open* – [Shriver] *won 1987* (d. McNeil/Stewart 6–3 7–6); *US Open* – [Navratilova] *won 1987* (d. Nagelsen/Annacone 6–4 6–7 7–6).

JAVIER SANCHEZ (Spain)

Born Pamplona, 1 February 1968; lives Barcelona; RH; 5ft 10in; 155lb; final 1990 ATP ranking 70 singles, 30 doubles; 1990 prize money $226,368.

Coached by Pato (Bill) Alvarez. Brother of Emilio and Arantxa. *1986:* No. 1 in ITF Jun world rankings. Won Orange Bowl 18s, US Open Jun singles and doubles (with Carbonell), r/u Wimbledon Jun singles and French Open Jun doubles (with Carbonell). *1987:* (110) R/u Madrid to his brother, Emilio. *1988:* (55) Won 1st GP titles at Buenos Aires in both singles and doubles; sf Itaparica and qf Bologna. *1989:* (51) Won both singles and doubles at Bologna, r/u Sao Paulo singles and took 3 more doubles titles with various partners. *1990:* Reached sf Madrid and last 16 French Open, unseeded. In doubles with various partners reached 6 f, winning 3. *1990 HIGHLIGHTS – SINGLES: Australian Open* 3r (d. Rahunen 6–0 6–3 6–1, Annacone 6–1 7–6 6–3, lost Paloheimo 7–5 6–4 3–6 6–1), *French Open* last 16, unseeded (d. Youl 6–1 3–6 6–2 7–6, Rebolledo 6–4 7–6 6–2, Kulti 6–4 6–4 6–3, lost Chang [seed 11] 6–4 6–4 6–2), *US Open* 1r (lost J. McEnroe 7–6 7–6 6–4); *sf* Madrid (d. Arrese 4–6 6–3 7–5, Costa 7–5 6–2, Baguena 6–3 6–1, lost Rosset 7–5 2–6 6–2). *1990 HIGHLIGHTS – DOUBLES:* (with Gomez unless stated) *won* Barcelona (d. Casal/E. Sanchez 7–6 7–5), [Winogradsky] *won* Kitzbuhel (d. Clavet/Skoff 7–6 6–2). [Casal] *won* Athens (d. Kempers/Krajicek 4–6 7–6 6–3); *r/u* Monte Carlo (lost Korda/Smid 6–4 7–6), *r/u* Madrid (lost Baguena/Camporese 6–4 3–6 6–3), [Camporese] *r/u* Gstaad (lost Casal/E. Sanchez 6–3 3–6 7–5).

FABRICE SANTORO (France)

Boris Paris, 7 December 1972, and lives there; RH; 5ft 9in; 140lb; final 1990 ATP ranking 62; 1990 prize money $127,027.

Nat champ in 12s, 14s and 16s. *1988:* (571) Won Orange Bowl 16s. *1989:* (235) Won

French Open Jun over Palmer and was No. 2 in ITF Jun rankings. Upset Gomez at Stuttgart. *1990:* Won Telford Challenger and then upset Gomez again *en route* to his 1st tour f at Toulouse. Qf Nice (d. Chesnokov) and Bordeaux. *1990 HIGHLIGHTS – SINGLES: French Open* 2r (d. Raoux 6–1 6–4 6–4, lost Arrese 4–6 6–3 6–2 6–2), *Wimbledon* 1r (lost Svensson [seed 10] 6–4 6–3 6–2), *US Open* 3r (d. Baron 6–2 6–4 6–4, Grabb 7–6 6–4 7–6, lost E. Sanchez 6–3 6–4 5–7 3–6 7–5); *won* Telford Challenger (d. Nyborg 6–3 5–7 6–4); *r/u* Toulouse (d. Gomez 6–2 3–6 6–3, Yzaga 6–2 6–2, Bergstrom 7–5 6–4, Agenor 7–6 6–3, lost Svensson 7–6 6–2).

LARISA SAVCHENKO (USSR)
Born Lvov, Ukraine, 21 July 1966; lives Urmala, Latvia; RH; 5ft 6½in; 138lb; final 1990 WTA ranking 87 singles, 7 (3) doubles; 1990 prize money $217,984.
1983: Ranked 10 on ITF jun list after reaching qf Wimbledon Jun and first Wimbledon doubles qf with Parkhomenko. *1984:* (138) Wimbledon doubles qf again. *1985:* (55) Third Wimbledon doubles qf and sf VS Denver in singles. Joined Fed Cup team. *1986:* (35) Showed affinity for grass courts, reaching sf Birmingham, qf Eastbourne, and upsetting Rehe at Wimbledon. Qualified with Parkhomenko for VS Champ doubles March and Nov.*1987:* (24) Won 4 doubles titles with Parkhomenko and ousted Navratilova/Shriver *en route* to sf Wimbledon. *1988:* (16) Upset Mandlikova and Sabatini as she swept to f VS California, upset Zvereva *en route* to sf Pan Pacific Open and Kohde-Kilsch *en route* to qf Eastbourne. Reached the same stage at US Open and Olympics and last 16 Wimbledon. In doubles with Zvereva r/u Wimbledon and·VS Champs for which she qualified in both singles and doubles. *1989:* (20) Upset Navratilova *en route* to f VS California but then, frustrated by her poor form in singles, she talked of retiring after US Open. However, there she reached last 16, upsetting Shriver, and followed up with sf Moscow and r/u VS Chicago. In doubles won French Open and r/u Wimbledon and VS Champs with Zvereva, reaching 9 more f and winning 4. Married Alex Neland, manager of USSR Nat tennis tream 21 Dec. *1990:* In singles qf Tokyo Toray and Birmingham. In doubles r/u French Open and won 3 titles with Zvereva, taking another with K. Jordan. Qualified for VS Champs with Zvereva but lost 1r to Adams/McNeil. *1990 HIGHLIGHTS – SINGLES: Australian Open* 1r, seed 12 (lost Tanvier 4–6 6–1 12–10), *French Open* 2r (d. Corsato 6–7 6–4 6–4, lost Meskhi 3–0 ret'd), *Wimbledon* 2r (d. Adams 5–7 6–4 6–3, lost Magers 6–3 6–4), *US Open* 3r (d. Rajchrtova 6–3 1–6 6–3, Cunningham 6–4 6–4, lost Wiesner [seed 15] 6–1 6–3). *1990 HIGHLIGHTS – DOUBLES:* (with Zvereva unless stated) *r/u French Open* (lost Novotna/Sukova 6–4 7–5); *won* Birmingham (d. Gregory/Magers 3–6 6–3 6–3), *won* Eastbourne (d. Fendick/Garrison 6–4 6–3), *won* Orlando (d. Bollegraf/McGrath 6–4 6–1), [K. Jordan] *won* Nashville (d. Schultz/Vis 6–1 6–2); *r/u* Sydney (lost Novotna/Sukova 6–3 7–5), [Sukova] *r/u* Hamburg (lost G. Fernandez/Navratilova 6–2 6–3). *CAREER HIGHLIGHTS – DOUBLES:* (with Zvereva) *French Open – won 1989* (d. Graf/Sabatini 6–4 6–4), *r/u 1990; Wimbledon – r/u 1988* (lost Graf/Sabatini 6–3 1–6 12–10), *r/u 1989* (lost Novotna/Sukova 6–1 6–2); *VS Champs – r/u 1988* (lost Navratilova/Shriver 6–3 6–4), *r/u 1989* (lost Navratilova/Shriver 6–3 6–2).

NAOKO SAWAMATSU (Japan)
Born Nishinomiya, 23 March 1973, and lives there; RH; 5ft 6in; 130lb; final 1990 WTA ranking 31; 1990 prize money $69.710.
Niece of Kazuko Sawamatsu, the 1975 Wimbledon doubles titlist. *1990:* Won Moulins satellite, then, a wild-card entry, she beat 3 seeded players to win Singapore, having reached sf Tokyo Suntory 2 weeks earlier. These results saw her breaking into the top 100 and then top 50 in April. *1990 HIGHLIGHTS – SINGLES: French Open* 2r (d. Harvey-Wild 6–1 4–6 6–2, lost Herreman 6–1 6–3), *Wimbledon* 1r (lost Dechaume 7–5 2–6 6–3), *US Open* 2r (d. Tarabini 6–1 6–3, lost Gildemeister 7–5 6–3); *won* Singapore (d. Bartlett 6–0 6–2, Paradis 3–6 6–4 6–3, Wasserman 6–2 6–7 6–4, Takagi 6–1 6–3, Kidowski 6–2 6–3, Loosemore 7–6 3–6 6–4); *sf* Tokyo Suntory (d. Hiraki 6–3 6–1, Louise Allen 7–6 7–5, Date 6–4 7–6, lost Smylie 6–1 6–2).

BRENDA SCHULTZ (Netherlands)
Born Haarlem, 28 December 1970; lives Heemstede; RH; 6ft 2in; 170lb; final 1990 WTA ranking 43; 1990 prize money $126,330.
Coached by Stanley Franker. *1987:* (150) Won Chicago on USTA circuit, qf Paris Open.

1988: (39) Won Wimbledon Jun over Derly and on the senior tour was a finalist at Oklahoma and Taipei. Upset Cecchini to reach last 16 French Open and also scored upsets during the year over Lindqvist, Hanika, Reggi and Fendick. *1989:* (85) Reached f Brisbane and last 16 Australian Open. *1990:* Reached last 16 Wimbledon, unseeded; sf Brisbane (d. Rinaldi); qf Tokyo Toray and Oklahoma (d. Reggi). *1990 HIGHLIGHTS – SINGLES: Australian Open* 2r (d. Pawlik 6–4 6–3, lost Date 7–5 7–6), *French Open* 2r (d. Garrone 6–4 7–6, lost Novotna [seed 11] 6–3 6–1), *Wimbledon* last 16, unseeded (d. Temesvari 6–2 6–0, McQuillan 6–4 3–6 7–5, Nagelsen 6–1 6–4, lost Zvereva [seed 11] 6–2 6–2), *US Open* 1r (lost Halard 6–2 6–4); *sf* Brisbane (d. Cammy MacGregor 7–5 6–3, Radford 4–6 6–3 6–3, Rinaldi 7–5 6–1, Godridge 7–5 6–3, lost Zvereva 6–4 6–1). *1990 HIGHLIGHTS – DOUBLES:* (with Vis] *r/u* VS Nashville (lost K. Jordan/Savchenko 6–1 6–2).

MONICA SELES (Yugoslavia)
Born Novi Sad, 2 December 1973; lives Sarasota, Fla.; LH; 2HF; 2HB; 5ft 9in; 118lb; final 1990 WTA ranking 2; 1990 prize money $1,637,222.
Coached by her Father Karolj; a cartoonist; travels with him and her mother Esther. Brother Zoltan (25) also trains her. Discovered by Nick Bollettieri at 1985 Orange Bowl; family moved to USA from Yugoslavia in 1986. Grew 5in between French Opens of 1989 and 1990. *1983:* At age 9, reached last 16 Sport Goofy singles. *1984:* Won Sport Goofy singles. *1985:* Won Sport Goofy singles and doubles. *1988:* (86) Upset Kelesi at VS Florida in 1st pro match, took Sabatini to 1s tb 1r LIPC and upset Magers and McNeil to reach sf New Orleans. *1989:* (6) Upset Savchenko and Manuela Maleeva at VS Washington, but had to default sf owing to injury, then won Houston over Evert and was r/u VS Dallas and Brighton. Unseeded at French Open she upset Garrison and Manuela Maleeva before extending Graf to 3s sf; reached last 16 Wimbledon and US Open and qualified for 1st VS Champs, where she lost qf to Navratilova. *1990:* Following her acrimonious split in March with Bollettieri, whom she considered was spending too much time coaching Agassi, she was coached only by her father. At 16 yrs 6 mths became the youngest French Open women's champion and second-youngest GS champion (after Lottie Dod, who was 15 yrs 10 mths when she won Wimbledon in 1897). She went into the French Open having won 5 consec tourns without dropping a set, but her unbeaten run of 36 matches was ended by Garrison in qf Wimbledon. She in turn had ended Graf's 66-match unbeaten run at Berlin, which she won in addition to LIPC, San Antonio, Tampa, Italian Open, Los Angeles and VS California – plus VS Champs, where she finished the season triumphantly by beating Sabatini in 5s in f. She beat Graf twice and Navratilova three times and by year's end had displaced Navratilova to finish ranked 2. Won WTA Most Improved Player award. *1990 HIGHLIGHTS – SINGLES: won French Open* seed 2 (d. Piccolini 6–0 6–0, Kelesi 4–6 6–4 6–4, Meskhi 7–6 7–6, Gildemeister [seed 16] 6–4 6–0, Maleeva Fragnière [seed 6] 3–6 6–1 7–5, Capriati 6–2 6–2, Graf [seed 1] 7–6 6–4), *Wimbledon* qf, seed 3 (d. Strandlund 6–2 6–0, Benjamin 6–3 7–5, A. Minter 6–3 6–3, Henricksson 6–1 6–0, lost Garrison [seed 5] 6–3 3–6 6–4); *won* LIPC (d. Harvey-Wild 6–1 6–4, Lapi 6–1 6–1, Fairbank Nideffer 6–3 6–4, Herreman 6–3 6–1, Tauziat 6–3 6–1, Wiesner 6–1 6–2), *won* San Antonio (d. A. Smith 6–3 7–5, Mandlikova 6–4 6–4, Fairbank Nideffer 6–3 6–0, Maleeva Fragnière 6–4 6–3), *won* Tampa (d. Collins 6–1 6–1, Faber 6–0 6–1, Sloane 6–2 6–0, Martinez 6–4 6–0, K. Maleeva 6–1 6–0), *won* Italian Open (d. Zrubakova 6–4 6–1, Paz 6–1 6–1, Maleeva Fragnière 6–0 6–2, Kelesi 6–1 6–2, Navratilova 6–1 6–1), *won* Berlin (d. Jagerman 6–1 6–0, M. Maleeva 6–2 6–3, Martinez 6–0 6–2, Cecchini 6–1 6–3, Graf 6–4 6–3), *won* VS Los Angeles (d. Keller 6–2 6–2, A. Smith 6–3 6–3, Frazier 2–6 6–2 7–5, M-J. Fernandez 6–1 6–0, Navratilova 6–0 6–7 6–4), *won* VS California (d. Temesvari 6–1 6–2, Rehe 6–1 6–2, Garrison 6–1 3–6 6–2, Navratilova 6–3 7–6), *won* VS Champs (d. Paulus 6–2 6–2, Sanchez-Vicario 5–7 7–6 6–4, M-J. Fernandez 6–3 6–4, Sabatini 6–4 5–7 4–6 6–4 6–2); *sf* VS Washington (d. S. Martin def., Shriver 6–2 7–6, lost Navratilova 6–3 6–0). *1990 HIGHLIGHTS – DOUBLES:* (with Kelesi] *won* Italian Open (d. Garrone/Golarsa 6–3 6–4). *CAREER HIGHLIGHTS – SINGLES: French Open – won 1990, sf 1989* (d. Reis, S. Martin, Garrison 6–3 6–2, Faull 6–3 6–2, Maleeva Fragnière 6–3 7–5, lost Graf 6–3 3–6 6–3); *VS Champs – won 1990;. LIPC – won 1990; Wimbledon – qf 1990.*

KIRRILY SHARPE (Australia)
Born Bankstown, 25 February 1973; lives Connenact; LH; 2HB; 5ft 5in; 135lb; final 1990 WTA ranking 164; 1990 prize money $36,352.

1990: Upset Reggi at French Open. In Jun game r/u Wimbledon (lost Strnadova 6–2 6–4) and won US Open doubles with Godridge, with whom she also took the title at Clarins on the senior tour. *1990 HIGHLIGHTS – SINGLES: Australian Open* 2r (d. Field 7–5 3–6 6–3, lost McQuillan 6–3 6–0), *French Open* 3r (d. Phelps 6–3 6–3, Reggi [seed 14] 6–4 6–2, lost Grossman 6–2 4–6 6–1). *1990 HIGHLIGHTS – DOUBLES:* (with Godridge) *won* Clarins (d. Dechaume/Herreman 4–6 6–3 6–1).

PAM SHRIVER (USA)
Born Baltimore, Md, 4 July 1962 and lives there; RH; 6ft; 150lb; final 1990 WTA ranking 66; 1990 prize money $50,976; career prize money $4,323,497.
Coached by Don Candy and Hank Harris, and at end 1988 by Bud Schultz. *1978:* (13) At age 16 upset top-seeded Navratilova to become youngest finalist in US Open. *1979:* (33) Troubled by nagging shoulder injury, lost 1r US Open. *1980:* (9) Won La Costa and r/u Sydney (d. Navratilova). *1981:* (7) Won first Wimbledon doubles title with Navratilova, sf Wimbledon and Australian Open singles (d. Austin in both) and won Perth. *1982:* (6) Sf US Open (d. Navratilova). *1983:* (4) Sf US Open and won Brisbane. *1984:* (4) Won VS Chicago and r/u Mahwah. *1985:* (4) Won Sydney, Melbourne and Birmingham. Completed double GS with Navratilova by collecting 8th straight GS title in Paris, but record 109-match winning streak broken in f Wimbledon by Jordan/Smylie. *1986:* (6) Won 5th Wimbledon doubles title in 6 years with Navratilova. Won Birmingham and Newport and reached sf VS Champs in Nov. *1987:* (4) Played no singles from March until June, returning to win Edgbaston, Canadian Open (d. Evert 1st time), VS Newport and New England, beating Evert again. With Navratilova won Australian and French Opens for 3rd GS in doubles, won US Open doubles, VS Champs for the 6th time and won French Open mixed doubles with E. Sanchez. *1988:* (5) In singles won Brisbane, Sydney, Pan Pacific Open and Zurich and reached 4 more f, including VS Champs, where she beat Evert in qf and Graf (suffering from flu) in sf. In doubles won Australian Open, French Open and 7th VS Champs with Navratilova and Olympic gold medal with Garrison. However, a form of mononucleosis restricted her performance at Wimbledon, and she lost 2r US Open to Meskhi. *1989:* (17) Struggling to find motivation, she suffered a lack lustre year in singles with r/u Newport her best showing and failed to reach VS Champs in singles, although she qualified again in doubles with Navratilova. Won 8 doubles titles with various partners, including Australian Open and VS Champs with Navratilova, who ended their partnership before US Open, where Shriver was r/u with M-J. Fernandez. Teamed with Navratilova again in winning US Fed Cup team v Spain. *1990:* Out of action from March having fractured her toe when she kicked a chair in frustration after a bad call and missed shot v Van Rensburg at Boca Raton. She then withdrew from Wimbledon following arthroscopic surgery for a shoulder injury suffered the previous Dec. Sf VS Chicago. *1990 HIGHLIGHTS – SINGLES: Australian Open* 3r, seed 11 (d. Sviglerova 6–3 6–4, Provis 1–6 6–2 9–7, lost Date 6–3 6–4); *sf* VS Chicago (d. Henricksson 6–3 6–4, Harvey-Wild 6–1 6–2, lost Navratilova 6–4 6–3). *1990 HIGHLIGHTS – DOUBLES:* [Mandlikova] *r/u* Brisbane (lost Novotna/Sukova 6–3 6–1). *CAREER HIGHLIGHTS – SINGLES: US Open – r/u 1978* (d. Reid, Hunt, Navratilova 7–6 7–6, lost Evert 7–5 6–4), *sf 1982* (d. Navratilova 1–6 7–6 6–2, lost Mandlikova 6–4 2–6 6–2), *sf 1983* (d. Jaeger 7–6 6–3, lost Navratilova 6–2 6–1); *VS Champs – r/u 1988* (d. Hanika, Evert 7–5 6–4, Graf 6–3 7–6, lost Sabatini 7–5 6–2 6–2), *sf 1984* (d. Mandlikova, lost Navratilova), *sf 1986* (lost Navratilova 6–2 4–6 6–4); *Wimbledon – sf 1981*, seed 7 (d. Ekblom, Little, Coles, Durie, Austin [seed 3] 7–5 6–4, lost Evert Lloyd [seed 1] 6–3 6–1), *sf 1987* (d. Hanika, Sukova 4–6 7–6 10–8, lost Graf 6–0 6–2), *sf 1988* (d. K. Maleeva, Garrison 6–4 6–4, lost Graf 6–1 6–2); *Australian Open – sf 1981* seed 6 (d. Desfor, Durie, Austin [seed 2] 7–5 7–6, lost Navratilova [seed 3] 6–3 7–5), *sf 1982* (lost Navratilova 6–3 6–4), *sf 1983* (d. Bassett 6–0 6–1, lost Navratilova 6–4 6–3). *CAREER HIGHLIGHTS – DOUBLES:* (with Navratilova unless stated) *French Open – won 1984* d. Kohde-Kilsch/Mandlikova 5–7 6–3 6–2), *won 1985* (d. Kohde-Kilsch/Sukova 4–6 6–2 6–2), *won 1987* (d. Graf/Sabatini 6–2 6–1), *won 1988* (d. Kohde-Kilsch/Sukova 6–2 7–5); *Wimbledon – won 1981* (d. K. Jordan/A. Smith 6–3 7–6), *won 1982* (d. K. Jordan/A. Smith 6–4 6–1), *won 1983* (d. Casals/Turnbull 6–2 6–2), *won 1984* (d. K. Jordan/A. Smith 6–3 6–4), *won 1986* (d. Mandlikova/Turnbull 6–1 6–3), *r/u 1985* (d. Mandlikova/Turnbull, lost K. Jordan/Smylie 5–7 6–3 6–4); *US Open – won 1983* (d. Fairbank/Reynolds 6–7 6–1 6–3), *won 1984* (d. Turnbull/Hobbs 6–2 6–2), *won 1986* (d. Mandlikova/Turnbull 6–4 3–6 6–3), *won 1987* (d. K.

Jordan/Smylie 5–7 6–4 6–2), [Stove] *r/u 1980* (lost King/Navratilova 7–6 7–5), *r/u 1985* (lost Kohde-Kilsch/Sukova 6–7 6–2 6–3), [M-J. Fernandez] *r/u 1989* (lost Mandlikova/ Navratilova 5–7 6–4 6–4); *Australian Open – won 1982* (d. Kohde-Kilsch/Pfaff 6–4 6–2), *won 1983* (d. Hobbs/Turnbull 6–4 6–7 6–2), *won 1984* (d. Kohde-Kilsch/Sukova 6–3 6–4), *won 1985* (d. Kohde-Kilsch/Sukova 6- 3 6–4), *won 1987* (d. Garrison/McNeil 6–1 6–0), *won 1988* (d. Evert/Turnbull 6–0 7–5), *won 1989* (d. Fendick/Hetherington 3–6 6–3 6–2), *r/u 1981* (lost K. Jordan/A. Smith 6–2 7–5); *Olympics – gold medal 1988* [Garrison] (d. Novotna/Sukova 4–6 6–2 10–8); *TS Champs – won 1982* (d. P. Smith/Reynolds 6–4 7–5); *VS Champs – won 1984* (d. Durie/Kiyomura 6–3 6–1), *won 1985* (d. Kohde-Kilsch/Sukova 6–7 6–4 7–6), *won 1986* (d. Kohde-Kilsch/Sukova 7–6 6–3), *won 1987* (d. Kohde-Kilsch/ Sukova 6–1 6–1), *won 1989* (d. Savchenko/Zvereva 6–3 6–2). *MIXED DOUBLES:* (with E. Sanchez) *French Open – won 1987* (d. McNeil/Stewart 6–3 7–6).

HORST SKOFF (Austria)
Born Klagenfurt, 22 August 1968; lives Kuehnstorf; RH; 5ft 9in; 155lb; final 1990 ATP ranking 26; 1990 prize money $247,239.
Coached by Gunther Bresnik. *1984:* (555) Won Orange Bowl 16. *1985:* (299) Won Austrian Nat Indoor. *1986:* (42) Austrian Nat Indoor Champ again, sf Barcelona, qf Kitzbuhel and Stuttgart. *1987:* (63) Upset Noah and Gomez *en route* to sf Monte Carlo. *1988:* (45) Won 1st GP title at Athens, following with Vienna. *1989:* (25) R/u Hamburg (d. Becker), Prague and Barcelona. *1990:* At Geneva won 1st tour title since 1988; also reached f Vienna and sf Kitzbuhel, upsetting Muster both times, and won 2 Challenger titles. *1990 HIGHLIGHTS – SINGLES: won* Geneva (d. Bergstrom 6–4 6–4, Cane 6–4 6–2, Furlan 7–6 7–6, Rosset 4–6 6–3 6–2, Bruguera 7–6 7–6), *won* Jakarta Challenger (d. Garner 7–6 4–6 6–1), *won* Salsburg-Bergheim Challenger (d. Altur 6–2 6–2); *r/u* Vienna (d. Antonitsch 3–6 7–5 6–2, Poliakov 6–7 6–4 6–2, Jonsson 6–3 6–4, Muster 6–2 7–6, lost Jarryd 6–3 6–3 6–1); *sf* Kitzbuhel (d. Saceanu 4–6 7–5 7–6, Carbonell 6–2 6–0, Muster 6–4 6–2, lost Novacek 6–4 4–6 6–4). *1990 HIGHLIGHTS – DOUBLES:* [Filippini] *r/u* Nice (lost Mancini/Noah 6–4 7–6), [Clavet] *r/u* Kitzbuhel (lost J. Sanchez/Winogradsky 7–6 6–2).

SUSAN SLOANE (USA)
Born Lexington, Ky, 5 December 1970, and lives there; RH; 2HB; 5ft 5in; 120lb; final 1990 WTA ranking 27; 1990 prize money $88,349.
Coached by Fritz Nau and Nick Bollettieri. *1984* R/u Orange Bowl 14s. *1985:* Ranked 3 in US 18s. *1986:* (88) Qf Indianapolis. *1987:* (111) Qf Arkansas. *1988:* (31) Upset McNeil *en route* 1st tour singles title at Nashville, reached sf Arizona and 4 other qf. *1989:* (39) Sf VS Kansas, VS Houston (upsetting McNeil) and VS Nashville. *1990:* R/u VS Nashville (d. Reggi); sf Wichita and VS Albuquerque. *1990 HIGHLIGHTS – SINGLES: French Open* 2r (d. Coetzer 6–4 6–3, lost Sabatini [seed 4] 6–0 5–7 6–1), *Wimbledon* 2r (d. Ferrando 1–6 7–6 6–3, lost Fendick 6–2 6–4), *US Open* 1r (lost Cioffi 7–6 6–3); *r/u* VS Nashville (d. Pampoulova 6–3 6–2, Keller 6–3 6–2, Reggi 6–3 6–3, Reinach 6–3 4–6 6–0, lost Medvedeva 6–3 7–6); *sf* Wichita (d. Vis 6–1 6–1, Hu Na 6–4 6–0, Frazier 7–5 3–6 6–3, lost Van Rensburg 6–2 7–6), *sf* VS Albuquerque (d. Henricksson 6–0 6–1, Cioffi 7–5 6–3, Van Rensburg 7–6 6–2, lost Gildemeister 6–2 6–2).

ANNE SMITH (USA)
Born Dallas, 1 July 1959, and lives there; RH; 5ft 5in; 120lb; final 1990 WTA ranking 33 singles, 17 doubles; 1990 prize money $113,042.
1976: R/u Orange Bowl. *1977:* Won Orange Bowl and became 1st American to win French Open Jun. *1978:* (20) Last 16 US Open. *1979:* (24) Last 16 US Open. *1980:* (24) With K. Jordan won French Open and Wimbledon doubles. *1981:* (16) With Jordan won US and Australian Opens and r/u Wimbledon. Won US Open mixed with Curren. *1982:* (13) R/u Washington, qf Wimbledon singles. With Jordan won French Open and r/u Wimbledon. In mixed won Wimbledon and US Open with Curren. *1983:* (28) After r/u French Open with Jordan, took a 6-month break to coach at Trinity Univ. *1984:* (Not ranked) Still coaching, but with Jordan won WTA Champs, r/u Wimbledon; with Curren won French Open mixed. Played Fed Cup. *1985:* (Not ranked) Playing sparingly, she reached last 16 Wimbledon. *1986:* (79) Won only 8 of 21 singles matches. *1987:* (40) At VS Indianapolis reached 1st f since 1982. *1988:* (53) Following rotator cuff surgery on her racket arm, she was out of action for 9 months, returning in July and reaching qf North California Open in her 2nd

tourn, then in Oct. upset Lindqvist and Potter to reach f New Orleans. *1989:* (42) Sf VS Dallas (d. Shriver and Fairbank) and VS New England (d. Kelesi and Martinez). *1990:* Sf VS Newport and Albuquerque; qf VS Washington and Birmingham in singles. In doubles with different partners reached 4 f, winning 3. *1990 HIGHLIGHTS – SINGLES: Wimbledon* 2r (d. Wood 6–3 4–6 6–2, lost Navratilova [seed 2] 6–2 6–3); *sf* VS Newport (d. Phelps 6–2 6–3, Hu Na 6–0 6–3, Smylie 6–1 7–6, lost Durie 6–4 6–1), *sf* VS Albuquerque (d. Werdel 7–5 6–1, Suire 6 4 7–5, Coetzer 6–2 6–1, lost Novotna 6–4 6–7 7–5). *1990 HIGHLIGHTS – DOUBLES:* (with McGrath unless stated) [Navratilova] *won* VS Chicago (d. Sanchez-Vicario/Tauziat 6–7 6–4 6–3), *won* VS Albuquerque (d. Louie Harper/White Prausa 7–6 6–4), *won* VS California (d. Fairbank Nideffer/R. White 2–6 6–0 6–4); [Fendick] *r/u* VS Newport (lost Gregory/Magers 7–6 6–1). *CAREER HIGHLIGHTS – DOUBLES:* (with K. Jordan unless stated) *French Open – won 1980* (d. Madruga/Villagran 6–1 6–0), [Navratilova] *won 1982* (d. Casals/Turnbull 6–3 6–4), *r/u 1983* (lost Reynolds/Fairbank 5–7 7–5 6–2); *Wimbledon – won 1980* (d. Casals/Turnbull 3–6 7–6 6–1), *r/u 1981* (d. Fairbank/Harford 6–1 6–2, lost Navratilova/Shriver 6–3 7–6), *r/u 1982* (d. Casals/Turnbull 6–4 fs, lost Navratilova/Shriver 7–5 6–1), *r/u 1984* (d. Potter/Walsh, lost Navratilova/Shriver 6–3 6–4); *US Open – won 1981* (d. Casals/Turnbull 6–3 6–3); *Australian Open – won 1981* (d. Navratilova/Shriver 6–2 7–5). *MIXED DOUBLES:* (with Curren unless stated) *French Open* – [Stockton] *won 1984* (d. Sayers/Stewart, A. Minter/Warder 6–2 6–4); *Wimbledon – won 1982* (d. Turnbull/J. Lloyd 7–5 fs); *US Open – won 1981* (d. Denton/Russell 6–4 7–6), *won 1982* (d. Potter/Taygan 7–6 fs).

ELIZABETH SAYERS SMYLIE (Australia)
Born Perth, 11 April 1963; lives Sydney; RH; 5ft 7in; 129lb; final 1990 WTA ranking 53 singles, 10 (14) doubles; 1990 prize money $258,904.
Coached by her husband, Peter (married 10 Nov. 1984). *1981:* Among world's top 10 jun. *1982:* (115) Won Sardinia on Italian satellite circuit and was ranked 7 in Australia. *1983:* (70) Won Kansas City. *1984:* (36) Ranked 2 in Australia behind Turnbull and played Fed Cup. Married Peter Smylie Nov. 10. *1985:* (43) Joined K. Jordan to beat Navratilova/Shriver in Wimbledon f, ending the record 109-match winning streak by world's top pair. *1986:* (80) Won only 6 of 20 singles matches including 7 straight 1r losses at start of year. Won LIPC mixed doubles with Fitzgerald. *1987:* (27) Qf Australian Open and won VS Oklahoma in Feb. in first singles f since Nov. 1984. In doubles r/u Wimbledon with Nagelsen and US Open with K. Jordan. *1988:* (172) Suffered a poor year in singles but won Eastbourne doubles with Pfaff. *1989:* (67) In singles reached f Tokyo and in doubles with various partners played 10 f, winning 5. *1990:* In doubles with K. Jordan won VS Champs and r/u Wimbledon, taking 2 other titles plus a 4th with G. Fernandez; in mixed won US Open with Woodbridge and was r/u Wimbledon with Fitzgerald. Her best showing in singles was r/u Tokyo Suntory. Voted WTA Comeback Player of the Year. *1990 HIGHLIGHTS – SINGLES: Australian Open* 3r (d. Hetherington 6–3 7–5, Reinstadler 6–2 6–4, lost Paulus 6–4 6–3), *French Open* 1r (lost Provis 6–1 6–3), *Wimbledon* 1r (lost Magers 6–1 7–6), *US Open* 1r (lost Paulus [seed 16] 7–5 6–1); *r/u* Tokyo Suntory (d. Wood 3–6 6–1 7–5, Wasserman 5–7 6–0 6–1, Okamoto 6–3 6–2, Sawamatsu 6–1 6–2, lost Lindqvist 6–3 6–2). *1990 HIGHLIGHTS – DOUBLES:* (with K. Jordan unless stated) *r/u Wimbledon* (lost Novotna/Sukova 6–3 6–4); [G. Fernandez] *won* Tokyo (d. Faull/McQuillan 6–2 6–2), *won* San Antonio (d. G. Fernandez/R. White 7–5 7–5), *won* Tokyo Suntory (d. Hu Na/Jaggard 6–0 3–6 6–1), *won* VS Champs (d. Paz/Sanchez-Vicario 7–6 6–4); *r/u* Strasbourg (lost Provis/E. Reinach 6–1 6–4). *1990 HIGHLIGHTS – MIXED DOUBLES:* [Fitzgerald] *r/u Wimbledon* (lost R. Leach/Garrison 7–5 6–2), [Woodbridge] *won US Open* (d. Zvereva/Pugh 6–4 6–2). *CAREER HIGHLIGHTS – SINGLES: Australian Open – qf 1987* (d. R. White, Sukova 7–5 3–6 7–5, lost Kohde-Kilsch 7–6 4–6 6–2). *CAREER HIGHLIGHTS – DOUBLES:* (with K. Jordan unless stated) *Wimbledon – won 1985* (d. Kohde-Kilsch/Sukova 5–7 6–1 6–4, Navratilova/Shriver 5–7 6–3 6–4), [Nagelsen] *r/u 1987* (lost Kohde-Kilsch/Sukova 7–5 7–5), *r/u 1990; VS Champs – won 1990; US Open – r/u 1987* (lost Navratilova/Shriver 5–7 6–4 6–2). *MIXED DOUBLES:* (with Fitzgerald unless stated) *US Open – won 1983* (d. Taygan/Potter 3–6 6–3 6–4), [Woodbridge] *won 1990, r/u 1984* (lost Manuela Maleeva/Tom Gullikson 2–6 7–5 6–4), *r/u 1985* (lost Gunthardt/Navratilova 6–3 6–4); *Wimbledon – r/u 1990*.

IRINA SPIRLEA (Romania)
Born 26 March 1974.
1990: Won French Open Jun doubles with Dragomir.

MILAN SREJBER (Czechoslovakia)
Born Prague, 30 December 1963, and lives there; RH; 6ft 8in; 216lb; final 1990 ATP ranking 85; 1990 prize money $191,197.
Coached by Vladislav Savrda. *1985:* (169) Won Finnish Challenger and was r/u Brazil Challenger. *1986:* (27) Began year brilliantly with win over Becker at LIPC after reaching f Toronto Indoor and followed with qf US Open. Helped lead Czech D Cup team to sf, defeating Oresar and Zivojinovic in qf and extending Edberg to 7–5 fs in sf. *1987:* (62) Less spectacular but reached sf US Pro Indoor, and collected wins over Connors and Vilas during the year. *1988:* (41) Returning after an 8-month lay-off with a foot injury, he upset Mecir to reach sf Milan and won 1st GP title at Rye Brook. *1989:* (97) Qf Wellington and won Copenhagen Challenger at end of year. *1990:* Won Heilbron Challenger and reached qf Milan and Seoul. *1990 HIGHLIGHTS – SINGLES: French Open* 2r (d. Wheaton 3–6 5–7 6–3 7–6 6–3, lost Courier [seed 13] 7–6 6–1 2–6 6–2), *Wimbledon* 2r (d. Reneberg 6–7 3–6 7–6 6–3 6–2, lost Pearce 6–3 6–3 6–1), *US Open* 2r (d. Steeb 7–5 7–6 6–3, lost Cahill 6–3 2–0 ret'd); *won* Heilbron Challenger (d. Mronz 7–6 4–6 7–6). *CAREER HIGHLIGHTS – SINGLES: US Open – qf 1986*, unseeded (d. Arias 7–5 6–0 6–3, Dyke, Yzaga, Witsken, lost Becker [seed 3] 6–3 6–2 6–1).

LOUISE STACEY (Australia)
Born 10 January 1972.
1990: R/u Australian Open Jun (lost M. Maleeva 7–5 6–7 6–1). *1990 HIGHLIGHTS – SINGLES: Australian Open* 1r (lost de Lone 6–4 7–5).

CARL-UWE (CHARLIE) STEEB (Germany)
Born Aalen, 1 September 1967; lives Stuttgart; LH; 6ft; 157lb; final 1990 ATP ranking 46; 1990 prize money $184,050.
Coached by Chris Lewis until end 1990. *1985:* (363). *1986:* (150) Won Hauptfeld and r/u Harren on German Satellite circuit; qf Buenos Aires. *1987:* (41) Upset Krickstein, Forget and Leconte to reach first GP sf in Stuttgart; qf Munich and Hilversum. *1988:* (73) Upset Zivojinovic *en route* to last 16 Australian Open and Jarryd to reach qf Olympics; sf Lorraine, qf Milan and Munich. Finished the year in style, beating Wilander in 5s as West Germany d. Sweden in D Cup f. *1989:* (15) Won his 1st GP title at Gstaad (d. Krickstein) and reached f Tokyo Seiko. *1990:* Upset Becker and Wilander back-to-back *en route* to f Sydney in Jan.; reached the same stage at Brussels and sf Brisbane, where he d. Wilander again. Pulled out of Paris Open in Oct. with a foot injury, requiring surgery. *1990 HIGHLIGHTS – SINGLES: Australian Open* 1r, seed 10 (lost Paloheimo 5–7 6–3 0–6 6–2 6–2), *US Open* 1r (lost Srejber 7–5 7–6 6–3); *r/u* Sydney (d. Lavalle 6–1 6–4, Fleurian 6–4 4–6 6–2, Becker 7–6 6–3, Wilander 6–3 6–2, lost Noah 5–7 6–3 6–4), *r/u* Brussels (d. Jelen 6–3 7–6, Hogstedt 7–6 4–6 6–2, Ivanisevic 6–3 3–6 6–4, Mecir 6–2 6–3, lost Becker 7–5 6–2 6–2), *sf* Brisbane (d. Wilander 6–2 6–3, Stolle 6–1 4–6 6–0, Kroon 7–5 7–5, lost Gilbert 5–7 6–3 6–4).

MICHAEL STICH (Germany)
Born Pinneberg, 18 October 1968; lives Elmshorn; RH; 6ft 4in; 175lb; final 1990 ATP ranking 42; 1990 prize money $280,823.
1986: Nat Jun champ. *1988:* (269) Won Munster Challenger. *1989:* (100) Played his 1st GP qf at Queen's, where he took Lendl to 3s, and reached the same stage at Bristol and Frankfurt. *1990:* Won his 1st tour title at Memphis, upsetting Chesnokov *en route* to becoming the 1st unseeded finalist there, and upset Volkov and Hlasek *en route* to qf Washington. In doubles reached 6 f, winning Munich and Vienna with Riglewski and Rosmalen with Hlasek. *1990 HIGHLIGHTS – SINGLES: Australian Open* 3r (d. Doohan 6–3 6–2 6–2, Lavalle 6–4 6–4 2–0 ret'd, lost Gomez [seed 9] 6–4 6–3 3–6 7–6), *French Open* 2r (d. Rive 6–4 6–1 6–1, lost Jaite [seed 10] 6–7 6–4 6–7 6–4 6–3), *Wimbledon* 3r (d. Dier 6–2 6–3 6–2, Rahunen 6–2 7–5 6–3, lost Forget [seed 11] 3–6 7–5 6–2 4–6 6–3), *US Open* 2r (d. Jonsson 6–4 6–2 7–5, lost Lendl [seed 3] 6–4 5–7 6–4 6–3); *won* Memphis (d. Connell 4–6 7–6 6–4, Everndon 6–1 6–2, Chesnokov 6–3 6–1, Washington 6–4 7–6, Muller 7–5 7–6, Masur 6–7 6–4 7–6). *1990 HIGHLIGHTS – DOUBLES:* (with Riglewski unless

stated) **won** Munich (d. Korda/Smid 6–1 6–4), [Hlasek] **won** Rosmalen (d. Grabb/P. McEnroe 7–6 6–3), **won** Vienna (d. Lozano/Witsken 6–4 6–4); **r/u** Memphis (lost Cahill/ Kratzmann 7–5 6–2), **r/u** Hamburg (lost Bruguera/Courier 7–6 6–2), **r/u** Long Island (lost Forget/Hlasek 2–6 6–3 6–4).

JASON STOLTENBERG (Australia)
Born Narrabri, 4 April 1970; lives Newcastle; RH; 6ft; 172lb; final 1990 ATP ranking 108; 1990 prize money $171,467.
1987: (413) 1st to become ITF Jun champ in both singles and doubles in the same year. Won Australian Open Jun singles and Australian and Wimbledon Jun doubles (with Woodbridge); r/u French Open and Wimbledon Jun singles. *1988:* (70) In Jun doubles won Australian Open, French Open and Wimbledon, all with Woodbridge. In the senior game reached last 16 Australian Open and qf Rye Brook and Brisbane. *1989:* (84) Upset Chang *en route* to his 1st GP f at Livingston. *1990:* In singles reached qf Orlando and Los Angeles. In doubles won 2 titles with Kratzmann and 1 with Woodbridge. *1990 HIGHLIGHTS – SINGLES: French Open* 2r (d. Schapers 6–4 6–3 6–1, lost Kroon 6–0 6–2 6–3), **Wimbledon** 2r (d. Woodbridge 6–3 7–5 7–6, lost Courier 6–2 7–6 6–4), **US Open** 2r (d. Riglewski 4–6 6–1 6–0 2–1 ret'd, lost Krickstein [seed 9] 6–4 6–2 6–4). *1990 HIGHLIGHTS – DOUBLES:* (with Kratzmann unless stated) **won** Singapore (d. Drewett/Woodbridge 6–1 6–0), **won** Manchester (d. N. Brown/Jones 6–3 2–6 6–4), [Woodbridge] **won** Brisbane (d. Garrow/Woodforde 2–6 6–4 6–4); [Woodbridge] **r/u** Seoul (lost Connell/Michibata 7–6 6–4).

ANDREA STRNADOVA (Czechoslovakia)
Born Prague, 28 May 1972 and lives there; 5ft 9in; 130lb; RH; 2HB; final 1990 WTA ranking 144; 1990 prize money $23,753.
1988: (374). *1989:* (199) Won Wimbledon Jun singles (d. McGrath 6–2 6–3) and in Jun doubles with Sviglerova won Australian Open and r/u Wimbledon to finish No. 1 in ITF Jun Doubles Rankings. In the senior game won Darmstadt on the German satellite circuit. *1990:* Won Wimbledon Jun singles (d. Sharpe 6–2 6–4) and doubles with Habsudova. Qf Leipzig in the senior game.

HELENA SUKOVA (Czechoslovakia)
Born Prague, 23 February 1965, and lives there; RH; 6ft 2in; 150lb; final 1990 WTA ranking 14 singles, 1 (2) doubles; 1990 prize money $562,715; career prize money $3,473,097.
Coached by Lada Travnicek until mid-1990; fitness coach Ivan Machytka. Travels with boyfriend Jaramir Jirik. Daughter of 1962 Wimbledon finalist, the late Vera Sukova, and Cyril Suk, former President of Czech Tennis Federation. Brother also named Cyril.
1981: (74) Beat Anne Smith and Barbara Potter to reach last 16 Australian Open at age 16. *1982:* (24) Qf Swiss Open, r/u US CC and Avon Futures Champs. *1983:* (17) Sf Sydney. *1984:* (7) R/u Australian Open (d. Navratilova) and won Brisbane. *1985:* (9) R/u VS Champ and Eastbourne. Qf Australian Open. Voted WTA Most Improved Player. *1986:* (5) Won Canadian Open and Hilversum and r/u US Open (d. Evert Lloyd first time in 15 career meetings). *1987:* (7) Sf US Open, qf Wimbledon, won Eastbourne (d. Evert and Navratilova back to back) and New Jersey in singles and Wimbledon doubles with Kohde-Kilsch. Qualified for VS Champs in singles and doubles. *1988:* (8) In singles qf Australian Open, French Open and Wimbledon; r/u Sydney, Pan Pacific Open and Berlin. In doubles r/u French Open with Kohde-Kilsch, won Olympic silver medal with Novotna, took 4 titles and reached 7 other f with various partners. Qualified for VS Champs in singles and doubles, reaching sf in both and beating Navratilova in qf singles. *1989:* (8) At Brisbane she won her 1st title for 18 months, following with r/u Australian Open (d. Navratilova qf), qf US Open and 5 sf to qualify for VS Champs, where she reached qf. Tore cartilage in right knee at Eastbourne, which kept her out for 2 months, although she played Wimbledon with knee taped and won doubles there with Novotna. Appeared in 7 other doubles f, winning 4. *1990:* Reached sf Australian Open, where she extended Graf to 3s, and was r/u Indian Wells, Birmingham and Brighton. Out for most of CC season undergoing treatment for Achilles' tendon problems, missing French Open singles and playing doubles there only at the request of her partner Novotna, with whom she won 8 of her 10 titles. They captured Australian Open, French Open and Wimbledon, but missed a GS in doubles when they lost US Open f to G. Fernandez/Navratilova. Qualified for VS Champs in both singles and

doubles, losing 1r singles to K. Maleeva and 1r doubles to Medvedeva/Meskhi. *1990 HIGHLIGHTS – SINGLES: Australian Open* sf, seed 4 (/d. Morton 6–4 6–3, Medvedeva 6–2 6–0, Loosemore 6–3 4–6 6–3, Date 6–4 6–3, K. Maleeva [seed 9] 6–4 6–3, lost Graf 6–3 3–6 6–4), *Wimbledon* last 16, seed 10 (d. Bollegraf 7–5 6–2, Jagerman 6–4 4–6 7–5, Dechaume 6–4 6–3, lost Garrison [seed 5] 6–3 6–3), *US Open* last 16 [seed 11] (d. Durie 1–6 7–6 7–6, Garrone 6–3 6–0, Stafford 7–5 6–1, lost Sabatini [seed 5] 6–2 6–1); *r/u* VS Indian Wells (d. Javer 4–6 7–6 6–0, Magers 6–4 5–7 7–6, Demongeot 6–4 6–3, Frazier 7–5 6–4, lost Navratilova 6–2 5–7 6–1), *r/u* Birmingham (d. Dahlman 6–3 6–2, Savchenko 3–6 6–3 6–2, Fairbank Nideffer 2–6 6–4 7–5, lost Garrison 6–4 6–1), *r/u* Brighton (d. Milvidskaia 6–4 7–6, M. Maleeva 6–4 6–1, Gomer 6–1 6–1, K. Maleeva 6–4 6–7 6–3, lost Graf 7–5 6–3). *1990 HIGHLIGHTS – DOUBLES:* (with Novotna unless stated) *won Australian Open* (d. Fendick/M-J. Fernandez 7–6 7–6), *won French Open* (d. Savchenko/Zvereva 6–4 7–5), *won Wimbledon* (d. K. Jordan/Smylie 6–2 7–6), *r/u US Open* (lost G. Fernandez/ Navratilova 6–2 6–4); *won* Brisbane (d. Mandlikova/Sukova 6–3 6–1), *won* Sydney (d. Savchenko/Zvereva 6–3 7–5), *won* VS Indian Wells (d. G. Fernandez/Navratilova 6–2 7–6), *won* VS Florida (d. Burgin/Turnbull 6–4 6–2), *won* LIPC (d. Nagelsen/R. White 6–4 6–3), [Tauziat] *won* Brighton (d. Durie/Zvereva 6–1 6–4), [G. Fernandez] *won* VS New England (d. M-J. Fernandez/Novotna 3–6 6–3 6–3); [Savchenko] *r/u* Hamburg (lost G. Feranandez/ Navratilova 6–2 6–3). *CAREER HIGHLIGHTS – SINGLES: Australian Open – r/u 1984* (d. Kohde-Kilsch, Shriver, Navratilova 1–6 6–3 7–5, lost Evert Lloyd 6–7 6–1 6–3), *r/u 1989* (d. Richardson, Ludloff, O'Neil, Tanvier 7–5 6–4, Navratilova [seed 2] 6–2 3–6 9–7, Cordwell 7–6 4–6 6–2, lost Graf [seed 1] 6–4 6–4), *sf 1990; US Open – r/u 1986* (d. Drescher, Gomer, Bonder, Garrison 6–4 2–6 6–4, Turnbull 6–4 6–0, Evert Lloyd 6–2 6–4, lost Navratilova 6–3 6–2), *sf 1987* (d. Hobbs, Kohde-Kilsch 6–1 6–3, lost Navratilova 6–2 6–2), *qf 1984* (d. K. Jordan, lost Navratilova), *qf 1989* (d. Langrova, Magers 6–2 6–7 6–2, A. Minter 1–6 6–2 6–1, Savchenko 4–6 6–1 6–2, lost Graf 6–1 6–1); *VS Champs – r/u 1985–86* (lost Navratilova 6–3 7–5 6–4), *sf 1986*; (lost Graf 7–6 3–6 6–1); *Wimbledon – qf 1986* (d. Parnell, Betzner, A. Minter, R. White 6–3 6–0, lost Evert Lloyd 7–6 4–6 6–4). *CAREER HIGHLIGHTS – DOUBLES:* (with Kohde-Kilsch unless stated) *Wimbledon – won 1987* (d. Nagelsen/Smylie 7–5 7–5), [Novotna] *won 1989* (d. Savchenko/Zvereva, 6–1 6–2), [Novotna] *won 1990; US Open – won 1985* (d. Navratilova/Shriver 6–7 6–2 6–3); *French Open –* [Novotna] *won 1990, r/u 1985* (lost Navratilova/Shriver 4–6 6–2 6–2), *r/u 1988* (lost Navratilova/Shriver 6–2 7–5); *Australian Open –* [Novotna] *won 1990, r/u 1984* (lost Navratilova/Shriver 6–3 6–4), *r/u 1985* (lost Navratilova/Shriver 6–3 6–4); *LIPC –* [Novotna] *won 1989* (d. G. Fernandez/McNeil 7–6 6–4), [Novotna] *won 1990; VS Champs – r/u 1984–85* (lost Navratilova/Shriver 6–7 6–4 7–6), *r/u 1985–86* (lost Mandlikova/ Turnbull 6–4 6–7 6–3), *r/u 1986* (lost Navratilova/Shriver 7–6 6–3), *r/u 1987* (lost Navratilova/Shriver 6–1 6–1); *Olympics* [Novotna] *silver medal 1988* (lost Shriver/ Garrison 4–6 6–2 10–8).

JONAS SVENSSON (Sweden)

Born Gothenburg, 21 October 1966; lives Kungsbaka; RH; 6ft 2in; 168lb; final 1990 ATP ranking 11; 1990 prize money $541,745.
Coach Tim Klein, psychologist Lars Ryberg. Fiancée Anne Galopp. *1978:* Won Swedish Nat. 12s outdoor and indoor. *1983:* (445) Sf Wimbledon Jun. *1982:* (741). *1985:* (122) Won Swiss Satellite and became full-time pro. *1986:* (21) Clearly the most improved player in the top 25, winning Cologne, narrowly losing to Noah in f Wembley, r/u Stuttgart and beating Jarryd, Zivojinovic and Mecir. *1987:* (30) Shortly after starting to work with psychologist Lars Ryberg, he reached last 16 US Open, won 1st GP title in Vienna and reached f Stockholm and Young Masters. *1988:* (22) Last 16 Australian Open, then reached his 1st GS sf in Paris, upsetting Lendl in ss, but was hampered in his performance at Wimbledon by a mystery virus infection. Won Lorraine and r/u Munich and Wembley. *1989:* (41) Upset, Becker *en route* to qf Australian Open and reached sf Lyon. *1990:* Enjoyed his best year to date, in which he reached last 16 Australian Open, then swept to sf French Open, unseeded on both occasions. Won Toulouse; r/u Rotterdam; sf Stuttgart, Munich and Paris Open, where he d. Lendl and E. Sanchez back-to-back. Competed GS Cup as No. 6 seed, lost 1r Gilbert 2–6 6–3 6–4. *1990 HIGHLIGHTS – SINGLES: Australian Open* last 16, unseeded (d. Hogstedt 6–2 7–5 7–5, Courier 2–6 6–2 6–3 6–2 [seed 14], Jonsson 6–4 7–5 3–6 4–6 6–2, lost Edberg [seed 3] 6–2 6–2 6–4), *French Open* sf,

Jonas Svensson of Sweden who enjoyed his most successful season since turning pro in 1985 by reaching his first Grand Slam semi-final in Paris and ending the year ranked No. 11 in the world. *(M. Cole)*

unseeded (d. Potier 6–4 3–6 6–1 6–2, Bruguera 2–6 2–6 6–4 6–4 6–0, Azar 5–7 6–4 6–1 7–6, Perez Roldan [seed 15] 2–6 6–4 6–2 6–2, Leconte 3–6 7–5 6–3 6–4, lost Agassi [seed 3] 6–1 6–4 3–6 6–3), *Wimbledon* 3r, seed 10 (d. Santoro 6–4 6–3 6–2, Washington 6–3 6–3 6–4, lost Wheaton 2–6 6–7 6–1 6–0 6–4), *US Open* 2r (d. Woodbridge 7–6 6–2 3–6 6–2, lost Wheaton 6–4 7–5 7–5); *won* Toulouse (d. Mattar 6–2 3–6 6–4, Paloheimo 7–5 6–0, Larsson 6–4 6–7 6–3, Mansdorf 6–7 6–4 6–3, Santoro 7–6 6–3); *r/u* Rotterdam (d. Nijssen 7–6 6–1, Novacek 7–6 7–5, Hogstedt 6–3 6–7 7–5, Hlasek 6–4 7–5, lost Gilbert 6–1 6–3); *sf* Stuttgart (d. Stich 7–6 7–5, Noah 6–2 6–4, Skoff 6–4 6–2, lost Becker 7–5 6–2), *sf* Munich (d. Sampras 0–6 6–1, Srejber 6–1 1–0 ret'd, Courier 3–6 6–3 6–4, lost Novacek 6–1 2–6 6–1), *sf* Paris Open (d. Champion 6–2 6–2, Lendl 3–6 6–4 6–2, E. Sanchez 7–5 6–4, lost Becker 4–6 7–6 6–1). *CAREER HIGHLIGHTS – SINGLES: French Open – sf 1988* unseeded (d. Miniussi, Champion, Nystrom 6–7 6–4 4–6 6–3 6–2, K. Carlsson 5–7 7–6 1–6 6–4 6–2, Lendl 7–6 7–5 6–2, lost Leconte 7–6 6–2 6–3), *sf 1990*.

EVA SVIGLEROVA (Czechoslovakia)
Born Plzen, 13 July 1971 and lives there; RH; 2HB; 5ft 7in; 134lb; final 1990 WTA ranking 95; 1990 prize money $50,953.
Coached by Jiri Hrdina. *1988:* (254). *1989:* (135) Sf Barcelona and r/u French Open Jun (lost Capriati 6–4 6–0) in singles. In Jun doubles with Strnadova won Australian Open and r/u Wimbledon. *1990:* Reached sf Tokyo Suntory and broke into the top 100 in Sept. *1990 HIGHLIGHTS – SINGLES: Australian Open* 1r (lost Shriver [seed 11] 6–3 6–4, *French Open* 3r (d. Rinaldi 6–2 5–5 ret'd, Van Rensburg 6–3 7–5, lost Novotna [seed 11] 7–5 6–2), *Wimbledon* 1r (lost Tanvier 6–2 6–4), *US Open* 1r (lost Van Rensburg 6–3 6–1); *sf* Tokyo Suntory (d. Kidowaki 6–7 6–3 6–3, Henricksson 6–1 6–2, Javer 6–1 6–4, lost Lindqvist 6–1 6–2).

ANDREW SZNAJDER (Canada)
Born Preston, England, 25 May 1967; lives Toronto; RH; 5ft 11in; 160lb; final 1990 ATP ranking 104; 1990 prize money $120,150.
Won Nat 14s, 16s, 18s outdoors. *1985:* (342). *1986:* (144) Qf Tel Aviv and won Nat Champs. *1987:* (246) Won Seattle Challenger and reached qf Tel Aviv again. All American at Pepperdine Univ. and joined Canadian D Cup squad. *1988:* (118) Won Las Vegas Challenger. *1989:* (56) Qf Montreal and Los Angeles; won Chicoutimi Challenger. *1990:* Reached his 1st tour singles f at Rio de Janeiro. *1990 HIGHLIGHTS – SINGLES: Australian Open* 2r (d. Nemecek 7–6 6–7 6–3 7–6, lost Mecir [seed 16] 2–6 6–1 6–0 6–2), *French Open* 2r (d. Pioline 7–6 6–3 6–1, lost Noah 6–4 5–7 6–4 6–4), *US Open* 1r (lost Krickstein 6–1 4–6 6–7 6–1 6–1); *r/u* Rio de Janeiro (d. Frana 6–3 6–2, Roese 6–3 6–3, Baur 7–5 6–1, Garrow 6–4 1–6 6–4, lost Mattar 6–4 6–4).

CATHERINE TANVIER (France)
Born Toulouse, 28 May 1965; lives Nice; RH; 2HB; 5ft 9½in; 129lb; final 1990 WTA ranking 96; 1990 prize money $62,129.
Coached by Patrice Hagelhauer and Steve Myers. *1979:* Won French Nat 14s. *1980:* (173) Won French Nat 16s. *1981:* (95) Sf Columbus. *1982:* (24) Won Wimbledon Jun over Sukova. In singles r/u Hershey and in doubles won Monte Carlo and Bakersfield. *1983:* (33) In singles won Freiburg, r/u Stuttgart and in doubles r/u Italian Open, Hittfeld and sf French Open. *1984:* (30) Sf German Open. *1985:* (39) Last 16 Wimbledon; sf US Indoor (d. Shriver). *1986:* (36) R/u Wimbledon and Wild Dunes. *1987:* (94). *1988:* (77) Last 16 French Open. *1989:* (65) Upset M-J. Fernandez *en route* to last 16 Australian Open and surprised Mandlikova *en route* to qf Brisbane. *1990:* Upset Savchenko 12–10 fs 1r Australian Open, advancing to last 16, unseeded, where she had to retire v Garrison. Sf Bayonne, where she won the doubles with Field. *1990 HIGHLIGHTS – SINGLES: Australian Open* last 16, unseeded (d. Savchenko 4–6 6–1 12–10, Inoue 6–4 6–4, Appelmans 7–6 6–0, lost Garrison 6–2 2–0 ret'd), *French Open* 1r (lost Zvereva [seed 10] 6–4 7–6), *Wimbledon* 3r (d. Sviglerova 6–2 6–4, Ludloff 6–3 6–4, lost Sabatini [seed 4] 6–4 6–2); *sf* Bayonne (d. Dahlman 7–5 6–2, Godridge 6–4 6–2, Paradis 7–5 6–4, lost A. Huber 6–0 6–4). *1990 HIGHLIGHTS – DOUBLES:* (with Field) *won* Bayonne (d. Faull/McQuillan 7–6 6–7 7–6).

PATRICIA TARABINI (Argentina)
Born La Plata, 6 August 1968; lives Tandil; RH; 5ft 5in; 135lb; final 1990 WTA ranking 55; 1990 prize money $87,768.

Coached by Patricio Apey. *1984:* R/u Orange Bowl 16s. *1985:* (305) No. 1 in ITF Jun World Rankings doubles after winning Italian Open Jun and r/u Orange Bowl singles, and winning French Open, Orange Bowl and r/u US Open Jun doubles (with Perez Roldan). *1986:* (125) Won French Open Jun, Orange Bowl and two titles on Italian circuit. *1987:* (69) Sf Berlin, qf Argentine Open and Athens. *1988:* (24) Upset Manuela Maleeva *en route* to sf Tampa, qf Houston and Nice. *1989:* (75) In singles reached f Strasbourg and sf Estoril; in doubles with Cecchini won Arcachon, Athens and Paris Open. *1990:* In singles r/u Guaruja and Clarins; sf Estoril. In doubles with various partners reached 4 f, winning 2. *1990 HIGHLIGHTS – SINGLES: French Open* 3r (d. Faull 6–0 6–4, Kohde-Kilsch 3–6 6–1 6–4, lost Maleeva Fragnière [seed 6] 2–6 7–5 6–0), *US Open* 1r (lost Sawamatsu 6–1 6–3); *r/u* Guaruja (d. Grousback 6–3 6–3, Ekstrand 6–4 7–6, Tiezzi 6–1 6–4, Baranski 6–2 6–2, lost Haumuller 7–6 6–4), *r/u* Clarins (d. Zardo 6–4 6–0, F. Romano 6–4 6–4, Langrova 6–4 6–3, Cecchini 6–4 7–5, lost Martinez 7–5 6–3), *sf* Estoril (d. Kschwendt 7–6 6–2, Vieira 6–4 6–2, Piccolini 6–2 4–6 6–2, lost Garrone 6–2 6–2). *1990 HIGHLIGHTS – DOUBLES:* (with Cecchini unless stated) [Paz] *won* Guaruja (d. Chabalgoity/Corsato 6–2 6–2), *won* Estoril (d. Bakkum/Jagerman 1–6 6–2 6–3); [Goles] *r/u* Barcelona (lost Paz/Sanchez-Vicario 6–7 6–2 6–1), *r/u* Kitzbuhel (lost Langrova/Zrubakova 6–0 6–4).

NATHALIE TAUZIAT (France)
Born Bangui, Africa, 17 October 1967; lives St Tropez; RH; 5ft 5in; 120lb; final 1990 WTA ranking 18; 1990 prize money $300,103.
Coached by Regis DeCamaret. *1985:* (112) Reached 3r French Open, upsetting 16th seed Casale, and played Fed Cup. *1986:* (67) Qf Hilversum. *1987:* (25) Last 16 French Open, sf Strasbourg, San Diego and Zurich and d. Rinaldi to reach qf LIPC. *1988:* (27) Last 16 French Open, r/u Nice and upset Zvereva and K. Maleeva *en route* to f Mahwah. In doubles with Demongeot upset Kohde-Kilsch/Sukova to win both Berlin and Zurich and qualified for VS Champs. *1989:* (25) Sf Italian Open (d. Manuela Maleeva) and San Diego. *1990:* In GS reached last 16 French Open, Wimbledon and US Open. Won her 1st primary circuit title at Bayonne; r/u Wichita and reached sf LIPC, Birmingham and Canadian Open (d. Maleeva Fragnière). Qualified for VS Champs, where she lost 1r to M-J. Fernandez. *1990 HIGHLIGHTS – SINGLES: French Open* last 16, seed 15 (d. Godridge 6–3 7–5, Hack 6–2 3–6 6–3, Lapi 6–1 2–6 6–1, lost Graf [seed 1] 6–1 6–4), *Wimbledon* last 16, unseeded (d. L. Field 6–1 6–1, Pfaff 6–2 6–1, Frazier 3–6 6–2 7–5, lost Sabatini [seed 4] 6–2 7–6), *US Open* last 16, unseeded (d. Dahlman 7–5 6–2, Zardo 6–4 4–6 6–2, Martinez [seed 10] 6–2 6–1, lost Garrison [seed 4] 6–1 7–5); *won* Bayonne (d. Strandlund 6–4 6–2, Wasserman 6–2 6–3, Dahlman 6–4 6–2, Van Lottum 6–2 6–1, A. Huber 6–3 7–6); *r/u* Wichita (d. McGrath 6–3 4–6 7–5, Ferrando 1–6 6–3 6–4, Bollegraf 6–1 6–2, Louie Harper 6–3 6–2, lost Van Rensburg 2–6 7–5 6–2); *sf* LIPC (d. Cammy MacGregor 6–2 4–6 6–3, Miyagi 6–1 6–4, Halard 6–4 6–3, Porwik 6–4 4–6 6–3, lost Seles 6–3 4–6 6–3); *sf* Birmingham (d. K. Jordan 5–7 6–3 7–5, Nu Na 7–5 6–2, A. Smith 6–1 6–2, lost Garrison 6–1 3–6 6–0), *sf* Canadian Open (d. Bowes 6–4 4–6 7–6, Hy 6–1 6–0, Maleeva Fragnière 6–3 6–2, lost Graf 6–2 6–2). *1990 HIGHLIGHTS – DOUBLES:* [Sukova] *won* Brighton (d. Durie/Zvereva 6–1 6–4); [Sanchez-Vicario] *r/u* VS Chicago (lost Navratilova/A. Smith 6–7 6–4 6–3).

MIKAEL TILLSTROEM (Sweden)
Born 5 March 1972.
1990: Won US Open Jun singles (d. Gaudenzi 2–6 6–4 7–6) and doubles with Renstroem.

MARIAN VAJDA (Czechoslovakia)
Born Povazska, 24 March, 1965; lives Bratislava; RH; 5ft 8in; 150lb; final 1990 ATP ranking 83; 1990 prize money $99,972.
Coached by Vladimir Zednik. Married 1988, daughter, Nicole born 14 Feb. 1988. *1985:* (52) A former Czech Nat Jun Champ, he came from nowhere to reach sf Kitzbuhel and qf Geneva. *1986:* (88) Qf Nice, Hilversum, Itaparica. *1987:* (46) After qualifying at Munich he upset Kriek and Nystrom in ss *en route* to f, following in Aug. with 1st GP title at Prague. *1988:* (72) Won Geneva (d. Carlsson in f) and reached qf Kitzbuhel. *1989:* (123) Reached f Bari and qf Kitzbuhel but slipped out of the top 100 for 1st time since 1984. *1990:* Qf Palermo, then in Oct. upset Muster *en route* to sf Athens. *1990: HIGHLIGHTS – SINGLES: French Open* 1r (lost Fleurian 6–2 6–4 6–1); *sf* Athens (d. Wohrmann 6–2 7–6, Muster 3–6 7–6 6–3, Carbonell 6–3 6–3, lost Davin 7–6 2–6 6–3).

NOELLE VAN LOTTUM (France)
Born Ameesfort, Netherlands, 12 July 1972; lives Paris; RH; 5ft 7in; 116lb; final 1990 WTA ranking 138; 1990 prize money $24,426.
1988: (275). **1989:** (410). **1990:** Sf Guaruja and Bayonne; r/u US Open Jun (lost M. Maleeva 7–5 6–2). **1990 HIGHLIGHTS – SINGLES: French Open** 1r (lost Sanchez-Vicario [seed 3] 6–1 6–3); **sf** Guaruja (d. Labat 3–6 6–4 6–3, Schwarz 6–2 6–7 7–5, Tessi 6–3 0–6 6–2, lost Haumuller 4–6 6–3 6–2), **sf** Bayonne (d. Etchemendy 6–4 6–2, Appelmans 7–6 6–4, Laval 6–1 7–5, lost Tauziat 6–2 6–1).

CHRISTO VAN RENSBURG (South Africa)
Born Uitenhage, 23 October 1962; lives Indian Wells, Cal.; RH; 6ft 1in; 160lb; final 1990 ATP ranking 61 singles, 61 doubles; 1990 prize money $210,540.
Coached by Peter Fishbach. No relation to Dinky. **1983:** (291) Won South African Jun. **1984:** (120) Formed partnership with Annacone in Dec. **1985:** (252) Moved into top 10 in doubles after winning 4 GP titles with Annacone, including first GS success at Australian Open. **1986:** (69) Reached sf Wimbledon doubles with Annacone but his appearance in last 16 singles there was more surprising. **1987:** (29) Won Orlando over Mayotte and Connors in 1st GP f. **1988:** (35) R/u Johannesburg, sf Sydney, Philadelphia and Tel Aviv. **1989:** (27) Won Johannesburg, r/u Queen's and reached last 16 both Australian Open and Wimbledon. Won 2 doubles titles with Annacone and qualified for Masters. **1990:** R/u Orlando; qf Queen's, Manchester and San Francisco; reached last 16 US Open, unseeded, and won 2 doubles titles. **1990 HIGHLIGHTS – SINGLES: Australian Open** 2r (d. Potier 6–2 5–7 7–15 6–3, lost Muster [seed 15] 1–6 7–5 7–5 2–6 8–6), **Wimbledon** 2r (d. Sampras [seed 12] 7–5 7–5 7–6, lost Volkov 7–5 6–4 7–6), **US Open** last 16, unseeded (d. Strelba 7–6 7–6 6–2, P. McEnroe 6–4 6–4 7–5, Mattar 6–1 6–4 5–7 6–4, lost Cherkasov 6–4 6–4 7–5); **r/u** Orlando (d. Zivojinovic 7–6 3–6 6–3, Periera 6–3 7–6, Stoltenberg 6–4 4–6 6–1, Pate 6–7 6–3 7–5, lost Gilbert 6–2 6–1). **1990 HIGHLIGHTS – DOUBLES:** [Kruger] **won** Basel (d. Broad/Muller 4–6 7–6 6–3). [Odizor] **won** Tel Aviv (d. Bathman/Bergh 6–3 6–4). **CAREER HIGHLIGHTS – DOUBLES:** (with Annacone) **Australian Open – won 1985** (d. Edmondson/Warwick 3–6 7–6 6–4 6–4); **LIPC – won 1987** (d. Flach/Seguso 6–2 6–4 6–4).

DINKY VAN RENSBURG (South Africa)
Born Salisbury, Rhodesia, 4 March 1968; lives Greatneck, NY; RH; 2HB; 5ft 7in; 123lb; final 1990 WTA rangking 30; 1990 prize money $131,803.
No relation to Christo. Coached by Gordon Birt. **1985:** R/u to Garrone at French Open Jun. No. 2 in ITF Jun rankings. **1986:** (69) Sf VS Tulsa and had wins over McNeil, Cecchini and Savchenko. **1937:** (95). **1988:** (54) Qf Oklahoma and Tampa, then reached her 1st tour singles f at VS Arizona. **1989:** (89). **1990:** Made an unexpected appearance in last 16 Australian Open then, again unseeded, won her 1st title for 3 years at Wichita. **1990 HIGHLIGHTS – SINGLES: Australian Open** last 16, unseeded (d. Ritter 6–0 6–0, Cioffi 6–0 6–4, Wasserman 6–4 6–2, lost Porwik 7–6 3–6 6–4), **French Open** 2r (d. La Fratta 6–4 6–2, lost Sviglerova 6–3 7–5), **Wimbledon** 2r (d. White Prausa 6–2 7–6, lost Nagelsen 2–6 6–4 6–2), **US Open** 3r (d. Sviglerova 6–3 6–1, Hanika 6–3 3–6 6–3, lost Maleeva Fragnière [seed 9] 6–1 6–0); **won** Wichita (d. A. White 7–6 7–5, Werdel 3–6 6–3 6–4, Daniels 6–1 4–6 6–2, Sloane 6–2 7–6, Tauziat 2–6 7–5 6–2). **1990 HIGHLIGHTS – DOUBLES:** [Field] **won** Geneva (d. Burgin/Nagelsen 5–7 7–6 7–5); [Henricksson] **r/u** VS Washington (lost Garrison/Navratilova 6–0 6–3), [Suire] **r/u** Zurich (lost Bollegraf/Pfaff 7–5 6–4).

DANIE VISSER (South Africa)
Born Rustenburg, 26 July 1961; lives Palm Desert, Cal. and Pretoria; LH; 5ft 11in; 175lb; final 1990 ATP ranking 197 singles, 1T doubles; 1990 prize money $322,665.
Wife Karen (married April 1989). **1984:** (72). **1985:** (143) Qf Livingston, last 16 Wimbledon. **1986:** (83) Sf Newport. **1987:** (136) Qf Stratton Mountain. **1988:** (143) Sf San Francisco in singles and won 2 doubles titles with Aldrich to qualify for Masters. **1989:** (141) Sf Newport in singles. In doubles with Aldrich won 3 titles, reached 3 more f and qualified for Masters, where they lost sf to Grabb and P. McEnroe. **1990:** In singles qf Memphis was his best showing. In doubles with Aldrich won 1st GS title at Australian Open, following with US Open and r/u Wimbledon, plus 2 more titles to qualify for IBM/ATP World Final. In mixed doubles r/u French Open with Provis. **1990 HIGHLIGHTS – SINGLES: Wimbledon** 2r (d. Connell 6–4 6–4 6–4, lost Gilbert [seed 7] 5–7 6–3 6–2 6–2). **1990 HIGHLIGHTS –**

DOUBLES: (with Aldrich) *won Australian Open* (d. Connell/Michibata 6–4 4–6 6–1 6–4), *r/u Wimbledon* (lost R. Leach/Pugh 7–6 7–6 7–6), *won US Open* (d. Annacone/Wheaton 6–2 7–6 6–2); *won* Stuttgart (d. Henricsson/Utgren 6–3 6–4), *won* Berlin (d. Curren/Galbraith 7–6 7–6); *r/u* Sydney (lost Cash/Kratzmann 6–4 7–5). *1990 HIGHLIGHTS – MIXED DOUBLES:* (with Provis) *r/u French Open* (lost Sanchez-Vicario/Lozano 7–6 7–6). *CAREER HIGHLIGHTS – DOUBLES:* (with Aldrich) *Australian Open – won 1990; US Open – won 1990; Wimbledon – r/u 1990. MIXED:* (with Provis) *French Open – r/u 1990.*

ALEXANDER VOLKOV (USSR)
Born Kaliningrad, 3 March 1967; lives Moscow; LH; 6ft 2in; 175lb; final 1990 ATP ranking 24; 1990 prize money $259,417.
In separate childhood accidents he broke each wrist. Originally played right-handed, then with either hand, and from 1985, when he broke right wrist, he has played left-handed. *1986:* (529) R/u Nat champs. *1987:* (104) Upset Gilbert *en route* to last 16 Wimbledon after qualifying, surprised Jaite at Paris Open and broke into top 100 Nov. *1988:* (79) Qf Sydney and won Munich Challenger. *1989:* (50) Sf Adelaide and Munich, then broke into top 50 after reaching 1st GP f at Milan. *1990:* R/u Rosmalen and Berlin; sf Vienna and Stockholm (d. E. Sanchez). In GS reached last 16 Wimbledon, unseeded, and upset top seed Edberg 1r US Open to move into the top 25. *1990 HIGHLIGHTS – SINGLES: Australian Open* 2r (d. J. Brown 6–3 6–3 6–1, lost Fleurian 6–4 1–6 7–5 2–6 6–2), *French Open* 3r (d. Pereira 6–4 6–0 4–6 6–4, Arias 1–6 6–3 6–3 4–6 6–1, lost Gomez [seed 4] 6–2 7–5 6–4 6–3), *Wimbledon* last 16, unseeded (d. Zivojinovic 6–7 7–6 7–6 6–1, Van Rensburg 7–5 6–4 7–6, Rosset 6–3 6–4 7–5, lost Curren 6–4 7–6 7–6), *US Open* 2r (d. Edberg [seed 1] 6–3 7–6 6–2, lost Witsken 6–2 6–2 6–3); *r/u* Rosmalen (d. Delaitre 6–2 6–1, Grabb 6–3 4–6 7–6, Layendecker 6–3 6–4, P. McEnroe 6–3 4–6 6–3, lost Mansdorf 6–3 7–6), *r/u* Berlin (d. Arias 6–3 6–4, Riglewski 6–3 6–3, Svensson 6–3 6–0, Mattar 6–3 6–2, lost Agenor 4–6 6–4 7–6); *sf* Vienna (d. Hogstedt 7–6 6–4, Wohrmann 7–5 6–3, Jaite 6–2 6–1, lost Jarryd 6–2 7–5), *sf* Stockholm (d. Steeb 4–6 6–4 6–3, E. Sanchez 7–6 6–3, Gustafsson 6–3 7–6, Kulti 6–2 6–1, lost Edberg 7–6 6–2).

MALIVAI WASHINGTON (USA)
Born Glen Cove, NY, 20 June 1969; lives Swartz Creek, Mich.; RH; 5ft 11in; 175lb; final 1990 ATP ranking 93; 1990 prize money $105,611.
Coached by his father, William. *1987:* R/u Easter Bowl. *1998:* (329) All-American at Univ. of Michigan. *1989:* (199) Won Seattle Challenger. *1990:* Reached sf Orlando after qualifying and appeared at same stage US CC. Upset Lendl in ss 1r New Haven in Aug. *1990 HIGHLIGHTS – SINGLES: French Open* 1r (lost Aguilera 7–5 4–6 6–1 6–2), *Wimbledon* 2r (d. Jonsson 6–2 6–3 6–1, lost Svensson 6–3 6–3 6–4), *US Open* 2r (d. Mancini 6–2 6–4 6–3, lost Curren 7–5 7–6 6–4); *sf* Orlando (d. Jones 6–3 6–2, Ross 6–1 7–5, S. Davis 6–3 7–5, lost Gilbert 6–2 7–5), *sf* US CC (d. Shiras 6–2 6–1, Lavalle 2–6 6–3 6–2, Wostenholme 6–4 4–6 6–3, lost Kaplan 6–3 6–2).

SANDRA WASSERMAN (Belgium)
Born Antwerp, 10 March 1970 and lives there; RH; 2HB; 5ft 8in; 136lb; final 1990 WTA ranking 100; 1990 prize money $46,413.
1986: (313). *1987:* (122) R/u Paris Open and extended M. Maleeva to 3s in 3r French Open. *1988:* (63) R/u Paris Open again, sf Bastad, qf Auckland, Barcelona, Sofia. *1989:* (69) Reached sf Wellington and Singapore. *1990:* Played her best tennis at beginning of year, when she upset Zvereva at Australian Open and reached qf Auckland and Wellington. *1990 HIGHLIGHTS – SINGLES: Australian Open* 3r (d. Langrova 7–6 7–5, Zvereva [seed 10] 7–5 6–1, lost Van Rensburg 6–4 6–2), *French Open* 1r (lost Strandlund 6–3 3–6 6–0), *Wimbledon* 1r (lost Wiesner [seed 14] 6–3 6–0), *US Open* 2r (d. Farley 1–6 6–3 6–3, lost Reggi 6–2 6–2).

ROBBIE WEISS (USA)
Born Chicago, Ill., 1 December 1966; lives Wheeling, Ill.; RH; 6ft; 165lb; final 1990 ATP ranking 89; 1990 prize money $66,559.
Wears a magnet strapped to his knee as a cure for tendonitis. Won 13 Nat Jun titles. *1984:* Won Wimbledon Jun doubles with R. Brown. *1985:* (338). *1966:* (668) Member of USTA Jun D Cup team for 3rd year. All-American at Pepperdine, helping them to NCAA finals.

1987: (954). *1988:* (492) All-American at Pepperdine again, becoming first from there to win NCAA singles (d. Garrow) and finishing the year ranked No. 1 collegiate player. *1989:* (169) R/u at 2 Challenger tourns. *1990:* Broke into top 100 in Oct. after winning his 1st tour title at Sao Paulo; qf Rosmalen, Brisbane and Newport (d. Mayotte). *1990 HIGHLIGHTS – SINGLES: won* Sao Paulo (d. Daufresne 6–0 4–6 6– 4, Bengoechea 6–4 6–4, Nido 6–4 6–3, Eltingh 7–6 4–6 7–6, Yzaga 3–6 7–6 6–3).

MARIANNE WERDEL (USA)
Born Los Angeles, Cal., 17 October 1967; lives Bakersfield, Cal.; RH; 2HB; 5ft 10in; 144lb; final 1990 WTA ranking 48; 1990 prize money $95,322.
1983: (221) R/u US Open Jun. *1985:* (122) Won USTA Key Biscayne and Fayetteville. *1986:* (32) Sf Puerto Rico, played Jun Fed Cup and was All-American at Stanford. *1987:* (59) Qf VS New Orleans and Tokyo and upset Shriver 1r VS Washington. *1988:* (103) After reaching sf Japan Open was sidelined for 2 months recovering from partially herniated disc. *1989:* (95) R/u Schenectady. *1990:* Upset Savchenko and Paz *en route* to f Schenectady. *1990 HIGHLIGHTS – SINGLES: Australian Open* 1r (lost Henricksson 4–6 6–4 6–4), *French Open* 1r (lost Burgin 6–3 6–3 6–4), *Wimbledon* 1r (lost Henricksson 7–5 6–2), *US Open* 1r (lost Martinez 2–6 7–5 6–2); *r/u* Schenectady (d. Savchenko 6–4 5–7 6–3, Ferrando 6–4 6–4, Reinach 5–7 6–4 6–4, Paz 4–6 7–5 6–3, lost A. Huber 6–1 5–7 6–4).

DAVID WHEATON (USA)
Born Minneapolis, Minn., 2 June 1969; lives Lake Minnetonka, Minn.; RH; 6ft 3in; 170lb; final 1990 ATP ranking 27; 1990 prize money $791,240.
Coached by Jerry Noyce. Spent time at Nick Bollettieri Tennis Academy. Travels with brother John, a lawyer. *1985:* US Jun D Cup squad 1985–87. *1986:* A freshman at Stanford, was r/u Nat Jun Champs. *1987:* (345) Extended Lendl to 3s at Washington and won US Open Jun singles over Cherkasov and US Nat 18s clay court over Courier. *1988:* (441). Played No. 1 singles and doubles for Stanford's NCAA winning team. *1989:* (66) Upset Agassi *en route* to sf Stratton Mountain and won Brasilia Challenger. *1990:* Reached qf Australian Open and US Opens and last 16 Wimbledon (lost Gilbert 13–11 5s), all unseeded, and with Annacone reached f doubles at US Open. Out of action 10 weeks early in year with stress fracture of leg, returning in May to win 1st tour title at US CC and broke into top 50. Reached sf inaugural GS Cup. *1990 HIGHLIGHTS – SINGLES: Australian Open* qf, unseeded (d. Ivanisevic 7–5 7–5 6–0, Larsson 6–3 6–2 3–6 6–1, Woodforde 6–3 4–5 ret'd, Krickstein [seed 5] 7–6 6–4 6–3, lost Edberg 7–5 7–6 3–6 6–2), *French Open* 1r (lost Srejber 3–6 5–7 6–3 7–6 6–3), *Wimbledon* last 16, unseeded (d. Larsson 7–6 6–4 6–2, Annacone 6–4 1–6 6–4 6–7 6–4, Svensson 2–6 6–7 6–1 6–0 6–4, lost Gilbert [seed 7] 6–7 3–6 6–1 6–4 13–11), *US Open* qf, unseeded (d. Arrese 6–3 6–1 6–0, Svensson 6–4 7–5 7–5, Annacone 6–2 7–6 6–3, Curren 7–5 7–6 4–6 6–4, lost J. McEnroe 6–1 6–4 6–4); *won* US CC (d. Matuszewski 3–6 6–1 7–5, Campbell 1–6 6–3 7–5, Tarango 6–2 6–7 7–6, Mronz 2–6 7–5 6–2, Kaplan 6–2 6–3); *sf* GS Cup, seed 8 (d. Noah 7–6 6–7 6–3, Lendl 6–2 7–6, lost Gilbert 6– 3 3–6 7–6 2–6 6–4). *1990 HIGHLIGHTS – DOUBLES:* (with Annacone) *r/u US Open* (lost Aldrich/Visser 6–2 7–6 6–2); *won* Canadian Open (d. Dyke/Lundgren 6–1 7–6). *CAREER HIGHLIGHTS – SINGLES: Australian Open – qf 1990; US Open – qf 1990. CAREER HIGHLIGHTS – DOUBLES:* (with Annacone) *US OPEN – r/u 1990.*

ROBIN WHITE (USA)
Born San Diego, Cal., 10 December 1963; lives Del Mar, Cal.; RH; 5ft 4½in; 125lb; final 1990 WTA ranking 59 singles, 12 (12) doubles; 1990 prize money $135,910.
Formerly coached by John Lloyd. *1984:* (105) R/u Wimbledon Plate. *1985:* (32) Last 16 US Open with win over Gadusek and won VS Hershey. *1986:* (20) Won 24 of 42 matches, upsetting Mandlikova and Sabatini to reach sf Eastbourne, and reaching last 16 Wimbledon. Qualified for VS Champ Nov. doubles with G. Fernandez. *1987:* (56) Qf New Orleans in singles and won 4 doubles titles. *1988:* (38) Upset Fendick to reach f North California Open. In doubles with G. Fernandez won US Open and Japan Open, reaching f on 4 other occasions to qualify for VS Champs. *1989:* (90) Qf San Diego was her best showing in singles, but in doubles she took 3 titles with G. Fernandez and won US Open mixed with Cannon. *1990:* In singles reached sf Auckland and in doubles reached 6 f with different partners, winning 2 titles. *1990 HIGHLIGHTS – SINGLES: Australian Open* 1r (lost Rinaldi 6–4 3–6 6–4), *Wimbledon* 3r (d. Myagi 6–2 6–1, M. Maleeva 4–6 7–5 6–4, lost

Capriati 7–5 6–7 6–3). **US Open** 3r (d. Temesvari 4–6 6–0 6–2, Halard 6–4 6–3, lost M-J. Fernandez [seed 8] 6–1 6–2); **sf** Auckland (d. Devries 4–0 ret'd, Wood 6–4 6–0, Durie 6–2 6–4, lost Meskhi 6–4 6–2). **1990 HIGHLIGHTS – DOUBLES:** [M-J. Fernandez] **won** Tokyo Nicherei (d. G. Fernandez/Navratilova 6–2 6–0), [Magers] **won** Moscow (d. Brioukhovets/Maniokova 6–2 6–4); [Hetherington] **r/u** Auckland (lost Medvedeva/Meskhi 3–6 6–3 7–6), [Nagelsen] **r/u** LIPC (lost Novotna/Sukova 6–4 6–3), [G. Fernandez] **r/u** San Antonio (lost K. Jordan/Smylie 7–5 7–5), [Fairbank Nideffer] **r/u** VS California (lost McGrath/A. Smith 2–6 6–0 6–4). **CAREER HIGHLIGHTS – DOUBLES:** (with G.Fernandez) **US Open – won 1988** (d. Fendick/Hetherington 6–4 6–1). **MIXED DOUBLES:** (with Cannon) **US Open – won 1989** (d. McGrath/R. Leach 6–7 7–5 6–4).

TAMI WHITLINGER (USA)
Born Neenah, Wis., 13 November 1968, and lives there; RH; 2HB; 5ft 6in; 118lb; final 1990 WTA ranking 81; 1990 prize money $60,379.
Coached by her father, Warren, and Ted Thomsen. **1986:** Won Nat 18s. **1988:** (626). **1989:** (129) Won 2 titles on USTA circuit and upset McNeil 1r Los Angeles. **1990:** Qf VS Chicago and VS Nashville and broke into top 100 1st time in Feb. **1990 HIGHLIGHTS – SINGLES: Australian Open** 3r (d. Suire 6–1 6–2, Phelps 7–5 6–3, lost G. Fernandez [seed 15] 7–6 6–3), **French Open** 1r (lost Rajchrtova 6–2 6–0), **Wimbledon** 2r (d. Field 6–3 6–2, lost Faull 6–2 6–3), **US Open** 1r (lost Zrubakova 7–5 6–2).

JUDITH POLZL WIESNER (Austria)
Born Hallein, 2 March 1966; lives Salzburg; RH; 5ft 7in; 138lb; final 1990 WTA ranking 17; 1990 prize money $251,446.
Husband Heinz (married April 1987). Coached by Karel Safarik. **1985:** (305). **1986:** (142) R/u Kitzbuhel and played Fed Cup. **1987:** (34) Sf Bastad and Athens and d. Bunge *en route* to both qf VS Arizona and 2r Italian Open. **1988:** (36) Upset Zvereva to reach f Strasbourg, Cecchini and Hanika as she won her 1st pro singles title at Aix-en-Provence, Kohde-Kilsch to reach sf Italian Open and McNeil *en route* to last 16 US Open. **1989:** (35) Reached last 16 Australian Open and won Arcachon. In doubles won Strasbourg and reached 2 other f. **1990:** The high spot of her year came when she beat Novotna, Maleeva Fragnière and Martinez to make an unexpected appearance in f LIPC; also reached sf Brisbane, Sydney, Barcelona, Hamburg and Kitzbuhel to qualify for VS Champs, where she lost 1r to Maleeva Fragnière. **1990 HIGHLIGHTS – SINGLES: Australian Open** 2r (d. Goles 7–5 6–2, lost Porwik 6–3 7–6), **French Open** 3r, seed 12 (d. Magers 6–4 6–0, Jaggard 6–3 6–1, lost Capriati 6–4 6–4), **Wimbledon** last 16, seed 14 (d. Wasserman 6–3 6–0, Quentrec 6–3 6–3, Gildemeister 6–2 7–6, lost Navratilova [seed 2] 6–3 6–3), **US Open** last 16, seed 15 (d. Daniels 6–3 6–1, Date 7–6 6–1, Savchenko 6–1 6–3, lost M-J. Fernandez [seed 8] 6–3 6–2); **r/u** LIPC (d. Werdel 7–6 0–6 6–3, Phelps 6–1 5–7 6–2, Novotna 7–5 5–7 6–3, Maleeva Fragnière 2–6 6–1 6–2, Martinez 7–6 6–2, lost Seles 6–1 6–2); **sf** Brisbane (d. Provis 7–6 6–2, Cunningham 6–2 2–6 6–4, Fendick 6–2 6–3, Novotna 7–6 6–3, lost McQuillan 6–3 7–6), **sf** Sydney (d. Quentrec 7–5 6–4, Bollegraf 6–3 6–2, Mandlikova 7–6 6–3, Porwik 6–3 4–6 6–3, lost Paulus 6–4 3–6 6–1), **sf** Barcelona (d. Sviglerova 6–4 6–0, McQuillan 6–0 6–2, lost Sanchez-Vicario 6–2 6–1), **sf** Hamburg (d. Frankl 6–1 6–0, Probst 6–3 6–2, Langrova 6–3 6–1, lost Graf 6–4 6–2), **sf** Kitzbuhel (d. Meier 6–3 6–4, Graham 6–1 6–1, Langrova 6–2 3–6 6–2, lost McQuillan 7–6 6–3). **CAREER HIGHLIGHTS – SINGLES: LIPC – r/u 1990.**

MATS WILANDER (Sweden)
Born Vaxjo, 22 August 1964; lives Greenwich, Conn., and Monte Carlo; RH; 2HB; 6ft 1in; 175lb; final 1990 ATP ranking 41; 1990 prize money $187,435; career prize money $7,310,656.
Formerly trained by Joe Breedlove and coached by Jan-Anders Sjogren. Married Sonya Mulholland 3 Jan. 1987. **1981:** (68) Won European Jun Champ and French Open Jun. **1982:** (7) Became youngest ever to win a GS event when he captured his first GP title at French Open aged 17 years, 9 months, 6 days with wins over Lendl, Gerulaitis, Clerc and Vilas. He was also the first unseeded player to win a GS event in the Open era. **1983:** (4) The only player in men's tennis to win tournaments on clay (6), grass (1) and cement (1), he won more tournaments than anyone else (9) including his second GS triumph at Australian Open over McEnroe and·Lendl. **1984:** (4) Retained his Australian crown and also won

Cincinnati and Barcelona. *1985:* (3) Won 2nd French Open as well as Boston and Bastad, and was r/u to Edberg at Australian Open. *1986:* (3) After winning at least one GS title for four straight years, he lost 3r French Open and 4r Wimbledon and US Open, but won Brussels and Cincinnati in singles, and in doubles with Nystrom won Wimbledon and reached f US Open. *1987:* (3) R/u to Lendl French Open, US Open, and Masters; qf Wimbledon, won his first Italian Open crown and titles in Brussels, Monte Carlo, Boston and US CC. *1988:* (1) The 1st man since Connors in 1974 to hold 3 GS titles in one year, he won Australian Open, French Open and became 1st Swede to win US Open. After that triumph he took over the No. 1 ranking from Lendl, who had held that position for 156 consecutive weeks. Also won LIPC, Cincinnati and Palermo, but reached no other f and fell in qf Wimbledon to Mecir. Suffering from shin splints, he was restricted at Masters and lost in D Cup f to Steeb as FRG d. SWE. *1989:* (12) Lacking in motivation he lost his No. 1 ranking to Lendl after Australian Open, where he fell to Krishnan 2r, and struggled for the rest of the year, reaching just 1 f (US Pro) and sf Monte Carlo, Cincinnati and Stockholm. Was unseeded in tourn for 1st time since 1982 at Paris Open in autumn and failed to qualify for Masters. *1990:* Began the year well with sf appearance in Australian Open, where he d. Becker before losing to Edberg. Took a 4-month break from the circuit from March to be with his father, who was dying of cancer, returning at Bastad in July. On Aug. 13, he slipped out of the top 50, but returned on 21 Oct. after f appearance at Lyon – his 1st f since Boston in 1989 and the 1st time he had won 2 consec matches since Australian Open. Followed with the title at Itaparica in Nov. Split with his long-time coach, Jan Anders Sjogren, in May, searching for new inspiration. *1990 HIGHLIGHTS – SINGLES: Australian Open* sf, seed 8 (d. Fromberg 7–6 7–5 7–5, Wostenholme 6–2 7–5 6–3, Masur 6–4 5–7 6–4 1–6 6–3, Paloheimo 7–5 6–4 6–0, Becker [seed 2] 6–4 6–4 6–2, lost Edberg [seed 3] 6–1 6–1 6–2], *US Open* 1r (lost Gilbert [seed 8] 6–4 3–6 6–3 7–5); *won* Itaparica (d. Wilkison 6–2 6–2, Cunha-Silva 6–2 6–2, Sznajder 6–1 6–0, Koevermans 6–4 6–3, Filippini 6–1 6–2); *r/u* Lyon (d. Cherkasov 6–2 3–6 6–3, Bloom 6–2 6–2, Svensson 4–6 6–4 6–3, Mronz 6–3 7–6, lost Rosset 6–3 6–2); *sf* Sydney (d. Rosset 6–4 6–2, Kroon 6–1 6–2, Sampras 6–7 7–6 6–0, lost Steeb 6–3 6–2). *CAREER HIGHLIGHTS – SINGLES: Australian Open – won 1983* (d. J. McEnroe 4–6 6–3 6–4 6–3, Lendl 6–1 6–4), *won 1984* (d. Curren 6–7 6–4 7–6 6–2), *won 1988* (d. Gustafsson, Saceanu, Jarryd 7–6 6–2 6–3, Edberg 6–0 6–7 6–3 3–6 6–1), Cash 6–3 6–7 2–6 6–1 8–6, *r/u 1985* (d. Kriek, Zivojinovic, lost Edberg 6–4 6–3 6–3), *sf 1990; French Open – won 1982*, unseeded (d. Lendl 4–6 7–5 3–6 6–4 6–2, Gerulaitis 6–3 6–3 4–6 6–4, Clerc 7–5 6–2 1–6 7–5, Vilas 1–6 7–6 [saving one s-p] 6–0 6–4), *won 1985* (d. Leconte, J. McEnroe [seed 1] 6–1 7–5 7–5, Lendl [seed 2] 3–6 6–4 6–2 6–2), *won 1988* (d. Zivojinovic 6–2 6–7 3–6 6–3 7–5, Agenor 6–1 7–6 6–3, E. Sanchez 6–7 7–6 6–3 6–4, Agassi 4–6 6–2 7–5 6–7 6–0, Leconte 7–6 6–2 6–1), *r/u 1983* (d. Sundstrom, J. McEnroe 1–6 6–2 6–4 6–0, Higueras, lost Noah 6–2 7–5 7–6), *r/u 1987* (d. Colombo, Annacone, Krickstein, Benhabiles, Noah 6–4 6–3 6–2, Becker 6–4 6–1 6–2, lost Lendl 7–5 6–2 3–6 7–6), *sf 1984* (lost Lendl 6–3 6–3 7–5); *US Open – won 1988* (d. Curren, Pernfors, Woodforde, E. Sanchez 3–6 7–6 6–0 6–4, Cahill 6–4 6–4 6–2, Lendl 6–4 4–6 6–3 5–7 6–4), *r/u 1987* (d. Ross, J. Carlsson, Pimek, Flach 6–3 6–3 7–6, Mecir 6–3 6–7 6–4 7–6, Edberg 6–4 3–6 6–3 6–4, lost Lendl 6–7 6–0 7–6 6–4), *sf 1985* (d. Annacone, Holmes, Jarryd 2–6 6–2 5–0 ret'd, lost J. McEnroe [seed 1] 3–6 6–4 4–6 6–3 6–3), *qf 1984* (lost Cash 7–6 6–4 2–6 6–3); *LIPC – won 1988* (d. Volkov, Woodforde, Krickstein 6–1 6–2 6–0, Noah 6–4 6–3 6–3, Connors 6–4 4–6 6–4 6–4); *Masters – r/u 1987* (d. Mecir, Cash, lost Edberg in rr, d. Edberg 6–2 4–6 6–3, lost Lendl 6–2 6–2 6–3), *sf 1983* (lost J. McEnroe 6–2 6–4), *sf 1984* (lost J. McEnroe 6–1 6–1). *CAREER HIGHLIGHTS – DOUBLES:* (with Nystrom) *Wimbledon – won 1986* (d. Donnelly/Fleming 7–6 6–3 6–3); *US Open – r/u 1986* (lost Gomez/Zivojinovic 4–6 6–3 6–3 4–6 6–3), *sf 1985* (lost Leconte/Noah 6–3 7–6 6–4); *Australian Open – r/u 1984* (lost Cash/Fitzgerald 6–4 6–4 2–6 6–3); *French Open – sf 1985* (lost Edmondson/Warwick 6–4 6–1 7–5).

TODD WITSKEN (USA)
Born Indianapolis, 4 November 1963; lives Carmel, Ind.; 5ft 11in; 165lb; final 1990 ATP ranking 58 singles, 21 doubles; 1990 prize money $250,624.
1983–84: Member of US Jun D Cup squad and All American at USC. *1985:* (218) Played three GP tournaments in time off from college. *1986:* (55) Stunned Connors in straight sets 3r US Open – the first time Connors had lost there before qf since 1972. *1987:* (158) Qf

Washington. *1988:* (67) Qf Australian Open (d. Leconte), sf Indianapolis. In doubles with Lozano won 3 titles and reached 5 more f to qualify for Masters, where they fell sf to R. Leach/Pugh. *1989:* (54) Sf Rio de Janeiro and Washington in singles. Won 4 doubles titles with 3 different partners, qualifying for Masters with Lozano, where they took 5th place. *1990:* R/u San Francisco (d. Krickstein); qf Washington (d. Mayotte) and Canadian Open (d. Gilbert). Reached 2 doubles f with Lozano, but won no title. *1990 HIGHLIGHTS – SINGLES: Australian Open* 1r (lost Oresar 6–4 6–1 6–4), *French Open* 1r (lost Bergstrom 6–1 6–2 6–0), *US Open* 3r (d. Nargio 6–3 6–7 7–6 6–4, Volkov 6–2 6–2 6–3, lost Curren 6–4 6–3 6–3); *r/u* San Francisco (d. Seguso 6–2 6–4, Muller 6–4 6–3, Reneberg 7–6 6–4, Rive 6–4 7–6, lost Agassi 6–1 6–3). *1990 HIGHLIGHTS – DOUBLES:* (with Lozano) *r/u* Washington (lost Connell/Michibata 6–3 6–7 6–2), *r/u* Vienna (lost Riglewski/Stich 6–4 6–4).

TODD WOODBRIDGE (Australia)
Born Sydney, 2 April 1971; lives Woolooware; RH; 5ft 10in; 150lb; final 1990 ATP ranking 50; 1990 prize money $253,992.
1987: (420) R/u Australian Open Jun to Stoltenberg with whom he won the doubles there and at Wimbledon. *1988:* (213) Won Tasmania and in Jun doubles with Stoltenberg won Australia Open, French Open and Wimbledon. *1989:* (131) Won Brisbane Challenger, upset Fitzgerald *en route* to sf GP event there and finished the year by winning Hobart Challenger. In Jun doubles won Australian and French Open with J. Anderson. *1990:* Upset Chang *en route* to 1st tour f at New Haven and Gilbert *en route* to sf Sydney Indoor. In doubles with various partners reached 4 f, winning 2, and took US Open mixed with Smylie. *1990 HIGHLIGHTS – SINGLES: Australian Open* 3r (d. Arrese 4–6 6–0 6–3 6–1, Pistolesi 6–3 6–2 6–2, lost Sampras 7–5 6–4 6–2), *French Open* 2r (d. Bahrami 2–6 6–1 4–6 6–3 8–6, lost Agassi 7–5 6–1 6–3), *Wimbledon* 1r (lost Stoltenberg 6–3 7–5 7–6), *US Open* 1r (lost Svensson 7–6 6–2 3–6 6–2); *r/u* New Haven (d. Hogstedt 6–3 1–6 6–3, Pearce 6–4 6–4, Masur 7–6 3–6 7–5, Woodforde 1–6 6–4 6–3, lost Rostagno 6–3 6–3); *sf* Sydney Indoor (d. Jones 6–4 6–0, Gilbert 7–6 6–3, Pearce 6–3 4–6 6–3, Connell 7–6 2–6 6–1, lost Becker 7–5 6–4). *1990 HIGHLIGHTS – DOUBLES:* (with Stoltenberg unless stated) [Youll] *won* Casablanca (d. Haarhuis/Koevermans 6–3 6–1), *won* Brisbane (d. Garrow/Woodforde 2–6 6–4 6–4); *r/u* Seoul (lost Connell/Michibata 7–6 6–4), [Drewett] *r/u* Singapore (lost Kratzmann/Stoltenberg 6–1 6–0). *MIXED DOUBLES:* (with Smylie) *won US Open* (d. Zvereva/Pugh 6–4 6–2). *CAREER HIGHLIGHTS – MIXED DOUBLES:* (with Smylie) *US Open – won 1990.*

MARK WOODFORDE (Australia)
Born Adelaide, 23 September 1965, and lives there; LH; 6ft 2in; 165lb; final 1990 ATP ranking 101 singles, 118 doubles; 1990 prize money $125,842.
Coached by Barry Phillips-Moore. *1984:* (385). *1985:* (127). *1986:* (181) Won 1st pro title at Auckland, sf Bristol. *1987:* (67) Last 16 US Open (d. Mayotte) after qualifying. *1988:* (42) Enjoyed a remarkable year, with success on all surfaces, in which he extended Lendl to 5 close sets in 4¾-hour 4r match at Wimbledon, conceding only 10–8 in 5s, upset Edberg and J. McEnroe to reach sf Toronto and beat McEnroe again *en route* to last 16 US Open, unseeded. Formed a useful doubles partnership with J. McEnroe in autumn. *1989:* (75) In singles won Adelaide and r/u Brisbane. In doubles won US Open with J. McEnroe and Monte Carlo with Smid. *1990:* Upset Chesnokov 2r Australian Open, but was forced to retire in 3r v Wheaton when he tore 2 ligaments in his ankle, requiring surgery. Out of action until June, when he progressed to last 16 Wimbledon, unseeded and a wild card, and in Aug. reached sf New Haven. *1990 HIGHLIGHTS – SINGLES: Australian Open* 3r (d. Altur 2–6 6–1 6–4 6–4, Chesnokov [seed 11] 6–3 6–2 7–5, lost Wheaton 6–3 4–5 ret'd), *Wimbledon* last 16, unseeded (d. Fitzgerald 7–5 6–2 6–4, Riglewski 6–7 6–4 6–4 7–5, Courier 7–5 5–7 7–5 6–4, lost Pearce 6–4 6–4 6–4); *sf* New Haven (d. Fitzgerald 6–4 7–5, Fromberg 6–1 2–6 6–4, Sevensson 6–3 3–6 6–4, Shelton 7–5 6–2, lost Woodbridge 1–6 6–4 6–3). *1990 HIGHLIGHTS – DOUBLES:* [Garrow] *r/u* Brisbane (lost Stoltenberg/Woodforde 2–6 6–4 6–4). *CAREER HIGHLIGHTS – DOUBLES:* (with J. McEnroe) *US Open – won 1989* (d. Flack/Seguso 6–4 4–6 6–3 6–3).

JAIME YZAGA (Peru)
Born Lima, 23 October 1967, and lives there; RH; 5ft 7in; 134lb; final 1990 ATP ranking 87; 1990 prize money $131,300.

Coached by Colon Nunez. Has suffered from recurring shoulder injury since 1982. *1981:* Won S. American 16s. *1983:* Won S. American 18s. *1984:* Joined Peruvian D Cup squad. *1985:* (45) Won French Jun and Wimbledon Jun doubles before bursting into last 16 US Open, after qualifying, where he was the only player to take a set off Lendl. *1986:* (64) Played D Cup for Peru, scored wins over Hlasek, Pecci and Pate and reached sf Tokyo. *1987:* (70) Won first GP singles title at Schenectady, following with Sao Paulo. *1988:* (65) Finished the year on a high note by winning Itaparica. Upset Gilbert at US Open and reached qf Italian Open, Florence and Sao Paulo. *1989:* (23) Upset Chang *en route* to f Tourn of Champs and Mecir at LIPC, as well as reaching sf Guaruja, Bordeaux, Orlando (d. E. Sanchez) and Itaparica. *1990:* R/u Sao Paulo and upset Berger at Monte Carlo. *1990 HIGHLIGHTS – SINGLES: French Open* 1r (lost Krickstein [seed 5] 6–0 2–6 6–3 6–3), *US Open* 1r (d. Novacek 7–5 7–6 6–3, Champion 6–1 3–6 6–3 6–2, lost Muster [seed 6] 6–2 6–2 4–6 5–7 7–6); *r/u* Sao Paulo (d. Marques 6–2 6–2, Saliola 6–2 7–5, Garner 7–5 7–5, Marcelino 6–4 3–6 7–6, lost Weiss 3–6 7–6 6–3).

EMANUELA ZARDO (Switzerland)
Born Bellinzona, 24 April 1970; lives Giubiasco; LH; 2HB; 5ft 4½in; 114lb; final 1990 WTA ranking 63; 1990 prize money $41,156.
1986: (294) Won Nat Jun Champ. *1987:* (254) Won 3 titles on satellite circuits and joined Swiss Fed Cup team. *1988:* (296). *1988:* (140) Won Oporto on Portuguese satellite circuit. *1990:* Reached sf Geneva, qf Wellington, Palermo and Estoril, and broke into the top 100 in June. *1990 HIGHLIGHTS – SINGLES: Australian Open* 1r (lost Pospisilova 6–4 6–1), *French Open* 1r (lost Cueto 7–6 6–0), *US Open* 2r (d. Caverzasio 6–1 4–6 6–1, lost Tauziat 6–4 4–6 6–2); *sf* Geneva (d. Krapl 6–1 6–3, Van Rensburg 7–5 6–7 6–1, Garrone 4–6 6–4 6–2, lost Paulus 7–5 6–3).

RADKA ZRUBAKOVA (Czechoslovakia)
Born Bratislava, 26 December 1970, and lives there; RH; 2HB; 5ft 6½in; 138lb; final 1990 WTA ranking 57; 1990 prize money $85,285.
1985: In Jun doubles with Holikova won US Open and r/u French Open. *1986:* (409) Won US Open Jun doubles with Novotna. *1987:* (143) Won Helsinki on satellite circuit. *1988:* (35) Last 16 Australian Open, sf Hamburg, qf Taranto, Berlin (d. Mandlikova) and Filderstadt. *1989:* (32) Won 1st tour singles title at Brussels, reached sf Adelaide and upset Sukova at Filderstadt. *1990:* Sf Bastad, upset Sukova again *en route* to qf Sydney and surprised Wiesner in reaching same stage at VS California. In doubles won Kitzbuhel with Langrova. *1990 HIGHLIGHTS – SINGLES: Australian Open* 1r (lost Miyagi 7–5 6–4), *French Open* 3r (d. Meier 6–1 6–2, Strandlund 6–1 7–6, lost Martinez 6–1 6–3), *Wimbledon* 1r (lost Jagerman 6–4 6–1), *US Open* 2r (d. Whitlinger 7–5 6–2, lost Fendick 6–2 6–3); *sf* Bastad (d. Tiezzi 6–4 6–2, Wood 6–1 6–4, Dopfer 6–2 6–4, lost Bartos 6–2 6–4). *1990 HIGHLIGHTS – DOUBLES:* [Langrova] *won* Kitzbuhel (d. Cecchini/Tarabini 6–0 6–4.

NATALIA ZVEREVA (USSR)
Born Minsk, 16 April 1971, and lives there; RH; 2HB; 5ft 8in; 138lb; final 1990 WTA ranking 12 singles, 5 (6) doubles; 1990 prize money $462,770.
Nicknamed Natasha. Coached by her father, Marat Zverev. *1985:* Won Bethesda on USTA circuit and World Jun Champs. *1986:* (92) In singles won Soviet Nat Champs (d. Savchenko), won Wimbledon Jun singles, USTA Bethesda, and was r/u to Rinaldi at VS Arkansas after qualifying, becoming youngest player to reach f of VS Series event, at 15 years 7 months. In doubles won French Open Jun and r/u Wimbledon Jun with Meskhi. *1987:* (19) ITF Jun Champ; won Nat Champ, Jun singles at French Open, Wimbledon and US Open and Jun doubles at French Open and Wimbledon with Medvedeva. Did not compete in Australian Open Jun. Last 16 Wimbledon, beating McNeil and extending Sabatini to 3s, won Taranto on Italian Satellite and reached f in Arkansas and Chicago in consecutive weeks. *1988:* (7) Played her best tennis to upset Navratilova last 16 French Open, but disappointed in her 1st GS f there, being totally outclassed 6–0 6–0 in 32 minutes by Graf. Last 16 Wimbledon, qf Olympics, r/u Eastbourne, New England and Montreal (d. Navratilova and Shriver back-to-back). In doubles with Savchenko r/u Wimbledon and won 2 titles. At VS Champs reached qf in singles and r/u in doubles. Voted WTA Newcomer of the Year. *1989:* (27) Was less successful in singles, winning no title, although she reached f FC Cup (d. Navratilova) and Moscow plus 3 more sf. However, in

doubles with Savchenko she won French Open, was r/u Wimbledon and VS Champs and reached 7 other f, winning 4. *1990:* Won 1st senior singles title at Brisbane (upset Sukova qf), following with Sydney the next week. Sf Washington, FC Cup, Amelia Island (extending Graf to 3s) and Berlin; qf Wimbledon. In doubles with Savchenko r/u French Open and won 3 titles; in mixed with Pugh won Australian Open and r/u US Open. Qualified for VS Champs in singles and doubles, losing 1r singles to Sanchez-Vicario and 1r doubles to Adams/McNeil. *1990 HIGHLIGHTS – SINGLES:* **Australian Open** 2r, seed 10 (d. Herreman 6–7 7–5 7–5, lost Wasserman 7–5 6–1), *French Open* last 16, seed 10 (d. Tanvier 6–4 7–6, Budarova 6–1 6–3, Martin 6–4 6–1, lost Maleeva Fragnière [seed 6] 6–4 6–2), *Wimbledon* qf, seed 11 (d. Harper 6–3 6–3, G. Fernandez 7–6 6–4, Magers 2–6 6–2 6–4, Schultz 6–2 6–2, lost Sabatini [seed 4] 6–2 2–6 8–6), *US Open* 2r, seed 14 (d. Quentrec 6–1 ret'd, lost Meskhi 6–4 6–0); *won* Brisbane (d. Jagerman 6–2 6–4, Inoue 7–5 6–4, Sukova 6–3 6–4, Schultz 6–4 6–1, McQuillan 6–4 6–0), *won* Sydney (d. Kijimuta 6–3 6–1, Golarsa 6–4 6–3, Demongeot 6–1 6–1, Halard 4–6 6–2 6–4, Frazier 6–3 2–6 6–2, Paulus 4–6 6–1 6–3); *sf* VS Washington (d. Cioffi 4–6 6–2 6–3, Provis 5–7 6–3 6–4, lost Garrison 6–2 3–6 6–3), *sf* FC Cup (d. Tarabini 6–4 6–2, Meskhi 6–2 6–1, Martinez 7–6 6–0, lost Capriati 6–0 6–4), *sf* Amelia Island (d. Grossman 6–2 6–2, Kanellopoulou 6–1 6–3, Garrison 6–1 2–6 7–6, lost Graf 7–6 6–7 6–1), *sf* Berlin (d. Grossman 4–6 6–3 6–2, Zrubakova 7–5 6–1, Wiesner 6–7 6–0 6–4, lost Graf 6–4 6–2). *1990 HIGHLIGHTS – DOUBLES:* (with Savchenko unless stated) *r/u French Open* (lost Novotna/Sukova 6–4 7–5); *won* Birmingham (d. Gregory/Magers 3–6 6–3 6–3), *won* Eastbourne (d. Fendick/Garrison 6–4 6–3), *won* Orlando (d. Bollegraf/McGrath 6–4 6–1); *r/u* Brisbane (lost Novotna/Sukova 6–3 7–5), [Paz] *r/u* FA Cup (lost Navratilova/Sanchez-Vicario 6–2 6–1), [Durie] *r/u* Brighton (lost Sukova/Tauziat 6–1 6–4). *1990 HIGHLIGHTS – MIXED DOUBLES: (with Pugh) won Australian Open* (d. R. Leach/Garrison 4–6 6–2 6–3), *r/u US Open* (lost Smylie/Woodbridge 6–4 6–2). *CAREER HIGHLIGHTS – SINGLES: Wimbledon – qf 1990. CAREER HIGHLIGHTS – DOUBLES:* (with Savchenko) *French Open – won 1989* (d. Graf/Sabatini 6–4 6–4), *r/u 1990; Wimbledon – r/u 1988* (lost Graf/Sabatini 6–3 1–6 12–10), *r/u 1989* (lost Novotna/Sukova 6–1 6–2); *VS Champs – r/u 1988* (lost Navratilova/Shriver 6–3 6–4), *r/u 1989* (lost Navratilova/Shriver 6–3 6–2). *CAREER HIGHLIGHTS – MIXED DOUBLES:* (with Pugh) *Australian Open – won 1990; US Open – r/u 1990.*

ALL-TIME GREATS

David Gray and John Barrett

WILMER LAWSON ALLISON (USA)
Born 8/1/04. Died 30/4/77. One of the greatest and most spectacular of American doubles specialists, he also gained some notable singles successes. Possessing a fierce smash, a serve 'with the kick of a Texas mustang', considerable power on the volley, and a fine backhand drive, he found an ideal doubles partner in John Van Ryn. They won at Wimbledon in **1929–30** and were runners-up in **1935.** They took the US title in **1931** and **1935** and reached the final in **1930/32/34/36.** His singles form was less consistent, but on his day could play brilliantly. He defeated Perry to win the US title in **1935,** and in **1930,** after beating Cochet, he was runner-up to Tilden at Wimbledon. Between **1929–35** he played in 45 D Cup rubbers, winning 18 out of 29 singles and 14 of his 16 doubles.

JOSEPH ASBOTH (Hungary)
Born 18/9/17. A stylish righthander whose victory in the **1947** French singles, when he beat Petra, Tom Brown and Sturgess, was Hungary's most important tennis success before their victory in the Saab King's Cup in 1976; 7 times nat champ; 6 times winner of the Hungarian int title; he played 1st at Wimbledon in **1939** and impressed those who saw him against Austin in 1 r. Lost to Bromwich in the **1948** sfs. From **1938–57** he played 41 D Cup rubbers in 16 ties.

ARTHUR ROBERT ASHE (USA)
Born 10/7/43. A cool, thoughtful, dogged competitor, he was the first black American to win the Wimbledon men's singles title and, in **1968,** playing as an amateur, he became the first US Open champion. Always happier on fast courts, he tried hard to succeed on clay but endured regular disappointments in Paris and never progressed further than the semi-finals **(1971)** in Rome. He was a semi-finalist at Wimbledon **1968–69** before surprising Connors in the **1975** final. He defeated Okker to win the US title in **1968** but in **1972** lost to Nastase after leading by two sets to one and 4–2 in the final. He won Australian singles **1970** and the WCT title **1975.** Refused a visa to South Africa in 1970, he broke through apartheid laws to play in Johannesburg **1973,** losing to Connors in the final and winning the doubles with Okker. After Missing most of the 1977 season, he regained his place among the leaders of the circuit in **1978** and reached match-point against McEnroe in the Masters final. Between **1963** and **1978,** he appeared in 18 Davis Cup ties, winning 27 out of 32 singles and one of two doubles. US Davis Cup captain **1980–85,** following his retirement from active play owing to a heart condition that had necessitated triple by-pass surgery.

CILLY AUSSEM (Germany)
Born 4/1/09. Died 22/3/63. Later the Contessa della Corta Brae. The first German to win the women's singles at Wimbledon. Her strokes were not strong but she was a model of steadiness and persistence. 'Quite small and more of a girl in appearance with round brown eyes and a cherub face', wrote Helen Wills. 'Her agility on court and the distance that she covers in spite of her shortness are really astonishing.' **1931** – when the Californian did not compete – was her best year. She beat Betty Nuthall in the French f and then defeated Hilde Krahwinkel in Wimbledon's only all-German final. That was a disappointing match, because both women were handicapped by blistered feet. Her victory compensated for an unlucky failure in **1930.** Then she slipped and sprained an ankle at 4–4 in the fs of her sf against Elizabeth Ryan and had to be carried from the court.

HENRY WILFRED AUSTIN (Great Britain)

Born 20/8/06. Bunny Austin's Wimbledon record was remarkable (and unlucky), but his most important contribution to British tennis was in the D Cup. The possessor of elegant groundstrokes, which compensated for a lack of power in his serving and smashing, he played many of the crucial singles, alongside Perry, in Britain's successful campaigns in the 1930s. A former Cambridge Univ captain, he played in 24 ties between *1929–37*, winning 36 of his 48 rubbers, all singles. He won 8 rubbers out of 12 and 5 out of 8 'live' rubbers in his 6 Challenge Rounds. At Wimbledon he failed only once to reach the qf or go further between *1929–39*. R/u to Vines *1932* and Budge *1938,* in sf *1929* and *1936/37,* and r/u to Henkel in *1937* French singles.

WILFRED BADDELEY (Great Britain)

Born 11/1/1872. Died 30/1/1929. Youngest winner – at 19 years, 5 months and 23 days – of Wimbledon singles in *1891* until Becker in 1985. Also won singles in *1892/95,* and doubles (with twin brother Herbert) *1891/94/95/96.*

MARCEL BERNARD (France)

Born 18/6/14. Shrewd and stylish, a canny lefthander with considerable touch, he is one of only two French players to have won in Paris since the days of the 'Musketeers' (the other is Noah, 1983); demonstrated his promise early, reaching the French singles sf and, with Boussus, the doubles in *1932,* still in sufficient form to be chosen for the French D Cup team in *1956.* In *1946* he won 5 set matches against Petra in the sf and Drobny in the final to take the French title; in sf on 3 other occasions; won the doubles with Borotra *(1936)* and with Petra *(1946)* and the mixed with Lollette Payot *(1935)* and Billie Yorke *(1936).* Between *1935–56* he played 42 D Cup rubbers in 25 ties and he has also served as president of the French Tennis Federation.

PAULINE MAY BETZ (USA)

Born 6/8/19. Now Mrs Addie. An agile, athletic competitor, who might have gained many more titles if the war had not interrupted international competition. She was ranked eighth in the US in *1939* and was the most successful player in wartime competitions there, winning the national title from *1942–44*. She won Wimbledon at a cost of only 20 games in *1946,* defeating Louise Brough 6–2 6–4 in the final. She and Miss Hart were runners-up to Miss Brough and Miss Osborne in the doubles and, if she was disappointed in Paris, where Miss Osborne beat her 1–6 8–6 7–5 in the final, after saving two match-points with drop-shots at 5–6 in the second set, she asserted her supremacy again at Forest Hills by defeating Doris Hart 11–9 6–3 in the final. Soon afterwards she turned professional.

BLANCHE BINGLEY (Great Britain)

Born 3/11/1863. Died 6/8/1946. Became Mrs Hillyard. One of the determined pioneers of women's tennis. She competed in the first women's tournament at Wimbledon in *1884* and lost to Maud Watson, the eventual champion, in sfs. The following year Miss Watson defeated her in f, but she avenged those failures by beating the champion in the challenge round in *1886.* That was the first of her six victories. Further successes followed in *1889, 1894, 1897, 1899* and *1900.* Only Lottie Dod, who retired in 1893, troubled her until Mrs Sterry ended her supremacy in 1901. Like many early players, her game was founded on a powerful forehand and strict command of length. A reluctant volleyer who invariably ran round her backhand, she was so quick and so fit that she was difficult to outmanoeuvre. She wore white gloves to give her a better grip and her follow-through on the forehand was said to have been so complete 'that her left shoulder was often a mass of bruises from the impact of the racket'. She married Commander G. W. Hillyard, secretary of the All England Club from 1907–24; altogether she competed in the championships 24 times.

PENELOPE DORA HARVEY BOOTHBY (Great Britain)

Born 2/8/1881. Died 22/2/1970. Became Mrs Green. One of the group of players from the county of Middlesex who dominated the early years of women's tennis at Wimbledon. She won one of the most exciting of the pre-1914 f, defeating Miss A. M. Morton 6–4 4–6 8–6 ('Few closer or more interesting struggles have ever been witnessed on the famous old court', wrote G. W. Hillyard) in **1909**, and lost the most dismal in the history of the championships to Mrs Lambert Chambers, who beat her 6–0 6–0, in the **1911** challenge round. Mrs Lambert Chambers had beaten her by the same score at the Beckenham tournament two weeks earlier and had allowed her only four games in the challenge round in **1910**. Somewhat fortunately she and Mrs McNair became Wimbledon's first women's doubles champions in 1913. They were down 2–6 2–4 to Mrs Lambert Chambers and Mrs Sterry in the final when Mrs Sterry fell and retired with a torn tendon. She and Mrs McNair were also semi-finalists in **1922**.

BJORN BORG (Sweden)
Born 6/6/56. One of the coolest match players the game has ever known, he matured early, winning his first important title, the **1974** Italian Open, shortly before his 18th birthday and the first of his six French Championships just after it. With fierce topspin on both his forehand and his double-handed backhand, a powerful serve and speedy court coverage plus an indomitable will to win, he was virtually invincible on European clay between **1974** and **1981** adding the French Open in **1975, 1978, 1979, 1980** and **1981** and a second Italian title in **1978** as well as the US Pro Championship on US clay in **1974, 1975** and **1976**. Never an instinctive volleyer, he confounded those observers who thought his game was unsuited to grass by setting a modern record at Wimbledon where he won five successive titles between **1976** and **1980**. Only William Renshaw, in the days of the Challenge Round, won more (1881–86). He learned to win indoors, taking the WCT title in **1976** and the Masters twice **(1979** and **1980)** and leading Sweden to their first D Cup success, a 3–2 victory over Czechoslovakia in Stockholm in **1975**. But he never solved the problems of the high, fast bounce and positive foothold of US hard courts. Four times he was beaten in the US Open final, twice by Connors **(1976, 1978)** and twice by McEnroe **(1980, 1981)**, the last three being on asphalt at Flushing Meadow. By the autumn of **1981** this great champion felt burnt out and virtually retired from the mainstream, restricting his play to exhibitions and special events. Although he attempted two comebacks, in **1982** and **1984**, he could no longer make the total commitment that had once made him supreme and turned to other interests. His legacy to Swedish tennis is immeasurable for he sparked the flame that has burned so brightly ever since through Wilander, Sundstrom, Jarryd, Nystrom and Edberg. His style of errorless, counter-attacking topspin inspired a whole generation of players around the world.–J.B.

JEAN BOROTRA (France)
Born 13/8/1898. A brilliantly agile volleyer and a shrewd player. One of the 'Four Musketeers' who won the D Cup for France from **1927–32**. Enthusiastic and popular, he continued to play competitive lawn tennis long past his 80th year, regularly appearing for France in International Club matches against Britain. Won Wimbledon singles **1924** and **1926** and doubles (with R. Lacoste) **1925** and (with J. Brugnon) **1932/33**. French singles **1924/31,** and doubles **1925/28/29/34/36**. Won Australian singles and doubles **1928**. Had long and spectacular covered court record, winning French singles title 12 times, British 11, and US 4. Played 54 D Cup rubbers **1922–47,** winning 36 in 32 ties.

MAUREEN CONNOLLY BRINKER (USA)
Born 17/9/34. Died 21/6/69. The most determined and concentrated of post-war women's champions she hit her groundstrokes with remorseless accuracy. Won US singles in **1951** at the age of 16 and thereafter lost only 4 matches – 2 to Doris Hart, one to Shirley Fry, and another to Beverley Fleitz – before she broke her leg in a riding accident in 1954 and retired. She was never beaten in singles at Wimbledon, winning **1952/53/54**. US singles **1951/52/ 53**. French singles **1953/54** and (with Mrs H. C. Hopman) doubles **1954**. Australian singles and doubles (with Julie Sampson) **1953**. Italian singles **1954**. She won all 9 of her W Cup rubbers and in **1953** she was the first woman to bring off the Grand Slam of the 4 major singles titles in the same year.

Above: (left) *Billie Jean King (USA) whose 20 Wimbledon titles are a record, and her old rival Margaret Court (AUS) who holds more Grand Slam crowns, 62, than anyone else.*
Below: (left) *Ilie Nastase twice a finalist at Wimbledon, and Bjorn Borg who beat him in 1976, the first of five consecutive victories for the Swede who plans to return to the men's circuit in 1991.* *(R & A Photofeatures)*

JOHN EDWARD BROMWICH (Australia)
Born 14/11/18. A gracefully unorthodox player whose career might have been even more successful if it had not been interrupted by World War II. Ambidextrous but using both hands on the forehand, he used a very light, softly strung racket to control the ball with great subtlety. He won the Australian singles in **1939** and regained the title from Quist in **1946.** Those were his only major singles victories, although he was agonisingly close to success in f of **1948** Wimbledon when he lost to Falkenburg after leading 5–2 in the fs and holding three match-points. But it was in doubles, mostly with Quist or Sedgman, that he earned most honours. He won at Wimbledon in **1948** (with Sedgman) **/50** (with Quist), took the US title three times, and he and Quist ruled in Australia from **1938–40** and **1946–50.** Won the Wimbledon mixed with Louise Brough, **1947/48,** and played in 53 D Cup rubbers between **1937–50.**

SIR NORMAN EVERARD BROOKES (Australia)
Born 14/11/1877. Died 10/1/1968. The first overseas winner of men's singles at Wimbledon. Left-handed and a notable volleyer, he lost to H. L. Doherty in Challenge Round on first visit to Wimbledon 1905. Won singles and doubles (with A. F. Wilding) **1907** and **1914** and Australian singles in **1911** and doubles in **1924** with J. O. Anderson. With Wilding won the D Cup for Australasia in **1907.** Between **1905–20** he played 39 rubbers and was 6 times a member of a side which won the Challenge Round. Returned to Wimbledon in **1924** at 46 and reached the 4r.

ALTHEA LOUISE BROUGH (USA)
Born 11/3/23. Now Mrs Clapp. An aggressive server and volleyer, she played a major part in establishing American domination of women's tennis immediately after World War II. Won Wimbledon singles **1948/49/50** and again in **1955** after the retirement of Maureen Connolly, who beat her in **1952** and **1954** f, US in **1947,** and Australian, **1950.** She and Margaret Osborne du Pont formed a redoubtable doubles partnership, winning 5 times at Wimbledon and 3 times in Paris, and holding the US title from **1942–50** and **1955/56/57.** She was mixed doubles champ at Wimbledon **1946/47/48/50** and took all 3 titles in **1948** and **1950.** She played 22 W Cup rubbers between **1946–57** and was never beaten.

JACQUES BRUGNON (France)
Born 11/6/1895. Died 20/3/1978. The doubles specialist of the 'Four Musketeers', he gained most of his early success with Cochet and then formed a partnership with Borotra, which was still capable of reaching the **1939** French f, when he was 44 and Borotra 40, and coming three times within a point of the title. He and Borotra returned to Wimbledon and reached the 3r in **1948.** Won Wimbledon doubles **1926/28** (Cochet) **/32/33** (Borotra). Between **1927–34** won French doubles 3 times with Cochet and twice with Borotra. Also Australian doubles (with Borotra) in **1928.** Reached singles sf at Wimbledon, **1926.** Played 31 D Cup doubles and 6 singles **1921–34.**

JOHN DONALD BUDGE (USA)
Born 13/6/15. The first player to bring off the Grand Slam of the 4 historic singles titles in one year – **1938.** A relentless competitor with a majestic backhand he won all 3 titles at Wimbledon in **1937** and **1938.** Won doubles (with G. Mako) and mixed (with Alice Marble). US singles **1937/38** and doubles (with Mako) **1936/38.** French and Australian singles **1938** and between **1935–38** won 25 out of 29 D Cup rubbers in 11 ties. Turned professional in **1938.**

MARIA ESTHER ANDION BUENO (Brazil)
Born 11/10/39. The most gracefully artistic of post-war women's champions. For nearly a decade her rivalry with Margaret Court provided the principal excitement of the women's game, but at the end she was plagued by injury. Won Wimbledon singles **1959/60/64,** and doubles (with Althea Gibson) **1958,** (with Darlene Hard) **1960/63,** (with Billie Jean King) **/65,** and (with Nancy Gunter) **/66.** US singles **1959/63/64/66** and doubles (with Darlene

Hard) **1960/62,** (with Nancy Gunter) **/66,** and (with Margaret Court) **/68.** French doubles (with Darlene Hard) **1960.** Australian doubles (with Christine Truman) **1960.** Italian singles, **1958/61/65.**

MAY SUTTON BUNDY (USA)
Born in Plymouth, England, 25/9/1886. Died 4/10/1975. In **1905** the first overseas player to win a Wimbledon title. The seventh and youngest child of a British naval officer, Captain A. de G. Sutton, she learnt tennis on asphalt courts after her family moved to California in 1893. She was forceful and vigorous with a disconcerting top-spin forehand. F. R. Burrow commented: 'She took a deep breath before every stroke and then hit the ball with all her force to the accompaniment of a very audible expiration.' After winning the US singles and doubles in **1904** she went, aged 18, to Wimbledon **1905** and defeated the holder, Miss Douglass, in the Challenge Round. Miss Douglass regained the title the following year, but then lost a third battle with the Californian in **1907.** After winning the US Clay Court singles **1912,** Miss Sutton married Thomas Bundy, 3 times a US doubles champ. She played doubles in the **1925** W Cup and in **1929** returned to Wimbledon at 42 to defeat Eileen Bennett, seeded 4, and reach the qf. She was still playing 44 years later. Her daughter Dorothy represented the US 3 times in the W Cup and won the Australian singles 1938 and a nephew, John Doeg, was US champ in 1930.

DOROTHEA LAMBERT CHAMBERS (Great Britain)
Born 3/9/1878. Died 7/1/1960. Née Douglass. The most successful British woman player before 1914, she won Wimbledon singles 7 times and lost dramatically to Suzanne Lenglen in **1919** Challenge Round after holding 2 match-points. Played in **1926** W Cup – 23 years after first success at Wimbledon. The daughter of an Ealing vicar, she became a coach in **1928.** Won Wimbledon singles **1903/04/06/10/11/13/14.**

HENRI COCHET (France)
Born 14/12/01. Died April 1987. The great instinctive genius of lawn tennis, swift and imaginative, a master of the volley and half-volley, whose play could rise to dizzy heights and sometimes slip to unexpected disaster. Won Wimbledon singles **1927/29** and doubles (with J. Brugnon) **1926/28.** US singles **1928.** French singles **1922/26/28/30/32** and doubles (with Brugnon) **1927/30/32.** With the other 'Musketeers', he played success-fully in 6 Challenge Rounds. Between **1922** and **1933,** when he turned professional, he won 44 D Cup rubbers out of 58 in 26 ties. After the war reinstated as an amateur.

JAMES SCOTT CONNORS (USA)
Born Belleville, Ill., 2/9/52. A pugnacious and competitive left-hander whose grand-mother and mother Gloria, herself a fine local player, brought him up to believe he could take on the world and win. Moving to California as a teenager he received expert help from the two Pancho's – Gonzales and Segura – as he won the NCAA singles in **1971** as a freshman at UCLA. Over the next eighteen years he set new standards of ground-stroke aggression that made him the best returner of the serve of his generation. His double-handed backhand and early ball forehand, both hit flat, fast and fearlessly for the lines, plus a boundless belief in his own ability that bordered on cockiness, brought him a record 109 professional tournament wins from his first in Jacksonville **1972** to his last in Tel Aviv **1989.** His two Wimbledon singles titles **1974/82** were further apart than any since Tilden's second and third wins **(1921/30).** In the first he destroyed 39-year-old Rosewall and then beat the little Australian again even more severely in the US Open final two months later to win the first of five US Open titles **1974/76/78/82/83.** He is the only man to have won that title on three different surfaces, grass **1974,** US clay **1976** and hard **1978.** He won the Australian Open **1974** on grass but was never prepared to compromise on European clay, a surface he failed to master despite frequent attempts. His 19 career doubles titles include two Grand Slam crowns, Wimbledon **1973** and US Open **1975,** both with Nastase whose outrageous behaviour on court he began to copy. His vulgar gestures and occasional out-bursts against authority were the only blemishes in a remarkably durable career that made

him the most popular player of the day and earned him the No. 1 computer ranking for a record 159 consecutive weeks 29th July *1974* – 16th August *1977* and 263 weeks altogether. He played only three years of *Davis Cup* tennis'. *1976/81/84* winning 10 and losing 3 singles rubbers in 7 ties.–J.B.

ASHLEY JOHN COOPER (Australia)
Born 15/9/36. A strong and determined competitor who maintained Australia's command of the international game after Hoad and Rosewall turned professional. After being overwhelmed by Hoad in the *1957* f at Wimbledon, he returned to beat Fraser in a stern test of endurance in *1958*. He was US champion *1958* and won Australia *1957–58*. His doubles victories included Australia *1958,* France *1957–58* and US *1958*. He played singles when Australia successfully defended the D Cup in *1957* and *1958,* winning one rubber in each match. He beat Seixas and lost to Mackay *1957* and beat Mackay and lost to Olmedo *1958*.

CHARLOTTE COOPER (Great Britain)
Born 22/9/1870. Died 10/10/1970. Became Mrs Sterry. One of the first successful women volleyers, she won at Wimbledon *1895/96/98/1901/08*. Overshadowed at first by Mrs Hillyard – her first three victories were gained in years when the older player did not compete – she defeated her at last in *1901,* the year of her marriage, after losing to Mrs Hillyard in four previous matches at the championships. In *1902* she lost in the famous re-played challenge round to Muriel Robb (they stopped at 4–6 13–11 on the first evening, then began again and Miss Robb won 7–5 6–1) and then regained the title in *1908* after beating Mrs Lambert Chambers in the quarter-finals. She reached the all-comers' final in *1912* and took Mrs McNair to 9–7 in the third set of a qf in *1913*. Her attacking spirit delighted her contemporaries. 'Her smiling good temper and sportsmanship made her as popular a player as ever went on to the Centre Court', wrote Burrow. 'She had a consti-tution like the proverbial ostrich. She never knew what it was to be tired and was never sick or sorry', said Hillyard.

BARON GOTTFRIED VON CRAMM (Germany)
Born 7/7/09. Died in car accident in Egypt 9/11/76. An elegant stylist and Germany's most successful player. Won French singles *1934/36* and doubles (with H. Henkel) *1937,* and German singles *1932/33/34/35/48/49* and doubles *1948/49/53/55*. Like F. S. Stolle, he was losing singles finalist at Wimbledon for 3 successive years – 1935–37. Won Wimble-don mixed (with Hilda Krahwinkel) *1933* and US doubles (with Henkel) *1937*. Won 82 D Cup rubbers out of 102 in 37 ties between *1932–53*.

JOHN HERBERT CRAWFORD (Australia)
Born 22/3/08. Classic stylist, he beat H. E. Vines in *1933* in one of the greatest of all Wimbledon f. Won Wimbledon doubles (with A. K. Quist) *1935*. French singles *1933* and doubles (with Quist) *1935,* Australian singles *1931/33* and doubles (with H. C. Hopman) *1929/30,* (with E. F. Moon) *1932,* and (with V. B. McGrath) *1935*. Won 36 out of 58 D Cup rubbers between *1928–37*.

DWIGHT FILLEY DAVIS (USA)
Born 5/7/1879. Died 28/11/1945. The donor of the D Cup, the trophy at stake in the international team championship. A Harvard undergraduate, he played against the British Isles in the first two matches of that competition, winning a single and partnering Hol-combe Ward successfully in the doubles in *1900* and, with Ward again, losing to the Dohertys in the doubles in *1902*. A lefthander, he won the US doubles with Ward from *1899–1901,* retiring undefeated, and also the all-comers' final at Wimbledon in *1901,* only to fall to the Dohertys. He was President of the US LTA in *1923,* US Secretary of War 1925–29 and later Governor-General of the Philippines.

MAX DECUGIS (France)
Born 24/9/1882. Died 6/9/1978. The first great French player. He spent his schooldays in England and won his first tournaments there. Short, quick, and wiry, he was an aggressive competitor, whom Lawrie Doherty described as 'the most promising young player in the world'. He dominated French tennis from *1903,* when he won in Paris for the first time, to the outbreak of World War I, winning the singles title 8 times in 12 years and the doubles from *1902–14* and again in *1920* when the Champs were resumed. He was still playing well enough to reach the singles final in *1923* when he was 41. By that time the age of the 'Musketeers' was dawning. Although he competed regularly at Wimbledon, he never progressed beyond the singles sf *(1911/12)* but, with Gobert, he gained France's first title by winning the doubles in *1911.*

CHARLOTTE DOD (Great Britain)
Born 24/9/1871. Died 27/6/1960. The first lawn tennis prodigy. Won the first of 5 Wimbledon titles in *1887* at the age of 15 years and 10 months. When she retired, she became an international golfer and hockey player. Nicknamed the 'Little Wonder', she won Wimbledon singles *1887/88/91/92/93.*

HUGH LAWRENCE DOHERTY (Great Britain)
Born London 8/10/1875. Died 21/8/1919. Learnt game with elder brother, Reginald Frank ('Reggie'), at Westminster School. Played for Cambridge Univ against Oxford in 1896–98 and developed into one of the most spectacular, aggressive, stylish, and successful of British players. 'Lawrie' Doherty was celebrated for smashing and volleying, and for speed about the court. With his brother, formed one of the greatest doubles partnerships in the history of the game. Won all-comers' singles at Wimbledon, *1898,* and singles champ *1902–06.* Doubles champ (with R. F. Doherty) *1897–1901, 1903–05.* First overseas player to win US singles, *1903,* and doubles, *1902/03.* In 5 D Cup challenge rounds, *1902–06,* he was never beaten, winning 7 singles rubbers and 5 doubles.

REGINALD FRANK DOHERTY (Great Britain)
Born London 14/10/1872. Died 29/12/1910. The senior partner of the great Doherty combination and the most notable stylist of early lawn tennis. Contemporary observers called his backhand, produced with back swing, full follow-through and remarkable touch, 'a model of perfection'. Was Wimbledon singles champ *1897–1900* and doubles champ *1897–1901* and *1903–05.* Reached the doubles challenge round at Wimbledon for first time with H. A. Nisbet in 1896. Thereafter he and his brother, H. L. Doherty, were beaten only by S. H. Smith and F. L. Riseley at Wimbledon. They lost to this pair in 1902, then beat them in the next three challenge rounds before falling to them again in 1906. The Dohertys won the US doubles in *1902/03.* Won South African singles and doubles, *1909.*

JAROSLAV DROBNY (Great Britain)
Born 12/10/21. Exiled himself from Czechoslovakia in 1949, became Egyptian subject in 1950 and a naturalised Briton in 1960. One of the great post-war clay court competitors with tremendous left-hand serve and smash, and delicate touch, he played in some of Wimbledon's most dramatic and emotional matches and eventually won the singles in *1954* at the age of 33. In *1946* he beat Kramer, the favourite; he lost to Schroeder in the *1949* f; in *1950* he let a two-set lead slip against Sedgman; Mottram surprised him in *1951;* he fell to Sedgman again in the *1952* f; and in *1953* he never recovered from beating Patty 8–6 16–18 3–6 8–6 12–10 in Wimbledon's second longest singles. The following year, when his chance seemed to be slipping away, he beat Rosewall, then 19, in f. He won in Paris in *1951/52* (after another series of dramatic failures), Italy *1950/51/53* and Germany *1950.* In *1946/47/48/49* he played in 43 D Cup rubbers, and won 37.

FRANCOISE DURR (France)
Born 25/12/42. Now Mrs Browning. The outstanding French woman player of the 1960s and 1970s. Shrewd and unorthodox, particularly in her serve and on the backhand, she

excelled in doubles. She gained her major singles successes in **1967** when she won the French and German titles and reached the US semi-finals, but in doubles won a host of titles with a variety of partners, including five successive French victories – with Gail Sheriff (later Mrs Chanfreau and now Mrs Lovera) **1967** and **1970/71,** and with Ann Jones, **1968/69.** Won US doubles **1972** with Betty Stove, and Italian and South African titles **1969** with Jones. She failed, however, in six Wimbledon doubles finals between **1965** and **1975.** Won Wimbledon mixed doubles with Tony Roche **1976** and the French with Jean-Claude Barclay in **1968, 1971** and **1973.**

ROY STANLEY EMERSON (Australia)
Born 3/11/36. A remarkable athlete, 'lean, keen, and trained to the last ounce', who led Australia's international challenge for five years after Laver turned professional in 1962. A Queenslander, he won Wimbledon singles **1964/65** but injury in 1966 spoilt his chance of equalling Perry's record of three successive titles. Won the doubles with Fraser **1959/61,** US singles **1961/64** and doubles **1959/60** (with Fraser) and **1965/66** (with Stolle), Australian singles **1961** and **1963/64/65/66/67** and doubles **1960/66.** On clay courts won the French singles **1963/67,** Italian **1959/61/66** and German **1967** and his most interesting doubles achievement was to take the French title from **1960/61/63/64/65** with five different partners, Fraser **1960/62,** Laver **1961,** Santana **1963,** Fletcher **1964,** and Stolle **1965.** He won 36 of his 40 D Cup rubbers and played in 9 successive challenge rounds between **1959** and **1967.**

CHRISTINE MARIE EVERT (USA)
Born Fort Lauderdale, Fl., 21/12/54. Now Mrs Andy Mill (married 30th July 1988). Coached by father Jimmy in Fort Lauderdale to become the most consistent back-court player of her generation: she won at least one Grand Slam singles title every year from **1974** to **1986** during which period her friendly rivalry with Martina Navratilova dominated the women's game. When she and Jimmy Connors (who were engaged at the time) won the two Wimbledon singles titles in **1974** with their double-handed backhands they legitimised the stroke and set a fashion that became a world trend. Her metronomic consistency, unshakeable concentration and fearless resolve to go for her shots were legendary and earned her more professional titles (157) than any other player, male or female, during the open era plus a fortune in prize money ($8,896,195). She competed for 19 consecutive years at the US Open and reached 9 finals, 8 semi-finals and was twice beaten in the quarter-finals, including her last year **1989** when she won her 101st match at these Championships, a record. As a sixteen-year-old, in **1971,** she reached the first of four consecutive semi-finals on grass at Forest Hills. In **1975/76/77** she won the title there on US clay and repeated that success on hard courts at Flushing Meadow in **1978/80/82,** by which time her first husband, John Lloyd (married 17th April 1979, divorced April 1987) had helped her to become a much better volleyer. In 13 challenges in Paris between 1973 and 1988 she won seven of the nine finals she contested (**1974/75/79/80/83/85/86**) and only in her last year failed to reach the semi-final, losing in the third round to Arantxa Sanchez-Vicario. She competed at Wimbledon every year from **1972** to **1989** and only in **1983** (when she was ill and lost to Kathy Jordan) did she fail to reach the semi-finals. She was the champion 3 times (**1974/76/81**), a finalist 7 times (**1973/78/79/80/82/84/85**) and a semi-finalist 7 times (**1972/75/77/86/87/88/89**). She competed in the Australian Open six times between **1974** and **1988**, winning the title in **1982** and **1984** and reaching the final in **1974/81/85/88.** Her 18 Grand Slam singles titles place her third behind Margaret Court (26) and Helen Wills Moody (19) on the list of great champions. Her streak of 125 consecutive wins on clay courts August **1973** – May **1979** is an all-time record and her prodigious achievement in reaching the semi-finals or better at 52 of her last 56 Grand Slams is unlikely ever to be equalled. She represented the United States eight times in the *Federation Cup* and won all but two of her 42 singles rubbers and 16 of 18 doubles rubbers in 42 ties between **1977** and **1989**. She was unbeaten in 26 Wightman Cup singles rubbers and won 8 of the 12 doubles rubbers she contested in 13 ties between **1971** and **1985**.–J.B.

ROBERT FALKENBURG (USA)
Born 29/1/26. Won the US Junior Championship in *1943–44* and came to Europe in *1947* with the reputation of possessing the fastest service in the US. He won at Queen's Club, but lost to Pails in qf at Wimbledon and then won the doubles with Kramer, defeating Mottram and Sidwell in f. The following year he won one of Wimbledon's most dramatic f, defeating Bromwich 7–5 0–6 6–2 3–6 7–5 after saving three match-points as 3–5 in 5s. He was born in New York, learnt most of his tennis in Los Angeles and moved to Brazil, for whom he played in D Cup on a residential qualification.

NEALE ANDREW FRASER (Australia)
Born 3/10/33. A consistently aggressive lefthander, with a plain, direct serve and volley game, he was trained by Hopman, winning 18 of 21 D Cup rubbers between *1958* and *1963,* and later captained the Australian team which recaptured the trophy at Cleveland in *1973* and at Melbourne in *1978/83.* Fraser started his Wimbledon career in the qualifying competition and ended by winning the singles in *1960* after a remarkable escape in the qf. Buchholz, who had held 5 match-points against him, retired with cramp. He won the doubles with Emerson *1959/61* and mixed with du Pont in *1962* – the year in which he and his brother, John, a Melbourne doctor, both reached the singles sf. Neither got through to the f. He won the US singles *1959/60* and doubles *1957/59/60,* the French doubles *1958/60/62,* and Australian doubles *1957/58/62.*

SHIRLEY JUNE FRY (USA)
Born 30/6/27. Now Mrs Irvin. A persistent competitor, whose most notable performances were in doubles. She was first ranked in the top ten in the US in 1944, but she did not gain her two major singles successes until *1956* when she won both Wimbledon and Forest Hills. Until then she had always been thwarted by fellow-Americans. She won the Wimbledon doubles from *1951–53* with Doris Hart, losing only four games in capturing the title in *1953* and beat Helen Fletcher and Jean Quertier 6–0 6–0 in sf and Julie Sampson and Maureen Connolly by the same score in f. They won the US title *1951–54.* Her other successes included the Wimbledon mixed, with Seixas, *1956,* the Australian singles and doubles, with Althea Gibson, *1957,* and the French singles, *1951,* and doubles, with Hart, *1950–53.* She played in six W Cup contests, winning 10 matches and losing twice.

ALTHEA GIBSON (USA)
Born 25/8/27. The first black player to dominate international lawn tennis, relying on fierce serving and considerable strength and reach. Won Wimbledon singles *1957/58* and (doubles (with Angela Buxton) *1957* and (with Maria Bueno) */58.* US singles *1957/58.* French singles and doubles (with Angela Buxton) *1956.* Australian doubles (with Shirley Fry) *1957.* Italian singles *1956.* W Cup *1957/58,* turned professional *1958.*

ANDRE HENRI GOBERT (France)
Born 30/9/1890. Died 6/12/1951. Wallis Myers described him as 'perhaps the greatest indoor player of all time'. With Decugis, he gained France's first Wimbledon title by defeating the holders, Ritchie and Wilding, in *1911.* Although they were beaten by Dixon and Roper Barrett the following year, the brilliant Gobert's compensation was a place in the all-comers' singles f in which he lost to the experienced A. W. Gore. He won the French covered court title from *1911–13* and again in *1920* and the British covered court event in *1911–12* and again from *1920–22.* He first played in D Cup in *1911* and his career ended when the 'Musketeers' arrived in *1922.* He also won two Olympic gold medals in *1912.*

RICHARD (PANCHO) GONZALES (USA)
Born 9/5/28. A dramatic and spectacular competitor, who was undoubtedly the best player in the world for most of the 1950s. He turned pro in 1949 after winning the US singles in *1948/49,* taking the US Clay Court title *1948/49,* the US indoor title *1949,* and winning the doubles in Paris and at Wimbledon – in his only amateur appearances there – in *1949* with Parker. Thereafter he played his brilliant, angry tennis away from the main arenas of the

game until, at last, open competition was allowed. By then he was 40, but he played one last great match for the Wimbledon crowd. In *1969* he beat Pasarell 22–24 1–6 16–14 6–3 11–9 in 5hr 12min – the longest singles seen at Wimbledon.

EVONNE FAY GOOLAGONG (Australia)
Born 31/7/51. Now Mrs Roger Cawley (married in 1975). One of the most naturally gifted of champions, she was the first of her Aborigine race to excel at the game. Suddenly in *1971* at the age of 19, 3 years before her coach Vic Edwards had forecast she would, she swept through both the French Championships and Wimbledon on a cloud of inspiration to win her first major titles. Although she reached the Wimbledon final again the following year and twice more, in *1975* and *1976*, it was not until *1980* that she won again – four years after the birth of her daughter, Kelly. This was the first win by a mother since Dorothea Lambert-Chambers's success in 1914. The nine-year gap between her championships was also the greatest since Bill Tilden's wins in 1921 and 1930. She was always more at home on faster surfaces where her beautifully instinctive volleying paid handsome dividends and she won her native Australian Open on that surface four times – *1974, 1975, 1976, 1978*. She was always a competent player on clay but tended to be rather erratic as her famous 'walkabouts' led to extravagant errors. Nevertheless, besides the French Open in *1971* she also won the Italian title in *1973*. The other highlights of her singles career were the victories in the South African Championships *(1972)* and the Virginia Slims Champs *(1974, 1976)*. She was a good doubles player and won once at Wimbledon *(1974)*, four times in Melbourne *(1971, 1974, 1975, 1976)* and twice in Johannesburg *(1971, 1972)*. In seven years of Fed Cup duty for Australia from *1971* to *1982* she won 33 of the 38 rubbers she contested in 24 ties. – J.B.

ARTHUR WENTWORTH GORE (Great Britain)
Born 2/1/1868. Died 1/12/1928. Wimbledon's oldest champ and probably the most persistent and industrious competitor in the history of the Champs. He played there for the first time in 1888 and although the Dohertys, Brookes, and Wilding were among his contemporaries, won the singles 3 times *1901* and *1908/09* and, at the age of 44 years and 6 months, won the right to challenge Wilding for the title in *1912*. That was his seventh appearance in the challenge round in 13 years. He was almost entirely a forehand player, hitting the ball flat with the racket in a dead line with his outstretched arm. His lightness of foot enabled him to protect his backhand which was no more than a safe push. He competed at every Wimbledon between *1888–1927* and captained the first British D Cup team at Boston in 1900, reaching sf US Champs on that trip.

KAREN HANTZE (USA)
Born 11/12/42. Now Mrs Susman. One of the new generation of aggressive Californians who arrived on the international scene at the start of the 1960s, she won the doubles at Wimbledon with the 17-year-old Billie Jean Moffitt in *1961* and then defeated Vera Sukova in the *1962* singles final. Marriage and motherhood restricted her tennis, but she won US doubles (again with Moffitt) *1964.* She played W Cup *1960–62* and *1965,* winning six of her nine matches, and Fed Cup *1965.*

DARLENE R. HARD (USA)
Born 6/1/36. An energetic volleyer, a shrewd tactician, and one of the best doubles players of her generation, she won the US singles in *1960* and *1961* and the French singles *1960,* but she failed in both her Wimbledon finals, losing to Althea Gibson in *1957* and Maria Bueno *1960.* She won the Wimbledon doubles, with Gibson *1957*, Jeanne Arth *1959* and twice with Bueno *(1960, 1963)* and the mixed in *1957* (with Rose), *1959–60* (with Laver). She won the US doubles six times and the French doubles three times. Perhaps her most surprising American success came in *1969,* some years after she had retired from regular competition, when she and Francoise Durr defeated Margaret Court and Virginia Wade 0–6 6–3 6–4 in f.

DORIS HART (USA)

Born 20/6/25. In spite of childhood illness which impeded her movement, she became one of the subtlest and most graceful of post-war competitors. Won Wimbledon singles *1951,* doubles (with Pat Todd) *1947* and (with Shirley Fry) *1951/52/53.* US singles *1954/55* and doubles (with Shirley Fry) *1951/52/53/54.* French singles *1950/52* and doubles (with Pat Todd) *1948* and (with Shirley Fry) *1950/51/53.* Australian singles *1949* and doubles (with Louise Brough) *1950.* Italian singles *1951/53* and South African singles *1952.* Also won many mixed titles, notably with E. V. Seixas at Wimbledon *1953/54/55.* Turned professional *1955.*

ADRIANNE SHIRLEY HAYDON (Great Britain)

Born 17/10/38. Now Mrs Jones. A shrewd, persistent lefthander, who reached sf at Wimbledon 7 times in 10 years, she captured the title at last in *1969* after beating Margaret Court in sf and Billie Jean King, to whom she had been r/u in *1967,* in f. She achieved international fame as a table tennis player, but decided to concentrate on lawn tennis after being r/u in three events in the 1957 World Table Tennis Champs. She won the French title in *1961/66,* Rome in *1966* and was twice r/u at Forest Hills *1961/67.* She took the French doubles (with Francoise Durr) in *1968/69* and won the Wimbledon mixed with Stolle in *1969.* Her W Cup record – 15 successful rubbers out of 32 in 12 matches – is another remarkable illustration of her tenacity and consistency.

ROBERT ANTHONY JOHN HEWITT (South Africa)

Born 12/1/40 in Sydney, Australia. He moved to South Africa in the early 1960s and started to represent that country when his residential qualification matured in 1967. A big brooding volcano of a man, he had deceptively fine touch and became one of the greatest right-court returners of the serve of modern times. He enjoyed two careers – first with fellow-Australian Fred Stolle and then with South Africa's Frew McMillan. With Stolle he won Wimbledon twice *(1962/64)* the Australian Championship twice *(1963/64)* and the Italian twice *(1963/64),* and with McMillan he added three more Wimbledon crowns *(1967/74/78)*, two German *(1967/70)*, one French *(1972)*, one US *(1977)*, one Masters :*(1977)* and one WCT *(1974)* title as well as the Italian in *1967* and four at home in South Africa *(1967/70/72/74)*. He registered four major mixed doubles successes with three different partners, winning in Australia with Jan Lehane in *1961*, in Paris with Billie Jean King in *1970* and twice at Wimbledon with his pupil, Greer Stevens, in *1977* and *1979*. He represented South Africa in D Cup *1967–74* and was a member of the successful team of *1974* that won by default from India. – J.B.

LEWIS ALAN HOAD (Australia)

Born 23/11/34. Capable of generating fierce power with great ease, he was one of the 'boy wonders' Harry Hopman produced to beat the US in the *1953* D Cup match. The other was Rosewall, 21 days his senior, who was to thwart his attempt on the Grand Slam in *1956* by beating him at Forest Hills, in the last of the 4 great f. That year Hoad had won the Australian and French titles, and had beaten Rosewall at Wimbledon. In *1957* he defeated Ashley Cooper in one of the most devastating Wimbledon f ever and then turned professional, but constant back trouble spoilt his pro career and also ended his attempt to return to the circuit when the game was opened to the pros. He won the Wimbledon doubles in *1953/55/56,* the US doubles in *1956,* the French doubles in *1953,* and the Australian doubles in *1953/56/57.* He won 17 rubbers out of 21 in D Cup play between *1953–56.*

HAZEL HOTCHKISS (USA)

Born 20/12/1886. Died 5/12/1974. Became Mrs G. Wightman. One of the most remarkable and enthusiastic competitors that the game has known. She was the donor of the W Cup and a considerable influence in American tennis for more than 60 years. She gained the first of her four US singles titles *(1909/10/11/19)* in 1909 and won the US indoor doubles for the 10th *(1919/21/24/27/28/29/30/31/33/43)* and last time in 1943. A remarkable volleyer with great speed about the court, she and Helen Wills were never beaten in doubles. They won the Wimbledon doubles in *1924* and the US doubles – a title which she had won on 4 other occasions – in *1924–28*. She captained the first US W Cup team in 1923 and between *1923–31* won 3 doubles rubbers in 5 matches.

HELEN HULL JACOBS (USA)
Born 6/8/08. A tenacious competitor, notable for duels with fellow-Californian, Helen Wills Moody, 5 times a Wimbledon finalist between *1929–39* but won only in *1936*. US singles *1932/33/34/35* and doubles (with Sarah Palfrey Fabyan) *1930/34/35*. Italian singles *1934*.

WILLIAM JOHNSTON (USA)
Born 2/11/1894. Died 1/6/1946. 'Little Bill', a Californian, small in physique but a brilliant volleyer and the possessor of a formidable top-spin forehand, was 'Big Bill' Tilden's principal rival at home in the first half of the 1920s. He defeated McLoughlin to win the US singles in *1915*, the first year at Forest Hills, lost to Williams in the *1916* final and then regained the title by beating Tilden in straight sets in *1919*. Tilden gained his revenge the following year and, although Johnston reached the final five times between *1920* and *1925*, Tilden always frustrated him. He beat Hunter in the *1923* Wimbledon final, losing only one set in the tournament. He won the US doubles with Griffin *1915/16* and *1920* and played in eight D Cup challenge rounds, winning 18 of his 21 D Cup rubbers.

BILLIE JEAN MOFFITT KING (USA)
Born 22/11/43. Perhaps the most important single figure in the history of tennis, as player, stateswoman, innovator and entrepreneur (usually with lawyer husband Larry King, whom she married in 1965), she has worked tirelessly to gain recognition and respect for the women's game. One of the founders of the women's pro tour in *1970*, twice President of the Women's Tennis Association, and the prime mover behind Team Tennis, she has been involved in most aspects of the game. As a player her natural exuberance and bubbling personality suited her attacking serve-and-volley game and made her a fearsome opponent. She will best be remembered for her 'Battle of the Sexes' against Bobby Riggs at the Houston Astrodome on 20 September, *1973* where the world's largest-ever crowd of 30,492 and some 50 million more around the world on TV, saw her win 6–4 6–3 6–3. In *1979* she achieved her 20th Wimbledon title to pass the record she had jointly shared with fellow-Californian Elizabeth Ryan who, ironically, had died on the eve of that unique achievement. Her unparalleled record comprises 6 singles – *1966, 1967, 1968, 1972, 1973* and *1975*; 10 women's doubles – *1961, 1962, 1965, 1967, 1968, 1970, 1971, 1972, 1973* and *1979*; 4 mixed doubles – *1967, 1971, 1973* and *1974*. She first played at Wimbledon in *1961* and won the doubles with Karen Hantze. At her last appearance in *1983* she was competing for the 22nd year (she had not entered in *1981*) and reached the mixed doubles final with Steve Denton when she played her 265th and last match at Wimbledon. It was also her 29th final and, as they lost to John Lloyd and Wendy Turnbull 7–5 in the final set, she was losing at that stage for only the 9th time. She was almost as successful in her own US Championships where she won 13 titles, 4 in singles – *1967, 1971, 1972, 1974*, five in doubles – *1964, 1967, 1974, 1978, 1980* and four in mixed – *1967, 1971, 1973, 1976* and, in addition she became the only woman to win US National titles on all four surfaces – grass, clay, hard and indoor – a feat she repeated in doubles with Rosie Casals with whom she had most of her major doubles successes. She won the French Open singles and doubles in *1972* and the mixed in *1967* and *1970* and was successful in singles and mixed at the Australian Open in *1968*, the first year of open tennis. Her 39 Grand Slam titles put her second only to Margaret Court who won 62. She was also the singles and doubles champion of Italy *(1970)* and of Germany *(1971)* and won the South African title 3 times *1966, 1967, 1969)*. With 21 winning rubbers from 26 played in 9 W Cup matches between *1961* and *1978*, plus 52 wins from 58 rubbers in 6 years of Fed Cup play from *1963* to *1979* she contributed hugely to American dominance in those team competitions. – J.B.

JAN KODES (Czechoslovakia)
Born 1/3/46. A dogged, industrious player with great strength and determination. He won his first major victories on clay, winning the French singles **1970/71** and reaching the Italian final **1970/71/72,** but he won the Wimbledon singles in the boycott year of **1973** and was runner-up in the US Champs **1971/73.** Having served his apprenticeship in European junior team competitions (he was on a winning Galea Cup team), he first represented Czechoslovakia in D Cup in **1966,** took them to the final in **1975** and was a member of their winning team in **1980.**

HILDE KRAHWINKEL (West Germany)
Born 26/3/08. Died 7/3/81. Became Mrs Sperling. A tall German, later Danish by marriage, whose dogged ability to retrieve from the back of the court turned her matches into long tests of endurance. She won the German indoor title in **1929** and then, emerging rapidly as an international player, lost to Cilly Aussem in the only all-German women's f at Wimbledon **1931.** She reached the final again in **1936,** losing 6–2 4–6 7–5 to Helen Jacobs, and altogether she was in qf (or better) 8 times. She won the French singles **1935–37,** defeating Mrs Mathieu in each of the three f, the Italian title **1935** and she was German singles champ **1933/35/37/39.** There was no competition in 1936. Her last important victory was in the Scandinavian indoor final in **1950.**

JACK ALBERT KRAMER (USA)
Born 1/8/21. A methodical and powerful exponent of the serve and volley game. Played for the US in the last pre-war D Cup challenge round against Australia. Won Wimbledon singles title in **1947** after losing dramatically to the then unknown Jaroslav Drobny in 1946. Won doubles **1946/47.** Won US singles **1946/47** and doubles **1940/41/43/47.** Turned pro **1947** and then controlled pro tennis for 15 years. Still appears occasionally as a television commentator and was executive director of ATP Sept. 1972–April 1975.

RENE LACOSTE (France)
Born 2/7/04. In spite of ill health, he became the best groundstroke player and most astute tactician of pre-war lawn tennis. Won Wimbledon singles **1925/28** and doubles (with J. Borotra) **1925.** Won US singles **1926/27,** French singles **1925/27/29** and French doubles (with Borotra) **1924/25/29.** Played in 51 D Cup rubbers between **1923–28** and won the crucial rubbers of the **1927** challenge round which brought France the trophy for the first time, when he beat Tilden and Johnston in the singles.

ARTHUR D. LARSEN (USA)
Born 6/4/25. A graceful, elegant lefthander with exquisite touch and some notable eccentricities, he was famous for his dressing-room superstitions, his physical twitches and his rituals on court. He was known as Tappy because he would have a lucky number for the day and would always tap the baseline, the umpire's chair – even his own toe – with his racket the required number of times before continuing. He won US singles **1950,** US Clay Courts **1952** and US Indoor **1953.** A motor-cycle accident in which he suffered severe head injuries ended his career in 1957.

RODNEY GEORGE LAVER (Australia)
Born 9/8/38. The first player to achieve the Grand Slam twice and the master of the old professional circuit, with Rosewall as his great rival, in its last days. A lefthander, red-haired like Budge, with a spectacularly aggressive style, he brought off the slam of the four major singles titles, as an amateur, in **1962** and then, as a professional, in **1969.** Disciplined, unassuming, quick and light in movement, he could produce sudden bombardments of shots, heavy with spin, which totally disconcerted his opponents. Born at Rockhampton, Queensland, 'Rocket' was a perfect nickname for the first tennis millionaire. If he had not turned professional in 1963, he would have won many more of the traditional titles. As it was, he won the singles at Wimbledon **1961/62** and **1968/69,** the doubles with Emerson **1971** and the mixed, with Darlene Hard, **1959/60.** He took the US singles and French

singles *1962* and *1969,* also winning the French doubles with Emerson and the mixed with Hard in *1961.* His Australian singles victories came in *1960, 1962* and *1969,* with doubles *1959/61* (Mark) and *1969* (Emerson). He was Italian singles champion *1962* and *1971,* German champion *1961/62* and a member of the undefeatcd D Cup team from *1959–62.* He returned to D Cup in *1973,* collecting three more rubbers in Australia's 5–0 victory over the US in the final at Cleveland.

SUZANNE LENGLEN (France)
Born 24/5/1899. Died 4/7/1938. The most exciting, and successful of women players. She survived 2 match-points to win at Wimbledon in *1919* against Mrs Lambert Chambers and thereafter lost only in a controversial match to Molla Mallory (US) in 1921 US Champs until her retirement in 1926. Quarrelled with the Wimbledon referee in 1926 and turned pro. Won Wimbledon singles and doubles (with Elizabeth Ryan) *1919/20/21/22/23/25.* French singles and doubles (with various partners) *1920/21/22/23/25/26.*

KATHLEEN McKANE (Great Britain)
Born 7/5/1896. Now Mrs Godfree. A fine match-player with a quick, aggressive game, she achieved the notable distinction of winning the Wimbledon singles twice – even though she was a contemporary of Suzanne Lenglen and Helen Wills. In Lenglen's absence, she beat the Californian (a feat which no other player achieved in the next 14 years at Wimbledon) in the *1924* final after trailing by a set and 1–4, and in *1926* she regained the title after being within a point of 1–4 in the third set against Lili d'Alvarez. She won the Wimbledon mixed (with Gilbert) in *1924* and in *1926* (with her husband, Leslie Godfree). She was r/u to Miss Wills at Forest Hills in 1925 after beating Elizabeth Ryan and Molla Mallory, and she won the US doubles in *1923* (with Mrs Covell) */27* (with Miss Harvey). She won 7 rubbers out of 17 in 7 W Cup matches between *1923–34.*

CHARLES ROBERT McKINLEY (USA)
Born 5/1/41. Died 11/8/86. An energetic and athletic match-player, who won the Wimbledon singles title in *1963* without meeting another seeded player in the course of the tournament. He was runner-up to Laver in *1961,* a disappointing competitor in *1962* but in *1963* bounced back to take the title. In the US Championships he never progressed further than the semi-finals, failing three times at that stage, but, with Ralston, he won the doubles in *1961* and *1963–64.* He played in 16 D Cup matches between *1960* and *1965* and won 29 of his 38 rubbers.

MAURICE EVANS McLOUGHLIN (USA)
Born 7/1/1890. Died 10/12/1957. The 'Californian Comet' was the first notable exponent of the cannonball service. Fiercely effective with volley and smash, he was US champ in*1912–13* and his appearance at Wimbledon was, as a contemporary remarked, a sign of the way the modern game was developing. His spectacular style had considerable appeal. When he met Wilding for the title in *1913,* 'there was such an indecent crush round the barriers of the Centre Court that, to avoid serious injury, several ladies had to be lifted over by policemen into the security of the arena'. Wilding beat him 8–6 6–3 10–8, but McLough-lin had the consolation of winning 2 rubbers in the American capture of the D Cup from Britain at Wimbledon. In the *1914* challenge round at Forest Hills he beat both Brookes and Wilding, but Australasia took the trophy. He did not play after the war. His aggressive style was said to have burnt him out.

FREW DONALD McMILLAN (South Africa)
Born 20/5/42 in Springs, a small Transvaal town. A gifted and unusual doubles player who invariably wore a peaked white cloth cap and held the racket with two hands on both sides to produce just the right blend of disguise, finesse and power. His partnership with expatriate Australian Bob Hewitt was particularly fruitful and they became one of the three greatest pairs of the post-Second World War years. Together they won their native South African title four times *(1967/70/72/74)* and succeeded at Wimbledon three times

(1967/72/78). They won once each the French *(1972)*, the US *(1977)*, the Masters *(1977* played in Jan '78), the WCT *(1974)* and the Italian *(1967)* titles and won the German twice *(1967/70)*. But it was in mixed doubles that he won his first and last major championships. In *1966* he partnered Annette Van Zyl to the French title and in *1981* he captured the Wimbledon mixed for the second time with Betty Stove, with whom he had been successful in 1978 – the same year they won a second US Open together *(1977/78)*. He played D Cup from *1965* to *1976* and was a member of the only team ever to win the famous trophy by default – from India in 1974. – J.B.

ALICE MARBLE (USA)
Born 28/9/13. Died 13/12/90. A brilliant server and volleyer whose career was interrupted by ill health and the war. Won Wimbledon singles *1939* and doubles (with Sarah Palfrey Fabyan) *1938/39.*US singles *1936/38/39/40* and doubles (with Sarah Palfrey Fabyan) *1937/38/39/40.* Turned pro *1941.*

SIMONE MATHIEU (France)
Born 31/1/08. Died 7/1/80. A formidable clay court player, she succeeded Lenglen as the leader of the women's game in France. She was junior champ – as a married woman – at 18, and 3 years later reached the French f, losing 6–3 6–4 to Wills. She was r/u again in *1933/36/37* before she won at last in *1938,* defeating Landry, and then retained her title *1939* against Jedrzejowska. She won the French doubles 6 times and the Wimbledon doubles twice with Ryan *1933/34* and once with Yorke *1937.* Her soundness from the baseline carried her 4 times to the singles sf.

HELEN WILLS MOODY (USA)
Born 6/10/05. Later Mrs A. Roark. Lenglen's successor as ruler of Wimbledon. A relentless baseliner, she won the singles 8 times in 9 attempts, losing only to Kitty McKane in 1924. (Between *1927–32* she won all the major singles champs, except Australia, without losing a set. Won Wimbledon singles *1927/28/29/30/32/33/35/38* and doubles (with Hazel Wightman) *1924* and (with Elizabeth Ryan) */27/30.* US singles *1923/24/25/27/28/29/31,* and doubles (with Mrs J. B. Jessup) *1922,* (with Hazel Wightman) */24/28,* and (with Mary K. Browne) */25.* French singles *1928/29/30/32* and doubles (with Elizabeth Ryan)*1930/ 31/32.*

ANGELA MORTIMER (Great Britain)
Born 21/4/32. Now Mrs Barrett. Britain's first post-war Wimbledon singles champ. Coached by Arthur Roberts at Torquay, she used an armoury of firmly controlled groundstrokes most effectively and considerable determination enabled her to overcome a certain frailty of physique. Her first notable success was the capture of the French title in *1955* – the first British victory in Paris since Peggy Scriven won in 1934 – and in the same year she won the Wimbledon doubles (with Anne Shilcock). She won the Australian title in *1958,* after travelling there to recover from illness, and 6 months later was r/u to Althea Gibson at Wimbledon. She won the title in *1961* by beating Christine Truman in the first all-British f of the modern Wimbledon. She won 5 rubbers out of 16 in 6 W Cup matches and became W Cup captain *1964–70* and Fed Cup captain *1967–70*

ILLIE NASTASE (Rumania)
Born 19/8/46. One of the most gifted shot-makers and fluid movers in the game's history, he never quite fulfilled his enormous potential. His two Grand Slam titles were won on different surfaces – on grass in New York in *1972* and on clay in Paris the following year. He could also play beautifully indoors as his four Masters titles in *1971, 1972, 1973, 1975* testify. Sadly for his many admirers, a childlike and sometimes mischievous streak was his undoing on many occasions, particularly towards the end of his playing days when he fell foul of authority for his behaviour. Throughout his career the showman in him struggled constantly with the athlete so that there was often a lack of steel about his match play. This failing, and an inability to put the ball away with his somewhat lightweight volleys, cost him

two chances to win the Wimbledon title – in *1972* when Smith beat him and in *1976* when Borg won the first of his five titles. His lightning reflexes made him an excellent doubles player and he won major titles in Paris *(1970)* and Rome *(1970* and *1972)*, at Wimbledon *(1973)* and in New York *(1975)*. He also won two mixed titles at Wimbledon with Rosie Casals *(1970, 1972)*. His biggest disappointment was his failure to lead Rumania to victory in the *1972* D Cup final against the Americans on clay in Bucharest where his loss to Smith in the opening rubber proved decisive. – J.B.

JOHN DAVID NEWCOMBE (Australia)
Born 23/5/44. The supreme exponent of the simple, rugged style in modern tennis. Splendidly confident and with great strength of personality, Newcombe relied upon a heavy service, forceful volleying and solid, powerful groundstrokes. His best singles successes were on grass – Wimbledon *1967, 1970/71,* US Championships *1967, 1973,* and Australia *1973, 1975* – but he also won, by doggedness and determination, the German *(1968)* and Italian *(1969)* titles. He and Roche formed the most successful of modern doubles partnerships, winning Wimbledon in *1965, 1968–70,* and *1974.* When Roche was injured in *1966,* Fletcher replaced him at short notice and he and Newcombe won the title. He won the US doubles with Roche *1967,* with Taylor *1971,* and with Davidson *1973,* France twice with Roche *(1967, 1969)* and once with Okker *(1973)* and Australia four times with Roche *(1965, 1967, 1971* and *1976)* and once with Anderson *(1973).* In *1981,* aged 37, he and Stolle (42) took McEnroe/Fleming to 5s tie-break in US Open sf. He first played in the Davis Cup in *1963* and finally against Italy in Rome, *1976,* but perhaps his best performance was in *1973* when he and Laver inflicted a 5–0 defeat upon the United States at Cleveland.

BETTY NUTHALL (Great Britain)
Born 23/6/11. Died 8/11/83. Became Mrs Shoemaker. An aggressive and attractive competitor, with a remarkable record as a junior, she never progressed beyond qf at Wimbledon but gained her most impressive victories abroad. At 16, after beating Molla Mallory, No. 6 seed, at Wimbledon in *1927,* she astonished the tennis world by reaching f at F Hills, where Helen Wills beat her 6–1 6–4. In *1930* she became the first British player to win that title with 6–4 6–1 victory over Mrs Harper. She won the US doubles *1930/31/33* and mixed *1929/31* and the French doubles *1931* and mixed *1931/32.* Her only British success in a nat singles event was the capture of the HC title in *1927.* She won the HC doubles *1926/28/31/32* and the mixed in *1927.* She played in 8 W Cup matches between *1927* and *1939,* winning 6 rubbers and losing 7.

ALEJANDRO OLMEDO (USA)
Born 24/3/36. The son of a groundsman in Peru, this superb natural athlete rose like a comet in *1958* to win D Cup for America in Brisbane almost single-handed. Selected by the captain, Perry T. Jones, Olmedo had rewarded him with two singles wins and a share with Ham Richardson in the doubles win that had sealed the victory. Success in the Australian Championships confirmed the quality of his play as he beat Neale Fraser in four sets. Six months later 'The Chief', as he was popularly known, won the *1959* Wimbledon from Rod Laver for the loss of only two sets, with one of the most competent displays of power tennis seen since the war. After taking part in the unsuccessful defence of D Cup where he lost to Fraser but beat Laver again, he reached the final of the US Championships but failed once more against Fraser. Immediately he turned professional. – J.B.

MANUEL ORANTES (Spain)
Born 6/2/49. A consummate artist on European clay whose exquisite touch and gentle, generous manners made him an international favourite. A left-hander who, after leading Spain to two Galea Cup victories in *1968* and *1969,* won his first two important titles in *1972* – the German and Italian Opens. His best year was *1975* for, besides winning a second German title, the Canadian Open and the first of his two US Clay Court crowns (he won the second in *1977*), he was triumphant on the clay at Forest Hills. After recovering

miraculously to defeat Vilas in a night-time semi-final, having trailed one set to two and 0–5 in the fourth, he was back on court 15 hours later to thrash Jimmy Connors 6–4 6–3 6–3 in a near-perfect display of the clay-court art. In *1976* he won the Spanish Open and at the year's end won Masters in Houston against Fibak with another brave recovery, coming back from one set to two and 1–4. He played in the losing Spanish team in the D Cup challenge round of *1967* in Brisbane but led his country to victory in the World Team Cup in Dusseldorf 11 years later. – J.B.

MARGARET OSBORNE (USA)
Born 4/4/18. Now Mrs du Pont. One of the finest of American doubles players and a formidably successful competitor in singles. With her splendidly consistent serving and her strength and skill at the net, she did much to set the pattern for the period of American supremacy in women's tennis, which began in 1946. Won Wimbledon singles in *1947* Forest Hills *1948/49/50* and Paris in *1946/49*. She and Louise Brough won the Wimbledon doubles in *1946/48/49/50/54.* They ruled the US doubles from *1942–50* and *1955–57,*and held the French title *1946/47/49.* She won the Wimbledon mixed with Neale Fraser in *1962* – 15 years after her first singles victory.

SARAH PALFREY (USA)
Born 18/9/12. Now Mrs Danzig, formerly Mrs Fabyan, and Mrs Cooke. A fine volleyor with a sweeping backhand and a notable doubles player, she partnered Alice Marble to victory at Wimbledon in *1938/39* and won the US doubles title with a variety of partners – Betty Nuthall, Helen Jacobs (3 times), Alice Marble (4 times) and Margaret Osborne – 9 times between *1930–41.* She won the US singles in *1941/45* and was r/u to Helen Jacobs in*1934/35.* She was the US mixed champion on 4 occasions. She played in 10 W Cup matches and won 14 rubbers out of 21.

ADRIANO PANATTA (Italy)
Born 9/7/50. Without doubt, 1976 was the *annus mirabilis* of Panatta's career. Until then he had always been dashing and stylish, but had never made full use of his talent. In *1976*, however, he lived dangerously and survived brilliantly. In Rome he became the first home player to win in Italy for 15 years after frustrating Warwick no fewer than 11 times at m-p in the first round. In Paris, against Hutka, he again faced a first-round m-p and again went on to take the championship. Four months later, when Italy won D Cup for the first time, Panatta played a major role in their victory. Paris, Rome and D Cup – this was Panatta's year! He was also the leading player in the Italian teams which reached the.*1977*, *1979* and *1980* D Cup finals. He reached the French sf in *1973* and *1975* and was runner-up in Rome *1978* and Hamburg *1972*.

GERALD L. PATTERSON (Australia)
Born 17/12/1895. Died 13/6/1967. Formidably aggressive with a cannonball service modelled on McLoughlin's, he was the dominating player when international competition was resumed in 1919. After being r/u to O'Hara Wood in the *1914* Australian singles, he became Wimbledon's first post-war champ by defeating Brookes in *1919*. He lost his Wimbledon title to Tilden in *1920* but regained it against Lycett in *1922*. R/u doubles in*1922* (O'Hara Wood) and *1928* (Hawkes) and won the mixed with Suzanne Lenglen in*1920*. He won the Australian singles in his fourth final in *1927*. Between *1919–28* he played 46 D Cup rubbers for Australia and Australasia and won 4 out of 12 challenge round rubbers. He was a nephew of Dame Nellie Melba and was the first man to win the Wimbledon singles by playing through when the challenge round was abolished there in 1922.

J. EDWARD PATTY (USA)
Born 11/2/24. An American who lived in Paris and developed his game there, 'Budge' Patty, with his elegant, effective forehand volley, was one of the great post-war sty-lists.*1950* – when he won both the Wimbledon and French singles – was the peak of his career, but his rivalry with Drobny captured the public's imagination. The most notable of

their long and dramatic matches was in the third round at Wimbledon in 1953. After 4½ hours Patty lost 8–6 16–18 3–6 8–6 12–10 after holding 6 match-points. He had beaten the Czech at Wimbledon in **1947** and 3 years later by 6–1 6–2 3–6 5–7 7–5 in his French f. The last of their meetings was in **1954**. Drobny, on his way to the title, won a 4-set sf. Patty won his last title there in **1957** when he and Mulloy, then aged 43, beat Hoad and Fraser to take the men's doubles. He won the Italian singles **1954,** and the German singles **1953/54** and doubles **1953/54/55.**

FRANK A. PARKER (USA)
Born 31/1/16. Shrewd, persistent, and accurate in spite of a certain lightness of shot, he shared with Trabert the distinction, rare for an American, of winning the French title twice. At his best on slow courts, he was ranked in the first 10 in the US for 17 consecutive years between **1933,** the year of the first of his 5 US Clay Court victories, and **1949** when he turned pro. His victories in Paris were in **1948/49**, and in **1949** he won the doubles in Paris and Wimbledon with Gonzales. He won the US singles in **1944** and **1945** as an Army sergeant and the doubles with Kramer in **1943.** He played in the D Cup challenge round against Britain in **1937** when the US regained the trophy after 10 years and in the **1939** and **1948** challenge rounds. He was beaten only twice in 14 D Cup rubbers.

FREDERICK JOHN PERRY (Great Britain)
Born 18/5/09. A US citizen. The most successful modern British player, an aggressive competitor with boundless self-confidence and a remarkable running forehand. Won Wimbledon singles **1934/35/36** – the first player since A. F. Wilding (1910–13) to take the title 3 years in succession – and mixed (with Dorothy Round) **1935/36.** US singles **1933/34/36.** French singles **1935** and doubles (with G. P. Hughes) **1933.** Australian singles **1934** and doubles (with Hughes) **1934.** Won 45 out of 52 D Cup rubbers, 34 out of 38 singles,between **1931–36.** Turned pro in **1936.**

YVON FRANCOIS MARIE PETRA (France)
Born 8/3/16 in Indo-China. Died 11/9/84. Wimbledon's first post-war men's singles champion. Reached mixed f at Wimbledon **1937** with Simone Mathieu and won French doubles**1938** with Destremau, defeating Budge and Mako in f. Between 1942, when he was released from a prisoner-of-war camp, and 1945, he consolidated his reputation as France's most aggressive competitor in wartime domestic competitions. At Wimbledon,**1946,** his strength, flair and, notably, the consistency of his heavy serving gained this formidably built player an unexpected title. Drobny beat Kramer, the favourite, in 4r. Petra disposed of Pails, the other expected finalist, in qf and then won 5s matches against Tom Brown and Geoff Brown. That was the peak of his career. Marcel Bernard beat him in the French sf – played in July that year – and his consolation was a doubles victory, partnered by Bernard, over Morea and Segura in f. Patty beat him easily on the second day at Forest Hills and in **1947** he lost to Tom Brown in qf at Wimbledon.

NICOLA PIETRANGELI (Italy)
Born 11/9/33. A master of the European clay court style, he was born in Tunis (of a French father and Russian mother) and between **1954** and **1972** played in 163 D Cup rubbers for Italy, more than anyone in history. Won most rubbers (120), played most singles (109) and won most (78), played most doubles (54), and won most (42), and played in most ties (66). Appeared in the **1960/61** challenge rounds against Australia, but won only one 'dead' singles. Won French singles **1959/60** and doubles (with Sirola), Italian singles **1957/61,** and German singles **1960.** Reached sf at Wimbledon, **1960,** and doubles final (with Sirola) **1956.**

DR JOSHUA PIM (Ireland)
Born 20/6/1869. Died 13/4/1942. A robust, determined competitor, regarded by contemporary critics as one of the great geniuses of early tennis. 'When Pim was at his best he was virtually unplayable', wrote Wallis Myers. 'It is scarcely exaggerating to say that he

could hit a coin placed anywhere on the court.' He reached sf at Wimbledon **1890,** losing to Hamilton, who became Wimbledon's first Irish champ, then lost in **1891** to Wilfred-Baddeley in the all-comers' f and again in **1892** challenge round. He gained his revenge, however, by beating Baddeley in the 2 following Wimbledon f. Pim won the Irish title for the 3rd and last time in **1895** but then played little first-class tennis until he was controversially picked for the D Cup match against USA at New York in 1902. He was preferred to Lawrie Doherty, lost both his singles badly and the British Isles were beaten 3–2. 'Although still very good, Pim had no more than a shadow of his former skill, but alas! a great deal more than the shadow of his former weight', wrote Commander Hillyard.

ADRIAN KARL QUIST (Australia)
Born 4/8/13. A shrewd, graceful doubles player, whose victories at Wimbledon were separated by a gap of 15 years. Won with J. H. Crawford in **1935** and, when almost a veteran, with J. E. Bromwich **1950.** Held Australian title from **1936–50,** winning twice with D. P. Turnbull and 8 times with Bromwich. Won US doubles (with Bromwich) **1939,** French doubles (with J. H. Crawford) **1935,** and Australian singles **1936/40/48.** Won 42 out of 55 D Cup rubbers in 28 ties between **1933–48.**

WILLIAM CHARLES RENSHAW (Great Britain)
Born 3/1/1861. Died 12/8/1904. The first great champ. Learnt on asphalt at school at Cheltenham with twin brother, Ernest, a more graceful but less determined competitor. They were the first spectacular players and their skill – particularly in volleying and smashing – brought crowds to Wimbledon and contributed considerably to the development of lawn tennis as a spectator sport. 'Willie' Renshaw was singles champ at Wimbledon from **1881–86** and in **1889.** He held the doubles, with Ernest, in **1884/85/86/88/89.** Ernest won the singles title in **1888** and was beaten by William in the challenge rounds of 1882 and 1883.

NANCY ANN RICHEY (USA)
Born 23/8/42. Later Mrs Gunter. A Texan, famous for her shorts and peaked cap, she was, like her brother, George Clifford Richey, a tenacious baseliner, impressive on clay. Her determination occasionally brought unexpected success on grass. She reached the **1969** US final, losing 6–2 6–2 to Margaret Court. She won Australia **1967,** beating Lesley Turner, another clay-court specialist, in the final. At Wimbledon she reached qf seven times in nine years **1964–72** but was semi-finalist only in **1968.** She won Wimbledon doubles with Maria Bueno **1966.** On clay she won French singles **1968,** beating Ann Jones to avenge a defeat in the **1966** final, but the best evidence of her quality was her record in US Clay Courts. She won Indianapolis from **1963–68** and even as late as **1975** led Chris Evert 7–5 5–0 in the semi-finals there, twice reaching match-point before retiring with cramp at 2–4 in the final set. She played Wightman Cup from **1962–68** and Federation Cup **1964–69.**

ROBERT LARIMORE RIGGS (USA)
Born 25/2/18. A shrewd, confident match-player, with remarkable versatility of shot, he won all 3 titles on his first appearance at Wimbledon in **1939.** He also won Forest Hills in **1939,** but lost to McNeill in the French f. He turned pro in 1941 and later became a notable competitor in veterans' events, but his greatest fame came at the age of 55. Profiting from the Women's Lib controversy, he challenged and beat Margaret Court 6–2 6–1 in a singles match in Ramona, Cal, and then lost to Billie Jean King 6–4 6–3 6–3, before a record television audience of almost 50 million and 30,492 paying spectators at the Houston Astrodome in September 1973.

ANTHONY DALTON ROCHE (Australia)
Born 17/6/45. Strong, rugged and a fine volleyer, he was the lefthander in one of Wimbledon's most successful doubles partnerships. He won the doubles with John Newcombe in **1965,** from **1968–70** (the first hat-trick of titles since the Dohertys 1903–5) and in **1974.** Other doubles victories included US **1967,** French **1967–69.** Australia **1965/67/71/76/77**

and Italy **1965/71.** He did not achieve as much as expected in singles, partly because of injury. The extraordinary operation on his left elbow, performed without knife or anaesthetic in the Philippines by a faith healer, received worldwide publicity. He never reached an Australian final in spite of numerous attempts, but was runner-up to Laver at Wimbledon in **1968** and lost two US Open finals: **1969** when Laver beat him to complete the Grand Slam and **1970** to Rosewall. His most successful year was **1966** when he won French and Italian titles. Played Davis Cup **1964–78** but did not play singles in a final until he beat Panatta in the opening match **1977.**

KENNETH ROBERT ROSEWALL (Australia)
Born 2/11/34. For a quarter of a century Rosewall's grace and easy, economical style delighted the connoisseurs and the only regret about his long and distinguished career is that, in spite of four finals over a period of 20 years, he never won the Wimbledon singles title. He began as a Hopman prodigy and it was not until the end of **1979** that he retired from Grand Prix tennis. In **1953,** aged 18, he won the Australian and French singles and, with Hoad, the French and Wimbledon doubles. In **1954** he lost to Drobny in the Wimbledon final. Hoad beat him in the **1956** Wimbledon final, but Rosewall avenged that defeat in the US final, frustrating Hoad in the last leg of his attempt on the Grand Slam. Turning professional in **1957,** he took over the leadership of the professional circuit from Gonzales until Laver's arrival in **1963.** Rosewall's skills endured. In **1968** he won the first open tournament at Bournemouth and then recaptured some of his former titles. He re-gained the French singles and doubles (with Stolle) in **1968.** In **1970** – after 14 years and aged 35 – he won the US title again and reached his fourth final at Forest Hills in **1974.** The gap between his Australian successes was even wider. After his victories in **1953** and **1955,** he won again in **1971** and **1972.** But Wimbledon always eluded him. Newcombe beat him in **1970,** his third final, and Connors overwhelmed him in the **1974** final.

DOROTHY EDITH ROUND (Great Britain)
Born 13/7/09. Died 12/11/82. Became Mrs Little. Determined and efficient, possessing a fine forehand drive and shrewd drop-shot, she was one of the two British women's singles champs at Wimbledon between the wars. She gained her first notable victory there against Lili d'Alvarez in **1931,** was r/u to Helen Wills Moody in **1933,** then beat Helen Jacobs to win the title in **1934** and regained it against Jadwiga Jedrzejowska in **1937.** She won the Australian singles in **1935** and the Wimbledon mixed in **1934** (with Miki) and **1935/36** (with Perry). She won 4 of her 13 W Cup rubbers between **1931–36.**

ELIZABETH RYAN (USA)
Born 5/2/1892. Died 6/7/1979. Suzanne Lenglen's doubles partner and the winner of 19 Wimbledon titles – 12 doubles and 7 mixed. A determined competitor with a cunningly chopped forehand and a great appetite for match-play, she was regarded by contemporaries as 'the best player never to win a great singles championship'. With a variety of partners, she won the Wimbledon doubles **1914/19/20/21/22/23/25/26/27/30/33/34** and the mixed **1919/21/23/27/28/30/32.** US doubles in **1926,** the French doubles **1930/32/33/34.**

JOHN WILLIAM VAN RYN (USA)
Born 30/6/05. Formed one of the most famous of all doubles partnerships with Wilmer Allison. Pat Hughes described their combination as 'a perfect blending of styles . . . Van Ryn dipped the ball over from the right court and his partner stepped in at the psychological moment for the final volley'. George Lott thought that their deep personal friendship and knowledge of each other's movements and reactions played an important part in their success. With Allison, Van Ryn succeeded at Wimbledon in **1929–30** and took the US title in **1931** and **1935.** He won Paris and Wimbledon with Lott in **1931.** In the **1929** D Cup challenge round he and Allison beat Cochet and Borotra and in the **1932** match they defeated Cochet and Brugnon. He was a member of the US team from **1929–36** and won 29 of his 32 rubbers in 24 matches. He lost only two of his 24 D Cup doubles.

MANUEL SANTANA (Spain)

Born 10/5/38. Learnt the game as a ballboy and, after a period in which he was the most admired clay court player in Europe, won US singles *1965,* and Wimbledon singles *1966.* Possesed a remarkable forehand and great delicacy of touch. Won French singles *1961* and *1964,* defeating Pietrangeli in both finals, and doubles (with Emerson) *1963,* and South African singles *1967.* The most successful Spanish player in history, he won 91 D Cup rubbers out of 119 between *1958* and *1973.*

RICHARD SAVITT (USA)

Born 4/3/27. His talent was discovered in the classic fashion by a complete stranger who saw him playing in a public park, and after a modest junior career he became a powerful exponent of the serve and volley game. Concentrating on tennis after a basketball injury in 1949, he rose rapidly on the US ranking-list, moving up from 16th to 6th after reaching sf at Forest Hills, *1950,* with victories over Seixas and Bromwich. His remarkable year was *1951.* He won both the Australian and Wimbledon titles, defeating McGregor in both finals. This was his first trip to Europe and he never achieved the same kind of success again, although he played some memorable matches, notably sf against Rosewall at Forest Hills, *1956,* and a vain defence of his US indoor title in a three-hour f in *1959.* He was a member of the US D Cup team in 1951, but was not chosen to play in the challenge round against Australia.

FREDERICK RUDOLPH SCHROEDER (USA)

Born 20/7/21. A powerful Californian whose aggressive serve-and-volley game brought him much success on fast surfaces. The US National Junior Champion in *1939*, he won the NC Championships from Stanford in *1942* and the same year won the US Championships, defeating Frank Parker in the final. In *1949* he reached the final again but lost in five sets to Pancho Gonzales. Earlier that same year, on his only visit to Wimbledon he had won the singles in heroic fashion after surviving four five-set matches. In the first round he had beaten his doubles partner, Gardnar Mulloy, 7–5 in the fifth (later they reached the doubles final and lost to Gonzales and Parker). In the quarter-finals he had been match-point down to Frank Sedgman and, despite being foot-faulted on his first serve, had followed in his second serve to hit a winning volley and finally won 9–7 in the final set. In all he played 291 games. Only two champions played more – Boris Becker (292) in 1985 and Ashley Cooper (322) in 1958. In doubles he won the US Championships with Jack Kramer in *1940, 1941* and *1947* and the mixed with Louise Brough in *1942.* A distinguished member of the US D Cup team between *1946* and *1951*, he played in six challenge rounds, winning eight of his 11 singles and one of his four doubles. – J.B.

FRANCIS ARTHUR SEDGMAN (Australia)

Born 29/10/27. A superb volleyer who seemed to glide about the court, he was Australia's first post-war Wimbledon singles champ and, with Ken McGregor, he achieved the grand slam of the 4 major doubles titles in *1953.* Won Wimbledon singles *1952* and doubles (with J. E. Bromwich) *1948* and (with McGregor) */51/52.* US singles *1951/52* and doubles (with Bromwich) *1950* and (with McGregor) */51.* French doubles (with McGregor) *1951/52.* Australian singles *1949/50* (with McGregor) doubles *1951/52.* Italian singles (and doubles with McGregor) *1952.* Won 25 D Cup rubbers out of 28 between *1949–52.* Turned pro in *1953.*

FRANCISCO 'PANCHO' SEGURA (Ecuador)

Born 20/6/21. An unorthodox showman who made his reputation in his pro years – he achieved little as an amateur. Won the US Clay Court title in *1944* and the US Indoor in *1946,* but made little mark at Wimbledon, losing to Tom Brown and to Drobny in his two singles appearances. He turned pro in 1947 and immediately became one of the great entertainers of the pro game. With his double-fisted forehand, his deadly lobs, his scuttling speed about the court, and his beaming smile, he was a most popular competitor for 20 years. If he did not win as many titles as he deserved, he was always capable of testing players of the quality of Kramer, Rosewall, and Gonzales.

ELIAS VICTOR SEIXAS (USA)

Born 30/8/23. A doggedly successful American competitor. Won Wimbledon singles *1953* and mixed *1953/54/55/56,* 3 times with Doris Hart and once with Shirley Fry. US singles *1954* and doubles (with M. G. Rose) *1952* and (with M. A. Trabert) */54.* French doubles (with Trabert) *1954/55.* Played in 7 successive D Cup challenge rounds and won 38 out of 55 rubbers in 19 ties between *1951–57.*

MARGARET SMITH (Australia)

Born 16/7/42. Now Mrs Court. In 1970 she became the second woman to achieve the Grand Slam of the major singles championships, having brought off a unique mixed doubles slam with Fletcher in *1963.* A powerful athlete, superbly fit, with a heavy service, great stamina and a formidable reach on the volley, she won a record number of 62 GS titles – and would have won more if she had not been afflicted by occasional and often inexplicable losses of confidence. Her major singles successes were Wimbledon *1963,1965, 1970,* US Championships *1962, 1965, 1969, 1970, 1973,* French Championships *1962, 1964, 1969, 1970, 1973,* and Australia *1960–66, 1969–71* and *1973.* She was also three times the holder of the Italian, German and South African titles. In addition, she won the doubles at Wimbledon twice and the mixed five times, the US doubles five times and the mixed on eight occasions, the French four times in doubles and mixed, and she held eight Australian doubles and two mixed titles. She toured successfully, with the help of her husband, Barry, with two children, but retired in 1977 when she found that she was expecting a third baby.

STANLEY ROGER SMITH (USA)

Born 14/12/46. The very epitome of the All-American boy with his tall straight-backed figure, his fair hair and his clean-cut good looks, he became a national hero in *1972,* as well as the world's No. 1 player, when he won a magnificent Wimbledon final against Nastase and then beat the Rumanian again in the opening rubber of the D Cup final on unfriendly clay in Bucharest to launch the United States towards an improbable victory against the odds. Earlier, in *1969,* he had won the US Nationals and the following year had beaten Laver and Rosewall to capture the first-ever Masters which, that year, was a round-robin competition. When he won the US Open in *1971* on the grass of Forest Hills he was perfecting the serve-and-volley technique that made him such an awkward opponent. Although his groundstrokes were never his strength, he used them intelligently to secure the few breaks of serve that were necessary as he blanketed the net to secure his own service games. His doubles partnership with Lutz was one of the best American pairings there has ever been. They are the only pair to have won US National titles on all four surfaces – grass, clay, hard and indoor. Four times they won the US Open – *1968, 1974, 1978, 1980* and in *1977* they were successful both in South Africa and the US Pro at Boston. In D Cup they are the only American pair to have won three Challenge Round rubbers and two in the Final Round. Overall his D Cup record is 34 wins and 7 losses in 23 ties. – J.B.

FREDERICK SYDNEY STOLLE (Australia)

Born 8/10/38. Former Sydney bank clerk, regarded primarily as doubles specialist, who by diligence and determination became one of the most successful singles players of the 1960s. Powerful serving and volleying, added to dogged consistency in return of service on the backhand, compensated for his lack of mobility and flexibility. Shared with Von Cramm the unlucky distinction of losing in 3 successive Wimbledon singles f, falling to McKinley *(1963)* and Emerson *(1964/65).* Was also r/u to Lundquist in *1964* Italian f, but won French singles *1965* and US and German titles *1966.* Established himself first as a doubles player with Hewitt. They won Australia *1963/64,* Wimbledon *1962/64* and Italy *1963/64.* With Emerson, who had dominated him in singles, won French and US doubles *1965* and Australia, Italy and US *1966.* In *1981,* aged 42, he and Newcombe (37) took McEnroe/Fleming to 5s tie-break in US Open sf. Became contract professional *1967* and reached

Wimbledon doubles f with Rosewall **1968**. Between **1964–66** he won 13 out of his 16 D Cup rubbers. Coached NY Sets to victory in World Team Tennis competition **1976**.

ERIC WILLIAM STURGESS (South Africa)

Born 10/6/20. South Africa's most successful singles competitor and their nat champ on no fewer than 11 occasions, beginning a sequence of victories in **1939/40** and continuing in **1945, 1948–54,** and **1957**. Outside Johannesburg his major achievement was the capture of the German singles **1952**; r/u in Paris **1947** and **1951** and lost to Gonzales in **1948** US f. Twice he was in Wimbledon sf, but in spite of speed, steadiness, and elegance, he lacked the weight of shot to win in the highest class and his second service was vulnerable. He won the French doubles with Fannin **1947** and a number of mixed titles, notably Wimbledon **1949** (with Sheila Summers) Land **1950** (with Louise Brough), and F Hills **1949** (with Brough).

WILLIAM F. TALBERT (USA)

Born 4/11/18. An expert in the practice, technique and strategy of doubles. The best right-court player of his generation, his most important victories were gained with Mulloy, with whom he won the US doubles **1942/45/46/48**, and a total of 84 out of 90 tournaments in ten years. With a variety of partners, he won US Clay Court doubles **1942/44/45/46** and the US Indoor Doubles **1949/50/51/52/54**. Abroad, with the young Trabert, also from Cincinnati, he won French and Italian doubles **1950**. He was runner-up to Parker in US singles **1944/45** and US Indoor champion **1948/51**. He won nine of his ten D Cup rubbers **1946–53**, from **1953–57** he captained the US D Cup team and later became Tournament Director of the US Open. All this was achieved despite the disability of diabetes.

WILLIAM TATUM TILDEN (USA)

Born 10/2/1893. Died 5/6/1953. For many critics the greatest player and student of match-strategy in the history of the game. Tall, with a long reach and a long stride, great strength and versatility of shot, and a powerful sense of drama, Tilden did not win a major title until he was 27. Then won Wimbledon singles **1920/21/30,** and doubles (with F. T. Hunter) **1927,** and US singles **1920/21/22/23/24/25/29**, and doubles **1918/21/22/23/27**. Was first Italian champ in **1930** and played D Cup from **1920–30** winning 34 rubbers out of 41 and 21 out of 28 in challenge rounds. Between **1920–26** won 13 successive challenge round singles. Turned pro in **1931**.

MARION ANTHONY TRABERT (USA)

Born 16/8/30. Won Wimbledon singles **1955** and US singles **1953/55** without losing a set. Won French singles **1954,** and doubles victories included US in **1954** (with E. V. Seixas), French **1950** (with W. F. Talbert) and **1954/55** (with Seixas) and Italian **1950** (with Talbert). Won 27 out of 35 D Cup rubbers between **1951–55**. Turned pro in **1955**.

CHRISTINE CLARA TRUMAN (Great Britain)

Born 16/1/41. Now Mrs Janes. Britain's most popular post-war player. She possessed a powerful forehand, a disconcerting ability to hit her way out of crises, a remarkable capacity for unorthodox volleying, and a temperament and court manners that made her a model for every schoolgirl in the country. She was always regarded as a potential Wimbledon champ and reached sf at the age of 16 at her first Wimbledon, where she lost to Althea Gibson, the eventual winner. Afterwards came a series of spectacular failures until she reached the **1961** f, only to fall to Angela Mortimer. Her best performances were a victory over Miss Gibson in the **1958** W Cup match, which helped to give Britain the trophy for the first time since the war, and the capture of the French and Italian singles titles in **1959**. Won **1960** Australian doubles with Maria Bueno. She and her sister, Nell, formed an aggressively effective – and sometimes erratic – doubles partnership. She won 10 rubbers out of 25 in 11 W Cup matches.

LESLEY ROSEMARY TURNER (Australia)

Born 16/8/42. Now Mrs Bowrey. Clever, strong and persistent, she gained her principal successes on European clay courts. In *1961* on her first European tour she lost to Maria Bueno in the Italian final and was runner-up again *1962* and *1964* before winning the title *1967/68.* She won the French singles *1963,* defeating Ann Jones, and *1965,* beating Margaret Court, and was runner-up *1962* and *1967.* She reached the Australian final *1964* and *1967.* In doubles, with Margaret Court, she won Wimbledon *1964,* Paris *1964/65* and Australia *1965.* Also took the Australian doubles title, with Judy Tegart, *1964* and *1967* and the US doubles, with Darlene Hard, *1961.* Won Wimbledon mixed doubles with Fred Stolle *1961* and *1964.*

H. ELLSWORTH VINES (USA)

Born 28/9/11. The possessor of a fine forehand and one of the fastest services of all time. Defeated Bunny Austin in *1932* 6–4 6–2 6–0 in one of the shortest Wimbledon f and lost title next year in a classic f against Jack Crawford. Won US singles *1931/32* and Australian doubles *1933.* Played D Cup *1932/33,* winning 13 rubbers out of 16. Turned pro *1934.*

SARAH VIRGINIA WADE (Great Britain)

Born 10/7/45. A spectacular and dramatic competitor, at her 16th attempt she finally achieved her ambition of winning the women's singles at Wimbledon in the Centenary year of *1977.* Until then her career had been an extravagant mixture of bitter disappointments, many of the worst endured at Wimbledon, and dazzling successes. Her first major success was gained at US Open *1968* when she defeated Billie Jean King 6–4 6–2 in the final. She won the Australian title, beating Evonne Goolagong, in *1972* and gained her only major clay-court success in *1971,* when she defeated Helga Masthoff in the Italian final. Her best doubles victories – France *1973,* US *1973/75,* Australia *1975* and Italy *1968* – were won with Margaret Court, but she also succeeded in Rome *1971* with Mrs Masthoff and *1973* with Olga Morozova. She also holds the record for the most appearances of any player of any nation in both Fed Cup (100 rubbers in 57 ties) and the W Cup (56 rubbers in 20 ties).

ANTHONY FREDERICK WILDING (New Zealand)

Born 31/10/1883. Killed in action in Belgium 9/5/1915. Coached by his father, a notable cricketer, he won the champ of Canterbury, New Zealand, at the age of 17 and went to Cambridge Univ for which he played *1904–05.* He became one of the great heroes of Edwardian tennis, winning the singles champ at Wimbledon *1910/11/12/13.* Won doubles (with N. E. Brookes) in *1907* and (with M. J. G. Ritchie) */08/10.* He won 21 of the 30 D Cup rubbers which he played for Australasia between *1905–14.*

SIDNEY BURR BEARDSLEE WOOD (USA)

Born 1/11/11. A nephew of the late Julian Myrick, a former President of the US LTA and the prime mover in 1913 in the development of Forest Hills as the national centre of tennis in the US, he made his first appearance at Wimbledon, aged 15, in *1927,* playing Lacoste on the Centre Court. In *1931,* aged 19 years and 243 days, he became Wimbledon's second youngest champion at the time. He won by default. Frank Shields fell in 4s of his sf against Borotra and damaged an ankle. Shields won, but was not fit enough to play in f. A shrewd strategist and a graceful stroke-maker, Wood was r/u to Allison at Forest Hills in *1935* but lost 6–2 6–2 6–3 in one of the tournament's most disappointing finals.

OBITUARIES 1990

Alice Marble, who died in December at her home in Palm Springs, California at the age of 77, won the Wimbledon singles title in 1939 on her third visit and was the outstanding woman player of the immediate pre-war years. Alice, a strong, natural athlete, had a profound effect upon the evolution of the sport. She was the first player to show that the serve-and-volley game could be executed successfully by a woman. She had won the first of her four singles and mixed doubles titles at the American Championships in 1936, two years after collapsing at the *Stade Roland Garros* in Paris while representing the USA in an international match against the French. Her illness was diagnosed as tuberculosis and Alice was told she would never play again. Having proved the doctors wrong she won the women's doubles at the US Championships in 1937 with Sarah Palfrey Fabyan and went on to claim the triple crown there in 1938, 1939 and 1940 – with Fabyan each time in women's doubles and with Don Budge, Harry Hopman and Bobby Riggs in mixed. With Fabyan and Riggs she equalled that feat in 1939 at Wimbledon where she had already won the mixed doubles the previous two years with Don Budge. In the post war years Alice's health deteriorated and she underwent several serious operations for cancer which failed to dim her enthusiasm or cheerfulness. Apart from her athletic expertise with the racket Alice Marble will also be remembered as the person who introduced shorts to women's tennis as well as the famous eyeshade that became fashionable as a symbol of style and elegance – and not just on the tennis court.

Lance Tingay, the distinguished tennis correspondent of the *Daily Telegraph* from 1952 until his retirement in 1981, died last March in London after having survived two previous heart attacks. He had begun his journalistic life with the Exchange Telegraph news agency and during the war served with the Royal Air Force. Tennis and Trollope were in his blood for, by dint of loving research, a lifetime spent watching the great tennis events and a rich understanding of the strengths and weaknesses of human nature, he made himself an expert in both fields. The sport's leading historian, who contributed each year a masterly précis of the world's tennis highlights for *Encyclopedia Britannica*, Lance wrote several learned books on the game including *100 Years of Wimbledon*, the official volume that was published to mark the centenary of The Championships in 1977, *The Guinness Book of Lawn Tennis Records* and *A History of Lawn Tennis in Pictures*. He also published, through his own Silverbridge Press, an anthology of Anthony Trollope's works and, over the years, built a fine collection of the master's works, including several first editions. So widely respected was Lance Tingay that he was made an honorary member of the All England Lawn Tennis Club, whose Championships he attended continuously for 43 years without missing a single day. He was also made a member of the International Lawn Tennis Clubs of Great Britain and France, an honour bestowed on few non-players. Lance was similarly honoured in the United States where he was voted into the Tennis Hall of Fame in Newport, Rhode Island.

Ted Tinling died on 23rd Mary 1990, one month before his 80th birthday, in a Cambridge hospital after a long fight against a lung disease that had left him very short of breath. Cuthbert Terrance Tinling, known to his friends originally as 'Teddy' and latterly as 'Ted' ('You've got to be with it', he had said when announcing the change), had been born in Eastbourne but, for reasons of health, spent much of his youth in the South of France where he developed a love affair with tennis that never died. While falling under the spell of Suzanne Lenglen, for whom he regularly umpired, he learned the skills of refereeing from George Simond and became his assistant. After the stormy departure of Suzanne from Wimbledon in 1926 Ted was appointed the following year as 'callboy' to The Championships, acting as liaison officer between players and committee, a role he was to return to in 1982 after 33 years in the wilderness. In pre-war London of the 1930's Ted had enjoyed his first commercial success as a dress designer. During the war he served with distinction as a Colonel in Intelligence and afterwards picked up the threads of his tennis life. He became the first and greatest tennis couturier and dressed most of the leading women players. The lace-edged panties he designed for 'Gorgeous' Gussie Moran in 1949 ensured him lasting fame. But the garment was ahead of its time. In the welter of publicity that surrounded this incident the Wimbledon committee dismissed Tinling and he remained persona non grata at the All England Club until his recall. From 1975 Ted made his home in Philadelphia and travelled extensively to tennis events all over the world for his employers, Virginia Slims. As a writer, broadcaster, publicist and, above all raconteur, Ted communicated his enthusiasm for the game with a sharp and sometimes wicked wit. His tall, stooping figure, dressed extravagantly for effect, was to be seen at all the major events, the shaven head with a diamond in the left ear, nodding sagely as each new champion emerged. He had seen them all, but we shall never see his like again.

CHAMPIONSHIP ROLLS

AUSTRALIAN CHAMPIONSHIPS

MEN'S SINGLES

	CHAMPION	RUNNER-UP	SCORE			
1905	R. W. Heath	A. H. Curtis	4–6	6–3	6–4	6–4
1906	A. F. Wilding	F. N. Fisher	6–0	6–0	6–4	
1907	H. M. Rice	H. A. Parker	6–3	6–4	6–4	
1908	F. B. Alexander	A. W. Dunlop	3–6	3–6	6–0	6–2	6–3
1909	A. F. Wilding	E. F. Parker	6–1	7–5	6–2	
1910	R. W. Heath	H. M. Rice	6–4	6–3	6–2	
1911	N. E. Brookes	H. M. Rice	6–1	6–2	6–3	
1912	J. C. Parke	A. E. Beamish	3–6	6–2	1–6	6–1	7–5
1913	E. F. Parker	H. A. Parker	2–6	6–1	6–3	6–2
1914	A. O'Hara Wood	G. L. Patterson	6–4	6–3	5–7	6–1
1915	F. G. Lowe	H. M. Rice	4–6	6–1	6–1	6–4
1916–18	*Not held*					
1919	A. R. F. Kingscote	E. O. Pockley	6–4	6–0	6–3	
1920	P. O'Hara Wood	V. Thomas	6–3	4–6	6–8	6–1	6–3
1921	R. H. Gemmell	A. Hedeman	7–5	6–1	6–4	
1922	J. O. Anderson	G. L. Patterson	6–0	3–6	3–6	6–3	6–2
1923	P. O'Hara Wood	C. B. St John	6–1	6–1	6–3	
1924	J. O. Anderson	R. E. Schlesinger	6–3	6–4	3–6	5–7	6–3
1925	J. O. Anderson	G. L. Patterson	11–9	2–6	6–2	6–3
1926	J. B. Hawkes	J. Willard	6–1	6–3	6–1	
1927	G. L. Patterson	J. B. Hawkes	3–6	6–4	3–6	18–16	6–3
1928	J. Borotra	R. O. Cummings	6–4	6–1	4–6	5–7	6–3
1929	J. C. Gregory	R. E. Schlesinger	6–2	6–2	5–7	7–5
1930	E. F. Moon	H. C. Hopman	6–3	6–1	6–3	
1931	J. H. Crawford	H. C. Hopman	6–4	6–2	2–6	6–1
1932	J. H. Crawford	H. C. Hopman	4–6	6–3	3–6	6–3	6–1
1933	J. H. Crawford	K. Gledhill	2–6	7–5	6–3	6–2
1934	F. J. Perry	J. H. Crawford	6–3	7–5	6–1	
1935	J. H. Crawford	F. J. Perry	2–6	6–4	6–4	6–4
1936	A. K. Quist	J. H. Crawford	6–2	6–3	4–6	3–6	9–7
1937	V. B. McGrath	J. E. Bromwich	6–3	1–6	6–0	2–6	6–1
1938	J. D. Budge	J. E. Bromwich	6–4	6–2	6–1	
1939	J. E. Bromwich	A. K. Quist	6–4	6–1	6–3	
1940	A. K. Quist	J. H. Crawford	6–3	6–1	6–2	
1941–45	*Not held*					
1946	J. E. Bromwich	D. Pails	5–7	6–3	7–5	3–6	6–2
1947	D. Pails	J. E. Bromwich	4–6	6–4	3–6	7–5	8–6
1948	A. K. Quist	J. E. Bromwich	6–4	3–6	6–3	2–6	6–3
1949	F. A. Sedgman	J. E. Bromwich	6–3	6–2	6–2	
1950	F. A. Sedgman	K. McGregor	6–3	6–4	4–6	6–1
1951	R. Savitt	K. McGregor	6–3	2–6	6–3	6–1
1952	K. McGregor	F. A. Sedgman	7–5	12–10	2–6	6–2
1953	K. R. Rosewall	M. G. Rose	6–0	6–3	6–4	
1954	M. G. Rose	R. N. Hartwig	6–2	0–6	6–4	6–2
1955	K. R. Rosewall	L. A. Hoad	9–7	6–4	6–4	
1956	L. A. Hoad	K. R. Rosewall	6–4	3–6	6–4	7–5
1957	A. J. Cooper	N. A. Fraser	6–3	9–11	6–4	6–2
1958	A. J. Cooper	M. J. Anderson	7–5	6–3	6–4	
1959	A. Olmedo	N. A. Fraser	6–1	6–2	3–6	6–3
1960	R. G. Laver	N. A. Fraser	5–7	3–6	6–3	8–6	8–6
1961	R. S. Emerson	R. G. Laver	1–6	6–3	7–6	6–4
1962	R. G. Laver	R. S. Emerson	8–6	0–6	6–4	6–4
1963	R. S. Emerson	K. N. Fletcher	6–3	6–3	6–1	

1964	R. S. Emerson	F. S. Stolle	6–3	6–4	6–2		
1965	R. S. Emerson	F. S. Stolle	7–9	2–6	6–4	7–5	6–1
1966	R. S. Emerson	A. R. Ashe	6–4	6–8	6–2	6–3	
1967	R. S. Emerson	A. R. Ashe	6–4	6–1	6–4		
1968	W. W. Bowrey	J. M. Gisbert	7–5	2–6	9–7	6–4	
1969	R. G. Laver	A. Gimeno	6–3	6–4	7–5		
1970	A. R. Ashe	R. D. Crealy	6–4	9–7	6–2		
1971	K. R. Rosewall	A. R. Ashe	6–1	7–5	6–3		
1972	K. R. Rosewall	M. J. Anderson	7–6	6–3	7–5		
1973	J. D. Newcombe	O. Parun	6–3	6–7	7–5	6–1	
1974	J. S. Connors	P. Dent	7–6	6–4	4–6	6–3	
1975	J. D. Newcombe	J. S. Connors	7–5	3–6	6–4	7–5	
1976	M. Edmondson	J. D. Newcombe	6–7	6–3	7–6	6–1	
1977 (Jan)	R. Tanner	G. Vilas	6–3	6–3	6–3		
1977 (Dec)	V. Gerulaitis	J. M. Lloyd	6–3	7–6	5–7	3–6	6–2
1978 (Dec)	G. Vilas	J. Marks	6–4	6–4	3–6	6–3	
1979 (Dec)	G. Vilas	J. Sadri	7–6	6–3	6–2		
1980 (Dec)	B. Teacher	K. Warwick	7–5	7–6	6–3		
1981 (Dec)	J. Kriek	S. Denton	6–2	7–6	6–7	6–4	
1982 (Dec)	J. Kriek	S. Denton	6–3	6–3	6–2		
1983 (Dec)	M. Wilander	I. Lendl	6–1	6–4	6–4		
1984 (Dec)	M. Wilander	K. Curren	6–7	6–4	7–6	6–2	
1985 (Dec)	S. Edberg	M. Wilander	6–4	6–3	6–3		
1986	*Not held*						
1987 (Jan)	S. Edberg	P. Cash	6–3	6–4	3–6	5–7	6–3
1988	M. Wilander	P. Cash	6–3	6–7	2–6	6–1	8–6
1989	I. Lendl	M. Mecir	6–2	6–2	6–2		
1990	I. Lendl	S. Edberg	4–6	7–6	5–2 ret'd		

	FIRST PRIZE (US $)
	5,000
	3,800
	10,000
	2,240
	8,750
	9,750
	12,489
	32,000
	32,000
	28,000
	41,000
	50,000
	65,000
	65,000
	70,000
	77,500
	100,000
	100,000
	103,875
	104,997
	140,000
	200,000

WOMEN'S SINGLES

	CHAMPION	RUNNER-UP	SCORE		
1922	Mrs M. Molesworth	Miss E. F. Boyd	6–3	10–8	
1923	Mrs M. Molesworth	Miss E. F. Boyd	6–1	7–5	
1924	Miss S. Lance	Miss E. F. Boyd	6–3	3–6	6–4
1925	Miss D. Akhurst	Miss E. F. Boyd	1–6	8–6	6–4
1926	Miss D. Akhurst	Miss E. F. Boyd	6–1	6–3	
1927	Miss E. F. Boyd	Mrs S. Harper	5–7	6–1	6–2
1928	Miss D. Akhurst	Miss E. F. Boyd	7–5	6–2	
1929	Miss D. Akhurst	Miss L. M. Bickerton	6–1	5–7	6–2
1930	Miss D. Akhurst	Mrs S. Harper	10–8	2–6	7–5
1931	Mrs C. Buttsworth	Mrs J. H. Crawford	1–6	6–3	6–4
1932	Mrs C. Buttsworth	Miss K. Le Messurier	9–7	6–4	
1933	Miss J. Hartigan	Mrs C. Buttsworth	6–4	6–3	
1934	Miss J. Hartigan	Mrs M. Molesworth	6–1	6–4	
1935	Miss D. E. Round	Miss N. M. Lyle	1–6	6–1	6–3
1936	Miss J. Hartigan	Miss N. Wynne	6–4	6–4	
1937	Miss N. Wynne	Mrs V. Westacott	6–3	5–7	6–4
1938	Miss D. M. Bundy	Miss D. Stevenson	6–3	6–2	
1939	Mrs V. Westacott	Mrs H. C. Hopman	6–1	6–2	
1940	Mrs N. Bolton	Miss T. Coyne	5–7	6–4	6–0
1941–45	*Not held*				
1946	Mrs N. Bolton	Miss J. Fitch	6–4	6–4	
1947	Mrs N. Bolton	Mrs H. C. Hopman	6–3	6–2	
1948	Mrs N. Bolton	Miss M. Toomey	6–3	6–1	
1949	Miss D. J. Hart	Mrs N. Bolton	6–3	6–4	
1950	Miss A. L. Brough	Miss D. J. Hart	6–4	3–6	6–4
1951	Mrs N. Bolton	Mrs T. D. Long	6–1	7–5	
1952	Mrs T. D. Long	Miss H. Angwin	6–2	6–3	
1953	Miss M. Connolly	Miss J. Sampson	6–3	6–2	
1954	Mrs T. D. Long	Miss J. Staley	6–3	6–4	
1955	Miss B. Penrose	Mrs T. D. Long	6–4	6–3	
1956	Miss M. Carter	Mrs T. D. Long	3–6	6–2	9–7
1957	Miss S. J. Fry	Miss A. Gibson	6–3	6–4	
1958	Miss A. Mortimer	Miss L. Coghlan	6–3	6–4	
1959	Mrs S. J. Reitano	Miss R. Schuurman	6–2	6–3	
1960	Miss M. Smith	Miss J. Lehane	7–5	6–2	
1961	Miss M. Smith	Miss J. Lehane	6–1	6–4	
1962	Miss M. Smith	Miss J. Lehane	6–0	6–2	
1963	Miss M. Smith	Miss J. Lehane	6–2	6–2	

1964	Miss M. Smith	Miss L. R. Turner	6–3	6–2		
1965	Miss M. Smith	Miss M. E. Bueno	5–7	6–4	5–2 ret'd	
1966	Miss M. Smith	Miss N. Richey	w.o.			
1967	Miss N. Richey	Miss L. R. Turner	6–1	6–4		FIRST
1968	Mrs L. W. King	Mrs B. M. Court	6–1	6–2		PRIZE
1969	Mrs B. M. Court	Mrs L. W. King	6–4	6–1		(US $)
1970	Mrs B. M. Court	Miss K. Melville	6–1	6–3		2,000
1971	Mrs B. M. Court	Miss E. Goolagong	2–6	7–5	7–6	700
1972	Miss S. V. Wade	Miss E. Goolagong	6–4	6–4		1,800
1973	Mrs B. M. Court	Miss E. Goolagong	6–4	7–5		1,200
1974	Miss E. Goolagong	Miss C. M. Evert	7–6	4–6	6–0	5,700
1975	Miss E. Goolagong	Miss M. Navratilova	6–3	6–2		9,000
1976	Mrs E. Cawley	Miss R. Tomanova	6–2	6–2		8,115
1977	(Jan) Mrs G. Reid	Miss D. Fromholtz	7–5	6–2		12,000
1977	(Dec) Mrs E. Cawley	Mrs H. Cawley	6–3	6–0		12,000
1978	(Dec) Miss C. O'Neil	Miss B. Nagelsen	6–3	7–6		9,000
1979	(Dec) Miss B. Jordan	Miss S. Walsh	6–3	6–3		6,000
1980	(Dec) Miss H. Mandlikova	Miss W. M. Turnbull	6–0	7–5		10,000
1981	(Dec) Miss M. Navratilova	Mrs C. Evert Lloyd	6–7	6–4	7–5	32,000
1982	(Dec) Mrs C. Evert Lloyd	Miss M. Navratilova	6–3	2–6	6–3	34,000
1983	(Dec) Miss M. Navratilova	Miss K. Jordan	6–2	7–6		40,000
1984	(Dec) Mrs J. M. Lloyd	Miss H. Sukova	6–7	6–1	6–3	75,000
1985	(Dec) Miss M.Navratilova	Mrs J. M. Lloyd	6–2	4–6	6–2	100,000
1986	*Not held*					100,000
1987	(Jan) Miss H. Mandlikova	Miss M. Navratilova	7–5	7–6		115,000
1988	Miss S. Graf	Miss C. Evert	6–1	7–6		115,000
1989	Miss S. Graf	Miss H. Sukova	6–4	6–4		135,000
1990	Miss S. Graf	Miss M-J. Fernandez	6–3	6–4		190,000

MEN'S DOUBLES

	CHAMPIONS	RUNNERS-UP	SCORE				
1905	R. Lycett/T. Tachell	E. T. Barnard/B. Spence	11–9	8–6	1–6	4–6	6–1
1906	R. W. Heath/A. F. Wilding	C. C. Cox/H. A. Parker	6–2	6–4	6–2		
1907	W. A. Gregg/H. A. Parker	H. M. Rice/G. W. Wright	6–2	3–6	6–3	6–2	
1908	F. B. Alexander/A. W. Dunlop	G. G. Sharpe/A. F. Wilding	6–3	6–2	6–1		
1909	J. P. Keane/E. F. Parker	C. Crooks/A. F. Wilding	1–6	6–1	6–1	9–7	
1910	A. Campbell/H. M. Rice	R. W. Heath/J. L. O'Dea	6–3	6–3	6–2		
1911	H. W. Heath/R. Lycett	J. J. Addison/N. E. Brookes	6–2	7–5	6–0		
1912	C. P. Dixon/J. C. Parke	A. E. Beamish/F. G. Lowe	6–0	6–4	6–2		
1913	A. H. Hedemann/E. F. Parker	H. Parker/R. Taylor	8–6	4–6	6–4	6–4	
1914	A. Campbell/G. L. Patterson	R. W. Heath/A. O'Hara Wood	7–5	3–6	6–3	6–3	
1915	H. M. Rice/C. V. Todd	F. G. Lowe/C. St John	8–6	6–4	7–9	6–3	
1916–1918	*Not held*						
1919	P. O'Hara Wood/R. V. Thomas	J. O. Anderson/A. H. Lowe	7–5	6–1	7–9	3–6	6–3
1920	P. O'Hara Wood/R. V. Thomas	H. Rice/R. Taylor	6–1	6–0	7–5		
1921	S. H. Eaton/R. H. Gemmell	E. Stokes/N. Breasly	7–5	6–3	6–3		
1922	J. B. Hawkes/G. L. Patterson	J. O. Anderson/N. Peach	8–10	6–0	6–0	7–5	
1923	P. O'Hara Wood/C. B. St John	H. Rice/J. Bullough	6–4	6–3	3–6	6–0	
1924	J. O. Anderson/N. E. Brookes	P. OHara Wood/G. L. Patterson	6–2	6–4	6–3		
1925	P. O'Hara Wood/G. L. Patterson	J. O. Anderson/F. Kalms	6–4	8–6	7–5		
1926	J. B. Hawkes/G. L. Patterson	J. O. Anderson/P. O'Hara Wood	6–1	6–4	6–2		
1927	J. B. Hawkes/G. L. Patterson	I. McInnes/P. O'Hara Wood	8–6	6–2	6–1		
1928	J. Borotra/J. Brugnon	E. F. Moon/J. Willard	6–2	4–6	6–4	6–4	
1929	J. H. Crawford/H. C. Hopman	R. O. Cummings/E. F. Moon	6–1	6–8	4–6	6–1	6–3
1930	J. H. Crawford/H. C. Hopman	J. Fitchett/J. B. Hawkes	8–6	6–1	2–6	6–3	
1931	C. Donohoe/R. Dunlop	J. H. Crawford/H. O. Hopman	8–6	6–2	5–7	7–9	6–4
1932	J. H. Crawford/E. F. Moon	H. C. Hopman/G. L. Patterson	12–10	6–3	4–6	6–4	
1933	K. Gledhill/H. E. Vines	J. H. Crawford/E. F. Moon	6–4	10–8	6–2		
1934	G. P. Hughes/F. J. Perry	A. K. Quist/D. P. Turnbull	6–8	6–3	6–4	3–6	6–3
1935	J. H. Crawford/V. B. McGrath	G. P. Hughes/F. J. Perry	6–4	8–6	6–2		
1935	J. H. Crawford/V. B. McGrath	G. P. Hughes/F. J. Perry	6–4	8–6	6–2		
1936	A. K. Quist/D. P. Turnbull	J. H. Crawford/V. B. McGrath	6–8	6–2	6–1	3–6	6–2
1937	A. K. Quist/D. P. Turnbull	J. E. Bromwich/J. E. Harper	6–2	9–7	1–6	6–8	6–4
1938	J. E. Bromwich/A. K. Quist	H. Henkel/G. Von Cramm	7–5	6–4	6–0		
1939	J. E. Bromwich/A. K. Quist	C. F. Long/D. P. Turnbull	6–4	7–5	6–2		
1940	J. E. Bromwich/A. K. Quist	J. H. Crawford/V. B. McGrath	6–3	7–5	6–1		
1941–1945	*Not held*						
1946	J. E. Bromwich/A. K. Quist	M. Newcombe/L. A. Schwartz	6–4	6–2	6–3		
1947	J. E. Bromwich/A. K. Quist	F. A. Sedgman/G. Worthington	6–1	6–3	6–1		

1948	J. E. Bromwich/A. K. Quist	C. Long/F. A. Sedgman	1–6	6–8	9–7	6–3	8–6
1949	J. E. Bromwich/A. K. Quist	G. Brown/O. W. Sidwell	6–8	7–5	6–2	6–3	
1950	J. E. Bromwich/A. K. Quist	J. Drobny/E. W. Sturgess	6–3	5–7	4–6	6–3	8–6
1951	K. McGregor/F. A. Sedgman	J. E. Bromwich/A. K. Quist	11–9	2–6	6–3	4–6	6–3
1952	K. McGregor/F. A. Sedgman	D. Candy/M. G. Rose	6–4	7–5	6–3		
1953	L. A. Hoad/K. R. Rosewall	D. Candy/M. G. Rose	9–11	6–4	10–8	6–4	
1954	R. N. Hartwig/M. G. Rose	N. A. Fraser/C. Wilderspin	6–3	6–4	6–2		
1955	E. V. Seixas/M. A. Trabert	L. A. Hoad/K. R. Rosewall	6–3	6–2	2–6	3–6	6–1
1956	L. A. Hoad/K. R. Rosewall	D. Candy/M. G. Rose	10–8	13–11	6–4		
1957	N. A. Fraser/L. A. Hoad	M. J. Anderson/A. Cooper	6–3	8–6	6–4		
1958	A. Cooper/N. A. Fraser	R. S. Emerson/R. Mark	6–5	6–8	3–6	6–3	7–5
1959	R. G. Laver/R. Mark	D. Candy/R. N. Howe	9–7	6–4	6–2		
1960	R. G. Laver/R. Mark	R. S. Emerson/N. A. Fraser	1–6	6–2	6–4	6–4	
1961	R. G. Laver/R. Mark	R. S. Emerson/M. F. Mulligan	6–3	7–5	3–6	7–9	6–2
1962	R. S. Emerson/N. A. Fraser	R. A. J. Hewitt/F. S. Stolle	4–6	4–6	6–1	6–4	11–9
1963	R. A. J. Hewitt/F. S. Stolle	K. N. Fletcher/J. D. Newcombe	6–2	3–6	6–3	3–6	6–3
1964	R. A. J. Hewitt/F. S. Stolle	R. S. Emerson/K. N. Fletcher	6–4	7–5	3–6	4–6	14–12
1965	J. D. Newcombe/A. D. Roche	R. S. Emerson/F. S. Stolle	3–6	4–6	13–11	6–3	6–4
1966	R. S. Emerson/F. S. Stolle	J. D. Newcombe/A. D. Roche	7–9	6–3	6–8	14–12	12–10
1967	J. D. Newcombe/A. D. Roche	W. W. Bowrey/O. K. Davidson	3–6	6–3	7–5	6–8	8–6
1968	R. D. Crealy/A. J. Stone	T. Addison/R. Keldie	10–8	6–4	6–3		
1969	R. S. Emerson/R. G. Laver	K. R. Rosewall/F. S. Stolle	6–4	6–4	6–4		
1970	R. C. Lutz/S. R. Smith	J. G. Alexander/P. Dent	6–3	8–6	6–3		
1971	J. D. Newcombe/A. D. Roche	T. S. Okker/M. C. Riessen	6–2	7–6			
1972	O. K. Davidson/K. R. Rosewall	R. Case/G. Masters	3–6	7–6	6–3		
1973	M. J. Anderson/J. D. Newcombe	J. G. Alexander/P. Dent	6–3	6–4	7–6		
1974	R. Case/G. Masters	S. Ball/R. Giltinan	6–7	6–3	6–4		
1975	J. G. Alexander/P. Dent	R. Carmichael/A. J. Stone	6–3	7–6			
1976	J. D. Newcombe/A. D. Roche	R. Case/G. Masters	7–6	6–4			
1977	A. R. Ashe/A. D. Roche	C. Pasarell/E. Van Dillen	6–4	6–4			
1977	(Dec) R. O. Ruffels/A. J. Stone	J. G. Alexander/P. Dent	7–6	7–6			
1978	(Dec) Fibak/K. Warwick	P. Kronk/C. Letcher	7–6	7–5			
1979	(Dec) P. McNamara/P. McNamee	P. Kronk/C. Letcher	7–6	6–2			
1980	(Dec) M. R. Edmondson/K. Warwick	P. McNamara/P. McNamee	7–5	6–4			
1981	(Dec) M. R. Edmondson/K. Warwick	H. Pfister/J. Sadri	6–3	6–7	6–3		
1982	(Dec) J. G. Alexander/J. Fitzgerald	A. Andrews/J. Sadri	6–4	7–6			
1983	(Dec) M. R. Edmondson/P. McNamee	S. Denton/S. E. Stewart	6–3	7–6			
1984	(Dec) M. R. Edmondson/S. E. Stewart	J. Nystrom/M. Wilander	6–2	6–2	7–5		
1985	(Dec) P. Annacone/C. Van Rensburg	M. R. Edmondson/K. Warwick	3–6	7–6	6–4	6–4	
1986	*Not held*						
1987	(Jan) S. Edberg/A. Jarryd	P. Doohan/L. Warder	6–4	6–4	7–6		
1988	R. Leach/J. Pugh	M. J. Bates/P. Lundgren	6–3	6–2	6–3		
1989	R. Leach/J. Pugh	D. Cahill/M. Kratzmann	6–4	6–4	6–4		
1990	P. Aldrich/D. Visser	G. Connell/G. Michibata	6–4	4–6	6–1	6–4	

WOMEN'S DOUBLES

	CHAMPIONS	RUNNERS-UP	SCORE		
1922	E. F. Boyd/M. Mountain	St George/H. S. Utz	1–6	6–4	7–5
1923	E. F. Boyd/S. Lance	M. Molesworth/H. Turner	6–1	6–4	
1924	D. Akhurst/S. Lance	K. Le Mesurier/P. O'Hara Wood	7–5	6–2	
1925	D. Akhurst/R. Harper	E. F. Boyd/K. Le Mesurier	6–4	6–3	
1926	E. F. Boyd/P. O'Hara Wood	D. Akhurst/M. Cox	6–3	6–8	8–6
1927	L. M. Bickerton/P. O'Hara Wood	E. F. Boyd/R. Harper	6–3	6–3	
1928	D. Akhurst/E. F. Boyd	K. Le Mesurier/D. Weston	6–3	6–1	
1929	D. Akhurst/L. M. Bickerton	R. Harper/P. O'Hara Wood	6–2	3–6	6–2
1930	E. Hood/M. Molesworth	M. Cox/R. Harper	6–3	0–6	7–5
1931	L. M. Bickerton/R. Cozens	A. Lloyd/H. S. Utz	6–0	6–4	
1932	C. Buttsworth/J. H. Crawford	K. Le Mesurier/D. Weston	6–2	6–2	
1933	M. Molesworth/V. Westacott	J. Hartigan/J. Van Ryn	6–3	6–3	
1934	M. Molesworth/V. Westacott	J. Hartigan/U. Valkenborg	6–8	6–4	6–4
1935	E. M. Dearman/N. M. Lyle	L. M. Bickerton/N. Hopman	6–3	6–4	
1936	T. Coyne/N. Wynne	M. Blick/K. Woodward	6–2	6–4	
1937	T. Coyne/N. Wynne	N. Hopman/V. Westacott	6–2	6–2	
1938	T. Coyne/N. Wynne	D. M. Bundy/D. E. Workman	9–7	6–4	
1939	T. Coyne/N. Wynne	M. Hardcastle/V. Westacott	7–5	6–4	
1940	T. Coyne/N. Bolton	J. Hartigan/E. Niemeyer	7–5	6–2	
1941–1945	*Not held*				
1946	M. Bevis/J. Fitch	Not available			
1947	N. Bolton/T. D. Long	M. Bevis/J. Fitch	6–3	6–3	

1948	N. Bolton/T. D. Long	M. Bevis/N. Jones	6–3 6–3	
1949	N. Bolton/T. D. Long	D./M. Toomey	6–0 6–1	
1950	L. Brough/D.J. Hart	N. Bolton/T. D. Long	6–3 2–6 6–3	
1951	N. Bolton/T. D. Long	J. Fitch/M. Hawton	6–2 6–1	
1952	N. Bolton/T. D. Long	R. Baker/M. Hawton	6–1 6–1	
1953	M. Connolly/J. Sampson	M. Hawton/B. Penrose	6–3 6–2	
1954	M. Hawton/B. Penrose	H. Redick-Smith/J. Wipplinger	6–3 8–6	
1955	M. Hawton/B. Penrose	N. Hopman/A. Thiele	7–5 6–1	
1956	M. Hawton/T. D. Long	M. Carter/B. Penrose	6–3 5–7 9–7	
1957	S. J. Fry/A. Gibson	M. Hawton/F. Muller	6–2 6–1	
1958	M. Hawton/T. D. Long	L. Coghlan/A. Mortimer	7–5 6–8 6–2	
1959	S. Reynolds/R. Schuurman	L. Coghlan/M. Reitano	7–5 6–4	
1960	M. E. Bueno/C. Truman	L. Robinson/M. Smith	6–2 5–7 6–2	
1961	M. Reitano/M. Smith	M. Hawton/J. Lehane	6–3 3–6 7–5	
1962	E. Ebbern/M. Smith	D. R. Hard/M. Reintano	6–4 6–4	
1963	R. Ebbern/M. Smith	J. Lehane/L. R. Turner	6–1 6–3	
1964	J. A. M. Tegart/L. R. Turner	R. Ebbern/M. Smith	6–4 6–4	
1965	M. Smith/L. R. Turner	R. Ebbern/B. J. Moffitt	1–6 6–2 6–3	
1966	C. Graebner/N. Richey	M. Smith/L. R. Turner	6–4 7–5	
1967	J. A. M. Tegart/L. R. Turner	L. Robinson/E. Terras	6–0 6–2	
1968	K. Krantzcke/K. Melville	J. A. M. Tegart/L. R. Turner	6–4 3–6 6–2	
1969	B. M. Court/J. A. M. Tegart	R. Casals/L. W. King	6–4 6–4	
1970	B. M. Court/D. Dalton	K. Krantzcke/K. Melville	6–3 6–4	
1971	B. M. Court/E. F. Goolagong	J. Emmerson/L. Hunt	6–0 6–0	
1972	H. Gourlay/K. Harris	P. Coleman/K. Krantzcke	6–2 6–3	
1973	B. M. Court/S. V. Wade	K. Harris/K. Melville	6–4 6–4	
1974	E. F. Goolagong/M. Michel	K. Harris/K. Melville	7–5 6–3	
1975	E. F. Goolagong/M. Michel	B. M. Court/O. Morozova	7–6 7–6	
1976	E. F. Cawley/H. Gourlay	W. W. Bowrey/R. Tomanova	8–1 (one set)	
1977	D. Fromholtz/H. Gourlay	B. Nagelsen/G. E. Reid	5–7 6–1 7–5	
1977	(Dec) E. F. Cawley/H. Cawley div'd with M. Guerrant/G. E. Reid			
1978	(Dec) B. Nagelsen/R. Tomanova	N. Sato/P. Whytcross	7–5 6–2	
1979	(Dec) D. D. Chaloner/D. R. Evers	L. Harrison/M. Mesker	6–2 1–6 6–0	
1980	(Dec) B. Nagelsen/M. Navratilova	A. Kiyomura/C. Reynolds	6–4 6–4	
1981	(Dec) K. Jordan/A. E. Smith	M. Navratilova/P. H. Shriver	6–2 7–5	
1982	(Dec) M. Navratilova/P. H. Shriver	C. Kohde/E. Pfaff	6–4 6–2	
1983	(Dec) M. Navratilova/P. H. Shriver	A. E. Hobbs/W. M. Turnbull	6–4 6–7 6–2	
1984	(Dec) M. Navratilova/P. H. Shriver	C. Kohde-Kilsch/H. Sukova	6–3 6–4	
1985	(Dec) M. Navratilova/P. H. Shriver	C. Kohde-Kilsch/H. Sukova	6–3 6–4	
1986	*Not held*			
1987	(Jan) M. Navratilova/P. H. Shriver	Z. Garrison/L. McNeil	6–1 6–0	
1988	M. Navratilova/P. H. Shriver	C. Evert/W. M. Turnbull	6–0 7–5	
1989	M. Navratilova/P. H. Shriver	P. Fendick/J. Hetherington	3–6 6–3 6–2	
1990	J. Novotna/H. Sukova	P. Fendick/M-J. Fernandez	7–6 7–6	

MIXED DOUBLES

	CHAMPIONS	RUNNERS-UP	SCORE	
1922	J. B. Hawkes/Miss E. F. Boyd	H. S. Utz/Mrs Utz	6–1 6–1	
1923	H. M. Rice/Miss S. Lance	C. St John/Miss M. Molesworth	2–6 6–4 6–4	
1924	J. Willard/Miss D. Akhurst	G. M. Hone/Miss E. F. Boyd	6–3 6–4	
1925	J. Willard/Miss D. Akhurst	R. E. Schlesinger/Mrs R. Harper	6–4 6–4	
1926	J. B. Hawkes/Miss E. F. Boyd	J. Willard/Miss D. Akhurst	6–2 6–4	
1927	J. B. Hawkes/Miss E. F. Boyd	J. Willard/Miss Y. Anthony	6–1 6–3	
1928	J. Borotra/Miss D. Akhurst	J. B. Hawkes/Miss E. F. Boyd	w.o	
1929	E. F. Moon/Miss D. Akhurst	J. H. Crawford/Miss M. Cox	6–0 7–5	
1930	H. C. Hopman/Miss N. Hall	J. H. Crawford/Miss M. Cox	11–9 3–6 6–3	
1931	J. H. Crawford/Mrs Crawford	A. Willard/Mrs V. Westacott	Not available	
1932	J. H. Crawford/Mrs Crawford	J. Satoh/Mrs P. O'Hara Wood	6–8 8–6 6–3	
1933	J. H. Crawford/Mrs Crawford	H. E. Vines/Mrs J. Van Ryn	3–6 7–5 13–11	
1934	E. F. Moon/Miss J. Hartigan	R. Dunlop/Mrs V. Westacott	6–3 6–4	
1935	C. Boussus/Miss L. Bickerton	V. G. Kirby/Mrs Bond	1–6 6–3 6–3	
1936	H. C. Hopman/Mrs Hopman	A. A. Kay/Miss M. Blick	6–2 6–0	
1937	H. C. Hopman/Mrs Hopman	D. P. Turnbull/Miss D. Stevenson	3–6 6–3 6–2	
1938	J. E. Bromwich/Miss J. Wilson	C. Long/Miss N. Wynne	6–3 6–2	
1939	H. C. Hopman/Mrs Hopman	J. E. Bromwich/Miss J. Wilson	6–8 6–2 6–3	
1940	C. Long/Mrs N. Bolton	H. C. Hopman/Mrs Hopman	7–5 2–6 6–4	
1941–1945	*Not held*			
1946	C. Long/Mrs N. Bolton	J. Bromwich/Miss J. Fitch	6–0 6–4	
1947	C. Long/Mrs N. Bolton	J. E. Bromwich/Miss J. Fitch	6–3 6–3	

1948	C. Long/Mrs N. Bolton	O. W. Sidwell/Mrs T. D. Long	7–5 4–6 8–6
1949	F. A. Sedgman/Miss D. J. Hart	J. E. Bromwich/Miss J. Fitch	6–1 5–7 12–10
1950	F. A. Sedgman/Miss D. J. Hart	E. W. Sturgess/Miss J. Fitch	6–3 2–6 6–3
1951	G. A. Worthington/Mrs T. D. Long	J. May/Miss C. Proctor	4–6 6–3 6–2
1952	G. A. Worthington/Mrs T. D. Long	T. Warhurst/Mrs A. R. Thiele	9–7 7–5
1953	R. N. Hartwig/Miss J. Sampson	H. Richardson/Miss M. Connolly	6–4 6–3
1954	R. N. Hartwig/Mrs T. D. Long	J. E. Bromwich/Miss B. Penrose	8–6 9–7
1955	G. A. Worthington/Mrs T. D. Long	L. A. Hoad/Miss J. Staley	6–2 6–1
1956	N. A. Fraser/Miss B. Penrose	R. S. Emerson/Mrs M. Hawton	6–2 6–4
1957	M. J. Anderson/Miss F. Muller	W. A. Knight/Miss J. Langley	7–5 3–6 6–1
1958	R. N. Howe/Mrs M. Hawton	A. Newman/Miss A. Mortimer	9–11 6–1 6–2
1959	R. Mark/Miss S. Reynolds	R. G. Laver/Miss R. Schuurman	4–6 13–11 6–1
1960	T. Fancutt/Miss J. Lehane	R. Mark/Mrs M. Reitano	6–2 7–5
1961	R. A. J. Hewitt/Miss J. Lehane	J. Pearce/Mrs M. Reitano	9–7 6–2
1962	F. S. Stolle/Miss L. R. Turner	R. Taylor/Miss D. R. Hard	6–3 9–7
1963	K. N. Fletcher/Miss M. Smith	F. S. Stolle/Miss L. R. Turner	7–5 5–7 6–4
1964	K. N. Fletcher/Miss M. Smith	M. J. Sangster/Miss J. Lehane	6–1 6–2
1965	J. D. Newcombe/Miss M. Smith div'd with O. K. Davidson/Miss R. Ebbern		
1966	A. D. Roche/Miss J. A. Tegart	W. W. Bowrey/Miss R. Ebbern	6–1 6–3
1967	O. K. Davidson/Miss L. R. Turner	A. D. Roche/Miss J. A. M. Tegart	9–7 6–4
1968	R. D. Crealy/Mrs L. W. King	A. J. Stone/Mrs B. M. Court	6–2 9–7
1969	M. C. Riessen/Mrs B. M. Court div'd with F. S. Stolle/Mrs P. F. Jones		
1970–1986	*Not held*		
1987	S. E. Stewart/Miss Z. Garrison	A. Castle/Miss A. E. Hobbs	3–6 7–6 6–3
1988	J. Pugh/Miss J. Novotna	Tim Gullikson/M. Navratilova	5–7 6–2 6–4
1989	J. Pugh/Miss J. Novotna	S. Stewart/Miss Z. Garrison	6–3 6–4
1990	J. Pugh/Miss N. Zvereva	R. Leach/Miss Z. Garrison	4–6 6–2 6–3

FRENCH CHAMPIONSHIPS

Up to 1924 entry was restricted to members of French clubs. In 1925 entry was open to all amateurs. The Championships became 'open' in 1968.

MEN'S SINGLES

1891	H. Briggs	1903–04	M. Decugis	1920	A. H. Gobert
1892	J. Schopfer	1905–06	M. Germot	1921	J. Samazeuilh
1893	L. Riboulet	1907–09	M. Decugis	1922	H. Cochet
1894–96	A. Vacherot	1910	M. Germot	1923	P. Blanchy
1897–1900	P. Ayme	1911	A. H. Gobert	1924	J. Borotra
1901	A. Vacherot	1912–14	M. Decugis		
1902	M. Vacherot	1915–19	*Not held*		

	CHAMPION	RUNNER-UP	SCORE			
1925	R. Lacoste	J. Borotra	7–5	6–1	6–4	
1926	H. Cochet	R. Lacoste	6–2	6–4	6–3	
1927	R. Lacoste	W. T. Tilden	6–4	4–6	5–7	6–3 11–9
1928	H. Cochet	R. Lacoste	5–7	6–3	6–1	6–3
1929	R. Lacoste	J. Borotra	6–3	2–6	6–0	2–6 8–6
1930	H. Cochet	W. T. Tilden	3–6	8–6	6–3	6–1
1931	J. Borotra	C. Boussus	2–6	6–4	7–5	6–4
1932	H. Cochet	G. de Stefani	6–0	6–4	4–6	6–3
1933	J. H. Crawford	H. Cochet	8–6	6–1	6–3	
1934	G. von Cramm	J. H. Crawford	6–4	7–9	3–6	7–5 6–3
1935	F. J. Perry	G. von Cramm	6–3	3–6	6–1	6–3
1936	G. von Cramm	F. J. Perry	6–0	2–6	6–2	2–6 6–0
1937	H. Henkel	H. W. Austin	6–1	6–4	6–3	
1938	J. D. Budge	R. Menzel	6–3	6–2	6–4	
1939	W. D. McNeill	R. L. Riggs	7–5	6–0	6–3	
1940–45	*Not held*					
1946	M. Bernard	J. Drobny	3–6	2–6	6–1	6–4 6–3
1947	J. Asboth	E. W. Sturgess	8–6	7–5	6–4	
1948	F. A. Parker	J. Drobny	6–4	7–5	5–7	8–6
1949	F. A. Parker	J. E. Patty	6–3	1–6	6–1	6–4
1950	J. E. Patty	J. Drobny	6–1	6–2	3–6	5–7 7–5
1951	J. Drobny	E. W. Sturgess	6–3	6–3	6–3	
1952	J. Drobny	F. A. Sedgman	6–2	6–0	3–6	6–3
1953	K. R. Rosewall	E. V. Seixas	6–3	6–4	1–6	6–2
1954	M. A. Trabert	A. Larsen	6–4	7–5	6–1	
1955	M. A. Trabert	S. Davidson	2–6	6–1	6–4	6–2

1956	L. A. Hoad	S. Davidson	6–4	8–6	6–3	
1957	S. Davidson	H. Flam	6–3	6–4	6–4	
1958	M. G. Rose	L. Ayala	6–3	6–4	6–4	
1959	N. Pietrangeli	I. C. Vermaak	3–6	6–3	6–4	6–1
1960	N. Pietrangeli	L. Ayala	3–6	6–3	6–4	4–6	6–3
1961	M. Santana	N. Pietrangeli	4–6	6–1	3–6	6–0	6–2
1962	R. G. Laver	R. S. Emerson	3–6	2–6	6–3	9–7	6–2
1963	R. S. Emerson	P. Darmon	3–6	6–1	6–4	6–4
1964	M. Santana	N. Pietrangeli	6–3	6–1	4–6	7–5

1965	F. S. Stolle	A. D. Roche	3–6	6–0	6–2	6–3	FIRST
1966	A. D. Roche	I. Gulyas	6–1	6–4	7–5		PRIZE
1967	R. S. Emerson	A. D. Roche	6–1	6–4	2–6	6–2	*(in French francs)*
1968	K. R. Rosewall	R. G. Laver	6–3	6–1	2–6	6–2	15,000
1969	R. G. Laver	K. R. Rosewall	6–4	6–3	6–4		35,000
1970	J. Kodes	Z. Franulovic	6–2	6–4	6–0		56,000
1971	J. Kodes	I. Nastase	8–6	6–2	2–6	7–5	48,000
1972	A. Gimeno	P. Proisy	4–6	6–3	6–1	6–1	48,000
1973	I. Nastase	N. Pilic	6–3	6–3	6–0		70,000
1974	B. Borg	M. Orantes	2–6	6–7	6–0	6–1	6–1	120,000
1975	B. Borg	G. Vilas	6–2	6–3	6–4		120,000
1976	A. Panatta	H. Solomon	6–1	6–4	4–6	7–6	130,000
1977	G. Vilas	B. E. Gottfried	6–0	6–3	6–0		190,000
1978	B. Borg	G. Vilas	6–3	6–1	6–3		210,000
1979	B. Borg	V. Pecci	6–3	6–1	6–7	6–4	208,200
1980	B. Borg	V. Gerulaitis	6–4	6–1	6–2		221,000
1981	B. Borg	I. Lendl	6–1	4–6	6–2	3–6	6–1	250,000
1982	M. Wilander	G. Vilas	1–6	7–6	6–0	6–4	400,000
1983	Y. Noah	M. Wilander	6–2	7–5	7–6		500,000
1984	I. Lendl	J. P. McEnroe	3–6	2–6	6–4	7–5	7–5	1,058,600
1985	M. Wilander	I. Lendl	3–6	6–4	6–2	6–2	1,338,200
1986	I. Lendl	M. Pernfors	6–3	6–2	6–4		1,397,250
1987	I. Lendl	M. Wilander	7–5	6–2	3–6	7–6	1,303,800
1988	M. Wilander	H. Leconte	7–5	6–2	6–1		1,500,240
1989	M. Chang	S. Edberg	6–1	3–6	4–6	6–4	6–2	1,791,390
1990	A. Gomez	A. Agassi	6–3	2–6	6–4	6–4	2,226,100

WOMEN'S SINGLES

1897–99	Mlle F. Masson	1906	Mme F. Fenwick	1915–19	*Not held*
1900	Mlle Y. Prevost	1907	Mme de Kermel	1920–23	Mlle S. Lenglen
1901	Mme P. Girod	1908	Mme F. Fenwick	1924	Mlle D. Vlasto
1902–03	Mlle F. Masson	1909–12	Mlle J. Matthey		
1904–05	Mlle K. Gillou	1913–14	Mlle M. Broquedis		

(Up to 1924 entry was restricted to members of French clubs. In 1925 entry was open to all amateurs.)

	CHAMPION	RUNNER-UP	SCORE		
1925	Mlle S. Lenglen	Miss K. McKane	6–1	6–2	
1926	Mlle S. Lenglen	Miss M. K. Browne	6–1	6–0	
1927	Mlle K. Bouman	Mrs G. Peacock	6–2	6–4	
1928	Miss H. N. Wills	Miss E. Bennett	6–1	6–2	
1929	Miss H. N. Wills	Mme R. Mathieu	6–3	6–4	
1930	Mrs F. S. Moody	Miss H. H. Jacobs	6–2	6–1	
1931	Frl C. Aussem	Miss B. Nuthall	8–6	6–1	
1932	Mrs F. S. Moody	Mme R. Mathieu	7–5	6–1	
1933	Miss M. C. Scriven	Mme R. Mathieu	6–2	4–6	6–4
1934	Miss M. C. Scriven	Miss H. H. Jacobs	7–5	4–6	6–1
1935	Mrs H. Sperling	Mme R. Mathieu	6–2	6–1	
1936	Mrs H. Sperling	Mme R. Mathieu	6–3	6–4	
1937	Mrs H. Sperling	Mme R. Mathieu	6–2	6–4	
1938	Mme R. Mathieu	Mme N. Landry	6–0	6–3	
1939	Mme R. Mathieu	Miss J. Jedrzejowska	6–3	8–6	
1940–45	*Not held*				
1946	Miss M. E. Osborne	Miss P. M. Betz	1–6	8–6	7–5
1947	Mrs P. C. Todd	Miss D. J. Hart	6–3	3–6	6–4
1948	Mme N. Landry	Miss S. J. Fry	6–2	0–6	6–0
1949	Mrs W. du Pont	Mme N. Adamson	7–5	6–2	
1950	Miss D. J. Hart	Mrs P. C. Todd	6–4	4–6	6–2
1951	Miss S. J. Fry	Miss D. J. Hart	6–3	3–6	6–3
1952	Miss D. J. Hart	Miss S. J. Fry	6–4	6–4	
1953	Miss M. Connolly	Miss D. J. Hart	6–2	6–4	

1954	Miss M. Connolly	Mme G. Bucaille	6–4	6–1		
1955	Miss A. Mortimer	Mrs D. P. Knode	2–6	7–5	10–8	
1956	Miss A. Gibson	Miss A. Mortimer	6–0	12–10		
1957	Miss S. J. Bloomer	Mrs D. P. Knode	6–1	6–3		
1958	Mrs Z. Kormoczy	Miss S. J. Bloomer	6–4	1–6	6–2	
1959	Miss C. C. Truman	Mrs Z. Kormoczy	6–4	7–5		
1960	Miss D. R. Hard	Miss Y. Ramirez	6–3	6–4		
1961	Miss A. S. Haydon	Miss Y. Ramirez	6–2	6–1		
1962	Miss M. Smith	Miss L. R. Turner	6–3	3–6	7 5	
1963	Miss L. R. Turner	Mrs P. F. Jones	2–6	6–3	7–5	
1964	Miss M. Smith	Miss M. E. Bueno	5–7	6–1	6–2	
1965	Miss L. R. Turner	Miss M. Smith	6–3	6–4		FIRST
1966	Mrs P. F. Jones	Miss N. Richey	6–3	6–1		PRIZE
1967	Mlle F. Durr	Miss L. R. Turner	4–6	6–3	6–4	(in French francs)
1968	Miss N. Richey	Mrs P. F. Jones	5–7	6–4	6–1	5,000
1969	Mrs B. M. Court	Mrs P. F. Jones	6–1	4–6	6–3	10,000
1970	Mrs B. M. Court	Miss H. Niessen	6–2	6–4		17,800
1971	Miss E. Goolagong	Miss H. Gourlay	6–3	7–5		13,500
1972	Mrs L. W. King	Miss E. Goolagong	6–3	6–3		13,500
1973	Mrs B. M. Court	Miss C. M. Evert	6–7	7–6	6–4	25,000
1974	Miss C. M. Evert	Mrs O. Morozova	6–1	6–2		40,000
1975	Miss C. M. Evert	Miss M. Navratilova	2–6	6–2	6–1	40,000
1976	Miss S. Barker	Miss R. Tomanova	6–2	0–6	6–2	30,000
1977	Miss M. Jausovec	Miss F. Mihai	6–2	6–7	6–1	35,000
1978	Miss V. Ruzici	Miss M. Jausovec	6–2	6–2		100,000
1979	Mrs C. Evert Lloyd	Miss W. M. Turnbull	6–2	6–0		126,900
1980	Mrs C. Evert Lloyd	Miss V. Ruzici	6–0	6–3		178,500
1981	Miss H. Mandlikova	Miss S. Hanika	6–2	6–4		200,000
1982	Miss M. Navratilova	Miss A. Jaeger	7–6	6–1		300,000
1983	Mrs C. Evert Lloyd	Miss M. Jausovec	6–1	6–2		375,000
1984	Miss M. Navratilova	Mrs C. Evert Lloyd	6–3	6–1		791,600
1985	Mrs C. Evert Lloyd	Miss M. Navratilova	6–3	6–7	7–5	1,262,700
1986	Mrs C. Evert Lloyd	Miss M. Navratilova	2–6	6–3	6–3	1,278,400
1987	Miss S. Graf	Miss M. Navratilova	6–4	4–6	8–6	1,178,840
1988	Miss S. Graf	Miss N. Zvereva	6–0	6–0		1,463,390
1989	Miss A. Sanchez	Miss S. Graf	7–6	3–6	7–5	1,593,175
1990	Miss M. Seles	Miss S. Graf	7–6	6–4		1,762,900

MEN'S DOUBLES

	CHAMPIONS	RUNNERS-UP	SCORE				
1925	J. Borotra/R. Lacoste	J. Brugnon/H. Cochet	7–5	4–6	6–3	2–6	6–3
1926	H. O. Kinsey/V. Richards	J. Brugnon/H. Cochet	6–4	6–1	4–6	6–4	
1927	J. Brugnon/H. Cochet	J. Borotra/R. Lacoste	2–6	6–2	6–0	1–6	6–4
1928	J. Borotra/J. Brugnon	R. de Buzelet/H. Cochet	6–4	3–6	6–2	3–6	6–4
1929	J. Borotra/R. Lacoste	J. Brugnon/H. Cochet	6–3	3–6	6–3	3–6	8–6
1930	J. Brugnon/H. Cochet	H. C. Hopman/J. Willard	6–3	9–7	6–3		
1931	G. M. Lott/J. Van Ryn	N. G. Farquharson/V. G. Kirby	6–4	6–3	6–4		
1932	J. Brugnon/H. Cochet	M. Bernard/C. Boussus	6–4	3–6	7–5	6–3	
1933	G. P. Hughes/F. J. Perry	V. B. McGrath/A. K. Quist	6–2	6–4	2–6	7–5	
1934	J. Borotra/J. Brugnon	J. H. Crawford/V. B. McGrath	11–9	6–3	2–6	4–6	9–7
1935	J. H. Crawford/A. K. Quist	V. B. McGrath/D. P. Turnbull	6–1	6–4	6–2		
1936	M. Bernard/J. Borotra	G. P. Hughes/C. R. D. Tuckey	6–2	3–6	9–7	6–1	
1937	G. Von Cramm/H. Henkel	N. G. Farquharson/V. G. Kirby	6–4	7–5	3–6	6–1	
1938	B. Destremau/Y. Petra	J. D. Budge/G. Mako	3–6	6–3	9–7	6–1	
1939	C. Harris/W. D. McNeil	J. Borotra/J. Brugnon	4–6	6–4	6–0	2–6	10–8
1940–1945	Not held						
1946	M. Bernard/Y. Petra	E. Morea/F. Segura	7–5	6–3	0–6	1–6	10–8
1947	E. Fannin/E. W. Sturgess	T. P. Brown/O. W. Sidwell	6–4	4–6	6–4	6–3	
1948	L. Bergelin/J. Drobny	H. C. Hopman/F. A. Sedgman	8–6	6–1	12–10		
1949	R. A. Gonzales/F. Parker	E. Fannin/E. W. Sturgess	6–3	8–6	5–7	6–3	
1950	W. F. Talbert/M. A. Trabert	J. Drobny/E. W. Sturgess	6–2	1–6	10–8	6–2	
1951	K. McGregor/F. A. Sedgman	G. Mulloy/R. Savitt	6–2	2–6	9–7	7–5	
1952	K. McGregor/F. A. Sedgman	G. Mulloy/R. Savitt	6–3	6–4	6–4		
1953	L. A. Hoad/K. R. Rosewall	M. G. Rose/C. Wilderspin	6–2	6–1	6–1		
1954	E. V. Seixas/M. A. Trabert	L. A. Hoad/K. R. Rosewall	6–4	6–2	6–1		
1955	E. V. Seixas/M. A. Trabert	N. Pietrangeli/O. Sirola	6–1	4–6	6–2	6–4	
1956	D. W. Candy/R. M. Perry	A. J. Cooper/L. A. Hoad	7–5	6–3	6–3		
1957	M. J. Anderson/A. J. Cooper	D. W. Candy/M. G. Rose	6–3	6–0	6–3		
1958	A. J. Cooper/N. A. Fraser	R. N. Howe/A. Segal	3–6	8–6	6–3	7–5	

1959 N. Pietrangeli/O. Sirola	R. S. Emerson/N. A. Fraser	6–3	6–2	14–12	
1960 R. S. Emerson/N. A. Fraser	J. L. Arilla/A. Gimeno	6–2	8–10	7–5	6–4
1961 R. S. Emerson/R. G. Laver	R. N. Howe/R. Mark	3–6	6–1	6–1	6–4
1962 R. S. Emerson/N. A. Fraser	W. P. Bungert/C. Kuhnke	6–3	6–4	7–5	
1963 R. S. Emerson/M. Santana	G. L. Forbes/A. Segal	6–2	6–4	6–4	
1964 R. S. Emerson/K. N. Fletcher	J. D. Newcombe/A. D. Roche	7–5	6–3	3–6	7–5
1965 R. S. Emerson/F. S. Stolle	K. N. Fletcher/R. A. J. Hewitt	6–8	6–3	8–6	6–2
1966 C. E. Graebner/R. D. Ralston	I. Nastase/I. Tiriac	6–3	6–3	6–0	
1967 J. D. Newcombe/A. D. Roche	R. S. Emerson/K. N. Fletcher	6–3	9–7	12–10	
1968 K. R. Rosewall/F. S. Stolle	R. S. Emerson/R. G. Laver	6–3	6–4	6–3	
1969 J. D. Newcombe/A. D. Roche	R. S. Emerson/R. G. Laver	4–6	6–1	3–6	6–4 6–4
1970 I. Nastase/I. Tiriac	A. R. Ashe/C. Pasarell	6–2	6–4	6–3	
1971 A. R. Ashe/M. C. Riessen	T. W. Gorman/S. R. Smith	6–8	4–6	6–3	6–4 11–9
1972 R. A. J. Hewitt/F. D. McMillan	P. Cornejo/J. Fillol	6–3	8–6	3–6	6–1
1973 J. D. Newcombe/T. S. Okker	J. S. Connors/I. Nastase	6–1	3–6	6–3	5–7 6–4
1974 R. D. Crealy/O. Parun	R. C. Lutz/S. R. Smith	6–3	6–2	3–6	5–7 6–1
1975 B. E. Gottfried/R. Ramirez	J. G. Alexander/P. Dent	6–2	2–6	6–2	6–4
1976 F. McNair/S. E. Stewart	B. E. Gottfried/R. Ramirez	7–6	6–3	6–1	
1977 B. E. Gottfried/R. Ramirez	W. Fibak/J. Kodes	7–6	4–6	6–3	6–4
1978 G. Mayer/H. Pfister	J. Higueras/M. Orantes	6–3	6–2	6–2	
1979 A. A./G. Mayer	R. Case/P. Dent	6–4	6–4	6–4	
1980 V. Amaya/H. Pfister	B. E. Gottfried/R. Ramirez	1–6	6–4	6–4	6–3
1981 H. Gunthardt/B. Taroczy	T. Moor/E. Teltscher	6–2	7–6	6–3	
1982 S. E. Stewart/F. Taygan	H. Gildemeister/B. Prajoux	7–5	6–3	1–1	ret'd
1983 A. Jarryd/H. Simonsson	M. R. Edmondson/S. E. Stewart	7–6	6–4	6–2	
1984 H. Leconte/Y. Noah	P. Slozil/T. Smid	6–4	2–6	3–6	6–3 6–2
1985 M. R. Edmondson/K. Warwick	S. Glickstein/H. Simonsson	6–3	6–4	6–7	6–3
1986 J. Fitzgerald/T. Smid	S. Edberg/A. Jarryd	6–3	4–6	6–3	6–7 14–12
1987 A. Jarryd/R. Seguso	G. Forget/Y. Noah	6–7	6–7	6–3	6–4 6–2
1988 A. Gomez/E. Sanchez	J. Fitzgerald/A. Jarryd	6–3	6–7	6–4	6–3
1989 J. Grabb/P. McEnroe	M. Bahrami/E. Winogradsky	6–4	2–6	6–4	7–6
1990 S. Casal/E. Sanchez	G. Ivanisevic/P. Korda	7–5	6–3		

WOMEN'S DOUBLES

	CHAMPIONS	RUNNERS-UP	SCORE		
1925	S. Lenglen/D. Vlasto	E. Colyer/K. McKane	6–1	9–11	6–2
1926	S. Lenglen/D. Vlasto	E. Colyer/L. A. Godfree	6–1	6–1	
1927	E. L. Heine/G. Peacock	P. Saunders/P. H. Watson	6–2	6–1	
1928	E. Bennett/P. H. Watson	S. Deve/A. Lafaurie	6–0	6–2	
1929	L. de Alvarez/K. Bouman	E. L. Heine/A. Neave	7–5	6–3	
1930	F. S. Moody/E. Ryan	S. Barbier/S. Mathieu	6–3	6–1	
1931	B. Nuthall/E. F. Whittingstall	C. Aussem/E. Ryan	9–7	6–2	
1932	F. S. Moody/E. Ryan	B. Nuthall/E. F. Whittingstall	6–1	6–3	
1933	S. Mathieu/E. Ryan	S. Henrotin/C. Rosambert	6–1	6–3	
1934	S. Mathieu/E. Ryan	H. H. Jacobs/S. Palfrey	3–6	6–4	6–2
1935	M. C. Scriven/K. Stammers	N. Adamoff/H. Sperling	6–4	6–0	
1936	S. Mathieu/A. M. Yorke	S. Noel/J. Jedrzejowska	2–6	6–4	6–4
1937	S. Mathieu/A. M. Yorke	D. Andrus/S. Henrotin	3–6	6–2	6–2
1938	S. Mathieu/A. M. Yorke	A. Halff/N. Landry	6–3	6–3	
1939	J. Jedrzejowska/S. Mathieu	A. Florian/H. Kovac	7–5	7–5	
1940–1945	*Not held*				
1946	L. Brough/M. Osborne	P. Betz/D. Hart	6–4	0–6	6–1
1947	L. Brough/M. Osborne	D. Hart/P. C. Todd	7–5	6–2	
1948	D. Hart/P. C. Todd	S. Fry/M. A. Prentiss	6–4	6–2	
1949	L. Brough/W. du Pont	J. Gannon/B. Hilton	7–5	6–1	
1950	S. Fry/D. Hart	L. Brough/W. du Pont	1–6	7–5	6–2
1951	S. Fry/D. Hart	B. Bartlett/B. Scofield	10–8	6–3	
1952	S. Fry/D. Hart	H. Redick-Smith/J. Wipplinger	7–5	6–1	
1953	S. Fry/D. Hart	M. Connolly/J. Sampson	6–4	6–3	
1954	M. Connolly/N. Hopman	M. Galtier/S. Schmitt	7–5	4–6	6–0
1955	B. Fleitz/D. R. Hard	S. J. Bloomer/P. Ward	7–5	6–8	13–11
1956	A. Buxton/A. Gibson	D. R. Hard/D. Knode	6–8	8–6	6–1
1957	S. J. Bloomer/D. R. Hard	Y. Ramirez/R. M. Reyes	7–5	4–6	7–5
1958	Y. Ramirez/R. M. Reyes	M. K. Hawton/T. D. Long	6–4	7–5	
1959	S. Reynolds/R. Schuurman	Y. Ramirez/R. M. Reyes	2–6	6–0	6–1
1960	M. E. Bueno/D. R. Hard	R. Hales/A. Haydon	6–2	7–5	
1961	S. Reynolds/R. Schuurman	M. E. Bueno/D. R. Hard	w.o.		
1962	S. Price/R. Schuurman	J. Bricka/M. Smith	6–4	6–4	

1963	P. F. Jones/R. Schuurman	R. A. Ebbern/M. Smith	7–5	6–4
1964	M. Smith/L. R. Turner	N. Baylon/H. Schultze	6–3	6–1
1965	M. Smith/L. R. Turner	F. Durr/J. Lieffrig	6–3	6–1
1966	M. Smith/J. A. M. Tegart	J. Blackman/F. Toyne	4–6	6–1	6–1
1967	F. Durr/G. Sheriff	A. M. Van Zyl/P. Walkden	6–2	6–2
1968	F. Durr/P. F. Jones	R. Casals/L. W. King	7–5	4–6	6–4
1969	F. Durr/P. F. Jones	M. Court/N. Richey	6–0	4–6	7–5
1970	F. Durr/G. Chanfreau	R. Casals/L. W. King	6–1	3–6	6–3
1971	F. Durr/G. Chanfreau	H. Gourlay/K. Harris	6–4	6–1
1972	L. W. King/B. Stove	W. Shaw/F. E. Truman	6–1	6–2
1973	M. Court/S. V. Wade	F. Durr/B. Stove	6–2	6–3
1974	C. Evert/O. Morozova	G. Chanfreau/K. Ebbinghaus	6–4	2–6	6–1
1975	C. Evert/M. Navratilova	J. Anthony/O. Morozova	6–3	6–2
1976	F. Bonicelli/G. Lovera	K. Harter/H. Masthoff	6–4	1–6	6–3
1977	R. Marsikova/P. Teeguarden	R. Fox/H. Gourlay	5–7	6–4	6–2
1978	M. Jausovec/V. Ruzici	N. Bowey/G. Lovera	5–7	6–4	8–6
1979	B. Stove/W. M. Turnbull	F. Durr/S. V. Wade	6–4	7–6
1980	K. Jordan/A. E. Smith	I. Madruga/I. Villagran	6–1	6–0
1981	R. Fairbank/T. Harford	C. Reynolds/P. Smith	6–1	6–3
1982	M. Navratilova/A. E. Smith	R. Casals/W. M. Turnbull	6–3	6–4
1983	R. Fairbank/C. Reynolds	K. Jordan/A. E. Smith	5–7	7–5	6–2
1984	M. Navratilova/P. H. Shriver	C. Kohde-Kilsch/H. Mandlikova	5–7	6–3	6–2
1985	M. Navratilova/P. H. Shriver	C. Kohde-Kilsch/H. Sukova	4–6	6–2	6–2
1986	M. Navratilova/A. Temesvari	S. Graf/G. Sabatini	6–1	6–2
1987	M. Navratilova/P. H. Shriver	S. Graf/G. Sabatini	6–2	6–1
1988	M. Navratilova/P. H. Shriver	C. Kohde-Kilsch/H. Sukova	6–2	7–5
1989	L. Savchenko/N. Zvereva	S. Graf/G. Sabatini	6–4	6–4
1990	J. Novotna/H. Sukova	L. Savchenko/N. Zvereva	6–4	7–5

MIXED DOUBLES

	CHAMPIONS	RUNNERS-UP	SCORE		
1925	J. Brugnon/Miss S. Lenglen	H. Cochet/Miss D. Vlasto	6–2	6–2
1926	J. Brugnon/Miss S. Lenglen	J. Borotra/Mrs Le Besnerais	6–4	6–3
1927	J. Borotra/Miss M. Broquedis	W. T. Tilden/Miss L. de Alvarez	6–4	2–6	6–2
1928	H. Cochet/Miss E. Bennett	F. T. Hunter/Miss H. Wills	3–6	6–3	6–3
1929	H. Cochet/Miss E. Bennett	F. T. Hunter/Miss H. Wills	6–3	6–2
1930	W. T. Tilden/Miss C. Aussem	H. Cochet/Mrs F. Whittingstall	6–4	6–4
1931	P. D. B. Spence/Miss B. Nuthall	H. W. Austin/Mrs D. C. Shepherd-Barron	6–3	5–7	6–3
1932	F. J. Perry/Miss B. Nuthall	S. B. Wood/Mrs F. S. Moody	6–4	6–2
1933	J. H. Crawford/Miss M. C. Scriven	F. J. Perry/Miss B. Nuthall	6–2	6–3
1934	J. Borotra/Miss C. Rosambert	A. K. Quist/Miss E. Ryan	6–2	6–4
1935	M. Bernard/Miss L. Payot	A. M. Legeay/Mrs S. Henrotin	4–6	6–2	6–4
1936	M. Bernard/Miss A. M. Yorke	A. M. Legeay/Mrs S. Henrotin	7–5	6–8	6–3
1937	Y. Petra/Mrs S. Mathieu	R. Journu/Miss M. Horne	7–5	7–5
1938	D. Mitic/Mrs S. Mathieu	C. Boussus/Miss N. Wynne	2–6	6–3	6–4
1939	E. T. Cooke/Mrs S. Fabyan	F. Kukuljevic/Mrs S. Mathieu	4–6	6–1	7–5
1940–1945	*Not held*			
1946	J. E. Patty/Miss P. M. Betz	T. P. Brown/Miss D. Bundy	7–5	9–7
1947	E. W. Sturgess/Mrs S. P. Summers	C. Caralulis/Miss J. Jedrzejowska	6–0	6–0
1948	J. Drobny/Mrs P. C. Todd	F. A. Sedgman/Miss D. Hart	6–3	3–6	6–3
1949	E. W. Sturgess/Mrs S. P. Summers	G. D. Oakley/Miss J. Quertier	6–1	6–1
1950	E. Morea/Miss B. Scofield	W. F. Talbert/Mrs P. C. Todd	w.o.
1951	F. A. Sedgman/Miss D. Hart	M. G. Rose/Mrs T. D. Long	7–5	6–2
1952	F. A. Sedgman/Miss D. Hart	E. W. Sturgess/Miss S. Fry	6–8	6–3	6–3
1953	E. V. Seixas/Miss D. Hart	M. G. Rose/Miss M. Connolly	4–6	6–4	6–0
1954	L. A. Hoad/Miss M. Connolly	R. N. Hartwig/Mrs J. Patorni	6–4	6–3
1955	G. L. Forbes/Miss D. R. Hard	L. Ayala/Miss J. Staley	5–7	6–1	6–2
1956	L. Ayala/Mrs T. D. Long	R. N. Howe/Miss D. R. Hard	4–6	6–4	6–1
1957	J. Javorsky/Miss V. Puzejova	L. Ayala/Miss E. Buding	6–3	6–4
1958	N. Pietrangeli/Miss S. J. Bloomer	R. N. Howe/Miss L. Coghlan	9–7	6–8	6–2
1959	W. A. Knight/Miss R. Ramirez	R. G. Laver/Miss R. Schuurman	6–4	6–4
1960	R. N. Howe/Miss M. Bueno	R. S. Emerson/Miss A. Haydon	1–6	6–1	6–2
1961	R. G. Laver/Miss D. R. Hard	J. Javorsky/Miss V. Puzejova	6–0	2–6	6–3
1962	R. N. Howe/Miss R. Schuurman	F. S. Stolle/Miss L. R. Turner	3–6	6–4	6–4
1963	K. N. Fletcher/Miss M. Smith	F. S. Stolle/Miss L. R. Turner	6–1	6–2
1964	K. N. Fletcher/Miss M. Smith	F. S. Stolle/Miss L. R. Turner	6–3	6–1
1965	K. N. Fletcher/Miss M. Smith	J. D. Newcombe/Miss M. Bueno	6–4	6–4
1966	F. D. McMillan/Miss A. M. Van Zyl	C. Graebner/Mrs P. F. Jones	1–6	6–3	6–2
1967	O. K. Davidson/Mrs L. W. King	I. Tiriac/Mrs P. F. Jones	6–3	6–1

1968	J. C. Barclay/Miss F. Durr	O. K. Davidson/Mrs L. W. King	6–1	6–4	
1969	M. C. Riessen/Mrs. B. M. Court	J. C. Barclay/Miss F. Durr	7–5	6–4	
1970	R. A. J. Hewitt/Mrs L. W. King	J. C. Barclay/Miss F. Durr	3–6	6–3	6–2
1971	J. C. Barclay/Miss F. Durr	T. Lejus/Miss W. Shaw	6–2	6–4	
1972	K. Warwick/Miss E. Goolagong	J. C. Barclay/Miss F. Durr	6–2	6–4	
1973	J. C. Barclay/Miss F. Durr	P. Dominguez/Miss B. Stove	6–1	6–4	
1974	I. Molina/Miss M. Navratilova	M. Lara/Mrs R. M. Darmon	6–3	6–3	
1975	T. Koch/Miss F. Bonicelli	J. Fillol/Miss P. Teeguarden	6–4	7–6	
1976	K. Warwick/Miss I. Kloss	C. Dowdeswell/Miss L. Boshoff	5–7	7–6	6–2
1977	J. P. McEnroe/Miss M. Carillo	I. Molina/Miss F. Mihai	7–6	6–3	
1978	P. Slozil/Miss R. Tomanova	P. Dominguez/Miss V. Ruzici	7–6	ret'd	
1979	R. A. J. Hewitt/Miss W. M. Turnbull	I. Tiriac/Miss V. Ruzici	6–3	2–6	6–3
1980	W. Martin/Miss A. E. Smith	S. Birner/Miss R. Tomanova	2–6	6–4	8–6
1981	J. Arias/Miss A. Jaeger	F. D. McNair/Miss B. Stove	7–6	6–4	
1982	J. M. Lloyd/Miss W. M. Turnbull	C. Motta/Miss C. Monteiro	6–2	7–6	
1983	E. Teltscher/Miss B. Jordan	C. Strode/Miss L. Allen	6–2	6–3	
1984	R. L. Stockton/Miss A. E. Smith	L. Warder/Miss A. Minter	6–2	6–4	
1985	H. P. Gunthardt/Miss M. Navratilova	F. Gonzalez/Miss P. Smith	2–6	6–3	6–2
1986	K. Flach/Miss K. Jordan	M. R. Edmondson/Miss. R. Fairbank	3–6	7–6	6–3
1987	E. Sanchez/Miss P. H. Shriver	S. E. Stewart/Miss L. McNeil	6–3	7–6	
1988	J. Lozano/Miss L. McNeil	M. Schapers/Miss B. Schultz	7–5	6–2	
1989	T. Nijssen/Miss M. Bollegraf	H. de la Pena/Miss A. Sanchez-Vicario	6–3	6–7	6–2
1990	J. Lozano/A. Sanchez-Vicario	D. Visser/Miss N. Provis	7–6	7–6	

WIMBLEDON CHAMPIONSHIPS

For the years 1913, 1914, and 1919–23 inclusive, these records include the 'World's Championship on Grass' granted to the LTA by the ILTF. This title was then abolished. Prior to 1922 the holder did not compete in the Championship but met the winner of the singles in the Challenge Round. The Challenge Round was abolished in 1922 and the holder subsequently played through. Modified 'seeding' was introduced in 1924. Full 'seeding', as we know it today, was first practised in 1927. The Championships became 'open' in 1968. From 1877–1921 the Championships were played at the Worple Road ground. Since 1922 they have been played at the present ground in Church Road.

There was a tie-break at 8–all in the years 1971–1978. Thereafter the tie-break was played at 6–all.

*Holders did not defend the title.

MEN'S SINGLES

	CHAMPION	RUNNER-UP	SCORE				
1877	S. W. Gore	W. C. Marshall	6–1	6–2	6–4		
1878	P. F. Hadow	S. W. Gore	7–5	6–1	9–7		
1879*	J. T. Hartley	V. St L. Goold	6–2	6–4	6–2		
1880	J. T. Hartley	H. F. Lawford	6–3	6–2	2–6	6–3	
1881	W. Renshaw	J. T. Hartley	6–0	6–1	6–1		
1882	W. Renshaw	E. Renshaw	6–1	2–6	4–6	6–2	6–2
1883	W. Renshaw	E. Renshaw	2–6	6–3	6–3	4–6	6–3
1884	W. Renshaw	H. F. Lawford	6–0	6–4	9–7		
1885	W. Renshaw	H. F. Lawford	7–5	6–2	4–6	7–5	
1886	W. Renshaw	H. F. Lawford	6–0	5–7	6–4		
1887*	H. F. Lawford	E. Renshaw	1–6	6–3	3–6	6–4	6–4
1888	E. Renshaw	H. F. Lawford	6–3	7–5	6–0		
1889	W. Renshaw	E. Renshaw	6–4	6–1	3–6	6–0	
1890	W. J. Hamilton	W. Renshaw	6–8	6–2	3–6	6–1	6–1
1891*	W. Baddeley	J. Pim	6–4	1–6	7–5	6–0	
1892	W. Baddeley	J. Pim	4–6	6–3	6–3	6–2	
1893	J. Pim	W. Baddeley	3–6	6–1	6–3	6–2	
1894	J. Pim	W. Baddeley	10–8	6–2	8–6		
1895*	W. Baddeley	W. V. Eaves	4–6	2–6	8–6	6–2	6–3
1896	H. S. Mahony	W. Baddeley	6–2	6–8	5–7	8–6	6–3
1897	R. F. Doherty	H. S. Mahony	6–4	6–4	6–3		
1898	R. F. Doherty	H. L. Doherty	6–3	6–3	2–6	5–7	6–1
1899	R. F. Doherty	A. W. Gore	1–6	4–6	6–2	6–3	6–3
1900	R. F. Doherty	S. H. Smith	6–8	6–3	6–1	6–2	
1901	A. W. Gore	R. F. Doherty	4–6	7–5	6–4	6–4	
1902	H. L. Doherty	A. W. Gore	6–4	6–3	3–6	6–0	
1903	H. L. Doherty	F. L. Riseley	7–5	6–3	6–0		
1904	H. L. Doherty	F. L. Riseley	6–1	7–5	8–6		
1905	H. L. Doherty	N. E. Brookes	8–6	6–2	6–4		
1906	H. L. Doherty	F. L. Riseley	6–4	4–6	6–2	6–3	

							FIRST PRIZE (£)
1907* N. E. Brookes	A. W. Gore	6–4	6–2	6–2			
1908* A. W. Gore	H. Roper Barrett	6–3	6–2	4–6	3–6	6–4	
1909 A. W. Gore	M. J. G. Ritchie	6–8	1–6	6–2	6–2	6–2	
1910 A. F. Wilding	A. W. Gore	6–4	7–5	4–6	6–2		
1911 A. F. Wilding	H. Roper Barrett	6–4	4–6	2–6	6–2 ret'd		
1912 A. F. Wilding	A. W. Gore	6–4	6–4	4–6	6–4		
1913 A. F. Wilding	M. E. McLoughlin	8–6	6–3	10–8			
1914 N. E. Brookes	A. F. Wilding	6–4	6–4	7–5			
1915–18 *Not held*							
1919 G. L. Patterson	N. E. Brookes	6–3	7–5	6–2			
1920 W. T. Tilden	G. L. Patterson	2–6	6–2	5–3	6–4		
1921 W. T. Tilden	B. I. C. Norton	4–6	2–6	6–1	6–0	7–5	
(Challenge Round abolished)							
1922* G. L. Patterson	R. Lycett	6–3	6–4	6–2			
1923* W. M. Johnston	F. T. Hunter	6–0	6–3	6–1			
1924 J. Borotra	R. Lacoste	6–1	3–6	6–1	3–6	6–4	
1925 R. Lacoste	J. Borotra	6–3	6–3	4–6	8–6		
1926 J. Borotra	Howard Kinsey	8–6	6–1	6–3			
1927 H. Cochet	J. Borotra	4–6	4–6	6–3	6–4	7–5	
1928 R. Lacoste	H. Cochet	6–1	4–6	6–4	6–2		
1929 H. Cochet	J. Borotra	6–4	6–3	6–4			
1930 W. T. Tilden	W. L. Allison	6–3	9–7	6–4			
1931* S. B. Wood	F. X. Shields	w.o.					
1932 H. E. Vines	H. W. Austin	6–4	6–2	6–0			
1933 J. H. Crawford	H. E. Vines	4–6	11–9	6–2	2–6	6–4	
1934 F. J. Perry	J. H. Crawford	6–3	6–0	7–5			
1935 F. J. Perry	G. von Cramm	6–2	6–4	6–4			
1936 F. J. Perry	G. von Cramm	6–1	6–1	6–0			
1937* J. D. Budge	G. von Cramm	6–3	6–4	6–2			
1938 J. D. Budge	H. W. Austin	6–1	6–0	6–3			
1939* R. L. Riggs	E. T. Cooke	2–6	8–6	3–6	6–3	6–2	
1940–45 *Not held*							
1946* Y. Petra	G. E. Brown	6–2	6–4	7–9	5–7	6–4	
1947 J. A. Kramer	T. Brown	6–1	6–3	6–2			
1948* R. Falkenburg	J. E. Bromwich	7–5	0–6	6–2	3–6	7–5	
1949 F. R. Schroeder	J. Drobny	3–6	6–0	6–3	4–6	6–4	
1950* J. E. Patty	F. A. Sedgman	6–1	8–10	6–2	6–3		
1951 R. Savitt	K. McGregor	6–4	6–4	6–4			
1952 F. A. Sedgman	J. Drobny	4–6	6–2	6–3	6–2		
1953* E. V. Seixas	K. Nielsen	9–7	6–3	6–4			
1954 J. Drobny	K. R. Rosewall	13–11	4–6	6–2	9–7		
1955 M. A. Trabert	K. Nielsen	6–3	7–5	6–1			
1956* L. A. Hoad	K. R. Rosewall	6–2	4–6	7–5	6–4		
1957 L. A. Hoad	A. J. Cooper	6–2	6–1	6–2			
1958* A. J. Cooper	N. A. Fraser	3–6	6–3	6–4	13–11		
1959* A. Olmedo	R. G. Laver	6–4	6–3	6–4			
1960* N. A. Fraser	R. G. Laver	6–4	3–6	9–7	7–5		
1961 R. G. Laver	C. R. McKinley	6–3	6–1	6–4			
1962 R. G. Laver	M. F. Mulligan	6–2	6–2	6–1			
1963* C. R. McKinley	F. S. Stolle	9–7	6–1	6–4			
1964 R. S. Emerson	F. S. Stolle	6–1	12–10	4–6	6–3		
1965 R. S. Emerson	F. S. Stolle	6–2	6–4	6–4			
1966 M. Santana	R. D. Ralston	6–4	11–9	6–4			
1967 J. D. Newcombe	W. P. Bungert	6–3	6–1	6–1			2,000
1968 R. G. Laver	A. D. Roche	6–3	6–4	6–2			2,000
1969 R. G. Laver	J. D. Newcombe	6–4	5–7	6–4	6–4		3,000
1970 J. D. Newcombe	K. R. Rosewall	5–7	6–3	6–2	3–6	6–1	3,000
1971 J. D. Newcombe	S. R. Smith	6–3	5–7	2–6	6–4	6–4	3,750
1972* S. R. Smith	I. Nastase	4–6	6–3	6–3	4–6	7–5	5,000
1973* J. Kodes	A. Metreveli	6–1	9–8	6–3			5,000
1974 J. S. Connors	K. R. Rosewall	6–1	6–1	6–4			10,000
1975 A. R. Ashe	J. S. Connors	6–1	6–1	5–7	6–4		10,000
1976 B. Borg	I. Nastase	6–4	6–2	9–7			12,500
1977 B. Borg	J. S. Connors	3–6	6–2	6–1	5–7	6–4	15,000
1978 B. Borg	J. S. Connors	6–2	6–2	6–3			19,000
1979 B. Borg	R. Tanner	6–7	6–1	3–6	6–3	6–4	20,000
1980 B. Borg	J. P. McEnroe	1–6	7–5	6–3	6–7	8–6	20,000
1981 J. P. McEnroe	B. Borg	4–6	7–6	7–6	6–4		21,600
1982 J. S. Connors	J. P. McEnroe	3–6	6–3	6–7	7–6	6–4	41,667
1983 J. P. McEnroe	C. J. Lewis	6–2	6–2	6–2			66,600
1984 J. P. McEnroe	J. S. Connors	6–1	6–1	6–2			100,000
1985 B. Becker	K. Curren	6–3	6–7	7–6	6–4		130,000

1986	B. Becker	I. Lendl	6–4	6–3	7–5			140,000
1987	P. Cash	I. Lendl	7–6	6–2	7–5			155,000
1988	S. Edberg	B. Becker	4–6	7–6	6–4	6–2		165,000
1989	B. Becker	S. Edberg	6–0	7–6	6–4			190,000
1990	S. Edberg	B. Becker	6–2	6–2	3–6	3–6	6–4	230,000

WOMEN'S SINGLE'S

	CHAMPION	RUNNER-UP	SCORE		
1884	Miss M. Watson	Miss L. Watson	6–8	6–3	6–3
1885	Miss M. Watson	Miss B. Bingley	6–1	7–5	
1886	Miss B. Bingley	Miss M. Watson	6–3	6–3	
1887	Miss C. Dod	Miss B. Bingley	6–2	6–0	
1888	Miss C. Dod	Mrs G. W. Hillyard	6–3	6–3	
1889*	Mrs G. W. Hillyard	Miss H. Rice	4–6	8–6	6–4
1890*	Miss H. Rice	Miss M. Jacks	6–4	6–1	
1891*	Miss C. Dod	Mrs G. W. Hillyard	6–2	6–1	
1892	Miss C. Dod	Mrs G. W. Hillyard	6–1	6–1	
1893	Miss C. Dod	Mrs G. W. Hillyard	6–8	6–1	6–4
1894*	Mrs G. W. Hillyard	Miss L. Austin	6–1	6–1	
1895*	Miss C. Cooper	Miss H. Jackson	7–5	8–6	
1896	Miss C. Cooper	Mrs W. H. Pickering	6–2	6–3	
1897	Mrs G. W. Hillyard	Miss C. Cooper	5–7	7–5	6–2
1898*	Miss C. Cooper	Miss L. Martin	6–4	6–4	
1899	Mrs G. W. Hillyard	Miss C. Cooper	6–2	6–3	
1900	Mrs G. W. Hillyard	Miss C. Cooper	4–6	6–4	6–4
1901	Mrs A. Sterry	Mrs G. W. Hillyard	6–2	6–2	
1902	Miss M. E. Robb	Mrs A. Sterry	7–5	6–1	
1903*	Miss D. K. Douglass	Miss E. W. Thomson	4–6	6–4	6–2
1904	Miss D. K. Douglass	Mrs A. Sterry	6–0	6–3	
1905	Miss M. Sutton	Miss D. K. Douglass	6–3	6–4	
1906	Miss D. K. Douglass	Miss M. Sutton	6–3	9–7	
1907	Miss M. Sutton	Mrs Lambert Chambers	6–1	6–4	
1908*	Mrs A. Sterry	Miss A. M. Morton	6–4	6–4	
1909*	Miss D. P. Boothby	Miss A. M. Morton	6–4	4–6	8–6
1910	Mrs Lambert Chambers	Miss D. P. Boothby	6–2	6–2	
1911	Mrs Lambert Chambers	Miss D. P. Boothby	6–0	6–0	
1912*	Mrs D. R. Larcombe	Mrs A. Sterry	6–3	6–1	
1913*	Mrs Lambert Chambers	Mrs R. J. McNair	6–0	6–4	
1914	Mrs Lambert Chambers	Mrs D. R. Larcombe	7–5	6–4	
1915–18	*Not held*				
1919	Mlle S. Lenglen	Mrs Lambert Chambers	10–8	4–6	9–7
1920	Mlle S. Lenglen	Mrs Lambert Chambers	6–3	6–0	
1921	Mlle S. Lenglen	Miss E. Ryan	6–2	6–0	
(Challenge Round abolished)					
1922	Mlle S. Lenglen	Mrs F. Mallory	6–2	6–0	
1923	Mlle S. Lenglen	Miss K. McKane	6–2	6–2	
1924	Miss K. McKane	Miss H. N. Wills	4–6	6–4	6–4
1925	Mlle S. Lenglen	Miss J. Fry	6–2	6–0	
1926	Mrs L. A. Godfree	Sta E. de Alvarez	6–2	4–6	6–3
1927	Miss H. N. Wills	Sta E. de Alvarez	6–2	6–4	
1928	Miss H. N. Wills	Sta E. de Alvarez	6–2	6–3	
1929	Miss H. N. Wills	Miss H. H. Jacobs	6–1	6–2	
1930	Mrs F. S. Moody	Miss E. Ryan	6–2	6–2	
1931*	Frl C. Aussem	Frl H. Krahwinkel	6–2	7–5	
1932*	Mrs F. S. Moody	Miss H. H. Jacobs	6–3	6–1	
1933	Mrs F. S. Moody	Miss D. E. Round	6–4	6–8	6–3
1934*	Miss D. E. Round	Miss H. H. Jacobs	6–2	5–7	6–3
1935	Mrs F. S. Moody	Miss H. H. Jacobs	6–3	3–6	7–5
1936*	Miss H. H. Jacobs	Mrs S. Sperling	6–2	4–6	7–5
1937	Miss D. E. Round	Miss J. Jedrzejowska	6–2	2–6	7–5
1938*	Mrs F. S. Moody	Miss H. H. Jacobs	6–4	6–0	
1939*	Miss A. Marble	Miss K. E. Stammers	6–2	6–0	
1940–45	*Not held*				
1946*	Miss P. M. Betz	Miss A. L. Brough	6–2	6–4	
1947*	Miss M. E. Osborne	Miss D. J. Hart	6–2	6–4	
1948	Miss A. L. Brough	Miss D. J. Hart	6–3	8–6	
1949	Miss A. L. Brough	Mrs W. du Pont	10–8	1–6	10–8
1950	Miss A. L. Brough	Mrs W. du Pont	6–1	3–6	6–1
1951	Miss D. J. Hart	Miss S. J. Fry	6–1	6–0	

Year	Champion	Runner-up	Score					FIRST PRIZE (£)
1952	Miss M. Connolly	Miss A. L. Brough	6–4	6–3				
1953	Miss M. Connolly	Miss D. J. Hart	8–6	7–5				
1954	Miss M. Connolly	Miss A. L. Brough	6–2	7–5				
1955*	Miss A. L. Brough	Mrs J. G. Fleitz	7–5	8–6				
1956	Miss S. J. Fry	Miss A. Buxton	6–3	6–1				
1957*	Miss A. Gibson	Miss D. R. Hard	6–3	6–2				
1958	Miss A. Gibson	Miss A. Mortimer	8–6	6–2				
1959*	Miss M. E. Bueno	Miss D. R. Hard	6–4	6–3				
1960	Miss M. E. Bueno	Miss S. Reynolds	8–6	6–0				
1961*	Miss A. Mortimer	Miss C. C. Truman	4–6	6–4	7–5			
1962	Mrs J. R. Susman	Mrs V. Sukova	6–4	6–4				
1963*	Miss M. Smith	Miss B. J. Moffitt	6–3	6–4				
1964	Miss M. E. Bueno	Miss M. Smith	6–4	7–9	6–3			
1965	Miss M. Smith	Miss M. E. Bueno	6–4	7–5				
1966	Mrs L. W. King	Miss M. E. Bueno	6–3	3–6	6–1			
1967	Mrs L. W. King	Mrs P. F. Jones	6–3	6–4				
1968	Mrs L. W. King	Miss J. A. M. Tegart	9–7	7–5				750
1969	Mrs P. F. Jones	Mrs L. W. King	3–6	6–3	6–2			1,500
1970*	Mrs B. M. Court	Mrs L. W. King	14–12	11–9				1,500
1971	Miss E. Goolagong	Mrs B. M. Court	6–4	6–1				1,800
1972	Mrs L. W. King	Miss E. Goolagong	6–3	6–3				2,400
1973	Mrs L. W. King	Miss C. M. Evert	6–0	7–5				3,000
1974	Miss C. M. Evert	Mrs O. Morozova	6–0	6–4				7,000
1975	Mrs L. W. King	Mrs R. A. Cawley	6–0	6–1				7,000
1976*	Miss C. M. Evert	Mrs R. A. Cawley	6–3	4–6	8–6			10,000
1977	Miss S. V. Wade	Miss B. F. Stove	4–6	6–3	6–1			13,500
1978	Miss M. Navratilova	Miss C. M. Evert	2–6	6–4	7–5			17,100
1979	Miss M. Navratilova	Mrs C. Evert Lloyd	6–4	6–4				18,000
1980	Mrs R. A. Cawley	Mrs C. Evert Lloyd	6–1	7–6				18,000
1981	Mrs C. Evert Lloyd	Miss H. Mandlikova	6–2	6–2				19,440
1982	Miss M. Navratilova	Mrs C. Evert Lloyd	6–1	3–6	6–2			37,500
1983	Miss M. Navratilova	Miss A. Jaeger	6–0	6–3				60,000
1984	Miss M. Navratilova	Mrs C. Evert Lloyd	7–6	6–2				90,000
1985	Miss M. Navratilova	Mrs C. Evert Lloyd	4–6	6–3	6–2			117,000
1986	Miss M. Navratilova	Miss H. Mandlikova	7–6	6–3				126,000
1987	Miss M. Navratilova	Miss S. Graf	7–5	6–3				139,500
1988	Miss S. Graf	Miss M. Navratilova	5–7	6–2	6–1			148,500
1989	Miss S. Graf	Miss M. Navratilova	6–2	6–7	6–1			171,000
1990	Miss M. Navratilova	Miss Z. Garrison	6–4	6–1				207,000

MEN'S DOUBLES

CHAMPIONS	RUNNERS-UP	SCORE				
1884 E./W. Renshaw	E. W. Lewis/E. L. Williams	6–3	6–1	1–6	6–4	
1885 E./W. Renshaw	C. E. Farrer/A. J. Stanley	6–3	6–3	10–8		
(Challenge Round instituted)						
1886 E./W. Renshaw	C. E. Farrer/A. J. Stanley	6–3	6–3	4–6	7–5	
1887* P. Bowes-Lyon W. W. Wilberforce	E. Barret-Smith/J. H. Crispe	7–5	6–3	6–2		
1888 E./W. Renshaw	P. Bowes-Lyon W. W. Wilberforce	2–6	1–6	6–3	6–4	6–3
1889 E./W. Renshaw	G. W. Hillyard/E. W. Lewis	6–4	6–4	3–6	0–6	6–1
1890* J. Pim/F. O. Stoker	G. W. Hillyard/E. W. Lewis	6–0	7–5	6–4		
1891 H./W. Baddeley	J. Pim/F. O. Stoker	6–1	6–3	1–6	6–2	
1892 H. S. Barlow/E. W. Lewis	H./W. Baddeley	4–6	6–2	8–6	6–4	
1893 J. Pim/F. O. Stoker	H. W. Barlow/E. W. Lewis	4–6	6–3	6–1	2–6	6–0
1894* H./W. Baddeley	H. S. Barlow/C. H. Martin	5–7	7–5	4–6	6–3	8–6
1895 H./W. Baddeley	W. V. Eaves/E. W. Lewis	8–6	5–7	6–4	6–3	
1896 H./W. Baddeley	R. F. Doherty/H. A. Nisbet	1–6	3–6	6–4	6–2	6–1
1897 H. L./R. F. Doherty	H./W. Baddeley	6–4	4–6	8–6	6–4	
1898 H. L./R. F. Doherty	C. Hobart/H. A. Nisbet	6–4	6–4	6–2		
1899 H. L./R. F. Doherty	C. Hobart/H. A. Nisbet	7–5	6–0	6–2		
1900 H. L./R. F. Doherty	H. A. Nisbet/H. Roper Barrett	9–7	7–5	4–6	3–6	6–3
1901 H. L./R. F. Doherty	D. F. Davis/H. Ward	4–6	6–2	6–3	9–7	
1902 F. L. Riseley/S. H. Smith	H. L./R. F. Doherty	4–6	8–6	6–3	4–6	11–9
1903 H. L./R. F. Doherty	F. L. Riseley/S. H. Smith	6–4	6–4	6–4		
1904 H. L./R. F. Doherty	F. L. Riseley/S. H. Smith	6–3	6–4	6–3		
1905 H. L./R. F. Doherty	F. L. Riseley/S. H. Smith	6–2	6–4	6–8	6–3	
1906 F. L. Riseley/S. H. Smith	H. L./R. F. Doherty	6–8	6–4	5–7	6–3	6–3
1907* N. E. Brookes/A. F. Wilding	K. Behr/B. C. Wright	6–4	6–4	6–2		

Year	Winners	Runners-up						Prize
1908*	M. J. G. Ritchie/A. F. Wilding	A. W. Gore/H. Roper Barrett	6–1	6–2	1–6	1–6	9–7	
1909*	A. W. Gore/H. Roper Barrett	S. N. Doust/H. A. Parker	6–2	6–1	6–4			
1910	M. J. G. Ritchie/A. F. Wilding	A. W. Gore/H. Roper Barrett	6–1	6–1	6–2			
1911	M. Decugis/A. H. Gobert	M. J. G. Ritchie/A. F. Wilding	9–7	5–7	6–3	2–6	6–2	
1912	C. P. Dixon/H. Roper Barrett	M. Decugis/A. H. Gobert	3–6	6–3	6–4	7–5		
1913	C. P. Dixon/H. Roper Barrett	H. Kleinschroth/F. W. Rahe	6–2	6–4	4–6	6–2		
1914	N. E. Brookes/A. F. Wilding	C. P. Dixon/H. Roper Barrett	6–1	6–1	5–7	8–6		
1915–1918	*Not held*							
1919*	P. O'Hara Wood/R. V. Thomas	R. W. Heath/R. Lycett	6–4	6–2	4–6	6–2		
1920*	C. S. Garland/R. N. Williams	A. R. F. Kingscote/J. C. Parke	4–6	6–4	7–5	6–2		
1921*	R. Lycett/M. Woosnam	A. H./F. G. Lowe	6–3	6–0	7–5			
(Challenge Round abolished)								
1922	J. O. Anderson/R. Lycett	P. O'Hara Wood/G. L. Patterson	3–6	7–9	6–4	6–3	11–9	
1923	L. A. Godfree/R. Lycett	E. Flaquer/Count de Gomar	6–3	6–4	3–6	6–3		
1924	F. T. Hunter/V. Richards	W. M. Washburn/R. N. Williams	6–3	3–6	8–10	8–6	6–3	
1925	J. Borotra/R. Lacoste	R. Casey/J. Hennessey	6–4	11–9	4–6	1–6	6–3	
1926	J. Brugnon/H. Cochet	H. Kinsey/V. Richards	7–5	4–6	6–3	6–2		
1927	F. T. Hunter/W. T. Tilden	J. Brugnon/H. Cochet	1–6	4–6	8–6	6–3	6–4	
1928	J. Brugnon/H. Cochet	J. B. Hawkes/G. L. Patterson	13–11	6–4	6–4			
1929	W. L. Allison/J. Van Ryn	I. G. Collins/J. C. Gregory	6–4	5–7	6–3	10–12	6–4	
1930	W. L. Allison/J. Van Ryn	J. H. Doeg/G. M. Lott	6–3	6–3	6–2			
1931	G. M. Lott/J. Van Ryn	J. Brugnon/H. Cochet	6–2	10–8	9–11	3–6	6–3	
1932	J. Borotra/J. Brugnon	G. P. Hughes/F. J. Perry	6–0	4–6	3–6	7–5	7–5	
1933	J. Borotra/J. Brugnon	R. Nunoi/J. Satoh	4–6	6–3	6–3	7–5		
1934	G. M. Lott/L. R. Stoefen	J. Borotra/J. Brugnon	6–2	6–3	6–4			
1935	J. H. Crawford/A. K Quist	W. L. Allison/J. Van Ryn	6–3	5–7	6–2	5–7	7–5	
1936	G. P. Hughes/C. R. D. Tuckey	C. E. Hare/F. H. D. Wilde	6–4	3–6	7–9	6–1	5–4	
1937	J. D. Budge/G. Mako	G. P. Hughes/C. R. D. Tuckey	6–0	6–4	6–8	6–1		
1938	J. D. Budge/G. Mako	H. Henkel/G. von Metaxa	6–4	3–6	6–3	8–6		
1939	E. T. Cooke/R. L. Riggs	C. E. Hare/F. H. D. Wilde	6–3	3–6	6–3	9–7		
1940–1945	*Not held*							
1946	T. Brown/J. A. Kramer	G. E. Brown/D. Pails	6–4	6–4	6–2			
1947	R. Falkenburg/J. A. Kramer	A. J. Mottram/O. W. Sidwell	8–6	6–3	6–3			
1948	J. E. Bromwich/F. A. Sedgman	T. Brown/G. Mulloy	5–7	7–5	7–5	9–7		
1949	R. A. Gonzales/F. A. Parker	G. Mulloy/F. R. Schroeder	6–4	6–4	6–2			
1950	J. E. Bromwich/A. K. Quist	G. E. Brown/O. W. Sidwell	7–5	3–6	6–3	3–6	6–2	
1951	K. McGregor/F. A. Sedgman	J. Drobny/E. W. Sturgess	3–6	6–2	6–3	3–6	6–3	
1952	K. McGregor/F. A. Sedgman	E. V. Seixas/E. W. Sturgess	6–3	7–5	6–4			
1953	L. A. Hoad/K. R. Rosewall	R. N. Hartwig/M. G. Rose	6–4	7–5	4–6	7–5		
1954	R. N. Hartwig/M. G. Rose	E. V. Seixas/M. A. Trabert	6–4	6–4	3–6	6–4		
1955	R. N. Hartwig/L. A. Hoad	N. A. Fraser/K. R. Rosewall	7–5	6–4	6–3			
1956	L. A. Hoad/K. R. Rosewall	N. Pietrangeli/O. Sirola	7–5	6–2	6–1			
1957	G. Mulloy/B. Patty	N. A. Fraser/L. A. Hoad	8–10	6–4	6–4	6–4		
1958	S. Davidson/U. Schmidt	A. J. Cooper/N. A. Fraser	6–4	6–4	8–6			
1959	R. Emerson/N. A. Fraser	R. Laver/R. Mark	8–6	6–3	1–6	9–7		
1960	R. H. Osuna/R. D. Ralston	M. G. Davies/R. K. Wilson	7–5	6–3	10–8			
1961	R. Emerson/N. A. Fraser	R. A. J. Hewitt/F. S. Stolle	6–4	6–8	6–4	6–8	8–6	
1962	R. A. J. Hewitt/F. S. Stolle	B. Jovanovic/N. Pilic	6–2	5–7	6–2	6–4		
1963	R. H. Osuna/A. Palafox	J. C. Barclay/P. Darmon	4–6	6–2	6–2	6–2		
1964	R. A. J. Hewitt/F. S. Stolle	R. Emerson/K. N. Fletcher	7–5	11–9	6–4			FIRST
1965	J. D. Newcombe/A. D. Roche	K. N. Fletcher/R. A. J. Hewitt	7–5	6–3	6–4			PRIZE
1966	K. N. Fletcher/J. D. Newcombe	W. W. Bowrey/O. K. Davidson	6–3	6–4	3–6	6–3		*(£ per*
1967	R. A. J. Hewitt/F. D. McMillan	R. Emerson/K. N. Fletcher	6–2	6–3	6–4			*team)*
1968	J. D. Newcombe/A. D. Roche	K. R. Rosewall/F. S. Stolle	3–6	8–6	5–7	14–12	6–3	800
1969	J. D. Newcombe/A. D. Roche	T. S. Okker/M. C. Riessen	7–5	11–9	6–3			1,000
1970	J. D. Newcombe/A. D. Roche	K. R. Rosewall/F. S. Stolle	10–8	6–3	6–1			1,000
1971	R. Emerson/R. Laver	A. R. Ashe/R. D. Ralston	4–6	9–7	6–8	6–4	6–4	750
1972	R. A. J. Hewitt/F. D. McMillan	S. R. Smith/E. Van Dillen	6–2	6–2	9–7			1,000
1973	J. S. Connors/I. Nastase	J. R. Cooper/N. A. Fraser	3–6	6–3	6–4	8–9	6–1	1,000
1974	J. D. Newcombe/A. D. Roche	Mr. C. Lutz/S. R. Smith	8–6	6–4	6–4			2,000
1975	V. Gerulaitis/A. Mayer	C. Dowdeswell/A. J. Stone	7–5	8–6	6–4			2,000
1976	B. E. Gottfried/R. Ramirez	Mr. L. Case/G. Masters	3–6	6–3	8–6	2–6	7–6	3,000
1977	R. L. Case/G. Masters	J. G. Alexander/P. C. Dent	6–3	6–4	3–6	8–9	6–4	6,000
1978	R. A. J. Hewitt/F. D. McMillan	P. Fleming/J. P. McEnroe	6–1	6–4	6–2			7,500
1979	P. Fleming/J. P. McEnroe	B. E. Gottfried/R. Ramirez	4–6	6–4	6–2	6–2		8,000
1980	P. McNamara/P. McNamee	Mr. C. Lutz/S. R. Smith	7–6	6–3	6–7	6–4		8,400
1981	P. Fleming/J. P. McEnroe	Mr. C. Lutz/S. R. Smith	6–4	6–4	6–4			9,070
1982	P. McNamara/P. McNamee	P. Fleming/J. P. McEnroe	6–3	6–2				16,666
1983	P. Fleming/J. P. McEnroe	T. E./T. R. Gullikson	6–4	6–3	6–4			26,628
1984	P. Fleming/J. P. McEnroe	P. Cash/P. McNamee	6–2	5–7	6–2	3–6	6–3	40,000
1985	H. P. Gunthardt/B. Taroczy	P. Cash/J. Fitzgerald	6–4	6–3	4–6	6–3		47,500
1986	J. Nystrom/M. Wilander	G. Donnelly/P. Fleming	7–6	6–3	6–3			48,500

1987	K. Flach/R. Seguso	S. Casal/E. Sanchez	3–6 6–7 7–6 6–1 6–4	53,730
1988	K. Flach/R. Seguso	J. Fitzgerald/A. Jarryd	6–4 2–6 6–4 7–6	57,200
1989	J. B. Fitzgerald/A. Jarryd	Mr. Leach/J. Pugh	3–6 7–6 6–4 7–6	65,870
1990	R. Leach/J. Pugh	P. Aldrich/D. Visser	7–6 7–6 7–6	94,230

WOMEN'S DOUBLES

	CHAMPIONS	RUNNERS-UP	SCORE			
1913	R. J. McNair/D. P. Boothby	A. Sterry/D. Lambert Chambers	4–6	2–4	ret'd	
1914	A. M. Morton/E. Ryan	G.annam/D. R. Larcombe	6–1	6–3		
1915–1918	Not held					
1919	S. Lenglen/E. Ryan	D. Lambert Chambers/D. R. Larcombe	4–6	7–5	6–3	
1920	S. Lenglen/E. Ryan	D. Lambert Chambers/D. R. Larcombe	6–4	6–0		
1921	S. Lenglen/E. Ryan	A. E. Beamish/G. Peacock	6–1	6–2		
1922	S. Lenglen/E. Ryan	K. McKane/A. D. Stocks	6–0	6–4		
1923	S. Lenglen/E. Ryan	J. Austin/E. L. Colyer	6–3	6–1		
1924	H. Wightman/H. N. Wills	B. C. Covell/K. McKane	6–4	6–4		
1925	S. Lenglen/E. Ryan	A. V. Bridge/C. G. McIlquham	6–2	6–2		
1926	M. K. Browne/E. Ryan	L. A. Godfree/E. L. Colyer	6–1	6–1		
1927	H. N. Wills/E. Ryan	E. L. Heine/G. Peacock	6–3	6–2		
1928	P. Saunders/M. Watson	E. Bennett/E. H. Harvey	6–2	6–3		
1929	L. R. C. Michell/M. Watson	B. C. Covell/D. C. Shepherd-Barron	6–4	8–6		
1930	F. S. Moody/E. Ryan	E. Cross/S. Palfrey	6–2	9–7		
1931	D. C. Shepherd-Barron/P. E. Mudford	D. Metaxa/J. Sigart	3–6	6–3	6–4	
1932	D. Metaxa/J. Sigart	H. H. Jacobs/E. Ryan	6–4	6–3		
1933	S. Mathieu/E. Ryan	F. James/A. M. Yorke	6–2	9–11	6–4	
1934	S. Mathieu/E. Ryan	D. B. Andrus/S. Henrotin	6–3	6–3		
1935	F. James/K. E. Stammers	S. Mathieu/H. Sperling	6–1	6–4		
1936	F. James/K. E. Stammers	S. Fabyan/H. H. Jacobs	6–2	6–1		
1937	S. Mathieu/A. M. Yorke	P. King/E. Pittman	6–3	6–3		
1938	S. Fabyan/A. Marble	S. Mathieu/A. M. Yorke	6–2	6–3		
1939	S. Fabyan/A. Marble	H. H. Jacobs/A. M. Yorke	6–1	6–0		
1940–1945	Not held					
1946	A. L. Brough/M. E. Osborne	P. M. Betz/D. J. Hart	6–3	2–6	6–3	
1947	D. J. Hart/P. C. Todd	A. L. Brough/M. E. Osborne	3–6	6–4	7–5	
1948	A. L. Brough/W. du Pont	D. J. Hart/P. C. Todd	6–3	3–6	6–3	
1949	A. L. Brough/W. du Pont	G. Moran/P. C. Todd	8–6	7–5		
1950	A. L. Brough/W. du Pont	S. J. Fry/D. J. Hart	6–4	5–7	6–1	
1951	S. J. Fry/D. J. Hart	A. L. Brough/W. du Pont	6–3	13–11		
1952	S. J. Fry/D. J. Hart	A. L. Brough/M. Connolly	8–6	6–3		
1953	S. J. Fry/D. J. Hart	M. Connolly/J. Sampson	6–0	6–0		
1954	A. L. Brough/W. du Pont	S. J. Fry/D. J. Hart	4–6	9–7	6–3	
1955	A. Mortimer/J. A. Shilcock	S. J. Bloomer/P. E. Ward	7–5	6–1		
1956	A. Buxton/A. Gibson	F. Muller/D. G. Seeney	6–1	8–6		
1957	A. Gibson/D. R. Hard	K. Hawton/T. D. Long	6–1	6–2		
1958	M. E. Bueno/A. Gibson	W. du Pont/M. Varner	6–3	7–5		
1959	J. Arth/D. R. Hard	J. G. Fleitz/C. C. Truman	2–6	6–2	6–3	
1960	M. E. Bueno/D. R. Hard	S. Reynolds/R. Schuurman	6–4	6–0		
1961	K. Hantz/B. J. Moffitt	J. Lehane/M. Smith	6–3	6–4		
1962	B. J. Moffitt/J. R. Susman	L. E. G. Price/R. Schuurman	5–7	6–3	7–5	
1963	M. E. Bueno/D. R. Hard	R. A. Ebbern/M. Smith	8–6	9–7		
1964	M. Smith/L. R. Turner	B. J. Moffitt/J. R. Susman	7–5	6–2		FIRST
1965	M. E. Bueno/B. J. Moffitt	F. Durr/J. Lieffrig	6–2	7–5		PRIZE
1966	M. E. Bueno/N. Richey	M. Smith/J. A. M. Tegart	6–3	4–6	6–4	(£ per
1967	R. Casals/L. W. King	M. E. Bueno/N. Richey	9–11	6–4	6–2	team)
1968	R. Casals/L. W. King	F. Durr/P. F. Jones	3–6	6–4	7–5	500
1969	B. M. Court/J. A. M. Tegart	P. S. A. Hogan/M. Michel	9–7	6–2		600
1970	R. Casals/L. W. King	F. Durr/S. V. Wade	6–2	6–3		600
1971	R. Casals/L. W. King	B. M. Court/E. Goolagong	6–3	6–2		450
1972	L. W. King/B. Stove	D. E. Dalton/F. Durr	6–2	4–6	6–3	600
1973	R. Casals/L. W. King	F. Durr/B. Stove	6–1	4–6	7–5	600
1973	E. Goolagong/M. Michel	H. F. Gourlay/K. M. Krantzcke	2–6	6–4	6–3	1,200
1975	A. Kiyomura/K. Sawamatsu	F. Durr/B. Stove	7–5	1–6	7–5	1,200
1976	C. Evert/M. Navratilova	L. W. King/B. Stove	6–1	3–6	7–5	2,400
1977	H. Gourlay-Cawley/J. C. Russell	M. Navratilova/B. Stove	6–3	6–3		5,200
1978	G. E. Reid/W. Turnbull	M. Jausovec/V. Ruzici	4–6	9–8	6–3	6,500
1979	L. W. King/M. Navratilova	B. Stove/W. M. Turnbull	5–7	6–3	6–2	6,930
1980	K. Jordan/A. E. Smith	R. Casals/W. M. Turnbull	4–6	7–5	6–1	7,276
1981	M. Navratilova/P. H. Shriver	K. Jordan/A. E. Smith	6–3	7–6		7,854
1982	M. Navratilova/P. H. Shriver	K. Jordan/A. E. Smith	6–4	6–1		14,450

1983	M. Navratilova/P. H. Shriver	Mr. Casals/W. M. Turnbull	6–2 6–2		23,100
1984	M. Navratilova/P. H. Shriver	K. Jordan/A. E. Smith	6–3 6–4		34,700
1985	K. Jordan/E. Smylie	M. Navratilova/P. H. Shriver	5–7 6–3 6–4		41,100
1986	M. Navratilova/P. H. Shriver	H. Mandlikova/W. M. Turnbull	6–1 6–3		42,060
1987	C. Kohde-Kilsch/H. Sukova	B. Nagelsen/E. Smylie	7–5 7–5		46,500
1988	S. Graf/G. Sabatini	L. Savchenko/N. Zvereva	6–3 1–6 12–10		49,500
1989	J. Novotna/H. Sukova	L. Savchenko/N. Zvereva	6–1 6–2		56,970
1990	J. Novotna/H. Sukova	K. Jordan/E. Smylie	6–3 6–4		81,510

MIXED DOUBLES

	CHAMPIONS	RUNNERS-UP	SCORE		
1913	Hope Crisp/Mrs C. O. Tuckey	J. C. Parke/Mrs D. R. Larcombe	3–6 5–3 ret'd		
1914	J. C. Parke/Mrs D. R. Larcombe	A. F. Wilding/Mlle M. Broquedis	4–6 6–4 6–2		
1915–1918	*Not held*				
1919	R. Lycett/Miss E. Ryan	A. D. Prebble/Mrs D. Lambert Chambers	6–0 6–0		
1920	G. L. Patterson/Mlle S. Lenglen	R. Lycett/Miss E. Ryan	7–5 6–3		
1921	R. Lycett/Miss E. Ryan	M. Woosnam/Miss P. L. Howkins	6–3 6–1		
1922	P. O'Hara Wood/Mlle S. Lenglen	R. Lycett/Miss E. Ryan	6–4 6–3		
1923	R. Lycett/Miss E. Ryan	L. S. Deane/Mrs D. C. Shepherd-Barron	6–4 7–5		
1924	J. B. Gilbert/Miss K. McKane	L. A. Godfree/Mrs D. C. Shepherd-Barron	6–3 3–6 6–3		
1925	J. Borotra/Mlle S. Lenglen	H. L. de Morpurgo/Miss E. Ryan	6–3 6–3		
1926	L. A./Mrs Godfree	H. Kinsey/Miss M. K. Browne	6–3 6–4		
1927	F. T. Hunter/Miss E. Ryan	L. A./Mrs Godfree	8–6 6–0		
1928	P. D. B. Spence/Miss E. Ryan	J. H. Crawford/Miss D. Akhurst	7–5 6–4		
1929	F. T. Hunter/Miss H. N. Wills	I. G. Collins/Miss J. Fry	6–1 6–4		
1930	J. H. Crawford/Miss E. Ryan	D. Prenn/Frl H. Krahwinkel	6–1 6–3		
1931	G. M. Lott/Mrs L. A. Harper	I. G. Collins/Miss J. C. Ridley	6–3 1–6 6–1		
1932	E. Maier/Miss E. Ryan	H. C. Hopman/Mlle J. Sigart	7–5 6–2		
1933	G. von Cramm/Frl H. Krahwinkel	N. G. Farquharson/Miss M. Heeley	7–5 8–6		
1934	R. Miki/Miss D. E. Round	H. W. Austin/Mrs D. C. Shepherd-Barron	3–6 6–4 6–0		
1935	F. J. Perry/Miss D. E. Round	H. C./Mrs Hopman	7–5 4–6 6–2		
1936	F. J. Perry/Miss D. E. Round	J. D. Budge/Mrs S. Fabyan	7–9 7–5 6–4		
1937	J. D. Budge/Miss A. Marble	Y. Petra/Mme S. Mathieu	6–4 6–1		
1938	J. D. Budge/Miss A. Marble	H. Henkel/Mrs S. Fabyan	6–1 6–4		
1939	R. L. Riggs/Miss A. Marble	F. H. D. Wilde/Miss N. B. Brown	9–7 6–1		
1940–1945	*Not held*				
1946	T. Brown/Miss A. L. Brough	G. E. Brown/Miss D. Bundy	6–4 6–4		
1947	J. E. Bromwich/Miss A. L. Brough	C. F. Long/Mrs N. M. Bolton	1–6 6–4 6–2		
1948	J. E. Bromwich/Miss A. L. Brough	F. A. Sedgman/Miss D. J. Hart	6–2 3–6 6–3		
1949	E. E. Sturgess/Mrs S. P. Summer	J. E. Bromwich/Miss A. L. Brough	9–7 9–11 7–5		
1950	E. W. Sturgess/Miss A. L. Brough	G. E. Brown/Mrs P. C. Todd	11–9 1–6 6–4		
1951	F. A. Sedgman/Miss D. J. Hart	M. G. Rose/Mrs N. M. Bolton	7–5 6–2		
1952	F. A. Sedgman/Miss D. J. Hart	E. Morea/Mrs T. D. Long	4–6 6–3 6–4		
1953	E. V. Seixas/Miss D. J. Hart	E. Morea/Miss S. J. Fry	9–7 7–5		
1954	E. V. Seixas/Miss D. J. Hart	K. R. Rosewall/Mrs W. du Pont	5–7 6–4 6–3		
1955	E. V. Seixas/Miss D. J. Hart	E. Morea/Miss A. L. Brough	8–6 2–6 6–3		
1956	E. V. Seixas/Miss S. J. Fry	G. Mulloy/Miss A. Gibson	2–6 6–2 7–5		
1957	M. G. Rose/Miss D. R. Hard	N. A. Fraser/Miss A. Gibson	6–4 7–5		
1958	R. N. Howe/Miss L. Coghlan	K. Nielsen/Miss A. Gibson	6–3 13–11		
1959	R. Laver/Miss D. R. Hard	N. A. Fraser/Miss M. E. Bueno	6–4 6–3		
1960	R. Laver/Miss D. R. Hard	R. N. Howe/Miss M. E. Bueno	13–11 3–6 8–6		
1961	F. S. Stolle/Miss L. R. Turner	R. N. Howe/Miss E. Buding	11–9 6–2		
1962	N. A. Fraser/Mrs W. du Pont	R. D. Ralston/Miss A. S. Haydon	2–6 6–3 13–11		
1963	K. N. Fletcher/Miss M. Smith	R. A. J. Hewitt/Miss D. R. Hard	11–9 6–4		
1964	F. S. Stolle/Miss L. R. Turner	K. N. Fletcher/Miss M. Smith	6–4 6–4		FIRST
1965	K. N. Fletcher/Miss M. Smith	A. D. Roche/Miss J. A. M. Tegart	12–10 6–3		PRIZE
1966	K. N. Fletcher/Miss M. Smith	R. D. Ralston/Mrs L. W. King	4–6 6–3 6–3		*(£ per*
1967	O. K. Davidson/Mrs L. W. King	K. N. Fletcher/Miss M. E. Bueno	7–5 6–0		*team)*
1968	K. N. Fletcher/Mrs B. M. Court	A. Metreveli/Miss O. Morozova	6–1 14–12		450
1969	F. S. Stolle/Mrs P. F. Jones	A. D. Roche/Miss J. A. M. Tegart	6–3 6–2		500
1970	I. Nastase/Miss R. Casals	A. Metreveli/Miss O. Morozova	6–3 4–6 9–7		500
1971	O. K. Davidson/Mrs L. W. King	M. C. Rieseen/Mrs B. M. Court	3–6 6–2 15–13		375
1972	I. Nastase/Miss R. Casals	K. Warwick/Miss E. Goolagong	6–4 6–4		500
1973	O. K. Davidson/Mrs L. W. King	Mr. Ramirez/Miss J. Newberry	6–3 6–2		500
1974	O. K. Davidson/Mrs L. W. King	M. J. Farrell/Miss L. J. Charles	6–3 9–7		1,000
1975	M. C. Riessen/Mrs B. M. Court	A. J. Stone/Miss B. Stove	6–4 7–5		1,000
1976	A. D. Roche/Miss F. Durr	R. L. Stockton/Miss R. Casals	6–3 2–6 7–5		2,000
1977	R. A. J. Hewitt/Miss G. R. Stevens	F. D. McMillan/Miss B. Stove	3–6 7–5 6–4		3,000
1978	F. D. McMillan/Miss B. Stove	R. O. Ruffels/Mrs L. W. King	6–2 6–2		4,000

1979	R. A. J. Hewitt/Miss G. R. Stevens	F. D. McMillan/Miss B. Stove	7–5	7–6		4,200
1980	J. R. Austin/Miss T. Austin	M. R. Edmondson/Miss D. L. Fromholtz	4–6	7–6	6–3	4,420
1981	F. D. McMillanP/Miss B. Stove	J. R. Austin/Miss T. Austin	4–6	7–6	6–3	4,770
1982	K. Curren/Miss A. E. Smith	J. M. Lloyd/Miss W. M. Turnbull	2–6	6–3	7–5	6,750
1983	J. M. Lloyd/Miss W. M. Turnbull	S. Denton/Mrs L. W. King	6–7	7–6	7–5	12,000
1984	J. M. Lloyd/Miss W. M. Turnbull	S. Denton/Miss K. Jordan	6–3	6–3		18,000
1985	P. McNamee/Miss M. Navratilova	J. Fitzgerald/Mrs E. Smylie	7–5	4–6	6–2	23,400
1986	K. Flach/Miss K. Jordan	H. P. Gunthardt/Miss M. Navratilova	6–3	7–6		25,200
1987	M. J. Bates/Miss J. M. Durie	D. Cahill/Miss N. Provis	7–6	6–3		27,900
1988	S. E. Stewart/Miss Z. Garrison	K. Jones/Mrs G. Magers	6–1	7–6		29,700
1989	J. Pugh/Miss J. Novotna	M. Kratzmann/Miss J. Byrne	6–4	5–7	6–4	34,200
1990	R. Leach/Miss Z. Garrison	J. Fitzgerald/Mrs E. Smylie	7–5	6–2		40,000

US NATIONAL CHAMPIONSHIPS 1881–1969

Holders did not defend the title

MEN'S SINGLES

	CHAMPION	RUNNER-UP	SCORE					
1881	R. D. Sears	W. E. Glyn	6–0	6–3	6–2			
1882	R. D. Sears	C. M. Clark	6–1	6–4	6–0			
1883	R. D. Sears	J. Dwight	6–2	6–0	9–7			
(Challenge Round instituted)								
1884	R. D. Sears	H. A. Taylor	6–0	1–6	6–0	6–2		
1885	R. D. Sears	G. M. Brinley	6–3	4–6	6–0	6–3		
1886	R. D. Sears	R. L. Beeckman	4–6	6–1	6–3	6–4		
1887	R. D. Sears	H. W. Slocum	6–1	6–3	6–2			
1888*	H. W. Slocum	H. A. Taylor	6–4	6–1	6–0			
1889	H. W. Slocum	Q. A. Shaw	6–3	6–1	4–6	6–2		
1890	O. S. Campbell	H. W. Slocum	6–2	4–6	6–3	6–1		
1891	O. S. Campbell	C. Hobart	2–6	7–5	7–9	6–1	6–2	
1892	O. S. Campbell	F. H. Hovey	7–5	3–6	6–3	7–5		
1893*	R. D. Wrenn	F. H. Hovey	6–4	3–6	6–4	6–4		
1894	R. D. Wrenn	M. F. Goodbody	6–8	6–1	6–4	6–4		
1895	F. H. Hovey	R. D. Wrenn	6–3	6–2	6–4			
1896	R. D. Wrenn	F. H. Hovey	7–5	3–6	6–0	1–6	6–1	
1897	R. D. Wrenn	W. V. Eaves	4–6	8–6	6–3	2–6	6–2	
1898*	M. D. Whitman	D. F. Davis	3–6	6–2	6–2	6–1		
1899	M. D. Whitman	J. P. Paret	6–1	6–2	3–6	7–5		
1900	M. D. Whitman	W. A. Larned	6–4	1–6	6–2	6–2		
1901*	W. A. Larned	B. C. Wright	6–2	6–8	6–4	6–4		
1902	W. A. Larned	Mr. F. Doherty	4–6	6–2	6–4	8–6		
1903	H. L. Doherty	W. A. Larned	6–0	6–3	10–8			
1904*	H. Ward	W. J. Clothier	10–8	6–4	9–7			
1905	B. C. Wright	H. Ward	6–2	6–1	11–9			
1906	W. J. Clothier	B. C. Wright	6–3	6–0	6–4			
1907*	W. A. Larned	R. LeRoy	6–2	6–2	6–4			
1908	W. A. Larned	B. C. Wright	6–1	6–2	8–6			
1909	W. A. Larned	W. J. Clothier	6–1	6–2	5–7	1–6	6–1	
1910	W. A. Larned	T. C. Bundy	6–1	5–7	6–0	6–8	6–1	
1911	W. A. Larned	M. E. McLoughlin	6–4	6–4	6–2			
(Challenge Round abolished)								
1912	M. E. McLoughlin	W. F. Johnson	3–6	2–6	6–2	6–4	6–2	
1913	M. E. McLoughlin	R. N. Williams	6–4	5–7	6–3	6–1		
1914	R. N. Williams	M. E. McLoughlin	6–3	8–6	10–8			
1915	W. M. Johnston	M. E. McLoughlin	1–6	6–0	7–5	10–8		
1916	R. N. Williams	W. M. Johnston	4–6	6–4	0–6	6–2	6–4	
1917†	R. L. Murray	N. W. Niles	5–7	8–6	6–3	6–3		
1918	R. L. Murray	W. T. Tilden	6–3	6–1	7–5			
1919	W. M. Johnston	W. T. Tilden	6–4	6–4	6–3			
1920	W. T. Tilden	W. M. Johnston	6–1	1–6	7–5	5–7	6–3	
1921	W. T. Tilden	W. F. Johnson	6–1	6–3	6–1			
1922	W. T. Tilden	W. M. Johnston	4–6	3–6	6–2	6–3	6–4	
1923	W. T. Tilden	W. M. Johnston	6–4	6–1	6–4			
1924	W. T. Tilden	W. M. Johnston	6–1	9–7	6–2			
1925	W. T. Tilden	W. M. Johnston	4–6	11–9	6–3	4–6	6–3	
1926	R. Lacoste	J. Borotra	6–4	6–0	6–4			
1927	R. Lacoste	W. T. Tilden	11–9	6–3	11–9			

1928	H. Cochet	F. T. Hunter	4–6	6–4	3–6	7–5	6–3
1929	W. T. Tilden	F. T. Hunter	3–6	6–3	4–6	6–2	6–4
1930	J. H. Doeg	F. X. Shields	10–8	1–6	6–4	16–14	
1931	H. E. Vines	G. M. Lott	7–9	6–3	9–7	7–5	
1932	H. E. Vines	H. Cochet	6–4	6–4	6–4		
1933	F. J. Perry	J. H. Crawford	6–3	11–13	4–6	6–0	6–1
1934	F. J. Perry	W. L. Allison	6–4	6–3	1–6	8–6	
1935	W. L. Allison	S. B. Wood	6–2	6–2	6–3		
1936	F. J. Perry	J. D. Budge	2–6	6–2	8–6	1–6	10–8
1937	J. D. Budge	C. Von Cramm	6–1	7–9	6–1	3–6	6–1
1938	J. D. Budge	G. Mako	6–3	6–8	6–2	6–1	
1939	R. L. Riggs	S. W. van Horn	6–4	6–2	6–4		
1940	W. D. McNeill	R. L. Riggs	4–6	6–8	6–3	6–3	7–5
1941	R. L. Riggs	F. Kovacs	5–7	6–1	6–3	6–3	
1942	F. R. Schroeder	F. A. Parker	8–6	7–5	3–6	4–6	6–2
1943	J. R. Hunt	J. A. Kramer	6–3	3–6	10–8	6–0	
1944	F. A. Parker	W. F. Talbert	6–4	3–6	6–3	6–3	
1945	F. A. Parker	W. F. Talbert	14–12	6–1	6–2		
1946	J. A. Kramer	T. P. Brown	9–7	6–3	6–0		
1947	J. A. Kramer	F. A. Parker	4–6	2–6	6–1	6–0	6–3
1948	R. A. Gonzales	E. W. Sturgess	6–2	6–3	14–12		
1949	R. A. Gonzales	F. R. Schroeder	16–18	2–6	6–1	6–2	6–4
1950	A. Larsen	H. Flam	6–3	4–6	5–7	6–4	6–3
1951	F. A. Sedgman	E. V. Seixas	6–4	6–1	6–1		
1952	F. A. Sedgman	G. Mulloy	6–1	6–2	6–3		
1953	M. A. Trabert	E. V. Seixas	6–3	6–2	6–3		
1954	E. V. Seixas	R. N. Hartwig	3–6	6–2	6–4	6–4	
1955	M. A. Trabert	K. R. Rosewall	9–7	6–3	6–3		
1956	K. R. Rosewall	L. A. Hoad	4–6	6–2	6–3	6–3	
1957	M. J. Anderson	A. J. Cooper	10–8	7–5	6–4		
1958	A. J. Cooper	M. J. Anderson	6–2	3–6	4–6	10–8	8–6
1959	N. A. Fraser	A. Olmedo	6–3	5–7	6–2	6–4	
1960	N. A. Fraser	R. G. Laver	6–4	6–4	9–7		
1961	R. S. Emerson	R. G. Laver	7–5	6–3	6–2		
1962	R. G. Laver	R. S. Emerson	6–2	6–4	5–7	6–4	
1963	R. H. Osuna	F. Froehling	7–5	6–4	6–2		
1964	R. S. Emerson	F. S. Stolle	6–4	6–2	6–4		
1965	M. Santana	E. C. Drysdale	6–2	7–9	7–5	6–1	
1966	F. S. Stolle	J. D. Newcombe	4–6	12–10	6–3	6–4	
1967	J. D. Newcombe	C. Graebner	6–4	6–4	8–6		
1968	A. R. Ashe	R. C. Lutz	4–6	6–3	8–10	6–0	6–4
1969	S. R. Smith	R. C. Lutz	9–7	6–3	6–1		

† Played as National Patriotic tournament.

WOMEN'S SINGLES

	CHAMPION	RUNNER-UP	SCORE				
1887	Miss E. Hansell	Miss L. Knight	6–1	6–0			
1888	Miss B. L. Townsend	Miss E. Hansell	6–3	6–5			
1889	Miss B. L. Townsend	Miss L. D. Voorhees	7–5	6–2			
1890	Miss E. C. Roosevelt	Miss B. L. Townsend	6–2	6–2			
1891	Miss M. E. Cahill	Miss E. C. Roosevelt	6–4	6–1	4–6	6–3	
1892	Miss M. E. Cahill	Miss E. H. Moore	5–7	6–3	6–4	4–6	6–2
1893*	Miss A. Terry	Miss A. L. Schultz	6–1	6–3			
1894	Miss H. Hellwig	Miss A. Terry	7–5	3–6	6–0	3–6	6–3
1895	Miss J. Atkinson	Miss H. Hellwig	6–4	6–2	6–1		
1896	Miss E. H. Moore	Miss J. Atkinson	6–4	4–6	6–2	6–2	
1897	Miss J. Atkinson	Miss E. H. Moore	6–3	6–3	4–6	3–6	6–3
1898	Miss J. Atkinson	Miss M. Jones	6–3	5–7	6–4	2–6	7–5
1899*	Miss M. Jones	Miss M. Banks	6–1	6–1	7–5		
1900*	Miss M. McAteer	Miss E. Parker	6–2	6–2	6–0		
1901	Miss E. H. Moore	Miss M. McAteer	6–4	3–6	7–5	2–6	6–2
1902	Miss M. Jones	Miss E. H. Moore	6–1	1–0	ret'd		
1903	Miss E. H. Moore	Miss M. Jones	7–5	8–6			
1904	Miss M. G. Sutton	Miss E. H. Moore	6–1	6–2			
1905*	Miss E. H. Moore	Miss H. Homans	6–4	5–7	6–1		
1906*	Miss H. Homans	Mrs M. Barger-Wallach	6–4	6–3			
1907*	Miss Evelyn Sears	Miss C. Neely	6–3	6–2			
1908	Mrs M. Barger-Wallach	Miss Evelyn Sears	6–3	1–6	6–3		
1909	Miss H. Hotchkiss	Mrs M. Barger-Wallach	6–0	6–1			

1910 Miss H. Hotchkiss	Miss L. Hammond	6–4	6–2	
1911 Miss H. Hotchkiss	Miss F. Sutton	8–10	6–1	9–7
1912* Miss M. K. Browne	Miss Eleanora Sears	6–4	6–2	
1913 Miss M. K. Browne	Miss D. Green	6–2	7–5	
1914 Miss M. K. Browne	Miss M. Wagner	6–2	1–6	6–1
1915* Miss M. Bjurstedt	Mrs G. W. Wightman	4–6	6–2	6–0
1916 Miss M. Bjurstedt	Mrs L. H. Raymond	6–0	6–1	
1917† Miss M. Bjurstedt	Miss M. Vanderhoef	4–6	6–0	6–2
1918 Miss M. Bjurstedt	Miss E. E. Goss	6–4	6–3	
(Challenge Round abolished)				
1919 Mrs G. W. Wightman	Miss M. Zinderstein	6–1	6–2	
1920 Mrs F. Mallory	Miss M. Zinderstein	6–3	6–1	
1921 Mrs F. Mallory	Miss M. K. Browne	4–6	6–4	6–2
1922 Mrs F. Mallory	Miss H. N. Wills	6–3	6–1	
1923 Miss H. N. Wills	Mrs F. Mallory	6–2	6–1	
1924 Miss H. N. Wills	Mrs F. Mallory	6–1	6–3	
1925 Miss H. N. Wills	Miss K. McKane	3–6	6–0	6–2
1926 Mrs F. Mallory	Miss E. Ryan	4–6	6–4	9–7
1927 Miss H. N. Wills	Miss B. Nuthall	6–1	6–4	
1928 Miss H. N. Wills	Miss H. H. Jacobs	6–2	6–1	
1929 Miss H. N. Wills	Mrs P. H. Watson	6–4	6–2	
1930 Miss B. Nuthall	Mrs L. A. Harper	6–1	6–4	
1931 Mrs F. S. Moody	Mrs F. Whittingstall	6–4	6–1	
1932 Miss H. H. Jacobs	Miss C. A. Babcock	6–2	6–2	
1933 Miss H. H. Jacobs	Mrs F. S. Moody	8–6	3–6	3–0 ret'd
1934 Miss H. H. Jacobs	Miss S. Palfrey	6–1	6–4	
1935 Miss H. H. Jacobs	Mrs S. P. Fabyan	6–2	6–4	
1936 Miss A. Marble	Miss H. HN. Jacobs	4–6	6–3	6–2
1937 Miss A. Lizana	Miss J. Jedrzejowksa	6–4	6–2	
1938 Miss A. Marble	Miss N. Wynne	6–0	6–3	
1939 Miss A. Marble	Miss H. H. Jacobs	6–0	8–10	6–4
1940 Miss A. Marble	Miss H. H. Jacobs	6–2	6–3	
1941 Mrs E. T. Cooke	Miss P. M. Betz	7–5	6–2	
1942 Miss P. M. Betz	Miss A. L. Brough	4–6	6–1	6–4
1943 Miss P. M. Betz	Miss A. L. Brough	6–3	5–7	6–3
1944 Miss P. M. Betz	Miss M. E. Osborne	6–3	8–6	
1945 Mrs E. T. Cooke	Miss P. M. Betz	3–6	8–6	6–4
1946 Miss P. M. Betz	Miss P. C. Todd	11–9	6–3	
1947 Miss A. L. Brough	Miss M. E. Osborne	8–6	4–6	6–1
1948 Mrs W. D. du Pont	Miss A. L. Brough	4–6	6–4	15–13
1949 Mrs W. D. du Pont	Miss D. J. Hart	6–4	6–1	
1950 Mrs W. D. du Pont	Miss D. J. Hart	6–4	6–3	
1951 Miss M. Connolly	Miss S. J. Fry	6–3	1–6	6–4
1952 Miss M. Connolly	Miss D. J. Hart	6–3	7–5	
1953 Miss M. Connolly	Miss D. J. Hart	6–2	6–4	
1954 Miss D. J. Hart	Miss A. L. Brough	6–8	6–1	8–6
1955 Miss D. J. Hart	Miss P. E. Ward	6–4	6–2	
1956 Miss S. J. Fry	Miss A. Gibson	6–3	6–4	
1957 Miss A. Gibson	Miss A. L. Brough	6–3	6–2	
1958 Miss A. Gibson	Miss D. R. Hard	3–6	6–1	6–2
1959 Miss M. E. Bueno	Miss C. C. Truman	6–1	6–4	
1960 Miss D. R. Hard	Miss M. E. Bueno	6–4	10–12	6–4
1961 Miss D. R. Hard	Miss A. S. Haydon	6–3	6–4	
1962 Miss M. Smith	Miss D. R. Hard	9–7	6–4	
1963 Miss M. E. Bueno	Miss M. Smith	7–5	6–4	
1964 Miss M. E. Bueno	Mrs C. Graebner	6–1	6–0	
1965 Miss M. Smith	Miss B. J. Moffitt	8–6	7–5	
1966 Miss M. E. Bueno	Miss N. Richey	6–3	6–1	
1967 Mrs L. W. King	Mrs P. F. Jones	11–9	6–4	
1968 Mrs B. M. Court	Miss M. E. Bueno	6–2	6–2	
1969 Mrs B. M. Court	Miss S. V. Wade	4–6	6–3	6–0

† *Played as National Patriotic tournament.*

MEN'S DOUBLES

*Holders did not defend the title.

CHAMPIONS	RUNNERS-UP	SCORE		
1881 C. M. Clark/F. W. Taylor	A. Van Rensselaer/A. E. Newbold	6–5	6–4	6–5
1882 J. Dwight/R. D. Sears	W. Nightingale/G. M. Smith	6–2	6–4	6–4

1883	J. Dwight/R. D. Sears	A. Van Rensselaer/A. E. Newbold	6–0	6–2	6–2	
1884	J. Dwight/R. D. Sears	A. Van Rensselaer/W. V. R. Berry	6–4	6–1	8–10	6–4
1885	J. S. Clark/R. D. Sears	W. P. Knapp/H. W. Slocum	6–3	6–0	6–2	
1886	J. Dwight/R. D. Sears	G. M. Brinley/H. A. Taylor	7–5	5–7	7–5	6–4
1887	J. Dwight/R. D. Sears	H. W. Slocum/H. A. Taylor	6–4	3–6	2–6	6–3 6–3
1888	O. S. Campbell/V. G. Hall	C. Hobart/E. P. MacMullen	6–4	6–2	6–4	
1889	H. W. Slocum/H. A. Taylor	O. S. Campbell/V. G. Hall	6–1	6–3	6–2	
1890	V. G. Hall/C. Hobart	C. W. Carver/J. A. Ryerson	6–3	4–6	6–2	2–6 6–3
(Challenge Round instituted)						
1891	O. S. Campbell/R. P. Huntington	V. G. Hall/C. Hobart	6–3	6–4	8–6	
1892	O. S. Campbell/R. P. Huntington	V. G. Hall/E. L. Hall	6–4	6–2	4–6	6–3
1893	C. Hobart/F. H. Hovey	O. S. Campbell/R. P. Huntington	6–3	6–4	4–6	6–2
1894	C. Hobart/F. H. Hovey	C. B. Neel/S. R. Neel	6–3	8–6	6–1	
1895	M. G. Chace/R. D. Wrenn	C. Hobart/F. H. Hovey	7–5	6–1	8–6	
1896*	C. B./S. R. Neel	M. G. Chace/R. D. Wrenn	6–3	1–6	6–1	3–6 6–1
1897	L. E. Ware/G. P. Sheldon	H. S. Mahony/H. A. Nisbet	11–13	6–2	9–7	1–6 6–1
1898	L. E. Ware/G. P. Sheldon	D. F. Davis/H. Ward	1–6	7–5	6–4	4–6 7–5
1899	D. F. Davis/H. Ward	L. E. Ware/G. P. Sheldon	6–4	6–4	6–3	
1900	D. F. Davis/H. Ward	F. B. Alexander/R. D. Little	6–4	9–7	12–10	
1901	D. F. Davis/H. Ward	L. E. Ware/B. C. Wright	6–3	9–7	6–1	
1902	H. L./R. F. Doherty	D. F. Davis/H. Ward	11–9	12–10	6–4	
1903	H. L./R. F. Doherty	L. Collins/L. H. Waldner	7–5	6–3	6–3	
1904*	H. Ward/B. C. Wright	K. Collins/R. D. Little	1–6	6–2	3–6	6–4 6–1
1905	H. Ward/B. C. Wright	F. B. Alexander/H. H. Hackett	6–3	6–1	6–2	
1906	H. Ward/B. C. Wright	F. B. Alexander/H. H. Hackett	6–3	3–6	6–3	6–3
1907*	F. B. Alexander/B. C. Wright	W. J. Clothier/W. A. Larned	6–3	6–1	6–4	
1908	F. B. Alexander/H. H. Hackett	R. D. Little/B. C. Wright	6–1	7–5	6–2	
1909	F. B. Alexander/H. H. Hackett	G. J. Janes/M. E. McLoughlin	6–4	6–1	6–0	
1910	F. B. Alexander/H. H. Hackett	T. C. Bundy/T. W. Hendrick	6–1	8–6	6–3	
1911	R. D. Little/G. F. Touchard	F. B. Alexander/H. H. Hackett	7–5	13–15	6–2	6–4
1912	T. C. Bundy/M. E. McLoughlin	R. D. Little/G. F. Touchard	3–6	6–2	6–1	7–5
1913	T. C. Bundy/M. E. McLoughlin	C. J. Griffin/J. R. Strachan	6–4	7–5	6–1	
1914	T. C. Bundy/M. E. McLoughlin	G. M. Church/D. Mathey	6–4	6–2	6–4	
1915	C. J. Griffin/W. M. Johnston	T. C. Bundy/M. E. McLoughlin	6–2	3–6	4–6	6–3 6–3
1916	C. J. Griffin/W. M. Johnston	W. Dawson/M. E. McLoughlin	6–4	6–3	5–7	6–3
1917	F. B. Alexander/H. A. Throckmorton	H. C. Johnson/I. C. Wright	11–9	6–4	6–4	
(Challenge Round abolished)						
1918	V. Richards/W. T. Tilden	F. B. Alexander/B. C. Wright	6–3	6–4	3–6	2–6 6–2
(Challenge Round restored)						
1919	N. E. Brookes/G. L. Patterson	V. Richards/W. T. Tilden	8–6	6–3	4–6	6–2
(Challenge Round abolished)						
1920	C. J. Griffin/W. M. Johnston	W. E. Davis/R. Roberts	6–2	6–2	6–3	
1921	V. Richards/W. T. Tilden	W. M. Washburn/R. N. Williams	13–11	12–10	6–1	
1922	V. Richards/W. T. Tilden	P. O'Hara Wood/G. L. Patterson	4–6	6–1	6–3	6–4
1923	B. I. C. Norton/W. T. Tilden	W. M. Washburn/R. N. Williams	3–6	6–2	6–3	5–7 6–2
1924	H. O./R. G. Kinsey	P. O'Hara Wood/G. L. Patterson	7–5	5–7	7–9	6–3 6–4
1925	V. Richards/R. N. Williams	J. B. Hawkes/G. L. Patterson	6–2	8–10	6–4	11–9
1926	V. Richards/R. N. Williams	A. H. Chapin/W. T. Tilden	6–4	6–8	11–9	6–3
1927	F. T. Hunter/W. T. Tilden	W. M. Johnston/R. N. Williams	10–8	6–3	6–3	
1928	J. F. Hennessey/G. M. Lott	J. B. Hawkes/G. L. Patterson	6–2	6–1	6–2	
1929	J. H. Doeg/G. M. Lott	R. B. Bell/L. N. White	10–8	16–14	6–1	
1930	J. H. Doeg/G. M. Lott	W. L. Allison/J. Van Ryn	8–6	6–3	4–6	13–15 6–4
1931	W. L. Allison/J. Van Ryn	R. B. Bell/G. S. Mangin	6–4	8–6	6–3	
1932	K. Gledhill/H. E. Vines	W. L. Allison/J. Van Ryn	6–4	6–3	6–2	
1933	G. M. Lott/L. R. Stoefen	F. A. Parker/F. X. Shields	11–13	9–7	9–7	6–3
1934	G. M. Lott/L. R. Stoefen	W. L. Allison/J. Van Ryn	6–4	9–7	3–6	6–4
1935	W. L. Allison/J. Van Ryn	J. D. Budge/G. Mako	6–4	6–2	3–6	2–6 6–1
1936	J. D. Budge/G. Mako	W. L. Allison/J. Van Ryn	6–4	6–2	6–4	
1937	G. Von Cramm/H. Henkel	J. D. Budge/G. Mako	6–4	7–5	6–4	
1938	J. D. Budge/G. Mako	J. E. Bromwich/A. K. Quist	6–3	6–2	6–1	
1939	J. E. Bromwich/A. K. Quist	J. H. Crawford/H. C. Hopman	8–6	6–1	6–4	
1940	J. A. Kramer/F. R. Schroeder	G. Mulloy/H. J. Prussoff	6–4	8–6	9–7	
1941	J. A. Kramer/F. R. Schroeder	G. Mulloy/W. Sabin	9–7	6–4	6–2	
1942	G. Mulloy/W. F. Talbert	F. R. Schroeder/S. B. Wood	9–7	7–5	6–1	
1943	J. A. Kramer/F. A. Parker	D. Freeman/W. F. Talbert	6–2	6–4	6–4	
1944	R. Falkenburg/W. D. McNeill	F. Segura/W. F. Talbert	7–5	6–4	3–6	6–1
1945	G. Mulloy/W. F. Talbert	R. Falkenburg/J. Tuero	12–10	8–10	12–10	6–2
1946	G. Mulloy/W. F. Talbert	G. Guernsey/W. D. McNeill	3–6	6–4	2–6	6–3 20–18
1947	J. A. Kramer/F. R. Schroeder	W. F. Talbert/O. W. Sidwell	6–4	7–5	6–3	
1948	G. Mulloy/W. F. Talbert	F. A. Parker/F. R. Schroeder	1–6	9–7	6–3	3–6 9–7
1949	J. Bromwich/O. W. Sidwell	F. A. Sedgman/G. Worthington	6–4	6–0	6–1	
1950	J. Bromwich/F. A. Sedgman	G. Mulloy/W. F. Talbert	7–5	8–6	3–6	6–1

1951	K. McGregor/F. A. Sedgman	D. Candy/M. G. Rose	10–8	6–4	4–6	7–5	
1952	M. G. Rose/E. V. Seixas	K. McGregor/F. A. Sedgman	3–6	10–8	10–8	6–8	8–6
1953	R. N. Hartwig/M. G. Rose	G. Mulloy/W. F. Talbert	6–4	4–6	6–2	6–4	
1954	E. V. Seixas/M. A. Trabert	L. A. Hoad/K. R. Rosewall	3–6	6–4	8–6	6–3	
1955	K. Kamo/A. Miyagi	G. Moss/W. Quillian	6–3	6–3	3–6	1–6	6–4
1956	L. A. Hoad/K. R. Rosewall	H. Richardson/E. V. Seixas	6–2	6–2	3–6	6–4	
1957	A. J. Cooper/N. A. Fraser	G. Mulloy/J. E. Patty	4–6	6–3	9–7	6–3	
1958	A. Olmedo/H. Richardson	S. Giammalva/B. McKay	3–6	6–3	6–4	6–4	
1959	R. S. Emerson/N. A. Fraser	E. Buchholz/A. Olmedo	3–6	6–3	5–7	6–4	7–5
1960	R. S. Emerson/N. A. Fraser	R. G. Laver/R. Mark	9–7	6–2	6–4		
1961	C. McKinley/R. D. Ralston	A. Palafox/R. H. Osuna	6–3	6–4	2–6	13–11	
1962	A. Palafox/R. H. Osuna	C. McKinley/R. D. Ralston	6–4	10–12	1–6	9–7	6–3
1963	C. McKinley/R. D. Ralston	A. Palafox/R. H. Osuna	9–7	4–6	5–7	6–3	11–9
1964	C. McKinley/R. D. Ralston	G. Stilwell/M. Sangster	6–3	6–2	6–4		
1965	R. S. Emerson/F. S. Stolle	F. Froehling/C. Pasarell	6–4	10–12	7–5	6–3	
1966	R. S. Emerson/F. S. Stolle	C. Graebner/R. D. Ralston	6–4	6–4	6–4		
1967	J. D. Newcombe/A. D. Roche	O. K. Davidson/W. W. Bowrey	6–8	9–7	6–3	6–3	
1968	R. C. Lutz/S. R. Smith	R. A. J. Hewitt/R. J. Moore	6–4	6–4	9–7		
1969	R. D. Crealy/A. Stone	W. W. Bowrey/C. Pasarell	9–11	6–3	7–5		

† *Played as National Patriotic tournament.*

WOMEN'S DOUBLES

Not recognised as an official Championship.

	CHAMPIONS	RUNNERS-UP	SCORE				
1887*	E. F. Hansell/L. Knight	L. Allderdice/Church	6–0	6–4			
1888*	E. C. Roosevelt/G. W. Roosevelt	A. K. Robinson/V. Ward	3–6	6–3	6–4		
1889	M. Ballard/B. L. Townsend	M. Wright/L. Knight	6–0	6–2			
1890	E. C. Roosevelt/G. W. Roosevelt	B. L. Townsend/M. Ballard	6–1	6–2			
1891	M. E. Cahill/Mrs W. F. Morgan	E. C. Roosevelt/G. W. Roosevelt	2–6	8–6	6–4		
1892	M. E. Cahill/A. M. McKinlay	Mrs A. H. Harris/A. R. Williams	6–1	6–3			
1893	H. Butler/A. M. Terry	A. L. Schultz/Stone	6–4	6–3			
1894	J. P. Atkinson/H. R. Hellwig	A. R. Williams/A. C. Wistar	6–4	7–5			
1895	J. P. Atkinson/H. R. Hellwig	E. H. Moore/A. R. Williams	6–2	6–2	12–10		
1896	J. P. Atkinson/E. H. Moore	A. R. Williams/A. C. Wistar	6–4	7–5			
1897	J. P. Atkinson/K. Atkinson	F. Edwards/E. J. Rastall	6–2	6–1	6–1		
1898	J. P. Atkinson/K. Atkinson	C. B. Neely/M. Wimer	6–1	2–6	4–6	6–1	6–2
1899	J. W. Craven/M. McAteer	M. Banks/E. J. Rastall	6–1	6–1	7–5		
1900	H. Champlin/E. Parker	M. McAteer/M. Wimer	9–7	6–2	6–2		
1901	J. P. Atkinson/M. McAteer	M. Jones/E. H. Moore	w.o.				
1902§	J. P. Atkinson/M. Jones	M. Banks/N. Closterman	6–2	7–5			
1903	E. H. Moore/C. B. Neely	M. Jones/M. Hall	6–4	6–1	6–1		
1904	M. Hall/M. G. Sutton	E. H. Moore/C. B. Neely	3–6	6–3	6–3‡		
1905	H. Homans/C. B. Neely	V. Maule/M. F. Oberteuffer	6–0	6–1			
1906	Mrs L. S. Coe/Mrs D. S. Platt	C. Boldt/H. Homans	6–4	6–4			
1907	C. B. Neely/M. Wimer	E. Wildey/N. Wildey	6–1	2–6	6–4		
1908	M. Curtis/Evelyn Sears	C. B. Neely/M. Steever	6–3	5–7	9–7		
1909	H. V. Hotchkiss/E. E. Rotch	D. Green/L. Moyes	6–1	6–1			
1910	H. V. Hotchkiss/E. E. Rotch	A. Browning/E. Wildey	6–4	6–4			
1911	H. V. Hotchkiss/Eleanora Sears	D. Green/F. Sutton	6–4	4–6	6–2		
1912	M. K. Browne/D. Green	Mrs M. Barger-Wallach/Mrs F. Schmitz	6–2	5–7	6–0		
1913	M. K. Browne/Mrs R. H. Williams	D. Green/E. Wildey	12–10	2–6	6–3		
1914	M. K. Browne/Mrs R. H. Williams	Mrs E. Raymond/E. Wildey	8–6	6–2			
1915	Eleanora Sears/Mrs G. W. Wightman	Mrs G. L. Chapman/Mrs M. McLean	10–8	6–2			
1916	M. Bjurstedt/E. Sears	Mrs E. Raymond/E. Wildey	4–6	6–2	10–8		
1917	M. Bjurstedt/Eleanora Sears	Mrs R. LeRoy/P. Walsh	6–2	6–4			
1918	E. E. Goss/M. Zinderstein	M. Bjurstedt/Mrs J. Rogge	7–5	8–6			
1919	E. E. Goss/M. Zinderstein	Eleanora Sears/Mrs G. W. Wightman	9–7	9–7			
1920	E. E. Goss/M. Zinderstein	H. Baker/E. Tennant	13–11	4–6	6–3		
1921	M. K. Browne/Mrs R. H. Williams	H. Gilleaudeau/Mrs L. G. Morris	6–3	6–2			
1922	Mrs J. B. Jessup/H. N. Wills	Mrs F. I. Mallory/E. Sigourney	6–4	7–9	6–3		
1923	Mrs B. C. Covell/K. McKane	E. E. Goss/Mrs G. W. Wightman	2–6	6–2	6–1		
1924	Mrs G. W. Wightman/H. N. Wills	E. E. Goss/Mrs J. B. Jessup	6–4	6–3			
1925	M. K. Browne/H. N. Wills	Mrs T. C. Bundy/E. Ryan	6–4	6–3			
1926	E. E. Goss/E. Ryan	M. K. Browne/Mrs A. H. Chapin	3–6	6–4	12–10		
1927	Mrs L. A. Godfree/E. H. Harvey	J. Fry/B. Nuthall	6–1	4–6	6–4		
1928	Mrs G. W. Wightman/H. N. Wills	E. Cross/Mrs L. A. Harper	6–2	6–2			
1929	Mrs L. R. C. Michell/Mrs P. H. Watson	Mrs B. C. Covell/Mrs D. C. Shepherd-Barron	2–6	6–3	6–4		

Year	Champions	Runners-up	Score		
1930	B. Nuthall/S. Palfrey	E. Cross/Mrs L. A. Harper	3–6	6–3	7–5
1931	B. Nuthall/Mrs E. F. Whittingstall	H. H. Jacobs/D. E. Round	6–2	6–4	
1932	H. H. Jacobs/S. Palfrey	A. Marble/Mrs M. Painter	8–6	6–1	
1933	F. James/B. Nuthall	Mrs F. S. Moody/E. Ryan	w.o.		
1934	H. H. Jacobs/S. Palfrey	Mrs D. B. Andrus/C. A. Babcock	4–6	6–3	6–4
1935	H. H. Jacobs/Mrs M. Fabyan	Mrs D. B. Andrus/C. A. Babcock	6–4	6–2	
1936	C. A. Babcock/Mrs J. Van Ryn	H. H. Jacobs/Mrs M. Fabyan	9–7	2–6	6–4
1937	Mrs M. Fabyan/A. Marble	C. A. Babcock/Mrs J. Van Ryn	7–5	6–4	
1938	Mrs M. Fabyan/A. Marble	J. Jedrzejowska/Mrs R. Mathieu	6–8	6–4	6–3
1939	Mrs M. Fabyan/A. Marble	Mrs S. H. Hammersley/K. E. Stammers	7–5	8–6	
1940	Mrs M. Fabyan/A. Marble	D. M. Bundy/Mrs J. Van Ryn	6–4	6–3	
1941	Mrs E. T. Cooke/M. E. Osborne	D. M. Bundy/D. J. Hart	3–6	6–1	6–4
1942	A. L. Brough/M. E. Osborne	P. M. Betz/D. J. Hart	9–7	6–2	6–1
1943	A. L. Brough/M. E. Osborne	P. M. Betz/D. J. Hart	6–4	6–3	
1944	A. L. Brough/M. E. Osborne	P. M. Betz/D. J. Hart	4–6	6–4	6–3
1945	A. L. Brough/M. E. Osborne	P. M. Betz/D. J. Hart	6–4	6–4	
1946	A. L. Brough/M. E. Osborne	Mrs P. C. Todd/Mrs M. A. Prentiss	6–1	6–3	
1947	A. L. Brough/M. E. Osborne	Mrs P. C. Todd/D. J. Hart	5–7	6–3	7–5
1948	A. L. Brough/Mrs W. D. du Pont	Mrs P. C. Todd/D. J. Hart	6–4	8–10	6–1
1949	A. L. Brough/Mrs W. D. du Pont	S. J. Fry/D. J. Hart	6–4	10–8	
1950	A. L. Brough/Mrs W. D. du Pont	S. J. Fry/D. J. Hart	6–2	6–3	
1951	S. J. Fry/D. J. Hart	N. Chaffee/Mrs P. C. Todd	6–4	6–2	
1952	S. J. Fry/D. J. Hart	A. L. Brough/M. Connolly	10–8	6–4	
1953	S. J. Fry/D. J. Hart	A. L. Brough/Mrs W. D. du Pont	6–2	7–9	9–7
1954	S. J. Fry/D. J. Hart	A. L. Brough/Mrs W. D. du Pont	6–4	6–4	
1955	A. L. Brough/Mrs W. D. du Pont	S. J. Fry/D. J. Hart	6–3	1–6	6–3
1956	A. L. Brough/Mrs W. D. du Pont	Mrs B. R. Pratt/S. J. Fry	6–3	6–0	
1957	A. L. Brough/Mrs W. D. du Pont	A. Gibson/D. R. Hard	6–2	7–5	
1958	J. M. Arth/D. R. Hard	A. Gibson/M. E. Bueno	2–6	6–3	6–4
1959	J. M. Arth/D. R. Hard	S. Moore/M. E. Bueno	6–2	6–3	
1960	M. E. Bueno/D. R. Hard	D. M. Catt/A. A. Haydon	6–1	6–1	
1961	D. R. Hard/L. Turner	E. Buding/Y. Ramirez	6–4	5–7	6–0
1962	M. E. Bueno/D. R. Hard	Mrs R. Susman/B. J. Moffitt	4–6	6–3	6–2
1963	R. Ebbern/M. Smith	M. E. Bueno/D. R. Hard	4–6	10–8	6–3
1964	Mrs R. Susman/B. J. Moffitt	M. Smith/L. Turner	3–6	6–2	6–4
1965	N. Richey/Mrs C. Graebner	Mrs R. Susman/B. J. Moffitt	6–4	6–4	
1966	M. E. Bueno/N. Richey	R. Casals/Mrs L. W. King	6–3	6–4	
1967	R. Casals/Mrs L. W. King	M. A. Eisel/Mrs D. Fales	4–6	6–3	6–4
1968	M. E. Bueno/M. Smith	S. V. Wade/Mrs G. M. Williams	6–3	7–5	
1969	Mrs B. M. Court/S. V. Wade	Mrs P. W. Curtis/V. Ziegenfuss	6–1	6–3	

† *Played as National Patriotic tournament.*
‡ *There is some doubt about the accuracy of this result.*
§ *5-set finals abolished.*

MIXED DOUBLES

Not recognised as an official championship

Year	CHAMPIONS	RUNNERS-UP	SCORE			
1887*	J. S. Clark/Miss L. Stokes	E. D. Faries/Miss L. Knight	7–5	6–4		
1888*	J. S. Clark/Miss M. Wright	P. Johnson/Miss A. Robinson	1–6	6–5	6–4	6–3
1889*	A. E. Wright/Miss G. W. Roosevelt	C. T. Lee/Miss B. L. Townsend	6–1	6–3	3–6	6–3
1890*	R. Beach/Miss M. E. Cahill	C. T. Lee/Miss B. L. Townsend	6–2	3–6	6–2	
1891*	M. R. Wright/Miss M. E. Cahill	C. T. Lee/Miss G. W. Roosevelt	6–4	6–0	6–5	
1892	C. Hobart/Miss M. E. Cahill	R. Beach/Miss E. H. Moore	6–1	6–3		
1893	C. Hobart/Miss E. C. Roosevelt	R. N. Willson/Miss Bankson	6–1	4–6	10–8	6–1
1894	E. P. Fischer/Miss J. P. Atkinson	G. Remak/Mrs McFadden	6–2	6–2	6–1	
1895	E. P. Fischer/Miss J. P. Atkinson	M. Fielding/Miss A. R. Williams	4–6	6–1	6–2	
1896	E. P. Fischer/Miss J. P. Atkinson	M. Fielding/Miss A. R. Williams	6–2	6–3	6–3	
1897	D. L. Magruder/Miss L. Henson	R. A. Griffin/Miss M. Banks	6–4	6–3	7–5	
1898	E. P. Fischer/Miss C. B. Neely	J. A. Hill/Miss H. Chapman	Not known			
1899	A. L. Hoskins/Miss E. J. Rastall	J. P. Gardner/Miss J. W. Craven	6–4	6–0	ret'd	
1900	A. Codman/Miss M. J. Hunnewell	G. Atkinson/Miss T. Shaw	11–9	6–3	6–1	
1901	R. D. Little/Miss M. Jones	C. Stevens/Miss M. McAteer	6–4	6–4	7–5	
1902	W. C. Grant/Miss E. H. Moore	A. L. Hoskins/Miss E. J. Rastall	6–2	6–1		
1903	H. F. Allen/Miss H. Chapman	W. H. Rowland/Miss C. B. Neely	6–4	7–5		
1904	W. C. Grant/Miss E. H. Moore	F. B. Dallas/Miss M. Sutton	6–2	6–1		
1905	C. Hobart/Mrs Hobart	E. B. Dewhurst/Miss E. H. Moore	6–2	6–4		
1906	E. B. Dewhurst/Miss S. Coffin	J. B. Johnson/Miss M. Johnson	6–3	7–5		
1907	W. F. Johnson/Miss M. Sayres	H. M. Tilden/Miss N. Wildey	6–1	7–5		

1908	N. W. Niles/Miss E. E. Rotch	R. D. Little/Miss L. Hammond	6–4 4–6 6–4
1909	W. F. Johnson/Miss H. V. Hotchkiss	R. D. Little/Miss L. Hammond	6–2 6–0
1910	J. R. Carpenter/Miss H. V. Hotchkiss	H. M. Tilden/Miss E. Wildey	6–2 6–2
1911	W. F. Johnson/Miss H. V. Hotchkiss	H. M. Tilden/Miss E. Wildey	6–4 6–4
1912	R. N. Williams/Miss M. K. Browne	W. J. Clothier/Miss Evelyn Sears	6–4 2–6 11–9
1913	W. T. Tilden/Miss M. K. Browne	C. S. Rogers/Miss D. Green	7–5 7–5
1914	W. T. Tilden/Miss M. K. Browne	J. R. Rowland/Miss M. Myers	6–1 6–4
1915	H. C. Johnson/Mrs G. W. Wightman	I. C. Wright/Miss M. Bjurstedt	6–0 6–1
1916	W. E. Davis/Miss Evelyn Sears	W. T. Tilden/Miss F. A. Ballin	6–4 7–5
1917	I. C. Wright/Miss M. Bjurstedt	W. T. Tilden/Miss F. A. Ballin	10–12 6–1 6–3
1918	I. C. Wright/Mrs G. W. Wightman	F. B. Alexander/Miss M. Bjurstedt	6–2 6–4
1919	V. Richards/Miss M. Zinderstein	W. T. Tilden/Miss F. A. Ballin	2–6 11–9 6–1
1920	W. F. Johnson/Mrs G. W. Wightman	C. Biddle/Mrs F. I. Mallory	6–4 6–3
1921	W. M. Johnston/Miss M. K. Browne	W. T. Tilden/Miss F. I. Mallory	3–6 6–4 6–3
1922	W. T. Tilden/Mrs F. I. Mallory	H. Kinsey/Miss H. N. Wills	6–4 6–3
1923	W. T. Tilden/Mrs F. I. Mallory	J. B. Hawkes/Miss K. McKane	6–3 2–6 10–8
1924	V. Richards/Miss H. N. Wills	W. T. Tilden/Mrs F. I. Mallory	6–8 7–5 6–0
1925	J. B. Hawkes/Miss K. McKane	V. Richards/Miss E. H. Harvey	6–2 6–4
1926	J. Borotra/Miss E. Ryan	R. Lacoste/Mrs G. W. Wightman	6–4 7–5
1927	H. Cochet/Miss E. Bennett	R. Lacoste/Mrs G. W. Wightman	2–6 6–0 6–2
1928	G. M. Lott/Miss B. Nuthall	H. W. Austin/Mrs B. C. Covell	6–3 6–3
1929	G. M. Lott/Miss B. Nuthall	H. W. Austin/Mrs B. C. Lovell	6–3 6–3
1930	W. L. Allison/Miss E. Cross	F. X. Shields/Miss M. Morrill	6–4 6–4
1931	G. M. Lott/Miss B. Nuthall	W.L. Allison/Mrs L. A. Harper	6–3 6–3
1932	F. J. Perry/Miss S. Palfrey	H. E. Vines/Miss H. H. Jacobs	6–3 7–5
1933	H. E. Vines/Miss E. Ryan	G. M. Lott/Miss S. Palfrey	11–9 6–1
1934	G. M. Lott/Miss H. H. Jacobs	L. R. Stoefen/Miss E. Ryan	4–6 13–11 6–2
1935	E. Maier/Mrs M. Fabyan	R. Menzel/Miss K. E. Stammers	6–3 3–6 6–4
1936	G. Mako/Miss A. Marble	J. D. Budge/Mrs M. Fabyan	6–3 6–2
1937	J. D. Budge/Mrs M. Fabyan	Y. Petra/Mme S. Henrotin	6–2 8–10 6–0
1938	J. D. Budge/Miss A. Marble	J. E. Bromwich/Miss T. Coyne	6–1 6–2
1939	H. C. Hopman/Miss A. Marble	E. T. Cooke/Mrs M. Fabyan	9–7 6–1
1940	R. L. Riggs/Miss A. Marble	J. A. Kramer/Miss D. M. Bundy	9–7 6–1
1941	J. A. Kramer/Mrs E. T. Cooke	R. L. Riggs/Miss P. M. Betz	4–6 6–4 6–4
1942	F. R. Schroeder/Miss A. L. Brough	A. D. Russell/Mrs P. C. Todd	3–6 6–1 6–4
1943	W. F. Talbert/Miss M. E. Osborne	F. Segura/Miss P. M. Betz	10–8 6–4
1944	W. F. Talbert/Miss M. E. Osborne	W. D. McNeill/Miss D. M. Bundy	6–2 6–3
1945	W. F. Talbert/Miss M. E. Osborne	R. Falkenburg/Miss D. J. Hart	6–4 6–4
1946	W. F. Talbert/Miss M. E. Osborne	R. Kimbrell/Miss A. L. Brough	6–3 6–4
1947	J. Bromwich/Miss A. L. Brough	F. Segura/Miss G. Moran	6–3 6–1
1948	T. P. Brown/Miss A. L. Brough	W. F. Talbert/Mrs W. D. du Pont	6–4 6–4
1949	E. W. Sturgess/Miss A. L. Brough	W. F. Talbert/Mrs W. D. du Pont	4–6 6–3 7–5
1950	K. McGregor/Mrs W. D. du Pont	F. A. Sedgman/Miss D. J. Hart	6–4 3–6 6–3
1951	F. A. Sedgman/Miss D. J. Hart	M. G. Rose/Miss S. J. Fry	6–3 6–2
1952	F. A. Sedgman/Miss D. J. Hart	L. A. Hoad/Mrs T. C. Long	6–3 7–5
1953	E. V. Seixas/Miss D. J. Hart	R. N. Hartwig/Miss J. A. Sampson	6–2 4–6 6–4
1954	E. V. Seixas/Miss D. J. Hart	K. R. Rosewall/Mrs W. D. du Pont	4–6 6–1 6–1
1955	E. V. Seixas/Miss D. J. Hart	L. A. Hoad/Miss S. J. Fry	9–7 6–1
1956	K. R. Rosewall/Mrs W. D. du Pont	L. A. Hoad/Miss D. R. Hard	9–7 6–1
1957	K. Nielsen/Miss A. Gibson	R. N. Howe/Miss D. R. Hard	6–3 9–7
1958	N. A. Fraser/Mrs W. D. du Pont	A. Olmedo/Miss M. E. Bueno	6–3 3–6 9–7
1959	N. A. Fraser/Mrs W. D. du Pont	R. Mark/Miss J. Hopps	7–5 13–15 6–2
1960	N. A. Fraser/Mrs W. D. du Pont	A. Palafox/Miss M. E. Bueno	6–3 6–2
1961	R. Mark/Miss M. Smith	R. D. Ralston/Miss D. R. Hard	w.o.
1962	F. S. Stolle/Miss M. Smith	F. Froehling/Miss L. Turner	7–5 6–2
1963	K. Fletcher/Miss M. Smith	E. Rubinoff/Miss J. Tegart	3–6 8–6 6–2
1964	J. D. Newcombe/Miss M. Smith	E. Rubinoff/Miss J. Tegart	10–8 4–6 6–3
1965	F. S. Stolle/Miss M. Smith	F. Froehling/Miss J. Tegart	5–2 6–2
1966	O. K. Davidson/Mrs D. Fales	E. Rubinoff/Miss C. A. Aucamp	6–1 6–3
1967	O. K. Davidson/Mrs L. W. King	S. R. Smith/Miss R. Casals	6–3 6–2
1968	P. W. Curtis/Miss M. A. Eisel	R. N. Perry/Miss T. A. Fretz	6–4 7–5
1969	P. Sullivan/Miss P. S. A. Hogan	T. Addison/Miss K. Pigeon	6–4 2–6 12–10

† *Played as National Patriotic tournament.*

US OPEN CHAMPIONSHIPS

Played at West Side Club, Forest Hills, New York, on grass courts 1968–74, on Har-Tru courts 1975–77. Played at National Tennis Centre, Flushing Meadow, New York, on cement courts, 1978 on.

MEN'S SINGLES

	CHAMPION	RUNNER-UP	SCORE					WINNER'S PRIZE ($)
1968	A. R. Ashe	T. S. Okker	14–12	5–7	6–3	3–6	6–3	14,000
1969	R. G. Laver	A. D. Roche	7–9	6–3	6–1	6–2		16,000
1970	K. R. Rosewall	A. D. Roche	2–6	6–4	7–6	6–3		20,000
1971	S. R. Smith	J. Kodes	3–6	6–3	6–2	7–6		15,000
1972	I. Nastase	A. R. Ashe	3–6	6–3	6–7	6–4	6–3	25,000
1973	J. D. Newcombe	J. Kodes	6–4	1–6	4–6	6–2	6–3	25,000
1974	J. S. Connors	K. R. Rosewall	6–1	6–0	6–1			22,500
1975	M. Orantes	J. S. Connors	6–4	6–3	6–3			25,000
1976	J. S. Connors	B. Borg	6–4	3–6	7–6	6–4		30,000
1977	G. Vilas	J. S. Connors	2–6	6–3	7–6	6–0		33,000
1978	J. S. Connors	B. Borg	6–4	6–2	6–2			38,000
1979	J. P. McEnroe	V. Gerulaitis	7–5	6–3	6–3			39,000
1980	J. P. McEnroe	B. Borg	7–6	6–1	6–7	5–7	6–4	46,000
1981	J. P. McEnroe	B. Borg	4–6	6–2	6–4	6–3		60,000
1982	J. S. Connors	I. Lendl	6–3	6–2	4–6	6–4		90,000
1983	J. S. Connors	I. Lendl	6–3	6–7	7–5	6–0		120,000
1984	J. P. McEnroe	I. Lendl	6–3	6–4	6–1			160,000
1985	I. Lendl	J. P. McEnroe	7–6	6–3	6–4			187,500
1986	I. Lendl	M. Mecir	6–4	6–2	6–0			210,000
1987	I. Lendl	M. Wilander	6–7	6–0	7–6	6–4		250,000
1988	M. Wilander	I. Lendl	6–4	4–6	6–3	5–7	6–4	275,000
1989	B. Becker	I. Lendl	7–6	1–6	6–3	7–6		300,000
1990	P. Sampras	A. Agassi	6–4	6–3	6–2			350,000

WOMEN'S SINGLES

	CHAMPION	RUNNER-UP	SCORE			WINNER'S PRIZE ($)
1968	Miss S. V. Wade	Mrs L. W. King	6–4	6–2		6,000
1969	Mrs B. M. Court	Miss N. Richey	6–2	6–2		6,000
1970	Mrs B. M. Court	Miss R. Casals	6–2	2–6	6–1	7,500
1971	Mrs L. W. King	Miss R. Casals	6–4	7–6		5,000
1972	Mrs L. W. King	Miss K. Melville	6–3	7–5		10,000
1973	Mrs B. M. Court	Miss E. Goolagong	7–6	5–7	6–2	25,000
1974	Mrs L. W. King	Miss E. Goolagong	3–6	6–3	7–5	22,500
1975	Miss C. M. Evert	Mrs R. A. Cawley	5–7	6–4	6–2	25,000
1976	Miss C. M. Evert	Mrs R. A. Cawley	6–3	6–0		30,000
1977	Miss C. M. Evert	Miss W. Turnbull	7–6	6–2		33,000
1978	Miss C. M. Evert	Miss P. Shriver	7–5	6–4		38,000
1979	Miss T. A. Austin	Miss C. M. Evert	6–4	6–3		39,000
1980	Mrs J. M. Lloyd	Miss H. Mandlikova	5–7	6–1	6–1	46,000
1981	Miss T. A. Austin	Miss M. Navratilova	1–6	7–6	7–6	60,000
1982	Mrs J. M. Lloyd	Miss H. Mandlikova	6–3	6–1		90,000
1983	Miss M. Navratilova	Mrs J. M. Lloyd	6–1	6–3		120,000
1984	Miss M. Navratilova	Mrs J. M. Lloyd	4–6	6–4	6–4	160,000
1985	Miss H. Mandlikova	Miss M. Navratilova	7–6	1–6	7–6	187,500
1986	Miss M. Navratilova	Miss H. Sukova	6–3	6–2		210,000
1987	Miss M. Navratilova	Miss S. Graf	7–6	6–1		250,000
1988	Miss S. Graf	Miss G. Sabatini	6–3	3–6	6–1	275,000
1989	Miss S. Graf	Miss M. Navratilova	3–6	7–5	6–1	300,000
1990	Miss G. Sabatini	Miss S. Graf	6–2	7–6		350,000

MEN'S DOUBLES

	CHAMPIONS	RUNNERS-UP	SCORE				
1968	R. C. Lutz/S. R. Smith	A. R. Ashe/A. Gimeno	11–9	6–1	7–5		
1969	K. R. Rosewall/F. S. Stolle	C. Pasarell/R. D. Ralston	2–6	7–5	13–11	6–3	
1970	P. Barthes/N. Pilic	R. S. Emerson/R. G. Laver	6–3	7–6	4–6	7–6	
1971	J. D. Newcombe/R. Taylor	S. R. Smith/E. van Dillen	6–7	6–3	7–6	4–6	7–6
1972	E. C. Drysdale/R. Taylor	O. K. Davidson/J. D. Newcombe	6–4	7–6	6–3		
1973	O. K. Davidson/J. D. Newcombe	R. G. Laver/K. R. Rosewall	7–5	2–6	7–5	7–5	
1974	R. C. Lutz/S. R. Smith	P. Cornejo/J. Fillol	6–3	6–3			
1975	J. S. Connors/I. Nastase	T. S. Okker/M. C. Riessen	6–4	7–6			

1976	T. S. Okker/M. C. Riessen	P. Kronk/C. Letcher	6–4	6–4			
1977	R. A. J. Hewitt/F. D. McMillan	B. E. Gottfried/R. Ramirez	6–4	6–0			
1978	R. C. Lutz/S. R. Smith	M. C. Riessen/S. E. Stewart	1–6	7–5	6–3		
1979	P. Fleming/J. P. McEnroe	R. C. Lutz/S. R. Smith	6–2	6–4			
1980	R. C. Lutz/S. R. Smith	P. Fleming/J. P. McEnroe	7–6	3–6	6–1	3–6	6–3
1981	P. Fleming/J. P. McEnroe	H. Gunthardt/P. McNamara	w.o.				
1982	K. Curren/S. Denton	V. Amaya/H. Pfister	6–2	6–7	5–7	6–2	6–4
1983	P. Fleming/J. P. McEnroe	F. Buehning/V. Winitsky	6–3	6–4	6–2		
1984	J. Fitzgerald/T. Smid	S. Edberg/A. Jarryd	7–6	6–3	6–3		
1985	K. Flach/R. Seguso	H. Leconte/Y. Noah	7–6	6–7	7–6	6–0	
1986	A. Gomez/S. Zivojinovic	J. Nystrom/M. Wilander	4–6	6–3	6–3	4–6	6–3
1987	S. Edberg/A. Jarryd	K. Flach/R. Seguso	7–6	6–2	4–6	5–7	7–6
1988	S. Casal/E. Sanchez	R. Leach/J. Pugh	w.o.				
1989	J. P. McEnroe/M. Woodforde	K. Flach/R. Seguso	6–4	4–6	6–3	6–3	
1990	P. Aldrich/D. Visser	P. Annacone/D. Wheaton	6–2	7–6	6–2		

WOMEN'S DOUBLES

	CHAMPIONS	RUNNERS-UP	SCORE		
1968	M. E. Bueno/Mrs B. M. Court	R. Casals/Mrs L. W. King	4–6	9–7	8–6
1969	F. Durr/D. R. Hard	Mrs B. M. Court/S. V. Wade	0–6	6–4	6–4
1970	Mrs B. M. Court/Mrs D. Dalton	R. Casals/S. V. Wade	6–3	6–4	
1971	R. Casals/Mrs D. Dalton	Mrs J. B. Chanfreau/F. Durr	6–3	6–3	
1972	F. Durr/B. Stove	Mrs B. M. Court/S. V. Wade	6–3	1–6	6–3
1973	Mrs B. M. Court/S. V. Wade	R. Casals/Mrs L. W. King	3–6	6–3	7–5
1974	R. Casals/Mrs L. W. King	F. Durr/B. Stove	7–6	6–7	6–4
1975	Mrs B. M. Court/S. V. Wade	R. Casals/Mrs L. W. King	7–5	2–6	7–5
1976	L. Boshoff/I. Kloss	O. Morozova/S. V. Wade	6–1	6–4	
1977	M. Navratilova/B. Stove	R. Richards/B. Stuart	6–1	7–6	
1978	Mrs L. W. King/M. Navratilova	Mrs G. E. Reid/W. M. Turnbull	7–6	6–4	
1979	B. Stove/W. M. Turnbull	Mrs L. W. King/M. Navratilova	7–5	6–3	
1980	Mrs L. W. King/M. Navratilova	P. H. Shriver/B. Stove	7–6	7–5	
1981	K. Jordan/A. E. Smith	R. Casals/W. M. Turnbull	6–3	6–3	
1982	R. Casals/W. M. Turnbull	B. Potter/S. A. Walsh	6–4	6–4	
1983	M. Navratilova/P. H. Shriver	R. Fairbank/C. Reynolds	6–7	6–1	6–3
1984	M. Navratilova/P. H. Shriver	A. E. Hobbs/W. M. Turnbull	6–2	6–4	
1985	C. Kohde-Kilsch/H. Sukova	M. Navratilova/P. H. Shriver	6–7	6–2	6–3
1986	M. Navratilova/P. H. Shriver	H. Mandlikova/W. M. Turnbull	6–4	3–6	6–3
1987	M. Navratilova/P. H. Shriver	K. Jordan/E. Smylie	5–7	6–4	6–2
1988	G. Fernandez/R. White	J. Hetherington/P. Fendick	6–4	6–1	
1989	H. Mandlikova/M. Navratilova	M.-J. Fernandez/P. H. Shriver	5–7	6–4	6–4
1990	G. Fernandez/M. Navratilova	J. Novotna/H. Sukova	6–2	6–4	

MIXED DOUBLES

	CHAMPIONS	RUNNERS-UP	SCORE		
1968	Not held				
1969	M. C. Riessen/Mrs B. M. Court	R. D. Ralston/Miss F. Durr	7–5	6–3	
1970	M. C. Riessen/Mrs B. M. Court	F. D. McMillan/Mrs D. Dalton	6–4	6–4	
1971	O. K. Davidson/Mrs L. W. King	R. R. Maud/Miss B. Stove	6–3	7–5	
1972	M. C. Riessen/Mrs B. M. Court	I. Nastase/Miss R. Casals	6–3	7–5	
1973	O. K. Davidson/Mrs L. W. King	M. C. Riessen/Miss B. M. Court	6–3	3–6	7–6
1974	G. Masters/Miss P. Teeguarden	J. S. Connors/Miss C. M. Evert	6–1	7–6	
1975	R. L. Stockton/Miss R. Casals	F. S. Stolle/Mrs L. W. King	6–3	7–6	
1976	P. Dent/Mrs L. W. King	F. D. McMillan/Miss B. Stove	3–6	6–2	7–5
1977	F. D. McMillan/Miss B. Stove	V. Gerulaitis/Mrs L. W. King	6–2	3–6	6–3
1978	F. D. McMillan/Miss B. Stove	R. O. Ruffels/Mrs L. W. King	6–3	7–6	
1979	R. A. J. Hewitt/Miss G. Stevens	F. D. McMillan/Miss B. Stove	6–3	7–5	
1980	M. C. Riessen/Miss W. M. Turnbull	F. D. McMillan/Miss B. Stove	7–5	6–2	
1981	K. Curren/Miss A. E. Smith	S. Denton/Miss J. Russell	6–4	7–6	
1982	K. Curren/Miss A. E. Smith	F. Taygan/Miss B. Potter	6–7	7–6	7–6
1983	J. Fitzgerald/Miss E. Sayers	F. Taygan/Miss B. Potter	3–6	6–3	6–4
1984	Tom Gullikson/Miss M. Maleeva	J. Fitzgerald/Miss E. Sayers	2–6	7–5	6–4
1985	H. Gunthardt/Miss M. Navratilova	J. Fitzgerald/Mrs E. Smylie	6–3	6–4	
1986	S. Casal/Miss R. Reggi	P. Fleming/Miss M. Navratilova	6–4	6–4	
1987	E. Sanchez/Miss M. Navratilova	P. Annacone/Miss B. Nagelsen	6–4	6–7	7–6
1988	J. Pugh/Miss J. Novotna	P. McEnroe/Mrs E. Smylie	7–6	6–3	
1989	S. Cannon/Miss R. White	R. Leach/Miss M. McGrath	3–6	6–2	7–5
1990	T. Woodbridge/Mrs E. Smylie	J. Pugh/Miss N. Zvereva	6–4	6–2	

ITALIAN CHAMPIONSHIPS

Staged in Milan 1930 to 1934. Moved to the Foro Italico in Rome in 1935. Not held 1936 to 1949 because of the Abyssinia War and World War II. In 1961 the tournament was staged in Turin. Men's and women's events were held at different dates in 1979. In 1980–1985 the women's events moved to Perugia.

MEN'S SINGLES

	CHAMPION	RUNNER-UP	SCORE				
1930	W. T. Tilden	H. L. de Morpurgo	6–1	6–1	6–2		
1931	G. P. Hughes	H. Cochet	6–4	6–3	6–2		
1932	A. Merlin	G. P. Hughes	6–1	5–7	6–0	8–6	
1933	E. Sertorio	A. Martin Legeay	6–3	6–1	6–3		
1934	G. Palmieri	G. de Stefani	6–3	6–0	7–5		
1935	W. Hines	G. Palmieri	6–3	10–8	9–7		
1936–49	*Not held*						
1950	J. Drobny	W. F. Talbert	6–4	6–3	7–9	6–2	
1951	J. Drobny	G. Cucelli	6–3	10–8	6–1		
1952	F. A. Sedgman	J. Drobny	7–5	6–3	1–6	6–4	
1953	J. Drobny	L. A. Hoad	6–2	6–1	6–2		
1954	J. E. Patty	E. Morea	11–9	6–4	6–4		
1955	F. Gardini	G. Merlo	6–1	1–6	3–6	5–6	ret'd
1956	L. A. Hoad	S. Davidson	7–5	6–2	6–0		
1957	N. Pietrangeli	G. Merlo	8–6	6–2	6–4		
1958	M. G. Rose	N. Pietrangeli	5–7	8–6	6–4	1–6	6–2
1959	L. Ayala	N. A. Fraser	6–3	1–6	6–3	6–3	
1960	B. MacKay	L. Ayala	7–5	7–5	0–6	0–6	6–1
1961	N. Pietrangeli	R. G. Laver	6–8	6–1	6–1	6–2	
1962	R. G. Laver	R. S. Emerson	6–1	1–6	3–6	6–3	6–1
1963	M. F. Mulligan	B. Jovanovic	6–2	4–6	6–3	8–6	
1964	J. E. Lundquist	F. S. Stolle	1–6	7–5	6–3	6–1	
1965	M. F. Mulligan	M. Santana	1–6	6–4	6–3	6–1	
1966	A. D. Roche	N. Pietrangeli	11–9	6–1	6–2		
1967	M. F. Mulligan	A. D. Roche	6–3	0–6	6–4	6–1	
1968	T. S. Okker	R. A. J. Hewitt	10–8	6–8	6–1	1–6	6–0
1969	J. D. Newcombe	A. D. Roche	6–3	4–6	6–3	5–7	6–3
1970	I. Nastase	J. Kodes	6–3	1–6	6–3	8–6	
1971	R. G. Laver	J. Kodes	7–5	6–3	6–3		
1972	M. Orantes	J. Kodes	4–6	6–1	7–5	6–2	
1973	I. Nastase	M. Orantes	6–1	6–1	6–1		
1974	B. Borg	I. Nastase	6–3	6–4	6–2		
1975	R. Ramirez	M. Orantes	7–6	7–5	7–5		
1976	A. Panatta	G. Vilas	2–6	7–6	6–2	7–6	
1977	V. Gerulaitis	A. Zugarelli	6–2	7–6	3–6	7–6	
1978	B. Borg	A. Panatta	1–6	6–3	6–1	4–6	6–3
1979	V. Gerulaitis	E. Dibbs	6–7	7–6	6–7	6–4	6–2
1980	G. Vilas	Y. Noah	6–0	6–4	6–4		
1981	J. L. Clerc	V. Pecci	6–3	6–4	6–0		
1982	A. Gomez	E. Teltscher	6–2	6–3	6–2		
1983	J. Arias	J. Higueras	6–2	6–2	6–1	6–4	
1984	A. Gomez	A. Krickstein	2–6	6–1	6–2	6–2	
1985	Y. Noah	M. Mecir	6–3	3–6	6–2	7–6	
1986	I. Lendl	E. Sanchez	7–5	4–6	6–1	6–1	
1987	M. Wilander	M. Jaite	6–3	6–4	6–4		
1988	I. Lendl	G. Perez Roldan	2–6	6–4	6–2	4–6	6–4
1989	A. Mancini	A. Agassi	6–3	4–6	2–6	7–6	6–1
1990	T. Muster	A. Chesnokov	6–1	6–3	6–1		

WOMEN'S SINGLES

	CHAMPION	RUNNER-UP	SCORE		
1930	Miss E. de Alvarez	Miss L. Valerio	3–6	8–6	6–0
1931	Mrs L. Valerio	Mrs D. Andrus	2–6	6–2	6–2
1932	Miss I. Adamoff	Miss L. Valerio	6–4	7–5	

1933	Miss E. Ryan	Miss I. Adamoff	6–1	6–1	
1934	Miss H. Jacobs	Miss L. Valerio	6–3	6–0	
1935	Miss H. Sperling	Miss L. Valerio	6–4	6–1	
1936–49	*Not held*				
1950	Mrs A. Bossi	Miss P. J. Curry	6–4	6–4	
1951	Miss D. J. Hart	Miss S. J. Fry	6–3	8–6	
1952	Miss S. Partridge	Miss M. P. Harrison	6–3	7–5	
1953	Miss D. J. Hart	Miss M. Connolly	4–6	9–7	6–3
1954	Miss M. Connolly	Miss P. E. Ward	6–3	6–0	
1955	Miss P. E. Ward	Miss E. Vollmer	6–4	6–3	
1956	Miss A. Gibson	Mrs S. Kormoczy	6–3	7–5	
1957	Miss S. J. Bloomer	Mrs D. P. Knode	1–6	9–7	6–2
1958	Miss M. E. Bueno	Miss L. Coghlan	3–6	6–3	6–3
1959	Miss C. C. Truman	Miss S. Reynolds	6–0	6–1	
1960	Mrs S. Kormoczy	Miss A. S. Haydon	6–4	4–6	6–1
1961	Miss M. E. Bueno	Miss L. R. Turner	6–4	6–4	
1962	Miss M. Smith	Miss M. E. Bueno	8–6	5–7	6–4
1963	Miss M. Smith	Miss L. R. Turner	6–3	6–4	
1964	Miss M. Smith	Miss L. R. Turner	6–1	6–1	
1965	Miss M. E. Bueno	Miss N. Richey	6–1	1–6	6–3
1966	Mrs P. F. Jones	Miss A. Van Zyl	8–6	6–1	
1967	Miss L. R. Turner	Miss M. E. Bueno	6–3	6–3	
1968	Mrs W. W. Bowrey	Mrs B. M. Court	2–6	6–2	6–3
1969	Miss J. M. Heldman	Miss K. Melville	7–5	6–4	
1970	Mrs L. W. King	Miss J. M. Heldman	6–1	6–3	
1971	Miss S. V. Wade	Mrs H. Masthoff	6–4	6–4	
1972	Miss L. Tuero	Mrs O. Morozova	6–4	6–3	
1973	Miss E. F. Goolagong	Miss C. M. Evert	7–6	6–0	
1974	Miss C. M. Evert	Miss M. Navratilova	6–3	6–3	
1975	Miss C. M. Evert	Miss M. Navratilova	6–1	6–0	
1976	Miss M. Jausovec	Miss L. Hunt	6–1	6–3	
1977	Miss J. Newberry	Miss R. Tomanova	6–3	7–6	
1978	Miss R. Marsikova	Miss V. Ruzici	7–5	7–5	
1979	Miss T. A. Austin	Miss S. Hanika	6–4	1–6	6–3
1980	Mrs J. M. Lloyd	Miss V. Ruzici	5–7	6–2	6–2
1981	Mrs J. M. Lloyd	Miss V. Ruzici	6–1	6–2	
1982	Mrs J. M. Lloyd	Miss H. Mandlikova	6–0	6–3	
1983	Miss A. Temesvari	Miss B. Gadusek	6–1	6–0	
1984	Miss M. Maleeva	Mrs J. M. Lloyd	6–3	6–3	
1985	Miss R. Reggi	Miss V. Nelson	6–4	6–4	
1986	*Not held*				
1987	Miss S. Graf	Miss G. Sabatini	7–5	4–6	6–0
1988	Miss G. Sabatini	Miss H. Kelesi	6–1	6–7	6–1
1989	Miss G. Sabatini	Miss A. Sanchez	6–2	5–7	6–4
1990	Miss M. Seles	Miss M. Navratilova	6–1	6–1	

MEN'S DOUBLES

	CHAMPIONS	RUNNERS-UP	SCORE				
1930	W. F. Coen/W. T. Tilden	H. L. de Morpurgo/P. Gaslini	6–0	6–3	6–3		
1931	A. del Bono/G. P. Hughes	H. Cochet/A. Merlin	3–6	8–6	4–6	6–4	6–3
1932	G. P. Hughes/G. de Stafani	J. Bonte/A. Merlin	6–2	6–2	6–4		
1933	J. Lesuer/A. M. Legeay	G. Palmieri/E. Sertorio	6–2	6–4	6–2		
1934	G. Palmieri/G. L. Rogers	G. P. Hughes/G. de Stefani	3–6	6–4	9–7	0–6	6–2
1935	J. H. Crawford/V. B. McGrath	J. Borotra/J. Brugnon	4–6	4–6	6–4	6–2	6–2
1936–49	*Not held*						
1950	W. F. Talbert/M. A. Trabert	J. E. Patty/O. W. Sidwell	6–3	6–1	4–6 ret'd		
1951	J. Drobny/R. Savitt	G. Cucelli/M. Del Bello	6–2	7–9	6–1	6–3	
1952	J. Drobny/F. A. Sedgman	G. Cucelli/M. Del Bello	3–6	7–5	3–6	6–3	6–2
1953	L. A. Hoad/K. R. Rosewall	J. Drobny/J. E. Patty	6–2	6–4	6–2		
1954	J. Drobny/E. Morea	M. A. Trabert/E. V. Seixas	6–4	0–6	3–6	6–3	6–4
1955	A. Larsen/E. Morca	N. Pietrangeli/O. Sirola	6–1	6–4	4–6	7–5	
1956	J. Drobny/L. A. Hoad	N. Pietrangeli/O. Sirola	11–9	6–2	6–3		
1957	N. A. Fraser/L. A. Hoad	N. Pietrangeli/O. Sirola	6–1	6–8	6–0	6–2	
1958	A. Jancso/K. Nielsen	L. Ayala/D. Candy	8–10	6–3	6–2	1–6	9–7
1959	R. S. Emerson/N. A. Fraser	N. Pietrangeli/O. Sirola	8–6	6–4	6–4		
1960	N. Pietrangeli/O. Sirola	R. S. Emerson/N. A. Fraser	3–6	7–5	2–6	11–11 ret'd	
1961	R. S. Emerson/N. A. Fraser	N. Pietrangeli/O. Sirola	6–2	6–4	11–9		
1962	N. A. Fraser/R. G. Laver	K. N. Fletcher/J. D. Newcombe	11–9	6–2	6–4		
1963	R. A. J. Hewitt/F. S. Stolle	N. Pietrangeli/O. Sirola	6–3	6–3	6–1		

1964	R. A. J. Hewitt/F. S. Stolle	A. D. Roche/J. D. Newcombe	7–5	6–3	3–6	7–5	
1965	A. D. Roche/J. D. Newcombe	C. Barnes/T. Koch	1–6	6–4	2–6	12–10 ret'd	
1966	R. S. Emerson/F. S. Stolle	N. Pietrangeli/E. C. Drysdale	6–4	12–10	6–3		
1967	R. A. J. Hewitt/F. D. McMillan	W. W. Bowrey/O. K. Davidson	6–3	2–6	6–3	9–7	
1968	T. S. Okker/M. C. Riessen	A. Stone/N. Kalogeropoulos	6–3	6–4	6–2		
1969	A. D. Roche/J. D. Newcombe	T. S. Okker/M. C. Riessen	6–4	1–6	ret'd		
1970	I. Nastase/I. Tiriac	W. W. Bowrey/O. K. Davidson	0–6	10–8	6–3	6–8	6–1
1971	A. D. Roche/J. D. Newcombe	A. Gimeno/R. Taylor	6–4	6–4			
1972	I. Nastase/I. Tiriac	L. A. Hoad/F. D. McMillan	3–6	3–6	6–4	6–3	5–3 ret'd
1973	J. D. Newcombe/T. S. Okker	R. Case/G. Masters	6–3	6–2	6–4		
1974	B. E. Gottfried/R. Ramirez	J. Gisbert/I. Nastase	6–3	6–2	6–3		
1975	B. E. Gottfried/R. Ramirez	J. S. Connors/I. Nastase	6–4	7–6	2–6	6–1	
1976	B. E. Gottfried/R. Ramirez	G. Masters/J. D. Newcombe	7–6	5–7	6–3	3–6	6–3
1977	B. E. Gottfried/R. Ramirez	F. McNair/S. E. Stewart	7–6	6–7	7–5		
1978	V. Pecci/B. Prajoux	J. Kodes/T. Smid	6–7	7–6	6–1		
1979	P. Fleming/T. Smid	J. L. Clerc/I. Nastase	4–6	6–1	7–5		
1980	M. R. Edmondson/K. Warwick	B. Taroczy/E. Teltscher	7–6	7–6			
1981	H. Gildemeister/A. Gomez	B. Manson/T. Smid	7–5	6–2			
1982	H. Gunthardt/B. Taroczy	W. Fibak/J. Fitzgerald	6–4	4–6	6–3		
1983	F. Gonzalez/V. Pecci	J. Gunnarsson/M. Leach	6–2	6–7	6–4		
1984	K. Flach/R. Seguso	J. G. Alexander/M. Leach	3–6	6–3	6–4		
1985	A. Jarryd/M. Wilander	K. Flach/R. Seguso	4–6	6–3	6–2		
1986	G. Forget/Y. Noah	M. R. Edmondson/S. E. Stewart	7–6	6–2			
1987	G. Forget/Y. Noah	M. Mecir/T. Smid	6–2	6–7	6–3		
1988	J. Lozano/T. Witsken	A. Jarryd/T. Smid	6–3	6–3			
1989	J. Courier/P. Sampras	D. Marcelino/M. Menezes	6–4	6–3			
1990	S. Casal/E. Sanchez	J. Courier/M. Davis	7–6	7–5			

WOMEN'S DOUBLES

	CHAMPIONS	RUNNERS-UP	SCORE		
1930	E. de Alvarez/L. Valerio	C. Anet/M. Neufeld	7–5	5–7	7–5
1931	A. Luzzatti/J. Prouse	Mrs D. Andrus Burke/L. Valerio	6–3	1–6	6–3
1932	C. Rosambert/L. Payot	Mrs D. Andrus Burke/L. Valerio	7–5	6–3	
1933	I. Adamoff/Mrs D. Andrus Burke	E. Ryan/L. Valerio	6–3	1–6	6–4
1934	H. H. Jacobs/E. Ryan	I. Adamoff/Mrs D. Andrus Burke	7–5	9–7	
1935	E. M. Dearman/N. Lyle	C. Aussem/E. Ryan	6–2	6–4	
1936–49	*Not held*				
1950	J. Quertier/J. Walker-Smith	B. E. Hilton/K. L. A. Tuckey	1–6	6–3	6–2
1951	S. J. Fry/D. J. Hart	L. Brough/T. D. Long	6–1	7–5	
1952	N. Hopman/ Mrs T. D. Long	N. Migliori/V. Tonoli	6–2	6–8	6–1
1953	M. Connolly/J. Sampson	S. J. Fry/D. J. Hart	6–8	6–4	6–4
1954	P. E. Ward/E. M. Watson	N. Adamson/G. Bucaille	3–6	6–3	6–4
1955	C. Mercellis/P. E. Ward	M. Muller/B. Penrose	6–4	10–8	
1956	M. Hawton/ Mrs T. D. Long	A. Buxton/D. R. Hard	6–4	6–8	9–7
1957	M. Hawton/ Mrs T. D. Long	Y. Ramirez/R. M. Reyes	6–1	6–1	
1958	S. J. Bloomer/C. Truman	M. Hawton/ Mrs T. D. Long	6–3	6–2	
1959	Y. Ramirez/R. M. Reyes	M. E. Bueno/J. Hopps	4–6	6–4	6–4
1960	M. Hellyer/Y. Ramirez	S. J. Brasher/A. Haydon	6–4	6–4	
1961	J. Lehane/L. R. Turner	M. Reitano/M. Smith	2–6	6–1	6–1
1962	M. E. Bueno/D. R. Hard	S. Lazzarino/L. Pericoli	6–4	6–4	
1963	R. Ebbern/M. Smith	S. Lazzarino/L. Pericoli	6–2	6–3	
1964	L. R. Turner/M. Smith	S. Lazzarino/L. Pericoli	6–1	6–2	
1965	M. Schacht/A. Van Zyl	S. Lazzarino/L. Pericoli	2–6	6–2	12–10
1966	N. Baylon/A. Van Zyl	Mrs P. F. Jones/E. Starkie	6–3	1–6	6–2
1967	R. Casals/L. R. Turner	S. Lazzarino/L. Pericoli	7–5	7–5	
1968	Mrs B. M. Court/S. V. Wade	A. Van Zyl/P. Walkden	6–2	7–5	
1969	F. Durr/ Mrs P. F. Jones	R. Casals/ Mrs L. W. King	6–3	3–6	6–2
1970	R. Casals/L. W. King	F. Durr/S. V. Wade	6–2	3–6	9–7
1971	Mrs H. Masthoff/S. V. Wade	Mrs L. Bowrey/H. Gourlay	5–7	6–2	6–2
1972	L. Hunt/ Mrs O. Morozova	Mrs G. Chanfreau/R. Vido	6–3	6–4	
1973	Mrs O. Morozova/S. V. Wade	M. Navratilova/R. Tomanova	3–6	6–2	7–5
1974	C. M. Evert/ Mrs O. Morozova	H. Masthoff/H. Orth	w.o.		
1975	C. M. Evert/M. Navratilova	S. Barker/G. Coles	6–1	6–2	
1976	L. Boshoff/I. Kloss	M. Simionescu/V. Ruzici	6–1	6–2	
1977	B. Cuypers/M. Kruger	B. Bruning/S. A. Walsh	3–6	7–5	6–2
1978	M. Jausovec/V. Ruzici	F. Mihai/B. Nagelsen	6–2	2–6	7–5
1979	B. Stove/W. M. Turnbull	Mrs E. Crawley/G. E. Reid	6–3	6–4	
1980	H. Mandlikova/R. Tomanova	I. Madruga/I. Villagran	6–4	6–4	

1981	C. Reynolds/P. Smith	Mrs J. M. Lloyd/V. Ruzici	7–5 6–1	
1982	K. Horvath/Y. Vermk	Mrs L. W. King/I. Kloss	2–6 6–4	7–6
1983	V. Ruzici/S. V. Wade	I. Madruga Osses/C. Tanvier	6–3 2–6	6–1
1984	I. Budarova/M. Skuherska	K. Horvath/V. Ruzici	7–6 1–6	6–4
1985	A. M. Cecchini/R. Reggi	P. Murgo/B. Romano	1–6 6–4	6–3
1986	*Not held*			
1987	M. Navratilova/G. Sabatini	C. Kohde-Kilsch/H. Sukova	6–4 6–1	
1988	J. Novotna/C. Suire	J. Byrne/J. Thompson	6–3 4–6	7–5
1989	E. Smylie/J. Thompson	M. Bollegraf/M. Paz	6–4 6–3	
1990	H. Kelesi/M. Seles	L. Garrone/L. Golarsa	6–3 6–4	

MIXED DOUBLES

	CHAMPIONS	RUNNERS-UP	SCORE		
1930	H. L. de Morpurgo/Miss E. de Alvarez	G. P. Hughes/Miss L. Valerio	4–6	6–4	6–2
1931	G. P. Hughes/Miss L. Valerio	A. del Bono/Mrs D. Andrus Burke	6–0	6–1	
1932	J. Bonte/Miss L. Payot	A. del Bono/Mrs D. Andrus Burke	6–1	6–2	
1933	A. M. Legeay/Mrs D. Andrus Burke	E. Gabrowitz/Miss Y. Orlandini	6–4	6–3	
1934	H. M. Culley/Miss E. Ryan	F. Puncec/Miss R. Couquerque	6–1	6–3	
1935	H. C. Hopman/Miss J. Jedrzejowska	G. P. Hughes/Miss E. M. Dearman	6–3	1–6	6–3
1936–49	*Not held*				
1950	A. K. Quist/Miss G. Moran	div'd with G. Cucelli/Miss A. Bossi	6–3	1–1	unf.
1951	F. Ampon/Miss S. J. Fry	L. Bergelin/Miss D. J. Hart	8–6	3–6	6–4
1952	K. Nielsen/Miss A. McGuire	E. Migone/Mrs M. J. de Riba	4–6	6–3	6–3
1953	E. V. Seixas/Miss D. J. Hart	M. G. Rose/Miss M. Connolly	6–4	6–4	
1954	E. V. Seixas/Miss M. Connolly	div'd with M. A. Trabert/Miss B. M. Kimbrell	3–6	11–9	3–3 unf.
1955	E. Morea/Miss P. E. Ward	div'd with M. G. Rose/Miss B. Penrose			
1956	L. Ayala/Mrs T. D. Long	G. Fachini/Miss S. J. Bloomer	6–4	6–3	
1957	L. Ayala/Mrs T. D. Long	R. N. Howe/Miss S. J. Bloomer	6–1	6–1	
1958	G. Fachini/Miss S. J. Bloomer	L. Ayala/Mrs T. D. Long	4–6	6–2	9–7
1959	F. Contreras/Miss R. M. Reyes	W. A. Knight/Miss Y. Ramirez	9–7	6–1	
1960	*Not held*				
1961	R. S. Emerson/Miss M. Smith	R. A. J. Hewitt/Miss J. Lehane	6–1	6–1	
1962	F. S. Stolle/Miss L. R. Turner	S. Davidson/Miss M. Schacht	6–4	6–1	
1963	*Not held*				
1964	J. D. Newcombe/Miss M. Smith	T. Koch/Miss M. E. Bueno	3–6	7–5	6–2
1965	J. E. Mandarino/Miss M. Coronado	V. Zarazua/Miss E. Subirats	6–1	6–1	
1966	*Not held*				
1967	W. W. Bowrey/Miss L. R. Turner	F. D. Mcmillan/Miss F. Durr	6–2	7–5	
1968	M. C. Riessen/Mrs B. M. Court	T. S. Okker/Miss S. V. Wade	8–6	6–3	
	Event ceased				

THE *DAVIS CUP*

The International Men's Team Championship of the World was initiated in 1900 when the British Isles, then comprising Great Britain and Ireland, challenged the United States for the trophy presented by Dwight F. Davis. The competition was enlarged in 1904 when Belgium and France took part. Each tie has comprised two players engaged in reverse singles plus a doubles match with the best of five sets throughout. In 1989 the tie-break was introduced for all sets except the fifth, in all matches.

From 1900 to 1971 the Champion Nation stood out until challenged by the winner of a knock-out competition between the challenging nations and had the choice of venue. The format was changed in 1972 with all nations taking part in a knock-out event. The format was amended in 1981, when the competition became sponsored by NEC. The Champion Nation was the winner of the World Group of 16 nations. Other nations competed in four zonal groups, two European, an American and an Eastern Zone, with the four winners earning promotion to the World Group. The four bottom nations of the top group, as decided by a relegation round, fell back to the zonal competition.

Between 1900 and 1990 the total number of participating nations was 93, including Hawaii and Estonia which have ceased to exist as distinct tennis nations. South Africa withdrew from the competition in 1979 and have not played since.

CHALLENGE ROUNDS (In playing order)

1900 USA d. British Isles 3–0, Boston: M. D. Whitman d. A. W. Gore 6–1 6–3 6–2; D. F. Davis d. E. D. Black 4–6 6–2 6–4 6–4; Davis/H. Ward d. Black/H. Roper Barrett 6–4 6–4 6–4; Davis div'd with Gore 9–7 9–9.
1901 *Not held*

1902 *USA d. British Isles 3–2, Brooklyn, New York:* W. A. Larned lost to R. F. Doherty 6–2 6–3 3–6 4–6 4–6; M. D. Whitman d. J. Pim 6–1 6–1 1–6 6–0; Larned d. Pim 6–3 6–2 6–3; Whitman d. R. F. Doherty 6–1 7–5 6–4; D. F. Davis/H. Ward lost to R. F./H. L. Doherty 6–3 8–10 3–6 4–6.

1903 *British Isles d. USA 4–1, Boston:* H. L. Doherty d. R. D. Wrenn 6–0 6–3 6–4; R. F. Doherty lost to W. A. Larned ret'd; R. F./H. L. Doherty d. R. D./G. L. Wrenn 7–5 9–7 2–6 6–3; H. L. Doherty d. Larned 6–3 6–8 6–0 2–6 7–5; R. F. Doherty d. R. D. Wrenn 6–4 3–6 6–3 6–8 6–4.

1904 *British Isles d. Belgium 5–0, Wimbledon:* H. L. Doherty d. P. de Borman 6–4 6–1 6–1; F. L. Riseley d. W. Lemaire 6–1 6–4 6–2; R. F./H. L. Doherty d. de Borman/Lemaire 6–0 6–1 6–3; H. L. Doherty w.o. Lemaire; Riseley d. de Borman 4–6 6–2 8–6 7–5.

1905 *British Isles d. USA 5–0, Wimbledon:* H. L. Doherty d. H. Ward 7–9 4–6 6–1 6–2 6–0; S. H. Smith d. W. A. Larned 6–4 6–4 5–7 6–4; R. F./H. L. Doherty d. Ward/B. Wright 8–10 6–2 6–2 4–6 8–6; Smith d. W. J. Clothier 4–6 6–1 6–4 6–3; H. L. Doherty d. Larned 6–4 2–6 6–8 6–4 6–2.

1906 *British Isles d. USA 5–0, Wimbledon:* H. L. Doherty d. R. D. Little 6–4 6–4 6–1; H. L. Doherty d. H. Ward 6–2 8–6 6–3; R. F./H. L. Doherty d. Little/Ward 3–6 11–9 9–7 6–1; Smith d. Ward 6–1 6–0 6–4; H. L. Doherty d. Little 3–6 6–3 6–8 6–1 6–3.

1907 *Australasia d. British Isles 3–2, Wimbledon:* N. E. Brookes d. A. W. Gore 7–5 6–1 7–5; A. F. Wilding d. H. Roper Barrett 1–6 6–4 6–3 7–5; Brookes/Wilding lost to Gore/Roper Barrett 6–3 6–4 5–7 2–6 11–13; Wilding lost to Gore 6–3 3–6 5–7 2–6; Brookes d. Roper Barrett 6–2 6–0 6–3.

1908 *Australasia d. USA 3–2, Melbourne:* N. E. Brookes d. F. B. Alexander 5–7 9–7 6–2 4–6 6–3; A. F. Wilding lost to B. Wright 6–3 5–7 3–6 1–6; Brookes/Wilding d. Alexander/Wright 6–4 6–2 5–7 1–6 6–4; Brookes lost to Wright 6–0 6–3 5–7 2–6 10–12; Wilding d. Alexander 6–3 6–4 6–1.

1909 *Australasia d. USA 5–0, Sydney:* N. E. Brookes d. M. E. McLoughlin 6–2 6–2 6–4; A. F. Wilding d. M. H. Long 6–2 7–5 6–1; Brookes/Wilding d. Long/McLoughlin 12–10 9–7 6–3; Brookes d. Long 6–4 7–5 8–6; Wilding d. McLoughlin 3–6 8–6 6–2 6–3.

1910 *Not held*

1911 *Australasia d. USA 5–0, Christchurch, NZ:* N. E. Brookes d. B. Wright 6–4 2–6 6–3 6–3; R. W. Heath d. W. A. Larned 2–6 6–1 7–5 6–2; Brookes/A. W. Dunlop d. Wright/M. E. McLoughlin 6–4 5–7 7–5 6–4; Brookes d. McLoughlin 6–4 3–6 4–6 6–3 6–4; Heath w.o. Wright.

1912 *British Isles d. Australasia 3–2, Melbourne:* J. C. Parke d. N. E. Brookes 8–6 6–3 5–7 6–2; C. P. Dixon d. R. W. Heath 5–7 6–4 6–4 6–4; A. E. Beamish/Parke lost Brookes/A. W. Dunlop 4–6 1–6 5–7; Dixon lost to Brookes 2–6 4–6 4–6; Parke d. Heath 6–2 6–4 6–4.

1913 *USA d. British Isles 3–2, Wimbledon:* M. E. McLoughlin lost to J. C. Parke 10–8 5–7 4–6 6–1 5–7; R. N. Williams d. C. P. Dixon 8–6 3–6 6–2 1–6 7–5; H. Hackett/McLoughlin d. Dixon/H. Roper Barrett 5–7 6–1 2–6 7–5 6–4; McLoughlin d. Dixon 8–6 6–3 6–2; Williams lost to Parke 2–6 7–5 7–5 4–6 2–6.

1914 *Australasia d. USA 3–2, Forest Hills, NY:* A. F. Wilding d. R. N. Williams 7–5 6–2 6–3; N. E. Brookes lost to M. E. McLoughlin 15–17 3–6 3–6; Brookes/Wilding d. T. C. Bundy/McLoughlin 6–3 8–6 9–7; Brookes d. Williams 6–1 6–2 8–10 6–3; Wilding lost to McLoughlin 2–6 3–6 2–6.

1915–18 *Not held*

1919 *Australasia d. British Isles 4–1, Sydney:* G. L. Patterson d. A. H. Lowe 6–4 6–3 2–6 6–3; J. O. Anderson lost to A. R. F. Kingscote 5–7 2–6 4–6; N. E. Brookes/Patterson d. A. E. Beamish/Kingscote 6–0 6–0 6–2; Patterson d. Kingscote 6–4 6–4 8–6; Anderson d. Lowe 6–4 5–7 6–3 4–6 12–10.

1920 *USA d. Australasia 5–0, Auckland:* W. T. Tilden d. N. E. Brookes 10–8 6–4 1–6 6–4; W. M. Johnston d. G. L. Patterson 6–3 6–1 6–1; Johnston/Tilden d. Brookes/Patterson 4–6 6–4 6–0 6–4; Johnston d. Brookes 5–7 7–5 6–3 6–3; Tilden d. Patterson 5–7 6–2 6–3 6–3.

1921 *USA d. Japan 5–0, Forest Hills, NY:* W. M. Johnston d. I. Kumagae 6–2 6–4 6–2; W. T. Tilden d. Z. Schimidzu 5–7 4–6 7–5 6–2 6–1; W. Washburn/R. N. Williams d. Kumagae/Shimidzu 6–2 7–5 4–6 7–5; Tilden d. Kumagae; 9–7 6–4 6–1; Johnston d. Shimizu 6–3 5–7 6–2 6–4.

1922 *USA d. Australasia 4–1, Forest Hills, NY:* W. T. Tilden d. G. L. Patterson 7–5 10–8 6–0; W. M. Johnston d. J. O. Anderson 6–1 6–2 6–3; V. Richards/Tilden lost to P. O'Hara Wood/Patterson 4–6 0–6 3–6; Johnston d. Pattersonp 6–2 6–2 6–1; Tilden d. Anderson 6–4 5–7 3–6 6–4 6–2.

1923 *USA d. Australia 4–1, Forest Hills, NY:* W. M. Johnston lost to J. O. Anderson 6–4 2–6 6–2 5–7 2–6; W. T. Tilden d. J. B. Hawkes 6–4 6–2 6–1; Tilden/R. N. Williams d. Anderson/Hawkes 17–15 11–13 2–6 6–3 6–2; Johnston d. Hawkes 6–0 6–2 6–1; Tilden d. Anderson 6–2 6–3 1–6 7–5.

1924 *USA d. Australia 5–0, Philadelphia:* W. T. Tilden d. G. L. Patterson 6–4 6–2 6–3; V. Richards d. P. O'Hara Wood 6–3 6–2 6–4; W. M. Johnston/Tilden d. O'Hara Wood/Patterson 5–7 6–3 6–4 6–1; Tilden d. O'Hara Wood 6–2 6–1 6–1; Richards d. Patterson 6–3 7–5 6–4.

1925 *USA d. France 5–0, Philadelphia:* W. T. Tilden d. J. Borotra 4–6 6–0 2–6 9–7 6–4; W. M. Johnston d. R. Lacoste 6–1 6–1 6–8 6–3; V. Richards/R. N. Williams d. Borotra/Lacoste 6–4 6–4 6–3; Tilden d. Lacoste 3–6 10–12 8–6 7–5 6–2; Johnston d. Borotra 6–1 6–4 6–0.

1926 *USA d. France 4–1, Philadelphia:* W. M. Johnston d. R. Lacoste 6–0 6–4 0–6 6–0; W. T. Tilden d. J. Borotra 6–2 6–3 6–3; V. Richards/R. N. Williams d. J. Brugnon/H. Cochet 6–4 6–4 6–2; Johnston d. Borotra 8–6 6–4 9–7; Tilden lost to Lacoste 6–4 4–6 6–8 6–8.

1927 *France d. USA 3–2, Philadelphia:* R. Lacoste d. W. M. Johnston 6–3 6–2 6–2; H. Cochet lost to W. T. Tilden 4–6 6–2 2–6 6–8; J. Borotra/J. Brugnon lost to F. Hunter/Tilden 6–3 3–6 3–6 6–4 0–6; Lacoste d. Tilden 6–4 4–6 6–3 6–3; Cochet d. Johnston 6–4 4–6 6–2 6–4.

1928 *France d. USA 4–1, Paris:* R. Lacoste lost to W. T. Tilden 6–1 4–6 4–6 6–2 3–6; H. Cochet d. J. Hennessey 5–7 9–7 6–3 6–0; J. Borotra/Cochet d. F. Hunter/Tilden 6–4 6–8 7–5 4–6 6–2; Lacoste d. Hennessey 4–6 6–1 7–5 6–3; Cochet d. Tilden 9–7 8–6 6–4.

1929 *France d. USA 3–2, Paris:* H. Cochet d. W. T. Tilden 6–3 6–1 6–2; J. Borotra d. G. M. Lott 6–1 3–6 6–4 7–5; Borotra/Cochet lost to W. Allison/J. Van Ryn 1–6 6–8 4–6; Cochet d. Lott 6–1 3–6 6–0 6–3; Borotra lost to Tilden 6–4 1–6 4–6 5–7.

1930 *France d. USA 4–1, Paris:* J. Borotra lost to W. T. Tilden 6–2 5–7 4–6 5–7; H. Cochet d. G. M. Lott 6–4 6–2 6–2; J.

Brugnon/Cochet d. W. Allison/J. Van Ryn 6–3 7–5 1–6 6–2; Borotra d. Lott 5–7 6–3 2–6 6–2 8–6; Cochet d. Tilden 4–6 6–3 6–1 7–5.

1931 France d. Great Britain 3–2, Paris: H. Cochet d. H. W. Austin 3–6 11–9 6–2 6–4; J. Borotra lost to F. J. Perry 6–4 8–10 0–6 6–4 4–6; J. Brugnon/Cochet d. G. P Hughes/C. H. Kingsley 6–1 5–7 6–3 8–6; Cochet d. Perry 6–4 1–6 9–7 6–3; Borotra lost to Austin 5–7 3–6 6–3 5–7.

1932 France d. USA 3–2, Paris: H. Cochet d. W. Allison 5–7 7–5 3–6 7–5 6–2; J. Borotra d. H. E. Vines 6–4 6–2 2–6 6–4; J. Brugnon/Cochet lost to Allison/J. Van Ryn 3–6 13–11 5–7 6–4 4–6; Borotra d. Allison 1–6 3–6 6–4 6–2 7–5; Cochet lost to Vines 6–4 6–0 5–7 6–8 2–6.

1933 Great Britain d. France 3–2, Paris: H. W. Austin d. A. Merlin 6–3 6–4 6–0; F. J. Perry d. H. Cochet 8–10 6–4 8–6 3–6 6–1; G. P. Hughes/H. G. N. Lee lost to J. Borotra/J. Brugnon 3–6 6–8 2–6; Austin lost to Cochet 7–5 4–6 6–4 4–6 4–6; Perry d. Merlin 4–6 8–6 6–2 7–5.

1934 Great Britain d. USA 4–1, Wimbledon: F. J. Perry d. S. B. Wood 6–1 4–6 5–7 6–0 6–3; H. W. Austin d. F. X. Shields 6–4 6–4 6–1; G. P. Hughes/H. G. N. Lee lost to G. M. Lott/L. Stoefen 5–7 0–6 6–4 7–9; Perry d. Shields 6–4 4–6 6–2 15–13; Austin d. Wood 6–4 6–0 6–8 6–3.

1935 Great Britain d. USA 5–0, Wimbledon: F. J. Perry d. J. D. Budge 6–0 6–8 6–3 6–4; H. W. Austin d. W. Allison 6–2 2–6 4–6 6–3 7–5; G. P. Hughes/C. R. D. Tuckey d. Allison/J. Van Ryn 6–2 1–6 6–8 6–3 6–3; Perry d. Allison 4–6 6–4 7–5 6–3; Austin d. Budge 6–2 6–4 6–8 7–5.

1936 Great Britain d. Australia 3–2, Wimbledon: H. W. Austin d. J. H. Crawford 4–6 6–3 6–1 6–1; F. J. Perry d. A. K. Quist 6–1 4–6 7–5 6–2; G. P. Hughes/C. R. D. Tuckey lost to Crawford/Quist 4–6 6–2 5–7 8–10; Austin lost top Quist 4–6 6–3 5–7 2–6; Perry d. Crawford 6–2 6–3 6–3.

1937 USA d. Great Britain 4–1, Wimbledon: F. A. Parker lost to H. W. Austin 3–6 2–6 5–7; J. D. Budge d. C. E. Hare 15–13 6–1 6–2; Budge/G. Mako d. C. R. D. Tuckey/F. H. D. Wilde 6–3 7–5 7–9 12–10; Parker d. Hare 6–2 6–4 6–2; Budge d. Austin 8–6 3–6 6–4 6–3.

1938 USA d. Australia 3–2, Philadelphia: R. L. Riggs d. A. K. Quist 4–6 6–0 8–6 6–1; J. D. Budge d. J. E. Bromwich 6–2 6–3 4–6 7–5; Budge/G. Mako lost to Bromwich/Quist 6–0 3–6 4–6 2–6; Budge d. Quist 8–6 6–1 6–2; Riggs lost to Bromwich 4–6 6–4 0–6 2–6.

1939 Australia d. USA 3–2, Philadelphia: J. E. Bromwich lost to R. L. Riggs 4–6 0–6 5–7; A. K. Quist lost to F. A. Parker 3–6 6–2 4–6 6–1 5–7; Bromwich/Quist d. J. R. Hunt/J. Kramer 5–7 6–2 7–5 6–2; Quist d. Riggs 6–1 6–4 3–6 3–6 6–4; Bromwich d. Parker 6–0 6–3 6–1.

1940–45 *Not held*

1946 USA d. Australia 5–0, Melbourne: F. R. Schroeder d. J. E. Bromwich 3–6 6–1 6–2 0–6 6–3; J. Kramer d. D. Pails 8–6 6–2 9–7; Kramer/Schroeder d. Bromwich/A. K. Quist 6–2 7–5 6–4; Kramer d. Bromwich 8–6 6–4 6–2 6–4; G Mulloy d. Pails 6–3 6–3 6–4.

1947 USA d. Australia 4–1, Forest Hills, NY: J. Kramer d. D. Pails 6–2 6–1 6–2; F. R. Schroeder d. J. E. Bromwich 6–4 5–7 6–3 6–3; Kramer/Schroeder lost to Bromwich/C. F. Long 4–6 6–2 2–6 4–6; Schroeder d. Pails 6–3 8–6 4–6 9–11 10–8; Kramer d. Bromwich 6–3 6–2 6–2.

1948 USA d. Australia 5–0, Forest Hills, NY: F. A. Parker d. O. W. Sidwell 6–4 6–4 6–4; F. R. Schroeder d. A. K. Quist 6–3 4–6 6–0 6–0; G. Mulloy/W. F. Talbert d. C. F. Long/Sidwell 8–6 9–7 2–6 7–5; Parker d. Quist 6–2 6–2 6–3; Schroeder d. Sidwell 6–2 6–1 6–1.

1949 USA d. Australia 4–1, Forest Hills, NY: F. R. Schroeder d. O. W. Sidwell 6–1 5–7 4–6 6–2 6–3; R. A. Gonzales d. F. A. Sedgman 8–6 6–4 9–7; G. Mulloy/W. F. Talbert lost to J. E. Bromwich/Sidwell 6–3 6–4 8–10 7–9 7–9; Schroeder d. Sedgman 6–4 6–3 6–3; Gonzales d. Sidwell 6–1 6–3 6–3.

1950 Australia d. USA 4–1, Forest Hills, NY: F. A. Sedgman d. T. Brown 6–0 8–6 9–7; K. McGregor d. F. R. Schroeder 13–11 6–3 6–4; J. E. Bromwich/Sedgman d. G. Mulloy/Schroeder 4–6 6–4 6–2 4–6 6–4; Sedgman d. Schroeder 6–2 6–2 6–2; McGregor lost to Brown 11–9 6–4 6–1.

1951 Australia d. USA 3–2, Sydney: M. G. Rose lost to E. V. Seixas 3–6 4–6 7–9; F. A. Sedgman d. F. R. Schroeder 6–4 6–3 4–6 6–4; K. McGregor/Sedgman d. Schroeder/M. A. Trabert 6–2 9–7 6–3; Rose lost to Schroeder 4–6 11–13 5–7; Sedgman d. Seixas 6–4 6–2 6–2.

1952 Australia d. USA 4–1, Adelaide: F. A. Sedgman d. E. V. Seixas 6–3 6–4 6–3; K. McGregor d. M. A. Trabert 11–9 6–4 6–1; McGregor/Sedgman d. Seixas/Trabert 6–3 6–4 1–6 6–3; Sedgman d. Trabert 7–5 6–4 10–8; McGregor lost to Seixas 3–6 6–8 8–6 3–6.

1953 Australia d. USA 3–2, Melbourne: L. A. Hoad d. E. V. Seixas 6–4 6–2 6–3; K. R. Rosewall lost to M. A. Trabert 3–6 4–6 4–6; R. Hartwig/Hoad lost to Seixas/Trabert 2–6 4–6 4–6; Hoad d. Trabert 13–11 6–3 2–6 3–6 7–5; Rosewall d. Seixas 6–2 2–6 6–3 6–4.

1954 USA d. Australia 3–2, Sydney: M. A. Trabert d. L. A. Hoad 6–4 2–6 12–10 6–3; E. V. Seixas d. K. R. Rosewall 8–6 6–8 6–4 6–3; Seixas/Trabert d. Hoad/Rosewall 6–2 4–6 6–2 10–8; Trabert lost to Rosewall 7–9 5–7 3–6; Seixas lost to R. Hartwig 6–4 3–6 2–6 3–6.

1955 Australia d. USA 5–0, Forest Hills, NY: K. R. Rosewall d. E. V. Seixas 6–3 10–8 4–6 6–2; L. A. Hoad d. M. A. Trabert 4–6 6–3 6–3 8–6; R. Hartwig/Hoad d. Seixas/Trabert 12–14 6–4 6–3 3–6 7–5; Rosewall d. H. Richardson 6–4 3–6 6–1 6–4; Hoad d. Seixas 7–9 6–1 6–4 6–4.

1956 Australia d. USA 5–0, Adelaide: L. A. Hoad d. H. Flam 6–2 6–3 6–3; K. R. Rosewall d. E. V. Seixas 6–2 7–5 6–3; Hoad/Rosewall d. S. Giammalva/Seixas 1–6 6–1 7–5 6–4; Hoad d. Seixas 6–2 7–5 6–3; Rosewall d. Giammalva 4–6 6–1 8–6 7–5.

1957 Australia d. USA 3–2, Melbourne: A. J. Cooper d. E. V. Seixas 3–6 7–5 6–1 1–6 6–3; M. J. Anderson d. B. MacKay 6–3 7–5 3–6 47–9 6–3; Anderson/M. G. Rose d. MacKay/Seixas 6–4 6–4 8–6; Cooper lost to MacKay 4–6 6–1 6–4 4–6 3–6; Anderson lost to Seixas 3–6 4–6 6–0 11–13.

1958 USA d. Australia 3–2, Brisbane: A. Olmedo d. M. J. Anderson 8–6 2–6 9–7 8–6; B. MacKay lost to A. J. Cooper 6–4 3–6 2–6 4–6; Olmedo/H. Richardson d. Anderson/N. A. Fraser 10–12 3–6 16–14 6–3 7–5; Olmedo d. Cooper 6–3 4–6 6–4 8–6; MacKay lost to Anderson 5–7 11–13 9–11.

1959 Australia d. USA 3–2, Forest Hills, NY: N. A. Fraser d. A. Olmedo 8–6 6–8 6–4 8–6; R. G. Laver lost to B. MacKay 5–7 4–6 1–6; R. S. Emerson/Fraser d. E. Buchholz/Olmedo 7–5 7–5 6–4; Laver lost to Olmedo 7–9 6–4 8–10 10–12; Fraser d. MacKay 8–6 3–6 6–2 6–4.

1960 *Australia d. Italy 4–1, Sydney:* N. A. Fraser d. O. Sirola 4–6 6–3 6–3 6–3; R. G. Laver d. N. Pietrangeli 8–6 6–4 6–3; R. S. Emerson/Fraser d. Pietrangeli/Sirola 10–8 5–7 6–3 6–4; Laver d. Sirola 9–7 6–2 6–3; Fraser lost to Pietrangeli 9–11 3–6 6–1 2–6.

1961 *Australia d. Italy 5–0, Melbourne:* R. S. Emerson d. N. Pietrangeli 8–6 6–4 6–0; R. G. Laver d. O. Sirola 6–1 6–4 6–3; Emerson/N. A. Fraser d. Pietrangeli/Sirola 6–2 6–3 6–4; Emerson d. Sirola 6–2 6–3 4–6 6–2; Laver d. Pietrangeli 6–3 3–6 4–6 6–3 8–6.

1962 *Australia d. Mexico 5–0, Brisbane:* N. A. Fraser d. A. Palafox 7–9 6–3 6–4 11–9; R. G. Laver d. R. H. Osuna 6–2 6–1 7–5; R. S. Emerson/Laver d. Osuna/Palafox 7–5 6–2 6–4; Fraser d. Osuna 3–6 11–9 6–1 3–6 6–4; Laver d. Palafox 6–1 4–6 6–4 8–6.

1963 *USA d. Australia 3–2, Adelaide:* R. D. Ralston d. J. D. Newcombe 6–4 6–1 3–6 4–6 7–5; C. R. McKinley lost to R. S. Emerson 3–6 6–3 5–7 5–7; McKinley/Ralston d. Emerson/N. A. Fraser 6–3 4–6 11–9 11–9; Ralston lost to Emerson 2–6 3–6 6–3 2–6; McKinley d. Newcombe 6–2 6–4 6–4.

1964 *Australia d. USA 3–2, Cleveland, Ohio:* F. S. Stolle lost to C. R. McKinley 1–6 7–9 6–4 2–6; R. S. Emerson d. R. D. Ralston 6–3 6–1 6–3; Emerson/Stolle lost to McKinley/Ralston 4–6 6–4 6–4 3–6 4–6; Stolle d. Ralston 7–5 6–3 3–6 9–11 6–4; Emerson d. McKinley 3–6 6–2 6–4 6–4.

1965 *Australia d. Spain 4–1, Sydney:* F. S. Stolle d. M. Santana 10–12 3–6 6–1 6–4 7–5; R. S. Emerson d. J. Gisbert 6–3 6–2 6–2; J. D. Newcombe/A. D. Roche d. J. L. Arilla/Santana 6–3 4–6 7–5 6–2; Emerson lost to Santana 6–2 3–6 4–6 13–15; Stolle d. Gisbert 6–2 6–4 8–6.

1966 *Australia d. India 4–1, Melbourne:* F. S. Stolle d. R. Krishnan 6–3 6–2 6–4; R. S. Emerson d. J. Mukerjea 7–5 6–4 6–2; J. D. Newcombe/A. D. Roche lost to Krishnan/Mukerjea 6–4 5–7 4–6 4–6; Emerson d. Krishnan 6–0 6–2 10–8; Stolle d. Mukerjea 7–5 6–8 6–3 5–7 6–3.

1967 *Australia d. Spain 4–1, Brisbane:* R. S. Emerson d. M. Santana 6–4 6–1 6–1; J. D. Newcombe d. M. Orantes 6–3 6–3 6–2; Newcombe/A. D. Roche d. Orantes/Santana 6–4 6–4 6–4; Newcombe lost to Santana 5–7 4–6 2–6; Emerson d. Orantes 6–1 6–1 2–6 6–4.

1968 *USA d. Australia 4–1, Adelaide:* C. Graebner d. W. W. Bowrey 8–10 6–4 8–6 3–6 6–1; A. R. Ashe d. R. O. Ruffels 6–8 7–5 6–3 6–3; R. C. Lutz/S. R. Smith d. J. G. Alexander/Ruffels 6–4 6–4 6–2; Graebner d. Ruffels 3–6 8–6 2–6 6–3 6–1; Ashe lost to Bowrey 6–2 3–6 9–11 6–8.

1969 *USA d. Rumania 5–0, Cleveland, Ohio:* A. R. Ashe d. I. Nastase 6–2 15–13 7–5; S. R. Smith d. I. Tiriac 6–8 6–3 5–7 6–4 6–4; R. C. Lutz/Smith d. Nastase/Tiriac 8–6 6–1 11–9; Smith d. Nastase 4–6 4–6 6–4 6–4 11–9; Ashe d. Tiriac 6–3 8–6 3–6 4–0 ret'd.

1970 *USA d. West Germany 5–0, Cleveland, Ohio:* A. R. Ashe d. W. Bungert 6–2 10–8 6–2; C. Richey d. C. Kuhnke 6–3 6–4 6–2; R. C. Lutz/S. R. Smith d. Bungert/Kuhnke 6–3 7–5 6–4; Richey d. Bungert 6–4 6–4 7–5; Ashe d. Kuhnke 6–8 10–12 9–7 13–11 6–4.

1971 *USA d. Rumania 3–2, Charlotte, NC:* S. R. Smith d. I. Nastase 7–5 6–3 6–1; F. A. Froehling d. I. Tiriac 3–6 1–6 6–1 6–3 8–6; Smith/E. Van Dillen lost to Nastase/Tiriac 5–7 4–6 8–6; Smith d. Tiriac 8–6 6–3 6–0; Froehling lost to Nastase 3–6 1–6 6–1 4–6.

Challenge Round abolished

FINAL ROUND SCORES

1972 *USA d. Rumania 3–2, Bucharest:* S. R. Smith d. I. Nastase 11–9 6–2 6–3; T. Gorman lost to I. Tiriac 6–4 6–2 4–6 3–6 2–6; Smith/E. Van Dillen d. Nastase/Tiriac 6–2 6–0 6–3; Smith d. Tiriac 4–6 6–2 6–4 2–6 6–0; Gorman lost to Nastase 1–6 2–6 7–5 8–10.

1973 *Australia d. USA 5–0, Cleveland, Ohio (indoors):* J. D. Newcombe d. S. R. Smith 6–1 3–6 6–3 3–6 6–4; R. G. Laver d. T. Gorman 8–10 8–6 6–8 6–3 6–1; Laver/Newcombe d. Smith/E. Van Dillen 6–1 6–2 6–4; Newcombe d. Gorman 6–2 6–1 6–3; Laver d. Smith 6–3 6–4 3–6 6–2.

1974 *South Africa w.o. India*

1975 *Sweden d. Czechoslovakia 3–2, Stockholm (indoors):* O. Bengtson lost to J. Kodes 4–6 6–2 5–7 4–6; B. Borg d. J. Hrebec 6–1 6–3 6–0; Bengtson/Borg d. Kodes/V. Zednik 6–4 6–4 6–4; Borg d. Kodes 6–4 6–2 6–2; Bengtson lost to Hrebec 6–1 3–6 1–6 4–6.

1976 *Italy d. Chile 4–1, Santiago:* C. Barazzutti d. J. Fillol 7–5 4–6 7–5 6–1; A. Panatta d. P. Cornejo 6–3 6–1 6–3; P. Bertolucci/Panatta d. Cornejo/Fillol 3–6 6–2 9–7 6–3; Panatta d. Fillol 8–6 6–4 3–6 10–8; A. Zugarelli lost to B. Prajoux 4–6 4–6 2–6.

1977 *Australia d. Italy 3–1, Sydney:* A. D. Roche d. A. Panatta 6–3 6–4 6–4; J. G. Alexander d. C. Barazzutti 6–2 8–6 4–6 6–2; Alexander/P. Dent lost to P. Bertolucci/Panatta 4–6 4–6 5–7; Alexander d. Panatta 6–4 4–6 2–6 8–6 11–9; Roche div'd with Barazzutti 12–12.

1978 *USA d. Great Britain 4–1, Palm Springs, California:* J. P. McEnroe d. J. M. Lloyd 6–1 6–2 6–2; B. E. Gottfried lost to C. J. Mottram 6–4 6–2 8–10 4–6 3–6; R. C. Lutz/S. R. Smith d. M. Cox/D. A. Lloyd 6–2 6–2 6–3; McEnroe d. Mottram 6–2 6–2 6–1; Gottfried d. J. M. Lloyd 6–1 6–2 6–4.

1979 *USA d. Italy 5–0, San Francisco (indoors):* V. Gerulaitis d. C. Barazzutti 6–3 3–2 ret'd; J. P. McEnroe d. A. Panatta 6–2 6–3 6–4; R. C. Lutz/S. R. Smith d. P. Bertolucci/Panatta 6–4 12–10 6–2; McEnroe d. A. Zugarelli 6–4 6–3 6–1; Gerulaitis d. Panatta 6–1 6–3 6–3.

1980 *Czechoslovakia d. Italy 4–1, Prague (indoors):* T. Smid d. A. Panatta 3–6 3–6 6–3 6–4 6–4; I. Lendl d. C. Barazzutti 4–6 6–1 6–1 6–2; Lendl/Smid d. P. Bertolucci/Panatta 3–6 6–3 3–6 6–3 6–4; Smid lost to Barazzutti 6–3 3–6 2–6; Lendl d. G. Ocleppo 6–3 6–3.

1981 *USA d. Argentina 3–1, Cincinnati (indoors):* J. P. McEnroe d. G. Vilas 6–3 6–2 6–2; R. Tanner lost to J. L. Clerc 5–7 3–6 6–8; P. Fleming/McEnroe d. Clerc/Vilas 6–3 4–6 6–4 4–6 11–9; McEnroe d. Clerc 7–5 5–7 6–3 3–6 6–3; Tanner div'd with Vilas 11–10.

1982 *USA d. France 4–1, Grenoble (indoors):* J. P. McEnroe d. Y. Noah 12–10 1–6 3–6 6–2 6–3; G. Mayer d. H. Leconte 6–2 6–2 7–9 6–4; P. Fleming/McEnroe d. Leconte/Noah 6–3 6–4 9–7; Mayer lost to Noah 1–6 0–6; McEnroe d. Leconte 6–2 6–3.

1983 *Australia d. Sweden 3–2, Melbourne:* P. Cash lost to M. Wilander 3–6 6–4 7–9 3–6; J. Fitzgerald d. J. Nystrom 6–4 6–2 4–6 6–4; M. R. Edmondson/P. McNamee d. A. Jarryd/H. Simonsson 4–6 6–4 6–2; Cash d. Nystrom 6–4 6–1 6–1; Fitzgerald lost to Wilander 8–6 0–6 1–6.

1984 Sweden d. USA 4–1, Gothenburg: M. Wilander d. J. S. Connors 6–1 6–3 6–3; H. Sundstrom d. J. P. McEnroe 13–11 6–4 6–3; S. Edberg/A. Jarryd d. P. Fleming/McEnroe 7–5 5–7 6–2 7–5; Wilander lost to McEnroe 3–6 7–6 3–6; Sundstrom d. J. Arias 3–6 8–6 6–3.

1985 Sweden d. West Germany 3–2, Munich: M. Wilander d. M. Westphal 6–3 6–4 10–8; S. Edberg lost to B. Becker 3–6 6–3 5–7 6–8; Wilander/J. Nystrom d. Becker/A. Maurer 6–4 6–2 6–1; Wilander lost to Becker 3–6 6–2 3–6 3–6; Edberg d. Westphal 3–6 7–5 6–4 6–3.

1986 Australia d. Sweden 3–2, Melbourne: P. Cash d. S. Edberg 13–11 13–11 6–4; P. McNamee lost to M. Pernfors 3–6 1–6 3–6; Cash/J. Fitzgerald d. Edberg/A. Jarryd 6–3 6–4 4–6 6–1; Cash d. Pernfors 2–6 4–6 6–3 6–4 6–3; McNamee lost to Edberg 8–10 4–6.

1987 Sweden d. India 5–0, Gothenburg: M. Wilander d. R. Krishnan 6–4 6–1 6–3; A. Jarryd d. V. Amritraj 6–3 6–3 6–1; Wilander/J. Nystrom d. An./V. Amritraj 6–3 3–6 6–1 6–2; Jarryd d. Krishnan 6–4 6–3; Wilander d. V. Amritraj 6–2 6–0.

1988 West Germany d. Sweden 4–1, Gothenburg: C.-U. Steeb d. M. Wilander 8–10 1–6 6–2 6–4 8–6; B. Becker d. S. Edberg 6–3 6–1 6–4; Becker/E. Jelen d. Edberg/A. Jarryd 3–6 2–6 7–5 6–3 6–2; Steeb lost to Edberg 4–6 6–8; P. Kuhnen w.o. K. Carlsson.

1989 West Germany d. Sweden 3–2, Stuttgart: C.-U. Steeb lost to M. Wilander 7–5 6–7 7–6 2–6 3–6; B. Becker d. S. Edberg 6–2 6–2 6–4; Becker/E. Jelen d. A. Jarryd/J. Gunnarsson 7–6 6–4 3–6 6–7 6–4; Becker d. Wilander 6–2 6–0 6–2; Steeb lost to Edberg 2–6 4–6.

1990 USA d. Australia 3–2, St Petersburg: A. Agassi d. R. Fromberg 4–6 6–4 4–6 6–2 6–4; M. Chang d. D. Cahill 6–2 7–6 6–0; R. Leach/J. Pugh d. P. Cash/J. Fitzgerald 6–4 6–2 3–6 7–6; Agassi lost to Cahill 4–6 6–4 ret.; Chang lost to Fromberg 5–7 6–2 3–6.

QUALIFIERS FOR WORLD GROUP

| 1990 | Belgium | Canada | France | Israel |
| | Mexico | Spain | Sweden | Yugoslavia |

FEDERATION CUP

International Women's Team Championship, staged on a knock-out basis at one venue with each tie comprising two singles and one doubles match.

FINAL ROUNDS

1963 USA d. Australia 2–1, Queen's Club, London, 18–21 June: D. R. Hard lost to M. Smith 3–6 0–6; B. J. Moffitt Yd. L. R. Turner 5–7 6–0 6–3; Hard/Moffitt d. Smith/Turner 3–6 13–11 6–3.

1964 Australia d. USA 2–1, Germantown Cricket Club, Philadelphia, 2–5 September: M. Smith d. B. J. Moffitt 6–2 6–3; L. R. Turner d. N. Richey 7–5 6–1; Smith/Turner lost to Moffitt/Mrs J. R. Susman 6–4 5–7 1–6.

1965 Australia d. USA 2–1, Kooyong Stadium, Melbourne, 12–18 January: L. R. Turner d. Mrs C. Graebner 6–3 2–6 6–3; M. Smith d. B. J. Moffitt 6–4 8–6; Smith/J. M. Tegart lost to Graebner/Moffitt 5–7 6–4 4–6.

1966 USA d. West Germany 3–0, Turin, 11–15 May: J. M. Heldman d. H. Niessen 4–6 7–5 6–1; Mrs L. W. King d. E. Buding 6–3 3–6 6–1; Mrs C. Graebner/Mrs King d. Buding/H. Schultse 6–4 6–2.

1967 USA d. Great Britain 2–0, Rot-Weiss Club, Berlin, 7–11 June: R. Casals d. S. V. Wade 9–7 8–6; Mrs L. W. King d. Mrs P. F. Jones 6–3 6–4; Casals/Mrs King div'd with Mrs Jones/Wade 6–8 9–7.

1968 Australia d. Netherlands 3–0, Stade Roland Garros, Paris, 23–26 May: K. A. Melville d. M. Jansen 4–6 7–5 6–3; Mrs B. M. Court d. A. Suurbeck 6–1 6–3; Court/Melville d. Suurbeck/L. Venneboer 6–3 6–8 7–5.

1969 Australia d. USA 2–1, Athens, 19–25 May: N. Richey d. K. A. Melville 6–4 6–3; J. M. Heldman lost to Mrs B. M. Court 1–6 6–8; J. Bartkowicz/Richey d. Court/J. M. Tegart 6–4 6–4.

1970 Australia d. West Germany 3–0, Freiburg, Germany, 19–24 May: K. M. Krantzcke d. Mrs H. Hoesl 6–2 6–3; Mrs D. E. Dalton d. H. Niessen 4–6 6–3 6–3; Dalton/Krantzcke d. Hoesl/Niessen 6–2 7–5.

1971 Australia d. Great Britain 3–0, Perth, Australia, 26–29 December 1970: Mrs B. M. Court d. Mrs P. F. Jones 6–8 6–3 6–2; E. F. Goolagong d. S. V. Wade 6–4 6–1; Court/L. Hunt d. W. M. Shaw/Wade 6–4 6–4.

1972 South Africa d. Great Britain 2–1, Ellis Park, Johannesburg, 19–26 March: Mrs Q. C. Pretorius lost to S. V. Wade 3–6 2–6; B. Kirk d. W. M. Shaw 4–6 7–5 6–0; Kirk/Pretorius d. Wade/Mrs G. M. Williams 6–1 7–5.

1973 Australia d. South Africa 3–0, Bad Homburg, Germany, 30 April–6 May: E. F. Goolagong d. Mrs Q. C. Pretorius 6–0 6–2; P. Coleman d. B. Kirk 10–8 6–0; Goolagong/J. Young d. Kirk/Pretorius 6–1 6–2.

1974 Australia d. USA 2–1, Naples, 13–19 May: E. F. Goolagong d. J. M. Heldman 6–1 7–5; D. L. Fromholtz lost to C. M. Evert 6–2 5–7 3–6; Goolagong/J. Young d. Heldman/S. A. Walsh 7–5 8–6.

1975 Czechoslovakia d. Australia 3–0, Aix-en-Provence, 6–11 May: M. Navratilova* d. E. F. Goolagong 6–3 6–4; R. Tomanova d. H Gourlay 6–4 6–2; Navratilova/Tomanova d. D. L. Fromholtz/Gourlay 6–3 6–1.

1976 USA d. Australia 2–1, Spectrum Stadium, Philadelphia, 22–29 August: R. Casals lost to Mrs G. Reid 6–1 3–6 5–7; Mrs L. W. King d. Mrs E. Cawley 7–6 6–4; Casals/King d. Cawley/Reid 7–5 6–3.

1977 USA d. Australia 2–1, Devonshire Park, Eastbourne, 13–18 June: Mrs L. W. King d. D. L. Fromholtz 6–1 2–6 6–2; C. M. Evert d. Mrs G. Reid 7–5 6–3; Casals/Evert lost to Reid/W. M. Turnbull 3–6 3–6.

1978 USA d. Australia 2–1, Kooyong Stadium, Melbourne, 27 November–3 December: T. A. Austin lost to Mrs G. Reid 3–6 3–6; C. M. Evert d. W. M. Turnbull 3–6 6–1 6–1; Evert/Mrs L. W. King d. Reid/Turnbull 4–6 6–1 6–4.

1979 USA d. Australia 3–0, Madrid, 30 April–6 May: T. A. Austin d. Mrs G. Reid 6–3 6–0; Mrs J. M. Lloyd d. D. L. Fromholtz 2–6 6–3 8–6; R. Casals/Mrs L. W. King d. Reid/W. M. Turnbull 3–6 6–3 8–6.

1980 USA d. Australia 3–0, Rot-Weiss Club, Berlin, 19–25 May: Mrs J. M. Lloyd d. D. L. Fromholtz 4–6 6–1 6–1; T. A. Austin d. W. M. Turnbull 6–2 6–3; R. Casals/K. Jordan d. Fromholtz/S. Leo 2–6 6–4 6–4.

1981 USA d. Great Britain 3–0, Tokyo, 9–15 November: A. Jaeger d. S. V. Wade 6–3 6–1; Mrs J. M. Lloyd d. S. Barker 6–2 6–1; R. Casals/K. Jordan d. J. M. Durie/Wade 6–4 7–5.

1982 *USA d. West Germany 3–0, Santa Clara, California, 19–25 July:* Mrs J. M. Lloyd d. C. Kohde 2–6 6–1 6–3; M. Navratilova d. B. Bunge 6–4 6–4; Lloyd/Navratilova d. Bunge/Kohde 3–6 6–1 6–2.

1983 *Czechoslovakia d. West Germany 2–1, Zurich, 18–24 July:* H. Sukova d. C. Kohde 6–4 2–6 6–2; H. Mandlikova d. B. Bunge 6–2 3–0 ret'd; I. Budarova/M. Skuherska lost to E. Pfaff/Kohde 6–3 2–6 1–6.

1984 *Czechoslovakia d. Australia 2–1, Sao Paulo, 15–22 July:* H. Sukova lost to A. Minter 5–7 5–7; H. Mandlikova d. E. Sayers 6–1 6–0; Mandlikova/Sukova d. W. Turnbull/Sayers 6–2 6–2.

1985 *Czechoslovakia d. USA 2–1, Nagoya, 7–13 October:* H. Sukova d. E. Burgin 6–3 6–7 6–4; H. Mandlikova d. K. Jordan 7–5 6–1; A. Holikova/R. Marsikova lost to Burgin/Jordan 2–6 3–6.

1986 *USA d. Czechoslovakia 3–0, Prague, 21–27 July:* Mrs J. M. Lloyd d. H. Sukova 7–5 7–6; M. Navratilova d. H. Mandlikova 7–5 6–1; Navratilova/P. H. Shriver d. Mandlikova/Sukova 6–4 6–2.

1987 *West Germany d. USA 2–1, Vancouver, 27 July–2 August:* C. Kohde-Kilsch lost to P. H. Shriver 0–6 6–7; S. Graf d. C. M. Evert 6–2 6–1; Kohde-Kilsch/Graf d. Evert/Shriver 1–6 7–5 6–4.

1988 *Czechoslovakia d. USSR 2–1, Melbourne, 7–11 December:* R. Zrubakova d. L. Savchenko 6–1 7–6; H. Sukova d. Zvereva 6–3 6–4; J. Novotna/J. Pospisilova lost to Savchenko/Zvereva 6–7 5–7.

1989 *USA d. Spain 3–0, Tokyo, 1–8 October:* C. Evert d. C. Martinez 6–3 6–2; M. Navratilova d. A. Sanchez 0–6 6–3 6–4; Z. Garrison/P. H. Shriver d. Martinez/Sanchez 7–5 6–1.

1990 *USA d. USSR 2-1, Atlanta, 22–29 July:* J. Capriati d. L. Meskhi 7–6 6–2; Z. Garrison lost to N. Zvereva 6–4 3–6 3–6; Z. Garrison/G. Fernandez d. N. Zvereva/L. Savchenko 6–4 6–3.

* M. Navratilova became a US citizen in 1981.

WIGHTMAN CUP

Women's team contest between USA and Great Britain, each match comprising five singles and two doubles, with reverse singles played between the two top players.

1923 *USA d. Great Britain 7–0, Forest Hills:* H. Wills d. K. McKane 6–2 7–5, d. Mrs R. Clayton 6–2 6–3; Mrs F. Mallory d. Clayton 6–1 8–6, d. McKane 6–2 6–3; E. Goss d. Mrs W. G. Beamish 6–2 0–6 7–5; Mrs G. W. Wightman/Goss d. McKane/Mrs B. C. Covell 10–8 5–7 6–4; Mallory/Wills d. Beamish/Clayton 3–6 2–6.

1924 *Great Britain d. USA 6–1, Wimbledon:* Mrs B. C. Covell d. H. Wills 6–2 6–4, d. Mrs F. Mallory 6–2 5–7 6–3; K. McKane d. Mallory 6–3 6–3, d. Wills 6–2 6–2; Mrs W. G. Beamish d. E. Goss 6–1 8–10 6–3; Covell/Mrs D. C. Shepherd-Barron d. Mrs M. Z. Jessup/Goss 6–2 6–2; McKane/E. Colyer lost to Mrs G. W. Wightman/Wills 6–2 2–6 4–6.

1925 *Great Britain d. USA 4–3, Forest Hills:* K. McKane d. Mrs F. Mallory 6–4 5–7 6–0, lost to H. Wills 1–6 6–1 7–9; J. Fry lost to Wills 0–6 5–7, lost to Mallory 3–6 0–6; Mrs R. Lambert Chambers d. Goss 7–5 3–6 6–1; Lambert Chambers/E. H. Harvey d. Mallory/Mrs T. C. Bundy 10–8 6–1; McKane/E. Colyer d. Wills/M. K. Browne 6–0 6–3.

1926 *USA d. Great Britain 4–3, Wimbledon:* E. Ryan d. J. Fry 6–1 6–3, lost to Mrs L. A. Godfree 1–6 7–5 4–6; M. K. Browne lost to Godfree 1–6 5–7, lost to Fry 6–3 0–6 4–6; Mrs M. Z. Jessup d. Mrs D. C. Shepherd-Barron 6–1 5–7 6–4; Jessup/E. Goss d. Mrs R. Lambert Chambers/Shepherd-Barron 6–4 6–2; Browne/Ryan d. Godfree/E. L. Colyer 3–6 6–2 6–4.

1927 *USA d. Great Britain 5–2, Forest Hills:* H. Wills d. J. Fry 6–2 6–0, d. Mrs L. A. Godfree 6–1 6–1; Mrs F. Mallory d. Godfree 6–4 6–2, d. J. Fry 6–2 11–9; H. H. Jacobs lost to B. Nuthall 3–6 6–2 1–6; E. Goss/Mrs A. H. Chapin lost to G. Sterry/Mrs J. Hill 7–5 5–7 5–7; Wills/Mrs G. W. Wightman d. Godfree/E. H. Harvey 6–4 6–3.

1928 *Great Britain d. USA 4–3, Wimbledon:* Mrs P. H. Watson lost to H. Wills 1–6 2–6, d. Mrs F. Mallory 2–6 6–1 6–2; E. Bennett d. Mallor 6–1 6–3, lost to Wills 3–6 2–6; B. Nuthall lost to H. H. Jacobs 3–6 1–6; E. H. Harvey/P. Saunders d. E. Goss/Jacobs 6–4 6–1; Bennett/Watson d. Wills/P. Anderson 6–2 6–1.

1929 *USA d. Great Britain 4–3, Forest Hills:* H. Wills d. Mrs P. H. Watson 6–1 6–4, d. B. Nuthall 8–6 8–6; H. H. Jacobs d. Nuthall 7–5 8–6, lost to Watson 3–6 2–6; E. Goss d. Mrs L. R. C. Michell 6–3 3–6 6–3; Wills/Goss lost to Watson/Michell 4–6 1–6; Mrs G. W. Wightman/Jacobs lost to Mrs B. C. Covell/Mrs D. C. Shepherd-Barron 2–6 1–6.

1930 *Great Britain d. USA 4–3, Wimbledon:* J. Fry lost to H. Wills 1–6 1–6, lost to H. H. Jacobs 0–6 3–6; Mrs P. H. Watson d. Jacobs 2–6 6–4, lost to Wills 5–7 1–6; P. Mudford d. S. Palfrey 6–0 6–2; Fry/E. H. Harvey d. Palfrey/E. Cross 2–6 6–2 6–4; Watson/Mrs L. A. Godfree d. Jacobs/Wills 7–5 1–6 6–4.

1931 *USA d. Great Britain 5–2, Forest Hills:* Mrs F. S. Moody d. P. Mudford 6–1 6–4, d. B. Nuthall 6–4 6–2; H. H. Jacobs d. Nuthall 8–6 6–4, d. Mudford 6–4 6–4; C. Babcock lost to B. Nuthall 6–4 6–2; Mrs L. A. Harper d. D. E. Round 6–3 4–6 9–7; S. Palfrey/Mrs G. W. Wightman lost to Mudford/Mrs D. C. Shepherd-Barron 4–6 8–10; Moody/Harper lost to Nuthall/Mrs Fearnley Whittingstall 6–8 7–5 3–6.

1932 *USA d. Great Britain 4–3, Wimbledon:* H. H. Jacobs d. D. E. Round 6–4 6–3, lost to Mrs Fearnley Whittingstall 4–6 6–2 1–6; Mrs F. S. Moody d. Fearnley Whittingstall 6–2 6–4, d. Round 6–2 6–3; Mrs L. A. Harper lost to Mrs M. R. King 6–3 1–6 1–6; Harper/Jacobs d. Mrs L. R. C. Michell/Round 6–4 6–1; Moody/Palfrey lost to Fearnley Whittingstall/B. Nuthall 3–6 6–1 8–10.

1933 *USA d. Great Britain 4–3, Forest Hills:* H. H. Jacobs d. D. E. Round 6–4 6–2, d. M. Scriven 5–7 6–2 7–5; S. Palfrey d. Scriven 6–3 6–1, lost to Round 4–6 8–10; C. Babcock lost to B. Nuthall 6–1 1–6 3–6; Jacobs/Palfrey d. Round/M. Heeley 6–4 6–2; A. Marble/Mrs J. Van Ryn lost to Nuthall/F. James 5–7 2–6.

1934 *USA d. Great Britain 5–2, Wimbledon:* S. Palfrey d. D. E. Round 6–3 3–6 8–6, d. M. Scriven 4–6 6–2 8–6; H. H. poJacobs d. Scriven 6–1 6–1, d. Round 6–4 6–4; C. Babcock lost to B. Nuthall 7–5 3–6 4–6; Babcock/J. Cruickshank lost to N. Lyle/E. M. Dearman 5–7 5–7; Jacobs/Palfrey d. Mrs L. A. Godfree/Nuthall 5–7 6–3 6–2.

1935 *USA d. Great Britain 4–3, Forest Hills:* H. H. Jacobs lost to K. Stammers 7–5 1–6 7–9, d. D. E. Round 6–3 6–2; Mrs E. B. Arnold lost to Round 0–6 3–6, d. Stammers 6–2 1–6 6–3; S. Palfrey d. Mrs M. R. King 6–0 6–3; Jacobs/Palfrey d. Stammers/F. James 6–3 6–2; Mrs D. B. Andrus/C. Babcock lost to N. Lyle/E. M. Dearman 6–3 A4–6 1–6.

1936 *USA d. Great Britain 4–3, Wimbledon:* H. H. Jacobs lost to K. Stammers 10–12 1–6, lost to D. E. Round 3–6 3–6;

S. Palfrey lost to Round 3–6 4–6, d. Stammers 6–3 6–4; C. Babcock d. M. Hardwick 6–4 4–6 6–2; Babcock/Mrs J. Van Ryn d. N. Lyle/E. M. Dearman 6–2 1–6 6–3; Jacobs/Palfrey d. Stammers/F. James 1–6 6–3 7–5.

1937 *USA d. Great Britain 6–1, Forest Hills:* A. Marble d. M. Hardwick 4–6 6–2 6–4, d. K. Stammers 6–3 6–1; H. H. Jacobs d. Stammers 6–1 4–6 6–4, d. Hardwick 2–6 6–4 6–2; S. Palfrey d. M. Lumb 6–3 6–1; Marble/Palfrey d. E.M. Dearman/J. Ingram 6–3 6–2; Mrs J. Van Ryn/D. M. Bundy lost to Stammers/F. James 3–6 8–10.

1938 *USA d. Great Britain 5–2, Wimbledon:* A. Marble lost to K. Stammers 6–3 5–7 3–6, d. M. Scriven 6–3 3–6 6–0; Mrs F. S. Moody d. Scriven 6–0 7–5, d. Stammers 6–2 3–6 6–3; S. Fabyan d. M. Lumb 5–7 6–2 6–3; Marble/Fabyan d. Lumb/F. James 6–4 6–2; Moody/D. Bundy lost to E. M. Dearman/J. Ingram 2–6 5–7.

1939 *USA d. Great Britain 5–2, Forest Hills:* A. Marble d. M. Hardwick 6–3 6–4, d. K. Stammers 3–6 6–3 6–4; H. H. Jacobs lost to Stammers 2–6 6–1 3–6, d. Hardwick 6–2 6–2; S. Fabyan lost to V. Scott 3–6 4–6; M. Arnold/D. M. Bundy d. B. Nuthall/N. Brown 6–3 6–1; Marble/Fabyan d. Stammers/Mrs S. H. Hammersley 7–5 6–2.

1940–45 *Not held.*

1946 *USA d. Great Britain 7–0, Wimbledon:* P. M. Betz d. Mrs J. Bostock 6–2 6–4, d. Mrs M. Menzies 6–4 6–4; M. Osborne d. Bostock 6–1 6–4, d. Menzies 6–3 6–2; L. Brough d. J. Curry 8–6 6–3; Brough/Osborne d. Bostock/Mrs M. Halford 6–2 6–1; Betz/D. Hart d. Mrs B. Passingham/M. Lincoln 6–1 6–3.

1947 *USA d. Great Britain 7–0, Forest Hills:* M. Osborne d. Mrs J. Bostock 6–4 2–6 6–2, d. Mrs M. Menzies 7–5 6–2; L. Brough d. Menzies 6–4 6–2, d. Bostock 6–4 6–4; D. Hart d. Mrs B. Hilton 4–6 6–3 7–5; Hart/Mrs P. C. Todd d. J. Gannon/J. Quertier 6–1 6–2; Brough/Osborne d. Bostock/Hilton 6–1 6–4.

1948 *USA d. Great Britain 6–1, Wimbledon:* Mrs W. du Pont d. Mrs J. Bostock 6–4 8–6, d. Mrs B. Hilton 6–3 6–4; L. Brough d. Hilton 6–1 6–1, d. Bostock 6–2 4–6 7–5; D. Hart d. J. Gannon 6–1 6–4; Brough/du Pont d. Mrs M. Menzies/Hilton 6–2 6–2; Hart/Mrs C. Todd lost to Bostock/Mrs N. W. Blair 3–6 4–6.

1949 *USA d. Great Britain, Merion Cricket Club, Philadelphia:* D. Hart d. Mrs J. Walker-Smith 6–3 6–1, d. Mrs B. Hilton 6–1 6–3; Mrs W. du Pont d. Hilton 6–1 6–3, d. Walker-Smith 6–4 6–2; B. Baker d. J. Quertier 6–4 7–5; Hart/S. Fry d. Quertier/Mrs N. W. Blair 6–1 6–2; G. Moran/Mrs P. C. Todd d. Hilton/K. Tuckey 6–4 8–6.

1950 *USA d. Great Britain 7–0, Wimbledon:* Mrs W. du Pont d. Mrs B. Hilton 6–3 6–4, d. Mrs J. Walker-Smith 6–3 6–2; L. Brough d. Hilton 2–6 6–2 7–5, d. Walker-Smith 6–0 6–0; D. Hart d. J. Curry 6–2 6–4; Hart/Mrs P. C. Todd d. Walker-Smith/J. Quertier 6–2 6–3; Brough/du Pont d. Hilton/K. Tuckey 6–2 6–0.

1951 *USA d. Great Britain 6–1, Longwood Cricket Club, Boston:* D. Hart d. J. Quertier 6–4 6–4, d. Mrs J. Walker-Smith 6–4 2–6 7–5; S. Fry d. Walker-Smith 6–1 6–4; lost to Quertier 3–6 6–8; M. Connolly d. K. Tuckey 6–1 6–3; Mrs P. C. Todd/N. Chaffee d. Mrs J. Mottram/P. Ward 7–5 6–3; S. Fry/D. Hart d. Quertier/Tuckey 6–3 6–3.

1952 *USA d. Great Britain 7–0, Wimbledon:* D. Hart d. Mrs J. Rinkel-Quertier 6–3 6–3, d. Mrs J. Walker-Smith–5 6–2; M. Connolly d. Walker-Smith 3–6 6–1 7–5, d. Rinkel-Quertier 9–7 6–2; S. Fry d. S. Partridge 6–0 8–6; Fry/Hart d. H. Fletcher/Rinkel-Quertier 8–6 6–4; L. Brough/Connolly d. Mrs J. Mottram/P. Ward 6–0 6–3.

1953 *USA d. Great Britain 7–0, Westchester Club, Rye, NY:* M. Connolly d. A. Mortimer 6–1 6–1, d. H. Fletcher 6–1 6–1; Hart d. Fletcher 6–4 7–5, d. Mortimer 6–1 6–1; S. Fry d. Rinkel-Quertier 6–2 6–4; L. Brough/Connolly d. Mortimer/A. Shilcock 6–2 6–3; Fry/Hart d. Fletcher/Rinkel-Quertier 6–2 6–1.

1954 *USA d. Great-Britain 6–0, Wimbledon:* M. Connolly d. H. Fletcher 6–1 6–3, d. A. Shilcock 6–2 6–2; Hart d. Shilcock 6–4 6–1, d. Fletcher 6–1 6–8 6–2; L. Brough d. A. Buxton 8–6 6–2; L. Brough/Mrs W. du Pont d. Buxton/P. Hird 2–6 6–4 7–5; S. Fry/Hart v. Fletcher/Shilcock not played.

1955 *USA d. Great Britain 6–1, Westchester Club, Rye, NY:* D. Hart lost to A. Mortimer 4–6 6–1 5–7, d. S. J. Bloomer 7–5 6–3; L. Brough d. Bloomer 6–2 6–4, d. Mortimer 6–0 6–2; Mrs D. Knode d. A. Buxton 6–3 6–3; Brough/Mrs W. du Pont d. Bloomer/P. Ward 6–3 6–3; S. Fry/Hart d. Buxton/Mortimer 3–6 6–2 7–5.

1956 *USA d. Great Britain 5–2, Wimbledon:* L. Brough d. A. Mortimer 3–6 6–4 7–5, d. A. Buxton 3–6 6–3 6–4; S. Fry d. Buxton 6–2 6–8 7–5, lost to Mortimer 4–6 3–6; Mrs D. Knode lost to S. J. Bloomer 4–6 4–6; B. Baker/Knode d. Bloomer/P. Ward 6–1 6–4; Brough/Fry d. Buxton/Mortimer 6–2 6–2.

1957 *USA d. Great Britain 6–1, Sewickley, Pennsylvania:* A. Gibson d. S. J. Bloomer 6–4 4–6 6–2, d. C. Truman 6–4 6–2; Mrs D. Knode d. Truman 6–2 11–9, d. Bloomer 5–7 6–1 6–2; D. R. Hard lost to A. Haydon 3–6 6–3 4–6; A. Gibson/Hard d. Bloomer/S. M. Armstrong 6–3 6–4; L. Brough/W. du Pont d. Haydon/A. Shilcock 6–4 6–1.

1958 *Great Britain d. USA 4–3, Wimbledon:* S. J. Bloomer lost to A. Gibson 3–6 4–6, lost to Mrs D. Knode 4–6 2–6; C. Truman d. Knode 6–4 6–4, d. Gibson 2–6 6–3 6–4; A. Haydon d. M. Arnold 6–3 5–7 6–3; Bloomer/Truman d. K. Fageros/Knode 6–2 6–3; A. Shilcock/P. Ward lost to Gibson/J. Jopps 4–6 6–3 3–6.

1959 *USA d. Great Britain 4–3, Sewickley, Pennsylvania:* Mrs B. Fleits d. A. Mortimer 6–2 6–1, d. C. Truman 6–4 6–4; D. R. Hard lost to Truman 6–4 6–2 3–6, d. Mortimer 6–3 6–8 6–4; S. Moore lost to A. Haydon 1–6 1–6; J. Arth/Hard d. S. J. Bloomer/Truman 9–7 9–7; J. Hopps/Moore lost to Haydon/Mortimer 2–6 4–6.

1960 *Great Britain d. USA 4–3, Wimbledon:* A. Haydon d. K. Hantze 2–6 11–9 6–1, lost to D. R. Hard 7–5 2–6 1–6; C. Truman lost to Hard 6–4 3–6 4–6, d. Hantze 7–5 6–3; A. Mortimer d. J. Hopps 6–8 6–4 6–1; Haydon/Mortimer lost to Hard/Hantze 0–6 0–6; S. J. Bloomer/Truman d. Hopps/Mrs D. Knode 6–4 9–7.

1961 *USA d. Great Britain 6–1, Saddle & Cycle Club, Chicago:* K. Hantze d. C. Truman 7–9 6–1 6–1, d. A. Haydon 6–1 6–4; B. J. Moffitt d. Haydon 6–4 6–4, lost to Truman 3–6 2–6; J. Bricka d. A. Mortimer 10–8 4–6 6–3; Al Hantze/Moffitt d. Truman/D. M. Catt 7–5 6–2; Mrs W. du Pont/M. Varner w.o. Mortimer/Haydon.

1962 *USA d. Great Britain 4–3, Wimbledon:* D. R. Hard d. C. Truman 6–2 6–2, d. A. Haydon 6–3 6–8 6–4; Mrs J. R. Susman lost to Haydon 8–10 5–7, d. Truman 6–4 7–5; N. Richey lost to D. M. Catt 1–6 5–7; Mrs W. du Pont/M. Varner d. Catt/E. Starkie 6–2 3–6 6–2; Hard/B. J. Moffitt lost to Haydon/Truman 4–6 3–6.

1963 *USA d. Great Britain 6–1, Cleveland Skating Club, Cleveland:* D. R. Hard lost to Mrs P. F. Jones 1–6 6–0 6–8, d. C. Truman 6–3 6–0; B. J. Moffitt d. Truman 6–4 19–17, d. Jones 6–4 4–6 6–3; N. Richey d. D. M. Catt 14–12 6–3; Hard/Moffitt d. Truman/Jones 4–6 7–5 6–2; Richey/Mrs D. Fales d. Catt/E. Starkie 6–4 6–8 6–2.

1964 *USA d. Great Britain 5–2, Wimbledon:* N. Richey d. D. M. Catt 4–6 6–4 7–5, d. Mrs P. F. Jones 7–5 11–9; B. J. Moffitt d. Jones 4–6 6–2 6–3, d. Catt 6–3 4–6 6–3; C. Caldwell d. E. Starkie 6–4 1–6 6–3; Caldwell/Moffitt lost to Catt/Jones 2–6 6–4 0–6; Richey/Mrs D. Fales lost to A. Mortimer/Starkie 6–2 3–6 4–6.

1965 *USA d. Great Britain 5–2, Clarke Stadium, Cleveland:* B. J. Moffitt lost to Mrs P. F. Jones 2–6 4–6, d. E. Starkie 6–3 6–2; N. Richey d. Starkie 6–1 6–0, lost to Jones 4–6 6–8; Mrs C. Graebner d. S. V. Wade 3–6 10–8 6–4; Graebner/Richey d. F. E. Truman/Starkie 6–1 6–0; Moffitt/Mrs J. R. Susman d. Jones/Wade 6–3 8–6.

1966 ***USA d. Great Britain 4–3, Wimbledon:*** N. Richey lost to Mrs P. F. Jones 6–2 4–6 3–6, d. S. V. Wade 2–6 6–2 7–5; Mrs L. W. King d. Wade 6–3 6–3, d. Jones 5–7 6–2 6–3; M. A. Eisel lost to W. Shaw 2–6 3–6; King/J. Albert lost to Jones/Wade 5–7 2–6; Richey/Eisel d. R. Bentley/E. Starkie 6–1 6–2.

1967 ***USA d. Great Britain 6–1, Clarke Stadium, Cleveland:*** Mrs L. W. King d. S. V. Wade 6–3 6–2, d. Mrs P. F. Jones 6–1 6–2; N. Richey d. Jones 6–2 6–2, d. Wade 3–6 8–6 6–2; R. Casals lost to C. Truman 6–3 5–7 1–6; Casals/King d. Jones/Wade 10–8 6–4; M. A. Eisel/Mrs C. Graebner d. W. Shaw/Mrs J. Williams 8–6 12–10.

1968 ***Great Britain d. USA 4–3, Wimbledon:*** Mrs C. Janes lost to N. Richey 1–6 6–8, lost to M. A. Eisel 4–6 3–6; S. V. Wade d. Eisel 6–0 6–1, d. Richey 6–4 2–6 6–3; W. Shaw lost to J. Bartkowicz 5–7 6–3 4–6; Shaw/Wade d. Eisel/Richey 5–7 6–4 6–3; Janes/F. E. Truman d. S. De Fina/K. Harter 6–3 2–6 6–3.

1969 ***USA d. Great Britain 5–2, Clarke Stadium, Cleveland:*** J. M. Heldman d. S. V. Wade 3–6 6–1 8–6, d. W. Shaw 6–3 6–4; N. Richey d. Shaw 8–6 6–2, lost to Wade 3–6 6–2 4–6; J. Bartkowicz d. Mrs C. Janes 8–6 6–0; Mrs P. Curtis/V. Ziengenfuss lost to Janes/F. E. Truman 1–6 6–3 4–6; Heldman/Bartkowicz d. Shaw/Wade 6–4 6–2.

1970 ***USA d. Great Britain 4–3, Wimbledon:*** Mrs L. W. King d. S. V. Wade 8–6 6–4, d. Mrs P. F. Jones 6–4 6–2; N. Richey lost to Jones 3–6 3–6, lost to Wade 3–6 2–6; J. M. Heldman d. Mrs G. Williams 6–3 6–2; Mrs P. Curtis/Heldman lost to Jones/Williams 3–6 2–6; King/J. Bartkowicz d. W. Shaw/Wade 7–5 6–8 6–2.

1971 ***USA d. Great Britain 4–3, Clarke Stadium, Cleveland:*** C. Evert d. W. Shaw 6–0 6–4, d. S. V. Wade 6–1 6–1; J. M. Heldman lost to Wade 5–7 5–7; V. Ziengenfuss d. Shaw 6–4 4–6 6–3; K. Pigeon lost to Mrs G. Williams 5–7 6–3 4–6; Mrs P. Curtis/Ziengenfuss d. Mrs C. Janes/F. E. Truman 6–1 6–4; Mrs C. Graebner/Evert lost to Wade/Williams 8–10 6–4 1–6.

1972 ***USA d. Great Britain 5–2, Wimbledon:*** W. Overton lost to Mrs G. Williams 3–6 6–3 3–6, lost to S. V. Wade 6–8 5–7; C. Evert d. Wade 4–6 6–3 6–3, d. Williams 6–2 6–3; P. S. A. Hogan d. C. Molesworth 6–8 6–4 6–2; Evert/Hogan d. W. Shaw/F. E. Truman 7–5 6–4; Overton/V. Ziegenfuss d. Wade/Williams 6–3 6–3.

1973 ***USA d. Great Britain 5–2, Longwood Cricket Club, Boston:*** C. Evert d. S. V. Wade 6–4 6–2, d. V. Burton 6–3 6–0; P. S. A. Hogan d. Burton 6–4 6–3, lost to Wade 2–6 2–6; L. Tuero d. G. Coles 7–5 6–2; Evert/M. Redondo lost to Coles/Wade 3–6 4–6; J. Evert/Hogan d. L. Beaven/L. Charles 6–3 4–6 8–6.

1974 ***Great Britain d. USA 6–1, Deeside Leisure Centre, Queensferry, North Wales (indoors):*** S. V. Wade d. J. M. Heldman 5–7 9–7 6–4, d. J. Newberry 6–1 6–3; G. Coles d. Newberry 4–6 6–1 6–3, d. Heldman 6–0 6–4; S. Barker d. J. Evert 4–6 6–4 6–1; Barker/Charles d. Newberry/B. Nagelsen 4–6 6–2 6–3; Coles/Wade lost to Heldman/M. Schallau 5–7 4–6.

1975 ***Great Britain d. USA 5–2, Public Auditorium, Cleveland (indoors):*** S. V. Wade d. M. Schallau 6–2 6–2; lost to C. Evert 3–6 5–7; G. Coles lost to Evert 4–6 1–6, d. Schallau 6–3 7–6; S. Barker d. J. Newberry 6–4 7–5; Mrs P. F. Jones/Wade d. Newberry/J. Anthony 6–2 6–3; Coles/Barker d. Evert/Schallau 7–5 6–4.

1976 ***Great Britain d. USA 5–2, Crystal Palace, London (indoors):*** C. Evert d. S. V. Wade 6–2 3–6 6–2, d. S. Barker 2–6 6–2 6–2; R. Casals lost to Barker 6–1 3–6 2–6, lost to Wade 6–3 7–3 ret'd.; T. Holladay d. G. Coles 3–6 6–1 6–4; Casals/Evert d. Barker/Wade 6–0 5–7 6–1; Mrs M. Guerrant/A. Kiyomura d. S. Mappin/L. Charles 6–2 6–2.

1977 ***USA d. Great Britain 7–0, Oakland, California (indoors):*** C. Evert d. S. V. Wade 7–5 7–6, d. S. Barker 6–1 6–2; Mrs L. W. King d. Barker 6–1 6–4, d. Wade 6–4 3–6 8–6; R. Casals d. M. Tyler 6–2 3–6 6–4; King/J. Russell d. S. Mappin/L. Charles 6–0 6–1; Casals/Evert d. Barker/Wade 6–2 6–4.

1978 ***Great Britain d. USA 4–3, Albert Hall, London (indoors):*** S. Barker lost to C. Evert 2–6 1–6, d. T. Austin 6–3 3–6 6–0; S. V. Wade d. Austin 3–6 6–3, lost to Evert 0–6 1–6; M. Tyler d. P. H. Shriver 5–7 6–2 6–3; S. Mappin/A. E. Hobbs lost to Mrs L. W. King/Austin 2–6 6–4 2–6; Barker/Wade d. Evert/Shriver 6–0 5–7 6–4.

1979 ***USA d. Great Britain 7–0, Palm Beach West, Florida:*** Mrs J. M. Lloyd d. S. Barker 7–5 6–2, d. S. V. Wade 6–1 6–1; T. Austin d. Wade 6–1 6–4, d. Barker 6–4 6–2; K. Jordan d. A. E. Hobbs 4–6 7 6–2; Austin/A. Kiyomura d. J. M. Durie/D. A. Jevans 6–3 6–1; Lloyd/R. Casals d. Barker/Wade 6–0 6–1.

1980 ***Great Britain d. USA 5–2, Albert Hall, London (indoors):*** Mrs J. M. Lloyd d. S. Barker 6–1 6–2, d. S. V. Wade 7–5 3–6 7–5; A. Jaeger d. W Rade 3–6 6–3 6–2, lost to Barker 7–5 3–6 3–6; K. Jordan lost to A. E. Hobbs 6–4 4–6 1–6; Lloyd/R. Casals d. Hobbs/G. Coles 6–3 6–3; A. E. Smith/Jordan d. Barker/Wade 6–4 7–5.

1981 ***USA d. Great Britain 7–0, International Amphitheatre, Chicago (indoors):*** T. Austin d. S. Barker 7–5 6–3, d. S. V. Wade 6–3 6–1; Mrs J. M. Lloyd d. Wade 6–1 6–3, d. Barker 6–3 6–0; A. Jaeger d. A. E. Hobbs 6–0 6–0; Jaeger/P. H. Shriver d. J. M. Durie/Hobbs 6–1 6–3; Lloyd/R. Casals d. G. Coles/Wade 6–3 6–3.

1982 ***USA d. Great Britain 6–1, Albert Hall, London (indoors):*** B. Potter d. S. Barker 6–2 6–2, d. J. M. Durie 5–7 7–6 6–2; Mrs J. M. Lloyd d. Durie 6–2 6–2, d. Barker 6–4 6–3; A. E. Smith d. S. V. Wade 3–6 7–5 6–3; R. Casals/Smith lost to Durie/A. E. Hobbs 3–6 6–2 3–6; Potter/S. A. Walsh d. Barker/Wade 2–6 6–4 6–4.

1983 ***USA d. Great Britain 6–1, Williamsburg, Virginia (indoors):*** M. Navratilova d. S. Barker 6–2 6–0, d. J. M. Durie 6–3 6–3; P. H. Shriver d. Durie 6–3 6–2, d. Barker 6–0 6–1; K. Rinaldi d. S. V. Wade 6–3 6–2; C. Reynolds/P. Smith lost to Barker/Wade 5–7 6–3 1–6; Navratilova/Shriver d. Durie/A. Croft 6–2 6–1.

1984 ***USA d. Great Britain 5–2, Albert Hall, London (indoors):*** Mrs J. M. Lloyd d. A. E. Hobbs 6–2 6–2; A. Moulton lost to A. Croft 1–6 7–5 4–6; B. Potter lost to J. M. Durie 3–6 6–7; Lloyd/Moulton d. A. Brown/S. V. Wade 6–2 6–2; Potter d. Hobbs 6–1 6–3; Lloyd d. Durie 7–6 6–1; Potter/S. A. Walsh d. Durie/Hobbs 7–6 4–6 9–7.

1985 ***USA d. Great Britain 7–0, Williamsburg, Virginia (indoors):*** Mrs J. M. Lloyd d. J. M. Durie 6–2 6–3; K. Rinaldi d. A. E. Hobbs 7–5 7–5; P. H. Shriver d. A. Croft 6–0 6–0; B. Nagelsen/A. White d. Croft/S. V. Wade 6–4 6–1; Shriver d. Durie 6–4 6–4; Lloyd d. Croft 6–3 6–0; Lloyd/Shriver d. Durie/Hobbs 6–3 6–7 6–2.

1986 ***USA d. Great Britain 7–0, Albert Hall, London (indoors):*** K. Rinaldi d. S. Gomer 6–3 7–6; S. Rehe d. A. Croft 6–3 6–1; B. Gadusek d. J. M. Durie 6–2 6–4; Gadusek/Rinaldi d. Croft/Gomer 6–3 5–7 6–3; Gadusek d. Hobbs 2–6 6–4 6–4; Rinaldi d. Durie 6–4 6–2; E. Burgin/A. White d. Durie/Hobbs 7–6 6–3.

1987 ***USA d. Great Britain 5–2, Williamsburg, Virginia (indoors):*** Z. Garrison d. A. E. Hobbs 7–5 6–2; L. McNeil d. S. Gomer 6–2 6–1; P. H. Shriver d. J. M. Durie 6–1 7–5; G. Fernandez/R. White d. Gomer/C. Wood 6–4 6–1; Shriver d. Hobbs 6–4 6–3; Garrison lost to Durie 6–7 3–6; Garrison/McNeil lost to Durie/Hobbs 6–0 4–6 5–7.

1988 ***USA d. Great Britain 7–0, Albert Hall, London (indoors):*** Z. Garrison d. J. M. Durie 6–2 6–4; P. Fendick d. M. Javer 6–2 6–1; L. McNeil d. S. Gomer 6–7 6–4 6–4; McNeil/B. Nagelsen d. Gomer/J. Salmon 6–3 6–2; Garrison d. C. Wood 6–3 6–2; McNeil d. Durie 6–1 6–2; G. Fernandez/Garrison d. Durie/Wood 6–1 6–3.

1989 **USA d. Great Britain 7–0, Williamsburg, Virginia:** L. McNeil d. J. Durie 7–5 6–1; J. Capriati d. C. Wood 6–0 6–0;
M.-J. Fernandez d. S. Gomer 6–1 6–2; McNeil d. Gomer 6–4 6–2; Fernandez d. Durie 6–1 7–5; B. Nagelsen/
Fernandez d. Gomer/Wood 6–2 7–6; P. Fendick/McNeil d. Durie/A. Hobbs 6–3 6–3.

EUROPEAN CUP

Formerly King's Cup

International Men's Team Championship on Indoor Courts. It was staged on a knock-out basis 1936–38,
1952–74, on a league basis 1976–83 with ties home and away. From 1984 the ties in each division were
held concurrently at one venue. The Challenge Round system was used in the two opening years, with
1937 the only Challenge Round.

FINALS

1936 **France d. Sweden 4–1, Stockholm:** J. Borotra d. K. Schroder 2–6 6–2 6–1 6–3, d. C. Ostberg 6–1 6–3 7–5; B.
Destremau d. Schroder 3–6 7–5 6–2 6–4, d. Ostberg 6–2 6–2 6–4; C. Boussus/J. Brugnon lost to Ostberg/
Schroder 2–6 6–3 4–6 6–3 4–6.

1937 **France d. Sweden 5–0, Paris:** B. Destremau d. K. Schroder 8–6 1–6 2–6 11–9 8–6, d. N. Rohlsson 1–6 1–6 6–3
6–1 6–0; Y. Petra d. Rohlsson 6–1 6–4 6–2, d. Schroder 6–3 3–6 6–3 6–4; H. Bolelli/J. Lesueur d. Schroder/H.
Wallen 10–8 6–4 6–4.

1938 **Germany d. Denmark 5–0, Hamburg:** R. Menzel d. H. Plougmann 6–3 6–2 8–6; H. Henkel d. I. Gerdes 6–4 6–0
6–3, d. Plougmann 6–2 6–1 6–3; R. Redl d. Gerdes 6–3 6–3 6–2; Henkel/Menzel d. Gerdes/Plougmann 6–0 6–4
6–2.

1939–51 *Not held*

1952 **Denmark d. Sweden 3–2, Stockholm:** K. Nielsen lost to S. Davidson 3–6 7–9 4–6; T. Ulrich d. T. Johansson 7–5
0–6 6–4 6–2; Nielsen/Ulrich d. Davidson/Johansson 6–2 2–6 4–6 8–6 7–5; Nielsen d. Johansson 6–3 6–4 6–1;
Ulrich lost to Davidson 6–4 4–6 1–6 6–1 2–6.

1953 **Denmark d. Sweden 3–2, Copenhagen:** T. Ulrich d. S. Davidson 14–12 11–9 1–6 11–9; J. Ulrich lost to T.
Johansson 0–6 2–6 7–9; J. Ulrich d. Davidson/N. Rohlsson 6–4 6–4 4–6 3–6 6–3; J. Ulrich lost to
Davidson 3–6 4–6 0–6; T. Ulrich d. Johansson 6–3 2–6 6–4 5–7 6–3.

1954 **Denmark d. Italy 3–2, Milan:** T. Ulrich d. G. Merlo 7–5 2–6 9–7 9–7; K. Nielsen lost to O. Sirola 5–7 6–8 8–6 6–2
3–6; Nielsen/Ulrich d. N. Pietrangeli/Sirola 2–6 2–6 11–9 6–1 12–10; Nielsen lost to Pietrangeli 5–7 6–3 9–7 3–6
5–7; Ulrich d. Sirola 7–5 10–8 6–4.

1955 **Sweden d. Denmark 4–1, Copenhagen:** S. Davidson d. J. Ulrich 7–5 12–10 6–1; U. Schmidt lost to K. Nielsen
3–6 2–6 6–4 4–6; Davidson/T. Johansson d. Nielsen/J. Ulrich 11–9 6–3 14–12; Davidson d. Nielsen 8–10 6–2 7–9
12–10 7–5; Schmidt d. J. Ulrich 7–9 3–6 6–0 8–6 6–3.

1956 **Sweden d. France 4–1, Paris:** S. Davidson lost to P. Darmon 7–9 6–2 5–7 6–8; U. Schmidt d. R. Haillet 6–1 /6–2
6–4; Davidson/Schmidt d. Darmon/P. Remy 8–6 3–6 6–1 6–4; Davidson d. Haillet 6–2 2–6 6–4 6–1; Schmidt d.
Darmon 6–1 10–8 6–3.

1957 **Sweden d. Denmark 3–2, Copenhagen:** J. E. Lundqvist d. K. Nielsen 4–6 6–3 10–8 6–4; U. Schmidt lost to T.
Ulrich 4–6 7–9 2–6; Lundqvist/Schmidt d. J. Ulrich/T. Ulrich 6–3 5–7 6–0 6–3; Lundqvist d. T. Ulrich 7–5 6–1 6–2;
Schmidt lost to Nielsen 6–4 4–6 2–6 5–7.

1958 **Sweden d. Denmark 3–2, Stockholm:** B. Folke lost to J. Ulrich 11–13 3–6 4–6; S. Davidson d. K. Nielsen 6–0 6–1
6–4; Davidson/T. Johansson d. Nielsen/J. Ulrich 10–8 1–6 6–3 6–8 6–3; Folke lost to Nielsen 4–6 3–6 3–6;
Davidson d. J. Ulrich 6–4 6–3 1–6 6–1.

1959 **Denmark won, Stockholm:** Denmark d. Italy 2–1, lost to Sweden 2–1, d. France 2–1 (12–11 sets); Sweden lost
to France 2–1, d. Denmark 2–1, d. Italy 2–1 (10–10 sets); Italy lost to Denmark 2–1, d. France 2–1, lost to Sweden
2–1 (11–11 sets); France d. Sweden 2–1, lost to Italy 2–1, lost to France 2–1 (10–11 sets). Danish team: K. Nielsen
and J. Ulrich.

1960 **Denmark d. West Germany 3–0, Paris:** J. Leschly d. B. Nitsche 6–4 8–6; J. Ulrich d. P. Scholl 6–2 6–3; Leschly/J.
Ulrich d. Nitsche/Scholl 6–8 6–2 6–0.

1961 **Sweden d. Denmark 2–1, Cologne:** U. Schmidt d. J. Leschly 6–4 6–2; J. E. Lundqvist d. J. Ulrich 6–3 6–1;
Lundqvist/Schmidt lost to Leschly/J. Ulrich 5–7 6–4 5–7.

1962 **Denmark d. Italy 3–0, Copenhagen:** J. Leschly d. G. Merlo 6–3 8–6; J. Ulrich d. N. Pietrangeli 6–4 6–2; Leschly/J.
Ulrich d. Pietrangeli/O. Sirola 9–7 7–5.

1963 **Yugoslavia d. Denmark 3–0, Belgrade:** Yugoslav team: B. Jovanovic and N. Pilic.

1964 **Great Britain d. Sweden 3–0, Stockholm:** M. J. Sangster d. J. E. Lundquist 13–15 10–8 12–10; R. Taylor d. B.
Holmstrom 6–3 9–7; Sangster/R. K. Wilson d. Holmstrom/L. Olander 4–6 12–10 6–4.

1965 **Great Britain d. Denmark 2–1, Torquay:** R. K. Wilson lost to J. Leschly 1–6 4–6; M. Cox d. C. Hedelund 6–4 6–3;
A. R. Mills/Wilson d. Leschly/Hedelund 3–6 6–2 6–4 12–10.

1966 **Great Britain d. Italy 3–0, Milan:** R. Taylor d. N. Pietrangeli 6–4 6–4; M. J. Sangster d. G. Maioli 7–9 6–4 11–9;
Sangster/R. K. Wilson d. D. di Maso/Maioli 6–4 6–1.

1967 **Great Britain d. Sweden 2–1, Stockholm:** R. Taylor d. O. Bengtson 2–6 6–3 9–7; R. K. Wilson d. M. Carlstein 8–6
6–2; M. Cox/Taylor lost to Bengtson/B. Homstrom 4–6 7–9.

1968 **Sweden d. Netherlands 2–1, Bratislava:** O. Bengtson lost to T. S. Okker 12–14 4–6; M. Carlstein d. J. Hordjik
6–4 6–3; Bengtson/Carlstein d. N. Fleury/Okker 1–6 4–6 7–5 6–3 6–4.

1969 **Czechoslovakia d. Sweden 2–1, Cologne:** V. Zednik d. H. Zahr 6–4A, 7–5; J. Kukal d. O. Bengtson 6–1 5–7 11–9;
Kukal/Zednik lost to Bengtson/H. Nerell 4–6 4–6.

1970 **France d. Denmark 2–1, Copenhagen:** J. B. Chanfreau d. J. Ulrich 6–3 8–6; G. Goven lost to J. Leschly 1–6 3–6;
Chanfreau/Goven d. Ulrich/Leschly 2–6 6–4 7–5.

***1971** **Italy d. Spain 2–1, Ancona:** A. Panatta lost to M. Orantes 2–6 3–6; N. Pietrangeli d. J. Gisbert 7–9 8–6 6–4; Panatta/Pietrangeli d. Gisbert/Orantes 4–6 8–6 6–3 6–4.*

***1972** **Spain d. Hungary 3–0, Madrid:** A. Gimeno d. S. Baranyi 10–8 6–2; J. Gisbert d. B. Taroczy 6–1 7–9 6–3; J. Herrera/A. Munoz d. R. Machan/Taroczy 6–4 3–6 7–5.*

***1973** **Sweden d. Italy 2–1, Hanover:** L. Johansson d. A. Zugarelli 6–4 6–3; B. Borg d. A. Panatta 4–6 6–2 8–6; Borg/Johansson lost to P. Bertolucci/Zugarelli 6–3 5–7 4–6.*

***1974** **Italy d. Sweden 3–0, Ancona:** A. Panatta d. R. Norberg 6–3 6–4; A. Zugarelli d. T. Svensson 6–3 6–4; P. Bertolucci/A. Panatta d. B. Andersson/Norberg 6–2 6–4.*

***1975** Not held*

***1976** **Hungary 11 wins, Great Britain 10 wins** (played entirely as round robin, each tie home and away). Hungarian team: P. Szoke, B. Taroczy. British team: M. Cox, J. M. Lloyd, C. J. Mottram, R. Taylor.*

***1977** **Sweden d. West Germany 5–1, Berlin:** R. Norberg d. U. Marten 6–2 4–6 6–4; K. Johansson d. K. Meiler 6–4 6–4; O. Bengtson/Norberg d. P. Elter/Meiler 6–2 6–2. **Linkoping:** Norberg d. U. Pinner 7–6 6–2; Johansson d. Meiler 6–7 6–2 6–3; Bengtson/Norberg lost to Elter/Marten 6–3 4–6 4–6.*

***1978** **Sweden d. Hungary 3–3 (9–7 sets), Uppsala:** T. Svensson d. P. Szoke 6–2 6–4; O. Bengtson lost to B. Taroczy 6–7 6–7; Bengtson/Svensson lost to Szoke/Taroczy 6–7 4–6; **Debrecen:** Svensson d. Szoke 6–2 6–2; Bengtson d. Taroczy 6–4 7–6; Bengtson/Svensson lost to Szoke/Taroczy 3–6 6–3 3–6.*

***1979** **Czechoslovakia d. Hungary 4–2, Pecs:** I. Lendl lost to J. Benyik 6–7 7–5 6–7; T. Smid d. B. Taroczy 5–7 6–3 6–4; P. Slozil/T. Smid d. P. Szoke/Taroczy 6–4 6–4; **Chrudin:** Lendl lost to Benyik 6–4 2–6 0–6; Smid d. Szoke 6–3 3–6 6–2; Slozil/Smid d. Benyik/Szoke 6–4 6–2.*

***1980** **Czechoslovakia d. Hungary 5–1, Chrudin:** T. Smid d. R. Machan 6–4 6–2; I. Lendl d. B. Taroczy 6–2 6–1; Smid/P. Slozil d. P. Szoke/Machan 6–4 7–5; **Debreden:** Smid d. J. Benyik 6–2 3–6 6–2; Lendl d. Machan 6–0 6–2; Smid/Slozil lost to Machan/Szoke 6–3 3–6 2–6.*

1981** **West Germany d. USSR 3–3 (9–7 sets), Moscow, 2–1, and Hamburg, 1–2.

***1982** **West Germany d. Czechoslovakia 2–1, Dortmund:** K. Eberhard lost to J. Navratil 4–6 1–6; U. Pinnder d. P. Slozilp 6–4 6–4; C. Zipf/H. D. Beutel d. Navratil/Slozil 6–3 6–4.*

***1983** **West Germany d. Czechoslovakia 2–1, Uppsala:** H. J. Schwaier lost to L. Pimek 6–4 2–6 3–6; M. Westphal d. J. Navratil 3–6 6–2 6–3; E. Jelen/W. Popp d. Navratil/Piimek 6–1 1–6 7–6.*

***1984** **Czechoslovakia d. Sweden 3–1, Essen:** M. Mecir d. J. Gunnarsson 7–6 6–4; L. Pimek lost to J. Nystrom 3–6 ⁻5–7; Pimek/J. Navratil d. Gunnarsson/Nystrom 3–6 6–2 6–4.*

***1985** **Sweden d. Switzerland 3–0, Essen:** T. Hogstedt d. R. Stadler 6–3 6–2; J. Gunnarsson d. J. Hlasek 7–5 4–6 6–2; S. Simonsson d. Hlasek/Stadler 6–3 3–6 6–3.*

***1986** **Switzerland d. Czechoslovakia 2–1, Queen's Club, London:** R. Stadler d. M. Vajda 6–4 7–5; J. Hlasek lost L. Pimek 7–5 3–6 5–7; Hlasek/Stadler d. Pimek/P. Korda 6–2 6–3.*

***1987** **Switzerland d. Great Britain 2–1, Hanover:** R. Stadler lost to M. J. Bates 6–7 2–6; J. Hlasek d. A. Castle 6–3 6–7 6–2; Hlasek/Stadler d. Bates/Castle 3–6 7–5 6–0.*

***1988** **Czechoslovakia d. Netherlands 2–1, Zurich:** P. Korda d. M. Oosting 6–3 7–6; doubles not played.*

***1989** **Czechoslovakia d. West Germany 2–1, Ostrava:** P. Korda lost to C.-U. Steeb 3–6 3–6; M. Srejber d. E. Jelen 7–5 6–3; Srejber/Korda d. P. Kuhnen/Jelen 7–6 7–6.*

***1990** **Germany d. USSR 2–1, Metz:** U. Riglewski lost to D. Poliakov 7–5 3–6 2–6; M. Stich d. A. Cherkasov 6–3 7–6; Stich/Riglewski d. A. Olhovskiy/V. Gabrichidze 6–3 7–6.*

WORLD TEAM CUP

Eight-nation men's team event, qualification by individual ATP rating. Formerly Nations Cup.

FINALS

Played at Kingston, Jamaica

***1975** **USA d. Great Britain 2–1:** R. Tanner d. R. Taylor 6–3 2–6 6–4; A. R. Ashe lost to C. J. Mottram 5–7 7–5 1–6; Ashe/Tanner d. Mottram/Taylor 6–1 1–6 6–4.*

***1976–77** Not held*

Played at Dusseldorf

***1978** **Spain d. Australia 2–1:** J. Higueras d. J. D. Newcombe 6–2 6–3; M. Orantes d. P. Dent 6–3 6–4; Higueras/Orantes lost to Dent/Newcombe 6–7 4–6.*

***1979** **Australia d. Italy 2–1:** J. G. Alexander d. C. Barazzutti 6–2 6–0; P. Dent lost to A. Panatta 3–6 3–6; Alexander/Dent d. P. Bertolucci/Panatta 6–3 7–6.*

***1980** **Argentina d. Italy 3–0:** G. Vilas d. C. Barazzutti 6–3 6–2; J. L. Clerc d. A. Panatta 7–6 6–3; Clerc/Vilas d. P. A. Bertolucci/Panatta 6–2 6–3.*

***1981** **Czechoslovakia d. Australia 2–1:** I. Lendl lost to P. McNamara 3–6 4–6; T. Smid d. P. McNamee 6–4 7–6; Lendl/Smid d. McNamara/McNamee 6–4 6–3.*

***1982** **USA d. Australia 2–1:** G. Mayer d. K. Warwick 7–6 6–2; E. Teltscher d. P. McNamara 6–4 7–6; Mayer/S. E. Stewart lost to M. R. Edmondson/McNamara 1–6 1–6.*

***1983** **Spain d. Australia 2–1:** J. Higueras d. M. R. Edmondson 6–2 6–4; M. Orantes d. P. Cash 6–3 6–2; A. Gimenez/Higueras lost to Cash/Edmondson 5–7 6–4 1–6.*

***1984** **USA d. Czechoslovakia 2–1:** J. P. McEnroe d. I. Lendl 6–3 6–2; J. Arias lost to T. Smid 6–4 6–7 4–6; P. Fleming/McEnroe d. Lendl/Smid 6–1 6–2.*

***1985** **USA d. Czechoslovakia 2–1:** J. P. McEnroe lost to I. Lendl 7–6 6–7 3–6; J. S. Connors d. M. Mecir 6–3 3–6 7–5; K. Flach/R. Seguso d. Lendl/T. Smid 6–3 7–6.*

***1986** **France d. Sweden 2–1:** H. Leconte d. A. Jarryd 6–3 3–6 6–1; T. Tulasne lost to M. Wilander 1–6 4–6; G. Forget/Leconte d. Jarryd/Wilander 6–3 2–6 6–2.*

1987 *Czechoslovakia d. USA 2–1:* M. Mecir d. J. P. McEnroe 7–5 2–6 2–1 disqual.; M. Srejber lost to B. Gilbert 4–6 7–5 4–6; Mecir/T. Smid d. Gilbert/R. Seguso 6–3 6–1.
1988 *Sweden d. USA 2–1:* S. Edberg d. T. Mayotte 6–4 6–2; K. Carlsson d. A. Krickstein 6–4 6–3; Edberg/A. Jarryd lost to K. Flach/R. Seguso 7–6 3–6 6–7.
1989 *West Germany d. Argentina 2–1:* B. Becker d. G. Perez Roldan 6–0 2–6 6–2; C.-U. Steeb lost to M. Jaite 4–6 3–6; Becker/E. Jelen d. J. Frana/G. Luna 6–4 7–5.
1990 *Yugoslavia d. USA 2–1:* G. Prpic d. B. Gilbert 6–4 6–4; G. Ivanisevic d. J. Courier 3–6 7–5 6–1; Prpic/S. Zivojinovic lost to K. Flach/R. Seguso 5–7 6–7.

GRAND SLAM CUP

A knockout competition held in Munich in December, for the 16 men who have amassed the most points in the four Grand Slam Championships of Australia, France, Great Britain and the USA. The competition administered by the Grand Slam Committee (the four Chairmen) and an Administrator, is promoted by an independent German company and offers prize money of $6 million. A further $2 million goes annually to the Grand Slam Development Fund, administered by the ITF.

	WINNER	RUNNER-UP	SCORE			FIRST PRIZE
1990	P. Sampras	B. Gilbert	6–3	6–4	6–2	$2,000,000

MEN'S GRAND PRIX WINNERS

	SINGLES	BONUS	DOUBLES	BONUS	SPONSOR
1970	C. Richey	$25,000			Pepsi-Cola
1971	S. R. Smith	$25,000			Pepsi-Cola
1972	I. Nastase	$50,000			Commercial Union
1973	I. Nastase	$55,000			Commercial Union
1974	G. Vilas	$100,000			Commercial Union
1975	G. Vilas	$100,000	J. Gisbert	$25,000	Commercial Union
1976	R. Ramirez	$150,000	R. Ramirez	$40,000	Commercial Union
1977	G. Vilas	$300,000	R. A. J. Hewitt	$85,000	Colgate
1978	J. S. Connors	*$300,000	W. Fibak	$90,000	Colgate
1979	J. P. McEnroe	$300,000	S. E. Stewart	$90,000	Colgate
1980	J. P. McEnroe	$300,000	S. R. Smith	$90,000	Volvo
1981	I. Lendl	$300,000	H. Gunthardt	$90,000	Volvo
1982	J. S. Connors	$600,000	S. E. Stewart	$150,000	Volvo
1983	M. Wilander	$600,000	P. Fleming	$150,000	Volvo
1984	J. P. McEnroe	$600,000	T. Smid	$150,000	Volvo
1985	I. Lendl	$800,000	R. Seguso	$165,000	Nabisco
1986	I. Lendl	$800,000	G. Forget	$165,000	Nabisco
1987	I. Lendl	$800,000	A. Jarryd	$165,000	Nabisco
1988	M. Wilander	$800,000	R. Leach	$165,000	Nabisco
1989	I. Lendl	$800,000	R. Leach	$165,000	Nabisco

* Neither Connors nor second-placed B. Borg had played enough tournaments to qualify for the bonus payment, which was awarded to third-placed E. Dibbs.

MEN'S GRAND PRIX MASTERS WINNERS

SINGLES

	VENUE	WINNER	RUNNER-UP	SCORE	FIRST PRIZE
1970	Tokyo	S. R. Smith	R. G. Laver	Round-Robin	$10,000
1971	Paris	I. Nastase	S. R. Smith	Round-Robin	$15,000
1972	Barcelona	I. Nastase	S. R. Smith	6–3 6–2 3–6 2–6 6–3	$15,000
1973	Boston	I. Nastase	T. S. Okker	6–3 7–5 4–6 6–3	$15,000
1974	Melbourne	G. Vilas	I. Nastase	7–6 6–2 3–6 3–6 6–4	$40,000
1975	Stockholm	I. Nastase	B. Borg	6–2 6–2 6–1	$40,000
1976	Houston	M. Orantes	W. Fibak	5–7 6–2 0–6 7–6 6–1	$40,000
1977*	New York	J. S. Connors	B. Borg	6–4 1–6 6–4	$100,000
1978*	New York	J. P. McEnroe	A. R. Ashe	6–7 6–3 7–5	$100,000
1979*	New York	B. Borg	V. Gerulaitis	6–2 6–2	$100,000
1980*	New York	B. Borg	I. Lendl	6–4 6–2 6–2	$100,000
1981*	New York	I. Lendl	V. Gerulaitis	6–7 2–6 7–6 6–2 6–4	$100,000
1982*	New York	I. Lendl	J. P. McEnroe	6–4 6–4 6–2	$100,000
1983*	New York	J. P. McEnroe	I. Lendl	6–3 6–4 6–4	$100,000
1984*	New York	J. P. McEnroe	I. Lendl	7 5 6–0 6–4	$100,000

1985*	New York	I. Lendl	B. Becker	6–2	7–6	6–3			$100,000
1986	New York	I. Lendl	B. Becker	6–4	6–4	6–4			$200,000
1987	New York	I. Lendl	M. Wilander	6–2	6–2	6–3			$200,000
1988	New York	B. Becker	I. Lendl	5–7	7–6	3–6	6–2	7–6	$150,000
1989	New York	S. Edberg	B. Becker	4–6	7–6	6–3	6–1		$285,000

* Played in January of the following year.

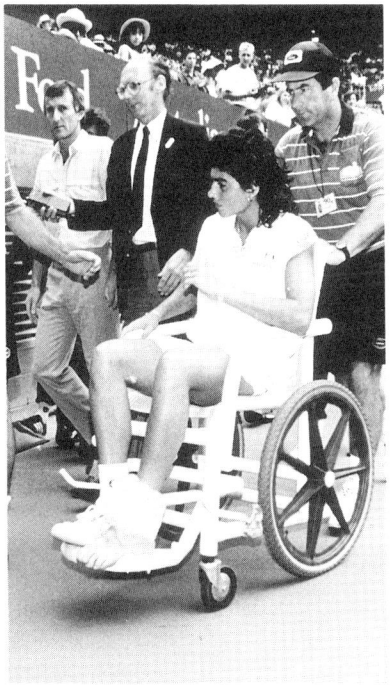 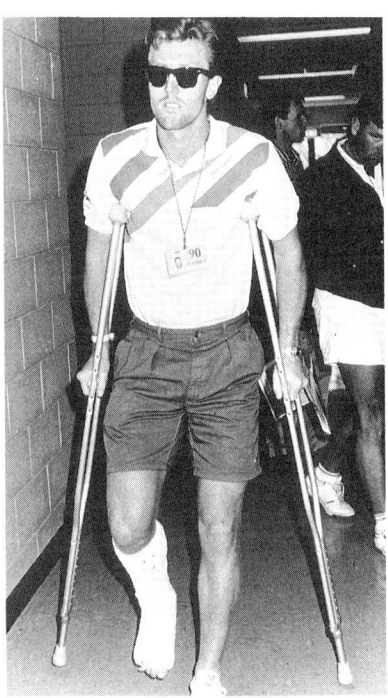

Within two hours on the middle Saturday in Melbourne both Gabriela Sabatini (left) and Mark Woodforde had been crippled with identical ankle injuries and carried from the court – two of the saddest pictures of 1990.   *(Professional Sport)*

DOUBLES

WINNERS	RUNNERS-UP	SCORE				
1970 S. R. Smith/A. R. Ashe	R. G. Laver/J. Kodes	Round-Robin				
1971–74 *Not held*						
1975 J. Gisbert/M. Orantes	J. Fassbender/H. J. Pohmann	Round-Robin				
1976 F. McNair/S. E. Stewart	B. E. Gottfried/R. Ramirez	6–3	5–7	5–7	6–4	6–4
1977* R. A. J. Hewitt/F. D. McMillan	R. C. Lutz/S. R. Smith	7–5	7–6	6–3		
1978* P. Fleming/J. P. McEnroe	W. Fibak/T. S. Okker	6–4	6–2	6–4		
1979* P. Fleming/J. P. McEnroe	W. Fibak/T. S. Okker	6–3	7–6	6–1		
1980* P. Fleming/J. P. McEnroe	P. McNamara/P. McNamee	6–4	6–3			
1981* P. Fleming/J. P. McEnroe	K. Curren/S. Denton	6–3	6–3			
1982* P. Fleming/J. P. McEnroe	S. E. Stewart/F. Taygan	6–2	6–2			
1983* P. Fleming/J. P. McEnroe	P. Slozil/T. Smid	6–2	6–2			
1984* P. Fleming/J. P. McEnroe	M. R. Edmondson/S. E. Stewart	6–3	6–1			
1985* A. Jarryd/S. Edberg	J. Nystrom/M. Wilander	6–1	7–6			
1986† A. Jarryd/S. Edberg	G. Forget/Y. Noah	6–3	7–6	6–3		
1987† M. Mecir/T. Smid	K. Flach/R. Seguso	6–4	7–5	7–6	6–3	
1988† R. Leach/J. Pugh	S. Casal/E. Sanchez	6–4	6–3	2–6	6–0	
1989† P. McEnroe/J. Grabb	A. Jarryd/J. Fitzgerald	7–5	7–6	5–7	6–3	

* Played in January of the following year.   † Played separately from the singles at the Royal Albert Hall, London.

ATP TOUR CHAMPIONSHIP

SINGLES

	VENUE	WINNER	RUNNER-UP	SCORE	FIRST PRIZE
1990	Frankfurt	A. Agassi	S. Edberg	5–7 7–6 7–5 6–2	$950,000

DOUBLES

	VENUE	WINNERS	RUNNERS-UP		FIRST PRIZE
1990	Sanctuary Cove, Australia	G. Forget/J. Hlasek	S. Casal/E. Sanchez	6–4 7–6 5–7 6–4	$225,000

WOMEN'S WORLD SERIES

	WINNER	BONUS	DOUBLES WINNERS	SPONSOR
1971	Mrs L. W. King	$10,000		Pepsi-Cola
1972	Mrs L. W. King	$20,000		Commerical Union
1973	Miss C. M. Evert	$23,000		Commercial Union
1974–76	*Not held*			
1977	Miss C. M. Evert	$100,000	Miss M. Navratilova/Miss B. Stove	Colgate
1978	Miss C. M. Evert	$100,000	Mrs G. E. Reid/Miss W. M. Turnbull	Colgate
1979	Mrs J. M. Lloyd	$115,000	Miss B. Stove/Miss W. M. Turnbull	Colgate
1980	Miss H. Mandlikova	$115,000	Miss K. Jordan/Miss A. E. Smith	Colgate
1981	Miss M. Navratilova	$125,000	Miss R. Casals/Miss W. M. Turnbull	Toyota
1982	Miss M. Navratilova	$130,000	Miss R. Casals/Miss W. M. Turnbull	Toyota
1983	Miss M. Navratilova	$150,000	Miss M. Navratilova/Miss P. H. Shriver	Virginia Slims
1984	Miss M. Navratilova	$150,000	Miss M. Navratilova/Miss P. H. Shriver	Virginia Slims
1985	Miss M. Navratilova	$150,000	Miss M. Navratilova/Miss P. H. Shriver	Virginia Slims
1986	Miss M. Navratilova	$200,000	Miss M. Navratilova/Miss P. H. Shriver	Virginia Slims
1987	Miss S. Graf	$225,000	Miss M. Navratilova/Miss P. H. Shriver	Virginia Slims
1988	Miss S. Graf	$400,000	Miss M. Navratilova/Miss P. H. Shriver	Virginia Slims
1989	Miss S. Graf	$400,000	Miss J. Novotna/Miss H. Sukova	Virginia Slims
1990	Miss S. Graf	$500,000	Miss J. Novotna/Miss H. Sukova	Kraft General Foods

WOMEN'S INTERNATIONAL SERIES CHAMPIONSHIPS

SINGLES

	VENUE	WINNER	RUNNER-UP	SCORE		FIRST PRIZE
1977	Palm Springs	Miss C. M. Evert	Mrs L. W. King	6–2	6–2	$75,000
1978	Palm Springs	Miss C. M. Evert	Miss M. Navratilova	6–3	6–3	$75,000
1979*	Landover, Maryland	Miss M. Navratilova	Miss T. A. Austin	6–2	6–1	$75,000

1980*	Palm Springs	Miss T. A. Austin	Miss A. Jaeger	6–2	6–2		$75,000
1981	East Rutherford, NJ	Miss T. A. Austin	Miss M. Navratilova	2–6	6–4	6–2	$75,000
1982	East Rutherford, NJ	Miss M. Navratilova	Mrs J. M. Lloyd	4–6	6–1	6–2	$75,000
1983*	Madison Square Garden, NY	Miss M. Navratilova	Mrs J. M. Lloyd	6–3	7–5	6–1**	$125,000
1984*	Madison Square Garden, NY	Miss M. Navratilova	Miss H. Sukova	6–3	7–5	6–4**	$125,000
1985*	Madison Square Garden, NY	Miss M. Navratilova	Miss H. Mandlikova	6–2 6–1**	6–0	3–6	$125,000
1986	Madison Square Garden, NY	Miss M. Navratilova	Miss S. Graf	7–6	6–3	6–2**	$125,000
1987	Madison Square Garden, NY	Miss S. Graf	Miss G. Sabatini	4–6 6–4**	6–4	6–0	$125,000
1988	Madison Square Garden, NY	Miss G. Sabatini	Miss P. H. Shriver	7–5	6–2	6–2**	$125,000
1989	Madison Square Garden, NY	Miss S. Graf	Miss M. Navratilova	6–4 6–2**	7–5	2–6	$125,000
1990	Madison Square Garden, NY	Miss M. Seles	Miss G. Sabatini	6–4 6–4	5–7	3–6 6–2	$250,000

*Played in the following year.   **Best of five sets.*

DOUBLES

	WINNERS	RUNNERS-UP	SCORE		
1977	Miss F. Durr/Miss S. V. Wade	Mrs H. Gourlay Cawley/Miss J. Russell	6–1	4–6	6–4
1978	Mrs L. W. King/Miss M. Navratilova	Mrs G. E. Reid/Miss W. M. Turnbull	6–3	6–4	
1979*	Mrs L. W. King/Miss M. Navratilova	Miss R. Casals/Mrs J. M. Lloyd	6–4	6–3	
1980*	Miss R. Casals/Miss W. M. Turnbull	Miss C. Reynolds/Miss P. Smith	6–3	4–6	7–6
1991	Miss M. Navratilova/Miss P. H. Shriver	Miss R. Casals/Miss W. M. Turnbull	6–3	6–4	
1982	Miss M. Navratilova/Miss P. H. Shriver	Miss C. Reynolds/Miss P. Smith	6–4	7–5	
1983*	Miss M. Navratilova/Miss P. H. Shriver	Miss J. M. Durie/Miss A. Kiyomura	6–3	6–1	
1984*	Miss M. Navratilova/Miss P. H. Shriver	Miss C. Kohde-Kilsch/Miss H. Sukova	6–7	6–4	7–6
1985*	Miss H. Mandlikova/Miss W. M. Turnbull	Miss C. Kohde-Kilsch/Miss H. Sukova	6–4	6–7	6–3
1986	Miss M. Navratilova/Miss P. H. Shriver	Miss C. Kohde-Kilsch/Miss H. Sukova	7–6	6–3	
1987	Miss M. Navratilova/Miss P. H. Shriver	Miss C. Kohde-Kilsch/Miss H. Sukova	6–1	6–1	
1988	Miss M. Navratilova/Miss P. H. Shriver	Miss L. Savchenko/Miss N. Zvereva	6–3	6–4	
1989	Miss M. Navratilova/Miss P. H. Shriver	Miss L. Savchenko/Miss N. Zvereva	6–3	6–2	
1990	Miss K. Jordan/Mrs E. Smylie	Miss M. Paz/Miss A. Sanchez-Vicario	7–6	6–4	

* Played in the following year.

WORLD CHAMPIONSHIP TENNIS
WCT FINALS, DALLAS

	WINNER	RUNNER-UP	SCORE				PRIZE
1971	K. R. Rosewall	R. G. Laver	6–4	1–6	7–6	7–6	$50,000
1972	K. R. Rosewall	R. G. Laver	4–6	6–0	6–3	6–7 7–6	50,000
1973	S. R. Smith	A. R. Ashe	6–3	6–3	4–6	6–4	50,000
1974	J. D. Newcombe	B. Borg	4–6	6–3	6–3	6–2	50,000
1975	A. R. Ashe	B. Borg	3–6	6–4	6–4	6–0	50,000
1976	B. Borg	G. Vilas	1–6	6–1	7–5	6–1	50,000
1977	J. S. Connors	R. D. Stockton	6–7	6–1	6–4	6–3	100,000
1978	V. Gerulaitis	E. Dibbs	6–3	6–2	6–1		100,000
1979	J. P. McEnroe	B. Borg	7–5	4–6	6–2	7–6	100,000
1980	J. S. Connors	J. P. McEnroe	2–6	7–6	6–1	6–2	100,000
1981	J. P. McEnroe	J. Kriek	7–6	6–3	4–6	0–6 6–4	100,000
1982	I. Lendl	J. P. McEnroe	6–2	3–6	6–3	6–3	150,000
1983	J. P. McEnroe	I. Lendl	6–2	4–6	6–3	6–7 7–6	150,000
1984	J. P. McEnroe	J. S. Connors	6–1	6–2	6–3		200,000
1985	I. Lendl	T. Mayotte	7–6	6–4	6–1		200,000
1986	A. Jarryd	B. Becker	6–7	6–1	6–1	6–4	200,000
1987	M. Mecir	J. P. McEnroe	6–0	3–6	6–2	6–2	200,000
1988	B. Becker	S. Edberg	6–4	1–6	7–5	6–2	200,000
1989	J. P. McEnroe	B. Gilbert	6–3	6–3	7–6		200,000

WORLD DOUBLES CHAMPIONSHIPS

VENUE	WINNERS	RUNNERS-UP	SCORE	PRIZE
1973 Montreal	R. C. Lutz/S. R. Smith	T. S. Okker/M. C. Riessen	6–2 7–6 6–0	$40,000
1974 Montreal	R. A. J. Hewitt/F. D. McMillan	J. D. Newcombe/O. K. Davidson	6–2 6–7 6–1 6–2	40,000
1975 Mexico City	B. R. Gottfried/R. Ramirez	M. Cox/C. Drysdale	7–6 6–7 7–6 7–6	40,000
1976 Kansas City	W. Fibak/K. Meiler	R. C. Lutz/S. R. Smith	6–3 2–6 3–6 6–3 6–4	40,000
1977 Kansas City	V. Amritraj/R. D. Stockton	V. Gerulaitis/A. Panatta	7–6 7–6 4–6 6–3	80,000
1978 Kansas City	W. Fibak/T. S. Okker	R. C. Lutz/S. R. Smith	6–7 6–4 6–0 6–3	80,000
1979 Olympia, London	J. P. McEnroe/P. Fleming	I. Nastase/S. E. Stewart	3–6 6–2 6–3 6–1	80,000
1980 Olympia, London	B. E. Gottfried/R. Ramirez	W. Fibak/T. S. Okker	3–6 6–4 6–4 3–6 6–3	80,000
1981 Olympia, London	P. McNamara/P. McNamee	V. Amaya/H. Pfister	6–3 2–6 3–6 6–3 6–2	80,000
1982 Birmingham	H. Gunthardt/B. Taroczy	K. Curren/S. Denton	6–7 6–3 7–5 6–4	80,000
1983 Royal Albert Hall, London	H. Gunthardt/B. Taroczy	B. E. Gottfried/R. Ramirez	6–3 7–5 7–6	80,000
1984 Royal Albert Hall, London	P. Slozil/T. Smid	A. Jarryd/H. Simonsson	1–6 6–3 3–6 6–4 6–3	80,000
1985 Royal Albert Hall, London	K. Flach/R. Seguso	H. Gunthardt/B. Taroczy	6–3 3–6 6–3 4–6 6–0	80,000

From 1986 this event was incorporated into the Masters Doubles.

GRAND SLAMS
The Grand Slam denotes holding the four championship titles of Australia, France, Wimbledon and the United States in the same year (shown in bold below). The list also includes consecutive wins, not in the same year.

MEN'S SINGLES

J. D. Budge: Wimbledon, US 1937, **Australia, France, Wimbledon, US 1938**
R. G. Laver: **Australia, France, Wimbledon, US 1962**
R. G. Laver: **Australia, France, Wimbledon, US 1969**

WOMEN'S SINGLES

Miss M. Connolly: Wimbledon, US 1952, **Australia, France, Wimbledon, US 1953**
Mrs B. M. Court: US 1969, **Australia, France, Wimbledon, US 1970**, Australia 1971
Miss M. Navratilova: Wimbledon, US, Australia 1983, France, Wimbledon, US 1984
Miss S. Graf: **Australia, France, Wimbledon, US 1988**

MEN'S DOUBLES

F. A. Sedgman: (With J. E. Bromwich) US 1950, **(with K. McGregor) Australia, France, Wimbledon, US 1951**, Australia, France, Wimbledon 1952
K. McGregor: **(With F. A. Sedgman) Australia, France, Wimbledon, US 1951**, Australia, France, Wimbledon 1952

WOMEN'S DOUBLES

Miss A. L. Brough: (with Mrs W. du Pont) France, Wimbledon, US 1949, (with Miss D. J. Hart) Australia 1950
Miss M. E. Bueno: **(With Miss C. C. Truman) Australia 1960, (with Miss D. R. Hard) France, Wimbledon, US 1960**
Miss M. Navratilova/Miss P. H. Shriver: Wimbledon, US, Australia 1983, **France, Wimbledon, US, Australia 1984**, France 1985; *Wimbledon, US 1986, Australia, France 1987
* *Miss Navratilova also won France 1986 with Miss A. Temesvari.*

MIXED DOUBLES

Miss M. Smith: (With F. S. Stolle) US 1962, **(with K. N. Fletcher) Australia, France, Wimbledon, US 1963**, Australia, France 1964
K. N. Fletcher: **(With Miss M. Smith) Australia, France, Wimbledon, US 1963**, Australia, France 1964
O. K. Davidson: (With Mrs D. Fales) US 1966, **(with Miss L. R. Turner) Australia 1967, (with Mrs L. W. King) France, Wimbledon, US 1967**
Mrs L. W. King: (With O. K. Davidson) France, Wimbledon, US 1967, (with R. D. Crealy) Australia 1968

JUNIOR SINGLES

E. H. Buchholz: **Australia, France, Wimbledon, US 1958** (*Note:* the US event was not then conducted as an international event)
S. Edberg: **France, Wimbledon, US, Australia 1983**

ITF VETERAN CHAMPIONSHIPS
MEN

	VENUE	35+ SINGLES	35+ DOUBLES	45+ SINGLES	45+ DOUBLES
1981	Sao Paulo			S. Davidson	S. Davidson/H. Stewart
1982	Poertschach			I. Gulyas	J. Morton/J. Nelson
1983	Bahia			I. Gulyas	K. Fuhrmann/F. Seeman
1984	Cervia			I. Gulyas	K. Fuhrmann/F. Seeman
1985	Melbourne			I. Barclay	A. Duestler/J. Nelson
1986	Poertschac			J. Lemann	J. Lemann/I. Ribeiro
1987	Garmisch-Partenkirchen			G. Rohrich	H. Gradischnig P. Pokorny
1988	Huntington Beach, Cal.	A. Gardiner	L. Levai/R. Machan	K. Diepraam	F./G. Krauss
1989	Vina Del Mar, Chile	A. Fillol	R. Machan/L. Levai	H. Elschenbroich	B. Nitsche/G. Krauss
1990	Umag, Yugoslavia	R. Machan	R. Machan/L. Levai	H. Elschenbroich	D. Johnson/J. Parker

	VENUE	55+ SINGLES	55+ DOUBLES	60+ SINGLES	60+ DOUBLES
1981	Sao Paulo	S. Clark	S. Clark/T. Johansson		
1982	Poertschach	R. McCarthy	A. Hussmuller/L. Legenstein	T. Johansson	T. Johansson/A. Ritzenberg
1983	Bahia	R. McCarthy	A. Hussmuller/L. Legenstein	—	—
1984	Cervia	G. Merlo	J. Morton/H. Stewart	—	—
1985	Melbourne	H. Stewart	J. Morton/H. Stewart	R. Sorlein	T. Johansson/V. Zabrodsky
1986	Poertschach	L. Maine	R. Howe/R. Seymour	M. McCarthy	O. Jirkovsky/J. Karlhofer
1987	Garmisch Partenkirchen	I. Gulyas	I. Gulyas/H. Stewart	R. Howe	L. Legenstein/A. Stolpa
1988	Huntington Beach, Cal.	I. Gulyas	S. Davidson/H. Stewart	R. McCarthy	R. Howe/R. McCarthy
1989	Vina Del Mar, Chile	I. Gulyas	C. DeVoe/J. Powless	R. McCarthy	R. Howe/R. McCarthy
1990	Umag, Yugoslavia	I. Gulyas	K. Sinclair/L. Main	S. Davidson	H. Stewart/S. Davidson

	VENUE	65+ SINGLES	65+ DOUBLES	70+ SINGLES	70+ DOUBLES
1982	Poertschach	F. Klein	J. Becker/F. Klein	—	—
1983	Bahia	R. San Martin	F. Barboza/H. Pizani	—	—
1984	Cervia	G. Mulloy	G. Mulloy/F. Klein	—	—
1985	Melbourne	J. Gilchrist	R. Ritzenberg/F. Klein	—	—
1986	Poertschach	T. Johansson	G. Mulloy/V. Hughes	—	—
1987	Garmisch-Partenkirchen	A. Swetka	B. Kempa/W. Kessler	—	—
1988	Huntington Beach, Cal.	T. Brown	L. Hammel/B. Sherman	F. Klein	G. Hippenstiel/G. Young
1989	Vina Del Mar, Chile	A. Vieira	A. Vieira/S. Verrati	A. Ritzenberg	A. Ritzenberg/F.Klein
1990	Umag, Yugoslavia	B. McCarthy	O. Jirkovsky/J. Karlhofer	W. Parsons	A. Swetka/A. Ritzenberg

WOMEN

	VENUE	40+ SINGLES	40+ DOUBLES	50+ SINGLES	50+ DOUBLES
1981	Sao Paulo	E. de Molina	N. Reed/M. S. Plante	A. Cury	—
1982	Poertschach	R. Drisaldi	*C. Hillebrand/N. Reed	E. Slytermann	E. Slytermann/I. Burmester
1983	Bahia	H. Masthoff	H. Masthoff/H. Orth	I. de Pla	G. Barboza/J. Borzone
1984	Cervia	H. Masthoff	H. Masthoff/H. Orth	C. Mazzoleni	H. Brabanec/P. Wearne
1985	Melbourne	H. Orth	J. Dalton/H. Orth	I. Michael	A. Fotheringham/A. Pilkinghome
1986	Poertschach	H. Masthoff	H. Masthoff/H. Orth	S. Brasher	S. Brasher/L. Cawthorne
1987	Garmisch-Partenkirchen	M. Pinterova	G. Lovera/M. Pinterova	S. Brasher	S. Brasher/L. Cawthorne
1988	Huntington Beach, Cal.	M. Pinterova	G. Lovera/R. Darmon	D. Matthiessen	J. Crofford/D. Matthiessen
1989	Vina Del Mar, Chile	M. Pinterova	M. Pinterova/H. Orth	I. Michael	N. Reed/B. Allendorf
1990	Umag, Yugoslavia	M. Pinterova	B. Mueller/L. Cash	M. Schultze	K. Schiavinato/J. Blackshaw

* held as 45+ event.

VENUE	60+ SINGLES	60+ DOUBLES
1988 Huntington	V. Glass	D. Cheney/C. Murdock
Beach, Cal.		
1989 Vina Del Mar, Chile	B. Pratt	D. Cheney/C. Murdock
1990 Umag, Yugoslavia	L. Owen	L. Stock/D. Young

DUBLER CUP
International Men's Team Championship for Over 45s

FINALS

	VENUE*	WINNERS	RUNNERS-UP	SCORE
1958	Monte Carlo	Italy	West Germany	3–1
1959	Zurich	Switzerland	Italy	4–1
1960	Merano, Italy	Italy	Switzerland	5–0
1961	Bologna	Italy	Austria	4–1
1962	Merano, Italy	Italy	France	3–2
1963	Merano, Italy	Italy	Belgium	4–1
1964	Merano, Italy	Italy	West Germany	5–0
1965	Merano, Italy	Italy	Sweden	3–0
1966	Florence	Sweden	Italy	4–1
1967	Avesta, Sweden	France	Sweden	3–2
1968	Paris	USA	France	5–0
1969	St Louis	USA	Sweden	4–1
1970	Cleveland	USA	Sweden	4–1
1971	La Costa, California	USA	Sweden	3–2
1972	Le Touquet	USA	France	4–1
1973	New York	Australia	USA	3–1
1974	New York	USA	Australia	3–2
1975	New York	Australia	USA	5–0
1976	Alassio, Italy	Italy	Canada	3–2
1977	New York	USA	France	4–1
1978	New York	USA	Australia	4–1
1979	Vienna	Austria	USA	3–2
1980	Cervia, Italy	Sweden	Austria	2–1
1981	Buenos Aires	USA	Great Britain	2–1
1982	Athens	USA	Great Britain	2–1
1983	New York	USA	West Germany	2–1
1984	Bastad	West Germany	USA	3–0
1985	Perth	West Germany	Australia	2–1
1986	Berlin	West Germany	Switzerland	3–0
1987	Poertschach	Italy	Austria	2–1
1988	Huntington Beach, Cal.	USA	West Germany	3–0
1989	Montevideo	USA	West Germany	2–1
1990	Bol, Yugoslavia	Germany	USA	2–1

* From 1958 to 1979 the early rounds were played zonally

AUSTRIA CUP
International Men's Team Competition for Over 55s

	VENUE	WINNERS	RUNNERS-UP	FINAL SCORE
1977	Baden b. Wien	Great Britain	Austria	2–1
1978	Brand (Austria)	USA	Sweden	2–1
1979	Brand (Austria)	USA	Sweden	3–0
1980	Brand (Austria)	USA	Sweden	2–1
1981	Poertsachach	USA	Sweden	3–0
1982	Cervia, Italy	Australia	USA	2–1
1983	New York	Australia	USA	2–1
1984	Poertschach	USA	Australia	2–1
1985	Perth	Australia	USA	3–0
1986	Poertschach	Australia	Canada	2–1
1987	Umag	Canada	Australia	3–0
1988	Huntington Beach, Cal.	Canada	West Germany	3–0
1989	Buenos Aires	Canada	USA	2–1
1990	Poertschach	Canada	USA	3–0

YOUNG CUP
International Women's Team Competition for Over 40s

	VENUE	WINNERS	RUNNERS-UP	FINAL SCORE
1977	Malmo	Argentina	Not available	
1978	Ancona	Italy	Not available	
1979	Cannes	West Germany	USA	3–0
1980	Bad Wiessee, Germany	West Germany	Italy	3–0
1981	Bad Wiessee, Germany	France	Italy	2–1
1982	Brand, Austria	France	Italy	3–0
1983	Cervia, Italy	West Germany	France	2–1
1984	Cervia, Italy	USA	France	3–0
1985	Poertschach, Austria	West Germany	France	3–0
1986	Brand	West Germany	USA	2–1
1987	Venice	France	USA	2–1
1988	Bagnoles de l'Orne, France	Great Britain	West Germany	3–0
1989	Poertschach	France	West Germany	3–0
1990	Keszthely, Hungary	France	USA	3–0

MARIA ESTHER BUENO CUP
International Women's Team Competition for Over 50s

	VENUE	WINNERS	RUNNERS-UP	FINAL SCORE
1983	Poertschach	Great Britain	USA	2–1
1984	Le Touquet, France	USA	France	3–0
1985	Bremen	USA	Great Britain	3–0
1986	Brand	USA	Great Britain	2–1
1987	Helsinki	USA	Great Britain	2–1
1988	Bahia	USA	Canada	2–1
1989	Bournemouth	USA	Great Britain	2–1
1990	Barcelona	Australia	Spain	2–1

ITALIA CUP
International Men's Team Competition for Over 35s

	VENUE	WINNERS	RUNNERS-UP	FINAL SCORE
1982	Cervia, Italy	Italy	USA	2–1
1983	Cervia, Italy	West Germany	USA	2–1
1984	Brand, Austria	West Germany	France	2–1
1985	Reggio Calabria, Italy	USA	Italy	2–0
1986	Normandy, France	West Germany	USA	3–0
1987	Grado	USA	Austria	2–1
1988	Bol, Yugoslavia	West Germany	USA	3–0
1989	Mainz, W. Germany	West Germany	USA	3–0
1990	Glasgow	Spain	Australia	2–1

BRITANNIA CUP
International Men's Team Competition for Over 65s

	VENUE	WINNERS	RUNNERS-UP	FINAL SCORE
1979	Queen's Club, London	USA	Great Britain	3–0
1980	Frinton-on-Sea	USA	Sweden	3–0
1981	Hurlingham Club, London	USA	Sweden	3–0
1982	New York	USA	Canada	3–0
1983	Poertschach	USA	Australia	3–0
1984	Poertschach	USA	Australia	3–0
1985	Poertschach	USA	Australia	3–0
1986	Bournemouth	USA	Norway	3–0
1987	Bastad	USA	Sweden	2–1
1988	Huntington Beach, Cal.	USA	France	3–0
1989	Umag	USA	France	3–0
1990	Bournemouth	USA	Australia	2–1

Who will ever forget the emotional scenes at centenary Wimbledon in 1977 when Virginia Wade at last won her national title at the 16th attempt in front of the Queen whose jubilee year it was? It was as if fate had decreed that this great athlete should be accorded one last triumph to crown a glittering but erratic career that had thrilled a nation for a full decade.
(R & A Photofeatures)

THE CRAWFORD CUP
International Men's Team Competition for Over 75s

	VENUE	WINNERS	RUNNERS-UP	FINAL SCORE
1983	Brand, Austria	USA	Sweden	3–0
1984	Helsinki, Finland	USA	Great Britain	3–0
1985	Brand, Austria	USA	Australia	3–0
1986	Seefeld, Austria	USA	France	3–0
1987	Poertschach	USA	Great Britain	3–0
1988	Keszthely, Hungary	USA	Great Britain	3–0
1989	Bol	USA	Brazil	3–0
1990	Brand, Austria	USA	Brazil	3–0

ALICE MARBLE CUP
International Women's Team Competition for Over 60s

	VENUE	WINNERS	RUNNERS-UP	FINAL SCORE
1988	Poertschach	USA	West Germany	3–0
1989	Brand	USA	West Germany	2–1
1990	Paderborn, Germany	USA	Germany	2–1

GOTTFRIED VON CRAMM CUP
International Men's Team Competition for Over 60s

	VENUE	WINNERS	RUNNERS-UP	FINAL SCORE
1989	Kempten	Australia	New Zealand	3–0
1990	Ontario	USA	Austria	2–1

AUSTRALIAN INTERNATIONAL JUNIOR CHAMPIONSHIPS
BOYS' SINGLES

1946	F. Sedgman	1956	R. Mark	1965	G. Goven
1947	D. Candy	1957	R. Laver	1966	K. Coombes
1948	K. McGregor	1958	M. Mulligan	1967	B. Fairlie (NZL)
1949	C. Wilderspin	1959	E. Buchholz (USA)	1968	P. Dent
1950	K. Rosewall	1060	W. Coghlan	1969	A. McDonald
1951	L. Hoad	1961	J. Newcombe	1970	J. Alexander
1952	K. Rosewall	1962	J. Newcombe	1971	C. Letcher
1953	W. Gilmour	1963	J. Newcombe	1972	P. Kronk
1954	W. Knight	1964	A. Roche	1973	P. McNamee
1955	G. Moss				

	WINNER	RUNNER-UP	SCORE		
1974	H. Brittain				
1975	B. Drewett (AUS)				
1976	R. Kelly				
1977	(Jan.) B. Drewett (AUS)				
1977	(Dec.) R. Kelly				
1978	P. Serrett (AUS)	C. Johnstone (AUS)	6–4	6–3	
1979	G. Whitecross (AUS)	C. Miller (AUS)	6–4	6–3	
1980	C. Miller (AUS)	W. Masur (AUS)	7–6	6–2	
1981	J. Windahl (SWE)	P. Cash (AUS)	6–4	6–4	
1982	M. Kratzman (AUS)	S. Youl (AUS)	6–3	7–5	
1983	S. Edberg (SWE)	S. Youl (AUS)	6–4	6–4	
1984	M. Kratzman (AUS)	P. Flyn (AUS)	6–4	6–1	
1985	S. Barr (AUS)	S. Furlong (AUS)	7–6	6–7	6–3
1986	*Not held*				
1987	J. Stoltenberg (AUS)	T. Woodbridge (AUS)	6–2	7–6	
1988	J. Anderson (AUS)	A. Florent (AUS)	7–5	7–6	
1989	N. Kulti (SWE)	T. Woodbridge (AUS)	6–2	6–0	
1990	D. Dier (FRG)	L. Paes (IND)	6–4	7–6	

GIRLS' SINGLES

1946	S. Grant	1956	L. Coghlan	1965	K. Melville
1947	J. Tuckfield	1957	M. Rayson	1966	K. Krantzcke
1948	B. Penrose	1958	J. Lehane	1967	A. Kenny
1949	J. Warnock	1959	J. Lehane	1968	L. Hunt
1950	B. McIntyre	1960	L. Turner	1969	L. Hunt
1951	M. Carter	1961	R. Ebbern	1970	E. Goolagong
1952	M. Carter	1962	R. Ebbern	1971	P. Coleman
1953	J. Staley	1963	R. Ebbern	1972	P. Coleman
1954	E. Orton	1964	K. Dening	1973	C. O'Neill
1955	E. Orton				

	WINNER	RUNNER-UP	SCORE
1974	J. Walker		
1975	S. Barker (GBR)		
1976	S. Saliba (AUS)		
1977	(Jan.) P. Bailey		
1977	(Dec.) A. Tobin (AUS)		
1978	E. Little (AUS)	S. Leo (AUS)	6–1 6–2
1979	A. Minter (AUS)	S. Leo (AUS)	6–4 6–3
1980	A. Minter (AUS)	E. Sayers (AUS)	6–4 6–2
1981	A. Minter (AUS)	C. Vanier (FRA)	6–4 6–2
1982	A. Brown (GBR)	P. Paradis (FRA)	6–3 6–4
1983	A. Brown (GBR)	B. Randall (AUS)	7–6 6–3
1984	A. Croft (GBR)	H. Dahlstrom (SWE)	6–0 6–1
1985	J. Byrne (AUS)	L. Field (AUS)	6–1 6–3
1986	Not held		
1987	M. Jaggard (AUS)	N. Provis (AUS)	6–2 6–4
1988	J. Faull (AUS)	E. Derly (FRA)	6–4 6–4
1989	K. Kessaris (USA)	A. Farley (USA)	6–1 6–2
1990	M. Maleeva (BUL)	L. Stacey (AUS)	7–5 6–7 6–1

BOYS' DOUBLES

	WINNERS	RUNNERS-UP	SCORE
1983	J. Harty (AUS)/D. Tyson (AUS)	A. Lane (AUS)/D. Cahill (AUS)	3–6 6–4 6–3
1984	M. Kratzman (AUS)/M. Baroch (AUS)	B. Custer (AUS)/D. Macpherson (AUS)	6–2 5–7 7–5
1985	B. Custer (AUS)/D. Macpherson (AUS)	C. Suk (TCH)/P. Korda (TCH)	7–5 6–2
1986	Not held		
1987	J. Stoltenberg (AUS)/T. Woodbridge (AUS)	S. Barr (AUS)/D. Roe (AUS)	6–2 6–4
1988	J. Stoltenberg (AUS)/T. Woodbridge (AUS)	J. Anderson (AUS)/R. Fromberg (AUS)	6–3 6–2
1989	J. Anderson (AUS)/T. Woodbridge (AUS)	J. Morgan (AUS)/A. Kratzmann (AUS)	6–4 6–2
1990	R. Petterson (SWE)/M. Renstroem (SWE)	R. Janecek (CAN)/E. Munoz de Cote (MEX)	4–6 7–6 6–1

GIRLS' DOUBLES

	WINNERS	RUNNERS-UP	SCORE
1983	B. Randall (AUS)/K. Staunton (AUS)	J. Byrne (AUS)/J. Thompson (AUS)	3–6 6–3 6–3
1984	L. Field (AUS)/L. Savchenko (URS)	M. Parun (NZL)/J. Masters (AUS)	7–6 6–2
1985	J. Byrne (AUS)/J. Thompson (AUS)	A. Scott/S. McCann	6–0 6–3
1986	Not held		
1987	N. Provis (AUS)/A. Devries (BEL)	D. Jones (AUS)/G. Dwyer (AUS)	6–3 6–1
1988	R. McQuillan (AUS)/J. Faull (AUS)	R. Stubbs (AUS)/K. McDonald (AUS)	6–1 7–5
1989	A. Strnadova (TCH)/E. Sviglerova (TCH)	N. Pratt (AUS)/A. Woolcock (AUS)	6–2 6–0
1990	L. Zaltz (ISR)/R. Mayer (ISR)	J. Hodder (AUS)/N. Pratt (AUS)	6–4 6–4

FRENCH INTERNATIONAL JUNIOR CHAMPIONSHIPS

BOYS' SINGLES

	WINNER	RUNNER-UP	SCORE		
1974	C. Casa (FRA)	U. Marten (FRG)	2–6	6–1	6–4
1975	C. Roger-Vasselin (FRA)	P. Elter (FRG)	6–1	6–2	
1976	H. Gunthardt (SUI)	J. L. Clerc (ARG)	4–6	7–6	6–4
1977	J. P. McEnroe (USA)	R. Kelly (AUS)	6–1	6–1	
1978	I. Lendl (TCH)	P. Hjertquist (SWE)	7–6	6–4	
1979	R. Krishnan (IND)	B. Testerman (USA)	2–6	6–1	6–0
1980	H. Leconte (FRA)	A. Tous (ESP)	7–6	6–3	
1981	M. Wilander (SWE)	J. Brown	7–5	6–1	
1982	T. Benhabiles (FRA)	L. Courteau (FRA)	7–6	6–2	
1983	S. Edberg (SWE)	F. Fevrier (FRA)	6–4	7–6	
1984	K. Carlsson (SWE)	M. Kratzman (AUS)	6–3	6–3	
1985	J. Yzaga (PER)	T. Muster (AUT)	2–6	6–3	6–0
1986	G. Perez Roldan (ARG)	S. Grenier (FRA)	4–6	6–3	6–2
1987	G. Perez Roldan (ARG)	J. Stoltenberg (AUS)	6–3	3–6	6–1
1988	N. Pereira (VEN)	M. Larsson (SWE)	7–6	6–3	
1989	F. Santoro (FRA)	J. Palmer (USA)	6–3	3–6	9–7
1990	A. Gaudenzi (ITA)	T. Enqvist (SWE)	2–6	7–6	6–4

GIRLS' SINGLES

	WINNER	RUNNER-UP	SCORE		
1974	M. Simionescu (RUM)	S. Barker (GBR)	6–3	6–3	
1975	R. Marsikova (TCH)	L. Mottram (GBR)	6–3	5–7	6–2
1976	M. Tyler (GBR)	M. Zoni (ITA)	6–1	6–3	
1977	A. E. Smith (USA)	H. Strachonova (TCH)	6–3	7–6	
1978	H. Mandlikova (TCH)	M. Rothschild (FRG)	6–1	6–1	
1979	L. Sandin (SWE)	M. L. Piatek (USA)	6–3	6–1	
1980	K. Horvath (USA)	K. Henry (USA)	6–2	6–2	
1981	B. Gadusek (USA)	H. Sukova (TCH)	6–7	6–1	6–4
1982	M. Maleeva (BUL)	P. Barg (USA)	7–5	6–2	
1983	P. Paradis (FRA)	D. Spence (USA)	7–6	6–3	
1984	G. Sabatini (ARG)	K. Maleeva (BUL)	6–3	5–7	6–3
1985	L. Garrone (ITA)	D. Van Rensburg (SAF)	6–1	6–3	
1986	P. Tarabini (ARG)	N. Provis (AUS)	6–3	6–3	
1987	N. Zvereva (URS)	J. Pospisilova(TCH)	6–1	6–0	
1988	J. Halard (FRA)	A. Farley (USA)	6–2	4–6	7–5
1989	J. Capriati (USA)	E. Sviglerova (TCH)	6–4	6–0	
1990	M. Maleeva (BUL)	T. Ignatieva (URS)	6–2	6–3	

BOYS' DOUBLES

	WINNERS	RUNNERS-UP	SCORE		
1983	M. Kratzman (AUS)/S. Youl (AUS)	A. Chesnokov (URS)/A. Olhovskiy (URS)	6–2	6–3	
1985	P. Korda (TCH)/C. Suk (TCH)	V. Godrichidze (URS)/V. Volkov (URS)	4–6	6–0	7–5
1986	F. Davin (ARG)/G. Perez-Roldan (ARG)	T. Carbonell (ESP)/J. Sanchez (ESP)	7–5	5–7	6–3
1987	J. Courier (USA)/J. Stark (USA)	F. Davin (ARG)/G. Perez-Roldan (ARG)	6–7	6–4	6–3
1988	J. Stoltenberg (AUS)/T. Woodbridge (AUS)	C. Coratti (ITA)/G. Ivanisevic (YUG)	7–6	7–5	
1989	J. Anderson (AUS)/T. Woodbridge (AUS)	L. Herrera (MEX)/M. Knowles (BAH)	6–3	4–6	6–2
1990	S. La Reau (CAN)/P. Le Blanc (CAN)	C. Marsh (AUS)/M. Ondruska (RSA)	7–6	6–7	9–7

GIRLS' DOUBLES

	WINNERS	RUNNERS-UP	SCORE		
1983	C. Anderholm (SWE)/H. Olsson (SWE)	K./M. Maleeva (BUL)	6–4	6–1	
1985	M.U Perez Roldan (ARG)/P. Tarabini (ARG)	A. Holikova (TCH)/R. Szrubakova (TCH)	6–3	5–7	6–4
1986	L. Meskhi (URS)/N. Zvereva (URS)	J. Novotna (TCH)/R. Rajchrtova (TCH)	1–6	6–3	6–0
1987	N. Medvedeva (URS)/N. Zvereva (URS)	M. Jaggard (AUS)/N. Provis (AUS)	6–3	6–3	
1988	A. Dechaume (FRA)/E. Derly (FRA)	J. Halard (FRA)/M. Laval (FRA)	6–4	3–6	6–3
1989	N. Pratt (AUS)/S.-T. Wang (TPE)	C. Caverzasio (ITA)/S. Farina (ITA)	7–5	3–6	8–6
1990	R. Dragomir (ROM)/I. Spirlea (ROM)	T. Ignatieva (URS)/I. Soukhova (URS)	6–3	6–1	

INTERNATIONAL WIMBLEDON JUNIOR CHAMPIONSHIPS

The event originated as an invitation tournament, boys' singles in 1947 and girls' singles in 1948. It became a championship event in 1975.

BOYS' SINGLES

1948	S. Stockenberg (SWE)	1957	J. I. Tattersall (GBR)	1966	V. Korotkov (URS)
1949	S. Stockenberg (SWE)	1958	E. Buchholz (USA)	1967	M. Orantes (ESP)
1950	J. A. T. Horn (GBR)	1959	T. Lejus (URS)	1968	J. G. Alexander (AUS)
1951	J. Kupferburger (RSA)	1960	A. R. Mandelstam (RSA)	1969	B. Bertram (RSA)
1952	R. K. Wilson (GBR)	1961	C. E. Graebner (USA)	1970	B. Bertram (RSA)
1953	W. A. Knight (GBR)	1962	S. Matthews (GBR)	1971	R. Kreiss (USA)
1954	R. Krishnan (IND)	1963	N. Kalogeropoulous (GRE)	1972	B. Borg (SWE)
1955	M. P. Hann (GBR)	1964	I. El Shafei (EGY)	1973	W. Martin (USA)
1956	R. Holmberg (USA)	1965	V. Korotkov (URS)	1974	W. Martin (USA)

	WINNER	RUNNER-UP	SCORE
1975	C. J. Lewis (NZL)	R. Ycaza (ECU)	6–1 6–4
1976	H. Gunthardt (SUI)	P. Elter (FRG)	6–4 7–5
1977	V. Winitsky (USA)	E. Teltscher (USA)	6–1 1–6 8–6
1978	I. Lendl (TCH)	J. Turpin (USA)	6–3 6–4
1979	R. Krishnan (IND)	D. Siegler (USA)	6–3 6–4
1980	T. Tulasne (FRA)	H. D. Beutel (FRG)	6–4 3–6 6–4
1981	M. Anger (USA)	P. Cash (AUS)	7–6 7–5
1982	P. Cash (AUS)	H. Sundstrom (SWE)	6–4 6–7 6–3
1983	S. Edberg (SWE)	J. Frawley (AUS)	6–3 7–6
1984	M. Kratzman (AUS)	S. Kruger (SAF)	6–4 4–6 6–3
1985	L. Lavalle	E. Velez (MEX)	6–4 6–4
1986	E. Velez (MEX)	J. Sanchez (ESP)	6–3 7–5
1987	D. Nargiso (ITA)	J. Stoltenberg (AUS)	7–6 6–4
1988	N. Pereira (VEN)	G. Raoux (FRA)	7–6 6–2
1989	N. Kulti (SWE)	T. Woodbridge (AUS)	6–4 6–3
1990	L. Paes (IND)	M. Ondruska (RSA)	7–6 6–2

GIRLS' SINGLES

1948	O. Miskova (TCH)	1952	ten Bosch (HOL)	1956	A. S. Haydon (GBR)
1949	C. Mercelis (BEL)	1953	D. Kilian (RSA)	1957	M. Arnold (USA)
1950	L. Cornell (GBR)	1954	V. A. Pitt (GBR)	1958	S. M. Moore (USA)
1951	L. Cornell (GBR)	1955	S. M. Armstrong (GBR)	1959	J. Cross (RSA)
1960	K. Hantze (USA)	1965	O. Morozova (URS)	1970	S. Walsh (USA)
1961	G. Baksheeva (URS)	1966	B. Lindstrom (FIN)	1971	M. Kroschina (URS)
1962	G. Baksheeva (URS)	1967	J. Salome (HOL)	1972	I. Kloss (RSA)
1963	D. M. Salfati (RSA)	1968	K. Pigeon (USA)	1973	A. Kiyomura (USA)
1964	P. Barkowicz (USA)	1969	K. Sawamatsu (JAP)	1974	M. Jausovec (YUG)

	WINNER	RUNNER-UP	SCORE
1975	N. Y. Chmyreva (URS)	R. Marsikova (TCH)	6–4 6–3
1976	N. Y. Chmyreva (URS)	M. Kruger (SAF)	6–3 2–6 6–1
1977	L. Antonoplis (USA)	Mareen Louie (USA)	6–5 6–1
1978	T. A. Austin (USA)	H. Mandlikova (TCH)	6–0 3–6 6–4
1979	M. L. Piatek (USA)	A. Moulton (USA)	6–1 6–3
1980	D. Freeman (AUS)	S. Leo (AUS)	7–6 7–5
1981	Z. Garrison (USA)	R. Uys (SAF)	6–4 3–6 6–0
1982	C. Tanvier (FRA)	H. Sukova (TCH)	6–2 7–5
1983	P. Paradis (FRA)	P. Hy (HKG)	6–2 6–1
1984	A. N. Croft (GBR)	E. Reinach (SAF)	3–6 6–3 6–2
1985	A. Holikova (TCH)	J. Byrne (AUS)	7–5 6–1
1986	N. Zvereva (URS)	L. Meskhi (URS)	2–6 6–2 9–7
1987	N. Zvereva (URS)	J. Halard (FRA)	6–4 6–4
1988	B. Schultz (HOL)	E. Derly (FRA)	7–6 6–1
1989	A. Strnadova (TCH)	M. McGrath (USA)	6–2 6–3
1990	A. Strnadova (TCH)	K. Sharpe (AUS)	6–2 6–4

BOYS' DOUBLES

	WINNERS	RUNNERS-UP	SCORE		
1982	P. Cash (AUS)/F. Frawley (AUS)	R. Leach (USA)/J. Ross (USA)	6–3	6–2	
1983	M. Kratzman (AUS)/S. Youl (AUS)	M. Nastase (RUM)/O. Rahnasto (FIN)	6–4	6–4	
1984	R. Brown (USA)/R. Weiss (USA)	M. Kratzman (AUS)/J. Svensson (SWE)	1–6	6–4	11–9
1985	A. Moreno (MEX)/J. Yzaga (PER)	P. Korda (TCH)/C. Suk (TCH)	7–6	6–4	
1986	T. Carbonell (ESP)/P. Korda (TCH)	S. Barr (AUS)/H. Karrasch (CAN)	6–1	6–1	
1987	J. Stoltenberg (AUS)/T. Woodbridge (AUS)	D. Nargiso (ITA)/E. Rossi (ITA)	6–3	7–6	
1988	J. Stoltenberg (AUS)/T. Woodbridge (AUS)	D. Rikl (TCH)/T. Zdrazila (TCH)	6–4	1–6	7–6
1989	J. Palmer (USA)/J. Stark (USA)	J.-L. De Jager (RSA)/W. Ferreira (RSA)	7–6	7–6	
1990	S. Lareau (CAN)/S. LeBlanc (CAN)	C. Marsh (RSA)/M. Ondruska (RSA)	7–6	4–6	6–3

GIRLS' DOUBLES

	WINNERS	RUNNERS-UP	SCORE		
1982	B. Herr (USA)/P. Barg (USA)	B. S. Gerken (USA)/G. Rush (USA)	6–1	6–4	
1983	P. Fendick (USA)/P. Hy (HKG)	C. Anderholm (SWE)/H. Olsson (SWE)	6–1	7–5	
1984	C. Kuhlman (USA)/S. Rehe (USA)	V. Milvidskaya (URS)/L. Savchenko (URS)	6–3	5–7	6–4
1985	L. Field (AUS)/J. Thompson (AUS)	E. Reinach (SAF)/J. Richardson (NZL)	6–1	6–2	
1986	M. Jaggard (AUS)/L. O'Neill (AUS)	L. Meskhi (URS)/N. Zvereva (URS)	7–6	6–4	
1987	N. Medvedeva (URS)/N. Zvereva (URS)	I. S. Kim (KOR)/P. M. Modena (HKG)	2–6	7–5	6–0
1988	J. Faull (AUS)/R. McQuillan (AUS)	A. Dechaume (FRA)/E. Derly (FRA)	4–6	6–2	6–3
1989	J. Capriati (USA)/M. McGrath (USA)	A. Strnadova (TCH)/E. Sviglerova (TCH)	6–4	6–2	
1990	K. Habsudova (TCH)/A. Strnadova (TCH)	N. Pratt (AUS)/K. Sharpe (AUS)	6–2	6–4	

US INTERNATIONAL JUNIOR CHAMPIONSHIPS

BOYS' SINGLES

	WINNER	RUNNER-UP	SCORE		
1974	W. Martin (USA)	F. Taygan (USA)	6–4	6–2	
1975	H. Schonfield (USA)	C. J. Lewis (NZL)	6–4	6–3	
1976	Y. Ycaza (ECU)	J. L. Clerc (ARG)	6–4	5–7	6–0
1977	V. Winitsky (USA)	E. Teltscher (USA)	6–4	6–4	
1978	P. Hjertquist (SWE)	S. Simonsson (SWE)	7–6	1–6	7–6
1979	S. Davis (USA)	J. Gunnarsson (SWE)	6–3	6–1	
1980	M. Falberg (USA)	E. Korita (USA)	6–0	6–2	
1981	T. Hogstedt (SWE)	H. Schwaier (FRG)	7–5	6–3	
1982	P. Cash (AUS)	G. Forget (FRA)	6–3	6–3	
1983	S. Edberg (SWE)	S. Youl (AUS)	6–2	6–4	
1984	M. Kratzman (AUS)	B. Becker (FRG)	6–3	7–6	
1985	T. Trigueiro (USA)	J. Blake (USA)	6–2	6–3	
1986	J. Sanchez (ESP)	F. Davin (ARG)	6–2	6–2	
1987	D. Wheaton (USA)	A. Cherkasov (URS)	7–5	6–0	
1988	N. Pereira (VEN)	N. Kulti (SWE)	6–1	6–2	
1989	J. Stark (USA)	N. Kulti (SWE)	6–4	6–1	
1990	A. Gaudenzi (ITA)	M. Tillstroem (SWE)	6–2	4–6	7–6

GIRLS' SINGLES

	WINNER	RUNNER-UP	SCORE		
1974	I. Kloss (SAF)	M. Jausovec (YUG)	6–4	6–3	
1975	N. T. Chmyreva (URS)	G. Stevens (SAF)	6–7	6–2	6–2
1976	M. Kruger (SAF)	L. Romanov (RUM)	6–3	7–5	
1977	C. Casabianca (ARG)	L. Antonoplis (USA)	6–3	2–6	6–2
1978	L. Siegel (USA)	I. Madruga (ARG)	6–4	6–4	
1979	A. Moulton (USA)	M. L. Piatek (USA)	7–6	7–6	
1980	S. Mascarin (USA)	K. Keil (USA)	6–3	6–4	
1981	Z. Garrison (USA)	K. Gompert (USA)	6–0	6–3	
1982	B. Herr (USA)	G. Rush (USA)	6–3	6–1	
1983	E. Minter (AUS)	M. Werdel (USA)	6–3	7–5	
1984	K. Maleeva (BUL)	N. Sodupe (USA)	6–1	6–2	
1985	L. Garrone (ITA)	A. Holikova (TCH)	6–2	7–6	
1986	E. Hakami (USA)	S. Stafford (USA)	6–2	6–1	

1987	N. Zvereva (URS)	S. Birch (USA)	6–0 6–3
1988	C. Cunningham (USA)	R. McQuillan (AUS)	6–3 6–1
1989	J. Capriati (USA)	R. McQuillan (AUS)	6–2 6–3
1990	M. Maleeva (BUL)	N. Van Lottum (FRA)	7–5 6–2

BOYS' DOUBLES

	WINNERS	RUNNERS-UP	SCORE
1982	J. Canter (USA)/M. Kures (USA)	P. Cash (AUS)/J. Frawley (AUS)	7–6 6–3
1983	M. Kratzman (AUS)/S. Youl (AUS)	P. McEnroe (USA)/B. Pearce (USA)	6–1 7–6
1984	L. Lavelle (MEX)/M. Nastase (RUM)	J. Icaza (PER)/A. Moreno (MEX)	7–6 1–6 6–1
1985	J. Blake (USA)/D. Yates (USA)	P. Flynn (USA)/D. McPherson (USA)	3–6 6–3 6–4
1986	T. Carbonell (ESP)/J. Sanchez (ESP)	J. Tarnago (USA)/D. Wheaton (USA)	6–4 1–6 6–1
1987	G. Ivanisevic (YUG)/D. Nargiso (ITA)	Z. Ali (IND)/B. Steven (NZL)	3–6 6–4 6–3
1988	J. Stark (USA)/J. Yoncey (USA)	M. Boscatta (ITA)/S. Pescosolido (ITA)	7–6 7–5
1989	W. Ferreira (RSA)/G. Stafford (RSA)	M. Damm (TCH)/J. Kodes (TCH)	6–3 6–4
1990	M. Renstroem (SWE)/M. Tillstroem (SWE)	S. LeBlanc (CAN)/G. Rusedski (CAN)	6–7 6–3 6–4

GIRLS' DOUBLES

	WINNERS	RUNNERS-UP	SCORE
1982	P. Barg (USA)/B. Herr (USA)	A. Hulbert (AUS)/B. Randall (AUS)	1–6 7–5 7–6
1983	A. Hulbert (AUS)/B. Randall (AUS)	N. Riva (URS)/L. Savchenko (URS)	6–4 6–2
1984	G. Sabatini (ARG)/M. Paz (MEX)	S. MacGregor (USA)/S. London (USA)	6–4 3–6 6–2
1985	R. Zrubakova (TCH)/A. Holikova (TCH)	P. Tarabini (ARG)/M. Perez Roldan (ARG)	6–4 2–6 7–5
1986	R. Zrubakova (TCH)/J. Novotna (TCH)	E. Brukhovets (URS)/L. Meskhi (URS)	6–4 6–2
1987	M. McGrath (USA)/K. Po (USA)	Il-Soon Kim (KOR)/Shi-Ting Wang (TPE)	6–4 7–5
1988	M. McGrath (USA)/K. Po (USA)	K. Caverzasio (ITA)/L. Lapi (ITA)	6–3 6–1
1989	J. Capriati (USA)/M. McGrath (USA)	J. Faull (AUS)/R. McQuillan (AUS)	6–0 6–3
1990	K. Godridge (AUS)/K. Sharpe (AUS)	E. deLone (USA)/L. Raymond (USA)	4–6 7–5 6–2

ITF JUNIOR WORLD RANKING LEADERS

BOYS' SINGLES
1978 Ivan Lendl (TCH)
1979 Raul Viver (ECU)
1980 Thierry Tulasne (FRA)
1981 Pat Cash (AUS)
1982 Guy Forget (FRA)
1983 Stefan Edberg (SWE)
1984 Mark Kratzman (AUS)
1985 Claudio Pistolesi (ITA)
1986 Javier Sanchez (ESP)
1987 Jason Stoltenberg (AUS)
1988 Nicolas Pereira (VEN)
1989 Nicklas Kulti (SWE)
1990 Andrea Gaudenzi (ITA)

GIRLS' SINGLES
1978 Hana Mandlikova (TCH)
1979 Mary-Lou Piatek (USA)
1980 Susan Mascarin (USA)
1981 Zina Garrison (USA)
1982 Gretchen Rush (USA)
1983 Pascale Paradis (FRA)
1984 Gabriela Sabatini (ARG)
1985 Laura Garrone (USA)
1986 Patricia Tarabini (ARG)
1987 Natalia Zvereva (URS)
1988 Cristina Tessi (ARG)
1989 Florencia Labat (ARG)
1990 Karina Habsudova (TCH)

BOYS' DOUBLES
1982 Fernando Perez (MEX)
1983 Mark Kratzman (AUS)
1984 Augustin Moreno (MEX)
1985 Petr Korda (TCH) and Cyril Suk (TCH)
1986 Tomas Carbonell (ESP)
1987 Jason Stoltenberg (AUS)
1988 David Rikl (TCH) and Tomas Zdrazila (TCH)
1989 Wayne Ferreira (RSA)
1990 Marten Renstroem (SWE)

GIRLS' DOUBLES
1982 Beth Herr (USA)
1983 Larisa Savchenko (URS)
1984 Mercedes Paz (ARG)
1985 Mariana Perez Roldan (ARG) and Patricia Tarabini (ARG)
1986 Leila Meskhi (URS)
1987 Natalia Medvedeva (URS)
1988 JoAnne Faull (AUS)
1989 Andrea Strnadova (TCH)
1990 Karina Habsudova (TCH)

WORLD YOUTH CUP

International Team Championship for boys and girls aged 16 and under. Early rounds played zonally.

BOYS' FINALS

1985 *Australia d. USA 2–1, Kobe Japan:* R. Fromberg lost to F. Montana 2–6 2–6; S. Barr d. J. A. Falbo 6–4 6–4; Barr/J. Stoltenberg d. Montana/Falbo 4–6 6–7 7–5.

1986 *Australia d. USA 2–1, Tokyo, Japan:* J. Stoltenberg d. J. Courier 6–2 6–4; R. Fromberg lost to M. Chang 4–6 4–6; Stoltenberg/T. Woodbridge d. Courier/Kass 7–6 6–2.

1987 *Australia d. Netherlands 3–0, Freiburg, West Germany:* T. Woodbridge d. P. Dogger 7–5 3–6 6–2; J. Anderson d. F. Wibier 6–0 6–1; J. Morgan/Woodbridge d. Dogger/Wibier 6–3 6–2.

1988 *Czechoslovakia d. USA 2–1:* J. Kodes d. J. Leach 7–6 6–2; M. Damm d. B. MacPhie 6–2 6–7 6–4; Damm/L. Hovorka lost to W. Bull/Leach 4–6 4–6.

1989 *West Germany d. Czechoslovakia 2–1:* S. Gessner lost to L. Thomas 5–7 5–7; G. Paul d. P. Gazda 6–4 6–4; Paul/D. Prinosil d. Gazda/Thomas 7–5 6–1.

1990 *USSR d. Australia 2–1:* D. Thomashevitch d. T. Vasiliadis 6–3 6–2; A. Medvedev lost to G. Doyle 6–2 4–6 5–7; E. Kafelnikov/Medvedev d. Doyle/B. Sceney 7–6 6–3.

GIRLS' FINALS

1985 *Czechoslovakia d. Australia 3–0, Kobe, Japan:* J. Pospisilova d. S. McCann 6–4 6–4; R. Zrubakova d. N. Provis 7–6 7–5; Pospisilova/Zrubakova d. Provis/W. Frazer 7–5 6–4.

1986 *Belgium d. Czechoslovakia 2–1, Tokyo, Japan:* A. Devries d. R. Zrubakova 6–3 6–4; S. Wasserman d. P. Langrova 6–4 7–5; Devries/C. Neuprez lost to Langrova/Zrubakova 4–6 2–6.

1987 *Australia d. USSR 2–1, Freiburg, West Germany:* J. Faull lost to N. Medvedeva 6–4 2–6 2–6; R. McQuillan d. E. Brioukhovets 3–6 6–2 6–3; Faull/McQuillan d. Brioukhovets/Medvedeva 6–3 6–1.

1988 *Australia d. Argentina 3–0:* K. A. Guse d. F. Haumuller 7–6 6–4; L. Guse d. C. Tessi 7–6 1–6 6–2; K. A. Guse/K. Sharpe d. I. Gorrachategui/Tessi 6–0 6–2.

1989 *West Germany d. Czechoslovakia 2–1:* M. Skulj-Zivec d. K. Matouskova 6–0 7–5; A. Huber d. K. Habsudova 6–0 6–3; K. Duell/Skulj-Zivec lost to Habsudova/P. Kucova 3–6 0–6.

1990 *Netherlands d. USSR 2–1:* P. Kamstra d. I. Soukhova 6–1 7–6; L. Niemantsverdriet lost to T. Ignatieva 0–6 6–1 4–6; Kamstra/Niemantsverdriet d. Ignatieva/Soukhova 6–3 4–6 6–1.

ORANGE BOWL

International 18 and Under Championship played in Miami each December.

BOYS' SINGLES

	WINNER	RUNNER-UP	SCORE				
1974	W. Martin (USA)	T. Smid (TCH)	6–7	4–6	6–2	6–1	7–6
1975	F. Luna (ESP)	B. E. Gottfried (USA)	6–4	6–4			
1976	J. P. McEnroe (USA)	E. Teltscher (USA)	7–5	6–1			
1977	I. Lendl (TCH)	Y. Noah (FRA)	4–6	7–6	6–3		
1978	G. Urpi (ESP)	S. van der Merwe (SAF)	6–3	6–1			
1979	R. Viver (ECU)	P. Arraya (PER)	7–6	6–4			
1980	J. Nystrom (SWE)	C. Castqtellan (ARG)	7–5	7–6			
1981	R. Arguello (ARG)	R. Joaquim (BRA)	6–2	6–1			
1982	G. Forget (FRA)	J. Bardou (ESP)	7–5	2–6	6–1		
1983	K. Carlsson (SWE)	E. Sanchez (ESP)	6–2	6–4			
1984	R. Brown (USA)	J. Berger (USA)	6–3	6–3			
1985	C. Pistolesi (ITA)	B. Oresar (YUG)	6–2	6–0			
1986	J. Sanchez (ESP)	A. Parker (USA)	6–3	6–4			
1987	J. Courier (USA)	A. Cherkasov (URS)	6–3	6–2			
1988	M. Rosset (USA)	S. Pescosolido (ITA)	7–6	3–6	6–1		
1989	F. Meligeni (ARG)	G. Lopez (ESP)	7–6	7–6			
1990	A. Medvedev (URS)	O. Fernandez (MEX)	6–4	2–6	6–2		

GIRLS' SINGLES

	WINNER	RUNNER-UP	SCORE		
1974	L. Epstein (USA)	C. Penn (USA)	6–1	6–2	
1975	L. Epstein (USA)	S. McInerny (USA)	6–2	6–1	
1976	M. Kruger (SAF)	A. .E. Smith (USA)	2–6	6–3	6–4
1977	A. E. Smith (USA)	H. Strachonova (TCH)	7–6	7–5	
1978	A. Jaeger (USA)	R. Fairbank (SAF)	6–1	6–3	
1979	K. Horvath (USA)	P. Murgo (ITA)	7–5	6–0	
1980	S. Mascarin (USA)	R. Sasak (YUG)	6–3	3–6	6–4
1981	P. Barg (USA)	H. Fukarkova (TCH)	6–2	6–3	
1982	C. Bassett (CAN)	M. Maleeva (BUL)	6–4	ret'd	

1983	D. Spence (USA)	A. Cecchini (ITA)	2–6 7–5 6–4
1984	G. Sabatini (ARG)	K. Maleeva (BUL)	6–1 6–3
1985	M. J. Fernandez (USA)	P. Tarabini (ARG)	7–5 6–1
1986	P. Tarabini (ARG)	B. Fulco (ARG)	6–2 6–2
1987	N. Zvereva (URS)	L. Lapi (ITA)	6–2 6–0
1988	C. Cunningham (USA)	L. Lapi (ITA)	6–0 6–1
1989	L. Spadea (USA)	S. Albinus (DEN)	6–0 6–3
1990	P. Perez (ESP)	S. Ramon (ESP)	6–1 7–6

GALEA CUP

International Men's Team Competition for players aged 20 and under.

FINAL ROUNDS

Played at Deauville

1950 Italy d. France 4–1: U. Bergamo d. R. L. Haillet 6–2 6–3, d. A. Lemyze 8–10 7–5 7–5; F. Gardini d. Lemyze 6–1 6–2; A. Parri lost to F. Nys 3–6 2–6; Gardini/H. Clerici d. Lemyze/Nys 6–1 6–3.

1951 France d. West Germany 5–0: A. Lemyze d. B. Pottinger 8–6 10–8; R. L. Haillet d. F. Feldbausch 6–4 6–4; G. Pilet d. C. Biederlack 1–6 6–2 6–2; P. Darmon d. J. Gulcz 6–4 1–6 6–1; Haillet/Lemyze d. Feldbausch/Pottinger 6–1 6–3 6–1.

Played at Vichy

1952 Italy d. France 4–1: N. Pietrangeli d. X. Perreau-Saussine 6–8 6–2 6–2, d. G. Pilet 7–5 6–1; A. Maggi lost to Pilet 3–6 6–2 3–6, d. Perreau-Saussine 6–4 7–5; Maggi/Pietrangeli d. J. N. Grinda/Pilet 10–8 6–3 6–3.

1953 France d. Italy 4–1: G. Pilet d. N. Pietrangeli 5–7 6–1 6–0, d. S. Jacobini 6–2 6–4; J. N. Grinda d. Jacobini 6–0 6–2, d. Pietrangeli 6–4 6–1; P. Darmon/Pilet lost to M. Pirro/Pietrangeli 3–6 5–7 7–9.

1954 Italy d. Yugoslavia 3–2: S. Jacobini d. L. Jagec 6–2 7–5, d. L. Backor 6–3 4–6 7–5; M. Pirro lost to Backor 6–3 4–6 4–6, lost to Jagec 0–6 5–7; Jacobsini/Pirro d. Backor/Jagec 10–8 4–6 6–4 6–3.

1955 Italy d. Spain 5–0: S. Jacobini d. A. Gimeno 3–6 6–3 6–4; F. Bonetti d. J. Moure 6–1 6–4; G. Morelli d. Moure 6–2 6–4; M. Drisaldi d. M. Santana 6–4 6–4; Drisaldi/Jacobini d. A. Arilla/Gimeno 6–3 6–4 2–6 6–1.

1956 Spain d. Italy 4–1: M. Santana d. F. Bonetti 6–3 5–7 7–5, d. G. Bonairi 4–6 6–5 7–5; A. Gimeno d. Bonetti 6–3 6–2, d. Bonairi 5–7 6–2 6–3: A. Arilla/A. Gimeno lost to M. Drisaldi/A. Maggi 6–1 4–6 3–6 3–6.

1957 Spain d. Italy 4–1: M. Santana d. G. Morelli 9–7 6–4, d. E. Casini 6–4 6–4; A. Gimeno d. F. Bonetti 6–3 6–4; J. L. Arilla lost to Morelli 3–6 6–8; A. Arilla/Gimeno d. Bonetti/Maggi 6–3 6–3.

1958 Spain d. West Germany 3–2: M. Santana d. W. Bungert 6–3 7–5 4–6 6–0, lost to D. Eklebe 1–6 5–7 6–1 3–6; A. Arilla d. Eklebe 6–1 9–7 4–6 7–5; J. Gisbert lost to W. Stuck 0–6 2–6 0–6; A. Arilla/Santana d. Eklebe/Stuck 7–6 6–3 6–3.

1959 West Germany d. USSR 4–1: W. Stuck d. A. Pontanin 6–3 6–0 6–1, d. T. Lejus 6–4 6–1 6–0; W. Bungert d. Lejus 6–2 6–3 6–2; L. Sanders lost to Pontanin 4–6 3–6 6–1 7–5 2–6; Bungert/Stuck d. Lejus/S. Likachev 6–4 5–7 3–6 7–5 6–4.

1960 France d. USSR 3–2: A. Bresson d. S. Likachev 6–3 6–2 6–4, d. T. Lejus 2–6 3–6 6–3 6–0 6–3; C. Duxin lost to Lejus 5–7 4–6 8–10, lost to Likachev 2–6 3–6 1–6; D. Contet/F. Jauffret d. Lejus/Likachev 8–6 6–2 4–6 6–2.

1961 France d. Spain 3–2: C. Duxin lost to J. Gisbert 1–6 3–6 2–6, d. T. Casado 6–2 6–1 6–1; F. Jauffret d. Casado 6–3 6–2 6–3, lost to Gisbert 6–1 4–6 3–6 6–4 3–6; D. Contet/Jauffret d. J. L. Arilla/Gisbert 6–2 6–0 6–2.

1962 France d. USSR 3–2: J. C. Barclay d. S. Mdzinarichvili 6–4 6–2 6–4, d. A. Metreveli 6–4 6–2 8–6; F. Jauffret lost to Metreveli 6–3 2–6 3–6 4–6, d. Mdzinarichvili 8–6 6–1 0–6 6–2; C. Duxin/Jauffret lost to Mdzinarichvili/Metreveli 8–6 3–6 4–6 5–7.

1963 Czechoslovakia d. Italy 3–2: S. Koudelka lost to G. Maioli 3–6 6–4 3–6 5–7; d. G. Di Maso 6–4 6–2 6–2; M. Holecek d. Di Maso 6–4 11–9 6–4, d. Maioli 6–0 6–3 8–6; Holecek/Koudelka lost to Di Maso/Maioli 6–8 4–6 9–7 7–9.

1964 USSR d. Czechoslovakia 3–2: A. Metreveli d. J. Kodes 6–3 6–3 4–6 17–15, d. S. Koudelka 6–1 6–4 6–1; A. Ivanov lost to Koudelka 6–4 8–10 6–8 2–6, lost to Kodes 7–5 6–4 8–10 6–8 3–6; Ivanov/Metreveli d. Koudelka/F. Pala 6–4 5–7 9–7 8–6.

1965 Czechoslovakia d. USSR 3–2: J. Kodes lost to A. Ivanov 5–7 6–3 6–3 2–6 1–6, d. V. Korotkov 6–2 5–7 7–5 6–1; M. Laudin d. Korotkov 6–2 9–7 6–0, lost to Ivanov 8–10 2–6 2–6; Kodes/J. Stoces d. Ivanov/Korotkov 6–2 6–3 6–1.

1966 Czechoslovakia d. USSR 4–1: J. Kodes d. S. Kakoulia 6–3 6–1 6–1; M. Laudin d. V. Korotkov 6–2 3–6 6–1 6–4, lost to Kakoulia 1–6 0–6 7–5 3–6; Kodes/J. Medonos d. A. Egorov/Korotkov 6–4 6–3 6–1.

1967 France d. Great Britain 3–1: J. B. Chanfreau d. G. Battrick 6–4 6–3 4–6 7–5, d. D. A. Lloyd 6–2 6–3 6–8 7–5; G. Goven d. D. A. Lloyd 3–6 6–3 6–2 6–2; Goven/Chanfreau d. Battrick/Lloyd 8–10 6–3 6–4 6–2.

1968 Spain d. France 3–2: M. Orantes d. G. Goven 6–4 6–2 6–3, d. P. Proisy 6–1 10–8 6–3; A. Munoz lost to Proisy 6–4 9–11 6–8 6–3 1–6, d. Goven 6–2 3–6 6–3 4–6 7–5; Munoz/Orantes lost to Goven/P. Dominguez 1–6 6–0 1–6 1–6.

1969 Spain d. Czechoslovakia 3–2: A. Munoz d. P. Hutka 1–6 6–3 6–1 6–3; M. Orantes d. J. Hrebec 6–2 6–4 7–5; J. Gisbert lost to Hutka 2–6 6–2 3–6 4–6; A. Muntanola lost to J. Pisecki 3–6 1–6 5–7; Munoz/Orantes d. Hrebec/Hutka 5–7 6–3 6–1 6–4.

1970 Czechoslovakia d. Spain 3–2: I. Pisecki lost to A. Munoz 7–5 4–6 4–6 2–6, d. A. Riba 6–1 6–2 6–2; J. Hrebec d. Riba 6–3 6–2 6–0, lost to Munoz 3–6 3–6 8–6 1–6; Hrebec/Pisecki d. Munoz/Riba 6–3 6–2 6–0.

1971 Sweden d. France 5–0: K. Johansson d. J. Lovera 6–1 0–6 6–1 6–3, d. E. Deblicker 10–12 6–4 6–3 1–6 7–5; T. Svensson d. Deblicker 6–2 6–2 6–2, d. Lovera 5–7 7–5 8–6; K./L. Johansson d. Naegelen/J. F. Caujoulle 6–4 6–4 6–2.

1972 Great Britain d. Spain 4–1: C. J. Mottram d. J. Herrera 6–1 4–6 6–0 2–6 7–5; S. Warboys d. J. Higueras 6–2 6–2 1–6 6–3, d. Herrera 6–3 6–2 0–6 2–6 7–5; J. M. Lloyd d. Higueras 6–2 10–8; Mottram/Warboys lost to Higueras/J. Moreno 6–3 3–6 4–6 6–1 5–7.

1973 *Spain d. Great Britain 4–1:* J. Higueras d. J. M. Lloyd 4–6 6–2 6–2 0–6 6–4; J. Moreno d. C. J. Mottram 3–6 3–6 6–3 6–1 6–3, d. Lloyd 6–1 6–1 6–3; Higueras/Moreno lost to S. Warboys/M. J. Farrell 7–9 3–6 2–6.

1974 *Czechoslovakia d. Spain 4–1:* P. Slozil d. S. Cabeza 6–4 6–2 6–1; T. Smid d. J. Soler 0–6 6–4 6–0 11–9, d. J. Garcia 6–3 1–6 6–3; J. Granat lost to A. Gimenez 4–6 2–6; Slozil/Smid d. Gimenez/Soler 6–4 6–2 6–4.

1975 *Czechoslovakia d. Spain 3–2:* T. Smid d. A. Gimenez 6–1 4–6 3–6 6–2 6–2, d. M. Mir 3–6 8–6 6–2 7–5; P. Slozil d. Mir 8–6 3–6 6–3 6–2, lost to A. Gimenez 4–6 8–6 1–6 5–7; Slozil/Smid lost to Gimenez/Mir 8–6 6–4 3–6 2–6 1–6.

1976 *West Germany d. Italy 3–2:* W. Zirngibl lost to F. Merlone 2–6 2–6 7–5 4–6, d. G. Ocleppo 6–1 6–1 6–4; P. Elter lost to Ocleppo 2–6 2–6 6–2 4–6, d. Merlone 6–3 3–6 6–4 6–4; U. Marten/K. Eberhard d. V. Vattuone/G. Marchetti 3–6 6–3 6–4 6–4.

1977 *Argentina d. France 3–2:* F. Dalla Fontana lost to C. Roger-Vasselin 4–6 6–1 4–6 4–6, d. C. Casa 6–3 7–6 6–3; J. L. Clerc lost to Casa 4–6 5–7 6–2 4–6 4; d. Roger-Vasselin 6–3 6–0 6–4; Clerc/A. Gattiker d. D. Bedel/Noah 2–6 4–6 7–5 6–1 6–4.

1978 *France d. Czechoslovakia 4–1:* Y. Noah d. D. Kulhaj 6–1 6–4 6–4; P. Portes d. I. Lendl 8–6 4–6 6–2 6–2; G. Morreton lost to Lendl 3–6 13–15; Portes d. M. Lacek 6–2 6–1; Morreton/Noah d. Kulhaj/Lendl 9–7 6–1 5–7 3–6 6–4.

1979 *France d. Czechoslovakia 3–2:* Y. Noah d. M. Lacek 6–3 6–1 6–1, d. D. Pohl 6–3 6–2 6–2; P. Portes lost to I. Lendl 1–6 3–6 5–7; T. Pham lost to Lacek 3–6 1–6; Noah/Portes d. Lacek/Lendl 14–12 5–7 8–6 7–5.

1980 *France d. Spain 3–2:* T. Tulasne d. A. Tous 6–4 6–3 6–2, d. J. B. Avendano 6–2 6–2 6–1; J. Potier lost to Avendano 6–8 2–6 2–6, lost to Tous 2–6 3–6; H. Leconte/Potier d. Avendano/Tous 6–0 7–5 3–6 6–1.

1981 *West Germany d. Australia 5–0:* C. Zipf d. G. Whitecross 5–7 7–5 9–11 6–2 6–2, d. C. Miller 8–6 3–6 11–9; H. D. Beutel d. Miller 3–6 8–6 6–2 6–1, d. Whitecross 6–4 6–2; Beutel/Zipf d. P. Doohan/Miller 6–4 7–5 6–2.

1982 *Australia d. Spain 3–2:* P. Cash d. A. Tous 4–6 6–2 8–10 6–4 6–1, lost to S. Casal 0–6 1–6; C. Miller d. Casal 6–4 1–6 9–7 6–3, lost to Tous 5–7 1–6; Cash/Miller d. Casal/M. Jaite 6–4 6–1 6–4.

1983 *France d. Spain 5–0:* G. Forget d. J. Bardou 6–2 6–2 5–7 4–6 10–8, d. M. Jaite 7–6 6–3; L. Courteau d. Jaite 6–4 10–8 3–6 6–2, d. Bardou 6–3 4–6 6 4; Courteau/Forget d. Bardou/Jaite 6–2 6–3 6–4.

1984 *Czechoslovakia d. Argentina 4–1:* M. Mecir d. G. Garetto 6–3 2–6 6–8 6–0 6–2, d. E. Masso 7–5 6–3; M. Vajda d. Masso 6–2 8–6 6–2, lost to Garetto 9–7 6–1; Mecir/K. Novacek d. Masso/Mena 6–4 6–4 6–1.

1985 *Italy d. USA 3–2:* P. Cane d. L. Jensen 6–2 6–1 8–6, d. R. Reneberg 6–3 6–0 6–4; C. Pistolesi lost to Reneberg 3–6 3–6 3–6, d. B. Pearce 10–8 4–6 4–6 6–1 6–1; Cane/M. Fioroni lost to Jensen/B. Pearce 1–6 6–3 1–6 2–6.

1986 *Spain d. Czechoslovakia 3–2:* J. Sanchez d. M. Strelba, d. P. Korda 6–2 6–3 6–2; F. Garcia lost to Strelba 4–6 12–14 8–10, d. Korda 1–6 6–4 6–4 6–1; Garcia/Sanchez lost to Korda/ C. Suk 11–13 4–6 3–6.

1987 *France d. Czechoslovakia 3–1:* O. Delaitre d. P. Korda 6–3 6–0, d. C. Suk 6–1 6–1; S. Grenier lost to P. Korda 7–6 2–6 11–13, d. C. Suk 6–3 6–2.

1988 *Australia d. Spain 3–2:* J. Stoltenberg d. J. Sanchez 6–3 3–6 6–4, lost to T. Carbonell 4–6 3–6; R. Fromberg lost to Sanchez 2–6 3–6, d. Carbonell 6–2 6–3; Stoltenberg/T. Woodbridge d. Carbonell/Sanchez 6–2 6–3.

1989 *France d. Australia 3–2:* A. Boetsch d. T. Woodbridge 6–1 6–1, d. J. Anderson 6–0 6–2; F. Fontang lost to Woodbridge 4–6 1–6, lost to Anderson 3–6 2–6; Boetsch/G. Raoux d. J. Morgan/Woodbridge 6–1 6–4.

1990 *Spain d. Czechoslovakia 3–2:* G. Lopez d. D. Rikl 7–6 6–3; d. C. Dosedel 6–3 6–2; J. Conde lost to Dosedel 6–7 5–7; E. Alvarez lost to D. Vacek 3–6 5–7; Lopez/Alvarez d. T. Zdrazila/Rikl 6–3 6–2.

VASCO VALERIO CUP

International Team Championship for boys aged 18 and under. Played zonally with the final stages in Lesa, Italy.

FINALS

1970 *Sweden d. France 4–1:* L. Johansson d. F. Caujolle 10–8 6–3; T. Svensson d. E. Naegelen 6–4 6–0; R. Norbeg lost to E. Deblicker 4–6 0–6; M. Stig d. A. Collinot 6–3 6–1; Johansson/Stig d. Deblicker/Naegelen 6–3 6–3.

1971 *Italy d. West Germany 4–0:* M. Consolini d. U. Pinner 6–2 1–0 ret'd; N. Gasparini d. R. Gehring 6–3 3–6 6–0; C. Borea d. A. Hongsag 3–6 6–4 6–3; C. Barazzutti v L. Jelitto 5–1 abandoned; Barazzutti/Gasparini d. Gehring/Jelitto 6–4 6–4.

1972 *Czechoslovakia d. USSR 3–2:* I. Hora lost to V. Borisov 6–4 7–9 5–7; P. Slozil d. A. Machavez 6–2 2–6 6–4; Slozil/J. Granat d. A. Bogomolov/Borisov 6–3 7–5; T. Smid lost to K. Pugaev 3–6 8–6 4–6; Granat d. Bogomolov 6–3 6–4.

1973 *Czechoslovakia d. USSR 4–1:* A. Jankowski lost to V. Borisov 6–4 2–3 ret'd; P. Slozil d. A. Machavez 6–3 5–7 6–4; J. Granat d. K. Pugaev 3–6 6–4 6–3; T. Smid d. V. Katsnelson 6–4 6–4; Jankowski/Slozil d. Borisov/Pugaev 6–8 10–8 6–3.

1974 *Spain d. Italy 3–2:* L. Fargas d. A. Meneschincheri 6–1 6–1; A. Capitan /M. Mir lost to A. Marchetti/A. Vattuone 6–3 4–6 3–6; M. Mir lost to G. Ocleppo 4–6 2–6; A. Torralbo d. Vattuone 9–11 6–4 6–3; Capitan d. G. Marchetti 8–6 3–6 6–3.

1975 *Italy d. USSR 3–2:* G. Ocleppo d. S. Baranov 7–5 6–5 ret'd; A. Spiga d. S. Molodoikov 6–4 6–8 6–0; A. Merlone d. V. Gruzman 6–2 0–6 6–3; A. Meneschincheri lost to S. Elerdashvili 9–11 4–6; Ocleppo/Merlone lost to Baranov/Gruzman 5–7 4–6.

1976 *West Germany d. France 4–1:* P. Elter d. P. Portes 6–3 6–2; W. Popp lost to Y. Noah 3–6 0–6; J. Henn d. J. Kuentz 6–2 6–2; A. Maurer d. G. Geniau 6–4 6–3; Elter/Popp d. G. Moretton/Noah 6–3 3–6 6–3.

1977 *Italy d. Rumania 5–0:* G. Rinaldini d. E. Pana 6–1 6–1; M. Rivaroli d. L. Mancas 6–2 6–4; N. Canessa d. A. Dirzu 6–3 2–6 6–4; P. Parrini d. F. Segarceanu 6–1 6–0; Canessa/Parrini d. Dirzu/Segarceanu 7–5 6–2.

1978 *Sweden d. Italy 3–2:* M. Wennberg d. F. Moscino 6–2 6–2; P. Hjertquist/S. Simonsson d. M. Alciati/C. Panatta 6–1 6–3; Hjertquist d. M. Ferrari 6–1 6–3; Simonsson lost to Alciati 4–6 1–6; A. Jarryd lost to Panatta 0–6 1–6.

1979 Sweden d. West Germany 4–1: S. Simonsson d. H. D. Beutel 6–4 6–0; T. Svensson d. C. Zipf 2–6 6–4 6–4; A. Jarryd d. K. Vogel 6–2 7–5; J. Gunnarsson d. A. Schulz 7–5 6–4; Simonsson/Svensson lost to Beutel/Zipf 3–6 6–2 6–8.
1980 Spain d. France 4–1: J. Aguilera d. T. Pham 6–4 1–6 6–3; A. Tous/S. Casal d. J. Potier/J. M. Piacentile 6–2 3–6 6–4; Tous lost to Potier 1–6 6–7; R. Mensua d. P. Kuchna 6–4 6–1; Casal d. Miacentile 6–1 6–1.
1981 Sweden d. Italy 3–2: H. Sundstrom d. S. Ercoli 6–4 6–2; J. Nystrom/M. Tideman lost to L. Botazzi/F. Cancellotti 6–1 3–6 4–6; Nystrom d. Botazzi 6–3 6–2; T. Hogstedt lost to Cancellotti 4–6 1–6; Tideman d. S. Colombo 6–2 7–6.
1982 Italy d. Spain 3–2: S. Ercoli lost to M. Jaite 2–6 6–7; M. Fiorini d. D. de Miguel 6–2 7–5; P. Cane d. E. Sanchez 6–1 3–6 6–4; M. Zampieri lost to J. Bardou 4–6 4–6; Cane/Fioroni d. Bardou/Jaite 4–6 6–3 8–6.
1983 Sweden d. Spain 4–1: J. Svensson d. G. R. Fernando 4–6 6–4 7–5; J./K. Carlsson d. D. de Miguel/J. Bardou 6–2 1–6 6–2; J. Carlsson lost to Bardou 4–6 2–6; K. Carlsson d. E. Sanchez 3–6 6–0 6–1; P. Lundgren d. L. F. Garcia 6–3 6–4.
1984 Italy d. France 3–1: F. Ricci d. G. Tournant 3–6 7–5; N. Devide d. P. Gardarein 6–3 6–4; I. Cappelloni d. O. Cayla 7–5 7–6; Gardarein/Winogradski d. Devide/Pistolesi 5–7 6–4 6–4.
1985 Italy d. Sweden 3–2: A. Baldoni lost to D. Engel 2–6 1–6; C. Pistolesi/S. Mezzadri d. C. Allgaardh/T. Nydahll 6–4 6–4; Pistolesi d. Allgaardh 6–3 6–4; U. Colombini d. C. Bergstrom 7–6 6–2; O. Camporese lost to U. Stenlund 0–6 3–6.
1986 Italy d. Spain 3–2: E. Rossi lost to J. Sanchez 6–7 4–6; O. Camporese lost to T. Carbonell 3–6 4–6; U. Pigato d. F. Anda 6–1 6–3; A. Baldoni d. F. Roig 7–5 6–4; Camporese/Rossi d. Carbonell/Sanchez 3–6 6–3 6–4.
1987 Czechoslovakia d. West Germany 2–0: D. Rikl d. C. Arriens 6–1 6–1; T. Zdrazila d. S. Nensel 6–1 4–6 6–2.
1988 Sweden d. Israel 3–0: N. Kulti d. R. Weidenfeld 7–6 6–2; L. Jonsson d. B. Merenstein 6–2 6–1; Kulti/M. Larsson d. Merenstein/O. Weinberg 6–3 6–4.
1989 Sweden d. West Germany 3–0: O. Kristiansson d. A. Kloodt 6–2 6–3; R. PettersAoson d. R. Leissler 6–2 6–1; D. Geivald/Kristiansson d. Kloodt/Leissler 6–7 6–1 6–2.
1990 Sweden d. USSR 2–1: M. Renstroem d. A. Rybalko 6–3 7–6; O. Ogorodov lost to R. Petterson 6–3 6–7 0–6; Renstroem/M. Tillstroem d. Ogordov/Rybalko 6–2 6–1

JEAN BOROTRA CUP

International Team Championship for boys aged 16 and under; originally the Jean Becker Cup. Finals played in Le Touquet.
1972 Spain d. France 4–1: M. Mir d. Ph. Gruthchet 6–3 6–2; F. Riba d. C. Freyss 6–2 1–6 6–4; A. Capitan d. R. Brunet 6–3 7–5; Masana/Mir lost to Frantz/Grutchet 6–4 6–7 3–6; Capitan/Riba d. Brunet/Freyss 7–5 3–6 9–7.
1973 Italy d. West Germany 3–2: M. Attolini lost to K. Eberhardt 1–6 1–6; G. Sileo d. P. Elter 7–5 6–4; M. Spiga d. U. Wellerdieck 6–2 7–5; Attolini/Sileo lost to Eberhardt/Elter 0–6 5–7; Mazzocchi/Spiga d. Liebthal/WellerAdieck 6–3 6–2.
1974 West Germany d. Italy 4–1: Buchbinder d. G. Rinaldi 6–2 6–2; P. Elter d. Risi 6–0 6–1; A. Maurer d. Gardi 6–7 7–5 6–1; Buchbinder/W. Popp lost to Gardi/Rinaldi 6–2 6–7 8–10; Elter/Maurer d. Risi/M. Rivarolli 6–0 6–3.
1975 Czechoslovakia d. Italy 3–2: M. Lacek d. G. Rinaldini 7–5 6–1; I. Lendl d. A. Ciardi 6–1 6–3; J. Kucera d. P. Parreni 6–4 6–4; Lacek/Kucera lost to Parreni/A. Rivaroli 4–6 4–6; Lendl/A. Vantuch lost to Ciardi/Rinaldini 6–1 4–6 3–6.
1976 Sweden d. Czechoslovakia 3–2: P. Hjertquist lost to I. Lendl 6–0 3–6 4–6; S. Simonsson d. A. Vikopa 6–3 6–0; H. Johansson d. T. Pitra 6–3 6–2; Simonsson/A. Fritzner lost to Lendl/J. Kerezek 6–4 3–6 1–6; Hjertquist/Johansson d. Pitra/J. Vikopal 6–3 6–2.
1977 Italy d. Sweden 3–2: A. Costa d. A. Jarryd 7–5 6–2; A. Giacomini lost to S. Simonsson 1–6 1–6; A. Moscino d. S. Svensson 6–4 6–4; Giacomini/A. Odling lost to Simonsson/Jarryd 3–6 4–6; Costa/Moscino d. Svensson/M. Wennberg 6–2 6–4.
1978 Sweden d. France 3–2: S. Svensson d. T. Tulasne 6–4 6–2; H. Simonsson lost to J. Potier 6–3 2–6 7–9 disqualified; J. Gunnarsson d. T. Pham 6–2 5–7 6–2; M. Wilander lost to J. L. Cotard 2–6 7–5 4–6; Svensson/ Simonsson d. Cotard/J. M. Piacentile 6–3 6–1.
1979 Sweden d. France 4–1: J. Windahll lost to T. Tulasne 2–6 1–6; M. Wilander d. H. Leconte 6–2 1–6 6–3; T. Hogstedt d. P. Kuchna 6–2 6–1; J. Sjogren d. J. M. Piacentile 6–1 6–1; Hogstedt/Wilander d. Leconte/Piacentile 3–6 6–3 6–4.
1980 Sweden d. Czechoslovakia 3–0: M. Wilander d. M. Mecir 3–6 6–1 6–1; A. Mansson d. K. Novacek 6–3 6–3; H. Sundstrom/Wilander d. Mecir/B. Stankovic 6–3 3–0 ret'd.
1981 France d. Sweden 3–2: T. Benhabiles d. S. Edberg 6–4 6–4; F. Hamonet d. J. B. Svensson 6–0 6–2; T. Chamsion lost to P. Svensson 3–6 6–2 0–6; O. Cayla lost to A. Henricsson 6–1 4–6 3–6; Hamonet/G. Forget d. Edberg/P. Svensson 6–4 1–6 6–2.
1982 Sweden d. Spain 4–1: J. Svensson d. J. Maso 6–2 6–2; S. Edberg d. F. Garcia 6–4 6–4; P. Svensson d. J. Oltra 6–2 6–1; J. Carlsson lost to S. Castello 5–7 1–6; Edberg/P. Svensson d. Garcia/Oltra 6–2 6–1.
1983 Sweden d. USSR 3–2: D. Engel d. V. Gabritchidze 7–5 6–1; K. Carlsson d. A. Volkov 6–2 6–4; C. Allgaardh d. A. Tchernetsky 7–5 6–3; C. Bergstrom lost to I. Metreveli 6–0 6–7 3–6; Carlsson/Allgaardh d. Volkov/Metreveli 6–3 6–7 6–3.
1984 Italy d. Sweden 4–1: P. Chinellato lost to T. Nydhal 4–6 6–4 3–6; O. Camporese d. H. Holm 6–4 6–0; A. Baldoni d. A. Rosen 6–4 6–0; S. Sorensen d. N. Utgren 6–2 6–4; Baldoni/E. Rossi d. T. Nydal/P. Henricsson 7–6 1–6 6–3.
1985 Sweden d. France 3–2: P. Henricsson lost to A. Boetsch 3–6 2–6; P. Wennberg d. P. Ventura 6–2 6–2; N. Utgren d. S. Blanquie 6–1 6–2; M. Zeile d. C. Sebastiani 6–1 6–3; Henricsson/Utgren lost to Boetsch/R. Pedros 2–6 6–3 4–6.
1986 Italy d. Netherlands 3–2: F. Mordegan lost to P. Dogger 5–7 6–3 1–6; D. Nargiso lost to J. Eltingh 5–7 2–6; C. Caratti d. J. Siemerink 7–5 6–0; R. Furlan d. R. Heethius 7–5 5–7 7–5; Caratti/Nargiso d. Eltingh/Siemerink 4–6 7–5 6–3.

1987 Austria d. Italy 3–2: T. Buchmayer d. F. Pisilli 6–3 6–1; O. Fuchs lost to S. Pescosolido 4–6 1–6; H. Priller d. M. Ardinghi 6–3 6–4; G. Bohm lost to M. Boscatto 6–2 1–6 6–8; Buchmayer/Priller d. Boscatto/Pescosolido 1–6 6–4 6–4.

1988 Sweden d. Czechoslovakia 3–2: J. Alven d. M. Damm 6–1 6–4; R. Pettersson d. J. Kodes 2–6 7–5 6–3; J. Sunnemark lost to L. Hovorka 6–3 0–6 3–6; M. Renstroem d. P. Gazda 6–1 2–6 6–2; Alven/Pettersson lost to Damm/Horkova 0–6 6–3 6–7.

1989 Czechoslovakia d. West Germany 4–1: P. Gazda d. A. Kriebel 7–5 6–3; R. Hanak d. D. Prinosil 6–0 6–4; L. Thomas d. J. Weinzierl 6–2 6–4; B. Galik d. M. Kohlmann 6–4 6–2; Gazda/Thomas lost to M. Kuckenbecker/ Prinosil 6–4 3–6 4–6.

1990 France d. Spain 3–2: N. Kischkewitz d. J. Gisbert 6–4 6–2; P. Lasserre d. A. Corretja 6–4 6–3; J. Hanquez lost to J. Martinez 7–6 5–7 2–6; O. Tauma d. G. Corrales 3–6 6–4 6–0; Kischkewitz/Tauma lost to Corretja/Gisbert 3–6 2–6.

DEL SOL CUP

International Team Championship for boys aged 14 and under. Played in zones with finals in Barcelona.

1979 Italy d. France 3–2: M. Fioroni d. M. Cartier 6–0 6–2; G. Possani d. G. Forget 6–7 7–5 6–3; A. Paris lost to T. Benhabiles 0–6 5–7; L. Baglioni lost to F. Hamonet 0–6 0–6; Possani/Paris d. Benhabiles/Hamonet 6–1 6–4.

1980 Sweden d. Italy 4–1: P. Svensson d. R. Salemme 6–4 7–6; S. Edberg d. F. Ricci 7–5 6–3; R. Lofquist d. F. Filippi 6–3 6–4; J. Svensson lost to P. Poggioli 4–6 2–6; Edberg/P. Svensson d. Filippi/A. Vacca 6–4 6–1.

1981 Sweden d. Israel 3–2: T. Johansson lost to A. Naor 2–6 6–7; C. Allgaardh lost to G. Blom 4–6 6–2 4–6; K. Carlsson d. R. Weinberg 6–0 6–0; C. Bergstrom d. M. Osherov 2–6 7–5 7–5; Allgaardh/Carlsson d. Blom/Osherov 6–2 6–1.

1982 Sweden d. West Germany 4–1: H. Kolm d. U. Kraft 6–1 6–0; K. Carlsson d. O. Sachau 6 0 6–0, P. Ekstrand lost to I. Kroll 0–6 2–6; T. Nydahl d. C. Guhl 6–0 1–6 6 1; Carlsson/Nydahl d. Guhl/Kraft 6–1 6–4.

1983 Sweden d. West Germany 3–2: U. Persson d. H. Stang 6–2 6–2; P. Henricsson d. P. Pfleger 6–4 6–1; U. Eriksson lost to U. Kraft 7–6 3–6 2–6; P. Wennberg lost to L. Orzessek 2–6 3–6; Henricsson/M. Urgren d. Kraft/Orzessek 6–2 6–3.

1984 West Germany d. Spain 4–1: S. Scheider d. F. Alfonso 6–3 4–6 7–5; F. Loddenkemper/A. Thoms d. J. Olivert/S. Bruguera 6–3 6–2; Loddenkemper d. Olivert 7–6 7–6; D. Richter d. A. Martinez 6–1 7–5; A. Thoms lost to Bruguera 3–6 6–2 4–6.

1985 Austria d. Italy 5–0: G. Bohm d. F. Casa 6–4 6–2; T. Buchmayer/O. Fuchs d. S. Pescosolido/F. Pisilli 6–2 6–3; Buchmayer d. Pescosolido 6–3 4–6 6–4; Fuchs d. Pisilli 6–3 7–6; H. Prilled d. M. Ardinghi 6–2 6–1.

1986 Sweden d. Yugoslavia 4–1: J. Alven d. S. Hirszon 6–3 6–4; R. Pettersson lost to B. Trupy 2–6 3–6; M. Ekstrand d. A. Tonejc 3–6 6–4 6–3; J. Henriksson d. S. Ban 6–4 7–6; Alven/Pettersson d. Hirszon/Trupej 6–2 6–4.

1987 West Germany d. Austria 4–1: J. Weinzierl lost to R. Wawra 3–6 2–6; G. Paul d. N. Patzak 6–0 6–1; S. Petraschek d. J. Knowle 3–6 6–2 6–2; A. Kriebel d. H. Kugler 6–2 6–3; Paul/Petraschek d. Knowle/Wawra 4–6 6–2 6–2.

1988 West Germany d. Spain 3–2: M. Kohlman d. A. Corretja 6–2 6–1; T. Ruhle lost to A. Bragado 0–6 3–6; J. Schors d. J. Martinez 6–2 6–0; K. Hecht lost to J. Velasco 6–0 5–7 1–6; Kohlman/M. Nacke d. Bragado/Corretja 7–6 7–6.

1989 France d. Sweden 4–1: N. Bertsch d. T.A Johansson 7–5 7–6; A. De Cret d. K. Bergh 6–4 6–2; S. Martinez d. P. Salasca 6–2 6–3; M. Dallay d. D. Winberg 7–5 6–4; Bertsch/De Cret lost to Johansson/Salasca 6–4 3–6 1–6 7–6 7–6.

1990 France d. Spain 5–0: M. Boye d. A. Pastor 7–6 3–6 6–4; N. Maurier d. J. Diaz 7–6 6–4; J. Van Lottum d. A. Gandarias 1–6 6–2 6–2; K. Dous d. E. Xapelli 6–4 6–1; Boye/Maurier d. Diaz/Pastor 6–2 6–2.

ANNIE SOISBAULT CUP

International Team Championship for women aged 20 and under. Played zonally with final stages in Le Touquet.

1965 Netherlands d. France 2–1: M. Jansen lost to J. Venturino 1–6 1–6; B. Stove d. C. Spinoza 6–1 1–6 6–3; Jansen/Stove d. Spinoza/Venturino 10–8 6–4.

1966 France d. Netherlands 2–1: A. A. Seghers lost to A. Bakker 4–6 7–5 2–6; J. Venturino d. M. Jansen 6–4 6–4; Seghers/Venturino d. Bakker/Jansen 7–5 6–8 6–4.

1967 Netherlands d. France 2–1: A. Bakker lost to O. de Roubin 3–6 0–1 ret'd; A. Suurbeck d. N. Cazeaux 8–6 6–2; Bakker/Suurbeck d. Cazeaux/de Roubin 6–0 6–0.

1968 USSR d. Czechoslovakia 3–0: O. Morozova d. M. Holubova 6–2 10–8; R. Islanova d. K. Vaneckova 7–5 6–2; Morozova/A. Eremeeva d. Holubova/Vaneckova 6–3 6–2.

1969 USSR d. Hungary 3–0: O. Morozova d. J. Szorenyi 6–0 6–1; S. Yansone d. A. Graczol 4–6 6–4 6–2; Yansone/E. Izopajitis d. Szorenyi/A. Barogh 8–6 6–1.

1970 USSR d. France 3–0: E. Izopajitis d. N. Fuchs 6–3 6–1; M. Kroshina d. A. M. Cassaigne 4–6 6–1 9–7; Izopajitis/K. Zincevic d. Fuchs/M. C. Brochard 6–4 2–6 6–3.

1971 France d. Czechoslovakia 2–1: N. Fuchs d. M. Kozeluhova 6–2 6–3; F. Guedy lost to R. Tomanova 4–6 1–6; M. C. Brochard/Fuchs d. Kozeluhova/Tomanova 1–6 7–5 6–3.

1972 USSR d. Great Britain 2–1: M. Kroshina d. G. L. Coles 6–3 6–4; E. Biriukova d. V. Burton 6–2 4–6 6–3; Biriukova/E. Granatuzova lost to L. J. Charles/Coles 3–6 2–6.

1973 Great Britain d. USSR 2–1: G. L. Coles d. M. Kroshina 7–5 4–6 6–3; S. Barker d. E. Granaturova 6–4 7–5; Barker/Coles lost to Granaturova/Kroshina 4–6 6–3 3–6.

1974 Czechoslovakia d. Great Britain 2–1: M. Navratilova d. G. L. Coles 6–1 6–2; R. Tomanova lost to S. Barker 3–6 2–6; Navratilova/Tomanova d. Baker/Coles 6–2 6–8 7–5.

1975 Great Britain d. Rumania 2–1: S. Barker d. V. Ruzici 4–6 6–4 6–2; L. J. Mottram lost to M. Simionescu 4–6 9–7 1–6; Barker/Mottram d. Ruzici/Simionescu 6–4 6–0.

1976 Czechoslovakia d. Great Britain 2–1: H. Strachonova lost to M. Tyler 7–5 4–6 4–6; R. Marsikova d. L. J. Mottram 6–2 6–4; Marsikova/K. Skronska d. Mottram/B. L. Thompson 6–3 8–10 6–1.
1977 Czechoslovakia d. Switzerland 3–0: H. Strachonova d. A. M. Ruegg 6–0 6–3; R. Marsikova d. M. SimmeAn 6–0 4–6 6–0; Marsikova/H. Mandlikova d. Ruegg/Simmen 8–6 6–4.
1978 USSR d. Switzerland 3–0: N. Chmyreva d. A. M. Ruegg 6–4 6–4; Eliseenko d. P. Delhees 7–5 6–4; Chmyreva/ Eliseenko d. Ruegg/M. Simmen 6–1 6–0.
1979 Czechoslovakia d. Great Britain 2–1: H. Mandlikova d. A. E. Hobbs 4–6 6–3 6–3; I. Budarova lost to J. M. Durie 6–8 6–4 6–8; Budarova/Mandlikova d. Durie/D. Jevans 1–6 6–2 6–3.
1980 Czechoslovakia d. Australia 2–1: I. Budarova d.S. Leo 6–4 6–4; M. Skuherska lost to D. Evers 0–6 3–6; Budarova/Skuherska d. Evers/M. Sawyer 6–3 6–3.
1981 Netherlands d. USSR 2–0: M. Van Der Torre d. J. Salnikova 6–1 6–4; N. Shutte d. O. Zaitzeva 6–1 6–4
1982 USSR d. Great Britain 2–1: O. Zaitseva d. S. Walpole 6–2 6–4; N. Reva d. A. Brown 6–1 6–3; J. Kashevarova/ Zaitseva lost to Brown/J. Salmon 6–2 2–6.
1983 France d. Czechoslovakia 2–1: P. Paradis d. H. Fukarkova 7–5 1–6 6–2; N. Herreman d. O. Votavova 6–4 6–0; Paradis/P. Thanh lost to Fukarkova/Votavova 6–4 3–6 4–6.
1984 USA d. Czechoslovakia 3–0: G. Rush d. O. Votavova 6–3 6–1; D. Spence d. A. Holikova 6–2 7–5; Rush/N. Kuhlman d. Votavova/Holikova 6–3 6–2.
1985 Czechoslovakia d. Argentina 3–0: A. Holikova d. P. Tarabini 3–6 7–5 6–4; O. Votavova d. M. Perez-Roldan 0–6 6–3 6–2; Holikova/J. Novotna d. Tarabini/Perez-Roldan 7–5 7–5.
1986 Czechoslovakia d. West Germany 2–1: R. Zrubakova d. M. Schropp 6–2 6–2; R. Rajchrtova d. A. Betzner 6–1 6–2; Rajchrtova/Zrubakova lost to Betzner/Schropp 6–7 2–6.
1987 Australia d. Czechoslovakia 2–1: N. Provis d. R. Rajchrtova 2–6 6–2 6–1; J. Byrne lost to J. Novotna 5–7 6–3 3–6; Byrne/Provis d. Novotna/Rajchrtova 6–4 0–6 6–3.
1988 Czechoslovakia d. Spain 2–1: R. Zrubakova d. C. Martinez 6–4 6–3; P. Langrova lost to A. Segura 2–6 1–6; Langrova/Zrubakova d. Martinez/N. Souto 6–3 2–6 9–7.
1989 Czechoslovakia d. Australia 2–0: J. Pospisilova d. J. Faull 6–4 3–6 6–4; P. Langrova d. R. Stubbs 6–0 6–2.
1990 USSR d. Australia 2–1: N. Medvedeva d. K. Sharpe 6–4 6–3; E. Brioukhovets d. K. MacDonald 6–1 1–6 6–3; N. Biletskaia/S. Komleva lost to MacDonald/R. Stubbs 1–6.

HM QUEEN SOFIA CUP

International Team Championship for girls aged 18 and under. Played zonally with the final stages in Spain.

FINALS
1972 Rumania d. West Germany 3–2: F. Mihai d. A. Spiedel 6–4 7–5; V. Ruzici/M. Simionescu d. B. Portcheller/B. Kasler 8–6 6–1; Ruzici d. Portcheller 2–6 6–0 6–1; Simionescu lost to Kasler 4–6 3–6; M. Neuweiller lost to K. Pohmann 4–6 3–6.
1973 Great Britain d. Spain 4–1: B. L. Thompson d. G. Nogues 6–4 6–4; L. J. Mottram d. J. Mateo 6–3 12–10; S. Barker d. J. Alvarez 7–5 6–0; Barker/Mottram d. Mateo/C. Chillida 6–2 6–2; J. Potterton lost to Chillida 3–6 0–6.
1974 Czechoslovakia d. France 4–1: L. Plchova d. M. Cozaux 6–4 6–1; Y. Brzakova lost to B. Simon 6–8 6–2 4–6; H. Strachonova d. C. Gimmig 6–3 6–0; R. Marsikova d. F. Thibault 8–4 6–4; Brzakova/A. Kulankova d. Thibault/A. Duguy 9–7 4–6 6–4.
1975 Great Britain d. Czechoslovakia 4–1: M. Tyler d. A. Kulhankova 6–1 3–6 6–3; C. Harrison d. J. Kopekova 6–3 6–3; L. J. Mottram d. H. Strachonova 2–6 11–9 6–3; J. Cottrell lost to K. Skronska 1–6 1–6; A. Cooper/Cottrell d. Skronska/Kulhankova 1–6 6–4 6–4.
1976 Great Britain d. Switzerland 3–1: J. M. Durie d. C. Jolissaint 4–6 6–3 6–4; A. Cooper lost to M. Simmen 6–4 0–6 4–6; C. Harrison d. A. Ruegg 6–4 6–7 6–2; M. Tyler d. P. Delhees 6–2 6–2.
1977 Czechoslovakia d. Sweden 5–0: H. Mandlikova d. M. Wiedel 6–2 6–2; I. Budarova d. H. Brywe 6–1 6–1; Mandlikova/Budarova d. A. C. Mansson/A. Nilsson 6–1 6–3; M. Skuherska d. Nilsson 6–0 6–4; H. Strachonova d. Mansson 6–3 7–5.
1978 Czechoslovakia d. Sweden 5–0: M. Skuherska d. L. Jacobson 6–3 6–2; H. Mandlikova d. H. Brywe 6–1 6–1; I. Budarova/Mandlikova d. Jacobson/L. Sandin 6–3 6–1; I. Petru d. A. Nilsson 6–1 6–2; Budarova d. Sandin 6–3 5–7 7–5.
1979 Czechoslovakia d. Switzerland 3–1: I. Bendlova d. P. Frey 6–1 6–1; M. Skuherska/I. Petru lost to C. Jolissaint/I. Villiger 3–6 4–6; Skuherska d. Villiger 3–6 6–1 6–1; I. Novakova d. Jolissaint 6–7 6–3 6–3; Petru v C. Pasquale 5–7 abandoned.
1980 Switzerland d. USSR 3–2: K. Stampfli d. J. Kashevarova 6–3 6–3; I. Villiger/L. Drescher lost to O. Zaitseva/S. Cherneva 4–6 5–7; Villiger d. Zaitseva 6–2 7–5; C. Pasquale lost to Cherneva 4–6 7–5 7–9; Drescher d. J. Salnikova 7–6 6–4.
1981 Sweden d. Czechoslovakia 3–2: B. Bjort d. P. Dutkova 6–2 6–3; M. Lindstrom/C. Lindqvist d. H. Sukova/M. Pazderova 6–3 6–3; C. Jexell lost to Pazderova 6–3 2–6 0 6; Lindqvist d. N. Piskackova 6–2 6–2; Lindstrom lost to Sukova 6–7 3–6.
1982 Italy d. Czechoslovakia 4–1: R. Reggi d. I. Petru 6–3 6–4; N. Virgintino lost to H. Fukarkova 7–5 2–6 3–6; A. Cecchini d. P. Dutkova 7–6 7–6; F. Bonsignori d. A. Souckova 6–3 6–0; Reggi/Virgintino d. Petru/Fukarkova 7–5 4–6 6–2.
1983 Italy d. Czechoslovakia 4–1: L. Ferrando d. A. Souckova 6–0 6–3; B. Romano/N. Virgintino d. A. Holikova/ Souckova 6–3 6–7 6–3; A. M. Cecchini d. O. Votavova 6–7 6–3 6–1; Virgintino d. P. Tesarova 6–3 6–1; S. Dalla Valle lost to Holikova 5–7 3–6.

1984 **Sweden d. Czechoslovakia 3–2:** H. Dahlstrom d. O. Votavova 6–3 6–3; A. Karlsson d. A. Holikova 6–3 6–0; A. Souckova d. M. Lundquist 7–5 7–5; K. Karlsson d. P. Tesarova 6–1 6–2; Votavova/Holikova d. Lundquist/Olsson 6–4 6–2.
1985 **Italy d.weden 4–1:** L. Lapi lost to C. Dahlman 0–6 1–6; L. Garrone/L. Golarsa d. A. K. Ollson/M. Lundquist 6–1 6–3; Garrone d. H. Dahlstrom 6–2 6–7 6–2; C. Nozzoli d. Ollson 6–4 6–4; Golarsa d. Lundquist 6–2 6–0.
1986 **Czechoslovakia d. Sweden 5–0:** R. Rajchrtova d. C. Dahlstrom 6–4 6–0; R. Zbrubakova d. J. Jonerup 6–3 6–3; J. Novotna d. M. Stradlund 6–4 6–2; D. Krajcovicova d. M. Ekstrand 6–3 7–5; Novotna/Rajchrtova d. M. Nilsson/Stradlund 6–0 6–1.
1987 **France d. Czechoslovakia 3–0:** A. Dechaume d. R. Zrubakova 6–4 6–3; E. Derly d. P. Langrova 7–5 6–1; Dechaume/S. Niox-Chateau d. Langrova/Zrubakova 6–7 6–4 6–3.
1988 **Spain d. USSR 2–1:** A. Sanchez d. N. Medvedeva 3–6 6–2 6–3; C. Martinez d. E. Brioukhovets 6–2 6–2; Martinez/Sanchez lost to Brioukhovets/Medvedeva 6–7 0–4 ret'd.
1989 **Spain d. Czechoslovakia 3–0:** A. Sanchez d. A. Strnadova 6–1 6–3; N. Avila d. J. Dubcova 6–3 6–0; S. Ramon/Sanchez d. K. Balnova/Strnadova 6–4 7–5.
1990 **Spain d. France 2–1:** P. Perez d. A. Zugasti 6–4 6–0; S. Ramon lost to A. Fusai 6–3 4–6 1–6; Perez/Ramon d. Fusai/Zugasti 7–5 6–2.

HELVETIE CUP

International Team Championship for girls aged 1 6 and under. Played zonally with final stages at Leysin, Switzerland.

FINALS
1977 **Italy d. Switzerland 3–2:** P. Cigognani lost to C. Jolissaint 0–6 3–6; B. Rossi d. I. Villiger 6–3 6–7 8–6; M. Calabria d. K. Stampfli 6–1 6–2; P. Murgo d. C. Pasquale 6–3 6–3; Rossi/Murgo lost to Jolissaint/Villiger 4–6 3–6.
1978 **Bulgaria d. West Germany 5–0:** M. Condova d. C. Kohde 1–6 6–3 6–1; A. Veltcheva d. Haas 3–5 7 6–4; I. Chichkova d. Hammig 6–3 6–0; I. Christova d. Wilmsmeyer 3–6 7–6 6–3; Condova/Veltcheva d. Kohde/Haas 3–6 6–2 6–2.
1979 **Sweden d. France 5–0:** C. Lindqvist d. I. Vernhes 6–7 6–3 6–0; B. Bjork d. C. Vanier 4–6 6–3 6–3; A. Flodin d. S. Gardette 6–0 6–1; H. Olsson/K. Marivall d. M. Callejo/Vanier 6–3 6–3; Olsson d. Calleja 6–2 6–1.
1980 **Sweden d. West Germany 3–2:** C. Anderholm d. M. Schropp 6–1 6–2; H. Olsson lost to K. Reuter 5–7 4–6; M. Schultz d. P. Keppeler 6–4 6–4; N. Nielson d. M. Reinhard 6–7 6–3 6–2; Olsson/Schultz lost to Reuter/Reinhard 6–1 4–6 5–7.
1981 **Sweden d. Italy 3–2:** A. Bjork lost to F. Sollenti 2–6 6–7; H. Olsson/C. Anderholm d. R. Reggi/F. Virgintino 0–6 6–2 6–1; Olsson d. A. M. Cecchini 6–4 7–5; Anderholm d. Reggi 6–3 3–6 6–4; I. Sjogreen lost to Virgintino 0–6 0–6.
1982 **USSR d. France 3–2:** I. Fishkina d. I. Demongeot 6–1 6–2; L. Savchenko/V. Milvidskaya lost to P. Paradis/N. Phan-Thanh 4–6 7–5 4–6; N. Bykova lost to Paradis 1–6 2–6; Savchenko d. Phan-Thanh 6–2 6–3; Mildvidskaya d. N. Herreman 6–1 6–4.
1983 **USSR d. Sweden 3–2:** A. Kuzmina d. A. K. Olsson 6–3 1–6 6–3; V. Milvidskaya d. H. Dahlmstrom 3–6 6–2 6–4; I. Fischkina lost to M. Lundquist 4–6 4–6; I. Fateeva lost to E. Helmersson 2–6 3–6; Fishkina/Mildvidskaya d. Dahlstrom/Lundquist 6–4 7–5.
1984 **Czechoslovakia d. West Germany 4–1:** R. Wlona lost to M. Gartner 7–6 3–6 4–6; J. Novotna/R. Rajchrotova d. S. Meier/R. Weiser 6–0 7–6; Novotna d. Meier 7–5 6–2; Rajchrotova d. Weiser 6–3 4–6 6–1; P. Sedkackova d. S. Hack 6–4 4–6 6–2.
1985 **West Germany d. Sweden 4–1:** M. Schurhoff d. M. Ekstrand 6–2 4–6 6–4; M. Gartner/S. Hack lost to M. Strandlund/M. Nilsson 3–6 3–6; Gartner/J. Jonerup 7–6 6–2; Hack d. Strandlund 6–1 6–1; W. Probst d. M. Nilsson 6–1 6–1.
1986 **Switzerland d. Czechoslovakia 3–1** (one rubber not played): E. Zardo d. M. Frimmelova 6–4 6–2; M. Strebel d. L. Laskova 7–5 6–1; S. Jaquet v. P. Langrova not played; M. Plocher d. E. Sviglerova 6–4 6–2; Jacquet/Plocher lost to Frimmelova/Langrova 6–0 1–6 5–7.
1987 **Netherlands d. Switzerland 3–2:** N. Van Dierendonck lost to S. Jacquet 6–7 3–6; B. Sonneveld lost to M. Plocher 6–2 3–6 4–6; Y. Grubben d. G. Villiger 7–5 7–6; E. Haslinghuis d. S. Bregnard 6–1 6–0; Sonneveld/Van Dierendonck d. Jacquet/Plocher 7–5 6–3.
1988 **West Germany d. Czechoslovakia 3–2:** V. Martinek d. K. Balnova 6–3 6–0; K. Duell lost to A. Strnadova 2–6 3–6; M. Skulj-Zivec d. H. Vildova 7–5 6–1; A. Popp lost to R. Bobkova 4–6 6–1 5–7; C. Hofmann/Martinek d. Balnova/Strnadova 7–5 7–5.
1989 **Czechoslovakia d. USSR 3–2:** R. Bobkova d. S. Komleva 6–2 6–1; K. Habsudova d. E. Makarova 7–6 6–0; K. Matouskova lost to M. Chirikova 3–6 6–3 5–7; K. Kroupova lost to T. Ignatieva 2–6 2–6; Bobkova/Matouskova d. Chirikova/Komleva 4–6 6–0 8–6.
1990 **USSR d. West Germany 3–2:** T. Ignatieva d. K. Freye 6–4 4–6 6–3; I. Soukhova d. S. Wachterhauser 7–5 6–2; V. Vitels lost to M. Babel 4–6 0–3 ret.; G. Beleni lost to P. Begerow 3–6 3–6; Ignatieva/Soukhova d. Babel/J. Dobberstein 6–4 6–4.

EUROPA CUP

International Team Championship for girls aged 14 and under.

FINALS
1981 **West Germany d. France 3–2, Winterslag, Belgium:** I. Cueto d. J. Clerin 6–3 2–6 6–1; R. Wieser lost to E. Folcher 1–6 6–3 1–6; S. Graf d. M. Phan-Thanh 7–5 6–3; S. Luidinant d. E. Grousseau 6–2 6–2; Graf/Wieser lost to Folcher/Grousseau 6–4 2–6 1–6.

1982 **Sweden d. West Germany 3–2, Mons, Belgium:** C. Dahlman d. S. Meier 7–5 7–5: H. Dahlstrom d. B. Herget 6–0 6–4; E. Helmersson lost to I. Cueto 3–6 7–6 0–6; I. Mattiasson lost to E. Walliser 5–7 2–6; Dahlstrom/Helmersson d. Cueto/Walliser 6–2 6–2.

1983 **West Germany d. France 3–2, Lee-on-Solent, Hampshire:** N. Vassen d. S. N. Chateau 4–6 6–3 6–2; W. Probst d. M. C. Rolet 7–5 5–7 ret'd; S. Hack lost to C. Bourdais 6–3 2–6 0–6; M. Gartner d. A. Dechaume 6–4 4–6 7–5; Gartner/Vassen lost to Bourdais/Dechaume 3–6 1–6.

1984 **France d. Sweden 4–1:** S. Dussault lost to R. Narbe 0–6 6–4 3–6; A. Dechaume/E. Derly d. M. Ekstrand/H. Johnsson 6–3 6–3; Dechaume d. Ekstrand 7–5 6–2; Derly d. Salsgard 6–4 3–6 6–1; M. Laval d. Johnsson 6–4 6–4.

1985 **USSR d. Italy 3–2:** N. Zvereva d. A. Dell'Orso 6–2 4–6 6–4; T. Tchernysova lost to F. Romano 3–6 2–6; E. Brihovec lost to S. Favini w.o.; A. Blumberga d. G. Boscheiro 6–3 4–6 6–4; Zvereva/Tchernysova d. Boscheiro/Dell'Orso 6–4 6–3.

1986 **Netherlands d. Italy 3–2:** Y. Grubben lost to Boscheiro 5–7 4–6; N. Van Lottum d. Favini 6–2 6–1; E. Markestein d. Migliori 6–4 6–4; E. Haslinghuis lost to Bertelloni 2–6 2–6; Grubben/Van Lottum d. Boscheiro/Migliori 6–2 6–2.

1987 **Czechoslovakia d. Austria 3–2:** P. Kucova lost to U. Priller 3–6 0–6; R. Bobkova d. D. Bidmon 6–2 6–4; P. Markova lost to N. Dobrovits 4–6 1–6; K. Matouskova d. S. Suchan 1–6 6–0 10–8; Bobkova/Kucova d. Dobrovits/Priller 6–4 4–6 7–5.

1988 **Hungary d. West Germany 3–2:** A. Foeldenyi d. A. Huber 6–0 3–6 8–6; B. Bathory lost to K. Denn-Samuel 0–6 3–6; M. Zsoldos d. P. Kemper 6–1 4–6 6–4; K. Kocsis lost to M. Kochta 6–4 1–6 1–6; Foeldenyi/Zsoldos d. Denn-Samuel/Huber 4–6 7–6 6–3.

1989 **Czechoslovakia d. Italy 5–0:** E. Martiucova d. R. Grande 7–6 6–3; I. Malkova d. G. Pizzichini 6–2 7–5; O. Hostakova d. S. Pifferi 5–7 6–1 7–5; M. Hautova d. A. Serra-Zanetti 6–0 6–2; Malkova/Martiucova d. Grande/Pifferi 6–1 6–4.

1990 **Czechoslovakia d. Yugoslavia 3–2:** S. Radevicova lost to I. Majoli 2–6 6–4 1–6; Z. Rebekova lost to T. Doric 5–7 4–6; A. Havrlikova d. S. Milas 6–1 6–2; A. Gersi d. D. Karadz 7–6 6–0; Havrlikova/Redevicova d. Doric/Majoli 6–3 7–5.

US INTERCOLLEGIATE CHAMPIONSHIPS

MEN'S SINGLES

WINNER	WINNER
1883 *Autumn:* H. A. Taylor (Harvard)	1920 L. M. Banks (Yale)
1883 *Spring:* J. S. Clark (Harvard)	1921 P. Neer (Stanford)
1884 W. P. Knapp (Yale)	1922 R. N. Williams (Yale)
1885 W. P. Knapp (Yale)	1923 C. H. Fischer (Phil. Osteo.)
1886 G. M. Brinley (Trinity, Con.)	1924 W. Scott (Washington)
1887 P. S. Sears (Harvard)	1925 E. G. Chandler (California)
1888 P. S. Sears (Harvard)	1926 E. G. Chandler (California)
1889 R. P. Huntington (Yale)	1927 W. Allison (Texas)
1890 F. H. Hovey (Harvard)	1928 H. Siligson (Lehigh)
1891 F. H. Hovey (Harvard)	1929 B. Bell (Texas)
1892 W. A. Larned (Cornell)	1930 C. Sutter (Tulane)
1893 M. G. Chace (Brown)	1931 K. Gledhill (Stanford)
1894 M. G. Chace (Yale)	1932 C. Sutter (Tulane)
1895 M. G. Chace (Yale)	1933 J. Tidball (UCLA)
1896 M. D. Whitman (Harvard)	1934 G. Mako (USC)
1897 S. G. Thompson (Princeton)	1935 W. Hess (Rice)
1898 L. E. Ware (Harvard)	1936 E. Sutter (Tulane)
1899 D. F. Davis (Harvard)	1937 E. Sutter (Tulane)
1900 R. D. Little (Princeton)	1938 F. D. Guernsey (Rice)
1901 F. B. Alexander (Princeton)	1939 F. D. Guernsey (Rice)
1902 W. J. Clothier (Harvard)	1940 D. McNeill (Kenyon Coll)
1903 E. B. Dewhurst (U of Penn)	1941 J. R. Hunt (US Naval Acad)
1904 R. LeRoy (Columbia)	1942 F. R. Schroeder (Stanford)
1905 E. B. Dewhurst (U of Penn)	1943 F. Segura (Miami)
1906 R. LeRoy (Columbia)	1944 F. Segura (Miami)
1907 G. P. Gardner (Harvard)	1945 F. Segura (Miami)
1908 N. W. Niles (Harvard)	1946 R. Falkenburg (USC)
1909 W. F. Johnson (U of Penn)	1947 G. Larned (Wm & Mary)
1910 R. A. Holden (Yale)	1948 H. E. Likas (U of San Francisco)
1911 E. H. Whitney (Harvard)	1949 J. Tuero (Tulane)
1912 G. M. Church (Princeton)	1950 H. Flam (USC)
1913 R. N. Williams (Harvard)	1951 M. A. Trabert (U of Cincinnati)
1914 G. M. Church (Princeton)	1952 H. Stewart (USC)
1915 R. N. Williams (Harvard)	1953 H. Richardson (Tulane)
1916 G. C. Caner (Harvard)	1954 H. Richardson (Tulane)
1917–18 *Not held*	1955 J. Aguero (Tulane)
1919 C. S. Garland (Yale)	1956 A. Olmedo (USC)

1957 B. McKay (U of Michigan)	1974 J. Whitlinger (Stanford)
1958 A. Olmedo (USC)	1975 W. Martin (UCLA)
1959 W. Reed (San Jose State)	1976 W. Scanlon (Trinity, Texas)
1960 L. Nagler (UCLA)	1977 M. Mitchell (Stanford)
1961 A. Fox (UCLA)	1978 J. P. McEnroe (Stanford)
1962 R. H. Osuna (USC)	1979 K. Curren (Texas)
1963 R. D. Ralston (USC)	1980 R. Van't Hof (USC)
1964 R. D. Ralston (USC)	1981 T. Mayotte (Stanford)
1965 A. R. Ashe (UCLA)	1982 M. Leach (Michigan)
1966 C. Pasarell (UCLA)	1983 G. Holmes (Utah)
1967 R. C. Lutz (USC)	1984 M. Pernfors (Georgia)
1968 S. R. Smith (USC)	1985 M. Pernfors (Georgia)
1969 J. Loyo-Mayo (USC)	1986 D. Goldie (Stanford)
1970 J. Borowiak (UCLA)	1987 A. Burrow (U of Miami)
1971 J. S. Connors (UCLA)	1988 R. Weiss (Pepperdine)
1972 R. L. Stockton (Trinity, Texas)	1989 D. Leaycraft (LSU)
1973 A. A. Mayer (Stanford)	1990 S. Bryan (Texas)

WOMEN'S SINGLES

WINNER	WINNER
1958 D. R. Hard (Pomona)	1975 S. Tolleson (Trinity, Texas)
1959 D. Floyd (Wm & Mary)	1976 B. Hallquist (USC)
1960 L. Vail (Oakland City)	1977 B. Hallquist (USC)
1961 T. A. Fretz (Occidental)	1978 S. Margolin (USC)
1962 R. Allison (Alabama)	1979 K. Jordan (Stanford)
1963 R. Allison (Alabama)	1980 W. White (Rollins)
1964 J. Albert (Stanford)	1981 A. M. Fernandez (Rollins)
1965 M. Henreid (UCLA)	1982 A. Moulton (Stanford)
1966 C. Martinez (San Francisco State)	1983 B. Herr (USC)
1967 O. Rippy (Odessa Jr)	1984 L. Spain (Georgia)
1968 E. Burrer (Trinity, Texas)	1985 L. Gates (Stanford)
1969 E. Burrer (Trinity, Texas)	1986 P. Fendick (Stanford)
1970 L. DuPont (N Carolina)	1987 P. Fendick (Stanford)
1971 P. Richmond (Arizona State)	1988 S. Stafford (Florida)
1972 J. Metcalf (Redlands)	1989 S. Birch (Stanford)
1973 J. Metcalf (Redlands)	1990 D. Graham (Stanford)
1974 C. Meyer (Marymount)	

Patty Fendick of the United States who won two doubles titles in 1990 and reached three other finals, including the Australian Open, with three different partners.
(Professional Sport)

THE INTERNATIONAL TENNIS FEDERATION

REGIONAL REPORTS
ITF JUNIOR RESULTS
ITF VETERAN TENNIS
NATIONAL RANKINGS

An historic moment in Melbourne as Ken Farrar **(right)**, *the ITF's chief Supervisor, prepares to disqualify John McEnroe during his fourth round match against Michael Pernfors of Sweden – the first such dismissal at a Grand Slam Championship in modern times.*

(Professional Sport)

THE INTERNATIONAL TENNIS FEDERATION

The International Tennis Federation
Palliser Road, Barons Court, London W14 9EN
Telephone: 071-381 8060. Cables: Intennis London W14. Telex: 919253 ITF G. Telefax: 071-381 3989

President 1989–91: Mr Philippe Chatrier.
Executive Vice-President: Mr Brian Tobin.
Honorary Life Vice-Presidents: Mr Jean Borotra, Mr Derek N. Hardwick (posthumously awarded), Mr Allan Heyman, Mr Pablo Llorens, Mr Giorgio de Stefani.
Vice-Presidents: Mr David Markin, Dr Heinz Grimm.
Honorary Life Counsellors: Mr Paolo Angeli, Mr Leslie E. Ashenheim, Mr Hunter L. Delatour Jnr, Mr Lazslo Gorodi, Mr J. Randolph Gregson, Mr Jack S. Harrison, Padma Bhushan R. K. Khanna, Mr Alvaro Pena, Mr Stan Malless, Mr Radmilo Nikolic, Mr W. Harcourt Woods.
Committee of Management 1989–91: Mr Philippe Chatrier, Mr Brian Tobin, Mr Olle Bergstrom, Mr Jim Cochrane, Mr Jean-Claude Delafosse, Dr Heinz Grimm, Mr Gordon Jorgensen, Mr Eiichi Kawatei, Mr David Markin, Mr Eduardo Moline O'Connor, Mr Ron Presley, Mr Francesco Ricci Bitti.
Honorary Treasurer 1989–91: Mr David Jude.
Auditors 1989–91: Messrs Ernst & Young, Becket House, 1 Lambeth Palace Road, London SE1 7EU.
Legal Counsel: UK: Wedlake Bell;
USA: Mr James W. Lillie.
Sub-Committees: *Davis Cup*; *Federation Cup*; Finance; Junior Competitions; Olympic; Rules of Tennis; Technical; Veterans.
Commissions: Media; Medical.
Secretariat: Mr Brian Tobin – Executive Vice President; Mr Mike Davies – Director of Marketing; Mr Thomas Hallberg – Director of Men's Tennis; Miss Sally Holdsworth – Director of Administration and Personnel; Miss Debbie Jevans – Director of Women's Tennis; Mr Doug MacCurdy – Director of Development; Mr Christopher Stokes – Director of Commercial Operations; Mr Bill Babcock – Tournament Administrator; Mr Ian Barnes – Media/Public Relations Administrator; Mr Leif Dahlgren – Development Administrator; Mrs Frances Deed – Financial Administrator; Mr Tony Gathercole – Veterans Administrator; Miss Jackie Nesbitt – Junior Tennis Administrator; Mr John Treleven – Computer Rankings Administrator.

GRAND SLAM COMMITTEE
Australian Open: Mr Geoff Pollard; **French Open:** Mr Philippe Chatrier; **Wimbledon:** Mr John Curry; **US Open:** Mr David Markin.
ITF Administrator: Mr Bill Babcock

WOMEN'S INTERNATIONAL PROFESSIONAL TENNIS COUNCIL
ITF Representatives: Voting Members – Mr Robert Cookson, Dr Heinz Grimm, Mr Brian Tobin, Miss Debbie Jevans, (Alternate: Miss Virginia Wade). **WTA Representatives: Voting Members** – Miss Peachy Kellmeyer, Miss Candy Reynolds, Mr Gerry Smith, Miss Wendy Turnbull (Alternates – Miss Lea Antonoplis, Miss Ana Leaird). **Tournament Representatives: USA: Voting Members** – Mr Jack Jones, Mr Bill Goldstein (Alternate – Mr Jerry Diamond). **European: Voting Member** – Mr George Hendon (Alternate – Mr Gunter Sanders). **Rest of World: Voting Member** – Mr Geoff Pollard (Alternate – Mr Jack Butefish). **Managing Director:** Mrs Jane Brown.
Kraft General Foods: Non-voting Representatives: Mr Tom Keim; Mrs Edy McGoldrick.
Virginia Slims: Non-voting Representatives: Miss Ina Broeman; Miss Anne Person.

WORLD CHAMPIONS PANEL
Mr Fred Perry, Mr Frank Sedgman, Mr Tony Trabert.

THE YEAR IN AFRICA

Competitive opportunities continued to increase in all areas of Africa for both juniors and adults. The year began with the ITF, West African Junior Championships/Air Afrique Trophy. The focus then changed to the *Davis Cup* by NEC where a record number of countries competed in the Euro-Africa Zone II. Zambia and Togo entered the competition for the first time. Morocco beat Zimbabwe to advance into Group I in 1991, whilst Ghana were relegated to Group II. By mid-year the emphasis was again on junior tennis when the World Youth Cup Qualifying was held in Accra and the East and Central Africa Junior Circuit in Botswana, Zimbabwe, Zambia and Kenya. Additionally, an ITF African Team competed in major events in Europe. Outstanding international results were registered by Karim Alami of Morocco and Tamer El-Sawy of Egypt.

Four Men's satellite circuits were held successfully in Morocco, Algeria/Tunisia, Ivory Coast/Togo and in Zambia/Botswana/Zimbabwe. Morocco and Kenya staged professional events at the Challenger Level. Women's satellite tournaments were held in Morocco, Algeria and Nigeria.

An ITF Development Officer for East Africa, Mr Angus Macaulay (USA) was appointed and is based in Nairobi. In addition, the first ITF African Training Centre was opened in September under the direction of Josef Brabenec, a former national coach of Canada. Mr Jean-Claude Delafosse, President of the *Federation Ivoirienne de Tennis* was elected president of the African Tennis Confederation.

EUROPEAN TENNIS ASSOCIATION

Once again, European players achieved outstanding results at Grand Slam Events in 1990: Steffi Graf and Monica Seles were the winners of the Australian and French Open respectively whilst Ivan Lendl and Stefan Edberg triumphed in Melbourne and at Wimbledon. In Team competitions, tribute must be paid to the splendid performance of Austria, semi-finalist in the *Davis Cup* by NEC, and to the USSR, finalist of the *Federation Cup* by NEC. Other extraordinary victories were scored by teams in the ITF NEC World Youth Cup: the Russian boys and the Dutch girls finally emerged among the best sixteen teams that competed in each category (boys and girls). The finals took place in Rotterdam.

In 1990 European Tennis registered an increase in international tournaments for all the categories of players, Professional, Junior and Veteran. In addition to the tournaments included in the major professional tours (ATP and General Kraft) the European Tennis Federation has scheduled the following tournaments: 35 challenger and 25 satellite (men) for a total prize money of $3.45 million, 77 Women's tournaments and 1 circuit (up to $50,000) where approximately $1.2 million are at stake, 136 Junior tournaments (18–16–14) and 101 International Veteran tournaments.

Team events also registered significant improvements in terms of numbers of competing teams as well as spectators and TV coverage. The European Men's Team Championship (with the new record entry of 28 nations) saw Germany win whilst in the equivalent Women's Championship (with 22 nations) USSR re-confirmed their 1989 success. The traditional Winter and Summer Cups for Juniors of all age groups assembled a total of 172 teams.

Veteran Team events also proved a success and for the first time a Club Competition for players aged 55+ was instituted. The traditional Champion Clubs Cup attracted many world class professional players.

In 1990 The European Tennis Association also assigned the distinction of 'European Championship' (indoor or outdoor) to three professional tournaments: Berlin Open (men) and Zurich and Geneva (women).

Finally, due recognition must be given to a new important development through an agreement reached with Eurocard. Eurocard has become official general sponsor of the Association and is expected to offer new interesting opportunities to European tennis at national and continental level.

THE SOUTH AMERICAN TENNIS FEDERATION

President: Nicolas Macchiavelo, *Vice president:* Eugenio Saller, *Members:* Vicente Calderon, Miguel Carresosa, Martin Rosenbaum (Secretary), *Honorary Int. Secretary:* Otto Hauser.

With the Secretariat established in Buenos Aires, working at full capacity, 1990 proved to be a very successful year for COSAT (Confederacion Sudamericana de Tenis). This was election year and two congresses were held. All nation-members participated and the future activity of the Federation as well as its programme was defined.

In the junior field, as usual, it was the organisation of the South American Junior Circuit, consisting of 10 first-class tournaments in Venezuela, Colombia, Ecuador, Peru, Bolivia, Chile, Argentina, Paraguay and Uruguay, which rank amongst the best in the world with grades A, 1, 2 and 3 that was the outstanding feature. Again a South American junior team was nominated to tour under the auspices of, and financed by, the ITF development office. They were guided by Ivan Molina and Ana Maria Arias with considerable success. Miss Labat of Argentina was crowned the under 18 girls World Champion, which shows the potential of some South American Nations, such as Argentina, in the junior's field. The Copa COSAT for juniors under 14 and 16 took place in 2 sections in Guayaquil (Ecuador) and Coquimbo (Chile). The final was played in Chile. The World Youth Cup, qualifying event in 1991 will be held in Argentina and Colombia.

This year, three complete men's satellite tournaments of $25,000 each and eight women's satellite tournaments of $10,000 were held. In 1991 these will be increased to 14 women's tournaments of $10,000 each and four men's of $25,000 each. In the Veteran field, nine South American Cups were organised in the category of 45, 55, 60, 65 (men) and 40, 50 and 60 (women) in Punta del Este (Uruguay) with most nations competing. Cups for men over 35 and women over 30 were played for in Cochabamba (Bolivia).

Officiating courses, conducted by the ITF officiating office, were held in Paraguay and Ecuador. As a result South America will now dispose of a number of first-class certified referees. Such courses will be held again in 1991 in Chile and Brazil.

Our official teaching team held successful courses in Uruguay, Chile, Brazil, Bolivia and Paraguay which many professionals attended. All in all an active and successful year.

THE PANAMERICAN TENNIS CONFEDERATION

President: Hector Pistelli (Argentina); *Secretary;* Gonzalo Mejia (Dominican Republic); *Treasurer:* Stanley Malless (USA); *Vice Presidents:* Jesus Topete Enrique (Mexico), Kurt Wodak (Colombia), Guzman Barreiro Ruis (Uruguay); *Spokesman:* Rolando Martinez Perez (Cuba), Jaime Mansilia (Guatemala), Nicolas Macciavello (Ecuador); *Honorary Members:* Ignacio Vega Alexander, Kenneth S. Niddrie, Ruben Velez Lebron.

Close to completing our twentieth anniversary, it is an appropriate moment to reflect. Our organisation was founded on 24 July, 1971, during the Panamerican Games (Cali, Colombia), and ODEPA acknowledged our existence during their eleventh General Assembly on 31 July 1971 (Cali, Colombia). In Santa Domingo (Dominican Republic), on 16 November 1971, the founder members met to discuss appointing the Heads of the organisation.

Since then the CPT has run the Panamerican Games, the Central American Games and the Caribbean Games. And to underline the importance that tennis has had in ODEPA and ODECABE, the game has been played in all the Central American Games and Caribbean Games since 1926, and in all the Panamerican Games since 1951.

During 1990 we concentrated on the organisation of the Central American and Caribbean Games (Mexico, 27 November 1990) and the next Panamerican Games (in Habana, Cuba, August 1991), plus the Stevens Cup for Veterans which took place in San Jose de Costa Rios on the 14 January 1991.

On the administrative front, there has not been a General Assembly this year (the distance being too great from the rest of America to Atenas, venue for the ITF meeting), but, despite this and the problems of distance, we have staged partial meetings for the Executive Committee, in which subjects of undisputed importance for the region have been dealt with.

REVIEW OF THE JUNIOR GAME 1990

Jackie Nesbitt

After one of the tightest competitions for several years, Andrea Gaudenzi (Italy), the French and US Open champion, became the Junior World Champion for boys' singles in the NEC Junior World Ranking. Andrea finished the year level on points with Leander Paes (India), a member of the ITF Grand Slam squad, capturing the title by virtue of his superior performances in the Group A events. If fact, so close was the competition that only 30 points separated the top five boys at the year-end, and any disappointment felt by Leander would have been tempered by several notable achievements including a runner-up position in the Australian Open and the prestigious title of Wimbledon Champion. In third place was Oliver Fernandez (Mexico) who performed consistently throughout the year. He was a semi-finalist at the Australian Open and runner-up in both the Italian Open and the Orange Bowl.

Just outside the top three places were Ivan Baron (USA) and Andrei Medvedev (USSR), fourth and fifth respectively. In his last year on the junior circuit Ivan met with reasonable success including victory in the Italian Open and a semi-final position at Wimbledon. Andrei started the year slowly but came good towards the end of the circuit. He led his team to victory in the NEC World Youth Cup Finals in Rotterdam, Netherlands in September, the Sunshine Cup in Florida, USA in December, and then took the final Group A title of the year with victory in the Orange Bowl. With a further two years possible in the juniors Andrei could certainly be a force to be reckoned with.

The girls singles title was awarded to Karina Habsudova (Czechoslovakia), who also claimed the girls doubles title. This feat has only been achieved once before, by Natalia Zvereva of USSR in 1987. Karina had a consistent year in the singles, winning the JAL Cup and reaching the semi-finals in both the Australian Open and Venezuela. The girls title chase was also extremely close with only 40 points separating the top four players.

Second placed Shi-Ting Wang (Chinese Taipei) reached the semi-final at the US Open but reached her position mainly due to her domination of the Asian Circuit, with wins in the Asian Closed, Thailand, Hong Kong and Japan Internationals. Equal on points in third and fourth positions respectively were Louise Stacey (Australia) and Ines Gorrochatequi (Argentina). Louise was the champion of the Canadian Open, quarter-finalist at the US Open and runner-up in her national Championships, the Australian Open. Ines Gorrochatequi kept up the tradition of fine achievement in the rankings by Argentinian players, thanks to a runner-up position in Venezuela and a semi-final at the Orange Bowl. Fifth place was taken by Tatiana Ignatieva who, like her compatriot Medvedev, could still compete for two more years on the circuit. She had a steady year which included a runner-up result in the French Open.

If the singles event were close run, the doubles were notable for their domination by the two champions. In the boys championships, Marten Renstroem (Sweden) completed his final year by taking the title in fine style after victories in the Australian Open, European Closed Championships, US Open, JAL Cup and Orange Bowl. Marten will, however, no doubt be grateful to his partner in the latter three events, Mikael Tillstroem (Sweden), who finished in second place. Mikael, partnered by other Swedish team mates dominated the early European indoor circuit, winning all four events entered.

The Canadian pair of Sebastian Le Blanc and Sebastian La Reau, ever present in the top positions of the doubles rankings throughout the year, finished in third and fourth position respectively. Together they were victorious at the French Open and Wimbledon, but Le Blanc with fellow Canadian, Greg Rusedski was also a runner-up at the US Open. With another year possible on the circuit the two Sebastiens could be strong contenders next year. Italian Open and Orange Bowl runner-up, John de Jager (South Africa) finished in fifth place.

Karina Habsudova took the girls doubles title following a memorable year in which she won the European Closed, Venezuela, Wimbledon and JAL Cup. This was an impressive collection of titles and the fact that they were achieved with a variety of partners demonstrates her great adaptability. The prospect of another possible year on the circuit will not please her opponents.

In joint second position were Tatiana Ignatieva and Irina Soukhova (USSR). Together throughout the year this young pair combined to form a formidable partnership winning the Italian Open and finishing runners-up at both the French Open and Orange Bowl. However, consistency was the key for fourth placed Catherine Barclay (Australia). Her achievements at major events were very impressive and included runner-up at the Italian Open, semi-finalist at the Australian, and quarter-finalist at the French Open and Wimbledon. Ruxandra Dragomir (Romania) finished in fifth place, again thanks mainly to a steady year. Her highlight, however, will be victory at the French Open with her compatriot Irina Spirlea.

The 6th NEC World Youth Cup in Rotterdam proved to be very successful for the home nation in the girls' event when the Dutch girls defeated USSR in the final. This was a memorable victory in view of the fact that the team from West Germany included Anke Huber, who had proved invincible last year. Netherlands defeated the top seeded Germans in the semi-finals and won a very closely contested final in the deciding doubles. The USSR boys were able to improve matters for their nation when they took the boys title against Australia, again clinching the trophy with success in the doubles.

Teamwork was very much the key for the USSR throughout the year. Their senior girls squad which included three former World Youth Cup finalists, took the Annie Soisbault Cup by defeating Australia. Not to be outdone, their younger girls squad captured the Helvetie Cup, with a hard fought victory over West Germany, and their boys defeated Canada in the final of the Sunshine Cup. One rare occasion when the boys were unsuccessful was against Sweden in the final of the Vasco Valerio Cup.

Continuing the European domination of all team events, Spain and France also met with great success. The Spanish girls and French boys collected two major titles each. Pilar Perez and Sylvia Ramon guided Spain to victory in the Queen Sofia Cup and Continental Players' Cup against France and Argentina respectively. The French found that success was to be gained in the younger age categories, winning both the Borotra Cup and the Del Sol Cup by defeating the Spanish.\ However, consolation was gained by Spain's senior boys who defeated Czechoslovakia in the Galea Cup when Emilio Alvarez and German Lopez won the crucial doubles rubber against David Rikl and Tomas Zdrazila, the 1988 joint world junior doubles champions. It is not often that Czechoslovakia complete a year without a team title in the junior game and 1990 was no exception. Despite losing the opening two rubbers of the five leg match, the Czechoslovakian 14 & Under girls squad finally came through to defeat Yugoslavia and win the European Cup.

NEC JUNIOR WORLD RANKING 1990

Only those players who qualified for a year-end ranking are listed. The minimum requirements for this were having played 6 NEC Junior World Ranking events, 3 of which were outside their own country and 3 of which were of Group A status.

BOYS' SINGLES

1 Andrea Gaudenzi (ITA); **2** Leander Paes (IND); **3** Oliver Fernandez (MEX); **4** Ivan Baron (USA); **5** Andrei Medvedev (URS); **6** Mikael Tillstroem (SWE); **7** Marten Renstroem (SWE); **8** Pavel Gazda (TCH); **9** Hernan Gumy (ARG); **10** Joshua Eagle (AUS); **11** Marcos Ondruska (RSA); **12** Dirk Dier (FRG); **13** Narathorn Srichaphan (THA); **14** Dinu Pescariu (ROM); **15** Sebastien Le Blanc (CAN); **16** David Witt (USA); **17** Daniel Nestor (CAN); **18** Oleg Ogorodov (URS); **19** Martin Damm (TCH); **20** Juan-Ignacio Garat (ARG).

GIRLS' SINGLES

1 Karina Habsudova (TCH); **2** Shi-Tang Wang (TPE); **3** Louise Stacey (AUS); **4** Ines Gorrochategui (ARG); **5** Tatiana Ignatieva (URS); **6** Petra Kucova (TCH); **7** Maria-Jose Gaidano (ARG); **8** Carla Rodriguez (PER); **9** Kirrily Sharpe (AUS); **10** Kaoru Shibata (JPN); **11** Andrea Strnadova (TCH); **12** Catherine Barclay (AUS); **13** Nathalie Baudone (ITA); **14** Eleonora Vegliante (VEN); **15** Aurora Gima (ROM); **16** Paula Cabezas (CHI); **17** Seong-Hcui Park (KOR); **18** Nicole Hummel (USA); **19** Nicole Pratt (AUS); **20** Kiyoko Yazawa (JPN).

BOYS' DOUBLES

1 Marten Renstroem (SWE); **2** Mikael Tillstroem (SWE); **3** Sebastien Le Blanc (CAN); **4** Sebastien La Reau (CAN); **5** John De Jager (RSA); **6** Oliver Fernandez (MEX); **7** Marcos Ondruska (RSA); **8** Robert Janecek (CAN); **9** David Witt (USA); **10** Juan-Ignacio Garat (ARG); **11** Brian MacPhie (USA); **12** Leander Paes (IND); **13** Johan De Beer (RSA); **14** Pavel Gazda (TCH); **15** Alistair Hunt (NZL); **16** Ivan Baron (USA); **17** Clinton Marsh (RSA); **18** Ernesto Munoz de Cote (MEX(: **19** Jamie Holmes (AUS); **20** Andrei Medvedev (URS).

GIRLS' DOUBLES

1 Karina Habsudova (TCH); **2**= Tatiana Ignatieva (URS), Irina Soukhova (URS); **4** Catherine Barclay (AUS); **5** Ruxandra Dragomir (ROM); **6** Petra Kucova (TCH); **7** Louise Stacey (AUS); **8** Nicole Pratt (AUS); **9** Eleonora Vegliante (VEN); **10** Seong-Heui Park (KOR); **11** Natasha Villarroel (BOL); **12** Shi-Ting Wang (TPE); **13** Carla Rodriguez (PER); **14** Jennifer Saret (PHI); **15** Maria-Jose Gaidano (ARG); **16** Nicole Hummel (USA); **17** Paula Cabezas (CHI); **18** Kiyoko Yazawa (JPN); **19** Wendy Martinez (MEX); **20** Elena Makarova (URS).

NEC JUNIOR WORLD RANKING 1990 – POINTS EXPLANATION

The NEC Junior World Ranking is a world-wide points-linked circuit of 104 tournaments, five continental championships and four team competitions in 60 countries, under the management of the International Tennis Federation. There are ten separate points categories covering three types of events. There is no limit to the number of tournaments in which a player may compete each year. The best six results from tournaments (Group A and 1–5), continental championships (Group B1–B3) and team competitions (Group C) count towards a player's final ranking. To qualify for a final ranking a player must have competed in at least six events, including at least three Group A tournaments and at least three outside his or her own country.

POINTS TABLE (Tournaments & Regional Championships)

SINGLES

	A	1	2	3	4	5	B1	B2	B3
Winner	200	100	70	55	40	30	150	100	55
Runner Up	150	80	55	40	30	20	100	80	40
Semi-Finalists	100	60	40	25	20	10	70	60	25
Quarter-Finalists*	70	40	25	15	10	5	45	40	15
Losers in last 16**	40	25	10	5	5	—	25	25	5
Losers in last 32***	20	10	—	—	—	—	10	10	—

* only if 16 or more players in draw
** only if 32 or more players in draw
***only if 64 or more players in draw

DOUBLES (each player)

	A	1	2	3	4	5	B1	B2	B3
Winners	150	80	55	40	30	20	100	80	40
Runners-up	100	60	40	25	20	10	70	60	25
Semi-Finalists*	70	40	25	15	10	5	45	40	15
Quarter-Finalists**	40	25	10	5	5	—	25	25	5
Losers in last 16***	20	10	—	—	—	—	10	10	

* only if 8 or more pairs in draw
** only if 16 or more pairs in draw
***only if 32 or more pairs in draw

POINTS TABLE (Group C – Team Competitions)

	No. 1 Singles Player Win	No. 2 Singles Player Win	Doubles Win Each Player
Final	100	80	80
Semi-Final	80	60	60
Quarter-Final	60	40	40

POINTS TABLE (Group A Bonus Points)

	Singles	Doubles
Winner of 4 or more Group A events	150	150

Magdelena Maleeva, 15, the youngest and potentially the best of the three Bulgarian sisters who are daughters of a former national champion, Julia Berberian, won the Grand Slam junior singles titles at the Australian, French and US Opens.

(Professional Sport)

ITF JUNIOR WORLD RANKING CIRCUIT 1990

DATE	TOURNAMENT	GROUP	BOYS' SINGLES FINAL	GIRLS' SINGLES FINAL
25 Dec–1 Jan	Casablanca Cup, Mexico	2	O. Fernandez d. I. Baron	L. Kimel d. V. Falter
27 Dec–1 Jan	African Closed, Ivory Coast	B3	K. Alami d. J-C. Nabi 6–2 6–0	S. Tawfik d. A. Vaughan 7–5 6–2
30 Dec–3 Jan	Queensland Girls', Australia	3		E. Pampoulova d. J. Hodder 6–0 6–3
31 Dec–4 Jan	South Australian Boys'	3	D. Dier d. G. Doyle 6–2 6–4	
1–6 Jan	Coqui Bowl, Puerto Rico	3	J. D. Jager d. M. Ondruska 6–4 7–5	M. Anderson d. J. Kruger 6–3 5–7 6–1
1–7 Jan	Banana Bowl, Brazil	2	D. Witt d. S. Le Blanc 6–2 6–2	P. Kucova d. M. Del Valls 6–0 6–2
2–7 Jan	Salk Indoor, Sweden	1	R. Leissler d. N. Lindstedt 7–6 6–3	C. Bernstein d. P. Soerensen 6–2 6–3
5–11 Jan	New South Wales, Australia	3	J. Kodes d. D. Nestor 6–3 6–1	J. Taylor d. L. Stacey 6–2 6–2
8–12 Jan	Vasteras Indoor, Sweden	4	M. Tillstroem d. C. Ruud 6–3 7–5	P. Soerensen d. M. Vallin 6–7 6–2 6–4
8–13 Jan	Coffee Bowl, Costa Rica	2	M. Ondruska d. J. De Jager 6–7 6–2 7–6	M. Anderson d. I. Petrov 6–0 4–6 6–1
8–14 Jan	Asuncion Bowl, Paraguay	2	B. Dabrowski d. A. Skrzypczak 6–2 6–2	P. Kucova d. M-C. Goy 6–4 6–1
8–14 Jan	South Pacific Closed, American Samoa	B3	G. Passi d. M. Kajer 7–5 2–6 6–3	W. Huynh d. T. Galeai 7–5 6–1
15–19 Jan	Victoria, Australia	2	G. Doyle d. B. Larkham 1–6 6–1 6–2	K. Habsudova d. K. Shibata 7–5 6–2
15–21 Jan	Carrasco Bowl, Uraguay	2	J-I. Garat d. C. Marsh 6–3 6–3	P. Kucova d. S-A. Siddall 6–2 6–2
22–28 Jan	Australian Open	A	D. Dier d. L. Paes 6–4 7–6	W. Maleeva d. L. Stacey 7–5 6–7 6–1
23–28 Jan	Argentina Cup, Buenos Aires	2	H. Gumy d. B. Dabrowski 6–3 6–0	M-J. Gaidano d. K. Kroupova 6–2 7–5
29 Jan–4 Feb	Milo Cup, Chile	3	C. Marsh d. P. Campana 6–1 6–4	M-J. Gaidano d. S. Ugarriza 6–3 7–5
5–11 Feb	Condor De Plata, Bolivia	3	C. Marsh d. A. Skrzypczak 6–2 6–2	M-J. Gaidano d. N. Villarroel 6–3 6–1
5–11 Feb	Indira Gandhi, India	5	L. Paes d. G. Natekar 6–2 0–6 6–0	J. Krishnamurthy d. A. Reddy 6–1 3–6 7–6
12–16 Feb	Qatar Champs	5	A. El-Sayed Ghonem d. M. Bhupathi 7–6 6–2	
12–18 Feb	Inka Bowl, Peru	5	A. Skrzypczak d. H. Gumy 6–1 6–4	A. Gima d. P. Cabezas 6–3 6–7 6–1
12–18 Feb	Start Indoor, Bulgaria	4	A. Akaladze d. D. Prchlik 6–2 6–2	A. Petrova d. M. Stuskova 6–4 6–1
19–25 Feb	Ecuador Cup, Quito	2	A. Medvedev d. H. Gumy 7–6 4–6 6–0	C. Rodriguez d. A. Gima 6–2 6–0
20–25 Feb	Czechoslovakian, Indoor	3	M. Tillstroem d. R. Kroll 6–4 6–2	A. Voinea d. L. Vojtkova 7–5 6–1
19–25 Feb	Asian Champs, Sri Lanka	B2	U. Walloopillai d. N. Scrichaphan 6–2 6–4	S-T. Wang d. Q. Bao 6–0 6–0
26 Feb–4 March	Inter-Continental Hotel, Sri Lanka	5	N. Srichaphan d. L. Paes 7–5 6–4	S-H. Park d. H-J. Park 6–2 6–1
27 Feb–4 March	Pony Malta Cup, Colombia	1	S. Le Blanc d. A. Medvedev 6–7 6–3 6–4	R. Bobkova d. M-J. Gaidano 6–1 6–0
28 Feb–4 March	Swedish Indoor	3	T. Enqvist d. J. Alven 6–3 4–6 6–3	P. Soerensen d. M. Vallin 5–7 7–5 6–4
5–11 March	Venezuelan Champs	A	P. Gazda d. H. Gumy 4–6 6–3 6–4	R. Bobkova d. I. Gorrochategui 6–3 6–1
5–11 March	Bavarian Indoor, Germany F.R.	5	D. Prinosil d. J. Knowle 7–6 1–6 6–4	V. Martinek d. S. Wachterhauser 6–3 6–0
6–11 March	Malaysian Champs	4	H. Kaneko d. A. Alcaraz 4–6 6–1 6–1	K. Nagatomi d. J. Saret 6–1 6–2
12–18 March	Sun Cup, Belgium	4	Y. La Marche d. A. Shvetz 4–6 6–2 6–3	S. Bentley d. D. Monami 7–5 2–1 rtd
12–18 March	Indonesia Int., Jakarta	4	A. Hunt d. C. Liggett 6–1 7–5	J-R. Sutedja d. K. Nagatomi 6–1 7–5
12–18 March	South American Closed, Venezuela	B2	J-I. Garat d. M. Achondo 6–4 6–2	C. Rodriguez d. P. Cabezas 6–3 6–1
19–25 March	Thailand Int., Bangkok	2	A. Hunt d. N. Srichaphan 6–3 7–5	S-T. Wang d. S. Martin 6–1 6–0
19–25 March	British Indoor	5	N. Adams d. P. Robinson 6–4 6–3	C. Hall d. V. Humphreys-Davis 7–5 4–6 7–6
26 March–1 April	Hong Kong Int.	2	A. Ito d. A. Hunt 2–6 6–4 6–3	S-T. Wang d. J. Saret 6–1 6–3
4–8 April	Katoro Cup, Yugoslavia	3	M. Damm d. R. Pettersson 6–2 6–1	R. Ritter d. B. Mulej 4–6 7–5 6–4
4–8 April	Phillipines Int., Manila	3	B. Wijaya d. J-W. Yun 2–6 6–4 6–2	J-R. Sutedja d. S. Tokiwa 6–4 6–0
11–15 April	Japan Champs, Tokyo	1	N. Srichaphan d. T. Enqvist 6–1 1–6 6–2	S-T. Wang d. K. Shibata 6–2 6–4
11–15 April	Pascuas Bowl, Paraguay	5	R. Alvarenga d. C. Nishiyama 6–0 6–1	S. Ugarriza d. V. Valdovinos 6–1 6–3

DATE	TOURNAMENT	GROUP	BOYS' SINGLES FINAL	GIRLS' SINGLES FINAL
11–16 April	Florence Int., Italy	2	D. Pescariu d. T. Van Houdt 6-2 4-6 6-2	K. Piccolini d. M. Maruska 5-7 7-6 6-1
15–21 April	Dubitzky Junior, Israel	4	A. Fadlun d. R. Eyal 6-7 6-3 6-4	I. Martin d. A. Vanc 6-3 2-6 7-6
16–22 April	Tashkent Int., USSR	3	O. Ogorodov d. E. Kremnev 6-4 4-6 6-4	M. Chirikova d. I. Sukhova 6-3 4-6 6-3
16–22 April	Grasse Int., France	4	S. Petraschek d. Y. La Marche 7-5 2-6 6-4	D. Monami d. D. Van De Zande 6-1 7-6
23–29 April	Sochi Int., USSR	3	A. Medvedev d. O. Ogorodov 5-7 6-4 6-0	I. Ignatieva d. I. Soukhova 6-2 2-6 7-6
26–29 April	Spring Bowl, Austria	2	R. Wawra d. R. Hanak 7-6 7-5	Z. Malkova d. E. Martincova 4-6 6-1 7-5
30 April–5 May	Salsomaggiore, Italy	4	A. Gaudenzi d. M. Valeri 3-6 6-3 6-3	I. Gorrochategui d. R. Dragomir 6-3 6-0
30 April–5 May	Panasonic Cup, Germany F.R.	2	D. Dier d. J. Renzenbrink 6-4 6-4	G. Anguelova d. C. Timm 7-5 3-6 6-0
8–12 May	Alessandria, Italy	2	A. Medvedev d. A. Rybalko 6-3 6-1	I. Gorrochategui d. I. Spirlea 6-3 7-5
14–12 May	Santa Croce, Italy	2	D. Scala d. M. Valeri 6-1 5-7 6-3	R. Dragomir d. T. Ignatieva 3-6 6-2 8-6
20–26 May	Italian Open	A	I. Baron d. O. Fernandez 7-5 6-1	S. Farina d. N. Baudone 6-1 6-2
28 May–2 June	Astrid Bowl, Belgium	1	M. Renstroem d. O. Fernandez 6-2 4-6 6-2	M-J. Gaidano d. N. Pratt 6-4 1-6 6-3
4–10 June	French Junior Open, Paris	A	A. Gaudenzi d. T. Enqvist 2-6 7-6 6-4	M. Maleeva d. T. Ignatieva 6-2 6-3
11–16 June	Flanders Cup, Belgium	2	L. Paes d. P. Delgado 6-3 4-6 6-1	S-H. Park d. P. Cabezas 2-6 6-3 6-0
11–17 June	Apple Bowl, Spain	4	J. Alven d. J-I. Garet 7-5 3-6 6-3	G. Leon d. E. Diez 6-1 7-5
13–16 June	Danubius Cup, Hungary	4	P. Bufka d. J. Trefil 6-4 6-3	N. Barkan d. A-M. Foeldenyi 6-4 6-0
19–24 June	LTA Int., Thames Ditton, England	2	L. Paes d. W. Kyriakos 7-5 6-3	K. Shibata d. C. Rodriguez 6-3 6-3
25–30 June	Danish Int.	4	R. Pawliska d. M. Eriksson 6-1 7-5	K. Kroupova d. M. Lincahl 6-3 6-1
26 June–1 July	LTA Int., Surbiton, England	1	M. Tillstroem d. L. Paes 6-2 6-3	S. Farina d. S-T. Wang 6-1 6-3
2–8 July	Wimbledon Junior	A	L. Paes d. M. Ondruska 7-5 2-6 6-4	A. Strnadova d. K. Sharpe 6-2 6-4
2–8 July	Netherlands Champs	4	M-A. Tardif d. K. Pettersson 6-1 3-6 6-4	L. Niemantsverdriet d. S. Rottier 6-3 3-6 6-4
9–15 July	German Junior Open	1	R. Hanak d. P. Gazda 6-1 6-4	L. Kucova d. C. Hofmann 6-2 0-6 6-4
16–20 July	Friendship Cup, Poland	4	B. Dabrowski d. A. Skrzypczak 6-0 6-3	A. Werblinska d. M. Wolff 6-1 6-2
16–21 July	Ebel Champs, Switzerland	3	T. El Sawy d. M. Achondo 5-7 7-6 6-4	J. Fauche d. C. Bernstein 0-6 6-2 6-3
16–21 July	Jamaican Int.	5	C. De Carish d. R. Robins 6-3 7-5	J. Rogan d. C. Walter 2-6 6-4 6-4
22–29 July	European Closed, Yugoslavia	B1	R. Wawra d. O. Ogorodov 6-2 7-5	M. Maruska d. K. Boogert 6-4 7-5
30 July–4 Aug	Slazenger Winchester, England	5	T. El Sawy d. L. Beckmann 6-4 6-0	C. Garner d. A. Driver 7-5 6-2
4–12 Aug	USTA Closed	1	I. Baron d. W. Bull 1-6 6-4 6-4 7-6	L. Raymond d. K. Phebus 6-2 4-6 6-0
6–11 Aug	Botswana Champs	5	Y. Auzoux d. R. Hasan	T. Attia d. A. Vaughan
6–11 Aug	Nigerian Int.	5	B. Galik d. G. Elawure 6-1 6-3	M. Olagundoye d. N. Uwakwe 6-7 6-2 6-0
6–12 Aug	Slovakia Cup, Czechoslovakia	3	O. Gross d. H. Wiltschnig 6-3 6-2	M. Stuskova d. D. Gorecka 2-0 w/o
8–12 Aug	Z Bank Cup, Austria	5	P. Gazda d. R. Hanak 6-1 6-1	C. Habernigg d. S. Haas 6-3 7-6
13–19 Aug	Crystal Cup, Czechoslovakia	2	V. Spadea d. J. Panagopoulous 6-1 6-3	P. Nelson d. M. Maruska 4-6 6-3 6-4
13–19 Aug	USTA Int. Grass, USA	5	J. Fikas d. J. Siuda 6-2 6-0	D. Foeldenyi d. N. Moll 6-3 6-4
14–18 Aug	Artex-Nyirfa Cup, Hungary	3	E. N'Goran d. Y. Auzoux 6-4 7-6	
20–24 Aug	Zimbabwe Champs, Harare	3	F. Lankford d. A. Urencio 6-2 6-4	L. Nhavene d. A. Vaughan 7-6 6-3
20–24 Aug	USTA Int. Hard, USA	5	A. Hameur-Laine d. S. Sargsian 6-4 6-4	M. Maruska d. S. Bentley 6-1 6-2
21–25 Aug	Zeralda Cup, Algeria	5	E. N'Goran d. R. Hassan 6-3 6-1	K. Kyrigian d. L. Alami 3-6 6-1 6-2
21–26 Aug	Zambia Champs	1	E. N'Goran d. Valeri 6-4 2-6 6-4	L. Nhavene d. Y. Attia 6-1 6-4
27 Aug–2 Sept	Canadian Open, Montreal	A	L. Roux d. M. Valeri 6-4 2-6 6-1	L. Stacey d. N. Hummel 7-6 6-3
28 Aug–2 Sept	Kenya Champs, Nairobi	5	E. N'Goran d. L. Ilou 6-4 6-3	A. Vaughan d. Y. Attia 3-6 6-4 6-4
3–9 Sept	US Open Junior, New York	A	A. Gaudenzi d. M. Tillstroem 6-2 4-6 7-6	M. Maleeva d. N. Van Lottum 7-5 6-2
3–9 Sept	Romanian Champs	5	A. Pavel d. S. Sargsian 6-3 6-2	A. Vanc d. I. Martin 6-2 6-3

DATE	TOURNAMENT	GROUP	BOYS' SINGLES FINAL	GIRLS' SINGLES FINAL
5-9 Sept	Luxembourg Champs	4	J. Bjorkman d. N. Lindstedt 6-2 6-4	O. Hostakova d. M. Hautova 7-5 6-3
10-16 Sept	Taipei Champs	2	S. Lapido d. F. Setiawan 7-6 6-0	Y-H. Liu d. S-P. Lin 6-2 6-2
10-16 Sept	Aphrodite Cup, Cyprus	5	S. Pospelov d. S. Barabov 6-4 7-5	R. Matokhniouk d. G. Belini 3-6 6-4 6-1
18-23 Sept	JAL Cup, Japan	A	M. Renstroem d. J. Eagle 6-2 3-6 6-3	K. Habsudova d. A. Sugiyama 4-6 6-4 6-2
20-23 Sept	Northern Territory, Australia	5	M. Hill d. R. Lonergan 6-4 3-6 6-2	N. Kenneally d. S. Carvin 6-3 6-1
27-30 Sept	Saloman Melnick, Chile	5	P. Delgado d. G. Prida 1-6 6-3 6-1	P. Cabezas d. M. Castro 6-1 6-3
1-6 Oct	Brunei Int.	4	S. Lapido d. E. Udozorh 7-6 4-6 6-4	K. Ishida d. A. Sugiyama 6-7 7-5 6-4
8-14 Oct	Mercu Buana, Indonesia	3	B. Wijaya d. N. Srichaphan 7-6 4-6 6-3	A. Sugiyama d. B. Sangaram 6-1 6-3
15-21 Oct	Singha Junior, Thailand	4	N. Srichaphan d. S. Ladipo 6-2 7-6	M. Yokobori d. B. Sangaram 6-4 6-0
22-27 Oct	Guangzhou Int., China	3	H-K. Song d. O. Borisov w/o	S-M. Kim d. J-Q. Yi 4-6 6-4 6-3
29 Oct-4 Nov	East Asian Champs, Hong Kong	3	Y-I. Wong d. N. Srichaphan 6-7 6-4 6-2	D-M. Chang d. Y-H. Yoo 6-4 7-5
5-11 Nov	Ershad Int., Bangladesh	5	N. Srichaphan d. S. Yongchantanasakul 6-2 6-4	S. Duangchan d. L. Fu 6-4 6-3
12-17 Nov	Pakistan Champs	5	J. Khan d. A. Shafiq 6-4 6-4	—
26 Nov-1 Dec	Yucatan Cup, Mexico	5	A. Urencio d. M. Osorio 6-3 6-4	S. Kagawa d. Starrett 4-6 7-6 7-5
3-8 Dec	Eddie Herr Int., USA	3	W. Bull d. D. Scala 7-6 6-2	T. Ignatieva d. L. Pugliese 6-3 6-1
17-23 Dec	Orange Bowl, USA	A	A. Medvedev d. O. Fernandez 6-4 2-6 6-2	P. Perez d. S. Ramon 6-1 7-6
24-30 Dec	Port Washington, USA	2	K. Alami d. J. De Jager 6-2 6-4	T. Ignatieva d. J. Kruger 6-3 6-1

GALEA CUP

Mens' 20 & Under International Team Championship
20 nations competed. Semi-finals and final played in Vichy, France, 10–14 July.
Quarter-finals: France d. USSR 4–0 (doubles not played); West Germany d. Australia 3–2; Spain d. Denmark 4–1; Czechoslovakia d. Italy 5–0. **Semi-finals:** Czechoslovakia d. France 3–2; Spain d. West Germany 4–0 (doubles not played). **3rd place play-off:** France v West Germany not played. **Final:** Spain d. Czechoslovakia 3–2 (G. Lopez d. D. Rikl 7–6 6–3; G. Lopez d. C. Dosedal 6–3 6–2; J. Conde lost to C. Dosedal 6–7 5–7; E. Alvarez lost to D. Vacek 3–6 5–7; Lopez/Alvarez d. T. Zdrazila/Rikl 6–3 6–2.

ANNIE SOISBAULT CUP

Womens' 20 & Under International Team Championship
11 nations competed. Played in Mimizan, France, 9–15 July.
Quarter-finals: USSR d. Denmark 3–0; Spain d. France 2–1; Australia d. Luxembourg 3–0; Czechoslovakia d. Netherlands 2–1. **Semi-finals:** USSR d. Spain 2–1; Australia d. Czechoslovakia 2–1. **3rd place play-off:** Spain d. Czechoslovakia 2–1. **Final:** USSR d. Australia 2–1 (N. Medvedeva d. K. Sharpe 6–4 6–3; E. Brioukhovets d. K. MacDonald 6–1 1–6 6–3; MacDonald/R. Stubbs d. N. Biletskaia/S. Komleva 6–1.

SUNSHINE CUP

Boys' 18 & Under International Team Championship
31 nations competed. Played in Weston, Florida, USA, 10–16 December.
Quarter-Finals: Mexico d. Italy 2–1; USSR d. Sweden 2–1; Argentina d. USA 2–1; Canada d. Spain 2–1. **Semi-finals:** USSR d. Mexico 2–0 (doubles not played); Canada d. Argentina 2–1. **Final:** USSR d. Canada 2–0 (A. Medvedev d. D. Nestor 1–6 6–3 6–3; O. Ogorodov d. S. La Reau 6–3 6–2; doubles not played).

MAUREEN CONNOLLY BRINKER CONTINENTAL PLAYERS' CUP

Girls' 18 & Under International Team Championship
27 nations competed. Played in Plantation, Florida, USA, 10–15 December.
Quarter-finals: Argentina d. Italy 2–1; Belgium d. Venezuela 3–0; Spain d. USA 3–0; USSR d. Netherlands 3–0. **Semi-finals:** Argentina d. Belgium 2–1; Spain d. USSR 2–0 (doubles not played). **Final:** Spain d. Argentina 2–0 (P. Perez d. I. Gorrochategui 6–4 5–7 6–2; S. Ramon d. M-J. Gaidano 2–6 6–2 6–1; doubles not played).

VASCO VALERIO CUP

Boys' 18 & Under International Team Championship
17 nations competed. Played in Novara (Lesa), Italy, 1–5 August.
Quarter-finals: Sweden d. Austria 3–0; Italy d. Yugoslavia 3–0; Spain d. France 3–0; USSR d. West Germany 3–0. **Semi-finals:** Sweden d. Italy 2–1; USSR d. Spain 2–1. **Final:** Sweden d. USSR 2–1 (M. Renstroem d. A. Rybalko 6–3 7–6; R. Pettersson lost to O. Ogorodov 6–3 6–7 0–6; Renstroem/M. Tillstroem d. Ogorodov/Rybalko 6–2 6–1).

HM QUEEN SOFIA CUP

Girls' 18 & Under International Team Championship
10 nations competed. Played in Lerida, Barcelona, Spain, 1–5 August.
Quarter-finals: Italy d. Czechoslovakia 2–1; France d. Sweden 2–1; Spain d. Romania 3–0; USSR d. Portugal 3–0. **Semi-finals:** France d. Italy 2–1; Spain d. USSR 2–1. **Final:** Spain d. France 2–1 (P. Perez d. A. Zugasti 6–4 6–0; S. Ramon lost to A. Fusai 6–3 4–6 1–6; Perez/Ramon d. Fusai/Zugasti 7–5 6–2.

JEAN BOROTRA CUP

Boys' 16 & Under International Team Championship
18 nations competed. Semi-finals and final played in Le Touquet, France, 19–21 July.
Quarter-finals: Austria d. Italy/USSR round-robin; France d. West Germany 4–1; Spain d. Sweden 4–1; Czechoslovakia d. Yugoslavia 5–0. **Semi-finals:** France d. Czechoslovakia 3–2; Spain d. Austria 4–1. **3rd place play-off:** Czechoslovakia d. Austria 3–2. **Final:** France d. Spain 3–2 (N. Kischkewitz d. J. Gilbert 6–4 6–2; P. Lasserre d. A. Corretja 6–4 6–3; J. Hanquez lost to J. Martinez 7–6 5–7 2–6; O. Tauma d. G. Corrales 3–6 6–4 6–0; Kischkewitz/Tauma lost to Corretja/Gisbert 3–6 2–6).

HELVETIE CUP

Girls' 16 & Under International Team Championship
19 nations competed. Semi-finals and final played in Leysin, Switzerland, 13–15 July.
Quarter-finals: Czechoslovakia d. France 3–2; West Germany d. Netherlands 3–2; USSR d. Italy 5–0; Romania d. Yugoslavia 3–2. ***Semi-finals:*** West Germany d. Czechoslovakia 3–2; USSR d. Romania 3–2. ***3rd place play-off:*** Czechoslovakia d. Romania 3–2. ***Final:*** USSR d. West Germany 3–2 (T. Ignatieva d. K. Freye 6–4 4–6 6–3; I. Soukhova d. S. Wachterhauser 7–5 6–2; V. Vitels lost to M. Babel 4–6 0–3 ret; G. Beleni lost to P. Begerow 3–6 3–6; Ignatieva/Soukhova d. Babel/J. Dobberstein 6–4 6–4).

DEL SOL CUP

Boys' 14 and Under International Team Championship
16 nations competed. Semi-finals and final played in Girona, Spain, 6–8 July.
Quarter-finals: France d. Czechoslovakia 3–2; Italy d. West Germany 4–1; Sweden d. Israel 5–0; Spain d. Netherlands/USSR round robin. ***Semi-finals:*** Spain d. Sweden 4–1; France d. Italy 5–0. ***3rd place play-off:*** Sweden d. Italy 4–1. ***Final:*** France d. Spain 5–0 (M. Boye d. A. Pastor 7–6 3–6 6–4; N. Maurier d. J. Diaz 7–6 6–4; J. Van Lottum d. A. Gandarias 1–6 6–2 6–2; K. Dous d. E. Xapelli 6–4 6–1; Boye/Maurier d. Diaz/Pastor 6–2 6–2).

EUROPA CUP

Girls' 14 & Under International Team Championship
15 nations competed. Semi-finals and finals played in Glasgow, Scotland, 5–7 July.
Quarter-finals: Yugoslavia d. France 4–1; Italy d. Hungary 5–0; USSR d. West Germany 4–1; Czechoslovakia d. Great Britain/Spain round-robin. ***Semi-finals:*** Czechoslovakia d. Italy 4–1; Yugoslavia d. USSR 3–2. ***3rd place play-off:*** USSR d. Italy 4–1. ***Final:*** Czechoslovakia d. Yugoslavia 3–2 (S. Radevicova lost to I. Majoli 2–6 6–4 1–6; Z. Rebekova lost to T. Doric 5–7 4–6; A. Havrlikova d. S. Milas 6–1 6–2; A. Gersi d. D. Karadz 7–6 6–0; Havrlikova/Radevicova d. Doric/Majoli 6–3 7–5).

The following tennis manufacturers
and other groups whose interest
lie in the sport are members of the
ITF FOUNDATION

Any commercial tennis organisation is welcome to
apply for membership – details of the
I.T.F. Foundation and the benefits it brings
to both sport and member can be obtained from:-

The ITF Foundation
International Tennis Federation
Palliser Road
Barons Court
London W14 9EN.

ITF VETERAN TENNIS

The challenge and enjoyment of Veterans Competitions is unique in some ways. As a junior you can only play in junior tennis in three categories, in senior tennis only one, over 18, until you feel you cannot compete on equal terms any longer. The Veterans game, however, offers a new challenge far more often. There are six categories for the men 35–45, 45–55, 55–60, 60–65, 65–70 and 70 onwards. The ladies have four, 40–50, 50–55, 55–60 and 60 onwards. Instead of being on the shelf you can be needed by your country in each of the age brackets for team events and you may compete in a new Age Group nearly every five years or will be able to in the not too distant future and so have something to aim for and someone to compete with on equal terms all your playing career. That is why the Veterans scene is so buoyant and is growing every year.

Apart from one team event it was Europe's turn to host 8 out of the 9 team competitions in 1990. The von Cramm Cup (Mens 60+) was held in Ontario, Canada. It was the first time Canada had organised and hosted a Veteran team event although they are well-known in team competitions and it proved to be a popular venue.

The USA continues to feature very strongly in the finals of these events. They won 4 out of 7 in 1990, one less than last year. Spain and Australia also did well by reaching two team finals for the first time in the same year when they played one another. Spain won the Italia Cup 2–1 and Australia the Bueno Cup by the same margin. Australia also reached the Britannia Final. West Germany took revenge for their last two defeats in the final of the Dubler Cup by beating the USA 2–1. Canada won the Austra Cup for the fourth consecutive year! No team yet has managed to wrest the Crawford or Britannia Cups away from the strangle-hold of the USA, although Australia kept the margin down to 2–1 in the Britannia.

The Veteran World Championships were held in Yugoslavia at the newly-built complex at Stella Maris in Umag, a beautiful and well appointed tennis centre of 16 clay courts which with the existing complex at Katoro, provided 32 match courts. Twenty-six nations were represented by 487 singles entrants. The welcome opening address was made on behalf of the ITF by the Executive Vice-President, Mr Brian Tobin, and it was good to see Fred Perry in attendance, a keen supporter of the Veterans game. The first two tournaments to be held in the USSR were also a success and we hope will go from strength to strength.

Many new and exciting events take place in 1991. One of these will be the first trial year of the new Veterans Computerised World Ranking Programme and the new 'Age Rule for Veterans' which allows a player to enter a competition who has reached *or will reach* the minimum age limit of the category on or before the 31st December of the year in which the competition is held. An exciting 1991 to look forward to!

ITALIA CUP

Men's 35 and over
GLASGOW, SCOTLAND, 8–14 JULY
Quarter-finals: Germany d. USA 2–1; Australia d. France 3–0; Great Britain d. Indonesia 3–0; Spain d. Austria 2–1.
Semi-finals: Australia d. Germany 2–1; Spain d. Great Britain 3–0.
Final: Spain d. Australia 2–1 (J. Moreno d. A. Rae 6–7 6–4 6–1; E. Vasquez d. R. Casey 6–1 6–3; Vasquez/J. Velasco lost to Casey/W. Cowley 1–6 6–7).

The legendary Mexican American, Pancho Gonzales, dominated the professional game in the 1950s and went on competing into his 40s as the game went open in 1968. The next year he won Wimbledon's longest match – a dramatic 5 hour 12 minutes marathon against Charlie Pasarell that spanned two days – an inspiration to veterans everywhere.

(R & A Photofeatures)

DUBLER CUP

Men's 45 and over
BOL, YUGOSLAVIA, 19–25 MAY
Quarter-finals: USA d. Netherlands 3–0; France d. Austria 2–1; Italy d. Australia 3–0; Germany d. Canada 3–0.
Semi-finals: USA d. France 3–0; Germany d. Italy 3–0.
Final: Germany d. USA 2–1 (H. Ploetz d. J. Parker 6–4 6–1; H. Elschenbroich d. P. Van Lingen 6–3 3–6 6–4; Ploetz/G. Krauss lost to E. Turville/D. Johnson 4–6 6–7).

AUSTRIA CUP

Men's 55 and over
POERTSCHACH, AUSTRIA, 10–16 JUNE
Quarter-finals: Canada d. Finland 3–0; Austria d. Australia 2–1; Germany d. France 3–0; USA d. Switzerland 2–0.
Semi-finals: Canada d. Austria 2–1; USA d. Germany 3–0.
Final: Canada d. USA 3–0 (L. Main d. C. DeVoe 6–3 6–4; K. Sinclair d. J. Perley 6–3 6–1; Main/Sinclair d. DeVoe/R. Garrido 6–3 1–6 6–1).

GOTTFRIED VON CRAMM CUP

Men's 60 and over
ONTARIO, CANADA, 19–25 AUGUST
Quarter-finals: Australia d. Canada 3–0; USA d. Argentina 3–0; Sweden d. France 2–1; Austria d. New Zealand 2–1.
Semi-finals: USA d. Australia 2–1; Austria d. Sweden 2–1.
Final: USA d. Austria 2–1 (J. Morton d. O. Jirkovski 6–3 6–1; B. Davis lost to L. Legenstein 4–6 5–7; Davis/D. Gale d. Legenstein/Jirkovski 6–7 7–5 6–3).

BRITANNIA CUP

Men's 65 and over
BOURNEMOUTH, ENGLAND, 20–25 MAY
Quarter-finals: USA d. Great Britain 3–0; Austria d. France 2–1; Sweden d. Germany 2–1; Australia d. Ireland 2–1.
Semi-finals: USA d. Austria 2–1; Australia d. Sweden 2–1.
Final: USA d. Australia 2–1 (T. Brown lost to B. McCarthy 6–3 1–6 5–7; F. Kovaleski d. B. Thompson 6–1 6–0; Brown/Kovaleski d. Lonergan/McCarthy 6–3 6–3).

CRAWFORD CUP

Men's 70 and over
BRAND, AUSTRIA, 20–25 MAY
Quarter-finals: USA d. Italy 3–0; Australia d. Canada 2–1; Great Britain d. Sweden 2–1; Brazil d. Germany 2–1.
Semi-finals: USA d. Australia 3–0; Brazil d. Great Britain 2–1.
Final: USA d. Brazil 3–0 (Pearson d. Bergmann 6–0 6–2; McGrath d. A. Juchem [score unknown]; A. Ritzenberg/A. Swetka d. Bergmann/Juchem [score unknown]).

YOUNG CUP

Women's 40 and over
KESZTHELY, HUNGARY, 10–16 JUNE
Quarter-finals: France d. Netherlands 3–0; Hungary d. Great Britain 3–0; USA d. Spain 3–0; Germany d. Italy 2–1.
Semi-finals: France d. Hungary 3–0; USA d. Germany 2–1.
Final: France d. USA 3–0 (G. Lovera d. M. Russo 7–5 6–0; N. Cazaux d. B. Mueller 6–2 4–6 6–2; Lovera/R. Darmon d. S. Adcock/Russo 6–1 6–1).

MARIA ESTHER BUENO CUP

Women's 50 and over
BARCELONA, SPAIN, 20–25 MAY
Quarter-finals: USA d. Austria 3–0; Australia d. Israel 2–0; Italy d. Great Britain 2–0; Spain d. Germany 2–1.
Semi-finals: Australia d. USA 3–0; Spain d. Italy 2–1.
Final: Australia d. Spain 2–1 (J. Blackshaw d. M. Pombo 6–0 6–2; K. Schiavinato lost to M. Schultze 4–6 1–6; N. Marsch/B. Grigg d. A. Estalella/Schultz 7–5 6–3).

ALICE MARBLE CUP

Women's 60 and over
PADERBORN, GERMANY, 20–25 MAY
Quarter-finals: USA d. Sweden 3–0; Australia d. Great Britain 2–1; Canada d. Mexico 2–1; Germany d. France 3–0.
Semi-finals: USA d. Australia 3–0; Germany d. Canada 3–0.
Final: USA d. Germany 2–1 (Rothfels d. Marczewski 6–4 3–6 6–1; L. Owen lost to K. Sorge 4–6 6–2 4–6; Owen/Rothfels d. B. Jung/Ambrosius 6–4 6–2).

ITF VETERAN CHAMPIONSHIPS

UMAG, YUGOSLAVIA, 26 MAY–3 JUNE
MEN'S OVER 35 SINGLES – Final: R. Machan (HUN) d. L. Levai (FRG) 6–0 7–5.
MEN'S OVER 35 DOUBLES – Final: Machan/Levai d. M. Mijuca/M. Wunschig (FRG) 6–2 6–3.
MEN'S OVER 45 SINGLES – Final: H. Elschenbroich (FRG) d. J. Parker (USA) 7–5 6–3.
MEN'S OVER 45 DOUBLES – Final: D. Johnson (USA)/Parker d. P. Pokorny (AUT)/H. Gradischnig (AUT) 7–6 6–4.
MEN'S OVER 55 SINGLES – Final: I. Gulyas (HUN) d. L. Main (CAN) 6–2 6–2.
MEN'S OVER 55 DOUBLES – Final: K. Sinclair (CAN)/Main d. Gulyas/W. Mertins (FRG) 6–2 3–6 6–4.
MEN'S OVER 60 SINGLES – Final: S. Davidson (SWE) d. H. Stewart (USA) 6–0 6–2.
MEN'S OVER 60 DOUBLES – Final: Stewart/Davidson d. L. Legenstein (AUT)/B. Ball (USA) 6–0 6–4.
MEN'S OVER 65 SINGLES – Final: B. McCarthy (AUS) d. A. Vieira (BRA) w/o.
MEN'S OVER 65 DOUBLES – Final: O. Jirkovsky (AUT)/J. Karlhofer (AUT) d. S. Verrati (FRA)/L. Lenart (HUN) 2–6 7–5 6–3.
MEN'S OVER 70 SINGLES – Final: W. Parsons (USA) d. A. Swetka (USA) 6–3 6–4.
MEN'S OVER 70 DOUBLES – Final: A. Swetka (USA)/A. Ritzenberg (USA) d. Parsons/M. Kizlink (GBR) 6–2 6–2.
WOMEN'S OVER 40 SINGLES – FINAL: M. Pinterova (HUN) d. H. Eisterlehner (FRG) 6–2 6–3.
WOMEN'S OVER 40 DOUBLES – FINAL: B. Mueller (USA)/L. Cash (USA) d. M. Oppenheimer (GBR)/Eisterlehner 6–2 1–6 6–3.
WOMEN'S OVER 50 SINGLES – Final: M. Schultze (ESP) d. K. Schiavinato (AUS) 6–0 7–5.
WOMEN'S OVER 50 DOUBLES – Final: Schiavinato/J. Blackshaw (AUS) d. B. Grigg (AUS)/N. Marsh (AUS) 7–6 6–4.
WOMEN'S OVER 60 SINGLES – Final: L. Owen (USA) d. M. Blom (HOL) 6–3 6–2.
WOMEN'S OVER 60 DOUBLES – Final: L. Stock (AUS)/D. Young (AUS) d. Owen/V. Gordon (USA) 6–2 6–2.

1990 ITF VETERAN WORLD RANKINGS

MEN

OVER 35
1 eq J. Moreno (ESP), E. Vasquez (ESP); **3** P. Torre (FRA); **4** R. Machan (HUN); **5** L. Levai (FRG); **6** M. Wunschig (FRG); **7 eq** E. Walter (AUT), M. Koek (HOL); **9** L. Petrov (BUL).

OVER 45
1 H. Elschenbroich (FRG); **2** H. Ploetz (FRG); **3** J. Parker (USA); **4** P. Polorny (AUT); **5** G. Krauss (FRG); **6** B. Nitsche (FRG); **7** G. Roehrich (ITA); **8** M. Leclerq (FRA); **9** F. Pierson (FRA); **10** P. Fuchs (AUT).

OVER 55
1 I. Gulyas (HUN); **2** K. Van Nostrand (USA); **3** L. Main (CAN); **4** J. Couder (ESP); **5** K. Sinclair (CAN); **6** C. Devoe (USA); **7** J. Powless (USA); **8** W. Mertins (FRG); **9** F. Hainka (AUT); **10** H. Hamza (AUT).

OVER 60
1 S. Davidson (SWE); **2** H. Stewart (USA); **3** J. Morton (USA); **4** B. Ball (USA); **5** L. Legenstein (AUT); **6** B. Howe (AUS); **7** A. Kendall (AUS); **8** P. Jalabert (FRA); **9** A. Hussmuller (FRG); **10** M. Monetti (ITA).

OVER 65
1 B. McCarthy (AUS); **2** T. Brown (USA); **3** F. Kovaleski (USA); **4 eq** L. Lenert (HUN), S. Verrati (FRA); **6** A. Vieira (BRA); **7** O. Jirkovsky (AUT); **8** M. Isidori (ITA); **9** V. Zabrodski (SWE); **10** A. Reich (FRG).

OVER 70
1 J. McGrath (USA); **2** W. Parsons (USA); **3** A. Swetka (USA); **4** A. Ritzenberg (USA); **5** J. Gilchrist (AUS); **6** S. Miloskovic (YUG); **7** A. Juchem (BRA); **8** M. Kizlink (GBR); **9** G. Henley (AUS); **10** A. Stegmann (FRG).

WOMEN

OVER 40
1 N. Cazaux (FRA); **2** M. Pinterova (HUN); **3** H. Eisterlehner (FRG); **4** H. Masthoff (FRG); **5** C. Creydt (FRG); **6** F. Szabo (HUN); **7** M. Russo (USA); **8** R. Schroeder (FRG); **9** M. Oppenhiemer (GBR); **10** M. Heeb (LIE).

OVER 50
1 M. Schultz (ESP); **2** Mayer-Zdralek (FRG); **3** S. Brasher (GBR); **4** Fuhrmann (FRG); **5** Castellucci (FRG); **6** J. Blackshaw (AUS); **7** K. Schiavinato (AUS); **8** B. Allendorf (FRG); **9** Rouire (FRG); **10** Beltrame (ITA).

OVER 60
1 L. Owen (USA); **2** B. Elsenstein (USA); **3** K. Sorge (FRG); **4** M. Blom (HOL); **5** K. Rothfels (USA); **6** V. Gordon (USA); **7** H. Brabenec (CAN); **8** J. Williams (GBR); **9** E. Szentirmai (HUN); **10** M. Marczewski (FRG).

The last mother to win at Wimbledon was Evonne Goolagong whose second victory in 1980, four years after the birth of daughter Kelly, came nine years after her first win and equalled the nine year gap of Bill Tilden, the champion in 1920, 1921 and 1930.

(R & A Photofeatures)

NATIONAL ASSOCIATIONS, RANKINGS AND CHAMPIONSHIPS

MEMBERS WITH VOTING RIGHTS (94)

Abbreviations: C. = Cable address; T. = Telephone number; TX. = Telex number.
Number following country's name denotes year of foundation.

ALGERIA (1962)

Fédération Algérienne de Tennis, Centre des Fédérations Sportives, Cité Olympique B.P. 88 El Biar, Algers 16030.
T. (2) 2790988/2793939; TX. 61379 KFS DZ; *Pres.* Col. Ali Tounsi; *Dir. Ex.* Mr Yahia Chettab.

ARGENTINA (1921)

Asociación Argentina de Tenis, av. San Juan 1315/17, (1148) Capital Federal, Buenos Aires.
C. Argtennis, Buenos Aires; T. (1) 26 1569/27 0101/26 4696; TX. 17336 ARGTEN AR; Fax (1) 3340296; *Pres.* Mr Juan Jose Vasquez; *Secs* Mr Juan Carlos Zamboni, Mr Francisco A. Turno.

AUSTRALIA (1904)

Tennis Australia, Private Bag 6060, Richmond South 3121, Victoria.
T. (3) 655 1277; TX. 36893 TENCRT AA; Fax (3) 650 2743; *Pres.* Mr Geoff Pollard; *Admin. Manager* Mr Mike Daws; *Tennis Manager* Mr Barry F. McMillan.
MEN: **1** Richard Fromberg; **2** Wally Masur; **3** Todd Woodbridge; **4** Darren Cahill; **5** Mark Kratzmann; **6** Pat Cash; **7** Mark Woodforde; **8** Jason Stoltenberg; **9** Simon Youl; **10** Broderick Dyke.
WOMEN: **1** Rachel McQuillan; **2** Nicole Provis; **3** Elizabeth Smylie; **4** Anne Minter; **5** Kristin Godridge; **6** Louise Field; **7** Michelle Jaggard; **8** Kirrily Sharpe; **9** Jo-Anne Faull; **10** Nicole Pratt.

AUSTRIA (1902)

Osterreichischer Tennisverband, Haekelstrasse 33, 1235 Wien, Austria.
C. Austriatennis, Vienna; T. (222) 8654506; TX. 131598 OETEN A; Fax (222) 86545065; *Pres.* Dr Theodor Zeh; *Sec.* Mr Peter Nader.
MEN: **1** Thomas Muster; **2** Horst Skoff; **3** Alexander Antonitsch; **4** Oliver Fuchs; **5** Gilbert Schaller; **6** Thomas Buchmayer; **7** Gerald Mandl; **8** Harald Mair; **9** Hans Priller; **10** Stefan Lochbihler.
WOMEN: **1** Barbara Paulus; **2** Judith Wiesner; **3** Beate Reinstadler; **4** Petra Ritter; **5** Sandra Dopfer; **6** Marion Maruska; **7** Ulrike Priller; **8** Nike Dobrovits; **9** Heidi Sprung; **10** Mirijam Schweda.

National Closed Championships

MEN'S SINGLES – Semi-finals: O. Fuchs d. T. Muster 7–5 1–0 w/o; A. Antonitsch d. S. Lochbihler 7–5 6–3.
Final: Fuchs d. Antonitsch 3–0 w/o.
WOMEN'S SINGLES – Semi-finals: M. Maruska d. M. Schweda 6–2 6–0; B. Reinstadler d. U. Priller 6–4 6–3.
Final: Reinstadler d. Maruska 6–4 0–6 6–3.

BAHAMAS (1947)

The Bahamas Lawn Tennis Association, PO Box N-10169, Nassau.
T. (809) 326 3000/326 1263; TX. 20170 BRITBEACH B; Fax (809) 363 3957; *Pres.* Mr J. Barrie Farrington; *Sec.* Ms Vicky Knowles.

BAHRAIN (1981)

Bahrain Lawn Tennis Federation, PO Box 26985, Bahrain.
C. Tennis, Bahrain; T. (973) 687236; TX. 8738 GPIC BN; *Pres.* Dr Tawfeeq Almoayed; *Sec.* Dr Yousif Abdul Ghafar Abdullah.

BANGLADESH (1972)

Bangladesh Tennis Federation, Tennis Complex, Ramna Green, Dhaka 1000.
C. Tennisfed, Dhaka; T. (2) 506650; TX. 642401 SHER BJ (Att. Tennis); *Pres.* Hussain Muhammad Ershad; *Sec.* Mr Masud H. Jamaly.

BARBADOS (1948)

Barbados Lawn Tennis Association, PO Box 615c, Bridgetown.
T. (809) 427 3661; *Pres.* Mr Bruce A. M. Hackett; *Sec.* Mrs Margaret Griffiths.

BELGIUM (1902)

Royal Belgian Tennis Federation, Passage International Rogier 6, BTE 522, 1210 Brussels.
C. Tennisfeder, Brussels; T. (2) 217 2365; TX. 24023 TENFED B; Fax (2) 217 6732; *Pres.* Mr Henri Denis; *Secs* Mr Walter Goethals, Mr Franz Lemaire.
MEN: 1 Eduardo Masso; 2 Bart Wuyts; 3 Xavier Daufresne; 4 Libor Pimek; 5 Filip Dewulf; 6 Denis Langaskens; 7 Guido Van Rompaey; 8 Christophe Delheille; 9 Gunther Vanderveeren; 10 Tom Van Houdt.
WOMEN: 1 Sabine Appelmans; 2 Sandra Wasserman; 3 Dominique Monami; 4 Ann Devries; 5 Ilse Veldeman; 6 Daphne Vandezande; 7 Caroline Wuillot; 8 Klaartje Van Baarle; 9 Vicky Maes; 10 Marianne Vermylen.

National Closed Championship
MEN'S SINGLES – Semi-finals: B. Wuyts d. D. Langaskens 6–3 3–6 6–4 6–1; L. Pimek d. P. Godfroid 6–2 6–2 3–6 5–7 7–6.
Final: Wuyts d. Pimek 6–4 6–4 6–7 6–3.
WOMEN'S SINGLES – Semi-finals: S. Wasserman d. A. Devries 6–2 6–4; S. Appelmans d. I. de Ruysscher 6–3 6–2.
Final: Appelmans d. Wasserman 6–4 6–4.

BOLIVIA (1937)

Federación Boliviana de Tennis, Calle Mexico no. 1638, Casilla Postal No. 14752, Cochabamba.
T. (2) 378769; TX. 2220 CAMPULP BV; *Pres.* Sr Vicente Calderon Zeballos.

BRAZIL (1956)

Confederacao Brasileira de Tenis , av. Paulista Nr. 352 – Sala 64, 6 Andar, Conjunto, 64 Cept – 01 310, Sao Paulo.
C. Cebetenis Rio de Janeiro; T. (11) 251 3920; TX. 113 2733 CTEN-BR; Fax (11) 289 9404; *Pres.* Mr Walter Elias; *Sec.* Marilia Silberberg.

BULGARIA (1930)

Bulgarian Tennis Federation, 18 Tolbouhin Boulevard, 1040 Sofia.
C. Besefese Tennis, Sofia; T. (2) 803710 or 808651 ext. 213/488; TX. 22723/22724 BSFS BG; Fax (2) 879670; *Pres.* Mr Roumen Serbezov; *Sec.* Mr Tzvetan Tzvetkov.
MEN: 1 Milko Petkov; 2 Ivailo Klashnov; 3 Krasimir Lazarov; 4 Orlin Stanoichev; 5 Ivan Keskinov; 6 Milen Velev; 7 Emil Kovachev; 8 Stefan Tzvetkov; 9 Ruslan Rainov; 10 Milen Ianakiev.
WOMEN: 1 Katerina Maleeva; 2 Elena Pampoulova; 3 Magdalena Maleeva; 4 Galia Angelova; 5 Dora Rangelova; 6 Tzvetelina Nikolova; 7 Ralitza Milorieva; 8 Borislava Tzvetkova; 9 Mariela Kraicheva; 10 Plamena Gogovska.

National Closed Championships
MEN'S SINGLES – Semi-finals: K. Lazarov d. S. Tzvetkov 6–4 6–3; M. Petkov d. R. Radev 7–5 6–3.
Final: Lazarov d. Petkov 7–5 7–5 7–6.
WOMEN'S SINGLES – Semi-finals: G. Angelova d. R. Milorieva 6–4 5–7 6–3; T. Nikolova d. P. Stoianova 6–3 7–5. **Final:** Angelova d. Nikolova 6–2 2–6 6–4.

CAMEROON (1966)

Fédération Camerounaise de Lawn Tennis, BP 1121, Yaounde.
C. Fecatennis-MJS-Yaounde; T. (237) 233860/1310 or 224329; TX. 8568 KN/MNFA 8261 KN; *Pres.*
Brig. Gen. James Tataw; *Sec.* Dr Noaki Mboulet.

CANADA (1890)

Tennis Canada, 3111 Steeles Avenue West, Downsview, Ontario M3J 3H2.
T. (416) 665 9777; TX. 02618419 CAN TENNIS TOR; Fax (416) 665 9017; *Pres.* Mr Robert H. Moffat;
Sec. Ms Shelley Evanochko.
MEN: **1** Andrew Sznajder; **2** Grant Connell; **3** Chris Pridham; **4** Martin Laurendeau; **5**
Martin Wostenholme; **6** Brian Gyetko; **7** Stephanne Bonneau; **8** Glen Michibata; **9** Doug Burke; **10**
Daniel Nestor.
WOMEN: **1** Helen Kelesi; **2** Patricia Hy; **3** Rene Alter; **4** Maureen Drake; **5** Carling Bassett Seguso; **6** Jill
Hetherington; **7** Teresa Dobson; **8** Susie Italiano; **9** Michelle Duda; **10** Laura Randmaa.

National Closed Championships
MEN'S SINGLES – Semi-finals: B. Gyetko d. A. Sznajder 6–7 6–4 6–4; G. Connell d. G. Michibata 7–6
6–4. **Final:** Gyetko d. Connell 7–6 3–6 7–6.
WOMEN'S SINGLES – Semi-finals: H. Kelesi d. J. Hetherington 6–2 3–6 6–1; P. Hy d. R. Simpson 6–1
6–2. **Final:** Kelesi d. Hy 7–6 4–6 6–1.

CHILE (1920)

Federación de Tenis de Chile, Almirante Simpson, No. 36 Providencia, Casilla 1149, Santiago.
T. (2) 2227279/342416; TX. 240976 COCH CL; Fax (2) 2229291; *Pres.* Mr Rogelio U Rojas; *Sec.* Mr
Rodolfo M. Salaue.

CHINA, PEOPLE'S REPUBLIC OF (1953)

Tennis Association of the People's Republic of China, 9 Tiyuguan Road, Beijing 100016.
C. Sportschine, Beijing; T. (1) 7012233; Fax (1) 7015858; TX. 22034 ACST CN/22323 CHOC CN; *Pres.*
Mr Lu Zhengcao; *Sec.* Ms Zhang Dacheng.
MEN: **1** Zbang Jiuhua; **2** Pan Bing; **3** Liu Xiaoohell; **4** Yu Menan; **5** Xia Jiaping; **6** Meng Qianghua; **7**
Shun Zhiwei; **8** Chen Huei.
WOMEN: **1** Chen Li; **2** Yang Lihus; **3** Lin Ning; **4** Zhu Yuyi; **5** Tang Min; **6** Wu Ying; **7** Tang Liyao; **8** Bi
Ying; **9** Li Yanlin; **10** Chen Jin.

CHINESE TAIPEI (1973)

Chinese Taipei Tennis Association, 2nd Floor, No. 285, Sec 4, Chung Hsiao East Rd, Taipei, Taiwan.
C. Sinovision, Taipei; T. (2) 7313026/7510051; TX. 22949 PACICON; Fax (2) 7711696; *Pres.* Mr M. C.
Chang; *Sec-Gen.* Mr Hu Cheng.
MEN: **1** Yu-Hui Lien; **2** Chung-Hsing Liu; **3** Chang-Rung Wu; **4** Huang-Jung Hsu; **5** Jinn-Yen Chiang; **6**
Yuen-Hong Lee; **7** Kuo-Long Ho; **8** Tze-Min Chung; **9** Chih-Jung Chang; **10** Chi-Ti Huang.
WOMEN: **1** Shi-Ting Wang; **2** Su-Lin Lai; **3** Ya-Hui Lin; **4** Fang-I in Lin; **5** Su-Ping Lin; **6** Mei-Chu Hsu; **7**
Yu-Shar Chiang; **8** Li-Chu Ding; **9** Su-Fong Kuo; **10** Lin-Ya Wu.

National Closed Championships
MEN'S SINGLES – Semi-finals: L. Yu-Hui d. H. Huang-Jung 6–3 6–2; W. Chang-Rung d. L. Chung-
Hsing 3–6 7–5 6–3. **Final:** L. Yu-Hui d. W. Chang-Rung 6–1 2–6 7–5.
WOMEN'S SINGLES – Semi-finals: W. Shi-Ting d. L. Ya-Hui 6–3 4–2 ret.; L. Su-Lin d. L. Fang-Lin 6–2
6–4. **Final:** W. Shi-Ting d. L. Su-Lin 7–6 6–0.

COLOMBIA (1932)

Federación Colombiana de Tenis, Apartado No. 10.917, calle 16 No. 9–64 Oficina 401, Bogota 1 D.E. C. Fedetenis, Bogota, T. (1) 282252; TX. 41275 ICJD CO; Fax (1) 2870936; *Pres* Mr Saulo Barac; *Exec. Sec.* Ms Hernando Ossa.

CONGO

Fédération Congolaise de Lawn Tennis, Stade de la Revolution BP 2061, Brazzaville.
T. (242) 833328; TX. 5414 KG; Fax (242) 835502; *Pres.* Mr Isidore Dinghat; *Sec.* Mr Antoine Ouabonzi.

COSTA RICA (1960)

Federación Costarricense de Tenis, PO Box 326-1005, Barrio Mexico, San Jose.
T. (506) 554793; TX. 2509 CODINCO; Fax (506) 214051; *Pres.* Mr Fred Thome; *Sec.* Mr Domingo Rivera.

COTE D'IVOIRE (1969)

Fédération Ivoirienne de Tennis, 01 BP V 273, Abidjan 01.
T. (225) 44 13 54; TX. 23493 IHCHOT CI; Fax (225) 44 00 50; *Pres.* Mr Jean-Claude Delafosse; *Gen. Sec.* Mr Kouame Kouadjo.

CUBA (1925)

Federación Cubana de Tenis de Campo, calle 13 NR 601 ESQ AC, Vedado Habana 4.
C. Olimpicuba, Habana; T. (7) 403581; TX. 511332 INDER CU; Fax (7) 328 350; *Pres.* Mr Rolando Martinez; *Sec.* Mr M. O. Rodriguez.

CYPRUS (1951)

Cyprus Tennis Federation, 20 Ionos Str., PO Box 3931, Nicosia.
T. (2) 366822/450875; TX. 5300 OLYMPIC CY; Fax (2) 464355; *Pres.* Mr Philios Christodoulou; *Sec.* Mr George Georgiades.
MEN: 1 Alkis Papamichael; **2** Yiannos Hadjigeorgiou; **3** Spyros Charalambous; **4** Simon Aynedjian; **5** Neoclis Neocleous; **6** Paris Christofides; **7** Jacques Heuchene; **8** Christodoulos Georgiades; **9** Antonis Indianos; **10** Constantinos Constantinou.
WOMEN: 1 Vanessa Xenopoullou; **2** Nicoletta Pericleous; **3** Eleni Pilava; **4** Sophie Sofocleous; **5** Natia Iacovou; **6** Percella Ioannides; **7** Mari Missirli; **8** Maro Malaou; **9** Anna Anastassiou; **10** Stalo Tritti.
National Closed Championships
MEN'S SINGLES – Semi-finals: A. Papamichael d. S. Aynedjian 6–4 6–3; Yiannos Hadjigeorgiou d. S. Charalambous 6–3 6–1. **Final:** Hadjigeorgiou d. Papamichael 6–1 6–4.
WOMEN'S SINGLES – Semi-finals: N. Iacovou d. N. Pericleous 6–3 6–0; E. Pilava d. P. Ioannides 6–3 6–1. **Final:** Pilava d. Iacovou 6–3 6–2.

CZECHOSLOVAKIA (1906)

Ceskoslovenska Tenisova Asociace, Ostrov Stvanice 38, 170 00 Prague 7.
C. Sportsvaz, Prague; T. (2) 2311484/2311678; TX. 122650 CSTVC; Fax (2) 2311717/2311868; *Pres.* Mr Jiri Lendl; *Sec.* Mr Michal Polak.

DENMARK (1920)

Dansk Tennis Forbund, Idraettens Hus, Broendby Stadion 20, 2605 Broendby.
C. Tennisforbund, Copenhagen; T. (4) 455555; TX. 33111 IDRAET DK (Att. Tennis); Fax (4) 456245; *Pres.* Mr Jorn Iversen; *Vice Pres.* Mr John Ahlstrand; *Gen. Sec.* Mr Hans Kristensen.
National Closed Championships (Indoor)
MEN'S SINGLES – Semi-finals: M. Tauson d. F. Fetterlein 6–0 7–5; M. Christensen d. T. Sorensen 6–3 7–5. **Final:** Tauson d. Christensen 6–3 6–1.

Andrei Chesnokov became the first Soviet player to pass the $1 million mark in career prize money as he won the tournaments in Monte Carlo and Tel Aviv and reached the fourth round at the French Open. *(M. Cole)*

WOMEN'S SINGLES – Semi-finals: T. Scheuer-Larsen d. P. Sorensen 6–4 6–1; M. Balling Stockmann d. K. Ptaszek 6–2 6–1. **Final:** Balling Stockmann d. Scheuer-Larsen 6–3 0–6 7–5.

National Closed Championships (Outdoor)
MEN'S SINGLES – Semi-finals: J. Larsen d. M. Tauson 7–6 6–3; F. Fetterlein d. N. Bendtsen 7–5 6–0. **Final:** Larsen d. Fetterlein 6–3 0–6 7–6.
WOMEN'S SINGLES – Semi-finals: L. Vandborg d. M. Dirch-Olsen 6–1 6–3; K. Ptaszek d. S. Gotil 6–1 6–4. **Final:** Ptaszek d. Vandborg 6–1 6–2.

DJIBOUTI (1978)

Fédération Djiboutienne de Tennis, rue Pierre-Pascal, BP 16, Djibouti.
C. PO Box 16, Djibouti; T. (253) 352286; TX. 5871 DJ PRESIDEN; *Pres.* Mr Houmed Houssein; *Gen. Sec.* Mr Araita Ahmed.

DOMINICAN REPUBLIC

Federación Dominicana de Tennis, Club Deportivo Naco, calle Central, Ens. Naco, Santo Domingo.
T. (809) 541 3685/3488; TX. 3460418 BONELLY; Fax (809) 688 7696/7441; *Pres.* Mr Gonzalo Mejia; *Sec.* Mr J. Ravello.

ECUADOR (1967)

Federación Ecuatoriana de Tenis, PO Box # 716, Guayaquil.
C. Fetenis, Guayaquil; T. (4) 313600; TX. 43482 NATURS ED; Fax (4) 313642; *Pres.* Mr Mario Canessa; *Sec.* Ms N. Guzman.
MEN: 1 Andres Gomez; 2 Giorio Canreade; 3 Raul Viver; 4 Andres Alarcon; 5 Pablo Campana; 6 Ernesto Lingen; 7 Luis Morejon; 8 Hugo Molina; 9 Carlos Huerta; 10 Erich Reich.
WOMEN: 1 Nuria Niemes; 2 Cecili Piedrahita; 3 Montserrat Martinez; 4 Maria Iciza; 5 Maria Campana; 6 Mercedes Ramos; 7 Maria Roberts; 8 Maria Cornejo; 9 Lourdes Serrano; 10 Paquita Freire.

EGYPT (1920)

Egyptian Lawn Tennis Federation, 13 Kasr el Nil Street, Cairo.
C. Gyplawnten, Cairo; T. (2) 753235; TX. 93697 SAFLM UN (Att. Tennis)/21554 STC UN/93000 OLYMP UN; Fax (2) 760345; *Pres.* Gen. Mohamed Tawfik; *Sec.* Prof. Hussein I. Nasr.
MEN: 1 Hassan El-Aroussy; 2 Khaled El-Salawy; 3 Hany Naser; 4 Moustafa Dalam; 5 Tamer Rahmy; 6 Naser Gharib; 7 Omar Haggag; 8 Khaled Abd El Rahman; 9 Ahmed Saied; 10 Adel El-Sayed.
WOMEN: 1 Shahira Tawfik; 2 Mona Saleh; 3 May Abdallah; 4 Hala Abd El-Wahab; 5 Linda Nagy; 6 Layla Abd El Salam; 7 Aida Serag.

National Closed Championships
MEN'S SINGLES – Semi-finals: H. El-Aroussy d. T. Rahmy 7–5 6–3; K. El-Salawy d. O. Hagag 6–1 6–7 6–0. **Final:** El-Aroussy d. El Salawy 6–1 6–2 3–6 6–4.
WOMEN'S SINGLES – Semi-finals: S. Tawfik d. H. Abd Elwahab 6–0 6–4; A. El Shishiny d. M. Saleh 6–4 6–2. **Final:** Tawfik d. El Elshishiny 6–0 6–3.

FINLAND (1911)

Suomen Tennisliitto, Radiokatu 12, SF-00240 Helsinki.
C. Tennisliitto, Helsinki; T. (0) 158 2301; TX. 121797 SVUL SF; Fax (0) 1582328; *Pres.* Mr Raimo Taivalkoski; *Sec.* Mr Eero Kiuttu.
MEN: 1 Veli Paloheimo; 2 Aki Rahunen; 3 Olli Rahnasto; 4 Kimmo Hurme; 5 Alexander Lindholm; 6 Janne Holtari; 7 Juha Pesola; 8 Juha Lemponen; 9 Tero Nissinen; 10 Pertti Vainikainen.
WOMEN: 1 Petra Thoren; 2 Nanne Dahlman; 3 Anne Aallonen; 4 Katja Kokko; 5 Anu Varpula; 6 Merikukka Forsius; 7 Minna Hatakka; 8 Marsa Kuurne; 9 Laura Mannisto; 10 Linda Jansson.

National Closed Championships
MEN'S SINGLES – Semi-finals: V. Paloheimo d. A. Lindholm 7–5 6–1; A. Rahunen d. V. Koho 6–2 6–3. **Final:** Paloheimo d. Rahunen 6–3 6–4.
WOMEN'S SINGLES – Semi-finals: K. Kokko d. M. Hatakka 6–3 6–3; P. Thoren d. L. Jansson 6–1 6–3. **Final:** Thoren d. Kokko 6–2 6–3.

FRANCE (1920)

Fédération Française de Tennis, Stade Roland Garros, 2 avenue Gordon Bennett, 75016 Paris, France.
C. Tenisfedet Paris; T. (1) 47 43 48 00; TX. TENFED 611871 F; Fax (1) 47 43 04 94; *Pres.* Mr Philippe
Chatrier; *Sec.* Mr Jean Claude Collinot.

GERMANY, DEMOCRATIC REPUBLIC OF

Deutscher Tennis-Verband der DDR, Storkower Strasse 118, 1055 Berlin.
T. (2) 54 98 533; TX. 114919 DTSB DD; *Pres.* Mr Hans-Joachim Petermann; *Sec.* Mr Wolfgang Joch.

GERMANY, FEDERAL REPUBLIC OF (1902)

Deutscher Tennis Bund e.V., Hallerstrasse 89, 2000 Hamburg 13.
T. (40) 411780; Fax (40) 4104480; *Pres.* Dr Claus Stauder; *Exec. Dir.* Mr Gunter Sanders.

National Closed Championships
MEN'S SINGLES – Semi-finals: H. Schwaier d. M. Rackl 6–3 6–2; R. Hass d. G. Marzenell 6–1 6–4.
Final: Schwaier d. Haas 5–7 3–6 7–6 7–6 7–5.
WOMEN'S SINGLES – Semi-finals: S. Hack d. B. Rittner 6–1 6–1; S. Gerke d. E. Schurhoff 6–2 6–2.
Final: Hack d. Gerke 6–0 2–6 6–0.

GHANA (1909)

Ghana Tennis Association, c/o National Sports Council, PO Box 1272, Accra.
C. Ghansport; T. (021) 663924/25/26/27; TX. 2519 GHANSPORT; Fax (021) 223910; *Pres.* Mr Edmund
Annan; *Sec.* Mr Gershon Komla Ayiih.
MEN: 1 Frank Ofori; **2** Samson Ahinakwa; **3** Kojo Atiso; **4** Kenneth Dowuona; **5** Noatey Dowuona; **6**
Emmanuel Paddi; **7** Eric Dowuona; **8** Isaac Nunoo; **9** Isaac Donkor; **10** Alex Amedjoe.
WOMEN: 1 Victoria Dowuona; **2** Mary Asigbetse; **3** Doris Acquah; **4** Sabine Mensah; **5** Jennifer Antwi;
6 Rahinatu Alldu; **7** Rebecca Kankam; **8** Ruth Ardayfio.

National Closed Championships
MEN'S SINGLES – Semi-finals: N. Dowuona d. S. Ahinakwa 7–6 4–6 8–6; K. Dowuona d. E. Paddi 6–7
6–3 8–6. ***Final:*** K. Dowuona d. N. Dowuona 6–2 7–6.
WOMEN'S SINGLES – Semi-finals: M. Asigbetse d. J. Antwi 6–0 6–1; V. Dowuona d. R. Alidu 6–2
6–3. ***Final:*** Dowuona d. Asigbetse 6–2 6–1.

GREAT BRITAIN (1888)

Lawn Tennis Association, The Queen's Club, West Kensington, London W14 9EG.
C. Lawntenna, London W14; T. (71) 385 2366; TX. 8956036 THELTA G; Fax (71) 381 5965; *Pres.* Mr
Ian A. King; *Exec. Dir.* Mr Ian D. Peacock; *Sec.* Mr John C. U. James.
MEN: 1 Jeremy Bates; **2** Nick Brown; **3** Danny Sapsford; **4** Andrew Castle; **5** Mark Petchey; **6** Chirs
Wilkinson; **7** James Turner; **8** Stephen Botfield; **9** Paul Hand; **10** Nick Fulwood.
WOMEN: 1 Joe Durie; **2** Sarah Loosemore; **3** Sara Gomer; **4** Monique Javer; **5** Samantha Smith; **6**
Clare Wood; **7** Julie Salmon; **8** Kaye Hand; **9** Belinda Borneo; **10** Sarah Bentley.

National Closed Championships
MEN'S SINGLES – Semi-finals: J. Bates d. S. Botfield 6–3 6–2; A. Castle d. L. Matthews 6–3 6–2.
Final: Bates d. Castle 6–3 6–2.
WOMEN'S SINGLES – Semi-finals: J. Durie d. J. Salmon 6–2 6–2; S. Gomer d. S. Loosemore 6–2
6–3. ***Final:*** Durie d. Gomer 6–3 6–4.

GREECE (1938)

Hellenic Tennis Federation, Fokionos Negri 9, 11257 Athens.
C. Efotennis, Athens; T. (1) 8654365/8654314; TX. 222415 EFOA GR; Fax (1) 8654365; *Pres.* Mr
Dimitris Stefanides; *Sec.* Mr Dionyssis Gangas.

National Closed Championships
MEN'S SINGLES – Semi-finals: G. Kalovelonis d. Th. Glavas 6–2 6–1; T. Bavelas d. J. Rigas 6–2 6–3.
Final: Bavelas d. Kalovelonis 7–5 4–6 6–3.

WOMEN'S SINGLES – Semi-finals: O. Tsarbopoulou d. H. Kagalou 6–1 6–0; C. Papadaki d. C. Zachariadou 6–3 6–3. **Final:** Tsarbopoulou d. Papadaki 6–4 7–6.

GUATEMALA

Federación Nacionale de Tenis, Palacio de Los Deportes, Zona 4, Guatemala City.
T. (2) 310261; TX. 6077 COG GU; Fax (2) 311152; *Pres.* Ing. Alfonso Padilla Juarez; *Sec.* Dr Adolfo Gomez Perez.

HAITI (1950)

Fédération Haitienne de Tennis, PO Box 1442, Port-au-Prince.
C. Joetienne, Port-au-Prince; T. (1) 51351; Fax (1) 51451/51461; *Pres.* Mr Frantz Liautaud; *Sec.* Dominique Carvonis.

HONG KONG (1909)

Hong Kong Tennis Association Ltd, Tennis Office, The Jubilee Sports Centre, Shatin, New Territories.
C. Tennis, Hong Kong; T. (0) 6023810; TX. 41224 JSCEN HX (Att. Tennis Ass.); Fax (0) 6915494 (Att. HKTA); *Pres.* Dr Philip Kwok JP; *Sec.* Mr Herman Hu; *Exec. Dir.* Mr Yan-pui Tsin.

HUNGARY (1907)

Magyar Tenisz Szovetseg, Dozsa Gyorgy ut 1-3, H-1143 Budapest.
C. Comsport Tennis, Budapest; T. (1) 25266872; TX. 225105 AISHK H; Fax (1) 1571304; *Pres.* Mr Bela Csabai; *Sec.* Mr Istvan Sauska.
MEN: **1** Sandor Noszaly; **2** Laszlo Markovits; **3** Kriztian Keresztes; **4** Istvan Gulyas; **5** Miklos Hornok; **6** Arpad Csizmarik; **7** Viktor Nagy; **8** Rudolf Fekete; **9** Peter Oroszpataki; **10** Zoltan Krasznai.
WOMEN: **1** Reka Szikszay; **2** Nora Koves; **3** Virag Csurgo; **4** Maria Zsoldos; **5** Greta Schmitt; **6** Petra Schmitt; **7** Katalin Kocsis; **8** Zsuzsa Turi; **9** Lilla Buza; **10** Agnes Muzamel.

National Closed Championships
MEN'S SINGLES – Semi-finals: J. Krocsko d. A. Csizmarik 6–3 6–0 6–1; L. Markovits d. J. Gulyas 6–0 6–4 6–3. **Final:** Markovits d. Krocsko 6–3 1–6 7–6 6–3.
WOMEN'S SINGLES – Semi-finals: V. Czurgo d. O. Dobo 6–0 6–1; A. Foldenyi d. B. Bathory 6–3 6–3. **Final:** Csurgo d. Foldenyi 6–4 6–2.

INDIA (1920)

All India Tennis Association, B-7/3 Asaf Ali Road, New Delhi 110 001, India.
C. TAX ASSIST NEW DELHI; T (11) 3275891/3274177/3274178; TX. 3163426 RKCO IN; *Pres.* Mr Kanwar Natwar Singh; *Gen. Sec.* Mr R. K. Khanna.

INDONESIA (1935)

Indonesian Tennis Association, Senayan Tennis Stadium, Jakarta 10270.
C. Tennis Indonesia, Jakarta; T. (21) 5707203; TX. 62794 PELTI IA; Fax (21) 5700157; *Pres.* Mr Moerdiono; *Sec.* Mr Suhardja Swy.

IRAN (1937)

Tennis Federation of Islamic Republic of Iran, Shahid Shirooki Stadium, Shahid Mofatteh St., Tehran.
C. Sportsiran; T. (21) 826999/832555; TX. 212691 VARZ IR; *Pres.* Mr M. Golsham Shirazi; *Sec.* Mr M. Sefatti.
MEN: **1** Kambiz Derafshi Javan; **2** Moharram Ali Khodaei; **3** Seyfollah Behzad Poor; **4** Abbas Kheil Tash; **5** Jahnbakhsh Soori; **6** Amin Estemrari; **7** Ahmad Reza Jamalian; **8** Mohsen Harandizadeh; **9** Ramin Reziani; **10** Mohammad Atshani.

IRAQ (1959)

Iraqi Tennis Federation, c/o Iraqi National Olympic Committee, PO Box No 441, Baghdad.
C. Iroq, Baghdad; T. (1) 7748261; TX. 213409 IROC IK; *Pres.* Mr Suhil N. Abdulla; *Sec.* M. Saadoun
Hasan.

IRELAND (1895)

Lawn Tennis Association, 54 Wellington Road, Ballsbridge, Dublin 4.
C. Irishtennis Dublin; T. (01) 681841; Fax (01) 683400; *Pres.* Mr Michael McCann; *Hon. Sec.* Mrs Mavis
Hogg; *Chief Exec.* Mr John Taylor.
MEN: **1** Eoin Collins; **2** Owen Casey; **3**= Peter Wright; **3**= Michael Nugent; **5** Garbhain O'Nuallian; **6**
Peter Lowther; **7** Stewart Doyle; **8** Liam Croke; **9** Victor Drummy; **10** John Rendina.
WOMEN: **1** Siobhan Nicholson; **2** Gina Niland; **3** Jennifer Thornton; **4** Fiona Long; **5** Carmel O'Sullivan;
6 Jennifer O'Brien; **7** Lisa O'Shea; **8** Nicola McCormick.

National Closed Championships
MEN'S SINGLES – Semi-finals: E. Collins d. S. Doyle 6–2 6–1; M. Nugent d. L. Croke 5–7 6–1 6–3.
Final: Collins d. Nugent 7–5 6–0.
WOMEN'S SINGLES – Semi-finals: S. Nicholson d. J. O'Brien 7–6 7–5; J. Thornton d. G. Niland 6–4
6–2. **Final:** Nicholson d. Thornton 6–7 6–4 6–4.

ISRAEL

Israel Tennis Association, PO Box 20073, Tel Aviv 61200.
C. ILTA, Tel Aviv; T. (3) 613911/625864; TX. 341118 BXTVIL; Fax (3) 5660319; *Chmn* Mr David Harnik;
Sec. Mr Zvi Meyer.
MEN: **1** Amos Mansdorf; **2** Gilad Bloom; **3** Shahar Perkiss; **4** Raviv Weidenfeld; **5** Boaz Merenstein; **6**
Amit Naor; **7** Michael Daniel; **8** Ohad Weinberg; **9** Ran Eyal; **10** Yuval Hirsch.
WOMEN: **1** Yael Segal; **2** Ilana Berger; **3** Dahlia Coriat; **4** Limor Zaltz; **5** Rona Mayer; **6** Yael Shavit; **7**
Mady Dadoch; **8** Anat Varon; **9** Tsipora Obziler; **10** Hagit Ohayon.

National Closed Championships
MEN'S SINGLES – Semi-finals: S. Perkiss d. A. Naor 6–1 6–4; R. Weidenfeld d. O. Weinberg 6–3 6–3.
Final: Perkiss d. Weidenfeld 6–4 6–4.
WOMEN'S SINGLES – Semi-finals: Y. Segal d. D. Coriat 2–6 6–2 6–1; H. Ohayon d. Y. Shavit 4–6 6–3
6–3. **Final:** Segal d. Ohayon 4–6 6–2 6–1.

ITALY (1910)

Federazione Italiana Tennis, viale Tiziano 70, 00196 Rome.
C. Italtennis, Rome; T. (6) 3960092/3966743; TX. 626343 FIT I; Fax (6) 36858166; *Pres.* Mr Paolo
Galgani; *Sec.* Mr Giuliano Annibali.
National Closed Championships
MEN'S SINGLES – Semi-finals: C. Pistolesi d. F. Cancellotti 7–5 7–6; M. Boscatto d. U. Pigato 7–5 5–7
7–5. **Final:** Pistolesi d. Boscatto 6–2 6–4 6–3.
WOMEN'S SINGLES – Semi-finals: F. Bonsignori d. L. Garrone 7–6 6–3; K. Piccolini d. S. D'Andrea
3–6 6–2 6–2. **Final:** Piccolini d. Bonsignori 6–7 4–0 ret.

JAMAICA

Jamaica Lawn Tennis Association, 2A Piccadilly Road, PO Box 175, Kingston 5.
C. Lawntenna, Kingston; T. New Kingston (809) 9295878; TX. 2441 JMTLNKN; Fax (809) 9292135;
Pres. Mr Ken Spencer; *Hon Sec.* Mr Andre The.

JAPAN (1921)

Japan Tennis Association, c/o Kishi Memorial Hall, 1-1-1 Jinnan, Shibuya-ku, Tokyo 150.
C. Niplotenis, Tokyo; T. (33) 481 2321; TX. 2428222 JTENIS J; Fax (33) 467 5192; *Pres.* Mr Tokusaburo
Kosaka; *Sec.* Mr Shin-ichi Shimizu.

JORDAN (1980)

Jordan Tennis Federation, PO Box 961046, Dahiat al Amir Rashed, Amman.
C. Tenfed, Amman; T. (962 6) 682796; Fax (962 6) 687950; TX. 24000 OLYMP; *Chmn* Dr Daoud Hanania; *Sec.* Dr Mohammed Sukhen.

KENYA (1922)

Kenya Lawn Tennis Association, PO Box 43184, Nairobi.
C. Tennis, Nairobi; T. (2) 745164; TX. 22119 MTSTRAV KE; Fax (2) 729277; *Chmn* Mr W. B. Katibi; *Sec.* Mr B. Aggarwal.

KOREA, REPUBLIC OF (1945)

Korea Tennis Association, Room 108, Olympic Gym. No. 2, 88-2, Oryun-dong, Songpa-gu, Seoul 138–678.
C. Kortennis, Seoul; T. (2) 420 4285/40 4286/40 3333 ext. 659/660; Fax (2) 420 4284; TLX. 24989 KOCSEL; *Pres.* Mr Choong-Kun Cho; *Sec.* Mr Yeoung-Moo Huh.
MEN: **1** Shin Han-Cheol; **2** Bae Nam-Ju; **3** Ji Seung-Ho; **4** Lee Jin-Soo; **5** Song Dong-Wook; **6** Lee Jin-Ho; **7** Chang Eui-Jong; **8** Kim Chi-Wan; **9** Kim Jae-Sik; **10** Ro Gap-Taik.
WOMEN: **1** Park Mal-Sim; **2** Kim Il-Soon; **3** Choi Jeom-Sang; **4** Sohn Mi-Ae; **5** Han Eun-Ju; **6** Pyo Hye-Jeong; **7** Im Sook-Ja; **8** Hwang Eun-Sook; **9** Lee Eun-Joo; **10** Choi Eul-Seon.

National Closed Championships
MEN'S SINGLES – Semi-finals: H-C. Shin d. S-H. Ji 6–4 5–7 6–3 7–5; C-W. Kim d. J-H. Lee 7–5 1–0 ret. *Final:* Shin d. Kim 6–4 6–3 6–1.
WOMEN'S SINGLES – Semi-finals: I-S. Kim d. S-J. Im 6–2 6–2; J-S. Choi d. Y-S. Kim 6–2 6–0. *Final:* Kim d. Choi 2–6 6–2 6–3.

KUWAIT (1967)

Kuwait Tennis Federation, PO Box 1462, Hawalli 32015.
C. Tennis Kuwait; T. (965) 2658148; TX. 23192 COMITE KT (Att. Tennis Ass); Fax (965) 2658149. *Pres.* Mr Khalid Al-Bannai; *Sec.* Mr Abdul Ridha Ghareeb.

LEBANON (1945)

Fédération Libanaise de Tennis, PO Box 113–5591, Hamra, Beyrouth.
C. Tennispong, Beyrouth; T. (961) 1342282; TX. 21665/20680 JOEINT LE (Att. E A Yazbeck); *Pres.* Mr Abdel Karim Matar; *Hon. Gen. Sec.* Mr Emile A. Yazbeck.
MEN: **1** Amin Khalaf; **2** Raymond Kattoura; **3** Nicolas Kanaan; **4** Hussein Badreddine; **5** Elie Aswad; **6** Wadih Sawaya; **7** Karim Aswad; **8** Toufic Zahlan; **9** Youssef Ghosteen; **10** Fadi Sabbah.
WOMEN: **1** Nahia Abu Khalil; **2** Aida Kaheel; **3** Sally Sawaya; **4** Sherifa Abuezzedine; **5** Lina Naser; **6** Sally Sawaya; **7** Muna El Murr; **8** Raya Zahlan; **9** Nada Sabra; **10** Fadia Dagher.

LIBYA (1947)

Jamahiriya Tennis Federation, Alfatah September Street, PO Box 2729, Tripoli.
C. Tennis Libya; T. (21) 39150/46883; TX. 20420 OLYMPIC LIBYA: *Pres.* Mr Omran Danna; *Sec.* Mr Mohamed Behelil.

LUXEMBOURG (1946)

Fédération Luxembourgeoise de Tennis, Boîte Postale 38, L 9201 Diekirch, Luxembourg.
C. Fédération Luxembourgeoise de Tennis, Luxembourg; T. (352) 81 75 41; Fax (352) 81 77 25; *Pres.* Mr Michel Wolter; *Gen. Sec.* Jean Goederich.
MEN: **1** Johny Goudenbour; **2** Jacques Radoux; **3** Serge Bruck; **4** Thierry Neiens; **5** Mike Van Kauvenbergh; **6** Paul Hoffman.
WOMEN: **1** Karin Kschwendt; **2** Marie-Christine Goy; **3**= Anne Kremer; **3**= Pascale Welter.

National Closed Championships
MEN'S SINGLES – Semi-finals: J. Goudenbour d. M. Van Kauvenbergh 6–3 6–2; S. Bruck d. P. Hoffmann 6–2 6–2. *Final:* Goudenbour d. Bruck 6–2 4–6 6–1.

Above: *Josef Brabenec, the Czech coach with a group of players from Togo, Cameroon, Guinee Conakry and Kenya at the ITF Training Centre, Abidjan.* **Below:** *Angus Macauley, the ITF Regional Development Officer for East Africa sets up a mini-tennis programme in Uganda.*

WOMEN'S SINGLES – Semi-finals: C. Goy d. P. Welter 6–1 6–0; K. Kschwendt d. R. Moyen 6–1 6–2.
Final: Kschwendt d. Goy 4–6 6–2 6–0.

MALAYSIA (1921)

Lawn Tennis Association of Malaysia, c/o National Tennis Centre, Jalan Duta, 50480 Kuala Lumpur, Malaysia.
C. Tennis Kuala Lumpur; T. (3) 2938070/2938050; Fax (3) 2925041; TX. NTC MA 28061; *Pres.* Hon. Mr Abdul Ghafar Baba; *Exec Sec.* Mr Syed Mohd Alkadry.

MALTA (1966)

Malta Lawn Tennis Association, PO Box 50, Sliema Post Office, Sliema.
T. (356) 512368/335728 (Secretary); TX. 623 MERGRU; Fax (356) 221135; *Pres.* Mr Joseph P. Galea; *Sec.* Mr G. J. Bonello.
MEN: **1** Christopher Gatt; **2** Gordon Asciak; **3=** Steve Schranz; **3=** Daryl Delicata; **5** Denis Galea.
WOMEN: **1** Carole Curmi; **2** Helen Asciak; **3** Elexia Stivala; **4** Katherine Cammilleri **5** Pat Attard.

National Closed Championships
MEN'S SINGLES – Semi-finals: G. Asciak d. S. Schranz 6–2 6–0; Ch. Gatt d. D. Delicata 6–2 6–3.
Final: Gatt d. Asciak 7–5 3–6 6–3.
WOMEN'S SINGLES – Semi-finals: C. Curmi d. B. Zammit 6–0 6–0; K. Camilleri d. K. Pace 7–5 6–4.
Final: Curmi d. Camilleri 6–1 6–2.

MEXICO (1952)

Mexican Tennis Federation, Miguel Angel de Quevedo 953, Mexico City 04330 DF.
C. Mextenis, Mexico City, T. (5) 689 6536; TX. 1761056 FMDTME; Fax (5) 689 6307; *Acting-Pres.* Mr Jesus Topete Enriquez; *Acting-Sec.* Mr Fernando Palafox Valadez.
MEN: **1** Enrique Herrera; **2** Leonardo Lavalle; **3** Francisco Maciel; **4** Jorge Lozano; **5** Agustin Moreno; **6** Eduardo Velez; **7** Roberto Lopez; **8** Oliver Fernandez; **9** Alain Lemaitre; **10** Jose Ayala.
WOMEN: **1** Angelica Gavaldon; **2** Aranzazu Gallardo; **3** Isabela Petrov; **4** Xochitl Escobedo; **5** Hortencia Hernandez; **6** Guadalupe Novelo; **7** Claudia Hernandez; **8** Alejandra Vallejo; **9** Mercedez Fernandez; **10** Karin Dalwitz.

National Closed Championships
MEN'S SINGLES – Semi-finals: F. Maciel d. A. Horeno 7–5 6–2 6–2; L. Herrera d. O. Fernandez 6–4 6–1 7–5. **Final:** Herrera d. Maciel 0–6 7–5 2–6 6–4 7–5.
WOMEN'S SINGLES – Semi-finals: A. Gavaldon d. I. Petrov 6–1 6–4; G. Novelo d. A. Gallardo 6–4 6–2. **Final:** Gavaldon d. Novelo 6–2 6–1.

MONACO (1927)

Fédération Monegasque de Lawn Tennis, 27 boulevard de Belgique, 98000 Monaco.
C. Fédération-Tennis-Monaco; T. (93) 30 01 02; TX. 469760 CONG MC (Att. LTA); Fax (93) 50 92 80; *Sec.* Mr Jean-Paul Samba.
MEN: **1** Gilles Ganancia; **2** Bernard Balleret; **3** Christophe Sebastiani; **4** Jerome Seguin; **5** Christophe Boggetti; **6** Djamel Boudjemline; **7** Jacques Vinceleoni; **8** Albert Viviani; **9** Christian Collange; **10** Jacques Guglielmi.
WOMEN: **1** Isabelle Demongeot; **2** Catherine Suire; **3** Nathalie Ballet; **4** Frederique Martin; **5** Alexandra Fusai; **6** Virginia Buzici; **7** Sandra Stella; **8** Agnes Barthelemy; **9** Samantha Etienne; **10** Frederique Hugonnet.

MOROCCO (1957)

Fédération Royale Marocaine de Tennis, Parc de la Ligue Arabe, BP 15794, Casablanca.
C. Tenisfede, Maroc; T. (212) 278731/262448/262855; TX. 23745 FRTENNIS; Fax (212) 262652; *Pres.* Mr Mohamed M'Jid; *Sec.* Mr Ahmed Mansouri.
MEN: **1** Younes El Aynaqui; **2** Karim Alami; **3** Mohamed Ridaoui; **4** Khalid Outaleb; **5** Arafa Chekrouni; **6** Yassine Lalaoui; **7** Mohamed Dlimi; **8** Abdelkalek Nadini; **9** Amine Kadiri; **10** Houcine Saber.
WOMEN: **1** Sanaa Belguezzar; **2** Rachida Ennajmi; **3** Mouna Kharchafi; **4** Yasmine Benziane; **5** Chamssi Filali; **6** Lamia Alami; **7** Salma Benzekri; **8** Soumia Islamy; **9** Hind Tajeddine.

National Closed Championships
MEN'S SINGLES – Semi-finals: A. Chekrouni d. Y. Lalaoui 6–0 2–0 ret.; Y. El Aynaoui d. M. Ridaoui 6–3 6–3. **Final:** El Aynaoui d. Chekrouni 6–2 5–7 6–1.
WOMEN'S SINGLES – Semi-finals: S. Belguezzar d. Y. Benziane 6–2 6–1; R. Ennajmi d. H. Tajjedine 6–1 7–5. **Final:** Ennajmi d. Belguezzar 6–2 6–0.

NETHERLANDS (1899)

Koninklijke Nederlandse Lawn Tennis Bond, PO Box 107, 1200 AC Hilversum.
C. Tennisbond, Hilversum; T. (35) 46941; TX. 43061 KNLTB NL; Fax (35) 40760; *Pres.* Mr Ruurd de Boer; *Vice Pres.* Mrs H. V. Mook-Grunberg; *Sec.* Mr Martin Mallon.
MEN: 1 Paul Haarhuis; **2** Mark Koevermans; **3** Jan Siemerink; **4** Michiel Schapers; **5** Richard Krajicek; **6** Jacco Elthingh; **7** Tom Nijssen; **8** Menno Oosting; **9** Ralph Kok; **10** Glen Schaap.
WOMEN: 1 Manon Bollegraf; **2** Brenda Schultz; **3** Nicole Jagerman; **4** Linda Niemantsverdriet; **5** Stephanie Rottier; **6** Hellas Ter Riet; **7** Miriam Oremens; **8** Heleen Van den Berg; **9** Carin Bakkum; **10** Caroline Vis.

National Closed Championships
MEN'S SINGLES – Semi-finals: P. Haarhuis d. R. Krajicek 4–6 6–0 7–6 7–6; J. Siemerink d. A. v d Zande 7–6 6–1 1–6 6–3. **Final:** Haarhuis d. Siemerink 6–0 6–7 6–1 6–4.
WOMEN'S SINGLES – Semi-finals: M. Reinders d. S. Schilder 7–6 6–2; L. Niemantsverdriet d. K. Boogert 6–3 1–6 6–2. **Final:** Niemantsverdriet d. Reinders 6–3 6–2.

NEW ZEALAND (1886)

New Zealand Lawn Tennis Association, PO Box 11541, Manners Street, Wellington.
C. Tennis, Wellington; T. (4) 731115; Fax (4) 712152; *Exec. Pres.* Mr Ian D. Wells.

NIGERIA (1927)

Nigeria Lawn Tennis Association, National Stadium, Syrulere, PO Box 145, Lagos.
C. Tennis Natsports, Lagos, T. (1) 83 0649; TX. 26559 ADEFNL NG; *Life Patron* Alhaji Raheem A. Adejumo; *Chmn* Col K. Fidelis; *Sec.* Miss Chinedu Ezealah.

NORWAY (1909)

Norges Tennisforbund, Haslevangen 33, PO Box 2870511, Oslo 5.
C. Norsktennis, Oslo; T. (2) 657550; TX. 78586 NIF N (Att. Tennis); Fax (2) 646409; *Pres.* Mr Dagfinn Holtan; *Sec.* Mr Jon-Erik Ross.
MEN: 1 Anders Haseth; **2** Christian Ruud; **3** Bent Ove Pedersen; **4** Arne Raabe; **5** Atle Willems; **6** Christer Francke; **7** Anders Rolfsen; **8** Kjetil Raanes; **9** Lars Hjarrand; **10** Erlend Efskind.
WOMEN: 1 Amy Jonsson; **2** Cathrine Instebo; **3** Therese Bakke; **4** Siri Mittet; **5** Astrid Sunde; **6** Christina Stangeland; **7** Christine Tuedt; **8** Helle Gimming; **9** Vibeke Hermanrud; **10** Ulrikke Evensen.

National Closed Championships
MEN'S SINGLES – Semi-finals: A. Haseth d. C. Rudd 6–3 0–6 6–2; B. Pedersen d. A. Raabe 6–3 6–4.
Final: Haseth d. Pedersen 6–0 6–3.
WOMEN'S SINGLES – Semi-finals: A. Jonsson d. S. Andersen 6–0 6–0; C. Instebo d. V. Bu 6–0 6–3.
Final: Jonsson d. Instebo 6–1 6–2.

PAKISTAN (1947)

Pakistan Tennis Federation, Wah Cantt, Pakistan.
C. Paktennis, Wah Cantt; T. (51) 66031/9 Ext. 2060; TX. 5840 POFAC PK; Fax (51) 584175; *Pres.* Lt General Talat Masood; *Sec.* Col. (Ret'd) M. A. A. Baig.
MEN: 1 Rashid Malik; **2** Hameed Ul-Haq; **3** Inam Ul-Haq; **4** Muhammad Khalid; **5** Mushaf Zia; **6** Usman Rahim; **7** Raza Ali Mirza; **8**= Ghulam Rasool; **8**= Hasan Mehmood; **8**= Jehanzeb Khan.
WOMEN: 1 Farah Khurshid; **2** Shahina Ahmed; **3** Rubina Hai; **4** Bushra Hussain; **5** Huma Mulji; **6**= Tahmina Mohteshim; **6**= Shah Rukh; **8**= Mrs Najim Abid; **8**= Saadia Rifaqat; **8**= Milaha Razzak.

PARAGUAY (1936)

Asociación Paraguaya de Tenis, Colón 1054, 1st Floor, Asunción.
T. (21) 97756; TX. 124 PY DIESA; Fax (21) 503721; *Pres.* Mr Miguel Carrizosa; *Exec. Dir.* Mr Daniel Lugo Llamosas.

PERU (1930)

Federación Peruana de Tenis, Cercado Campo de Marte, s/n Jesus Maria, Lima.
T. (14) 249979; TX. 25056 PE FPTENIS; Fax (14) 420015; *Pres.* Mr Yolvi Senno; *Sec.* Mr Alfredo Perez Mendoza.

PHILIPPINES (1946)

Philippine Tennis Association, Rizal Memorial Sports Complex, Vito Cruz Street, Manila.
C. Philta, Manila; T. (2) 583535/588248; TX. 23297 ALTIS PH/40255 ALTA PM; Fax (2) 5220229; *Pres.* Col Salvador H. Andrada; *Sec.* Mr Armando P. Alcaraz.
MEN: **1** Felix Barrientos; **2** Danilo Pila; **3** Roland So; **4** Manuel Tolentino; **5** Julio Carluen; **6** Rod Rafael; **7** Andres Battad; **8** Camoy Palahang; **9** Jun Alerre; **10** Nilo Natividad.
WOMEN: **1** Jennifer Saret; **2** Dorothy Suarez; **3** Sarah Castillejo; **4** Diane Castillejo; **5** Joanna Feria; **6** Emily Roque; **7** Francesca La'o; **8** Tonia Cook; **9** Michelle Pangilinan; **10** Carol Roque.

National Closed Championships
MEN'S SINGLES – Semi-finals: F. Barrientos d. R. Rafael 7–6 6–1; D. Pila d. R. So 6–2 6–1. *Final:* Barrientos d. Pila 6–4 6–4.
WOMEN'S SINGLES – Semi-finals: J. Saret d. D. Castillejo 6–1 6–4; S. Castillejo d. T. Cook 6–2 4–6 6–2. *Final:* Saret d. Castillejo 6–3 6–2.

POLAND (1921)

Polski Zwiazek Tenisowy, ul. Marszalkowska 2, 3rd Floor, 00-581 Warsaw.
C. Poltenis, Warsaw; T. (22) 21 80 01/29 26 21; TX. 816494 PAISP PL/812466 COS PL; *Pres.* Prof. Kazimierz Doktor; *Dir.* Mrs Teresa Jaczewska.
MEN: **1** Wojciech; **2** Lech Bienkowski; **3** Bartlomiej Dabrowski; **4** Tomasz Iwanski; **5** Krzysztof Ganszczyk; **6** Maciej Kost; **7** Wojciech Jomroz; **8** Lech Sidor; **9** Pawel Ostrowski; **10** Tomasz Lichon.
WOMEN: **1** Katarzyna Nowak; **2** Iwona Kuczynska; **3** Magdalena Mroz; **4** Katarzyna Teodorowicz; **5** Sylwia Czopek; **6** Renata Skrzypczynska; **7** Beata Gumula; **8** Hanna Kuklinska; **9** Anna Gabzdyl; **10** Dorota Muras.

National Closed Championships
MEN'S SINGLES – Semi-finals: W. Kowalski d. K. Ganszczyk 6–3 6–1; M. Kost d. M. Luczak 7–5 6–3. *Final:* Kowalski d. Kost 7–6 6–7 6–3 6–7 6–3.
WOMEN'S SINGLES – Semi-finals: K. Nowak d. M. Starosta 6–3 6–1; T. Wojtkiewicz d. K. Teodorowicz 6–4 6–4. *Final:* Nowak d. Wojtkiewicz 6–4 6–4.

PORTUGAL (1925)

Federacao Portugesa de Tenis, Estadio Nacional, Apartado 210, 2 796 Linda-a-Velha Codex, Portugal.
C. TENIS PORTUGAL; T. (1) 4151356/4151394; TX. 65257 TENFED P; *Pres.* Mr Jose Castro Rocha; *Sec.* Mr Daniel Duarte Silva.

National Closed Championships
MEN'S SINGLES – Semi-finals: J. Cunha-Silva d. J. Nunes 6–2 6–1 6–1; N. Marques d. P. Coelho 6–1 6–2 6–1. *Final:* Marques d. Cunha-Silva 6–2 7–6 6–3.
WOMEN'S SINGLES – Semi-finals: S. Prazeres d. E. Mendonca 6–1 6–0; T. Couto d. J. Pedroso 6–3 6–3. *Final:* Prazeres d. Couto 6–4 1–6 6–3.

ROMANIA (1929)

Federatia Romana de Tennis, Str. Vasile Conta 16, 70139 Bucharest.
C. Sportrom, Bucharest; T. (0) 119787; TX. 11180 SPORT R; Fax (0) 119869; *Pres.* Mr Constantin Iurea; *Sec.* Prof. Lucian Vasiliu.

SAUDI ARABIA (1956)

Saudi Arabian Tennis Federation, PO Box 4674, Riyadh 11412.
C. Koratawla, Riyadh; T. (1) 4820188/4822829; TX. 404130 TENNIS SJ; *Pres.* Mr Soliman Aljabhan; *Sec.* Mr Saud Ali Abdulaziz.
MEN: 1 Al Mokial Bader; 2 Saleh Fahmey; 3 Fitiani Khalid; 4 Oshban Gamal; 5 Al Anzi Osman; 6 Mashour Moutaz; 7 Sagis Abed Allah; 8 Ibrahim Tawfik; 9 Amoudy Habil; 10 Mohafa Mohamed.
National Closed Championships
MEN'S SINGLES – Semi-finals: M. Bader d. O. Gamal 6–4 7–5; S. Fahmey d. F. Khalid 7–6 6–4. **Final:** Bader d. Fahmey 6–4 6–7 6–4.

SENEGAL (1960)

Fédération Sénégalaise de Tennis, Sporting Club, 28 avenue Roosevelt, BP 510, Dakar.
T. (221) 210239; TX. 61159 SG CTDSENE; *Pres.* Mr Mamadou Bary; *Sec.* Layti Ndiaye.

SINGAPORE (1928)

Singapore Lawn Tennis Association, 4 Normanton Park, # 07-115, Singapore 0511.
T. (65) 7600200 Ext 202; TX. 35467 NASTAD RS; Fax (65) 2722704; *Pres.* Dr Ong Leong Boon; *Hon. Sec.* Maj. S. Uthrapathy.

SPAIN (1909)

Real Federación Española de Tenis, avda Diagonal 618 3 D, O8021 Barcelona.
C. FEDETENIS Barcelona; T. (3) 2005355/2010844/2005878/2015586; Fax (3) 2021279; *Pres.* Mr Agustin Pujol; *Sec.* Mr Tomas Garcia Balmaseda.
MEN: 1 Emilio Sanchez; 2 Juan Aguilera; 3 Javier Sanchez; 4 Sergio Bruguera; 5 Jorge Arrese; 6 Tomas Carbonell; 7 Jose Francisco Altur; 8 Francisco Roig; 9 Fernando Luna; 10 Carlos Costa.
WOMEN: 1 Arantxa Sanchez-Vicario; 2 Conchita Martinez; 3 Immaculada Varas; 4 Maite Martinez; 5 Rosa Bielsa; 6 Neus Avila; 7 Ana Maria Segura; 8 Virginia Ruano; 9 Ninoska Souto; 10 Ana Larracoechea.
National Closed Championships
MEN'S SINGLES – Semi-finals: E. Sanchez d. J. Sanchez 6–3 6–3; S. Bruguera d. S. Casal 6–4 7–6. **Final:** Bruguera d. Sanchez 6–2 7–6 6–4.
WOMEN'S SINGLES – Semi-finals: A. Sanchez-Vicario d. N. Avila 6–2 7–6; P. Perez d. I. Varas 6–4 6–4. **Final:** Sanchez-Vicario d. Perez 6–2 6–3.

SRI LANKA (1915)

Sri Lanka Tennis Association, 45 Sir Marcus Fernando Mawatha, Colombo 7.
C. Tennis, Colombo; T. (1) 686174; TX. 21537 METALIX CE; Fax (1) 580721; *Pres.* Mr D. L. Seneviratne; *Sec.* Mr Dhyan Peiris.

SUDAN (1956)

Sudan Lawn Tennis Association, PO Box 1553, Khartoum.
T. (11) 70081; TX. 22345 ARART SD/22558 DIGES SD; *Pres.* Mr Mohamed Ahmed Giha; *Sec.* Dr Fatih Hasabrasoul.

SWEDEN (1906)

The Swedish Tennis Association, Lidingovagen 75, 115 37 Stockholm.
C. Svenstennis; T. (8) 6679770; TX. 12235 TENNIS S; Fax (8) 6646606; *Pres.* Mr Olle Bergstrom; *Gen. Sec.* Mr Rolf Levin.
MEN: 1 Stefan Edberg; 2 Magnus Gustafsson; 3 Jonas Svennson; 4 Mats Wilander; 5 Jan Gunnarsson; 6 Magnus Larsson; 7 Niclas Kroon; 8 Mikael Pernfors; 9 Thomas Hogstedt; 10 David Engel.
WOMEN: 1 Catarina Lindqvist; 2 Cecilia Dahlman; 3 Maria Strandlund; 4 Jonna Jonerup; 5 Maria Ekstrand; 6 Maria Lindstrom; 7 Annika Narbe; 8 Anna-Karin Olsson; 9 Michaela Pazderova; 10 Catharina Bernstein.

SWITZERLAND (1896)

Schweizerischer Tennisverband, Talgut Zentrum 5, CH 3063, Ittigen/BE.
C. Suissetennis, Bern; T. (31) 587444; TX. 911391 STVCH; Fax (31) 582924; *Pres.* Mrs Christina Ungricht; *Sec.* Mr Daniel Gundelfinger.
MEN: **1** Jakob Hlasek; **2** Marc Rosset; **3** Claudio Mezzadri; **4** Zoltan Kuharszky; **5** Roland Stadler; **6** Stefano Mezzadri; **7** Marc Walder; **8** Thierry Grin; **9** Emmanuel Marmillod; **10** Sandro Della Piana.
WOMEN: **1** Manuela Maleeva; **2** Emanuela Zardo; **3** Csilla Bartos; **4** Celine Cohen; **5** Eva Krapl; **6** Sandrine Jaquet; **7** Christelle Fauche; **8** Michele Strebel; **9** Gabrielle Villiger; **10** Monica De Lenart.

National Closed Championships
MEN'S SINGLES – Semi-finals: Z. Kuharsky d. St. Mezzadri 7–6 6–4; R. Stadler d. M. Walder 6–1 6–2.
Final: Kuharsky d. Stadler 6–4 6–2 6–7 7–6.
WOMEN'S SINGLES – Semi-finals: E. Zardo d. Ch. Fauche 6–3 6–0; C. Marty d. E. Krapl 6–1 1–6 6–2.
Final: Zardo d. Marty 6–2 6–0.

SYRIA, ARAB REPUBLIC (1953)

Syrian Arab Tennis Federation, PO Box 421, Damascus.
T. (11) 225026/34/52; TX. 411578 SPOFED SY; *Pres.* Mr Ahmad Al Hamed; *Sec.* Mr Mustafa Hendi.

THAILAND (1927)

The Lawn Tennis Association of Thailand, c/o Sports Promotion Organisation of Thailand, Hua Mark, Bangkok 10240.
C. Thai Tennis, Bangkok; T. (2) 3140808/3146142; TX 84828 TH; Fax (2) 2714800/2554158; *Pres.* Mr Varin Pulsirivong; *Sec.* Mr Danai Chulajata.
MEN: **1** Tharakorn Srichaphan; **2** Vorapol Thongkhamachu; **3** Narathorn Srichaphan; **4** Panomkorm Pladcheunil; **5** Wittaya Samrej; **6** Noppadol Sricharoen; **7** Jirawat Rakkarnphat; **8** Siri Thamairiboon; **9** Paradorn Chinchaona; **10** Tomorn Chantra.
WOMEN: **1** Orawan Thampenari; **2** Tosapron Summa; **3** Benjamas Saengaram; **4** Kritsana Summa; **5** Suwimol Duangohand; **6** Ohawisa Rarerng; **7** Orathai Thampenari; **8** Rungnapha Surachet; **9** Nutohanan Wimonnit; **10** Rachada Thanadirek.

National Closed Championships
MEN'S SINGLES – Semi finals: N. Srichapan d. V. Thongkhamchu 6–0 6–4; T. Srichaphan d. N. Sricharoen 6–1 6–4. *Final:* N. Srichaphan d. T. Srichaphan 4–6 6–3 6–4.
WOMEN'S SINGLES – Semi-finals: B. Saengaram d. T. Summa 6–4 7–5; O. Thampenari d. S. Duangohand 6–2 6–1. *Final:* Saengaram d. Thampenari 7–6 7–6.

TOGO (1955)

Fédération Togolaise de Tennis, BP 3601, Lome.
T. (228) 215965/210320/210920/210607; TX. 5442 GRD TG; Fax (228) 210607; *Pres.* Mr Kwao Aquereburu; *Sec.* Mr Koffi Galokpo.

TRINIDAD AND TOBAGO (1948)

The Lawn Tennis Association of Trinidad and Tobago, 16 S^ott Street, St Augustine, Trinidad.
C. Lawntenna, Port of Spain; T. (809) 662 5876; Fax (809) 627 5278; *Pres.* Mr Ken A. Mark; *Sec.* Mr Emile Elias.

TUNISIA (1954)

Fédération Tunisienne de Tennis, Cité Nationale Sportive – El Menzah, 1004 Tunis.
T. (1) 238 144; TX. 14637 TOPMED TN; Fax (1) 786 188; *Pres.* Mr Fathi Farah; *Sec.* Mr Hanafi Salah.

TURKEY (1923)

Turkiye Tenis Federasyonu, Ulus Is Hani, Ankara.
C. Tennis Sport, Ankara; T. (41) 3103960/261; TX. 44 531 BTGM TR; *Pres.* Mr Ertan Cireli; *Sec* Mr Yener Dogru.

USA (1881)

United States Tennis Association Inc., 12th Floor, 1212 Avenue of the Americas, New York, NY 10036.
C. Ustennis, New York; T. (212) 302 3322; TX. 424499 ULTA UI; Fax (212) 764 1838; *Pres*. Mr David
Markin; *Sec*. Mr J. Howard Frazer.

USSR (1932)

Lawn Tennis Federation of the USSR, Luzhnetskaya Naberezhnaya 8, 119270 Moscow.
C. Sportkomitet, Moscow; T. (095) 201 08 64; TX. 411287 PRIX SU; *Pres*. Mr I. Volk; *Gen. Sec*. Mr
Victor Yanchuk.
MEN: **1** Andrei Chesnokov; **2** Andrei Cherkasov; **3** Alexander Volkov; **4** Andrei Olhovskiy; **5** Dmitri
Poliakov; **6** Andres Vysand; **7** Vladimir Gabrichidze; **8** Sergei Scakun; **9** David Kacharava.
WOMEN: **1** Natalia Zvereva; **2** Leila Meskhi; **3** Larisa Savchenko; **4** Natalia Medvedeva; **5** Elena
Brioukhovets; **6** Eugenia Maniokova; **7** Victoria Milvidskai; **8** Agnese Blumberga; **9** Natalia Biletskaia.

National Closed Championships
MEN'S SINGLES –Semi-finals: A. Olhovskiy d. V. Gabrichidze w/o; D. Poliakov d. D. Kacharava 6–4
6–2 6–2. **Final:** Poliakov d. Olhovskiy 6–4 4–6 7–5 7–5.
WOMEN'S SINGLES – Semi-finals: E. Makarova d. E. Brioukhovets ret.; E. Maniokova d. N. Biletskaia
3–6 6–4 6–4. **Final:** Maniokova d. Makarova 6–3 6–2.

URUGUAY (1915)

Asociación Uruguya de Tennis, Galicia 1392, CP 11.200, Montevideo.
C. Urutennis, Montevideo; T. (2) 91 50 20; TX. 22333 CADE UY; Fax (2) 96 04 10; *Pres*. Mr Carlos Rymer
Estrada; *Sec*. Glauco Peirano Siri.

VENEZUELA (1927)

Federación Venezolana de Tenis, Apartado 70539, Los Ruices, Caracas 1070-A.
C. Fevetenis, Caracas; T. (2) 9792421/9791487; TX. 28465 FVT VC; Fax (2) 9792694; *Pres*. Mr Fermin
Perez; *Sec*. Mr Alfredo Lanciani.

YUGOSLAVIA (1922)

Tenis Savez Yugoslavije, Terazije 35, 11000 Belgrade.
C. Tesaj, Belgrade; T. (11) 33 33 36; TX. 12595 SFKJ YU; *Pres*. Mr Petar Marinkovic; *Sec*. Mr Zoran
Peric.

ZAMBIA (1975)

Zambia Lawn Tennis Association, PO Box 32604, Lusaka.
T. (1) 221767; TX. 45820 ZA; Fax (1) 221914; *Pres*. Mr Moses S. Mulenga; *Sec*. Miss S. Kapulile.

ZIMBABWE (1904)

Tennis Association of Zimbabwe, PO Box No. A575, Avondale, Harare.
T. (4) 35073; TX. 22648 M'GAMBA; Fax (4) 62670; *Pres*. Mr Norman Gurr; *Sec*. Mrs Christine Greener.

Associate Members without voting rights (64)

AFGHANISTAN   Afghan Lawn Tennis Association, c/o National Olympic Committee of Afghanistan,
Ghasi Stadium, Kabul.
C. Olympic Kabul; TX. 20579; *Pres*. Mr Ghulam Sakhi Hassani; *Sec*. Mr Nematullah Mangal.

AMERICAN SAMOA (1985)   American Samoa Tennis Association, PO Box 28, Pago Pago, American
Samoa 96799.
T. (684) 633 4075; Fax (684) 633 5315; *Pres*. Mr Bill Satele; *Sec*. Mr Pat Galeai.

ANDORRA   Federacio Andorrana de Tenis, San Antoni, 5 Entresol A. Escaldes, Principaute d'Andorre.
T. (628) 26728; *Pres.* Mr Alexandre Escale; *Sec.* Mr Claudi Sala.

ANGOLA   Federacao Angolana de Tenis, PO Box 3677, Luanda.
T. (1) 361152/350961; TX. 3121 EMISSORA AN/3052 INTSER AN; Fax (1) 330281; *Pres.* Mr Luis Lopes; *Sec.* Mr Nelson Assis.

ANTIGUA (1982)   The Antigua and Barbuda Tennis Association, PO Box 1419, St John's, Antigua.
T. (809) 461 0631; *Pres.* Mr Glen Edwards; *Sec.* Mr Norris Franker.

ARUBA   Aruba Lawn Tennis Bond, Seru Pretu 25, PO Box 1151, Paradera, Aruba, Netherlands Antilles.
T. (8) 32593/23120; Fax (8) 27946; *Pres.* Mr Albert Pouson; *Sec.* Mr Winston Kock.

BENIN   Fédération Béninoise de Lawn Tennis, BP 2709, Cotonou 1.
C. Lawn Tenkning; T. (229) 300123/330448; TX. 5342 COTONOU; Fax (229) 314684; *Pres.* Mr Edgar-Yves Monnou; *Sec.* Mr M. F. Adedjouma.

BERMUDA   Bermuda Lawn Tennis Association, PO Box HM 341, Hamilton HM BX.
C. Ernstaudit, Bermuda, T. (29) 295 0319/295 7272; TX. 3680 ERNST BA; Fax 295 5193; *Pres.* Mr Gordon K. Harris; *Sec.* Mrs Gill Butterfield.

BHUTAN (1976)   Bhutan Tennis Federation, PO Box 103, Thimphu.
C. Olympic; *Pres.* Mr T. Dorji; *Sec.* Mr L. Tsering.

BOTSWANA (1964)   Botswana Lawn Tennis Association, PO Box 1174, Gaborone.
T. (31) 373193; TX. 2424 BD; Fax (31) 4108; *Pres.* Dr Quill Hermans; *Sec.* Mrs Jenny Hayzelden.

BRITISH VIRGIN ISLANDS (1982)   British Virgin Islands Tennis Association, PO Box 665, Road Town, Tortola.
C. Veritatem Tortola; T. 49 45471; TX. 7918 PMMBVI VB; Fax 49 45477; *Pres.* Dr Ken Adamson; *Sec.* Mr Noel Barton.

BRUNEI DARUSSALAM (1967)   Brunei Darussalam Lawn Tennis Association, PO Box 1300, Bandar Seri Begawan 1913, Brunei.
T. (2) 225344; TX. BERSATU BU 2357; Fax (2) 223897/229355; *Pres.* Mr Tom Butcher; *Sec.* Mr John Chia.

BURKINA FASO (1970)   Fédération Burkinabe de Tennis, BP 1765, Ouagadougou 1.
Fax (226) 306116; TX. 5268 CHAMCOM; *Pres.* Mr Issoufou Zongo; *Sec.* Mr Oumdouba Ouedraogo.

BURMA (1949)   Burma Tennis Federation, Aung San Memorial Stadium, Kandawgalay Post Office, Rangoon.
C. Ubsped, Rangoon; T. (1) 0171731; *Pres.* Mr Joe Ba Maung; *Sec.* Mr A. Thein.

CAPE VERDE (1986)   Federacao Cabo-Verdiana de Tenis, Ministerio da Informacao, Cultura e Desportos, Rua 5 de Julho, Praia.
T. 613309; TX. 6030; *Pres.* Mr Antero Barros; *Sec.* Mr Antonio Ferreira.

CAYMAN ISLANDS (1973)   Tennis Federation of the Cayman Islands, PO Box 689, George Town, Grand Cayman Islands.
T. (1 809 94) 92077; TX. 4310 CORPSER CP; *Pres.* Mr David Bodden.

COOK ISLANDS (1947)   Cook Islands Tennis Association, PO Box 72, Rarotonga.
T. (682) 22327; TX. 62026 SSIRARO; Fax (682) 20979; *Pres.* Mr Brian R. Baudinet; *Sec.* Mr Tupou A. Faireka.

DOMINICA (1960)   Dominica Lawn Tennis Association, c/o The President, PO Box 199, Canefield Industrial Estate, Canefield.
T. 448 3000/3011; TX. 8655 DOMLEC DO; Fax 449 2051; *Pres.* Mr Ninian Marie; *Sec.* Mr Thomas Dorsett.

ETHIOPIA (1972)   Ethiopian Lawn Tennis Federation, c/o Sports Commission, PO Box 3241, Addis Ababa.
C. Addis Ababa (c/o Sports Commission); T. (1) 156795; TX. 21377 NESCO ET; *Pres.* Mr Hailu Ballha; *Sec.* Mr Wereky Ferede.

FIJI (1934)   Fiji Lawn Tennis Association, PO Box 2399, Government Buildings, Suva.
T. (679) 315988/300280; TX. 2276 USP FJ; Fax (679) 300482; *Pres.* Mr Cliff Benson; *Sec.* Ms Daphne Mar.

GABON (1988)   Fédération Gabonaise de Tennis, BP 3623, Libreville, Gabon.
T. (241) 733218; TX. 5219 CENATEC GO; *Pres.* Mr A. Paul-Apandina; *Sec.* Mr Jean-Jacques Massima Landji.

GAMBIA (1938)   Gambia Tennis Association, PO Box 570, Banjul, The Gambia.
C. SSHOKSECURITY; T. (220) 28688; TX. 2274 SSHOFIC; *Pres.* Mr Demba A. N'dow; *Sec.* Mr Geoffrey M. Renner.

GRENADA (1973)   Grenada Lawn Tennis Association, PO Box 221, St George's, Grenada.
T. (440) 2434; *Pres.* Mr E. Gresham; *Sec.* Mr R. L. Hughes.

GUAM   Tennis Association of Guam, PO Box 4379, Agana, Guam 96910.
C. Chelsea, Guam; T. (671) 734 2624; Fax (671) 477 4826; *Pres.* Pat Ching; *Sec.* Mrs Jean Taniguchi.

GUINEE CONAKRY (1984)   Fédération Guinéenne de Tennis, Au Secrétariat d'État à la Jeunesse et aux Sports, BP 262.
C. FGT BP 262, Conakry Guinee; T. 441962; TX. 22302 MJ GE; *Pres.* Mr Aly Sylla; *Sec.* Mme Magass Malado Diallo.

GUYANA (1933)   Guyana Lawn Tennis Association, PO Box 10205, Georgetown.
C. Lawntenna, Georgetown. T. (2) 64217 (Pres) (2) 61971 (Sec); TX. 3054 REPBANK; *Pres.* Mr John Tracey; *Sec.* Mr Duane Lopes.

ICELAND (1987)   Icelandic Tennis Association, Ithrotamidstoedinni i Laugardal, 104 Reykjavik.
T. (1) 83377; TX. 2314 ISI-IS; Fax (1) 678848; *Pres.* Ms Gudny Eiriksdottir; *Sec.* Mr Sigurduir Asgeirsson.

KOREA, PEOPLE'S DEMOCRATIC REPUBLIC (1945)   Tennis Association of the Democratic People's Republic of Korea, Munsin-Dong, Dongdaewon Dist. Pyongyang.
C. Tennis Pyongyang; T. (82) 62386/63998/73198/22386/23998; TX. 5472 KP; *Pres.* Mr Kim Ju Yong; *Sec* Mr Li Won Gun.

LESOTHO (1920)   Lesotho Lawn Tennis Association, PO Box 156, Maseru 100.
C. LIPAPALI; TX. 4330 FOREIN LO; Fax (266) 310047; *Pres.* Mr E. M. Khali; *Sec.* Mr C. M. Notsi.

LIBERIA (1987)   Liberia Lawn Tennis Association, PO Box 1742, Monrovia.
T. (231) 222877/262932; Fax: (231) 261257 *Pres.* Dr W. Taylor Neal; *Sec.* Mr Clemenceau Urey.

LIECHTENSTEIN (1968)   Liechtensteiner Tennisverband, Bartlegroschstrasse 36, 9490 Vaduz.
T. (75) 56659; Fax (75) 56518; *Pres.* Mr Walter Walser; *Sec.* Mr Werner Schaechle.

MALAWI (1966)   Lawn Tennis Association of Malawi, PO Box 1417, Blantyre.
T. (265) 670033; (Chmn); TX. 44114; Fax (265) 670808; *Chmn* Mr George Banda; *Sec.* Mrs Ann Carter.

THE MALDIVES (1983)   Tennis Association of the Maldives, c/o Maldives Olympic Committee, Male.
T. 322443; TX. 77039 MINHOM MF; Fax 324739; *Pres.* Mr Ahmed Aslam.

MAURITIUS (1910)   Mauritius Lawn Tennis Association, PO Box 46, Rose Hill.
C. Tennis, Mauritius; T. (230) 45922/47011/47812; TX. 4729 SPORTS IW (Att. MLTA); *Pres.* Roger de Coriolis; *Sec.* Mlle C. de Maroussem.

MONTSERRAT (1984)   Montserrat Tennis Association, PO Box 209, Plymouth, Montserrat, British West Indies.
T. (491) 2478; *Pres.* Ms Candia Williams; *Sec.* Mr George Barratt.

MOZAMBIQUE (1979)   Federacao Mocambicana de Tenis, Caixa Postal 4351, Maputo.
C. JOFIRES, MAPUTO; T. (258) 27027; TX. 6614 BMS MO; Fax (258) 420349; *Pres.* Mr Pedro Figueiredo; *Sec* Mr Victorino Nhabangue.

NAMIBIA (1930)   Namibia Tennis Association, PO Box 479, Windhoek 9000.
T. (61) 224478; Fax (61) 229884; *Pres.* Dr Pietie Loubser; *Sec.* Mr Patrick Gardner.

NEPAL (1968)   All Nepal Tennis Association, PO Box 2090, Dasarath Stadium, Kathmandu.
T. (977) 211732/215712; TX. 2390 NSCNP/2614 INSURE NP; *Pres.* Mr Siddheshwar Singh; *Sec.* Mr Sarad Lama.

NETHERLANDS ANTILLES   Nederlandse Antilliaanse Tennis Federatie, PO Box 3571, Emmastad, Curacao.
T. (9) 44192; Fax (9) 81423; *Pres.* Mr Maximo Rufino Paula; *Sec.* Mr Hilberto Thomas.

NIGER (1988)   Fédération Nigerienne de Tennis, BP 10 788, Niamey, République du Niger.
T. 735893; TX. 5460 NI; *Pres.* Mr Ahmed Ousman Diallo; *Sec.* Mr Boubacar Djibo.

NORTHERN MARIANA ISLANDS Northern Mariana Islands Tennis Association, Caller Box PPP, Saipan, MP 96950.
T. (234) 8438; TX. 236503484285 MCIUW; Fax (234) 5545; *Pres.* Mr Terry Saltiban; *Sec.* Ms Faye Crozat.

OMAN (1986) Oman Tennis Association, PO Box 5226, Ruwi, Sultanate of Oman.
T. (968) 703461; Fax (968) 798846; *Pres.* Mr Hamood Bin Faisal Bin Saeed; *Sec.* Mr Majeed Bin Adbullah Alasfoor.

PANAMA, REPUBLIC OF (1964) Federación Panamena de Tenis, Apartado 6-6717, El Dorado.
T. 60 0019/26 2785/60; TX. 2534 INDE PG or 3429 OLIMPAN PG; *Pres* Mr Emilio Palomo; *Sec.* Mr Winston Arosemena.

PAPUA NEW GUINEA (1963) Papua New Guinea Lawn Tennis Association, PO Box 5656, Boroko.
Fax (675) 213367; *Pres.* Michael Lee; Mr Paul Briggs.

PUERTO RICO (1952) Puerto Rico Tennis Association, PO Box 40456, Minillas Sta. Santurce, PR 00940.
T. 765 7711; TX. 345 4212 PRTA PD; Fax 765 3182; *Pres.* Mr Ruben Jordan; *Sec.* Mirtza Rodriguez.

QATAR (1984) Qatar Tennis and Squash Federation, PO Box 4959, Doha.
C. QATSF DOHA; T. 351629/351631/454444; TX. 4749 QATFOT DH; Fax 351626; *Pres.* Jassim Al-Nusf; *Sec.* Mr Mohammed K. Al-Binali.

RWANDA (1984) Fédération Rwandaise de Tennis, B P 1958, Kigali.
T. (250) 74032; Fax (250) 74031; TX. 90922517; *Pres.* Mr Gaspard Musabyimana; *Sec.* Mr Vedaste Nkanika.

ST KITTS AND NEVIS (1962) St Kitts Lawn Tennis Association, c/o Denise Morris, St Kitts and Nevis Port Authority, PO Box 186, Basseterre, St Kitts.
T. (465) 8121; Fax (465) 6661; *Pres.* Mr Nigel Rawlins; *Sec.* Ms Denise Morris.

ST LUCIA St Lucia Lawn Tennis Association, c/o PO 308, Castries, Saint Lucia, West Indies.
T. (1 809 45) 22434; *Pres.* Mr Ornan Monplaisir.

ST VINCENT AND GRENADINES (1972) St Vincent and the Grenadines Lawn Tennis Association, PO Box 604, Halifax Street, St Vincent.
Pres. Mr Michael Nanton; *Sec.* Miss Diane DaSilva.

SAN MARINO (1950) Federazione Sammarinese Tennis, Casella Postale no. 2, Dogana, 47031 Republic of San Marino.
C. Piazza M Tini n 15-47031 DOGANA; T. (39-549) 905303; TX. 284 CONSMAR SO; Fax (39-549) 908187; *Pres.* Mr Remo Raimondi; *Sec.* Maria Teresa Righi.

SEYCHELLES (1955) Seychelles Tennis Association, PO Box 602, Victoria, Mahe.
T. (248) 47414; TX. 2305 MINED SZ; *Pres.* Mr John Adam; *Sec.* Kingsley Pouponneau.

SIERRA LEONE (1965) Sierra Leone Lawn Tennis Association, c/o National Sports Council, PO Box 1181, Freetown.
T. (22) 40562/40167/41340; *Pres.* Mr Henry Moore; *Sec.* Mr E. T. Ngandi.

SOMALI Somali Amateur Tennis Association, PO Box 7536, Mogadishu.
T. (1) 21073/36635; *Pres.* Mr Y. H. Yousaf; *Admin. Off.* Abdulkadir I. Haji.

SURINAM (1936) Surinaamse Tennisbond, PO Box 2087, Zinniastraat 3, Paramaribo.
T. 97279/76727; TX. 240 LBBANK SN; *Pres.* Mr C. Pigot; *Vice Pres.* Mr E. Samson Sr; *Sec.* Mrs Shirley Relyveld.

SWAZILAND (1968) Swaziland Tennis Union, Box 2397, Manzini.
T. 52935 (Sec.); TX. 2036 WD (Pres.); Fax 43275; *Pres.* Mr Satch Khumalo; *Sec.* Mr Bheki Nsibande.

TONGA (1959) Tonga Amateur National Tennis Association, c/o Tonga Sports Association, PO Box 1278, Nuku-Alofa.
T. (676) 21 283/21 288; TX. 66295 TASNOC TS; Fax (676) 24105; *Pres.* Mr Sitiveni Finau; *Sec.* Fuka Kitekeiaho.

UGANDA (1948) Uganda Tennis Association, c/o National Council of Sports, PO Box 9825, Kampala.
Telegrams. LUGOGO; T. (41) 259121; TX. 61069 OPM UGA; *Chmn* Mr Paul Bakashabaruhanga; *Sec.* Mr P. Jemba-Kaggwa.

UNITED ARAB EMIRATES (1982) United Arab Emirates Tennis Association, PO Box 87, Dubai.
T. (4) 690393; TX. 46347 FAGEN EM; Fax (4) 521802; *Pres.* Mr Hassan Khansaheb; *Sec.* Mr Nasser Madani.

US VIRGIN ISLANDS (1973)   Virgin Island Tennis Association, PO Box 11181, St Thomas, USVI 00801.
T. 774 8547; Fax 776 0310; *Pres.* Mr William F. McComb; *Vice Pres.* Ms Virginia Angus; *Sec.* Joyce Wisby.

WESTERN SAMOA (1955)   Western Samoa Lawn Tennis Association, PO Box 2025, Apia.
T. (685) 22202; TX. 245 SAMSHIP SX; Fax (685) 20912/20026; *Pres.* Mr George Vaeau; *Sec.* Mrs Helen Mihaljevich.

YEMEN (1902)   Yemen Tennis Federation, PO Box 4601, Aden.
C. Madhrab, Aden; T. 53244/53639; *Pres.* Mr Ali Nasser Fadle; *Sec.* Mr Mohamed Ebrahim Gabal.

ZAIRE (1984)   Fédération Zairoise de Lawn Tennis, BP 20750 Kin 15, Kinshasa.
T. (12) 30546/30080/78053; TX. 21160 SGA KIN ZR; Fax (12) 30546; *Pres.* Mr Kanyama Mishindu; *Sec.* Mr Eleko Botuna Bo'osisa.

With the help of her new Czech born coach, the naturalised Australian Hana Mandlikova, Jana Novotna won in Albuquerque and reached the semi-finals in Paris, Eastbourne and Zurich to give promise of a push towards the top ten in 1991.   (M. Cole)

INDEX